John Williams

John Williams

A Composer's Life

Tim Greiving

OXFORD
UNIVERSITY PRESS

Oxford University Press is a department of the University of Oxford.
It furthers the University's objective of excellence in research, scholarship,
and education by publishing worldwide. Oxford is a registered trade mark of
Oxford University Press in the UK and certain other countries.

Published in the United States of America by Oxford University Press
198 Madison Avenue, New York, NY 10016, United States of America.

© Tim Greiving 2025

All rights reserved. No part of this publication may be reproduced, stored in a retrieval system, transmitted, used for text and data mining, or used for training artificial intelligence, in any form or by any means, without the prior permission in writing of Oxford University Press, or as expressly permitted by law, by license or under terms agreed with the appropriate reprographics rights organization. Inquiries concerning reproduction outside the scope of the above should be sent to the Rights Department, Oxford University Press, at the address above.

You must not circulate this work in any other form
and you must impose this same condition on any acquirer.

Library of Congress Cataloging-in-Publication Data
Names: Greiving, Tim, author.
Title: John Williams : a composer's life / Tim Greiving.
Description: New York : Oxford University Press, 2025. | Includes index.
Identifiers: LCCN 2025015913 (print) | LCCN 2025015914 (ebook) |
ISBN 9780197620885 (hardback) | ISBN 9780197620908 (epub)
Subjects: LCSH: Williams, John, 1932– | Composers—United States—Biography. |
Motion picture music—United States—History and criticism. | LCGFT: Biographies.
Classification: LCC ML410.W71335 G74 2025 (print) | LCC ML410.W71335 (ebook) |
DDC 780.92 [B]—dc23/eng/20250404
LC record available at https://lccn.loc.gov/2025015913
LC ebook record available at https://lccn.loc.gov/2025015914

DOI: 10.1093/oso/9780197620885.001.0001

Printed by Sheridan Books, Inc., United States of America

The manufacturer's authorized representative in the EU for product safety is
Oxford University Press España S.A., Parque Empresarial San Fernando de Henares,
Avenida de Castilla, 2 – 28830 Madrid (www.oup.es/en or product.safety@oup.com).
OUP España S.A. also acts as importer into Spain of products made by the manufacturer.

The John Williams score brought *Indiana Jones* to life. Without that music it wouldn't have been much of a movie. It's the music which makes Indy come alive.

—**Bob Dylan**

John Williams has been the single most significant contributor to my success as a filmmaker.

—**Steven Spielberg**

Contents

Introduction: Dreaming Backward — 3

PART I. HOLLYWOOD

1. The Ancestral Home, 1877–1932 — 15
2. Very First Adventure, 1932–1950 — 31
3. Leaving Home, 1951–1956 — 57
4. Love Theme, 1957–1968 — 74
5. In Search of Unicorns, 1969–1974 — 123
6. The Beginning of a Friendship, 1972–1976 — 168
7. Binary Sunset, 1977 — 201
8. Death on the Carousel, 1978–1979 — 223
9. The Miracle of the Ark, 1980–1983 — 243

PART II. TANGLEWOOD

10. Cadillac of the Skies, 1983–1987 — 283
11. Somewhere in My Memory, 1988–1991 — 315
12. Journey to the Island, 1991–1996 — 355
13. Duel of the Fates, 1997–1999 — 396
14. Where Dreams Are Born, 2000–2003 — 426
15. Confluence, 2004–2008 — 456
16. Simple Gifts, 2008–2014 — 478
17. Old Friends, 2015–2019 — 508
18. Reunion and Finale, 2020–2024 — 535

Epilogue: Heartwood   **552**

Acknowledgments: Close Encounters with the White Goddess   557
Notes   563
Index   619

atavistic | ˌadəˈvistik | ▶ **adj.** relating to or characterized by reversion to something ancient or ancestral

I've never been an artist, Tim. I am a simple musician.
—**John Williams, 2022**

Introduction
Dreaming Backward

"If everything's ready here on the dark side of the moon... play the five tones." A technician at the synthesizer console obeys, keying a sequence of five simple notes which seem to spell out a greeting as colored lights synchronously flash with each tone on a large board behind him; the giant, hovering spacecraft answers with belching bass notes—and slowly, miraculously, the two species begin a conversation purely in music. A sheriff at his dinner table, haunted by a recent awful death, notices his tiny son silently imitating his every hand gesture; tenderness is communicated without words and accented with a halting, compassionate phrase for duetting harp and piano, which hovers over a slightly troubled pedal note on low strings. Having lulled an ugly, waddling creature from outer space into his suburban bedroom, a nervous young boy wipes his mouth and lifts his fingers to his lips, and the little creature mimics in kind—their wordless exchange accompanied by a fluttering harp solo, a melody that softly suggests the beginning of a unique kind of love story.

In each scene a third party is invisible, but his presence is keenly felt. With notes and orchestral color, John Williams said what these characters could not. He was the omnipresent narrator, the magician behind the curtain. Actors may convey love in their facial expressions, or express suffering or panic in their eyes, but the music tells the ultimate truth and provides faith in these make-believe stories. The score—John Williams—is their soul.

Film music is the invisible art of subtext and emotion and atmosphere, of what John Williams called "underdialogue." "The unspoken, nonliteral things between characters, between adversaries, or between lovers or battling forces," he explained, "those are the things that I try to pick up on." John Williams made himself invisible as a way of being. For the most part he lived like a monk, keeping to his unshowy home or his simple writing studio. He didn't flaunt his considerable wealth or his status as the great composer of the cinema age and perhaps the most famous composer of the last hundred years. There were small signs of a remarkable life in his little bungalow office on the Universal Studios lot: a framed photo with President Barack Obama, or evidence of the man who gave him this office, Steven Spielberg, who worked a few dozen yards away. But there was no grand display case of his five Academy Awards, no props from the uber-famous films he scored, no status symbols of success or ego. It was mostly just the Steinway grand piano and a humble writing desk, sharpened pencils, and stacks of score paper—the archaic tools of a lost art. His quiet working life and his soft, unassuming demeanor made sense: this humble cobbler's workshop was an appropriate place for someone who toils *behind* the scenes and *under* the celebrity film stars and directors.

What made less sense, in theory, was his own celebrity; the nearly 18,000 people—of all ages, genders, and colors—who flocked to his three sold-out concerts at the Hollywood Bowl every summer, who erupted with fan-crazed fervor when their favorite tunes came blasting from the orchestra. As John Williams got older, the flame of fandom only got hotter. It flared up not just in Hollywood but in Boston and Chicago and New York, and it caught fire around the world—in Tokyo, Berlin, Vienna, and Milan. The deafening sound those fans made when Williams brought his music to concerts was the sound reserved for a pop idol or a cultural icon.

How did a career accompanist, a film composer—this invisible man—become *both*?

* * *

John Williams quipped that his biography should be titled *Lucky Man*. Certainly luck was a factor: he was born to a father who not only spurred his musical education but surrounded him with ace performers, provided him with the best teachers, and brought him into the factories of popular entertainment; he had brilliant peers and mentors who generously helped shape his inquisitive mind and nascent creativity; as a young man he had ready access to some of the best players in the country—conservatory-trained band kids and crackerjack recording musicians—and to the industry where film music was being forged at the highest level; he joined the scoring workforce when composers were in high demand and live session players were guaranteed; and, at the moment where his career could have easily been relegated to a much more invisible shelf of film trivia, he caught the ear of a young Spielberg—who then gave John Williams "a big canvas," Spielberg says, "to be able to do what he was born into this life to do."

Many composers would kill to have his luck. But, from the time he was an adolescent, his Olympian work ethic set him apart, as did his relentless curiosity and pursuit of excellence. He could have easily "settled" as a band arranger or concert pianist or studio musician—all areas where he was gifted and appreciated—but something drove him to *create* music for symphony orchestra, music that told stories and wove spells, music that touched millions of ears, even if it was often subconscious. Something drove him to push his craft harder and farther, not just to absorb and master new styles and genres and techniques, but to raise the level of compositional integrity in a field of music that was typically treated as perfunctory. And once he had done all of *that*, something drove him to a new metamorphosis: to be a concert conductor, as well as a classical composer. With each development, he achieved public acclaim and access to new worlds, perpetually growing, ascending. The *something*—the force within that propelled him higher and higher—was not luck or good timing or inherited talent. It was extraterrestrial.

Or, at the very least, *ancient*. John Williams may not have been from another planet—though he accompanied a shocking abundance of aliens—but he *was* a man from out of time. In his thirties he became very interested in poetry and mythology, especially after an extended season in England in the early 1970s, and he gradually developed a philosophy—informed by psychologist Carl Jung and mythologist Robert Graves—about the collective unconscious and the way in which we are all linked to each other and to our ancestors. Music is part of that link, he believed, and it makes us react and feel the way it does because it reminds us of natural sounds heard by our Neanderthal selves, or ceremonial sounds heard by medieval serfs, or bandstand tunes heard by our grandparents. Music is spiritual and psychological; it is a communion between the present and the past. John Williams had a deep reverence for the past: for the great composers of yesterday, as well as for the trees that unite our own timeline with the humans from centuries ago. He read biographies and collected antique music stands. Like an archaeologist, he studied the past for clues and timeless treasures—and his music became a reliquary of his most enchanted finds. "Antiquity lives in us," he said:

> It isn't gone. It's in our bodies. We remember our experience cutting lumber for a slave ship that we had to row on. I don't know what it means, but I believe if we get it right musically, and the performance is right, and the listener is in the right frame and has some background, if possible, we complete the triad—the triad being the composer, the interpreter, and the audience. I think when something strikes me, that's *why* it strikes me—because I've struck something in me that will strike something in you. And it's because our brains are the same thing, the same one.

He had the gifts of a wizard—of conjuring moods and sympathetic magic—and, according to many friends and colleagues, a personality to match. He has been alternately likened to a British conductor from another century, a teacher in a bygone Vermont schoolhouse, and Santa Claus's brother. "He is like Santa Claus in the sense that his eyes sparkle when he speaks," says Yo-Yo Ma. "He has a glint in his eyes. And he gets fascinated by something, so you see his very expressive eyes." But he was also the earthbound product of New England before and during World War II: his proper manners and proper speech betrayed this, as did his work ethic and wartime sense of patriotism and love of country. He was a son of jazz—a hepcat who called his friends "baby" and who made everything swing. And he was an old man even when he was a young man, a serious disciple of serious music who, given his druthers, would prefer to cocoon himself indoors with his piano and his score paper. If he hadn't married a socialite actress who pushed him out to parties and introduced him to the movers and shakers in the film and recording worlds of the 1960s, his career would likely have played out very differently. He was not a showman or self-promoter, and if he hadn't befriended exuberant sponsors and cheerleaders like André Previn and Lionel Newman, his trajectory would not have been so visible, so triumphant. He was permanently engraved by a great tragedy at a pivotal moment in his story arc, and his music, which was suddenly infused with profound emotion, became even more all-consuming. And if he had not found the young film score geek with very nostalgic taste, who also happened to make the most popular movies of his generation, there's no telling how quickly the name *John Williams* may have been forgotten—if it would have ever been learned.

Luck, timing, mysterious force, circumstance, connections: the recipe for any successful life. But what catapults a person beyond mere success and onto a higher plane of not just planetary fame and familiarity, but almost universal *love*?

* * *

John Williams located the cultural pressure point of nostalgia. He wrote music that caused people to "dream backward," as he once put it. He was not an iconoclast in any sense; he did not set out to invent a new musical language or overthrow the rules of his predecessors. He communicated completely and unabashedly in iconography, in half-remembered echoes of history. Some of his crabbier critics confused his work for theft, but in fact it was a very conscious and sophisticated synthesis of past symbols and touchstones, metabolized into a new energy that shot directly into the collective heart and psyche, and *always* with a personal fingerprint and idiosyncratic passion that transcended mere pastiche. His music was drawn from the well of music past, but it was always completely *his* music.

Of all the classical composers, he related the most to Brahms. As Jan Swafford wrote in his 1997 biography, "Brahms was a traditionalist who worshipped the masters of the past, but he took for granted that he must bring something original to his tradition. He was a craftsman among craftsmen, doing his job as best he could in all humility, though to him the work was not ordinary but something at the highest level of human endeavor. Music was Brahms' religion—but music as a private spiritual and intellectual quest, and a shared undertaking" (p. 181). Every word applies to John Williams.

That he possessed a staggering and seemingly endless ability to craft the most infectious earworms is undeniable. His tunes, again and again, leapt out from the soundtrack and into memory traces, pursed lips, pianos, marching bands, and orchestras, all the way from elementary schools to the halls of high culture. "It's not even a songwriter," says composer John Powell. "It's a *hit*-writer." John Williams joined an elite club of prolific creators of instantly recognizable, unforgettable melodies: Jerome Kern, Paul McCartney, Elton John. The list is a matter of debate, but it's not terribly long. It must be conceded that his melody seeds were carried on the winds of blockbusters like *Star Wars* and *E.T.* and *Harry Potter*, finding purchase in fertile soil far and wide, young and old, for years and years and years. But that does not explain away the intrinsic power of the tunes—and would these cinematic myths have been nearly as beloved and potent *without* his themes? "The true genius of John Williams," according to *Star Wars* creator George Lucas, "is that these are mediocre works which John made great."

And as critical as the themes were to his cultural reach, they were only the most obvious pillars of entire, long-form scores that developed those themes like a great symphonist, scores that infused every pore and riveting moment of the films they accompanied. "I think the true genius of what he does, if you look at his scores, is the way that he dramatically rides the smaller scenes," says director Rian Johnson—"his instincts as a storyteller." John Williams has such an elegant, dramaturgical mind, filmmaker George Miller says, that "he could write a thesis on the characters, but particularly on the underlying themes." Under the glinting surface of those indelible tunes were oceans of deep feeling and subtext and dramatic action and comedic ballet and religious climax. Whether the average audience member noticed these grand operas below, or whether it was a kind of hypnotic spell cast without their conscious knowledge, their viscera and their nostalgia registered the effect. Many millions forged a powerful connection to these stories and characters, and when they heard the music their tear ducts filled, and their hearts dreamed backward.

John Williams was a conductor of our collective memory. Initially the music reminded us of something else—a memory from our childhood, or our culture's childhood—and triggered an emotional response. "It's like when you smell bread baking and you think of your mother's kitchen," he said. "It's that kind of sensual connection, an aural memory. That's a successful score." But then the scores forged *new* memories: of Elliott asking E.T. to stay; of Darth Vader striding past imposing rows of Storm Troopers; of young Jim running to the rooftop, euphoric, as American bombers fly through his POW camp; of a mother crumbling to her knees at the sight of a priest in her driveway; of a mother driving away, in tears, from the artificial "son" she abandons in the woods. John Williams frequently scored larger-than-life myths or legendary moments in history, so the canvases were open to grand gestures and powerful aural memories. He scored some of the foundational dreams and cinematic religious moments of the 20th and 21st centuries, and his scores created transcendence and formed permanent grooves in the cultural recall.

Film scores are inherently referential; they need to communicate an idea or a feeling with shorthand, and the most effective way to do that is often by reminding the audience of something they already know. But John Williams used nostalgia—which he defined as "laundered history"—to an end of pure emotional catharsis and spiritual awe. And he meant every note. "The most important observation to make about his music is that he believes in it and it is honest," *Boston Globe* critic Richard Dyer wrote in 1993. "You can't write heroic music if you don't believe in heroism; it would ring hollow. You can't write patriotic music if you don't have patriotic feelings. In a way, a mass-media composer like Williams is a truer successor to populist composers like Verdi than most operatic composers today."

Less attention was paid to his concert works, although they were highly coveted commissions by some of the eminent soloists of the day: Yo-Yo Ma, Anne-Sophie Mutter, Emanuel Ax. They, too, reverberated with history—but a more ancient, atavistic past. They were explorations of mystical glens and forests, the homes of spirits and Druids. On the surface, especially to fans of his popular film scores, they were less accessible and less entertaining, certainly less *tuneful*. But underneath his seemingly simple film tunes was great complexity, and underneath his seemingly complex concert music was deep emotion and lyricism. In both cases, deeper excavation brings greater rewards. For Jim Svejda, a veteran classical radio broadcaster, "it's the greatest series of instrumental concertos written by an American composer—*period*."

* * *

John Williams is, to a great extent, unknowable. He retreated into his music-making and did not bare his soul or interrogate his feelings in interviews or even in private conversation. "We don't get to hear him, necessarily, talking about his rich inner life," says Ma, his friend. "But we can *hear* it." As the composer himself admitted: "I'm defined by my work, by the details of the process of making music. My work is what I am." To drop in on John Williams at almost any point in his life was to watch him silently crouched over a desk or piano, *writing* music, or else find him in a recording session or a concert, *making* music. All else in his life took a back seat to the work; music was where he expressed his emotions, communicated with the world, collaborated with other artists, and it was the ocean where he plunged to escape or cope with grief. His life was music, and music was his life.

And for that reason, this biography began as a fool's errand. Its subject had never authorized or participated in a book or documentary about his life, and he was resolutely against any biographical project even happening. He was eloquent about music and film in a sizable body of interviews given over his 70 years in the public eye, but he revealed little about himself. I attempted to cobble together an account from these scraps, and to interview everyone I possibly could who had any association with or memories of the man—from high school classmates and youthful bandmates and family members to famous directors and producers he worked with, from studio musicians and concert musicians to fellow film composers young and old. A consistent portrait emerged: he wasn't as square or serious as he appeared—he had a buoyancy and a sense of humor, and he didn't take himself too seriously—but he was also *extremely* serious about his craft and the making of music. His self-deprecating humility wasn't false, and it might even be laced with a dash of self-loathing. There were no enemies, no skeletons, no smoking guns. I was on the trail of a man whose kindness and stainless reputation put him in the company of pop culture saints like Tom Hanks and Fred Rogers. In a way, this lack of drama—of sex, drugs, or rock 'n' roll—might have made him a *boring* subject.

But as I investigated further, the music started telling me more stories: of religion and relics, pride and exultation, literature and poetry, mischief and joy, sorrow and regret. These feelings obviously came from the stories he was accompanying, but they also clearly came from within. I found a man marked by dramatic pain, a composer who was in many ways self-educated and self-made, a seeker with insatiable curiosity. The deeper I plumbed John Towner Williams, the more fathoms I discovered.

And then, miracle of miracles ... he decided to let me in. He slowly thawed from total resistance to reluctant helpfulness to generous participation, and the stories—about his childhood, his father, his most important music teacher, his relationships, his career, his philosophies about music and life, his disappointments, his peculiar sensitivities and defensiveness, his worries about the future of music—came trickling out. Stories about the incredible *Zelig* plot of his life, which spanned from the era of big band and radio and Old Hollywood to New Hollywood to whatever this modern Hollywood is, and which orbited the stars of Frank Sinatra, Mahalia Jackson, Alfred Hitchcock, Audrey Hepburn, Clint Eastwood, Ted Kennedy, Leonard Bernstein, Seiji Ozawa, Kobe Bryant, and Queen Elizabeth II—to name just a few.

He was a formidable intellect, a voracious reader who could hold forth on politics and world history as well as music history. He loved vocabulary and used to keep an enormous dictionary next to his bed; he often chided me for not knowing what certain obscure words meant. He revered the novelist John Updike and the poet Hart Crane. He held a soft spot for *The White Goddess*, a bizarre and dense book by Robert Graves which catalogued Celtic myths and poetry and world religions, which John said he couldn't understand and also that he had been reading for 40 years. He particularly loved *Doctor Faustus*, the 1947 novel by Thomas Mann—a fictional biography of an invented German composer, but really a commentary on musical genius and on the madness of the Second World War. John said he related to the composer, Adrian Leverkühn, as a person completely consumed by music: "It puts its arm around you, and then you can't get it off—you're trapped," he said. "Most journeyman composers like myself feel a little bit of that, at a different level." The centerpiece of that novel is a feverish conversation between Leverkühn and the devil, in which the former sells his soul to the latter and all his artistic ingenuities and mortal disasters begin. John said he once had a dream exactly like that: "When I arrived at that section of the book, I thought: *my God, I've been here myself.*" (He was shocked when I told him that his classmate, Susan Sontag, had visited Mann at his Los Angeles home while the author was working on that book during their sophomore year at North Hollywood High.)

He was both more normal than I expected—he always took the rocking chair opposite the couch when I visited his studio, and it felt like I was just having a chat with my grandfather—and more complex and fascinating. Here was a man who prided himself on politesse and especially *dignity*, and who was famous for never saying an unkind word about anyone—and yet whose best friend, Lionel Newman, had tangy nicknames for everybody and a notoriously foul mouth and dirty sense of humor, whose party trick was making lifelike phallus shapes with table napkins. John had been married to his second wife since 1980, but she was rarely seen with him in public and lived in a different home several hours away. When the subject of his critics came up, John waved them away with a smile and in the same moment displayed clear frustration at their small-mindedness.

One day, early in our meetings, he mused: "I wonder if music was better in the ages when people believed in miracles."

He knew his work mattered to a vast number of people, and he also wondered why anyone would want to read about his life; there was no plot, he said. He gave his daughter, Jenny, his blessing to talk to me—and she candidly shared dramatic revelations about her father, her mother, and the pain and tragedy and love and laughter inside her childhood. Little by little, he let down his guard and shared his inner life.

Never *completely*—John Williams remains a mystery to me, and he will likely remain a mystery when you finish reading this book. But he also came into much sharper focus. Here was a seemingly unremarkable New York boy born during the Great Depression, a jazz kid and self-proclaimed piano "nerd" who ended up in Hollywood as a teenager but wanted to play Rachmaninoff with the New York Philharmonic, who didn't care for movies and didn't harbor dreams of being a composer but who, by some strange force, fell sideways into becoming the doyen of film composers. Here was a story of magical ability harnessed by a slave to perfection with an indefatigable drive and thirst for knowledge, of ordinary tools pushed to their most extraordinary limits, of a talented tunesmith with an instinct for dramaturgy and human psychology—who fortuitously collided with some of the great mythmakers and storytellers of the past 60 years. An average American kid who became America's composer and united the world with his invisible "background music." His music, says clarinetist Anthony McGill, is "the music of *all* of us. It's humanity's soundtrack. Like, the *one* thing we can agree on is pretty much John Williams."

In a very true sense, John Williams—what an ordinary name—was just an ordinary music cobbler; anyone could conceivably follow in his footsteps. "I am a simple musician," he told me earnestly. Simple, yes, quiet—invisible. But he was also much, *much* more (Figure I.1).

A note to the reader: The chapter titles in this book are all derived from the names of cues in the film scores of John Williams (he named his own cues) or of his concert works, and they correspond to the particular period in discussion or perhaps simply poetically apply. There are also terms sprinkled throughout the text ("inamorata," the White Goddess) which are allusions to either his music or work that played a significant role in his life. The goal here was not to be cute, but to suffuse the entire book with the language of John Williams.

Figure I.1. "Come, come." Williams in the studio, ca. 1980 (Photographer unknown, Courtesy of John Williams).

PART I
HOLLYWOOD

Is it kind of a slow development? An unanticipated future that hadn't been planned out? I never went to anybody and said, "I want to be a film composer."

—John Williams[1]

1
The Ancestral Home, 1877–1932

> *My father, I must say, was an extraordinary creature. Disappointed greatly. Had a very difficult time. But quite astonishing abilities, on little or no education.*
>
> —John Williams[1]

The music began in an ancient forest. Most of Maine, 90 percent of the state, is forest. Hardy Norway maple, white ash, American elm, and Northern white cedar made the state's central coast a banquet for shipbuilders. When the first Europeans stepped on the soil of present-day Bath in the summer of 1605, Captain George Weymouth immediately recognized this area—with its bustling river lanes, natural docks, and treasury of timber—as an excellent hub for ships. The region's gold was its white pine, which was felled and skidded across New England to make masts for the Royal Navy. Bath became known as the "City of Ships," and in the prosperous 1800s "the busy shipyards attracted workmen from outside," according to a history by Edward Clarence Plummer, "and the romance of the sea drew many of the native young men to a seaman's career." By midcentury, the city boasted multiple churches, mansions, and a theater. The Civil War asked Bath for gunboats and spent 200 of its sons, and in the war's wake there was a brief depression; men were out of work and vagrants roamed the streets.[2]

It was during this civic low tide, on April 19, 1877, that Thomas Michael Nagle was born.[*]

But as Nagle grew up, the city boomed once again. During the first decade of his life the shipyards roared with activity, and in 1889 the Bath Iron Works was founded with an eye on the future of mechanical ships—creating jobs for generations of Bath men, including one of Thomas's older brothers. The Nagles (sometimes spelled *Neagles*) lived in a house on Water Street, just between the iron works and the center of town. Thomas's parents, Richard and Hanora Nagle, were both born in Ireland. Richard left his west coast village of Lios Ceannúir—a place with few trees, but one that boasted the sheer Cliffs of Moher and the healing Well of St. Brigid—departing for America when he was 16 amid the great potato famine, arriving in Boston in 1853 and heading immediately for Bath. He was a laborer all his life, but managed to earn enough to purchase, in 1890, a Keller Brothers piano for the family home.

---

[*] Some records show 1876.

Thomas was the youngest of eight children. Three of his siblings died at the age of 12, 22, and 35, respectively, all buried in the local Oak Grove Cemetery. Still, despite the hardships, a young Bath man's life in the 1890s was a charmed one. "The odor of pine chips and tarred rigging still pervaded the docks and shipyards," wrote Plummer, "as did that of homely virtue and New England idealism the firesides and meeting places of the people." The shipwrights of Bath, Plummer noted, had developed a national reputation: "These were largely men who had grown up in the local yards, who had the traditions of a century and a half of shipbuilding inbred in them, and who took more pride in the quality of their work than satisfaction in the pay envelope. *They were artists rather than laborers.*" By the end of the century the city had reached a population of 10,000, and Bath was now one of the wealthiest in the area, bustling with gaiety and glamor. Roller skating was the new fad, and like every other sizable town in Maine, Bath had its own large skating rink—the Alameda—which occupied almost the entire block between Centre and Vine Streets. A bandstand was suspended over the center of the rink, and the Alameda doubled as a performance venue and arena for balls and political gatherings. A trolley line opened in 1893, and Bathites went for joy rides in open cars. In the summer, steamers carried folks between town and the thicket of islands immediately to the east. Churches and other groups took daylight and moonlight excursions to nearby Popham Beach, where young people danced and roller skated, made love and music, and—like a scene straight out of *Carousel*—slaked their worked-up appetites with clambakes on the beach. (The 1956 movie version of that Rodgers and Hammerstein musical was filmed in Boothbay Harbor on these islands.)

Balls at the Alameda required live music for polkas, waltzes, two-steps, and several varieties of square dances. A proper Maine ball in the Gay Nineties was the real deal: "Five hundred people or more could and did dance with comfort in the Alameda at one time, with a thousand more in the galleries looking on," wrote Plummer. "At such times the best orchestra in the State was none too good. The dancing began at eight and concluded at three or four the next morning." If you surveyed the band at one of these occasions you might find a young Thomas Nagle, who was never destined for the life of a shipbuilder or logger or firefighter or any of the other reliable professions that called the boys of Bath. Nagle was, for better and for worse, a *musician*—at a moment when music was in high demand. He played both piano and the drums; by age 19 he was providing piano entertainment for parties, and in his early twenties he organized a small band that furnished music for balls and dances in Bath and neighboring Brunswick. In 1898 he became a member of the Columbia Theatre Orchestra and played drums in concerts and at school dances, balls, and church events at his local Catholic parish, St. Mary's. Making an actual *living* as a musician proved tough, and Nagle earned some of his wages by cutting hair at his cousin's barber shop. But he had an itch to make musical entertainment on a grand scale, and he had a performing company right at his feet: the laity of St. Mary's. After leading his band at the annual church fair—a lavish multi-day event in the fall of 1902—Nagle, now 25 (Figure 1.1), helmed a committee to

MR. THOMAS M. NEAGLE,
Manager of the Minstrel Show Given By
St. Cecilia Club.

Figure 1.1. Portrait of Thomas Nagle, age 25, in the *Lewiston Evening Journal*, February 25, 1903 (Courtesy of the *Lewiston Sun-Journal*).

produce an amateur minstrel show the following February with nearly 100 performers on the big stage at the Columbia Theatre.

"Amateur minstrel performers," the local paper proclaimed, "are getting to be quite the fad in Bath." Minstrel shows were America's first true invention in the performing arts, a direct prefigure of burlesque and vaudeville and a homegrown outgrowth of opera which rejected that art form's highfalutin European airs and instead developed a more down-home personality. For the entire second half of the 19th century, minstrel shows were the locus of American pop culture. "Our best poets and authors contribute to the progress of this our only original American Institution," boasted one minstrel performer in 1863. "Its songs are sung by Fifth Avenue belles and are hummed by modest serving-girls. Brass bands march through streets playing songs the newsboys will soon be whistling." They also capitalized on crude stereotypes of the distinctive patois, personas, and music of America's enslaved Africans. White men wore blackface, using makeup to exaggerate big eyes and huge, gaping lips, and spoke in flamboyantly "negro" dialect—costumed and moving about in wild colors for comedic effect. When Nagle started producing his own minstrel shows in the early 1900s, the form had baked into a formula: every opening act featured a song and dance with a chorus circling an interlocutor, the master of ceremonies whose precise and haughty English provided fodder for the blackface "end men" to mock. "Audiences could indulge their anti-intellectualism and antielitism by laughing at him," Robert C. Toll wrote in his book *Blacking Up*. "But when he patiently corrected the ignorant comedians with their malaprop-laden dialects, audiences could feel superior ... and laugh with him." Not everyone in the cast wore blackface, and this opening act also featured non-affected songs as well as improvised jokes and social commentary specific to the audience at hand. At Nagle's first show, "the jokes by the end men and girls were new, and many of them being of a local hue, did not fail to bring forth many peals of laughter, and will give the Catholics of Bath many enjoyable moments as they think about them during the Lenten season." America's Irish Catholics had eagerly adopted minstrelsy, largely as a way to escape their *own* status as a minority pariah. Negroes took the comic role in American theater that the ignorant Irish servant occupied over in England, and the newly immigrated Irishman sought to align with his white neighbors by taking part in these all-American productions—often hosted and produced by churches like St. Mary's—distinguishing himself from African Americans by making entertainment at their expense.[3]

These were elaborate entertainments, and Nagle did it all: prompter, stage manager, chorister, and general supervisor, as well as devising the costumes and laying out the scenery. The *Bath Independent* reported on his first big show: "When the big curtain rang up at 8.15, the audience saw a beautiful clearing in a wooded scene, with 70 people in the background elevated by four tiers of raised seats." The opening act included the numbers "My Pliney Waltz Song," "Laughing Song," and "Ebony Belles." It was followed by a variety section or *olio*—a series of sincere ballads performed by parishioners, some buck-and-wing dancing (a precursor of tap), and finally a vaudeville showcase featuring Jimmy Devine, "the boy wonder," in a unicycle stunt show, Frank Lamar and his baton swinging and acrobatic dancing, and John Carr doing some impressive hand balancing "and the sensational slide for life on a wire." Music was provided by an orchestra led by Nagle's friend, Edward Gaudreau, a young violinist who played in the Maine State Orchestra.[4] Nagle produced another minstrel show with 40 participants a few months later, coupled with a street parade, and then took that same show to Boothbay Harbor.

Thomas Nagle was a budding entrepreneur. He learned the skills of piano tuning and repair at a local school, and in January 1904 he opened his own music shop in the center of Bath at the high meeting of Front and Centre Streets. T. M. Nagle's store was stocked with everything in the music line: elegant new pianos—which the owner could tune, re-felt, and re-string for you—mandolins, guitars, banjos, sheet music, phonographs, and the largest lot of records in the city. It also served as headquarters for Gaudreau's Concert Orchestra. Nagle's retail experiment revealed his ambition and a desire to marshal large musical forces, but it also further exposed the difficulty of making a stable living in music.

He now lived with his mother in a house at 987 Middle Street, a few blocks from the heart of town—and less than a half mile up the very same street lived a young woman named Katie. Katherine Christine Duffy was born in Bangor on June 1, 1877—the daughter of Francis and Margaret Duffy, both American-born children of Irish immigrants. Her father was a stonemason who died before her fifth birthday. She grew up in a house on Pleasant Street, an ironic name for a home to four girls and their widowed mother struggling to survive. Margaret remarried a boilermaker, and Katie moved with them to Bath in the mid-1890s when she was a teenager.† Katie was only 18 when her mother died. Her grandchildren remembered her as a tough, mean woman—but many of her formative experiences were tough and mean.

Katie was an active member of the St. Mary's society and their annual fairs, and on a stormy week in 1901 she was helping out at the Children of Mary's prize table at the Alameda where Thomas Nagle, who was also performing in the Columbia Orchestra at the fair, won a picture from her table. A few months later, St. Mary's threw a big "coffee party" where Katie served as a waitress and Nagle played the drums. Perhaps it was little more than proximity and shared community that drew the restless young musician and this stoic tomboy together, but somehow a courtship was formed. They were married at St. Mary's on May 24, 1904, Katie wearing "a becoming gown of pongee silk with hat to match."[5] They honeymooned in nearby Portland and Boston, and when the newlyweds came home they were met with a serenade by the Bath Band, a new musical group whose members included Nagle and his friend Gaudreau.

So why did Nagle immediately abandon his music shop and move with his new bride up the coast to Rockland? He left us no explanation, but we know he rented a tenement house at 10 Grace Street and found employment in the Farwell Opera House orchestra, making his debut in September 1904 in a production of a new comic opera, *The Way of the Transgressor*. He advertised his piano-tuning services in the Rockland newspaper and found additional work playing snare drum in the Maine State Band—a 28-piece orchestra composed of the best musicians in the area—as well as instructing percussionists in the Sons of Veterans drum corps and supplying music for balls and dances at the Samoset Hotel in Rockland's Bay Point. (In one Samoset performance, Thomas was conducted by August Kuntz, a violinist in the Boston Symphony.) He directed minstrel shows at the local parish of St. Bernard's, and even acted as an end man. Then, on November 15, 1905, Katie gave birth to their son; she named him John Francis (after her father). But Nagle, the boy's father, was long gone.

* * *

---

† Her sister Nellie remained in Bangor, where at one point she was robbed and attacked by a drunken vagrant from New Brunswick. ("Mr. Welch Has Stumbled Again," *Bangor Daily News*, October 7, 1904.)

For a short, heavy-set man, Thomas Nagle sure was slippery. His mother, Hanora, died in 1906—"a generous, large-hearted, Christian woman" according to her obituary—and she left the family home in Bath to her son, but Nagle was nowhere to be found; he was sued by the First National Bank of Bath and the house was sold in a public auction.[6] He slipped across the Canadian border to Ottawa, where he found work playing drums in the pit at the Bennett vaudeville theater. "Two hours and a half without a yawn" was the Bennett's motto, and acts included musical comedy, blackface comedians, dogs doing tricks, Emir the musical horse, a telepathist, and "catchy moving pictures." Nagle directed a minstrel show at Bennett's, and he also ventured into a new side enterprise—operating his own picture shows outside Ottawa. (At one showing, the film caught fire.) Nagle and his drums were next in the orchestra at the grand opening of the brand-new Family Theater in October 1910—Ottawa's first continuous home for vaudeville. Electric lights, murals, and mahogany chairs upholstered in black leather adorned this 1,200-seat palace on Queen Street, which offered four shows a day. Attractions included dramatic sketches, singing, comedy, head and hand balancing—and motion picture reels.[7]

Pictures had been in motion in North America since the fall of 1888, when Thomas Edison filed a patent for a device that would do "for the eye what the Phonograph does for the ear." He called his contraption the Kinetoscope, and in 1894 two brothers from Ottawa opened the first Kinetoscope parlor in New York City. These peephole picture machines were single use, often installed in rows, and the reels lasted only around 30 seconds. A hidden phonograph played a non-synchronized soundtrack through ear tubes. It was a newfangled wonder with obvious limitations, and the quest to project these images on a wall for a larger audience was quickly underway. Vaudeville theaters were the obvious venue for this new curiosity, and within a few years many of them began installing projectors that could throw the images on wide screens that hung above the proscenium. Movies became one act among all the others on a given bill. Theater managers liked them for their novelty, and movie producers liked vaudeville theaters for their captive middle-class patrons. Companies like Biograph, Edison, and Vitagraph sold a full-service package of projectors, projectionists, and their own house-made motion pictures, but by 1907 there was a buzzing film exchange market that catalyzed the creation of narrative films. Moviemaking was quickly becoming an industry, and audiences were beginning to form a habit.

Canada's wealthy Allen family cashed in on the movie business, forming a company out of Calgary to build or renovate deluxe movie palaces and securing the exclusive rights to distribute films by the newly established Universal Film Manufacturing Company—locking up both exhibition and distribution of an art form which *some* felt was a passing fancy but others believed was the future of entertainment. The Allens invested in luxury and talented staff, and elevated the moviegoing experience by treating the design of their theaters as a production unto itself—drawing inspiration from grand opera houses and European temples. They obtained quality, family-friendly films from Paramount Pictures and Goldwyn, and accompanied them with expensive pipe organs and high-class musicians. One of Canada's very first luxury movie palaces was the Allen Theatre on 8th Avenue East in Calgary, which seated 840 moviegoers and opened its gleaming doors on November 15, 1913—which was, incidentally, the eighth birthday of Nagle's son. (He would miss them all.)[8]

Styled after a Venetian palazzo, the Allen had onyx balusters, two marble staircases, and an auditorium with Axminster carpets and large opera seats dressed in red velour. It boasted an 18-by-13-foot bowed screen, and a magnificent pipe organ designed by the same Chicago firm that built one for the Mormon Tabernacle in Salt Lake City. Thomas Nagle, aspiring maestro, seized his moment: in 1914 he took command of the Allen Theatre orchestra—selecting, arranging, and conducting the musical accompaniments for feature films. One news article marked him as "perhaps one of the first orchestra leaders in a Calgary picture house and, as an interpreter of motion picture playing, has few superiors."[9] The films he accompanied included a documentary about the British army, a swashbuckling adventure romance called *The Port of Missing Men*, and an early Cecil B. DeMille picture, *Brewster's Millions*. "Music lovers and those who appreciate good music are unanimous in their praise," wrote the Calgary *Daily Herald*. "Every member of the orchestra is a soloist."[10] When they weren't playing along to films, Nagle and his 10-piece band played the pops—songs like "Evening Star" from Wagner's *Tannhauser*, "If I Had Someone Like You at Home," and medleys of English, Irish, and Scotch folk songs. They also did request nights. The following April, and right next door, the equally resplendent Empress Theatre opened its doors under new management and with new renovations—the ceiling covered in pressed tin, the side walls decorated in gilt and green—showing Keystone comedies and other feature pictures. "Special mention may be given to the concert orchestra," wrote the *Herald*, "which is a feature of the house, and Tom Nagle, the leader, and his five pieces render excellent music, cueing the pictures to perfection."[11]

* * *

But the world was at war, and Nagle—now almost 40 and considerably overweight—enlisted in the Canadian army in April 1916. On his attestation paper, which held him to solemnly swear that his answers were true, he claimed he had been born in Ottawa. Asked if he had any children, he wrote "None." Required by the army to draw up a will, he left everything he owned to Ben Cronk, manager of the Allen. Nagle was placed in the Bantam Battalion, a special unit for men under the standard height requirement of 5-foot-4, and he served as bandmaster of the 143rd Battalion—even organizing and directing a minstrel show in Victoria. His unit was sent to England and then France in the spring of 1917, just ahead of the entry of Americans into the war; in Belgium he complained about back and leg pain, and in November he was discharged. He told friends he had been injured in battle, a fib, writing a letter to his sister in Bath: "Yes this war is Hell but we are on the last lap of it now. After another year Fritz will be pretty much in."[12] After recovering in Edmonton, Nagle came back to Ottawa—"just as fat as ever," observed the Ottawa *Citizen*, but with "the same smile that did much in winning friends."[13]

Nagle lived alone in various hotels, and he formed a "Home Brew Jazz and Novelty Band," playing at parties and accompanying dance classes at venues in Ottawa. The itinerant music man found his way to a resort in Ontario—Fort Frances, right on the American border—accompanying vaudeville acts. In 1926 he took direction of his own theater, the Capital in Ottawa, programming more feature films "with high class music."[14] But that venture only lasted one year. Nagle spent the rest of his life managing a resort and amusement park in Winnipeg Beach on the southwest shores of Lake Winnipeg. The park boasted a wooden roller coaster, toboggan slide, Ferris wheel, bowling alley, and a dancing pavilion. It was the site of the Empress Hotel, where Nagle lived and where he also hosted a variety of musical groups and held a regular battle of bands. Every year he oversaw improvements and additions to the park.

He died on January 4, 1935, of natural causes, at age 60. He left behind a second wife, Albina (née Perreault), and had most recently been living in the Montreal neighborhood of Ville St. Pierre. Being a veteran, he was buried at the National Field of Honour Cemetery in Pointe-Claire, with his Canadian Expeditionary Force credentials etched on the stone.

He also died likely knowing nothing about his two-year-old grandson who lived in New York and bore an adopted name. Thomas Nagle was the paternal grandfather of John Williams, who spent most of his life completely unaware of Nagle's existence. Nagle was an all-around musician and a pioneer in the art of film scoring—an art form his famous grandson would one day dominate and perfect.

* * *

When Nagle deserted his wife and newborn child in Rockland back in 1905, Katherine (Katie) immediately went home to Bangor. "My mother told me she was separated from Nagle because he 'wasn't nice,'" said Christine Cameron, Katherine's great-niece. "In those times no one talked about these issues. It was spoken about in whispers."[15] Katherine and her son, Johnny Francis, moved in with her stepfather and his sister in a house on Pine Street. She took a job as a salesclerk at the big department store in town, Freese's—fondly referred to as "Fifth Avenue in Maine"—where she worked for the next 40 years.

Johnny Francis Nagle prophesied his own career when he was a little boy, toddling away from his mother's clutch and falling in with a parade marching down Oak Street while banging away on a toy drum. He never knew his drummer father, but trees can be enchanted and roots are powerful, and he picked up the beat all the same. Katherine said she "never gave Johnny so much as a quarter toward his musical education," but she also didn't discourage his interests. "He got hold of drum sticks when he was very young and from that time on he was at anything in the house that would give a sound," she told a reporter years later. "Why, he had that mantel right there all scarred up. And many times he'd start drumming on just one beat until I'd have to rush into the room and beg him to try something else for a while to give us some relief."[16]

Katherine was 38 when she took a new husband, Henry D. Williams—who was 67—a prominent Republican in Bangor politics and chairman of the police examining board. Both were divorced. Williams's father owned a different department store on Main Street before it was purchased by A. Langdon Freese and absorbed into

Freese's much bigger establishment. On November 23, 1916, Henry and Katherine filed official adoption papers for her son with the State of Maine, legally changing his name to John Francis Williams. Then, just 13 months after Katherine married Henry, the old man died. In his will he left a single dollar to a daughter from his first marriage, and the rest of his estate to Katherine—and in the case of *her* death, to Johnny Francis. The widow and her son were now comfortably residing at Williams's house on Leighton Street, a spacious two-story home wrapped in wooden shingles and located just a mile from Freese's. Katherine never remarried, and she lived at Leighton with her Irish stepfather, John Judge, and her mother's sister, known to all as "Aunt Kate." Katherine had the world's worst luck with marriage, but perhaps she had no need for male companionship. She raised Johnny Francis with Aunt Kate and never married again. Some of her descendants wondered if she might have been lesbian, but whatever her sexual orientation, she certainly bucked the conventions of meek femininity of the time. She wore buttoned-up, androgynous clothes, and was a hardworking, independent buyer of children's clothing who would travel by herself to New York for new acquisitions. "She certainly behaved in the world like a successful man," said her great-granddaughter, Jenny. "By today's standard it wouldn't be any big deal. But *then* it was."[17] Johnny Francis's mother used him as a model for the children's clothing she sold, both for boys *and* girls. He reluctantly obliged.

One of Johnny Francis's first jobs was a paper route that took him past a house where a lady would always give him a cookie, and another house that—according to his childhood friend, Tom Kane—was an infamous brothel. "There's a little short street that went down to the Kenduskeag Stream," Kane's daughter recalled, "and the whorehouse was there. Every Friday they would say, 'Maybe today they'll invite us in!' My father said, 'Every damn Friday, that manicured hand would come out and drop a quarter in our hands. We'd have to leave, going away disappointed.' "[18] A boy's life in Bangor, the one-time "lumber capital of the world" which claimed to be the home of legendary woodsman Paul Bunyan, involved many outdoor activities. Growing up in this river-split land of ancient towering oaks, white pine, and Northern white cedar (species *arborvitae*, the "tree of life"), Johnny Francis particularly loved fishing and hunting, and he became quite a skilled marksman. His tutor in the great outdoors was his grandfather, Katherine's stepfather, whom he affectionately called "Goppy." During World War I, when American children were asked to contribute anything they had to the effort, Johnny Francis sacrificed a pair of binoculars. He received a thank you letter from the Secretary of the Navy, Franklin D. Roosevelt.

By the time he arrived at Bangor High School, teenage Johnny Francis couldn't read music but played the drums "altogether by ear," his mother said, "teaching himself and picking up bits of instruction whenever he could get near an experienced drummer." It was the Roaring Twenties—the Jazz Age—and the hot new music had wafted up from New Orleans and gotten into the blood and toes of all the young white boys and girls of Maine. This was the era of foxtrots and swingy waltzes and Dixieland, and he formed his own band—Johnny Williams' Happy Six—which played dance music at school functions like the annual Freshman Hop, as well as grown-up dances at City Hall and the Chateau Ballroom. "It was a great shock to me when he told me he was going away from Bangor to get into the musical profession," said Katherine. "I had wanted him to finish high school but he was determined that the best course was to stop." Johnny Francis dropped out of school at 17, and he left home with nothing but a collapsible drum, a change of clothes, and enough money to pay his carfare to Portland, where he kept time all summer for tourists at a resort on Kennebunk Beach.

He was offered a musical chair by violinist Tom Kane, his old friend from the paper route who, slightly older, was now a World War I veteran with his own traveling dance band based in Bangor. "Tom gave me my first job," Johnny Francis said. "We played all over the state of Maine, from weddings to bar mitzvahs." Tom Kane's Society Orchestra frequently kept the college kids in motion at the University of Maine in nearby Orono, where Johnny Francis enrolled but never cracked a book, he said. "I just played drums."‡[19] At first he didn't stray far from Bangor, and he made an even bigger impression when he joined a local all-star group, Pete Rogers and His Rainbow Club Orchestra, earning praise as "one of the best drummers in New England."[20] This popular society orchestra often played at the Chateau, and they were even broadcast on local radio station WABI, "the Pine Tree Wave." Then came his best offer yet: a spot in the dance orchestra of Joe Herlihy, a big name all over New England, who discovered future headliners Rudy Vallée and trombonist Jerry Colonna, who would later turn comedian and play second banana to Bob Hope. Colonna and Johnny Francis were instantly best friends. Herlihy's "Collegians" played in dance halls up and down the coast, and Johnny Francis joined the 12-man crew, along with Pete Rogers, in the summer of 1925 during their residency at the Hampton Beach Casino in northern Massachusetts. The group migrated down and settled in Boston, broadcasting on the radio from Music Box Hall in the Back Bay area. They even recorded a few songs.

Until now, phonograph recordings were still being made acoustically and manually, with musicians playing into a horn on the wall and singers often using megaphones to be heard above the orchestra. Thanks to technological advances during the war, the condenser microphone and vacuum-tube amplifier were invented and the first electrically produced recordings were released in early 1925. The advertising boys at the Victor Talking Machine Company, the biggest name in gramophones, pronounced November 2nd "Victor Day" with the deployment of its new electric Orthophonic Victrola. Americans were spending millions on records, and the hottest genre was jazz—although what passed for "jazz" records in the 1920s was often a very pale-skinned stretch of the term. "Everything with a beat and bluesy tonality was regarded as *jazz*," historian Gary Giddins explained, adding that it was used as a synonymous word for "exciting or devilish dance music." On the day *before* Victor Day, Harry Warner—of the famous Warner brothers—acquired the Vitagraph company and its sound-picture technology. The talkies were coming.[21]

* * *

---

‡ The school has no record of his enrollment.

Boston was thrumming with music in the late 1920s when Johnny Francis arrived and made the city his new home. Along "Cultural Mile," which boasted the Opera House and the New England Conservatory of Music, the Boston Symphony Orchestra (BSO) was premiering new works by Aaron Copland at Symphony Hall under the baton of music director Serge Koussevitzky, a Russian emigrant who championed new music and who was fundamental in the institution of the Tanglewood Music Center.[§] Italian conductor Alfredo Casella led the BSO's summer ensemble, the Boston Pops, although by the end of the decade he was succeeded by a young pianist in the orchestra, Arthur Fiedler, who remained Pops conductor for half a century.

Meanwhile, in the city's cabaret district, nightclubs pulsed with society bands and floor shows, liquefied by booze that patrons brought in themselves. Prohibition was in full force, and you could only purchase a glass with ice and a mixer from the menu. (The U.S. Supreme Court soon cracked down on the serving of cracked ice and ginger ale, padlocking a few Boston clubs who broke the law with these flagrant highball kits.) The Lido-Venice club, located on the second floor of an old church on Warrenton Street, was home to the orchestra of "Jacques Renard," a glamorous stage name for a short Jewish violinist with glasses, whose real name was Jacob Staviski. In 1927 the popular bandleader was approached by a shady California investor about building a glitzy new nightclub, and the Cocoanut Grove—its name taken from the famous club in Los Angeles—opened in October with tuxedoed waiters, a fancy French chef, and top-shelf music performed by Renard's band. The main dining room sat 500 patrons, its sides terraced with a Spanish tile covering and the ceiling decorated like a star-strewn sky. After recording two songs with Herlihy in New York in the summer of 1927, Johnny Francis was invited to join Renard's group in Boston, where he also took music classes at the New England Conservatory for one semester and studied percussion with George Lawrence Stone, a classical drummer who wrote a book on technique called *Stick Control*. He was performing with Renard at the Cocoanut Grove one night when, among the floor show dancers, he spotted a petite girl with dark hair and light features and a slightly crooked smile that formed a diamond in her cheeks. Her eyes were pools of kindness, and he was besotted.

Esther Towner's roots went back to England by way of Colonial America. Her great-great-grandfather, Ithiel Towner, was born in 1742 in Connecticut Colony. The son of a British Navy man, Towner was so loyal to the Crown that he joined the British army as a militiaman in 1777 during America's Revolutionary War, then abandoned his home in New York to live across the Canadian border in the town of St John's. (The Towners were also fourth cousins of Hannibal Hamlin, a congressman and senator from Maine who served as Abraham Lincoln's first vice president.) Towner's descendants lived in Quebec until David J. Towner—a towering man at six-foot-six who spoke fluent French—immigrated to America from Montreal in 1879 by train to Vermont. David Towner was a carpenter, and when the Boston Symphony commissioned its new home

---

[§] Copland was the soloist in his own piano concerto premiere in Boston in January 1927, and his use of saxophones and jazz rhythms created a minor scandal within the upper-crusty crowd.

at the corner of Huntington and Massachusetts Avenues at the end of that century, he was on the construction crew. "The family story," according to his grandson, "was that while working on Symphony Hall up in one of the upper interior walls, he dropped his hammer—with his initials 'D.T.' on it—and the hammer just fell down into the lower works and disappeared, and is probably still there."[22] Symphony Hall opened its doors in October 1900, and Henry Lee Higginson—the philanthropist who founded the BSO and personally financed the new "temple" of music—told its first audience: "Whether this hall can ever give so much joy to our people as the old Music Hall no one can tell. Much depends on the public."[23]

Towner married another Canadian expat, Ada Bridget Hennessey, and they were renting a house in the Roxbury neighborhood when Esther Gertrude—the youngest of their 13 children—was born on March 19, 1909. Esther's children would always celebrate her birthday on the 17th, Saint Patrick's Day, with a joint party. The Towners moved into a rental house at 3 Farnum Place—which was later razed and repurposed by the campus of Northeastern University—mere blocks from Symphony Hall. Little Esther became a student of Gertrude Dolan-DePetro—a Boston native who ran a girls' dance studio in Roxbury with her husband, and whose pupils performed in annual recitals, as well as minstrel shows and revues on the same bills as silent films. Esther was dancing in recitals at 13, and soon after she was entering beauty contests. In her late teens she found employment with Lou Walters, the Booker of Boston. "Vaudeville was king in the prosperous post–World War I giddiness known as the Roaring Twenties, and my father owned the keys to the kingdom, at least in New England," wrote Barbara Walters, TV journalist, in her memoir. Louis Walters, her father, was an English émigré who had his own booking agency by the time he was 20. "Magicians, dancers, comics, big stars, little stars," Barbara Walters wrote, "my father had them all."[24] He would lose his fortune when the Great Depression hit and the talkies emptied vaudeville stages, turning them into movie palaces, but just before the crash Walters was booking the Lido-Venice and most of the other nightclubs in Boston—and Esther was one of his dancing girls. She was afraid of water, and when she was asked to go to Europe with a troupe of dancers, she refused.

The ambitious drummer fell in love with the graceful dancer (Figure 1.2). They were married in a Boston church on June 2, 1929, with Jerry Colonna—Johnny's best friend—as his best man.

Johnny Francis kept moving up. He changed tempo from Renard to Leo Reisman's orchestra, a "corking" big band which held a standing spot in the grand Egyptian Room at Boston's Brunswick Hotel.[25] (Both groups broadcast locally on station WNAC.) Reisman was a conservatory-trained violinist who brought a classical elegance to his society dance music, and his admirers included the French composers Maurice Ravel and Darius Milhaud. He had the first recording band in Boston—a star for the Columbia Phonograph Company—which expanded his popularity across state lines. Soon New York came calling. After a short-term summer engagement in Manhattan on the rooftop of the Waldorf-Astoria, Reisman was signed by Vitaphone

Figure 1.2. Johnny Francis Williams and Esther Towner on their honeymoon, 1929 (Courtesy of Paula Arlich).

to star in a series of short films—now equipped with Vitaphone sound. In 1929, he took his 16-piece "Hotel Brunswick Orchestra" to Brooklyn and filmed a handful of musical shorts that ran for weeks at a time in movie houses across the country—like *Rhythms*, which captured the bandleader and his men in stylized silhouettes, playing a medley that included Duke Ellington's sultry "The Mooche" and a violin solo by Reisman in a close-up shot with his 24-year-old drummer gently tapping waltz time behind him. It was Johnny Francis's first appearance in a motion picture.[26]

Colonna was also in the orchestra with Johnny Francis, and Reisman became their ticket to the Big Apple. Esther—friends called her "Essie"—was equally close with Colonna's girlfriend, Flo, and together they all decided to chase the big time and move to New York. The young couples were inseparable—always laughing, playing music, and horseback riding on weekends together. The subway line had just been extended to the Queens neighborhood of Flushing, which was booming with a population of 55,000, and Johnny Francis and Esther rented an apartment on Parsons Boulevard— just a few blocks from all the action at Northern and Main, where the Keith-Albee vaudeville theater would quickly transform into RKO Keith's movie palace. Outside the downtown area, Flushing was mostly abandoned farms, mud flats, and dirt roads, and also the home of a giant marsh teeming with vermin and sewage—the dump site for all of Brooklyn's garbage.

Johnny Francis and Esther arrived there just as the national economy imploded. The stock market crashed on a fateful Thursday in October, and the country fell into its Great Depression. Suddenly entertainment and escapism were more important than ever, and Johnny Francis was completely insulated from the crash because his supply was in great demand. Just two days after Black Thursday, Reisman's group was hired as the official orchestra of the RKO Hour on NBC. Johnny Francis joined the local musicians' union on December 5, 1929, and there was work in abundance. His most exciting job site yet was the newly opened Central Park Casino. This nightlife wonder, located off East 72nd Street just inside New York's famous park, boasted an art deco ballroom with a ceiling full of crystal chandeliers and black mirrors that reflected the likes of Mayor Jimmy Walker—who was there almost every night—and the cream of New York's high society all dressed to the nines. "As I looked around the room," wrote a young broker, "I figured that Cartier had delivered their jewels by the barrel."[27] (Because of Prohibition, guests would leave bottles of booze in their cars; when they were ready for more, the maître d' would signal to their chauffeurs.) The Casino's ceiling wasn't just visually splendid, it was acoustically brilliant. Only the very best dance band would do, and Leo Reisman was offered what was arguably the most glamorous bandstand in the country. *Variety*'s breathless report singled out the music: "Proving that dance music alone, regardless of name value, is still the paramount issue in making or breaking a dine-and-dance place, tremendous success of the Central Park Casino is a vast tribute to Leo Reisman and his Victor recording orchestra. Coming to New York, virtually unknown and unheralded . . . [Reisman] whammed the smart group with his best stepping music."[28] Raved the *Brooklyn Daily Eagle*: "Good orchestras may come and good orchestras may go, but none of 'em have ever equaled lion-maned Leo Reisman's, for what it takes to make your collar-wilt."[29] The great American songwriter Jerome Kern called Reisman's orchestra "the string quartet of dance bands."[30] Johnny Francis provided rhythm for Reisman at the Casino for more than two years, and also appeared with him in vaudeville sets. The orchestra was even booked at the Paramount theater on Broadway to play music on either side of motion pictures like *Follow the Leader* starring Ed Wynn, and an adaptation of *Tom Sawyer* with Jackie Coogan. (For some of these theater engagements, Reisman hired a young pianist and composer named Johnny Green, future head of music at MGM.) One of the films Reisman's orchestra played alongside was *The Right to Love*, in January 1931, and the *New York Times* made special mention of this being "the first picture to be presented by the recently discovered process whereby all noises, such as grating, popping, and other surface sounds, are eliminated.... The excluding of bothersome noises is highly successful, for, because of the background of silence the players' voices are more life-like than ever."[31]

On June 22, 1930, the very same day the ill-fated Lindbergh baby was born, Johnny Francis and Esther welcomed their first child. They named her Joan Katherine, after his mother, and the young parents moved into a brand-new house in Flushing. Esther faithfully attended Sunday mass at St. Mary's Catholic Church, an A-frame colonial building on nearby Parsons Boulevard under the pastorship of Father Hugh Lynch. Esther Williams was "the very definition of benignity, and sweetness, and thorough goodness," according to her son. "Long-suffering and patient." She was a devout churchgoer for her entire life, and "in the strictest sense of the word, she had *faith*."[32] That could not be said of Johnny Francis. *His* religion was forever and always music, and men in the Williams family playfully poked fun at Esther's piety; a running phrase was "Get thee to a nunnery." Johnny Francis had now signed with Meyer Davis, a bandleader who also led one of the largest booking organizations for dance orchestras in the United States. He left Reisman's outfit to play with Roger Wolfe Kahn, prodigy son of a wealthy German arts baron, Otto Hermann Kahn. The younger Kahn was a popular composer and jazz leader whose hot band included Adolph Deutsch, Perry Botkin, and Manny Klein—all of whom figure later in this story—as well as Leo Arnaud, who wrote the famous "Bugler's Dream" associated with the modern Olympics. More and more work was coming from radio, where endless hours of performed music were sponsored by America's booming retail industry. Johnny Francis played on the *Lucky Strike Hour*, the Listerine program with baritone singer Russ Columbo, and the Edgeworth Tobacco program with Arnold Johnson's orchestra. The audio medium was exploding in popularity, with listeners tuning in for an average of four hours a day.[33] In the depressed period between 1930 and 1932, movie attendance plummeted—everyone was at home with their free entertainment, which provided everything from comedy to drama to the best singers and "orks" in the country.

* * *

In February 1932, Herbert Hoover was president of the United States, unknowingly in the final months of his only term. The Winter Olympics were happening upstate in Lake Placid, New York. Later that year, *Buck Rogers in the 25th Century* would debut on the radio, and Franklin Roosevelt would be elected president in a landslide. In December, Radio City Music Hall opened its doors in New York City. It was a baby boom year for prominent figures of the twentieth century, including four future film composers: Michel Legrand (*The Umbrellas of Cherbourg*) and Francis Lai (*Love Story*), both from France, and Lalo Schifrin (*Mission: Impossible*) and Gato Barbieri (*Last Tango in Paris*) from Argentina.

There was a cold snap on Monday night, February 8. That evening, Ignacy Paderewski—pianist and former prime minister of Poland—played a concert at Madison Square Garden, and Sergei Rachmaninoff gave a recital at The Town Hall in the theater district. Future film composer Bernard Herrmann was finishing his studies at Juilliard, and present film composer Max Steiner was composing a milestone score for *Symphony of Six Million* using leitmotifs—melodies or musical phrases assigned to characters and story elements—and developing them in an intentional way, an approach that was soon embraced as the major template for this new art form.[34]

It was on February 8, 1932, that John Towner Williams arrived on Earth. He was born during an extremely fertile cultural period, and his debut accompanied the birth of the modern motion picture with its attendant musical score. In an auspicious adumbration, the new house that John was delivered to was located on Hollywood Avenue.

2
Very First Adventure, 1932–1950

> *Boy, we yanked the nucleus right out of that Hollywood High band. We were pretty rough at first—everybody fighting for their own salad.*
> —Curly Williams, *Time Magazine*, 1949[1]

> *The* Time Magazine *thing was a total misquote of me. It put me off journalists at an early age.*
> —John Williams, 2023[2]

The first music John Williams ever heard was his mother singing: "When the sun goes down, the tide goes out. The people gather round and they all began to shout. Hey hey, Uncle Dud, it's a treat to beat your feet on the Mississippi mud." Esther Williams would sing this to him as a baby, "before I knew what she was doing," he said, "like how you play bunting with the baby's feet." "Mississippi Mud" was a catchy foxtrot written in 1927 by Harry Barris and recorded by Bing Crosby and Paul Whiteman's Rhythm Boys. John Williams, in other words, was born listening to jazz. "Tommy Dorsey and Benny Goodman and Glenn Miller were friends of my father's," he said. "Paul Whiteman, who premiered *Rhapsody in Blue* ... I shook his hand." John grew up with the feeling that his parents were part of a musical *royalty*. And, he added, "I didn't hear any classical music until I was in my teens."[3]

From the start, living in the house at 149-30 Hollywood Avenue, John's parents dressed him just like his big sister. He had curly locks, and they liked to bundle him up in a dark peacoat and a beret. His cherubic Irish face glinted with bright blue eyes, and his terrapin mouth was in a constant smile. From a window box in the Hollywood house he could see the magnificent buildings of Queens College over the treetops, and the family dream was that he would study there one day. His childhood was carefree and blissfully unworried about the economic pain in the rest of the country's depression, spoiled with a loving mother and a working father and a doting sister, surrounded by laughter and love and, always, music. John grew up in a front row seat to his father's business: *show* business.

From his mother, John inherited kindness and dignity. He did not assume her religion, but "probably I have carried some sense of Catholicism and the medieval attraction of the art in it, and the superstition and spirituality of what's in it."[4] From his father he came by an unflagging work ethic and an omnivorous hunger for knowledge, a sideman's ethos—a stalwart accompanist who supports another person's story and does not require the glory of a star—and music coursing through his veins. His father could be a jokester and liked to give everyone nicknames, and despite his serious persona John, too, could be very silly, and his nicknames for people were gifts. Johnny Francis was a heavy smoker and drinker, and under the influence he was prone to anger—whereas John developed a much more moderate and controlled temperament. But he adored his father and imitated his enterprise. "I need to work all the time," John said. "It could go back to some kind of Puritanism in my family. Maybe the hedonists sitting under a palm tree have us all beat. But I think work's the best way to feel that you're making a contribution, to keeping sane."[5]

* * *

The summer after John was born, Johnny Francis played the drums in a series of short films starring Morton Downey, a silky tenor and radio star. In August, the old man brought his young family home to Bangor to visit his mother, where he received a hero's welcome. He and Jerry Colonna were both rising names in the world of radio, and the childless Colonnas were a constant in young John's life. Colonna was just beginning to develop a comic persona that would later make him famous on radio, then TV, culminating in a character dubbed "Professor Colonna," and he tried his shtick out on his friend's giggling children. Little Johnny and Joanie especially loved it when he would smear his big mustache with pie meringue, and they would often toddle over to the Colonna house, crawling through the milkman flap to unlock the door, and enjoy hot cinnamon toast and milk prepared by Flo.[6] Colonna introduced John to authentic Italian food, and also gave him the nickname "Bud," which John's family called him for decades to come.

In 1935, Johnny Francis bought a new home at nearby 143-40 Poplar Avenue in Flushing. (Many of the adjoining avenues—Ash, Beech, Cherry—were also named for trees.) The house was just a few blocks south of St. Mary's Church and right above Kissena Park, a wooded green space that contained a lake and a cemetery. It was a handsome and spacious, three-story white home with an attic and a side garden, and the scene of John's sylvan childhood. David Towner, Esther's father, died in December 1936, and Esther's mother moved into the Poplar house. St. Mary's opened a brand-new school that fall, a two-story brick building on the adjacent lot, with 13 classrooms and a capacity for 800 students. In a speech at the cornerstone-laying ceremony, Reverend Martin Fitzpatrick (from a neighboring church in Corona) decried the public school system, which "eliminates all idea of religion from the classroom and it hopes that this deficiency will be made up in the home or in the church. The Catholic Church rejects the atheistic system," the priest proclaimed, "because that system rejects all thought of God."[7]

By 1936, both Johnny Francis and Jerry Colonna had earned coveted seats in the CBS Radio Orchestra, an all-purpose band that played over the airwaves between ads for cigarettes and the wondrous new invention of baking powder. The band ranged from 10 to 20 rotating musicians at any given time, pooled from the best white jazzmen in New York. "They were basically the house band," said music historian Irwin Chusid. "They were there to accompany vocalists, they could be there to provide music between shows, to fill in a gap—whatever they needed to do, they were on call in the studio, just musicians who could sight read, who knew the standards, who were very good on their instrument."[8] "All the musicians tried to get into radio where the money was," said Johnny Francis, who earned a weekly salary of $500. "I was doing 22 radio shows a week, and hardly ever got to see my wife."[9] Johnny Francis sailed his family through the troubled waters of the Great Depression on a luxury cruiser. Young John's life was comfortable and, compared with other kids he knew, close to extravagance. The musicians at CBS had contracts for unsponsored shows, and received an extra check for the Lucky Strike– and Philip Morris–sponsored programs. "They were almost like plutocrats," said John, whose father took him hunting and fishing, took him to baseball and football games, and bought him bicycles and instruments. "I think I had a sense of privilege, I have to confess," John said, "that we were better off than our neighbors."[10]

The orchestra director at CBS was Mark Warnow, who in 1932 hired his younger brother, Harry, to join the orchestra as staff pianist. Harry was a middling player, but he liked to write little ditties, and his brother would promote his music on the air. Harry had his first hit in 1932 with "Christmas Night in Harlem," but "it was a bit sticky for [Mark] to be playing my music," he said—so Harry Warnow rebranded himself "Raymond Scott," a moniker plucked from the Manhattan phone book because "it had good rhythm to it."[11] "That's *one* story that Raymond told," said Chusid. "A lot of people think he just didn't want to be identified as Jewish." "Scott" was frustrated with playing the same tired music all the time ("They used the best musicians in New York," said clarinetist Artie Shaw, "for some of the worst music"[12]), and he expressed as much to his boss, a producer at CBS, who finally told him: "Okay, wise guy, we'll give you some of the fellows from the band and let's see what you can do.'"[13] Having played with the group every day for years, Scott already had an all-star team in mind. He enlisted bass player Louis Shoobe, tenor saxophonist Dave Harris, clarinetist Pete Pumiglio, Bunny Berigan on trumpet—and on drums, Johnny Francis. He gave his group the misleading name "Raymond Scott Quintette" because, he said, he didn't like the word "sextet." "Someone told me about this wild guy ... who had been rehearsing one song for eight months," recalled a producer at the Master record label. "I went over to CBS to listen to them—they were rehearsing 'The Toy Trumpet' for Mark Warnow's Christmas show—and they absolutely knocked me out."[14] The Quintette debuted "The Toy Trumpet" on *Saturday Night Swing Session* on December 26, 1936, and Scott's music became an overnight sensation. Scott wrote several pieces in a similar vein: short little scenes with evocative titles in what might be considered descriptive pop music. It wasn't, however, *jazz*. "The members of the Quintette were actually not principally great jazz artists," John argued. "They were very fine, technically trained musicians, all five of them, who *played* jazz." The Quintette, he said, "lived on that border between novelty and quasi-jazz."[15] Among Scott's quirks: he didn't write the music down, and did not allow improvisation. He would pick out one bar or phrase at a time on the piano and have each musician play it back to him, then edit or save it, and slowly—painfully—mason a two- or three-minute song together, brick by brick. Everyone memorized their sanctioned part and no one could deviate, which drove the other guys crazy. Scott later became obsessed with electronics, and Johnny Francis quipped: "All he ever had was machines—only we had names."[16]

"The fact that he didn't want improvisation immediately puts him in opposition with the whole principle of what jazz really is," said John. "The musicians would grouse about Scott's rehearsing hour after hour, and coming back and rehearsing some more. He was obsessive-compulsive, obviously, about all this. Whereas in the idiom of jazz, freedom was the thing that everyone sought. And he wasn't willing to give them much of that."[17] Scott rehearsed the group at his studio on the 24th floor of the RKO Building, and recorded *everything*. He liked to record at night, and in addition to the microphones in his high-ceilinged studio he put one in the hallway outside and another inside the tiled men's bathroom, enhancing his five-man group with a wallop of reverb long before Phil Spector's famous "wall of sound." They churned out a dozen tracks at the top of 1937, and the first record they released—which contained "Twilight in Turkey" and "Minuet in Jazz"—sold out in a week. "Turkey" opened with a rapid-fire drum solo by Johnny Francis, and was made to capture "a crowded square," Scott explained. "Twilight is setting in ... Arab barters with Arab ... prayer time is approaching ... camels are resting ... a group of dancing girls are entertaining ... an Englishman gets lost ... traffic is heavy ... the afternoon heat is still felt...."[18] Despite the agony in making the music, or perhaps because of it, Scott's group began cranking out one hit after another. The *New Yorker* counted among Scott's admirers Cab Calloway, Duke Ellington, Jascha Heifetz, and even Igor Stravinsky.[19] In a way, he was writing crude—and often crudely *ethnic*—miniature film scores without a film, with names like "War Dance for Wooden Indians" and "Dinner Music for a Pack of Hungry Cannibals." More specifically, it was *cartoonish* film music, a literal imitation of a visual scene. In fact, Scott's music outlived its vogue in the 1930s because it was co-opted by *Looney Tunes* and several other cartoon shows in subsequent decades. His most enduring number was "Powerhouse," a toon staple, which he wrote to sound like the inner workings of a power plant.

Johnny Francis was an essential part of the Quintette sound. He didn't just use a standard drum kit—he also played cowbells and woodblocks and chau gongs, and even had a plain Boy Scout drum modified with timpani tuning handles. His contributions were part of the musical storytelling and often played for humor, but always with superior skill and even *elegance*. "Johnny's drumming, to me," said Chusid, "was more distinctive in that it was more playful, it was more animated, it was more geared towards novelty effects. Certainly more so than any drummer I can think of, with the exception of Spike Jones, who came later." Lindley Armstrong "Spike" Jones was a Hollywood-based contemporary who used cowbells, car horns, and dog barks in his zany novelty music. "I really think Spike Jones was influenced by Johnny Williams," said Chusid. "One of the hallmarks of Johnny's playing is that, despite the fact that he was hitting anything within reach and there was a novelty aspect to it, there was restraint, there was *taste*."[20] One Scott number that predated the Quintette was "Piano and Pistol Duel," which featured Raymond Scott and Johnny Francis and, as the radio announcer joked, conductor Leith Stevens "wearing a bulletproof vest." It was one of several silly little pieces that Johnny Francis played during his early CBS days, something to fill time in the loosely structured gaps between shows. The "pistol" was Johnny firing his drum, no doubt inspired by his own affinity for guns. Johnny Francis could almost sound like a drum machine—or a machine *gun*. "He sounds like World War II instead of World War I," noted Jeff Winner, a producer of Scott's archives.[21] Johnny Francis made a handsome profit from Scott's quirky hits, which caught fire partly thanks to the exploding popularity of nickel-operated automatic phonograph machines. In the years 1937–1938, an estimated 200,000–400,000 machines were in operation nationally in restaurants, cafés, bowling alleys, and roller-skating rinks.[22] The drummer begrudgingly accepted that Scott made him a better player: "All that discipline helped," Johnny Francis said. "It had to. I developed a technique way beyond what I'd had."[23] With a taste of fame and some name recognition, he recorded two songs of his own as "Johnny Williams and his Swing Sextet" in the summer of 1936. On piano was Claude Thornhill, "a funny-looking gent," according to Artie Shaw, "with that potato nose and round German face," and reddish hair that stuck up like straw.[24] A sophisticated arranger and composer of impressionistic jazz, Thornhill became a good friend of the Williams family, and he made an indelible impression on young John.

* * *

It was no surprise that Scott's highly visual music attracted Hollywood. After the Quintette made one of their first public appearances at Cafe Trocadero on the Sunset Strip in October 1937, there was a studio bidding war for the group and its famous tunes—which was won by Darryl F. Zanuck and 20th Century Fox. The Quintette was placed under contract just like a movie star, and they were reportedly offered $100,000 for a year's work. Johnny Francis brought his whole family out to Los Angeles that fall, including his newest baby, Gerald—nicknamed "Jerry" after Colonna—who was born one day after John's fifth birthday. They found a home near the Fox lot, a Spanish-style house on Dunleer Drive in the neighborhood of Cheviot Hills, which overlooked a great, mostly empty valley. Standing on the street corner, John could see all the way down to MGM Studios, and from the backyard he could see the Pacific Ocean. "It looked to me like I was standing on a Himalayan peak," he said. John was enrolled in his first year of school at Overland Elementary, located in easy walking distance. On the corner of Overland Avenue and Pico Boulevard was a pony ride, where Johnny Francis would take John and Joan for some pint-sized recreation. All of this was within blocks of Fox, where Johnny Francis entered every workday through the west gate on Tennessee Avenue.[25]

The Quintette's first major appearance was in the Eddie Cantor picture *Ali Baba Goes to Town*, where they played "Twilight in Turkey"—dressed in stereotypical "Arabian" turbans and harem pants—as accompaniment to two belly dancers. Onscreen, Johnny Francis starts the number with a pounding lead-in, and the camera focuses on some stick-twirling action and a short close-up of him mugging behind a fake goatee, although audiences were more likely watching the thinly veiled beauties in front of the band. Their next movie was *Rebecca of Sunnybrook Farm*, starring nine-year-old Shirley Temple as a budding radio performer. The Quintette doesn't actually appear on camera in the final cut, with the exception of a fleeting shot of Johnny Francis's hands rolling a snare drum, but they did back Temple with an extended performance of "The Toy Trumpet," which she sings and taps for the big finale. Temple was enthralled by Scott's drummer, and after a rehearsal Johnny Francis showed her how to work the bass drum and cymbals. The film's director, Allan Dwan, thought this was cute and decided to add a moment where his little star joined the band (Figure 2.1). "He ordered a set of traps delivered to the cottage for practice," Temple recalled. "Williams finally had set up my drums in our kitchenette and every noontime thereafter came over to demonstrate some new trick—how to crisscross my arms while drumming or some rapid-fire sequence on cymbals, bell, and wood block. Thumping and clanging was dessert to me, but Mother just got headaches. The more proficient I became, the more she despaired, finally complaining to Dwan that my posture was unladylike, sitting there with legs apart, bouncing around and banging at cymbals."[26] Screenwriters in the neighboring bungalows also complained, so Temple's drum kit was thrown out, along with the sequence. John and Joan loved hanging around the Fox lot. Temple played with Joan and even invited her to the star's birthday party. "She had a little bungalow with a picket fence," John remembered, "where she could stay with her mother and her dresses, and being a child I was more interested in where Shirley Temple's bungalow was than anything else."[27]

In addition to other film appearances, the Raymond Scott Quintette continued to broadcast on CBS's *Saturday Night Swing Club* from a studio in Hollywood. In

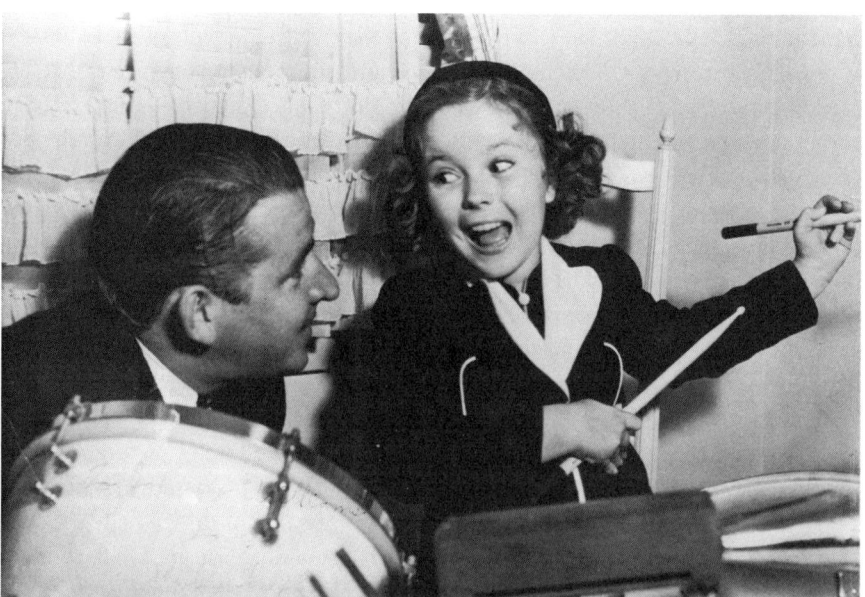

Figure 2.1. Johnny Francis with Shirley Temple during the making of *Rebecca of Sunnybrook Farm*, 1937 (Courtesy of Paula Arlich).

November 1937 they played a tribute to Eddie Cantor, celebrating his 25 years in showbiz, alongside Judy Garland and Jacques Renard's orchestra, for a room full of stars at the Ambassador Hotel. The Quintette was scheduled to perform a live show with Cantor in February 1938, but Johnny Francis was put out of commission when his car was struck from behind and, in the days before seatbelts, the knock to his head put him in a hospital for a day. Scott's band was part of an audition for a new CBS program hosted by Milton Berle, and in the summer of 1938 they also performed on *Hollywood Showcase* out of the Hollywood Hotel every Friday night. (That program was soon replaced by Orson Welles's *Mercury Theatre of the Air*, featuring Bernard Herrmann's orchestra.) Johnny Francis and the Quintette were in Los Angeles for an entire year—long enough to make a lasting impression on John, who turned six during that magical season. But a restless Raymond Scott was all too happy to return to New York in the fall of 1938, and so the Williams family moved back, too. It was a source of some sadness; Esther wanted to stay in L.A.

When they returned to New York, the Quintette played a series of concerts at the Paramount Theatre backed by Mark Warnow's orchestra in their live vaudeville debut. On Christmas Day, 1938, they performed in a massive concert at Carnegie Hall, sharing a bill with Louis Armstrong, Artie Shaw, and other musicians playing music by Duke Ellington, George Gershwin, Richard Rodgers, and Fred Van Eps—a virtuoso banjo player and patriarch of a family of noteworthy musicians. John never cited Scott or his pocket film scores as an influence, but it was Scott who gave John his first taste of movie magic, his first steps on a studio lot. Far more influential, in John's mind, was the *radio*. It was always on, either as background music while his mother washed the dishes, or as appointment entertainment for the whole family. John tuned in to serials like *The Adventures of Superman* and *The Shadow*, which initially starred Orson Welles as the title vigilante; the program used a piece of music by Camille Saint-Saëns for its theme, but was scored with organ music by Rosa Rio and Elsie Thompson, two of the lone women in the music department at CBS. Herrmann's music was also in the airwaves, and John wondered if perhaps the style of descriptive, storytelling movie scoring he later developed came from listening to "stories being told where you couldn't see anything. You had to imagine it. Theater of the mind."[28] Then again, he remembered listening to far more comedy and musical programs than dramas. One composer's name he looked forward to hearing was Edgar "Cookie" Fairchild, a pianist and music director for Eddie Cantor's radio show. "Each week he would do an orchestra number," John said, "and I used to wait for that."*[29]

Most significantly, John absorbed the popular music of his day. He didn't go to classical concerts or listen to much classical music as a child, but he *did* imbibe the songs of Jerome Kern, George Gershwin, Irving Berlin, and Harold Arlen. "If I find myself humming tunes that aren't my own," he said, "it's probably something that I've heard in childhood, some Gershwin melody my mother hummed."[30] His favorite of

---

* Fairchild started scoring films at Universal in the 1940s.

all was Kern, who wrote airborne, reflective songs like "All the Things You Are" and "The Song Is You." The latter is "about as good as an American popular song can be," John said. "The modulatory processes in it—that wonderful climax after the middle section that rises on a halftone back to the tonic where it's not supposed to go at that point." John paid special attention to the greatest melodists and song-crafters of the early 20th century, and it can't be overstated how much his musical genes were modified by these composers: "There's no question that these lyrical songwriters influenced me. I wanted to know their pieces, learn them—which I did."[31]

* * *

John's old neighborhood had been utterly transformed into the "World of Tomorrow" while he was in Los Angeles. Under the direction of Robert Moses, the infamous city planner who utterly remade the city of New York using less-than-democratic means, the fetid ash dump just a mile west of the Williams house on Poplar (Figure 2.2) was converted into the site of the New York World's Fair. This utopian showcase opened on April 30, 1939, and it was symbolized by the Trylon and Perisphere structures, which contained a giant model of the "city of the future." For the next two years, some 44 million people came to the Fair to marvel at feats of futuristic design and be entertained by marionette shows, aquatic extravaganzas, and thrill rides. "I could look out my mother's bedroom window," John said, "and I could see the Trylon and Perisphere being constructed. And to this day, the colors of blue and orange spark me: *these were the colors of the World's Fair*."[32]

Figure 2.2. The Williams house at 143-30 Poplar Avenue, Flushing, Queens (Courtesy of Paula Arlich).

John resumed his elementary education at St. Mary's, where the Sisters of St. Joseph provided a godly education for all the Catholic boys and girls of Flushing. He never forgot the name of his most serious teacher: Sister Varner. He loved the house on Poplar and could still walk through it in his memory for the rest of his life—beginning in the basement, which had an upright piano and an ornate bar that Johnny Francis and Jerry Colonna built by hand, featuring a brass rail and mirrors, an entrance on the side, and plumbing. "He wanted to be an architect," said John. "That was his dream. He was a fantastic woods craftsman." Johnny Francis pursued that dream at one point by taking courses at Columbia University, where he earned high marks in architectural mathematics. The basement also included a shooting range, where Johnny Francis—who made his own bullets—practiced for pistol competitions, which he regularly won. Esther successfully kept her children and guests from wandering into the range when it was in use, and there were never any accidents. On the ground floor was a dining room, kitchen, pantry, and living room where the Williamses entertained their friends, most of whom were musicians. Upstairs were three bedrooms, including John's—and a stairway to an attic. The yard was a great place for John to play baseball, and he could easily hop down to Kissena Park to form a team.[33]

Once Johnny Francis returned to New York, he formed a musical group of his own. He wanted to record 10 singles with the band, and *Variety* reported that he was hiring people to dance during rehearsals: "Williams has a team of shagsters, fox trot duo, and a rhumba pair, hopping to his embryo tempos to help him set proper paces."[34] Billed as "Drummer Man Johnny Williams," he cut a few tracks for the Vocalion label, including "Memory Lane" and "Clarinet Marmalade." That year he also earned the cover spot on *Leedy Drum Topics*—the percussion maker's magazine—which touted him as "one of the finest, and one of the busiest drummers in the country."[35] Johnny Francis was on the verge of breaking out as his own bandleader, building a full-size dance band under manager Ted Collins, booked by the Music Corporation of America (MCA), and landing a deal with Columbia Records.

But marquee stardom never happened. In January 1940, Johnny Francis called off his band rehearsals and shelved recording plans because he was "unable to unearth the caliber of men he wanted," according to *Variety*, which assured that he would pick back up in the summer.[36] Instead, he spent the next 10 years in New York in the rhythm section at CBS, playing on *Your Hit Parade* under Mark Warnow and accompanying singer Kate Smith.

An unlikely sensation, Smith was a plus-sized contralto from Washington, D.C., who went from being mocked for her weight during four years on Broadway to becoming "the undisputed first lady of radio."[37] Thanks to her tireless manager, the aforementioned Ted Collins, Smith found gold in the airwaves, and beginning in 1937 she expanded her reach into America's homes through a musical variety show, the *Kate Smith Hour*, and the daytime talk show *Kate Smith Speaks*, where she dispensed folksy, patriotic wisdom in between selling millions of dollars' worth of cigars, automobiles, and coffee. Smith's largest legacy was her definitive interpretation of "God Bless America," which Irving Berlin wrote just for her (repurposing an old tune). She

Figure 2.3. Joan, Jerry, and John at Rye Beach, summer 1943 (Courtesy of Paula Arlich).

sang it for the first of countless times on her nightly show on November 10, 1938, for an Armistice Day special, and it was quickly adopted as a second national anthem. The first season of the *Kate Smith Hour* introduced America to Bud Abbott and Lou Costello, including their smash act "Who's on First," which launched them to international fame and a successful movie career. Johnny Francis joined in the show's second season, accompanying a parade of celebrity guests including Henny Youngman, Jackie Gleason, Gene Kelly, and dramatic performances by Lee Cobb and Elia Kazan. *Variety* singled out the house band, "a hot ensemble with Johnny Williams to behave a little demented as the head fireman."[38] Johnny Francis's accompanist ethos was captured in a quote he gave to *Radio Mirror* in 1940: "The drum should be a foundation instrument and should be kept in its place and not made the object of annoyance and disturbance as has become the modern habit."[39] *Pinocchio*, Walt Disney's second animated feature film, opened on the eve of John's eighth birthday. The design of the pool hall on Pleasure Island was a playful homage to the Trylon and Perisphere structures at the World's Fair, which did resemble a pool cue and eight ball, and a few weeks earlier Johnny Francis sat in with singer Chick Bullock and a freelance band to record a foxtrot version of the film's big tune, "When You Wish Upon a Star."[40]

* * *

John was now old enough to sit still and keep quiet, so Johnny Francis started bringing his eight-year-old son to rehearsals at the CBS Radio Theatre on Broadway, an enormous venue situated between West 53rd and West 54th Street.† "My fascination with orchestration came from sitting quietly in a corner while the conductor rehearsed," John said. "It became my mission to understand what happened when the bows went up and down, why the brass came in only at certain points, and even why everyone played exactly when they did. On the way home I asked my father many questions, and he gave me one book on music after another."[41]

Johnny Francis fixed John up with his first piano teacher, Jacob Louis Merkur, a member of the CBS band and a composer in his own right. At Merkur's recommendation, they purchased an Altenburg piano. "I struggled with that thing," John said. "At the time I didn't know the Altenburg wasn't very good." Merkur would come to the house and give both John and Joan piano lessons. "My sister was always a better player than I was," John admitted. "We gave our first recital at Steinway Hall in New York City, and I went on second. She was older. She was also more serious."[42] Joan worked more diligently than her younger brother, but she was given far less encouragement—a symptom of this patriarchal age in American culture. "The boys were revered and the women were in the kitchen serving up the men," said Joan's daughter, Paula. "My mom was as gifted as any of them—classically trained, incredible person as far as the talent was there—but unfortunately she didn't get all the kudos." Joan would make a two-hour subway commute for her piano lessons, all by herself, and come all the way home, only to get asked to make dinner.[43] By contrast, after his Saturday morning piano lessons, John was invited to sit in the back of his father's orchestra where he marveled at the French horn and the flute and how they waited minutes at a time for the right moment to make their distinctive sounds. "I was fascinated with the orchestra," he said, "never dreaming I would write music for an orchestra, but having an interest in seeing how people did it. A state of blissful unconsciousness, if you like, that maybe goes with children."[44] The powerful sound, majesty, and seemingly limitless colors of this collective musical body was "the biggest single turn-on. The orchestra became my passion."[45]

Johnny Francis taught his son how to read music, and he actively stoked John's musical curiosity. John began a daily practice on the Altenburg in the living room, but to spare his mother he went down to the jangly upright in the basement when he wanted to play with Jerry—who took after his father on the drums—and neighbor kids who would bring over their brass and wind instruments for jam sessions. A moment of enlightenment came when one neighbor boy brought his trumpet over, and "I began to play the song, and he played, and it was terrible," said John. "My father explained to me, 'Well, a trumpet is in B-flat. It has to be written up a tone.' So he gave me some manuscript paper, and I went up a tone, and we played together.... This was like *Eureka!* What a magical thing to be able to do."[46] To John it felt like a miracle, that "something I had put down with my hand, even though it wasn't my

---

† The theater, built in 1925 by Arthur Hammerstein—uncle of lyricist Oscar Hammerstein II—was home to CBS radio broadcasts and their audiences during this period; it later became a familiar stage on television screens as the famous Ed Sullivan Theater.

own music, made it possible for us to play together. The fun of that, and the sense of discovery that one could adjust, manipulate, arrange music and then have the joy of doing it with someone else was, I think, one of the most profound experiences I had as a young person studying music."[47] Soon John was teaching himself orchestration and arranging. His father's extensive home library included books on composition and counterpoint by Percy Goetschius, a star teacher at the turn of the century.‡ Johnny Francis inscribed a volume on Bach to his son: "From Dad, whose Bach is worse than his bite." There were also books by Arthur Lange and Hector Berlioz, as well as Nikolai Rimsky-Korsakov's highly regarded *Principles of Orchestration*. John would sit in the basement "and pore over orchestration books. I applied Rimsky-Korsakov to the pop tunes of 1940 and 1941."[48]

Perhaps his most important orchestration "teacher" was Claude Thornhill. Friend and former bandmate of Johnny Francis, Thornhill founded his own big band which featured, unusually, French horns and the perfume of French impressionism. His compositions—most famously the piece "Snowfall" from 1941—tended toward the slow and dreamy, and he was a mentor to Gil Evans, who later became an arranger for Miles Davis. (Davis's seminal *Birth of the Cool* album, from 1957, "came from some of the sessions we did trying to sound like Claude Thornhill's band," wrote Davis, who added: "We were trying to sound like Claude Thornhill, but he had gotten his shit from Duke Ellington and Fletcher Henderson."[49]) When Thornhill enlisted in the Navy in 1942, where his band played in the Pacific Theater, he left all of his clothes and belongings in trunks that were stored in the Williams's attic, which is where John discovered a trove of Thornhill's handwritten scores. "One of the pieces there, with his delicate handwriting, was 'Name It and You Can Have It.'" John would sit in the attic and pore over these scores, and the cool seeped in. "If I have any reference to anybody," he said, "it would be Claude Thornhill—not Debussy. The use of French horns and so on has always been a big part of what my idea of orchestration should have been."[50]

And though he would always claim to be apathetic about film, John did develop a brief movie habit during his golden childhood. Loew's Prospect Theatre was a huge, single-screen movie palace at 41-10 Main Street in downtown Flushing, built in 1928 originally as a home for vaudeville. He would go almost weekly with his sister or his friends—and mostly he was listening to the music. "I might have developed some sort of sense," he admitted, "some sort of intuitive sympathy." The names of these films slipped from his memory, but "I remember being very, very moved by one or two war films, with these guys machine gunning. These were frightening things, but very compelling."[51]

* * *

The war played an outsized part in John's boyhood. It was a seminal experience that helped shape his pure love of country and respect for the military. "I was ten through

---

‡ Goetschius was to harmony, Richard Rodgers said, what Henry Gray was to anatomy. (Meryle Secrest, *Somewhere for Me: A Biography of Richard Rodgers* [2001]).

thirteen in the years of the war," he said, "and I remember the 18-year-olds all being drafted out of our neighborhood, and watched the progress of the armies and the navies all through the war. It was the most dramatic event in my young life. And of course I remember the music, and of course I remember the country's spirit at the time. And how, in my young mind, the effort really defined who we were at that point, completely, 24 hours a day. It was our mission to complete this, get through this difficulty."[52] Esther, whom John affectionately called "Duck," volunteered the side garden in the lot next to their house and enlisted her son in the war effort. "My mother and I had a victory garden," said John, "where we grew tomatoes and string beans by the ton, bushels of them. And then she, with a pressure cooker, stored them all for the winter's use and gave them to neighbors. She turned out to be a good farmer, and I was her assistant."[53]

Johnny Francis was too old to fight, but he accompanied Kate Smith as she sold war bonds and fanned patriotic fervor, and he also put his expert marksmanship to use by driving down to Quantico in Virginia and training Marines how to shoot .45 Colt handguns. During the war years he played on many other CBS shows, but the most prominent was *Your Hit Parade*—a hugely popular Saturday night roundup of the moment's top songs, arranged for a big band of 45 musicians and conducted by Mark Warnow. Sponsored by Lucky Strike cigarettes—which liberally gifted unlimited packs to the musicians—these hits were determined through a survey conducted by the American Tobacco Company and the Lord & Thomas advertising agency.[54] The program hosted many celebrity vocalists, including two of John's future collaborators: Frank Sinatra and lyricist Johnny Mercer.

As a boy, John loved the book *Johnny Tremain*. Written in 1943 by a New England woman, it told the coming-of-age story of a boy named Johnny who lives in Boston during the Revolutionary War and interacts with many of the heroes from that period. "I read it over and over again," John said (Figure 2.3).[55] He turned 13 in 1945, and a few months later the war ended. That summer was a rite of passage that permanently rewired his worldview:

> I was awakened in 1945 by two things. The pictures of the Holocaust. We had no idea: what the hell is this? All these living corpses, and *piles* of corpses. I'm looking at this thing, I'm 13 years old. And the same week or two later comes the atomic bomb—which scared everybody to death. And the two or three or four years that followed that, I looked and I could see not only these horrible things, but that the United States was sitting on the very top of the whole world. It was a Gemini beyond anything you could possibly imagine. It was the only currency in the world worth anything.[56]

In February 1946, John enrolled at Bishop Loughlin Memorial High School, an institution with roots dating back to 1851, where most of the faculty were religious brothers. "My parents wanted me to go to Fordham, and that was the route to it," John said of the famed Catholic university in the Bronx. "So I had a very short exposure to the beginnings of a real Jesuit education—which I never got. Which may be a good thing, I don't know." The high school was located at 357 Clermont Avenue in Brooklyn, which required two subway rides from his house on Long Island and back, and John would always get home late at night.[57] He only attended the school for a single semester, but he received good marks; his lowest grade was in music.[58]

Then Johnny Francis suddenly decided to open a gift shop in Floral Park, six miles east of Flushing, that sold greeting cards and records. He sold the house on Poplar for $12,000, and in September he moved his family into an apartment behind the store at 255-05 Hillside Avenue. (Jerry Colonna attended the grand opening and signed autographs.[59]) This sudden move was motivated by the war being over, said John: "I think he felt that his work in radio was being reduced by the waves of young musicians coming out of the service. He felt that his future was a little less secure than he would like. I think that was a very, very tough decision for him. He was very worried, financially."[60] John transferred to nearby Jamaica High, his Jesuit days abruptly halted.

Esther enjoyed running the store, but it was a fleeting venture. *Your Hit Parade*, under pressure from its new vocal star, Andy Russell, relocated to Los Angeles that November—and Johnny Francis decided to move with it.[61] In the spring of 1947, he put all his drums in the back of his small Jeep and drove from New York to Hollywood. "I'd never seen such beautiful country," said John, his only passenger. "The brand new Pennsylvania Turnpike, and into Illinois and Ohio, down to Arkansas and out to Oklahoma. See the oil wells and that vast space of the West—day after day of this. Spotting Tucumcari in New Mexico and guessing how far it was from the car. I would say 'five miles,' and he'd say, 'No, it's probably more like 75 or 100 miles.'" Those five days in the car with his father stayed with John for the rest of his life. He paid attention to all of the young GIs, freshly back from the war and working as attendants at gas stations, converting their Army shirts into work shirts simply by removing the chevrons. John saw an old Black man sitting in a broken-down train station in the middle of Iowa, strumming and slapping an out-of-tune steel-front guitar:

> It was the era of hobos, the era of old guitar players sitting out in the woods entertaining themselves, and the era of vast, empty spaces—some of them kind of dirty, the old trains going. It wasn't the Madison Avenue country of the USA that I knew. And now I carry all that nostalgia with me for a period that, at the time, I certainly didn't understand. In a child's eye, what does patriotism mean? Well, "buy war bonds," or "contribute your worn-out pencils" or whatever—the way a 10-year-old would think about it.

When they entered California, he saw an enormous date farm that "looked like I imagined Egypt must have been—an oriental world of light." John's vision of America was a country endlessly stretching and on top of the world. He admittedly had never heard of Jim Crow at this point in his life; all he saw was optimism and togetherness, an arm-linked march into a future pregnant with potential. His patriotism was forever shot through with the *nostalgia*—"laundered memory"—that he felt for this period in his and his country's life.

Also on this road trip, John's father played the part of teacher and wise mentor. Johnny Francis always had a didactic impulse, and would take young drummers under his wing and give them advice. Now he was strongly encouraging his 15-year-old son to give up the trombone and focus seriously on piano. "He talked about and almost nothing less than: I have to read, and I have to practice the piano eight hours a day, the way he did with his instruments when he was younger. And, actually, I wasn't *awake* yet. But he began to probe and poke and repeat all the ideas that a father, a good father at that time, would do."[62]

Johnny Francis Williams, a largely self-taught drummer who climbed his way from the backwoods of Maine to playing with the major dance bands of the 1920s and then to the heights of popular recording and national radio in New York, was taking the next big leap in his career. He was moving to the recording stages of Los Angeles, and he was about to enter the world of Hollywood film music as a session player. "My father, I must say, was an extraordinary creature," said John. "Disappointed greatly. Had a very difficult time. But quite astonishing abilities, on little or no education. An avid reader. Student of French. He did so many interesting things."[63]

One thing the old man never did was *compose* music. But he did offer his teenage son a kernel of wisdom: "He once advised me to 'Write it down before you forget it. *It may be better than you think*.'"[64]

* * *

The odd thing about the world's most famous movie composer is that John Williams never really cared about movies. He grew up in an era where there was no television set in the house, and as he bluntly put it, "I was never particularly a fan of movies."[65] But the movies loved *him*, and had a kind of tractor beam pull on his talents. Having tasted a drop of the motion picture business as a child, John suddenly found himself living in its backyard as a teenager, with his father's professional life converging on cinema. John never pursued Hollywood ... but Hollywood grabbed him and wouldn't let him go.

Johnny Francis's move from New York to the West Coast represented an industry shift. He came out to Los Angeles with *Your Hit Parade*, but the days of radio orchestras were on the wane. Mark Warnow died suddenly of a heart attack in October 1949, the day after conducting his 493rd episode of the show, and Raymond Scott took over its full transition to television and back to New York.[66] Suddenly unmoored in Southern California, and with many of his friends playing on film scores, Johnny Francis was approached with an offer from the house conductor at Columbia Pictures and soon found himself in the staff orchestra at a minor movie studio that was on the cusp of major success. Within a few years he was playing percussion on the scores for *All the King's Men*, *From Here to Eternity*, and *On the Waterfront*. He was now in the orbit of musicians and composers for films and television, many of whom became good family friends.

The Williams family settled in North Hollywood, purchasing a small, two-bedroom house with a detached garage at 5259 Vantage Avenue. Joan, unhappily uprooted in her senior year of high school, got the second bedroom; John was her date at the senior prom. Johnny Francis converted the detached garage into a studio apartment for John and Jerry—which immediately became both dorm and music studio. Once the lonely frontier town of Toluca, North Hollywood was the home of Universal Pictures—located just a few miles south of the Williams house—and also home to many movie and recording stars. During the war years it was one of the fastest-growing cities in the United States: the Lockheed Corporation in adjacent Burbank produced fleets of war planes, and many of its 50,000 employees bought houses in North Hollywood. The surge in car traffic required a massive highway extension through the Cahuenga Pass, and when the war ended, veterans came home to the city by the thousands—the population boom actually caused the city's Chamber of Commerce to discourage further growth.[67] Houses were in short supply, and Lankershim Boulevard and the Cahuenga Freeway were clogged with vehicles. When John's family arrived, teenagers were wrecking their cars in staggering numbers, and the parents of North Hollywood petitioned their high school to offer driving lessons.[68]

John was 15, and he looked the perfect hybrid of his mother and father. His hair was red and curly, a gift from his Irish ancestors. His bright face was a long oval with a prominent chin, handsome and just a little feminine, with plump lips casing an easy smile. He transferred as a sophomore to North Hollywood High School, located just a few blocks east from his new house. In the New York school system John had been in the "third grade," the first year of high school being grades 1 and 2 and the second year grades 3 and 4. "So I went to the admissions office at North Hollywood, and the woman said to me, 'What grade are you in?' I said, 'The third grade,' and of course all the kids had a little joke about that. I didn't know what they were laughing at."[69]

John jumped in the best way he knew how, by joining the school orchestra. His favored instrument was still the trombone—inspired by ace bandleaders and arrangers like Tommy Dorsey and Nelson Riddle. Before the move from New York, his father had set him up with a teacher named Robert Paolucci, an esteemed trombonist in the CBS orchestra, and in California John studied with Bill Atkinson, a prominent freelancer and principal trombone player in Alfred Newman's orchestra at Twentieth Century Fox. So John played trombone in the North Hollywood High orchestra, accompanying the fall play, graduation, and other occasions in an ensemble that also included Susan Sontag—future prize-winning commentator on American society. "Sue" was also in one of John's favorite non-musical classes, Civics, and "she spoke more than the teacher," he said.[70] Sontag edited the school newspaper before graduating early at 15, and she later painted a highly critical portrait of North Hollywood High: an intellectual desert where used condoms littered the lawn, Christian students led boycotts against the biology textbook, and the 11th grade English teacher assigned copies of *Reader's Digest* while she knitted at her desk.[71] Sontag told the latter story often, and when a former physical education teacher read about it in an *L.A. Times* article in the 1990s, the teacher responded with a letter to the editor: "She was a supercilious student, and it seems that she hasn't changed. North Hollywood was academically good then. Many of the students' families were movie industry professionals; others were talented musicians. The music department put on quite professional concerts, seasonal programs and musicals.... It's hard to make valid judgments when you're busy looking down your nose and sneering."[72]

Indeed, the school's nickname was "Bingville," owing to Bing Crosby's warm relationship from when he lived in the neighborhood from 1936 to 1943; the singer would drop by with a cigar and watch students rehearse. The school "had a very stout theatrical department," said Richard Hein, John's classmate who starred in their sophomore-year production of Sigmund Romberg's operetta *The New Moon* and the next year's production of Gilbert and Sullivan's *The Mikado*.[73] The school was stuffed with talent—it would soon produce both *West Side Story* stars Russ Tamblyn and Richard Beymer—not surprising, considering its proximity to the film and music factories and the profession of many of the students' parents. John's closest friends were all musicians: Perry Botkin, Jr., who was the son of Bing Crosby's guitar player; Gene Estes, whose father, "Ace" Estes, was a professional drummer; and Don Ingle, son of musical comedian "Red" Ingle, who played saxophone with Spike Jones. Several future actors were also on campus, including Martin Milner (*Route 66*), Susan Morrow (*Cat-Women of the Moon*), and Barbara Ruick—daughter of the bandleader-actor Mel Ruick and Lurene Tuttle, a popular character actress who was once considered "The First Lady of Radio."[74] Ruick and Tuttle were divorced, and Barbara was living with her mother in nearby Studio City. A natural performer from birth, she was as extroverted and involved in high school society as John *wasn't*: she was a member of the Vagabonds sorority and the Treble Clef singing club, acted in plays and skits, and sang every chance she got. Barbara also loved the drums.

John enjoyed French class, and his dad helped him get through math "like a breeze"—but he didn't really get involved in campus life. "He just wasn't a joiner from what I could surmise," said classmate Vince Piazza. All the boys in the class of 1950 wore either white dress shirts or T-shirts and Levi's jeans, Piazza said, "and you always tried to rip off the guy's red tag on those Levi's."[75] Nicknames were a big thing. Botkin came to high school already saddled with "Bunny" since he was born on Easter Sunday. "I could have killed my parents for having named me that," Botkin said. "All the way through high school I guarded against that name. Oh Jesus, I hated that."[76] John's new friends took to calling him "Curly" because of his hair; the name stuck, and he adopted it as a stage moniker.

John attended his very first symphonic concert in January 1948. The Los Angeles Philharmonic performed three nights under guest conductor Charles Munch, a star in France who was making waves in America. (He became music director of the Boston Symphony in 1949.) At the Philharmonic Auditorium in downtown L.A., Munch guided the local orchestra through Gabriel Fauré's suite of incidental music from *Pelléas et Mélisande*, Arthur Honegger's new Symphony no. 2, and César Franck's Symphony in D minor.[77] John had composed "little pieces" as a child, but now he was beginning to orchestrate his own music. "I didn't have an idea in my mind until well into my teenage years that one could be a composer professionally," he insisted.[78] Applying the skills he had taught himself, John wrote arrangements for some of the school orchestra's productions, and he also occasionally conducted. "The whole time I wondered how I could get better at doing both, so I bought books and read a lot to find out."[79] He continued to play trombone in the school band during his junior year, pepping up sporting events; he also learned the rudiments on trumpet, clarinet, bassoon, and tuba. But his father kept nudging him toward the piano, arguing that it would be much better for his writing and overall musicianship. Like most kids his age, John loved jazz—but he also began entertaining the idea of becoming a serious concert pianist. "Late in life, really, for an idea like this," he thought.[80] He started taking lessons with Sara Compinsky, a Russian-born pianist who had a popular trio with her siblings, Manuel and Alec. Compinsky would make tea with a samovar, a Russian metal contraption that boils water, and her piano lessons were gentle. "You'd play something you know pretty well, *she* would play it, and you would see an interpretive breadth that a kid my age certainly wouldn't have had."[81]

Far more significantly, he studied piano with Robert "Bobby" Van Eps, whose famous musical family knew Johnny Francis from New York.[§] Van Eps was a classically trained pianist, composer, and conductor who toured with the Dorsey brothers before moving to Los Angeles in the 1930s—where he wrote concert works but earned his living in the music department at MGM playing piano and arranging. (His eclectic interests also included audio engineering, and he invented a special phonograph tone arm that eliminated tracking distortion.[82]) He even wrote a piano concerto which he sent to Vladimir Horowitz, "who never played it, but he said he admired it," said John. "Very romantic, almost Chopinesque." A respected teacher, Van Eps later poured his expertise into an original textbook, *The Physics of Piano Technique*, which he self-published in 1954.

"The truly great performer is given to the world only when Mother Nature sees fit to endow a single human being with talent, industry, and intellect—all three, and each in generous measure," Van Eps wrote in his introduction. "It is not mechanics, but talent and intellect which defy precise appraisal and may perhaps be classified as mysteries. This is why we often hear it said that musicians are born, not made. Be that as it may, one point is certain: industry, born of the will to conquer, makes up, many times over, for lack of talent."[83] His idiosyncratic technique was based on the laws of physics, and because of that he had a completely unorthodox approach to the keyboard, fingers, and scales. In his mind, the "assets" of the human hand—short fingers and long fingers and a thumb that sits lower on its own axis—are matched with the "liabilities" of the keyboard—long levers and short levers, white keys extending below black keys—like a jigsaw puzzle. This is why, to Van Eps, the C major scale is the most difficult to play.

"It's very true," John agreed.

---

§ Fred Van Eps, Jr., Bobby's brother, was an arranger who worked on *Your Hit Parade*, and another brother, George, was a renowned jazz guitarist.

For hundreds of years, billions of piano students have been taught that middle C is the center of the piano keyboard, but Van Eps trained John to see that, in fact, *D* is the true center—"because you have to see C sharp and E flat as being a pair, with the center in the middle of the pair." It was a totally different orientation to the instrument, but it conformed Mother Nature's design to the clavier's, and allowed for better mirroring between the two hands, more fluid motion up and down the keyboard. "Original, as far as I know," said John. "He was kind of a nerd—but right, actually. The hands knew better—this one what was happening here, a mirror of this one going up at the same time. Has to be two keys. If it's two sharps going up, it's two flats going down. If it's four flats going up, it's four sharps going down. That's not the way people teach the piano, that I've ever heard of—but it's wonderfully efficient."[84]

* * *

In his first year at North Hollywood High, John's trombone was recruited by The Starlighters—a 15-piece big band composed of current students and alumni, founded by Ernie Star, a recent graduate and, in John's mind, a "near professional kid." In February 1948 they were crowned "Most Professional" at an area battle of the bands. Barbara sang with the band, and she and John quickly became best friends, inseparable. "I was in love with Barbara, I think, at age 15," said John. And who could blame him? She was cute, bubbly, funny, outgoing, and a great singer. "All of our adult friends expected us to be living life together," he said. "And I think both of us would have agreed with that."[85] It was Barbara who inspired John's first foray beyond mere *interpretation* and into musical *invention*:

> I would go to her house and I would improvise on the piano. She would ask me to do a "portrait" of Orson Welles, or a portrait of Mickey Mouse, or a portrait of her Uncle Walter or Uncle Norman, the doctor. What's the difference between Walter and the doctor? Well, Walter's a drinker, and the doctor's a wonderful surgeon. That was a game that we played, and I had no preparation for it at all.[86]

John soon left the Starlighters and the school band and started his own combo (Figure 2.4), switching to the piano and betraying a latent desire to lead. "When it began to look more like a rut than a groove, 17-year-old Piano Player Johnny ('Curley') Williams (named after his drummer father) broke away and formed his own quintet," *Time* magazine reported in October 1949, in the first national article about our John Williams. It listed his bandmates as Sidney (Mel) Pollen, "a bullfiddle slapper like his dad, Al Pollen," Botkin, Estes, and Ingle, and included several colorful quotes: "'Boy,' says Curley, 'we yanked the nucleus right out of that Hollywood High band.' As Curley, the boss of the juvenile jazzbos, puts it, 'We were pretty rough at first—everybody fighting for their own salad.' Now, when they play together, they like to 'get casual.'" When John read the article, he was perplexed. "A total misquote," he said. "*Where did this come from?*"

But jazz and its hepcat lingo *were* part of John's vocabulary; he continued to call musicians and friends "baby" and "angel" throughout his life. And he leaned into

CURLEY WILLIAMS (LEFT) & BAND
A fight for the salad.

Figure 2.4. John and his high school combo (*TIME*, October 31, 1949).

the persona of "Curly" (as it was normally spelled), tickling the ivories with his new band at school functions and growing in fame on campus. In April 1949, Curly Williams was the school paper's Personality of the Week: "His father is a musician and has been a great musical influence on him," *The Arcade* reported. "Curly appears to be a very ambitious boy as he claims to practice the piano four hours every day.... After graduating from high school, Curly plans on attending UCLA and majoring in music. He would like to go on the road after college and look around for opportunities. Curly Williams, our personality of the week, is very interested in his career, and he has the talent to go ahead."[87] The band's fame outgrew the pages of the *Arcade* when they helped launch the Dri-Nite Club, a teens-only joint instituted in the spring of 1949 by the Van Nuys Optimists (a do-gooder organization that sponsored Boy Scout troops and baseball teams). The Optimists renovated a run-down building on Gilmore Street in Van Nuys, leased from the Los Angeles Board of Education, and hosted a hundred teenagers there every Saturday night from 8 to 11:30 p.m. "The music is as hot as they like. The floor show completely their own. There's plenty to drink at the bar," the *Los Angeles Mirror* reported. "The newest version of the newest dance gets a tryout. The wallflowers don't last very long. The price of admission is no strain—it's only half a buck.... You see, the club presents all the fun of nightclubbing without the big tab—or hangover. The bar serves only soft drinks, the music is by Curly Williams's North Hollywood high school band, and the floor show talent comes from among those present."⁸⁸ The club attracted a "high type of teenager," as one of the grownups in charge put it. "The young people are always neat and well-behaved," another chaperone bragged. "To encourage this, we do not admit boys who wear jeans or other work clothes. It is only fair to the girls that they dress suitably on Saturday nights."⁸⁹ The scene was way too square for *some* teens. "I never made it to the Dri-Nite Club," Vince Piazza said drily. "I was too busy drinking beer at the Victory Drive-In theater."⁹⁰

Barbara emceed the programs and acted in skits, and Curly and his combo accompanied her vocal group, the Melodairs. (She was also the band's banker.) During their senior year the shows were broadcast twice a week on the Valley radio station KGIL in a program called *Teen Time*. As hostess, Barbara introduced "celebrity guests," including 1949's Miss Burbank: Debbie Reynolds. "At that time Debbie wanted to be a gym teacher, and she thought me a bit wild because I sang with a band," Barbara said.⁹¹ (The two became friends.) In addition to hosting slightly more *humble* teen talents, like "Julie Tait and her dancing dog," the young performers also called on their famous parents and friends. Johnny Francis and Jerry Colonna surprised a record crowd in July 1949, sitting in with Curly and the Melodairs. By October, Curly's band was noteworthy enough to attract that attention from *Time*:

> Last week, devoutly following in their fathers' solid-beat footsteps, the famous sons' five were the hottest band in Hollywood. They were playing only three nights a week; schoolwork kept them from doing more. Since July they had been packing fans into Van Nuys' elaborate teenagers' Ciro's, the Dri-Nite Club, and making more than pocket money doing it (about $45 a week). By last week, they had spread out to playing one-nighters here & there, for fraternity dances and Hollywood highlifers such as Columnist Jimmy Fidler. But the surest sign that they were really arriving was the hushed way the fans listened when the boys sat in with jazzbos like Drummer Zutty Singleton out at the Club 47, a Ventura Boulevard bistro where the best of Hollywood's radio and movie musicians go after work to jam.⁹²

Curly's combo, almost always with Barbara, played everything from a square dance in Glendale to a Yom Kippur dance at the West Valley Hebrew Center in Reseda to a polio drive at the Valley March of Dimes in Sherman Oaks. In March they supplied music for a St. Patrick's Day Dance in Reseda, where Desi Arnaz and Lucille Ball provided entertainment. All the while John was writing charts for his band, "always noodling around," and gaining invaluable experience as both a public performer and arranger.

* * *

To understand John Williams as a composer, one first has to appreciate him as an *arranger*. "I did more arranging than composing early on," he said. "For me, it seemed like a very natural thing."⁹³ Conductor Leonard Slatkin, a longtime friend, said he did the same thing in high school: "A lot of us get our chops when we're young by doing that—especially if we have a bit of jazz in our background somewhere." Arranging allows a budding composer "to stretch your wings a little bit," Slatkin said. "You can't change the melody—of course not—and you can't change the words. But what you *can* change are the harmonies that go under it, and the colors if you're using other instruments. That's one of the ways you learn to find your voice."[94] Alex Ross, classical music critic for the *New Yorker*, agreed there can be a hugely inventive element to arranging: "The song is basically there, and you recognize the chord changes, but then there are these inflections and shadings and nuances that are brought into it." Ross noted that, by absorbing the Great American Songbook and jazz repertoire of the day, John was actually receiving a great education in the nuances of 20th-century harmony,

> whether or not he was sitting down and studying Bartok as such, or Debussy, or Prokofiev. Because that language had spread so far and wide, and those composers had also learned from popular traditions and folk traditions. So he didn't seem to lose much from not having that sustained kind of study of classical composition from a very early age, because he was learning the craft anyway.
>
> Arrangement can be a very rich creative craft in itself, because of the enriching of harmony, and the use of orchestration—not just to create atmosphere, but *in* the orchestration you introduce variations and echoes of the motifs that are being heard on the top line, the melodic line, and that adds a lot of *depth of field* to the listening experience.[95]

John was listening intently to other arrangers. "From 1910 to 1950 there was this arc of American genius," he said, and it was musical minds such as Cole Porter, George Gershwin, Irving Berlin, and Conrad Salinger "who created the other part of this arc." As an example, John cited the 10-minute arrangement of the Porter song "Begin the Beguine" as arranged by Eddie Powell for the film *Broadway Melody of 1940*. "'Begin the Beguine' is a great piece," John said, "but *this* is an extended masterpiece."[96] In high school John heard the work of other great orchestrators at his infrequent trips to the movies—he praised the penmanship of Albert Sendrey and Murray Cutter, Leo Arnaud, and Robert Franklyn. "My fellow young music students that I used to go to these movies with thought, as I did, that the MGM musical was so much better achieved than Warner Bros. and 20th Century Fox."[97] One of the all-time great pop music arrangers had come to Hollywood around the same time as the Williams family. The year 1946 saw the disbanding of many famous big bands, the result of a postwar dip in interest, and a whole army of "carpetbagger" players migrated to the West Coast studios for work. Among them was Nelson Riddle, best known for his impressionistic, silky beds for Frank Sinatra. Riddle took a job at NBC in April 1947, and Johnny Francis was so impressed with the arrangements Riddle wrote for *Your Hit Parade* that he made sure to introduce Riddle to his teenage son. At this point John was on a trajectory that could have made *him* the next Nelson Riddle, still a viable path.

* * *

By sixteen, John's piano was so good that his father took him along to the music stage at Columbia Pictures, located in "Gower Gulch" at the corner of Sunset Boulevard and North Gower Street, where select members of the studio orchestra had formed a casual "kicks" band (as in, *not for work, just for kicks*) that played jazz and dance music on Wednesday nights. The staff pianist, George Greeley, wasn't interested, so "I would go and kibitz," John said.[98] His social life, such as it was, consisted entirely of music. "As far as going to the beach or bowling or something... no," said brother Jerry. "His recreation, his fun and everything else was always music. If he was going to go out—and we did—we would go to hear a group." John took Jerry to hear jazz pianist Oscar Peterson at Sardi's, the popular nightclub on Hollywood Boulevard, and trumpeter Harry James and his big band at the Palladium on Sunset Boulevard, "because Dad knew a lot of the players in the band," Jerry said.[99] Perry Botkin, Jr., remembered teenage John as someone who "wasn't having a whoop-de-doo time. He was really serious about what he was doing." Did he have any interests *other* than music? "Yeah," Botkin answered, "*girls*. That was it. Otherwise it was all music."[100]

When Barbara ran for the student office of safety commissioner in the spring of 1949, an effusive petition ran in *The Arcade*: "Whatta gal! Whatta gal! Those are the only words that I can think of to describe Barbara Ruick. She is the type of girl who has a marvelous, wonderful, great, super, colossal, personality. She is always smiling, cheerful, and helpful."[101] The ad was signed: *Curly Williams, Campaign Manager*. Curly's band played the Sadie Hawkins Dance in November of his last semester, and the school promoted the lead-up as "Beaver Week"—a gimmick that culminated with a prize given to the boy with the most "novel" beard. "Curly, after many weeks of bitter experimentation, discovered he was not the type for a natural beard," the *Arcade* reported in a tone of teenage wit. "Out of pure sympathy, the *Arcade* Staff obtained one for him and featured him as Beaver of the Week" (Figure 2.5).[102]

To Bobby Van Eps, John's affection for Barbara was an obstacle. When John began taking piano lessons with Van Eps, the teacher said he would need to practice four hours every single day if he wanted to be great. Young, serious, and already obsessed with excellence, John heeded his advice. "So here's 'Curly Williams' at daytime in high school," John said, who then was "a nerd at home for four hours before he went to bed, catching up with Chopin, Rachmaninoff, Bach, and Beethoven, and whatever I had to do—and killing myself to learn how." But John was more than merely a *nerd*: he was a virtuoso of self-motivation, insatiably curious for more and more knowledge and skill. One of Van Eps's methods for improving sightreading was for John to tie a bedsheet around his neck like a bib and drape it over the keyboard so it was no longer visible. His lessons at Van Eps's house in Glendale were only supposed to be an hour:

> So I would go there at whatever time of day... and I'd be there all day. We'd have the piano lesson, and then he would play for me, talk to me, and so on, and then he would take me to the kitchen table where he was orchestrating something for some film. And I'd sit there, and he would take me to the piano and show me what he was doing—like a mentor and a teacher and a father all together.
>
> He really didn't want me to marry Barbara. He was completely against it. He didn't want me to do anything but study. He said, "You can be a great pianist. You can be a great musician. Why do you do this? Why do you do that? It's beneath your talent." I wasn't flattered by it, because I hardly knew what he was saying. I said,

Figure 2.5. "Beaver of the Week" (*The Arcade*, November 18, 1949) (Courtesy of North Hollywood High School).

"How could my marrying her hurt my piano career?" Well, he was right, of course. If I did, I wouldn't study anymore. It would be an entirely different mindset. Actually, I really think I would have been more uncomfortable if I'd done exactly what he wanted me to do, but that was his wish.[103]

Really, Van Eps was training John like an Olympic athlete. *"What are you eating? How much exercise do you get? You're practicing too much—you hurt your hand here."* John wanted to please this musical father, and he was equally motivated by his real father's expectations of discipline and a fear of disapproving his old man. He cooped himself up in the garage studio day in and day out in order to master his instrument, which his brothers remembered with amusement. (Donald Joseph Williams, John's youngest brother, was born on April 27, 1948—a bit of a surprise addition to the Williams clan after a prolonged fermata. He, too, took up the drums.) "I'd say, 'Well, let's go out and get something,'" Jerry said. "*Yeah, as soon as I finish this, I'll be right there.* Mom would call him for dinner. *Yeah, I'll be right there—I just have to finish this one thing.*"[104] John was *such* a slave to practice that his mother began to worry about his health. "It is daunting," John admitted. "It does get to the point where it becomes work and not fun anymore. And if you want to get ahead here, you have to spend so much time at it. Train your body like an athlete to do all this stuff, and your mind to be able to sight read and do all the things you have to do."[105] Van Eps later said John was the most serious student he ever had.[106]

John's teacher was especially fascinated with fugues and counterpoint, and he wrote beautiful fugues himself. "We examined Bach a lot for piano playing," John said. "But he was very, very focused on contrapuntal aspects and writing contrapuntally. He was a real *craftsman*. He thought of music as *engineering*, almost, as some of the earlier practitioners may have." John's own contrapuntal skills were awakened—the magical dance between different melodic lines—and he also absorbed lessons in orchestration and arranging from Van Eps while the teacher plugged away at his side job with MGM. Many of these lessons included things John already knew "because I'd been in those books since I was 14 years old," he said. "But this was a living demonstration by somebody who was willing to talk about it verbally and share it with me. 'This is too thick. Don't do this.' He would orchestrate beautifully for strings." Looking back, John said, "90 percent of what I know about music I owe to Van Eps. The other 10 percent, certainly maybe more than that, would be to my father who actually taught me to read music." John started to dream that he might actually pursue a career as a concert pianist; Van Eps saw his remarkable talent and drove him as hard as he did because he believed it was within John's grasp. "I think I loved him," John said. "And I understood from my father that I needed the discipline if I was going to survive as a pianist—or as anything. So I had, I guess, responsibility. It's like someone who's going to study medicine. There's only one way to do it, and that is: *do the work.*"[107]

* * *

John graduated from high school in February 1950 with the Winter class (each class at North Hollywood High was divided into two seasons), although he continued to perform at school events with members of his combo. He had actually taken on a few piano students of his own—among them a boy named Gil Garfield, whose father owned a chain of drug stores in Los Angeles. "A marvelously gifted kid," John said. But Garfield couldn't write music, so when he came up with songs and lyrics for an original musical called *Raise the Roof,* John wrote out the songs, arranged them for the school orchestra, and conducted the production—which also starred Barbara— in the Bingville auditorium.**[108] All of this while John was now a freshman at the

---

** After high school, Garfield teamed up with his classmate Bert Convy to form The Cheers, a doo-wop group that had hits with the songs "I Need Your Lovin (Bazoom)" and "Black Denim Trousers and Motorcycle Boots."

University of California Los Angeles (UCLA), a picturesque campus in Westwood on the city's west side, where he studied harmony, theory, and composition.[109] He continued to perform as "Curly Williams" at UCLA school dances, and he also joined the school's Reserve Officers' Training Corps (ROTC). Barbara was crowned queen at North Hollywood High's annual Spring Festival and she graduated in June near the top of her class. Instead of college, Barbara enrolled in the TV variety show *College Bowl*, a new ABC production filmed in New York and led by Chico Marx. When she arrived on the East Coast, she wrote a letter to her high school friend, Richard Hein: "I learned one thing, and that is when you're going to interview with Chico Marx you better prepare to keep your legs crossed."[110] In Manhattan she shared an apartment with several young women, including actress Tippi Hedren.[111] John transferred to Los Angeles City College (LACC) for the fall semester, where he took more music classes, but his formal education was in jeopardy. The Korean War was heating up, and both UCLA and LACC featured robust debates about the draft in their student newspapers; 6 percent of City College's student body dropped out during the fall semester to join the military.

At 18, John composed his first "serious" piece of music: a Prokofiev-inspired piano sonata which "was never a sonata," he admitted.[112] He became enamored of the Soviet greats around this time, particularly Shostakovich. The first person he ever played it for was Claude Thornhill, who had moved to Los Angeles to try his hand at film scoring. John was giving serious thought to becoming a concert pianist, already dreaming of studying with the country's premier teacher: Madame Rosina Lhévinne at the Juilliard School. But Uncle Sam had other plans. When John received his draft notice, "it was frightening," he said.[113] Conscription was imminent, and he was faced with a dilemma: as an ROTC cadet, John *could* choose to finish his undergraduate degree, then serve two years active duty, followed by six years reserve in the military—or he could *enlist* and only serve four, avoid combat in the safety of the band program, and resume his musical education at age 23. He decided to enlist. As he was departing, he was given a cigarette lighter inscribed from his friends in "the Columbia Pictures Dance Band," which he carried in his pocket for the next four years.[114]

In January 1951, just before his 19th birthday, he headed to Texas for basic training. His hometown paper published an announcement: "A former band musician, he will play in the Air Force band."[115]

3
Leaving Home, 1951–1956

I wanted to play Rachmaninoff with the New York Philharmonic.
—John Williams, 1980[1]

A torrent of teenagers enlisted in the Air Force in 1950. North Korea invaded South Korea that June, igniting a conflict known in the United States plainly as the Korean War. As allies of the southern nation and vehement anti-communists, the U.S. joined the fray in July, and throughout John's short time in college the newspapers were preoccupied with the action. "If ever we were unprepared for a war, we were on this occasion," said General Matthew Ridgway, commander of the U.S. Eighth Army in Korea. "Our armed forces had been economized into ineffectiveness." The Air Force had become a much smaller and sleepier body after World War II—before the Korean War commenced, the branch had less than half a million people in uniform. Suddenly they needed twice as many. Several bases across the country were used for basic training, but the "Gateway to the Air Force" was Lackland Air Force Base (AFB) in San Antonio, Texas. Opened in the final days of World War II, Lackland admitted women for the first time in October 1948, and eight months later integrated Black members into its regular units. The quiet base was jolted awake in the summer of 1950, and it could barely handle the thousands of new recruits flooding into San Antonio. When China joined its communist brethren in North Korea in November, the Air Force took the cap off its recruiting quota and the bottle exploded.[2] The universal draft was still in effect and was rumored to start ramping up; young people like John were eager to join the fight on their own terms. By enlisting, he could elect to join the band program and stay out of harm's way.

Like thousands of his peers, John waited until after Christmas to enlist. A surge of sign-ups started at the end of December, and by January 9, 1951, the Air Force had to impose a limit of 1,000 recruits per day in order to regulate the flow into Lackland. The rush crescendoed on January 16, 1951, when a record high of 7,746 recruits arrived at the Air Force gateway. "By rail, air, and road, enlistees converged on Lackland from all corners of the nation," an *Airman* magazine article recounted. "At one time, about 60 percent of the Pullman railroad cars in the nation were tied up around San Antonio." Lackland was only built to accommodate 20,000 trainees; by January, it hosted 73,000. Staff worked around the clock to process 4,000 arrivals each day, which meant there was a huge backlog in waiting. Some were diverted to the Sheppard and Sampson bases, but still too many were pouring into Lackland. Squad tents were constructed to house the overflow when the Korean conflict started, and by the time John arrived there were several thousand of these 32-by-16-feet shelters, packing twelve men apiece into what was one of the largest tent cities in American military history. It was the middle of winter, which in San Antonio was relatively mild, albeit wet—until a cold, six-degree blast of snow and sleet hit the camp on January 29. Trainees lucky enough to have steel cots and mattresses were given two blankets; the ones on canvas cots were issued four. Some covered themselves with newspapers, and when the temperature plummeted they burned broomsticks, tool handles, and slices of their tent poles to stay warm. This massive influx forced the Air Force to cut basic training down to a mere 14 days—which wasn't training, it was said, so much as sending "inoculated civilians" to their next duty stations.[3]

At the end of John's cold but fleeting stay at Lackland, he received his assignment: *medical service*. He was terrified all over again, "so of course I called my father. I said, 'Oh my god, what do I do? They're going to put me in the medical thing for years.'" Johnny Francis told Jerry Colonna, and it was either Colonna or his friend Bob Hope, who made a call to the general at Lackland; both entertainers had visited the major military bases many times and knew the commanding officers. John's fate was nearly that of a character on the show *M*A*S*H*—"Yeah," he quipped, "I'd be good at giving injections"—but not for the first or last time, showbiz changed his fortune.[4]

John was assigned to Davis-Monthan Air Force Base in Tucson, Arizona, where he joined the 775th Air Force Band, along with several of his friends from back home—like John Bambridge, Jr., who was a year older and a graduate of Van Nuys High. Bambridge was an "absolute class A woodwind player," John said, and his father was a classical tuba player in the Warner Brothers orchestra; John Bambridge, Sr., actually produced a few recordings of his son's trio—which included John—at Radio Recorders in Hollywood, not for commercial release but just for fun.[5] Bambridge, Jr., was studying at Juilliard when he, too, enlisted in January 1951—and he proved an invaluable young teacher on John's journey toward composing.

The Air Force encouraged cadets to take classes at the University of Arizona, which John did throughout the year he was there. He discovered that Arthur Olaf Andersen, a composer from Rhode Island who wrote what John regarded as the definitive book on harmony, was head of the music theory department. So John took composition lessons with Andersen, showing him the piano sonata and a few other pieces. "What I got from him was some encouragement," John said. "That's pretty much all."[6] In March, Leonard Bernstein came through town on a tour with the Israel Philharmonic, and John saw the great American conductor for the first time in a concert at the university auditorium.

John was still playing trombone, but "he had ruined his chops over-practicing, and he'd crack a lot of notes," said Bill Peterson, a trumpeter and graduate of San Bernardino High who arrived at Davis-Monthan at the same time. "He never practiced the thing except in the band rehearsals. We went out every day to take the flag down: the band marched, they took the flag down, we came back—we were done for the day." John, Peterson, Bambridge, and Mel Pollen all palled around in the barracks when they weren't playing music for parades or dances for enlisted men or officers—and in their free time, jazz. Peterson and John saw *An American in Paris* when it came to town, then went back to the barracks, where John played George Gershwin's dreamy "Love Is Here to Stay" from the film.[7]

Music continued to dominate John's life. "He was attuned to everything that was going on," said Peterson. "I remember practicing one day, something out of a book, and it was a note that was tied to another note. He heard me play that as he walked by my room, and he came back and said, 'You're late getting off that first note.'" There was an open-air band shell and amphitheater on base that had a stage with a spinet piano, and John was given a key. While his friends went to play tennis or swim, John would go over to the open-air auditorium—with temperatures often in the 100s—wearing his formal fatigues. Peterson would gather him at lunchtime: "I'd knock on the door, and it would open . . . and by this time he was down to his skivvies." Walking back from the amphitheater to the chow hall one day, Peterson asked John what he was working on all those hours, and John simply pumped his ring finger up and down: "*That.*"

The L.A. friend group often piled into a car and drove home on weekends, where John would take a lesson with Van Eps and come back to the base with a composition assignment, something eccentric like "a piece for six clarinets." John had so many good players at his disposal that the only limit was his imagination. "He just wanted to soak it all up," said Peterson, "*now.*"[8] John later lamented how the Korean War would be eclipsed in America's cultural memory by the war in Vietnam, its many sacrifices too easily forgotten, but one of its unique qualities was the influx of highly skilled musicians. "All these conservatory kids came running out," said John, avoiding combat by opting into the band program like he did, "and we had in my barracks all these kids that were all future symphony orchestra players. I would ask someone, 'How do you play that trill on a flute?' and he would show me. So I perhaps had a better school than I would have had if I had been able to go to Juilliard."[9]

John was specifically learning orchestration for *band*—only woodwinds, brass, and percussion—and in that, the most influential teacher he had was his friend, John Bambridge, Jr. "He would write wind stems all the way down," John said, drawing a vertical line with his finger, "if they were in sync with the brass stems. Which you wouldn't normally do—I mean, it's something that a kid would do. But it gave me a visual concept of these divided sections. [Bambridge] and I were practically roommates in the Air Force, and I learned so much about voicing and harmonization from him. I think he taught me more about band arranging than anybody." Bambridge's father took a shine to John, and—with some kind of prophetic sight—recognized his writing potential. He gifted John a copy of Frank Skinner's 1950 book *Underscore*, the composer's technical guide to film scoring. For some reason the old man gave it, not to his son, "who was more advanced than I," but to *John Williams*. "And it's with me forever, and my debt to him is great, because I studied it."*[10]

---

* The younger Bambridge was recruited to the Air Force's premier band in Washington, D.C., where in January 1953 he participated in President Dwight D. Eisenhower's inauguration ceremonies. When Bambridge married a Wisconsin girl in Studio City that fall, John was his best man. ("Neenah Girl Says Vows with Airman," *Post-Crescent* [Appleton, WI], September 14, 1953.)

Bob Hope and Jerry Colonna came to Tucson in February 1952 to raise money for charity and to entertain the troops, and John and the 775th played at a taping of *The Bob Hope Show* on base.[11] One month later, John was reassigned to the outer limits of Newfoundland and the Pepperrell Air Force Base, located in the city of St. John's on the easternmost tip of North America. It was charming but freezing cold, and "the population was not healthy, and the diets were not good," said John. "A lot of tuberculosis and graveyards full of kids." Pepperrell was built in 1941, a strategic site between the United States and Great Britain during the Second World War, and it boasted modern barracks on Quidi Vidi Lake, complete with large recreation rooms, a mess hall, barber shop, rifle ranges, and sports fields. There was also a good café and a movie theater where the band would sometimes play concerts. Each room had two occupants, and the barracks were well built to withstand the harsh northern weather. The officer in charge of the post exchange was a young man named Lee Sherman, who became John's friend and future roommate. Pepperrell had "vast open rooms, one big enough that we could have our whole 60-piece band rehearsing in there," John said. "There was another wing where I used to have little rehearsals for the wind group and the brass group that I would conduct . . . not *conduct*," he demurred, "but count measures."[12]

John spent two memorable years with the 596th Air Force Band in Newfoundland. It was a *very* good band that boasted French horns, trumpets, and two virtuoso flutists. John was an all-purpose pianist and a brass doubler, and he played all manner of ceremonies and regattas with the 50-piece concert band, which serviced all of the bases on Newfoundland, Labrador, Iceland, and Greenland, but he was also appointed to the Starlighters—a prestigious, 16-person dance orchestra that dressed up and played for upscale occasions on the Pepperrell base as well as the Canadian Air Base. "Same personnel, different clothes," John explained. "There's a picture of the Starlighters in their uniforms and me in a tux, because I had written some show material for somebody's wife on the base, conducted it and so on. I don't know *where* I got the tuxedo."[13] It wasn't long before the other musicians realized that John was the only airman at Pepperrell who knew how to arrange—and they put him to work. "Published arrangements were available, but I could perhaps advance the harmonizations, or add some tricks," he said. "I remember a situation where we had a wind quintet and the available music was not great, and so: *well, I'll write a wind quintet.*"[14] The dance band played summer concerts in a gazebo where the base commander would request his favorite songs, and John also played in various jazz combos on the side.

The only *action* John saw in the service was musical, although he did take one trip in a B-25 bomber—"the loudest airplane I have ever heard," he said. "It's a two engine plane, and the radio bubble is in the top, which is where I was stuck."[15] But he credited his time in the military for some of the daily working disciplines he maintained for the rest of his life. Living on base with his peers also gave him some of the fraternal college experience he'd missed out on. "I was quite happy about it," he said. "We were living with these young players—some of whom I had known from Los Angeles. And certainly the best way, I think, to learn instrumentation is to live with and play with and study other people as they study their instruments."¹⁶ Harold Hanson, an officer and bassoon player, would let John stay at his apartment when John couldn't get quiet time to practice in the barracks. Hanson also tried to teach John bassoon. "I sat next to him at rehearsals," John said. "He played first, and I played whatever I could."¹⁷† Sitting around on the base, John started listening to classical music in earnest. "I *loved* the Soviets," he said, referring to Sergeis Prokofiev and Rachmaninoff. "I discovered the Shostakovich Fifth when I was in the Air Force, age 20. And I wanted to go study with Ben Britten at that time, I admired his music so much. I was greatly interested in ballet and ballet music."¹⁸

In January 1953, John saw *The Quiet Man* at the local Paramount Theatre. The John Ford film, set in Ireland and starring John Wayne as an American boxer who falls in love with an Irish lass played by Maureen O'Hara, strongly impressed him with its score by Victor Young, which was rooted in Irish folk song. Young adapted "The Rakes of Mallow" throughout the film, sometimes using it to accentuate the comedy of fight scenes, other times "in a very passionate and romantic way," John said, "such as the first time Wayne sees O'Hara across a field and wonders if what he sees is real. It's very inspiring music." For John, it was one of the first scores "that turned me on to the idea of writing music for the movies."¹⁹

* * *

Among the charts John wrote for his Air Force bands were arrangements of Newfoundland folk songs, which he included in concerts on the base in the summer of 1953.‡ Members of a German-Canadian industrial film company were in the audience on one of these occasions, and "no sooner is the concert over than a representative of the Newfoundland Tourist Development Board comes backstage and wants me to write an underscore based on a Newfoundland theme for a picture the government of Newfoundland is producing," John wrote in a letter to his parents a few days later.²⁰ Atlantic Films had gathered footage of attractions and attractive people all over the island—from Signal Hill's overlook of the city to boat racing on Quidi Vidi Lake—and wrapped their 20-minute commercial, titled *You Are Welcome*, around a corny conceit: the adventures of a traveling suitcase named Sammy Sealskin. It was narrated by "Mr. Canada," a nickname for Canadian Broadcasting Corporation newsman John Fisher.

This was the canvas for John's very first film score. It was exactly the kind of institutional film that *Mystery Science Theater 3000* would later send up, and it inspired music of that ilk. But this humble little movie curiously found John Williams—who insisted he had never before now entertained the idea of scoring movies—and gently woke up the craft that would come to define him. The music for *You Are Welcome* bounces along with a daffy jaunt in the vein of children's theater, running through

---

† Decades later, John repaid the favor by giving Hanson's Las Vegas woodwind octet free use of his film scores.

‡ When Elizabeth II was crowned Queen of the United Kingdom that June, the band accompanied a fireworks show in her honor. ("Coronation Fireworks at Quidi Vidi," *The Daily News* [St. John's], June 4, 1953.)

variations on Newfoundland folk songs—mainly "Feller from Fortune," but also "Jack Was Ev'ry Inch a Sailor," "The Ode to Newfoundland," and "The Squid Jiggin' Ground," all sea shanties with Irish DNA. The score only occasionally relaxes into a more pastoral or romantic mode, with one brief nod to jazz during a montage of St. John's nightlife. Several times a xylophone glissando cartoonishly accents a golf club swinging or a person jumping into water. "It was not an original score," John stressed. "I did not have a clue or an idea on how to do that."[21] The assignment required permission from John's commanding officer, which he was duly granted. He wasn't allowed to take payment for the job, but he was relieved of all service duties to pen the score—and he also got permission to record it with his bandmates. He wrote music for 12 players, including five woodwinds, two French horns, a trumpet, piano, string bass, and percussion. They recorded at the Atlantic Films studio on Prescott Street in downtown St. John's, and the occasion was marked with a photograph taken by John's friend and fellow arranger, Sy Johnson (Figure 3.1).

"Someday the words 'Music by Johnny Williams' will flash on your local theater screen." That was the prescient lede of an article that ran in *The Beacon*, an airman newspaper, on August 27, 1954 (Figure 3.2), which went on to note how the score "lacked the ever present 'lush' string section [which] necessitated Johnny to call upon his former training to gain proper utilization of the limited instrumentation and intricate scoring to give the overall effect of a large orchestra."[22] *You Are Welcome* premiered in

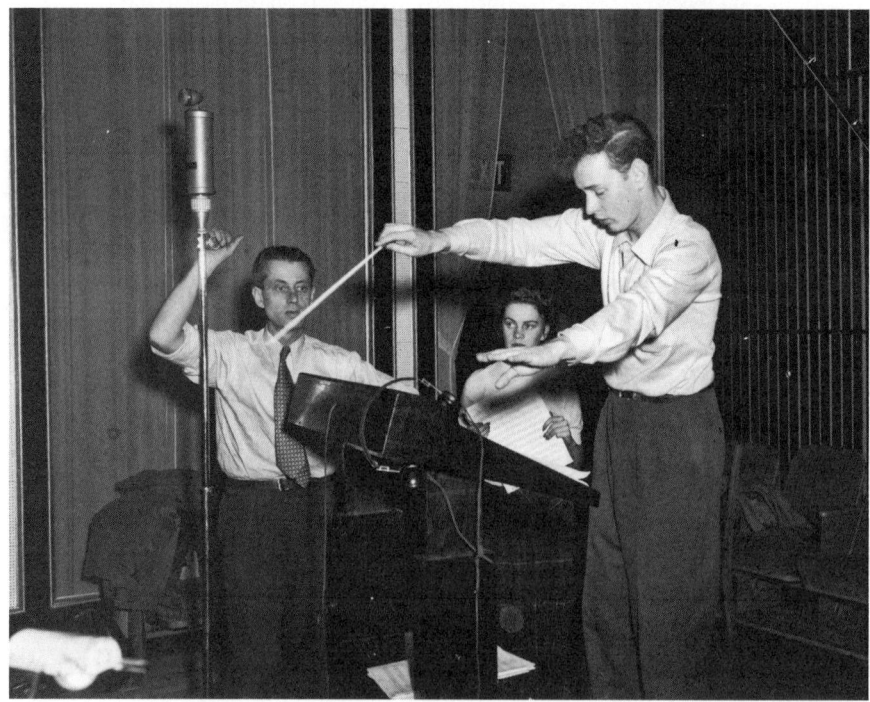

Figure 3.1. John conducting the score for *You Are Welcome*, 1953 (Photograph by Sy Johnson, Courtesy of John Williams).

Toronto at an international trade fair and had its hometown debut that November at the Paramount Theatre. "It was a profound experience to write music for my bandmates and then to rehearse and conduct it for the recording in the film studio," John said. "This was certainly one of the most significant events in that period of my life."[23]

MUSICIAN, COMPOSER AND ARRANGER A/1c John Williams puts finishing touch on another score.

Figure 3.2. John at piano with score (*The Beacon*, August 27, 1954).

* * *

John's tour in Newfoundland ended in the summer of 1954, when his final transfer took him back to Southern California and the March Air Force Base in Riverside, just an hour east of Los Angeles. There he joined the 523rd Band, continuing to play the usual service club dances, but his proximity to L.A. also enabled him to jump back into show business. He wrote arrangements for trumpeter Pete Candoli—a young but road-tested big band musician who lived next door to John's family in North Hollywood.[24] Candoli had a rehearsal band that practiced at the Local 47 musicians' union building on Vine Street, and John lent his piano prowess as well as his charts. "I felt quite the celebrity, coming from March Field to be able to play with Pete Candoli and his group," John said.[25] He also did some arranging for Horace Heidt's popular radio revue show, *The American Way*, which featured a big band with strings. He was back in Southern California just in time for his sister's wedding. On August 14, 1954,

Joan Williams married a Marine who served in the Korean War, William Russell Warren, at a Catholic church in Studio City. The reception at Eaton's Restaurant featured Jerry Colonna singing "You're My Everything" with backing by Pete Candoli, Bobby Van Eps, and John the celebrity airman.[26] On the weekends John kept meeting with Van Eps, and he also started going to a composition teacher in North Hollywood named Max Rossi. John played him the piano sonata "with the fourth chords that I thought I invented," and Rossi told John's father: "You have to get him with Mario. He needs a real teacher."[27]

Mario Castelnuovo-Tedesco, an Italian émigré, was a respected concert composer best known for a guitar concerto written for Andrés Segovia, but like so many other conservatory-trained refugees in Hollywood, he earned his living as a ghostwriter on film scores at MGM. Perhaps his greatest legacy, though, was his role as "the teacher du jour in Hollywood," according to Jerry Goldsmith, a contemporary of John's who studied with Tedesco.[28] So did André Previn, Nelson Riddle, Henry Mancini, and many Newmans—Alfred, Lionel, and Randy. Tedesco took students at his house on South Clark Street in Beverly Hills, charging them 15 dollars an hour and teaching orchestration by assigning a piece that was written for solo piano—something by Brahms or Debussy—and having them flesh it out for orchestra. He was meticulous but gentle, and "provided a safe haven for young composers," said James Westby, a Tedesco authority. "Many of the European teachers were very regimented in their teaching style. Mario had an incredible way of taking the student, finding exactly what was missing and filling that in. In doing so, he empowered the student in very important ways."[29] Previn described him as "one of the kindest, gentlest, most adorable men I ever met."[30] John simply said, "I think he really taught everyone that ever amounted to anything at all out there in those years," but he minimized the actual education he received in Tedesco's home in the fall of 1954. "I sat with him, and he talked, and he looked at my music. I spent very little time with Mario. It was very like Arthur Andersen—the same thing. I think probably, in terms of conversation, I wasn't prepared enough. Pretty broad and erudite man, and he wanted to give me instructions in harmony, which I didn't feel I needed, but I paid attention to it. It was all too brief."[31]

When Van Eps was asked to play piano for an engagement at Eugene Loring's ballet company in Hollywood, he recommended John instead. Loring had choreographed Aaron Copland's groundbreaking Americana ballet, *Billy the Kid*, in 1938, and moved on to straddle the worlds of Hollywood and high art: his film credits included the children's fantasy musical, *The 5,000 Fingers of Dr. T.*, and later *Sabrina* and *Funny Face*, and he also received the first ballet commission for American TV with *The Capital of the World*, with an original score by George Antheil.§ Van Eps recommended John to both Antheil and Loring, and for a short time John accompanied ballet rehearsals as well as performances at various colleges, where Loring's students gave demonstration revues of classical ballet, modern dance, and jive to

---

§ The self-proclaimed "Bad Boy of Music," Antheil scandalized audiences in the 1920s with his avant-garde works written for car horns and airplane propellers.

music by Antheil as well as Copland, Paul Hindemith, Benjamin Britten, and Erich Wolfgang Korngold. "I enjoyed it," John said. "I met Antheil a number of times."[32]

At last, John was discharged from the Air Force in January 1955. The *Beacon* article claimed that he was planning to pick up his studies at UCLA, "with a goal of writing and playing for motion pictures."[33] Curiously, John would later dispute this idea, claiming he never had any notion of scoring films. For now, freed from the Air Force, he was set on getting to New York to study with the best piano teacher in the country.

* * *

During John's airman years, his high school sweetheart took flight in her own field. After six months in New York with parts on Chico Marx's show and a few soap operas, Barbara returned to Hollywood and landed a regular spot on *The Jerry Colonna Show*. The premiere episode of that ABC variety series featured a sketch with Colonna as a barber and Italian crooner Frankie Laine as his customer, as well as a barbershop quartet performance of "Sweet Adeline" assisted by this "blond dish."[34] That was the kind of press Barbara was getting in the trades: "a delectable little blonde," "decorative appearances by a cutie named Barbara Ruick were an eyeful easy to take."[35] With her lithe figure and almost cartoonishly expressive face, Barbara was very good at physical comedy, and her honeyed alto attracted the attention of an agent, Milton "Milt" Ebbins—who signed Barbara with MGM as both an actress and a singer on the studio's record label. She recorded flirty love songs like "Retreat (Cries My Heart)" and "You Couldn't Be Cuter," earning decent reviews, with some comparing her to Doris Day.

But her talents were being squandered on the MGM film stages. "You can't blame them for waiting to see how I sell on records before letting me sing before cameras," said Barbara, who had bit parts, often uncredited, in a dozen now-forgotten dramas—*Scaramouche*, *Fearless Fagen*, *Apache War Smoke*—playing everything from a pregnant young mother to a cowgirl.[36] She finally got a chance to sing on screen in the summer of 1953, co-starring with her friend Debbie Reynolds in *The Affairs of Dobie Gillis*. One of Barbara's few films that outlived its era—thanks to classic movie TV—this campus comedy was a fluffy, hokey confection that stitched together a few random song-and-dance numbers with sitcom hijinks. On the call sheet below lead Bobby Van as the fun-loving Dobie and Reynolds as his girlfriend, Barbara played the lively Lorna, a soubrette whose more extroverted and flirtatious personality fails to woo Dobie. The movie offered a vivid portrait of the exact kind of scene Barbara and Curly had ruled a few years earlier—dances in a school gymnasium, radio broadcasts with a band—and it's easy to see how she had once charmed the bobby socks off North Hollywood's teens when she bursts into a performance of "You Can't Do Wrong Doin' Right" for a rapt audience in a campus dining hall. Onscreen, Barbara moves beguilingly, throwing a catlike growl into her vocals—even as her co-star, Bob Fosse, literally dances circles around her. Her mother, Lurene Tuttle, was also in the film—though ironically playing Debbie Reynolds's mother.

Like any other starlet, Barbara's love life was the subject of gossip. She was reportedly dating a stage actor twelve years her elder in December 1951, the same month she traveled to Newfoundland and Labrador with a troupe of performers to entertain servicemen at several Christmas shows.[37] (John arrived only a few months later.) In her company was another rising MGM star, Carleton Carpenter—who "fell absolutely ass over teakettle in love" with her, as Carpenter wrote in a memoir that also detailed his secret dalliances with men. He and Barbara spent all of their free time together, and "we talked often of marriage," Carpenter wrote, "but it was difficult setting an exact time. When I was hot for the altar, it wasn't right for her; when she was ready, I wasn't." They were invited by songwriter Frank Loesser to record demos for his new movie musical, *Hans Christian Andersen*, and they released one of the songs—"No Two People"—on wax. Friends nicknamed them "Barbass and Carltass."[38] Barbara adored Carpenter and freely accepted his bisexuality, and she showed a similarly liberal warmth to Conrad Salinger, a closeted gay arranger at MGM who became a close friend around the same time. In August 1952, Barbara secretly married a crooner named Frank Howren, but the marriage was "just as secretly annulled in Morales, Mexico, on grounds that [it] was never consummated," according to the gossip mill.[39] Columnist Dorothy Kilgallen suggested that MGM actively tried to kill the affair so they could groom a romance with their new star, Robert Horton, whom Barbara married on August 22, 1953, at the Flamingo Wedding Chapel in Las Vegas.[40] Horton had been in the 1952 western *Apache War Smoke* with Barbara, and he later became famous for a starring role in the TV western *Wagon Train*. It was Horton's second marriage, and Barbara painted a rosy picture for the trades—but Horton, too, was closeted.[41] It was a studio-arranged union without any romance.

In truth, John and Barbara had never lost their flame for each other: "We were a couple since we were children," John said. "Horton recognized that also, very sweetly." John would pick Barbara up on dates, and Horton would simply smile and say, "Well, you kids go off and have a good time!"[42] Barbara eventually slipped free of her MGM contract, tired of playing thankless, non-singing parts and wanting the freedom to perform in nightclubs and on television, and in December 1954 she signed a contract with CBS.[43] She was featured in the pilot for *The Johnny Carson Show*, a short-lived variety program that foreshadowed Carson's reign as a talk show host, although she didn't last beyond the first episode.[44] Then, in August 1955 she signed with 20th Century Fox and was given her best role to date in the Rodgers and Hammerstein musical *Carousel*, which was set to star Shirley Jones as Julie Jordan and Frank Sinatra as Billy Bigelow.[45] (Sinatra famously backed out after they arrived in Boothbay Harbor, Maine, and was hurriedly replaced by Gordon MacRae.) Barbara had the supporting part of Julie's best friend, Carrie Pipperidge. It was a lavish studio feature, and she got her own solo number—"When I Marry Mr. Snow"—and lots of CinemaScope screen time. Riding high, Barbara signed a five-year contract with Columbia Records that summer.[46]

As her career was picking up and she was spending more and more time with John, who was now out of the service, she set to breaking up her prop marriage to Horton. They were formally separated by the time she landed *Carousel*, and Barbara initiated divorce proceedings, then flew to set on Boothbay Harbor the day after the court hearing.[47] (The gossip columns reported neglect and even abuse by Horton, which was the official cover story.) Barbara didn't want alimony or property—she just wanted *release*. She didn't tell the judge what she really wanted: to marry Mr. Williams.

* * *

Madame Rosina Lhévinne, a Russian pianist who taught at the Juilliard School from 1925 until her death in 1976, was, at this time, the most widely respected piano teacher in the United States.[48] Juilliard, the most revered music school in the country, was celebrating its 50th anniversary in 1955. It was still in its old location on Claremont Avenue in Morningside Heights—a campus today occupied by the Manhattan School of Music—in the 24th Precinct on the Upper West Side. This was the same year Robert Moses, the notorious urban planner, was given city approval to raze several neighborhoods on the Upper West Side, home to many Puerto Rican and Black communities, to make way for Juilliard's new home in San Juan Hill—a scene that later served as the backdrop for *West Side Story*.

John saw Juilliard as the Mecca for music study and, for him, Lhévinne was the "high watermark of piano pedagogy. My idea was that she was the best there was, and that somehow I needed to study with her."[49] But first he had to audition. John knew Morris "Mo" Goldenberg, a percussion teacher at Juilliard and former radio musician—not through his father, but through his own networking in the New York theater scene.** Goldenberg secured an audition for John in the spring of 1955, which took place in Lhévinne's apartment, and he even suggested some repertoire.

"Probably the best piano playing I ever did in my life was the day on which I auditioned for her," John said. "But I worked up that program, because I wanted to be accepted by her so much." He played a Bach prelude and fugue, a movement from one of Beethoven's sonatas, Chopin's lightning-fast Étude in C-sharp minor ("a party piece of mine"), and a fugue piece by Van Eps. "She interrupted me from time to time," he said. "I think I began with the Bach, and she came over and stopped me and she said to one of her assistants, 'Look at this boy's hands. Beautiful hand position.' I remember I was pleased with that. I had no idea what she thought of my playing." As he was playing the Bach, "she pointed to the music and said to me, 'What is that?' And I said, 'That's like a canon.'" "'Vy do you say it is *like* a canon,' she said in her Russian accent, 'ven it *is* a canon?'"[50] *Like* or not, Lhévinne agreed to take John as her student. "The proudest day of my life," he said.[51]

John found a basement apartment near the corner of West End and 88th, where he roomed with his friend Lee Sherman from the Air Force. He rented a piano from Steinway Hall, and he and Sherman liked to play *Rhapsody in Blue* with four hands. He made appointments with Lhévinne by phone and met her at a practice room at Juilliard for private lessons.[52] He never enrolled in courses at Juilliard, and he didn't earn a degree there—in fact, John Williams never obtained a college degree. He also didn't take part in Lhévinne's renowned weekly master classes, which were "like going to a mini Carnegie Hall recital for those of us who played in the class," said Daniel

---

** Goldenberg's son, Billy, became a successful television composer who scored Steven Spielberg's feature-length debut, *Duel*, in 1971.

Pollack, another Lhévinne student at the time.[53] Her students in 1955 also included two soon-to-be famous virtuosos: John Browning and Van Cliburn. "The other students there were, then as now, younger and prodigious, sometimes genius level youngsters that come in to play," John said, "which I certainly was not."[54] He always downplayed his piano talent, but "to be accepted to the class of Madame Lhévinne was quite stupendous, frankly," said Pollack. John could at least admit that he played *well*, and worked very hard. He later loved to recite the story of being in a practice room one day, "and hearing some thundering octaves coming down from the next room or the room up the hall. And I had to stop and listen to this. I thought, *my God, that's at a technical level I could never achieve.* 'Who is that?' I asked someone. And they said, 'That's John Browning,' who I also knew was a student of Rosina's, who was probably at that time 17.... And we all remember—it's recognizably human—that when you're 20 years old or so, and someone is five years younger, that's a cosmic difference."[55] In truth, Browning was only one year younger than John—but his confidence was sufficiently shaken.

Lhévinne, who turned 75 that March, focused less on fundamentals with John and more on feeling and humanity, a holistic approach to musical performance. "My memories of it had more to do with a kind of nurturing or maternal quality," John said. "I think she was very attached to her late husband. She talked about him all the time."[56] Josef Lhévinne was a world-renowned Russian prodigy on the piano, and also a master teacher from the founding of Juilliard. He died from a heart attack in December 1944, and his widow never remarried. Early on, she gave John an autographed recording of Josef's arrangement of *Stars and Stripes Forever* for solo piano— "the damnedest thing you've ever heard," John said.[57] "I think her great grief and her love, all directed towards her husband, all sort of revolved around and was directed towards her students." John concluded that Madame Lhévinne "was certainly one of the great influences in my life."[58]

The Fall 1955 issue of the *Juilliard Review* contained an article about the current economic plight of performing musicians. The author warned about the increasing "automation" of musicians in the form of recordings. "In place of the 22,000 employed in silent movie houses in 1929, the seven major studios in 1954 employed only 303 full-time musicians in Hollywood to put sound track on film." Granted, those select musicians earned a plush $8,677 a year on average, the highest wage in any field for members of the American Federation of Musicians (AFM). Jobs were equally shrinking in radio, television, and live classical performance, the article went on—but one bright spot was that "the men who play in night clubs and in traveling dance bands earn a full-time living, although their employment is also sporadic. There are approximately eight hundred traveling dance bands, varying from small combinations of three and four up to name bands of thirty. These men are the very life blood of the AFM."[59]

* * *

Living in Manhattan cost money, and John paid his bills that spring playing dance dates in clubs and hotels around town, sitting in with bebop clarinetists—Tony Scott and Buddy DeFranco—at places like the famous Minton's Playhouse in Harlem. He also accompanied vocal auditions at the Winter Garden Theater for Broadway legend Richard Rodgers, who at the time was developing the lesser-known show, *Pipe Dream*. It was a halcyon time to *hear* shows: John could bop around New York and listen to Miles Davis, Stan Getz, Duke Ellington, or Count Basie. "I saw and heard them all. Had great interest in them—loved the music, of course."[60] Through Tony Scott, who was also a music director and arranger, John landed a job with singer Harry Belafonte. He played piano in the pit orchestra for a well-received Broadway revue, *3 for Tonight*, which co-starred the dancing couple Marge and Gower Champion and featured original songs by Belafonte and music by composer Walter Schumann. The revue ran for 85 performances from April through June at the Plymouth Theatre, and it was captured for a CBS broadcast at the end of its run.[61]

Back in Los Angeles that summer, John was invited to lay down his first piano tracks on a professional recording: over two days in August 1955, he played on a series of Belafonte songs at Radio Recorders, a studio at 7000 Santa Monica Boulevard in Hollywood that would become one of John's regular haunts.[62] He was especially excited to play with trumpeter Maynard Ferguson, a Canadian alumnus of Stan Kenton's outfit. Some of the songs came from the revue—"Matilda," "Scarlet Ribbons"—and one of them, "Man Smart (Woman Smarter)," made the cut as the closer for *Calypso*, the bestselling 1956 album that catapulted Belafonte's career.

John continued studying with Lhévinne in L.A. in the summer of 1955, where she taught at the short-lived Los Angeles Conservatory on Figueroa Street, downtown. He even chauffeured her to the beach in his car.[63] One day she asked John: "What do you do?" "And I said, 'Well, I do some orchestration.' She said, 'You know how to orchestrate?' And I said, 'Oh, yes, I've been doing that since I was 14-years-old.' … She said, 'Well, that's fantastic. If you can orchestrate, that's what you should do!'" John smiled at the memory: "I think indicating to me that probably she understood that I wasn't going to have a top career as a pianist. Certainly that was clear." Between Browning's "thundering octaves" and Lhévinne's comments, John began to think: "*Maybe she's right—I should have a career writing music rather than playing it.* And at the time, of course, I didn't realize that that would be the ultimate outcome of things for me. But she was prophetic in that."[64]

* * *

Vic Damone was a popular draw of the time, an Italian-American crooner who had a hit in 1947 with the song "I Have But One Heart."[††] He had been working with Burt Bacharach as his pianist and conductor, but they parted ways over creative differences; in the summer of 1955, Damone's manager Milt Ebbins—who also happened to manage Barbara—held auditions for a new pianist in the New York office of George Wood, Damone's agent. "The first one came in and started playing as if he were in a concert hall, showing off all the pyrotechnics he had," Damone recounted:

[††] The fictitious crooner Johnny Fontane later sang that song in *The Godfather*, in a part that Damone turned down.

The second one was so tentative I could hardly make out what song he was playing. As the third candidate came in and sat down, I went off to the side to talk to George and Milt. "Who are these guys?" I said. "I need somebody who can accompany and conduct and maybe do some arranging. Those two didn't have a clue." While we were talking, the third one started doodling around on the piano, just to keep himself occupied until I was ready for him. But the chords he was playing were so beautiful, I stopped talking. "Wait a minute," I said to George and Milt. "Wait a minute. Listen to that. This might be the right guy." I went over to the piano.

"God, those are beautiful chords you're playing. What's your name?"

"Thank you," he said. "I'm John Williams. Would you like to sing a song?"

"Yes. How about 'Embraceable You' "? It's Gershwin. Everybody knows it. He hit a note.

"The key all right?" he said.

"Yes, fine." I started: "Embrace me / You sweet embraceable you." I'm listening to what he's playing against what I'm singing. He waits for me. "Just one look at you." I stopped, waiting to see what he would do. He played something to round out the phrase, and ended with the chord. I could have come in right then or an hour from then. I had the chord. The man was completely attuned to what I was doing. He was breathing with me. "Oh," I said, "that's beautiful. Just right. Do you arrange?"

"Yes."

"Can you conduct?"

"Yes."

"Well, you've got the job, Mr. Williams."[65]

John joined Damone's traveling retinue as a pianist, playing in clubs from L.A. to Houston to Florida. In November they had a 12-day stand at the Cocoanut Grove; John was dinged in *Variety*'s review for failing to give the orchestra their beat.[66] But the singer couldn't have been happier—and as an *arranger* John's taste was "unerring," Damone said. In fact, John's taste had a major hand in the crooner's biggest hit. In February 1956, *My Fair Lady*, the new musical by Lerner and Loewe, was in its test run in Philadelphia with stars Rex Harrison and Julie Andrews, and Damone's record label, Columbia Records, had first dibs on its songs. Mitch Miller, the influential A&R man at Columbia, sent the scores to Damone for him to pick one. "I was doing shows at the Copacabana just then," Damone recalled, "and John and I were staying at the St. Moritz in New York in a two-bedroom suite with a piano, so we could rehearse. When Mitch sent over the score, we went through the whole thing. I especially liked the song 'I've Grown Accustomed to Her Face.' But John said, 'No, that's a nice song, but this is the song for you: 'On the Street Where You Live.'' He played it for me and I sang it. I thought, *Yes, this is interesting.* John had already pictured what I might be able to do with it."

Miller informed them that unfortunately the show's producers were actually taking that song out, so they needed to pick another. He invited them to his office to discuss, where they met Columbia's house arranger, Percy Faith. John and Damone both looked at each other and marveled at the fact that Faith worked at a desk and not a piano.‡‡ Faith reluctantly agreed to hear John and Damone's interpretation of "On the Street Where You Live," and said: "You're right. That's too good not to do." "We've got to record this quickly," Miller said. "If it's a hit, they'll have to keep it in the show." Two days later, they recorded Faith's arrangement of the song with an orchestra at the Columbia studio on Thirtieth Street. They did only two quick takes. When the song came out, it was a top ten hit for weeks. "They did have to keep the song in the show," Damone bragged, "and it was the record that did it."[67]

* * *

Barbara made a big impression in *Carousel* as a sweet, if naive, young woman who's ready to settle down with a man who smells like fish, and who defends Julie against her ne'er-do-well husband, Billy Bigelow. Director Henry King called her "one of the greatest young talents I have seen in the past 30 years."[68] So it was confusing, and disheartening, when Fox dropped her option that March. She was living with Shirley Jones, her best friend in real life, in a Tudor-style apartment building on South Beverly Glen, just a few blocks west of the Fox lot. Jones remembered John paying frequent visits: "He was *wild* about Barbara. The way he looked at her ... I mean, you could tell he was just absolutely head over heels."[69]

In the spring of 1956, "we discovered that Barbara was expecting," said John, who was a virgin before he courted his childhood sweetheart. "And the awkward thing was that she was married at the time." Enter Mickey Rudin, Frank Sinatra's lawyer-agent who "had a lot of clout, and understood how things were done in certain circles," as John put it. Milt Ebbins pointed John and Barbara to this Hollywood heavy who had a history of arranging "Mexican divorces" for his celebrity clients. Rudin told John it was easy: "It's possible in the state of Chihuahua to have a divorce and a marriage at the same time that is recognized in California. You can't go to Nogales to do this, because California will not accept it. So if you go to a certain lawyer in El Paso, Texas, he will take it to a court in Chihuahua—and you can be divorced and married on the same day." So John and Barbara were married in secret. "Now," John said, "we had been *like* we were married since we were 15 years old—not in any sexual sense in those years at all—but we were older now, and we were at a stage in life where such things happen, and they're appropriate. And so it worked out fine. I'm very indebted to the memory of Mickey Rudin."[70] In September, Hollywood gossip columnist Louella Parsons revealed that not only had John and Barbara eloped, but that she was expecting their first baby in the spring.[71] "When we got together then," John said, "we knew each other so well that it wasn't like we were starting at the beginning of our relationship. It was just like a continuation."[72]

* * *

When John Williams reflected on his unusual education, he had neither regrets nor feelings of inferiority. He acquired a king's wealth of knowledge from the fugato exercises and Olympian piano training with Bobby Van Eps, from teaching himself

---

‡‡ John would write at a desk for most of his composing life, though he didn't attribute this practice to Faith.

orchestration through books and beginning to compose, and from the Air Force—which was its own kind of conservatory, a hothouse full of first-rate musicians who taught John everything he needed to know about their instruments, where he could write charts and dance arrangements and adaptations of folk tunes and have it all played back to him in real time. This was a musical boot camp, learning in the trenches, and it would live on in his mastery of brass and wind writing, as well as his penchant for marches and martial fanfare. Band arranging is technically very challenging, John noted, because the clarinets and piccolos are all in completely different keys. "Bandstration, as we call it, is as difficult as orchestration, or maybe more. Strings in an orchestra don't have to *breathe*. So by the time I was out of the Air Force, playing the best I ever played, and had enough experience compared to my jazz or studio players—I was quite a good arranger already, without any conservatory training."[73]

He likened himself to Claude Debussy, who avoided formal studies at the Paris Conservatory with the arch conservative Luigi Cherubini and was largely self-taught

Figure 3.3. Williams in studio, age 24, ca. 1956 (Provided by Black Film Center & Archive, Indiana University, Bloomington, Indiana).

as a composer. "Debussy is a god—I'm just a cobbler," John insisted. "But there are similarities I think."[74]

If the Korean War had never interfered and he could have pursued a "serious" education at Juilliard like he had dreamed of, John would have no doubt been funneled into a philosophy and style of writing that dominated the 20th century after the Second World War—a language of serialism and atonality, anti-populist and anti-melody. He would have had to conform. "No question," he said. "That probably would be the direction I would have *wanted* to go," he admitted, "and I might have been very well put in a box."[75] (Figure 3.3).

4
Love Theme, 1957–1968

> *She was very instrumental in everything that he did. And he's told me forever that he owes a lot of his success to their early relationship and her connections.*
>
> —Jenny Williams, on her mother[1]

That John's heart was both generous and tender would eventually become evident in the feelings he invested in his popular film music, and in the feelings he evoked from his audience. These emotions were not a sham or a put-on; they grew organically in the garden of his own heart. "He's an extremely sensitive, empathic individual," said Jenny, the daughter who became a psychotherapist. "Always has been. And *sometimes* those kinds of people have to build walls because of their sensitivity—and not walls in a negative way, but just like *protection*. I just think he's very sensitive, and in a really good way, in a way that really, really serves him. But he has to also protect it, because it's very raw."[2] John shared his heart with his family and closest friends, although it was never enough. Barbara would lament with her girlfriends that he wasn't as emotionally available as she wanted him to be. And sometimes he erected a wall between himself and others after a certain point—a major life change, for example, or a tragedy—and those friends might feel abruptly cut off, cut *out*. It hurt, but no one really resented him because they knew it didn't come from a place of anger, or ego, or a petty sense of superiority. It was more often than not a means to stave off pain—to protect himself.

There were three key objects of his heart's devotion, three great loves that all emerged in the prime of his early adulthood. One was a wife, one was a best friend, and one was the White Goddess he was devoted to forever and above all: *music*. These inamoratas would help take him, slowly but steadily, to astounding heights of fame and deep fathoms of feeling. John had loved Barbara Ruick from the moment he met her at age 15. She was gorgeous, outgoing, funny, worldly, and constantly in motion. She *was* music. Now they were married and expecting their first baby and feeling the mutual need to settle down and create a home. The first chapter of John's professional career unfolded the way it did largely because of that practical need, and a lot of it also came directly from Barbara's connections and her active social conducting, nudging her introverted husband into the right parties with the right people. It was *Barbara* who introduced John to Alfred Newman, who subsequently introduced John to his brother, Lionel—another great love of John's life. Lionel Newman became John's confidant and beloved brother, his "Tootsie," and Newman also recognized the talent in his younger friend and, as head of the music department at Fox, he had the power to champion and promote it—in time.

As for music—music was there from the very beginning, from the drumbeats in the forests of Maine and the Kern tunes wafting through the ornate console radio, to the swinging rhythms John kept in the Dri-Nite Club and the Officers Clubs in the Air Force. Music was his master and his muse, his vocation and his universe. He bowed before it, served it, and communicated through it. John was too enamored and awed by music to ever claim mastery of it, and there was always so much more to learn about music and its mysteries that "a lifetime was not enough"—a Sergei Rachmaninoff quote he repeated like scripture. John set out on a lifetime quest to plumb its depths, and he loved and obeyed it, sometimes to the detriment of the other loves in his life. "In the exercise of what I do, a lot of things get neglected," he admitted.[3] *Music consumes your life*, he said.[4]

* * *

John was 24 and still flirting with a life on the road; besides his adventures with Vic Damone, he also led an orchestra accompanying singer Howard Keel at the Copa Room in the Sands Hotel in Las Vegas. Likewise, Barbara was enjoying a new life on the stage: she made her Broadway debut as Bianca/Lois Lane in a revival of the Cole Porter musical *Kiss Me, Kate*, which opened at New York City Center in May and ran for 23 performances. Immediately afterward she went to Cincinnati, where she starred in a Summer Playhouse production, *Champagne Complex*, as a woman who disrobes to polka-dotted underwear at the taste of bubbly. The local *Enquirer* found her "extremely animated, mercurial, and sometimes zany."[5] In public she was still being coy about her marital status, but she couldn't hide her love affair with John for long. She was already on to her next play—*Plain and Fancy*, a summer stock show in Long Island—when the news hit gossip pages and she had to withdraw because her new role as a real mother was rapidly approaching.[6] On January 3, 1957, Jennifer Williams was born at St. John's hospital in Santa Monica.

John was an artist, but he was also a pragmatist. Six days after Jenny was born, he was at the Sands Hotel in Vegas accompanying Keel—and he was back there again in May—but as the bio on one of his early solo albums put it: "John Towner Williams chose not to take the night club glory road to fame, but decided to accept the comparative obscurity but far greater security that is the lot of a Hollywood 'studio' musician."[7] When André Previn later asked what led him into film work and John said it was the birth of Jenny, the more cynical Previn responded wryly: "So it was venal to begin with." In a filmed interview conversation, captured in 1988, John scrunches his face up in a wince.

"Eh, I don't know if it's a word I would use, but..." John says, laughing nervously.

"All right," Previn says, "*financial*."

"It was a sudden, urgent necessity," allows John.[8]

The movies were much more venal for Previn, the wunderkind composer who, only three years older than John, was already famous scoring movies and earning Oscar nominations for movie musicals like *Three Little Words* and *Kiss Me, Kate*. John admired Previn from the moment they met, and saw in this urbane renaissance man a model for the kind of career he could have: recording pianist, arranger, composer, and conductor all in one. "I tried to emulate André," John said, and he did in a host of ways with far-reaching consequences—but only to a point. There was an ever-present cockiness and elitism in Previn's attitude toward Hollywood and movie producers and many of the hands that fed him, which was something John never copied. Too, John said, "somewhere along the line he had learned much more *about* jazz than I would ever know about it, yet somehow I thought I was a better jazz *player* than he was."[9] Previn recognized John's talent immediately, and adopted him not just as a close friend but a protégé. "For quite a few years," John said, "if he couldn't make a jazz date he would send me as a substitute, or he would hire me as a pianist for his orchestra, or even recommend me to producers of a couple of big films that I did."[10] "Johnny seemed to be almost the younger brother, the way he looked up to André," said actress Mia Farrow, who was later married to Previn. "It was really, really sweet."[11]

John needed a stable income, so studio life was very appealing—and he had a head start with his connections in the film and recording industries. But his early years were mostly characterized by what John counted as dues-paying work. "You wouldn't imagine the things I would do for 20 dollars," he said. He was hired by a bandleader and composer named Phil Moore to accompany singer Leda Annest, a soprano with a "semi operatic voice," in arias and Jerome Kern songs. A lot of his work came through referrals from Van Eps, who was friends with a bandleader named Tommy Jones; when Van Eps didn't want to play a given dance date at a club with Jones, "'Bud' was elected," said John, who played endless club dates along with numerous odd-job sessions, commercial jingles, and "every possible kind of scut work you can imagine."[12]

But he found his true calling in the movies.

* * *

The first act of John's career was an apprenticeship in an old world—playing music for veteran film composers and with elder musicians, learning the ropes in an old fashion. "I was working with people in their fifties and sixties," he said, "and I was out of a generation the whole time."[13] The music was written with pencils and paper, synchronized to picture using a big clock and stripes painted on frames of film. Scores were still orchestral and neoclassical and more than often melodramatic. Movies were still "pictures," and the session musicians were all men. It was the twilight of the studio system, an era of movie moguls and contract stars and bustling music departments with patriarchal music directors and house orchestras on staff on every studio lot in town. And it was all about to implode.

It's worth noting that John did not burst onto the scene with a youthful hunger to reinvent or rebel against tradition. He had talent galore and a desire to prove it, but he made himself a diligent pupil of the orthodox craft and a student of some of the very masters who architected the art of scoring films. He did not, like some of his colleagues, rage against the machine—he *absorbed* the machine. The lessons and ethos he learned as a casual disciple of Franz Waxman, Dimitri Tiomkin, Alfred Newman, and others would stick with him for the rest of his life.

One of his best connections was at Columbia Pictures, where his father was still playing with John's old friends from the "kicks" band. The studio boasted a vibrant music department, directed by a violinist-conductor from Philadelphia named Morris Stoloff, with a stable of staff composers and a contracted orchestra of 35–40 men. The majors, like Warner Bros. and Fox, had larger ensembles and a higher profile—John thought MGM's orchestra was the best of all—not to mention bigger, nicer rooms. But Stoloff had been a good enough musician to perform with Jascha Heifetz, and his group was a "very high level orchestra," John said, one that included concertmaster Marshall Sosson, a virtuoso from the Chicago Symphony, and principal trumpeter Manny Klein, an old New York friend of John's father. The piano bench was suddenly open with the departure of George Greeley, who had moved into composing, so John auditioned. "The principal requisite there was sight reading," John said. "I was a good sight reader, and what I couldn't read I could generally fill in a little bit." Stoloff simply told John to *play something*, so he played a prelude by Van Eps. Stoloff stopped him right in the middle of the piece and put a stubby paper card on the piano: "Can you read this?" It was an old-school production card, a four-line reduction of a full score. "I played whatever I played, and he said, 'You have the job.' " Contrary to later conjecture, John was never actually on staff at Columbia, but he was now one of their first-call keyboard players and would get frequent calls from their orchestra contractor, Dave Klein. "I had no *orchestral* experience as a pianist," John emphasized, but he caught on immediately. "At that very tender age I was sitting four days and sometimes five days a week—because the volume of production in the studio was such that the orchestra was busy all the time."[14] Out on the scoring stage, each movie was projected on a giant screen at the back of the room. The film was marked with "streamers," lines that moved across the image to indicate when to stop and start every cue, as well as "punch marks" which gave the conductor a heads-up about a moment they needed to hit. It was a daily masterclass with real masters of the craft of film composition. "The thing that excited me about working in the studios was that I was playing new music every day," John said. "The ink was still wet, so to speak. Some of it was good, some not so good—but when you were finished with one thing, you moved right on to the next."[15]

In his first year in the studios—1956—he played on numerous B-movie scores for Les Baxter, the bandleader who helped popularize the exotica genre, and also for Marlin Skiles, a prolific provider of music for the B hive at Allied Artists.* Skiles was one of these composers who "churned them out," John said,[16] and it was Skiles who gave John his first crack at actually writing a cue—for a United Artists detective thriller, *My Gun Is Quick*, in April 1957. John also played piano on the score. But John quickly left the slums, thanks to two lightning bolts that struck very early in his session-playing days and catapulted him from being a "kid just out of the Air Force," as he put it, to the upper echelons of film studio recording.

---

* Skiles had also orchestrated for Leonard Bernstein's one and only film score, *On the Waterfront*, and would later write a textbook on film scoring.

Bobby Helfer was an agent at MCA who represented composers including Previn and Elmer Bernstein, and he had recently assumed the role of hiring their orchestras for recording dates. Helfer asked Bobby Van Eps to play a piano concerto by Phil Moore on a studio date, but instead Van Eps referred his gifted former student. Moore was a trailblazing Black pianist and arranger from Seattle who, in the 1940s, had leveraged his nightly work with a rickety touring band into Hollywood success. After writing uncredited arrangements on Disney's *Dumbo*, Moore took a job at MGM, where he met Van Eps and where he accompanied Gene Kelly and Judy Garland, orchestrated some 40 films, was Lena Horne's pianist, and wrote the hit song "Shoo-Shoo Baby." But MGM wouldn't hire a person of color as one of their music directors, so Moore left the studio and made himself a director—arranging for Frank Sinatra, forming his own recording group, the Phil Moore Four, and founding the Modern Classics Orchestra, a blended ensemble of both classical and jazz musicians, Black and white.[17] That ensemble premiered his Concerto for Piano and Orchestra in 1947, and it was later recorded with pianist Calvin Jackson—another Black arranger who took Moore's old job at MGM (and who had a bit part in one of the first films that John scored: *I Passed for White*). John learned the jazz concerto and performed it with a contract orchestra at Radio Recorders.† Helfer was knocked out. "He decided I was the *best pianist he had ever heard*," John said, quoting the contractor's excited pronouncement, and overnight Helfer began hiring John for primo recording dates with Bernstein—John's first session for the composer was *Sweet Smell of Success* in May 1957—and other top-tier composers.[18]

The other bolt landed when Alexander "Sandy" Courage, a journeyman composer and orchestrator who later became famous for his *Star Trek* theme, invited John to Capitol Records to improvise some jazz on Chopin's Prelude in A Major. Courage, too, thought John was fantastic, and connected him with composer Adolph Deutsch.[19] John had known Deutsch as a boy—the London-born composer was in Roger Wolfe Kahn's band with Johnny Francis before winning Oscars for his work on *Oklahoma!* and *Seven Brides for Seven Brothers*—and at Courage's enthusiastic recommendation Deutsch hired John to play piano on a scoring session for *Funny Face*, the Stanley Donen picture starring Audrey Hepburn and Fred Astaire. On the morning of September 19, 1956, John sat with the Paramount orchestra and performed on the scores for both *Funny Face* and Dimitri Tiomkin's *Gunfight at the O.K. Corral*.[20]

Still another auspicious connection came through Barbara. On *Carousel* she had worked with Alfred Newman, the legendary composer and music director at Fox—a man who had helped establish the sound and technique of film scoring in Hollywood and played an outsized role in its development—and she introduced Newman to her husband. Newman liked John from the moment he heard him at a piano, and

---

† Moore described his piece as a party where classical and jazz struggle to understand each other, giving way to an "orgiastic revel." Several spots in the piano solo were marked "ad lib," leaving room for improvisation. Moore also did some scoring work, and John's earliest dates on the Columbia stage included playing calliope and celeste on episodes of an animated TV series, *The Gerald McBoing-Boing Show*—based on a Dr. Seuss character—that were scored by Moore.

he hired John to play on a pre-record session for the new film adaptation of *South Pacific* in January 1957. "I was very much a green kid on the street," said John, "and one of the nice things about Alfred, and flattering things, was that when I met him he seemed to already know me. He would come over to the piano and talk to me." Newman welcomed John not only into the Fox musical family, but the expansive Newman dynasty—his brothers Lionel and Emil were both film composers. He also, according to Newman's regular collaborator Ken Darby, gave John his very first offer to score a feature film. "And as the story goes, I refused this, what was then a very generous offer and good opportunity," said John, who couldn't recall this would-be start of his film composing career. "I was *so* young—really just out of school, 23, 24 years old—and I was writing music, but I don't think with the kind of confidence that I felt I would have needed.... In those years I thought of myself as a pianist." But, "instead of being the great man from on high," John said, "he made *me* feel as though I were somebody, and he was interested in what I gathered he took to be my talent." Newman developed a warm, mentoring relationship with John, and over the years John would sit in Newman's bungalow and chat—"this was like talking to the Pope to a young musician." Newman was paternal with John, supportive and encouraging "in a way that I must tell you surprised me. I really had no idea, at that time, that I would go as far in film composing." Newman wouldn't have known that either, John said, "but there was some kind of special empathy that I felt from him that made me feel very special."[21]

John would go on to become a regular at Newman family holiday parties, and eventually a very dear friend of Alfred's brother, Lionel.

* * *

John and Barbara moved into a house on Bloomfield Street in Toluca Lake. When he wasn't getting calls by Helfer or Klein for a film date, John was getting calls to play jazz. In November 1956, he was invited to record four contributions for *Modern Jazz Gallery*, an all-star showcase for West Coast jazzers. He was already in that orbit and in their league, and he and his quartet—which included his brother Jerry on the drums—supplied two musical theater standards, including Cole Porter's "Anything Goes," and two originals credited to "John Towner"—one of several professional monikers he was trying out. Inspired by the likes of Previn, John decided to take a swing at becoming a marquee recording artist. Possibly through Phil Moore, he met Albert Marx, an itinerant record producer and freelance repertoire scout for the budget Kapp Records (which released *Modern Jazz Gallery*), and John cut two records under his own name. *The John Towner Touch*, released in July 1957, opened with a quicksilver piano arrangement of "The Most Beautiful Girl in the World," a jazz standard from the Rodgers and Hart musical *Jumbo*. On the LP, John's fingers fly through a series of his own uptempo arrangements of sunny showtunes, supported by acoustic guitar, bass, brush percussion, and a string orchestra conducted by Russell Garcia—capping it all off with his one original tune, "Hello." *Variety* called the album "tasty" and a "varied and delightful session at the 88."[22] That October, John recorded *World on a String*, a tribute to the songs of Harold Arlen, which included his small combo arrangements of "Over the Rainbow," "Come Rain or Come Shine," and "That Old Black Magic." "They didn't sell," John quipped.[23]

But his keyboard prowess was undeniable, and it was soon valued by big names in popular music. John joined an orchestra under Nelson Riddle's baton for three numbers: "Blues in the Night," "What's New?," and "Gone with the Wind." They were the finishing touches on *Frank Sinatra Sings for Only the Lonely*, a number one album nominated for a Grammy and considered by both Riddle and Sinatra as their best work. John became friendly with Riddle, and played on a few of his sessions at Capitol with singer Nat King Cole that featured on the Cole album *To Whom It May Concern*. John was nervous, "because Nat was such a great natural pianist," and when Cole came over to the piano to introduce himself, John stammered: "I feel very uncomfortable in your presence, playing piano for you." Cole said breezily: "No, no, no—it's fine. You just go ahead and do what you want to do."[24] John also played keys on albums by Henry Mancini, Pete Candoli, Dave Pell, and Jerry Fielding. On reflection, John lumped all of this into the category of "scut work," and when confronted as an elder with vinyl copies of his pop past, he called it "schadenfreude." "That's the way I see them. I don't think you could make anything serious out of that except as a result of a *possibility*. Most of it's just irritating remembrances of a juvenile life."[25]

* * *

In hindsight, it was only a matter of time before John Williams started scoring pictures. He was feeling more and more restless at the piano during scoring sessions, and "I began to absorb, by osmosis really, at least the performance practices and the accepted conventions of what would have been done for those films in those years," he said. Stoloff started to ask him, "Can you orchestrate these fifty bars for Thursday?" And "with the temerity of youth" John said, "Yes, I'll do it." Because he was good and quick, he increasingly got asked to do orchestrations for other composers in "last-minute pressure situations."[26] There was, he admitted, an element of pride motivating his leap from the piano bench to the podium. "I sat there at age 24, callow, inexperienced, and largely stupid," he told Previn in that 1988 interview, "and as I was playing and having a few bars' rest, I began to look at the film, and I began to see the conductor over here, and think to myself..."

"*I can do this*," Previn interjects. They both laugh.

"Not only *I can do it*," says John, "but with the temerity of youth, again, *I can do it better than he can do it*."

"That's right," says Previn.

"And one thinks that," John says. "I suppose it's a healthy thing. If ambition or if temerity doesn't belong to the young, who does it belong to?"[27]

John had written plenty of charts for bands and other small ensembles. But, he said,

> Naturally I was still nervous. The most important thing, though, was being a member of those orchestras and sitting there day after day through the good stuff and the bad stuff. You learn pretty quickly. I wasn't over-confident—that's not in my nature—but I accepted, trembling, at the same time knowing that I could probably

make as good a job of it as the next fellow. It was a natural progression, and, as I look back on it now, pretty fast.[28]

Orchestration was an organic stepping stone to full-on composition—and in the annals of Hollywood history, those credited as orchestrators often ghostwrote whole segments of film scores, so the dividing line was already a blur. John admired the work of Edward B. Powell, Alfred Newman's right-hand orchestrator, but he credited one man above all for influencing his early film orchestration: Conrad Salinger. A good friend of Barbara's from when she was in New York doing *Kiss Me, Kate*, Salinger quickly became close with the young couple. "I learned a tremendous amount from him," John said, "mostly from looking at his scores.

> He principally did musicals—he was the architect of what you might call the "MGM sound," that marvelous glow that the orchestra had. It really came from his writing. His scores were highly idiosyncratic: he'd have the third trombone way up in tenor clef, and trumpets low down doing some funny thing.... No one quite had his touch....
>
> I think I learned more from Conrad Salinger than anyone else, even though I don't write anything like him, and not through any specific instruction—just from a kind of osmosis, by being around him.[29]

John orchestrated on everything from *Gidget*, the beach party movie starring Sandra Dee, to Dimitri Tiomkin's theme song for the show *Gunslinger* and his Oscar-nominated score for *The Guns of Navarone*, a World War II picture starring Gregory Peck and David Niven. Everything in Tiomkin's sketch was written in the bass clef, so John asked a friend how he was supposed to orchestrate it. "Throw some of it out," his friend replied.[30]

John's burgeoning and obvious talent as an orchestrator coalesced with a sheer *need* for composers in the exploding field of television. It was the tail end of live TV, and in March 1958 John was hired to score his very first program: an episode of the prestige anthology drama *Playhouse 90*. So called for its 90-minute runtime, the show helped launch the careers of many acclaimed writers, including Rod Serling, and directors Arthur Penn and Franklin J. Schaffner, a former military man and documentarian who went on to forge a creative alliance with Jerry Goldsmith. Schaffner directed the episode "The Right Hand Man," a thinly veiled story about the William Morris Agency, which starred Dana Andrews, Anne Baxter, and Leslie Nielsen. It was shot in Studio 43 at CBS Television City with actors (and cameras) running between 10 sets, jumping over cables and stressing over the red light and the only shot they had at getting it right.[31] John had less than four days to write the music after a Saturday run-through for the live premiere on Thursday, March 20. He chose to write the score as a four-hand piano duet and performed it with Walter Ruick, Barbara's uncle, who had played in a theater orchestra with Glenn Miller before becoming a pianist and arranger at Paramount and then MGM, where he accompanied and wrote dance arrangements for Eleanor Powell, Fred Astaire, and Doris Day, and even composed his own songs.‡ The two pianists accompanied the teleplay in real time in a basement beneath the stage. "You could time the rehearsal," John explained, "and if the scene were a minute and 30 seconds in rehearsal, it might be a minute 40 in the performance, or less—but it was close. You had a monitor, and you worked from a script. You marked the script, and you had the cues—the dialogue scenes that were scored. Exactly the way you would score a radio show."[32]

* * *

John struck up several important friendships as he was finding his professional footing. Besides Previn there was Bernard Herrmann. "Friendship is a difficult word to use with Benny," John said, "because there were always adversarial aspects with every relationship; if they weren't there, he put them there. But I can use the word 'friendship' with Benny. He was quite warmly friendly to me, more so than most people." John and Barbara often socialized with Herrmann, and she had "a wonderful way of handling Benny if he began to become abusive. She would say, 'Oh, Benny, stop that! Behave yourself! Use your napkin!' He would giggle and get all flustered—even blush sometimes."[33] His other pals included two jazz composers who were slightly older, Pete Rugolo and Henry Mancini. "They were young and silly together," said Mancini's wife, Ginny. "They used to hang out in Pete's apartment and read dirty limericks."[34] Mancini was about to become a household name as both a popular conductor and recording artist, and the match that lit the fire was his soundtrack for a TV show created in 1958 by director Blake Edwards. *Peter Gunn*, starring Craig Stevens, kicked off a wave of shows about detectives for the hepcat age—and Mancini's score was central to its cultural catchiness.

Jazz had been slinking its way into film, beginning with Alex North's slinky score for *A Streetcar Named Desire* in 1951. At Columbia Pictures, Marlon Brando's insistence to have music by Milton "Shorty" Rogers in *The Wild One* opened the minds of old school music directors to the idea that jazz musicians could, in fact, read music and weren't *all* "dope fiends," according to Milt Bernhart, a trombonist who was a mainstay at The Lighthouse Café in Hermosa Beach where arrangers like Rogers were concocting what became identified as "West Coast Jazz." Skeptically at first, Morris Stoloff welcomed Bernhart and his fellow West Coast jazzbos onto the scoring stage, where the conservatory-trained musicians sniffed them out like strange dogs and found that they actually got along. "Shorty's writing fit a lot of films like a glove," said Bernhart, "especially films about boys in the big cities who were in trouble, druggies. It just seemed to work." Suddenly, Bernhart said, "anybody who could play bebop and read music started to get calls on motion pictures."[35] Soon came standouts like Elmer Bernstein's savagely jazzy score for *The Man with the Golden Arm*, the 1955 drama starring Frank Sinatra as a drummer and a heroin junkie. *Peter Gunn* was directly inspired by the kind of music Shorty Rogers was making—the series featured an in-world jazz club

---

‡ John and his uncle-in-law also recorded a four-hand piano album in 1958, with John's arrangements of the *South Pacific* songbook. Ruick died from cancer eight years later.

called "Mother's"—and it opened the floodgates for this musical language to become synonymous with crime and cool on the small screen. "It was an idea that, I think, was obvious," Mancini said. "Blake had set it in a jazz club. The minute that hit, the rest of it all fell into place."[36] *The Music from Peter Gunn* went to the top spot on Billboard's popular album chart for several weeks and it cleaned up at the inaugural Grammy Awards, where it won the first ever "Album of the Year." Mancini's swaggering main theme opened with a low, infectious piano riff that acted like a siren song for audiences to run to the television set—a riff that was performed by John Williams.

There was a symbiotic relationship between Hollywood and the local jazz scene. L.A. culture writer Scott Timberg argued that the studio musician system made West Coast Jazz possible,[37] and Mario Castelnuovo-Tedesco half-jokingly referred to himself as the Father of West Coast Jazz, considering how many Hollywood composers of this era he taught, Rogers among them.[38] John's bandmates on *Gunn*—Ronnie Lang, Gene Cipriano, Ted Nash and Dick Nash, Pete Candoli, Rolly Bundock, Jack Sperling, and Shelly Manne—were some of the best jazzmen in town, and when they weren't on the scoring stage they were lighting fires in local clubs. It was such a hot sound that movie studios quickly wanted to cash in on the craze: in the 1957 movie *Hot Rod Rumble*, which was scored by Sandy Courage, the musicians—including Manne, Candoli, and John—got their own special screen credit. "West Coast Jazz" was more than just a reference to its place of origin—it was a difference in *attitude*. The other coast was dominated by the likes of Miles Davis and John Coltrane, and one broad distinction was that "West Coast fire, the West Coast jazz, was more under palm trees, and the East Coast fire was more under the train station," according to Ron Carter, a double bass player who ran with Miles Davis. "That kind of impact, that kind of fire, that kind of *make a mistake and don't care*. California had more sand, they had no snow, they were kind of comfortable with the weather—and they played that kind of jazz."[39] Another obvious difference: most of the West Coasters were white. In New York the music of cats like Coltrane and Cannonball Adderley was "real intense, no holds barred, and greasy and bluesy," explained sax player Dan Higgins, whereas "the West Coast is more Dave Brubeck, more arranged things, quieter, more sophisticated chord changes, and playing somewhat *pale*."[40] "It was *all* jazz," said Ronnie Lang. "I think it was a little more polite out here. Some of the people in the East Coast thought it was too constrained."[41]

* * *

The scoring musicians of Los Angeles, members of the American Federation of Musicians (AFM) Local 47, went on strike in February 1958, the same month Harry Cohn, president of Columbia Pictures, died. Precipitated in part by the Red Scare and the McCarthy witch hunt, the studio system was crumbling and the whole notion of staff players was being re-evaluated. There were 11 different film studios, and each had its own orchestra—which meant there were about 650 fully employed musicians with salaries, health benefits, and pensions. The argument against this policy, Leonard Slatkin pointed out, "was that it prevented other musicians from getting work and therefore was considered a 'closed shop.'" So the AFM and the studios proposed doing away with contracts and hiring musicians on a film-by-film basis. Slatkin's parents, Eleanor and Felix, were against that idea and sided with a movement that birthed a *new* union, the Musicians Guild of America. But the old system collapsed all the same, and in the fall of 1958 the contract orchestras were formally eliminated and all of these former staff players were suddenly forced to go freelance. This was bad news for many musicians, because what in fact happened was a sharp consolidation of players getting called for jobs—from 650 down to about 200.[42]

But *just* as this was happening, musicians pressured AFM president James C. Petrillo to resign, and under new leadership the union struck a deal with the studios that guaranteed an abundance of original music for television. Before this deal, most shows were "scored" using a library of canned tracks from earlier episodes or other existing sources. The new arrangement relaxed the residual percentages that studios would owe in exchange for a minimum requirement of new music—nine hours of recording for every half-hour series consisting of 39 episodes, and so on— which resulted in a gold rush for composers and studio musicians.[43] The biggest goldmine of all was Revue Studios, the largest single producer of television shows in the 20th century, which immediately began investing in quality original music. Revue was the television division of Universal Pictures, which had recently been purchased by MCA—the biggest talent agency in Hollywood. Under its shrewdly capitalist president Lew Wasserman, MCA courted corporate sponsors to foot part of the bill and maintained ownership of their shows, thereby keeping all of the syndication profits. The small screen was still anathema to most movie stars, and film studio moguls kept TV production far away in New York—but MCA cracked the market in L.A. by convincing the president of the Screen Actors Guild, Ronald Reagan, to give MCA a blanket waiver that would allow Revue to produce TV shows without any Guild interference—despite the obvious conflict of interest it was for a talent agency that represented actors to be making the films they starred in. Soon MCA was making ungodly gains from its TV division, selling shows to all three networks, hiring its own talent at discounted rates—and attracting unwanted attention from the United States Justice Department. When MCA bought Universal in December 1958, it turned the struggling studio into a cash machine—luring celebrity directors like Alfred Hitchcock into making movies—and even television, with the anthology show *Alfred Hitchcock Presents*. MCA's pitch to wary clients was: "If Hitchcock can do it, why can't you?"[44]

Universal made a record profit in 1959, and its three biggest film hits were all MCA packages, including *Some Like It Hot*.§ Adolph Deutsch scored that hit Billy Wilder comedy, starring Jack Lemmon and Tony Curtis as musicians who dress in drag and tour with an all-female band, and John played piano on the sessions in January 1959—which meant he got to "accompany" Marilyn Monroe. The sultry star had already pre-recorded her songs, so really John just played while listening to her singing

---

§ Billy Wilder included a wink at his film's corporate parent in a scene where Tony Curtis's character, a musician, pops his head into an office with an "MCA" sign.

"I Wanna Be Loved by You" through headphones. He picked up a valuable lesson from Deutsch, who

> always used to say that music shouldn't try too hard to be funny itself, otherwise one would have something on the level of *Tom and Jerry*. I think I believe this. I think music is very rarely funny in and of itself. If a scene in a film is funny, I would almost prefer to leave it unscored, unless, of course, it is some kind of slapstick or burlesque where music can provide, in a balletic sense, tempo.[45]

Stanley Wilson was a trumpeter and arranger from New York who played in the resident band at the Cocoanut Grove before the war, worked as a welder at Lockheed Aircraft during it, and afterward became an arranger at MGM and then a composer at Republic Studios, where he cranked out scores for dozens of low-rent westerns. "My great claim to fame is that I did the music for some of the serials," Wilson said. "There's a cult of nuts around the world who still sit and watch old Republic serials ... like *Commando Cody* and *The Space Machine*."**[46] His eclectic career culminated in his appointment as music director at Revue in 1953, which he turned into a vibrant farm system for film composers. The scoring stage on the Universal lot was abuzz with three-hour sessions three times a day, sometimes seven days a week. There were more composers working in film and television than at any time in history, and "Stanley was looking for *anybody* who could write *anything*," said John, "the need was so great."[47]

In the fall of 1958, John signed a seven-year contract with Revue.[48] It effectively obligated him to scoring 39 one-hour programs every year, on a smorgasbord of different shows—many of them anthologies with a new cast and storyline from week to week. "Meaning," John said, "that one week I had to do an hour comedy, the next week I had to do an hour western ... and I mean the *next week*. Given if they had 25 minutes of music ... the requirements of the job would be that you had to write music, orchestrate it, and conduct it. And so that was a school like no other."[49] John wagered that he scored some 45 reels a week: "Cue music, real factory-line work. A great opportunity for a young man with a family to earn a living and gain experience."[50] The first show John scored under his new contract was *M Squad*, starring Lee Marvin as Lieutenant Frank Ballinger in one of many G-men series at the time. The show's swaggering, horn-heavy theme tune was written by Count Basie, "but it was too large a sound to carry through the rest of the show," Stanley Wilson said. "That's when I looked up two really top jazzmen, Benny Carter and Johnny Williams."[51] The appointment made Carter the first Black composer to receive screen credit on primetime television, and he and John both performed with a brass-heavy band on their own scores. On Friday, October 24, 1958, John received his first real screen credit—as "John T. Williams,

---

** One of these nuts was a young Steven Spielberg.

Jr."—on "The Trap," an early episode in the show's second season about a kid who accidentally kills a pawnbroker.

By 1960, Wilson had at least 13 composers on staff at Revue—including Cyril J. Mockridge, Conrad Salinger, Pete Rugolo, and Gerald Fried. (Later additions would include Quincy Jones and Dave Grusin.) "The majors had let everybody go," said John. "It was very difficult for people like Herb Spencer and Salinger, because they were let go just at the end of a year or two before they would have had their 30-year pension. So they lost that as well, and they were bitter about it, of course. And so many of them ended up here working for Stanley Wilson." John kept soaking up knowledge from his elders, particularly "Cy" Mockridge—an English pianist and composer who had been in the trenches in World War I before joining the music publishing company Chappell-Harms doing piano reductions for Richard Rodgers's music, then scoring movies at 20th Century Fox for Alfred Newman. "He had a wonderful touch, not unlike Salinger," said John. "Cy and Connie were like two rooms away from my 'cell.'" The Revue composers all worked in a row of small, windowless offices—described by John as "prison cells with pianos"—in a low building just inside the main entrance of the Universal lot. Each room had a little spinet piano, and a music editor sat in the last room in the hall. Working in the old tradition of Hollywood film scoring, the music editor would take detailed notes about where music was to enter and exit, and a secretary would type up the dialogue and describe the action, together yielding "cue sheets," which were John's guide as he set to composing cues timed to the tenth of a second.[52] He worked this way, essentially, for the rest of his career. These composer cells were first come, first served, and when Quincy Jones joined the cohort he got stuck with a room labeled "Sprinkler Drain," a former storage closet of the studio's fire sprinklers. "Film scorers back then," Jones said, "were at the bottom of the Hollywood food chain."[53]

John didn't ask the old-timers questions so much as look at their sketches and listen attentively on the scoring stage. Mockridge was especially meticulous, John said:

> Most of us were rushing, because we had so much to do. Poor guy would sit here till midnight, and it was even very hard on his health. He had to stop after a while. He was not young, and he was heavy. But I have to say, I learned so much just being in proximity to those guys, who were in my mind then *ancients*. And I could hear what the ancients had done the same day or later in the week.[54]

Wilson ran the operation, spotting every episode to determine where music needed to go and for how long, and he went to bat for the composers he hired and in many cases discovered. He also composed several show themes himself, including *Tales of Wells Fargo*.[††] "In the flurry and heat of battle, as a youngster with not a lot of experience," John said, "I was just very busy, extremely focused, and did my best to keep up

---

[††] When the studio was still using canned music, it was Wilson who chose Charles Gounod's "Funeral March of a Marionette" to open every episode of *Alfred Hitchcock Presents*.

with the work."⁵⁵ In the ashes of the old film studio system, Revue was a small-screen echo: a cohort of composers *in house*, working side by side in an environment that was both collegial and competitive. "We were all trying to outdo each other and do something unique and different, but it was all very exciting and a very creative time," said Jerry Goldsmith, a rising star who joined the crew in 1960.

> I was working all night to do one show a week. We took such pride in it and it was really very exciting, and we'd all listen to each other—I'd be outside Dave Grusin's office listening to what he was writing and thinking, "Hmm," and they'd be outside my office listening to what I was writing, but there was a friendly camaraderie at the same time and it was very exciting.⁵⁶

John was given a never-ending stream of film-sized assignments, with a recording studio and staff orchestra at his disposal—much like the Alfred Newmans and Max Steiners before him. He hired his father to play on many of his TV scores, and had to figure out a way to address the old man: "I couldn't say 'Percussion, what's wrong?' And I couldn't say 'Papa, you're a bar early!' So my nickname for him was 'Vibes,' being vibraphone, which he was playing a lot of at the time.... 'Vibes, that's a little too loud'—that's the way we communicated."⁵⁷ John's father never had a pension, and his financial insecurity became John's concern. Besides giving him work at Revue, John would use his earnings to help his parents with a house payment, for instance, or an operation for his mother. Johnny Francis "was insecure in nature," John said, "and he was very limited in his experience, musically.

> He didn't have great experience playing orchestral repertoire of a broad nature. He was more of a swing band jazz musician, with very limited areas of a musical point of view to work. And that worried me very much, and his struggles to move from where he was musically in his career to where he thought he needed to be. So he went into studies of mallets, and he worked very, very hard. But he was already in his late 40s, I think, and never *really* mastered it in the way that someone 19 years old can do.
>
> And so, until the advent of dear Stanley Wilson, he really wasn't working. I don't want to over-credit myself, but there were some issues, a little bit larger than household, that I was able to take care of early on. Which was no great suffering for me, and nothing that shouldn't have been expected and freely given—and it was. His later years were tough. He had emphysema and so on. But he always had great humor, and normally behaved himself very well. And so I felt, at a very young age, that I had to help.⁵⁸

John respected his elders in every respect, including how he developed his voice and instincts as a composer for the screen. Playing in the studio orchestras and breathing the air of so many veteran film composers as he did, "I felt that I needed to follow in their path," he said, "that there was a path going forward about how these people can compose in film, that it's something I needed to learn to do." He applied the skills he had learned from observing Van Eps and from Frank Skinner's book *Underscore*, and took from his elder colleagues lessons about craft, "and how to sync, and the *mécanique* of the thing."[59] He was the respectful pupil of a fairly young but already conventional art form—and he spent the next decade learning its ropes.

* * *

John scored his very first feature film in 1959. *Daddy-O* was the definition of a B-movie: a black-and-white 1950s teen exploitation flick, more disposable than popcorn at a drive-in theater, where in June 1959 you could catch it on a double bill with *Roadracers* for 50 cents—its scant 84 minutes packed with stale hepcat slang, unknown actors giving stiff performances, and casual sexism.‡‡ It was a production of American International Pictures, and co-produced by the Kansas-based Imperial Productions, which launched the career of director Robert Altman. Directed by Lou Place, a first- and only-time filmmaker whose other credits included production management on such titles as *Teenage Doll* (1957) and *She Gods of Shark Reef* (1958), it gave a starring role to "heartthrob accordionist" Dick Contino. As the truck-driving crooner Phil Sandifer, nicknamed "Daddy-O," Contino's hairy-chested charisma translated decently to the screen, but compelling drama mostly evaded him. The *Los Angeles Times* was actually quite kind, praising the star power of its two leads and the "generally sharp script" by David Moessinger, which "is cool enough, man, in the teen dialogue department and not bad on characters."[60] No mention was made of the jazzy score composed by an unknown cat named "John Williams." (He started going by "Johnny Williams" in his screen credits immediately thereafter.) John's debut film score hewed closely to the sound of other teenybopper and hot-rod pictures of the moment, with rat-a-tat hi-hat motors, fast-walking upright bass lines, and cool piano licks. As a work of dramatic film scoring it was primitive, and the movie foreshadowed John's first decade of film assignments, which mostly centered on immature teenagers or 20-something lovers. He was often getting higher quality material for the small screen.

His next film was about L.A. high school students loving and fighting and singing and dancing, all overseen by a new teacher played by America's deejay, Dick Clark. John was hired to score *Because They're Young* in December 1959, and "there was a budget of about $3.50 for the music," he joked.[61] A proto–*American Graffiti*, the Columbia film tapped into the popular surf rock of which Clark was national spokesman via his TV showcase, *American Bandstand*. The movie laced scenes of teen drama and puppy love with songs emanating from car radios and performed by a cast that included singer James Darren, fresh off *Gidget*. John's score had to weave around those songs, and in some cases quote them. Darren performs the title song, which John did not write, at a school dance. John arranged the tune sweetly under romantic

---

‡‡ It had the ignominious honor of being beamed aboard the "Satellite of Love" and roasted in an early episode of the cult movie-riffing series *Mystery Science Theater 3000*. When John's credit appears on screen, the wisecracking robot Tom Servo jabs: "Oh no, John Williams before he heard Stravinsky."

scenes and gave it heroism for the finale. Much of this first phase of John's film-scoring career was saddled with tunes by other composers. Partly thanks to the advent of the long-playing record, the 1960s was the age of the pop title song—epitomized by the James Bond films but hardly exclusive to them—and the waning of the grand, classically influenced orchestral scores that defined the golden age of movies.[62] John, an adept arranger with jazz bona fides, navigated these waters gracefully, but there was a growing fear among composers that big symphonic scoring might never come back.

He was hired to score a more dramatic film that same year, but it was barely a step up in quality. *I Passed for White* was adapted from a 1955 book by Mary Hastings Bradley, based on the true story of a mixed-race woman in Chicago (dubbed "Reba Lee") who was raised by her Black family in a Black community, but who *passed for white* and so decides to run away and try life as a white girl with a white husband. It was a sensational and provocative conceit for a society just waking up to the Civil Rights Movement, and the story is, in retrospect, surprisingly compassionate—albeit stuck in a time when "Negro" was still the nomenclature and interracial marriage a social taboo. Aesthetically the film had the visual style and dialogue of pedestrian television, helmed by director Fred M. Wilcox of *Forbidden Planet*. A white actress played Bernice, whose Black life was represented by a jazz club called the Green Cat, and for once John got to provide the onscreen source music himself. His main theme was a melancholy, romantic ballad in the spirit of David Raksin's *Laura*, performed by solo saxophone in both the main title and also diegetically on the club stage. In the film noir tradition, there was something both seductive and resigned about the melody—a comment on Bernice's desirability and the ill fate of her short-lived tour of the white world. John also wrote a mysterious theme for French horn that played over swirling, dreamlike strings in the opening sequence as Bernice regards herself in a mirror brushing her hair. This recurring idea often accompanied the character examining her own reflection, and it lent an eerie, almost science-fiction quality to this tale of a traveler between two racial planets. The score wobbles and quivers under her new mother-in-law's suspicions ("She's not natural," the old woman says, "like a cat in a strange attic"), and keeps pace with the too-muchness of the film's histrionic climax involving the stillbirth of Bernice's baby and a return to her old life.

John interviewed for a far superior film in 1959—*Anatomy of a Murder*—but director Otto Preminger gave the job to Duke Ellington. "There was no mention at that point of Duke," John said, "but I guess it must have meant that he was looking for a jazz-influenced score."[63]

* * *

As he started his film-composing career, John and Barbara started a family. After Jenny came Mark, born April 25, 1958. Joseph Stanley arrived on September 4, 1960. John referred to the kids as his "little trio,"[64] and he bought a house on Hayvenhurst Avenue in Encino, where they lived not far from the likes of Shelly Manne, Henry Mancini, and Elmer Bernstein. A *Valley Times* article in April 1962 lamented how there were no jazz clubs in the San Fernando Valley despite the fact that roughly 2,650 of the 16,000 members of Local 47 musicians lived in or near the Valley, and "a sizable proportion of these must be jazzmen."⁶⁵ Barbara paused her career to raise the trio, but her irrepressible talents continued to find expression. In early 1959 she appeared in a musical comedy play, *The Boy Friend*, at the Ivar Theatre in Hollywood. "Miss Ruick," wrote the *Hollywood Reporter*, "in delivering the hoary gems of musical stage dialogue given her with more or less a straight face, or singing and dancing up a storm, is a sheer delight."⁶⁶ She also took part in comedy sketches at the Composers and Lyricists Guild of America's annual dinners, and joined a group called SHARE—"Share Happily and Reap Endlessly"—a charity performance organization created by wives of the Rat Pack and populated by Hollywood's "better halves." When she and John occasionally traveled to Europe, they would go to jazz clubs at night, "and with unimagined temerity and chutzpah," John said, "I would go to the piano during the pianist's break, secure enough to do that, and she would sing—which she did brilliantly."⁶⁷

"I'm sure if it wasn't for us she would have been working a lot more," said Jenny, who remembered Barbara preparing for her latest musical productions by blasting the cast album and singing along. Barbara was hardly ever *not* singing.⁶⁸ "I think she would have had a great career had she not married John," admitted her friend, Edye Rugolo. "She would have gone on to Broadway." Edye, also a singer, married Pete Rugolo in 1959, and she and Barbara hit it off at a time when they were both having babies. The SHARE ladies rehearsed on the Paramount and MGM lots, working with top arrangers; in one show, Barbara sang "Take Back Your Mink" from *Guys and Dolls*. "She was just a kick," said Edye. "She was very, very sensuous—very sexy girl—and she stole the show." The Rugolos were part of a social scene that included other composers—Previn, Mancini, Goldsmith—and "we all went out together all the time," Edye said. "We had dinners in a restaurant in the Valley called Monty's, and we went to small clubs."⁶⁹

John and "Babs," his pet name for her, were great social company and great hosts, mostly thanks to the effervescent and extroverted Barbara. Ginny Mancini said Barbara was "the most fun person you could have in a room." These were light, carefree years: Barbara would organize group outings for their friends, buying subscriptions to the Doolittle Theater—the hot Hollywood playhouse that was across the street from the hip Hollywood restaurant, the Brown Derby. "She was instrumental in getting us all out," said Edye. John went along with all of it, although "from then till now," said their friend Bob Klein, "Barbara was the social life. When there was a party at the house, Barbara social directed the whole thing—and Johnny was charming. Even at that time, there was nobody that didn't love John Williams. He just was likable. Everybody felt that way about him."⁷⁰

* * *

The buffet of Revue shows garnished by John included *Wagon Train, Bachelor Father, Markham, Tales of Wells Fargo, Checkmate, General Electric Theatre, Alcoa Premiere, Wide Country, Kraft Mystery Theatre, Kraft Suspense Theatre*, and *Bob Hope Presents: The Chrysler Theatre*. They ran the full gamut of genres, and as a neophyte composer in the heat of merciless deadlines, John typically conformed to the established templates for each genre—a character actor slowly finding his own voice. This "graduate school," as he called it, taught him several lifelong lessons: a discipline of measuring the total amount of music required and writing enough minutes each day to meet that goal; how to write *and* orchestrate on demand, very quickly; and the importance of not only *spotting* music but also dramatic storytelling through music. What he didn't know instinctively he asked his fellow composers or Stanley Wilson—but mostly he learned the art of scoring through sheer repetition, volume, and variety. "I wrote 20 to 25 minutes of music every week for 39 weeks a year," John said. "After five years I had a technique."[71]

Barbara kept up with John's shows and she wrote little poems about them—"silly, but personal," said John, who framed a quartet of these poems. "It's between the two of us."[72] His music for *Wagon Train*—which starred Barbara's ex-husband, Robert Horton—adhered to the basic western formula established by the likes of Jerome Moross by way of Aaron Copland, but some of John's action cues foreshadowed the staccato brass figures in his more mature scores to come, and his plucky music for pizzicato strings anticipated his later approach to comedy scoring. John learned a valuable, humbling lesson about his new craft at the very beginning:

> When you are done, you become only a part of a total experience—you can be covered up by a bit of conversation, or the squeak of a wagon wheel, or the squoosh of a spaceship. But even when you can't actually hear the music, you can tell that it has contributed something indefinable to the total experience if the composer has done a good job—you miss it if it isn't there. What a composer can never forget is that what he is doing is *musique practique*, music made-to-measure.[73]

Bachelor Father epitomized another genre: the sitcom. John Forsythe (future *Dynasty* star) played a single lawyer charged with raising his teenage niece in Beverly Hills and in between his dates with pretty women. It aired on NBC at 9 p.m. on Thursdays, sponsored by American Tobacco. The comedy wasn't sophisticated, but it was sweet, and John's music hugged it with bouncy flute lines, swaying strings, and lots of xylophone. Of all his TV work, in fact, *Bachelor Father* was actually the most representative of John's early feature film résumé: light comedy, quippy dialogue, and relational antics. A less prestigious genre, but one for which his nimble touch and the experience he was building in his side career—as a conductor and arranger creating a soft bed for contemporary singers—made him particularly well suited. He worked closely with Conrad Salinger on the show, who took the middle season of *Bachelor Father* in between John's first and third, writing in adjacent cells. Salinger and his common-law husband were frequent dinner guests at the Williams home. "Connie was entertaining," John said, "and he was funny, and just so delightfully and flamboyantly *gay* at a time when this was very difficult to be. It caused Connie a lot of pain." Salinger died in June 1962 from an overdose of sleeping pills at the age of 59. "He had great brilliance," John said, "and great highs, and equally great lows."[74]

Barbara could relate.

* * *

John finally graduated to steering his own series in 1960. Produced by Dick Berg, who had written the "Right-Hand Man" episode of *Playhouse 90*, *Checkmate* rode the wave of jazzy crime-solving shows unleashed by the popularity of *Peter Gunn*. That wave also included *Johnny Staccato*, a series created by Berg and starring John Cassavetes as a jazz pianist cum detective—which was scored by Elmer Bernstein but with piano licks played by John; in fact, John actually appeared onscreen in the pilot episode in September 1959, tapping in for Johnny Staccato for a set at the jazz club Waldo's. Jennings Lang, a young executive at Revue, was the man responsible for *Staccato*, and Blake Edwards was furious at his gall to create such a blatant *Gunn* rip-off. Hank Grant, picking up on the trend, quipped in the *Hollywood Reporter*: "These days, when our hero snaps a heavy's arm, the bass man sforzandos a sharply plucked G-flat while the brass section glisses down from a high B-flat to emphasize the victim's groans."[75]

Checkmate was created by the British mystery novelist Eric Ambler, and it starred Anthony George and Doug McClure as the team at Checkmate, Inc.—a detective agency in San Francisco, where some of the show was filmed, on a mission to prevent crimes from happening with help from a local criminologist played by Sebastian Cabot. Despite some bad reviews, it was one of the year's top 10 new shows, premiering on CBS on Saturday, September 17, at 8:30 p.m. after *Perry Mason*, with special guest Anne Baxter, and announced with a slick, *Gunn*-like theme song composed by John. Shelly Manne, Ronnie Lang, and many of his *Gunn* mates performed on the track, which rolled an addictive electric guitar groove under a mysterious, angular horn motif. John was an obvious choice for *Checkmate*—a cat whose natural habitat was cool, intellectual jazz. It was "my first responsibility as a show," said John, which "meant that I had to produce a lot more music than I had been used to doing, and had to be on the stage every week." It was also his first opportunity to establish a thematic identity and tone for a whole series, and he adapted his main theme into various action and suspense cues. He wrote to the potential of his all-star bandmates: Lang was one of his versatile doublers, picking up a bass flute or a saxophone as needed, and Manne played percussion and "could always be relied upon for imaginative sounds," said John, who persuaded Wilson to let him record the main recurring cues—the front and end titles and "bumpers" played every week—at the Hollywood pop temple, Western Recorders, because he felt it "would give us the brilliant jazz sound that we needed."[76] "God," said sax player Gene Cipriano, "when you got a call to work with John Williams, that was it. That'd be the highlight of the week."[77]

John scored every episode of the show's highly rated first season, and like *Gunn* the music took on a life of its own. RCA wanted the album rights, but Columbia Records beat them to it—releasing an album in early 1961 composed of new arrangements of tunes from the show, along with a few additional charts. "We knew that John was an up-and-coming composer," said the album's producer, James Harbert.[78] Columbia was the top label in the world, run by Goddard Lieberson, a conservatory-trained musician who knew Aaron Copland and promoted music by Schoenberg and Stravinsky. Lieberson liked orchestras and vocalists and jazz, but he was allergic to rock 'n' roll—calling it "prepubertal singers singing about post-pubertal problems."[79] He was responsible for introducing the long-playing record in 1948, an innovation by an engineer at the label. The 33 revolutions-per-minute "LP" required electric amplification, which meant consumers had to invest in new equipment, but it allowed artists to record 17 minutes on each side—the equivalent of an entire "album" of 78s. Columbia initially used the technology for classical music, recording symphonies in their entirety and in hi-fi. One of Lieberson's other major successes was the Broadway show tune album. He convinced parent company CBS to stage a production of *My Fair Lady*, which became a smash hit, as did the accompanying cast album. (Vic Damone recorded "On the Street Where You Live" for Columbia.) Show albums were suddenly all the rage, and Lieberson practically printed money with the cast recordings for *South Pacific*, *The Sound of Music*, and *West Side Story*. In 1957 he tried something a little more daring, resurrecting an old George and Ira Gershwin show from 1926—*Oh, Kay!*—solely for a new recording. He handpicked the cast, led by Shirley Jones's new husband, Jack Cassidy, and Barbara Ruick—the album's top-billed star who performed the standout number, "Someone to Watch over Me."[80] Once again, it was Barbara who introduced John to an important career connection. They met the tall, dapper Lieberson for lunch in New York and a few times in L.A. "Very elegant guy," said John. "Seemed to be a great friend of Stravinsky."[81] Lieberson had recently expanded Columbia's footprint to the West Coast by opening a new recording center in Los Angeles, and he put a producer named Irving Townsend in charge of all things California and the label's pop division. John was one of the first new artists Townsend signed, along with André Previn and the New Christy Minstrels. John's previous pop records had been made for budget labels—Kapp, Bethlehem, Tops—but now he was married to the best in show.[82]

Much of Columbia's West Coast efforts involved soundtrack albums, and *Checkmate* was John's first featured record after signing. His theme was released as a single, which *Billboard* deemed "interesting jockey wax."[83] The *Tucson Citizen* declared the music to be an integral part of the show's success in a profile of John the following August, when the show launched its second season. "There's a great surge of interest in good music in America," John told the reporter. "Young composers have a great responsibility to create lucid and enjoyable music for a discerning public."[84] The album earned John his first Grammy nomination, for Best Sound Track; he lost to Mancini's immortal score for *Breakfast at Tiffany's*. Shelly Manne dug the *Checkmate* music so much he started featuring it at his Hollywood jazz club, the Manne-Hole on Cahuenga Boulevard, and recorded his own LP of *Checkmate* arrangements in October 1961. For the first time it was *John* being interpreted by an admirer. "What attracted me to the music," Manne said, "was the mood the pieces create—you might call it a 'modal' mood." He also praised John's melodies: "They are good jazz lines. He didn't conceive of *Checkmate* as a jazz score, but because Johnny is also a jazz musician, he knows how to write lines which lay just right for jazz blowing."[85]

* * *

But the main reason John was signed to Columbia was to accompany the label's West Coast singers as an arranger and conductor. After his early work writing charts for

Vic Damone, he landed studio gigs with several now-forgotten vocalists on smaller record labels—among them *Remembering with Marjorie Lee* (1957), *Yvonne de Carlo Sings* (1957), and Johnny Desmond's *Swings* (1958). Columbia opened its new office on Sunset Boulevard largely in response to the migration of so many singers and musicians to Hollywood, and after Townsend produced the *Checkmate* album he assigned John to accompany Pam Garner on her 1960 album *Pam Sings Ballads for Broken Hearts*, where John wrote appropriately smoky, cocktail-clinking arrangements for the sultry lounge singer from Texas on songs including "Willow Weep for Me" and "Lilac Wine."

Columbia wanted to give a lush new sound to their gospel queen, Mahalia Jackson, and Jackson didn't want to record with any other white person than Townsend, John said, joking that Lieberson then hired "the whitest composer-conductor to work with that he could find."[86] John wrote out choral parts in the formal SATB (soprano, alto, tenor, bass) divisions, and he was surprised and a little worried when Jackson brought in some of her own, untrained singers to join the professional studio choir. But Jackson's crew fell in just fine, bringing authentic color and texture to the sound. Beginning in 1960 with *I Believe*, John arranged and conducted a total of four albums with Jackson—all collections of spiritual songs as well as a Christmas album: *Silent Night*. The LPs *Every Time I Feel the Spirit* and *Great Songs of Love and Faith* both won Grammys for Best Gospel Album, and John cherished working in a genre that he felt was "true music, truly inspired, and truly unusual and unique to the group of worshipers."[87] Working for Jackson meant working with Mildred Falls, her plus-sized pianist "who could drown out my whole sixty-piece orchestra," John said. "I took everything down from the way Mildred played, because Mahalia believed the way she did it was the way the Lord meant it to be."[88] Jackson liked John as a leader, but "recording with any orchestra was like a girdle," according to her biographer Laurraine Goreau, and the singer worked herself into a state trying to nail her vocal while also shouting out parts to her lay choristers. During one intense session Jackson tripped on a microphone stand and broke her foot, which sent her to the hospital. She insisted on coming back to the studio, and lay flat on her back on a motel mattress to finish the sessions.[89]

John also made four albums with Frankie Laine, an Italian-American crooner who previously had a hit with the song "That's My Desire" and had now morphed into the voice of the Old West thanks to popular theme songs he recorded for the shows *High Noon*, *Rawhide*, and *Gunslinger* (which John arranged for Tiomkin). John's albums with Laine, from *Hell Bent for Leather!* in 1961 to *Wanderlust* in 1963, kept the cowboy flavor. "We would do these whip-cracking things and these folk songs that he would bring into his style," John said. "A pleasant and joyful man to work with."[90]

"It was a circus of a time," John reflected. "A twelve-song LP would take a week to write and record and edit. Compare that to a rock album, where it takes three or four months to get thirty-five minutes worth of music."[91] All of this pop arranging and conducting work suggested an intriguing career alternative—albeit one that would have been difficult to maintain in the emerging world of The Beatles—but in time John dismissed it as mere scut work.

* * *

The occasional theatrical film that came John's way was still B grade, but he was finally offered a serious drama with some grown-up action in December 1960. As the Cold War chilled Europe, a film crew traveled to Austria and Switzerland to shoot a tale of espionage and escape from the Communist regime in Hungary; based on a novel by Alistair MacLean, who also wrote *The Guns of Navarone*, the film featured stunning scenery and mostly European actors around an American protagonist played by Oscar-winner Richard Widmark. But *The Secret Ways* was chock full of "thoroughly outmoded style and a pack of visual clichés," wrote *Variety*, voicing the consensus opinion when the movie came out in May 1961, calling it "a poor man's *Third Man*."[92] Still, it was a nice canvas for music. After a silent prologue on the Austrian-Hungarian Border in 1960 that ends in violent death, John introduced a downcast, Eastern European motif on tack piano over revving celli. The main theme, which plays as the opening credits shimmer on pools of black water, is a restless, racing search that whips into excitingly dark, embellished adventure before calming back down into the tack piano motif sighing over twitching strings. John's ability to transport audiences to a faraway location would become much more sophisticated, as would the movies he was offered, but the score evoked the Iron Curtain and its thrilling dangers nicely, judiciously sprinkling in that zither-like sound as well as accordion. Different facets of the main theme are reprised throughout the film, spinning a web of secretive suspense in a score that slithers and prowls, with just a little romance and action between all of the sneaking. John's score heroically tried to enliven a fundamentally inert action picture, and several critics noticed: "Johnny Williams' theme music adds an appropriately ominous note," wrote *Variety*, and *Hollywood Reporter* found it "distinctive."[93] In its scathing review of the film, the *New York Times* sounded a rare complaint: "Oddly enough, the music here, too, provides the tip-off... it soon becomes loudly insistent, telegraphing most of the incidents."[94]

It was back to the stifling confines of comedy, where John was pigeonholed for most of the decade. "I became a little bit frustrated," he said.[95] At least *Bachelor Flat* marked the beginning of his long and significant relationship with 20th Century Fox, and while the movie was as silly and lowbrow as anything he ever scored, it did yield a beautiful tune in "Tuesday's Theme." Named for actress Tuesday Weld rather than her character in the film (Libby), it was the first theme where John was especially inspired by a beautiful and talented leading lady. It's also the bright, earnest spot in a score that otherwise has to pogo between a goofy Revolutionary War sketch and the situational comedy antics of a middle-aged Brit and a young American stud played by *West Side Story* star Richard Beymer. Weld, in mischievous coquette mode, pretends to be a criminal on the lam in order to get to know her mother's fiancé, played by the British comic actor Terry-Thomas, an older, gap-toothed archaeology professor who inexplicably has every single young woman in town all hot and bothered. Beymer, by contrast, is a hopeless bachelor who lives in a trailer in the professor's beachside driveway.

The cartoonish film was directed by *Looney Tunes* veteran Frank Tashlin, and the material was lower-brow than much of John's TV work at the time. "Lots of brass chords on cuts to brassieres," he said, "that sort of thing."[96] Indeed, after Beymer's character sees a pair of women's underwear hanging out to dry in front of the professor's house, he goes out for a drive on his moped along the Pacific Coast Highway and suddenly realizes what he saw—helpfully superimposed on screen next to him—to the sound of a clanging cymbal. John wrote a bouncy, sitcom-worthy main theme that gets a lot of varied mileage throughout, as well as comic marches and a big band mambo for the lengthy sequence of a small dachshund dragging a gigantic dinosaur bone along the beach. By contrast, "Tuesday's Theme" is sweet and curious and almost childlike in performances on solo flute or electric guitar over swaying strings and muted trombones—a wonderfully whistle-able melody that treats the character with more respect than the screenplay.

John recorded the music in August 1961—the same month he finished playing piano on the film sessions for *West Side Story*, a massive musical project he had been performing on since the previous year. The celebrated screen version of Leonard Bernstein's masterpiece was one of the very last things John did as a studio pianist. He went home and said to Barbara, "If I could possibly earn enough money for our family working at Universal, I don't want to play anymore." Session work, he said, was no longer challenging.[97] Among his hundreds of credits as a session player were Jerome Moross's western score for *The Big Country*, Previn's adaptation of George Gershwin's *Porgy and Bess*, the comedy *Bell, Book and Candle* (scored by George Duning), the nuclear apocalyptic drama *On the Beach* (Ernest Gold), and the Dean Martin showbiz film *Career* (Franz Waxman). John played the prominent piano solos and did some arranging on Adolph Deutsch's score for *The Apartment*, the Billy Wilder comedy about office affairs. His last date on record was a pre-record session for *The Birds*—the Hitchcock film that famously had no score. John played the piano solo that Tippi Hedren mimes when she visits Rod Taylor and his family before the birds go fully nuts.

"I always say to people who are composers, if you can possibly play in the orchestra for a year or two or three, or even a concert band, do it," John insisted. "The opportunity as a youngster playing for Bernard Herrmann in the orchestra, though he may be screaming at me ... was a good preparation [for] the opportunities that came later."[98] John's time in the orchestra shaped so much of the film composer he became, from the way he ran his sessions to the way he wrote. It was another critical piece of his unusual education.

* * *

Slightly higher art soon came John's way in several prestigious anthology dramas. *General Electric Theater* was a long-running series hosted by Ronald Reagan with a theme by Elmer Bernstein, airing on CBS Sunday nights at 9 p.m. John scored a half dozen episodes beginning in the show's eighth season. More significant was *Premiere Theatre*, a series that aired for two seasons on ABC Tuesdays at 10 p.m.—sponsored by the aluminum company Alcoa and hosted by Fred Astaire. "I had come to trust in Johnny," said series producer Dick Berg. "He was dependable, and there simply wasn't a lot of time for philosophical decisions. People like Johnny were pretty much left to their own devices."[99] *Alcoa Premiere* debuted on October 10, 1961. John wrote the main theme—an opulent overture—and he composed an original, bespoke score for almost every single one of its 60 episodes, which alternated between a half hour and hour in length, now with the canvas and budget for a larger orchestra. This was a higher grade of meat to sink his teeth into: the second season premiere, "Flashing Spikes," starred Jimmy Stewart as a disgraced baseball player, featured a cameo by John Wayne, and was directed by John Ford—in the same year that all three made *The Man Who Shot Liberty Valance*. The *Alcoa* episode wasn't nearly on that level, but it did inspire a pastoral drama score, including some bandstand nostalgia, worthy of America's national pastime. John wrote his first atonal music for "The Jail," from a science-fiction story by Ray Bradbury set in the distant future of 2002. *Alcoa Premiere* boasted guest stars like Charlton Heston, William Shatner, and a very young Robert Redford. ("I remember commenting to people in the projection booth about what a telling figure this unknown young man became when you put him on the screen," John later bragged.[100]) The series also earned John his first acclaim from his fellow TV composers, with a Primetime Emmy nomination both seasons.

John encountered several of his future filmmaker collaborators in the minor leagues of television. He scored episodes directed by both Sydney Pollack and David Lowell Rich on *Premiere*, and he crossed paths with Irvin Kershner and Robert Altman on *Kraft Suspense Theatre*. He first met Altman on *Kraft Mystery Theatre*, a summer offshoot of the long-running anthology sponsored by the maker of Cheez Whiz—*Kraft Television Theatre*—which ran from 1961 to 1963. John composed the non-cheesy theme and scored several episodes. Altman "was very different from other directors," John said. "I didn't meet them; there wasn't contact. But once I was assigned to Bob he practically lived over in the music department with me—inviting me to his house, wanting to have drinks after work. I was fascinated with him because he showed so much unaccustomed interest in what I was doing. He became a collaborator in a way that wasn't usual in those days in TV."[101]

John also composed the theme for *Bob Hope Presents: The Chrysler Theater* and scored several episodes of the hour-long drama anthology that aired on NBC. *Chrysler* was one of Revue's most expensive and prestigious products, and its distinguished alumni included writers Rod Serling and Edward Anhalt (whose screenplay for the film *Becket* was produced around this time). John's theme for the show was an important-sounding syncopated fugal fanfare, which gave way to a lush, romantic curtain-raiser. Episodes included "One Day in the Life of Ivan Denisovich," based on a new short novel and starring Jason Robards as a prisoner in a Soviet labor camp. John's score was armed with militaristic brass, snare drum, and timpani suspense, and featured a lonely clarinet solo for the men waiting out in the cold. Another episode was "War of Nerves," directed by Pollack, which met its Parisian café setting with slinky saxophones and romantic, Gallic suspense. More variety, more deadlines—more experience.

* * *

Meanwhile, John kept trying to make a splash as a name recording artist—a more exciting prospect than the weekly grind of television and flimsy film assignments—and his strongest effort of all was *Rhythm in Motion*. In late April 1961 he went into Columbia's studios to record an album that would show off their new stereo technology, using 14 condenser microphones, as well as his arranging chops. He took several bygone showtunes ("The Surrey with the Fringe on Top," "Let's Do It") and breathed syncopated, playful new life into them with a large orchestra—one that included his friends Shelly Manne, Pete Candoli, the Nash brothers, and both his father and Jerry on percussion. John's charts "combine smoking big band writing with soaring horn countermelodies, helter-skelter woodwind passages, and inventive use of percussion," wrote Williams scholar Jeff Eldridge, who noted how the muted brass and "cartoon-style woodwind" effects became staples of John's 1960s comedy scores.[102] "It was the year that stereo was getting very big," recounted the album's producer, James Harbert, who was planning a whole series of "in Motion" stereo albums. "That fad passed rather quickly."[103] Harbert was a trumpet player and all-around musician from Oklahoma City who had studied piano and composition at the Curtis Institute of Music, then gave up his early dreams of joining a symphony orchestra and returned to his home state to earn a degree in journalism. A brief stint in advertising took him out to Los Angeles, where he then became Doris Day's rehearsal pianist and a pop songwriter. "He was a man of considerable parts," said John—and they became good friends. John made several radio appearances to promote the album, even in Denver, but sales and airplay didn't live up to his or Columbia's hopes—even though it found fans. *Disc* magazine called it "one of the occasional happy surprises which come out of the blue and catch your ear and hold it solid from the first bar to the last." Composer David Shire bought *Rhythm in Motion* when it first came out, and it became one of his all-time favorites. "He is master of so many different styles and genres," Shire marveled, "and he doesn't just dabble in them—he is a *master* in all of them."[104] Eldridge posed an interesting question: What if the album had been a blockbuster? Could that have steered John away from the path of movies? Then again, what future *was* there for a jazzy orchestra arranger by the end of the decade?

John and Barbara were visiting New York in February 1964, staying at the Sherry-Netherland, when they attempted to leave the hotel during the middle of the day and "there was a sea of humanity, all the way up to the entrance of the Plaza," he said. "Impassable." So they were forced back into the hotel, and John asked someone what was going on. He was told some pop group called "the Beatles" were in town and going on Ed Sullivan's show that night. When John heard a Beatles record for the first time, "I would hear Ringo play drums and I thought: *well, I've been working with Buddy Rich and Shelly Manne and Alvin Stoller. This kid sounds like a rank amateur to me.* What possibly could be so good about these kids—that would then take the place of Harold Arlen and Cole Porter? I wasn't as enlightened as Lenny Bernstein, and I didn't immediately hear their genius."[105] As the sixties rolled on, neither John nor Barbara listened to the Beatles, the Beach Boys, or Bob Dylan—although Barbara loved Janis Joplin for her unique voice. It was almost always jazz playing in the house.

"I didn't really hear much of classical music," said Jenny, "but I remember my father *reading* a lot of it."[106] In the evenings, John was prone to curl up with a written score of Beethoven or Brahms and read it like a book.

Rhythm in Motion was the last full-length album reserved exclusively for "Johnny Williams and His Orchestra," although Columbia allowed John to cut a few singles—"Tuesday's Theme," "Montreal" by Peter Knauer, a new rendition of "The Black Knight" from *Checkmate*, and "Augie's Great Piano," an original composition with John on the keys—before letting his contract expire in July 1964.[107] During that time he also did a number of arrangements for André Previn on albums that showcased film music both old and new. But by now Previn had more than one foot out the door, with his toes pointed toward the classical world, and he was anxious to take John with him. The pop album with the most staying power was John's jazzification of *My Fair Lady*. Prompted by the release of the new movie adaptation and instigated by Shelly Manne, *My Fair Lady with the UN-original Cast* featured John's playfully hep, syncopated charts of the Lerner and Loewe songbook with cheeky vocals by Jack Sheldon and Irene Kral. John wrote an instrumental overture and his new interpretations included "On the Street Where You Live"—the song he was partly responsible for keeping in the show. (On tuba was John Bambridge, Sr., the man who had given him the book *Underscore*.) The album arrived on October 5, a few weeks before the film. John met Alan Jay Lerner and Frederick Loewe shortly thereafter. "They didn't forgive me immediately," he joked.[108] John, Manne, and much of that same band gave a similar treatment to George Gershwin's canon the following spring. *Manne—That's Gershwin!* was released on Capitol Records in May 1965. It was quickly followed by another Previn album of film themes which John supplied arrangements for—the last strictly pop or jazz album John would make.

***

John was finally offered his first decent movie in May 1962. Like *I Passed for White*, it dealt with racial prejudice and interracial romance head-on, this time on the lush islands of Hawaii—but *Diamond Head* tackled those themes with a first-rate cast and a witty script by Marguerite Roberts, adapted from a 1960 novel by journalist Peter Gilman. Producer Jerry Bresler had hired John for *Because They're Young* and, right after this, *Gidget Goes to Rome*; all three movies featured singer James Darren, an Italian American who in *Diamond Head* played a brown-toned native Hawaiian named Paul—the most blatant instance of brownface in a film where his mother was played by an actress of Russian-Jewish-Scottish heritage and his half-brother by *West Side Story*'s George Chakiris, the son of Greek immigrants.[§§] The casting does somewhat undermine the power of the plot, which some critics derided as a soap or "pineapple" opera. But *Diamond Head* largely transcended its flaws with a sensitive, engaging story about a wealthy baron named King—played with gusto by Charlton Heston, three years after his Oscar-winning performance as Judah Ben-Hur—who

---

[§§] John had previously arranged several songs for Darren on the singer's *Album No. 1* in 1959.

reacts badly when his little sister Sloane announces her engagement to Paul. King is running for Congress to represent the newest addition to the United States, and his high-minded speeches about equality are betrayed by his visceral objection to the family line being sullied with native blood. ("It had to come into my home before I knew what I really believed," King says through clenched teeth.) He's also a hypocrite, engaged in an affair with the beautiful Mai Chen, who adds to his woes when she informs King she's carrying his child. By the end of the story, Paul and Mai are dead, both victims of King's racist ego in their own way. The more melodramatic elements were mostly grounded by the fine performers and director Guy Green, a British cinematographer who won an Oscar for lensing David Lean's *Great Expectations* before moving to the director's chair. Green took full advantage of his location shoot on the island of Kauai, and the film was so scenically beautiful that the state of Hawaii was glad to use it as a promotion for tourism.

It was also, ironically, a missed opportunity for John. Bresler had gotten so hooked on a Hugo Winterhalter cantata called "Diamond Head" that he named the film after it and appointed the song its main theme.*** Darren recorded "Diamond Head" for Columbia's Colpix Records—although the sung version didn't make it into the movie for some reason. John elegantly adapted the sighing, romantic tune, giving it a trotting pulse and brass embellishments for scenes of King riding his land, squeezing passion from it for Sloane and Paul's happier moments, and using a French horn to make it as forlorn as the prematurely widowed Sloane walking the beaches alone. The most interesting cue in the score accompanied the weirdest scene: a dream Sloane has in her fevered, drunken sleep where she imagines herself riding a white horse and then bathing nude by a waterfall, beckoning romantically to Chakiris, who then morphs into Paul, who then turns into her *brother*. John treated the fantasy with mysticism and aquatic romance that then spirals wildly along with Sloane. But beyond that, there was more source music in the film than underscore—cues for soft Hawaiian dances, lounge piano music for upscale restaurants, and a pounding drum beat for an engagement party that turns deadly. John recorded the score in August 1962 with his friends in the Columbia orchestra, and the film had its big premiere gala in Honolulu that December. John's contribution got a curt, sterile mention in *Hollywood Reporter*'s review as being "effective,"[109] whereas *Variety* deemed it "unobtrusive."[110] Now boasting its own dedicated record label, Columbia Pictures rode the wave of soundtrack releases with an album featuring Darren's song and a collection of rearrangements by John that were loosely tied to the actual score. Though an odd representation of his work, it was the first soundtrack LP for a John Williams film score.

Bresler and Darren immediately went on to make the far more disposable *Gidget Goes to Rome*. The teen series was running out of narrative steam by its third entry, which took the character on a poor man's *Roman Holiday*. Once again, John was required to work with someone else's songs: Darren performed "Gegetta" and "Grande

---

*** Winterhalter was best known as a bandleader and arranger for singers like Sinatra and Doris Day, but he also contributed several albums to the popular "exotica" genre.

Luna Italiana," both written by George David Weiss and Al Kasha, and John made liberal use of the bouncing "Gegetta" tune, drizzling it in a light spaghetti sauce of accordion and tremolo guitar. There are some lovely champagne arrangements in the film's more relaxed moments of the group touring Rome, and reflective passages where Gidget is feeling melancholy or heartbroken. John wrote a few Italianist source cues for restaurant bands and parties, often using "Gegetta," and when Gidget jumps into the Trevi Fountain to retrieve a gold coin she inadvertently tossed in to make a wish, John showered the moment with a spirited, sparkling take on the tune as a guard drags her out of the water. But most of the score plays in a much broader key, with parody *Cleopatra* music and some mischievous writing for woodwinds, brass, and pizzicato celli that would become hallmarks of his approach to light comedy. *Variety* called *Gidget Goes to Rome* the third and poorest in the teen series, and listed John as "among those who contributed their skills to this losing cause."[111]

His next two film assignments were equally lost causes. Revue hired director Don Siegel (*Invasion of the Body Snatchers*) to make a feature-length TV movie that would launch a new anthology series for NBC. *Project 120* was a reference to the two-hour length, and the idea was to be as big in concept and execution as cinema. *The Killers* ultimately went to movie theaters instead of TV screens anyway, but only because it was judged too sexy and violent. Based very loosely on the Ernest Hemingway story, the project was notable for being Ronald Reagan's last film as an actor and his lone turn as a bad guy—a ruthless mob boss who at one point slaps a woman. (Reagan came to hate the movie.[112]) It began shooting on November 21, 1963, and the next day the company got news on set of JFK's assassination.[113] John wrote a blaring, percussive main title theme for the opening credits, all scuzzy and harsh, but the song anchor in the film, "Too Little Time," was actually composed by Henry Mancini. This slow lounge ballad was performed by Nancy Wilson and introduced diegetically for an early scene of Johnny—the ill-fated racecar driver played by John Cassavetes—dancing with a femme fatale named Sheila. John quotes the tune in a lovey-dovey setting as the couple necks and drinks champagne, then in a melancholy way after Johnny crashes during a race and wakes up in a hospital with damage to his eyes. It crops up whenever the romantic pair reunites, often in flashbacks, but there isn't much time for love. There are long stretches of the film without any score, and the occasional crime-jazz action cues don't have much personality—which suited the movie.

A talented filmmaker, J. Lee Thompson had made *The Guns of Navarone* and *Cape Fear*, as well as several serious pictures about exotic foreign lands such as *Taras Bulba*, which is perhaps why he was chosen for one of the most bizarre, misbegotten concepts ever for a movie—and easily the biggest turkey John ever scored. *John Goldfarb, Please Come Home* was "inspired" by the true story of an American spy pilot shot down over Soviet Russia and held prisoner, a fraught episode in the early days of the Cold War. Screenwriter William Blatty, the novelist who would write *The Exorcist*, inexplicably played the idea as a farce about an untalented ex-footballer whose plane goes down in the Middle East and is forced by an Arab king to coach the natives in a match with Notre Dame on a gridiron in the middle of the desert. Notre Dame sued 20th Century Fox for exploiting their good reputation for something so crass, and the lawsuit held the film's release up for months.[114] It was an oafish, laugh-free slog featuring British actor Peter Ustinov in brownface as King Fawz doing a broad Arab imitation and driving around his palace in a kitted-out golf cart, ogling the beautiful and predominantly white women in his harem. The marquee star was Shirley MacLaine—her husband produced the film—as a Lois Lane–style feminist reporter who agrees to go undercover as a harem girl in order to write about the king. She's assured the king is old and impotent, but quickly learns that he does, in fact, make use of his harem, and she spends most of the film in various states of undress, clownishly trying to avoid the king's bed. Richard Crenna played the title character, who winds up in a keffiyeh trying hopelessly to teach Bedouins how to throw a touchdown. The production was offensive not only because of its camp caricatures of another culture but also for its garish plastic sets, and for a movie about a horny despot and full of women in spangly bikinis, its attempt at a romance between Crenna and MacLaine was downright flaccid.

There was almost *nothing* for John to work with, and he was forced to do his own crude stereotyping of Arabian idioms and belly dancing music; he also spoofed American military music and football fight songs, and threw some silent-film ragtime piano at a scene where the king triggers an exploding toy train in MacLaine's bedroom and comes in with a firehose to blast her with water. The climactic football match devolves into the Bedouins biting Notre Dame players and goats running onto the field, butting heads with the Fighting Irish and spraying them with milk. At the very least, John got to work with James Harbert, who had by now left Columbia Records to begin his own arranging career. John hired Harbert as an orchestrator on several TV scores at Revue, and *Goldfarb* was the first of several film projects they did together at Fox. "I went to the Curtis Institute and John went to Juilliard, so we always joked about that," Harbert said. "He'd hand me sketches that were pretty well voiced, and I'd tell him, 'I could just hand this over to a copyist; you don't need me.' But he'd say, 'I want you to give it some of your Curtis snobbery.' He also liked my manuscript, which he called 'Danish modern.' Later I actually saw a behavioral therapist so I could learn to notate faster ... John saw my scores and insisted I didn't write them. He told me to please go back to my Danish modern!"[115] The only piece of beauty John pulled from this muck was a pretty love theme for flute and timid strings. He got to write his own title song for a change, but "John Goldfarb, Please Come Home" doesn't sound like he was too excited about it. MacLaine sang the number, a weird, uncatchy hybrid of fuzz rock and Arabia that opens the film; John also turned the tune into Fawz U's marching band fight song. Incredibly, MacLaine's screeching rendition of "John Goldfarb" was released as a single while the film itself was stuck in limbo. When the courts finally allowed the film to open in March 1965, critics jumped on it with extra glee. The *New York Times*' Bosley Crowther said it "not only makes Notre Dame look foolish in a familiar low-comedy way but it also demeans the prestige of movie humor and, indeed, of the human race."[116] John's reputation was mercifully untarnished, and the one true blessing to come out of *John Goldfarb* was the beginning of his relationship with Fox producer Richard D. Zanuck. Because of Fox, and its TV music director Lionel Newman, his luck was about to turn. "I remember being very frustrated, talking to Lionel and Barbara and others," John said. "You know, *This is not going anywhere*. But things happened."[117]

John's contract with Revue was up by 1965, and he was more than ready to leave the prison cell of television. Besides the regular anthology series, he had also scored several pilots, some of which—like *McHale's Navy*—were ordered to series and scored by other composers. One of the last things he composed at Revue was the pilot and theme music for *Gilligan's Island*. That original pilot never aired, and the theme was replaced by one written by show creator Sherwood Schwartz. Still, John's theme *was* recycled several times in the series as underscore. As goofy and disposable, and in some cases *godawful*, as many of the assignments were, John owed so much of his scoring craft and process to this formative season of his career—"I could say *all* of it," he said.

> I certainly learned a lot, and it was a sort of miniature mirror of what we had to do in feature films—one week a comedy, another week a western. You had to change your style and some of your grammar and all the rest of it—quickly and weekly and so on. But frankly I didn't think much about it. These were weekly assignments that I just did, as well as I could do. For a lot of those times I felt that I could do the work better than some of the older colleagues. Whether that's just temerity of youth or there was some objective truth in it, I don't know.

It was a vocational school like no other, one that demanded versatility and speed. It also rewarded, or at least encouraged, a certain amount of Hollywood classicism—the traditions of scoring films and television that were established by a previous generation. As opposed to his more radical peers like Jerry Goldsmith, whose "orchestration was Jerry's entirely," said John—"he'd have one flute and one electric saw"—John wasn't out to invent a new musical language or wildly subvert genre expectations. The old ways were his inheritance, and "it seemed like a very natural environment to me," he said.

> My father was working in a studio every day and talking about it every night—*this composer, that composer*. I visited the stage. Somebody coming out here from Missouri from a music school to start working in TV wouldn't be acclimatized the way I must have been. I knew all the musicians, I played in the orchestra before I started to write. It was the most natural progression in the world. I might have joined something that was in motion—moving it *forward*, I hope, to some degree. It was already there, and I joined it in the best way I could.[118]

* * *

The Williams family moved again in 1963, settling into a beautiful two-story house on High Valley Road in Encino. Downstairs was the kitchen, den, dining room, living

Figure 4.1. John and Barbara by the pool, 1965 (Courtesy of Paula Arlich).

room, and master bedroom. Upstairs was the kids' domain: three bedrooms and a playroom. The backyard pool was in constant use; Barbara loved the sun (Figure 4.1). The kids made fast friends with their new neighbors who lived behind the house, and John coordinated with their mother to build a small gated passage that connected the two yards. They called it "the dirty way," said Jenny, "which meant we didn't have to go down the street and go all the way around." The Williams family had a cat, Mitchell, and a white standard poodle named Big, "but because he lived with us in the backyard he was more like a dusty brown," said Jenny. Barbara wasn't a great cook, but she was a good *fixer*—making standard kid food like hot dogs, hamburgers, lamb chops, and macaroni and cheese. Family dinners were rare, and on many evenings the kids would hover at the top of the stairs to hear the soundtrack of chatter and clinking cocktail glasses that accompanied regular parties hosted by Barbara, with music provided by John and his talented friends.[119] John also loved to host and perform in chamber concerts at the house—often with Edgar Lustgarten, a veteran cellist of the St. Louis Symphony—paired with a Sunday brunch. "It was very civilized," John said. "We served Bloody Marys and Eddie and I would play these pieces. Seemed to be longer days with time in between for that kind of music, which I loved doing."[120]

There wasn't a soul who didn't adore Barbara, a woman who would *sing* conversation to her kids as often as she would speak it. But her bubbly personality masked a more complex character. "My mom struggled with depression," said Jenny, "and as the only daughter and the oldest child, I was very in touch with and in tune with what she was going through. From a very, very early age I felt very protective and responsible for my brothers, because I really wanted to make sure Mom was okay and not burdened by us." Jenny was a classic tomboy, and unlike her brothers, she loved to play catch every day with Dad. They would also sit and read together at night, forming a deep bond that never broke. "Even in the very beginning, he was always the parent I would go to," Jenny said.[121] After John left Revue, he worked from home. "There was a little room off the kitchen that was like his work room," said Joseph, the youngest, "and it had a little stand-up piano and a nice desk for him to write. I remember the smell of pencils being sharpened."[122] There was a family rule not to enter the office when John was working, but it wasn't enforced with any severity. "I used to pass notes under the door—'Hey man!'" said Jenny, "and draw pictures and stuff, and he would smile and get back to me. But we knew that he was working, and so we respected that. I think he was always so happy when he had a studio to go to so that he could get away from the frenetic household, from kids and everything."

If John really likes you, "he changes your name," said Edye Rugolo, who earned the nickname "McGiffy."[123] Jenny was "Sister Varner," after the most serious nun from his primary school in Flushing. John called Lionel Newman "Tootsie," because he always had candy on his desk. Robert Altman went by "The Flying Dutchman," although John usually just called him Bob. John didn't have a nickname for Previn, but Previn forever called him "Babe." John, so demure and dignified, was strangely drawn to larger-than-life personalities, raconteurs, and jokesters—Altman, Previn, Newman—who were much more openly arrogant or crude or cynical than he was. "He's always had friends like that," said Jenny. "I think it's because he's a great audience, and he's very entertained by their personalities. And they all loved him. I just think he was a great audience for their boisterousness, their being crude—all the things he may not do himself. He loved being around them."[124]

Barbara returned to the stage in 1964 with a supporting role in *She Loves Me* at MelodyLand Theatre in Anaheim. Her co-stars were James Darren and Dorothy Collins—the young second wife of Raymond Scott. Barbara and Collins were good friends, and John found himself reuniting with his dad's old bandleader on double dates. The Scotts lived on Long Island, and John and Barbara visited with them on several occasions. "We reminisced about the 1930s when I was a little eight-year-old following the Quintette around," John said.[125] "My mom loved how kooky Barbara was," said Collins's daughter, Deborah, who was struck by Barbara's "great big heart, and her very open face. [It was] almost clownlike—she could be very expressive and emotive with her face."

> Barbara was definitely larger than life. She was just one of those people who you just felt like she would listen to you. She had this big sort of outward kind of thing, but she was very dear. You felt warm around her, because she was so warm and funny. She would dress in really fun ways. Her hair was red, in like a bouffant bob with bangs. She wore wild clothes like leopard prints, just kind of jazzy stuff.[126]

Barbara made a campy return to the screen on February 22, 1965, in another Rodgers and Hammerstein musical. *Cinderella* was the duo's only show written for television, originally premiering in 1957 with Julie Andrews. For the revival production, Barbara played the wicked stepsister Esmerelda, an ungainly bimbo who compulsively flutters her eyelashes and who, paired with the comic actress Pat Carroll, tortures Leslie Ann Warren's Cinderella. There were three weeks of rehearsals and a week of taping, with all songs performed live on set. "If it lives up to all our expectations it should be an annual event around CBS, maybe for the next five years," Barbara said. "That would suit me fine. I'm tired of seeing the *Wizard of Oz*." A *Valley Times* article noted how she had paused her performing career to raise her children. "Now," she said, "when millions (including producers) see tonight's show they'll know I'm back in action."[127] Motherhood had only strengthened her voice, she said: "The volume comes from screaming at the kids."[128]

* * *

John turned 33 in February 1965, and his music was also starting to mature. Besides concentrating on feature films over television, he was also dipping his pencil into the classical stream. The first public performance of one of his "serious" concert works occurred on March 29. Famed jazz bandleader Stan Kenton formed the Los Angeles Neophonic Orchestra, which commissioned and performed contemporary music that fused jazz with classical and featured many of John's friends. Kenton opened the final, sold-out concert of their inaugural season with John's Prelude and Fugue at the Music Center in downtown L.A. Dedicated to Claude Thornhill, his stylistic influence and father's old friend, the piece was a more dissonant and sophisticated but still relentlessly groovy application of John's jazz style, and it "adhered faithfully to the classical form," as Harvey Siders wrote in the *Los Angeles Evening Citizen*, building "to a logical fugal climax."[129] In an overall lukewarm review of the evening, the *Los Angeles Times* stacked John's piece in the column of "worthwhile" selections, "based on brooding chromaticisms of a melodic tone row."[130][†††]

In December, André Previn conducted the premiere of John's most ambitious concert work yet, the eight-minute *Essay for Strings*, performed by the Houston

---

[†††] Kenton and company recorded the piece on an album for Capitol Records.

Symphony Orchestra—the first symphony orchestra program of a John Williams classical work. As he would tend to do, John wrote a rather technical program note:

> The work, for string orchestra, is in one movement and its character is essentially dramatic. After a quiet introduction, the main "row like" theme appears. This is followed quickly by just a suggestion of the driving sixteenth-note "motor" figure which eventually, after other development, moves the work into its final section. It is here that the main theme joins the "motor" figure and they combine to propel the piece to its conclusion.[131]

Previn took the piece to Pittsburgh the following December, and John flew out to hear the city's orchestra perform it on a program with Brahms's D Minor piano concerto under the hands of Israeli soloist Daniel Barenboim.[‡‡‡] The *Pittsburgh Post-Gazette* critic Donald Steinfirst judged the *Essay* "a work of unusual merit. String writing of orchestral dimensions is not particularly easy and Mr. Williams has undoubted mastery of his craft.... It also proves that twelve-tone writing need be neither dissonant nor raucous and if the program notes had not mentioned the fact, it is doubtful that the dodecaphonic technique would have been recognized, certainly not by me."[132] *Essay for Strings* was later selected by the Rockefeller Foundation in an attempt to promote modern music, and performed at several American universities: in the summer of 1967 the St. Louis Symphony performed it at the local Washington University, and the Los Angeles Philharmonic under conductor Zubin Mehta performed it at USC, UCLA, and Occidental College.[133]

Previn was doing everything he could to shed his Hollywood skin, and he used his new platform as a symphony conductor to promote—and nudge—John's classical inclinations.

* * *

John had the bizarre distinction of scoring the one and only film directed by Frank Sinatra. The Vietnam War was heating up in 1965, and *None But the Brave* was an antiwar film about World War II and an unlikely co-production between Sinatra's Artanis Productions/Warner Bros. and the Japanese studio Tokyo Eiga. The joint screenplay by American John Twist and Japanese Katsuya Susaki stranded a contingent from each country on an island in the Pacific, forced to arrive at an uneasy truce and, in the process, experiencing the other's humanity. Sinatra, now 50, played a grizzled, drunken combat medic who in the film's most harrowing scene operates on a wounded Japanese soldier in exchange for food and water for his men. The film compassionately centered and humanized the Japanese, who speak their own (subtitled) language, and Sinatra often cut between nighttime conversations going on in each camp that reveal the nations as two sides of the same worthy coin. It was one of the sturdiest projects John had

---

[‡‡‡] While in Pittsburgh, John, Previn, and Barenboim went together to see a stage production of *A Midsummer Night's Dream*. ("Praise by Previn," *Pittsburgh Post-Gazette*, December 15, 1966.)

been given to date, and he was signed in September 1964 after the film finished shooting on location in Hawaii. The music was supervised by John's old boss, Morris Stoloff, who was now music director at Sinatra's label, Reprise, and a good friend of the singer. Stoloff might have been the one who recommended John for the job. "I was very surprised about that," John said, "because Frank Sinatra knew all the musicians in Hollywood and could have had anyone he wished. I felt at the time, and still do, that I was a very lucky person to have that assignment." Sinatra couldn't have been nicer, John said. "Maybe you wouldn't want him for an enemy, but he is a marvelous friend. He's a very compelling character; he can give you the impression he is completely alone in the world."[134] After the music was recorded, Sinatra sent John a thank you note and gifts.

It was not a great film, but it inspired John's most ambitious and cohesive score to date. The main theme was his first serious Americana melody for a motion picture—aspirational in a Copland-like setting, punctuated with jagged counterpoint on French horns and a rising bass line on low strings. It was clearly a product of its era, but full of the romantic heroism with a hint of danger that became one of John's trademarks. Just as the script and performances didn't demean the Japanese characters, John's music was culturally specific—relying on block percussion, flutes, and a pentatonic scale—without dipping into crude orientalism. The score has extended cues of martial suspense, brassy combat, and tropical atmosphere—not at the level of infectiousness or searing personality that his later adventure scores would have, but hinting at his potential. An emotional standout comes in the quiet nighttime conversation between Captain Bourke and Lt. Kuroki, where a gentle breeze blown by clarinet and flutes ushers in a reflective piece of koto music for Kuroki's fond reminiscence of his beautiful home; a lone French horn emerges out of this nostalgic cloud as a symbol of war and manly allegiance as we see Kuroki in uniform, leaving his wife. The anguished string and angular horn writing when the Americans and Japanese are forced to go their separate ways in the unavoidable fate of war presaged John's soured patriotic scores for Oliver Stone, as did the ending: a lonely, Taps-like trumpet statement of the main theme as the camera hovers over bloody corpses of Japanese soldiers, then a passionate string and trumpet extension of the tune as Sinatra surveys dead Americans—all culminating with a lovely reprise of the theme as the director's unsubtle thesis appears on the screen in bold text: "NOBODY EVER WINS." Such noble intentions were sabotaged by generic staging and a confusion in tone—with some broad, goofball acting by Tommy Sands in particular. *None But the Brave* opened on February 24, 1965, and Bosley Crowther spoke for most critics: "If the threat of Frank Sinatra as a film director is judged by his first try ... it is clear that there need be no apprehension among the members of the Screen Directors Guild. A minimum show of creative invention and a maximum use of cinema clichés are evident in the staging of this war film."[135] The rare acknowledgment of John's score in reviews praised it as "excellent background" and "unobtrusively useful."[136] It was the first of many films that John would score about the American military and the agony of war.

John was reluctantly lured back to television by producer Irwin Allen, who was making an adventure series at Fox that transposed *Swiss Family Robinson* into outer space in the distant year of 1997. As music director of TV at Fox, Lionel Newman was a czar much like his brother Alfred had been, with the power to promote and empower composers he liked. "My dad was a great mentor," said Lionel's daughter, Carroll Newman. "He pushed, and he navigated, and he stood up to producers and directors and studio executives to say, 'No, *this* is who's going to do this.'" Newman was blunt, tough, and foul-mouthed—a cigar-smoking musical mafioso from a bygone time, equally loved and feared. "Dad wasn't interested in mediocrity, or mediocre composers and musicians," said Carroll. "I think he just didn't have any time for it."[137] He met John through Alfred and was impressed with the scores he heard—and especially the *Rhythm in Motion* album—and he was eager to hire John, who was 16 years his junior, and champion this new prizefighter on the rise. "Johnny served a tough apprenticeship," Newman said. "He did cops-and-robbers movies, writing Fender-bass things with bongos. It didn't take him long to grow out of that."[138] If nothing else, it was a smart business decision on John's part. "Why *not* befriend Lionel?" said nephew David Newman, Alfred's oldest son. "It's a good idea, even if you didn't like him, because Lionel could get you work—particularly at Fox."[139]

Lost in Space was a high-concept melodramatic sitcom for the whole family, with a talking robot and two precocious kids and a snide villain who mugged for the camera and all but twirled a mustache. The series predated *Star Trek*, and in some of its broad strokes it prefigured *Star Wars*—another Fox production. John scored the premiere episode, "The Reluctant Stowaway," and three more from the first season—music that was tracked into many subsequent episodes—and he wrote its jaunty, manic main theme. Unlike the big, heroic brass fanfares in his later space adventures, the *Lost in Space* theme was a goofy, stuttering distress signal with shrill glissandos created by an electronic, theremin-like instrument that was invented by a trombonist, Paul Tanner. John's underscore was more sinister and dramatic, underlining the schemings of evil Dr. Smith and the many unforgiving threats in the cold reaches of outer space, with flavors of his Prelude and Fugue. John admitted his music could be "kind of campy. I remember doing some silly waltzes with four flutes and things. That just seemed right for this kind of carrying on that Irwin had there. It did get a little bit broad fairly quickly."[140] His orchestra was larger than the one he had at Revue, with a substantial brass section and an emphasis on horns and winds. The most emotional score was for his final episode, "My Friend, Mr. Nobody," in which Penny Robinson befriends an unseen presence in a cave. John composed a flute-forward tone poem and some heart-churning anxiety pounded along by timpani. When the show entered its third season, John composed a new main theme—a bright, uptempo fanfare with a dash of go-go energy.

Allen was a good friend of Goddard Lieberson, and the two could not have been in more stark contrast. Lieberson was "elegant, and tailored from St. James," said John, "and Irwin with the worst toupee ever and orange shirts—everything was orange in his office."[141] But the comparatively vulgar Allen valued John's cultured contributions so much that he asked John to lay the musical groundwork for his next two shows: *The Time Tunnel* and *Land of the Giants*. John wrote theme songs and scored the pilots for both series, which premiered in 1966 and 1968, respectively. He brought a similar "comic book" style of scoring, as he would describe it, to each show's larger-than-life danger and derring-do. It wasn't glamorous work, and harmonica player Tommy Morgan marveled at John's grace under frustration: "We were at Fox on a session one time doing the pilot for a series," Morgan said. "They recut it and never told him. So about two or three hours into it John would say, 'Well, let's see what they did to this one.' But he never blew up. And he had an absolute right to show anger at that point, because when you crafted a score to fit the way John did and they change the picture on you, you've just thrown away a man's work for a week. And he kept his temper."[142]

John later admitted he hated a lot of this work, but for all their silliness, the Allen TV scores were some of the most widely heard of John's early career, and they portended the blockbuster adventures that catapulted his career in the following decade. But just as importantly, they nurtured a relationship between John and Lionel Newman. "He looked over my shoulder at various TV shows that I was scribbling out as fast as I could," said John, "and he said: 'You're really good at orchestration.'"[143] Newman made sure John had the best players in his orchestra, like studio legends Felix and Eleanor Slatkin. But very quickly it was more than just a collegial friendship or business partnership. David Newman said they were "blood brothers." It was, in Carroll Newman's words, "a love story." Lionel and his wife, Beverly, became close with John and Barbara. John and "Tootsie" would talk on the phone in the evenings, and Carroll remembered "the joy that I would see on my dad's face. There was always the conversation—my mom saying, 'So what did *Johnny* do today?' It was like Dad telling about his boyfriend, like two girls talking. I just remember seeing the joy in this intimacy that they had ... just something different spark in him when he would talk with Johnny or about him."[144] John relied on Newman's counsel and support, "especially in the early years of our friendship," John said, "when I couldn't get what I thought was a good job. He would say, 'Just wait, keep working ... stay in love with music ... and keep working. Everything will come'"[145] (Figure 4.2).

* * *

Westerns are always a prime grade of movie steak for a composer, with their scenic vistas, equestrian motion, and mythical archetypes—and John was assigned two in 1966. *The Rare Breed* starred James Stewart as a middle-aged rodeo bulldogger who gets roped into escorting a widowed Englishwoman, her daughter, and their prized bull "Vindicator," the rare Hereford from the title. Andrew V. McLaglen had just directed Stewart in *Shenandoah*, and the film reunited *The Parent Trap* adult stars Maureen O'Hara and Brian Keith, along with Juliet Mills—older sister of *Parent Trap* heroine Hayley Mills—as O'Hara's daughter. Broad comedy and a bifurcated nature compromised the film—the first half with the rodeo and dangerous journey across western plains was far superior to the soundstage-bound sitcom with Keith—but it did give John a chance to write a rousing, catchy theme in the Moross tradition, a theme that alternates from a gentle trot to an exuberant, bouncing gallop. There was a donnybrook cue, some staccato brass action, a sinister motif for the film's villain, and a foxhunt-type scherzo as horse riders chase bulls through the valley. The film sits

Figure 4.2. Illustration by Ken Wannberg (Courtesy of Carroll Newman).

in its feelings just long enough for John to plumb a little deeper, as in the sad death march when Mills takes Vindicator out to release him into the wild—a cue that grows into a string adagio when the parting proves difficult, with tragic brass and strings as the animal runs off. The slow-burning romance between Stewart and O'Hara is treated with timid, sweet, and finally heroic variations of the main theme. The film opened in February 1966, a flawed vehicle for a fun, sticky cowboy score that anticipated John's more mature "oater" music for *The Reivers* and *The Cowboys*.

The Plainsman was a much wobblier carriage, driven by comic depictions of Calamity Jane, Wild Bill Hickock, and Buffalo Bill Cody in what Universal originally created as a two-hour pilot for a proposed new TV series. As steered by plainman David Lowell Rich, a staff director for Universal TV, the movie was full of bland cowboys-and-Indians fare, unfunny shtick, dull action, and cheap-looking production that all betrayed its small-screen origins. The pilot was meant to air in February 1966, but CBS wasn't satisfied, so Universal decided to release it theatrically even with its obvious commercial breaks. John had far less meat to chew on: the show's lighthearted tone influenced his seriocomic approach, but he was increasingly unwilling just to crank out cheap music by the foot, and the more sophisticated and thoughtful passages in his score wrestled with some less inspired action cues and suspense music. The main theme took its cue from a Civil War battle which opens the film, a romantic bugle call that resembles the John Williams of later Americana scores, when he would really get the chance to let his music leave the barn.

The score John considered his first major work was for yet another comedy—but this one finally had *class*. *How to Steal a Million* was directed by William Wyler, the three-time Oscar-winner of some of the greatest pictures in mid-century Hollywood—*The Best Years of Our Lives*, *The Big Country*, *Ben-Hur*—and it reunited Wyler with his *Roman Holiday* star Audrey Hepburn, whose character falls in cahoots and in love with Peter O'Toole as a man she believes to be a dashing art thief. Nicole (Hepburn) is at wit's end with her father, an expert art forger who cavalierly auctions and profits off his work. When his fake Benvenuto Cellini statue of Venus goes on display at the local museum and an insurance examination threatens to bring his whole charade down, Nicole convinces Simon (O'Toole) to help her break in and steal it to keep her father from going to jail ... unaware that Simon is an undercover forgery examiner and a museum security specialist. This potentially ludicrous concept was done with the precision of a master forger and the elegance of a world-class burglar, and Hepburn and O'Toole crackled with glamorous chemistry and wit. The Paris locations and 1960s style, from Hepburn's wardrobe to O'Toole's car, made it all the more appealing and certainly the finest romantic comedy in Phase One of John's career.

Lionel Newman recommended John for the job, and John stole off with this little jewel in a score that fizzes with flirtatious bubbles and bloodless crime. His main theme opens the film with a jumpy, broken-chord piano groove that rolls under a swaying melody for saxophone and strings. It's as whimsical and cosmopolitan as Hepburn herself, hinting at the heist but mostly acknowledging the easygoing, flirtatious nature of the proceedings. John used it liberally throughout—sometimes whisking through the Paris streets in a car with the central pair, or relaxing into a woozy, besotted state when Simon surprises Nicole with a druglike kiss. From start to finish, the score is overflowing with ear-tickling melody and graceful orchestration. The Venus and Nicole's father are represented by a dreamy, drunken tune for muted trumpet and harpsichord; even the funny music is a little more *serious* in its funniness, more cohesive as music than his earlier comedies. There is a recurring, inquisitive line for alto sax, and Nicole gets her own jazzy theme, which John also turned into piano lounge music for scenes in a hotel restaurant. There's even a taste of James Bond with a fuzzy electric guitar motif that accompanies Simon and Nicole casing the museum for the big heist. John was in his element and on fire, decorating his platter of delicious tunes like a huge spread of candied desserts. He was proud of the score, and rightly so.

He turned the love theme into a song, "Two Lovers," which is how he came to meet an English lyricist named Leslie Bricusse. "Really we were kind of forced upon each other," Bricusse said, "because I was a resident lyricist at Fox, and he was the resident composer. So it was a kind of natural thing," and the beginning of a long and fruitful collaboration. "Everybody knew early on that he was the one," Bricusse said. "André Previn, who was my great friend before he left, said, 'You know, if you're going to work with anyone, work with John Williams.'"[146] John recorded the score at Fox in late April 1966, with his dad on percussion and his youngest brother, Don—who had just come home from college at Curtis—providing handclaps and finger snaps. ("I didn't get paid," Don said. "I was just happy.")[147] Newman oversaw the sessions, and gave his protégé one suggestion John never forgot:

> I had just finished recording a love scene with Audrey Hepburn and Peter O'Toole. I'd done what I thought was a pretty good job, and was about to dismiss the orchestra, when Lionel stepped on the podium and whispered in my ear, "You know in the scene, just before they kiss, make just one more take, with a slight diminuendo just before the final embrace, and then bring the orchestra to a full climax just as the two lovers come together." He also whispered, "Don't worry about the overtime ... just try it." I re-recorded the scene with Lionel's suggested nuance, and it turned what was an ordinary orchestral accompaniment into a moment of magic.[148]

John enjoyed working with Wyler, the 63-year-old warhorse who grew up in Switzerland and began working at Universal when he was 19 at the invitation of his famous cousin—Carl Laemmle, who owned the studio. Wyler was hard of hearing by now, and although he was "not a gruff person," John said, he was "very direct and also very quiet."[149] The film had its world premiere at the Egyptian Theatre in July, and at the afterparty Barbara prodded John to introduce himself to Igor Stravinsky, but John was too nervous: "I was convinced that he probably would have said to me, 'So *you're* responsible for the rubbish I just heard for these two hours.'"[150]

Hollywood loves pigeonholes, and a batch of less successful and less romantic comedies followed. *Not with My Wife, You Don't* was little more than a silly string of gags about two American airmen—played by Tony Curtis and George C. Scott—vying for the same Italian woman. Several scenes were filmed at March Air Force Base in Riverside, where John spent his last year in the service, and featured some of his successors in the 523rd Air Force Band playing his music onscreen. The comedic concoction was a major downgrade from the Hepburn-Wyler vintage, but John made the most of its smorgasbord of tones and scenarios—writing part of a fiery violin concerto (performed onscreen by an animated green "jealousy monster"), marching band music, surf rock, an over-the-top patriotic piece for a servicemen bar fight, comical suspense for electric guitar and trombone, a sendup of Italian New Wave film music, and an opera spoof he cutely titled "Foney Poochini." Many of these comic cues were short and "sitcommy," but John was obviously having fun. The most substantive parts of his score were anchored by two song melodies: "Big Beautiful Ball," an acrobatic tune that plays under the main titles, and the love ballad, "My Inamorata," which swings between seductively sweet and melancholy modes. It was John's first collaboration with one of America's most revered lyricists, Johnny Mercer, whom he had met in New York as a 13-year-old boy when Mercer sang on *Your Hit Parade*. John recorded the score in July 1966, with both his dad and brother Jerry in the orchestra.[§§§]

John was now the go-to composer for fizzy capers and bedroom farces, which led to the Arthur Hiller film *Penelope*, starring Natalie Wood as a young housewife who reacts to her husband's disinterest by robbing his bank. (A young Peter Falk was the detective on her trail, a slightly more suave and clean-cut preview of Lieutenant Columbo.) John wrote a surf-rock style theme song with lyrics by Bricusse, performed by an off-brand Beach Boys group called The Pennypipers. The score featured fuzzy electric guitar, electric piano, and muted brass for a load of carbonated sixties hijinks. Like John's other cartoonish comedies from this period, the film was full of skit-like flashbacks and sidebars, an opportunity for broad genre pastiches. It's an ever-present score that accented Penelope's antics in a flirtatious, romantic, champagne style—though not consistently, since the film itself was so schizoid. John wrote a special theme for Penelope's yellow dress, and gave his main theme a lush, languid arrangement for the rare moments of suspended romance. *Variety* called *Penelope* "'cute' in the best-accepted use of the term,"[151] whereas *The Record* said it might be the worst film of the year.[152] In his review of the soundtrack, Allen Macauley at *The Morning Call* wrote: "What a pity this movie score by Johnny Williams isn't utter trash, so that one could dismiss it and be on to better things. The problem here is posed by Williams' own skill. He's much too good to be wasted on a potboiler like this. His writing is evocative and properly slick, and he deserves a fresh chance at better material. One hopes he gets it."[153]

He wouldn't for a little while longer. *Penelope* was followed by *A Guide for the Married Man*—in which Walter Matthau hankers for an affair in a world filled with pert, jiggling temptations and is "guided" by an adultery guru played by Robert Morse. Directed by none other than Gene Kelly, the comedy took a vaudevillian, juvenile approach to grownup subject matter that was completely out of touch with a new generation—one that produced *The Graduate* that same year. John was actually interviewed by director Mike Nichols to score that generation-defining film, but the job—which was ultimately one of adapting Simon & Garfunkel's songs into underscore—went to Dave Grusin, one of John's old Revue cellmates. John scored Kelly's bouncing dance of infidelity with balletic comedy music, and his title song, with words by Bricusse, was performed by The Turtles—who had just landed their biggest hit with "Happy Together." "He would have saved himself probably a lot of

---

[§§§] John also recorded a new batch of album arrangements for a soundtrack LP, which Warner Bros. Records released in November. The film fizzled on impact when it came out, but the music lived on when Tony Bennett recorded "My Inamorata" for his 1972 album, *Summer of '42*, and continued to perform the song in concert.

time *not* including us," cracked Turtle co-founder Mark Volman. "I think we were not even 20, 21. It was just so fun to be treated like adults."[154] The band held their own with other session musicians, and they included the song on their most successful album, *Happy Together*, occasionally performing it in concert. Scoring yet another parade of sketches—this time featuring all-star cameos by Lucille Ball, Carl Reiner, and Jack Benny—John wrote spoofs of ancient caveman music, ancient Roman music, and stuffy baroque music, along with drunken trombone lines and all kinds of lustful jazz. The movie was basically a cartoon about horny men trying to satisfy their urges, human versions of Tex Avery's panting wolf, and John scored it accordingly. It was a rewarding experience inasmuch as he got to work with the dancing legend; Kelly was demanding and hands-on, John said, and "would stand over the moviola and talk about tempo, where it should increase when the comedy does this and that, and almost kind of directing the composition of the music the way that a choreographer would do, dealing principally with aspects of speed and dynamics."[155] The project also commenced another important relationship: Herbert Spencer became John's trusty orchestrator for the next several decades. An American who grew up in Chile, Spencer had written arrangements for *Your Hit Parade* before joining the top-tier arrangers in Hollywood in the 1930s. He was nearly three decades older than John. Spencer later recounted doing "some God-awful pictures like *A Guide for the Married Man*—I mean absolute bombs," but right away he was impressed with the quality of John's writing: "Very up-town. Here he gets these lousy pictures and he writes this kind of stuff. But he was just trying to get his nails into something.... Since he never really had a real good picture to work on, you couldn't really tell what he could do."[156]

John was assigned still *another* burlesque caper comedy that year. *Fitzwilly* starred Dick Van Dyke as a butler who scams rich companies to patronize charities on behalf of his once-wealthy mistress. It was based on a novel, *A Garden of Cucumbers*, and the film premiered at Gimbels department store in New York—a bold move considering the finale had "Fitzwilly" pulling a con on Gimbels, distracting their security by creating a shopping-frenzied mob and stealing their money. It was directed by Delbert Mann, who won an Oscar in 1955 for his very first feature, *Marty*, but whose film career was on a downward slide. Producer Walter Mirisch initially wanted Previn to score the film, but Previn was firmly eyeing his exit by now and he recommended John for the job. Mirisch remembered John's elegant piano playing on *The Apartment* and promptly agreed. In addition to the many faux-baroque comic set pieces, John wrote a swaying ballad that appears in dreamy, swooning arrangements for flirting and kissing scenes, then turns into a song ("Make Me Rainbows") with lyrics by Alan and Marilyn Bergman—the husband-and-wife team that came to dominate soundtracks in the 1960s and 1970s and who wrote several songs with John. "Make Me Rainbows" was recorded by Vic Damone, Carol Burnett, and even Ella Fitzgerald, and it stands as one of the finest songs John wrote in this or any era.

Mann loved the score, and he and John became good friends.

* * *

John found his first Oscar nomination in, of all places, the *Valley of the Dolls*. Based on a soapy, lurid novel by Jacqueline Susann—a thinly veiled tattle tale about Marilyn Monroe and Judy Garland drowning in a world of sexual exploitation and mouthfuls of amphetamine and barbiturate capsules (or "dolls")—it starred Patty Duke as the Garland figure, a singing naïf named Neely O'Hara; Barbara Parkins played the put-upon ingénue, Anne Wells, and Sharon Tate the lithe beauty, Jennifer North, who sells her body to a French pornographer. It had everything: showbiz scandal ripped straight from the dressing rooms of Hollywood, drugs, sex, and suicide—a backstage musical with chronic depression. Somehow, André Previn was persuaded by director Mark Robson to write five songs for the film, with lyrics by his wife Dory. Mrs. Previn was wandering her own valley at the time, and their marriage was collapsing under the weight of her husband's infidelities and her attendant mental breakdown. They were the perfect mess to serenade this messy melodrama, but their songs were lacking in luster, and Previn—who had just accepted a position as conductor of the Houston Symphony—was so halfhearted about participating that he bailed on arranging the songs and composing the score. For that, he referred Robson to John.

Judy Garland was meant to play the has-been veteran Helen Lawson, and John actually conducted a session with the singer in his arrangement of the glam belter "I'll Plant My Own Tree." But Garland, who was still suffering from the addiction and psychological demons that would take her down within two years, hated Previn's songs and left the project.[157] John screened the film with Robson in August 1967 and wrote an assortment of sophisticated arrangements for the songbook—splashy Broadway stylings for "It's Impossible," smoky café backing in "Come Live with Me," and a dreamy, nostalgic perfume for the title song—giving these middling tunes a champagne bubble bath that made them *almost* intoxicating, even if the Previn vintage was cheap and left a headache. John also composed a sparkling source cue for Anne's cosmetics commercial, a steamy gallic cue for the French nudie film Jennifer stars in, and a connective underscore that delicately wove in and out of the songs with high class. His music, mostly adapted from the Previn tunes, begins the film in a lush reverie that matches the beautiful opening montage of Anne taking a train from her snowy New England home. It tracks the bright-eyed romance, the heady kaleidoscope of fame, and the tragic downfall of the three women. Neely's breakdown is scored with a tortured string adagio, and her time in the sanitarium was made extra eerie by John's first experiment with a brand-new invention: the Moog synthesizer.[158] The title song reprises in snippets throughout the film, performed by R&B singer Dionne Warwick. Released as a record, "(Theme From) Valley of the Dolls" was a hit, and John's work outshone both the tunes *and* the film. Robson expressed his delight to Fox president Richard Zanuck, and Zanuck replied in a memo: "I couldn't agree more, nor be more pleased. I think Johnny Williams is one of the most talented young composers we have in California. I think it would be to our benefit if we tied Johnny up for two pictures over a period of 18 months. He is tremendously versatile and would be a big asset to our organization."[159]

The music editor on *Dolls* was Kenneth Wannberg, who first met John at a cocktail party in the late 1950s when he was dating a singer friend of Barbara's. A pianist and composer in his own right, Wannberg charted a path just a beat off from John's: he grew up in Venice, California, enlisted in the Air Force just a few months ahead of John in October 1950, where he also did his basic training at Lackland, then played piano in nightclubs on the East Coast after the service. A friend told him he should apply for a music editing job at 20th Century Fox, and some of his earliest jobs were on *The King and I* and *South Pacific*.[160] Wannberg was a wizard with splicers in a prehistoric era when the job title was actually "music cutter" because that's exactly what they did. Wannberg's catch-all role as music editor included spotting the film with John, taking detailed notes about where music should enter and exit and what kind, then staying nearby while John wrote—running a noisy moviola in an adjacent room and checking John's cues-in-progress against picture to make sure they fit. He would be there at recording sessions, a trusted second pair of ears, reading along with the score and helping John choose which takes were the best. And then he would edit: using a literal splicer to cut magnetic tape, either to stitch different takes together for the most ideal performance of any given cue, or editing bars in or (more often) out to conform to the picture, which may have been further cut down after the score was recorded. He became John's devoted music editor, a role that was more than just an associate: it was an everyday companion in the office, an intimate collaborator, an ally in the spotting session *and* the mixing room (Wannberg attended all final mixes, fighting for John's score)—a wingman from takeoff to landing, and a dear friend. They ate lunch together every day, and every afternoon Wannberg met John on the ninth hole for drinks. Lionel Newman nicknamed him "Wampi," and the name stuck. On this, their maiden voyage, "John was all very serious musically," Wannberg said. "It was no nonsense. The picture didn't do very well, but John did a marvelous score. He always transcends the picture."[161] For his exceptional work on *Dolls*, John was nominated for his first Academy Award, in the adapted score category, alongside his mentors and friends: Alfred Newman and Ken Darby (for *Camelot*), Lionel Newman and Alexander Courage (*Doctor Dolittle*), Frank De Vol (*Guess Who's Coming to Dinner*), and André Previn and Joseph Gershenson (*Thoroughly Modern Millie*). Newman and *Camelot* took the prize that night, but John had finally climbed out of the valley and into the big leagues of motion picture scoring.

* * *

But to really break out in Hollywood, John had to *get* out of Hollywood. The opportunity came from Delbert Mann, whose directorial dry patch took him back into television, where Mann got his start in the early 1950s. The Oscar-winning filmmaker was initially reluctant, but NBC won him over by offering a location shoot in Europe and a prime-time slot for a TV movie adaptation of the classic Swiss novel *Heidi*. At first, Mann wanted to hire Jerry Goldsmith, with whom he'd worked on the 1963 Rock Hudson film, *A Gathering of Eagles*.[162] But Goldsmith was committed to another movie, so Mann went to his *Fitzwilly* composer. This unplanned, unexceptional pairing was going to spark a fire in John's pen.

John was hired even before the million-dollar production commenced shooting in the Swiss Alps in September 1967, mainly because Mann needed a song on set and felt that "one of the principal elements of this score should come from a little folk song that Heidi was to sing," Mann wrote in his memoir.[163] The company was abroad when John came up with "Heidi's Song," a sweet little yearning lullaby. Screenwriter Earl Hammer wrote a lyric "expressing Heidi's longing to have a place she could call her own, a theme that ran strongly throughout the script," Mann wrote. Jenny Williams was now 10, the same age as the little girl playing Heidi—Jennifer Edwards, daughter of *Peter Gunn* creator Blake Edwards—so John taped *his* Jenny singing the tune and sent the tape and a lead sheet to Mann in Switzerland. "It had exactly the old simple folk song quality I had wanted," Mann wrote. "It was, simply, magic."[*****] Retitled "A Place of My Own," Heidi's song formed the melodic heart of John's score. But when he got the picture back from Mann, with its breathtaking vistas of snow-capped peaks and rolling green fields and babbling creeks, John was inspired to write something even grander—a kind of alpine opera. Even though *Heidi* was made for television, it was painted on a large canvas in stunning images that invited an equally large and stunning musical response. It was also a purely storybook story, a theatrical children's tale about an orphan girl and her crotchety grandfather, a journey from a confined life of abandonment into a much larger world of beauty and love. At last liberated from puerile sex comedies and filmed plays on tiny sets, John had—for the first time in his decade-old career—a story epic enough for his epic talents. He responded with "a big, sort of Mahlerian score," and the best thing he had ever composed for the screen.[164] The movie itself, aside from those magnificent images, was mediocre—the child performances stagy, and the narrative trapped within TV conventions like act breaks for commercials. NBC originally planned it as a 90-minute special, but Mann convinced them "we had enough good film for a two-hour slot." The end result was both too thin *and* too padded. But the inherent strength of Johanna Spyri's timeless story and the sincerity of Mann's intentions were enhanced by John's utterly sincere score.

He wrote a splendid, sparkling overture as if this were a lavish roadshow musical, and he took a theatrical approach to the whole score—underlining action and even dialogue scenes with lyrical recitative that matched the emotion and atmosphere, then bursting into big instrumental arias when the story called for it. Heidi's reaction to the Alps was reflected in a romantic, sweeping statement of her theme, punctuated by a Bavarian horn figure that serves as an emblem of the time and setting. Her theme is a constant presence in the score, channeling her uncertainty when she first arrives at her grandfather's cottage, her sweet innocence as she falls asleep cuddling a baby goat, her sadness when she's later missing her grandfather, and a kind of dreaminess as she talks with her invalid friend, Klara. There are comic interludes when Heidi and her friend Peter milk goats and later when a monkey gets loose at a dinner table, a mystically romantic theme for Klara's father and her governess, played

---

[*****] The two Jennifers remained friends for life.

by Jean Simmons, and a climatic cue when Klara has a breakthrough and learns to walk again—an anti-death march as she stiffly crawls through the grass, with sparkling glockenspiel and hopeful horns gradually layered in, then swelling strings as she sees her father, building and building into passionate chords as she takes her awkward first steps, and finally a *religioso* resolution when she embraces her father.

The score was not only chock full of such dramatic apexes, it was a completely cohesive work of symphonic drama—a logical and emotional large-scale composition that was in perfect harmony with the onscreen storytelling but equally powerful and descriptive on its own. It perfectly served the picture even as it transcended the picture—the first major example of what would become John's signature. All John could offer by way of an explanation for this milestone achievement was: "I was very free at that moment."[165]

The larger-than-life score was recorded in Hamburg, and John took his whole family to Germany during the holidays in anticipation of the sessions, scheduled for January 1968. They rented a house for two weeks and navigated Germany together, with Jenny going on walks with John and his film friends around Hamburg. Her little brothers refused to eat anything other than hamburgers and fish sticks, "and we didn't understand the language," said Jenny, "so I just remember it was very comical to watch my mother try to negotiate with these grocers—like, 'How do we get these things? Because that's the only way I'm going to get my kids to eat.'"[166] It was in Hamburg where John heard Richard Wagner's music for the first time. He had lunch with Wolfgang Sawallisch, conductor of the Hamburg Symphony Orchestra, and heard that ensemble perform the first parts of the Ring Cycle. John didn't think the musicians were quite as good as the best American orchestras, but he was flooded with the romance of their playing and the spellbound attention of the audience. "I loved the French horns," John said. "They had a Waldhorn kind of sound—very different than what we did. They would blow those Austrian horns, and it was thrilling. I looked around the audience with Barbara and thought: *my god*. Their people were like *more* than in church—some kind of a spooky vibe. The way that German and Austrian people feel about music, it's different than here. It's hard for us to even grab—something in the language, something in the whole lifestyle."[167]

John's recording orchestra for *Heidi* was composed of players from the Hamburg Opera. "I met some of them before we recorded; I had gone to a few of the productions of the opera and heard them play, and I was inspired by that," said John. "I did my best to write a score that would allow the orchestra to show some of their beautiful sound, to the degree that the film allowed the space to do that."[168] The score was recorded in the Deutsche Grammophon studio in Hamburg, "which was technically very advanced," John said, "so the original recordings were, I would say, superior to what I'd been used to getting in Hollywood. The whole experience was a happy one."[169] Mann wasn't able to attend the sessions, but his producing partner Frederick Brogger wrote him an ecstatic letter: "After two days of scoring, all I can tell you is that we had both better try to contract with Johnny for life. His music is not only beautiful, and dramatically and thematically so marvelous, but in great taste. You were absolutely correct!!"[170]

NBC chose to hold the completed film for the fall, with dreams of turning it into a perennial classic. Back at home, John celebrated his 36th birthday with a party attended by Henry Mancini, Johnny Mercer, and other showbiz pals. Everyone gave John 36 of something; one friend gave him 36 Blackwing pencils—every film composer's favorite at the time—another gave him 36 baby turtles.[171] John set to work on a special *Heidi* soundtrack album for Capitol Records, which he recorded in London at Cine-Tele Sound (CTS) Studios in May. The resulting double LP featured narration by Edwards and Sir Michael Redgrave, who played Heidi's grandfather, as well as special arrangements of John's love theme and a new rendition of "A Place of My Own" with lyrics by Rod McKuen. The deluxe album was released in time for the telefilm's premiere: November 17, 1968. On that particular Sunday evening, the Oakland Raiders were playing the New York Jets in what turned out to be a nailbiter. Mann was sitting in a screening room at 30 Rockefeller Center in New York, and he was convinced his film would be delayed until the game was over, thereby messing with all of the commercial breaks and possibly confusing or losing the young audience he wanted. The Jets were leading the Raiders 32–29 and had possession of the ball when "the clock's sweep second hand moved up to the appointed hour," Mann recalled.

> I could feel my apprehension rising. Suddenly, miracle of miracles, the game went off the air, with one minute and five seconds to play. Commercials and station identification follow. Then, to my relief and joy, here came the opening beauty shots of the Alps and Johnny Williams' soaring music. I knew a lot of people would be angry and I, too, wanted to see the finish of the game, but I downed these thoughts and settled back to enjoy what I was sure was one of my best shows.[172]

As Heidi softened her grandfather's hardened heart and Klara struggled with her infirmities, chyrons occasionally appeared at the bottom of the screen, infuriating Mann and updating irate football fans that the Raiders had miraculously returned a fumble and scored *two* touchdowns to make an incredible comeback and win the game 43–32. Enough angry people flooded NBC with calls that night that the network's switchboard blew out. Still, ratings were remarkably high and reviews were good. The *Boston Globe* said *Heidi* was "told without a false or maudlin note . . . a small classic that deserves annual exposure as an example of TV inspiration at its finest."[173] Several critics, including the *Philadelphia Inquirer* and the *New York Daily News*, singled out John's score. NBC ran a full-page ad the next week filled with positive quotes, culminating with: "I didn't get a chance to see it, but I hear it was great. —Joe Namath, New York Jets."[174]

The much richer legacy was that, with *Heidi*, John's style and craft had taken a giant leap into maturity.

* * *

Lionel Newman was so fond of John, so excited to advance John's career, that he offered John his own studio on the Fox lot just so they could be near each other. It was a convenient commute, since the Williamses moved into a new house on Dalehurst

Avenue in Westwood in 1968, just a few blocks from the UCLA campus and less than three miles from Fox. John and Newman socialized before work every morning with donuts, cigars, and coffee, and they celebrated the end of every day with drinks and more cigars. John's office was in a bungalow just inside the Tennessee gate on the west side of the lot, near Alfred Newman's old bungalow (and, before that, Shirley Temple's).

"Lionel's office was a kind of a circus," said John, and it was also a stark depiction of how different these two men were. Richard Nixon was the new president, and Newman had novelty Nixon phalluses attached to all his light switches. (Newman was also famous for making penises out of paper napkins, a skill he taught his three daughters.) John vividly remembered a day when the refined wife of the esteemed English conductor, Sir George Solti, visited Fox and he was stuck with the task of giving her a tour of the music building since Newman was out of town. John quickly hid all the bawdy figurines and toys that Newman had amassed over the years in his office, then desperately tried to stand between Lady Solti and the light switches where, he said, "you couldn't avoid touching a 'Nixonian' protuberance if you wanted to turn on the lights."[175]

Not everyone appreciated Newman's ribaldry—particularly women. A young female orchestra contractor arrived early to a session at Fox one day and asked Newman where she could find the restroom. "You're doing a man's job," Newman spat. "Use the men's room." "I don't know how I had the wherewithal to say this," the woman recalled, "but I said, 'Oh, so every horrible thing people have said about you is true.' John loved him—they were so close—and I just could never understand it. Coarse, vulgar ... I just did not like it at all." Lionel's nephew Randy Newman, who started working in the Fox music library in the 1960s, noted that he "wasn't *just* a vulgarian. He could be charming. You wouldn't say he was dignified, but he was funny—very funny."[176] Jenny was around Newman a lot at the studio, and "he was always incredibly kind and sweet to me," she said, "so I didn't see the part of him that everybody else saw—which was the sort of acerbic, offensive side. He was always very, very, very sweet."[177]

But the bond between John and Newman, as inexplicable as it was to some, was affectionate, deep, and full of laughter and advice and brotherly love. "My dad had a lot of really good friends, but the intimacy between the two of them was significant," said Carroll Newman, who likened it to two people in love. "It really is a love story. They used to kid about it and everything—but they had each other's hearts."[178]

* * *

Things were really starting to cook. With the minor leagues of TV behind him, and a crystallization of his identity—not as a pianist or a bandleader or a recording artist, but an honest-to-God *film composer*—John's star was rapidly ascending. The Oscar nomination may not have been for his own original melodies, but it was a formal recognition from his peers and the industry that served as a kind of anointing. His unique voice as a composer had slowly emerged and taken shape over the course of the past decade, his absorption of all manner of styles and genres had filled his library of imagination to the brim, and he was poised to unleash all of his pent-up talent on bigger and better assignments—which were, indeed, just around the bend. While he was in Hamburg recording *Heidi*, John received a telegram from his agent Marc Newman—Lionel's brother—with news about his next major project: arranging and orchestrating an opulent period musical starring Peter O'Toole and Petula Clark. *Goodbye, Mr. Chips* was an even more significant accelerant in his career than *Heidi*. Within just a couple of years, John was going to win his first Oscar *and* write the scores that caught the ear of his most important collaborator ... strapping him to a rocket that would propel him to the highest strata of popular culture. His number was finally about to get called.

But also, unbeknownst to John, the worst thing imaginable would happen first.

5
In Search of Unicorns, 1969–1974

> *I was in love with London—and I felt I had a new life. No Hollywood studios, no dubbing sessions to go to. It was one of the happiest times of my life.*
> —**John Williams**[1]

John's first violin concerto is a shock to anyone who knows John Williams as the "*Jaws* and *Star Wars* guy." In this defiantly modernist work, which he began writing in 1974, the protagonist string searches a barren, hostile wasteland, asking questions that are never answered, itching with discomfort and crying for help—then running for it. In the second movement, over heaving chords, the violin sings an aching lament that is lyrical, but unresolved. At points, the orchestra bursts into loud and profound keening before the violin retracts back into a kind of bittersweet stillness. In his otherwise mostly technical program notes, John described this movement as having "an elegiac melodic subject" and being "introspective." Without elaborating, he concluded: "It is dedicated to the memory of my late wife."

* * *

"Johnny Williams" became *John Williams* in 1969. Against the backdrop of seismic changes in American culture—Vietnam and Nixon in politics, *Easy Rider* and *2001* at the movies—he emerged that year with two scores that revealed a new depth and maturity in his writing and foreshadowed the world-famous composer he was about to become. Both projects are full of his recognizable handwriting, packed with prefigures of later scores. One was a path he went down for several years but ultimately abandoned: musicals. The other was a widescreen, family-geared adventure that activated his brand of extra-melodic, symphonic Americana and his flair for converting a familiar style into something new. *That* was a path he would stay on.

Goodbye, Mr. Chips was a beloved 1934 book by James Hilton about a beloved teacher at an English boarding school, which became a beloved 1939 film that won Robert Donat an Oscar for best actor—which then became a bloody headache for MGM when André Previn and his wife Dory attempted to turn it into a musical in the 1960s. By 1967, Previn was jonesing for the exit on both Hollywood and his marriage, and after years of false starts on the project, MGM and producer Arthur P. Jacobs decided to drop the Previns's completed *Chips* songbook, "principally because they felt the idiom of the lyrics was not sufficiently English," Leslie Bricusse explained.[2] Jacobs had just produced *Doctor Dolittle* with Bricusse's songs, and he hired the Englishman to write a new song score for *Chips* from scratch. On his way out, Previn made one last note: hire John Williams as arranger.

John was no stranger to arranging by now, of course, and he had often played caretaker to other composers' melodies and spun them into underscore—most recently for Previn's tunes in *Valley of the Dolls*. But he had never taken on a full-blown *musical*, which has its own unique set of demands: arranging and orchestrating a book's worth of tunes in a way that honors the composer's voice while also furthering the storytelling; working with singers in rehearsals and pre-records and sometimes even more; and finally gluing the entire work together with dramatic underscore, stitching the songs to the book and removing the seams—not to mention composing an overture, entr'acte, and exit music. He nearly had his *first* opportunity to do so just before *Chips*—with Francis Ford Coppola. "He was suggested to be musical director for *Finian's Rainbow*," Coppola said. "I had very specific attitudes to Broadway shows, feeling that Hollywood often did not adhere to the feel and style of the originals, and I rejected the possibility of John Williams out of hand." Looking back on that decision decades later, Coppola said it was "one of the great mistakes of my career. He never accepted a project with me afterwards."[3]

John took the *Chips* assignment in January 1968, and this decision would alter the next few years of his life, along with his approach to music. It required him to spend months on this one assignment, in *London*, and often alone. Bricusse wrote a batch of athletic songs knowing he had a songbird in Mrs. Chips—played by English pop singer Petula Clark, who had ironically just starred in *Finian's Rainbow*—and in the titular Mr. Chips he had an actor with incredible *emotional* range ... but not much in the way of music: Peter O'Toole. "Not that I was expecting or wanted it to be Howard Keel or Mario Lanza," Bricusse wrote in his witty memoir. "I just wanted someone who could carry a tune. I knew that Peter could carry a bottle of scotch with no problems, but if he had a musical background it was even further in the background than his first sighting of Omar Sharif in *Lawrence of Arabia*."[4]

John flew to London in April to record demos and playback versions of Bricusse's songs with the film's cast. He worked tirelessly with O'Toole, one wobbly note at a time, on his two big songs—"Where Did My Childhood Go?" which a weary Chips sings to himself early in the film, and the much giddier "What a Lot of Flowers" after he marries Petula Clark's character, Katherine Bridges. "Peter loved to sing," said Clark. "I used to go out with Peter to have dinner, and we always finished up a little bit tiddly because that's the way it was, and he used to break into song. I mean, he knew all the good old Irish songs and all the Beatles songs. But I think when he got into a studio it was a different cup of tea."[5] O'Toole remembered those painstaking days with John in London's CTS Studios, joking that John would be lucky to salvage a single note out of nearly 49 takes of one song.[6] But the actor had two big helps. One was that, largely to appeal to a hip 1969 crowd, Jacobs and Bricusse elected to make this a largely *interior* musical—so instead of O'Toole and his co-stars bursting into song onscreen, their voices hover overhead like internal dialogue as they go about their business. O'Toole was also able to hide behind the creakier voice of his aging schoolteacher. But the real ace up his sleeve was John Williams. In his arrangement for "Childhood," John cushioned O'Toole's unsteady tenor with delicate flutes and a soft cloud of strings, and he flew alongside Bricusse's melody with a wistful, infectious piano lick of his own creation. Every song in *Chips* is masterfully arranged—from the organ-powered Brookfield school anthem ("Fill the World with Love") to the love songs Katherine sings—but nowhere is John's sensitivity and indispensability as a musical caretaker more evident than in O'Toole's songs. "And, oh-my-God, did he make me sound good," Bricusse wrote. "At the famed CTS Studios in London's Notting Hill, he recorded the string of glorious arrangements that flowed from his unerring pen, setting the unmistakable style and creating the unique and distinctive sounds that were to become his signature in the 1970s, making him the greatest film composer of all time." Bricusse had struggled with the show's big love song, and finally came up with two: the studio-favored "You and I," a conventional ballad, and his own favorite, "Tomorrow with Me." "I persuaded the ever sanguine John to write arrangements for both songs, and Pet to sing them both, on the understanding that the priority be given to 'You and I' on the single three-hour recording session allotted to us," he recalled. "John pre-recorded the orchestra. Predictably, the 'You and I' arrangement was top-class vintage Williams. The orchestration for 'Tomorrow With Me' was something more, quite simply the most stunning chart for any song I have ever written."[7]

"Tomorrow with Me" is, indeed, the better song. It's edgier, *cooler*, and John gave the strings an insistent, syncopated pulse under Bricusse's swooping anthem, along with little low piano accents, then brought in a searching oboe, then chimes, then horns—with the whole orchestra gradually flowering and exploding with brass and percussion and Clark belting out the lyrics. They recorded the song at the last minute of that single session, and it went unused—despite Bricusse trying to find a home for it throughout the rest of his career. "What he and Pet Clark brought to that song that afternoon elevated its status and made it the best song I have ever written," Bricusse said. John "was obviously very good with singers," said Clark. "And that's a very special thing, because there are some arrangers who are just brilliant, but they're not brilliant when it comes to accompanying singers—which is a very different thing. But he can do it all."[8]

* * *

John took a short break from *Chips* to score *Story of a Woman*, a Universal project—executive produced by Jennings Lang, musically supervised by Stanley Wilson—that attempted to ride the European New Wave with a melodramatic story about infidelity and love triangles in glamorous locales. It was the first English-language film for Swedish actress Bibi Andersson, playing a Swedish pianist in Rome who falls in love with a young, married Italian medical student—then flees home to marry an older American diplomat, her heart broken and tugged in two different but equally scenic directions. It was written and directed by Leonardo Bercovici, an Italian who went to work in Hollywood in the 1930s before the Red Scare exiled him back to Italy in the 1950s. Fellini or Bergman this was *not*, but the sunny Rome and snowy Stockholm locations gave John a chance to find his inner Ennio Morricone, and he ladled Bercovici's stale pasta with a dreamily romantic, quasi-baroque score that incorporated washy electric guitar and pop percussion.

The score was based on a melancholy theme tune that stirs with almost angry passion in the chorus. Marilyn and Alan Bergman wrote a lyric ("Whatever I am, whatever I was / Whatever will happen to me / I owe to a love, a long-ago love / Who showed me what love ought to be!") which was translated into Italian for the opening song ("Uno di qua, l'altra di la"). John accompanied Karin's (Andersson) pensive memories of making love to Bruno (James Farentino) with a setting of the theme for French horns, strings, and hazy harp arpeggios that climaxes with a pop backbeat. He struggled to maintain any kind of narrative cohesion or consistent emotional tone in this awkward, accident-prone cinematic romance, mostly reprising the main theme in various guises. The standout cue is a romantic musical storm when Karin and Bruno kiss, which turns joyful under a montage of them skiing together and watching a series of winter sports, but the theme evolves and dramatically electrifies as Karin begins to look less and less happy, its worried heart rate accelerating with snare drums and insistent horns on slow motion shots of skiers, horns barking and strings roiling tensely as the exaggerated intensity of a bobsled race triggers Bruno's memory of his anger on the night his wife died. The sequence doesn't work, but not for lack of John's dexterous support.

It was a quick and thankless assignment, but he at least got to record the music in Rome. *Before* that trip, John had flown to Houston for the world premiere of his Symphony No. 1. It was the biggest "serious" composition he had ever attempted, written two years earlier "partly to prove to myself that I *could*, partly to learn the process," he said. Also: "I had some time on my hands."[9] John was at the sketch phase of the symphony when he had lunch with Bernard Herrmann one day and was complaining about wanting to write music other than film scores. To which Herrmann replied: "Who's stopping you?!" "His answer was so blatant and direct," John said, "and *right*—that I went home and spent the requisite four or five months writing this piece. In my life, I suppose he represented some kind of avuncular push that that remark illustrates well—a man of few words, but the right ones at the right time for a young person."[10] He completed the symphony in December 1966.

As the new music director of the Houston Symphony, André Previn now had a platform in which to champion his protégé—Previn was actively encouraging John to emigrate from Hollywood with him—and he premiered John's symphony on October 21 and 22, 1968, on a program that also featured Mozart, Mahler, and Barber. (John dedicated his three-movement work to Previn.) Woodwinds introduce the symphony's main idea, a four-note motive woven throughout the sonata. The second movement features a theme played by bells, piano, vibraphone, harp, and triangle. In the finale ("Maestoso"), timpani pounds out an inversion of the principal motive, followed by variations on clarinet, oboe, then flute. "While Williams employs chromaticism and dissonance freely in this work," the program note explained, "the symphony does not appear to employ serial techniques or other devices of the current avant-garde. It is strongly rhythmic and its themes are distinctive."[11]

Before returning to London, John came home to jot off a new score for Mark Robson. *Daddy's Gone A-Hunting* was somehow even trashier than Robson's *Valley of the Dolls*, a low-rent thriller featuring amateur actors and a story by B-moviemaker Larry Cohen about a psychotic ex-boyfriend tormenting the young woman who aborted his baby. It was directed and photographed without panache, events unfold incoherently and inertly and, despite the fact that the central threat is an infant being thrown off a skyscraper, it is completely devoid of suspense and scares. The most intriguing thing in the film is a sex scene reflected in the eye of a prop cat. It wouldn't be long before John turned down such dreck—he presumably took the job out of loyalty to Robson—and his score sounds like passionless obligation … cheap, shocking schlock and light flower-power romance. He wrote the title song with Dory Previn, a Bond song imitation performed by singer Lyn Roman. The only noteworthy aspects of the score are hints of the weird aleatoric effects that John would explore much more effectively with *Images* three years later.

John was meant to score a *CBS Playhouse* TV movie for Delbert Mann called *Saturday Adoption*—to be recorded in New York in November—but instead he found himself sitting in a hotel room in gray, overcast London, summoned back to arrange a new version of "London Is London" for *Chips*. After jetting home to spend Christmas with his family, John rented a flat in January 1969 in the Belgravia neighborhood of London, at 74b Eaton Place—where he holed up for the next five months to compose and orchestrate the film's instrumental score. Barbara and the kids came for a two-week visit in April ("country outings, visiting monuments, etc.," John reported in a letter to Stanley Wilson), and his dad flew over in April ("wandering about London viewing all of the art")—but otherwise John was alone.[12]

So was Barbara. The *Valley Times* ran a cutesy article that May about her "playing both mommy and daddy" while her hubby was away and how, while in the midst of rehearsing for SHARE's star-studded annual fundraiser, Boomtown Party, she broke her nose helping 11-year-old Mark build a toy rocket in the backyard.[13] But she was more deeply alone than most people realized. Her exuberant, life-of-the-party charisma was an unpredictable counterpart to her frequent depressions. When she was low, she was *very* low. John couldn't fathom why—she had kids, friends, and a beautiful home, and was adored by movie stars and musicians in abundance. "It was just impossible to completely understand," said Jenny, who watched her mother repeatedly crash, "because we didn't know much. In those days therapy was about blaming your parents for everything." Barbara did bear scars of emotional abandonment and extremely low self-esteem, added to the fact that she suffered from facial acne for her entire adult life—which made onscreen parts much harder to come by. She had wanted to be a mother, but she also wanted a career, and there was a tension in that impossible balance, always. The weather at home was unpredictable, and no one in her family knew how to control it.

John cared for her the best that he could, rescuing her from the depths whenever he could—but the love of his life was suffering on a level he could not comprehend. And he blamed himself.[14]

* * *

Alone in London, John didn't even have the luxury of his trusty orchestrator, Herbert Spencer, who was on assignment in L.A. In one of many letters he wrote during that time, John told Lionel Newman to give his regards to Herbie, "who I miss desperately and whose hand I miss holding. I am doing most of the orchestrating myself and this writer's cramp certainly can't help my piano playing. Can it?"[15] He signed the letter "Little Dimy," one of Newman's affectionate nicknames for him. Dimitri Tiomkin was called "Dimy," John explained, "and 'Dimy' was famous for going over budget. When I started to do films at Fox, Lionel was always present, and apparently I was always going over time picking little things."[16] John described himself as "the world's busiest gentile" in the leadup to recording with orchestra in April 1969—"the usual madness," he wrote to Newman," but it all seems to be going quite well and I think in the end we will have quite a nice score. Eternal optimism!!" He wrote to both Newman and Previn about his thrill at meeting the English composer William Walton, having been invited to attend the recording sessions for Walton's score for *Battle of Britain*.* "A wonderfully simple man," John told Newman. "He reminds me so much of Cy Mockridge—with the same stoop resulting, I am sure, from centuries of bending over the score page. It was one of my more pleasant days which I couldn't wait to recount to you—thrilling to meet such celebrities—I respond like a schoolgirl and still only 37! At this astonishingly slow rate I should live to be 700."[17]

He may have felt like a "schoolgirl," but the deep flow he entered to write the score for *Chips* was a kind of graduation. The tunes themselves may not have been his own, but he dressed them in such sumptuous, ornate garments as to elevate what were mostly rather flimsy and forgettable melodies into something much, much grander. Bricusse persuaded Jacobs and director Herbert Ross to have an overture so they could "take advantage of John Williams' particular talents,"[18] which John used to create a dazzling sunrise of orchestration and showcase his knack for melodic interplay; he introduced several Bricusse tunes amidst galloping, very English string runs, cascading waterfalls of harp and electric harpsichord, and counterpoint lines and harmonies that are as vital as the song melodies. It was a bath bomb of orchestral beauty, and a debutante ball for the mature John Williams. The entire score is an ear feast: when Chips runs after Katherine at the end of act one to the instrumental strains of "You and I," John has the French horns soaring with noble romance; the score ends with what became a John Williams trademark—a fake-out coda, with the orchestra dropping to expose a tolling school bell, then sweeping back in with its final, satisfying chords.

John's team included music supervisor Ian Fraser, a British renaissance man, and an American music editor, William Saracino, whose credits dated back to *The Wizard of Oz* and *Pinocchio*. Saracino nicknamed John "The Nit Picker" because of how fastidious he was on the recording and mixing stages. "John was very finicky, very sort of particular," said Saracino's assistant, John Grover. "If he wasn't quite happy with it, they would do it while on the scoring session, and just make slight changes. It was

---

* Walton's score would be unceremoniously thrown out and mostly replaced with one by English film composer Ron Goodwin.

a really happy time. Didn't seem to be short of money. It wasn't all kick bollock and scramble—it was moviemaking!" When the film was later recut in Culver City for its 70mm roadshow presentation, John requested the original six-track recordings be brought over from London; any new piece of score he wrote to fit the new cut, contractually, had to be recorded in London—so Grover was tasked with making multiple red-eye flights between continents in the span of a few days. Grover's wife knitted a small square out of quarter-inch tape as a gift for the "Knit Picker." "He was absolutely tickled pink," said Grover. "I think he had it framed." (John reciprocated with an engraved watch for Grover.)[19]

With typical modesty, John downplayed his contribution to the score, which earned an Oscar nomination alongside O'Toole's performance. "Just say that I do the window dressing," he told *Today's Cinema*. But Bricusse knew better: "For me, if you look at the whole body of his work, I think that he became John Williams on *Goodbye, Mr. Chips*."[20]

* * *

John came home at last in June 1969—but he was still abroad when he won his first Emmy earlier that month for *Heidi*. Barbara and Jenny went to the ceremony, hosted by Bill Cosby at the Santa Monica Municipal Auditorium, in his stead, and when his name was announced Barbara leapt up and let out a loud squeal of joy. "I was so embarrassed," said Jenny, who was 12. "I thought she was in pain or something. But then they gave the trophy to her, and she let me hold it all night. I was so proud." In hindsight, Jenny appreciated the emotion behind Barbara's wild yelp: "She had been *building* this with him."[21]

The Williams family had just relocated from the Valley to their house at 334 Dalehurst Avenue in the "Little Holmby" pocket of Westwood. John finished work on the *Chips* soundtrack album for MGM Records, which included a photo of him, now balding, with a red goatee and a new look he was trying out: a black turtleneck. In August, he gave a lecture at the Eastman School of Music. The school's wind orchestra had premiered John's newly composed Sinfonietta for Wind Ensemble in April while he was still in London, which the local *Democrat and Chronicle* called an "eardrum-tester," meant mostly as a compliment. "A frankly atonal work that often jars the senses but does develop a musical shape even as it goes on to a deafening climax. It sounds a little like electronic music—that is, music created by arbitrary sounds—yet set to musical notes that convey definite reactions. It has been put together carefully and seemed to us a definite improvement over much that we hear today."[22]

John asked his contact at MCA for a tape of the concert, and he seemed a little ruffled at the man's understanding of the piece: "It doesn't surprise me when you comment that the work is difficult and I'm sure you are aware I've never thought of the piece as a student work," John wrote. "It seems to me it would only be of interest to performance ensembles of the highest professional quality."[23] John may have been self-effacing about his work in public comments and interviews, but he wanted his serious music to be taken seriously. He confided to Previn that he was frustrated about having to put his "musical life" on hold, and he was depressed about leaving England.²⁴ Previn had just been appointed principal conductor of the London Symphony Orchestra, and he was constantly coaxing his friend to flee the land of cue sheets and idiot producers. "André was complicated in terms of the way he had left movie composing, the way he felt about 'Hollywood,'" said Mia Farrow, Previn's new girlfriend at the time. "And he felt he had stepped into a world that demanded more of him, and that was serious music. He just thought Johnny had such an immense musical talent as a composer that he shouldn't be 'wasting it' on movies, was his perspective. And he never let go. That was the bone he worried throughout his entire life. 'Is he still doing those movies? Oh my God.'"²⁵

In a letter to Previn on June 19, John wrote: "My projects for the rest of the year will simply be some composing and rest. I want to avoid pictures like the plague for at least a few months. Also I am getting the predictable itch to do a little conducting. You don't know of a situation that can use the services of a low cost neophyte conductor with a good ear, and Tiny Kahn-like† sense of time and a glowing red beard?" His classical inklings would have to wait; once again, the movies needed him too much.

* * *

The other major score from this *annus mirabilis* was, in fact, an eleventh-hour replacement score. Mark Rydell, an actor-turned-director from New York, made a film from William Faulkner's final novel, starring Steve McQueen and Rupert Crosse as *The Reivers* (an old Scottish word for thieves), who conscript young Lucius and his grandfather's fancy yellow car, a Winton Flyer, into a rite of passage trip to Memphis—where Lucius meets prostitutes in a bordello, encounters an openly racist sheriff, ends up in prison, wins an important horse race, and essentially comes of age. The film was shot on location in Mississippi, and Rydell hired composer Lalo Schifrin for the score. The Argentine jazzman ruled Sunday nights on CBS with his music for *Mission: Impossible*, and he was quickly becoming the hot new flavor in Hollywood. He scored Rydell's first film, *The Fox*, and McQueen's most iconic vehicle, *Bullitt*. For *The Reivers*, the Bergmans wrote the lyric for an original Schifrin song ("The World Is Open Wide"), and the composer's score—with parts for banjo, gut string guitar, harmonica, Fender bass, kazoo, and saxophones—was recorded in August 1969.²⁶

"But it became clear after hearing his work that Schifrin, who did such a wonderful job on *Bullitt*, wasn't the right fit for *The Reivers*," said executive producer Robert Relyea, McQueen's business partner (and coincidentally the cousin of John and Barbara's old schoolmate, Richard Hein). "We were out of time—just as Schifrin bailed us out with twelve days left on *Bullitt*, we had to find a composer willing to start from scratch and bail us out on *The Reivers* with less than two weeks left to the premiere. So we turned to John Williams."²⁷ ‡ It was either the Bergmans or Mort

---

† Tiny Kahn was a drummer in the West Coast jazz scene.
‡ Schifrin spun his own version of events when he was asked a few years later if he'd ever had a score thrown out: "No. I never get to that point, but I was going to start a film, and when I felt that the difference of concept was such that I knew it would be trouble—unless I would sacrifice my artistic integrity—I walked out before it started." (Irwin Bazelon, *Knowing the Score* [1975].)

Abrahams, associate producer on *Chips*, who recommended John to Rydell—and it was an instantly happy marriage. "He had a quality which was very open," said Rydell, who was himself a pianist and had studied at Juilliard. "I saw right away that he was brilliant. He is warm, friendly, and full of ideas. I suggested that we make it a really big score, with a big orchestra. And he was delighted that I was going to be behind him for that, because the studio automatically tried to reduce everything. And I somehow, in my arrogance in those days, said, 'No, no, we need a big score here.'"[28] Many of the same musicians who played on Schifrin's rejected score also played on John's sessions, which were held at CBS's Radford Studio Center.

There's a scene early in the movie with McQueen's Boon and Lucius singing "Camptown Races" on a joyride in the Winton Flyer, and John took that famous Stephen Foster tune—and the basic milieu of the early 20th-century South—as the prompt for his score, a rich mélange of folk Americana with ragtime and blues and the occasional comical sliding trombone. The homages aren't hidden; the back of the soundtrack LP even says that the score "was written by John Williams—with just a little help from Stephen Collins Foster."[29] But John took those references out of their barn and rode them into a full, jubilant gallop. He let their idioms inform his most tune-filled score to date, with a lazy-summer theme for harmonica and other folksy instruments that grows into a bucolic anthem for full orchestra. "I find all of Rydell's pictures especially musical," John said. "The fact that the little boy in the film looked exactly like my youngest son at the time of the creation of the movie may have had something to do with the affinity I felt for the film."[30]

The Reivers isn't a children's movie, by any means—Rydell actually had to cut some lines and part of the bordello sequence to avoid an X rating—but it does have a *children's theater* quality, with Burgess Meredith's nostalgic narration and a larger-than-life depiction of events. John matched that tone with theatrical scoring, like the sparkling pageantry when the Flyer is first debuted, the way he imitates an old car horn with honking trombones, and the horny striptease trombones that accompany the boys' arrival in Memphis. When Lucius sees his first pair of breasts in a graphic painting, John treats it like a mystical fantasy with vibrating bells and mysterious, dreamy string chords. By contrast, Lucius's innocent affection for the kindhearted hooker, Corrie, is scored with music for a fairytale princess. This big, storybook style attended a film that didn't quite have the endearing charm to pull it off, but Rydell unwittingly gave John Williams his best and biggest canvas yet. There was no reason to hide *underneath* the movie; John could really let his inner romantic storyteller fly. There is evident gleeful abandon in the way he played with his super-sticky tunes, like a child playing with action figures. Action sequences for motorcars and horses are goosed with incendiary banjo solos, barroom tack piano, furious country fiddlin', mouth harp, and tuned jugs and cowbells. *Stylistically* he may have been "grokking"—a sixties-era musician term for ingesting the language and manners of some existing music—but he metabolized those references into a new kind of energy, and the melodies, the playful spirit, and the elegant interweaving of every element was pure John

Williams. Even more so than *Chips*, *The Reivers* announced his distinct voice as a film composer, and it also began a phase of harmonica-heavy, rustic-orchestral Americana scores.

When the film came out on Christmas Day 1969, many critics noticed the score. "With its elements of ricky-tick country music and ragtime," wrote *Variety*, "[it] reinforces the mood without intruding."[31] ("Intrusion" was one of the only measuring sticks that film critics used on scores at the time, if they even bothered to comment on them at all.) Even more prescient was the *Hollywood Reporter*'s John Mahoney, who was knocked over by John's contribution. "The score is the second outstanding one this year from John Williams, and one of the increasingly few fully developed and organically related scores about." In one of the most elegant, spot-on summations of John's unique gift, Mahoney called it "a score that is alternately a reliquary of period and rambunctious evocation of its spirit."[32] Not everyone loved it. Pauline Kael, the *New Yorker* critic whose opinions had an outsized footprint in the culture during Hollywood's new auteur era, complained that when Rydell "isn't sure how to do things, he overdoes them. He's good with the actors and he obviously loves the material, but he grabs at our emotions with arch closeups and forces the incidents to be too beguiling, so at times *The Reivers* seems to be rogue Disney." She went on, pinpointing what would soon become a common film critic's gripe against John's scoring: "The movie is sweet enough and rollicking enough without the score's constantly reminding us to appreciate how darling everything is; the music is like a fungus that cheeps and chirrups."[33]

But in fact, the film had tapped into one of John's superpowers: *nostalgia*—the power of music to recall echoes of bygone days, to tickle our unconscious collective memory and spiritually reunite us with our ancestors. To move us, to transport us, to a *feeling* of a romanticized past—splashing in sun-dappled lakes, our first ride in a car with the top down, our earliest and most innocent stirrings of sexual desire. He did this with idioms and instrumentation that were familiar and associated with yesteryear, but all in service of his own wizardry as a melody-writer and dramatic musical orator. A portal had opened. The sleeper had awakened. John Caps, a writer and radio producer who corresponded with John in the early 1970s, elegantly pondered this awakening in a 1991 essay. John's earlier scores had been well crafted and contained tasty tunes, Caps argued, but they were structured piecemeal and without "narrative authority." "The orchestra successfully reiterates what is already happening on screen but makes no real attempt to take over the storytelling," Caps wrote. "Its function is to serve as host." Yet here, he marveled, just one year after *A Guide for the Married Man*, John wrote *The Reivers*, "whose musical language is so consistent, whose central emotional line is so expressive, and whose presence in the film actually takes on a narrative quality. How did that happen? Where did it come from?" Caps cited a Serge Koussevitzky comment about always looking for the "central line" in any great work of music, and proposed that with *The Reivers*, "as though by some timely decision," John had found the Central Line:

> The music score assumes an American tone of such freshness and affection that the whole setting feels immediately like our own nostalgia, even if we are foreigners there.... The main theme [is] an airborne expression of great freedom and the sort of affirmation of life which is the Central Line of this film....
>
> The body of the score is about that Central Line, which Judith Crist described in her review at the time: "a joyous sense of life and laughter and the good things that generations give." And as the line develops, the score moves with it.... This is movie scoring which is at once pictorial and pertinent, music which proceeds with, alters alongside, and ultimately even drives the narrative. Williams' music becomes the conscience of the characters for us and comes to represent a time and place we might not have otherwise understood.... *The Reivers* was Williams' first consistent and cohesive score for a film. It is perhaps the greatest of compliments that by now the film and its music seem inseparable.

Caps wondered if perhaps John was motivated by Previn's impatience "to find something more solid, something more respectable to do with his talents" than film scores. "In their friendship, did Williams find the model for his own discontent? Previn moved on to a triumphant conducting career with all the leading symphonies. Is that when and is that why Williams moved on to *The Reivers*," and a more compositionally serious, cohesive, and *indispensable* mode of film scoring?[34] John himself acknowledged this was a milestone score that marked a significant turning point in his career and his method, but he wasn't entirely sure how or why it happened. "Good opportunity. Faulkner," he mused quietly. "I guess at the time it seemed the most natural thing. It was all written very quickly. Wish I could tell you it was anything *conscious* that I did. It just seemed to be what was required. Might it have anything to do with listening to radio plays as a child? Stories being told where you couldn't see anything—you had to imagine it. Theater of the mind. It's *possible*."[35] He had also just come back from England, a life-giving and creatively stimulating experience.

As a piece of *music*, this was the first score John felt fully, truly proud of. "In every film score, there may be a nice little tune or a good turn of phrase," he said in 1980. "So much creative juice goes flowing into a film score that here and there there are sixteen good measures in the middle of some necessary window dressing or folderol. Benny [Herrmann] had the sense to put those good bits into order and work them into pieces that could stand on their own. He recorded them then—and on those records he has left something of himself. I have tried to do that with some of my own music—and I've been encouraging my colleagues to do the same thing."[36] John also noted how Lionel Newman would push him: "Try to make every cue an entity. Make it a piece. Make it a statement. Have it have a beginning and an ending, if you can—and some development, even, within the thing itself." Which is actually a helpful tool, John said, "rather than having a clean slate all the time, if bar 34 can be a relative of bar 14, in some way. Certainly that's going to be a unifying thing, at some very deep and unconscious or subconscious level that the audience may be listening. I don't think you can prove any of it. But I believe it."[37]

The Reivers held two further adumbrations for John. It forged a friendship with Rydell that yielded several more collaborations. "We hung out a lot," said Rydell. "We became very close friends after that."[38] Even more significantly, John packaged a stellar soundtrack album for Columbia Records—which was purchased by a 23-year-old Steven Spielberg, who had collected soundtracks ever since he was a teenager in Arizona and who was currently trying to get his directing career going. Spielberg had never heard of John Williams *or* seen the film, and he mainly picked up the LP because it had Steve McQueen on the cover. He wrote the screenplay for *Ace Eli and Rodger of the Skies*, a story about barnstorming in the 1930s, while listening to *The Reivers*; the Winton Flyer music was perfect inspiration for its flying scenes. In a way, Spielberg said, the screenplay "was based on the music, which I heard so often I wore the record out and had to buy another one. The script never got made. Back then nobody was interested in my big inspirations. I thought, 'If I ever get a shot at directing a movie, I really want to see if this guy will write the score.'"[39]

* * *

But America was simply not in the mood for the throwback, earnest theatricality of *Goodbye, Mr. Chips* and *The Reivers* in 1969. Both films did poor business, and the best picture Oscar for that year went to *Midnight Cowboy*, an X-rated symbol of the New Wave of directors in Hollywood and a countercultural reaction to the state of affairs both on college campuses at home and jungles abroad. *Reivers* did earn John his first Oscar nomination for *original* score, but he lost to a zeitgeist, poppy score by Burt Bacharach for the hippie western *Butch Cassidy and the Sundance Kid*. (John's adapted score for *Chips* was also nominated for an Oscar, but lost to Lionel Newman's *Hello, Dolly*.) It was the year after *2001: A Space Odyssey*, in which Stanley Kubrick threw out an original score by Alex North in favor of his temp score of classical needle-drops. And it was the year of *Easy Rider*, a low-budget longhair fantasy that used rock 'n' roll songs as score and became a generational touchstone. Both films were harbingers of a new approach to film music, one that did away with traditional, customized orchestral scoring in favor of ironic reappropriation or, simply, music "the kids" were actually listening to. A new class of young filmmakers had stormed into town and were taking over, and they didn't want their grandmothers' melodramatic, classical scores.

John actually admired *2001* and what it said about the role of cultural association in music. "What I think Kubrick has shown so wonderfully well is that the associations can be dispelled," he said in 1973.

> Take a thing like the Strauss waltz in *2001*. The whole thing about a waltz is grace, and you see that the orchestra can achieve this. Kubrick takes what is the essence of courtly grace, the waltz, and uses it to accompany these lumbering but weightless giants out in space during their kind of sexual coupling. And even though the Strauss waltz in my mind, probably in yours too—it's the Danube, it's Viennese awful chocolate cakes and ghastly Viennese coffee. You know what I mean? But Kubrick says to us, "Watch the film for more than five seconds and forget those associations, and it will stop being nineteenthcentury Vienna," and in the hands

of [Herbert] Von Karajan the music becomes a work of art that says "look," that says "air," that says "float" in beautiful orchestral terms, and if you go with this film, the film helps dispel all of these associations, and we're into a new audio-visual world.[40]

Nevertheless, some Hollywood composers were beginning to panic. With the proven success of films using existing music tracks, and a growing orchestral allergy among hip directors and producers, were their careers in jeopardy? John was actively swimming against that tide with his work … and pretty soon his peers were going to credit him for reversing it.

* * *

Fiddler on the Roof was a stage phenomenon around the world. Based on the stories of Sholem Aleichem about life in a shtetl in Soviet-occupied Ukraine, the 1964 musical by Jerry Bock and Sheldon Harnick endeared Jews and gentiles alike with its heartfelt blend of humor—about poverty, generational tensions, relationships—and genuine pathos and drama about having to leave home and say goodbye to the ones you love. Immediately producer Walter Mirisch and United Artists Studios, the team that brought *West Side Story* to the big screen, were eager to adapt *Fiddler* as a movie.

Norman Jewison—who was not Jewish, despite his name—saw the stage show in New York on its opening week, and even though he had never made a film musical, he had just directed the Oscar-winning *In the Heat of the Night* for United Artists and was keen to take this on.[§] Jewison hedged his inexperience by hiring a stellar support team, and right away knew he needed "a brilliant conductor/composer."[41] John met with Jewison in the fall of 1969, and expressed that he wanted the job as badly as Jewison wanted him. "It's a fabulous show with a great score," John said. "To put it on film is to be given the opportunity to immortalize it, and we all felt it had to be made as well as human hands could make it."[42]

John joined Jewison on a trip to Tel Aviv in October to meet with Topol, who played Tevye the milkman in the Israeli stage production of *Fiddler*, and he accompanied the singer on piano for a few of the show's songs. John and Jewison also went to Jerusalem, where the director could consult about culture and period details and John could conduct research. "It was a wonderful opportunity for me to go to the music department at the university, and spend a couple of days listening, and taking a few notes," said John. "All of this put me in a frame of mind, I guess you could say, or a mode of listening, or a *remembering* that I needed—not only to try to contribute to what Jerry Bock did, brilliantly, on Broadway, but also to deal with the Russian aspects of what the story had."[43] He listened to tapes of shtetl bands, and with Jewison he also spent several days watching Jewish films from Russia and Poland at a museum in Haifa. John was also at the cast auditions in both Los Angeles and New York in late 1969 and early 1970, listening keenly to the vocals. Michele Marsh, under

---

[§] Jewison *had* directed TV musicals in his native Canada, as well as specials like *The Judy Garland Show* in 1962—which featured a few of John's arrangements. (Barbara Isenberg, *Tradition!* [2014].)

consideration to play the middle daughter Hodel, was asked to work one-on-one with John before being cast. "Norman was a little concerned about the breathiness in my voice," Marsh recalled, "but Johnny said: 'We can work with that.'"⁴⁴

The challenge, and the opportunity, was to stretch this story beyond its proscenium and take advantage of having a 70mm-sized epic. Jewison worked with Joseph Stein, who wrote the Broadway book, to add scenes and action that would have been impossible on stage, and he made the important decision to shoot on location in Yugoslavia to create an authentic recreation of the fictional village of Anatevka. John, too, thought about *scale*. "The orchestra in the theater may have been 30 players," he said. "We probably had 80. People would ask, 'Well, why would you want to take a little chamber piece like that and expand it to 80?'" The assignment, as John saw it, was to "broaden it out. In Norman's film, you can actually see the countryside, you can see the Cossacks, and the weight of the horses, and the size of the events, and so on. So there's a trip that has to be made between what's confined in the theater and put into a 70 millimeter, multi-channel sound medium … and still be faithful to the original work."⁴⁵

John had been eager to return to London—which explains why he took the enormous leap of relocating there, with his whole family, for the better part of two years. In June 1970, they moved into a rented flat at 21 Tregunter Road in Kensington, a flat that belonged to Miriam Spencer of the Marks & Spencer department stores.** The flat had a grand piano in the front room, where John would compose and play with friends.⁴⁶ The other musical bases for *Fiddler* were Pinewood Studios, the famed home of James Bond productions, located an hour west of London—where song and dance numbers were rehearsed and the film's interiors were shot—and Anvil Studios, which John selected as the place to record. He picked a team of his own, including recording engineer Eric Tomlinson and his old friend Sandy Courage to help with song orchestration.

While John was abroad, two of his professional father figures—orchestra contractor Bobby Helfer and Revue music director Stanley Wilson—died premature deaths within weeks of each other. Helfer had been suffering from mental distress in the wake of a painful divorce, and on June 13, 1970, he locked himself in a room at Universal's hotel and ended his own life.⁴⁷ One month later, while vacationing in Colorado with Revue alumnus Dave Grusin, Wilson died of a heart attack. Both men were only 53.††

Much happier was the Williams family adventure in London, which Jenny characterized as "one of the best experiences I've ever had in my life." She was 13, and she went to an English school—"which was fantastic. I'm a person that loves structure, and I've always loved school, and the English system is very structured, kids are in uniforms, super traditional—but way ahead of where I was as an American student."

** Mrs. Spencer had priceless artwork hanging around the apartment, which she stored away before the Williams clan barreled into her property. (JW to TG, November 4, 2022.)

†† Some years later, John persuaded Universal to name the street that ran behind the old Revue music building "Stanley Wilson Avenue."

She caught up and fell in love with England life, to the point where she even begged her parents to stay when their departure was approaching.[48] John loved it, too. He and Barbara spent a lot of time with André Previn and Mia Farrow in their Surrey home—a modified old tavern with an immense fireplace and half-moons carved in the front door. Farrow, nearly twenty years younger than Previn, was intimidated by his new-found classical life and urbane friend group, but "of all of André's friends," she said, "I felt closest to John." It was really the only friendship Previn had retained from the old country of Hollywood, and it ran deep. "They were both extremely smart, well read, had good senses of humor," Farrow said. "They had a past that they shared." Previn would reliably, *insistently* berate John for staying in Hollywood and continuing to score movies. It wasn't playful jabbing, either. "André was genuinely disappointed," Farrow said, "as ironic as that sounds. He was genuinely annoyed. He was vexed and perplexed that Johnny kept wanting to do what André considered to be a second-rate form, at best."

John would always just laugh. "Any grousing came from André having such immense respect for Johnny's talent," Farrow added. Previn's perspective was warped by his own frustrating experiences in Hollywood and the many mediocre films he worked on, and "he felt that Johnny would be wasting his gift." While Previn and John talked music and literature, Farrow and Barbara would chat about their children and home life. Barbara confided some of her disappointments and depressive lows. "I think that John didn't know how to reach her during those," Farrow mused. "It was kind of before everybody had shrinks and stuff, and before meds had evolved to a certain point where they were common. She did talk about that, about being low, and that there's a loneliness, a solitude to depression."[49]

Living in London, John would play chamber music concerts in parlors with local players and old friends. With Edgar Lustgarten he even recorded a duo for cello and piano that the cellist had commissioned from an American composer, David Ward-Steinman. The album, released on the Orion label, also included Prokofiev's Sonata in C for cello and piano, and the front cover was a photo of John sitting at his piano in the Kensington flat. Though he performed chamber music often, it was the rare *recording* John made as a classical pianist, and the duo was a difficult part—full of fast runs and crunchy, 20th-century chords. One of his new friends was the violinist Desmond Bradley, an Australian virtuoso who was making a name for himself as a soloist in London and who played on sessions for both *Chips* and *Fiddler*. In one of his house concerts, John played the G Major Sonata by Brahms, and Previn said, "What about the A major and the D minor? You can't stop there." So John learned all three sonatas, and Bradley told him, "Anytime you want to play, come—we'll play the Brahms." So they read through the sonatas together, and even performed one on a recital. During a scoring session one day, Bradley was reading a book that purported to be a work of poetry and mythology analysis, written by the English novelist Robert Graves. Bradley told John, "You've *got* to read it," so John bought himself a copy of *The White Goddess*—"and became quite in love with the whole idea of Celtic poetry and its decline." The book seriously turned him onto poetry, "word magic," as John called it, "the ability to invent music with language, change order, and actually create things that don't exist by the use of our greatest tool, which is language." John fell for English poets like William Wordsworth, but particularly for Americans including Emily Dickinson, Carl Sandburg, Walt Whitman, and Hart Crane. (He thought Crane's poem "The Bridge" was his best.)[50]

More than that, he became obsessed with *The White Goddess*—a mystifying tome densely packed with Celtic, Greek, Jewish, and Christian myths, a meticulous "history" of ancient poets who encoded their secrets into riddles that manifested in a poem about a "Battle of the Trees," where the trees were, in Graves's telling, actually metaphors for *letters*. Bizarrely compelling, historically dubious, and rich with imagination and story, the book lit up John's theories about a shared cultural memory and our mystical relationship with trees, and it would seed many song lyrics and concerti down the road. "I found it resonating," said John—who was becoming a poet himself. No longer merely an accompanist or a workaday cue-mason, undergirding stories with notational infrastructure, he was beginning to explore his powers of enchantment and sympathetic magic. He was learning that he could, with a certain melodic turn of phrase or succulent chord change or mixture of instrumental potions, make an audience *feel* something profound. Consider this passage from Graves:

> The test of a poet's vision, one might say, is the accuracy of his portrayal of the White Goddess and the island over which she rules. The reason why the hairs stand on end, the eyes water, the throat is constricted, the skin crawls, and a shiver runs down the spine when one writes or reads a true poem is that a true poem is necessarily an invocation of the White Goddess, or Muse, the Mother of All Living, the ancient power of fright and lust—the female spider or the queen-bee whose embrace is death.[51]

John had discovered her.[‡‡]

* * *

Unlike with *Chips*, the score for *Fiddler* was already set in stone and more or less "sacrosanct," in John's words. This was a job of handling with care. "Jerry Bock's creation, the blood of all of this, was almost enough," he said. "The score was very rich, and with both its influence and my research, I was comfortable working with the material." After studying the theatrical score, he set it aside and began thinking about how to tailor his song accompaniments to the film's singers and to Jewison's unique staging and choreography of numbers. He played piano at rehearsals, where Jewison would act out all of the parts himself for the cast. "He could actually sing the parts," John said.[52]

One only needs to hear the original 1964 cast recording of *Fiddler on the Roof* to appreciate the pixie dust of John Williams. Take "Sunrise, Sunset," the lullaby-like

---

[‡‡] With a wink, John suggested I call this book *Close Encounters with the White Goddess*.

wedding song where parents and children muse about the circle of life. The original arrangement is a small wedding band of accordion, bouncing bass, and tremolo mandolin. But in the film: a cold, mysterious gust of strings and chimes carries in the melancholy vocals, with Hebraic flute and fiddle lines accentuating the lyric and the string orchestra heaving underneath with a rising tide of emotion. It's bigger and more *cinematic*, yes, but it's also more emotional—without ever falling into *schmaltz*. John added to his 85-piece orchestra several folk instruments, including cimbalom and zither, and a Russian balalaika band he found in London. That ancient Siberian stringed instrument supplies both celebration in the cross-cultural dance that breaks out in "To Life," as well as a broken heart under Hodel's farewell to her father in "Far from the Home I Love." John adorned the entire score with little touches like this, gracing Bock's melodies with Jewish and Russian detail and feeling. He also answered Jewison's call for musical extensions throughout, easing the transition from stage to screen and filling the wide horizons of Anatevka. John wrote original dramatic score for new scenes with the Russian military storming Motel and Tzeitel's wedding and later Perchik's political sermon in Kyiv. He wrote a new stoic theme for the Russians, first heard on organ in "Tradition" when the camera pans past the Orthodox church, and employed again when Chava meets her Russian husband-to-be and when an anxious Golde runs to the church to look for her missing daughter.

John was also tasked with writing new music for the fiddler himself. To accompany the opening credits, he composed a lengthy cadenza for the film's silhouetted symbol of tradition. Jewison asked him: "Who is the best fiddler in the world?" John immediately answered: "Isaac Stern." So Jewison flew to Chicago where the Polish-American virtuoso was performing, and his impassioned plea eventually wooed Stern to come to London for three days in July 1970, at considerable cost, and perform the opening violin showcase as well as several solos John composed to be dotted throughout the film.[53] Anxious and excited for the sessions, Jewison "dressed as if for an evening performance. Stern wore his old sweatpants."[54] The actual fiddler *on screen* was an actor-dancer named Tutte Lemkow,[§§] who mimicked Stern's parts—and "Nit Picker" John insisted on working with the man to ensure accuracy. "I remember John Williams rehearsing this guy for hours with his fingering," said Jewison. "When I said, 'John,' he's going to be up on a roof,' he told me, 'I know you. You'll end up with a close-up, and his fingers will be on the wrong goddamn key. All the musicians will know it's a fake.'"[55]

While Jewison was off shooting the film in Yugoslavia, John had time to take another job: a TV movie adaptation of Charlotte Brontë's *Jane Eyre*, directed by his friend Delbert Mann. (He was supposed to score Mann's in-between literary TV special, *David Copperfield*, but *Fiddler* had intervened.) It was the fall of 1970, and John suddenly had a two-month break which "worked out beautifully," he said, "just the right amount of time."[56] John and Barbara even drove several hours up to the film's locations in Yorkshire "to get the feel and flavor of the place," Mann recalled. "I have

---

[§§] Lemkow later turned up as an imam in *Raiders of the Lost Ark*.

never had a composer do this and it was undoubtedly a strong factor in the quality of Johnny's music for the film."[57]

Despite the rich, authentic settings and a talented cast—English Susannah York as Jane and American George C. Scott, fresh from his role as General Patton, playing the tormented Rochester—the movie suffered from dull direction and a stuffy, leaden tone, boxed in by the smallness of the screen. Yet, somehow, it inspired the most romantic, thematically rich score John had ever written—an even more assured and romantic work than *The Reivers*. He wrote several themes before viewing a frame of film—something he very rarely did—drawing purely from the novel, script, and his own time on the moors. He wrote a yearning, bittersweet tune for Jane—which the character plays herself on piano in the film—and a secretive, slightly ominous theme for Thornfield Hall, where Rochester and his painful past reside. Harpsichord and piano root the score in the fire-warmed rooms of 19th-century England, and the music of the moors is appropriately full of windswept beauty and danger. There are hints of the exotic, pagan suspense found in some of John's later scores in his music for the scene of young Jane and her sickly friend Helen talking late one night. Jane's push-pull dynamic with Rochester is treated with alternating romance and fear, her horse-powered flights across the countryside charged with rip-roaring strings and flyaway flute lines, and her late relationship with the stern St. John scored with a very buttoned-up and very English tune. When Jane finally returns to Rochester, now blinded from the torching of Thornfield by his psychotic wife, a timid harpsichord and piano underline their cautious reunion; her theme plays tenderly on flute over mannered harpsichord figures, and then impassioned string chords send amorous blood flowing into an elegant finale.

"I love English music," John said.

> I have a very atavistic feeling towards it, and I poured this love into the score. At least to me, as an American, the score seems very English; I don't know if it does to English sensibilities in quite the same way. But, for me, something like that is the easiest thing to do and one of the things I love doing more than anything else. I just love the whole English musical idiom: in the end, when science is put aside, I guess real music is "Greensleeves" and suchlike. That's the spirit of music. Musical phrases like that just seem to come out of the bowels of the earth.[58]

He insisted that he didn't need to study scores by English composers like Ralph Vaughan Williams because he had an innate sense of the musical terroir—though he did meet Vaughan Williams's widow, Ursula, around this time. "She was introduced to me by Bernard Herrmann, and we went to a few concerts together. When Adrian Boult played his F minor symphony, I said to Ursula, 'That's fabulous.' And she said to me, 'No, no, no—you should have heard *Ralph* conduct it.'"[59]

Delbert Mann thought *Jane Eyre* was one of John's "very best pieces of writing and it may well be the best and richest score written for any of my films. It contributes so much to the atmosphere of the picture and to the characters and their conflicts."[60] When the movie played on NBC's *Bell System Family Theatre* on March 24, 1971—and then in theaters in Europe—critics perked up at the score, which "heightened the effectiveness of several scenes, much more than Mann's direction," according to the *Pittsburgh Press*.[61] The *Calgary Herald*'s critic wrote: "As for John Williams' restrained, unobtrusive score, it is a refreshing change from so much contemporary film music which tends to smother the action with heavy-handed comment."[62] Regular viewers from Miami to Kansas, and even Nottingham, England, wrote their local papers to inquire about it. "Please tell me where I can get a recorded copy of the haunting piano music," pleaded one in Queens.[63] *Jane Eyre* was one of the first John Williams scores to leap from the background and into the ears of people anxious to listen to it on its own.

Fortunately for them, John recorded an album of suites at Anvil Studios in October 1970—his 60-piece orchestra supplemented by organ and both electric and standard harpsichord. The soundtrack was released by Capitol Records when the movie aired, and it became one of the first must-have score albums for a small but growing Williams fanbase. John's inner romantic and his love for England translated into a score that remained one of his personal favorites, and one he played in concert for decades to come—although initially he balked at that possibility. "You couldn't really," he said in 1973, "because it's a pastiche of another style."[64] Once he did begin programming it, though, John said the score for *Jane Eyre* "is very close to my musical heart. It's created folk music, if you like, and I like to play it because it is gratifying for the orchestra and melodic in a very colorful and atmospheric way. And if one could say that one's heart lies with one's own music and still be in acceptable taste, then I can say that something of my heart lies with some of that music."[65] When John thought about why his style might have matured and metamorphosed in the period between *Heidi* and *Jane Eyre*, he surmised: "I was very free at that moment. I was in love with London, and I felt I had a new life. No Hollywood studios, no dubbing sessions to go to—I left that to [Mann]. It was one of the happiest times of my life."[66]

* * *

John and family moved back to Los Angeles in August 1971, and into a rental house in Beverly Hills. A few months later, John purchased a handsome, French colonial home in Little Holmby for the price of $187,500. Built in 1935 by an attorney, Frank Forrester Chase, it had 10 rooms, dormer windows with wooden shutters, a shingled roof, and a brick walkway that connected the street to the front door. (A photograph of the home and its interiors actually landed on the front page of the *Los Angeles Times* when it was first completed.) Nestled among several trees with a pool in the backyard, the house was spacious but not ostentatious, with an elegantly curved stairway connecting the two floors. John kept his grand piano, which he nicknamed "Stella Steinway," in the front living room and, despite all the dramatic changes and adventures to come, he never moved again.

His busy schedule kept him from scoring Mann's next novel adaptation for TV, *Kidnapped*, and *Jane Eyre* would prove to be their final collaboration. (John expressed his regrets in a letter to Mann's producing partner, Frederick Brogger, and he also thanked Brogger for shutting down an aspiring lyricist from putting words to the *Jane*

Eyre theme: "I feel a bit jealously possessive about this material and appreciate your stopping his 'fooling around.' I will mention to him that I am sending the material to Johnny Mercer and that should put a finish to that."[67]) His conflict, aside from finishing *Fiddler*, was Mark Rydell's new film.

The counterculture had invaded the Wild West by the early 1970s, which saw revisionist "oaters" like Robert Altman's *McCabe and Mrs. Miller*, Arthur Penn's *Little Big Man*, and Sydney Pollack's *Jeremiah Johnson*. The latter was a product of Pollack and Rydell's new joint venture, Sanford Productions. Rydell's first film out of that office, *The Cowboys*, was also a western that played with the seventies generational clash—but at heart Rydell was a romantic, even a kind of classicist. So even though his cowboy movie had a psychopathic longhair, played by 1970s madman Bruce Dern, outright *killing* the symbol of tradition—John Wayne—*The Cowboys* was really a rather sweet, old-fashioned steers-and-vistas picture about an aging man and his team of adopted sons. Wayne played Wil Andersen, a rancher whose cowhands abandon him for the gold rush just when he needs them for a critical cattle drive. He's forced to hire local schoolboys (giving the film its very literal title), and their long trek becomes a rite of passage which exposes them to their first Black man (Roscoe Lee Brown, as a traveling cook), prostitutes, hard work, and ultimately death; in its broad strokes, the film was a spiritual brother to *The Reivers*.[***] Dern angered an entire generation of older moviegoers by being "the man who killed John Wayne," and some critics took issue with the film's brutal ending—where the boys avenge their surrogate father's death by offing Dern and his posse. Rydell fended off critiques that the film was too violent, and also that it was a "rightist" agenda film like *Dirty Harry*. "Generally speaking," Rydell said, "I find that the people who resist my work are people who resist feelings. I love feelings. I think they're the raw material of art. When you can move somebody, when you're not reaching through their heads, but you're kind of reaching at them through their viscera—that's the material I look for."[68]

With its sentimental core and gorgeous New Mexican landscapes photographed by Robert Surtees, whose credits included *Ben-Hur* and *Oklahoma*, *The Cowboys* inspired John's career-best western score. Going against the grain of many of his New Wave peers, Rydell welcomed a large symphonic score that trafficked in the traditions established by Aaron Copland, Jerome Moross, and Elmer Bernstein. "We talked about themes," said the director. "'How do you like this for here?' and he would play it on the piano. I wanted him to do what he thought was right."[69] Starting work in the fall of 1971, John wrote a whole herd of themes: a rootin' tootin' adventure theme with bow-sizzling string runs, a syncopated rodeo theme for the boys' training, an ominous bad guy motif for moaning electric harmonica, and a reflective sunset tune for Wayne's character. Rydell's canvas was wide, and John filled every inch.

[***] Both were written by the married duo, Irving Ravetch and Harriet Frank, Jr.

Just as he had done with *The Reivers*, John took a theatrical approach—the film even has an overture, entr'acte, and exit music. There is comedy for the boys' naivete mingling with Wayne's grizzled skepticism—John recognized the humor in doubling a low tuba with high flute, and he also exploited the harmonica's comic potential—but overall there is an earnestness that pervades the onscreen drama. As Wil stares out at the horizon one night before the drive, his theme aches on a French horn with long years, regret, and suspended notes that find delicious resolution. A haze of high strings hovers overhead, and both the melody and its orchestration prefigured John's approach to other lone, noble father figures in future films. This theme is given a heroic treatment, a folksy campfire rendition on harmonica and guitar, and a final, sentimental reprise as Wil's words echo in the boys' heads after he dies.

The toe-tapping adventure theme gets a full workout, occasionally interrupted by the music for Dern's character. John gave Wayne's killer a creepy, low, whining motif that was performed by harmonica wiz Tommy Morgan. "Our skull session lasted like ten minutes, because he knew what he wanted and I played it," said Morgan. "I had never played that type of thing before—I created that for the picture. I used an old lip embouchure in order to be able to control the bend of the notes. And you hear moaning, but there's some echo involved."[70] This was achieved by the Echoplex tape delay machine, a popular device among film composers at the time. Once again, John acted as the paternal storyteller with a colorful cast of leitmotifs: the villain motif; a mysterious, slightly scary cue for electric harpsichord for when the boys meet their first Black man and he indulges them with a harrowing tale; woozy music for the boys after a hard day's work followed by their first hangover; and endangered but fun action music when they enact their revenge. In many ways, this was a proto–*Star Wars* approach but in western mode, with a similar playfulness in the use and counterpoint of leitmotifs and many orchestrational gestures that would become John's signatures. The score also found John going deeper emotionally, and more expansive and mature musically, owing to his advancing skills, as well as the wideness of the genre giving him room to explore this much romanticism before outer space would. It was also another leap forward in his spotting finesse and dramaturgy, felt in the way John let cues linger from one scene into the next and elegantly anticipating and lubricating the narrative. For a story about cow-boys becoming cow-men, it was an appropriate field for his own evolution.

John recorded his 69-piece orchestra in mid-November. "I think that sometimes I make films so I can go to scoring sessions," Rydell said. "There's nothing quite so exciting as coming onto a scoring stage with John Williams and a hundred musicians, and hearing for the first time the overture to *The Cowboys*—which to this day I remember as being one of the most exciting moments of my life."[71] The film opened in January, but it had the unfortunate luck of running against *The Godfather*. Reviews were mixed, with the *New York Times*' Vincent Canby calling it a parody, "formica Western,"[72] and Roger Ebert mostly liking it ... until the implausible ending, "during which every one of the range-wise, hardened, experienced, jailbird gunmen is killed and not a single kid gets nicked, even. Let me tell you, it takes a lot of heroic music to paper over this ending."[73] But the music was too good to let expire, and a few years later André Previn convinced John to adapt the overture into a concert suite—which he would continue to revisit for decades.

* * *

Hollywood's composers went on strike in the winter of 1971. Elmer Bernstein, president of the Composers and Lyricists Guild of America, led the charge against the Association of Motion Picture and Television Producers and 15 production companies in a $300 million suit claiming the industry was illegally preventing music men from their rightful residuals.[74] For a few months, many composers set down their pencils and hoisted picket signs. The strike prevented John from writing a full score for his final TV movie assignment—which was arguably for the best. *The Screaming Woman* boasted a story by Ray Bradbury and the legendary Olivia de Havilland in her first small screen appearance, but its tale about an aged lady discovering a woman buried alive and no one believing her was stretched far too thin into feature length, and Jack Smight's direction was as unimaginative as his contemporary work on *McCloud*. Airing on ABC in January 1972, the movie was mostly scored with stock music from old shows like *Thriller*, but John did supply a main theme written for crazed, swirling strings and harpsichord.

That April, the Eastman Wind Ensemble premiered John's *Nostalgic Jazz Odyssey* at its annual gala concert. "Williams, a television and motion picture composer with every right to call himself a 'serious' composer, has written a 15-minute 'Odyssey' which encapsulates many of the currents which have given jazz such life-giving vitality," wrote Theodore Price for the local *Democrat and Chronicle*, who described the piece as beginning "with a series of cascading false-starts by a saxophone quintet. The entire ensemble indulges in a curtain-raising, improvisatory free-for-all. Then quickly follow episode after episode, climaxed by a cool 'Big Band' pool of sound that melts into a peppery swing style, a free-flow stream of jazzy consciousness cued by five solo saxes and a final nostalgic chorale, which the composer calls 'a Requiem for jazz-type hymn.'"[75] When John was faced with inspiration starvation—à la *The Screaming Woman*—he could always turn to the concert hall.

His symphony was performed twice by the LSO in Nottingham three months later, and Mia Farrow sat next to John at both concerts conducted by Previn. *The Guardian* deemed the symphony "one of the more successful attempts to combine jazz with symphony." "It is not the melodic material, functional if unremarkable, which causes the doubts," the doubtful critic went on. "It is more to do with the construction of these two movements and the way they leap into climaxes which are so little motivated and so little prepared that the listener has no opportunity to become involved. Or perhaps Mr. Previn was trying too hard to create non-stop excitement."[76] The local *Evening Post* was more flattering:

> Scored with an expert resourcefulness, richly variegated in texture, color and dynamic contrast, it turned out to be a much more demanding composition than many

may have expected…. It's not every day that Nottingham is exposed to a live composer of such musical scope, and when two gentlemen made a conspicuous exit from the hall after the first movement, one began to fear the worst. However, despite the unfamiliar idiom of the work, some of its vitality evidently rubbed off on the listeners, and John Williams himself stood up to take several bows from the stalls.[77]

Bernard Herrmann was living in London by now, and although he told John and Previn he wouldn't be coming to the performance, they caught him sneaking in. Herrmann called John the next morning and said: "It's a good piece. I like the first movement, you have a good tune in there—what did ya cover it up for with all those effects, all that excessive orchestration?!"[78] A few years later John said: "I want to re-work the Symphony some time. I like the first movement but there are some glaring flaws in the second movement and the last part of the finale which I think I can now put right."[79]†††

John was starting to feel a symphonic conductor itch of his own, and that September he led the Burbank Symphony Orchestra in a selection of his film scores at the Starlight Bowl. The cello soloist was Edgar Lustgarten, and the program included John's impressive music from *Fiddler*, *The Reivers*, *The Cowboys*, and his latest achievement—the most insane film score he ever composed.[80]

* * *

Images was an idea Robert Altman had in Santa Barbara back in 1968, about "a woman who loved her husband more than herself, so she killed him." "I plan to scare the hell out of the world with it," he told *Variety*.[81] He was all set to shoot the film in Vancouver in the fall of 1969—he had his cast, cinematographer, and locations picked out—but he ran afoul of the Canadian film union and the project fell apart.‡‡‡ *Images* was turned down by every major studio, so Altman produced it himself through his Lion's Gate Films, with additional financing from the London-based Hemdale Group, and he finally shot it in Ireland in late 1971. (When Altman edited the film in London, he lived in John's old *Fiddler* flat.[82]) Altman shared the script with John early on, with a novel idea for the score—he said, "Write a piece of music first, and I'll film the score." "That didn't happen," John said. "I didn't have time to write the music, and he went off on another picture, and the whole thing matured a couple of years later. But I'd been thinking about it and thinking about the schizophrenic quality of this film and this character. Here was a girl who one moment was in touch with reality and the next moment went out of touch altogether. And it seemed to me that the music should be done in two parts and it should have a duality for those reasons."[83]

††† He never touched it again, it was never recorded, and John discouraged other interested orchestras from performing it. Looking back on it in his senior years, he referred to the symphony as an *oeuvre jeunesse*. Then, leafing through its pages for the first time in decades, he paused: "I don't think it's that bad." (JW to TG, March 9, 2023.)

‡‡‡ In the meantime, Altman made his biggest career hit, which was scored by a different jazzman-cum-scorer named Johnny: surname Mandel. It's possible Altman first asked John to score *M*A*S*H*—decades later, John couldn't remember for sure—but it was John who, at a preview screening, was the first person to tell Altman he'd made a classic. (Dyer, "Downturn Hasn't Slowed This Diva," *Boston Globe*, October 18, 2002.)

John remembered an exhibition at UCLA a few years earlier where he first encountered sculptures by the French brothers François and Bernard Baschet—otherworldly steel and glass contraptions that also made unique musical noises when struck or vibrated. A perfect sound for this character's psychotic breaks, he thought, and he asked Previn if there were any musicians around who could play these sculptures. Previn recommended Stomu Yamash'ta, a Japanese avant-garde percussionist who played concerts around the world and who had just performed on Peter Maxwell Davies's score for the Ken Russell film *The Devils*. (As a teenager, Yamash'ta also played on the score for Akira Kurosawa's *Yojimbo*.) John phoned Yamash'ta, who lived in Paris, and the 24-year-old musician invited John to come see the sculptures in person at the Baschets' studio.

Yamash'ta was immediately surprised by how kind John was, after meeting many composers with much more forceful personalities. "I could relate very easily with John—with many subjects besides music," Yamash'ta said. "I was very friendly, to start, with John, and he was very sincere." Yamash'ta demonstrated the sculptures' potential, and John picked out a few to rent. He also attended shows at Yamash'ta's theater company, Red Buddha, where he witnessed the musician making unusual growls and moans with his voice—which John decided also belonged in his schizophrenic score. The next big question was how to *notate* Yamash'ta's parts. John wanted the randomness of these bizarre sounds, but he also wanted them to be as intentionally performed and placed as everything else in his score. In Paris, he said, "I made little notes for myself about the instruments: what they would do; what we would call them; a little, simple method of graph notation to time out these percussion effects with either the conventional music or the film action it was to correspond with." He had to find a whole new approach to writing, said Yamash'ta, who saw John's imagination catch fire inside the Baschet studio: "It went [to a] totally different dimension." Yamash'ta also referred John to a Tōru Takemitsu piece he had been playing which used *colors* as description.[84]

Altman's film played with the audience's mind just as much as that of its lead character, played by *Jane Eyre*'s Susannah York. Cathryn keeps getting phone calls from a mysterious woman who claims her husband Hugh is having an affair, and Hugh begins appearing to her as other men. They get away to their cottage in the country, and her hallucinations intensify—she sees the ghost of an old flame, a real friend of her husband's who openly flirts with her, and her brain scrambles all three men, even in the midst of sex, to the point where she can't keep reality straight. She's also haunted by her own doppelganger, and is eventually whipped into such a psychotic frenzy that she throws that woman off a cliff ... but the dead body turns out to be her husband. The film is more cerebral than scary, but it is a stylish, Altmanesque head-trip. The director's freewheeling, improvisatory approach to filmmaking led him to incorporate wind chimes as a recurring audiovisual motif, a suggestion which came from his editor, Graeme Clifford. York, who was pregnant at the time of filming, came to set with a children's book she'd written—which Altman then turned into a central element of the script.

John sharply juxtaposed Yamash'ta's aleatoric scrapings and clackings and moans and heavy breathing and wild shakuhachi notes with pastoral, storybook music for the sequences where Cathryn narrates passages from her book, *In Search of Unicorns*, which are married on screen to bucolic imagery of the Irish forest. Half of the score is demonically shrill and unpredictable, mirroring Cathryn's psychosis and even misdirecting the audience as to what she might or might not be imagining; the other half is melancholy, melodic, and exquisitely beautiful. "I think it twists the audience's head around 360 degrees plus more," said Graeme Clifford. "It was a psychological thriller going in, but I think that the score contributed so much to that movie that the average viewer probably isn't even aware of it. The music, to me—more than most movies—blends itself in with the visuals and the soundtrack to such a degree that half the time you don't know whether you're listening to music or what's going on on the location, or what's going on inside the characters' heads. It got *inside* the movie in a way that I've rarely seen happen."§§§ Clifford observed John and Altman's relationship as "pretty pal-sy wal-sy. I always felt they were sort of men of the same cut, so to speak. They could have been brothers, really. And they just seemed awfully close—more so than the usual director-composer relationship." He could tell John was an "interior person. He was pretty quiet. I wouldn't say introverted, but a lot was going on within, I felt, that was never expressed. And he was just a very gentle soul. But there was a gentle soul in Bob, too. I found them very compatible with one another."[85]

The score was recorded with a 29-piece orchestra at CTS Studios in London in March 1972. Altman loved the unorthodox sessions with Yamash'ta: "We had an old piano carcass, and he would throw a rock into it, onto the strings and onto the sounding board, and it went [*makes crashing sound*]. But John Williams wrote those into the score, specifically, and what they were. The score itself I have framed, and it's just a gorgeous—it should be in a book—because you see this, in the staffs … suddenly it'll say, 'Hiss like an angry snake' or he'll have these kind of sound descriptions [that] Stomu would perform."[86] John considered Yamash'ta so significant to the score that he deserved his own screen credit. At the musician's request, instead of *percussion*, the credit was: "Sounds by Stomu Yamash'ta."

Images was, by far, the most *un*–John Williams score that John Williams ever wrote. It was atonal, experimental, unfriendly, and unmelodic—except when it's not. A cue like "Dogs, Ponies and Old Ruins," a misty nocturne for lute, guitar, marimba, and strings, is as tonally beautiful as anything he ever composed. But owing to the subject matter and Altman's openness to the unconventional, John was able to let his own freak flag fly. "Bob Altman is great to work for," John said when the film was finished. "He imposed no demands or restrictions. A lot of exciting developments are taking place because of this new way of working. Composers are more involved, but they also have more musical freedom." He went on, cleanly articulating his own newfound ethos as a film composer:

---

§§§ Clifford was so impressed with Stomu Yamash'ta that, a few years later, he brought him in to contribute music to *The Man Who Fell to Earth*, starring David Bowie.

> It gets to the point where you are writing to satisfy yourself as well as to satisfy the commercial requirements of a movie. One has to make a living out of film composing, in order that a serious musician like myself can devote time to composition for my own satisfaction and development. It's really great that the two things are coming closer and closer together.[87]

The film premiered at Cannes in May. Critics were divided, but many were seduced by its arthouse chills. "*Images* is Altman's most challenging film to date; it is a stunning job all around," wrote the *Independent Film Journal*'s critic, Lloyd Ibert, who didn't mention John's score at all.[88] But when the film finally ran in the United States in 1973, several reviews *did*. "John Williams' haunting music effectively underscores the film's climate of despair and doom," wrote Jeanne Miller at the *San Francisco Examiner*. "The film is a dazzling exercise in mood and style."[89] Joe Baltake of the *Philadelphia Daily News* observed that John's "tinkling music punctuates every nuance and bit of action,"[90] whereas R. H. Gardner of the *Baltimore Sun* found the score intrusive.[91] The *Tucson Citizen*'s Micheline Keating argued that the "eerie background score put the finishing touches on this extraordinary movie.... If anything, it is almost too fine a film and there is no relaxation in it. On the contrary, Altman demands constant attention from his audience."[92]

That audience mostly failed to turn up. Columbia bought the distribution rights after every other studio passed, and "when it wasn't a runaway success, they buried it," Altman complained to *Variety*.[93] "*Images* I thought was perfect," he later reflected. "I said, 'Oh boy, this is it. Everybody in the world is going to see this.' Nobody did."[94] Still, Judith Crist of *New York* magazine named it among the best films of 1972, Altman's script was nominated for a Writers Guild of America award, and among its cult following were some of Altman's fellow auteurs. Stomu Yamash'ta was friends with both Michelangelo Antonioni and Federico Fellini, and "these people love the film," he said. "Not [the] majority, but many artists, they like the film, because the film made an enormous possibility for the future."[95]

John was so proud of his score that he created a soundtrack album which combined cues from the film with pieces he composed but didn't make it in. He wrote his own liner notes detailing the background of using the Baschet sculptures and Yamash'ta's unique involvement, along with his thought process about how to address the story's duality:

> When Altman first showed me his film in London in January of 1972, I was overwhelmed by the picture and the atmosphere he created. It did seem to me, however, that some contrast between the "real" and the "unreal" might be achieved musically—not for the purpose of cueing the audience, but more to get inside of Cathryn's head, so to speak, and musically accompany her state of mind rather than her physical condition or behavior. I wanted to contrast the sad, loveless, childless greyness of her "real" life with the terrifying encounters of her "other" existence. For her real-life music I composed a simple, sad, G-minor tune, but with

peculiar Prokofiev-like shiftings of key center, and contrasted with a 6/8 running-in-the-woods kind of figure. All of this is presented in a very conventional way, set for piano and string orchestra, without giving any hint of the horrors Cathryn is to experience. I also tried to give this "real" music a quality of great age so that it would accompany Cathryn as she composed her stories for children, which seemed to be made up of characters from an epoch long forgotten.... Combined with string orchestra and keyboards, Yamash'ta's playing served to accompany Cathryn's flight from reality.[96]

When the film fizzled at the box office, that album release was scrapped—although it still found its way onto vinyl, and John gave copies to his friends.[****] That included members of the Academy's music branch, who nominated the score for an Oscar alongside *The Poseidon Adventure*. John loved talking about the score, and several pages in composer Irwin Bazelon's 1975 book, *Knowing the Score*, were devoted to a discussion on the topic. Christopher Palmer, an English composer who went on to assist Bernard Herrmann and Miklós Rózsa, interviewed John in April 1972 and praised him for "making the sound of today's films relevant to the films themselves. Which means borrowing elements, without prejudice, from whatever musical disciplines and traditions readily suit his purpose." "He rates his new score for *Images* as a major breakthrough," Palmer went on, then quoting John directly: "It's many years since I felt so excited over a project. I do feel that the film music of the future is going to spring from the blending and coalescing of 'traditional' notions with avant-garde techniques and pop."[97]

This score represented a road John *could* have gone down. "It had a debt to [Edgard] Varèse, whose music enormously interested me," he said. "If I had never written film scores, if I had proceeded writing concert music, it might have been in this vein. I think I would have enjoyed it. I might even have been fairly good at it. But my path didn't go that way."[98] Instead, he mostly reserved his experimental Mr. Hyde for concert works—he even considered turning *Images* into a percussion concerto—but by detaching from avant-Altman, as he was about to do, and hitching his wagon to populist stars like Spielberg and George Lucas, he would lean into the romantic, lyrical storyteller that showed up in *The Cowboys* and was about to take over almost completely. The split personality within *Images* is a great metaphor for the two composers inside John—and whether for commercial reasons or personal preference, he threw the "crazy" one off a cliff.

* * *

Images was born during a heady time. John turned 40 on February 8, 1972.[††††] He won his first Academy Award on April 10 for *Fiddler on the Roof*. When his name was called inside the Dorothy Chandler Pavilion, he had to scoot past several

---
[****] He signed one for Bob Klein, his and Barbara's friend: "Ghostly noises from 'Images' with affection from your greatest fan."
[††††] Max Steiner, one of John's most obvious industry forebears, died six weeks earlier.

friends and collaborators, having won over Richard and Robert Sherman's song score for *Bedknobs and Broomsticks*—Robert stood to let him out and warmly shook his hand—Leslie Bricusse's *Willy Wonka & the Chocolate Factory*, and his old boss Dimitri Tiomkin's score for the Russian biopic *Tchaikovsky*. With mullet-length hair on the back of his head bobbing behind him as he jogged to the stage—his pate pretty much bald by now—John delivered a short, no-nonsense acceptance speech: "I want to thank, for all of us, Sheldon Harnick and Jerry Bock for their marvelous score of *Fiddler on the Roof*, which I think has enriched all of our lives. And for myself, my thank-you list goes from here to the parking lot, but I do want to mention Norman Jewison, my Canadian friend; Isaac Stern; and my colleague Sandy Courage. Thank you very much."[99]

The final two John Williams scores of 1972 further symbolized the crossroads he was at. One was a gentle "people" picture, sparingly scored, with an eye toward the pop idiom of the seventies. The other—a big effects extravaganza for the whole family that kicked off a rash of disaster movies, of which John became the master—was a preview of coming attractions that were about to destroy box office records and conquer the world. Director Martin Ritt was an old-timer drawn to gentle human stories like *Sounder*, which was actually his introduction to John. That portrait of a Southern Black family during the Depression was originally scored by John's good friend, Alex North, but Ritt felt that North's score did not suit the movie, and tossed it out. Ritt asked Taj Mahal—the blues guitarist who had an acting part in the film—to replace it with a new score, improvised, like Miles Davis had done in 1958 for *Elevator to the Gallows*. John was hired as a consultant for this unorthodox arrangement, and he attended a spotting session where he gave suggestions about cueing and tempo, which music editor Norman Schwartz then conveyed to Taj Mahal on the scoring stage.[100] Ritt was impressed, and he hired John for his next film. *Pete 'n' Tillie* was adapted by *Casablanca* screenwriter Julius J. Epstein from a 1968 novella, and among the film's flaws is mannered dialogue that always sounds conspicuously *written*. The casting was also strange: Walter Matthau, then 52, as the casually sexist, unfaithful "Pete," and lanky comedian Carol Burnett, 39, as his put-upon wife "Tillie." What begins as an awkward love story without much chemistry and *zero* heat becomes a melodrama when their nine-year-old son dies from a malignant disease. The film features such oddities as Matthau playing ragtime in the nude, Burnett—until now giving an extremely muted performance—shouting at the heavens through tears, "Mother of Mercy, I spit on you!" and then getting into a slapstick water fight with another woman.

John described Ritt as "tough, serious, realistic, theatrically oriented—if you have ten minutes of music in one of his films you've done well, because he doesn't like the cosmetic distraction of music."[101] Indeed, *Pete 'n' Tillie* only has about 20 minutes of score, and most of it variations on John's gentle love theme. Full of aching suspensions and a few big leaps, it's a melancholy ballad that is often performed on piano and bears some resemblance to the song work he did in the 1960s. The tune lent itself to lyrics, which were supplied by his friends the Bergmans.‡‡‡‡ The film was released at Christmastime, and several critics received it as a gift. "This is the wittiest, warmest and most ingratiating movie to appear in a long time, with a beautifully sustained and muted edge of sadness," gushed Howard Thompson at the *New York Times*.[102] *Variety* found it to be a "generally beautiful, touching and discreetly sentimental drama-with-comedy ... told with compassion."[103] The *L.A. Times* called John's score "carefully enhancing,"[104] and *Motion Picture Daily* said it was "appropriately heart-tugging."[105] While the film was still in theaters, it was announced that Ritt would be directing a movie adaptation of the book *First Blood*, which did not pan out—but in an alternate universe, there is perhaps a *Rambo* score by John Williams.

The highest grossing film of 1972, outdoing even *The Godfather*, was *The Poseidon Adventure*. Director Ronald Neame later noted that the film "was aimed to a very young audience. People between the age of 10 and 15 absolutely loved it. Our more sophisticated critics absolutely hated it. And when it was finished, the press slaughtered us, and I thought we had a flop on our hands. But history has proved me wrong."[106] John's association with such films, a recipe for unprecedented success, was just beginning. It didn't matter that star Gene Hackman felt he was "slumming it," according to Neame, or that the director allowed his cast—which included Ernest Borgnine, Shelly Winters, and Roddy McDowall—to overact against his better judgment, or that they ran out of money before shooting the big rescue finale and had to settle for a "rather diminutive end," in the director's words, on the Fox backlot. The spectacle of movie stars climbing, swimming, and dying on their way up toward the bottom of an overturned ocean liner proved a titanic hit. Producer Irwin Allen proudly said the film was geared to a mass audience turned off by excessive pornography, profanity, and violence. The zeitgeist was still effectively split, with daring adult movies like *Deliverance*, *Cabaret*, and *Lady Sings the Blues* all debuting in 1972. *Frenzy*, a seedy murder mystery, featured the first nudity in an Alfred Hitchcock film, and *Last Tango in Paris* blurred the line between art film and hard pornography. John was firmly aligning himself with more family fare.

Allen was simply taking his winning formula from small to silver screen—ordinary people in extraordinary danger—and naturally he wanted to retain his lucky composer. After hearing John's score for *Poseidon*, Allen excitedly wrote an associate: "I think the music will be responsible for yet another great improvement in the overall finished product."[107] Neame was a British cinematographer who also produced David Lean's early films, and he had recently directed *Scrooge*, Leslie Bricusse's musical version of *A Christmas Carol*. He and John spotted *Poseidon* conservatively, and even still, Neame ultimately dropped several cues that were written and recorded, feeling that the drama worked well enough on its own. "Music is another dimension," Neame said, "and it's terribly important to a film ... provided the music is in the right place and isn't used too much. If you use music too much, then it becomes boring and you

---

‡‡‡‡ The sung version wasn't used in the film, but Matthau made his singing debut with a Decca release of "Love's the Only Game in Town," with John's instrumental on the B-side.

don't bother to listen to it."[108] This was the prevailing attitude among directors of the time, and most films had ample white space in their soundtrack. John himself thought many of his films to come were overscored.

The film's main theme, a worried but resolute brass anthem over a string figure bobbing like the ocean, sets the tone under the opening credits—and then there is no score for the next 25 minutes as characters and their different personalities and relationships are introduced before the Poseidon capsizes. That catchy rhythmic figure rolls under much of the score, and the theme reprises heroically and sternly as Hackman's reverend leads his motley band of survivors through the ship's own levels of hell. It's mostly mystery and suspense in between, with tense brass clusters, angsty violins, and watery harp arpeggios. When Winters's character dies in Hackman's arms, John sends her off with a string adagio. Hackman's self-sacrifice is honored with a determined statement of the main theme, which builds as his diaspora moves toward the hatch—and as they're rescued, the bobbing rhythm buoys a grand, relieved restatement of the tune which blossoms and sparkles under the end credits and concludes with a classic Williams fake-out. John was saddled with a lame 1970s sundress of a love song, "The Morning After," written by Joel Hirschhorn and Al Kasha (who had written "Gegetta" for *Gidget Goes to Rome*) and lip-synced on screen by actress Carol Lynley. John interpolated this tune into his score in a few places, cleverly counterpointing his own theme with a piece of the melody in the end credits. Every time John did a session for Irwin Allen, the producer would take the podium at one point for a big inside joke. John would hand him the baton, Allen gave the players a downbeat—and the orchestra would make the worst, loudest, nastiest sound they could muster. "The worse it sounded, the more he would laugh," said John. "He loved it. Everyone had to give him a raspberry on their horns. *Every* session. That was part of the routine."[109]

Poseidon feels like 1970s TV in mostly all the worst ways—with obvious, flat staging and direction, slack pacing, and a prosaic tone. These pre-Spielberg adventure films—including *The Cowboys*—were great platforms for John to stretch his proverbial legs and flex his muscles as he discovered his voice as the heroic narrator, but visually and dramatically they were like flat soda. Still, John was providing noble subtext and elevating the picture. John Caps was impressed by how the score "stayed away from the action and the characters per se. . . . It was following, and indeed can be said to have established without help from the film script, the film's Central Line: *Man against Fate*."[110]

"Probably the commercial hit of the New Year," the unnamed *Independent Film Journal* critic shrugged in December after the film opened. "Surefire adventure film notion has a number of Hollywood's hammier pros trapped in an ocean liner that's capsized. Their slow progression toward escape may get a bit hokey, but today's audiences like that, and they'll be on the edge of their seat throughout anyway. If this one can't make it at the boxoffice, then the genre's dead."[111] *Variety*'s rave review—"Allen has produced some of the most exciting sequences seen in years"—called John's music out, only to deem it . . . "appropriate."[112] "The Morning After," sung by Maureen McGovern and nominated for an Oscar, was released as a single, but no score album was released. John competed against himself at the 45th Academy Awards in January 1973, with both *Poseidon* and *Images* up for Oscars in one of the stranger music years in the Academy's history. Nino Rota's instant classic score for *The Godfather* was nominated, then *un*-nominated after his Italian colleagues spread word to Hollywood that Rota had recycled a theme from one of his earlier films—and what ended up winning the award was Charlie Chaplin's score for *Limelight*, a film made in 1952 but only just now eligible for Oscar consideration because it had finally screened in Los Angeles.[113] John was asked to direct the orchestra at the ceremony, which he did for the first of several times. Bobby Helfer's instruction to any composer who was both conducting at the Oscars *and* nominated for an award was to hand the baton to Helfer, who would be sitting on a stool next to the podium. Helfer wasn't around anymore … and this particular year, John didn't need to hand off the baton.

Poseidon won at the bank, though, becoming the most profitable film in 20th Century Fox's history and kicking off several more lucrative disaster films with scores by John Williams—charting his course to blockbuster fortune and glory.

* * *

What turned out to be John's last project with Robert Altman was just as experimental as their other collaborations. Following his European art thriller *Images*, Altman went back to Hollywood and classic film noir—adapting a story about Raymond Chandler's famous private eye, Philip Marlowe, and working with screenwriter Leigh Brackett, who decades earlier had penned *The Big Sleep* with Humphrey Bogart as Marlowe. Naturally there was an Altmanesque twist: with his mumbly *M*A*S*H* star Elliott Gould, Altman reimagined the 1940s private dick as a Rip Van Winkle type who "wakes up" in the 1970s and stumbles through a world of pot smoke and hippies, topless women doing yoga, and a Los Angeles obsessed with its own movie history. Inspired by a scene he shot for *Images*, Altman kept his camera continually roaming, zooming in and out, and dollying—partly, he explained, to make the audience into a voyeur, but also because Altman never did things the normal way.

His eccentricities extended to the music. "I've always said at the beginning of conceiving a film, I'd love the music to be indigenous, so that there's not going to be any violins that you can't see, that it won't come from nowhere," Altman said:

> I've never completely achieved that, though in *The Long Goodbye* the music became a character in itself. The reason we have to have music in films is to put a cocoon around it, so the audience doesn't become conscious of other people or embarrassed by being there. The music is a kind of tunnel to help keep your focus. I don't understand music, but it's something that can be so visceral and inside you, and I try not to lead what the action is going to be—I mean, we don't hit those chords so you think, "Oh, I'm going to get scared." One day I'll do a film without any music.[114]

Altman's clever idea was to have the same tune playing diegetically and repeatedly throughout the film in different quotidian forms. So John's original melody—a nostalgic, minor key torch song—becomes a pop vocal on the car radio, instrumental Muzak in the grocery store where Marlowe goes for cat food, a doorbell tone, a lonely piano inside a bar, a psychedelic sitar piece, an uptempo jazz number, and even a flimsy Mexican funeral band processional that was played live on location. Altman even cut between different versions of the song, always perfectly on the musical phrase, as he cut between Marlowe and the movie star who fakes his own death. Performers included singers Jack Sheldon and Clydie King, Dave Grusin and his trio, and John himself on solo piano. At one point, Mark Rydell—who came out of acting retirement to play a savage crime boss—sings the song to himself in his skyscraper office. "I thought that was another brave idea," said Rydell. "To make that song the whole score. A million different ways it was played ... I love that idea. See, Bob was always brave. He was audacious. He had a unique, creative spirit that was willing to go anywhere."[115]

John obviously had to write the song, "The Long Goodbye," before Altman shot the film, which he did in the summer of 1972. It reunited him with lyricist Johnny Mercer, who lent the song some Old Hollywood authenticity. "One of his really great songs, I think," said John. "It's a beautiful, sad, very recognizably Mercer piece."[116]§§§§ There's no question why John loved working with Altman: Who else would come up with such an oddball idea and give their composer so much creative leeway? "We would go into a dentist's office or an elevator and there would be this ubiquitous and irritating music playing," said John, who constantly lamented how pervasive music had become in every corner and store and dinner party in modern society. "It was threaded through, kind of like an unconscious wallpapering technique. I think it's completely unique. I don't think anyone has tried it quite the same way before or since."[117]

The film opened in Los Angeles in March 1973, and it was immediately pounced on. "You don't have to admire Raymond Chandler to regret the movie, but it helps," Charles Champlin wrote in his acidic review for the *L.A. Times*, adding that "John T. Williams did the very vigorous score."[118] *Variety* called it an "uneven satire. . . . Good production, confusing story. . . . There are several running gags. The John Williams-Johnny Mercer title tune recurs in every conceivable tempo and arrangement."[119] It was a financial bomb, and Altman blamed the United Artists marketing campaign, which depicted Gould suavely holding a gun, for giving audiences the wrong impression. He actually had the studio pause the release and he went to Jack Davis of *MAD Magazine*, who came up with an eye-catching and clearly satirical cartoon ad with the film's cast of kooky characters.[120] When the movie opened in New York that fall, it was hailed as a masterpiece. "Altman's goodbye to the private-eye hero is comic and melancholy and full of regrets," wrote the *New Yorker*'s Pauline Kael.

> It's like cleaning house and throwing out things that you know you're going to miss—there comes a time when junk dreams get in your way. *The Long Goodbye* reaches a satirical dead end that kisses off the private-eye form as gracefully as *Beat the Devil* finished off the cycle of the international-intrigue thriller. Altman

---

§§§§ Mercer died in 1976. John was pleased when Harry Connick, Jr., covered the song several decades later, and John also arranged the tune for Anne-Sophie Mutter's solo violin.

does variations on Chandler's theme the way the John Williams score does variations on the title song, which is a tender ballad in one scene, a funeral dirge in another. Williams' music is a parody of the movies' frequent overuse of a theme, and a demonstration of how adaptable a theme can be.[121]

One of the big contradictions in Altman "was that he was always fighting with the studios," John said, "but he sought acceptance. He sought praise of the establishment in his own way as hard or harder than any other people did. He craved the approval of the people out here. His bad-boy-naughtiness character not to the contrary. He didn't want to play the game as he saw it being played. Maybe that has connections to his gambler roots."[122] An apt metaphor, since the next time their paths crossed was on a movie about gambling—with the heaviest loss imaginable.

* * *

John was ready to give musicals a rest after *Fiddler on the Roof*, but Arthur Jacobs convinced him to slip back into his showtune shoes one last time—to assist Richard and Robert Sherman on their musical retelling of *Tom Sawyer*. The Sherman Brothers specialized in "simple, singable" songs that often involved wordplay and were especially appealing to small children. They found fame as Walt Disney's in-house song team, and their work at the studio culminated in two Oscars for *Mary Poppins* in 1965. These affiliations "might make people feel that their work wasn't sophisticated," John said. "Whatever hierarch types there may be that criticize popular songwriting at every level, whether it's Irving Berlin or the Sherman Brothers, who will criticize the idiom, will be critical of composers in a wide range that do this work. But I think there's a ground that's higher than what professionals recognize, and that is that if you get high enough in any kind of work—good enough, put it that way—the issue of style becomes unimportant. You get beyond that."[123]

In the wake of Disney's death, *Tom Sawyer* had become a passion project for the brothers, who applied lessons they learned on *Mary Poppins* to weave together different episodes from Mark Twain's 1876 novel, anchored to a central, emotional theme. They realized "the key to it was what Mark Twain had written at the end of this series of stories," Richard Sherman explained. "He said, 'I can't write about Tom Sawyer anymore, because now he's a young man.' And we said, 'Oh my God! Oh my God! That's the story! That's the key to this whole thing.' We realized we had gotten our 'Feed the Birds,' [which] was the key to *Mary Poppins*.... In this case: Only once in a boy's life is he carefree."[124] From there they wrote "River Song," a soaring folk ballad, performed on the soundtrack by country artist Charley Pride.

John was much more collaborative with the Shermans than was possible on *Fiddler*—coming in before the shoot as they were still developing the songbook—and the material was less precious. He sat with them at the piano, devising possible arrangements, joined them for rehearsals with the cast, and helped them pre-record the vocals. The Shermans had worked with an arranger, Irwin Kostal, on several prior films, and they trusted John completely with their tunes. "John Williams is a hero," said Richard Sherman. "He's so great. He made everything smooth and just perfect.... A great scoring man, when he's working with a musical, will take the songwriter's work and compose with it, and make it work for the film. So he would be composing with our themes, and doing wonder—bending and switching and fiddling around. It was a wonderful, masterful piece of work."[125] Don Taylor, who had directed episodes of several of John's TV shows (including *Alcoa Premiere*, *Checkmate*, and *Wagon Train*), shot the film on location in Missouri. Full of rich period detail, with some hammy acting aside, it was a sweet time machine to an adventure-filled Indian Summer in a bygone era. The Shermans' songs weren't quite as sticky as their best work, but pleasant and varied enough, and John enriched them with spirited, Americana arrangements; *Tom Sawyer* thus joined a class with *The Reivers* and other folksy, harmonica-heavy scores he composed during this period. He indulged the burlesque nature of the song "Gratifaction" with a ragtime piano solo; handled the puppy romance between Tom and Becky with sweet, uptempo harpsichord and plucked strings in the song "How Come?"; created a playful hoedown for "Hannibal Mo," a big, happy, nostalgic picnic anthem that concludes with an almost hymnal setting of the cast singing a satisfied, full-belly coda; and he made the bookending "River Song" alternately pastoral, poppy with a drumkit beat, and ultimately fully orchestral and sentimental as a symbolic steamboat takes Tom into adulthood. He also worked these tunes into a fairly substantial underscore, which gracefully settles the Sherman numbers into the organic world of the film and also into some original narrative music of his own. Beyond the rousing overture, there is brass adventure and delicious orchestral folk, plucky comedy for tuba and pizzicato strings, sinister and mysterious music for the murderous Injun Joe, and tenderness at the emotional finale. "He really did a great job," said Richard Sherman. "Still was recognizably, many times, our tune. But it's the way he handled it. It was so great."[126]

Tom Sawyer was an Easter attraction in 1973, and it earned mostly positive reviews. A soundtrack album, packed with photographs and the full lyrics, was released by United Artists Records, and together the Shermans and John received both Golden Globe and Oscar nominations. Even before the film finished shooting, the creative team decided to follow immediately with a *Huck Finn* musical, and the Shermans asked John if he would come along for another adventure. But John was ready to stop singing and dancing for a while.

* * *

John's flute concerto, which he gave the name *Design*, premiered on March 5, 1973—although it was actually composed in late 1969. It was inspired by his exposure to the shakuhachi, a Japanese flute. "I wanted to create something for the conventional modern flute," he wrote in his program note, "that would reflect the atmosphere evoked by the Shakuhachi flutists. I wanted the solo part to sound 'improvised' and decided to make the flute the only wind instrument employed in the piece. The accompaniment is provided by strings, percussion, piano, celeste, and harps, as they make mysterious sounds like the snapping of branches, while we explore some imaginary mythical forest."[127] This was the first of *many* times he would invoke trees in a concert piece.

John was a regular concertgoer at the Glendale Symphony, and he was impressed with their principal flutist, Sheridon Stokes—a virtuoso who, at 20, had been the youngest musician to join Alfred Newman's orchestra at Fox, and who had also played on John's scores for *Lost in Space*. John asked a receptive Stokes if he would premiere his new concerto—and other than mentioning the shakuhachi, which Stokes did his best to imitate, John mostly gave Stokes free rein, knowing he was at home in modern music as a staple at L.A.'s famous Monday Evening Concerts, which Igor Stravinsky often attended. "I'd play very avant-garde music," Stokes said. "I would take a piece like John's, then I would decide what I wanted to do with it and use all the experimental techniques that I had, and the sounds and so forth, to make it into an interesting work of music."[128] The four-movement, 14-minute piece was premiered by the UCLA Chamber Orchestra under conductor Mehli Mehta at the university's Schoenberg Hall, just a few blocks from John's house. The *L.A. Times* sent a critic, who wrote that "*Design* evinces deft craftsmanship, but on first hearing the score seems more distinguished for the variety and skill of its orchestration than for the depth of its musical content."[129]

The concerto was pure 20th century: string harmonics, metal plates, tone clusters, and flutter-tonguing. John said he was always very much "interested in the avant-garde expressions of what was going on in music.... I was never rejecting any kind of future growth on my part."[130] John distinguished Beethoven and Brahms, two of his favorite composers, by noting that the former was all about the future possibilities of music—he called Beethoven "the Robert Oppenheimer of composers"—and the latter was about honoring the traditions of the past. "I was certainly more Brahmsian," he said, "in the sense of taking my inspiration from what went *behind* me, rather than to discover what's coming *forward*."[131] That was true in his film music, by and large, but when writing away from screen stories he was clearly charting a path in the realm of *Die Reihe*—the mid-century German music journal which John used as a shorthand for the whole class of postwar, academic thinking that only atonal, nonmelodic, serialist, Schoenbergian sequencing was worthy music in modern times. For John, *Die Reihe* was the whole "mind fix, the prejudice, the Catholicism if you like, of these people who won't like what I do." He firmly insisted that he was not cowing to or trying to impress these cultural gatekeepers—the critics, the conductors, the musicians—by writing concert music in a markedly different and less easily digestible style than his film music. "I don't feel *any* pressure," he said almost defensively. "What pressure is it that I would feel? To seek the approbation of people who wouldn't offer it in any case? It's certainly not something I worry about when I'm writing. Then we're slaves to something as simple as style, you know, *fashion*. You would think of that pressure as the manifestation of a stylistic fetish, which doesn't deserve your time or mine."[132]

But others disagreed with his self-analysis. John Mauceri, a conductor apprentice of Leonard Bernstein who championed film music in the concert hall, believed John was most likely influenced or persuaded by André Previn to split his musical personalities for these two worlds.[133] Another colleague of John's privately intimated that, especially early on, John cared *very much* about what classical critics thought of him: "He wanted the legitimacy of being accepted by them."

* * *

The most intelligent, subtle, and handsomely photographed film John scored to this point in his career was *The Paper Chase*—the story of a young Harvard law student, played by Timothy Bottoms, who is both intimidated by his brilliant professor and obsessed with impressing him. John Houseman won an Oscar for his performance as Professor Kingsfield; the warm, wooden university classrooms and dorms in Toronto and the crisp autumnal and wintry beauty of Cambridge were captured by Gordon Willis, the "Prince of Darkness" cinematographer who painted *The Godfather* and *All the President's Men*; and the film was to higher education what *President's Men* was to journalism: a cozy, seductive valentine to academic excellence.

It also didn't need much score. Director James Bridges, who hired John in early March 1973, had his studious characters listening to classical music by Bach and G. P. Telemann in their dorm rooms, and used that refined music—sometimes ironically—as de facto score. John adapted these pieces as needed. Bridges also opted for plenty of still air, and there isn't an original score cue until 35 minutes into the film, when John introduces his love theme for James Hart (Bottoms) and Susan (Lindsay Wagner), whom Hart is shocked—and then delighted—to discover is Kingsfield's daughter. That revelation takes their fling into a new direction, and as Hart admires her beauty with an endearingly innocent look on his face, John's 1970s pop-baroque melody underscores their flirtation with harpsichord and flutes. That theme is the heart of his score; sometimes fragile, other times romantically swooning. When Kingsfield unexpectedly returns to his house one night, John scored the comedy of Hart running out of Susan's bedroom and the house into the cold night air in his boxers with an uptempo comic dance for harpsichord and strings. Later, Hart sneaks into the secret part of the Harvard law library to snoop through Kingsfield's own student notes, which John treated like an enchanted entrance into the Holy of Holies. A feverish study session montage is accompanied by a fast-churning string dance that interrupts dainty harpsichord runs with stray electric guitar and drum kit notes for an odd, discordant effect. But the love theme prevailed in a score emblematic of the gentler "people" pictures that John did so well, but received little attention for.

The studious film was previewed for the American Bar Association in Washington, D.C., in August, the same month it screened at Richard Nixon's White House at the request of his daughter, Julie.[134] But neither critics nor audiences were eager to enroll in Kingsfield's class in the fall of 1973, not after the fun, laid-back summer of *American Graffiti*. George Lucas's teen cruising movie, even with its throwback rock 'n' roll soundtrack, felt more in line with youth culture, and when *The Paper Chase* entered theaters, it ran against two other juggernauts: *The Sting* and *The Exorcist*. But it did seem like cynicism was slowly giving way to fun sincerity, and a *Variety* article published in September 1973 reported, almost offhandedly, that Lucas "will direct and script a scifier called *The Star Wars*."[135]

Somewhere in the uncanny valley between the unwashed counterculture and Lucas's laundered nostalgia was *The Man Who Loved Cat Dancing*, yet another attempt to square old western tropes with the new social order. According to its screenwriter, Eleanor Perry, it was "the first women's lib western"—a bold if unsubstantiated claim.[136] Based on a novel by an Indiana housewife, it starred Burt Reynolds as Jay Grobart, a charming scofflaw who lost his Native American wife, Cat Dancing, and ends up unintentionally kidnapping a new love, Catherine Crocker, an unsatisfied married woman. There were deaths, train robberies, and furtive glances at undressed bodies during a river bath—but the film, directed by TV western warhorse Richard Sarafian, was mostly an aimless, dull effort with a confusing tone. It was also a plagued production and a rushed post, with two teams of editors hired to finish the film in time for its black-tie Hollywood premiere on June 26.[137] Michel Legrand was an unusual hire for the score, but the Parisian melodist had successfully crossed over from French fare like *The Umbrellas of Cherbourg* to Hollywood with films such as *The Thomas Crown Affair* and *Brian's Song*. He recorded his score the first week of June, an experimental and mystical approach to the film that included Shoshone chants, cimbalom, ocarina, sarod, electric guitar, and Legrand himself chanting. In a time when producers and directors only heard their score on the day of the (expensive) recording session, Sarafian immediately regretted hiring Legrand. The composer was dismissed, others were interviewed the next day, and John was hired to write and record a 40-minute score—with less than a week to do so.[138]

These circumstances explain John's relatively simple theme-and-variations score, although his achievement under such pressure was no less impressive (and brought back memories of his intense episodic TV days). To match the film's contemporary attitude, John wrote a poppy main theme for tack piano, cool bass, and electric guitar that rides on top of a syncopated guitar groove and uptempo drumbeat, lushed out with strings and harmonica, which was once again performed by Tommy Morgan. Some of the studio musicians found John hard to work for, Morgan recalled, but not he: "All you had to do was play great and not make mistakes. That's the way *he* was, and he expected it from the people around him. In Hollywood you're surrounded by the finest musicians in the world, so John just assumes everybody was in that league."[139] Besides the many variations of the theme, which occasionally faded out like a song on the radio (likely owing to the post-production rush), John wrote individual themes for Jay and Catherine, hoedown action music, queasy string music for *multiple* attempted rapes of Catherine, and mystically tender music for the Shoshone tribe. There are also some lovely French horn and trumpet solos and a cool firing-squad timpani and snare motif for some of the finale—but the score is largely a tour of the main theme's possibilities on rambling acoustic guitar, flutes, or harmonica.

"The film's poetry is as numbing as its violence," wrote Vincent Canby, whose review called the film "a kind of festival of incompetence."[140] To help with sales, the studio hired popular singer-songwriter Paul Williams to turn John's theme into an actual pop song. Williams—no relation—used part of John's melody as a verse for his slow ballad, "Dream Away," which he debuted on *The Tonight Show* with Johnny

Carson in July and included on his 1974 album, *Here Comes Inspiration*—featuring many of the same musicians from the score, with John conducting that one track. "Although the film inspired the lyrics, it didn't really fit as an end title song," Paul Williams explained. "The melody was certainly gorgeous. The happy ending to that story is that Mr. Sinatra was kind enough to include it in his *Ol' Blue Eyes Is Back* album."[141] Despite their many crossed paths over the years, this was the one and only time Frank Sinatra recorded a song by John Williams. One review praised it as "a minor classic, firmly in the Sinatra mold—melodic, thoughtful, and read with the composer's intent in mind."[142]

John re-teamed with Paul Williams in a bigger way on his next odd job. *Cinderella Liberty* was his third outing with Mark Rydell, an offbeat story about a sailor whose rectal cyst and missing papers put his service on pause; stranded in Seattle, he falls in love with a sex worker whose chosen career and young Black son prove challenges to an easy romance. James Caan, fresh off *The Godfather*, was cast as the lead. (Francis Ford Coppola visited the Seattle location to watch a scene.) Rydell felt this was "an honorable, grown-up love story," and he couldn't wait to work with John again. The only problem was that John didn't want to do it. "It's too personal," John said, according to Rydell. "It's too intimate. I don't know … it's not right for me." But "I convinced him, and pushed him, and pressed him," Rydell said, "and he wrote this wonderful score. It's so romantic, and so touching, and so directed to the heart of the film."[143]

It was a long way from the wistful Americana of their previous collaborations—although all *three* films featured prostitutes—but once again, John featured harmonica solos throughout, this time with the Belgian jazzbo Jean "Toots" Thielemans. John responded to the film's contemporary setting with music for a small, pop-flavored orchestra with spotlighted guitar, upright bass, and electric piano. He and Paul Williams wrote five songs together, and Paul sang two that were used in the film: "Wednesday Special," a scuzzy blues bar number with a drunken gait and Rydell himself making "vocal mischief"—Rydell said he was channeling the hero's discomfort from his cyst—and the much calmer, lovelier "Nice to Be Around," a melancholy love song that formed the basis of John's score. Rydell could not have been happier: "John Williams never made a fucking mistake. Every cue was right, every song. The songs were wonderful. 'You'd be so nice to be around.' He understood right away that it was a critical kind of love story."[144] After nearly an hour into the film without any score, John debuted the tune on Thielemans's harmonica and acoustic guitar as Baggs (Caan) and Maggie (Marsha Mason) make love for the first time. A flute takes up the melody, joined by electric piano, while Baggs talks about his religious background; the music builds romantically as they open up to each other and he notices a scar on her back and begins kissing it, and she cries to the strains of a gentle piano and strings reprisal of the theme. The tune gently resurfaces when Baggs visits Maggie in the hospital after she gives birth—Rydell courted controversy by filming an actual live birth—but there is no score when the baby dies. A depressive pall hangs over the rest of the film, as Maggie goes back to hooking and drifts away from Baggs, accompanied by sad versions of the theme, sung by either Williams or Thielemans's harmonica.

"An honor to collaborate with such genius," Paul Williams said (Figure 5.1). "John was nice enough to write a gorgeous arrangement for my recording of the song. My memories are of his kindness—often lovingly addressing the orchestra as children. 'Now children, at bar 348 the oboes....'"[145] The film opened in December, and it made Charles Champlin's list of 1973 favorites. "John Williams has done music which perfectly reflects the latter-day gin-mill atmosphere in which much of the movie takes place," Champlin noted.[146] *Variety* judged it "an earthy but very touching story," and the score "excellent, and Paul Williams' singing of his own lyrics to some songs is tops."[147] Less impressed was Gene Siskel: "All that's salvageable in this wreck are a pair of quiet, tender scenes between Caan and Mason, and a John Williams theme that probably will be nominated as 'best song.'"[148] "Nice to Be Around" was indeed nominated for an Oscar, along with the score for *Cinderella Liberty*. For some reason, actor Telly Savalas—Kojak himself—sang the song on the big night in April 1974, in the same bizarre ceremony where a hippie streaker ran onstage behind presenter David Niven who, without missing a beat, quipped about the man's "shortcomings." John lost in all categories to Marvin Hamlisch, who swept the field with *The Way We Were*, both song and score, and Hamlisch's adapted Scott Joplin ragtime score for *The Sting*.

Figure 5.1. Paul Williams, Mark Rydell, and John during the sessions for *Cinderella Liberty*, 1973 (Courtesy of John Williams).

The *Cinderella Liberty* score had a small life beyond its original vehicle. Maureen McGovern had a minor hit with "Nice to Be Around" in the spring of 1974, and it was recorded also by Helen Reddy and Rosemary Clooney. Unlike many of his other songs from this period, John, too, kept the tune alive. Thielemans was becoming a fixture on movie and TV soundtracks—he played his versatile chromatic harmonica on *Midnight Cowboy* as well as the theme song for *Sesame Street*—but he was also a jazz virtuoso who hung with Oscar Peterson, Benny Goodman, and Quincy Jones, who called the Belgian cat "one of the greatest musicians that ever lived. Oh, he's a king."[149] John felt the same way, and he used Thielemans on another score he recorded in 1973, *The Sugarland Express*—John's first film with Steven Spielberg. "Steven stole him and gave him everything," said Rydell, with a laugh, who wouldn't get to work with John again for more than a decade. "When you were in John's presence, you knew you were in the presence of a major artist. You felt it. You could see it. And Spielberg swallowed him, and they were inseparable after that. I actually was angry. I felt like I had been robbed. But it was okay. He had a wonderful career with Steven." Rydell may have been a romantic filmmaker like Spielberg, but his tastes were much more idiosyncratic. "When I reflect on the pictures that I made," he said, "they all seem to me to be unusual, not the *run of the mill* kind of films."[150] Rydell would later lament how cinema suddenly changed in the mid-1970s at the loss of human behavior movies, and instead be replaced with a blockbuster mentality and "things that will attract the 11-year-old audience."[151]

Perhaps it simply wasn't meant to be. Just like he drifted away from Altman, John began gravitating toward more populist, surefire, commercial entertainment. He remained friends with Rydell, and at one point they were developing a movie together about a subject close to home for both of them: music conservatories.***** "John is a miracle of a composer, and a wonderfully decent man," said Rydell. "I enjoyed every moment I spent with him. As a matter of fact, I used to say that if I was lost on a desert island, and I couldn't have a woman with me, I would ask for John Williams to be with me—because we had that kind of intimate, friendly, wonderful, creative relationship."[152]

Right when *Cinderella Liberty* was shooting in Seattle, *Conrack* was filming on the island of St. Simons, Georgia, where Governor Jimmy Carter personally facilitated locations and supplied local schoolchildren for Martin Ritt's newest production.[153] The script, by Irving Ravetch and Harriet Frank, Jr., was based on the true story of a "latter-day Mr. Chips" named Pat Conroy, a white schoolteacher who was misnamed "Conrack" by his classroom of rural Black children. New York actor Jon Voight, star of *Deliverance* and *Midnight Cowboy*, was yet again playing a Southerner with a dubious accent—although this time in a much more uplifting, inspirational family movie. True to form, Ritt didn't want much score—but John wrote enough to

---

***** Rydell mentioned the conservatory project in 1979: "It will focus in on a form of the arts most people have little awareness of," he said. It never came to pass. (Marilyn Beck, "Sonny Bono Strives to Be a Solo Success," *The Daily Breeze* [Torrance], January 14, 1979.)

be noticed in numerous reviews. Jay Samuels at the New Jersey *Courier-Post* wrote that "John Williams, whose haunting score for *The Reivers* enhanced the Old South lyrical quality of that film, has done the same here, with a country simplicity and heartful understanding."[154] Unaware of just how prescient his observation was, Tony Macklin at the Dayton *Journal Herald* noted that the music was by "the ubiquitous John Williams."[155]

John wrote another amblin', country-fried tune that was in the same wheelhouse as *Cat Dancing* and *Sugarland*. It captured the film's rustic Georgia atmosphere in a generally warm, friendly mood, and once again highlighted harmonica as well as some virtuoso writing for acoustic guitar. Tommy Tedesco, one of the Wrecking Crew musicians who helped define the sound of California pop, played all of the lead parts—a difficult sight-reading job that yielded a few slips and slides. John told him not to worry: they'd overdub his part later. After a few days of studying the music, Tedesco came back and played it all perfectly. But now John thought the flawless performance sounded too "sterile," remembered Tommy Morgan, who was playing harmonica on the score. "John preferred the parts where Tom was ... not *struggling* with them, but he was playing them for the first time. They were just better on the original sessions than the so-called 'overdub perfection.'"[156] Outside of variations on the main theme, John wrote a sweet kind of madrigal for recorder and harpsichord for a sequence where the students go trick-or-treating on the mainland. He was still deep in his harpsichords-and-harmonicas phase; John Caps described the *Conrack* score as "hillbilly baroque."[157] John also composed a snippet of swashbuckling source music for a scene where Conroy brings out a projector and shows the kids a pirate movie, *The Black Swan*. That 1942 Tyrone Power film was scored by Alfred Newman, but for whatever reason—likely owing to rights—John wrote new source score to fit the action, his first swashbuckler. The film had its premiere in Atlanta on March 14, 1974, with Jimmy Carter and the real Pat Conroy in attendance. "I kinda liked the movie," said the real Conroy, "because I pretended I wasn't associated with it at all. As far as I'm concerned, the movie is a fantasy."[158]

* * *

A few weeks earlier, Barbara went to Reno, Nevada, to play a small role in Robert Altman's new film. She was as dear to him and Kathryn Altman as John was; when the Altman marriage was on the rocks during the making of *The Long Goodbye* and Kathryn was contemplating leaving her husband over his flagrant affairs, Barbara advised her to see a family therapist.[159][†††††] The Altmans celebrated Thanksgiving that year with the Williams family. "Bob really liked Barbara," said Altman's daughter, Konni Corriere, who was a teenager at the time. "He liked Johnny too, but Johnny is so kind of withdrawn and within himself, you know. He's shy, and I'm shy, and a

---

[†††††] Kathryn gave Altman an ultimatum, and he eventually came back begging on his knees. "It was like a little boy who had done wrong and knew it and wanted to make amends," she said. They remained together until the director's death in 2006. (Zuckoff, *Robert Altman*.)

shy person can always spot another shy person across the room. Even at 14, I knew he was."

John was *so* shy, so inhibited, that Barbara felt he was a bit uptight. She once told him that what he should do is take off all his clothes and run down Sunset Boulevard naked. In the early weeks of 1974 she tried to loosen him up by giving him a gift: a vibrantly colorful, pop expressionist painting of a nude redheaded woman, crouching with her rear in the air and her large breasts hanging above a handwritten phrase: "I have a butterfly in my ass." It was the kind of thing John would *never* display in a public space—even though his best friend Lionel happily would—but he reluctantly agreed to hang the painting in the living room as long as he could paper over the lewd caption. Babs was constantly trying to pull him out of himself and embrace the wilder side of life. "They were really an interesting couple, because they didn't seem to have anything in common," said Corriere. "And it was just sweet the way they interacted. But he would always be on his own, you know, composing somewhere, *off*, and she would be the one socializing and doing all the talking.

> Bob loved Barbara so much. He hired her for *California Split* and everything—even though it was a little part, he wanted to have her around. So it was both of them, but I think it was mainly Barbara, to tell you the truth. She was flittering and fluttering all over the place, and John was slow and moving into his little hole. But you just knew there was something there that my parents did not have in a million years—that they had it, and I could feel it, and it was just lovely. It was nice to be around.[160]

California Split was very nearly a Steven Spielberg film. Joseph Walsh, a former child actor from the early days of television, was friends with the young director and they had been developing a script for months about the misadventures of two gambler buddies. MGM green-lit the film, but Walsh butted heads with the head of the studio and pulled out. "People said, 'You are one of the great morons of all time. You should do what they want,'" Walsh recalled. "But to me I couldn't do it." His agent sent the script to Altman, who loved it and made a deal with Columbia to produce. Years later, Spielberg said to Walsh, "I could have made millions of dollars with the movie," and that he would have built up the climax "to the greatest orgasm in town. The foreplay would have been so unbelievable that when the orgasm came the audience would have been on the edge of its seat." "It would have been," Walsh said, "a totally different movie."[161] (John later said Spielberg never told him about this strange connection.)

Altman cast Barbara in a bit part—a hardened bartender in the back room of a Reno casino at the end of the trail for Elliott Gould and George Segal's lay-about gamblers. She greets the two men wearing a white cowboy hat and low-slung glasses. (A running gag in the film is that multiple women are named Barbara, which Segal came up with on his own after noticing several of the actresses and women working behind the scenes shared the name.[162]) Gould waxes on about how to read a poker table, and Barbara stands behind the two men smirking and smoking a cigarette. She had *just* found a makeup she liked that covered her chronic acne, and "she told me she had seen the dailies," recalled her friend Edye Rugolo, "and she said, 'Guess what, I actually looked good.' And that made me so happy, that she had that confidence back."[163] Emotionally, though, Barbara was in a terrible state. "I've seen that movie a couple times," said Jenny, "and whenever I see her, I'm like: *wow, she wasn't doing well*."[164] Altman shot the scene, which also featured local poker legend "Amarillo Slim" Preston, on a snowy Thursday afternoon in the Sky Room of the 12-story Mapes Hotel, located along the riverwalk in the heart of Reno. "It was stunning," said Gould. "They built the casino on the roof. We didn't actually shoot *in* the casino. I don't think we were allowed to. So Leon Ericksen, who was the art director, built the casino, and we worked in it. I think there were like maybe two nights—maybe we got it all in one day."[165]

On Saturday night, March 2, 1974, John was at Leslie and Evie Bricusse's home having dinner. He and Bricusse were developing a musical for Gene Kelly based on the French play *Ondine*. They all spoke on the phone with Barbara, who was staying in Room 418 of the Mapes Hotel, and John told her goodnight. The next morning, Altman and Gould were shooting craps before starting work. "I don't even know *how* to shoot craps," said Gould, "but Bob was covering all the numbers. And someone whispered something to Bob, and there was like a ripple over the table. It was like some energy or something that happened."[166]

It was a frigid day in Reno, high of 35. In Los Angeles, the newspapers were concerned with Watergate and gas lines. John had just turned 42. And Barbara, 41, was dead.

"We crapped out," said Gould. "We couldn't play anymore. That was a very shocking, very disturbing event." "I was in the bathtub," remembered Edye Rugolo. "My husband walked in and said, 'I have terrible news for you.' I said, 'What?'—not expecting in a million years that blow. And he said, 'Barbara's dead.' And I said, 'What??' and I started to cry. I think I cried all night long." "I just have this memory of walking down Madison Avenue with all the traffic and things," said Bob Klein. "I was in New York on business, and I got a call—and I can't remember who called with the news. Said, 'Bob ... *Barb died*.' It was so totally out of the blue, the shock on the set—all of that got shared amongst the people I knew. But it was totally unexpected. Barbara was as healthy as anybody I ever knew." "Everybody just really lost it, *hard*," said Altman's son, Bobby. "It was, I guess, really unexpected."[167]

Jenny was home alone that Sunday morning when the phone rang. It was Kathryn Altman asking for John. Jenny said he was out somewhere. "Okay," Kathryn said. "Tell him when he gets home he's got to call me, because it's important." "I knew something was weird," said Jenny, "so I remember going downstairs and going: *wow, I wonder what the fuck happened*. And then Dad came home. I said, 'You've got to call Kathryn.' So he calls Kathryn ... and then he finds out.... It totally shook him to the floor." John came out and told Jenny the upsetting news, and said: "I need to walk around." Jenny was given the awful task of finding her brothers and telling them each individually what had happened. "It was a bad day," she said.[168]

Alone in her hotel room the previous night, wearing a pink nightgown and her wedding ring studded with three diamonds, Barbara had a blood clot burst in the left hemisphere of her brain. The official cause of death, determined by an autopsy performed the next day, was a "ruptured berry aneurysm ... with massive intracerebral hemorrhage."[169] The exact same thing happened to Quincy Jones just a few months later; he said "it felt like somebody shot a shotgun through my head. I could feel the blood wobbling around in my body."[170][‡‡‡‡‡] "It was just heartbreaking," said Corriere, "because she *was* life. She just ... encapsulated life. She was so full of joy and exuberance."[171]

"I remember every second" of that day, said Joe, who was 13. "And it's too long—too long and deep a story. Maybe I'll write about it at some point."[172] Mark and Joe took it the hardest of anyone, and it permanently shaped their very core.

John immediately traveled to Reno, along with Barbara's longtime physician, Dr. Alvin Sellers, to deal with the aftermath. His reaction to this impact event "initially was very physical," John said. "Certainly the most profound experience of my life, of losing my partner from childhood and mother of my children, in this cruel way. Depriving her of everything that happened since then—everything. My whole life would have been hers. And I felt very sick. I didn't *get* sick, but I felt very uncomfortable."[173] It was a physical manifestation of grief that lasted for weeks. Compounding the sadness, John refused to talk about it, even with his children. There was inexplicably no funeral, no discussion—no closure. The message, Jenny said, was: "Let's not talk about this anymore."[174] Jenny never learned what happened to the body; decades later, she arranged for a memorial plaque in Forest Lawn Cemetery in Glendale.[175] It was a profound and violently sudden loss, and John wasn't there to save Barbara. "The most devastating thing about that whole event was how it affected my dad," said Jenny. "He really, truly felt like it was his fault. Even to this *day*, I think he has a hard time not believing that somehow it *was* his fault, and that all of her troubles leading up to her death were his fault. Maybe it has something to do with Catholic guilt."[176]

* * *

John was on the cusp of unprecedented success, fame, and musical magnificence. No one who watched—and listened to—his meteoric rise with Spielberg and *Star Wars* would have guessed that he had just suffered the most horrific tragedy imaginable, because he kept that wound hidden from the world. He simply didn't talk about it—certainly not publicly, but also not with his friends or even his children. This was the moment when his guard fully went up, and he became a man of intense privacy.

The only friend John *could* open up to, it seems, was Lionel Newman. Carroll Newman would ask her mom: *What's Dad feeling? And what is Johnny feeling?* "Or I'd hear Dad on the phone with Johnny, and it would be soft and sweet. I didn't hear John speaking, but from what Dad was saying it was like letting him know: 'You're gonna

---

[‡‡‡‡‡] Jones was given a miniscule chance of surviving, and his friends actually organized a memorial concert before he remarkably recovered. (Quincy Jones, *Q: The Autobiography of Quincy Jones*, [2001].)

get through this. It's gonna be all right.' I remember my dad saying, '*Go to your piano.*' Dad was advising him to put it into the music."[177]

At a panel discussion in July 2014, John—now 82—finally, *subtly* revealed to the public how this awful event affected him:

> When I was about 40 years old, I lost somebody very, very, very close to me unexpectedly. And before that point in my life, I didn't know what I was doing. But after that point, in my writing, in my approach to music, in everything that I was doing, I felt clear about what it is I was trying to do, and how I could do it with whatever small gift I may have been given. It was a huge emotional turning point in my life—let's leave it there—but one that resonates with me still, and taught me about who I was, and what I was doing, and what it meant.
>
> And this is a deeply emotional thing—and in a way, that was the greatest gift ever given to me, if I can put it that way, by anyone. And so that's the best answer I can give you. And certainly a pivotal moment in my thinking, in my living of my life, and approaching the blank page absolutely. I immediately knew where to go with this emotionally.[178]

He later elaborated: "As a composer, I felt suddenly so much stronger. I don't know why that is. What I used to tell myself is that she was helping me from someplace else, and that I felt a new assurance, and a new power, and a new ... *something*."[179] "You know that he believes that his success has to do with her somehow?" said Jenny. "That her spirit lives on. He also says, in a very sort of sad way, that he wishes so much that she had been able to enjoy his success—because he attributes his beginnings, and his connections, with *her*."[180]

6
The Beginning of a Friendship, 1972–1976

> *I was a traditionalist in terms of music. I wanted the scores to make my movies bigger than I had made them. And Johnny made all my movies bigger than the films I intended.*
>
> —**Steven Spielberg**[1]

"Steven took me to a very fancy restaurant in Beverly Hills for lunch, in the days of these martini lunches. It was like going with a teenager who had never ordered wine before and didn't quite know what to do with the silver. He was so young, a little older than my children but not a whole lot. And seemed to know more about my music than I did. He would sing third themes from some remote western."[2]

When these two stars aligned in the fall of 1972, Steven Spielberg was 25. John Williams was 40. The father of three teenagers—a serious, old-soul musician with nearly 20 years in the business—found himself seated across from an excitable, nerdy wunderkind who had just been offered his first feature after wowing the brass at Universal with *Duel*, a white-knuckle TV movie about a mysterious big rig hunting an everyman in the California desert. John, who never paid much heed to the films or TV of his own youth, was encountering a kid from Arizona who worshiped movies and had been collecting soundtracks since he was 10 and who whistled "Make Me Rainbows" for John during lunch. Spielberg was, in his own words, "one of those fanboys of motion picture scores."[3]

* * *

Spielberg's mother, Leah, trained as a concert pianist and sacrificed a career in music to raise her children, but she still played classical piano for her son in utero and as an infant. "Steven always had a highly developed imagination," Leah said in 1986. "He was afraid of everything. When he was little he would insist that I light the top of the [piano] so he could see the strings while I played. Then he would fall on the floor, screaming in fear."[4] Spielberg's parents took him to concerts at the nearby Philadelphia Orchestra, where he sat "trapped in between them," he said. "When I wanted to leave, I couldn't. And it wasn't because I was bored. It was because I was *terrified*—because of the power of Stravinsky, the power of Prokofiev, the power of Mahler." It was

> a kind of aural experience that took me to the unknown, and terrified me—but also fascinated me and made me curious. So when I started to see movies, even before

I was noticing what the films were about I was noticing what the film *sounded* like, what the musical scores were like. I saw a number of pictures as a kid in movie theaters where the music was more memorable than the films.[5]

The first soundtrack album Spielberg's parents bought him was Leith Stevens's score for *Destination Moon*, the 1950 sci-fi movie directed by George Pal. "I remember listening to that score and falling in love with it, especially how *misterioso* it was." The second was Miklós Rózsa's eerie, romantic score for theremin and orchestra for the 1945 Alfred Hitchcock film *Spellbound*. The needle was in; another film score junkie was born. "I amassed, right through my teenage years, a *tremendous* collection of soundtracks," Spielberg said. "So I had already been properly inducted into the language of movie music before I ever heard *The Reivers*, and therefore was able to compare John's score to Korngold and Steiner and Tiomkin and Alex North and Miklós Rózsa and Hugo Friedhofer and Benny Herrmann. I just felt that this was one of the best composers I had ever listened to, and I already had this entire context by which to make that judgment."[6]

This early education also permanently shaped the filmmaker's taste in the style and role of music—how extroverted and tuneful and dominant it could be in a film—separating him from many of his peers in the 1970s. "I've always made movies about the things that scare me and, musically, I was attracted to the kind of music that frightened me when I was three, four, five years old," he explained. He was a traditionalist, in that he wanted scores "to make my movies bigger than I had made them."[7] Spielberg once said his favorite movies were made between 1932 and 1952, and he was also, like John, influenced by radio dramas and the heavy narrative role of music inside the theater of the mind. "When I look at a film all put together, it's dead," Spielberg said in 1980.

> It's like lively death. The film moves, and it's action paced, but there's sometimes nothing behind the eyes of the movie. And for me music has always brought out a kind of spirit, and the soul of the movie is evident once there was music to encourage it along. I've always felt that music was ... an integral part of movies. And I think in the 1960s people got away from that. They began to equate realism with *lack* of musical sound, the absence of music. And those were the days of the social commentary, when young filmmakers were afraid to be too theatrical or too sentimental.[8]

Spielberg played clarinet in his school bands, tooting John Philip Sousa in his marching band and accompanying high school musicals. His collection of film soundtracks grew alongside his boyhood obsession with making movies, and the two flames fed each other. Pulling from his collection of old Alfred Newman and Tiomkin scores, he would take his 8mm camera and "make a movie *to* the music." In 1964, at 17, he scored his own feature-length debut, *Firelight*, composed on clarinet and transposed for his high school orchestra with help from his mother. "If I weren't a filmmaker," Spielberg confessed, "I'd probably be in music. I'd play piano or I'd compose. I'd probably be a starving composer somewhere in Hollywood right now, hopefully not starving, but I probably would not have been successful."[9]

In 1968, having finagled his way into an apprenticeship on the Universal lot, where he hung out in cutting rooms and networked with future mentors and sponsors, Spielberg directed a romantic short film, *Amblin'*. He brought a record player and a stack of his soundtrack albums into the editing room, and for two weeks, day and night, he would pace the room listening to music while constructing his movie. *Amblin'* earned the teen whiz a seven-year contract at Universal—an echo of John's career start—where he directed episodes of TV series like Rod Serling's *Night Gallery* and *Columbo*.[10]

But he had his heart set on making features, and in 1969 he was writing a spec script for *Ace Eli and Rodger of the Skies* while listening to John's score for *The Reivers* on repeat.* That same year Spielberg read an *Associated Press* article about a married couple who kidnapped a Texas highway patrolman and led a massive police chase across the state in hopes of getting their children back. He tried to sell the idea as a movie to Universal, but the studio kept him in the salt mines of television. In the summer of 1971, Spielberg directed the pilot and arguably best episode of *Columbo*, the beloved Peter Falk detective series. "Murder by the Book" was scored by Billy Goldenberg, a theater-turned-TV composer from New York (whose father had helped John get into Juilliard nearly 20 years earlier). A few months later, Spielberg got his big shot to make *Duel*, based on a short story by *Twilight Zone* alumnus Richard Matheson. It, too, was scored by Goldenberg, "one of the best scores ever written for one of my movies," Spielberg later said. Both scores were taut, inventive thrillers that sounded uniquely of the time—Goldenberg helped popularize the avant-baroque-mystery sound that became a trademark of 1970s film and TV—and it's interesting to imagine an alternate universe where it was *Spielberg & Goldenberg* reigning at the box office.

"But everything changed," Spielberg said, "when I met Johnny."[11]

* * *

Elmer Bernstein, the great American composer of films such as *To Kill a Mockingbird* and *The Great Escape*, penned an essay in 1972 for the magazine *High Fidelity*, titled "What Ever Happened to Great Movie Music?," in which he lamented that "the events of the past few years in the field of film scoring seem to indicate that any discussion of this great art may indeed have to be a historical summary at the end of its era of greatness."

"I find it inconceivable that this sophisticated art has in such a short time degenerated into a bleakness of various electronic noises and generally futile attempts to 'make the pop Top 40 charts,'" he wrote. "It appears the king is dead and the court jester has been installed in his place." He continued, waxing about the potential power of his art form:

---

* *Ace Eli* was eventually bought by Fox, but directed by TV veteran John Erman in 1973. It was, in Fox president Richard D. Zanuck's opinion, terrible. (McBride, *Steven Spielberg*.)

> Music is the art that begins where words and images leave off—which is what makes it so effective in films. Sonic vibrations set part of the body in motion and touch the listener in an almost purely visceral manner. Music can stimulate the greatest possible range of moods, shades, and fantasies. Also, it is an art that envelops the listener who cannot escape it save by leaving the area. Unlike the written word or visual image, there is no need to intellectualize its existence. That its source is unseen and that it can enter and leave at almost imperceptible levels makes music an invaluable tool with which the skilled film composer can practice emotional seductions upon the viewer of a movie.

Bernstein pegged two culprits for the beginning of the end: Dimitri Tiomkin landing a hit song with *High Noon*, and Bernstein's own score for *The Man with the Golden Arm*—combined with Mancini's *Peter Gunn*—leading to a proliferation of "pop sounds" in film and TV music. In today's terrifying, violent world, Bernstein sighed,

> art tends to become sensation, aesthetics becomes a belief that the way to protest brutality is to reflect it in art. In motion pictures we are treated to an onslaught of violence and sensation, without form, without art, and without humanity. In this atmosphere the quality of film scores is being strangled by the search for effect, for "new sounds" without content and form on the part of the artist, and by avarice on the part of the producer. Today the once proud art of film scoring has turned into a sound, a sensation, or hopefully a hit. How ironic that in an era in which music enjoys its greatest popularity as an art, film producers are demonstrating the greatest ignorance of the use of music in films since the beginning of that medium's history.[12]

Clearly, Elmer Bernstein had never met Steven Spielberg.

* * *

Thanks to *Duel*, which was a hit on TV screens in America and also in European movie houses, Spielberg was finally eligible for the big leagues. He had forged several important relationships with the higher-ups at Universal—including Jennings Lang, who put up the money for Spielberg to develop an outline of the Texas chase story with a young screenwriting duo, Hal Barwood and Matthew Robbins. The studio balked at their screenplay, which was called *Carte Blanche* in reference to the leeway that local law enforcement offered the married kidnappers. But when the hot new producing duo of Richard Zanuck and David Brown signed an exclusive deal with Universal, they put the film into production, now called *The Sugarland Express*.[13]

Jennings Lang was instrumental in the genesis of *Sugarland* as well as *Jaws*, but perhaps his greatest legacy, or at least the one with the biggest cultural footprint, was setting the lunch date between John Williams and Steven Spielberg (and possibly being the one who picked up the tab). Lang had known John since the early Revue days, and he produced several Universal films that John scored; his second wife, actress-singer Monica Lewis, was a close friend of Barbara's from their shared adventures at MGM in the 1950s, and the foursome often socialized. In their Beverly Hills mansion, the Langs would host parties and screen movies on the weekends, and John would play piano. He was impressed by Lang's teenage son, Michael, who was already showing promise on the keys.

It was sometime around December 1972, before Spielberg traveled to Texas to film *Sugarland*, when Lang booked a table for the nervous young filmmaker and the veteran composer at that posh Beverly Hills restaurant at Spielberg's request. Spielberg had just cast Goldie Hawn as the lead in his first feature film, and he was determined to have her western adventures scored by the man who had made *The Reivers* and *The Cowboys* levitate off the ground. "When I heard both scores, I had to meet this modern relic from a lost era of film symphonies," Spielberg said. "I wanted a real Aaron Copland sound for my first movie."[14] But there was a wrinkle in time that might have prevented what happened next—and possibly created an alternate Hollywood history. Charles Fox, a New York composer who studied music with Nadia Boulanger in Paris before a prolific career writing songs and scoring television and films, had co-written the ballad "Killing Me Softly with His Song," which Roberta Flack turned into a gigantic hit when her version came out in January 1973. Spielberg heard it on the car radio driving to set every day, and fell in love with the song. Back in L.A., the young filmmaker gave Fox a call. "I'd love to talk to you about doing my first film, *Sugarland Express*," he said. So Fox invited Spielberg over to his house in Encino for lunch—Fox's wife, Joan, made tuna fish salad—and they discussed the project. Spielberg left a copy of the script and Fox said he would love to score the film; they met again at least once at Spielberg's Universal office. In Fox's memory, one day Spielberg called and said, "I'm awfully sorry. I thought you'd score my picture, but Zanuck and Brown have talked with John Williams." "He apologized to me in a very nice way," Fox recalled. "Said, 'I hope we'll work together again.' I said, 'I look forward to it,' and I wished him good luck. That was it." Fox held no bitterness about his brush with Spielberg glory: "John Williams and Steven Spielberg gave the world a gift," he said later. "John Williams did more for music and film than any other composer."[15]

Spielberg, who over the years *never* mentioned this other (potential) parallel universe, confirmed that the meeting took place. "It's true," he said—offering no more details.[16] What most likely happened was that John was always his first choice, and that John gave Spielberg a conditional yes before seeing the film; in the meantime, Spielberg met with Fox because he knew he would need a backup if John said no. John must have screened the film in the spring of 1973 (it finished shooting in March). When he saw his very first Steven Spielberg film, John "thought it was very good, especially the second half."[17] He agreed to compose the score. Spielberg said he wanted a full orchestra with "a colossal string section. But John politely said *no*, this was for the harmonica and a very small string ensemble."[18]

The Sugarland Express opens with a bus pulling to a stop on a rural Texas road chilled by winter. The camera descends and reorients from its godlike POV to human-height, and Hawn's character, Lou Jean, disembarks and walks down a perpendicular road toward the prison that holds her husband. John scored the moment with a simple acoustic guitar arpeggio grooving under his main harmonica theme—a sweet, reaching melody with a singable pop structure, soon joined by sympathetic strings and contemporary percussion. It was a lovely but unremarkable beginning to a partnership that became associated with large-scale adventure, majesty, and awe. What *was* evident and auspicious right from the start was Spielberg's faith in lyricism and unembarrassed sentiment—which John gladly provided.

And right from the start, Spielberg was accused of being overly sentimental. Critics found fault in his compassionate characterization of this would-be Bonnie and Clyde, the hapless patrolman they kidnap, and the kind Captain Tanner who leads the hunt but with a kind of fatherly love. Critics also found Spielberg manipulative. "Everything is underlined," Stephen Farber sneered in the *New York Times*:

> Spielberg sacrifices narrative logic and character consistency for quick thrills and easy laughs. He has a very crude sense of humor, indicated by his obsession with toilet jokes, and an irrepressible maudlin streak. Early on Spielberg lingers over a shot of the couple's baby playing with a dog, and after the final tragedy, he moves in for a close-up as a police car drives over a discarded teddy bear. It's depressing to see a young director who is already so shameless.[19]

But others, like the influential Pauline Kael, saw the debut of a master. "*The Sugarland Express* is like some of the entertaining studio-factory films of the past (it's as commercial and shallow and impersonal), yet it has so much eagerness and flash and talent that it just about transforms its scrubby ingredients," Kael wrote in the *New Yorker*. "Composition seems to come naturally to him, as it does to some of the young Italians; Spielberg uses his gift in a very free-and-easy, American way—for humor, and for a physical response to action. He could be that rarity among directors a born entertainer—perhaps a new generation's Howard Hawks. In terms of the pleasure that technical assurance gives an audience, this film is one of the most phenomenal debut films in the history of movies." "If there is such a thing as a movie sense," Kael declared, "Spielberg really has it."[20] The critical response to *Sugarland* was the Spielberg conundrum in a nutshell: he was a technical filmmaker undeniably talented at entertaining, at composing actors and choreographing action like music—Kael called him a *wizard*—but for others he was also "shameless," "shallow," and "slick." John had no such qualms: "I thought, *my god, this kid is really a great filmmaker.*"[21]

Sparsely applied, as with most dramatic films of the time, John's score was appropriately small and countrified. Toots Thielemans's playful harmonica jammed with pedal steel guitar (to be performed "with Hank Williams feel," John marked on the score), Fender bass, and a shuffle rhythm created with coconut shells and scat vocals in cues that cast the initial action in a playful, almost ludicrous light. John gave Tanner and his armada of cop cars a martial motif for snare drum, timpani, low piano, and drawled but urgent strings; these are neither villains nor heroes, simply men of the law doing their job. The film's quiet but growing tension is scored with a haze of high strings, alternately worried and weary. But it's the singable harmonica theme—"haunting and wonderful," in Spielberg's words, and "so evocative of that part of Texas"—that persists and foregrounds the gentle humanity in every main character.[22] When the kidnap car runs out of gas, the outlaw couple persuades Tanner to push them to a filling station. The humor of the situation, acknowledged by shuffle rhythm and twangy harmonica, gives way to an ingenious split-screen effect with Tanner's eyes seen in his rearview mirror at the top of the frame, and naive Lou Jean looking tenderly at the lawman through the rear window in the lower half. John brought in soft acoustic guitar and a sleepy version of his harmonica theme as their eyes meet with compassion. In this post-Vietnam, post-Watergate moment, when Spielberg's contemporaries were questioning authority and expressing a cynical, paranoid worldview, he saw only good in his law-enforcing characters (a trend that continued in his next two films). Where most of his classmates of the Hollywood New Wave had a sour outlook, Spielberg found sweetness. That flavor was *saccharine* for some filmgoers, but one reason he and John became unshakably simpatico was that John, too, saw mostly sweetness and nobility in the world. John scored a handful of cynical films in his long career, but he gravitated toward the romantic and the redemptive—qualities embodied by the films of Steven Spielberg.

The *Sugarland Express* score was recorded in July 1973 at Universal, and it's most likely that Barbara attended some of the sessions. Spielberg got to know her a little during that year: "Oh, she was a beautiful person, a beautiful human being," he said. "Very, *very* attentive to John's needs, and yet had a completely independent life, creative life, of her own. And John adored her."[23] Thielemans, who once described his playing sound as being "in that little space between a smile and a tear," played his usual chromatic harmonica.[24] Joining him were Buddy Emmons on pedal steel guitar, Jerry Williams and Emil Richards on percussion, Joe Porcaro and Tommy Tedesco on guitar, and Carol Kaye—another one of the famed Wrecking Crew—on Fender bass. "I never wanted to be hired because I was Jennings Lang's son," said Mike Lang, who played piano on the score. "To some extent that's uncontrollable, because we interface with some of the same people. But thank God for my own security of being okay with who I was. I was in a profession where you couldn't really get a job and keep it through nepotism—you have to actually play the piano."[25] (John would go on to hire Lang on many future scores.) Spielberg was a kid in a candy store. "I'm a very controlling person as a director," he said. "I think most directors have to be. But I decided to abdicate all my control when John threw in with me."[26] Spielberg admitted that, in this first outing, "I was a fanboy and he was my hero. I don't believe I settled into my friendship with Johnny until around *Jaws*, because I was so enamored and in awe of him. I just know that what impressed Johnny about *me*, to the best of *my* recollection, was my knowledge of film scores from the past." John invited Spielberg to join him at a dinner at the home of composer Alex North, and "I couldn't help myself," Spielberg said—"I hummed the entire opening main title from *Spartacus* to Alex. I probably embarrassed *everybody* in the room, but I was in a fugue state of adulation, because here I had Johnny Williams *and* Alex North in the same room."[27]

"He struck me as a very juvenile personality," said John,[28] who described their relationship as "the result of a lot of very compatible dissimilarities."[29] "I had already worked with William Wyler, and Robert Altman, and Martin Ritt—and they were all older than I was," he said. "So *I* was the kid, in a way, working for these older people that I admire so much. Suddenly this was a complete flip-flop, and I was working with somebody who was younger than I was, so he was set apart by age, and by a seeming contradiction in taste—where you expect him to be listening to only rock 'n' roll records."[30] Spielberg said he simply felt "a kind of alchemy between us that I've never questioned, and I've never really looked at it very carefully because I tend not to look a gift horse in the mouth." Lopsided by age and personality, they were never natural playmates. André Previn could talk eruditely about classical music and make urbane wisecracks about Hollywood. Lionel Newman could crack John up with his creatively profane tongue. Spielberg was the first to admit: "I'm not a funny guy. I don't make a lot of jokes. I can't even remember how to *tell* a joke because I can't remember the joke."[31] It didn't matter. John said the day he met Spielberg was "one of the luckiest days of my life." Both men described it as a marriage. *The Sugarland Express*, which tolled the wedding bells, premiered in late March 1974—just weeks after Barbara died and turned John's world upside down. John and Barbara had been married for 18 years. One union was suddenly, horrifically over, just as this new creative matrimony commenced—and it seems the intensity of the one can only be fully appreciated by the intense loss of the other.

Spielberg shook his head, uncomfortable drawing the marriage metaphor quite that far. "I'm not sure I associate it with that kind of a bond," he said. "We had the kind of bond that often occurs with composers and lyricists as opposed to husbands and wives. I provided him the libretto to score. I did feel an affinity to John that Hammerstein must have felt to Rodgers."[32] Spielberg, who had a complex relationship with his own father at the time, always looked for mentors, "men that are in positions of power, that he has looked up to," said Kathleen Kennedy, who later became a producer and close colleague of Spielberg's. That was true both artistically and in business: "He's always been enormously respectful of that kind of a relationship. And I just think he had, right from the beginning, this incredible respect for John. So it wasn't collegial in that, you know, they're punching each other on the shoulder and that kind of thing—because that's not who John is. But there's an intimacy between the two of them."[33] Said Jenny: "Certainly in the beginning, I think it was a little bit similar to a father-son relationship. And I think they both needed that at the time. I think it was important and valuable for them to be in those positions at the time, just psychologically."[34]

* * *

Barbara's death left a crater in John's life. He went deeper inside, retreating from many of the friends who were inextricably tied to her. "He became almost reclusive," said Shirley Jones, whose children used to play with the Williams kids. "I tried to see him after Barbara passed away, and he wasn't very receptive to that. I think he was in such mourning that he just didn't want to see the friends that they had had together. He needed to sort of remove himself for a while."[35] "He and I never talked about Barbara after she died," said Bob Klein. "It was almost as if John would rather I didn't bring it up. I can understand that. So I won't. My feeling is that his private life became much *more* private and even heavier work oriented after Barb died."[36] "When we lost Barbara," said Ginny Mancini, "John became ... oh, I don't know. How do you withstand a tragedy like that, when you have three young children and have to bear the brunt of that sadness? It's hard to describe. The lightness disappeared for quite a while."[37]

Jenny, who was 17, had to step up and take on some of Barbara's role as both mother to her little brothers—who were 16 and 13—and social manager for John. She was on John's arm just a few weeks after Barbara's death when he attended the Academy Awards on April 2, 1974, with three total nominations for *Tom Sawyer* and *Cinderella Liberty*. In a photo taken before they drove to Dorothy Chandler Pavilion (Figure 6.1), their easy smiles masked a deep cavern of sadness and unspoken feelings. With her red hair and movie star smile, Jenny was the spitting image of her mother. Pete Rugolo told his wife: "It must break John's heart when he sees Jenny, because she resembles her mother so much. It makes *me* cry when I see her."[38]

Jenny didn't cry, didn't grieve. "I went right into: *Gotta make sure Dad's okay, gotta make sure my brothers are going to school, that there's food in the house, they're eating, they're going to bed*," she said. "So I went right into that mode and never really had a chance to grieve." Mark and Joe, both momma's boys, were destroyed—in ways that reverberated for the rest of their lives. But no one would talk about it. Lurene Tuttle, Jenny's "Gaga" whom she adored, refused to speak on the subject. "It was not talked about, not dealt with," said Jenny. "All of us individually had to go through our own process, and be on our own paths with the loss. We all had very different kinds of experiences and recoveries. She was the center of the family." The house in Little Holmby was suddenly "very eerie," said Jenny. "It was very empty. I just remember having to be on hyper *alert* mode, because I was concerned about my dad, I was *very* worried about my brothers—I needed to be responsible for them—and that continued on for many, many years. They're both incredible people—the sweetest men you could ever meet—but they were really young, and they needed help. I tried to do my best."[39] Within days of Barbara's death, Kathryn Altman came over with a friend and went through Barbara's closets and things, "which I just was not in any kind of shape to do," said John. "I didn't even go into that part of the house for a while."[40]

John never worked with Robert Altman again, although he did consider scoring the director's futuristic *Quintet* a few years later. "He was a crazy, crazy, man, and I loved him dearly," John said. "When Barbara died, we broke up a little bit. It was not intentional. I think it just was painful. Life does these things, you know."[41] Their temperaments, both artistic and personal, were always a strange mix, and without Barbara's lubricating joy those differences likely became starker. "I drifted away from working with him, not through any intentional decision or conscious decision," John said. "I got busy with other directors and other projects. Bob chided me about going Hollywood and getting successful. He would chide me or tease me or censure me about pursuing

Figure 6.1. John and Jenny going to the Oscars, March 1974 (Courtesy of Jenny Williams).

overly commercial projects—probably my work with Spielberg. He saw that artistically as a kind of betrayal of some kind of bohemian artistic principles he clung to."[42] John also never worked with Delbert Mann again after 1974, nor Irwin Allen. And he didn't work with either Rydell or Ritt again for more than a decade. It was a shedding year, the vestiges of John's "second base" career—and the one tied to Barbara—shaking loose as he began a new life with Spielberg and all their partnership would lead to. John dove even further into his work, and the emotions in his music became noticeably deeper and more profound. The new intensity of his drive and maturation of his style, not coincidentally, were rocket fuel for his fast-approaching explosion of success.

Personal trauma "makes or breaks people," John said. "I was young and my wife was very young. Had I been 20 years older, I would've been less able to restart my life. Immediately thereafter, I did feel differently about working, especially with music. I can't quantify or describe what it did. But we do change. All life experience does that. We have accidents. We have happy things. Having three teenage children at the time required a lot of focus and strength, being a single parent.... We could talk for a week about this."[43]

Six weeks after Barbara's death, on April 13, John took the podium at Dorothy Chandler to conduct his flute concerto with the Glendale Symphony, a group composed of mostly film session players. "His wife had just died, and he was pretty upset," said flutist Sheridon Stokes, who had asked John to conduct *before* the tragic event took place. "I said, 'Well, you don't have to.' And he said, 'No, that's fine—it'll be good for me.'"[44] But John did take some time off from film-scoring assignments "and tinkered around with the violin concerto," he said, which is where he poured his feelings of love and grief for his childhood sweetheart. The concerto "was an ode to her, without question," said Jenny, "so he put a lot of emotion into that. It was good for him to have that project."[45]

* * *

While Spielberg was away on Martha's Vineyard shooting *Jaws*, John scored two more disaster movies. They both served as warm-up blockbuster scores, although Spielberg's film would instantly render their inert direction and hokey special effects as antediluvian relics. *Earthquake* was John's last film with Mark Robson, and it followed the typical disaster formula of throwing a huge all-star cast—in this case, Charlton Heston, Ava Gardner, George Kennedy, and Richard Roundtree—into a violent crisis that lasts half of the running time and claims a few famous victims. *Earthquake* was executive produced by Jennings Lang (his wife, Monica Lewis, had a small part), who came up with a gimmick to lure audiences away from their TV rooms at home: "Sensurround," a special control rack installed in theaters that emitted loud, seat-shaking "tremor simulator" sounds timed to the film's soundtrack. *The Godfather* novelist Mario Puzo co-wrote the screenplay, which featured Heston in a bitter, loveless marriage with Gardner—and having an affair with a much younger Geneviève Bujold—Roundtree as a stunt motorcyclist, and a real-life former Pentecostal preacher named Marjoe Gortner playing a psychotic Army volunteer who murders survivors after the quake and tries to rape a young woman. Neither family friendly nor particularly mature, this motley premise was clearly an excuse to lay Los Angeles to waste like a sandcastle and cash in on the latest craze.

John agreed with Robson that the score should focus on characters rather than the catastrophe, especially since his music would have been swallowed by the Sensurround cacophony during the earthquake itself. He wrote a romantically anxious theme for French horns that suited the film's contemporary L.A. setting with syncopated pop percussion and a low bass and piano groove, "a long-line melody to match the sweep of the film," he explained, "under which I could inject rhythms to represent the feverish day-to-day activities of the great city, teeming with life."[46] There's a gentle love theme for Heston and Bujold that symbolizes the only real softness in the story. John wrote some obviously *Shaft*-inspired music for Roundtree's character, with a funky rhythm jiving under muted brass, wah-wah guitar, and psychedelic electric piano. Tension was scored with watery piano and chimes for seismic activity at the dam, tense clusters of high violins, and low staccato notes on piano. Gortner's deranged character is accompanied by an unhinged baroque figure on electric piano. In general, music served mainly as an aftershock.

The film premiered in November and received mostly positive press. *Variety* called *Earthquake* "an excellent dramatic exploitation extravaganza" and "surprisingly above average for this type film,"[47] and Charles Champlin at the *L.A. Times* wrote that the "superior score is molto agitato and immense."[48] When picking his favorite scores for the Academy Awards a few months later, Champlin singled this one out: "the eerie diabolic dissonances for *Earthquake* were just what the seismologist ordered."[49] More and more, reviewers and audiences were paying attention to John's scores. *Earthquake* and his next project served, if nothing else, as advance publicity for the disaster film to end all disaster films.

Irwin Allen had escaped a capsized ocean liner with a heap of booty, and he decided to set a high-rise on fire to generate even more. *The Towering Inferno* was a more impressive effort than *The Poseidon Adventure* in terms of stars and spectacle, but it followed the same warmed-over recipe—all the way down to having a live band playing an original song with lyrics that hinted at death. "We May Never Love Like This Again" was performed onscreen by Maureen McGovern, who sang *Poseidon*'s "The Morning After"—both written by Al Kasha and Joel Hirschhorn—and it, too, won an Oscar. Why mess with success?

The production was also a feat that brought together two major studios, Warner Bros. and 20th Century Fox, in what the producers touted as "the block-buster of the century."[50] When reporters asked him if the public would ever get tired of disaster pictures, Allen shot back: "Not disaster! It's a *crisis* picture. Crisis. Crisis. Disaster has another meaning. I should think this type of picture could continue being made as a way of getting people away from their television sets. But it better damn well be a good story. There would never be an end to Westerns. There would not be an end to comedies. Why then would there be an end to crisis pictures?"[51] *Inferno* boasted two of Hollywood's biggest stars: Paul Newman and Steve McQueen. Surviving and dying alongside them were Faye Dunaway, William Holden, Fred Astaire, Richard Chamberlain, Robert Vaughn, and former footballer O. J. Simpson. Amalgamated from two separate novels (*The Glass Inferno* and *The Tower*), Stirling Silliphant's script introduced yet another variety pack of characters, here gathered to celebrate the completion of San Francisco's latest architectural wonder. Corners were cut, a fire starts, and for the better part of two hours these movie stars run through flames, shimmy down blasted stairwells, swing from elevator cables, argue, love, and burn.

There was much more demand for music than in *Earthquake*, though still plenty of noisy effects. Allen "loves music from start to finish," John said, "there can't be too much for him. He's theatrical, an extrovert, so he likes it big in the Hollywood tradition—which is fun."[52] John wrote a main anthem to open the film with a nightly news-like quality and pop rhythm; adventure and urgency and romance all swirl together, and an interlude with open fifth chords relate this to his other Americana scores. The film feigned at being a lofty paean to the heroes who fight fires for real, and John's main title included a noble horn solo for the placard dedicating the movie to their sacrifice. From there it was a towering score filled with love themes, original lounge Muzak, brassy fanfares—and then anxiety, slow-cooking drama, and scorching alarm. John scored the fire but he always kept his eye on the humans inside, their worry, their heroism, and their tragic ends. A standout cue accompanies the scene where secret lovers (played by Robert Wagner and Susan Flannery) are trapped in a room engulfed by flames. A frantically rising clarinet line is punctuated by horn blasts, comingling with the Kasha-Hirschhorn song melody, and it all whips into a tense lament for strings and semi-automatic trumpet notes. Various trials culminate in McQueen's fire chief and Newman's architect exploding water tanks at the top of the building to douse the fire—and once the ensuing biblical flood and explosions subside, the main theme gently ebbs back in as the last survivors stir, various character melodies flowing together with a rising but wearied coda. In retrospect, the action music was a dry run for both *Jaws* and *Star Wars*, a banquet of melodic stress in service of a movie with far less magic. Overall the music was less thematically cohesive and sturdily built as a musical narrative than John's later adventure scores—probably because the film was as flimsily constructed as the skyscraper itself. Far too long, the movie dragged and sagged with too many characters to fully invest in. Knowing where to even *put* music must have been an exhausting chore.

But the film elevated John's stature even higher. When it opened in December 1974, inhaling $50 million and eight Oscar nominations, *Variety* called it "a big film [with] a big John Williams soundtrack to go with it."[53] Champlin praised the score as "very potent stuff, ominous and urgent, fully underlining everything we watch, in a return to an earlier-day Hollywood regard for music's role in heightening drama."[54] John's score was nominated for an Oscar against Jerry Goldsmith's *Chinatown*, Richard Rodney Bennett's *Murder on the Orient Express*, and Nino Rota's *The Godfather: Part II*. (The latter won.) Noting the surplus of disaster films in theaters that Christmas, Gene Siskel expressed his concern about a trend that, to a great degree, bore out: "Stories with mass appeal will be the ones that get financed. Action will dominate thought as a script component. The movie actor will be re-established as a principal drawing card. Hollywood's brief, insincere love affair with directors' artistic aspirations will be terminated, pronto. In short, the movies will return to their origins as populist entertainment."[55] Even while the film was in production, Allen announced that his next "crisis" was going to be a swarm of killer bees, and, sure enough, John was attached to score *The Swarm* up through the summer of 1977. But *The Towering Inferno* would turn out to be the last of his old-school disaster pics; there were much bigger fish to fry.

* * *

John never scored a James Bond film, but he came pretty close. Spielberg was vocally eager to direct a Bond movie after *Sugarland*—which didn't happen, but Indiana Jones was partly conceived out of that want. *The Eiger Sanction*, a 1972 novel by the American author Trevanian, was a spy-adventure thriller about a "super anti-hero" with a strange mix of Bond and proto–Indiana Jones qualities: Jonathan Hemlock is an art collector/assassin/mountain climber who globetrots and kills ("sanctions") his marks in exotic locales when he isn't teaching at a university. "It's really a male fantasy," Clint Eastwood said in 1975. "He appeals to all the elements a man would like to be."[56] An early scene in the film, which Eastwood starred in and directed, was like a grimy funhouse mirror of *Raiders of the Lost Ark*: college girls moon over Hemlock, a hot adventurer professor in glasses, as he lectures about antiquity—only *this* hero smacks one of his students on her butt after rejecting an offer of sex to improve her grade. Pulpy and politically incorrect, the story put Hemlock in debt to his crime boss, an evil albino named Dragon; in love with a Black femme fatale named Jemima Brown, leading to several cringeworthy Aunt Jemima jokes; a gay assassin played to the hilt by Jack Cassidy, who has a little dog named for a gay slur; a Native American woman named George who trains Hemlock for his big climb by running ahead of him in short shorts and occasionally flashing him—then sleeping with him, then trying to murder him—and that's all *before* the actual extended climb up the Swiss mountain in the film's title. It was almost a parody of Bond tropes, but told with mostly utter sincerity and 1970s scuzz. Paul Newman was originally cast as Hemlock, but he didn't like the script and pulled out.[57] Produced by Zanuck and Brown and supervised by Lang, the production ran concurrently with *Jaws* and John recorded his score in January 1975, just two months before recording the latter. There was a stark contrast between the visual storytelling skills of Eastwood and Spielberg, to say nothing of the redemptive, more family-friendly thrills of *Jaws*—but John was nonetheless inspired to compose a baroque-mystery score for *Eiger* with a killer main theme that shared traits with, of all things, his melancholy music for *Jane Eyre*.

Once again, he used modern electric instruments—guitar, harpsichord, piano, wah-wah—to perform fugal and ornamented lines evoking the distant past. "We were filming both in Europe [and] America," said Eastwood. "In America I wanted more modern music, and then in the European stuff we had more classical so that we could separate it."[58] Springing up from the suspense and murderous tension was a well of melody: beyond the main theme, which is alternately applied to espionage adventure and romance, John wrote a timid sonatina for acoustic guitar and harpsichord for a character named Felicity (whose scenes were eventually cut); a running theme for Hemlock's sweaty pursuit of George in the scenic beauties of Arizona—yet another baroque dance for harpsichord, guitar, and orchestra that *should* feel over-mannered for these contemporary escapades but instead lends the shallow proceedings some majesty; and an ascendant, triumphant motif for Hemlock's summit of an imposing rock tower, decorated with sparkling harpsichord notes and brass fanfare. When Hemlock finally arrives at the Eiger and the promised icy expedition begins, there are plenty of stunning vistas on screen but shallow crevices where compelling drama should be. The film's final hour was an obvious excuse to show Eastwood clambering up dangerous-looking peaks on location in Switzerland, but it was John Williams who did the heavy lifting—pulling leaden bodies up a beautiful mountain, supplying most of the tension and doom-laden rhythm toward a catastrophic crescendo and, at last, a relieved reprise of the melancholy main theme.

John enjoyed working with Eastwood, who was just two years older. "I never went through a dubbing session so breezily," John said. "He went, 'More of this. Less of that.' And that's as far as he'd ever go. He was right."[59] The film had its "hometown" premiere on May 15, 1975, in Carmel, California, where Eastwood and his family lived. The *L.A. Times* called it a "splendid high adventure, done with much wit and style," and praised the "formal, even elegiac score by Leonard Rosenman."[60] (The paper ran a correction the following day.) Less enthused were the *New York Times* ("a long, foolish but never boring suspense melodrama"[61]) and the *Ottawa Journal* ("The monumental stupidities that are evident in *The Eiger Sanction* make it a candidate for the dumbest movie of the year"[62]). The film "is intended as escapist fun," wrote Wayne Harada at the *Honolulu Advertiser*. "It is far better a visual experience—vistas of the mountains are exquisitely photographed—than a verbal one—the script is so bland, it might've been subbed with nothing but John Williams' effective, mood-provoking music."[63] In its review of the soundtrack album, *Variety* said the film "wasn't as good as the score John Williams composed and conducted. Williams is becoming, or has become, one of the best in the film music business and this album adds to his laurels."[64] Enough heat was bubbling about the *Jaws* score when the shark film went into previews that MCA rushed John back into the studio—four whole months after recording his *Eiger Sanction* score—to produce an album of arranged suites and cues for an *Eiger* LP.

And for the first time, John drew the attention of the *New York Times*, which ran an article about the new class of film composers. "A handsome, self-confident clan, they dress very expensively, eat at the best restaurants, live in luxury houses or apartments, drive costly cars, and mingle with the chic Hollywood set," reported Charles Higham, an Englishman who became infamous for his juicy celebrity biographies. "Unlike most 'concert' composers, they are not struggling and anguished, fighting to achieve perfection; the secret of their success is speed, slickness, and the ability to dash off scores in a week or two, with a minimum of fuss." The May 1975 article asserted that a top-flight movie composer today made $25,000 per score plus percentages of album sales, and earned an annual income of $100,000 and up. John was profiled alongside Lalo Schifrin and David Shire, and Higham offered qualified praise:

> Williams, 43, may not be as consistently inventive as Schifrin, but he is every bit as popular with Hollywood producers. Subdued and self-effacing, with fair hair and a blond beard, he is known as one of the most cooperative composers in the industry. His first major feature was *The Reivers*, in which he supplied a cheerful pastiche of

Stephen Foster tunes, and an attractive waltz theme expressing the romanticism of Steve McQueen's love for a car. His offbeat score for Robert Altman's *Images*, about a sexually disturbed girl's fantasies, was full of eerie, dissonant effects. In *The Towering Inferno*, he combined a series of water chimes and four Peking gongs to achieve atonal results one would not expect to find in a conventional "disaster" epic.

John told Higham: "Film scoring may be very rewarding, but it's also agony. Film composers are not their own masters. They are working for corporations. You accept that as part of the job."[65] This was one of his rare public complaints about Hollywood, a sure echo of Previn's attitude. It wasn't just that John would learn to parse his words more carefully and become more diplomatic; he was on the cusp of working for music-loving filmmakers who offered him a freedom he could never have imagined.

* * *

Just before he attained Hollywood immortality, John took a big, hard swing at West End glory: he wrote an original stage musical. It was an understandable itch to come out of playing custodian to so many other composers' showtunes for so many years. He had graduated from a musical theater apprenticeship like no other, and his own music had an innate, unlimited lyricism that all but begged for a libretto. But the result proved to be far more of a disaster than anything Irwin Allen ever cooked up—one of the rare and total belly flops in John's career.

Jim Harbert, his friend since their early days at Columbia Records, had the idea of adapting a stage musical from the stormy tale of the relationship between King Henry II and Thomas Becket, Archbishop of Canterbury, which had been adapted into plays by both T. S. Eliot and Jean Anouilh. "Now, how do you make a musical out of *that*?" John said, years later. "You've got to be a little bit crazy." John liked Harbert's concept of framing the story as an allegorical chess game of political intrigue, "and through various moves, beginning with the affectionate bond between Henry and Thomas as young nobles hunting and doing things together—with even homosexual undertones—it would grow through the various steps on the chessboard to where a murder is the final result. Could be an intriguing idea."[66] Harbert took a crack at the show's book, but it "was considered too serious," he said, "and so other writers came in and changed it."[67] His lyrics remained, but the book was ultimately rewritten by none other than Edward Anhalt, the gruff New Yorker who had written the screenplay for the 1964 film adaptation of Anouilh's play, *Becket*, starring Richard Burton and Peter O'Toole. With John on board, it seemed like an all-star team destined for greatness. They found an eager impresario in Sam Grossman, an endearingly smooth real estate tycoon who grew up in Beverly Hills and went to high school with André Previn. "I had a musical background of absolutely no repute. I mean, no repute—none, zero," said Grossman, who nonetheless enjoyed producing shows in high school and college. "I produced all kinds of shit—and that's what it really, basically was. But it was fun." Grossman hit it off right away with John: "He had written three or four songs, as I recall, and he played them for me. And naturally I thought: *holy shit, this is pretty good stuff.*"[68] Grossman "had a *vision*, he thought," said John, "and *damn all the torpedoes*, he will see to it we arrive at the vision."

This was around 1973, and for two years Grossman, John, and Harbert sang for their supper—hosting countless auditions for potential backers, either at John's house or Grossman's, or sometimes at a rented studio. "We had a lot of fun doing those run-throughs—we did at least 50 or 60 of them—Harbert and I doing our best to sing, John playing the piano," said Grossman, who was dating Barbra Streisand around this time. "I wish to hell I had some film of that." When they presented at John's house, teenage Jenny would usually sing the female parts; she couldn't believe it when Groucho Marx came over to hear the show one day. John and company even auditioned for Hal Prince in New York, but Grossman was looking beyond Broadway and setting his torpedoes on London. Why? "M-O-N-E-Y," he said, spelling out the word. "In New York it would cost twice as much as in London. Literally twice as much. And so naturally, the businessman that I am: 'Shit, we've got to do it in London. Besides, it's an English piece.' *Besides, besides, besides.* All of which proved to be the dumbest thing I ever did in my life. If it had opened in New York, I think we'd have had a nice run. As it turned out it opened in exactly a hundred percent of the wrong place—for which I take the responsibility."

The bullish Yanks traveled to London in early 1975 to cast and rehearse *Thomas and the King*, which was booked for an October debut at the historic, 1,200-seat Her Majesty's Theatre in the Haymarket. Grossman began a hype campaign declaring it was going to "knock over the West End, and it was going to be bigger than *Camelot*, it was going to be bigger than *Ben-Hur*"—at least that's how James Smillie remembered it. The Australian actor had recently moved to London, playing Tony in a revival of *West Side Story* and most recently Petruchio in *Kiss Me, Kate* at the Oxford Playhouse. "I got a call from my agent to say, 'Can you rush down to London and sing for this musical called *Thomas and the King*?'" Smillie recalled:

> I didn't pay it much heed. Anyway, I got in there, went on, sang the first one: "Where's the life that late I led? / Where has it gone? Totally dead. / Where's the fun I used to ..." Got about that far into it and the casting director—who, it appeared, was the only person there—she said, "Hang on, hang on, hang on." She ran out, and about five minutes later, unbeknownst to me, John came back, Jimmy, Eddie ... I think the whole lot. They were hailing a cab to go to the airport.

After learning and singing Henry II's big number, "Man of Love," Smillie—who was going by "Jim Smilie" at the time—got the part. Edward Fox, who had just starred in *The Day of the Jackal*, was allegedly considered for the role of Becket, as was John Castle from *The Lion in Winter*—who probably *should* have gotten it, said Smillie. Instead, the role went to Royal Shakespeare Company veteran Richard Johnson. Things began favorably, and everyone was excited. "On the opening day of the rehearsals, they were all there," said Smillie. "John sat down and played the piano—I remember it to this day, the shock of red hair, the beard, the little red cheeks and everything. And he's singing all these blinking songs, and Jimmy Harbert's going, 'We shall do it! We shall do it! Change this kingdom....' It was fantastic. Absolutely fantastic."[69]

But then cracks began to form. Braham Murray, the show's director, walked out over creative differences, and choreographer Norman Maen was hastily promoted, "so he was nervous as a kitten," said Smillie. And it was clear almost immediately that the all-important role of Thomas was miscast. "Richard really couldn't sing it," said Smillie. "He had this really difficult part in the second act, and he's saying something about, 'God, please ... I don't understand. He's calling me back. Should I go? Should I not?' And the entry points were Sondheim-like—it was really difficult. And Richard ... he could never get to it, and he hated the whole thing." Casting Eleanor of Aquitaine, the leading lady, also proved a challenge. "If we'd have done this show in New York, we'd have had 50 young ladies standing, *begging* to sing the part—and all 45 out of the 50 could have really blown it away," said Grossman. "We spent three weeks nonstop, every day, trying to find anybody in England who could sing. The chances of that were two: slim and none. Right there I should have packed it up and gone home." The role went to Dilys Hamlett, who had been in many of Murray's previous shows. "Doing a show in London in those years was crazy," said Grossman. "They had no ears. Absolutely no ears. They may have gotten some since. I know a six-year-old kid who can play chopsticks on the piano better than these guys know about music. As you can see, I'm still a little bitter."

John was in Los Angeles during most of the rehearsal period, but when the company decided the opening number wasn't working, he flew back to London to write a new one in just a few days. "It didn't really work," Smillie admitted. "It wasn't really particularly good, and it was a very slow start. It needed to be a punchier start." Still, Smillie maintained his optimism, savoring the melodies he genuinely liked and riding high on the promises that this would be his ticket to the big time. "John was saying to me, 'You'll be singing with the San Francisco Light Opera Company!' You know, 'I'm doing pictures for this young guy called Steven. I'm about to do a thing called *Jaws*,' and all this sort of thing. 'Any minute now you'll be working with Brando and Jack Nicholson!'" When the show opened on October 16, the London critics had already sharpened their teeth—and they went straight for the jugular. *The Stage and Television Today* called it "the sort of show one comes away from 'humming the costumes.' ... Here we have the Becket and Henry the Second drama reduced to postage stamp size. You would hardly think that the tension, passion, and tragedy of it could be almost totally destroyed, but this is so here." After excoriating the book and lyrics, the review went on: "The music by John Williams isn't much either; synthetic film score material with not a song to remember with any pleasure."[70] In an absolute tour de force of vitriol, Charles Lewsen opened his salvo in *The Times* by calling *Thomas and the King* a "puny pinprick in the buttock of the theatrical season." "This fargo, this omnifutile, pasteboard, and plasti-coated bladder of blather is based on no work of art but on the barefaced assumption that, in the theatre, you can get away with any formless, illogical, unconscionable twaddle, provided you do it to music." (It's a truism among critics that pans are the most fun to write.) Lewsen added that "the composer who regards a change of key as an adequate substitute for melody is John Williams (no, not the guitarist)."[71]

Beyond the show's missteps in casting, and besides having no workshop period in smaller markets that might have refined the material, it was also true that John's songs did not rise to his highest standards. As deeply as he loved England and its musical language, the tunes in *Thomas* weren't as noble or indelible as those in *Jane Eyre*. The orchestration was characteristically vibrant—there were even hints of *Jaws*-like menace in the show's nightmare number, "Will No One Rid Me?"—but it was weakened for a small, thin ensemble, and simply never as interesting as the pixie dust he sprinkled on *Chips* and *Fiddler*. (Herbert Spencer contributed to the orchestration for *Thomas*.) The songs themselves slanted toward comical and arch, and the outcome was often merely annoying, whereas the serious numbers didn't have enough gravity. "It's probably horrible," John said on reflection. "It would have to be. Although there was a tune or two in there that wasn't so bad. But it's something that didn't need to be done."

Smillie argued the main problem was with the book, and that there was terrific promise in the music. "I enjoyed singing 'Improbable as Spring,'" Smillie said, "but it was kind of cliché in a way. The one that I *really* loved was 'Man of Love.' The lyrics were better, and I could show off. And also the end where he says, 'We can solve these problems. We can solve the world. I didn't mean to kill you, but we'll go on. You're martyred. We're going to do it—we'll make the world a better place....' That used to reduce me, and it always used to get a standing ovation, even if you had 20 or 30 people there. They stood up at the end and proclaimed that. Because it came out of that *Jaws*-like inferno, the nightmare of him being smitten by these four knights." The show ran for two weeks and folded after 27 performances. "I mean, the nonsense that was going on before it—up we opened and we had film directors and film stars and all that sort of thing in the audience," said Smillie, shaking his head. "As soon as we got the reviews, we saw no one. Everyone disappeared. I remember being really depressed and putting on about two stone in weight afterwards. I ate everything and didn't want to do anything and closed myself in a dark room." (Decades later, Smillie could at least laugh about the whole affair.)

A group of John's friends flew from L.A. to see *Thomas and the King*. "I loved the show," said Bob Klein. "I knew there was still a lot of work to do on the book, but it was working for me."[72] John and Grossman remained friends, and for years they talked about restaging the show—"taking it to Los Angeles and going into the Ahmanson," Grossman said. "We got fairly serious about it, but it didn't go anywhere. Mostly because John was up to his ass in about 15 film scores."† Klein went on to launch the Foundation for New American Musicals, and he kept telling John it should be

---

† In 1981, after John became a household name, That's Entertainment Records gathered most of the original cast into a London studio with a small orchestra and captured the musical for posterity on a limited edition LP. Richard Johnson had no desire to reprise his role, so another Australian, Lewis Fiander, sang the part of Thomas. John reportedly wasn't happy with the recording.

remounted. "I know it's a lot of Lerner and Loewe influence, which may bother John as being not original enough," said Klein. "But there are songs in there that are knockouts." "We worked on that show for three years," John said, "and it lasted for about three weeks. That may be the reason why I've never written for the stage since."[73] And he never did—although in the immediate wake of *Thomas* he did consider adapting a musical from George Bernard Shaw's 1882 novel, *Cashel Byron's Profession*, a social drama about a boxer. Several magazine articles reported that Don Black (writer of many famous James Bond songs) was writing the lyrics and that it was being booked for a London run in 1977.[74] John was in dialogue with the British poet Tony Harrison, who came to L.A. with his son in August 1976 and watched John record the score for *Black Sunday*. But according to Harrison, "John Williams and I came to a mutual decision that we weren't really suited to each other and my Hollywood career ended forever."[75]

Writing musicals just wasn't "my cup of tea," John said in 1983, "although some little part of my brain back here, in my soul or heart—as we all do, I suppose, anyone in the entertainment business is interested in the theater.

> I might be able to do something, I don't know. I think it's a special feel, too, particularly in New York theater. I think of somebody like Marvin Hamlisch, for example, who's younger than I am, but he's grown up in New York City, and he worked in the theater in pits, and it's in his blood, and he's been a rehearsal pianist and a songwriter.... I think there's a certain kind of street knowledge that comes from being in the milieu that can only be earned that way. And that's something that I've never really gotten.

He added: "I've never really been a *vocal* composer."[76] Many lyricists and singers would beg to differ.

* * *

"When I occasionally play the *Jaws* theme, and play the opening two notes, people laugh," John said in 2017. "This I would love someone to explain to me—some psychologist perhaps will do it."[77] But the very first time he played the opening notes of *Jaws*, a half-step interval between E and F, Steven Spielberg laughed, too. "I thought he was pulling my leg," the director said. "And he played it again. And then he played it until I stopped laughing."[78]

John was hired to score *Jaws* in the fall of 1974. Spielberg was nearly devoured by the long, exhausting shoot on open waters near Martha's Vineyard, beset by a finicky mechanical shark that he feared would *only* inspire laughter. The suits at Universal were equally worried; when studio president Sid Sheinberg saw a rough cut, he sat stony-faced in the screening room. Producer David Brown nervously asked him what he thought, and Sheinberg said: "It's okay." After an arduous, expensive, 159-day production, that response "was like being given one-half a star," Brown said. But Brown knew Sheinberg was right: "*Of course* it was only okay. It didn't have Johnny Williams' music."[79] In that first cut of the film, the coloring was still wonky and the pneumatic burps from hoses inside the animatronic shark were still audible. It was hard not to laugh.

Jaws was one of those near-disaster productions where everything seemed to go wrong but somehow every element was perfectly right, all melting into a miraculous alchemy. Its naive director was, in Spielberg's own words, the right mixture of stupid and courageous at the age of 27, and he not only wrangled the logistical action required to make *Jaws* a nail-biting thrill ride, but he also breathed its warm embers of humanity to life and made it so much more. The great chemistry between the story's unlikely trio, who sail out on the rickety *Orca* to capture the great white terrorizing the island of Amity, was obviously due to the casting of Roy Scheider as the put-upon police chief, Richard Dreyfuss as the nebbish oceanographer, and Robert Shaw as the battle-scarred shark hunter. But under Spielberg's direction, their scenes crackle with humor and charisma, taking the audience joyously along for the ride and securing our investment in their fate. It's the quiet moments between jolts that elevate *Jaws* far above other "disaster" or monster movies, and which deepen the experience of watching it over time. Scheider's Chief Brody is a dimensional, introspective protagonist, and we share his frustration at the town's foolish mayor and suffer with him after a little boy is eaten on his watch. When the boy's mourning mother slaps Brody, it stings. Sitting at his dinner table, shaken and bereft, his own young son briefly lifts his spirits by spontaneously imitating Brody's body language. It's tender and real and beautiful, and grace notes like that are sprinkled throughout. Still, even today, *Jaws* is scary as hell. Spielberg learned how to create tension from suspense masters like Alfred Hitchcock, teasing the audience with rhythmic and arrhythmic cuts and adding his own visual virtuosity to make watching his film a full-body experience. His conspirator in the editing room was Verna Fields, a legend who earned the nickname "Mother Cutter" and who had recently worked on both *Sugarland Express* and George Lucas's *American Graffiti*. It was partly the prop shark's failures that made Spielberg rely on *inferring* its presence in much of the film, but the result was a masterclass in making the audience do half the work, our imaginations flooding with nightmare fuel. Contrasting *The Poseidon Adventure* with *Jaws*, on the surface a similarly waterbound disaster movie, dramatically reveals the importance of directors. Almost all of John's movies before this were like flat cola. Spielberg's films, by contrast, *fizzed*.

But Spielberg knew that only music would make the thing swim. He had in his mind avant-garde horror music, and he temped in some of John's freaky, cerebral score for *Images*. John told him that was all wrong, and instead he devised something that was as brainless as the shark: "All instinct," John said, "meaning something could be very repetitious, very visceral, and grab you in your gut, not in your brain." He came up with a simple bass ostinato, "just repeating those two notes, and introduce a third note when you don't expect it."[80] And because the shark itself was often only implied, he explained, "the beauty of that little ostinato is you can play it softly—the shark is far away. You can keep playing it louder and louder—there's no shark there, but you can feel it. It can be deafening—it can accelerate as it comes to you. Or it can ritard as it goes away. You can paint a whole choreography without seeing anything."[81] John played his brainless notes. Spielberg laughed. John said, "Oh no, this is serious. I mean it. This is *Jaws*." Spielberg reflected: "At first I thought it was too primitive. I wanted something a little more melodic for the shark, and then Johnny said, 'What you don't have here is *The L-Shaped Room*.[‡] ... You have made yourself a popcorn movie.' And he was absolutely right."[82] "Sometimes," the director said, "the best ideas are the most simple ones—and John had found a signature for the entire score."[83]

The first time John watched the film, Spielberg was actually in Hawaii with some friends, and "I came out of the screening so excited," John said. "I had been working for nearly 25 years in Hollywood but had never had an opportunity to do a film that was absolutely brilliant. I had already conducted *Fiddler on the Roof*, and I had worked with directors like William Wyler and Robert Altman and others. But *Jaws* just floored me."[84] John spotted the film with Fields and Spielberg, who both weighed in on where music should start and stop. "I would say that John's decisions were probably the prime ones," said Fields. "When I edited the picture I had no idea where or when there should be music. It was a good picture before it was scored, but the score did tremendous things for it."[85] *Spotting* was the area where John's talents really began to shine during this period. Deciding *when* and *how* music enters and exits, where music is *absent*, and which scenes and moments should be fused together by score is a cinematic storytelling skill unique to a small strata of film composers. By now John was totally fluent in the language of film; he had an innate sense for how to accompany it. "Part of the genius of John Williams is not just that he is the greatest composer of film music since Max Steiner," said Spielberg, who started calling John "Max" during the course of *Jaws*—but "the art of film composition is the placement of that composition. For instance, in the case of *Jaws*, John did not want the music to celebrate a red herring—he wanted it to signal only the actual arrival of the shark."[86]

The simple ostinato, which dominates the first third of the movie as the shark preys on Amity, immediately became one of the most recognizable motifs in musical history. But, as composer Hans Zimmer pointed out, "nobody knows what an unbelievable feat of 20th century avant-garde music everything *past* those two repeating notes is. The scary thing about *Jaws* is those two notes, but the scary thing to any would-be composer is everything that happens *outside* those two notes."[87] With that idée fixe[§] planted in the score's amygdala, John composed a complete popcorn symphony with its own imagery and its own narrative logic, the culmination of his quest to make an effective film score that was also an inherent musical opus. He wrote a comically classical *promenade* for the scene of hapless humans crowding the beach, which he gave the winking cue title "Tourists on the Menu." In a subtle touch of genius, he scored the tender dinner table scene with a Lydian harp phrase repeated over a low

---

[‡] *The L-Shaped Room* was a 1962 British social drama, largely scored with Brahms's first piano concerto.
[§] John's definition of an idée fixe was "when a musical motif or identifying melodic phrase is used repeatedly to suggest the character or suggest the obsessive." (Jeff Bond, "God Almighty!" *Film Score Monthly*, January 2003.)

bass pedal, and "it just lifted the space into this kind of childlike wonder," observed composer Thomas Newman. "It was not trying very hard to do much, but accomplishing so much at the same time, and that was a small but really valuable lesson to me."[88] Speaking about that moment, Spielberg noted that John "doesn't find his music mathematically, scientifically, or intellectually. He just opens up his mojo and it rains down on him."[89]

John saw the remainder of the film as a huge, over-the-top "pirate movie with a touch of *Fantasia*."[90] Spielberg let him score it as such, where most of his contemporaries would have cringed at the notion of having sea shanties and swashbuckling music for their tense thriller. *This* was the moment—more so than *Sugarland*—when John Williams and Steven Spielberg chemically bonded. John's grand, romantic instincts were welcomed by a director with equally outsized romantic instincts, who decided to release his own preconceptions and trust this veteran composer he admired. "Stupid" and courageous, together they created a masterpiece of tension and euphoria.

The sessions for *Jaws* took place in March 1975 on the Fox scoring stage. Producer Richard Zanuck had been banished from a leadership position at the studio a few years prior by his father, Daryl Zanuck, so he had to sneak onto the lot to listen. He hid in the shadows, according to *Jaws* co-writer Carl Gottlieb, "laughing to himself."[91] John wrote several challenging solos for tuba, which he cast as "the voice of the shark." "What I had in mind were the lower instruments of the orchestra, those capable of plunging the sonic depths," he explained, "that would represent the shark in music. The tuba was one of the instruments that could create that atmosphere. It's a difficult tuba part, and players need to be on their toes to do it."[92] This was unbeknownst to the principal tuba player, Tommy Johnson, who was running frantically late for the session on Wednesday, March 5. There was a rare, dramatic downpour in L.A. that day, and Johnson was stuck in gridlock traffic from an accident on the 405 freeway. He arrived at Fox 35 minutes after the session began, "and you're *never* late for a scoring session in L.A., not more than once or twice in your life," pianist Ralph Grierson said, "because you won't be there again if you are."[93] An embarrassed Johnson, sopping wet and lugging his tuba, sat down in his chair and opened the score—and the first cue on the agenda was his formidable solo. "When you're late like that, you're just really all upset," Johnson said. "This solo kept recurring in almost every cue. I found out later that was the theme for the shark."[94] But the orchestra rose up to support him, and "Tommy played it with great facility and ease," said John. "He always did."[95]

The other voice for the shark, brainlessly chugging in the orchestra's lower fathoms, was Edgar Lustgarten's principal cello. Another member of the *Jaws* orchestra was Jacob Krachmalnick, who had been concertmaster with the Philadelphia Orchestra when Spielberg was a little boy. This was Spielberg's first recording session with a large orchestra, and he invited his mother to come—"and she was much more impressed by the fact that Krachmalnick was in our orchestra," said John, than that her son "had made a film and had a full orchestra at his own disposal."[96] Even the director joined the ensemble. The Fourth of July sequence on the beach featured a school marching band playing in a gazebo in the background—"march music, pop tunes, stuff like that to give an air of celebration," said John. "It's barely audible on the soundtrack but it's there all the time."[97] John recorded this source music in a separate session where the musicians all detuned their instruments to sound like an amateur school band. After a few bars, Spielberg told them to stop. "I played in a band like that," he said. "Can one of you guys give me your clarinet?" Someone did, and he started to play, "and it was godawful," recalled Ronnie Lang. "He said, '*That's* what I want you guys to sound like.'"[98]

When *Jaws* was loosed in the summer of 1975, advanced by a massive ad campaign and unusually opening in hundreds of theaters simultaneously across the country, it obliterated every previous box office record and became the most successful film of all time. "*Jaws* fever" swept the nation, infiltrating everything from Johnny Carson's *Tonight Show* to political cartoons to licensed merchandise. It did for lakes and swimming pools what *Psycho* had done for showers; no one could get it out of their head. It was a genuine cultural phenomenon, widely attributed with creating the modern summer blockbuster—and John's sticky, scary music was attached at the brainstem. When Gilda Radner answered the door in the *Saturday Night Live* sketch "Landshark," John's score sold the joke. More than that, when people said *Jaws* scared them out of the water, "it was Johnny who scared them out of the water," Spielberg argued. "His music was scarier than seeing the shark."[99] The director always contended that John's score was responsible for at least *half* of the film's success, "because he gave that shark musical teeth."[100] John would humbly demur: "I think to myself: the film also made the music. If you played that music without reference to the film, I don't think we'd pay much attention to it. It was a joining of elements at a moment that really worked in terms of popular entertainment."[101]

MCA released a soundtrack album in June, and the theme made it onto the Billboard Hot 100 chart, reaching number 32 in September.[102] The score was nominated for several awards, and in March 1976 it won a BAFTA, a Grammy, *and* an Academy Award. At the age of 44, after paying his dues for nearly two decades, John finally won an Oscar for best original score. He hopped right on stage from the pit, since he was also music director for the ceremony; his acceptance speech was brief and grateful to others.

It would be hard to overstate just how transcendent the score for *Jaws* became. John's ability to dream up its indelible signature, a musical idée fixe, turned a film score tune into a Pavlovian signal of dread that penetrated the entire planet. When *Time* magazine asked Leonard Slatkin who the most influential composer of the 20th century was, he didn't hesitate. He said: "I can't name another composer who has influenced more people than John. In classical music, if you say 'I can name that tune in four notes'"—Slatkin hummed the theme from Beethoven's Fifth Symphony—"everybody knows that. But with John he had it with"—and Slatkin hummed the *Jaws* motif. "*Two notes*, you know what that is. There's somebody whose legacy is assured."[103] The effect of *Jaws* was profound and far-reaching. When Stanley Kubrick wanted to scare young Danny Lloyd on the set of *The Shining*, he played John's score. (It was *so* effective that he only did it once and never again.[104]) Stephen Sondheim credited *Jaws* for his idea to create a continuous, ominous score for *Sweeney Todd*. "John Williams is responsible for *Jaws*, not Steven Spielberg," said Sondheim. "That's not to put down Spielberg, just that I remember sitting in that theater, and the screen lit up, and there was this underwater shot, and those double-basses started, and I was terrified. I didn't even know what I was looking at. Music can do that. Music doesn't have any particular literary context, but it does have the ability to stir a certain kind of emotion." Sondheim added: "All I know is that John Williams frightened me to death."[105]

* * *

Jaws was the big bang that expanded the galaxy of John's career, and the aftermath was exciting and occasionally messy. John was suddenly the film composer du jour, which meant he was offered high-profile crap along with high craft. In the surrounding months, several would-be projects were announced that never came to pass: Spielberg was planning to follow *Jaws* with a science-fiction film called *Clearwater*, written by Barwood and Robbins, and he was also committed to make a film about the Negro baseball leagues, *The Bingo Long Traveling All-Stars & Motor Kings*—but when post-production on *Jaws* ran long, he had to drop out.** After winning his Oscar, John was announced in the trades as composer for the adaptation of another underwater thriller by *Jaws* novelist Peter Benchley: *The Deep*. (John Barry ended up scoring the film, for director Peter Yates.) At the same time, he was also signed by Universal to score *The Sentinel*, an urban horror movie directed by Michael Winner—a gig that ultimately went to composer Gil Mellé.

Almost every big shot in town wanted to work with John, from whiz kid directors to cinema legends. And it was a thrilling day indeed when John received an invitation to meet with none other than the Master of Suspense. Alfred Hitchcock was on his 53rd film, initially called *Deceit* but later christened *Family Plot*—or *Alfred Hitchcock's Family Plot* in full, a winking title if there ever was one. The film, which turned out to be Hitchcock's last, literally ended with the lead actress *winking* at the camera. It's a rollicking romp of a suspense film, unabashedly cheeky and unworried about newfangled filmmaking techniques. The script, based on a novel called *The Rainbird Pattern*, was written by *North by Northwest* scribe Ernest Lehman—and it contains some of that earlier film's spirit of wordplay and hijinks. It was shot in the summer of 1975, and launched with a media luncheon on the Universal lot in a make-believe graveyard, complete with a church organist playing cocktail music and guest's names printed on little gravestones. The studio was riding high on the success of *Jaws*—as was Hitchcock, who had significant stock points with MCA. Spielberg, who was thrown off the set of *Torn Curtain*, wanted another chance at observing the master at

---

** John Badham eventually directed the film.

work, and he showed up on the soundstage one day during the shoot of *Family Plot*. According to Spielberg, Hitchcock never even turned around but had him quietly removed: "It was actually quite thrilling. That was the closest I came to Hitchcock. I learned that he had eyes in the back of his head."[106] According to Bruce Dern, one of the film's stars, Hitchcock couldn't face Spielberg out of embarrassment. "Isn't he the boy that made the fish movie?" Hitchcock said. "I could never sit down and talk with him." "Why not?" asked Dern. "Because I look at him and feel like such a whore," Hitchcock said. The veteran director had accepted a million dollars from Universal to voice the *Jaws* ride at the studio's theme park. "I can't sit down and talk to the boy who did the fish movie," he repeated.[107]

Hitchcock was famously wedded to Bernard Herrmann on most of his best films, but that relationship broke up in 1966 during the making of *Torn Curtain*. After a few years in exile, Herrmann was now living in London and working with young fanboys like Brian De Palma and Martin Scorsese. When John was asked to score *Family Plot*, he was thrilled but also worried about how Benny—a man not exactly known for his gracious temperament—would take it. At his interview for the job, John said: "Mr. Hitchcock, wouldn't the film world be thrilled if Benny Herrmann and you worked together again?" Hitchcock said, "No, put that out of your mind—I want you to do the score. Mr. Herrmann and I won't work together again, so you should have no feelings of delicacy about doing the picture." John heard the director's version of why that great partnership ended, but drew his own conclusion—which was that Hitchcock's personality "may have been such that he might not have liked the idea that his pictures were not as good without Bernard Herrmann's music. That may be doing Hitchcock an injustice, but it was just something I felt." John also asked for Herrmann's blessing, and received it. He spoke to his old friend on the phone in late December 1975, while Herrmann was actually in a Burbank studio to record his score for *Taxi Driver*—John was planning to attend a session—and besides getting the green light, he also overheard Herrmann yelling at the mixer. The next day, Spielberg actually visited the scoring stage and screwed up the courage to talk to Herrmann. "I admire your music a lot!" he blurted out. "Well, if you admire my music so much," the old man replied, "why do you always use John Williams for your pictures?!"[108] Herrmann recorded the final notes for *Taxi Driver* that day, December 23, and that night he died of heart failure in his hotel room. John attended the memorial a few days later. "The irony in his death," wrote *Variety*, "is that the symphonic film score, largely out of vogue for the past decade, has begun to emerge again, and he would have been in the forefront of that field in whatever pix he chose to score for many future years."[109]

It's fascinating, and appropriately macabre, that the death of Bernard Herrmann hovered over the one film John scored for Alfred Hitchcock. It was a pleasant experience for John; they would meet over lunch, with Hitchcock always taking a sirloin steak and red wine. ("He said he wanted to counteract the animal fat with acid," John recalled, "and he must have known what he was doing.")[110] At their first meeting, John asked Hitchcock how he got along with Ernest Lehman, whom he and Barbara had gone to dinner with at one point. Hitchcock unbuttoned his shirt and pointed to the scar where his pacemaker had been installed a year earlier. "Ernie Lehman did this to me," Hitchcock said.[111] They talked a lot about British music, "of Vaughan Williams, Benjamin Britten, William Walton, and others," John said. "He was a man full of marvelous stories and history. He was a lover of Elgar, I think, more than anything."[112] Hitchcock also had very specific ideas about spotting and the type of music he wanted for *Family Plot*. Perhaps his sparring days with composers were behind him now that he was 76 years old and in declining health; John found him "very easy and congenial" and his musical direction strong and clear. Hitchcock loved offstage choruses, and he specifically referenced Debussy's *Sirènes*—a tone poem with mystically swirling female voices—as a sound for Blanche Tyler (Barbara Harris) and her phony seances. John obliged, and his own choral idea gave the score much of its identity.[113] There was a playful tone to the whole film, which has Blanche and her cab driver boyfriend George (Dern) swindling an elderly widow who reveals that, years ago, she had her sister's illegitimate child taken away and now she wants to find her long-lost nephew and give him her vast fortune. Blanche and George set out to find the man, Arthur, who turns out to have murdered his adopted parents and faked his own death and is now a successful jewel thief (William Devane) in league with his girlfriend, Fran (Karen Black). One scheming duo becomes entangled with another, escalating with several attempted murders and some suspense, but none of it ever very serious. John initially conceived some darker fear in his music, but Hitchcock told him, "Mr. Williams: murder can be *fun*."[114]

John wrote music that was mostly straight and dramatic, but in a way that supported the film's light tone. He prominently featured harpsichord, which plays a mystery theme under Fran's initial appearance—one of the film's few shocks—as she suddenly appears and marches in a dark disguise toward a police station. Harpsichord also plays John's main theme, a devilishly uptempo tune that captures the film's playful spirit. *Family Plot* has more detractors than fans, but for its admirers it is a genuinely entertaining wild ride with four game actors, double entendres galore, and a jolly good plot with unexpected but satisfying twists and turns. Hitchcock wasn't trying to outdo himself or improve on his tropes—he kept repeating that "self-plagiarism is style" while promoting the film—and it is best enjoyed as a throwback amusement or a sweet cocktail. With John's delicious, ironic, and genuinely beautiful music flowing underneath, the film goes down smoothly indeed.

When *Family Plot* opened in April 1976, critics were fairly split—some were charmed, others felt Hitchcock had lost the plot—and many contrasted it with Hollywood's new master of suspense. Referring to the set piece where George and Blanche careen down a mountain road in a car without breaks, achieved with obvious rear projection, the *New Times* critic wrote: "Steven Spielberg could have filmed it with one eye tied behind his back. In fact, the failure of *Family Plot* only underlines the lessons in suspense filmmaking that Spielberg, with *Jaws*, proved he had learned at 25, and which Hitchcock at 75 has sadly forgotten."[115] John was once asked to compare Hitchcock and Spielberg. "Both were very comfortable with music, very happy to have the orchestra playing a lot," he said thoughtfully, "both interested in intimate details like tempo and spotting. Much of their filmmaking style has to do with their use of music—music that has an idiosyncratic stamp. Steven is a very different personality, sunnier, more optimistic, less skeptical—a very different view of life. But where music is concerned and its function, they are very similar."[116]

* * *

Where Hitchcock was operatic with his music, Arthur Penn was austere. The Oscar-nominated director of *Bonnie and Clyde* and *Little Big Man* had just made another cynical, revisionist western—*The Missouri Breaks*—a project that generated hot anticipation with its pairing of New Wave star Jack Nicholson and legendary method man Marlon Brando.[††] Brando ran away with Penn's film, and not in a *good* way. Nicholson played a horse thief who falls for the daughter of a wealthy rancher he stole from, and the rancher hires a hitman (Brando) to go after whoever is picking off his herd—a fairly standard western plot, but in Penn's telling drained of any conventional optimism or mythicizing. The film was darkly lit, shapeless, and shaggily acted by a posse that included Harry Dean Stanton, and the vibe was pure seventies grunge. Brando doesn't appear until 36 minutes into the film, but he immediately sucks it into his extraterrestrial orbit. Sporting an alien-Irish brogue and a wardrobe of strange outfits, including full-on pioneer drag, Brando teeters through the movie like a drunk gremlin—chewing carrots and scenery, gleefully picking off the horse thieves with increasing violence, taking a bubble bath, and even farting on camera.

John's score was fittingly weird, and he only used six instruments. "Penn is a theater director principally—although he's done a number of distinguished films—and he's not a man, I think, who is comfortable with opulent scores," John said. "He wanted *The Missouri Breaks* to be spartan, personal, so I tried to achieve that with a small ensemble. He seemed to like it very much; it seemed to fit his preconceptions of what the sound ought to be. He didn't want any large orchestral, Coplandesque, *Big Country* sound at all; he was very specific about that."[117] Matching the film's offbeat gait, John's main theme is a peg-legged and tipsy ramble for guitar, electric bass, rock drums, and harmonica that keeps switching tones. Nicholson and his merry band of rustlers were scored with more joyous and upbeat blues music—John scored the giddy comedy of their robbing a train with a catchy folk ditty. There's an innocent, almost childlike love theme for Nicholson and the naive Jane (Kathleen Lloyd), performed on acoustic guitar, electric piano, and harmonica over a pop rhythm. Brando's assassin is often watching his prey through binoculars from afar, accompanied by an electronic harpsichord effect, *Images*-style watery percussion, and a low electric harmonica moan reminiscent of the villain motif in *The Cowboys*—achieved the same way with an Echoplex and again by Tommy Morgan. John asked Morgan to come to New York for the recording sessions, which Penn insisted on holding in his hometown. "A very difficult score," said Morgan. "I was pushed to the limits. John wrote that way. He

---

[††] Oddly enough, Robert Altman was making his own revisionist western at the same time. *Buffalo Bill and the Indians* was scored by Richard Baskin.

would take you right to the edge, and sometimes guys fell off." Morgan pointed out the "Train Robbery" cue:

> The harmonica is a very difficult part. Generally, as the note goes up a big leap, you turn around and you come down. In John's piece it kept going, so it was hard to play. I asked John if I could move one note an octave, and then an impossible part became playable. And he was absolutely supportive of that. He didn't want to see you crash. He didn't push you to the wall and just do it. He did it because he wanted that sound. I have just nothing but the highest regard for his abilities... my god.[118]

"Corned beef and ham hash," was *Variety*'s opinion of *The Missouri Breaks* when it opened in the summer of 1976, but "John Williams' spare and low-key score is good."[119] *Boxoffice* labeled it "Strange on the range."[120] The film found one fan at the *Arizona Republic*, Mike Petryni, who called it *magnificent*: "Its humor is offbeat: expected 'classic' lines are left unsaid. Expected confrontations are thrown away. Yet it is magnificent if only because it disappoints expectations—because it does the unexpected.... The brilliant musical score by John Williams, who did the score for *Jaws*, also helps Penn provide the intensity that ultimately makes *The Missouri Breaks* a tense, exciting achievement."[121]

On the complete opposite pole of New Hollywood was a rah-rah Dad Movie released in the nostalgic summer of the country's bicentennial. *Midway* was a proto–*Top Gun* for Baby Boomers; it even ends with a message of gratitude to the U.S. Navy. John scored the film out of loyalty to producer Walter Mirisch, who called him and said, "You must do this. There's a great march waiting to be written by you." John felt that much of his recent success was owed to Mirisch and *Fiddler*: "He was a wonderful entrée for me in that period, and was the catapult for the things that followed."[122] John would score a great many films about the war that fascinated him as a child, but *Midway* was the dullest of them all. Despite a cast that boasted Charlton Heston, Henry Fonda, Glenn Ford, and Hal Holbrook, the film was confusingly plotted with pages of boring war dialogue, its action encrusted with obvious rear projection as well as grainy stock footage of dogfights from old Japanese films. Based on "the greatest naval battle in World War II," according to the marketing department at Universal, the film was originally to be directed by *The Towering Inferno*'s John Guillermin, but due to a scheduling conflict he was replaced by *Airport 1975* director Jack Smight.[123] *Midway*, like *None But the Brave*, was at least admirable for its sensitivity toward Japanese characters, and it didn't indulge in creaky stereotypes. In the film's final line, Fonda sighs: "Were we better than the Japanese, or just luckier?" But the road to movie mediocrity is paved with good intentions.

John's score is noteworthy for being his first openly and heroically *patriotic* film music; just as the United States was celebrating its 200th birthday, he took his first step on the trail of John Philip Sousa and other composers who turned their love of country into a catchy tune. The main theme for *Midway* was also his first prominent *march*, a reminder of his Air Force Band days and another soon-to-be-staple in his career—and this two-step was as ear-wormy as any of them. His other major theme was a warm and serene hymn for the fallen. The action music was built mostly from these two melodies, and *Midway* served as a runway for the aerial action he would perfect in a galaxy far, far away. The *many* sequences of battle strategizing and dogfights—including *Star Warsian* lines like "Rainbow leader! Come in rainbow leader!"—were great practice in composing the architecture of lengthy set pieces that crosscut between different ships and teams, making it all cohesive with musical continuity and without crudely Mickey-Mousing the action. Stylistically, too, the suspenseful adventure music was brassy and percussive with imperial fanfare and flourish. Unfortunately, the score had much less inspiring and kinetic visuals to accompany, and it also had to contend with noisy sound effects and the rumblings of Sensurround. But John clearly enjoyed the assignment, bringing to bear all of the "baggage" from his youth of following troop movements during the war and writing military band music. The historic Battle of Midway was "a pretty horrifically sad day, a great loss of life out there on both sides," he said, "but it also had a kind of romantic aspect to it. The further we get away from these great naval battles, and the further we get away from the tragic elements of them, they become more romantic pages in a history book." He delicately admitted that the movie "belongs to an earlier period, I think, in its style of filmmaking."[124]

Variety noted an upsurge in World War II films—which besides *Midway* included *A Bridge Too Far*, *MacArthur*, and many others in the pipeline—and attributed this trend to a fading disillusionment about the Vietnam War.[125] George Lucas's space opera, in the works, was a direct reaction to the pessimism that had dominated the decade. But ironically, John's last assignment before *Star Wars* was a dark, hard-boiled time bomb of a movie about an American POW who survived torture in Vietnam, and who wants to cause maximum damage to his home country by teaming up with the Palestinian terrorist outfit, Black September—and killing everyone at the Super Bowl. *Black Sunday* was adapted from a new novel by Thomas Harris, who would go on to create the character of Hannibal Lecter. Ernest Lehman co-wrote the screenplay and John Frankenheimer, a director who made popular films like *The Manchurian Candidate* before falling out of Hollywood favor, was hoping to make his comeback with this film. He nearly did. Robert Evans, hotshot producer at Paramount who struck gold with *The Godfather* and *Chinatown*, was convinced he had another jackpot on his hands. The final act involved a Goodyear blimp carrying explosives, a helicopter chase, and a football stadium filled with 80,000 extras. "You should have seen John handle the crowds and the blimp," Evans bragged. "He was like Eisenhower landing at Normandy."[126] The film starred Robert Shaw as an Israeli agent on the trail of Black September; during a bloody raid on their base he spares a beautiful woman played by Marthe Keller, and unwittingly lets the terrorist plot thicken. Keller has recruited Bruce Dern's character, a Goodyear pilot who has a boiling desire for carnage under his jovial surface. There are suspenseful cat-and-mouse chases on the water, in the streets, and in quiet hospital corridors—along with introspective political conversations—all leading to the explosive game day.

John's score was an extension of the method that proved so tensely effective in *Jaws*. His new idée fixe was a neurotic motif for the deadly plot—a dark thought on an endless loop in the movie's brain. It is simple and predatorial like *Jaws*, only a little more *human*. The palette was also more contemporary, with electric piano and drum kit and with none of the earlier film's seafaring musical joy—although even here there was a formal classical fugue for the montage of police sweeping the stadium before the Super Bowl. The filmmaking style was much less formal and fun, and John used murky, hazy tension to accompany the slow burn of Frankenheimer's handheld images and unglamorous lighting and framing, which created an intentionally messy, almost verité effect. The plot motif creeps and crawls from beginning to end on furtive celeste, on flutes, and sometimes on top of a low, insistent groove provided by baritone piano and marimba. A smear of high, queasy strings keeps everything feeling *wrong*. As game time draws nearer, the motif becomes more urgent and, frankly, very cool. John added horns and harmonies and doubled the rhythm underneath, accelerating his own blimp to its chaotic, spectacular, and ultimately doomed climax. There are seeds of the adrenaline-fueled tension of his later danger scores in a swirling, worried string figure and frantic, syncopated rhythms heard as the blimp lifts off—the score sits on the stylistic edge between his old disaster films and a new emerging sound— and John's use of the *Dies Irae*, an ancient motif of death from the Latin Mass, foreshadowed its appearance in *Close Encounters*. John recorded the score at Paramount in August 1976. There were several last-minute changes; some cues were dropped and others were recorded at a later session.[127] "Structuring a suspense movie is like writing a musical composition," Evans told the *New York Times*. "As we approached the Super Bowl, the music got louder and the cutting quicker. There were 181 cuts in the three minute sequence between the time the blimp entered the stadium and the end of the picture. Some of those cuts were only four frames—one sixth of a second. Subliminal cuts. I wanted the audience overwhelmed. I wanted them part of the crowd. I wanted them to feel a total sense of panic."[128]

When the film finally came out in March 1977, it did so in the wake of a Universal film called *Two-Minute Warning* about a terrorist loose in a football stadium; it was also saddled with an R rating against Evans and Frankenheimer's objections. *Black Sunday* failed to find the *Jaws*-sized audience that Paramount anticipated, even though it received mostly positive reviews. *Hollywood Reporter* highlighted that "the infallible John Williams has underlined all with a suitably ominous score."[129] "John Williams, who sometimes seems to have scored all our melodramas," wrote Charles Champlin, "has done *Black Sunday*, too, and his music, with its heartbeat pulsations and its rising urgency, is worth 50 pages of exposition. It is invaluable."[130] There was no soundtrack album—although, as part of a growing fad, a 12-inch disco version of the theme was independently produced. There were no major award nominations for the film or its score, and *Black Sunday* was quickly forgotten.

It was 1977, and Frankenheimer's downer film was competing with the more uplifting likes of *Rocky* and *Annie Hall* and, very soon, *Star Wars*. The last gasps of countercultural disenchantment and grime were running headlong into old-school, romantic heroism and inspiration ... and John was poised to catch the countervailing wave. Film music was about to be redefined, and the movie industry upended entirely.

* * *

John's rocket to unprecedented success and global fame was on the launchpad, roaring and ablaze. He turned 45 in February 1977, and after years of toiling in relatively quiet obscurity, learning the ropes and discovering his powers, the stars were aligning to carry his lyrical, storytelling genius into the dreams and eardrums of an entire generation across the planet. Of course, Barbara was still gone—which "made a lot of this not very important, to be quite honest," John said.[131]

But, he had also found new romance.

The Newmans had all attempted to play Cupid with their daughters. Marc Newman, John's agent, tried to set John up with his daughter Melissa, and Lionel and Beverly protested: "Not Melissa—if it's going to be anybody, it should be Jennifer!" "It was just always so weird to me," said Jennifer's older sister, Carroll. "But they were serious!"[132]

Norman Lloyd, the veteran actor of several Hitchcock films and a prolific TV producer, was an executive producer and occasional director for *Hollywood Television Theatre*, an anthology series of teleplays produced by L.A.'s PBS affiliate, KCET. In the year following Barbara's sudden death, Lloyd asked John to compose a new musical signature for the series; John responded with a rousing, rat-a-tat horn fanfare and *Cowboys*-like string figure that would announce the show for two seasons.‡‡

Assisting Lloyd was a young woman named Samantha. Born Hannah Jane Winslow in October 1944, Samantha was the daughter of Willet "Pete" Winslow, a native of Orange, California, who worked his way up through the ranks in Orange law enforcement to become the county marshal. Her maternal grandfather, William Ruff, was a Lutheran reverend who played piano and spoke German. Samantha graduated from Orange High in 1962 ("considers not having any enemies her biggest accomplishment," according to the school yearbook) and attended Concordia Lutheran College in Austin, Texas. She ran marathons, loved improving houses—and was intensely private, even more so than John.[133] She was 30 years old, once divorced with no children, a pretty, doe-like brunette with a reserved smile. John was instantly smitten:

> I thought she was the most beautiful girl I'd ever seen in my life. We crossed paths several times in the process of doing this project with Norman, and eventually it led to some dinner dates and so on, and I became so much attracted and very deeply in love with her.
>
> She was enormously helpful to me—not in any professional way at all. But you can imagine me, being as busy as I was with three teenage children in the house. I had a woman, of course, cooking and looking after all of us—Samantha didn't do any of that. But she became a great partner. She's a fantastic person. She is the other half of my life.[134]

---

‡‡ Jerry Goldsmith composed a new theme for the series in 1976.

Samantha could never replace Barbara, nor was John looking for her to do so. She made John *happy*, said Jenny, so "I was really happy for him."[135] Carroll Newman suggested that, in the wake of Barbara's death, there was a void in John's life—"and it wasn't that he needed another *woman* to love, in my opinion. He needed more of *himself* to love, more work to love."[136] John, who was never very physically affectionate or emotionally expressive with his loved ones, poured his heart into music.

And, oh, how that garden grew—almost entirely thanks to John's unlikely friendship with a merit-badge movie nerd who basked in old-fashioned symphonic scoring and was a wizard with a movie camera. Had Steven Spielberg never come along, or if he had sought out a different composer, John's destiny—*both* of their destinies—would have been unimaginably different. But the movie gods saw fit to bind their fates and change the fate of cinema altogether. John "was a thoroughbred just stuck in a gate, waiting for somebody to open it," said Spielberg.

> And I'm really happy I got a chance to open the gate with my movies.
>
> Because those were the movies John always wanted to score—without me even knowing it, but him certainly sensing that I was giving him a landscape, a big canvas to be able to do what he was born into this life to do. Which is the reason I called George Lucas on the first day of scoring *Jaws* over at Fox, and held the phone up to the speakers and said, "You've got to use this guy for *Star Wars*."[137]

7
Binary Sunset, 1977

> *I just thought it'd be really cool to have aliens and humans communicating by what reaches us quicker than anything... which is the passion of music.*
> —**Steven Spielberg**[1]

George Lucas was in distress. He had come to the final stages of a years-long journey to bring his ambitious space opera to the screen, and it was all in shambles. "We were very, very worried about him when he came back from that shoot," said Matthew Robbins, Lucas's old pal from USC, "because he was so depressed and exhausted." Lucas often stayed at Robbins's house when he was in Los Angeles, and here he was, sitting on the guest room bed, despondent. "I only got 10 percent," Lucas groaned. "I only got 10 percent."[2] When the 32-year-old director screened a rough cut of *Star Wars* for several close friends in February 1977, their reaction was overwhelmingly negative. Brian De Palma tore the movie to shreds. Lucas's wife, Marcia, openly sobbed. Only Steven Spielberg recognized its promise—but Lucas felt doomed.[3]

A few weeks earlier, Lucas had screened the same cut for the composer who came strongly recommended by Spielberg. John went up to San Anselmo in Marin County, California, to watch the film, along with Lionel Newman and Ken Wannberg, then sequestered in his studio at Fox to write the score. His first downbeat was just two months later—March 5, 1977—at Anvil Studios in the town of Denham just outside London. Lucas pulled himself away from managing effects shots at Industrial Light & Magic and recording James Earl Jones's voiceover in order to oversee the scoring sessions. "He was sort of damaged by the battles that he'd had with the studios," said Robbins, "and I think he was ready for more and worse with the executives at Fox and all the rest of it. It was *only* after the first day of scoring that George really got excited about what he had made. It was when he got to see the fairy dust of John Williams—it was like the sun came out again. He was the old George."[4]

Other than Lucas, John Williams was the person "most singularly responsible for the enormous impact" *Star Wars* had on culture. This according to the man who played Luke Skywalker. "He gives a sort of epic status," said Mark Hamill, "that we certainly wouldn't have without his music."[5]

John took two trips to the stars in 1977, and these twin voyages permanently altered the course of his career and Hollywood itself. One spawned the most lucrative and enduring entertainment brand he would ever be associated with, and the dominant entity most people would forever associate with *him*. The other sealed his spiritual communion with Spielberg and set the stage for their many decades of adventures to come. These two films were quite different in tone, content, and sophistication, and they inspired very different scores. But both were a reaction to the 1970s blues and paranoia felt so keenly in American culture and in movies of the time. Both filmmakers were young, romantic idealists who wanted to conjure new dreams of old-fashioned heroes and benevolent aliens. They were both inspired by the childlike fantasias of Walt Disney—and both men surrendered completely to the power of John's music.

These three disparate artists, none of them religious, came together to form a trinity and created pop *religioso* cinema—complete with prophecies and visions, icons and scripture, psalms and hymns—which immediately inspired zealous fervor and an enormous congregation, one that continues to grow to this day.

* * *

Lucas listened to classical music while he wrote the screenplay for *Star Wars*, and again while he was editing picture. He originally thought about following Stanley Kubrick's example and needle-dropping this old music *as* the film's score. Part of Lucas's genius was conceiving of this futuristic universe of wizards and spaceships and Wookies as an *ancient* civilization—a "used future." Every object looks rusty and beat-up, conversations reference events from the distant past, and the celestial dogfights are modeled after documentary footage from World War II. This "familiar but unfamiliar" conceit transported audiences to incredible and fantastical destinations that, strangely, felt nostalgic. Setting his far-fetched images to antique music, Lucas figured, would help sell the illusion. When he hired Paul Hirsch, a film editor from New York who had just cut De Palma's hit horror movie, *Carrie*, the director asked Hirsch if he knew anything about classical music. Hirsch knew quite a lot, it turned out, and he suggested temping several scenes with passages from Stravinsky's *The Rite of Spring*. Lucas had already used "Mars" from Gustav Holst's *The Planets* for the opening, Dvořák's *New World* symphony for the medal ceremony finale, and *Les Préludes*—a Franz Liszt piece that accompanied many scenes from *Flash Gordon Conquers the Universe*, an obvious inspiration for *Star Wars*—in the sequence where Luke breaks into Leia's cell, as well as Miklós Rózsa's theme for the 1952 film *Ivanhoe* to underscore the main titles.[6]

But Lucas realized he really needed a live composer to help him achieve his vision. It's somewhat ironic that he had just made *American Graffiti*, a film that perfected the use of rock songs instead of original score—a trend many felt was threatening the extinction of Hollywood's composers. He reached out to his friend for advice during post-production on *Jaws*. "I want a classical score," Lucas said. "I want the Korngold kind of feel about this thing. It's an old-fashioned kind of movie, and I want that grand soundtrack that you used to have on movies." His friend didn't even hesitate. "The guy you've got to talk to is John Williams," Spielberg gushed. "I love him. He's the greatest composer who ever lived."[7]

John met Lucas for the first time in the spring of 1975, on the Universal lot, more than a year before he would see any footage.[8] John broke with his usual preference and read the script, but in the meantime he scored *Family Plot* and *Black Sunday* and finished his violin concerto. The concerto wouldn't premiere until 1981, but his musical memory of Barbara was occupying his thoughts during this pivotal time, and he was proud of the piece. John felt it was "about the closest I've been able to come to a genuine, idiosyncratic expression. As I was working on that, I was just beginning to feel my wings." He believed it was more refined, cohesive, and better organized than his symphony or any other concert works to date, and went so far as to call it "the best music I've written. For the first time in my life, at a relatively late age, I began to feel some kind of real crystallization of personal idiom."[9]

It was just after New Year's Day, 1977, when John and his small entourage first screened the unfinished print of *Star Wars* at Lucas's house in San Anselmo.[10] It was an interesting scene: Lucas, Hirsch, and producer Gary Kurtz all in their 30s, and John, Wannberg, and Newman all middle-aged, closely bonded and jovial, with Newman cracking his usual acerbic jokes.[11] They spotted the film over the course of two days, with Wannberg taking notes and Lucas referencing his classical temp to communicate what he wanted the score to feel like. Lucas told John: "I'm basically doing a silent movie, and I need to have the discipline of the way silent movie music was written." "It's done in a very old-fashioned style," Lucas later explained—"the music kind of tells the story."[12] John had, unintentionally, been preparing for this moment ever since the leap forward he made on *Heidi*. He finally had his most cosmic canvas yet—a widescreen opera of archetypal heroes and villains, of larger-than-life space battles and noble deaths and damsels in distress. Here was a fusion reactor of ripened skill and rich opportunity.

John convinced Lucas not to imitate *2001*, explaining the benefits of a fully original, tailor-made score. "I felt that the film wanted thematic unity," John said. "I believed we needed melodic themes of our own which I could sort of bend around and put through all the permutations that I would need in the dramatic situations." If Lucas took music from *The Planets* and played it at the beginning of the film, John argued, "it would not necessarily fit in the middle nor at the end of the film. On the other hand, I did not want to hear a piece of Dvořák here, a piece of Tchaikovsky there, and a piece of Holst in another place." But John did find the temp useful: it convinced him "George was right about the idiom of the music," that instead of a clichéd futuristic, electronic approach, "the music should be on fairly familiar emotional ground. I think what George's temp track did was to prove that the disparity of styles was the right thing for this picture."[13]

But as John went back to Fox to compose a score, nobody saw *Star Wars* as anything more than a throwback kiddie serial. "George always described it to me as a kids' picture, a little Disney film," Spielberg said, "that he didn't think anyone would want to see, but *he* wanted to see it."[14] "He always said he was making it for 10-year-old boys," said Marcia Lucas, who also co-edited the film. "He was into making the toys before we even started shooting the movie."[15] Watching it on his rattling moviola, John scrutinized awkward scenes of laser sword fights and actors stomping around in black helmets and furry costumes; decades later, he confessed he wasn't all that interested in *Star Wars*, and that there was another film at Fox that tempted him more.* Spielberg's

---

* John later claimed this was *A Bridge Too Far*, the star-studded World War II picture directed by Richard Attenborough and released by United Artists in June 1977.

insistence convinced John to do *Star Wars*, but he always thought of it as something "kids would go to on a Saturday afternoon, and that it had a kind of cartoon-like character, and the orchestra and the music should somehow be in that genre, whatever that is. I thought: *I have to grab the attention of the ten-year-olds with this.*"[16]

* * *

John had done plenty of operatic, storyteller scoring by now, assigning leitmotifs to specific characters and locations and acting out their adventures on the stage of his score—but never as ambitiously or audaciously as he did in *Star Wars*. He drew on every molecule of the orchestration expertise, melody craft, and cinema sense he had developed over the past two decades to narrate a massive musical story for an audience of children, à la *Peter and the Wolf*. That meant a lot of simple tunes, delineating between characters (and forces) good and evil—but, John admitted, "these genuine, simple tunes are the hardest things to uncover."[17]

The first thing he did was create a robust cast of character themes. Lucas was very clear about this being a fairy tale, so John wrote a romantic fairy princess melody for Princess Leia, which also served as the score's love theme. John had actually known Carrie Fisher, the actress who played Leia, since she was a baby; Barbara and Debbie Reynolds had remained friends since their high school days, and John and Barbara went to see Reynolds's infant girl in 1956.[18] (Also, Jenny Williams grew up going to Fisher's birthday parties.) Luke Skywalker marvels at Leia's beauty when he sees her for the first time, so John wrote an accordingly beautiful tune that leapt like a heart in love. For Luke he composed a melody "that reflected the brassy, bold, masculine, and noble qualities I saw in the character. When the theme is played softly, I tended towards a softer brass sound. But I used fanfarish horns for the more heraldic passages." His theme for Obi-Wan "Ben" Kenobi reflected not only the Alec Guinness character but *all* Jedi, and it "also serves to represent the Force, the spiritual-philosophical belief of the Jedi Knights, and the Old Republic. Like the Princess' Theme, it has a fairy tale aspect rather than a futuristic aspect. There is a lot of English horn in Ben's Theme which is often heard under dialogue. At other times, the melody becomes the heroic march of the Jedi Knights." John composed a villainous tune for Darth Vader, who "represents the bad side of the Force. For his theme, I used a lot of bassoons and muted trombones and other sorts of low sounds." It was an effectively imposing, mustache-twirling idea, played *a la marcia* (in a martial style), and if it feels slight today it's only because it was later supplanted by the Imperial March—the theme to end all themes. John also provided a tune for the Jawas, the aliens who gather scrap and sell R2-D2 and C-3PO to Luke's uncle, as well as a motif for the Death Star. "I felt the use of all these themes and the orchestrations give the score a kind of classic operatic quality," John explained in his liner notes for the soundtrack album.[19]

The composer most associated with leitmotif opera was Richard Wagner, whose 19th-century fairy-tale epics were immersive entertainments that strongly anticipated motion pictures. But John dismissed any conscious influence from Wagner. The first time he heard the *Ring* cycle was in 1968 at a performance by the Hamburg Opera while he was in town for *Heidi*, and he "found it somewhat inaccessible, mostly because I didn't know German," he said. "I don't really know the Wagner operas at all.

> People say they hear Wagner in *Star Wars*, and I can only think: it's not because I put it there. Now, of course, I know that Wagner had a great influence on Korngold and all the early Hollywood composers. Wagner lives with us here—you can't escape it. I have been in the big river swimming with all of them.[20]

Lucas insisted on opening his film with the old 20th Century Fox logo, with its iconic edifice lettering and searchlights and the accompanying fanfare by Alfred Newman, which had fallen almost completely out of use. So John wrote his main title music, with its blinding brass salvo, in the key of B-flat to match the Newman piece—effectively turning the Fox fanfare into the *Star Wars* fanfare. As the prologue text rolled up the screen against a starry void, John's main theme recalled the bygone days of Korngold and swashbuckling derring-do. Hamill was initially disappointed when he saw a track list on the *Star Wars* album and didn't see a theme for Luke, but John explained the main theme *was* his[21]: Luke's theme is adapted from the pomp and circumstance of the opening crawl into a small but noble French horn solo when we first meet the character on Tatooine. It's heard in warm and intimate settings as his narrow world begins to expand with new revelations of the Force and Darth Vader and the battle against the Empire, and it plays hopefully as he and Obi-Wan make it to Mos Eisley and team up with Han Solo—the only major character who did not get his own leitmotif. John followed Luke's adventures with alternately vulnerable, brave, and urgent variations on his theme—facing off against the Imperial motif as our heroes exchange fire with stormtroopers, swinging over a chasm with Korngoldian swash, and mingling with an exciting action theme as they escape the Death Star in a dogfight. The trench-run climax finds Luke's theme oscillating between a state of worry, determination, and Force-guided majesty, and it finally jettisons back into magnificent fanfare for the end credits—an audience-thrilling tradition that John would carry into all future *Star Wars* installments.

Obi-Wan's theme became the fundamental thread in the *Star Wars* tapestry, and much more associated with the Force itself. It probes the mysteries and ancient magic of this "energy field that binds the galaxy together" with searching and longing, brimming with wonder, and often appears on French horn as characters discuss or invoke the Force with hushed reverence. But John also mobilized the tune for battle, played it as an elegy, and converted it into a conquering, triumphant anthem for the medal ceremony—played *allegro con fuoco*, "fast and fiery," like its Dvořák reference. This arrangement also recalled *Orb and Sceptre*, a regal march commissioned for the 1953 coronation of Queen Elizabeth II and composed by Sir William Walton—a doff of the cap to one of John's English heroes. Besides Luke's theme, the Force melody is quoted more than any other in the *Star Wars* score—and never more gloriously than in the iconic "Binary Sunset" scene, where it soars with deep and distant beauty as Luke peers out into the galaxy beyond his desert home. John wrote an early draft of this cue without the Force theme, which, though surging with equal wistfulness, wasn't nearly as indelible. It was Lucas who suggested revising it around "Ben's theme," and "in the end he was very right," John admitted.[22] When Obi-Wan tells Luke about the Force, the theme sparkles and shimmers underneath, and in both urgent action and sympathetic lament it is ever-present as Luke mourns his aunt and uncle, as he and Obi-Wan begin their space adventure together, and when Obi-Wan lets himself be killed by Vader. When Luke's mentor returns again as a spirit, guiding him to use the Force to fire the fatal blow against the Death Star, the Force theme levitates majestically on strings.

Leia's theme is introduced in a fragile state on solo trumpet as she records her hologram message. It's a theme of feminine, royal beauty, full of not only the pining she would inspire in Luke and Han but also the grace and fire she exhibits as a rebel leader. When Luke sees her for the first time as a flickering hologram, asking Obi-Wan for help, her theme is played delicately on oboe—then flute and French horn—over shivering strings. This early scene is mirrored when Obi-Wan dies: Leia's theme erupts in anguish as her "only hope" sacrifices himself to help her and her companions escape. "I felt it had the most sweeping melody of all the themes in the score," John explained. "This wildly romantic music in this tragic setting represents Luke's and the Princess' reaction to leaving Ben behind."[23] During the end credits, which John treated like an encore to bring his principal cast of melodies out for a bow, the cellos sing Leia's theme in its grandest guise over swirling strings and flute fragments of Luke's theme.

There was no filler music in *Star Wars*—no folderol. C-3PO and R2-D2 earned their own whimsical leitmotif for woodwinds. The Jawas have their mischievous, mysterious march, and the Sand People a "brutal attack" (per John's score instructions) on anvil and tuned drums. John's prototype Vader theme is a sinister melody that slithers along the corridors of the Death Star, often surrounded by menacing brass. John gave the aerial showdown between the Millennium Falcon and swarming TIE Fighters its own infectious dance melody, which somehow managed to hit all of the action beats perfectly while retaining its own internal musical logic. Even the *source* music commanded attention: Lucas shot his cantina sequence with a band of goofy-looking aliens "playing" fake instruments, and he told John the track should sound as though alien musicians found an old Benny Goodman arrangement under a rock and tried to play it in their own style; so John wrote an absurdly catchy ditty using "tinny saxophones and those Trinidad steel drums, which kind of in a way imitate Lionel Hampton of the 1930s," he said.[24]

John had been building toward this ideal in his film work—creating a score with total thematic and melodic continuity, narratively developed, with no junk or throwaway bits. *Star Wars* proved a perfect opportunity to achieve this feat, and Lucas gave him free rein to do it. Film scores are so often fragmentary and disjointed, and what amazed Ken Wannberg about John was how every unit of his score was proper *music*. "It won't be a cue. It becomes a piece of music that can be played as a concert piece. They could have been very vertical, very like film music cues, but John always managed, *always* managed, to make his stuff very musical. I think that's probably one of his greatest techniques."[25] The end result wasn't just an effective dramatic score that accompanied the onscreen odyssey, not just a majestic and sophisticated score that ennobled these silly and implausible characters—although it certainly *was* all of that. The score made "a mind-boggling difference," said Carroll Ballard, Lucas's friend who shot second-unit footage. "It gave the hokey characters a certain dimension. When you saw the film without the score, you couldn't take it seriously."[26] But even more than that, John created a long-form work of program music that made absolute sense *away* from picture, telling its own compelling story even when you removed the film. *Star Wars* wasn't the first, but on the most cosmic scale yet, it finally and completely unlocked John Williams as a symphonic storyteller and a *filmmaker* in his own right. The music was bigger than the movie.

* * *

The *Star Wars* score baptized a legion of John Williams followers, and has continued to do so in perpetuity—but it was also ground zero for a host of John Williams *detractors*. Ever since 1977, critics have pointed out the evident vocabulary of Holst, Stravinsky, Dvořák, and Korngold as though they had discovered the smoking gun that would lead to John's arrest for grand larceny. As recently as 2015, the *L.A. Times* critic Mark Swed wrote that John "all but lifted the core idea of his soundtrack score from the Scherzo of Erich Korngold's Symphony in F-sharp Minor."[27] John's conspicuous nods to the classical repertoire, for many judges, undermined the originality and value of his score, and this musical "crime" has often been extrapolated to the rest of John's work.

But this criticism is ignorant, and for many reasons. *Star Wars*—which was later rechristened as *A New Hope*—was the one episode in this long-running series that was most nakedly indebted to its classical references—which was, again, all part of the aesthetic and conceptual foundation of the entire film. Just as Lucas was taking archetypes from ancient myths, westerns, and Akira Kurosawa films and remixing them into an outer-space, techno myth of his own creation, John remixed recognizable tropes from the concert hall and old movie scores for *effect*. He wasn't, in other words, trying to hide the Holst. As for the composer of *King's Row* and *The Sea Hawk*, "people always say I'm a grandchild of Korngold," John said quizzically, "and I never even heard those films."[28] Furthermore, the melodies in *Star Wars*—those indelible earworms that were inseparable from their assigned characters—were *completely* his own. He took these original creations, these miniature masterpieces of hard-won simplicity, on a journey through the orchestrational and idiomatic atmospheres of various classical masters. *Star Wars* transcends pastiche, synthesizing all these disparate allusions into a unified whole and emerging as a work that sounds defiantly like ... John Williams. This score was admittedly the most primitive of the film series as far as metabolizing its ancient echoes into a new energy, but John nonetheless codified an inchoate "*Star Warsian*" language that far outgrew its roots and formed the heart of what would grow to be a nine-cycle space opera that remains unrivaled by any film composer before or since. "Holst could never have written that score," John said in a rare moment of self-defense. "Nor could Strauss. And Strauss' music was German. Holst is English. *Star Wars* is American, if you really look at it."[29]

"To accuse Williams of plagiarism," Alex Ross wrote in a 2016 essay for the *New Yorker*, "brings to mind the famous retort made by Brahms when it was pointed out that the big tune in the finale of his First Symphony resembled Beethoven's *Ode to Joy*: 'Any ass can hear that.'"[30] Of course, this same critic had his *own* change of heart: in 1998, Ross called John "an accomplished pasticheur" and "a master of his art, even if he has no style to call his own."[31] Reflecting on that article decades later, Ross admitted: "I know more about film music now and am not so happy with some of the more sweeping, off-the-cuff judgments here."[32] It was a certain academic, conservatory type—teachers and students and hardened professional critics—who pounced on John for his supposed sins, and Ross was one of his many critics whose verdict evolved over time.

Frank Lehman, the first musicologist to take the *Star Wars* scores seriously as a prominent academic—cataloging and analyzing every single motif—addressed John's accusers this way: "I hate to say this, but if you looked at those Holst and Stravinsky pieces that you're accusing Williams of plagiarizing, you'll find that those are modeled on other works as well. There's no end to the chain of referentiality." "I don't think Williams would ever *deny* the influence," Lehman elaborated:

> It's all very up front and lovingly done, and always with a bit of a Williams twist, too. It's never simply regurgitation—unlike some other film composers. There are examples of film composers who I think are far less ingenious when it comes to channeling the voices of other composers. And, it's never at the expense of the integrity of Williams' own artistic product. Otherwise I don't think that he would be performing these things as frequently as he does. There's certainly no embarrassment or concealment of the fact that there's *Mars* during the "Imperial Attack," or Walton's *Orb and Sceptre* during the throne room, because he performs these things in concerts all the time.
>
> It's only really for *A New Hope* where those references are so overt. And actually, the majority of the score *isn't*—it's just a few isolated moments, plus the overall idiom, which is much more eclectic than people generally admit.[33]

Still, the pall of supposed plagiarism and pastiche has followed John ever since the summer of 1977. It made him easy to dismiss by classical snobs, a folded-arms rebuttal to his immense popularity. Even some film critics started knocking him by wryly naming composers they were reminded of in any given score; sometimes different critics would cite two completely different composers John allegedly stole from when brushing off the *same score*. John's youngest brother, Don, wondered if this perpetually circling vulture made John wary of critics and journalists, if it was part of what made him so guarded. "I wish that the art of music criticism would be *higher*," John confessed, "that the writing would be finer and more educated, broadly."[34] His own relationship to this whole question was complicated. At times he would freely talk about his quotations and homages, even going so far as minimizing his work as a film composer altogether: "I don't think of myself as a kind of ivory-tower experimentalist, or a musical scientist," he told an interviewer in 1985. "My work is in the area of pastiche, it's theatrical, it's occasional music. It doesn't serve the same function as 'art' music."[35] But for John, there was a large and important distinction between *pastiche* and *plagiarism*, and he considered pastiche not only a large part of the film composer's job but also a potential element in any great music. "How do you differentiate art from pastiche?" he said. "It's a big question. Ravel's *La Valse* is a deliberate satirical pastiche of a Viennese customary waltz. Given its mastery, does that disqualify it as art?" When he did let his guard down, he clearly found this charge irritating—especially when it was uneducated:

> I think I've got 35 themes in *Star Wars* that have nothing to do with Korngold or anybody else. And it is unforgivable vanity, I suppose, but whether what I've done is art, or pastiche, or rubbish, or whatever it is, much of it is known around the world by people and performed everywhere all over the world. And I'm not taking credit for it, because I didn't write this with manipulation in mind, or mercenary reward, or anything at all—except covering my rear end, trying to do a film with two hours of music that will be accepted and will work. What takes it from there to where it is now? Not me.[36]

When John read Laurie Winer's book, *Oscar Hammerstein II and the Invention of the Musical*, he highlighted a passage from the introduction:

> Cultures roil forward, as artists of all kinds respond not just to the world but to each other, borrowing from what came before, benefiting from forces much larger than themselves. And because we understand that art depends on evolution, on restatement, on remixing all the bits and pieces of the past, we no longer can credit anyone with being the inventor of anything.[37]

"Now," he said, looking up from the book, "I think that's the best answer to these questions I've ever heard."[38]

* * *

Star Wars was the first score John recorded with the London Symphony Orchestra—a relationship brokered by their music director, André Previn—and it resulted in a mutual love affair and a long collaborative relationship. "I think they played beautifully, particularly the brass section," John said. "It has such nobility and such a wonderful heraldic sound. I think it really brings something to the film."[39] John conducted the orchestra over the course of 14 packed sessions for a total of 42 hours. Lucas reveled in the music and the gravity it was lending his pictures, and at one point he excitedly called Spielberg and held the phone out for 30 minutes to share the scoring in progress.[40] (This became a common practice for the two men with their shared maestro.)

Lucas had made several cuts to the film since John first spotted it and wrote his score. "You know this is going to affect the music," Hirsch told Lucas, and Lucas replied: "I know. It can't be helped." Hirsch kept a detailed rundown of all the changes they made to the picture, and a day or so before the sessions in London, he sent a Telex to Wannberg with the list. Wannberg called Hirsch from London "apoplectic and stuttering," Hirsch recalled, and said, "You know we can't do anything about this! We have to score to the version that you gave us."[41] Thankfully Wannberg was a true music *editor*, and his innate musicality and gift with a splicer enabled him to seamlessly manipulate a piece of actual recorded tape into a compositionally cohesive edit that fit most picture changes. Wannberg later told director George Miller that he made 147 musical edits on *Star Wars*. Asked how he worked his magic, Wannberg laughed: "Well ... just being a music editor! I don't know what more to say." Occasionally there would be changes that were impossible for him to edit, "and John would have to write an extension," Wannberg said. "He called them 'musical plugs.'"[42]

Wannberg's role as John's deputy also included attending the dub, one of the final stages in post-production where the mix of all sound was decided. That meant squaring off with Ben Burtt, creator of the signature humming lightsabers, screaming TIE fighters, and musically beeping droids. "The *Star Wars* [films] are heavy on effects," Wannberg said. "Ben Burtt, who's a friend of mine, he's a talented guy ... we had some pretty good, friendly fights." "Well, that does happen," Burtt admitted. "It does happen a lot. I mean, I wouldn't say a *fight*. I'm sure we frustrated each other on occasion."[43] Wannberg found the dub (any dub) tortuous, John said, fighting for John's music "with all the sound effects roaring away. He had a wonderful relationship with George Lucas, because everyone said 'yes' to George. George would say, 'How was the reel?' and everybody would say, 'It's great, George.' And Ken would sit in the corner and say, 'I think it stinks!' George somehow loved that, the contrarianism there, the anti-authoritarian aspect of it. Ken and George became an inseparable duo."[44] John and Wannberg had by now established a warmth and creative partnership that would carry them for several decades; to John, Wannberg was "Wampi," and Wannberg started calling John "Lord Vader." "He's a very gentle person, and very soft spoken," said Wannberg. "Never raises his voice. And he's just Class A, all the way down the line. Nothing at all seamy about John. He commands your friendship, and he's a decent, decent, decent man. I was really lucky to latch onto John. What I like about him, aside from his talent—which is huge—is really how caring he is."[45]

John's support team on *Star Wars* also included no less than *four* orchestrators: Herb Spencer, Angela Morley, Arthur Morton, and Al Woodbury. Spencer was another wingman, someone who was in the Fox office along with Wannberg most days John was writing. "He's an expert orchestrator," said John, "but he's also a guy I can live with for the length of time it takes to do a picture." But John insisted that, at the end of the day, he was his own orchestrator:

> It's more of a personal thing. I don't want to minimize the contribution of orchestrators but, on the other hand, I try to be *very* careful about my sketches so that

I get just what I want: winds on two or three staves, horns, brass, low brass, piano, percussion, etc., in the middle, and then three or four staves for strings, so that on eight or ten staves you can get almost a note-perfect accurate score. But the sheer labor of laying it out in full score for symphony orchestra would greatly slow me up, so here orchestrators help. When you consider that *Star Wars* had some 90 minutes of orchestral music and had to be written in some six-plus weeks ... about half the length of an opera ... well, to do that without even stenographic help from an orchestrator would be physically impossible.[46]

Among the myriad other things it generated, *Star Wars* kicked off a spate of dense, "notey" orchestral scores that would increasingly define John's corpus—and which all but forced him to delegate stenographic orchestration work. But he took great pride in his finely detailed sketches, leaving almost no harmonic or coloristic decisions to other hands. On *Star Wars* there were 800 pages of score; Spencer orchestrated 500, while the other three deputies did about 100 apiece. "I hope it's a compliment to my sketches," John said, "that you can't tell who did what."[47]

* * *

Every fear and hopeful expectation alike was upended when *Star Wars* opened on May 25, 1977. Lines formed around blocks all across the United States, then the rest of the world, and in those darkened theaters minds were blown and new dreams were born. The film's financial success broke every record in Hollywood history, and the blueprint for making movies was permanently rewritten. For some film lovers, it was the death knell of the challenging, human, auteur cinema that had, until now, characterized the 1970s; film critics and grumpy grownups would blame Lucas for hijacking the movie industry for juvenile entertainment and turning it into a fast-food franchising machine.

But *Star Wars* equally inspired a generation of future directors, writers, and artists of all kinds. Improbably, the story took root in popular culture and grew into a modern myth and even a kind of religion, populating a global consciousness with new heroes and villains and spirituality, arousing cultic devotion. And this new faith was hymned by John Williams—it was impossible to separate the power of one from the other. Harrison Ford, who played Han Solo, said the music gave *Star Wars* "gravitas and sophistication and focus and energy and emotion."[48] Hamill said: "It's just impossible to overstate his contribution. Because everything he does with his music just renders everything that much more exhilarating, that much more relatable. It provides connective tissue. It's just mind-boggling. I'm sure they could devote entire studies to his contributions to the culture."[49]

The double LP soundtrack album was released in June on 20th Century Fox Records; with the iconic *Star Wars* logo in stark white against a black background, retailing at nine dollars, it went platinum within a month of release. "The label is feverishly pressing as many copies of the LP as possible to get them to distributors and into the stores," the *Hollywood Reporter* wrote that July. "If we've got the movie of the year, we can also have the album of the year," said one marketing executive. Before long, it was the highest selling non-pop album of all time.[50†] The album sales lined John's pockets, as did the 1 percent of the film's abundant profits that Lucas generously gave him (Lucas also gave "points" to the principal cast, Kurtz, and a few others)—a gift that kept on giving.[51]

The soundtrack album was a fascinating artifact not just for its commercial success, but for the bounty of information contained inside. The paper insert listed credits for the entire orchestra, along with recording dates—as well as thorough liner notes by John that detailed his glossary of leitmotifs, his thoughts on the value and pitfalls of temp tracks, why he didn't like to read scripts before composing, and his architectural process. His notes culminated with a breakdown of each track included on the album, and how and why certain themes were employed and where. It was almost as if John *anticipated* that this soundtrack would be the gateway drug for millions of future composers, musicians, and film score fans. "I think I sensed that it was better than the usual thing that I had been doing," he admitted many years later.[52]

Other musical artists surfed the *Star Wars* wave. Ernie Freeman and the Graffiti Orchestra put out a disco dance version of the main theme in July. That same month, Meco, the pseudonym for a trombonist from Pennsylvania named Domenico Monardo, released a disco-fied 15-minute collage of music from the score, laced with spacey sound effects. Meco's version of the main theme was released as a single which sold 2 million copies and sat at the top of the Billboard chart for two weeks.[53] "I hadn't heard of either Disco or Meco," John admitted in 1979.[54]

Star Wars is "the closest a young composer has come to re-creating the Steiner/Korngold style of scoring," wrote *Screen International*. "Williams has produced one of the best scores to come out of Hollywood in recent years. Most importantly, because it has sold in such large quantities, it has demonstrated that the symphonic score can be commercially viable. Let's hope it's a sign that it will all continue for another 50 years."[55] Alexandre Desplat was one of many future composers whose life was changed: "I was in a car with a friend who had offered me a double vinyl of *Star Wars*, the black one," Desplat said. "I remember having said to him, 'Hmm … *Music composed and conducted by John Williams*. That's what I want to do.'"[56] Andrew Stanton, future director of the Pixar films *Finding Nemo* and *Wall-E* and a self-avowed film score geek, said he was "like many others of my age, where once I heard *Star Wars*—and I couldn't go see it again—I had to at least buy the soundtrack, and embed it into my brain so that it was the closest I could be to watching the movie again."[57]

Music from the film was programmed in concerts almost immediately, and persistently. It cannot be overstated just how responsible this score was for the resurgence and rescue of orchestral music in film—and of the classical ensemble as a whole. André Previn said bluntly that John single-handedly revived the symphony orchestra in movie scores.[58] Alex Ross wrote that "*Star Wars*, exuberantly blasted out

---

† The last available tally was that the album sold more than 4 million copies, although record sales data from the era preceding SoundScan were hard to verify. (Jeffrey Paul Smith, *The Sounds of Commerce: Marketing Popular Film Music* [1998].)

by the London Symphony, made the orchestra seem essential again."[59] *Star Trek* had inspired a generation of kids to become scientists and astronauts; *Star Wars* inspired a generation of kids to become *musicians*.

Star Wars changed John's life, and his contribution changed many others—not to mention popular culture and the future of music. And all for what he considered a "Saturday afternoon movie for kids."

* * *

George Lucas visited the set of his friend's new film while in the midst of editing *Star Wars*. At Steven Spielberg's rental house in Mobile, Alabama—where the big finale of *Close Encounters of the Third Kind* was being shot inside a giant hanger—the director would entertain his dinner guests with an organ, picking out tunes from his favorite movie scores, and he and François Truffaut, the French director who had an acting role in *Close Encounters*, played a running game of "Guess which movie this song is from?"[60]

Growing up, Disney movies were among the few that Spielberg was allowed to watch, and they left a permanent sunburn on his psyche. "I was probably more influenced by Walt Disney than by anybody else," he said in 1977. "I was more frightened by the 'Night on Bald Mountain' sequence in *Fantasia* than by anything I ever saw in a movie before or since."[61] (It was no coincidence that his new, deeply personal film ended with a night encounter on a bald mountain.) He began dreaming about bright lights and visitors from the stars as a child, and that motif haunted his entire career: his first feature-length movie, *Firelight*, was an amateur high school production that directly prefigured the subject of *Close Encounters*. He began seriously developing his UFO movie even before *Jaws*, and enlisted top talent from *Taxi Driver*: married producers Michael and Julia Phillips, and screenwriter Paul Schrader. A Protestant student of theology who almost became a preacher, Schrader devised a story about a "modern-day St. Paul" who works for the government to debunk stories about alien encounters . . . until he has one himself. Spielberg rejected that screenplay, and wound up writing one himself.[62] There was a whiff of Watergate in his script, with U.S. government officials trying to cover up the visitation of extraterrestrials. But at his core, Spielberg was an optimistic dreamer, not a paranoiac, and he made his protagonist what he called a "Mr. Everyday Regular Fella"—played by his cinematic stand-in, Richard Dreyfuss—who has a holy encounter with a UFO and becomes entirely obsessed with making direct contact, an obsession that hurtles him down a road away from his wife and children and spiritually summons him to the mountaintop at Devil's Tower in Wyoming. It was, in many ways, a story about Spielberg himself.

A central motif in his script was the aliens' mode of communication: lights, colors, and *music*. "I don't know where that came from," he said. "I just thought it'd be really cool to have aliens and humans communicating by what reaches us quicker than anything—which is the passion of music." An old friend of the Spielbergs, Millie Tieger, knew right away where it came from: "I thought, There's Leah with the music and Arnold with computers. That's Steve, the little boy," Tieger said. "Steve wrote a movie about Mommy and Daddy."[63] With music at the heart of his story, Spielberg knew how important it was "that John become a major character," and John read the script long before a frame had been shot.⁶⁴ His first task was to come up with a five-note musical "signal" that would commence a conversation between species. John asked if he could have *six or seven* notes, but Spielberg believed anything more than five became a melody: he wanted the equivalent of a doorbell, a simple "hello." John racked up some 200 different five-note motifs, and he and Spielberg became paralyzed trying to decide which was the *right* one, so Spielberg called a mathematician friend of his to find out just how many possible five-note variations there were within the 12-note chromatic scale, and the answer was something like 134,000. So John stopped adding to the pile, and together they landed—somewhat arbitrarily and "for purely aesthetic reasons"—on one that went *re-mi-do-DO-sol*. "It has no mystic meaning, as far as I know," John said, but he later recognized the benefit of the phrase ending on a fifth—the equivalent of ending a sentence with the word "and." "It's unfinished," he explained. "You can either repeat it *ad infinitum* or go on to something else. That was one thing in its favor—it didn't resolve. Another thing was the octave drop, with the result that you have to *ascend* to the fifth."⁶⁵ Yet another benefit, he said, was that "the interval of the perfect fifth also rattles our memories of antiquity."⁶⁶ Spielberg played the motif for Julia Phillips, which she recounted in her spicy tell-all memoir: "I tell myself these five notes are worth every penny of the fifty plus thousand I have had to pay John Williams. In fact I had to pay John Williams his fee times two, since we ran out of time on the previous deal."⁶⁷

Spielberg sprinkled this motif all throughout his film. The little boy Barry taps it out on his xylophone just before his abduction. A congregation of 3,000 Indians sings it in unison. Spielberg hired a local choir leader for that sequence who kept singing the wrong five notes. Bob Balaban, who played the translator for Truffaut's character, observed the whole comic scene:

> ADs rush over to him and sing the correct notes in his ears. Unfortunately, they keep giving him the wrong notes. He gets upset. He is carrying a religious prayer gourd, and as the cameras reload he removes a pair of thick eyeglasses and a pack of Camels from it. He lights up and nervously studies his music. Filming begins, and he stuffs everything back into the gourd. He never does get the notes right, and all three thousand extras spend several hours following him in the incorrect response.⁶⁸

It was John's idea to translate these five notes into hand signals, using a system devised for young children by the Hungarian composer Zoltán Kodály. "We didn't know whether the E.T.s could hear the notes or not if we played them. That was the conception," John said. "And when the little E.T. made a signal with his hand back, we knew we were communicating. It's fantastic." Truffaut was in charge of learning and teaching these hand signs in the movie, and John came to the set on August 5, 1976, to observe, with Spielberg singing the motif for his cast. "There's something inevitable about the sequence," Balaban wrote. "As we practice our hand signals we sing along with appropriate notes." A few days later, they began shooting the climactic scene where the earthlings have a musical dialogue with the alien mothership, which begins with the five notes and quickly escalates into a breathless, avant-garde, overlapping conversation. Phil Dodds, the technician who installed the ARP synthesizer console on the Mobile set, was promoted to playing the machine live onscreen. John had pre-recorded "The Dialogue" music at Fox in June, and Dodd simply mimicked it on the ARP, which was rigged so that certain notes would trigger corresponding colored lights on a huge switchboard. John stayed on to oversee the sequence, and even though Dodds wasn't producing any of the sounds himself, "he's a little nervous," Balaban observed.[69]

Truffaut, the revered director of French New Wave films including *The 400 Blows* and *Day for Night*, had led the movement to recognize Alfred Hitchcock as a great artist and helped popularize *auteur theory*—the notion that, even though films are collaborative, they should ultimately bear the artistic stamp of their *author*: the director. "John was the one who made me realize that François Truffaut was wrong," said Richard Dreyfuss, who spent some time observing the *Jaws* score in progress and felt keenly just how integral it was to that film's success and aesthetic. According to Dreyfuss, when he met Truffaut for the first time he said: "It's an honor to meet you, Mr. Truffaut ... and there's no such thing as *auteur*." Truffaut laughed, "and we had a great six months arguing about it," said Dreyfuss. "But it was John who made me realize."[70]

* * *

John returned from Alabama to write *Star Wars*. When that film opened and blew *Jaws* out of the financial waters to become the highest-grossing film in history, Spielberg bought an ad in *Variety* that showed R2-D2 hooking his great white shark with a fishing pole.[71] Spielberg said he thought *Star Wars* was the greatest score he had ever heard, "and I couldn't understand how any creative entity, or any creative genius, could do a score like he did for George Lucas and *still* have something in his reserve tanks for me and *Close Encounters*. And it really worried me."[72]

Like *Jaws*, the *Close Encounters* score is often remembered for its handful of iconic notes—both were instant signatures that got stuck in the public brain. Hans Zimmer worshiped the *Close Encounters* score, "and I don't mean those five notes," he said. "I mean everything else." Zimmer likened the five-note signal to the use of the *Marseillaise* in Tchaikovsky's *1812 Overture*. "Yeah, okay, we know it's coming and we know we're going to hang a lot of it onto this," but he pointed beyond it to John's ingenious use of the *Dies Irae*, that downward spiraling fragment of requiem mass music—a shorthand for the day of wrath.[73] The tune had been appropriated in concert and movie music before, but John was arguably the first to exploit its full potential in a film score. And according to John, it was completely unconscious: "People said, '*Dies Irae*. Why did you use that in the score?' I didn't know what they were quite talking about. My connection is entirely involuntary, unconscious, and accidental."[74] Deliberate or not, it was utterly brilliant to take this medieval motif and plug it into a science-fiction film, constantly exclaiming, "The world is going to end! The world is going to end!" and "playing up the paranoia," said Zimmer, "and the religious or the spiritual fanaticisms that pervade this film." The ancient phrase pervades the entire score: Right after Roy Neary's first encounter with a UFO, as he sits inside his truck on a rural road, violins pluck the motif over an agitated bed of strings; it sounds brighter as Roy and others witness a flyby a few nights later; as his spiritual fever heats up and the call to Devil's Tower grows louder, the *Dies Irae* develops into a muscular, brass action theme, then escalates with anxiety when Roy is apprehended in Wyoming. When Roy finally sees "The Mountain" in real life, the *Dies Irae* transforms from an ominous specter into a sparkling, major key ostinato—like a winged fairy beckoning him to the mountaintop.

As dissimilar as John's two 1977 space scores are, there's something to be said about the fact that both *Star Wars* and *Close Encounters* open with a blinding chord, a sudden orchestral big bang. In *Close Encounters,* a slow-boiling chord of dissonance explodes into resolution as Spielberg's dark screen turns blindingly white and the story begins—like an opera, as filmmaker Denis Villeneuve observed.[75] John played with 20th-century atonality and atmospherics, borrowing language from cacophonists like Arnold Schoenberg and Krzysztof Penderecki for the chaos and mystery that dominate the first third of the film. He channeled the choral clusters of György Ligeti—whose music made Kubrick's vision of *2001* so terrifying—for the kidnapping of Barry, while later extending his more tonal and ethereal siren vocals from *Family Plot*. As the U.S. military evacuates the area surrounding Devil's Tower, the score becomes a martial adventure movie, with Neary and his fellow traveler, Jillian (Melinda Dillon), sneaking out of government custody on their madcap quest to the tower, and the pulsing horn figures here are reminiscent of Herrmann's running-man music in *North by Northwest*. The score's grand finale begins with the five-note signal and the diegetic musical conversation, then swells into pure cosmic opera—resolving its avant-garde disorder into rapturous, symphonic exultation. When the extraterrestrials step out of the mothership, "the tone-clusters involve all the twelve notes of the chromatic scale," John explained, "then you take one strand away, then another, so the music grows more and more consonant—until you end up with a pure, liturgical E major."[76] The score concludes with a wondrously theatrical, romantic presentation of the five-note motif. When John arranged his score into a concert suite soon after, the first four minutes had "every manifestation of *klangfarben*," he said—a German term associated with Schoenberg, meaning "color making"—"full of the most screeching dissonances that overlap into other screeching dissonances, with brass figures and every kind of manifestation of avant-garde noise you can think. And *suddenly* a 180 is turned, and you get a beautiful, E major weightless waltz." André Previn joked that he should call the piece *Penderecki Gets a Passport*.[77]

John had to score much of the last act without seeing any of Douglas Trumbull's spectacular visual effects. Using a grease pencil, Spielberg drew rough ideas on a film strip of the barnstorming lights and the descent of the mothership. "When a light went from red to blue," John said, "we wanted the orchestra to go from one harmonic color to another, and to time that thing—very difficult to do without a completed film."[78] "A challenge to both of us," Spielberg agreed, "but it liberated John to score freely—*sans coitus interruptus*—and inspired me in reconstructing certain visuals to the final music."[79] Spielberg always knew he was going to let John's music take the wheel for the film's final stretch, and he "opened the shots up so John would be able to create a more operatic sound," and even choreographed some of his visual action *to* the music.[80] The director was surprised when John told him that creating a score for a finished picture "is far and away more frustrating than creating an original symphonic composition that never has to conform to the beats, measures, and boundary layers of a screen story, but instead flows freely from the composer's imagination as he tells his own story from start to finish," Spielberg wrote in his liner notes for the soundtrack LP. "This is perhaps why much of John's music for [*Close Encounters*] is so airborne and awe inspiring." This radical appreciation of music and the deference of director to composer are at the heart of why John showed such devotion to Spielberg, and why the scores he composed for Spielberg's movies rose above the ordinary—why they were able to take flight into a liminal, spiritual space and capture the imagination of so many people around the world. Spielberg turned background music into *foreground* music, designing sequences or revising them with the explicit intention of handing the narrative and emotional reins to his exalted composer. If John needed an extra frame or two of film to complete a musical thought, Spielberg would give it to him.[81] (This was almost never true with George Lucas. "We tended to shorten everything after Johnny had written the score," said producer Howard Kazanjian, "taking out a few frames, taking out eight seconds."[82])

Spielberg also gave John *free* rein, trusting his composer's instincts and inviting John to be his co-filmmaker. John had firmly found his voice as a composer by this time, and Spielberg gave him canvas after sprawling canvas to express it; no emotion was too sincere or too big. This was anathema to *some* critics: with John's big-hearted music front and center, Spielberg's films were dismissed as maudlin, melodramatic, or manipulative. Paul Schrader was one of those critics: "I never understood Steven's obsession with that schmaltzy kind of folded-in score," he said. "When you hire a guy like John Williams, you know what you're going to get. And *Steven* knows what he's going to get. Steven doesn't even have to show up. I can't bear to listen to it."[83]

But for the rest of us, Spielberg's unabashed romanticism and emotionalism were divinely matched by John's gift for majesty and lyricism, and a host of believers were smitten and enchanted—drawn to their Hollywood mountain.

* * *

Spielberg always planned to end his film with the classic recording of "When You Wish Upon a Star" by Ukulele Ike, who voiced Jiminy Cricket in Disney's *Pinocchio*. That song "was the coat hanger on which I designed the movie," he said.[84] (John once joked that Spielberg had "a *Pinocchio* fetish."[85]) The song plays on a music box as our introduction to the Neary family, and Roy extols the greatness of *Pinocchio* to his kids; the big payoff was going to be a full, rapturous reprise over the end credits after the mothership flies off with Neary inside. Balaban discovered that Spielberg had obtained the rights to the song during production:

> Steven plays the song on the organ as we all sing along in Jiminy Cricket's squeaky voice. When we get to the high note on "... no request is too extreme..." we break into a falsetto yelp that makes Elmer [Spielberg's dog] leave the room. I think it's a wonderful idea to end the movie with this sweet song.[86]

Hollywood reporters were desperate for any scrap of information about the mystery-shrouded production, anything that might reveal what the plot was or whether the film was a disaster that would bankrupt Columbia Pictures. After it previewed in Dallas in October, Balaban wrote that "*US Magazine* has been begging me to tell them about the movie, but I am sworn to secrecy. They are trying to find out what song is played at the end of the film. It feels like something out of Watergate. Phone conversation: 'Is it a song from a children's movie? Don't answer if the answer is 'yes.' If it's 'no,' keep talking.'"[87] Spielberg previewed the film with and without the song in the credits, and the reaction in Dallas convinced him to take it out. He came to realize the song implied that "everything up until the last thirty minutes was a fantasy," Spielberg said. "The people who liked it didn't *love* it—they *liked* it. The people who didn't like it were *adamant*." "It diminished the film," said Trumbull. "It was too cornball and too referential to something else that took you out of the mood that had been created for the film."[88] Spielberg's solution was to have John interpolate the melody into the climax of the score. It was a subtle but deft nod to Jiminy Cricket's ballad, suggesting rather than explicitly stating that dreams come true when you wish on a star. "A kind of memory trace," John said—"a Jungian trip."[89] Spielberg admitted that, when sung, it "was an overstatement of innocence." But, Richard Dreyfuss observed, "if you ever need an insight into Steven, that song is it."[90]

* * *

John's score was recorded at Burbank Studios in June 1977. Spielberg and producer Michael Phillips showed up every day in blue jeans; John wore a turtleneck sweater and suede shoes. "He is the gentlest of souls, as everybody will attest," said Phillips, "but he also had an impish sense of humor, which he displayed a lot. He used to dub everybody with a nickname. Spielberg was 'The Little Stinker,' and I was 'The Prince of Darkness.' I don't know why"—Phillips laughed—"I'm a nice guy. And I dubbed him back 'The Boston Fop,' or 'Fop' for short—because he dressed rather foppishly compared to us. We had a very intense series of pool games, with a lot of cheating, a lot of taunting as we rotated. It was a happy time."[91]

With this film, "John became more than just a composer for hire," Spielberg said. "He was a creative collaborator in all phases of post-production, spending every day for fifteen weeks in the mixing studio and editing rooms. He taught me about under-rated Russian composers and good German wines, and I taught him how to pace the hallways and how to eat junk foods."[92] On this project, the two became one creative soul—which may account for why John often said, when pressed, that this might be his favorite score. Love was back in his life.

Close Encounters of the Third Kind premiered in New York on November 15, 1977. It wasn't the box office or cultural sensation that *Star Wars* was—although at

$116 million, it was the third-highest grossing film of the year. And for budding intellects like Alex Ross, the future author of *The Rest Is Noise: Listening to the Twentieth Century*—who was nine when he saw the film five times at a theater in Washington, D.C.—this film was clearly superior: "I irritated friends by insisting that it was better than *Star Wars*, and followed the box-office grosses in the forlorn hope that my favorite would surpass its rival." "*Close Encounters* still strikes me as an amazing creation," Ross wrote in an essay comparing these binary stars of 1977:

> A one-off fusion of blockbuster spectacle with the disheveled realism of nineteen-seventies filmmaking. It has a wildness, a madness that is missing from Spielberg's subsequent movies. The Disneyesque fireworks of the finale can't hide the fact that the hero of the tale is abandoning his family in the grip of a monomaniacal obsession. Looking back, though, I'm sure that what really held me spellbound was the score....
>
> I was a full-on classical-music nerd, playing the piano and trying to write my own compositions. I'd dabbled in Wagner, Bruckner, and Mahler, but knew nothing of twentieth-century music. *Close Encounters* offered, at the start, a seething mass of dissonant clusters, which abruptly coalesce into a bright, clipped C major chord, somehow just as spooky as what came before. The *Star Wars* music had a familiar ring, but this kind of free, frenzied painting with sound was new to me, and has fascinated me ever since.[93]

The story in *Close Encounters* was a revealing one for Spielberg—a portal into his childhood dreams and fears, of divorce as much as of aliens. But it also served as a powerful metaphor for his faith in music and, by proxy, in John Williams. Music is the divine link, the message from beyond. "John certainly brings audiences closer to the stars," Spielberg said.[94] Denis Villeneuve, one of the young directors greatly changed by the film, said there are "a few movies where you feel the strong adequation between the narrative and the score, but never like in *Close Encounters of the Third Kind*—where the score is not only a perfect dance with the storytelling, but is more. It's a language." Villeneuve would make his own homage with *Arrival*, and what he found powerful, and hopeful, about the implicit moral of *Close Encounters* is the idea that different civilizations can be linked by the power of culture and art.[95] Hans Zimmer considered John's score in "the same class as Stravinsky's *Firebird*—as a great piece of 20th century concert music."[96]

"*Close Encounters*, I think, added up to more than a piece of celluloid," said John. "It had a soul."[97]

*　*　*

The year 1977 was a supernova. The blinding phenomenon of *Star Wars* and the deafening roar of its score marked a permanent notch on the timeline of film history: there was *Before Star Wars* and there was *After Star Wars*. That, combined with the celestial glory of *Close Encounters*, took John Williams into a new sphere altogether. He was the most famous Hollywood composer since Henry Mancini—but this was a different kind of prestige: he was somehow both a pop star and a modern Mozart, wielding a classical orchestra to make massive hits. This was highbrow populism, *serious fun*. John was at the epicenter of popular culture; he was the king of film music. He had been quietly and perhaps unconsciously gravitating toward this reign for 20 years, and while some film fans had been paying attention prior to *Star Wars*... now *everybody* noticed.

In November, Zubin Mehta conducted the Los Angeles Philharmonic in suites from both scores in a space-themed program at the Hollywood Bowl. According to reports, the sold-out audience "went out of their minds."[98] "We did it first as a children's concert," said Mehta, the Indian music director of the LA Phil. "We used lasers, so those were really gimmicks. But I only did it once. Then it caught on in America."[99] The *San Francisco Examiner* noticed that it seemed "this space-program-cum-movies is going to put symphonic organizations into the orbit of rock concerts."[100] It was the vision of Ernest Fleischmann, the forward-thinking general manager of the LA Phil. Like just about everyone else on planet Earth, he saw *Star Wars* on opening weekend with his kids: "I thought, 'God, this score—!' It's really the score and the sound effects that have made that movie what it was. It was almost Wagnerian."[101] Fleischmann went to John's house to make the case that *Star Wars* should be performed, and convinced Mehta to do the laser concert and then a recording of the suites for an album on London Records. Jim Svejda, a veteran classical radio broadcaster, argued that it was the first time a major American orchestra took film music seriously: "I think it made a very dramatic statement."[102] It was also Fleischmann who convinced John to conduct *Star Wars* himself the following summer.

In February 1978, John was invited to London to conduct the LSO in selections from his two space scores for a packed Royal Albert Hall (Figure 7.1). He was presented with gold and silver discs for *Star Wars* album sales while in England,[103] where a few weeks later he attended the annual Royal Film Performance for the UK premiere of *Close Encounters*—along with Spielberg, Dreyfuss, Harrison Ford, and Truffaut—and shook the hand of Queen Elizabeth II.[104] He conducted music from both scores in March with the Pittsburgh Symphony, which was taped for an episode of his friend's new local PBS show, *Previn and the Pittsburgh*. André Previn was now the music director in Steel City, and he continued to use his platform to promote John. By March, the *Close Encounters* soundtrack album had gone platinum, and a variety of other artists continued to release their own versions of these sci-fi symphonies. Music from *Star Wars* was performed more than 400 times in the 1978–1979 season. "I told Zubin I couldn't understand it," John said. "I have no pretensions about that score."[105]

Outside the Dorothy Chandler Pavilion on Monday, April 3, 1978, members of the Palestine Liberation Organization and reactionaries dressed like Nazis scuffled with members of the Jewish Defense League who were protesting actress Vanessa Redgrave, Oscar-nominated for her supporting role in *Julia*, for taking part in a documentary called *The Palestinian*.[106] Meanwhile, inside the theater, John jogged to the stage to collect his third Academy Award. *Star Wars* bested his own nominated

Figure 7.1. John and C-3PO outside Royal Albert Hall, February 1978 (Photograph by Anthony Haas, A.H.P. Films Limited, Courtesy of John Williams).

score for *Close Encounters*, as well as scores by Maurice Jarre, Georges Delerue, and Marvin Hamlisch. The category was presented by two of John's old bosses—Johnny Green and Henry Mancini—and his name was announced by Olivia Newton-John. Mancini, who would reportedly grow quite jealous of his former pianist's symphonic success, embraced John and kissed him on the cheek. John meekly and hurriedly thanked George Lucas and Gary Kurtz, Lionel Newman, the LSO and engineer Eric Tomlinson—"and for myself, ladies and gentlemen, my warmest thanks for this very treasured award and marvelous moment."[107]

Star Wars was a phenomenon beyond anyone's wildest dreams, and over the next few decades it would continue to grow, swell, and bloat. John would never leave its ancient, faraway galaxy—and now he was in another stratosphere altogether.

8
Death on the Carousel, 1978–1979

> *I'm always looking for something that will bring the best out of me, and that I can give more to. It's not always the best pictures. Sometimes a lesser one will offer me more opportunities.*
>
> —**John Williams, 1978**[1]

For every artist there is a tension between *art* and *commerce*, between bold self-expression and giving the public—or the producer—what they want.

Now that John had found his "wings," and simultaneously found filmmakers who gave him the freedom to really fly, the movies began to carry much of his own soul and self. The movie scores might grok[*] other styles here and there, and they were certainly affected by the boundaries of scene and storytelling demands. But by the late 1970s, John took every film—even the clunkers—as an opportunity for serious creative exploration and feeling. Even as a hired gun, even as he aimed to please crowds and directors, he was a true *composer* ... and he couldn't help but reveal himself.

This dualism is even evident, perhaps, within the same melody. Most big John Williams movie tunes have an A and a B part, and Hans Zimmer posited that the A part is always "extraordinarily catchy, and he writes it for *them*—the director, the audience, those people who will on the first note go, 'Wow!' And then the B part usually gets more reflective, gets more intricate, gets more complicated, gets more beautiful. There's more craftsmanship and just genius involved. I have a feeling he writes the B part for himself."[2]

In one of his first in-depth interviews, conducted in February 1978, John said he would take it as a good sign "if more of my private self was creeping into my commercial work. I think my commercial work must be getting better for it. That sounds a wildly egotistical thing to say, but if what you write is true, if it isn't a lie or a compromise, when you're working on commission or in a commercial medium, then I think you're doing better than just journalistic work."[3]

* * *

If John was now in the Hollywood stratosphere, the artistic merit of assignments that immediately came his way did not exactly reflect it. He dodged two bullets by backing out of Irwin Allen's *The Swarm*, a disaster movie about African killer bees that Janet

---

[*] Randy Kerber, who became a go-to session pianist for John, explained this term in the way 1960s musicians used it: "It's like ingesting the entire concept and meaning and feeling of the thing, and then from that he creates what he'd like to do. So it's not copying. It's ... *grokking*."

Maslin called "the surprise comedy hit of the season,"[4] and Robert Altman's *Quintet*—a Paul Newman film set in a future ice age which Vincent Canby deemed "the most aggressively self-indulgent motion picture made in the last 20 years by a major American director."[5] John also wisely steered clear of the *Star Wars Holiday Special*, which featured Carrie Fisher singing a "Life Day" song set to his main theme—just one of a thousand cringe-worthy moments in an infamously misbegotten 90 minutes of television. It was also a rare example of him ever allowing such a thing to happen: "I resist people putting lyrics to those things, because it fixes a meaning in the mind of people," he said. "We had a lot of requests to make lyrics to, for example, the princess theme in *Star Wars*."[6]†

But the films he *did* score in the immediate wake of *Star Wars* and *Close Encounters* were a huge step down, a crop of expensive lemons. And still the music was consistently excellent. "I'm always looking for something that will bring the best out of me, and that I can give more to," he said. "It's not always the best pictures. Sometimes a lesser one will offer me more opportunities."

Brian De Palma, a friend of both Lucas and Spielberg, had a big hit in 1976 with *Carrie*, and he chased it with *The Fury*—another story about a young woman with paranormal powers who gets bullied at school. The convoluted plot had Kirk Douglas playing Peter, a former CIA agent whose partner tries to have him killed while stealing his teenage son, Robin, who has psychic abilities; Peter hooks up with Hester, a woman who works at a school for psychically gifted young people including Gillian—played by Amy Irving—whose second sight leads her to Peter, and Peter to Robin . . . leaving behind a trail of exsanguinated bodies, a demolished carousel, and an exploding head. De Palma's lurid aesthetic and gimmicky camerawork only made the overwrought story more laughable—which was indeed the reaction of many audiences at the head-blowing climax. "I like stylization, I try to get away with as much of it as possible until people start laughing at it," the director admitted. "I go as broad as you possibly can go and get away with it, making as many audacious choices as you can without becoming ridiculous. It is a very thin line that you're balancing on."[7]

Balance was not a word fit for *The Fury*, but for John this was the young director who had rejuvenated his old friend. "I'd admired Brian De Palma's last few films, particularly *Obsession*, which had a Bernard Herrmann score I liked very much (so like *Vertigo*)," he said. "I thought Brian had served Herrmann's music better than anyone in so many years. I wrote to him and thanked him for that." John later met De Palma through Spielberg—who was now, incidentally, dating Amy Irving. De Palma popped into John's office at Fox one day and said, "Look, we're doing this picture, *The Fury*, and alas poor dear Benny isn't with us and Amy's the star—would you do the score?" John answered: "With great pleasure." John screened the picture in New York, where De Palma was editing with Paul Hirsch, then spotted it on his own back in L.A. He sent De Palma a typewritten list of the scenes he thought should have music; De

---

† This didn't prevent parodies, of course; Bill Murray, as "Nick the Lounge Singer," famously created a less-than-poetic lyric for the *Star Wars* theme on *Saturday Night Live* in January 1978.

Palma called and asked if three additional scenes could be scored, "so he wanted more music than even I intended."[8] De Palma had given Herrmann free rein, "just handing over total responsibility for the soundtrack to the composer," said Hirsch. "Brian got used to working that way, and I think he basically treated John with similar respect."[9]

Much like he had done with *Family Plot* for Hitchcock, John stepped into Herrmann's void with a score that began in Herrmann's language but quickly developed into a distinctly Williams score—packed with sticky melodies and grand emotion and ennobling some very shallow seventies schlock. It's hard to see on the screen what attracted John *other* than all of the personal connections, but John offered that De Palma "loves music; he can't have enough of it.

> He loves to play it out loud, and I think that's wonderful from my own point of view. He's also a good filmmaker: as I studied the timing of the film on the moviola I realized what great expertise was involved. He's a great student of Hitchcock, of course; every shot is planned—there's none of this willy-nilly editing from here to there. It's rhythmic, it's very musical in that sense; the scenes will almost play themselves. So many directors are jealous of their realistic sounds—they want exactly what was there in the scene. Not with Brian! He'll have an opera playing in the background if he likes it! He's theatrical, he has flair, he's musical.[10]

John's main theme is a swirling, obsessive figure that begins in the low woodwinds like many of Herrmann's scores—an idea Martin Scorsese referred to as a psychological or emotional vortex—but unlike Herrmann, John developed it into a more lyrical melody that is both seductive and terrifying, a tragic opera that shared some blood with his upcoming score for *Dracula*. John often assigned this theme to an ARP synthesizer meant to imitate a theremin, and the legato melody line was well suited to the theremin's ghostly wail.‡ This melancholy theme hovers over most of the film, rising and falling like a troubled mental tide; occasionally John activated it into a plucky, staccato heartbeat over a pumping horn rhythm for chase scenes. John also gave the ill-fated Hester a romantic adagio that resolves into a soulful oboe melody. For the montage of Gillian's idyllic early days at the Paragon Institute, John wrote a sweetly lilting ballet with graceful solos floating out from its plucky dance rhythm. The idyll is quickly shattered when she begins having visions of her psychic twin, Robin, being abused by people at Paragon, and John troubled her innocent motif accordingly. For the scene where a mopey Robin uses telekinesis to spin a carousel wildly out of control, John adapted his main theme into a major key for calliope—which spins faster and faster on the soundtrack in disharmony with a terrific crescendo of doom. Queasy suspense and elevated elegy attend the surviving characters as they're driven toward an inevitable, explosive conclusion. Herrmann's ghost can be felt in the primordial oozing of contrabassoons, the baying horn figures, and the endless repetition of the hypnotic vortex figure. Once again, John was speaking with the slight

---

‡ Herrmann famously used two theremins in his score for *The Day the Earth Stood Still*.

accent of another composer—in this case, a friend and mentor—while telling a new story in his own increasingly unmistakable voice. The score was recorded at Fox in January 1978.[11] Lionel Newman oversaw the sessions, and at one point he started a war of teasing remarks with the film's producer, Frank Yablans. It quickly escalated, and Yablans said, "Lionel, we better stop right here before one of us wounds the other." "It was a little tense in the booth while this was going on," said Hirsch.[12]

John co-wrote two soft rock source songs, "Hold You" and "I'm Tired," with lyrics and high tenor vocals by his 17-year-old son, Joe, who was beginning to sow his own career in rock 'n' roll. "I think it was just a means of maybe being able to spend time together," said Joe,[13] who had until now been sowing a harvest of wild oats ever since Barbara's death, hanging out with older troublemakers and getting deep into marijuana, alcohol, and hallucinogens. "I kept getting booted out of schools," Joe said. John was at a loss, and he often had his own parents stay over at the house to help keep an eye on his youngest. "He was very, very busy," Joe said, "but he was also at the same time very present for me.

> I think that all three of us kids had our issues, but mine were maybe a little bit more pronounced. I had troubles with the law a lot. The loss of my mother *angered* me, more than anything. I think my sister was devastated in her way. My brother sort of froze up after that experience. And my reaction was one of rage. I think maybe personality-wise I'm a little bit more boisterous, so I would do crazy things.... People would dare me to do crazy things.[14]

The third time John collected Joe from a police station, he was angry—and by the fourth time, John sent Joe, 14 years old, off to The Athenian School, a boarding school 25 miles inland from the Bay area. Joe's time there, particularly with an inspiring teacher, lit a fuse of musical ambition which provided a healthier outlet for his fury and his feelings—something his father had modeled in his own way.

The Fury was mostly skewered by critics when it came out on March 15. DePalma "has taken a nose dive," Ron Pennington wrote in the *Hollywood Reporter*. "John Williams helps build what little suspense and tension there is through his musical score, which is in the lush, romantic suspense tradition."[15] One critic who loved the film was, improbably, Pauline Kael, who gushed about its visual poetry and power, and who also singled out "what may be as apt and delicately varied a score as any horror movie has ever had. [Williams] scares us without banshee melodramatics. He sets the mood under the opening titles: otherworldly, seductively frightening. The music cues us in. This isn't going to be a gross horror film; it's visionary science-fiction horror."[16] To each their own; but John's music undeniably had a seductive, telekinetic effect.

***

Sequels were once considered as childish as space adventures and stories about supermen flying around in tights—but by 1978, all three things were being reevaluated by the film industry. Hollywood was learning that child's play could, in fact, be incredibly lucrative; the *Planet of the Apes* sequels revealed the financial potential of serialized feature films—what was later called a "franchise," a term co-opted from fast food chains. For his part, Spielberg dismissed the notion of a second *Jaws* as a "cheap carny trick." "Doing a sequel is really like operating a slot machine knowing you're going to get three cherries every time," he told a crowd at the San Francisco Film Festival in October 1975. "It reduces moviemaking as an art to just a science."[17]

But after the enormous box office bite of *Jaws*, Zanuck and Brown and Universal were all licking their lips at the thought of another meal. Spielberg, still shivering from the wet hell of making the first film, flatly declined. The producers hired screenwriter Howard Sackler, who initially proposed making a prequel based on the chilling, real-life story that Quint told about the U.S.S. *Indianapolis*—but Sid Sheinberg vetoed that idea.[18] Studios and writers were beginning to grapple with the basic conundrum of sequels: How do you make something *more of the same but different*? With some hesitation, John agreed to score *Jaws 2*—in part because he learned his themes would be used regardless, and he wanted control. He cheerfully related his assignment to the old Hollywood serials: "If you had Roy Rogers or the Lone Ranger, you would always have the same signature music." It was the first sequel John ever scored—the first of many—and he admitted that *Jaws* "doesn't suggest itself as a candidate for a series of films in the same way that Buck Rogers would, for example. I think that perhaps makes it unique. But the tradition of revisiting themes in a film was certainly not new—I think just new to this genre."[19]

Production began on Martha's Vineyard in June with director John Hancock, who had just made the Robert De Niro baseball movie, *Bang the Drum Slowly*. Hancock had the bold idea of making this an eerie ghost movie in a bereft, haunted Amity, but there was a creative clash right from the start, and within three weeks Hancock was removed from the picture and most of his footage flushed.[20] Carl Gottlieb, co-writer on the first *Jaws*, received a frantic phone call to quickly rework the script, and he mapped a plot much closer to the original—Roy Scheider's Brody is still the sheriff, more people are eaten by a shark, and the town still won't listen—simply adding the vogue element of teenage cruising culture, but on the open seas. Zanuck and Brown desperately solicited several directors, and at this point Spielberg actually offered to pick up the baton, but only if he could have several months to retool the script.[21] There wasn't time. So this hot potato landed in the hands of Jeannot Szwarc, a French director who actually shared an office with Spielberg when they were both young men making TV at Universal.[§] *Jaws 2* was always going to be a fool's errand for whichever poor fool ended up with it—an unnecessary second helping that xeroxed the beats of the first film without any of the magical alchemy between Scheider, Shaw, and Dreyfuss. Szwarc's direction had none of Spielberg's flair, the teen cast lacked the charisma of their obvious counterparts in *American Graffiti*, and the phony shark looked

---

[§] According to Rocky Lang, son of Jennings Lang, Szwarc passed on directing *Duel*. (Rocky Lang, *Growing Up Hollywood: Tales from the Son of a Movie Mogul* [2014]).

even phonier in its indulgent screen time. Where Spielberg's film had been a tense, tightly controlled highwire act, this spool of film was slack and soggy.

But John was now firmly in the business of elevating everything he took on, even bona fide turkeys. Maybe it was just his unfailing work ethic, or because he was often on a picture owing to a personal relationship he wanted to honor—or perhaps it was because he now had a reputation of his own to uphold, which the reviews for *Jaws 2* certainly validated as a motive. "As always," wrote the *Hollywood Reporter*, "Williams' contribution to the film is both estimable and inestimable."[22] Soon enough he would be much pickier about the films he attached his name to, but for the time being he was going to give an A+ effort for some C- movies.

Because of the frenzied production schedule, John had to start working on his score even before the picture was finished. Szwarc had a general discussion with him about the film, "and I told him that there's more at sea," Szwarc said, "so there would be more of an element of adventure … a swashbuckling element." The director showed John his roughly edited footage, "and then whatever I didn't have I would describe to him," Szwarc said. "I'd show him the storyboards, and he read the script."[23] Timings had to be guessed, but John rose to the challenge. He decided to compose a new theme for the sequel—a patiently ticking, strummed riff for harp suggesting fate, with echoes of the watery impressionism in Debussy's *La Mer*. This fate motif was more of a mysterious atmosphere than the first film's predatory heartbeat, but it was equally simple, repetitive, and catchy. It opens the film with wandering, aquatic flute and oboe lines as two divers explore the ocean floor. When the camera acknowledges that the wrecked ship they find is indeed the *Orca*, John quoted his pirate shanty from the first film—the first time he ever quoted an old musical friend from one of his earlier scores as a tool of narration; to some degree, his film work was about to become a long conversation with itself. Naturally, the classic *Jaws* motif was also used throughout the sequel score, developed in mostly rich and not redundant ways; unlike its visual analog, John was careful not to swim it completely into the ground. Instead of a shanty adventure theme, John complemented this film's teen sailors with a jaunty, sunny promenade for strings that served as the score's secondary theme. The teens are obliviously happy in several inert scenes, but John adorned their adventure theme with lots of lovely, elegant flourishes. Like for the first film, he wrote a lightly comic classical dance for more "tourists on the menu," here accenting a closeup shot of women's butts with a tuba solo. After Brody freaks out and clears the beach over a false alarm, he is comforted with a sympathetic trumpet melody that aches with good intentions as a little boy helps him retrieve bullet shells on the beach—a lovely score moment the film itself doesn't earn. John's score heroically maintains its energy and melodic continuity as the plot limps toward another flammable climax, suggesting a much better film when listened to on its own. An anticlimactic ending abruptly gives way to the end titles, which John graced with a pastoral theme of relief. On the score he wrote the performance direction "NOBLY."

MCA Records launched a marketing campaign for the soundtrack, which was released on June 12 in line with the film—complete with a giant cardboard shark sent to hundreds of stores.[24] John's "background music" had become big business. In his film review for the *L.A. Times*, Charles Champlin noticed that "Williams returns with ominous murmurings in the basses and tranquil melodies in the woodwinds and flutes to suggest the menace and the raptures of the deep. His music is again extremely contributory."[25] When Universal ran "For Your Consideration" ads for a futile Oscar campaign, all their pull quotes from reviews highlighted the score—the film's only redeeming element. *Jaws 2* only made $81 million, compared with its predecessor's $260 million, but it was enough to yield two more sequels with ever diminishing returns. John was wise enough to stay out of the water.

"If you were to give me a choice of doing a sequel to a film that I've already done or to do a new score, my choice would be to do the new score," John said. But, he added, sequels did at least give him the chance to ask himself: *Have I done as well this time, or maybe even better?*[26] He was always looking for ways to improve, and grow.

* * *

John was in London in July when he got a call from the Los Angeles Philharmonic asking if he could drop everything and conduct two concerts at the Hollywood Bowl.[27] Arthur Fiedler, the 83-year-old conductor of the Boston Pops, was too sick to fly to L.A., and John—who had before now shown little desire to conduct in public—quickly packed his baton and flew home to step in for Fiedler: an adumbration of future events. The program included Mozart, Weber, Berlioz, Vaughan Williams, and selections from *The Cowboys*, *Jaws*, and *Star Wars*; the latter were quickly added to take advantage of the celebrity substitute conductor. The *L.A. Times* critic, Lewis Segal, was not impressed with John's scores—"Each is baldly derivative"—or his conducting.[28] It was the beginning of a long hostility from the classical culturati in the local paper; no prophet is accepted in his hometown ... at least not by its critics. John returned to London, where he sat for a conversation about his flourishing career at the National Film Theatre. In between clips, he explained the mechanics of film scoring—illustrating music's power to supply "hidden dialogue" in *Jane Eyre*—and offered a few hints about the superhero score he was currently working on.[29]

When John agreed to score *Superman* in the fall of 1977, it was reported to be the highest price ever paid for a film score. "He will make even more from royalties," noted the *New York Daily News*.[30] John received $52,500 for 10 weeks of work, as well as $1,050 a week "as a contribution towards his accommodation and living expenses," according to his contract, which also guaranteed him first-class air travel, a chauffeur, and a mention in all of the movie's ads.[31] Richard Donner had been shooting his extravagant comic book film since March, before the shock wave of *Star Wars*. His first choice for composer was Jerry Goldsmith, who had recently written the Oscar-winning, hair-raising score for Donner's *The Omen*. But when production went over schedule, Goldsmith became unavailable. "And due respect to Jerry," said Donner, "there could have been no better choice for me at that moment than John."[32] The film was further delayed because of unfinished special effects, moving it from a summer 1978 release to Christmas. John began working on the score well before seeing anything final. "I keep a musical notebook by my piano," he said, and when he had a few weeks in the fall of 1977 he started coming up with character themes. "Whether or not they'll end up in the film, I can't say at this stage." He anticipated that the style would be tonal, "and kind of ceremonious and heraldic—C major to D major-ish, if you know what I mean. The triumph of good over evil—not unlike *Star Wars*, I suppose."[33] When the film came out, some critics griped that *Superman* did sound too much like *Star Wars*. There was no question that the film's producers, Alexander Salkind and his son Ilya, were taking a giant page out of the *Star Wars* playbook. Their business model was to get investment money from European bankers, buy the services of the hottest writers, directors, stars, and composers, then go to a U.S. company and raise more millions by selling distribution rights. "This produces movies that are influenced by other hit films," *Newsday* reported, "which is why the music of *Superman* sounds derived from *Star Wars*."[34]

One of the common gibes against John, once he entered the star field of success, was that *all his scores sound the same*. Bombastic, heroic, old-fashioned adventure music, all. And while there were some obvious, surface similarities in the heraldic heroism of these two scores, primarily in their respective main themes, that accusation ignores the vast majority of *Superman*—which begins as a cosmic tone poem in Krypton, becomes an Americana elegy as it follows Kal-El to Kansas, then flies to urban Metropolis, where it conforms to villain buffoonery, romantic comedy, and, yes, brassy, triumphant action. If anything, the score had a few *too many* personalities, owing to Donner's tonally split and overstuffed comic book movie. Matthew Robbins, screenwriter of *The Sugarland Express*, put it bluntly: "It upset me that John was lending his talent to second-grade, B-minus-at-best filmmaking. But he took it very seriously, and he comes very close"—Robbins laughed—"to *almost kind of* lifting that crap."[35]

Donner's conceit was to take the *Superman* legend, so familiar to generations of children through comic books, radio serials, and the George Reeves TV series—and tell it earnestly. So even though there are characters named Zod and Jor-El, a baby who crashes on Earth in a spaceship and who can lift cars above his head, and a man who can run faster than a train and fly through the air but goes weak in the knees when exposed to a glowing green rock … it would all be treated with a straight face, even reverence. Jor-El would be played by one of the greatest American actors of all time, Marlon Brando, Clark Kent's father by Western icon Glenn Ford, and bad guy Lex Luthor by New Wave hero Gene Hackman. Expensive, ornate sets would be numerous and vast, deaths would be lamented with intensity, and the audience would be completely convinced that a man could fly. Some of these gambits paid off—Brando and Ford both gave dignified, even touching performances, and the film's highlights are the hero's two fathers each bestowing their son with wisdom and courage, scenes that John scored with tenderness and passion. The *religioso* quality in the music for Jor-El's benediction is a perfect example of John's holy touch, and why so many people came to feel a spiritual bond with his music: he took these popcorn myths as seriously as church, and wrote music as for the Lord. There is a real mystique to the prologue on Krypton, which John enhanced by evoking Richard Strauss in passages of otherworldly impressionism. Ilya Salkind specifically asked John to reference *2001: A*

Space Odyssey in his music for Krypton: "I felt that would give the planet a sense of an ascended society that the audience would make a connection with, maybe subconsciously," the producer said.³⁶ The chromatic Krypton motif follows Kal-El to Earth, acting like a siren call when teenage Clark investigates the glowing mystery in his Kansas barn (accompanied by cryptic female vocals which recall *Family Plot* and *Close Encounters*)—and then maturing Clark into a super *man* as he follows his existential mystery to the icy Fortress of Solitude. "The music accompanying the Krypton aspects of the film uses modalities that are a little less tonal—more dissonant and more dense in construction," said John, who contrasted that with the scenes in Kansas: "In the Rockwellian areas there is a more open texture of the harmonies and in the melodic structuring."³⁷ John wrote a tune for Ford's character, Jonathan Kent, that harkened back to his theme for another Western archetype: John Wayne in *The Cowboys*. Jonathan's theme embodies sturdy, sensitive manhood, wearily staring into a setting sun. The *Superman* score peaks early when Jonathan suddenly collapses from a heart attack; playful, pastoral father-son music gives way to a low pedal, a twilight haze of string chords, and a tolling bell acknowledging the tragic event, which resolves into a tribute statement of Jonathan's theme on French horn attending his funeral. The sound of heartland beauty now suffers as Ma Kent watches Clark standing in their field at sunrise, and when they say goodbye, the theme rises and rises as Donner's camera glides around behind them and upward into the sky.

John is "emotionally involved," Donner said with a kind of awe. "He's not just writing notes on a piece of paper because it fits the visual. He's *inside* the characters."³⁸

The rest of the movie never matches the height of that poignant scene, even as Christopher Reeve finally flies in as adult Superman almost an hour into the runtime. The mood is a stark, grubby contrast in Metropolis, and the broad comic tone of the villains repeals the seriousness from the film's first hour; responding in kind, John wrote a goofy villain march for solo tuba. From here, the score is dominated by comic book action and John's *Superman* theme—a march. It opens with a three-note fanfare, which "established a kind of modus operandi," John explained, "that each time he [revealed] the shirt, there was this musical, balletic preparation."³⁹ Donner was stunned when he heard the fanfare for the first time. John was recording the main title music, as all of the film's credits go whooshing by, and Donner was in the control room:

> And it came to the word "Superman," which came zooming out from behind and onto the screen—and when it did, if you listen, John Williams' music says the word "Superman." He actually created the word with the music. And we were so blown away when it happened, and I got so excited I ran out onto the music stage just to hug him. And I didn't even think, because I fucked up the whole music take. And that was only the beginning! But as soon as I heard that, I thought: *Oh my god, do we have a score.*⁴⁰**

** This anecdote was fun, if an embellishment of the truth.

After the majesty of Krypton and Kansas, once the action moves to Metropolis and the Superman theme kicks into high gear, "I tried to have the music constructed in such a way that it would be heroic and big and operatic—but not take itself seriously," said John, who thought the movie had a "kind of theatrical camp," and that if he "could strike a level of theater and sleight of hand and tongue in cheek in the creation of the themes, that it might be the right idea."[41] Which is not to say that John's music didn't ennoble the camp in Metropolis. It did. But there was an undeniably exaggerated quality to the *Superman* theme—clearly sentient of the *Adventures of Superman* TV theme by Leon Klatzkin, a sparkling brass march with a downward-walking bass figure—which isn't *quite* so blatant in *Star Wars*. There was a tension in just how committed Donner and company were to the spandex-wearing, cat-saving patriot, and John responded by giving the character an iconic signature—one that came to define the all-American god for decades—but with a wink.

There was more earnestness in his love theme for Superman and Lois. Hinted at during their first scene together and further developed when he rescues Lois from a near-fatal fall from a high-rise, it was a romantic, airborne aria so lyrical that it practically begged for words. Sure enough, Donner asked John to turn it into a song for the big showcase when Superman takes Lois for a scenic glide above the clouds. Their mutual friend Paul Williams supplied a lyric:

> Just inside my soul
> There's a love and a light I never knew
> Just inside my soul
> There's a world that I saved for you
> Like tonight.... It is lovely and love swept
> Not a dream, but a promise that time kept
> To a love, beyond time, that'll never end
> That'll come again
> Come again
> When you hear me calling

"John's melody was gorgeous, as they always are," said Paul Williams. "The lyric related to the most powerful and touching moment in the film to me, when Superman flies supersonically around the earth and turns back time to save Lois' life. Richard Donner, who was terrific and a friend before the job, did not love what I wrote. Actually he wouldn't love anything except his idea, which was to use the title, 'Can you read my mind.' I was young and truly impressed with what I had written ... and refused to change it." Reflecting on the episode decades later, Williams said: "I was 49 when I got sober, and almost anytime after that I would've thought: your job is to serve Mr. Donner's vision, so at least try writing what he wants. I wasn't that person yet."[42] With time running out, John quickly phoned his friend Leslie Bricusse, "embarrassed to tell me that two or three people had tried to put a lyric to it, but nothing seemed to work," Bricusse recounted. "I was not overly flattered to be what turned out to be the fourth choice for this little chore, but it did have the upside of giving me the chance to write an 'I'll show 'em' lyric." Bricusse screened the film with John and Donner in London, and he was taken with the "fabulous flying sequence" that gloried in "this most glorious melody, one of the greatest John has ever composed."[43]

Bricusse crafted a lyric anchored to the phrase "Can You Read My Mind" that hit very specific beats of Superman and Lois exchanging glances, acting as unspoken dialogue. ("Here I am like a kid out of school / holding hands with a god / I'm a fool. Will you look at me, quivering like a little girl, shivering / You can see right through me.") He was proud of it, and John and Donner were pleased. Bricusse was informed that Toni Tennille, from the married pop duo Captain and Tennille, was going to record it. He thought: "John and I had at the very least an Oscar nomination locked up." Then Donner had a last-minute idea, a *crazy* idea, to have Margot Kidder record the lyric herself. John said, according to Bricusse's memory, "It won't work, but I've agreed to spend Sunday morning in a studio with him and Margot Kidder, with her trying to do the voiceover. She can't sing a note, and the whole thing is a complete waste of time, but there it is."

Assured he had nothing to worry about, Bricusse showed up excited for the film's world premiere on December 10 at the Kennedy Center in Washington, where President Jimmy Carter was in attendance. "The magic moment arrived when Superman lifted Lois Lane up [and] swirled her up and away across the city for their enchanted aerial circuit of the Statue of Liberty," Bricusse recounted.

> John's great theme established itself ever more strongly and kept them aloft until they arrived there and at the start of the vocal simultaneously. I knew it frame by frame. I waited for Toni Tennille's golden vocal chords to hit the opening title line of the song. And nothing happened. I sat bolt upright in my seat and glared along the row at John Williams, who was four or five places away.
>
> About a bar and a half late, to my total horror, I heard the whining, toneless, flat speaking voice of Margot Kidder declaim the line "Can you read my mind?" as though she were lodging a complaint. I sat transfixed as her far-from-dulcet Canadian tones ... droned endlessly on through what now seemed the interminable song, slowly annihilating it as she went, never once in time with the music, always dragging behind it, and therefore never once synching my lyric to the visuals, which I had gone to such painstaking lengths to achieve.

Bricusse said he watched the rest of the film "in abject misery" and silently confronted John afterward. "He was beyond embarrassed, flustered for the only time in all the years I have known him." When Maureen McGovern recorded the song a few months later and it became a top 10 hit on the Adult Contemporary chart, "it was unfortunately far too little far too late," Bricusse said. "I love Dick Donner and I love John Williams, but on that nightmare occasion they both came perilously close to losing a significant percentage of my high regard." (Bricusse may have felt betrayed, but this was essentially exactly what these same two artists had done with Peter O'Toole's interior numbers in *Goodbye, Mr Chips*.)

John composed most of the *Superman* score in June 1978, and he recorded it the next month with the LSO at Anvil. A self-proclaimed "John Williams devotee," Mark Hamill attended one of the sessions.[44] John produced a double LP for Warner Bros. Records with the film's blocky logo glinting against a star black background just like the best-selling *Star Wars* album, which likely fueled the snarky critics who thought the two scores sounded the same. The film itself had a mixed response. Champlin noted that John "has become the musical voice of space and assorted epics, and whose work this time, too, is heroic, symphonic, significantly useful and good to hear,"[45] but Kael found *Superman* to be "a cheesy-looking film, with a John Williams 'epic' score that transcends self-parody—cosmic fanfares keep coming when there's nothing to celebrate"; she dismissed it all as "not much more than a 70-mm. version of a kiddie-matinée serial."[46] Roger Ebert loved *Superman*, calling it "a pure delight, a wondrous combination of all the old-fashioned things we never really get tired of: adventure and romance, heroes and villains, earthshaking special effects, and—you know what else? Wit. That surprised me more than anything: That this big-budget epic … would turn out to have an intelligent sense of humor about itself."[47]

For a legion of children, *Superman* was a blastoff from beginning to end, and John's score another highly descriptive storybook full of indelible tunes that permanently defined the Man of Steel. The main theme accompanied Superman's further adventures in three subsequent chapters with Reeve, as well as a late sequel directed by Bryan Singer. When Hans Zimmer was faced with a new iteration of the character in Zack Snyder's *Man of Steel* in 2013, he was frozen. "For three months, I did nothing," Zimmer said. "I just sat there like a deer in front of the headlights." *How do you replace the John Williams Superman theme?* Snyder eventually told him, "It's just a movie!" which effectively broke Zimmer free. "I found a completely different way into it than John did," he said. "Absolutely the opposite." Where John's theme loudly and proudly declared this was Superman from the get-go, Zimmer went in the opposite direction. "But you can understand that everything John had done was haunting me. It wasn't John, and it wasn't even his music. It was the *fans*—the rabid fans."[48]

John was planning to score *Superman II* immediately, which Donner had begun directing in tandem with the first film. But the director clashed with the Salkinds and departed the project, and Richard Lester was brought in to finish the job. In October 1979, John watched the film with Lester, the British-based American director who made two hit films with the Beatles. But after the screening he told Ilya Salkind: "I'm sorry, but I don't think I can work with him." John "was very calm and professional, as he always is, but that was the end of it," said Salkind. "I don't know exactly what was said, but I knew from working with Michel Legrand and Lalo Schifrin on the *Musketeers* pictures that Richard is very opinionated when it comes to music in his films."[49] English composer Ken Thorne adapted John's themes for films II and III, and Sandy Courage did the same for *Superman IV: The Quest for Peace*, as the series imploded with ridiculousness.†† After *Jaws 2*, John became more intentional about quality control.

Giorgio Moroder predicted that John would be nominated for an Oscar, "but I don't think he'll win because he won last year for *Star Wars*." The Italian pop songwriter and producer, who helped invent disco before transitioning to film, was actively campaigning for his dancey electronic score for *Midnight Express*. "I used to dream of Hollywood like it was Christmas," he said, "and the Oscar means so much. If you win one, you're kind of a legend in Europe."⁵⁰ Moroder was right: *Superman* was nominated, but *Midnight Express* won—overcoming several traditional orchestral scores and signaling a wave of electronica at the movies, as well as film scorers from outside the conservatory. This would change the art form significantly, but it never posed a direct threat to John.

Superman added another globally recognized tune to the melodic pantheon John was building, a status undoubtedly juiced by the character's popularity and success of the picture—as with *Star Wars*, though, it's impossible to separate the film's triumph from the power of the music. John always harbored affection for *Superman*, "a wonderful illustration of a very big idea," he said. "The idea of a creature coming from another planet who would look like a human, but wouldn't have any of the restrictive elements placed upon him like gravity or anything else, this super creature, superhero, would be able to transcend all of that and have no restrictions placed upon him. It's a big idea—you may be able to call it an epic idea—and these big ideas, these epic things, I think, can be illustrated, supported musically." Likening it to the larger-than-life ideas that were once the domain of opera, he added: "It's a perfect subject to take a symphony orchestra and paint with a big move of the brush all the emotions and the great feats that we're seeing and experiencing."⁵¹

* * *

John was at risk of getting pigeonholed in outer space. He agreed to score *Meteor*, an asteroid disaster picture starring Sean Connery and Natalie Wood and directed by *Poseidon Adventure*'s Ronald Neame. Early posters ran with his name in the billing block, and he mentioned the assignment in an interview with the English magazine *Films & Filming*—but it fell through because of scheduling, or perhaps because John simply smelled another rotten egg. In that same interview, John also mentioned that he might do *Alien*. Ridley Scott asked John to score his seminal space horror film, but John simply didn't have the time ("or maybe I was tired," he posited⁵²), and the job went to Jerry Goldsmith.‡‡

Instead, John's next project would be yet another flying legend. Walter Mirisch, his old producer patron, saw the 1977 stage production of Bram Stoker's *Dracula* on

---

†† John composed three new character themes for *Superman IV*—an exuberant melody for a schoolboy named Jeremy, a sensual theme for a new love interest, Lacy, and a villain theme for Nuclear Man—mostly as a gift to Courage.
‡‡ Goldsmith had a bumpy ride with Scott, a notoriously challenging collaborator for composers, but emerged with a terrifyingly majestic work that stood among the composer's best.

Broadway and was enchanted—not by its creaky, campy script from the 1920s, but by Frank Langella's riveting lead performance. John Badham, fresh off directing the smash *Saturday Night Fever*, agreed to make a film version with Langella so long as there was an entirely new script. Badham made several changes to Stoker's plot with screenwriter W. D. Richter, who had recently retooled *Invasion of the Body Snatchers* for a new generation, and turned Count Dracula into a much more sensual, sympathetic bloodsucker.[53] The film was shot on stunning locations in Cornwall, England, and at Shepperton Studios, populated with a young cast of unknown British actors alongside Donald Pleasance as the asylum doctor and Sir Laurence Olivier as Professor Van Helsing, who in this version is the father of Mina, one of Dracula's first victims. Langella refused to wear fake fangs or anything cheesy, and he held every scene with a controlled, charismatic performance charged with sex appeal, his irises flickering like candle flames. (This was in fact a nervous tic, but Badham loved the effect.) The film's marketing campaign was aimed at young women. "We're taking a very romantic interpretation of the vampire," said Badham, "making it a very appealing sort of evil."[54]

This approach was catnip for John, a chance to write a wordless opera of gothic sensuality that broke him out of Saturday morning adventure mode while still letting him have big, memorable themes and a huge orchestra. Mirisch suggested John to Badham, who had been a fan of the composer since *The Paper Chase* and was all too glad to have him, and John was hired before production even began. Badham visited John at Fox to discuss his ideas for the film, and John suggested several pieces of classical music for the temp track—an unorthodox arrangement which gave John outsized influence on the film's tone. "I wanted his help," said Badham. "He was very instrumental in directing me toward the composer Penderecki. Really dark, strange, strange music." The Polish composer had influenced some of the chaotic *klangfarben* in *Close Encounters*, and John thought his music would serve *Dracula* well. He also suggested Wagner's heaving romantic tragedy, *Tristan und Isolde*, which had been a major inspiration for Herrmann's score for *Vertigo*—another story of dangerous obsession. In the history of Hollywood it was quite an anomaly for the composer to select the temp music, but "I didn't want to pick something that he was going to be stuck with," Badham explained. "I wanted him to help me pick something that he would be happy with—because you know the phenomenon of falling in love with the temp music."[55]

John confessed that he had never seen a vampire film, and Badham was delighted: "How fortunate to have the pre-eminent film composer of the day arrive with no advance notions of the kind of ketchup and thunder music that prevails in the horror film genre."[56] When Badham returned to Los Angeles in the spring with his film, they screened it together and John asked to watch it multiple times. When he asked, "Where would you like music?" Badham said, "Wherever you think it's appropriate." The director elaborated:

> Here I've got the privilege of having John, who will take a theme and work it fabulously throughout the whole picture. It's like going to an artist and saying, "Oh, on that portrait you're doing of me, don't use any *green* paint. I like lots of orange." I'm

going to take advantage, give him as much creative freedom as possible, and let him know that I absolutely trust him, all the way. I felt it would be presumptuous of me to give him exact spotting notes.[57]

Sexually speaking, John scored very few *adult* films in his life—especially after leaving the R-rated fare of Altman and Rydell for the PG adventures of Lucas and Spielberg. And while there was no explicit nudity or sex in *Dracula*, it stands as one of the most libidinous films in John's catalog. "I always felt that *Dracula* was a very erotic story," said John, who tended to blush whenever he spoke about sex. "Certainly the way that John Badham directed it, I felt that that was so. And wonderful subject for music, really, for the sweep and arc of a kind of romance in areas that we are uncertain about, and odd worlds that we're attracted to but we may be a little bit afraid of at the same time."[58] This was also one of the only *romantic villains* John ever scored. He typically communicated a lot about character with the opening interval of his themes—a heroic fifth for Luke Skywalker and Superman, a pining but innocent sixth for Princess Leia. For Dracula he chose a devious, charged *seventh*. His main theme begins with that bold, bloodlust declaration, then flutters around in a minor key—like the Count in bat form—declares again, then flutters. The melody is offset by a figure on barking horns and a low string motif sliding up and down like the tide of an upset ocean, and the whole score perfectly captures the image of "a dark and stormy night." Fear and sensuality hold hands from the very beginning; strings ooze and drip and then twitch under Dracula's theme as he slowly approaches young Mina in her bed from the side of the building, scratching at her window like a creature of the night. John responded with slow-building horror infused with lustful anticipation, the orchestra rising and throbbing as Mina opens her blouse for her nocturnal visitor. This union doesn't bode well for Mina, whose funeral is attended with lonely nobility on solo trumpet in a heartfelt elegy for the character. Lucy, although betrothed to Jonathan Harker, finds herself drawn to the Count—and when Dracula seduces her on his balcony, John mined his theme for ever more lust over ominous low strings. Despite the appearance of Van Helsing, on a course to avenge his daughter's death and bring down her killer, Dracula works his magic on Lucy, appearing at her window in a swirl of pouring fog, his shirt billowing open. Their love scene is impressionistic rather than explicit, silhouettes shot against red laser light, and after some orchestral foreplay John cooked his theme up to a full-boil climax—violins cascading up and down as Dracula slits his chest and has Lucy drink from it. "It was all more implied eroticism than literal," said Badham. "About the biggest amount of skin you get is when Frank rips his shirt open. But oh my god, it just makes me gasp when I hear it, because John composed the internal feelings of what it might have been like." Initially, Badham thought John might have gone *too* far, "that maybe the love scene might have been getting a little too dark for my taste," he said. He mentioned this to John, who agreed to compose a toned-down alternative. "And as we worked with it on the dubbing stage," Badham said, "I realized I was just bloody wrong. We worked our way, bit by bit, back to what John gave us in the first place."[59]

John spent several weeks finishing the score in London, holed up in a suite with a piano at a posh hotel, Claridge's, in Mayfair. Whenever he could, Badham lured John out for dinner at one of the nice Chinese restaurants in the area. John brought his faithful orchestrator with him, Herb Spencer. "I always thought of him as John's Renfield," Badham laughed.[60] The LSO recorded the score at Anvil in April 1979, and Badham was ecstatic. "The nineteenth century romantics could all say they had a descendant living late in the 20th Century," he wrote in the album notes. Less thrilled was editor John Bloom, who felt "the music was too bombastic for the film," Bloom later said. "I felt it should be more subtle, more eerie. But John's style is to give it all."[61] Bloom "is very conservative," said Badham. "Brilliant editor, but very conservative in his tastes."[62]

The film, which was released in July, drew positive reviews, with extra attention on the score. Ron Pennington at the *Hollywood Reporter* praised Langella's performance and John's music, "which ranks as one of his most impressive achievements."[63] Janet Maslin agreed: "John Williams has contributed yet another ravishing score."[64] The *Washington Post*'s Gary Arnold called the film a "dazzler," and commenting on the love scene, he wrote that "Williams is turned loose on his most transporting musical theme, expanding the ecstatic illusion until it promises to lift you into another dimension."[65] The *Democrat and Chronicle*'s critic loved the film and praised John's "magnificent score—one of the best from this talented man who has quickly become a giant among film composers."[66] But it wasn't enough to seduce audiences. The film's weak box office was partly attributed to the Dracula parody starring George Hamilton, *Love at First Bite*, out at the same time. (Werner Herzog's *Nosferatu the Vampyre* was also released in 1979.) And despite receiving an album on MCA Records, the score slipped into the mist of public consciousness along with the film—never as widely known as others from this period. But as Badham himself recognized, it was a powerful work purely as a listening experience. "Film music and the films they go with often cannot stand alone," the director wrote. "They are weakly interdependent. This is never true of John's score which stands on its own—as do all his scores."[67]§§

* * *

Steven Spielberg was a brilliant director with exquisite mastery of his craft, a wise business sense, an uncanny understanding of the public, and occasionally very bad taste. He was a movie nerd and a total square who nonetheless wanted to be part of the cool gang—which explains why several of his friends were stand-up comedians, why he was an instant devotee of *Saturday Night Live* (and often present at tapings), and why he went trapshooting on Wednesdays with the macho moviemaker John Milius. He was never going to abandon himself to drugs or the self-destructive hedonism of his contemporaries, but he did want to belong.[68] One of his worst influences was John

---

§§ A few years later, Badham asked John to score his techno-thriller *WarGames*, but John's busy schedule wouldn't allow it. (Badham to TG.)

Landis—a friendship that would have lethal consequences—who unleashed a plague of juvenile adult comedies with *National Lampoon's Animal House* in 1978. Now, on a hot streak at the Hollywood poker table after *Close Encounters*, Spielberg decided to cash in all his chips on a zany comedy in the Landis mode, but with his own knack for cinematic spectacle. The resulting film, as Champlin put it, had "the winsome appeal of scrofula and croup rolled into one ... the most conspicuous waste since the last major oil spill, which it somewhat resembles." At least, Champlin added, "John Williams' score is heroic."[69]

Before settling on making *1941* (a project formerly known as *The Night the Japs Attacked*), Spielberg considered following *Close Encounters* with a variety of interesting what-if projects: an Errol Flynn–style pirate movie; a spooky story about a ventriloquist and his evil dummy, which he discussed making with Robert De Niro (*Magic* was ultimately snagged by Richard Attenborough, who cast Anthony Hopkins); and a live TV production of *Twelve Angry Men*.[70] After befriending "the Bobs," Robert Zemeckis and Bob Gale—recent graduates of the USC film school—he decided to direct their script about a set of kids growing up in suburbia. Spielberg changed the setting of *Growing Up* from Chicago to the more autobiographical Phoenix—but it was a crude, R-rated script that his friend Caleb Deschanel found "disgusting," and Spielberg chickened out. "The movie that he really wanted to make about kids turned out to be *E.T.*," said Deschanel.[71] Ultimately, Spielberg opted to make a *different* crude comedy by the Bobs—about the citizens of Los Angeles freaking out after the Japanese attack on Pearl Harbor. Milius, who almost directed *1941* himself, referred to it as a "multi-million dollar *Three Stooges* movie." "It was like a pie fight from the old silent movie era," said Spielberg, "and what's wrong about sticking a pie in the face of the Statue of Liberty from time to time if it's in the spirit of humor?"[72] Charlton Heston, John Wayne, and James Stewart all declined to be in the film due to its irreverence about America—which was far from the real problem with *1941*. Taking a page from Landis, Spielberg borrowed some of the hot young stars from *SNL*—John Belushi and Dan Aykroyd—in an overstuffed cast of characters and multiple plot threads which confused chaos and explosions and building-sized pie fights for comedy. It's not that Spielberg couldn't do humor; there are hilarious visual gags and funny moments in most of his films. The difference was that these moments were all perfectly timed drops of levity *within* action or drama, whereas *1941* tried to be a capital C Comedy from beginning to end. ("I'm comically courageous when comedy isn't home plate," Spielberg later admitted.[73]) But he was also, simply, working with an unfunny script. Belushi storms around the film firing guns, scratching his crotch—which squeaks due to a strategically stored chew toy—and erratically flying his plane. An overreliance on pratfalls ranges from someone planting their face in a cake to an entire paint factory getting demolished by a tank. Racial differences are played for laughs in the interplay between angry Japanese officers, a Nazi captain, and a country bumpkin played by Slim Pickens. The story whiplashes from the sexual innuendo and escapades of a horny airman and his secretary to Eddie Deezen's bargain-shelf Jerry Lewis and his ventriloquist dummy. A Ferris wheel rolls off a pier and an entire house slides into the ocean ... and none of it is remotely funny.***

The highlight of the film, other than watching Spielberg pulverize millions of dollars on screen with outrageous practical stunts and impressive miniatures, was a choreographed musical-brawl set piece at the Hollywood U.S.O. In fact, Spielberg blamed the film's failure partly on his inability to commit to his original idea: "I always thought of *1941* as an old-fashioned Hollywood musical, and had fantasized with John Williams about doing eight musical song and dance numbers, all based on big band music—Tommy Dorsey, Benny Goodman, and that sort of feel of the big band era.... John was enthusiastic about this." Spielberg wanted to replace several lines of dialogue with lyrics, including a big song and dance number by the old Hollywoodland sign, and make a retro, roadshow attraction. "But I didn't have the courage of my convictions, or even the courage of my innermost dreams," he said. "So inside *1941* we have ... the jitterbug sequence, which was sort of a fragment of what I wanted to do."[74] It was the first of *many* times Spielberg would only flirt with making one of his films sing. Dancers rehearsed to a recording of "Sing Sing Sing," the famous finale of Benny Goodman's 1938 concert at Carnegie Hall. ("There was a great uproar in the press that the world of music was contaminated by jazz, that he had the temerity to bring jazz into Carnegie Hall, this sacred temple of art," said John—whose first jazz albums were produced by Albert Marx, the man who recorded that concert.[75]) John wrote a "kind of parody," he said, which he cheekily called "Swing, Swing, Swing," a lively big band number that was meticulously timed to the movements of swinging bodies and fists (and ample faces planted in crotches). It was basically a ballet, and "the nice thing about doing an original piece," John said, "was we didn't have to distort Benny Goodman's music so much out of shape in order to accommodate these choreographic gestures of a punch as a brass chord, and somebody slipping and falling to some other gesture in the woodwinds, and so on."[76] The sequence was a showcase for Spielberg's virtuosic choreography of human and camera movement—he said directing it was the best part of making *1941*—and John added a big, satisfying string lift to the band as the sequence crescendoed.

In December 1978, well before he wrote anything else, John composed an original score for an early teaser trailer shot by Milius. Footage of Belushi talking to the audience as Wild "Wayne" Kelso (his name was later changed to Bill) inspired John to write an over-the-top patriotic march and some orientalism as Kelso outlines the Japanese threat before taking to the skies. Bob Gale was at this session with a hand recorder, "and I was running around for a couple of weeks playing it for anybody," he said. " 'Listen to how great this is!' "[77] John took a similar tack when he sat down to compose his film score the following summer, but came up with a different histrionic

---

*** Jenny Williams, now 21 and out of college, was taking a stab at acting—encouraged and coached by her grandmother, Lurene. She affected an Irish brogue in a Shamrock Shake commercial for McDonald's, and landed bit parts in a few TV movies. Spielberg gave her a small role as a U.S.O. girl in *1941*, and she spent 10 weeks in her trailer waiting to be called for her scene—which was shot but ultimately cut. (Jenny Williams to TG, March 10, 2023.)

march for Kelso. John and Spielberg both agreed the Belushi character "should be characterized by a typical World War II march, of the kind that I grew up with as a child," John said, a march with a "jazzy, almost southern swagger to it.... The American drill sergeant of World War II was always some guy from the deep south, with a 'you all' accent, and all this kind of very down-home swagger to him. It's jazzy, and the accents are tilted, and the sync-ups are a little bit off, and it's a little bit impertinent in its character—as some of the kids with their uniforms were when they were soldiers."[78] Kelso's theme became the "March from *1941*," the unifying thematic idea for the film. It was a delectable piece of ear candy, never overstaying its welcome, and while there is a straight earnestness to the music on its own, it becomes comic by association with Belushi's blustering hijinks—and builds toward an exaggerated finale complete with cannon blasts, like it's the William Tell Overture on the Fourth of July. Spielberg always said it was his favorite of John's marches, even above the one for *Raiders of the Lost Ark*.[79] The beautiful secretary and her lust for airplanes inspired a shimmering, wondrous motif, a satirical cousin to some of the serious flight-loving characters John scored in later films. Following Elmer Bernstein's approach to *Animal House* and a slew of bawdy comedies that followed, John scored *1941* with a straight face; emotions of awe, patriotism, and action were all treated with serious intent. The only winks come in the form of comically exaggerated music for the Japanese characters—which avoided being racist insofar as it was mocking the Americans' daft perception of their enemy—or whenever John goosed the march with extreme vim and orchestration. And as misguided as his comedic instincts were, Spielberg was at least audacious enough to make fun of *himself*—giving John opportunities to send up his own scores for both *Jaws* and *Close Encounters* to accompany the director's self-spoofs.

After recording the score at Warner Bros. in August (the musicians reportedly laughed like crazy at several scenes[80]), John previewed his new march in a concert called "The Magic of Film Music" at Dorothy Chandler on October 29—alongside music by the late Alfred Newman conducted by his brother Lionel, and David Raksin, Hugo Friedhofer, and Miklós Rózsa, who were all in attendance. The program was performed by The Orchestra, a new 86-piece group comprised of L.A. studio musicians. In a review, *Billboard* noted it was "more the kind of program one would associate with the Boston Pops."[81] Spielberg previewed the film at his "lucky" theater in Dallas, the Medallion—and it was an unmitigated disaster, with a vacuum of laughter. John's score was now Spielberg's only hope. "Johnny's been overwriting over my overdirection over Zemeckis and Gale's overwritten script," he nervously wisecracked.[82] Spielberg made some last-minute cuts and changes, but the film was received no better at the Hollywood premiere in December—and critics went to town on the boy wonder's first belly flop. "*1941* is less comic than cumbersome," wrote Canby, "as much fun as a 40-pound wristwatch."[83] "The movie finally reduces itself to an assault on our eyes and ears," wrote Ebert, "a nonstop series of climaxes, screams, explosions, double-takes, sight gags, and ethnic jokes."[84] "Billed as a comedy spectacle," wrote *Variety*, "*1941* is long on spectacle, but short on comedy."[85]

The film, which cost $26.5 million, way overreached its budget as well as Spielberg's Midas touch. He was duly chastened by the experience, and he immediately whipped around to make an under-schedule, under-budget action-adventure masterclass. "Hopefully *1941* is the last movie I make that celebrates the boy in me," he sighed. "And then hopefully I can go on from here and do something more adultlike and perhaps more boring."[86]

* * *

John emerged from *1941* unscathed, as he did all of these duds and bombs. *His* contribution was nearly always distinguished positively in a negatively reviewed film, and through a combination of good fortune and good gambling, he was about to hit one of Hollywood's longest hot streaks.

The 1970s, a decade that took him from the minor leagues to the majors—a decade that began with Barbara and ended without her—were over. The kids were grown and all in college or working. John was approaching 50, and the world was his oyster.

In May 1979, he guest-conducted another concert with the Boston Pops, once again stepping in for Arthur Fiedler—who was dying. Suddenly, the Pops needed a new director. And even though John was already engaged to lead them in a concert in January at Carnegie Hall, he "was not one of the expected candidates," said Thomas Morris, general manager of the Boston Symphony. "He was known as a film composer, but he was not known as a conductor. A lot of people didn't even know what he looked like."[87]

Besides, John had other things on his mind—like getting married again, and how to score another *Star Wars* adventure.

9
The Miracle of the Ark, 1980–1983

> *John: "It's shameless. Will we get away with it?"*
> *Spielberg: "Movies are shameless."*[1]

John often claimed he never had designs on being a conductor, that he only started doing it in the studio out of "self-defense" after seeing other hands bungle his music. As his composing career progressed, he was invited to guest conduct orchestras at home in Glendale and Burbank, and further afield in cities like Pittsburgh and Atlanta. But even as late as 1976, after he conducted the Royal Philharmonic Orchestra in several selections of his film scores at the Royal Albert Hall as part of their "Filmharmonic" variety concert, he told an inquiring fan: "I don't concertize—it's just not part of what I do professionally, whereas Mancini and Elmer Bernstein and Michel Legrand and some of these other chaps do that as a way of earning money."[2] But Ernest Fleischmann could see John's potential on the podium, as could André Previn.

After John whisked in for Arthur Fiedler at the Hollywood Bowl in 1978, he was one of a dozen conductors invited to sub for the ailing maestro in the Pops' 1979 season. These were really covert auditions for Fiedler's successor, and a search committee graded John's two appearances on baton technique, musicianship, style, personality, and programming skill.[3] Fiedler was a living legend in Boston, and one of the most *public* conductors in the country. He led the Boston Pops for a staggering 50 years, appearing on television screens across America with the debut of the PBS series *Evening at Pops* in 1970. With his Einstein-like white hair and mustache, aristocratic style, and playful persona, "Mr. Pops" was such an icon of conducting that he even inspired his own Muppet.[4] His concerts consistently sold out, and his recordings sold in the millions. When he died on July 10, 1979, it was the death of an era—and the Boston Symphony brass worried that the Pops might die with him. Thomas Morris asked John to step in for the group's already scheduled appearance at Carnegie Hall in January 1980. "When you have a high profile concert like that, for a healthy fee with a name conductor like Arthur Fiedler, you need a substitute, and you need a *name* conductor," said Morris, who had worked for the Boston Symphony Orchestra (BSO) since 1969 and was recently promoted to the role of general manager. "John Williams was a name."[5] John's teenage dream of playing Carnegie Hall had finally come true— just not the way he originally conceived it.

But *no one* considered John a serious contender for Fiedler's shoes. Richard Dyer, classical critic for the *Boston Globe*, went to all of the guest conductor concerts in the summer of 1979—except John's. "Because," Dyer explained, "I thought, like everyone else, why on earth would he be interested in this?"[6]

Founded in 1885, the Boston Pops was in actuality the BSO, simply without the first chairs. It was originally created to let the European principal players go home during the summer while keeping the other musicians employed between regular seasons.[7] Most people born after 1929 would have been shocked to discover that Fiedler was, in fact, the *eighteenth* director of the Pops. During his half-century reign, Fiedler was synonymous with the summer band, and he codified its identity. The Pops was fundamentally about atmosphere and repertoire: for 12 weeks every May through July, six nights a week, the BSO players shed their formal black suits for blue sports coats and played long programs of light classical and contemporary pop music while merry Bostonians ate and drank and talked, often loudly. The Pops primarily played in Symphony Hall, where during the summer the theater rows were replaced with tables and chairs, turning the place into a glorified beer hall. They also played special shows outdoors in the Hatch Shell on the Charles River near Boston Common, and once every summer at the BSO's seasonal home at Tanglewood— a rural outpost for picnic audiences and music students on the western border of Massachusetts. When you bought a ticket to a Pops concert, you were essentially paying for a dinner show. "In the Fiedler years, programs were announced *maybe* a week ahead of time," said Morris. "You bought a ticket to go to the *Pops*. It was an institution."[8]

It was all at once a less prestigious post for a conductor, popular and highly visible, and exhausting. "I had no conception of the enormity of what [Fiedler] did until I was invited to conduct in Boston," John reflected. "This amount of conducting, on a purely physical level, would be equivalent, say, to pitching five or six major league baseball games each week ... a daunting workload even for a person several decades younger than Fiedler."[9] With his burgeoning, blockbuster film work and comfortable life split between Little Holmby and London, why *would* John be interested?

Morris claimed he was the only person who saw it before anyone else. After a *Boston Globe* article listed John among those being considered, John wrote Morris a letter to say he was flattered. Morris called Previn in October 1979 for his thoughts, "and Previn strongly suggested John, and really talked about how 'You should not underestimate what John Williams can do. He's not just a film composer. He's a *musician.*'"[10] Other names at the top of the BSO's list were Erich Kunzel, conductor of the Cincinnati Pops, and John Covelli in Flint, Michigan.[11] John was the candidate with the least public performance experience, and also the only one who would potentially, occasionally need to give up million-dollar movie assignments in order to do the job.

But after a months-long cloak-and-dagger campaign—with Morris and assistant manager Peter Gelb flying back and forth from London, where John was recording *The Empire Strikes Back*, meeting with John in hotel rooms under false names, conferring with BSO music director Seiji Ozawa, and negotiating with John's agent, Marc Newman—he was announced as the new conductor of the Boston Pops in a surprise press conference at London's Savoy Hotel on January 10, 1980, signing a two-year contract.[12]

"In Boston," reported *Newsweek*, "they compared it to choosing a new Pope."[13]

* * *

Not everything that swells improves, as evidenced by *Jaws 2*, and John's career was soon to be littered with sequels and prequels—repeat visits to the slot machines that kept spitting out billions of quarters. But *The Empire Strikes Back* was, without question, a vast improvement on *Star Wars*. Not only did George Lucas have more control over the entire enterprise this time out, he also wisely delegated screenwriting and directing duties to better qualified collaborators. Stakes heightened, the tone darkened, and in the hands of writer Lawrence Kasdan and director Irvin Kershner the emphasis was placed on character development and relationships. Kershner compared it to the second movement of a symphony.[14] Han and Leia's salt-and-vinegar love story dominated, and Luke's growth as a Jedi forced him to confront harsh realities. Even his extended communion with a frog-like Muppet was handled with dramatic weight and poignancy.

In turn, John took his scoring to another level, and there are many who consider *Empire* his magnum opus. There were the obvious new inventions: a yearning love theme for Han Solo and Princess Leia, a sage ballad for Yoda—and the Imperial March, possibly the most famous melody John would ever write. Effectively Darth Vader's theme, the tune became an immediate staple of marching bands and sports games everywhere. "It's very military in an ominous and aggressive sense," John said. "That is probably why they use it the way they do."[15] It would become John's inevitable encore in concerts for the rest of his life—his "Hey Jude"—and audiences in every part of the world went wild on the first beat every single time. This dark anthem, belted out on brass, imperiously vaulting up and down a modified minor scale, evoked the sense of legion boots marching toward some inescapable, evil end. It was an instant shorthand for "bad guy" music—but it was also just plain *cool*.

"Sometimes themes come very painfully after hours of holding my head in my hands at the piano," John said.

> Days can go by and I'll think it is never going to come. Then I'll sit down at the piano and it sort of pops into my mind. After two weeks of frustration it just appears out of nowhere. Other times I might think about a theme for a character and get it straight off. It is a strange and mysterious and frustrating process, almost impossible to describe.[16]

John retained and matured most of his themes from the first film, but shed the conspicuous allusions to Stravinsky and Holst, further developing his own unique idiom for Lucas's faraway universe. His score kept pace with the story's action, from the noisy snow battle on Hoth to Han's daredevil flight through an asteroid field. This meant lots and lots of *notes* and an emphasis on tempo, but it was John's most refined effort yet in the art of melodic action—conveying urgency and hitting crucial beats through the deployment of his army of leitmotifs. The music was always grounded in storytelling and never crudely Mickey-Mousing. He scored the film's action sequences like ballets, with a syncopated scherzo choreographed to the stomping metal legs of the AT-ATs, Luke's theme ringing out nobly and imperiled in the heat of the dance. The Asteroid Field cue is a masterclass in writing to a highly kinetic and beat-specific set piece, matching every exploding space rock and careening TIE fighter within a piece of music that was so tuneful and structured it seemed like it must have preexisted the visuals. John had mastered the art of tailoring unified score to action without any musical seams.

The *Star Wars* films proved the perfect canvas for his hyper-melodic, balletic approach. And even though he frequently waved off this style of writing as simply demanded by the popcorn antics of the films ("It's almost like a cartoon, because music accompanies the gestures and movements all the time"[17]), he clearly had fun doing it and he gave it his all. "I have had to write active music which can be orchestrated with a flourish, a lot of decoration, a quick tempo," he said. "As these are heroic films, the music necessarily reflects the heroic element. It must underlie the emotional content and have an epic sweep to it. It's not a crutch but a sustaining element in films of this kind—and it's very stimulating to compose."[18]

Empire also opened up the storyline with quiet character moments. Even as they flee gunfire on Hoth and dance with death aboard the Millennium Falcon, Han and Leia still find time for combative, flirtatious repartee and hushed intimacy. Their tune is a classic John Williams love theme, incredibly singable and full of soaring lift and pining suspensions and anticipations. He expertly developed it from their early comedic banter to their first kiss aboard the Falcon, and to the high drama of Han's not-quite-fatal execution scene. Once they're entrapped by Vader in Cloud City, the melody's inherent sorrow surfaces even as its romance blooms. It activates with urgency and heroism with Leia's last-ditch attempt to save Han, then cries out with pain and desperation as she tearfully watches his frozen body disappear in Boba Fett's ship. With John's music carrying this emotional climax in its arms, the film was elevated from children's theater to grand opera.

The major new character was Yoda, a green puppet credibly brought to life by Frank Oz and just a few more serious pitches away from his Miss Piggy or Grover. Yoda is equally quirky, lovable, and wise—and John's theme captured all of those qualities. It "begins in a kind of piquant way," he explained, "and develops into a more profound, more noble piece."[19] Introduced timidly and somewhat comically on top of plucked strings, the melody begins to reveal its depth as Luke learns who Yoda really is, and it is unveiled in all its glory when Yoda uses the Force to lift Luke's X-wing out from the swamp, soaring over a magical flute figure and finally crescendoing with a big fanfare. It turns mournful as Luke decides to leave his training to save his friends, and John cleverly turned the theme into a breathless action motif as Luke sneaks into Cloud City—an afterglow of Yoda's counsel. The Imperial March dominated in its first outing, often serving as a sudden turn of the page from action elsewhere back to Vader and his fleet. It is first hinted on high piccolo as the Star Destroyer sends a probe down to Hoth, and it figures prominently in the snow battle, stomping through the abandoned rebel base with Vader and competing with active, heroic statements of Luke's theme as he and his companions fend off encroaching AT-ATs. Bold and brassy, it hunts down the Falcon, chokes a parade of Imperial officers, and threatens to swallow Han and Leia in Cloud City. When Vader fatefully reveals he is Luke's father, his theme hits with the sucker punch gravity of that revelation. When he later implores his son telepathically to join him, it hovers above queasy, swirling strings as Luke struggles to digest what he has just learned. The march held court over the end credits suite in its most regal, elegant rendition yet. The Hoth battle and the Rebel army waging it have their own martial, heroic tunes. For that sequence John deployed five piccolos, five oboes, a battery of eight percussion, two grand pianos, three harps, and even Wagner tubas, in addition to the full London Symphony Orchestra "in order to achieve a bizarre, mechanical, brutal sound" for the Imperial Walkers.[20] Boba Fett elicited a pulsing, menacing motif on low bassoon; Cloud City is represented with a deceptively sunny theme, as Lando gives Han and Leia a cheery tour of what is about to become a place of suffering; and a somber death march plays as Han's frozen body is led down the halls of Lando's palace to Boba Fett's ship.

The most potent legacies from the first film were John's themes for Luke and Obi-Wan Kenobi, the latter now simply acting as a theme for the Force. Luke's march grew in subtlety along with the character: it wanders in on French horn when he first reveals himself, traces the highs and lows of his escape from the wampa monster and the Battle of Hoth, and turns inward during his time on Dagobah—revealing the sadness and confusion that come with his deeper encounters with the Force. The versatile Force theme also deepens and expands along with Luke's facility with the mystical energy field: it appears during the early visitation of Obi-Wan's ghost in the snow, becomes endangered during the snow battle, and is both fragile and forceful over the course of Luke's training. The tune rises majestically as Obi-Wan and Yoda counsel Luke not to give in to hate as he leaves for Cloud City, finishing on a sad cello coda because they know what awaits him.

All told, it was just under two hours of music: a genuine popcorn symphony. John spent the winter of 1979 composing, and once again relied on Herb Spencer for the vast and detailed orchestration work. "I suppose composers for centuries have complained about this," John said while in the thick of working on *Empire*. "I think of Mozart having to produce a mass for Sunday for the archbishop, or Haydn writing something for Esterházy on demand. 'Let me have a new symphony for Thursday night's dinner.' I suppose it's as old as the art of writing music."[21] He compared this project to "the equivalent of several Lisztian tone poems." "Or a couple of symphonies," his interviewer responded. "Yes, except that it's not really a fair comparison," John demurred, "because this kind of incidental music is quicker to write than an organic piece like a symphony."[22]

A BBC film crew captured the score's creation, from the spotting sessions in San Rafael to the writing desk in John's office at Fox to the Anvil stage in London. The resulting documentary, *Star Wars—Music by John Williams*, featured charming footage of Spencer in a suit and tie, calling for "John T." to come and look at something on his manuscript. "Right here," John says, entering from the other room in a burgundy sweater over a white collared shirt and smiling. By now his hair has abandoned the top of his head altogether but is still reddish on the sides. In another scene, John and Ken Wannberg stand over a moviola watching and rewatching a black-and-white print of the sequence where Han and Leia slowly realize the cave they're hiding in is actually a gigantic space slug. The work in John's little factory is delightfully quaint and simple, even cozy—where the only tools are a piano, pencils and paper, and spools of physical film. The documentary, which aired in May 1980, gave the public its first glimpse into the life and work of this hermetic composer, who was getting more famous by the hour. It included shots of his house, both exterior and interior, and captured John accompanying an opera singer at the piano; he likes to play chamber music with friends for fun, he says, and that making music with his own hands makes him a better composer. He sat for an interview next to Spielberg, and they discussed granular details about the music in *Jaws* and *Close Encounters*. Clips from *How to Steal a Million* and *Jane Eyre* were also played and discussed, providing context for a man most people only knew for his recent blockbusters.[23]

The *Empire* score was recorded at Anvil Studios in December 1979 through January 1980. Richard Dyer flew to London, primarily to cover the burbling news of John's appointment with the Pops, but he also sent home a revealingly detailed dispatch about the *Empire* sessions. Posted outside the door to the giant scoring stage was a sign: "Do Not Interfere with Studio Set-up Otherwise the Empire Will Strike Back," signed by Darth Vader. Inside the booth, Lucas sat next to Lionel Newman. "Gents," John said to the orchestra at one point, "I think it's clean enough to do a DT"—a "dirty track," meaning a complete run-through of a cue that they would then go back and make any corrections needed. Dyer witnessed the scoring of the pivotal scene where Han is lowered into a carbon chamber:

> Take 145 is over. Williams moves to the control room. He isn't happy yet with the synchronization between the music and the screen. He admits the playing has a way to go. Furthermore, there is too much detail in his orchestration. The chimes and harp have to go. Lionel Newman doesn't like one bell passage; "It sounds like fire engines." Out it goes; John Williams laughs and says, "Avon calling." Lucas disagrees with the mood of one passage. Williams explains, "I was trying to give her a cold shiver." Lucas says, "No, I want her sad, romantic, plaintive." Williams will have to write some new music to drop into those measures later; he knows how to do it.
>
> It is time to do the passage again. There is a delay. The recording engineer, it is explained over the booming intercom to the amusement of all, "went to get rid of his beer." Williams takes this opportunity to point out that one section is going to have to be slower "now that I have seen the tempi." ... Another take. This time Lucas feels there needs to be some kind of extra nudge when Darth Vader comes on to the screen. "It sounds like in-the-middle music." John Williams turns to the

trombone section and rewrites their part on the spot; it is instant orchestration. The next time Darth Vader comes on to the screen there will be a nudge.[24]

John could "change things around to make them sound better and on the fly," Dyer marveled decades later. "I've never seen anybody else do that."[25]

* * *

John's appointment to the Pops was a national event. He was interviewed, profiled, and analyzed by dozens of publications, becoming a visible celebrity overnight. Most people wanted to know *why*—why a hotshot Hollywood composer in the prime of his career would want to spend almost every night of his summer conducting light classical music. In his first press conference, John answered: "This is an opportunity to make music on a level I haven't had before. The art of music for me has been a life-long love affair, a real passion, for more than 40 years. I know only a fraction of what exists, and my excitement now is that I have the instrument for exploring what there is more fully. You could say my position is ideal."[26] He kept referring to the Pops as an "instrument," and he also compared it to a Rolls-Royce: "You feel responsiveness, reserves of power and energy. They can increase volume without having the tune get noisy. They haven't got a vulgar sound in their whole repertory."[27]

Previn was his usual feisty self, explaining why *he* thought it was a great idea:

> Anybody who thinks John Williams is "just a Hollywood musician" is completely wrong. He is such a good musician, so thorough, so completely schooled. John is damned fortunate at this stage of his career that the job at the Pops should be open. As I said to him recently, "Why do you want to spend the rest of your life in a frightening goddamn city like Los Angeles? You've got nothing left to prove out there."
>
> At the same time the Pops is lucky that John is available. He is a first-class pianist, and he knows a terrific amount of music. Furthermore, he knows the orchestra from the point of view of the man with the pencil, and that means intimately. He can make superlative arrangements of pop materials, and he can edit, fix, handle anything that comes up in someone else's arrangement, make it better, and all in a matter of minutes. That's quite rare among conductors. Did I say rare? That's being polite. It's unique.
>
> He is also a very efficient conductor; the players of the London Symphony Orchestra, who have recorded several film scores with him, are full of admiration. They say there's no nonsense about him, that he knows what he wants and he knows how to get it.[28]

John later admitted he took the job, in great part, "because André wanted me to be a conductor. *Silly* reason."[29] But John was also adamant that he was not following Previn's path out of Hollywood in exchange for a career as an *important maestro*. "I leave that to André," he said. "If I had his talent I might consider it. But truthfully, I love film work. For me it is really fun."[30] This was purely a chance for John to stretch himself even more as a musician, a chance to dive into the library of classical music and go swimming, a chance to "invigorate my composing," he said.[31] It was a challenge to himself, to see if he had what it took to be like his friends Previn and Leonard Slatkin. It was an opportunity to step away from the writing desk and his hermit's cave, and to play and exercise with other musicians for a few weeks every year. It was a homecoming to the town where his parents met, to the hall his grandfather helped build and where his mother grew up just a few blocks away.

On some level, he also saw it as a chance to evangelize the art of film music, and to persuade a classical audience in Boston—and across the United States, thanks to PBS—to take that music and its composers *seriously*:

> I find it disappointing that some of the greatest musical minds of the century have shied away from film music. When you consider the kind of audience you can reach, the sheer numbers of people, it's a shame that Stravinsky, for example, never wrote film music. I say this with complete awareness of the dangers of easy popularization. Prokofiev wrote splendid music for films, and it never endangered his art. There's commercialization in a healthy sense as well as an unhealthy sense. Maybe that's why I find the Boston Pops programming idea congenial. A lot of it is light and fluffy, but some of it is the best music there is. The same audience digests it all to one degree or another. It shows what can be done in a popular forum.[32]

He suggested that it was possible for him to "bring prestige to the best film music by presenting it in a concert format. Only one half of one percent of the music written in the 19th century is anything we ever hear today; surely there must be at least that percentage of good music written for films."[33] In 1980, the wall separating the concert hall and film music was impossibly high and barb-wired at the top. The only way to get it into Symphony Hall was to remove the serious leather seats and serve it with sandwiches and beer. It was all right for the Hollywood Bowl and those Filmharmonic evenings, but when John dared to take it inside the Dorothy Chandler with the Los Angeles Philharmonic or any other "serious" venue, he was met with fangs among the appointed tastemakers and gatekeepers. When he conducted the Pops in Detroit that February, the *Free Press* critic sneered: "His compositional style ranges from Copland mimicry ... through pompous, brassy open fourths and fifths (*Superman* and *Star Wars*) to weak imitations of the contemporary Hungarian composer György Ligeti (*Close Encounters of the Third Kind*). While it may suit the films it accompanies, it can't stand on its own too well."[34] A *pops* orchestra was the only viable option for making a concerted effort at programming film music in the hall—and even then it had to contend with clinking silverware and noisy chatter. That was one of the hardest things for John to get used to: "People told me I waited too long between numbers. I kept waiting for the din from the audience to die down, but it never did."[35]

When the concept was first introduced, "pops" simply referred to *light* classical music—overtures, waltzes, marches, and pleasant symphony movements. In time the category grew to embrace Broadway show tunes and later the orchestral—or big band—music that was popular in nightclubs and on the radio. Before the 1960s, most pop music *was* orchestral. But Fiedler didn't draw a line when the radio started to fill with rock 'n' roll: he commissioned orchestral arrangements of Beatles tunes and invited Karen Carpenter to sing with the Pops. John made the irrefutable case that, of all things, *movie scores* were the organic inheritor of the "pops" mantle: orchestral music, fun and emotional and catchy, heard by millions of people around the world.

For the most part, John was welcomed with open arms by Boston and the BSO, who were excited to have such a starry yet modest celebrity at the helm. Only a tiny minority of naysayers spoke up when his hiring was announced. "Williams made no impression on me whatsoever," said Jordan Whitelaw, producer of *Evening at Symphony*—the "serious" counterpart to *Evening at Pops*. "His music shouldn't happen to a dog. I don't think anyone in the orchestra could have conceived that he would have been named conductor. So, mazel tov."[36] One anonymous violinist said of John's tryout: "He didn't make a strong impression. He seemed a relatively unremarkable conductor. It seemed obvious there were other reasons why he was at the Pops."[37] Jenny, who was now 23 and in premed school at USC, later said it was "very, very brave to do something like that in the middle of his career, and also have to deal with understanding the minutia and workings of the Brahmin Boston crowd."[38*] And while the embrace was an overall warm one, John had an uphill battle ahead. The musicians had grown complacent and bored under Fiedler. They were contractually forced to play the Pops summer season, and many did not hide that they were there under duress. They were used to performing the same old tired music, much of which they neither respected nor enjoyed. And now here comes Mr. Hollywood, with almost no public conducting experience, bringing in a stack of *movie music*. There was a pool of low-level discontent that would bubble for a few years ... and eventually boil over.

* * *

Two scoring assignments were announced in January 1980 amidst the hubbub of the Boston news. Director Michael Cimino engaged John to write a big, traditional, Copland-style score for his western epic, *Heaven's Gate*—which turned into an epic disaster—but that job was one of the sacrifices John made in light of his new conducting workload.[39†] John was also signed by producer Mitsuhari Ishii and director Terence Young to score *Inchon*, a big-budget film starring Gregory Peck, about General MacArthur's amphibious invasion during the Korean War—a decisive battle that occurred just a few months before John joined the Air Force. The *Hollywood Reporter* announced that he would record it with the London Philharmonic in the spring.[40] That, too, was dropped. "Williams got smart," quipped Jerry Goldsmith, who picked it up.[41] Whether it was purely a scheduling conflict that forced John to eject from these two bombs, or a last-minute judgment call, he *was* getting choosier

---

[*] Boston Brahmins, a term coined by Oliver Wendell Holmes, were the city's upper class—wealthy, educated aristocrats, many of whom descended from the English Puritans. Stereotypical adjectives would include "strait-laced" and "hide-bound."

[†] Actor-musician David Mansfield wound up taking the soundtrack in a much leaner direction.

about how to spend his increasingly precious time—and his batting average at the box office mostly reflected it. "John is very, very aware of the business that he's in," said a close friend who knew that John kept tabs on the box office fate of his films. "He's a businessman—don't forget."[42] John hedged on this, saying he only started paying attention when people began pointing out numbers *to* him. But we do try to be good gamblers, he admitted. "If we could pick hits—either songs, musicals, opera, or film—we would be Sol Hurok times 10," he said, referring to the self-made classical impresario of the 20th century. "I don't think anybody wants to be that, by the way."[43]

John cleared the rest of 1980 for Pops work, which involved studying a mountain of music. In just the first week, he was tasked with conducting Henryk Wieniawski's second violin concerto with Isaac Stern, and Camille Saint-Saëns's second violin concerto with Emanuel Borok, among two dozen other classical works both large and small. Eugene Ormandy, longtime conductor of the Philadelphia Orchestra, told John, "Oh, you know all this music." John said, "No, sir. I don't know it all." Ormandy said, "Well, you're gonna *learn* it." "It was a real work challenge," John said. "I never put a score down. If I went to the bathroom I took Saint-Saëns with me. Psychologically I felt, in many ways, inferior to the orchestra, because they had mastered so much repertoire that I had not. I can't say that they were not helpful, because they were."[44]

His monumental new job also included courting celebrity guest artists, going on a charm offensive with the Boston press, and getting ready for his primetime television debut. "I don't think of myself as a public person—certainly not the way Arthur Fiedler was," he told Ellen Pfeifer, music critic for the *Boston Herald American*. "It was never my wish to be a public performer. That was never one of my goals. I never used to give interviews because they didn't seem necessary. I was always happy being a behind-the-scenes person and felt you should talk less and work more." Pfeiffer pointed out the many differences between the old maestro and this new one:

> With thinning red hair and a red beard, wearing the same functional black turtleneck and gray slacks he seems to favor for leisure, he has none of the instant recognition factor of Fiedler. He is attractive in an unremarkable way, gentle, and soft-spoken, but you wouldn't be likely to recognize him if he walked down the street. There is none of the dark, rakish, matinee-idol handsomeness Fiedler had when he took over the Pops. Nor does he appear to have Fiedler's compulsive flair for publicity. You can't imagine Williams posing for Scotch commercials or dressing up in outlandish costumes for record album jackets. Instead, he comes across as a thoroughly nice human being (in contrast to the curmudgeonly Fiedler) with a strong sense of privacy and reserve.[45]

John and Samantha moved into a rented house in the upscale neighborhood of Beacon Hill, stocked with a Baldwin piano.[46] After John conducted a fundraising preview concert, the 96th Pops season officially commenced on April 29, 1980; 2,300 people paid $50 apiece[47] to see the orchestra's new conductor—wearing white slacks and a blue jacket with a white carnation—as he led the orchestra in music from *The*

Cowboys and *Star Wars*, including a new piece called the "Imperial March." (*Empire* had not even opened yet.) Burgess Meredith reprised his role as *The Reivers* narrator and read material from Faulkner's book during the *Reivers* suite, and Isaac Stern performed excerpts from *Fiddler on the Roof*. Anthony Daniels waddled out in his C-3PO costume and a baton to conduct the *Star Wars* theme. In the audience were Gary Kurtz, Gene Shalit, Mark Hamill, and a 24-year-old cellist; Yo-Yo Ma's first impression of John was "this incredibly gracious gentleman who's like everybody's favorite uncle."[48]

There were also television cameras: the whole evening was broadcast live on *Evening at Pops*. "I think he *hated* that part of it," said Susan Dangel, a producer for the PBS program:

> He didn't quite realize how iconic Arthur Fiedler was in Boston, and what it was to step into that—the demanding nature, and what people expected. There's an Arthur Fiedler statue on the Esplanade. There's an Arthur Fiedler footbridge. I don't think John quite realized that, and he was self-conscious about it. I think he felt like if you wanted someone to be an actor on camera then you should hire an actor. We expected John to really be able to turn and talk. And then we tried to find ways around it, and he just wasn't happy doing it.[49]

"He didn't like looking at himself," said Bill Cosel, the producer and creator of *Evening at Pops*, who assured John he was easy to watch. "But I'm not like Seiji Ozawa, who's so balletic and so physical," John said. "I feel like a lump. I feel like a lox." John would grow more comfortable as a television personality and spokesperson, but this first summer was a baptism by limelight. Cosel had produced many showboating and often silly appearances with Fiedler, and he came up with an idea for a trailer introducing John to PBS audiences: a cartoon of a bearded conductor parachuting into Symphony Hall—the invasion of Hollywood by air. John said no immediately—he wasn't a showman like Fiedler.[50] "I am more a musician than a man of Hollywood," he insisted.[51] He also had real disdain for the medium. "Television is so disappointing," he told a Boston reporter. "Tawdry? It is tawdry. A national disgrace, really."[52] But, he also recognized and appreciated the potential *importance* of TV, just as he knew how powerful film was for spreading the gospel of orchestral music. Leonard Bernstein used television to educate and promote classical music to new audiences, as had Previn in both Pittsburgh and London—and this was John's chance to do the same for film music.‡

That first concert broadcast was a bit misleading; the televised portion was *all* John's music and did not include the Wieniawski concerto and music by William Walton and Stephen Sondheim that were also performed in Symphony Hall. In his first season, John did not actually program his own music very often. He retained

---

‡ Saturday night Pops concerts were also broadcast live on local FM radio.

Fiedler's "tripartite" structure, which typically only left room in the final third of any concert for contemporary pop music or film scores. "And of that," Morris said, "John was very self-effacing."[53] He was on a mission to legitimize the *best* of film music, and to spotlight the composers and arrangers of the great American songbook, as well as newer Broadway talents like Sondheim. In his first season, he programmed film music by Herrmann and Erich Wolfgang Korngold—whose son George Korngold would soon produce John's Pops albums—as well as contemporaries Maurice Jarre, Marvin Hamlisch, and John Barry. (In June, Lionel Newman flew in to guest conduct an evening of "Music from Hollywood.") Here and there, John peppered in a single theme or a suite from one of his scores, but just as often left himself off the set list.

John's music *did* dominate his debut recording—*Pops in Space*—which quickly became the best-selling album in Philips Records history.[54] And the gimmickry of his debut concert was a portent of the sweet-and-sour nature of his life in classical halls. In May, he conducted music from *Superman*, and an actor dressed as a burglar wove through the audience stealing sips of champagne on his way to a safe on the stage, out of which sprang WGBH president David O. Ives dressed as the Man of Steel.[55] Beeping droids and Stormtroopers would never be far from the conductor's podium from this moment on.

But did John care?

"I think *that* he's amused by, the Stormtroopers," said Dangel.[56]

The Pops role crystallized an interesting paradox: John was bringing film music into hallowed halls, asking classical audiences to take it seriously—while that seriousness was constantly being punctured and undermined. "Popular music played by a symphony orchestra doesn't have to be trashy," he insisted. "It can always be done in a stellar way." His unique attitude about this was influenced by a recent experience he had in Vienna—"a concert of Strauss waltzes and other light things. The musicians were smiling and having a good time, but there was also seriousness in their faces as they played with felicity, subtlety, and perfection of ensemble. There isn't an English word to express that attitude of *combining seriousness and fun*, though there may be one in German, but that's what I think the Pops should be. And that's what I'll strive for—everyone having a wonderful time and making an exemplary musical presentation."[57]

One thing he hoped to do with his new personal orchestra was to record new film scores, which he did right away—albeit on a small scale. After the success of *Close Encounters* saved Columbia from bankruptcy, Steven Spielberg convinced the studio to give him $2 million to shoot several new scenes which budget and schedule initially forced him to leave out. He also cut or trimmed several old scenes and edited in footage already shot—including a moment where Roy has a panicked episode in his bathtub. The studio's only condition for this "Special Edition" was that he had to take his audience inside the mothership. Spielberg resented that compromise, and most audiences agreed it was a mistake. The only upside was that it necessitated a new score cue, "Inside," which John wrote in the spring and recorded with the Pops and the

Tanglewood Festival Chorus at Symphony Hall on June 13.[58] Carrying on from the ethereal string chords and female choir from his original finale, this short tone poem accompanied Roy's awestruck reaction to the techno set and optical light show, and featured another interpolation of "When You Wish Upon a Star." Spielberg also reinstated the 1977 recording of John's original end credits cue, which culminates with an even more explicit and extended orchestral statement of the Pinocchio tune.

But because of the Pops' busy summer schedule, including nightly concerts and recordings, John was rarely able to take advantage of having his own orchestra to record complete new scores. "To do a large-scale film, you need 19 sessions in nine or ten full working days," he said. "To get this orchestra for ten days any time of the year is very difficult."[59]

* * *

In a rare public comment, Samantha spoke to the *Boston Globe* on the evening of John's big premiere concert: "We have been so busy since John was named conductor of the Pops that we haven't had time for anything else. After tonight, we're going to sit down and figure out a date for the wedding."[60]

John waffled on whether to get married again. When Richard Dyer first met Samantha, she was introduced as John's secretary.[61] Sandy DeCrescent, John's orchestra contractor for decades, claimed it was *she* who introduced Samantha to John—as his assistant.[62] Lionel Newman would say: "Look, you have her around so she can carry your music and your batons. But it's not fair. Either marry her or say goodbye."[63] John roundly refuted this narrative. "It's not true that she ever worked for me," he said. "Someone suggested that, and it's not true."[64] Regardless, the ever colorful Lionel advised John: "*Either shit or get off the pot.*"[65]

On June 9, John and Samantha were married at King's Chapel, a Unitarian church in the city center not far from where his parents had exchanged vows in 1929. "It was a very private and quiet affair," he said.[66] There was no music, and the only two guests were Lionel and Beverly Newman. "I have pictures right after the wedding," said Carroll Newman. "My mom and Samantha are walking in back of John and my dad—who are holding hands. I mean, it was very telling."[67]

For many of John's friends, Samantha was an enigma. Where Barbara had been vivacious and the life of the party, Samantha was quiet and guarded. "She was very sincere and sweet, and a little shy," said Mia Farrow. "Which I understood completely, since I too was a little shy. But I didn't have that kind of connection that I had with Barbara—who *wasn't* shy, and was very open."[68] Some of John's old friends, especially the ones who were close to Barbara, felt he withdrew from those legacy relationships—but then, Barbara was always the social force pulling John out of his introverted artist's shell. "I don't know Samantha very well," Ginny Mancini said. "They have a strange marriage. She's hardly ever around."[69] Edye Rugolo, who liked Samantha, remembered an occasion where they were all three having dinner at Trader Vic's—a tiki restaurant and one of John's favorite spots in Beverly Hills. "I'd had too much to drink," Rugolo said, "and I told him how much I miss Barbara. And he shushed me. He was uncomfortable about that."[70] Leonard Slatkin felt that John continued to harbor great affection for Barbara, "and that makes the second marriage, perhaps, a little more difficult."[71]

Samantha did become friendly with Alex North's young wife, Annemarie. The two went for walks together in the hills of the Pacific Palisades, and would have rich conversations with their husbands over dinner and cocktails (Figure 9.1). "Samantha had very strong points of view," said Alex North's son, Steven. "She demonstrated them very articulately, and John always gave her all the space she needed. They were a very tight couple. They were very, very warm and, shall I say, intellectually stimulating."[72]

Figure 9.1. John and Samantha with Alex and Annemarie North, ca. 1980 (Photographer unknown, Courtesy of John Williams).

She made John *happy*, said Jenny.[73] That was all that mattered. John wasn't sad anymore. Marc Newman, Lionel's older brother and John's agent, died of cancer in August 1980.[74] John invited Tom Morris to L.A. with him for the funeral, since Morris was the one who had negotiated the Pops deal with Newman. The day after the funeral, Morris went to lunch with John and Lionel at the Fox commissary. "John was already starting to express his ambivalence about the Boston position, because he was nervous," said Morris. "It was a lot of work, it was the first time—it was all new." John told Morris: "I don't know if I'm really right for this."

They were sitting there and eating among Hollywood legends like Mel Brooks, when in walked Fox president Sherry Lansing, who brought along several investors to stargaze. She came over to John's table, Morris said: "And 'Oh, John!' 'Oh, Sherry baby,' you know, *kiss, kiss, kiss*. And Sherry says to the two suits: 'I want you to meet John Williams, *conductor of the Boston Pops*.' They were all pleased—and never mentioned once that John had eaten lunch in there for 30 years, never mentioned *Star Wars*, never mentioned *Jaws*. He was 'conductor of the Boston Pops' in his world. And that was big news. That was the moment I said: 'I'm not going to worry about his ambivalence.'"[75]

John, in kind, brought Hollywood to Massachusetts. Every summer, the BSO migrated to Tanglewood—the musical institute in a forested campus in the rolling hills of Lenox, founded by Serge Koussevitzky in 1937, where talented students played music with masters like Aaron Copland and learned from legends like Leonard Bernstein, where classical giants gathered and made music and dined together. Tanglewood was a classical greenhouse, a hotbed of new art music—and a symbol of the high cultural center of the United States. Every summer, thousands of individuals and families descended from all over New England to picnic and watch concerts in a massive, partly outdoor venue called The Shed; one annual tradition was "Tanglewood on Parade," a daylong festival with multiple conductors, a jumbo-sized orchestra combining the BSO and student ensembles, and always ending with the "1812 Overture" by Tchaikovsky—which John conducted in his first Tanglewood on Parade as new Pops conductor, on Friday, August 22. He told the young staffers he had some guests coming and asked if they could be escorted backstage. "Of course," a staff member answered. "How will we know them?" "Well, you'll probably recognize them," John said. It was Steven Spielberg and Amy Irving.[76]

John's life was expanding, socially and creatively. It now spanned from the home of popular cinema to the heart of American classical music. But unlike Miklós Rózsa's frustrated "double life," as Rózsa called it in his memoir—irreconcilably split between philistine Hollywood producers and the rarefied concert hall—John wanted to find a way to harmonize these two themes.

* * *

Indiana Jones was a creative love child conceived on a Hawaiian beach while Spielberg and Lucas awaited box office results from the opening of *Star Wars* in 1977. Spielberg had always wanted to direct a James Bond movie, and Lucas said he had an even better idea about a globetrotting archaeologist who goes searching for ancient, mystical treasure. Like *Star Wars*, it was a trail mix of the popcorn and candy from their childhoods—primarily Saturday matinee serials like *Tailspin Tommy*, *Masked Marvel*, and *Commando Cody*. "I always wondered why Hollywood hadn't done anything to revive the genre of the outdoor adventure," Spielberg said, "of narrow misses and close calls. It was just amazing to me that it hadn't been done before."[77]

As he prepared to scout locations for *Raiders of the Lost Ark* in the deserts of Tunisia and other far-flung locales, Spielberg was talking to his producer—Howard Kazanjian, who had incidentally produced *Family Plot* for Alfred Hitchcock—about John's best scores and other film music he loved. Spielberg had just purchased a brand-new Sony Walkman, the portable cassette player introduced in 1979, and Kazanjian suggested he should have his enormous library of scores transferred to cassette. Frank Marshall, a young producer working with Spielberg for the first time—and who incidentally had known John since childhood; his father, Jack Marshall, was a TV composer at Revue—went on the location scout trips carrying two large gray cases filled with cassettes so Spielberg could listen to his scores on the go; and during principal photography, Spielberg would listen to music between takes. The Well of the Souls sequence—where Indy finally discovers the Ark of the Covenant, only to be sealed in with it—was one where he was already thinking about the kind of music he wanted.[78]§ After his own globetrotting adventures shooting the film, Spielberg spotted it with John in December. "I have absolute trust and faith that John is right," Spielberg said. "When he sees my movie for the first time, which I have already seen dozens of times, John's first impressions of my films are the impressions that I listen to. And then I get to hear how much John loves the movie, because he goes and musically enhances it and takes it to an entirely different level."[79] John recognized *Raiders* as another Saturday popcorn picture; he noted how the action was always *comedy* action with a wink and a "slight camp edge," and he referred to Spielberg's approach as Comic Book "with a capital C and B."[80] He scored it accordingly—but with his unfailing commitment to *serious* fun.

When he was ready, John called Spielberg over to his office at Fox to audition theme ideas on the piano. He had written two main theme possibilities, and he played the first—an upward galloping, jaunty tune, "which I freaked out over," Spielberg said. "I loved it so much." Then he played his other idea, which had a more yearning lilt. "My only input was to say, 'Can't you use *both*?' And he did! He made the latter the bridge, and he made the former the main theme."[81] John confessed that this "simple little sequence of notes" was probably the hardest part of scoring *Raiders*:

---

§ Spielberg was at the same time developing a musical he wanted to make called *Reel to Reel*, a metamemoir about a young filmmaker trying to make his first film: a science-fiction musical. John would almost certainly have written the songs. Spielberg even flew back to L.A. from the set of *Raiders* to present it to Sid Sheinberg, who turned it down. (McBride, *Steven Spielberg*.)

> I spend more time on those little bits of musical grammar to get them just right, so that they seem inevitable—seem like they've always been there, they're so simple. And you think it's almost like, "Eureka! Of course, there it is—it *has* to be that." I don't know how many permutations I will go through with a six-note motif like that, one note down, one note up, and spend a lot of time on these little simplicities which are often the hardest things to capture, I think for anybody. It's not difficult to obfuscate, to complicate, to add layers of things. But to peel layers off to get to an essential phrase, that speaks directly and succinctly and clearly, they're hard to find. And I always have fun with Steven going over these things, because he loves to come to the piano, and I'll play, and we experiment around.[82]

John wrote yet another old-fashioned, singable love theme for Indy's old flame, Marion Ravenwood, played by Karen Allen. He likened it to "As Time Goes By," a ballad made famous in the movie *Casablanca*, and other romantic tunes from old Warner Bros. films.[83] Marion's theme opened with the same interval as Han and Leia's love theme, clearly cooked in the same kitchen during the same season, but it had a slightly more curious, even glamorous personality. "I loved her spunk and spirit," John said.

> I didn't know where this love story was going to go, if anywhere, but in spite of their spiky relationship I thought that there was a real spark between the two of them, and a real sort of potential love story was there.... I thought if the music were lyrical and emotional and warm, and the orchestra could sing this love theme—even if we didn't have *love* love scenes—that it might be permissible to interject that kind of musical emotion in their relationship.[84]

The whole score was another embarrassment of melodic riches. John wrote a motif for the medallion Indy needs from Marion—a mysterious breeze on English horn blowing in from eastern deserts—another for the Ark—a hauntingly *religioso* chorale—and yet another for the comical basket chase in Cairo. The latter cue was a mode John categorized as *burlesque*, in the sense of exaggerated imitation. John said he loved working with Lucas and Spielberg because they both used score "in a very theatrical way. That gives the music an opportunity to project itself, and gives *me* an opportunity to support the architecture of their pieces in the thematic way, to the extent that wouldn't be possible in all kinds of films."[85] Some critics complained that Spielberg and Lucas movie romances were sexless, but John excelled at supplying hidden dialogue—and implied intercourse. His music was better than sex.

The film opens with a *misterioso* introduction to the adventuring archaeologist, mid-quest in a South American jungle in 1936. This first cue "paints a picture," director Rian Johnson observed. "If it were the overture to an opera, for instance, it could play in the dark with the curtain closed for the opening, and when the curtain goes up and you see the jungle set, it would make perfect sense to you."[86] Mostly, *Raiders* is one big, cliffhanging set piece after another, and John's primary concern, once armed with his character melodies, was to map out the correct tempo for each one. After Indy's suspenseful exploration of a cave full of booby traps, his escape from blow-dart-wielding natives is accompanied by comedic pizzicato and orchestral flourishes—a deft ballet of action, danger, humor, and heroism, sincere but not overly straight, hitting *just* the right notes along with Spielberg's camera and Harrison Ford's committed-but-comical performance, and finally debuting the Raiders march as his getaway plane takes off. John was quite conservative with his deployment of that theme, which doesn't fully leave the barn until Indy dukes it out with a brawny Nazi in front of a rotating airplane late in the picture. Spielberg admired John's discerning use of Indy's theme: "When he uses it, it allows us to root for the hero. And when he doesn't use it, we're worried about our hero."[87] The march finds an entirely new groove in the big truck chase that follows, where Indy takes on an entire Nazi motorcade with just a horse and his bare knuckles. John cleverly alternated the tempo, from insistent trot to gallop to stampede, to match the action—and he kept finding ways to ratchet up the excitement, vary the pace, and then bring in the heroic Raiders theme at just the right moment of triumph. "There's a musical progression that includes an amazing kind of accelerated ostinato," said Spielberg, "when Johnny actually sort of tells all of us when to really get excited. The music says, 'Okay, *now* you're gonna see something.' He makes the promise, and it's my job to keep the promise. And if I can't, it's his job to write better music than I directed so he can keep the promise for me," Spielberg laughed.[88]

As unbelievably tuneful as John's scoring was—a technicolor candy store of sticky confections—he insisted that *rhythm* might be the most important aspect of his job:

> The speed of the film, and sensitivity to it, and the ability of a composer to help the speed of a film, and give it rhythm, and give it timing ... in my mind is even more important than the melody and the big tune. Because you cut film for speed, you cut it for tempo. The director shoots it for tempo.... *Everything*, every movement of the body, of machine, of all of that, needs to be given thought relative to time.[89]

A two-minute sequence in a film, he explained, can feel half as fast or twice as long depending on how it's scored. "The music affects the sense of continuum of time and the way the eye perceives the film." Lawrence Kasdan, who wrote the screenplay for *Raiders*, was most impressed with how John could change pace and tone on a dime, "quickly and economically. You'll be going along and it's gigantic—it's a chase, it's a fight—and then all of a sudden there'll be this quiet moment. Which is sort of what I prided myself in my writing, that it should mix it up like that. It's just like throwing different pitches all the time, and the quicker you can write the transition and have it be effective, the better. John has a *genius* for that. And it's not like he's just covering it. He's got something beautiful for it."[90]

John briefly stepped away from working on *Raiders* to conduct his first holiday Pops concerts, which included selections of Handel's *Messiah*, *The Nutcracker*, and Christmas carols by Alfred Burt. He wore a burgundy jacket and stood under a giant snowflake; an ersatz Santa Claus brought out John's first Boston Christmas gift: a pair of red socks. "Williams has grown a much more confident conductor in the course of his year with the Pops," Dyer reported, "much more expansive, much more at ease with the public."[91] He finished the *Raiders* score and was supposed to return to Boston for the annual New Year's concert—but had to cancel at the last minute when he came down with the flu.

He flew to London in February to record *Raiders* with the LSO. The Anvil company had lost its scoring stage in Denham, and had just moved its operation into the historic but moribund recording studio on Abbey Road in St. John's Wood. Things had gotten so bad at the old EMI Studios, where artists from Edward Elgar to the Beatles once made legendary recordings, that many of its materials were sold off and its owners considered turning the giant Studio One into a car park. It was a literal lifesaver when Anvil moved in, installing 35mm projectors and an eight-foot screen to equip the stage for movie scoring. "I think about Abbey Road as being a kind of mother of the music that's been performed there," John said. "She has preserved it for us."[92] But where John spoke of it as a spiritual environment, others found it a bit suffocating. Composer Trevor Jones, who tried to record his score for *The Dark Crystal* with the LSO there a few months later, said there was no ventilation in the control booth, which was already confining and crowded with just a few bodies—and where recording engineer Eric Tomlinson smoked a pipe. The situation was further exacerbated by the speaker monitors inside the booth, Jones said: "When the music was a particular volume too loud, the speaker would just automatically pop and cut out dead."[93] The facility greatly improved in time, and became a recording destination—particularly for Hollywood.

When the orchestra took down John's main theme for the first time, Lucas leaned over to Kazanjian and Spielberg and muttered: "It sounds like *Hogan's Heroes*." "Maybe he was looking for record sales," Kazanjian laughed, "or a march that schools could use at football stadiums."[94] The filmmakers stuck around for seven days, then left the rest of the work—including new arrangements for a soundtrack LP—in the capable hands of Lionel Newman. *Raiders of the Lost Ark* came out in June and immediately redeemed Spielberg after the debacle of *1941*. John's new march *did* enter the pop canon, another immediate staple of band rooms everywhere. But "I was never writing something thinking, *This is gonna sell and make a big hit*," John said. "Can't possibly be a motive."[95]

Just as Sondheim contended it was John who made *Jaws* scary, the great American poet Bob Dylan argued that John's score "brought *Indiana Jones* to life. Without that music it wouldn't have been much of a movie. It's the music which makes Indy come alive."[96]

* * *

As John was composing *Raiders* in December, he also put the finishing touches on his violin concerto. "There was no hope of a performance," he remarked. "I never expected one, frankly. I just put it in a drawer and let it sit there."[97]

John dreamed of having Isaac Stern perform this deeply personal work; they had become friendly through *Fiddler on the Roof*, and Stern came over to John's house after Barbara died, where John played sections of the concerto for him. "He was very empathetic about the whole situation that I faced," John said, "and as a result became interested in the piece."[98] John's second choice was Itzhak Perlman, but the honor went to Mark Peskanov, a young Russian violinist on the rise who had recently played a concert with Slatkin—who was now music director of the St. Louis Symphony. Slatkin and Peskanov offered to premiere the concerto in St. Louis. "John wasn't confident enough, yet, to want to conduct it himself," said Slatkin.[99]**

Peskanov was thrilled to receive his first new concerto by a living composer—"a major, major, major concerto *from scratch*," he gushed. They met only once, for a few hours in the office of Juilliard professor Dorothy DeLay. Peskanov practiced the work diligently, and even publicly on a California recital tour with his cousin, a pianist. "I just loved this concerto so much," Peskanov said, "so I would start to play maybe a movement, like the first movement, because it sounded very nice with the piano as well, to my ears. And I saw the peoples' reactions: they really enjoyed it." John did not discuss the origins of his piece in any detail, but Peskanov knew it was about his late wife: "So I always felt there was some kind of tragedy in there. I just felt this pain, and then at the same time great love, and passion—and some joy. But it's a very *inner* piece. Although there is a climax, finally, in the last movement—a great, great, big climax. It was an incredible emotional experience every time I would play this piece."[100] John evaded discussing the ways in which Barbara inspired the work—at times even saying it wasn't *about* her, but simply motivated by her love of the violin and constant prompting him to write something for the instrument. "It's not elegiac," he later argued. "It's a virtuosic piece I think she would have liked. It's joyous, actually, in its mood. It doesn't reflect anything funereal. It celebrates one woman's life."[101] But for Jenny, who attended the premiere, it was an ode to Barbara "without question. He put a lot of emotion into that. It was good for him to have that project. I hear *her*— especially in the second movement. Beautiful, sad, complex, stunning, entertaining, powerfully emotional. That music said so much about her."[102]

The concerto premiered on January 29, 1981, at the orchestra's Powell Hall. In his review for the *St. Louis Globe-Democrat*, James Wierzbicki deemed it "so craftily paced and so seductively orchestrated that those who hear it have little choice but to give in to its emotive power."[103] When Slatkin, Peskanov, and the St. Louis Symphony took the piece to Carnegie Hall a week later, the New York critics were less kind. Edward Rothstein of the *New York Times* wrote that John "had few ideas, and the Bergian, Hindemithian violin line was tiresomely monotonous."[104] Bill Zakariasen of the *Daily News* described it as "a dreary piece ... predictable notespinning of no profile whatsoever."[105] But Peskanov said he and John were both very happy with the

---

** Slatkin claimed that Tom Morris offered him the Pops position before going to John. "I thought: if I do that, it's going to be difficult to get out of that particular straitjacket, for want of a better word," Slatkin said. "So I turned it down." (Slatkin to TG.)

Carnegie performance, which was attended by Stern: "I felt very inspired that particular night. And I remember we talked with John, and John said, 'Oh God, I wish we would have a recording of that.'" Maybe, Peskanov wondered, that performance "just had exactly all the emotions that he felt."[106]

The concerto was recorded shortly thereafter, in December 1981, with Peskanov and the LSO at Anvil Abbey Road. George Korngold produced the album for Varése Sarabande Records, which paired the piece with John's flute concerto, performed by LSO principal flutist Peter Lloyd. Previn had given the flute concerto its American premiere in Pittsburgh over the summer; John gave a talk at Heinz Hall beforehand, "and captivated Pittsburgh composers and serious students of music with his articulate and intelligent comments on music and composing," Carl Apone reported in the *Pittsburgh Press*:

> The concerto, however, was much less winning to these ears, although the audience received it warmly. Judging from the concerto, Williams has a completely different approach to classical music than he does to his movie music. The concerto is complex, driving, strident, percussive, atonal, and more daring than anything he attempts in his screen music, although the slashing sounds in the concerto are reminiscent of the sounds in *Close Encounters of the Third Kind*. But in his concerto, the music director of the Boston Pops has nothing like the engaging melodies we remember from his movie music....
>
> In this, he and Previn apparently are on similar wave lengths. They seem so concerned with being labeled commercial or Hollywood that they are determined their classical music will be esoteric, ultra-modern. Williams admits classical music is "a way of stretching myself and getting rid of certain impulses I couldn't get rid of in any other way." Perhaps if he did not stretch himself quite so far from his movie music, and were not so afraid of melodies when he puts on his classical music hat, the results would be more satisfying and pleasurable for audiences.[107]

This developed into a common theme in response to John's concert music, though not always expressed as a complaint. John stressed that he never felt any pressure to conform to the postwar language of atonality and serialism in order to be taken seriously in a concert music setting,[108] but several composers and conductors who knew John stressed that there *absolutely* was pressure to conform in order to be accepted.

In a 2022 essay for *Gramophone*, Andrew Farach-Colton wrote: "If one encounters Williams' concert music having only heard his film music, the experience can be a jolt. The surprise is not so much that he's continued to employ 12-note techniques (for even as early as the First Violin Concerto, he sews tonality and atonality together quite seamlessly); what I imagine will be most disconcerting is the relative lack of memorable tunes and motifs of the sort that are so plentiful in his film scores."[109] But Slatkin, who was interviewed for that same article, concluded that "I don't differentiate all that much between his film music and his concert works. I hear too many threads that interact and I think they end up influencing each other. After all, they both come from the same soul."

* * *

John spent most of 1981 away from film, saving his energy for the concerto and a second, grueling season with the Pops. At their annual Fourth of July concert at the Hatch Shell, he had an audience of 225,000 people. "You don't really feel much connection with it onstage because of the lights," he said.

> But the first time I turned around at the end of the first number, there was still some natural light—it was early in the evening—and I could see all the way up the Charles River. There was this multitude of people, and the only word I could think of for it was "biblical." It was sort of like a multitude crossing the sea—something like that. No way to describe the feeling of standing in front of that number of people. The Pope maybe could tell you something about it.[110]

But the honeymoon period in Boston was waning slightly. Pops concerts were not consistently selling out that summer, and people weren't sure if John was going to stick around after his contract expired. Some felt he just wasn't *Boston* enough: "His white tie and tails look as though he bought them rather than inherited them," sneered *Boston Magazine*'s Michael Ryan. "It might have been unreasonable to expect that he should be a graduate of the Latin School, like Arthur Fiedler, but one has the horrifying feeling that he has never even heard of the old Mechanics High School."[111]

John also made the choice to program even less of his film scores than in his first season. "I've been criticized for playing too *much* of my own music, and some people are disappointed that I haven't played *enough* of it," he said that summer. "So it works a little bit both ways. The part that I've taken seriously, though, is at the end of a lot of concerts some little tots come in wanting autographs, and they always say, 'Why don't you play *Star Wars*?' Every concert, you know—and that's nice."[112] That summer he rented a home in the Berkshires near Tanglewood—"Heavenly," he said. Playing the part of the gracious first lady backstage or hobnobbing with wealthy donors, Samantha gave herself the nickname "Maestro Babe."[113] Besides being a photographer—John displayed her work in his office at Symphony Hall—she was also a marathon runner. She was one of a gaggle of people in jogging suits who ran through the hall during a Pops arrangement of the *Chariots of Fire* theme that summer (Figure 9.2); John's surprise was caught by a photographer. "I used to run a little with her, but I don't get very far, I'm afraid," he said.[114]

The lone film John took on that year was an act of kindness for a friend. "It's a charming piece about robots who fall in love and make babies out of old spare auto parts," he told a curious reporter.[115] The movie was called *Heartbeeps*. "It was floundering, and we were not testing well, and the studio was already at it with scissors, recutting," said producer Michael Phillips, who met John on *Close Encounters*. "I called John and asked him as a favor if he would try to breathe some life into this

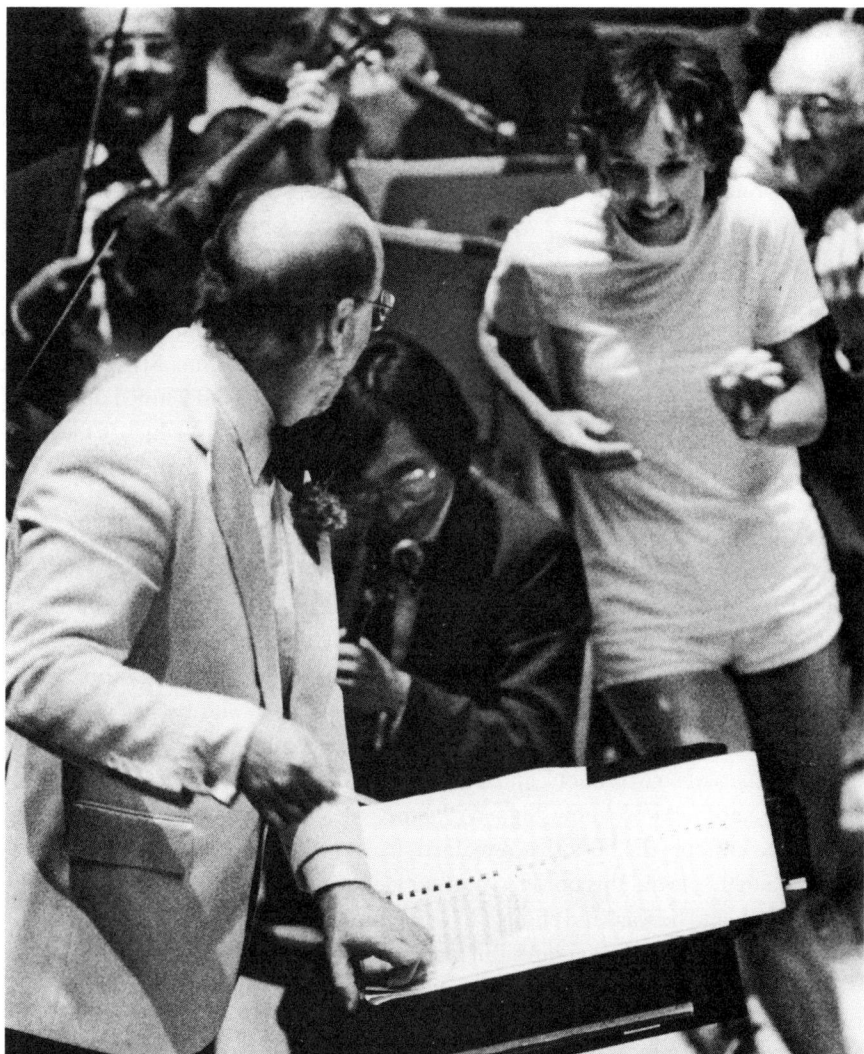

Figure 9.2. Samantha jogs on stage at a Boston Pops concert, June 1982 (Photo by Michael Quan, Courtesy of the Boston Globe Library collection at Northeastern University Archives and Special Collection).

film—which was suffering. I knew that it wouldn't beckon him creatively. I just put it on a very personal level: 'Please, can you help me out?'"[116]

Heartbeeps was an undeniably flawed film with an identity crisis. Director Allan Arkush, a graduate of the Roger Corman school of moviemaking, was hired off the success of his punk musical film *Rock 'n' Roll High School*, and the suits at Universal expected a wacky comedy about robots starring Andy Kaufman. "I had a very, very different idea of the movie," said Arkush. "I thought I was doing a silent movie about first love. I don't know what I was thinking, but it explains a lot about the movie." The resulting film, set in the far-off future of 1995, jerked wildly between broad comedy and poetry: when it wasn't following the antics of a tank-like robot called Crimebuster blowing up houses or a young Christopher Guest riding another giant robot as a raccoon comically covers its eyes, *Heartbeeps* surprisingly slowed down with languid scenes of Kaufman's Val and Bernadette Peters's Aqua—two servant robots who fall in love and go on an adventure with their scrap robot "baby." At times, it is a patient exploration of the beauty of nature and human intimacy. Arkush was influenced by the silent film *7th Heaven* by Frank Borzage. "I don't think I ever told the *studio* I was doing an homage to Frank Borzage—I was not stupid," said Arkush. "The problem is that *I* didn't have the skills to make that silence, and that dynamic. My blocking, in many cases, was too rudimentary, and not involving enough, and I ended up putting it all in an airless world where it doesn't seem anything else exists—which is the fairytale aspect of it." Looking back on it, Arkush made the same comment Spielberg had made about *1941*: "Many times, the film was directing *me*."[117]

Arkush temped his movie with a lot of Brian Eno and Talking Heads music, logically leaning in the direction of electronics. He had Grateful Dead's Jerry Garcia "perform" the voice of the robot baby Phil with his guitar, so as to distinguish it from R2-D2's beeps and bloops. Universal was not happy with his first cut, and the previews were disastrous—so the studio kicked Arkush out of the editing room and off his own movie. Verna Fields, "Mother Cutter," swooped in and hacked *Heartbeeps* down to an anemic 75 minutes with an emphasis on the wacky. "It was a sweet love story between two robots, and they took all the action sequences and comedy sequences and ... I don't know," sighed Phillips: "Meat grinder." He desperately called on John to ennoble the husk that remained. Universal flinched, but agreed to John's fee of $85,000. "He did this on very short notice," said Phillips. "He had a little gap in his schedule, and he was kind enough to write this—probably knowing that it was not going to be one of his great credits. But *thank you, John, for coming through*."[118]

Arkush only met John once, at the spotting session. The producers and studio took John out to dinner beforehand "and I was not invited to that," the exiled director said. "So I just sat there and watched them talk about what they were going to score, and threw in my two cents. But by then it was such a different movie."[119] In the midst of this white-hot, rocket-to-the-moon period of *Star Wars* and Indiana Jones, *Heartbeeps* bore some of the same hyper-motivic, theatrical DNA, but it was exceptional for being one of the most synth-centric scores of John's entire career. In that way, it quickly became one of his most *dated*—locked to a very specific moment in time and the analog, monophonic sounds that were available. John was never too comfortable writing for electronics: after using a Moog for an effect in *Valley of the Dolls,* he began incorporating synths into his scores in the 1970s, but mostly just as additional voices in the orchestra as opposed to lead instruments, and usually conceived as sonic equivalents to a traditional, acoustic instrument. Michael Boddicker, who began working with John on *Close Encounters*, remembered session dates with John as somewhat frustrating for him and his fellow synthesists: "*Obviously* there's nothing I could possibly say negative about John's ability as a leader, John's ability as a conductor, John's ability as an orchestrator, John's ability as a composer. He's phenomenal. But his knowledge of synthesizers is, like, *zip*." When Boddicker turned up for a session, the music on his stand listed "Sound No. 1," "Sound No. 2," "Sound No. 3." He kept trying to get John's attention and ask what *kind* of sound was intended for each of these parts. Finally John said, "Michael, Sound No. 1 is a voice, Sound No. 2 is a bell, Sound No. 3 is a harpsichord. Okay, let's go for a take!"[120]

John's main theme was a heroic little anthem that opens with a classic Williams groove on a synth bass voice, then nobly sings out on a brassy synth lead. It's surrounded by electronic sparkle and shimmer, with a rapid sequenced heartbeat (*beep*)—but it's all mostly treated like a traditional orchestra rather than pure electronica. And before long, a real orchestra sweeps in with familiar human warmth. The main title overture also introduced a love theme on French horns, romantic but innocent in keeping with the story's childlike robo-lovers. This ballad tune was performed by Nyle Steiner on his own invention, the electronic valve instrument, or EVI; John would simply write "Steiner" on his score part. The film's quiet early scenes were scored with a glassy, celestial ambience—like a breeze blowing through wind chimes, an idea John would turn to again in several films. He also brought back an angelic female choir to accompany the pair's awakening love. The score overflows with Prokofievian leitmotifs; it's basically *Peter 2000 and the Wolf-bot*. There's a sweet little cantilena on oboe for the trio who leave the robot factory to learn more about the world (Val and Aqua are joined by a wisecracker named Catskil), and a lightly comical but slightly endangered adventure theme as they sneak out and commandeer a van. They spend the rest of their quest pursued by the destructive, talkative Crimebuster who gets his own villainous march, like a more synthy, pulsing Imperial March with a rock drum backbeat. The robot's incessant incursion into *Heartbeeps*, jabbering away about law enforcement and throwing missiles, is one of the film's most annoying attributes—but his driving, syncopated earworm theme is, by contrast, always welcome. Phil was given a Coplandesque melody of curiosity and cuteness; despite the futuristic characters and instrumentation, John treated much of the forest-set story like an Americana pastoral. The recording sessions took place in November, and the deposed director "liked how gentle it was, and melodic," Arkush said. "It was one of the things about the movie, at that point, that I took some solace in."[121] The film did tank, but Phillips was grateful for the favor. It was the last time he and John collaborated—although there was a tantalizing adaptation of Isaac Asimov's remarkable *Foundation* trilogy that the producer was attempting to sell at the time—with Spielberg, George Roy Hill, and the English writer David Wood each meant to direct. "It's another one," Phillips sighed, "that got away."[122]

John turned 50 in February 1982, which he celebrated with a party at Sam Grossman's house, with music performed by Count Basie and his band.[123] It felt a little like getting old, although John liked to point out that the talking picture was itself only about 50, a relative infant. "College cinema departments didn't exist in my student years, but every campus seems to have one now, and interest in film has become a passion," he said. "Whatever opera was to the nineteenth century, film is to the close of the twentieth. If we had a Wagner in this century, he would be a DeMille making his own pictures."[124]

* * *

The first preview of *E.T.* was like a religious experience, Sid Sheinberg said. The president of Universal Studios, and one of Spielberg's early mentors, witnessed the audience response in Houston, and it was "a little bit like the way people feel if they feel they've seen God."[125]

What started life as a semi-sequel to *Close Encounters* (what if one of those little creatures got off the mothership and stayed on Earth for a while?) turned into an intimate and deeply personal Spielberg film about a young boy in a suburban house rocked by divorce, lonely and scared, who is visited by a magical being from the stars—and is healed. With the additive powers of screenwriter Melissa Mathison, who was dating Harrison Ford at the time, the story evolved to include a psychic-emotional bond forming between the boy and the alien. As his older brother Michael describes it to a grown-up: *"Elliott feels his feelings."* Spielberg characterized *E.T.* as a "tiny epic" and, at its heart, a love story.

E.T. is the glowing red heart of the Spielberg-Williams collaboration. It distilled everything great about their mutual aesthetics into the purest form—an alchemy of childlike simplicity, theatricality, unabashed emotionalism, grandeur, religious parable and, finally, airborne exultation. Both men were at the peak of their powers and completely in sync with each other, and the bond in the story doubled as a beautiful metaphor for their own: *John felt Steven's feelings.* As Spielberg himself said, "John Williams *is* E.T."[126] Where else did this man with his strange gifts come from if not the stars? This wise, gentle being who reveals almost nothing about himself, but makes planets spin and touches peoples' hearts just by waving his hands. This profound channeler and director of emotions, who through some mystery can make us feel fear, or cause us to weep.

John knew the film was something special the first time he saw it. "I can always tell when John is happy," Spielberg said, "because we don't have a lot of musical discussions. He already has themes running through his mind."[127] It was already powerful *without* music, John said, "but obviously very empty."[128] "It sets the most magical story in the most mundane of circumstances: the suburbs, a broken marriage, interesting kids. This little creature hidden in the bedroom, falling in love with these young Earthlings and vice versa—an unbelievable story told so skillfully, so expertly, that you buy it completely."[129] It was indeed a tiny epic, a suburban fairy tale mostly taking place inside an ordinary middle-class house or in the forest just beyond, filled with rich homelife bric-a-brac and texture, visually told from a child's point of view. John, who spent three months composing the music, approached it as such: his score was pure fairy tale, a vividly descriptive tone poem where a brief shot of a rabbit is accompanied by a quizzical oboe line, where the fluttering of a harp accents a reading of *Peter Pan and Tinkerbell*. The orchestra swoons right alongside a drowsy Elliott and E.T., and when they get drunk, so does the music. From the very first frame, so much of the story's intention is communicated with music: wordless images of waddling creatures exploring the forest fauna, when touched by John, become mystical and wondrous. His adagio pipe organ chords turn this ordinary environment into an enchanted forest and an imposing cathedral (*religioso* was his direction to musicians), and the musical mood establishes the benevolence of the extraterrestrials just as it identifies the not-quite-evil threat of the faceless men who suddenly arrive in their trucks. *Without* score, the opening sequence is creepy but emotionally opaque. In John's hands, it is the overture to a spiritual odyssey.

E.T. was the score John would always cite to illustrate his masterful method of breadcrumbing a theme. Once he had sculpted his main "flying" theme—a constantly reaching lullaby melody that rides a steady harmonic surge—he began dropping hints and pieces of it, much like Elliott's Reese's Pieces, in choice moments throughout the film. The enigmatic flute call heard at the very beginning of the film is a related fragment, but open-ended and unresolved. "I first wrote the clarion call," John said of this motif, which also closes the film. "The clarion call had to do with a little boy looking out of a window, and he's trying to make contact with a creature from the other world. I want to compose first a signal, not a melody. The clarion call is the basis for the *E.T.* theme."[130] Pieces of this theme are eked out as E.T. slowly reveals his telekinetic powers and his desire to "phone home," as his and Elliott's spiritual link intensifies, and more still as he constructs a crude communication machine. And then, finally, with this pregnancy of perhaps unconscious anticipation, the melody euphorically explodes when E.T. causes Elliott's bike to lift off and fly across the face of the moon. "You hear three notes of it, then six notes of it, then seven notes of it," said John, "so you're kind of getting to know it. But when the bicycle takes off and you hear all twelve notes of the melody, it's a wonderful sense of rightness of the arrival, the delivery of something that has been fated. We haven't drifted into this—it's been *decreed* somehow."[131] If there was a recurring, defining trait in all of John's disparate music for the movies, it was this sense of *lift*. "I think that's who he is," said Constantine Kitsopoulos, who would conduct many of John's scores live to picture. "When there's a moment that requires a lift, often what happens right before it is a harmonic tension that leads to a resolution. It's not a dominant-tonic resolution that says 'here's the cadence.' It lands on a harmony, and you wonder where it could go, and then there's a resolution." With resolution comes euphoria—something rare in modern cinema, argued Kitsopoulos, who compared the technique to Beethoven: "I get my students to look at the opening of the Beethoven Seventh; we're used to it, but you always have to look at it in the context of surprise at the premiere. The first time you see those bicycles take off in *E.T.*, it's mind-blowing."[132]

But the *E.T.* theme is really a love theme, explained John: "It's not sensual in the way a love theme would be, but it develops as their relationship develops. It starts with a few notes, they look at each other a little bit uncertain. And it grows and becomes more confident, and more lyrical as E.T. begins to communicate with the boy. At the end it's kind of a full-blown sort of operatic aria when E.T. goes away." John likened it to "a moment in opera when two lovers are being separated. I build to that kind of musical denouement."[133] Spielberg agreed that the last 15 minutes of *E.T.* was close to an opera, "because of John Williams' contribution."¹³⁴ John would occasionally worry about a modulation in the music that felt too emotionally punchy, too manipulative. "It's shameless," he worried to Spielberg. "Will we get away with it?" Spielberg's answer: "Movies *are* shameless."

The score's other themes almost all relate to the central melody.†† An active quest motif, with similar intervals but a feeling of anxious determination, is first heard when Elliott leaves his candy-coated bait for the wrinkled creature who terrified him the night before, and it returns on urgent brass in their breathless bicycle escapades. John wrote a separate friendship theme for E.T. and Elliott that opens with the same vaulting fifth but is more intimate and internal, expressed ever so delicately on solo harp as their love story begins, and on solo oboe when Elliott declares: "I'm keeping him." There's also a rat-a-tat "bad guy" theme for the mysterious Keys and his fellow scientific G-men, which sounds menacing early on but never outright *mean* or predatory. When the motif gets handed to a solo flute as the men monitor Elliott's conversation from inside a surveillance van, it's increasingly clear they are just grown-up children themselves, longing for their own close encounter. The gloomy organ theme, which initially lent a strangely religious majesty to the image of E.T. walking in the woods, comes back and haunts the moment when E.T. begins to grow weak, and again when he dies. When the story crescendoes toward a death and resurrection, the so-far vaguely Christlike allegory is no longer vague. (Spielberg chafed at the suggestion, insisting he was a good Jewish boy.¹³⁵) On boyish solo oboe, the flying theme pleads along with Elliott for E.T. to "*stay with me*," and the orchestra keens at his passing—strings wilting with sorrow as Elliott and his family look on helplessly. Elliott's tearful parting words are scored with heartbroken affection, a reprise of the love theme on celeste and crying oboe—and the rapturous moment when E.T. comes back to life warrants a springing fountain of the flying theme.

John recorded *E.T.* at MGM in late March 1982. He wanted to record in Boston, but the BSO's merciless schedule simply didn't allow it.¹³⁶ The L.A. session players took a brief hiatus during the scoring dates for the Academy Awards ceremony, where John's old-fashioned score for *Raiders* lost to the newfangled, anachronistic synth tunes in *Chariots of Fire*. *E.T.* culminates in a tour de force set piece where Elliott and Michael sneak E.T. out of their house in a stolen van, meet Michael's buddies in the park, and commence a daring bicycle journey to the forest while pursued by armed government men, climaxing with another magical escape by air. The lengthy cue John composed was chock full of beats and sync points—not only emotional and comedic ones, but musical acknowledgments of the bicycles swooping down hills and other kinetic hits. As legend has it, John tried this 15-minute cue with the orchestra a few times, but just couldn't get it perfectly synchronized with every bit of choreography—so Spielberg stopped the projector and told John just to play it freely, organically feeling the tempo, and offered to recut the sequence to match the music. David Newman, who was playing in the violin section that day, had a different take on this oft-recounted

---

†† Now, it wasn't just *sequels* where John's scores were in communication with each other: a trick-or-treater dressed as Yoda in *E.T.* gave him the chance to cameo one of his musical characters from a separate universe.

story: "It seemed more for show to me," Newman said. "And then the benevolent Spielberg shut off the film and said, 'Just do it.' I mean, it's not like a really fast piece of music. There was much harder stuff to sync in the movie—it was just the most important cue. It's better to play it over and over and over and over for the director so they get used to it." Newman added: "What I know now, looking back, is that I think John was very calculating about everything he did. I don't think he did anything without some sort of calculation for it. But that is simply my opinion, only anecdotally."[137]

There was certainly plenty of *musical* calculation going on. After this heart-stopping action came the tear-jerking goodbyes and E.T.'s ship lifting off and leaving a rainbow in its wake. The issue of synchronization was not just a logistical one for John; he recognized it as utterly critical for the audience's relationship to the film: "What people can't possibly realize is the amount of ... kinetic detail that is put into film music. They would only understand it if you took it away.

> Every phrase—not only is the length of it important, but the loudness of it, the relative dynamic of it, or softness of it, the kind of push and shove thing that it has. . . . The ship goes up, and it goes up to a certain point, and then it whooshes across the sky and becomes a rainbow, and does something else. I mean, that's one little event that maybe is, I don't know, ten seconds at the end of a whole reel of music that's 10 minutes long. But if the orchestra builds just in the right way, and just has a *luft*‡‡ as the spaceship goes off, and then shifts into another gear as it whooshes off to the left and becomes the rainbow, the sequence is successful. But if I miscue it, if the orchestra's late on the takeoff and early on the whoosh across, the eye goes crazy. The eye and the ear don't match. But once it's exactly in sync, the viewer can sit back and listen and enjoy the experience—and not even realize that the ear has been manipulated as precisely as the eye has been.[138]

Having written such a grand and passionate finale, John decided to strip everything back and score the end credits with a solo piano rendition of his flying theme. Ralph Grierson remembered John popping by the scoring stage for another movie one day and asking if he was available for *E.T.* "Oh, great!" John said when Grierson confirmed he was—"I'll write something for you." Two weeks later, Grierson showed up on the scoring stage, he recalled, "and I'm looking through the book—and there is this piece of music that looks really difficult, which is the end credit piano solo. And so every day I'm like, *Oh shit*, you know—it's like, *This may be the time that I don't make it*."[139] But Grierson succeeded, amply, and the solo piano reprise was a virtuosic showpiece.

Educated listeners have noted the taste of Howard Hanson in *E.T.* The film's editor, Carol Littleton—who was on loan to Spielberg while Michael Kahn was concurrently editing *Poltergeist*—used the fast final movement from Hanson's second symphony for

---

‡‡ The pause right before a downbeat.

the boys taking off on their bikes and the adagio movement for the final goodbye. She also used the largo movement from Shostakovich's sixth symphony for the opening sequence in the forest.[140] No one tried to hide these ingredients; Spielberg told *American Cinematographer* about the temp selections in an interview: "We were very successful in putting some of our images to music and then taking the music out so Johnny Williams could have a fair shot at imagining his own themes."[141] The terroir of these classical works remained in the final dish, "but it's innovative," composer John Powell insists: "Because nobody else sounds like that. If you look at *E.T.*, it's like, okay, you can see there's a bit of Howard Hanson, and there's a bit of this and there's a bit of that. But fuck it! As a whole, *nothing* else could be that score. So I can't see that as anything other than just unique and innovation in itself."[142] Is it sacrilege to suggest that John Williams did Howard Hanson better than *Howard Hanson*? (Just one man's thought.)

On its surface, there was something so unapologetically direct and literal about the scoring of *E.T.*—but John's musical commentary was so sophisticated, so *right*, that it vibrated in perfect harmony with Spielberg's visual fantasia and only added depth and insight. This was emotional ballet, music finely choreographed to each feeling and movement of the characters. It was the current of melancholy and the painful ache of loving and losing that runs under the entire film, and it was the pixie dust that makes the bicycles—and the movie itself—levitate into the night sky. Structurally, the score obviously could not follow sonata form—but in terms of its sophistication, musical challenge, thematic development, and sweep, it was, for all intents and purposes, a *symphony*. The French conductor Stéphane Denève, who was the same age as Elliott when the film came out and who wept when he saw it, later studied the score in depth. "Following so many cues, especially in action scenes, it *should* sound like cartoon music," Denève marveled, "like following the action and just building the suspense.

> But that's the mystery, and I think what makes his music *so* strong and so special, is that he never—without even thinking about it, I think—forgets the inner logic of the scenes and of the harmony behind it. When I studied *E.T.,* I was amazed that it was very much a kind of symphonic work, just happening to follow some streamlines.[143]

John was sweating out his third season with the Pops when *E.T.* opened and summarily destroyed every box office record that Spielberg and Lucas had previously set. It reigned at the top for more than a decade. Thanks in enormous part to John's music, the film played audiences like a fiddle and beckoned them to keep coming back for more. When the score won John his fourth Academy Award, he simply thanked the director and the local musicians who had brought the music to life.[144]

E.T. and *Close Encounters* were spiritual brothers, and John usually said that one or the other was his own favorite score—but that *E.T.* was the film he most enjoyed scoring.[145] Looking back on his collaborations with Spielberg decades later, John said: "I think maybe it's his masterpiece."[146] The director felt the same feelings. "John's score to the movie *E.T.* is unlike any of his others," Spielberg wrote in 1982. "It is soothing and benign. It is scary and suspenseful and, toward the climax, downright operatic. For me, this is John Williams' best work for the movies."[147] Asked in 2003 what he would like to be remembered for, John said it would probably be *Star Wars*—"but *E.T.* would mean even more."[148]

* * *

From the ecstatic highs of that experience, John came smack down to earth for his next picture. At one point, Martin Ritt was going to direct a film called *Monsignore*, based on a novel by the French writer Jack-Alain Léger about the corruption and secret life of a Catholic priest in Rome. Ritt described it as "a pragmatic look at the Vatican" in 1979, "very theatrical and possibly very commercial," and he even traveled to Rome to scout locations, with plans to begin shooting in the summer of 1980.[149] Perhaps Ritt's early involvement explains why John took the assignment—because nothing in the movie does. Ultimately *Monsignor* (as the title was now spelled) was directed by Frank Perry and produced by Frank Yablans, the duo behind the ridiculed *Mommie Dearest*. The film offered Christopher Reeve a chance to chip away at his Superman image and play an enterprising priest whose background as an army chaplain allows him to covertly collaborate with the Mafia, running a racket to profit the Vatican. Father Flaherty has an affair with a postulant nun named Clara, played by Geneviève Bujold, who only knows him as an American army man but learns his priestly identity during a ceremony with the Pope. The film clearly wanted to be *The Godfather* of clergy movies, but it was so weakly scripted, acted, and directed that it tripped on its own cassock and face-planted into a baptistry of soapy clichés. John's score earned him his one and only Razzie nomination—guilt by association. "The self-serious pic teeters on the brink of being an all-out hoot through much of its running time," *Variety* wrote. "Williams' score is okay, but not one of his major achievements."[150] Still, a lot of critics singled out the score as one of the film's only positive attributes, even as many of them laughed at the music's seriousness and heft in light of the film's inert gas. "[Perry] wanted to do a film with spectacle and tone, but all he's managed is parody," wrote the *Baltimore Evening Sun*'s Lou Cedrone.[151] Exhibit A was a scene where Clara finds out who Flaherty really is, extravagantly accompanied by an original liturgical mass for orchestra, church organ, and a choir shouting "Gloria!" "Chance brings them to the same papal ceremony, and uncool Clara starts a traffic jam in the center aisle of the cathedral by staring in prolonged amazement at Flaherty in his priestly uniform," wrote the *Washington Post*'s Gary Arnold. "One of the funniest recognition scenes in theatrical history, it's immeasurably enhanced by the solemnity of the occasion, a wittily timed choral selection orchestrated in the background by John Williams and the exquisite back-and-forth of Bujold's accusing gawk and Reeve's averted glance."[152]

Taken on its own, "Gloria" was a majestic—if just a *little* overwrought—faux church anthem. John was clearly trying his damnedest to save this wayward soul. He wrote the score quickly after wrapping the 1982 Pops season, and he actually recycled a "comedy overture" he had originally intended as a piece for the Pops, using it to accompany Flaherty and his American partner-in-crime as they drive around

Italy.[153] John's main tune for *Monsignor* had a glimmer of *The Godfather* theme by Nino Rota—a melancholy waltz for solo trumpet with a rich Sicilian flavor. The tune represented "the futility, sadness, and great conflict that characterizes the relationship of Flaherty and Clara," John explained.[154] It opens the film, sung over an inquisitive harpsichord figure (throwing back to the days of *Family Plot* and *Eiger Sanction*), then taken up by harpsichord and cellos. The theme resurfaces much later, slowly and sensually, when Flaherty and Clara make hungry eyes at each other, get naked, and fall in love. It regrettably disappears with Clara's character with plenty of running time remaining, but waltzes back in for the end credits in a grand finale with a stunning horn pulse motif as the waltz crescendoes to a close. When Flaherty is first called to the Vatican, John accompanied his awe with a brief but mighty French horn melody and a haze of penitent string chords. The melody from "Gloria" quietly attends Flaherty as he picks olives and talks to an elder priest, Santoni, in the guise of a delicate and uplifting adagio—a highlight in a sumptuous score full of highlights. The music was recorded in London in August, and John recorded a separate soundtrack LP in October. He was able to milk the experience further by programming "Gloria" in concert with the Pops beginning in the summer of 1983—but this score, which immediately followed the glorious *E.T.*, was quickly forgotten. In many ways, the music for *Monsignor* was just as *religioso* as *E.T.*, but its almost instant obscurity proved just how important the accompanying celluloid liturgy was for making proselytes.

John tentatively agreed to score another rotten egg: Franklin Schaffner's *Yes, Giorgio*, a romantic comedy starring opera star Luciano Pavarotti in his film debut. Scenes were even shot at Hatch Shell in Boston, with 100,000 "extras" enjoying a free concert in the summer of 1981.[155] But neither John nor the Pops could make the time to participate, so Emerson Buckley—Pavarotti's personal baton—conducted The Opera Company of Boston Orchestra for the sequence. In the end, John only composed one song for the film: "If We Were in Love," with lyrics by the Bergmans—the closest thing to musical theater he had done since *Thomas and the King*. Pavarotti performed the extroverted pop aria in the film, and an instrumental version sat on the soundtrack, alongside a parade of classical arias and a score by Welsh composer Michael J. Lewis. A TV special, *Pavarotti and Friends*, aired in March 1982, featuring footage of the tenor rehearsing the song and chatting with John at the piano. *Yes, Giorgio* opened in September and was roundly flayed by critics and ignored by audiences. *Variety* found John's song "hokey but rather lovely,"[156] while Janet Maslin described it as a "painfully lighthearted new ballad."[157] John included the instrumental on his next Pops album, *Aisle Seat*, which also featured music from *E.T.*, *Raiders*, and film work by other composers.

The *New York Times* gave *Aisle Seat* good marks in an article that also took stock of the growing Pops catalogue under John's leadership, and of his scoring work overall. The reviewer, Theodore W. Libbey, Jr., called him the "pre-eminent soundtracker of our day," and attributed John's success to "one of the most acute compositional talents in the business."

It has been rightly pointed out that Mr. Williams is an eclectic, that his muse borrows frequently from the works of well known composers. What has not been pointed out as often is that Mr. Williams has flair, inventiveness and a genuine melodic gift, and that his music can be surpassingly effective in its evocation of mood. It succeeds, sometimes with surprising eloquence, in conveying the sense of wonder and excitement at the heart of today's high-budget, high-tech box office blockbusters.[158]

* * *

"I have at least one more space film to do," John said in August 1982. "But beyond that I can't say."[159]

There was never any doubt that John would score *Return of the Jedi*, which closed the *Star Wars* trilogy and a roller-coaster chapter of his career. He involved himself early, when it was still called *Revenge of the Jedi*, making a trip up north in the fall of 1981 to listen to Japanese taiko drummers in the ILM parking lot along with George Lucas and Lionel Newman; Lucas needed music for the Ewok drummers at the film's celebration finale ahead of shooting, and was considering taiko as a possible style. In January 1982, John recorded a spacey baroque source piece for Lucas to use on set in a scene at Jabba's palace.[160]

Once again, Lucas abstained from directing. Several deputies were considered, and one of the strongest—and strangest—candidates was David Lynch. The surrealist filmmaker had most recently made *The Elephant Man*, a surprising success with eight major Oscar nominations. Lynch was offered the *Jedi* job—and took it—but then panicked and backed out. "David told me he didn't want to do the picture because he didn't want John Williams," said Kazanjian. "I was stunned." The other reason Lynch gave Kazanjian was that he didn't want to work with Ben Burtt; he had his own sound guy. But most likely, the producer surmised, it was because "he felt that George Lucas was going to be looking over his shoulder."[161] Instead, the job fell to Welsh director Richard Marquand, a journeyman hired off the strength of his 1981 wartime romance, *Eye of the Needle*. But John's primary collaborator continued to be Lucas, who was currently going through a heart-crushing divorce. For its critics, *Jedi* was the nadir of the original trilogy, a cash-in filled with shameless toy marketing—namely the Ewoks—and tired performances. Even some of its participants agreed. "I thought it was the weakest one," said Carrie Fisher. "I was glad to see that costume for the last time," said Ford. "I don't think it had a very successful ending, with that teddy bear picnic."[162]

But looking beyond its "teddy bear" antics, *Jedi* was at once the grossest *and* most soulful of the three acts. It begins with an enormous, oozing space slug capturing Princess Leia and putting her in chains and a metal bikini, and it ends with Luke Skywalker in a battle for his very soul. It is deliciously haunted by Emperor Palpatine, a terrifying, cackling agent of the devil who somehow makes Darth Vader seem sympathetic. The story was certainly the stuff of opera, and John rose to the material's grandest intentions, composing a score that provided an emotionally weighty and satisfying coda to the series (albeit a temporary one). "The jump from *Star Wars* to

Empire to *Jedi* for me was not a great one," John said. "It felt like one piece, one continual experience." For Lucas, the voluminous music John wrote for the series was "the underpinning, a grease that each movie slides along on, as well as a glue that holds it together so that you can follow it. There's always been a scene or a moment in which the music connects so strongly with the visual that it sends shivers up my spine every time I see it."[163] Where Spielberg was a hyperactive film music geek who spoke about melody and musical emotion with gusto, Lucas was a car and tech nerd whose vocabulary on the subject was much smaller. For Lucas, it was high praise to say that John was "right up there with Buddy Holly and the Drifters."[164] "I think George is a more quiet person with Johnny," Kazanjian said. "Oftentimes they'd get into discussions about the future, technology. I was there for some of that. Although similar in age, Steven acts like he's 15, 20 years younger. He's more excitable, he's more articulate, he talks faster, he thinks faster, he directs faster. And Johnny accommodates that. With George, they both kind of slow down."[165]

John spotted the film with Lucas in November 1982. Burtt suggested leaving music out of the speeder bike chase through the forests of Endor, because it would be more intense "if we surprised the audience with just a point-of-view reality of visceral bike sounds," Burtt argued. "I felt it was unnecessary to have music tell the audience that it was exciting. Johnny Williams agreed, so George threw up his hands and said, 'Okay, if you guys say so.'" The film's special effects were behind schedule, so Lucas sent John what reels were finished, one or two at a time, and John scored it piecemeal.[166] As usual, Newman was John's second pair of ears at the spotting and scoring sessions—and for this score, yet another Newman was brought into the fold: 27-year-old Thomas Newman, Alfred's youngest son. "He threw me a bone," Newman said. "I mean, *he* would not put it that way." Newman orchestrated one pivotal cue—when Darth Vader dies. "It was an amazing thing to do," Newman said, "but in the end his sketches are so complete, you find yourself just saying, 'Okay, here's where he writes *tuba*, and here's where I'm going to orchestrate tuba.'"[167] "My debt to the elder Newmans, Alfred and Lionel, is very great," John said.[168]

John organically built on the style he had established in the first two films, finding novel ways of developing old melodies and giving themes to the film's major new characters. From the moment of Vader's arrival on the new Death Star, the music in *Jedi*, while retaining some of its bombast and *Buck Rogers* "popcorn" villainy, was more mature and subtly sinister. The opening shot mirrored that of *Star Wars*—a Star Destroyer looming overhead—but this time it was set to mysterious high strings and ghostly melody fragments. The Imperial March is teased in gloomy harmonies before the brass bay it out in full force, and the dark tune commingles with an elegant, swirling new motif as Vader walks with his cowering subordinate. Vader's theme is still mighty in this score—grandly unfurled when he welcomes the Emperor to the new Death Star—but it evolves in sophisticated and emotionally complicated ways. When Yoda confirms Vader's paternity to Luke, a lone French horn sings a sad variation. It plays quietly against the Force theme when Luke approaches Endor and he and Vader sense each other's presence, and again as Luke appeals to his father's goodness before their audience with Vader's master. When that goodness finally breaks free and Vader sacrifices himself to save Luke from the Emperor, Vader's theme is redeemed. Weakened and strained as Anakin/Vader looks at Luke with his own eyes, it breathes its last on solo horn and finally on a lone, delicate harp. A tune that once struck fear into the hearts of the galaxy ultimately becomes surprisingly, vulnerably beautiful.

John conjured pure evil with his theme for Emperor Palpatine—a dark, quasi-Gregorian chant for wordless male choir. The melody bore some relation to Vader's theme with its leaping minor intervals, but where Vader's theme is often about military might, the Emperor's is more pagan and liturgical: it is the hate he tries to seduce Luke with, the moral rot at his core. The chant haunts the Emperor's conversations with Vader about his plans for Luke, then underscores their lengthy battle of wills inside the royal chamber. It taunts Luke with the revelation of the Emperor's cunning trap, then explodes in brassy crescendo when Luke gives in and fights his father—competing with the Force theme, much like Obi-Wan's influence is competing with the Emperor's for Luke's fate. When Vader baits his son, threatening to seduce Leia to the dark side, Luke lashes out with a terrified fury, and those same male voices now sing a new song—a heartbreaking, fiery lament. Brass and chorus combine forces as the Emperor assaults Luke with Force lightning and his theme rises and rises with intensity ... but is ultimately overpowered by the stalwart Force theme as Vader turns on his master.

The film's initial villain, Jabba the Hutt, has a Prokofiev-like theme that's appropriately fat and slimy. His melody rises and falls in the low register of a tuba, grotesque and slightly comic at first, then more sinister as he interrupts Han and Leia's reunion and summons Leia to his icky fold. John's theme for the Ewoks reflected their quirky personality: accompanied by jungle percussion and often performed on pan flute and high woodwinds, it appears with the introduction of Wicket—and although it's cute and cuddly at the outset, it reveals a resourcefulness and bravery that goes into action with militarized variations during the Battle of Endor, a battle that toggles between spirited hijinks against the Empire and tragic Ewok casualties; John eulogized the latter with a pained string motif.

He introduced a new theme for Luke and Leia—who we learn are brother and sister—a warm, lyrical melody with an undercurrent of sadness. In its shape, the tune is a sister to Luke's theme, only slower and more ruminative. Princess Leia's original theme makes a few appearances, as when Obi-Wan reveals their sibling relationship to Luke; when Luke timidly shares this information with Leia, the Force theme plays hesitantly over quivering strings, and their new sibling theme blossoms on celli against a slightly mystical figure as she realizes: "Somehow I've always known." When the Empire is defeated, and Leia finally tells Han about being Luke's sister, the two themes for the two men in her life play together again ... only this time with sweet relief. The saga's oldest themes, for Luke and the Force, are a constant presence in variations of heroism and sadness and the constant call to virtue. Yoda's theme returns for Luke's brief visit to his Jedi master—this time in a sadder, weaker form to match the ancient Jedi's dying state. John sends Yoda off with Taps-like French horn and an aching lament for strings. This moment is symbolic of the *Jedi* score overall, which has a strong sense of familiarity as well as finality. Old friends die, character arcs come to an end. The dark side is at its darkest, and even the action has a weariness to it. John took his themes to the edge of the abyss—but in the end, good triumphs over evil.

John wrote an Ewok celebration song for the finale and his son Joe wrote the lyrics, which Burtt then translated into "Ewokese." (At one point, Lucas considered commissioning a song from the band Toto[169]—which Joe would actually join a few years later as their new lead singer.) This upbeat folk anthem was catchy and triumphant... and just a little bit silly... with a choir singing nonsense words ("Yub Nub!"), accentuated by shots of the cuddly warriors using beheaded Stormtrooper helmets as percussion; Lucas was sufficiently embarrassed by it to have it later replaced. One of the stranger source cues John ever wrote was "Lapti Nek," a funky disco number performed by Jabba's house band and sung by a puppet. The English lyrics were also written by Joe, who was coming into his own as a songwriter, having released his debut pop album in 1982—John and Joe even appeared together on *The Today Show* that June—and the vocal was performed by Michelle Gruska, sister of Jenny's new husband, Jay Gruska.[§§]

The LSO recorded John's Act Three score in January 1983. Ian McDiarmid, who played the Emperor, came to one of the sessions at Abbey Road and "at one particular point," the Scottish actor said, "it was just the music and the actors involved, with no dialogue, and I said to George, 'God, you know, it reminds me of a silent movie.' And he said, 'Well, in many ways it is.' And I knew exactly what he meant, that the dialogue is not of paramount importance."[170] Lucas kept snipping the film down even after the score was recorded, which meant Wannberg had to snip the music. "George takes things out," said Kazanjian. "Steven, I'm sure, will give the guy a break."[171] John wrote a cue for Luke building his new lightsaber and hearing Vader's voice, but the scene was dropped. Recuts to the climactic lightsaber duel at one point sacrificed a stunning musical transition, and Kazanjian begged Wannberg to shift the cue over just a little so they could retain the passage.[172] Wannberg was also battling Burtt, whose spaceship sounds and crackling lightsabers kept drowning out John's music. "The music editor's job is to save the music, so to speak," said Wannberg. "Music is kind of a mystery to a lot of people. They don't know how to handle it. And we had some pretty good, friendly fights over the concept of music versus sound effects."[173] Burtt "always felt that his sound was covered up," said Kazanjian. "Ultimately, if you were asking George, George would say music over sound if there was a conflict. The boss would say: 'We're going with John.'"[174]

* * *

When *Jedi* came out in May 1983, it was the closing of a circle. Lucas was exhausted, and he would not return to the Skywalker universe for more than a decade. John put the Jabba and Ewok themes in rotation in his Pops concerts, but this third score slid

---

[§§] For the film itself, Lucas opted to use the pre-recorded vocals by the film's sound department assistant, Annie Arbogast. (Rinzler, *The Making of Return of the Jedi*.)

a little further into the cultural mist than the first two. (He did nickname his Boston assistant, Nancy Knutsen, "my little Ewok."[175]) The soundtrack album—which featured an illustration of Lucas's hands holding a blue lightsaber[176]—was released on LP, cassette, and the novel compact disc, but it sold less copies than either *Star Wars* or *Empire*. John's score was nominated for an Academy Award the following spring, but lost to Bill Conti's *The Right Stuff*.

So much had changed in the past six years. John had now scored the five highest-grossing films in history, and he was the most famous and successful film composer in the world—celebrated by the National Association of Theatre Owners as "the first billion-dollar musical composer of the cinema."[177] In February 1983, Jenny gave John his first grandchild: a girl named Barbara.

John ended speculation about his future with the Pops by signing a five-year, "evergreen" contract that was a little more forgiving on his schedule. "You may find it hard to believe," he told the orchestra, gathered to rehearse for their Christmas concert in December 1982, "but I find you collectively irresistible."[178] He had mostly adjusted to the demands of the job and the publicity that came with it, and had improved his control and technique as a conductor. "I don't want to be complacent about it, about my own appointment, or about the orchestra's success, about the audience's connection to the Pops," he said. "Complacency is something we don't want. And I want to be here as long as it's working well. It's not a kind of ego trip for me.... It's something that I want to do if it's a healthy thing for all concerned."[179] He continued to wrestle with how much of his own music to program in Pops concerts, but Susan Dangel's young daughter said something incisive one day. "She'd be watching the shows or watching the editing," the *Evening at Pops* producer recalled, "and out of a little voice came: 'Did you ever notice he's only really happy when he's playing his own music?'"[180]

John's status as both a composer and conductor was growing by the day—and although the musicians in Boston generally liked him, a thoughtless hiss was going to light the fuse for one of his biggest and only public explosions. He had triumphed to become the world's greatest film composer ... but many in the classical world still did not respect him (Figure 9.3).

Figure 9.3. John and Ewoks (Photographer unknown, Courtesy of John Williams).

PART II
TANGLEWOOD

I think the high place in American musical life is Tanglewood. This is a sort of Vatican.

—**John Williams**[1]

10
Cadillac of the Skies, 1983–1987

> *To them, it's playtime—but to me it's serious.*
> —John Williams[1]

John spent the summer of 1983 in another merciless grind at the Pops—conducting seven shows a week for 12 weeks, taping multiple concerts for PBS, and recording three new albums. Only one rehearsal was allotted for each performance. "When I see Seiji get four rehearsals for a program of one concerto and one symphony," John said, "I think: *If I could only have half that!*"[2]

But no amount of rehearsal time could save John from the scorn of Martin Bernheimer, the curmudgeonly critic for the *Los Angeles Times*, who wrote a scathing review of John's concert that winter with the Los Angeles Philharmonic. Ernest Fleischmann, the orchestra's czar whose faith in John after *Star Wars* helped launch his conducting career, invited John to make his first podium appearance at the city's sacred temple of art, the Dorothy Chandler Pavilion (where just a few months earlier John picked up his Oscar for *E.T.*). Bernheimer wouldn't have it: "[Why] entrust a presumably serious winter-season program to John Williams, an amiable musician whose claims to fame and fortune are predicated on movie-score bombast and Boston Pops bagatelles?" he oozed. "Why would anyone think that what is good for the Hollywood Bowl goose is good for the Music Center gander? Why would the Philharmonic, which has virtually abandoned prime-time exploration of important modern music, squander a precious third of a program on the West Coast premiere of Williams' gnarled, innocuous Violin Concerto anno 1974?" Bernheimer went on to complain about how the *hoi polloi* who came to the concert applauded after every movement ("it was one of those nights"), and to describe the conductor as an "efficient musical traffic cop, despite a disconcerting tendency to gild the expressive lily with excessive facial choreography." He skewered the violin concerto's "frantic, patently ungrateful, bravura fiddling, sometimes offset by listless orchestral doodling and noodling," and shamelessly admitted that he left at intermission, before John conducted *The Planets* suite by Holst.[3] Incredibly, Bernheimer was objecting to John's very *person*—there wasn't a single piece of his film music on the program.

The background to this episode was that the LA Phil was actively looking for its next music director, and Fleischmann was auditioning potential candidates with guest conducting concerts. That was not the case here, John insisted: "I wouldn't have had the breadth of repertoire. He knew that. He would know that that was not a job for me."

The critic must have assumed John was under consideration for the job, "and I think Bernheimer's idea was to put an end to that thing, to stop it right now."[4] In reality, Fleischmann's list of potential candidates included everyone from Leonard Bernstein to Leonard Slatkin; John's name was not on it.[5] Bernheimer was notoriously nasty, and he had been a vocal critic of former music director Zubin Mehta. "Bernheimer is envious," Fleischmann once said flatly. "He's a failed conductor, and Zubin is a big success, and they're the same age."[6] *Times* readers sent in a stack of letters complaining about the rude, vitriolic review—which prompted the critic to double down in another screed. "I object," he huffed, "to our fine orchestra playing so much tired, candy-coated, third-rate, pre-digested music when so much lively, adventurous, challenging, second-rate music remains ignored."[7] This stirred an even *stronger* clapback from readers, like Richard Friday in Woodland Hills: "I must say I have never read a more self-indulgent, infantile piece of snob journalism."[8] Only one letter was printed in solidarity: "God bless Martin Bernheimer," wrote Mark Kent Bridgeford in Van Nuys. "The music of John Williams merits no credibility outside the comic-book social circle."[9]

The gulf between "serious" connoisseurs of orchestral music and the general public remained remarkably deep. Somehow, John took it in stride.

His egoless cool came in handy again in March 1984, when Frank Sinatra asked John to conduct the New York Philharmonic in an all-star, black-tie concert at Radio City Music Hall. Diana Ross and Luciano Pavarotti also performed, and the event raised 3.5 million dollars for the Sloan-Kettering Memorial Cancer Center.[10] The rehearsal for the 8 p.m. performance ended around 5 p.m., and as the musicians were dismissed for dinner, the orchestra manager came over to John and said, "Frank wants to see you right away in his room." John duly went to Sinatra's dressing room, and the blue-eyed crooner said: "John, you know the last tune we did?"

"Yes, Frank."

"Tonight it has to be a half tone lower."

"Well, Frank, it's 5 o'clock. Everyone's gone. You've got 85 musicians—they all have separate sheets. It's going to be impossible to transpose that down."

Sinatra shook his head, and "he looked at me with these *assassin* eyes," John recalled, and said: "John, you don't understand. *Tonight it has to be a half tone lower.*"

John was terrified, and he explained his predicament to the orchestra manager—who jumped into action and phoned three men who worked in the library at the Metropolitan Orchestra, who hastily took down the whole song and re-transposed it on the spot. The concert went off without a hitch, and by the end of the evening Sinatra was in tears of joy when representatives from Sloan-Kettering draped him with a gold medal. John laughed at the memory. "He couldn't be sweeter," John said of the singer he had known since his boyhood, the director who hired him to score *None But the Brave* in 1965. "When I did the movie for him, he was dear, sending presents and all this stuff. But he could be *terrifying*." There was "a sense of Mafia power in the room which I think any *dolt* would pick up," John said. "*This* dolt picked it up."[11]

* * *

Spielberg had gone through hell producing *Twilight Zone: The Movie*. Actor Vic Morrow and two Vietnamese children were killed by a crashing helicopter, on camera, in a stunt gone horrifically wrong. It happened under the watch of director John Landis, who neglected child labor laws and set safety practices—but Spielberg suffered the psychic trauma and was caught up in a five-year investigation against Landis and his associates for involuntary manslaughter. Coming on the heels of *E.T.*, Spielberg described this period as "a mixture of ecstasy and grief. It's made me grow up a little more."[12] He distanced himself from Landis and abandoned the darker chapter he had planned to direct for the anthology film, instead making the saccharine, danger-free story, "Kick the Can." And, for the first time since *The Sugarland Express*, Spielberg collaborated with a composer other than John: Jerry Goldsmith, with whom he had also worked closely on *Poltergeist*.* Goldsmith was just a few years older than John, and their careers ran on closely parallel tracks; they were friendly rivals who often socialized at dinner parties, playing four-hand piano together for the other guests. Goldsmith was a genius at dramaturgy and musical world-building; he was an expert tunesmith and could wield a classical orchestra as well as anyone, but he also favored more idiosyncratic instrumentation and dove headlong into electronics. There was, and continues to be, a lively debate among film score fans about whether Goldsmith or Williams was the greatest of all time, but one major handicap was that Goldsmith rarely got the kind of plum assignments or major hits or Midas filmmakers that John did. Spielberg liked to say: "If you're looking for a composer, get John Williams. If you can't get John Williams, get Jerry Goldsmith. And if you can't get Jerry Goldsmith, *wait*."[13]

Lucas was reeling from a hell of his own—a painful divorce from his wife Marcia—when the two men saddled up again for *Indiana Jones and the Temple of Doom*, which helps explain why the prequel's storyline went shockingly dark. Set before the events of *Raiders*, *Temple of Doom* threw Jones and his loyal kid sidekick, Short Round (Ke Huy Quan), together with the ditzy Willie (Kate Capshaw) into India, where the quest for a fabled stone stolen from a village takes them into the fiery bowels of a mysterious palace, and the home of an ancient cult which practices human sacrifice, uses cursed blood to control minds, and enslaves children for manual labor. The sight of a bloody, still-pumping heart pulled from a terrified man's chest cavity and the sounds of whipped children screaming pushed the limits of the Motion Picture Association of America's (MPAA) PG rating, and the PG-13 was born as a direct response. But *Doom* was also a funny and emotional rollercoaster ride, with Short Round making pint-sized wisecracks without ever irritating, physical comedy and sight gags as bubbly as any Spielberg ever concocted, and genuine pathos within the hellfire. The movie was a five-course feast for John, and like a master chef, he set about composing a buffet of new character motifs and action set pieces.

---

* *Poltergeist* was officially directed by Tobe Hooper, but it has long been contended that Spielberg was the one calling the shots, and Goldsmith confirmed that Spielberg was his sole collaborator on the score.

John retreated into his Fox studio after Labor Day to begin scoring *Temple of Doom*—although there were two pieces he had to complete before principal photography. Spielberg opened the film with a song-and-dance number in the style of Busby Berkeley, with Capshaw leading a chorus of showgirls in a Mandarin translation of "Anything Goes" by Cole Porter. John wrote the flashy arrangement, a delectable blend of heyday MGM and Chinese seasoning. Spielberg also needed a bloodthirsty chant for the Thuggee cult that he could play back on set; he sent John a lyric in Sanskrit and John convened 30 singers from the Tanglewood Festival Chorus and 10 members of the Pops percussion section—playing African log drum, *prempensua*,[†] *dondos*,[‡] and *gyli*[§]—to record a five-minute piece which John called "Sanskrit Sacrifice."[14]

After that Cole Porter curtain-raiser, John's score continues on with extreme choreography. Strings swirl in time with the lazy Susan used to pass around a large diamond and antidote for the poisoned cocktail that Indy drinks at Club Obi-Wan in Spielberg's most blatant James Bond homage to date. The score segues from suspenseful to comical as the antidote and diamond are kicked around the dance floor under a crowd gone berserk, and John sent the high-stepping "Anything Goes" melody into the fray as the score rolls along with a giant gong Indy uses for cover, pops with the tommy gun fire, and plummets from a window with Indy and Willie. They land in a moving car driven by an adorable kid with blocks on his feet to reach the pedals; Short Round's introduction is accompanied by his plucky, easternized motif—like a more caffeinated cousin of Yoda's theme. A light quote of Indy's familiar tune plays as the trio arrives at the airport for their getaway, but charming heroism turns to worry as a smirking Indy shuts the plane door, which reveals that it belongs to his would-be killer, and then the Raiders March returns triumphantly as the plane takes off into night sky. It was pure crowd-pleasing, leave-the-theater-whistling theatricality, and the entire *Doom* score is finely, explicitly calibrated this way—offering some of John's most sophisticated, tuneful cartooning ever.

He composed an old-fashioned love theme for Willie, more swooning than yearning in nature, as well as a whole cast of exotic motifs for the action-packed adventure—from the syncopated scherzo for their mountain slalom on an inflatable raft, to an atmospheric sitar for the Indian village missing its magical stone and its children, to an intimidating brass fanfare for the imposing mysteries of Pankot Palace. It was an embarrassment of leitmotifs, obviously but expertly synchronized to all of the twists, turns, and sudden drops of this mine car chase of a movie. John had a ball with the love theme, adapting it into a comic ballet between Indy and Willie, horny and haughty in their "nocturnal activities" at the palace: as Indy gets waylaid by brutes trying to murder him in one room, Willie is impatiently awaiting her would-be paramour in the other, and John went full burlesque. But these ticklish pizzicatos soon give way to inky black darkness.

[†] A lamellaphone, or box piano, from Ghana.
[‡] Talking drums, also from Ghana.
[§] A Ghanaian xylophone.

For the moment when the human sacrifice appears, John wrote in his score that the chorus should slowly change pitch "with demented delight!!" and he had the percussion imitate a heartbeat in sync with the heart on screen. The theme he wrote for the "slave children" initially plays as an anguished and stern motif, accompanying their chained and miserable plight. After Indy is captured and forced to drink the blood of Kali, he nearly murders Willie in a ritual sacrifice before Short Round scorches his side and breaks the spell—giving way to the sidekick's motif, warmly embraced by Indy's theme on cellos. The emotion crescendoes, Willie says, "Let's get out of here," and Indy fixes his gaze and answers: "Right ... *all* of us," cueing a syncopated, steroidal stomp of the Slave Children theme. It's an ingenious feat of characterization—you can hear the clanking chains in the rhythmic motor and the weary but heroic heart of these kidnapped kids—bottled into a piece that grooves like a toe-tapping march. Pound for pound, *Temple of Doom* might paradoxically be the heaviest, lightest, catchiest, most dense, and most deliriously fun score of John's career.

He recorded the score in Los Angeles on the MGM stage. No one realized it at the time, but with the *Star Wars* trilogy already completed, this film marked the end of what one Lucasfilm employee called the "Periclean age." From 1977 to 1984, "the hits just kept on coming," said Louis Friedman, who wore many hats at the company. "I thought: *This is how it always is*. You work for a company, and every picture you work on is huge."[15] It was also an endpoint of sorts for John, whose focus would turn to different kinds of projects and a modified approach to scoring after 1984. Recording mixer Ben Burtt would always play a game during these years: when John's scores came back to him for the mix, he would try and guess which cue was meant for which scene without looking at the labels. With *Temple of Doom*, Burtt said he could guess about 90 percent of the cues:

> Of all the films we worked on, *Temple of Doom* has, to me, the most Steiner-esque score. It's got more different themes for locations and places, and transitions to places, and characters that are articulate and really interesting themes unto themselves. There's an elephant theme, and there's an arrival at the castle theme, and there's a go-into-the-caves theme, and there's a Willie theme, and an Indy theme, and a Short Round theme. I just love that score. I think there was a period there in the '80s ... where we had the music really hitting things so perfectly.[16]

When the film opened in May 1984, it was criticized for being too depraved, too reliant on special effects, too noisy. "What with John Williams' incessant score and the library full of sound effects, there isn't a quiet moment in the entire picture," *Variety* groused, "and the filmmakers have piled one giant setpiece on top of another to the point where one never knows where it will all end."[17] Arthur Knight at the *Hollywood Reporter* called the music "wall-to-wall" and "full-throated."[18] The score was nominated for an Oscar the following spring, but ironically lost to a David Lean epic set in the same region—*A Passage to India*, with music by Maurice Jarre. Spielberg would later disparage and even regret *Temple of Doom*, and he immediately began to look for more "grown-up" pictures to make. John had given it his very best—but he, too, was ready for a change of pace.

* * *

John Williams simply was not a man who lost his temper. Even when he was demanding high standards of musicianship and professionalism, he was diplomatic, patient, *stoic*. Whenever there had been discipline issues among studio players during a scoring session, he would often delegate his anger to Lionel Newman, who had no problem cracking heads. At one illustrative session when John was becoming secretly frustrated with the musicians, Newman spoke into his headphones from the booth: "I'm gonna come in and be Lionel. We're gonna get them going." Newman stormed out onto the stage and started playfully cursing: "Fuck you! What the hell! You got grease on your fingers?" The orchestra relaxed. "I think they just get tense because they know the composer's getting tense," said Carroll Newman. "My dad would do that often." John would just say he needed "a Lionel moment."[19] In Boston, John always worked "quickly yet calmly," concertmaster Emanuel Borok said in 1983. "He doesn't rehearse what doesn't need to be rehearsed and he has an amazingly sensitive ear. Even under the most frantic conditions—which happens very often at Pops rehearsals—he is incredibly efficient and he is also one of the friendliest conductors I have ever seen. He has this very special warmth in his eyes whenever he talks with musicians."[20]

So it was exceedingly strange when on Tuesday, June 12, 1984, John's frustration with the listless Pops players flared up, first as a stern lecture—and then him storming out and announcing his resignation. He put his baton down, walked off the stage, and said: "I don't have to take this anymore."[21]

John had a full Pops slate planned for the summer of 1984, including concerts at nearby Foxboro Stadium with special guests Peter, Paul and Mary, Tony Bennett, Rosemary Clooney, and Linda Ronstadt. He had already recorded a Pops album with Jessye Norman, conducted Wynton Marsalis in a Haydn trumpet concerto, and opened the new *Evening at Pops* season with Big Bird and other characters from *Sesame Street*. The latter concert was just one week before *the hiss*. The players could sense something was wrong. "He was very upset with our attitude," said bass player John Salkowski. At one point John, exasperated, asked the orchestra: "Why aren't you enjoying this?"[22]

The Boston musicians liked John. A lot. But many of them hated the Pops repertoire, felt it was beneath them. They resented the relentless schedule. In Fiedler's day, players would express their boredom by sailing paper planes overhead, or once even letting a live lobster onto the stage. One of their scampish traditions, when they played through an arrangement they didn't care for, was to hiss their displeasure.[23] Fiedler had a complicated relationship with the group—he believed they hated him, and they referred to the Pops as "Fiedler's Concentration Camp"—but he ignored their disrespect and soldiered on for 50 years.[24] The pressure, the frustration, the boredom, and the contractual obligation were all simmering well before John arrived. But on this particular Tuesday morning, John got onto the musicians in a way he had never done before. "He's never gotten angry," said Pasquale Cardillo, a veteran clarinetist who was about to retire. "He's never said a harsh word on the stage to anybody." It was nearing intermission and John stopped the orchestra because they were talking and not paying attention; he expressed his disappointment with their poor performance of the overture from Glazunov's ballet *Raymonda*, as well as Ray Henderson's "The Varsity Drag." Then, after intermission, the orchestra tried one of John's new compositions: "America, The Dream Goes On" was a sweet, bouncy, patriotic chorale with words by the Bergmans and which was, to some ears, a cheesy expression of national pride. That was clearly how some of the Boston players felt when a small but vocal band of tongues expressed their distaste.

"He's an extremely sensitive man," said Cardillo. "I can understand, even if he had no intention of leaving, that a man who is this sensitive could very well have said, 'This is an absolute indignity to me. Goodbye.'" Still, Cardillo insisted that discipline under Williams was "1,000 percent" better than it was with Fiedler, and that "the whole orchestra is being blamed for something just a few people did."[25] The news of John's sudden resignation erupted in Boston and around the country. John released a clinical statement about "artistic and creative differences," but columnists and readers alike blamed the unruly Pops. "I go to the gas station," said Cardillo, "and the attendant says, 'What did you do to John?'" The players went into a panic, cramming into John's office and begging him not to leave. Bill Moyer, orchestra manager, described it as a very emotional meeting "where grown men were crying."[26] But John stood firm. The hiss was simply "the straw that broke the camel's back," said Craig Nordstrom, chairman of the Players' Committee.[27] The Pops situation was teetering on the edge of untenable, and *no one* was happy about it. The strain inevitably created morale and discipline problems, but unlike John's contract orchestras in the studios, he had no power to fire or replace troublemakers. Those around John wondered if "Popsgate" (as the event got dubbed in the press) finally gave him an excuse to slip out of a deal he had never really bargained for—a position that was far more public and exhausting than he realized, in an environment that was much more of a party than a serious performance showcase. "I would rewind this whole thing and say I think he quit because, way down deep in his heart and soul, he didn't really like the idea of what's required," said Bill Cosel, the producer of *Evening at Pops*, who had become a personal friend of John's. "I think he began to realize what the Boston Pops audience was all about. And he's not against that—my god, he's written commercial film music for all kinds of things. But standing up there and doing it is a different matter. It's not a recording session. It's an entertainment."[28] John had avoided playing a Fiedler-type clown, but the Pops was still a circus.

The hiss event was a stark demonstration of how seriously John took music, *all* music. As Pops assistant conductor Harry Ellis Dickson observed: "John thinks every musician should be as engrossed in the music as he is."[29] John awkwardly conducted through a few more concerts in Boston after the announcement—his Fourth of July concert packed a quarter-million people along the Charles River[30]—and he waved farewell to the city in his last performance at Symphony Hall on July 8. One audience member gathered signatures during intermission, petitioning John not to leave, and sent the card to him backstage. At the end of the night, Richard Buell reported, the audience was on its feet for several minutes "cheering and applauding John Williams:

> The orchestra joined the demonstration as well. In his final curtain call Williams made a point of waving goodbye—first to the right balconies, then to the floor, then to the balconies on the left. No one doubted that the demonstration would have continued even longer if the conductor had not taken concertmaster Roger Shermont by the hand and led him offstage—a signal for the orchestra to disperse.[31]

Privately, John was *angry*—which he expressed in letters to Newman—but the only way he knew how to deal with it was to walk away. "I remember my dad saying that when John would get angry, he just didn't know how to do it," Carroll Newman said. "If it was business where my dad could be involved, my dad would say, 'Well, *this* is what you say,' or my dad would write somebody a letter—one of his letters—and say, 'What the hell are you doing?' My dad would speak for him. Not because John couldn't speak ... but in a way, he *couldn't*. He just didn't have that ability."[32]

* * *

Quitting the Pops was no sacrifice for John as far as money and employment were concerned; the BSO was well aware they needed *him* more than he needed them. John had no shortage of work waiting for him back in Hollywood. He had already written a new "Fanfare and Theme" for the Olympic Games—commissioned by event producer David L. Wolper—which was first heard on May 8 at a press preview of the opening and closing ceremonies for the Summer Games in Los Angeles. He gave the piece its first big public outing in a July 27 concert at the Hollywood Bowl called "Prelude to the Olympics."

Olympics fever gripped the city in the summer of 1984, and even though the hotshot producers of *Flashdance* summoned a parade of famous musical contributors, including Giorgio Moroder and Toto, for an official album of the games, it was John's *Olympic Fanfare and Theme* that resounded the loudest and longest. His fanfare heralded the opening ceremonies on July 28, with John conducting 150 trumpets to a crowd of 88,000 people inside the Memorial Coliseum downtown, President Ronald Reagan and several movie stars among them.[33] The fanfare attended every medal ceremony, and a few weeks later the orchestral theme accompanied victors in a closing ceremony that also included an after-dark laser show set to action music from *Return of the Jedi* and a lighthearted homage to *Close Encounters*, where a "spaceship" above the stadium communicated by synthesizer with trumpets on the ground, both parties singing John's new fanfare.[34]

After its ubiquitous presence in TV broadcasts of the games, schools and colleges around the country began performing the Olympic theme at local sporting events that fall. It won a Grammy in 1985 for best instrumental composition, and went on to become utterly synonymous with the Olympics through NBC's regular coverage for decades to come. John had written fanfares for plenty of fictitious ceremonies and occasions, but this was his first major composition for real-life action heroes. His involvement was certainly owed to the fact that these games were hosted by *Hollywood*, but the 1984 Olympics had the powerful effect of tying his music to *America*—on an international stage—like nothing else before. John's knack for lyrical heroism and brass band writing, and his ability to condense a powerful feeling of pride and triumph into a sticky, pop-sized anthem, now transcended popular entertainment and became wedded to the culture itself. The Olympic theme rightly earned its place as a fixture—patriotism without corn, and genuinely stirring—and this was the moment when John started to become his country's unofficial composer laureate.

A coronation which was keenly, painfully felt back in Boston.

* * *

In the lull between giant Lucas and Spielberg events, John was now free to return to old pastures and smaller character pictures. He got a call from his old comrade Mark Rydell, who was following his popular film *On Golden Pond* with a movie about the plight of American farmers. *The River* had Mel Gibson, Sissy Spacek, and Scott Glenn in the cast, a convincing flood sequence shot in the farmlands of Tennessee—and the misfortune of coming out on the heels of two other movies about the plights of American farmers: *Country* and *Places in the Heart*.

John screened the film with Rydell in July, right after he quit the Pops. The director described his own filmmaking style as "poetic realism,"[35] and he had made a film with plenty of room for John's melodic poetry, "very pastoral and very different from the space films," said John,[36] who was ready for a break from all the busy Saturday morning escapism. This was a chance to revisit the Americana of *The Reivers* and *The Cowboys*, albeit in a musical landscape changed by time. There were echoes of the Appalachian rodeoing from those earlier scores, as well as the bluesy soloing from *Conrack*, but *The River* was a contemporary tale set in the 1980s, and as such it invited electronics into the orchestra. As a composer, John too had changed, and this score anticipated some of his more sober dramas ahead. There is a worn-out, battle-scarred quality to the music; John could no doubt relate to Gibson's Tom Garvey, an old-school farmer beaten down by years of hard work but stubbornly refusing to modernize. In many ways, like Garvey, John was a man out of time.

He composed four major themes: a melancholy birdsong for the farmland and the river itself, which opens the film on solo flute; a simple folk anthem for the Garvey family; a lightly sensual love theme for Tom and Mae (Spacek), often heard on solo trumpet; and a noble, matriarchal oboe melody for Mae. The film opens with a bucolic scene of the young Garvey boy fishing and quickly disrupted by a storm, which John painted with a mysterious tone poem—introducing the family and land themes within a moody river that mixed his standard ensemble with a country-style 12-string guitar as well as electric guitar, electric harpsichord, and synthesizer. Tom's tractor overturns as the river swells, and John scored the frantic flooding sequence with a low piano ostinato and repeating tense chords. Rydell opted to use an alternate version of this cue, which laid strangely triumphant quotes of the family theme over a poppy backbeat, and the sometimes awkward presence of electronics in the score was an apt metaphor for the intrusion of modernity and industry into the old-school farmer's way of life—but it was still peculiar hearing John's gentle symphonic tunes propped up by a drum machine.

An admitted Luddite, John was never quite in his element with synthesizers and electronics. Why did an earthy film like *The River* even need them? Then again, this wasn't so different from the infusion of contemporary pop instrumentation and attitude in some of his 1970s scores, or the 1960s scores before *that*. After the tidal wave of classical symphonic scores for Spielberg and Lucas, it was easy to forget that John used to keep at least one toe in the musical zeitgeist. But it's very often those nods that curdle with age, perhaps because they were so unnatural for him. "He never got into synthesizers," said Ralph Grierson, who played on *The River*. "But he trusted the people who were making the sounds to come up with something, because we had to basically create a sound from a description on the part that would say, you know, 'Magico.' What does that mean? Or 'Brilliante'—all these Italian kind of things. You'd open up the part when you were playing synths, and it would be these very delightful descriptions of the sound."[37]

Still, the *River* score also brims with virtuosic solo parts for acoustic guitar, flute, and trumpet, performed by Tommy Tedesco, Jim Walker, and Warren Luening, respectively, who each got their own credits on the soundtrack album. Tedesco's fast-pickin' guitar played the family theme in its most bucolic setting for a montage of family life on the farm. Walker serenaded Tom and Mae's kissing scenes with John's noirish, body-aching love theme—which is interrupted by a pop-folk version of the family theme featuring tack piano and Fender Rhodes in the rhythm section under Tedesco's fancy fretwork. The score frequently straddles between idyllic and sensual; Rydell said he realized just how electric Gibson and Spacek's chemistry was while on the set. "*The River* is going to rattle everyone's bones," he said.[38]

But Rydell was not a bone-rattling director, and after years of playing in a kinetic sandbox with Steven Spielberg, John had to musically provide much more of the liquid current to Rydell's flat, plain staging and camerawork. The director admitted he was most interested in actors and performance, and the result was a lack of visual dynamism—despite the fact that *The River* was lensed by the same cinematographer who shot *Close Encounters*. There are long stretches in the film without any music— Rydell dropped several cues in the final mix—but after Tom returns from working in a steel mill to supplement the family income, a musical tide rises with the surging river in a majestic piece John called "The Ancestral Home." Facing off with his nemesis, a character who embodies industrial evolution, Tom and his family begin defiantly stacking sandbags to dam the water, with Mae's theme joining in—and the stoic ancestral melody lifts even higher as the Garveys are aided by their friends and neighbors.

At its best, Rydell's film was an almost mythic ode to the American farmer, and this climactic heartland ballad was the perfect encapsulation of that intention. John's loyalty to old friends like Rydell was admirable, but his music was rarely complemented or well served with the non-Spielberg directors. It was the last film he would ever score for Mark Rydell.

* * *

The marriage in Boston was not so easily annulled. Behind the scenes, John had gathered all 100 orchestra members for two marathon meetings, and after several summits with the orchestra's board of trustees and administration, he agreed to reconsider his resignation. On August 1, 1984, mere weeks after he exited the stage at Symphony Hall, John reclaimed the helm for the Pops' centennial season. He released a statement:

> I have only the greatest admiration and genuine affection for the orchestra and its members. Our recent differences have been put behind us and I look forward to conducting the 1985 season as well as working on proposed changes which will be of great benefit to the orchestra and the quality of its music-making.[39]

John had incredible new leverage, and he used it to negotiate several changes: a more forgiving rehearsal and performance schedule for the BSO musicians, who were now allowed to play Pops concerts on a voluntary basis; a greater reliance on the freelance Pops Esplanade orchestra in the summer season; and a less raucous atmosphere in Symphony Hall, which translated to everything from servers wearing quieter shoes to audience members only being permitted to enter the hall between pieces. He was discreet with the press. "It is not necessary to discuss private matters in public; that is beneath the orchestra's dignity," John said, effectively summarizing his philosophy about all things *infra dig* and private.[40] He was the antithesis of his outspoken friends and colleagues, casual bad-mouthers like Previn, and he was the cheery diplomat when he returned to Tanglewood to conduct his Olympic theme in August, blaming the recent "bumpy weather" and "contretemps" on "a morale slump, the result of overwork." "It was not a discipline problem," he insisted. "What happened this spring was that adversity brought out the best in everybody. For the first time, all of us—the orchestral players, Seiji Ozawa, the management, myself got together and did a lot of talking. In the past few weeks, these talks have brought out a lot of gripes and problems that wouldn't have come out otherwise. We've cleared the air."[41] Changing the subject, he said he was glad to come back because Samantha loved running in New England with its absence of smog, and because he had formed deep attachments in the city.

The BSO was more than relieved to have their star conductor back in time for the Pops's 100th birthday. Between concerts and records, the Pops was generating $2.3 million in revenues each season. "The few people who were acting childish will be very careful about it now, knowing how sensitive he is," said Dickson. "John Williams belongs here," said Tom Morris.[42] The *Berkshire Eagle*'s Milton R. Bass wrote a less reverent column, noting how the orchestra and John released statements "that were as carefully worded as a United States invitation to a disarmament conference."[43] There remained a very small, rotten subspecies of apples within the orchestra who would grumble about John under their breath, but Ann Hobson Pilot, the BSO's longtime harpist, said it was "the same contingency that disliked everything that happened, that disliked Seiji Ozawa, that disliked in later years James Levine.

> There was just this little group of bitter people who were probably bitter in their own lives. I can remember some of the young folks that came to sub with the BSO but didn't have the job—they were right out of school—and they were all excited. It was the best thing that ever happened to them. And they really played well and all. Then they got the job, and then *everything* was awful—they hated the job, they hated the conductor, they hated this and hated that. It was like a personality thing. I think they were just unhappy people, and so they were unhappy with everything.[44]

But it was the last time they would ever disrespect John so flagrantly. He had earned their respect, and he was actively reshaping the Pops into something more like him—something more dignified. Richard Dyer believed the reason John came back to the Pops was because he had not yet finished what he set out to do: he was on a mission to legitimize film music in the concert hall.[45]

In February 1985, John was commissioned to write new theme music for NBC's *Nightly News with Tom Brokaw*. "We wanted something that serves as an attention-getting melody," he said, "a statement that is accessible and hopefully not banal."[46] Much like his Olympic theme, the resulting anthem—"The Mission"—saturated the American consciousness through its nightly living room presence on a major network's primetime news hour. John said he was inspired by memories of his father tapping out Morse code signals, as well as "the clatter of ticker tape."[47] The theme opens with a pulsing call-to-action string rhythm, which gives way to a gently soaring tune—a cinematic climb on strings answered with varying urgent brass mottos. The B section is a syncopated horn signal that became the oft-used shorthand for the show; John's gift for "doorbell" motifs in movies was now employed to alert home viewers of real-life action. He said he wanted to write something with nobility of purpose and consistency, and "the dignity that our networks can achieve and deserve."[48] (There was that word again: *dignity*.) He actually composed multiple themes for NBC, including a scherzo for the *Today Show*, a "Pulse of Events," and a "Fugue for the Changing Times," along with several bumpers for commercial breaks, etc. But the *Nightly News* theme was the one that stuck around and landed like the best of his film themes. "We wanted to get away from synthesizer sounds forever," said NBC executive Tom Wolzien—who wrote the check for an 80-piece orchestra, which was recorded in April in an all-day session at Paramount.[49]

John later recorded it with the Pops, and it is likely the only TV news theme to enter the concert repertoire.

* * *

Spielberg had been circling the idea of a Peter Pan musical since *E.T.*, a film that featured a mother reading *Peter Pan* to her daughter. At various points it was reportedly going to star his friend Michael Jackson—John squashed this rumor[50]—and then a cast of unknown children. John mentioned the project several times to reporters that summer, explaining it would have nothing to do with either the 1953 Disney animated movie or the 1954 Broadway version starring Mary Martin. "I think by Christmas time we'll already be working with some of the kiddies," he said, estimating that the film would be out by the end of 1986 or the summer of 1987.⁵¹ John spoke of writing the songbook with Alan and Marilyn Bergman, but in fact started working on it with Leslie Bricusse; they produced at least one song. But Spielberg's heart was never fully in the project, and in December 1986 he let his rights to the property lapse.** Several years later, John would resurrect the idea of a Pan musical with Spielberg, but in a different form.

There were at the same time discussions about an *E.T.* sequel, though that was mercifully abandoned, and Spielberg was also mulling an adaptation of Thomas Keneally's historical novel, *Schindler's Ark*. Instead, the director's next project was a film version of *The Color Purple*—which was scored by Quincy Jones, one of the film's producers and a more obvious fit for the African American story. "Certainly Steven *wanted* John to do that," said producer Kathleen Kennedy, "but Quincy was a producer from the get-go. I would say that was a little fraught—but it was really Quincy from day one."⁵² Spielberg followed that with an ambitious anthology series that brought him back to Universal television. *Amazing Stories*, a reference to the old pulp magazine, harkened back to *The Twilight Zone* and some of the anthology shows John scored in his youth. With Spielberg's blank-check power, it was also one of the most expensive shows that had ever been attempted. NBC was so confident in his Midas touch that they committed to producing and airing 44 episodes, sight unseen, with a budget of roughly $1 million per half-hour program.⁵³ Spielberg wanted to use the show as a farm system for young filmmakers, but he also roped in some of his famous friends—including Martin Scorsese and Clint Eastwood—and gave everyone carte blanche to tell their own "amazing story" however they wanted. Naturally, he also made sure there was money for live orchestral scores, which were by now verging on extinction in television's neon age of synthesizers. "NBC has got a lot of guts," Spielberg said, "to let me run with this experiment."⁵⁴

He directed two episodes himself, a chance to relive his boyish beginnings in TV, but this time with his trusty composer in tow. John hadn't scored a television project (other than the nightly news) since *The Screaming Woman* in 1972, and this would surely be of a much higher caliber. But as it turned out, 1985 was the year that the Spielberg and Lucas rockets both began to sputter. Lucas was responsible for laying a notorious rotten egg, *Howard the Duck* (which was scored by John Barry), and *Amazing Stories* fared almost as badly. The pilot episode, "Ghost Train," was a simple idea—an old man warns his family that they've built their house on the path of a train that crashed when he was a boy—but even at 24 minutes, the conceit seemed stretched and padded. Spielberg ballooned his other episode to a full hour, but "The Mission" did not justify its runtime; not even young Kevin Costner and Kiefer Sutherland could prop up the tale of a World War II airman who gets trapped in the belly turret

---

** They were snapped up by Disney and "international entrepreneur" Dodi Fayed. That production also never materialized. (Marilyn Beck, "'Peter Pan' Film to Fly—Sans Steven & Michael," New York *Daily News*, December 23, 1986.)

of a plane without its landing gear and literally *draws* himself out of danger by manifesting cartoon wheels. Every episode opened with a title sequence featuring cavemen around a fire and computer-animated books, knights, and spaceships, with an original theme by John—a spirited boy's adventure tune for brass with some primitive percussion to acknowledge the cavemen onscreen. John also composed an end title for every episode, which borrowed the sparkling piano arpeggios from *E.T.*'s end title for a sentimental sendoff. The episodes themselves were scored in John's highly theatrical style, which was even more pronounced because of their concentrated length.

He composed two primary motifs for "Ghost Train," a twirling groove that could either be mysteriously sunny or cloudy, and a more noble, reaching lullaby-like theme. For "The Mission," he had more time to fill and a bigger orchestra. He made the most of Spielberg's clunky canvas, which with its live G.I. Joe action figures and plane talk had echoes of *1941* without any of the attempted humor, but much of the same lifelessness. It was a talky hour of television, confined to different sections of a flying bomber, and John complemented the constant thrum of the engine with a curious French horn motif flying through a fog of strings and a steady feeling of wondrous suspense. The bomber takes enemy fire, which destroys its landing gear and seals off the belly turret, and as the gunner Jonathan realizes his doomed predicament, John empathized with a string adagio. He quickened the pulse with some Indiana Jones–like action rhythms, and the hour built toward a ticking time bomb of the plane landing, a priest reading the Bible over a loudspeaker, and Jonathan furiously scribbling the wheels of his salvation on a doodle pad—all culminating in a fairytale finale.

The pilot premiered on September 29 in the primetime spot of Sunday at 8 p.m., and after so much hyped anticipation and secrecy, critics were simply not impressed. "More belly-flop than hoopla," wrote *Hollywood Reporter*'s Richard Hack.[55] "The Mission" aired in November, and by now the series was limping in the ratings; it ended the season in 35th place—a massive disappointment for both NBC and Spielberg.[56][††] For all his filmmaking brilliance, business savvy, and commercial instinct, Spielberg proved to have poorer taste when it came to many of his protégés and the projects he produced for other directors. This era launched a parade of flops and stinkers stamped with his name, including *Young Sherlock Holmes*, *The Money Pit*, and *Harry and the Hendersons*. None of these films were scored by John—Spielberg wanted to keep his lucky charm all for himself—but other composers were dying to work with Spielberg. Like James Horner, a rising young star who scored many Spielberg side projects, including **batteries not included*. That film's director, Matthew Robbins, said one of the main reasons Horner took the assignment was "because he really wanted to meet and spend time with Steven. But Steven really was loyal to John Williams. He wasn't about to switch over to James Horner, who I think was lurking." Horner rightly pegged Spielberg as a filmmaker who made immersive, powerful cinema that bowed to extroverted, emotional, *melodic* music—cinema where "you are in another kind of state,"

[††] Some tonal course correction was attempted in the second season, which featured no episodes directed by Spielberg or scored by John, but the costly series was put out of its misery in 1987.

said Robbins. "*Any* composer who met Steven would have a glancing dream of: *Oh my god—this is a guy who would put me front and center the way he did John Williams.*"⁵⁷

* * *

Bygones were bygones when John returned to Boston in the summer of 1985, and he renewed his vows to the Pops in glorious fashion. To celebrate their 100th anniversary, the Pops embarked on the most ambitious tour in the group's history: a 15-city parade across the United States. John conducted every program—the tour caravan included a Winnebago camper where he could have privacy and keep his orange juice and Perrier water chilled—and they drew record crowds at the Blossom Festival, summer home of the Cleveland Orchestra, and at the Chicago Symphony's outdoor Ravinia Festival.⁵⁸‡‡ 50,000 people crowded around the Reflecting Pool in Washington for the concert at the Lincoln Memorial on July 14—some climbed trees for a better look. John conducted a few patriotic classics, led a chorus of 350 singers in "Battle Hymn of the Republic," and was joined by singer John Denver for "America, The Dream Goes On." Nancy Reagan, who had just learned that her husband needed surgery for a cancerous growth on his colon, attended a Pops concert on the South Lawn of the White House with George H.W. Bush at her side.

John seemed completely reinvigorated by his comeback. Speaking to a reporter on a stop in San Diego, John articulated his personal mission:

> Whatever I am composing or conducting—a film score or a concerto, a jazz group or a symphony—I approach the work with the same rigorous standards of professionalism. Of course, I'm not saying that I don't hear any difference between Duke Ellington and Mozart, or that I believe each of these composers to have equal intellectual weight, but I have respectful regard for both. . . .
>
> As a composer I know that capturing spirit and mood with simplicity is extremely difficult. For me, all music is serious, although I recognize that some music is intended to entertain, and other music is meant to edify. These are different objectives, but for professional musicians all music must be seriously prepared and performed as well as possible.⁵⁹

He had been suffering problems with his lower back—the disc slippage and muscle spasms got so bad that he spent 10 days in the hospital that spring—and it motivated him to lose some weight. He showed off his loose pants when he got to Boston that summer, and said: "I'm convinced if I hadn't been conducting, my back trouble would have happened four or five years ago." A trainer for the Los Angeles Rams football team gave him floor exercises to do twice a day for 20 minutes, "a new religion," he called it, "though it doesn't impress [Samantha] very much."⁶⁰

---

‡‡ If not for the tour, John likely would have scored *Out of Africa*, Sydney Pollack's romantic epic starring Robert Redford and Meryl Streep, set in colonial Kenya. Pollack asked, and John said he would have happily done it if he had the time. (JW to TG, June 2, 2023.) John Barry earned an Oscar nomination for his lush, airborne score.

John came back to the Pops with a gift: a new concerto for principal tuba player Chester Schmitz. "I don't really know why I wrote it," John shrugged—"just urge and instinct. I've always liked the tuba," he said, noting the solos he had written for *Fitzwilly* and *Jaws*. "It's such an agile instrument, like a huge cornet."[61] John spotted Schmitz's talent early on, writing a two-minute tuba solo in his *Reivers* suite to imitate the story's yellow motorcar, as well as an extended concert version of Jabba the Hutt's rotund theme. Schmitz remembered their very first meeting at a rehearsal in 1980: John said, "Oh Chester, I heard you play Sibelius' First Symphony last January and I was greatly impressed with your playing, so I've written you a little something in this piece this morning." That's when Schmitz learned that "a little something" from John was something you had better take a look at ahead of time. The only thing in the classical repertoire as *challenging* as John's music for tuba were Elgar's symphonies, Schmitz said: "All of a sudden you jump up an octave and you play something with the horns, a big solo." John had taken his four-movement *Return of the Jedi* suite around the country, and in October 1984 he called Schmitz and told him: "I really liked the way you played Jabba. The past three or four months I've turned down a couple of movie scores, and I've just been fooling around with this tuba concerto." With his typical modesty, John said: "I wondered if you would do me the honor of allowing me to dedicate it to you."[62]

It was the first serious showpiece for tuba since the concerto composed by Ralph Vaughan Williams in 1954, and John and Schmitz premiered the piece on May 8, 1985. Unfolding in three movements, it hewed close to the style of his populist film writing, full of tonal fun, lyricism, and humor in a way his flute concerto and other concert music had largely dodged. "I've put passages in it for some of my pets in the orchestra—solos for the flute and English horn, for the horn quartet and for a trio of trumpets," John said. "It's light and tuneful, and I hope it has enough events in it to make it fun."[63] In his review, Dyer called it "a piece for the Pops, but not a Pops piece—this is not a cute, condescending 'Tubby the Tuba' sort of effort; there are no rude noises and crude jokes. It is a virtuoso workout for the soloist and for the instrument; of course it is effectively, unusually, and at points even sumptuously orchestrated. More to the point, it is actually good music in which interesting ideas are put through their paces, spankingly."[64]

Reviewing the concerto a few years later, Anthony Tommasini agreed that it was "no gimmicky Pops piece but a work of seriousness:

> The first movement is a peppery dialogue for soloist and orchestra with offbeat compound rhythms and jaunty tunes. It's a nice touch to cushion the moody cadenza for the solo instrument with four supportive horns. The slow movement is languid and melancholic, harmonically reminiscent of David Diamond or Paul Creston. The perky finale is announced with a Stravinskian brass fanfare. Some of the brainy academic composers could learn a thing or two from Williams about giving pieces real rhythmic thrust. If the work is not strikingly original, it's handsome, well-made, and appealing, though the audience, it seemed, did not particularly

respond to it. To many Pops goers, the concerto must have sounded suspiciously like a piece of modern music, which it is.[65]

"It was a major contribution to the tuba repertoire," said Schmitz. "Everybody's playing this thing. First it was just tuba players, but shortly then the bass trombone players got in on the act."[66] John brought the piece home in a September concert at the Hollywood Bowl with the LA Phil's principal tuba, Roger Bobo. In his *L.A. Times* review, Marc Shulgold complained there was little of substance, that "the instrument is simply not a grateful concerto voice, and the composer could not dispel that conception in this aimless, tuneless offering despite his urgent podium proddings."[67] Nonsense. If anyone wants to look for the joyful, lyrical John Williams they know from the movies in one of his concert works, they should start with his tuba concerto.

That fall, Previn came home to assume directorship of the LA Phil. It was an uneasy relationship from day one: Fleischmann expected Previn to bring some of Hollywood into the hall, but Previn refused. In his first interviews with the *L.A. Times,* he insulted the entire film industry by saying he had forgotten where his four Oscars even were until he found them recently while packing. "They're all tarnished and ancient-looking," Previn said. "I think that must be symbolic."[68] He frequently clashed with Fleischmann, and he also drew complaints from orchestra subscribers. Previn blamed the slow-motion disaster on his popcorn past: "Some critics will forgive you for being an axe murderer, but never for scoring a film.... The movies are not a part of my life anymore, or a part of my thinking. Only in Los Angeles does this remain a crucial part of my biography. It is ridiculous."[69] John remained as close to Previn as ever, and was glad to have him nearby again. But while his friend tried to prove his own seriousness by disowning film, John continued to bring seriousness to *his* chosen art form.

In September, Lionel Newman retired from Fox after almost 40 years. John attended the retirement party thrown by his new agent—Michael Gorfaine—along with Henry Mancini and Lionel's nephew, Randy, who was coming into his own as a film composer.[70] In an exit interview with the *L.A. Times*, Lionel said he was going to keep working with John, who "changed the scope of film music. He made it big again. He made it thrilling."[71] But with Newman's departure, John abandoned his office at Fox of nearly 20 years. Without his friend to eat lunch and kibitz with every day on the lot, there seemed simply no point. Besides, John had an office waiting for him at the newly built Amblin offices on the Universal lot—an architectural ode to the Taos Pueblo in New Mexico—where Spielberg could now easily pop by to hear John's newest themes. As he was leaving, John looked at the Steinway 200,000 series grand piano—"probably the best Steinways ever made in the United States," he said—which Fox had bought around 1930, and which had once belonged to Alfred Newman. It was the piano he wrote *Jaws* and *Star Wars* and *E.T.* on. He said to Lionel, "I can't leave that," so Newman arranged for John to purchase the piano, soaked in decades of film music history and cigar smoke, and take it with him to Amblin.[72]

On October 19, 1985, Johnny Francis Williams died. A lifelong smoker and alcoholic, he had suffered poor health and emphysema for years, and the lung condition finally brought him down just shy of his 80th birthday. Johnny Francis had witnessed his son's incredible ascendancy, and although he was a complicated man who could be very tough with his criticism and high standards, he was the greatest influence on John's becoming a composer, and the reason for his insatiable, self-learning drive. "I think my siblings would agree that I got the best of my father," John said.[73]

* * *

In January 1986, John was busy writing music for a fictional film about a female teacher and a crew of kids who accidentally take a NASA shuttle into space. Then, on January 28, the actual Space Shuttle *Challenger* launched and, because the O-ring seals inside one of its rocket boosters had hardened undetected in the cold weather the previous night, a pressurized gas leak suddenly and violently ignited one of the propellant tanks. The shuttle exploded in full view of the entire world, killing a crew of seven, including the first civilian on board a space flight: a female teacher.[74] It was a national tragedy—and it also put a curse on the prospects of John's new project: *SpaceCamp*.

When Spielberg's first child, Max,[§§] was born and he decided to ground the Peter Pan flight ("I didn't want to go to London and have seven kids on wires in front of blue screens swinging around," he said[75]), it suddenly opened up John's winter schedule. *SpaceCamp* was the feature directing debut of Harry Winer, a Detroiter who abandoned a path toward law school and politics to write and direct for television. Winer was surrounded by veteran crew members and lots of youthful talent; the cast featured Lea Thompson, Kelly McGillis, and a baby-faced Joaquin Phoenix (going by "Leaf" at the time) as a boy whose obsession with *Star Wars* filled the film's screenplay with quotes from John's space trilogy.[***] Kate Capshaw played a pilot named Andie, who dreamed of going into space since she was a little girl but is presently stuck teaching kids about space on the ground in Alabama. The film begins like a high school comedy, albeit skewing younger with the antics of Phoenix and his robot friend, Jinx; their hijinks accidentally launch an actual space shuttle with the teen astronauts on board, turning the film into a tense survival mission. It was a cute after-school adventure with heart, sold with sincerity by Winer and his committed cast, and it harmonized with America's excitement about the *Challenger* mission: "The whole notion of the space shuttle taking the first layperson up into space, the teacher, was something that was invested with everyone's hopes and dreams," said Winer, "that it wasn't just going to be the rarefied few—the fighter pilots and engineers and scientists—who were going to get a chance to go up into space, but every one of us. It was going to be a doorway through which each of us could walk."[76] John was touched by this optimistic story, and

---

[§§] John wasn't sure if the name was an indirect nod to Spielberg's pet name for *him* … but it must have been.

[***] *Star Wars* was so culturally ubiquitous that it now frequently invaded other movies. Also, in the summer of 1986, John learned that a Russian astronaut had brought a tape of his *Star Wars* music into space and listened to it while watching Earth storms from above. (Dyer, "'You Can Choose Your Own Country,'" *Boston Globe*, June 22, 1986.)

he agreed to work with the first-time director—"a *huge*, huge coup," Winer admitted. It was produced by ABC's new film division, which actually shuttered shortly after the film was shot, and the project was adopted by 20th Century Fox. John insisted on recording his score there—one last ride into space with Newman.

John "had no ego, that I experienced," said Winer. "He was generous. And his approach to his work, which is the kind of approach that I always fantasized was the height of the creative process, was to understand who the characters were, what the story was, what the filmmaker's intention was, and start from that place—in addition to his own instinctive response to the scenes." John latched onto the opening shot of young Andie staring at the stars from her lawn, declaring she'll go up there one day, and this childhood dream formed the heart of his score; even as danger ensues and chaos unfolds, John musically fulfilled the payoff when her dream comes true. He opened the film with a "call" à la *E.T.*—a twinkling motto on electronic keyboard. But *unlike E.T.* or the other space adventures he had recently done, the music for *SpaceCamp* was less about fantasy and more about science and pragmatism. John's themes were more internal; they take off, but without any pixie dust. At one point, producer Leonard Goldberg turned to Winer during the mix and said, "Where's the catchy musical phrase?" Goldberg wanted something as instantly, magically identifiable as *E.T.* or *Star Wars* or *Raiders*. Winer gave John carte blanche, and "somehow John tended away from that into what felt more of an aspirational, character-driven journey than a heightened reality."[77] Stylistically, the score was more an outgrowth of John's patriotic Pops and Olympics music than the Lucasfilm fairytales. It was dreamy Americana, introduced with his theme for Andie's dream in the opening titles. Another main idea was for Max and Jinx, a gently rising and yearning motif that comes to life alongside their budding friendship and Jinx's hyper-literal reaction when Max, bullied and misunderstood, wishes he was in space. Jinx goes into the control room, lights up and starts spinning—like a genie granting a wish—which John scored with restrained majesty.

Andie's theme comes to represent the kids and their mission, and during their early training montage it bounces in a hilariously 1980s arrangement for funky synths and electric bass. John's pop education had formally ended with West Coast jazz, and his attempt at a "cool" bop for the MTV generation was endearingly unhip. (Perhaps this track was a communication with his son Joe, who contributed a modern pop song of his own to the soundtrack.) John was much more in his element in a lofty, awed presentation of Andie's theme during the team's approach and exploration of the shuttle, complemented by exciting horn lines and climaxing with a dramatic crescendo as the shuttle, to everyone's surprise, actually launches. The theme turns into a dreamy tone poem when the gang reaches orbit and gawks at Earth below, but they quickly realize they don't have enough oxygen on board to last through re-entry, and John scored their anxiety with agitated melody lines. The score's palette grows more synthesized in this middle act, more in line with the adult dramas he was moving into; likewise, the suspense was not treated like John's Saturday space operas—it's more subdued and interior. There is a languid, slightly static quality to the film once the characters become lost in space, and John's score grows similarly sleepy. The orchestra stirs back to life after the teens figure out how to get home, with grand, heroic reprises of the main themes and lots of virtuosic flourish. John had always loved ornamenting his scores and liberally handing out shiny solos—but by now it was almost like he was writing parts of his scores *knowing* they would be performed in concert. The end credits version of his main theme was a Pops-ready showstopper in the spirit of the Olympic theme, with the same rhythmic motor as his upcoming *Liberty Fanfare*.

"I trusted this man like few others I've come in contact with in my life," Winer said. Every conversation was deep: "We'd go beneath the surface, and he was right there for anywhere that you want to take the conversation—and sometimes *led* it there. But it was always about what would serve the story, and his insights would elevate the material rather than minimize it." When the real *Challenger* blew up—a sickening and televised blow for the students of beloved teacher Christa McAuliffe, and a gut punch to the entire world—there was a lot of handwringing at Fox about whether to simply shelve the film. But the studio decided to forge ahead with a summer release. Capshaw called Winer right after the tragedy and asked: "Do you think we have a problem?" Winer replied: "No, no, this is a fantasy. This has nothing to do with what just occurred." He laughed darkly at the memory of his naivete: "But it did."[78]

In April, a few weeks after the *SpaceCamp* sessions, John's own beloved teacher died. He had seen less and less of Bobby Van Eps since his busy career took off, although he would occasionally visit Van Eps at his brother George's house, and they would always ask "Bud" to play the piano. John attended the funeral for Van Eps, deceased at 87. Like John's father, this man had been a complicated and intense but hugely formative figure in his life. "I think I loved him," John said.[79]

The doomed opening of *SpaceCamp*, on June 6, 1986, unfolded just as feared. "I went on opening night," said Winer, "and the theater was empty pretty much."[80] Appreciating the impossible situation, some critics softened their blows, but most found the movie to be juvenile, shallow, and derivative. Several reviews noted the presence of the composer, tying this film to Lucas's universe. "Unfortunately it's being sold as if it's this year's *Star Wars*. And there's no way it can live up to the hype," Jimmy Summers wrote in *Boxoffice*. "Even some of the on-screen trappings, especially John Williams' bombastic score, seem part of a plan to sell the movie as something it's not. It's not, for instance, a movie for adults, at least not for adults who appreciate plausibility in their movies."[81] Winer carried "the burden of the disappointment" with him for decades, but he felt some delayed vindication when he was celebrated at the real Space Camp in Huntsville, Alabama, on the film's 30th anniversary and several people told him it had inspired them to go into the space program. He cherished his collaboration with John, and felt the score totally captured "the grandeur of dreaming." Thinking even beyond the *SpaceCamp* score, Winer noted that John's music altogether instills a feeling of possibility, "that we're justified in having faith that there's a larger reality.

> And that's what makes us feel good, I think. It allows our hearts to soar. I guess part of it is that life's an adventure, and he gets that.... There's something heartful about John's music, and grand about his music, that makes us all feel bigger than how we feel on a day to day basis.

It's not even just a matter of dreaming. It's about the possibilities that dreams can be achieved. That's where the hope lies. That's what inspires the hope, I think. He makes those dreams real, in a certain sort of way, but never loses touch with the fact that it's a grand dream. It's never small. It's not surprising that his movies are many times in space or related to space, because he can fill that space. Not just fill it in; he can create the feeling of the vastness through his music, of worlds that we want to explore, and that we have the capacity to. That's why people respond. There's something we're inspired by, because now we want to taste that grandeur. And for this one fleeting moment, an hour and a half of our lives, we are tasting that grandeur, and we can take that with us after we leave the theater—and maybe that'll inspire us to pursue grander dreams in our own lives.[82]

* * *

The Statue of Liberty turned 100 in 1986, and to celebrate her new renovation, David Wolper and TV impresario Norman Lear threw a televised, Olympics-style birthday party.[83] John was commissioned to write a new fanfare, and also asked to play host for a big Fourth of July concert on the New Jersey lawn facing Lady Liberty. As with the Olympics, a recording of his fanfare was used in ABC's television coverage of the multi-day festivities before John unfurled the piece live, in grand style, with buglers wearing plumed hats and blue capes. Leading the Boston Pops Esplanade band, he wore a black tux and a chunky TV broadcaster's headset; ABC cut between the musicians and formations of men marching around in Colonial American garb, carrying flags, in a rather kitschy patriotic pageant for the Reagan-Epcot era. (President Reagan was there to kick off the ceremonies.) (Figure 10.1.)

This new piece was another entry in John's growing canon of brass-heavy American anthems for an empire at peace—it was also one of his best. A dramatic bugle herald and some ceremonial gongs introduce the first half, which sounds like a fox hunt through a fireworks show; the middle section relaxes into a wistful, pastoral string melody—"like thinking back about our parents," John said, "and everyone who came through the immigrant experience"[84]—which is punctuated by the excited main staccato motto; the fanfare modulates with emotion into a now-galloping charge, eases back into serenity, then explodes. It was a splendid orchestral exhibition on a special occasion, but also an astounding amount of narrative and feeling packed into four minutes. The fanfare actually premiered a month earlier at Symphony Hall, at the BSO's annual President's Night fundraiser. Reviewing for the *Globe*, Anthony Tommasini called it "a humdinger.

> It's got two great tunes: a brassy and boisterous fanfare riff, all roulades and flourishes and forward motion; and a long-lined tune for hushed-up strings that sounds like lots of others Williams has composed for Hollywood, but still gets you right in the back of the throat. This is not surprising. Like the "Waltz King" Johann Strauss Jr. and the "March King" John Philip Sousa, Williams knows how to write music for occasions that is effective, well-fashioned, uncontroversial, and wildly successful. This is not as easy as it looks. Just think of Johannes Brahms, who all his

Figure 10.1. John rehearsing with the Pops Esplanade in front of the Statue of Liberty, July 4, 1986 (Photographer unknown, Courtesy of John Williams).

life despaired of ever writing a waltz as good as any of those by Strauss. Williams has mastered the time-honored technique of composing music with "interchangeable parts," a technique applied with equal success to automobile assembly by that granddaddy of corporate presidents, Henry Ford.[85]

John looked mostly at ease when he turned to address the horde on the Jersey lawn, beamed into the homes of millions of Americans, the wind whipping into his microphone as he introduced Bernstein's *Candide* overture. He and John Denver gave each other a thumbs up before another performance of "America, the Dream Goes On," this time backed by a large choir of service members. The event was a little old-fashioned, corny, and Hollywood—but it only solidified John's status as the new Sousa ... maybe even the new Bernstein, whom John was just getting to know.

John and "Lenny," the great American evangelist of music, started to cross paths at Tanglewood every summer. That September, they both took part in a concert celebrating the 350th anniversary of Harvard at the university's gigantic stadium. It had been a busy summer: John also wrote a fanfare for the centennial of Texas, premiered by the Houston Symphony, and he went on another national tour with the freelance Esplanade orchestra—which was documented by a Japanese film crew as part of the country's preparation for a five-city visit from the Pops, scheduled for the winter of 1987. After the whirlwind Pops season and his usual concert at the Hollywood Bowl in September, John took the rest of the year off. He gave a tribute to Spielberg in December when his friend received the Scopus Award from the American Friends of the Hebrew University. In his acceptance speech, Spielberg said: "How do we stay innocent and trusting in a world that makes us more cynical? The American Dream is based on innocence and trust—I'll keep on making films that reflect a universe I believe in."[86] Having just written an earnest, optimistic valentine to the Statue of Liberty, John could not have agreed more. These two innocents were about to collaborate on their first feature since *Temple of Doom*—and with *The Color Purple* and fatherhood launching him out of fantasyland, Spielberg was ready to tell his most serious story yet.

* * *

In the spring of 1987, John wrote a short score for the new "Omnimax" theater at the Boston Museum of Science, a commission from local philanthropist David Mugar.[87] The film, titled *New England Time Capsule*, was like a cutting-edge echo of John's very beginnings with the Newfoundland travelogue *You Are Welcome*—this one showing off the natural wonders and culture of New England for a screen several stories high, with narration by Leonard Nimoy. John's score, a sprightly, flying homage to his motherland, was performed by a small band and synths; he later arranged it for orchestra as *Hymn to New England*, which he premiered with the Pops that May.[†††]

[†††] In May, he also premiered a new theme for the Special Olympics and their 1987 Summer Games—a bouncing, uptempo ditty that was ready-made for marching bands. He attended the opening ceremonies in South Bend, Indiana, conducting the United States Navy Band in his new tune: *We're Lookin' Good*. (Guy Livingstone, "Chatter: Boston," *Variety*, May 13, 1987.)

John then got to write a more *devilish* hymn to New England, in a much-needed variation from all of the sincere pomp and positivity. In *The Witches of Eastwick*, Jack Nicholson played an outrageous, repulsive, and lustful incarnation of the devil who seduces three lonely women—played by Cher, Michelle Pfeiffer, and Susan Sarandon—in a small Massachusetts town aghast at their bacchanal. Adapted from the 1984 novel by John Updike and directed by *Mad Max*'s George Miller, it was a wicked satire filled with R-rated double entendres and gooey special effects, and John—already an Updike fan—gobbled it up like a Rhode Island clambake. "I'm very taken with it," he told Dyer that summer. "The script simplifies the novel—there are fewer characters and a different ending—but it is beautifully written." He explained that one of his tasks was to write different music for "three large-scale seduction scenes. One of the women is a cellist, and at one point the climax of the Dvořák Concerto sweeps into the Love Theme from *The Witches of Eastwick*. I hope Tony Dvořák won't mind!"[88] While there was no explicit nudity or sex in the film, it was the bawdiest thing John had worked on for quite some time.

Miller had a miserable time making the film, which he blamed on producer Jon Peters and studio dynamics at Warner Bros., "and it filtered right through the middle production people," Miller said. "It was just a crazy, and quite frankly *corrupt* production. It was the Eighties. It was all the worst behavior. Madness. It was irrational ... that's why I kept thinking cocaine—or psychosis." With some coaching from the sage Nicholson, Miller eventually put his foot down and gave the studio ultimatums: Peters had to stay off the set, Miller would cut the film not on the Warner Bros. lot but in a separate facility—a converted barn on King Vidor's former estate in Beverly Hills—and he would finish post-production in Australia without any studio interference. Miller was a longtime fan of John's—he considered *The Long Goodbye* one of the most extraordinary scores he'd ever heard—and when he learned that John wanted to score *Eastwick*, he was thrilled: "Just look at his scores. He can adapt to anything. He can do anything." From the moment they met, "it was as though we had been discussing this film a long time," Miller said. "He's a man who's not only elegant in his manner, but an extremely elegant mind. His assessments, his diagnostics, were so acute that *I* didn't have to do the talking." After John screened the film privately, he met Miller for a spotting session at the Vidor barn. They had the "usual conversations" about the function of music in different scenes, Miller said:

> And we only got, I think, less than halfway through the movie when I realized: there's no point in me talking—because he already understands all the subtext, all the underlying dynamics in the movie. So not only was he a great composer, he was a great *dramaturg*. That's, I think, why he's had such an enduring legacy: he could write a thesis on the characters, but particularly on the underlying themes.

In the middle of their session, Miller said to John, "Look, you really understand it already. Why don't you just go and work on it?"[89]

John's main theme for the trio of witches was a mischievous danse macabre, unveiled during the opening credits in an overture for orchestra, bell-like synths, and sampled harpsichord. (The hybrid electronic-orchestral palette was another nice metaphor for ancient evil visiting modern society.) When the ladies unwittingly cast a spell and manifest their ideal man one night, the theme blows in like a storm with baying horns and a buzzing bass line—which was created by the twang of an Asian idiophone aptly called a *devil chaser*. The mysterious Daryl Van Horne has his own "love" theme—a sinister aria that comes in furtively on midi harpsichord, then flowers into operatic orgasm when he seduces the first of the three heroines, replete with synthesizer voices that John characterized in his written score as "Devil's Wind" and "Devil's Breath." Nicholson's devilry was also given voice by frenzied fiddling, a nod to the legend of Old Scratch who shows up to offer a wish in exchange for your soul and knows his way around the violin.[‡‡‡] Having read the Updike novel, one of John's intuitions about the Van Horne character was that he was not the devil of the Bible. "He started off basically as a Pan figure, a satyr in pagan times," said Miller.

> In all cultures, the seasons were defined by female goddesses, and the satyr or the Puck-like character would come along and impregnate them, and that would lead to the spring. So it was a very, very pagan devil, as it were. And that's where Jack went, and that's what John saw immediately. The first thing he said was, "I'm thinking of an Irish jig, impish quality, more than a dark thing."[90]

The second seduction begins with a fiery duet between Sarandon's cello and Nicholson's fiddle in Dvořák's B minor cello concerto, which climaxes with an ornamented quote of the love theme. The third seduction is foreplayed by a tennis game featuring all three ladies and an enchanted tennis ball, and John scored the match with a burlesque dance for piano and strings and flitting winds. The final seduction is a dream-like sequence inside Van Horne's ballroom filled with pink balloons; Miller shot the scene with playback of a Pavarotti recording of "Nessun Dorma" from the Puccini opera *Turandot*, in keeping with Van Horne's weaponization of classical music. Miller left this source cue in the final cut, and John said to him: "I really adore 'Nessun Dorma,' but in terms of the rest of the score it doesn't connect . . . it doesn't flow through," as Miller recalled. "He's incredibly polite, and he said, 'Would you mind if I had a crack, not on 'Nessun Dorma,' but doing something that would replace it, in time and so on?' I said, 'Yeah, go for it.' He said, 'If you don't like it, don't worry. Don't even bother.'" John wrote a sumptuous ballad for strings and strummed harp with Puccini amounts of romance, an impassioned French horn solo, a glittering bridge, and a flowering (or rather *deflowering*) finale. It fit the timing of the scene and into the rest of the score, but it just "didn't do what 'Nessun Dorma' had done" for Miller—so he kept the source track in and simply crossfaded into the latter part of John's cue.

[‡‡‡] Old Scratch was depicted in a 1941 film scored by Bernard Herrmann, *The Devil and Daniel Webster*.

"Puccini did it, somehow, in the mind," said Miller. "I think now they call it 'temp love,' but that's what happened."[91] The foursome's wicked bliss is threatened by wagging town members, led by the prudish Felicia, and Van Horne curses her with a mouth full of cherry pits—a gross-out comedy sequence scored with slithering cellos and sliding winds. After Felicia dies and the ladies turn their backs on Van Horne, the story escalates with his fury and mounting special effects; the score goes deeper into hell, imitating skittering insects and squirming snakes, much like John had done for Indiana Jones. The music almost dips into aleatoric *Images* territory as Van Horne's true dark colors are on full display, but it never loses touch with whimsical fiddling and fun.

John hired Ian Underwood, a pop session player who graduated from Frank Zappa's Mothers of Invention, to play synths on the score. In an unusual move for John, he asked Underwood if it was possible to create musical samples of various sounds—among them a pair of snipping scissors. "Because if I could play it, he could write something for it," said Underwood—"rhythmically, or it could be used in a musical context of some kind." John wrote a few "scissor" solos, particularly for the climactic "Destruction of Daryl" cue. Underwood also sampled a real devil chaser: "If you do that, you can play it higher or lower—you don't have to play the one sound that the devil chaser makes. You can play it lower on the keyboard, and then it's a devil chaser *basso*."[92]

The witches theme returns in a scurrying dance form as the women cook up a voodoo doll to destroy Van Horne while he's off in town to buy ice cream. Before he starts getting telekinetically tortured, Van Horne appears to whistle part of the main theme—but it was actually *John's* lips providing the whistle.[93] The gleeful torment of the devil is accompanied by a magical cyclone carrying fragments of the major themes, and then the witches' theme is fully unleashed in a delightfully demented showcase featuring the giant pipe organ at Fox as Van Horne furiously drives home to confront his defecting harem. This cue was the basis for John's concert version, "The Devil's Dance," and one only had to see his enormous grin when conducting it with the Pops to see how much fun he had composing this score. "He's actually really, really funny," said Susan Dangel, who thought that of all of John's scores, the "Devil's Dance" was "the music that makes me think most: *there he is*. Because he is sort of devilish, funny—he's playing it straight and looking like he's not."[94] It was one of the cheekiest scores John ever wrote, and even though it didn't enter the cultural Mount Olympus, he kept a special place for it in his mischievous heart. "He definitely has a twinkle in his eye," said Miller, "and obviously to be as free as he is an artist, and so eclectic—there's no question that the score comes out of the person who writes it."[95]

The *Witches* score was recorded in April at Fox.§§§ Miller was impressed that John conducted most cues without a click track, to get a more fluid performance, and he was in awe of John's ears, "the granular acuity of his hearing and understanding,

---

§§§ That same month, John traveled to Houston to conduct his violin concerto with Alexander Treger, along with *Essay for Strings*. He was supposed to conduct his symphony, but swapped it out with film themes. (The symphony was never performed after 1972.) "More people hear the music to *Star Wars* in a year than will ever hear my violin concerto in a lifetime," he told the *Houston Post*. "I feel I can contribute as much or more as a film composer than I can as a symphonic writer. So we have to prioritize things. Life does a lot of that for us." (Carl Cunningham, "Podium Part-Time Home to John Williams," *Houston Post*, March 29, 1987.)

whether it was rhythm, or the picture's wrong... he would make those small adjustments." For Miller, John was "a profound intellect and a profound intuition working in some sort of interplay—one feeding the other. So you can get the great analytical mind, and you can get the completely free, intuitive mind. But the synergy that happens when the two are together is in John Williams."[96]

Eastwick claimed the top box office spot when it opened in June and became the year's tenth-highest grossing film. Most critics found it a disappointing adaptation of Updike's incisive commentary on Puritanism and sex, and Janet Maslin thought it "brings a broad, obvious, punchy style and a lot of special effects to bear upon a story of seduction that is much too frail to support this kind of gimmickry."[97] Jack Garner of *Gannett* argued that "filmgoers are also manipulated by John Williams' robust and bouncy score that stresses the would-be whimsy of the piece, while contributing to its lack of subtlety."[98] Many reviews ignored the score altogether—which, in Miller's mind, was to ignore the depth of the story: "A film is apprehended by the audience as a whole body experience," he said. "It happens in the viscera, it happens in the heart, in the intellect. There's an anthropological dimension to film, there's a mythological or spiritual or philosophical level, and all of those things are happening at once. You're looking for it to hit all of those things." Miller compared the deepest films to icebergs, and argued that music is often best at handling the invisible berg beneath the water—all the subtext and "deeper resonances" that ought to be *felt* rather than overtly displayed. When making a film, Miller usually wouldn't have time to discuss these deeper elements with his actors, cinematographer, editor, and so on. But, he said, "when you first have the conversation with the composer, you go back to those deep subtextual conversations, because they can add that dimension to a film."[99]

Almost as if he were hexed with the devil's cherries himself, John had to back out of his planned 10-concert tour with the Pops Esplanade in July 1987 when he was hospitalized with an intestinal infection. "It was a garden-variety illness," he said, "but it dragged on for a couple of weeks."[100] Filling in for him at the last minute was John Mauceri—a protégé of Bernstein's who was a vocal champion of film music in concert. An affable showman, Mauceri was openly discussed as a natural candidate for the Pops position, should it ever open again.[101]

* * *

John had composed grand opera and spiritual euphoria for Steven Spielberg in the service of fantastic adventures and fairy tales. With *Empire of the Sun*, he finally had an opportunity to do the same for a more grounded historical subject. Spielberg's uneasy portrait of wartime atrocities, frantic crowds in panic, and ashen, haunted human beings was a potent echo of the Holocaust—a subject he was still timidly contemplating for a future project—and *Empire of the Sun*, along with *The Color Purple*, effectively broke his reputation as a Peter Pan filmmaker and gave him the confidence to make a movie about the Shoah.**** But *Empire* was more than merely a stepping

---

**** A Hebrew word for the Holocaust, literally meaning *catastrophe*.

stone to *Schindler's List*; it was the culmination of his maturity as an artist, a variation on themes he kept coming back to, an exercise in restraining his impulse to dazzle and entertain while still taking full advantage of his virtuosity with visuals and emotions. "It's an unusually serious picture for Steven Spielberg to have made, but I think it is a good one," John said at the time. "He shoots everything so wonderfully well: the big scenes of the invasion of the city are quite remarkable. And although the story is very serious, it is also very beautiful."[102]

Based on the 1984 novel by J. G. Ballard, whose fictional tale was fed with real memories of his own childhood, the film cast 13-year-old Christian Bale as Jamie "Jim" Graham, a British schoolboy living in opulence in Shanghai just before the Japanese attack on Pearl Harbor; traumatically separated from his family when the war breaks out, Jim is forced to wear out his youth behind barbed wire in a series of internment camps. At its core, this was the same story as *Pinocchio* and *E.T.*—about a young boy abandoned, who "dies" and comes back to life—but told through the prism of World War II, which had obsessed Spielberg since his own boyhood. It was an expert blend of the filmmaker's recurring motifs: G.I.s and airplanes, a precocious boy with an outsized imagination, refusing to grow up but also growing up too fast ... wondering if we're all alone in the universe. "I had never read anything with an adult setting—even *Oliver Twist*—where a child saw things through a man's eyes as opposed to a man discovering things through the child in him," Spielberg said. "This was just the reverse of what I felt—leading up to *Empire*—was my credo. And then I discovered very quickly that this movie and turning forty happening at almost the same time was no coincidence—that I had decided to do a movie with grown-up themes and values, although spoken through a voice that hadn't changed through puberty as yet." Some critics complained that there was still too much redemption and storybook sheen on the horrors he depicted in the film, and even Spielberg admitted that "I don't think I've made a dark movie. But it's as dark as I've allowed myself to get, and that was perversely very compelling to me."[103]

John scored *Empire of the Sun* like a religious experience. The film opens inside a church, in a scene of Jim singing a solo in the ancient Welsh carol "Suo Gân" ("Sleep, my darling") with a boys' choir, and this hymn-like lullaby becomes a major theme in the film.†††† John's original theme for Jim is also a lullaby—first heard timidly on flute and electric piano in a nursery-like setting as Jim lies in bed talking to his mother: "Perhaps God is our dream," the pensive boy muses, "and we're his." Jim's religion isn't Christianity—he announces early in the film that he's an atheist—but *flight*. In his sheltered paradise before the fall, Jim stumbles on a downed fighter plane and lives out his fantasy inside the cockpit, a moment John scored with serenity and heavenly choir (writing his trademark "RELIGIOSO" in the score). These angelic voices, a combination of women and boys, provide wordless emotional narration throughout Jim's odyssey, almost always connected with airplanes and boyhood innocence. But

---

†††† Kathleen Kennedy and Frank Marshall happened on "Suo Gân" while shopping for choral music with James Horner at a Tower Records in London. (Kennedy to TG.)

as darkness descends, that beatific beauty takes on a ghostly pall. The first sight of Japanese military prompts aleatoric percussive effects and an animalistic shakuhachi, calling to mind the musical disturbances in *Images*. When Jim is literally pulled from his childhood bedroom and out into the terrifying streets of Shanghai, the childlike tones in his motif are abandoned for spare, clustered tension and orchestral anxiety, and this terrifying sequence culminates with trumpets wailing in disturbed dissonance as Jim stands above a sea of humanity and cries out for his mommy.

Jim braves the outside world and finds a substitute father in Basie, a Fagin-like American expat played by John Malkovich. Spielberg demonstrated admirable patience and maturity in letting scenes unfold, often without dialogue; "I've been looking for a visual narrative—a motion-picture story—that could be told nearly exclusively through visual metaphors and non-pretentious symbolism," he said.[104] The film is also absent of score for many scenes, letting lonely coughs and the sad cacophony of war fill the soundtrack; when it *is* present, it's often lean and ambiguously fraught. So when the orchestra does swell, or Jim's theme returns, it's desperately meaningful—a cry from the distant past, a teardrop on an emaciated cheek. When Jim arrives at the labor camp where he will unknowingly spend the next few years, he sees a Japanese plane and reaches out to embrace it—his boyish silhouette, like Peter Pan's shadow, dramatically lit from behind by a welder's sparks. John scored it as a sacred moment. Jim's theme tiptoes in on fragile chimes and harp, hugged by strings and then horns, as a trinity of pilots walk over; Jim salutes them and they salute back in what Spielberg referred to as a "holy communion," sanctified by choir.[105]

Years elapse without comment, and a plucky adventure theme announces Jim's new life as he runs through the camp bartering various items and interacting with his neighbors—a surge of boyish optimism and imagination inside this hellhole, and a dance piece John earmarked for future Pops concerts. Jim's high-stakes mission to retrieve a pheasant outside the camp fence was scored with more wild shakuhachi and percussion, and his triumphant march to claim his reward—a bunk in the American men's dormitory—accompanied by the fife and drum march of "The British Grenadiers." There is little humor in the film, something Spielberg had to bite his tongue to avoid, but this small bit of buoyancy in the film's middle is welcome relief. As the war draws to a close, Jim watches as kamikaze pilots sing a Japanese hymn during their last rites and joins in with his nostalgic "Suo Gân" solo. Everyone in the camp looks on with confused awe, his young boy's voice joined by invisible chorus;[‡‡‡‡] the camp's defeated guard tears up at the beauty of the song and the stupid futility of war. Suddenly American planes whiz through the camp and Jim runs up to a rooftop in ecstasy, jumping up and down and waving maniacally. John's heavenly choir matched the surreal image of a plane flying by in slow motion, its pilot waving, and Jim lets out a shout of exultant joy—a holy fool. John named this magnificent cue "Cadillac of the Skies" after Jim's shouted nickname for the P-51 bomber, and

---

[‡‡‡‡] The voice actually belonged to an English chorister named James Rainbird.

the euphoric, *religioso* music abruptly sickens when Jim tells the camp doctor that if they had died, their bones would be in the runway; he begins to cry and says, "I can't remember what my parents look like," and the score's heart breaks from euphoria to anguish in an instant, with the choir continuing hauntingly as the doctor carries Jim down from the roof like a toddler, the camp exploding behind them. "He's in a fugue state of delirium and insanity," Spielberg remarked.

> Johnny understood that, and Johnny brought the voices into that sequence—which made the whole scene feel suspended. Not only was the P-51 flying, but Jim was off the ground as well, musically. John just had a sixth sense about creating something that was not only the right *fit*, but something that was going to raise the stakes of the story, of the suspense, of the drama, of the pathos, to elevations or altitudes I had not even envisioned. Which is why I have often said that Johnny does the final rewrite to all of my films.[106]

Though liberated, Jim and the other refugees now wander the wasteland without food or aid, and John accompanied this passage with a somber death march and emphatic string adagio. The ghost choir lingers over a stadium full of raided belongings and consecrates the moment when Mrs. Victor dies and Jim thinks the atom bomb light is her soul going up to heaven. The choir and Jim's theme ebb and flow with his fate—he trudges on, then finds a cache of American food, then trudges on again. Jim's happy reunion with his young Japanese counterpart is cut short when Basie and his gang shoot and kill the boy, and as Jim pumps his friend's chest (repeating "I can bring everyone back" with fervor), John's score treats it like a sacred rite with utter conviction—suddenly the boy he's trying to resurrect is his old self in his old red schoolboy uniform. In a callback to an earlier scene at his home, Jim rides a found bicycle through his old camp to the strains of a spunky, jubilant chorale that John composed for the film. The Latin words in "Exultate Justi" are about praising and rejoicing in the Lord, and the choir sings "Alleluia" right as missiles filled with food parachute through the roof and Jim laughs like a little boy again. (This ecclesiastic anthem entered John's Christmas Pops repertoire that December.)

John recorded the score in October at MGM with an enormous orchestra and choir. ("Suo Gân" had been recorded in London before production, by The Ambrosian Singers.) It was his first collaboration with recording engineer Shawn Murphy, who had previously worked for Disney on productions for its new theme park in Orlando, Epcot Center. "I had done some big scores prior to that," said Murphy, "but with John Williams you want to be absolutely on top of your game. So that picture was the education." Murphy caught on right away, proving himself handier than the typical engineer because he could also read music—until now, Lionel Newman had served as the "booth monitor" who handled that aspect—and he became an indispensable member of John's core team. Murphy was surprised to learn that John liked to balance everything live in the room and record it all at once, and since he was his own orchestrator "he knows what it's supposed to sound like," Murphy said. John also preferred to *live*

Plate 1. John, graduation day at St. Mary's, age 12, 1944 (Courtesy of John Williams).

Plate 2. John, age 18, in his garage apartment/studio (1950) (Courtesy of John Williams).

Plate 3. John during the Air Force years, 1952 (Courtesy of John Williams).

Plate 4. Regatta Day, St. John's, August 1952 (Courtesy of John Williams).

Plate 5. John at work in his Encino home, ca. 1959 (Courtesy of Jenny Williams).

Plate 6. John and baby Jenny, 1957 (Courtesy of John Williams).

Plate 7. John rehearsing with singer Leda Annest, ca. 1957 (Provided by Black Film Center & Archive, Indiana University, Bloomington, Indiana).

Plate 8. Barbara, expecting Joseph, at baby shower with her mother, Lurene Tuttle, August 1960 (Courtesy of Paula Arlich).

Plate 9. A domestic scene circa 1960; John with Barbara, Jenny, and Mark (Courtesy of John Williams).

Plate 10. John relaxing by the pool at his house in Encino, 1960 (Courtesy of John Williams).

Plate 11. John and Barbara in Calais, France, 1970 (Courtesy of Jenny Williams).

Plate 12. John and Jenny having fun in the pool, 1973 (Courtesy of Jenny Williams).

Plate 13. John with his father, Johnny Francis Williams, ca. 1980 (Courtesy of John Williams).

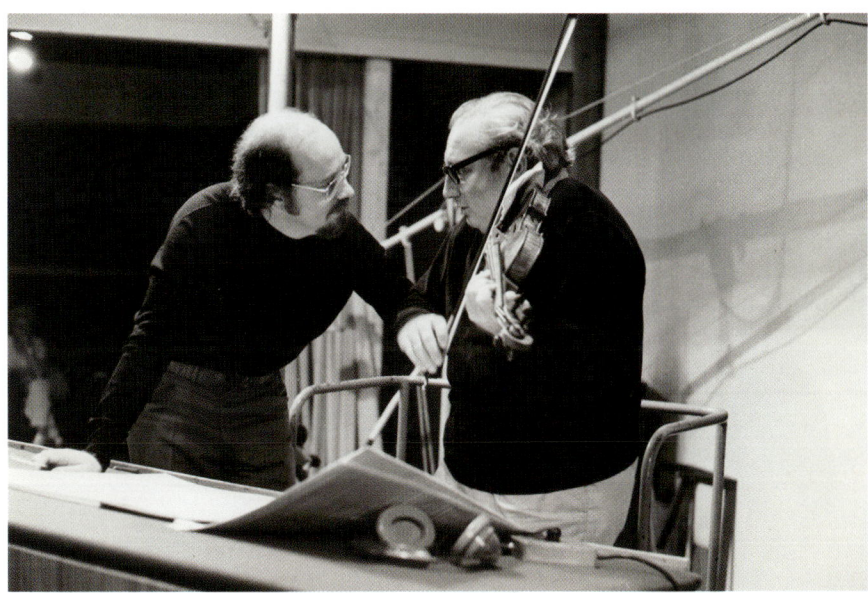

Plate 14. John and Isaac Stern in studio recording *Fiddler on the Roof*, July 1970 (Photo by David James, Courtesy of John Williams).

Plate 15. Toots Thielemans, Spielberg, and John at the *Sugarland Express* sessions, July 1973 (Photographer unknown, Courtesy of John Williams).

Plate 16. Recording the score for *Jaws* at Fox, May 1975 (Courtesy of John Williams).

Plate 17. Spielberg and John at work on *Close Encounters*, 1977 (Courtesy of John Williams).

Plate 18. John happy at the podium, ca. 1977 (Courtesy of Carroll Newman).

Plate 19. John at the piano with Lionel Newman, Jerry Goldsmith, and Carol Goldsmith, ca. 1976 (Photo by Alexander Courage. Alexander Courage Collection, Sibley Music Library, Eastman School of Music, University of Rochester).

Plate 20. John meets Queen Elizabeth II at the Royal Film Performance of *Close Encounters*, March 13, 1978 (Photo by Harry Myers/Shutterstock).

Plate 21. John basks in the response to his debut as new Boston Pops conductor, Carnegie Hall, January 22, 1980 (Associated Press).

Plate 22. Seiji Ozawa, Yo-Yo Ma, Tom Morris, and John at Tanglewood on Parade, August 1984 (Photographer unknown, Courtesy of John Williams).

Plate 23. John Denver, John, and Kim (Smedvig) Taylor before the Lincoln Memorial concert, July 1985 (Photographer unknown, Courtesy of John Williams).

Plate 24. John conducts the Pops on the South Lawn of the White House for Nancy Reagan, George H.W. Bush, and Barbara Bush, among 400 others, July 1985 (Courtesy of John Williams).

Plate 25. John and Lionel Newman in London, 1979 (Courtesy of Carroll Newman).

Plate 26. John with André Previn and his son, Matthew, ca. 1978 (Courtesy of John Williams).

Plate 27. John and Ken "Wampi" Wannberg at the moviola, ca. 1995 (Courtesy of John Williams).

Plate 28. John and Leonard Bernstein with the Boston Symphony Orchestra, 1989 (Photographer unknown, Courtesy of the BSO Archives).

Plate 29. President Barack Obama and John, February 25, 2010 (Courtesy of John Williams).

Plate 30. Spielberg and John backstage in the later years (Courtesy of John Williams).

Plate 31. John at work in his Amblin studio, ca. 1992 (Photo by Alexander Courage. Alexander Courage Collection, Sibley Music Library, Eastman School of Music, University of Rochester).

mix his score—"record it, and listen to it, and he'll make edits based on performances from take to take. Remixing is not really a big part of his world."[107]

Empire of the Sun was admired by a majority of critics, but some felt conflicted about its more operatic elements. "Art and artifice play equal parts in the telling of this tale," wrote Maslin. "And the latter, even though intrusive at times, is part and parcel of the film's overriding style." She noted the presence of a poster for *Gone With the Wind* in the film, and suggested that the 1939 movie was "a useful comparison, at least in terms of subject and style. The makers of that film didn't really burn Atlanta; that wasn't their method. They, too, as Mr. Spielberg does, let the score sometimes trumpet the characters' emotions unnecessarily."[108] David Stratton of the *Sydney Morning Herald* was much harsher: "When Jim salutes a trio of Japanese pilots, about to take off on a mission, or joins in singing a Japanese hymn, Spielberg films him as if shooting a mystical experience, and the usually reliable composer, John Williams, provides an execrable choral music score which reduces the whole scene to an embarrassing miscalculation."[109] But the chorus of praise prevailed. "Spielberg weaves this epic tapestry with grace and precision, threading throughout his own indelibly optimistic signature, spelled, of course, through the clear eyes of a wise and impressionable child," wrote Duane Byrge at the *Hollywood Reporter*. "Williams' resonant and triumphant score superbly augments this simple and complex narrative."[110] Vincent Canby put *Empire* in his top 10 of 1987, and deemed it "the best film ever made about childhood by a director born and bred in this country, where movie makers tend to take a safely revisionist view of childhood, one that's limited by expectations of what audiences want to believe about themselves."[111] Time and distance proved that this film was, indeed, the grown-up graduation of Spielberg into a new David Lean, anchored by a miraculous performance by Bale and transubstantiated by John's spiritual score. "John is the poet in me," Spielberg wrote at the time.[112]

Fittingly, John actually went to Japan just as *Empire* was being shipped to theaters. He took the Pops Esplanade on a five-city tour—to Osaka, Shizuoka, Yokohama, Tokyo, and Nagoya—where their repertoire of Broadway medleys, overtures, and John's film music was met with sold-out crowds. (The December 5 concert in Tokyo was broadcast on television across the nation.) Samantha joined him, and the whole company celebrated Thanksgiving together in Osaka.[113] John was having lower back pain again, and the Japanese music promoter, Yoshito Yamazaki, persuaded train conductors to allow John to lie on the floor of baggage compartments; at one point he gave John a piggyback ride down a flight of stairs at a train station.[114] John surmised his trouble was the result of bad posture at the writing desk, leaning to his right for more than 30 years, and he soon found a therapist in Boston who helped straighten him out. "I now write on the left side," he laughed. "Which actually, silly as that is, changed things."[115]

This tour was the beginning of a love affair between John and the people of Japan, who clearly already adored his music, and immediately there were talks of bringing the Pops back for another tour. The most obvious cultural difference with local audiences was how quiet and attentive they were during each piece—but when the concert ended, the ovations went on for as long as 25 minutes. "There's so much applause we can't get off the stage," said concertmaster Joseph Scheer, who observed that John was demonstrably proud of some of his own music: "He would *never* say that, of course, but you can tell by the way he conducts some of it, the music from *E.T.* and *Close Encounters* especially. When we're playing *Jaws*, there's a tongue-in-cheek feeling to it, but when we play the others, there's a sense of communication among all of us, and you can feel how important it is to him. When the audience responds that same way to his music, you can *see* how happy and touched John is."[116]

* * *

"I am committed to doing another *Indiana Jones* film," John told Dyer as he prepared for Japan, "but that comes later.

> I look at scripts all the time, and people are always suggesting projects to me, but I find it's increasingly harder to find something that's just right. There's no point in just doing some average kind of thing. People are always asking me what I think of the new movies, and I don't know what to say. After I've spent whole days in screening rooms, the last thing on earth I want to do is go and sit in the dark and watch another movie. I don't like to go and see my own films in the theater—I can't bear it. Usually the print is scratchy, and one of the speakers is full of static and another speaker is down, and I sit there in agony.

"Steven Spielberg is one of the few people who knows my secret," John added. "I never go to the movies."[117]

11
Somewhere in My Memory, 1988–1991

> We need to do the best work that we can and have others call it art or pop or trash or great or whatever it is going to be. I think to approach it with a mindset that it is beneath our dignity or beneath art, or any such attitude, is to be self-defeating from the first day.
>
> —**John Williams, 1991**[1]

John very nearly scored *Rain Man*. Spielberg spent months developing the project with actors Dustin Hoffman and Tom Cruise and screenwriter Ronald Bass—the story of a self-centered man who re-enters the life of his severely autistic older brother out of greed, but redemption ensues. Spielberg's new production designer, Rick Carter, prepared a whole "bible" of concept art that would have constructed a world from the autistic character's unique point of view.[2] But the script wasn't working well enough when Spielberg set off on his third adventure with Indiana Jones in the spring of 1988, so he had to let it go. Looking back, he called it one of the biggest regrets of his life.[3] Barry Levinson assumed the mantle, and his film won four Oscars—including best picture and best director. *Rain Man* also ignited the career of composer Hans Zimmer, whose synthesized pop licks and world music grooves signaled a stark departure from the symphonic, classical complexity of John's work.

Suddenly Zimmer became the exciting new flavor in Hollywood, courted by macho rock 'n' roll directors like the British brothers Ridley and Tony Scott. "They all thought Jerry Goldsmith and John Williams were has-beens, and it was time to do completely different things," Zimmer said. The new MO was: *Don't sound like John Williams*. "Orchestra was thought of as a very old-fashioned sound," said Zimmer, whose early work embodied that attitude—although he never agreed with it. "I remember having a Walkman and a cassette of *Close Encounters* and saying to this radical filmmaker, when nothing was going on, 'Hey, I've got this really interesting piece of music. Do you want to have a listen to it?'" Zimmer didn't tell him what it was, but had the director listen to the whole score. "That's really amazing. Who is it?" the director asked. "*John Williams*," Zimmer answered, to the director's shock. "Once I took the *Star Wars* baggage away, they could hear it."[4] Another composer on the rise was Danny Elfman, whose bombastic, gothic score for *Batman* drew some comparisons to John's super scores. But Elfman was a punk rocker and, like Zimmer, he had no classical training. This dramatic sea change had already started with the likes of untrained synth wizards, namely Vangelis and Giorgio Moroder, earlier in the decade—but the reign of old-school composers, educated in counterpoint and fugues, and who wrote and orchestrated their own music with pencil and paper, was rapidly dwindling.

As digital overtook analog in every aspect of filmmaking, musicians with electrical wiring had a distinct advantage. Zimmer helped pioneer the practice of synth mock-ups, crude but representative demos which mostly eliminated scoring-stage surprises for directors; this also killed off the quaint tradition of composers demonstrating their themes and ideas on a piano … as well as the luxury and freedom of being left to their own devices until the recording date. Film scoring quickly became a much more highly collaborative project with directors, which yielded positive fruit but also made it prone to micromanagement and endless rewriting. The move to digital film editing, which began in earnest in the late 1980s, made cutting and tweaking pictures infinitely easier, which made the cuts handed to composers less and less *locked*. This ever-fluid state began to favor—and perhaps even necessitate—Zimmer's brand of minimal, repetitive, groove-based scores, which could easily be snipped and shifted around to fit new edits. Once again, the film industry and its pundits were beginning to wonder if the old style of scoring—*John's* style—was still relevant.

Even outside of film, orchestras were in trouble. Symphonies in Oakland, San Diego, Vancouver, and Nashville were canceling their seasons and filing for bankruptcy, which in 1987 prompted longtime LA Phil manager Ernest Fleischmann to tell a graduating class of musicians in Cleveland bluntly: "The orchestra as we know it is dead." Paul Harvey, the folksy cultural commentator who told Americans true stories over the radio for 50 years, wrote a syndicated opinion column in March 1988 about the worrisome state of classical music, and he offered a diagnosis:

> Historically, a primary requisite of concert music was that it must appeal to somebody outside the professional music field. Audiences mostly. Perhaps an isolated, individual patron. But one way or another, concert music, to justify itself, had to reach out to human hearts beyond the footlights. Today we have composers capable of doing that. John Williams is one. So capable is he of stirring our emotions that his work is regularly commissioned to enhance America's finest motion pictures. Yet, such is the arrogance of right-now concert programmers that they will accept the theater music of a teenage Mendelssohn on a "serious" program while rejecting the incidental music of John Williams.[5]

When composer William Bolcom won the Pulitzer Prize for his piece "12 New Etudes for Piano" in 1988, he spoke about the difficulty of making a living as a composer, and noted how John smartly recognized that film was "what makes the bucks. And he got knocked down by other composers, because they're a jealous lot. This century is the only one in which composers are essentially judged by their peers, and the parochialism that brings about has created a lot of difficulty."[6]

* * *

Samantha was looking at vacation homes, and she ended up designing one from scratch in Colorado, near Telluride. At one point, she had considered purchasing

Cole Porter's old house in Williamstown, Massachusetts—but it was too far from Tanglewood to be of much use for John. "This man's just not interested in anything but music," she said, "so I'd never see him. He'd always be heading for Lenox."[7]

The year 1988 was full of fanfares. John was commissioned by NBC to write new music for the Summer Olympics in Seoul; he wrote a *Fanfare for Ten Year Olds* for the tenth anniversary of the Young Charleston Theatre Company in South Carolina; and by year's end he also gave an athletic piece to his new neighbors in Colorado, a fanfare for the Alpine World Ski Championships in Vail, which was recorded by local brass players and percussion in Denver. None of these pieces captured the culture's ear like his previous event tunes, and their moment was about as ephemeral as the 1988 presidential campaign of Michael Dukakis, longtime governor of Massachusetts, for whom John *also* wrote a fanfare. Dukakis was married to Harry Ellis Dickson's daughter, Kitty, and Dickson—veteran assistant conductor of the Pops—approached John about writing a piece "very hesitatingly." But John said: "I'll do anything in the world for Mike. It would be an honor." "If Mike is elected," Dickson said, "I think we'll have some wonderful concerts in the White House."[8] *Fanfare for Michael Dukakis* premiered at the Democratic National Convention in Atlanta, with Dickson leading a local 35-piece band of brass, drums, and electric guitar.[9] It had some of the spunky spirit from *Amazing Stories* and the Mission Theme, but sounded corny in a weak performance as it heralded the party's ill-fated nominee ahead of his acceptance speech, which included the electrifying line: "This election isn't about ideology. It's about competence." John watched the performance from home on TV. "I hope it's suitably celebratory and magisterial and in the spirit to match the moment," he said.[10] Reporting on the convention for *L.A. Weekly*, John Powers referred to John as "that most Reaganoid of film composers."[11] Asked whether he was a Democrat, John replied, through a spokesperson: "I'm uncomfortable with labels, but I'm comfortable with Michael."[12]

That spring, John conducted a concert of film music at UCLA alongside an all-star roster of composers—including Goldsmith, Georges Delerue, Maurice Jarre, Ennio Morricone, Newmans David and Randy, Alex North, and Miklós Rózsa[13]—as well as an evening of his scores in Orange County. The Pops kicked off its 1988 season with special guest Dionne Warwick, whom John had known since she sang on *Valley of the Dolls*, and that summer they hosted Ray Charles, Perry Como, and the Smothers Brothers. "I think the orchestra is in the best shape it's been in since I came here," said John, who was proud of new acoustic and lighting improvements inside Symphony Hall.[14] The summer culminated in a gigantic 70th birthday celebration for Leonard Bernstein at Tanglewood, and John conducted some of the four-hour, globally televised concert alongside Seiji Ozawa, John Mauceri, and Michael Tilson Thomas—though he was practically lost in the sea of guest musicians, opera stars, and celebrities which ranged from Quincy Jones to Lauren Bacall. Standing in the wings of a concert stage as John was about to walk on, Bernstein, without any warning, reached down and grabbed John by the testicles and whispered in his ear: "Don't fuck this up!" (This became an amusing anecdote in the Williams family.)[15] At the end of the night, everyone huddled on stage and sang "Happy Birthday" to the honoree, and a teary Bernstein hugged and kissed the lot.

An afterparty was held at the nearby Blantyre, a Gilded Age–era castle and resort where John was staying the night. He regularly lodged here during his Tanglewood retreats, claiming the former "ice house," which had been converted into a cozy cottage, complete with a grand piano and verdant views. He had a concert in Saratoga Springs the next evening, so he hadn't planned to attend the party or even the curtain call, but for Bernstein's sake he decided to stick around and leave for Saratoga early the next morning. John had a new assistant at the BSO, 30-year-old Diane Read, and he put her up in the room adjacent, where Jenny often stayed. "My alarm goes off at, I don't know, 5:30 in the morning or some insane time like that," Read recalled. "I hear this little knock on the door that was between my room and John's room, and I crack it open and he whispers: 'Angel, I ordered pancakes!'" After breakfast they drove an hour north to Saratoga Springs, where that night John conducted the Philadelphia Orchestra at the new Saratoga Performing Arts Center. The air was so chilly that steam was visibly emanating from John in his exertion. One of Read's new tasks was to hand John a dry shirt during intermissions; no one could imagine "how soggy this man's shirts are after just one set on stage," she said. (When fans wrote to John and asked why he always wore a black turtleneck, he explained: "Conducting is rigorous work. Black doesn't show perspiration.") Samantha was a very health-conscious person, said Read, "so it was really naughty of him to send me out to go get a Big Mac and fries" after the concert. They got in the car to drive back to Tanglewood, and John said: "Oh, angel, we need a little something-something for the road." "So we pull into this Mini Mart," said Read, and get the grossest stuff:

> Pretzels and licorice sticks and just crazy, *jack your blood sugar and drive in the middle of the night back to where you came from* kind of thing. In a 24-hour period I've gone from Bernstein to pancakes to a concert where he's steaming and a Big Mac, and now we're loading up on crap to drive back home. And I remember the moon was full. There was something very otherworldly about it, kind of out-of-body.

From then on, John and Read gave each other junk food nicknames. "I send mail to his house: 'Maestro Enrico Donutti,'" she said, "and he calls me his 'Little Cruller,' or 'The Donut Lady.'" On a later Pops tour, they even dreamed up a fictional business called Donut Man Donuts. "Our motto was 'Take a bite out of this,'" said Read. "One year for his birthday, I made him a Donut Man Donuts uniform vest. Of *course* he was going to write a theme song."[16]

* * *

But that summer wasn't all donuts and pancakes. A long-gestating lawsuit against John by composer Les Baxter, his one-time employer, went to trial in downtown Los Angeles. Baxter first sued John in 1983, alleging that the main theme from *E.T.* was stolen from an exotica instrumental called "Joy" from Baxter's 1953 album, *The*

Passions. He wanted a piece of *E.T.*'s enormous profit, not damages, and claimed John had to have known "Joy," since John played that piece with Baxter's orchestra at the Hollywood Bowl in the 1960s. The district court dismissed it using a simple layperson test: "The Court cannot hear any substantial similarity between defendant's expression of the idea and plaintiff's." But Baxter appealed, and the Ninth Circuit Court of Appeals granted him a trial. What followed was a total waste of John's time—as well as an incredible opportunity for others to hear John dissect his process at a granular level ... because the defendant was also a lead witness.

For two weeks in late August, Judge Harry Hupp and a jury heard both "Joy" and *E.T.* played over and over. They watched the 1982 film in its entirety. Philip Springer, a composer and witness for the plaintiff, testified that he thought John repeated *himself* when he wrote the *E.T.* theme after the *Star Wars* theme. "I never tell a lie," he told John's attorney, Ronald Rosen. "Many composers do repeat themselves, don't they?" said Rosen. "Yes, but not with quite such banal material," Springer replied. "You consider Mr. Williams's material to be banal?" "I consider the *Star Wars* theme to be banal, yes.... [But] I think corny is a better word."[17] Snooty condescension about John's music was now playing out in a court of law.

John sat at a piano in the courtroom and gave a robust, but always dignified, defense against Baxter's claims. Not only was Baxter unable to supply any evidence that John ever actually played "Joy" at the Bowl, but John whipped the notion that there was any conscious similarity between the one tiny phrase in "Joy" and his *E.T.* theme. He compared it to reading sentences from two different books—"I took the bus to Bakersfield," and "We took the bus to Toronto." "What's common is 'took the bus,'" he said. "That's what you heard as being similar.... It's not 'Joy,' it's not *E.T.* It's been microscoped out of context." John also walked the jury through his creation of the *E.T.* score, explaining how the opening "clarion call" was the basis for the main theme, and how "the psychology of the fifth belongs to our collective human memory. It's a call to battle." Professor Williams also emphasized the difference between *emotions* in the two tunes:

> In *E.T.*, when the bicycle takes off—remember E.T. and his little friends racing the bicycle, straining with great effort to break gravity and to fly?—the composer has to create an emotion that is not joy ... We need to make a distinction that's subtle but of the essence. We know what joy is. Nicely described in Mr. Baxter's music. In the *E.T.* theme, I'd like to use the word *exaltation*, the theme is exalting. We know what joy is, it's happiness. Do we know what exaltation is? Exaltation is happiness, but it's more. It's like when you bust your gut running a race, marathon even, and you come through the finish line and that feeling of success after tremendous struggle, tremendous tension to win something, when you break the ... That is exaltation. That's more than joy.
>
> Now, how do I define exaltation musically? It's got to have some weight.... The basic tempo is the same, but the meter, the kinetic, the energy of both melodies is totally different. That's why one is written in quarter notes, and the other is written in half notes. Mine has long notes, it has to give us exaltation. The end of the B

theme, which you haven't heard yet in *E.T.* ends like this [*plays piano*]. It's great tension, unresolved, great expectation to go [*plays piano*]. That's not joy—that's exaltation. If I made my piece the same rhythm as Baxter's, it would be like this [*plays and sings*]. Then we are coming to the big tune, and it will be [*plays*]. The length of the notes is absolutely of the essence. That's the reason it's in 3/2 and not 4/4. I don't want to again take the time to write this out. I hope you all remember that the *E.T.* music is written in 3/2 and the notes were big and they were round.

Now, to conduct "Joy" [*plays piano*], a well-titled piece [*sings*], it has a bounce to it, that's why he's got *da-da-da-dum*, it's always marked separate—separate bows, marcato and woodwinds and so on—*da-da-da-da-da-de-da-bum-bum*. It's not the same emotion as *da-de-da-da-da-da-da-dum*. It won't work if the notes are too short. It won't work if the tempo doesn't have a broad kinetic to it. *E.T.* will not work if I shorten those notes. The length of the note is of the essence in determining what the emotional meaning is.... The psychology behind the two compositions is completely different. If I'd ever heard Baxter's music, which I never have, I wouldn't possibly connect it with—

MR. BLANCHARD: "I think he's arguing again, Your Honor."
ROSEN: Now, Mr. Williams if you could—
COURT: Okay. Let's stick with the musical opinions.
WILLIAMS: Sorry.

John continued to excitedly play and sing to demonstrate his points, and kept tripping into accidentally "arguing."

When are you going to resolve it? When the bicycle goes up [*plays piano*] or whatever the relevant action is. And we time it on the screen exactly. I wait for that moment. The orchestra plays this [*plays*]. Now when that bicycle goes off, we play tonic, home, mother chord [*plays*]. We can't play [*plays*]. It doesn't resolve yet, it's too late. It's impossible to use a dominant chord at that point. So our pieces are insufficiently alike, intervallically in their melody. That is insufficient to identify either piece.... So you've been asked to look at one little fragment out of context, you've been asked to look at "have rode the bus"—

COURT: Slow down. I think you are getting into argument now.
WILLIAMS: Sorry, sorry. I beg your pardon, Your Honor, I've never been in court before.
COURT: I understand.
WILLIAMS: I'm not a teacher. I'm doing my best to be clear.

A few minutes later, he was too excitable for the stenographer:

And then a little bit later he has a harmony that goes [*plays*]. The orchestra is playing very loud, and underneath the tubas and the trombones and trumpets—
COURT: Wait a minute. Slow down, please.

WILLIAMS: Okay. Underneath—
COURT: Slow down and keep your voice up loud enough to be heard over the music because—
WILLIAMS: How about if I say first what's going to happen?
COURT: —because the Reporter has to hear what you're saying as well as the Recorder over here has to get it on the recording machine.
WILLIAMS: I've been chastised for this before.
COURT: Well, it's not a chastisement.
WILLIAMS: No, it's proper. I apologize. In the third stage, there is a long chord....

In the end, the court ruled that there was no copyright infringement. Baxter appealed, unsuccessfully. "The only person whom I ever heard say anything unflattering about John was Les Baxter," said singer Michael Feinstein. "But Les was, from my perspective, kind of cuckoo."[18] The lawsuit "was certainly a nuisance," John admitted.[19]*

* * *

John's new *Olympic Spirit* theme papered NBC's 19-day coverage of the 1988 Summer Games in Seoul, which kicked off in September. ABC still held the exclusive rights to Leo Arnaud's *Bugler's Dream*, the fanfare that Americans had associated with the Olympics since 1968, and which John used to precede his 1984 Olympic theme. (Arnaud was actually an old acquaintance of John's father, having played trombone in Roger Wolfe Kahn's band.) This new piece—another bugler's dream, leading into a more stately, grand expression over a rapid-fire snare pulse—was very good, but quickly forgotten, perhaps because NBC's ratings were much lower than four years earlier. John also wrote 50 short new bumpers for NBC news and election coverage, an election which saw Dukakis lose in a landslide to George H.W. Bush. "It's very difficult to devise music for television," John confessed, "in part because the sound is so bad. People leave the set on all the time, and so it becomes nothing more than the source of a constant noise level. So, I write fanfares in the hope of catching people's attention. Actually, these days, synthesizer music is on television almost 24 hours a day. So when you write acoustic music, the way I do, you automatically get attention!"[20]

He wanted to take a hiatus from movies, but then along came a little gem he simply couldn't turn down. *The Accidental Tourist* was based on a novel by Anne Tyler about a man who writes guidebooks for business travelers that eliminate all foreign surprises and discomforts. Macon is grieving the death of his child, which breaks up his marriage, when he meets an eccentric dog trainer named Muriel who slowly begins to pump blood back into his broken heart. Lawrence Kasdan directed the film, starring William Hurt and Geena Davis, casting the whole story in shades of gray.

---

* Eight years later, a plastic surgeon in Irvine sued John, MCA, and Amblin, claiming that the theme for *Jurassic Park* was a blatant theft of an unpublished song the doctor wrote in 1991 after the death of his daughter. The case was dismissed. (Zan Dubin, "Hollywood Stole His Tune, Irvine Man Says," *Los Angeles Times*, June 14, 1996.)

"The thought of that kind of loss was overwhelming to me," Kasdan said. "So, while I thought the movie could be very funny—and for me, at least, *is*—it's also sad. I think even Anne Tyler was a little shocked by how sad I found the whole thing. I don't know if it's because she doesn't have children.... But to me it's one of the saddest books ever written." Kasdan hired Bruce Broughton, one of several younger composers who found work operating in a Williams-esque mode—who had previously scored the director's 1985 western *Silverado*. Broughton "really wanted to do the job," Kasdan said. "But I think I had something in my head that was so strong which I identified at the time as *Bach*. No one knows less what that means than me, but I had liked Bach, and I thought that was the right feeling for *Accidental Tourist*. I think he was mystified by that, and I'm sad that I had to say, 'I'm gonna move on.'" Facing a void, Kasdan said: "The thought that I could get *John* was astounding to me."[21]

In late August, amidst Bernstein's 70th birthday party and the lawsuit, John heard about Kasdan's film and asked if he could screen it. "I *loved* this movie when I first saw it," John said. "It's a beautiful love story. It's a story about sadness, and happiness, and family, and a beautiful little boy. So it's basic, wonderful human values. I was so touched with it." John also saw it as a refreshing oasis, a chance to break away from all of the space adventures that require extroverted "brass and cymbals and fanfare and so on; great for music, swashbuckling and all of that. But having done a dozen or so of those, along comes *Accidental Tourist*, which is quiet and touching and sweet. And a wonderful opportunity to create music. It had a gentle, atmospheric, nostalgic feeling."[22] When Kasdan made his reference to Bach, John understood immediately—and even though Macon's family is a kooky lot who feel like they belong to another era and maybe even another country, Kasdan said it wasn't so much about the *oldness* of Bach's music. It was the idea that "there were a lot of delicate notes dancing around something that was very heavy.

> I don't know if that even describes Bach, but in *my* mind that's what Bach could do. There's such detail. Tiny little moments, with enormous speed, where you say, "*Oh*, what am I feeling now? What am I feeling now? What change just happened?" I think that's what I was looking for. Because the hero, Macon, is dancing between the grief just killing him and ending his chances in life, and this possibility of some sort of second life—that he could recover.[23]

John's main theme for *The Accidental Tourist*, typically performed on piano, has some Bach-like ornamentation in its hypnotic, looping staircase of grief. It's always in motion, almost obsessively, carried along by a rolling river of piano arpeggios. It tries to rise, but keeps falling back down. "The creation of a tune like this, while it seems simple and while it is direct, can take lots of time," said John. "It's like so many things in life: if you press for it, if you get writer's cramp ... it won't work. You have to be easy, let it come to you, and in that sense you don't court the muse. You wait for it and she comes. The harder you search for it, the more difficult will be the connection."[24] It was one of his simplest and most economical scores—he essentially repeated this one theme again and again. The film opens with the four chords at the heart of this theme, played haltingly on electric keyboard—a motto which hovers over the rest of the score like the ghost of Macon's son, Ethan.

This central dance of grief hints at hope when Macon first meets Muriel, and the tune has a cheery exterior and an up tempo as their relationship progresses—it works well for budding romance, sometimes handed from piano to sonorous woodwinds, but remains stuck and unable to escape its intrinsic melancholy. The tone grows warmer as Macon begins to bond with Muriel's own son, but he panics at the prospect of a new, messy life with another family and messily rebounds with his first wife, Sarah. Their misguided rekindling is scored with a romantic but troubled repetition of that ghostly motto; they can't escape the pain they share. The atmosphere is hazy and mystical when Macon finally breaks it off with Sarah and runs away to Paris. John's opening motto plays timidly on keyboards as Macon lugs his suitcase down a Paris street, it picks up momentum—then holds on a pregnant string sustain as he sets down his suitcase and symbolically abandons his baggage. A mysterious interlude accompanies him hailing a cab, when he suddenly sees the visage of his son in a French boy who helps him. The tune slowly gathers steam as he starts for the airport, but it's nearly swallowed by anguish as he passes the boy in slow motion and begins to weep. And then he sees Muriel, and the melody surges and blooms with romance as they lock eyes—and Macon finally *smiles*. The end credits explode into a gleeful, liberated development of the theme dancing on top of a sprightly brass rhythm. "The last scene in the movie is a masterclass in film scoring," said David Newman. "A theme that is hardly ever developed in the score begins to unfold and flower, just like the Macon Leary character. It's wonderful."[25]

"I love dualities," said Kasdan, "and that theme expresses such duality. Because it's the tragedy and the grief. And the grief, in my mind, couldn't be controlled like a dog. He goes looking for some way to control this uncontrollable thing that's haunting him, and he finds someone who can help him do that. But the duality of that sadness and melancholy ... plus this thing up here which is like: *there's still hope*."[26]

The Accidental Tourist was a critical darling, and the film earned Oscar nominations for best picture, screenplay, and score. John lost to the music from Robert Redford's offbeat southwestern fantasy, *The Milagro Beanfield War*, composed by Dave Grusin—who didn't even bother to come to the ceremony because he thought he "was the longest shot of the evening," Grusin said. "I figured John Williams would win again."[27] John seemed especially proud of this score when he played selections and discussed it with Gene Shalit on *Today* ahead of the Oscars, but he strangely let it expire soon after. "I've tried a million times to get him to let me do that final scene" in concert, said Newman. "He just doesn't like it."[†][28]

* * *

There was a slight feeling of obligation when Spielberg finally fulfilled his promise to George Lucas to direct *three* Indiana Jones pictures. He had all but disowned the second film—"There's not an ounce of my own personal feeling in *Temple of Doom*,"

[†] Newman finally got his chance in 2022 when he conducted an evening of John's music in San Diego.

Spielberg said[29]—and by 1988, he was on to less "popcorny" adventures and seemed a bit tired of the whip and wise cracking. Chris Columbus, the promising young screenwriter of *Gremlins*, was hired to write the third film in 1984—but his *Indiana Jones and the Monkey King* was rejected, and Jeffrey Boam (who had written *Innerspace* for Amblin) came in and cracked a story about the Holy Grail, centered on Indy's discordant relationship with his father. With the brilliant casting of Sean Connery as Henry Jones, Sr., *Indiana Jones and The Last Crusade* openly acknowledged the series' sonship to James Bond and became a comic, odd couple road movie with a tender heart, which also followed the basic blueprint of *Raiders*.

John thought it was the best film of the trilogy,[30] and he spent the latter half of 1988 working on his score. There was plenty of cartooning, beginning with the lengthy prologue featuring River Phoenix's young Indy stealing an ancient cross from tomb raiders and escaping via moving circus train. John gave the Cross of Coronado its own Spanish-inflected motif, and he choreographed the ensuing chase with a plucky new adventure theme—an elaborate set piece so fun and so melodic that one could actually hum the whole thing.‡ As the cue gallops merrily along, John accented a moment with snakes, a rhino gets its own low brassy motif, and many of the thuds and beats are punctuated, yet the whole piece flows like a liquid ballet without ever lazily Mickey-Mousing. The first hint of the *Raiders* march comes hesitantly when Indy picks up a whip and gives himself his identifiable chin scar, and then it rouses heroically as Indy runs away from the train. John liked this cue so much, especially as a demonstration of the vital role music plays in film, that he began regularly conducting it in concert to picture.

His major new themes were for Henry Jones and the Holy Grail. The Grail motif is a stoic hymn, more reverently grown-up and weary than the childlike fear-and-wonder of the Ark theme from *Raiders*. This tune solemnly plays as Donovan, the story's covert villain, tells Indy a "bedtime story" about the grail—but then it gives way to Henry's theme when the conversation turns to Indy's missing father. Tender, paternal, and English, this theme was the soft heart of the film. Between the Boy Scout adventures and the major theme of a father-son reconciliation, Spielberg was clearly plumbing territory close to home. There was also a new Nazi motif, but Elsa—Indy's latest love interest, played by Alison Doody—forfeited her right to a love theme by betraying our hero.

Much like Spielberg was at this point in his life, the *Last Crusade* score straddles a line between popcorn-buttered boyhood escapades and the acceptance of responsibility and the all-importance of family. The balancing act works, thanks to the undeniable comic chemistry between Connery and Ford, and John gave their father-son exploits a syncopated scherzo which begins when they're tied up by the Nazis and, having escaped a room they accidentally set on fire, revs up as they lead a frenzied motorcycle chase from still more Nazis. John always felt the action in *Indiana Jones* movies had a wink, and he gave the latter piece the cheeky title "Scherzo for Motorcycle

---

‡ Cartoon character Peter Griffin did just that in a 2011 episode of *Family Guy*. The show's creator, Seth MacFarlane, was a huge John Williams fan.

and Orchestra"—which became another evergreen favorite of his in concerts. An even more comedic, burlesque act accompanies the scene on a blimp when Nazis search for the Jones boys. They collide with Donovan and his goons in the desert, in a tank-versus-horse chase that visually echoes the truck chase from *Raiders*, but John scored this action with a more lumbering, sinister rhythm befitting the villains' Panzers. Having taken a few years off from this kind of hyper-balletic scoring, John's replenished energy was apparent in the multitude of busy-but-catchy action cues—including an early boat chase in Vienna with strummed mandolin for local flavor and a time-bomb-ticking climax as Indy's boat is being chopped to pieces by a giant blade.

The story concludes not with a chase or explosive fight, but a hushed obstacle course inside an ancient temple, where Indy has to rely on his father's religious knowledge and his own faith. The atmosphere here is far more internal and relational than merely suspenseful—because the stakes are personal: Henry has been shot, and Indy must retrieve the Grail if he wants to save his father's life. John reverently developed the holy Grail hymn as Indy spells "Jehovah" correctly and proceeds to the final test, where choir and swirling melody attend his arrival at a staggering chasm. The Grail theme repeats on strings in an anxious variation as Marcus Brody pleads for Indy to come quickly; the music builds and then holds for a sustained chord as Indy takes a leap of faith—rewarded with a firm footing on an invisible bridge and chords of mystical relief.

All throughout the journey, John judiciously scattered warm, familial statements of his respective themes for Henry and Indy; after Henry sees his son go over the edge of a cliff and believes him to be dead, their grateful hug is marked with a slow, noble variation of Henry's theme, which quickly turns animated as Henry pluckily marches on, and Indy's tune floats on solo flute as a sweet punchline when his hat miraculously rolls by. Their evolving relationship gives the film its emotional resolution: after Elsa falls to her death trying to grab the Grail, Henry reaches out for his son and, using his boy's preferred name for the first time, gently says: "*Indiana*. Let it go"—a moment made all the more beautiful by a duet between Henry's father-knows-best theme and a soft cello rendition of his son's theme. The film ends with warmth and humor and a ride into the sunset, and John trotted out his major melodies in a grand suite for the end credits.

"This is my commencement music," Spielberg said as he listened to the score being recorded at MGM in February 1989. "It feels like the end of an era, and the end of a quest."[31] The film did expectedly great business when it opened in May, and while some critics felt it showed signs of fatigue and repetition, others saw signals of maturity. "It once seemed as if Spielberg films were prompted entirely by other films, and that they had no real connection to a world outside," Vincent Canby wrote. "With *Empire of the Sun* and *Indiana Jones and the Last Crusade*, it is clear that his movies are growing up."[32]

* * *

John flew to Tucson that January for a concert to benefit the Jewish Federation of Southern Arizona. It had been almost 40 years since he was stationed at Monthan Air Force Base, and the town was unrecognizable to him.[33] The clarinetist for the Tucson Symphony, John Denman, used to play for the National Philharmonic Orchestra in

London and had played on several of John's early scores. "I noticed that his stick technique has changed and he is much more the symphonic conductor than the movie conductor that I remember," Denman said. "But there was one thing I missed in seeing him more recently. When he was young, he always used to conduct with a large cigar sticking out of his mouth."[34] John did the Tucson concert, of mostly his film music, as a favor to the local chapter's president: Deborah Newman Sharpe. He had known Lionel's daughter since she was a little girl.

Just two weeks later, on February 3, Lionel Newman died from cardiac arrest at Cedars-Sinai Medical Center. He was 73.[35] John was recording a session for *Last Crusade* that day; the funeral was held on, of all days, John's birthday. He gave the eulogy for his best friend, and spoke about Newman's childhood and how he had inherited personality traits from his mother:

> Like Luba, Lionel's wit and humor was forged by a thousand years of Russian Jewish experience. When he talked to agents on the telephone, he could resemble a canny 12th century Byzantine. He was colorful, and he could set your imagination running wild. Frank Sinatra, in his biography, says that Lionel was one of the funniest men in Hollywood. Sinatra was right. Marilyn Monroe adored him ... it was impossible not to.[36]

John spoke of the profound impact the Newman family had on American culture ("The story of this family is the story of our country," he said, "and it would take at least an E. L. Doctorow to do it justice"), and he won laughs as he detailed Newman's collection of crude novelties and his infamous mouth: "If the control of words can command legions, and the pen is mightier than the sword, then Lionel's mouth was more potent than anything the Pentagon could shoot at you." But John also detailed how profound Newman's advice and friendship were for him personally, how Lionel had given him just the right direction during a session of *How to Steal a Million*—and how "for years, I discussed every project I did with him, and the message was always the same: Do a good job, don't let me down. I NEED to be proud of you!"

"We were really close friends," John added, "and when I would get a little depressed, he would always exhort me to love life, to celebrate it. He used to say to me over and over again: 'The world is still beautiful, even with all the traffic, the injustice, the noise, the wars. The world is still beautiful. It's all we have and we should celebrate it.'"[37] John had lost one of the other great loves of his life, and no one ever quite filled the particular void that Newman's death created. "I think Lionel Newman gave John endless hours of entertainment," said Spielberg, who admitted he wasn't funny himself and couldn't do that for John. "Lionel was talented, but he was crass, and he was crude, he was inappropriate—not only for *this* time, but for *all* time. And yet he was completely amusing, and there's nothing that he wouldn't say if he felt like saying it. And I think John admired his chutzpah. I think also John would sit there in a room with Lionel, and probably to himself there, say: *There but for the grace of God go I.*"[38] Many of John's friends wondered how John—so dignified, so proper, so tactful—could have loved such a man so deeply. Bill Cosel figured "it was that Lionel was so outrageous, on all levels, that it amused John to think that somebody could actually do that. Because *he* wouldn't. He would not behave like that. And I know when we've had phone conversations and would pass jokes back and forth, I've sometimes let a blue word slip out—and he'll laugh. And I realize it's probably not part of his day anymore. He doesn't have Lionel."[39]

When Carroll Newman went to see John at the Hollywood Bowl that September, she started crying: "What I saw was Johnny moving so much as he conducted. He started dancing. That's what my dad did. I had never seen John conduct that way."[40]

* * *

Against all odds, John had arrived at his tenth season with the Boston Pops. His guests in the summer of 1989 included soprano Kathleen Battle and saxophonist Branford Marsalis in a tribute to Duke Ellington; Loretta Lynn and Crystal Gayle in an evening of country music; Mandy Patinkin and Barbara Cook in a Broadway showcase; and Previn performing Gershwin's piano concerto. In June, he conducted a program with Leonard Bernstein. "It takes a conductor who doesn't know the meaning of fear to share the podium with Bernstein," Dyer wrote. "Williams acquitted himself with his usual unassuming honor."[41] John had cut back significantly on his weekly commitments, but he did take the Pops Esplanade out on a 10-city tour. Reflecting on his milestone tenure, John said:

> So much has changed—and so little. That's the way tradition works; change comes in very small increments. I don't think it's complacent to point out that the popularity of the Pops does not seem to have diminished at all. But we have to be alert to the danger signs. The traditional source of the Pops repertory is the Broadway stage, and now there's very little new music that people want to live with, that they want to keep. So we have to keep up the search for a repertoire, finding new things, and discarding things that no longer work. The Pops is famous for delivering a certain glowing good feeling that it must produce each and every time out. The amazing thing is that it does.[42]

In an interview that ran on the Fourth of July, John volunteered more introspective and philosophical musings than he ever did with a reporter:

> Music is very intoxicating, very seductive. It can hold your attention longer than reading. When I'm working, I don't think of myself. I think only of the music. I don't set out to lose myself, but I do. I abandon myself to the music. If you concentrate completely on subject X, your own adrenaline anesthetizes you from subject Y. The pursuit of excellence is what life ought to be about. It's trying to get closer to God, to imitate the perfect state. The odyssey to find perfection should define humanity. This thought comes into my consciousness when I'm working. If I forge my music better, if I shape it better, if I make it better, I am happier than if I hadn't tried. To me it's like this: If you bust your gut and you lose, you feel badly. But if you don't bust your gut and you lose, you feel much worse....

> Discipline is essential to creativity. Rarely is anything right the first time. Maybe, *maybe* you get it on the fifth try. Discipline involves tenacity and steadfastness. It has to be applied vigorously every day. Music is athletic. You have to train every day in order to perform. If you get lazy, you get weak. Musicians are like joggers. If you jog every day, you get to a higher level. Success is the result of sustained effort.
>
> Music is a basic human need. We communicate verbally. We communicate with body language. But there comes a time when a shepherd picks up a flute or a hunter picks up a drum and plays out his joy or his pain. Music is an essential nutrient. Without it, we are incomplete.

"I'm never frustrated by music," John added. "What can be frustrating is not being able to solve problems in a given piece. You have to address yourself to your own inadequacies. The joy of music doesn't come often to me. Most things are flawed. Maybe I'm being too hard on myself. The ideal always seems to elude me. I always want to do better. After all, I'm defined by my work, by the details of the process of making music. My work is what I am."[43]

* * *

John had watched a rough cut of *Born on the Fourth of July*, and he was "staggered" by it. "It may be the most powerful film I have ever seen. It sounds pretentious to say I was 'inspired,' but I knew immediately I had to do it, and I knew immediately how to do it. I want to score it for trumpet and strings."[44]

Something just clicked when John met Oliver Stone, a filmmaker who, despite his seeming gruffness and cynicism about America, was actually a gooey romantic at his core. Stone had been disillusioned about his country after serving in the Vietnam War, and he started making films from his disillusionment that were amazingly popular, beginning with *Platoon* in 1984. Long before that, Stone had wanted to tell the true story of Ron Kovic, a patriotic kid from Massapequa, New York, who volunteered to serve in Vietnam, where he was paralyzed from the waist down in combat, then came back to a country that spat on him and turned a blind eye, converting Kovic into an activist. Back in 1978, it was going to star Al Pacino and likely be directed by someone other than Stone.[45] It took another decade, and the successful launch of Stone's filmmaking career, to make it a reality. Stone cast the young star of *Rain Man*, Tom Cruise, to play a mostly wheelchair-bound, long-haired Kovic. If *Platoon* was the *Iliad*, Stone said, *July* was the *Odyssey*: he had to get the soldiers back home.[46]

It was Budd Carr, Stone's music editor, who suggested John should score the film. "I don't think that'll work, because he's a big shot," Stone told him, but Carr said, "No, I think he'd be interested." John "was known then for his summer performances with the Boston Pops," Stone reflected, "with a classic Fourth of July concert, and also, of course, with his work for sci-fi films and Spielberg. He was regarded, at that point, as *the* American composer. And this, as Budd pointed out, was truly an American film."[47] Stone arranged a meeting with John in February, and then screened a five-hour version of the film for him in April. John immediately cottoned to this warrior from New England:

I felt greatly in sympathy with him. Maybe if I hadn't been in the Air Force I wouldn't have had quite the same feeling. He seemed one of my brothers, in a sense. He'd been through a lot of the same experience … although what I was playing in, writing music for a band, that's hardly being in Vietnam. But Oliver's a man of action. He would be up on the battlements.[48]

And even though Stone's temperament was a far remove from innocent, sincere Spielberg, John recognized Stone as another Romantic: "He could have a cape! A wonderful character."[49]

When he screened *Born on the Fourth of July*, John said he thought "some sequences in the film are as good as anything I have ever seen. Tom Cruise has matured remarkably and he is brilliant in it. But I know people are going to find it difficult to watch some of this film, and whether the American public is ready to embrace something so strong, I don't know. But it is an important film and to my mind the best of the Vietnam films."[50] Stone's movie gave John a chance to explore the underbelly of America and the tragedy of misplaced or perverted patriotism. It was the *tragedy* John responded to most. This wasn't mere pessimism or nihilism; Stone painted the glowing nostalgia of what America once was, or at least *felt* like it once was, and lamented how the country had failed to live up to its highest ideals. It was the lament of a true believer, a patriot. "The Vietnam War caused so much pain and did such violence to the nation's psyche that it's probably something we'll revisit decade after decade," John said. "The beautiful thing about *Born on the Fourth of July* is that it's really the story of one man's experience. It personalizes the war and its aftermath in a way that gives the movie a very sharp point. When I looked at this film for the first time, I was enormously moved—almost to the point of tears a couple times."[51] He channeled those tears into a profoundly moving composition. "I knew immediately I would want a string orchestra to sing in opposition to all the realism on the screen," John said, "and then the idea came to have a solo trumpet—not a military trumpet, but an American trumpet, to recall the happy youth of this boy. And I knew I wanted Tim."[52]

Tim Morrison joined the BSO in 1980, the same year John took over the Pops. He left for a few years to play with a brass quintet, then returned in 1987 to become the Pops's principal trumpet. John thought Morrison had an "American sound" and "a real serenity in his playing."[53] Like many of John's scores, *Born* opens with a call—in this case, Morrison's lone trumpet singing a plaintive, Taps-like motif (which John marked "Misterioso"), answered by agitated cellos. This musical cry sets the film's tragic tone and foreshadows Ron's fate—but first Stone creates a portrait of the hero's happy childhood, playing war with his friends in the woods, kissing the pretty blonde girl as fireworks go off, hitting a home run, and soaking up John F. Kennedy's inspirational inauguration speech. Stone and his cinematographer, Robert Richardson, shot it all as amber-hued myth, and John scored it with warm, lyrical Americana and a melody for Morrison's trumpet that aches with nostalgia. "Yeah, it's sentimental," Stone admitted. "But it's the *good* corn, you know. That's what you need in a movie. You have to have good corn, and you have to dress up the cliché."[54]

The "good corn" is countered from the start with John's main theme for Ron—an aching adagio for strings that juxtaposes the revelry of an Independence Day parade where veterans from earlier wars are shown wincing at explosives and walking by without limbs ... ghosts of Ron's future. Stone had liberally used Samuel Barber's Adagio for Strings in *Platoon*, and John alluded to that piece's style and mood with an anguished elegy that went to deeper emotional places than almost anything he had ever written, yet still leapt with hopefulness.§ "The inevitable destiny that seems to invade Ron's life is in that music," said Stone. "It's very Beethoven-like."[55] The trumpet cry returns when a now-teenage Ron listens to a Marine recruiter at his school inspiring and challenging him to serve his country. John's adagio darkens the following diner conversation about prom with Ron's friends, who don't understand why he would want to go to Vietnam. Stone closes this chapter with exquisite sentimentality on a shot of Ron running to the prom in the rain and clutching one last dance with his childhood crush to the strains of Henry Mancini's "Moon River." The sudden whiplash to a battle in the Cua Viet River is stark and blinding, and John scored the confusion of war with distant, non-musical drums that sound almost like artillery fire. All of the romanticism has bled out, and the moment where Marines realize they've killed a hut full of women and children is queasy and nightmarish, with portamento string sliding and clusters, aleatorically intensifying as Ron runs outside and exchanges gunfire in a chaotic haze.

"You hear the baby crying, the smell of blood, you hear weird sounds," said Stone, "and Williams helps the battle, makes it effective—because in a sense the music has no destination and no sense of direction. Confusion ... the battle is on top of you."[56] Strings suddenly go limp when Ron shoots one of his own men, Wilson, running over the dune. The trumpet dirge returns as the sun sets on a silhouette of Ron, crouched in the sand as Wilson's body is dragged away. This psychic injury is followed by a physical one, and John uses his adagio, swelling to grandeur, when Ron gets hit in the leg. Inside the purgatory of a medical tent, surrounded by an ugly cacophony of squirting blood, open wounds, and men moaning in agony, the hummed chords of a synth chorus (notated by John as "VOICES OF THE DAMNED") are joined by feverish "Ghostly Voices," whispering what sounds like the word "Wilson" over and over. This was actually *John's* voice, sampled by synth player Randy Kerber and creepily played back through a keyboard with added haunting effects.[57] The grim hospital sequence that follows was unscored—instead, Ron's hour in the depth of hell was soundtracked ironically with contemporary pop songs.

When he returns home in a wheelchair, the sunny "Early Days" trumpet melody valiantly tries, like Ron, to act like everything is fine. But the adagio is at its heels when Ron's mother comes out to the driveway to welcome him. "Williams hit it here," said Stone, "the romantic yearning of this mother to have her son back, but she wants her son whole—and no matter what she says or does, he knows that *she* knows that she can't

---

§ Likewise, Barber's violin concerto served as a model for this score's warm nostalgia theme.

live with this. It breaks her heart."⁵⁸ When Ron is asked to speak at a Fourth of July parade, the trumpet cry and elegy that score his PTSD and the mockery of disapproving hippies were a marked reversal of so many celebratory Fourth concerts that John led by the Charles River. Ron unravels at home and escapes to Mexico for a life of drinking and debauchery with another paralyzed vet (played by Willem Dafoe). Adding to his misery, Ron is a virgin with now useless genitals, and his encounter with a kind sex worker is grieved with a lonely melody for English horn. After hitting rock bottom, he decides to come home, confess to Wilson's family, and protest the war; his decision triggers a stirring reprise of the Early Days trumpet theme (John's performance note: *"With freedom and nostalgia"*) encouraged by a determined drum machine beat and a synthesizer acting as "rock-like bass." The adagio reveals its uplifting side as Ron goes off to join demonstrators at the Republican National Convention in Miami, and then at the Democratic National Convention where he is welcomed with open arms.

Stone brought a gun with him to the Fox scoring stage in August; he quipped it was in case the recording didn't go well. "I thought he was going to shoot *me*," John said, laughing at the memory, and Stone said, "No, I'll shoot *myself*."⁵⁹ It was Stone's first big orchestral session as a filmmaker, and when he heard John's music for the first time, "I was agog," Stone said. "He is a metronome. And very generous and kind—he's not a screamer or anything like that. He doesn't even act like a disciplinarian. He's just very easygoing." On the first day, Morrison laid down the six-minute, virtuosic overture and main title; when it was finished, the entire orchestra gave him a standing ovation. John's themes for *Born on the Fourth of July*, Stone said, "had gravitas, and they had ardor and poetry in them. I was young, and I was learning the ropes. He gave me tremendous confidence."⁶⁰ John wrote roughly 55 minutes of music—a quarter of which was left out of the final film. "'Like most of my colleagues, I sometimes feel that the best things we write end up on the cutting-room floor,'" John said. "You may end up with half of what you've written ultimately not on the soundtrack, and a third of that may not be very well heard."⁶¹ What score remained, though, was prominent—and powerful.

For a two-and-a-half-hour movie about grisly injuries and the horrors of war and the awfulness of humanity and the United States, it was a surprising hit. Critics were in awe. "Stone has shown America to itself in a way it won't forget," gushed *Variety*'s Amy Dawes, who called it "the most gripping, devastating, telling, and understanding film about the Vietnam era ever.... With John Williams' moving score rising behind the action, it becomes clear Stone is not telling this story to evoke nostalgia."⁶² Maslin was won over, almost despite herself:

> It's easy to fault Mr. Stone's films for their sheer hot-bloodedness, for their eagerness to manipulate and their utter disregard of quieter, more considered tactics. It's also easy to resent feeling so thoroughly pummeled, pounded, and overwhelmed by what is, at least nominally, a work of popular entertainment. And it's particularly easy, in light of such responses, to overlook how terrifically expert Mr. Stone has become in achieving these effects. In *Born on the Fourth of July*, Mr. Stone

reaches out instantly to his audience's gut-level emotions and sustains a walloping impact for two and a half hours.

Maslin called John's score "majestically mournful."[63]

John had not lost an ounce of his own patriotism, but he also wasn't so blinded by it that he couldn't participate in criticism of his country—especially when it was motivated by love. "I wanted to convey a sense of requiem for what the country was before the Vietnam War, for what we've lost and what we've learned," he said. "For me it was a resonant subject that had to do with all the unconscious atavism we carry with us from childhood about our language and culture and music."[64] He also wanted to convey a sense of redemption: "I see the music as an elegy; it's kind of a requiem; and in the end, it's very positive and it celebrates this country."[65] The soundtrack album, which featured several period pop songs, was a top seller. MCA Records released John's theme as a single, and the company even sent a music video to MTV and VH1 featuring Tim Morrison in the studio. Morrison's trumpet became John's pet on several scores to follow, eventually convincing the musician to relocate to Hollywood. The score for *July* "remains one of the benchmarks for trumpet writing in film," Morrison said. "It was an extraordinary score in that respect."[66]

"I hope that people will like the music," John said. "I deeply hope that they'll want to go see the film. Now if all the media attention being paid to the movie as well as to the music has a positive effect on the Oscar voting, I say that's all to the good. I don't think the commercial aspects of this thing should be seen as evil."[67] When the score was expectedly nominated for an Oscar, a survey of John's fellow composers put it at the top of the heap. Elfman, overlooked that year for *Batman*, said it was his favorite of the nominees, as did Zimmer.[68] Of the film's eight nominations, Stone won for directing. John's score, along with *Last Crusade*, lost to *The Little Mermaid* by Alan Menken—whose long reign at the annual ceremony was just beginning. John began programming the *July* theme in his concerts, and two years later American figure skater Nancy Kerrigan did a routine to this theme at the 1992 Winter Olympics. "John outdid himself for me on this," said Stone, "until I heard *JFK*."[69]

John swung from Stone's youthful vim back to a collaborator from his past when he scored Martin Ritt's *Stanley & Iris*. Scripted by Harriet Frank Jr. and Irving Ravetch, the screenwriting couple behind *The Reivers*, *The Cowboys*, and *Conrack* (coming out of retirement here in their 70s), the film cast Robert De Niro as an illiterate man who finds a friend in Jane Fonda's widowed food assembly worker. It was an examination of America's woeful illiteracy problem and a portrait of life in the working class—while also subtly folding in a host of indignities such as domestic abuse, teen pregnancy, crime, and assisted living. It was deliberately small in scale and social in purpose, and failed at being much more, but it did offer an intimate stage for John to write a light, leisurely score, much as he had done almost 20 years earlier for *Pete 'n' Tillie*—another Ritt drama about an odd couple. John once commented that a composer was lucky to get 10 minutes of score into a Ritt film because he "doesn't like the cosmetic distraction of music." Perhaps the director had softened in his old age, because there was substantially more than 10 minutes in *Stanley & Iris*. Still, there are many long stretches *without*, and John's work was spare and emotionally restrained. On a relatively small music budget of $250,000, he composed a handful of themes that gave a handful of soloists notes to really *sing*. The main theme, introduced under the opening titles, is a pastoral birdsong for solo flute that warbles above a gently rolling piano groove, setting a lovely, undisturbed mood for shots of picturesque Waterbury, Connecticut.

John assigned the flute to Iris, and the trumpet to Stanley, and the two instruments play in unison on a friendly theme over another babbling piano current as Stanley takes Iris home on his bike. Stanley's theme is built on open fifths performed by piano, simple yet inquisitive like the character; a French horn picks up the melody during a montage of Stanley working odd jobs. Another montage has him spending time with his elderly father at a nursing home, and John wrote a bittersweet melody for piano and strings, not unlike the kind of music Randy Newman specialized in around this time (including a score the following year for *Awakenings*, which starred De Niro as another taciturn man in need of help). When Stanley drunkenly stumbles into Iris's house late one night, the softness of the scene and Iris's reception are scored with Stanley's piano chords and theme on clarinet, and the tune stirs with new hope after their first late-night reading lesson. John's main theme reprises on childlike celeste as Stanley shows off his new knowledge about trees to Iris's son, and again on clarinet when he offers to help Iris with her ironing and they begin to forge a family. But the optimism is disrupted when Stanley gets lost on an assignment from Iris to read street signs—eliciting a frightened variation of the main theme, wandering around in a fog of strings. That turns to a cloud of wonder when Iris discovers that Stanley is a clever inventor, and the main theme expresses her affectionate awe on clarinet. Moving toward romance alongside Stanley's growing confidence, John introduces an airy dance theme he called "Reading Lessons" that helps keep the story in motion. But Iris is still stuck on her deceased husband, and John scores the sadness in her tearful lovemaking to Stanley one night with teary, tense string chords. "Three people in bed are one too many for me," a resigned Stanley says, and his stoic trumpet echoes through the cut across time that follows. In the end, Iris is able to move on romantically and Stanley puts it all together literately, and John treats their climactic moment inside a library with a grand cello melody (reminiscent of Luke and Leia's theme) which gives way to a dressed-up reprise of the film's main theme as Stanley reads triumphantly and loudly. Iris puts Stanley on a plane to Detroit, and her flute dialogues with his trumpet as he writes her a series of letters and she daydreams of him. The score and film both conclude with gentle, rosy romance.

Stanley & Iris came and went without much attention—most of the media focus was on people continuing to protest "Hanoi Jane"—and it was to be John's last collaboration with Martin Ritt, who died in December 1990, and the end of an era in his film career.

* * *

When Spielberg saw *A Guy Named Joe* as a teenager, it made him cry.[70] With its tale of a World War II airman who dies in combat but returns as a spirit to guide his successor in life and love, the 1943 film commanded a special hold on the director's heart, and he talked about remaking it ever since he started making movies. Richard Dreyfuss was another softie for the afterlife movie, and he aggressively courted the lead part formerly played by Spencer Tracy. Numerous scripts were written throughout the 1980s, and at one point Spielberg was looking at casting Paul Newman and Robert Redford with Debra Winger as the gal of their mutual affections.[71] He finally landed on a draft he liked, loaded with comedic repartee, and he cast Dreyfuss as Pete the pilot, with Holly Hunter as Dorinda, and newcomer Brad Johnson as Ted. The biggest revision from the original film, written by Dalton Trumbo, was exporting the drama from World War II to modern-day firefighter pilots. That change, for many, was a fatal flaw. "This was an homage—and it didn't work," Dreyfuss said bluntly, looking back on the film.

> They had the Nazis to fight, and the war was not over, and there were things that could happen that could turn the war into a tragedy [*snaps fingers*] like *that*. And there was nothing that we could do that would equivalent out to that comparison. I said to Steven: "Put it back in World War II." We talked a lot about it, and I didn't win, and that was that. The problem is that a fire is not something you have an emotional feeling about. You're not going to lose civilization. And that was too big a decision to get wrong.[72]

But for its admirers, *Always* was chock-full of delights: the quippy banter and offbeat chemistry between Dreyfuss and Hunter (who makes fun of her co-star's donkey-like laugh); John Goodman as their helium-filled third wheel; Audrey Hepburn in her final role as the divine "Hap" who counsels Pete in the afterlife; magnificent vistas of airplanes in flight and forests on fire captured with Spielberg's airborne virtuosity; and a spiritual-romantic tone poem by John. It was a corny, old-fashioned, at times openly goofy romantic comedy with a grounding of tragedy and unrequited love, and simultaneously a weightless sense of life-affirming spirituality—and John locked right onto its wavelength. Unusually for a Spielberg film, his score waited in the wings for the first act as the potent compound of Pete's daredevilry and Dorinda's feistiness is established and they wind up dancing to "Smoke Gets in Your Eyes"—*their song*.** It's when Dorinda is walking back to their cozy cottage that night, and sees Pete's plane in an ominous blue light, that John's delicate, ethereal score floats in—with a mystical keyboard motif that returns a little later when that same blue light falls on Pete (from an open refrigerator) and Dorinda senses that something bad is about to happen. John blessed their romance with a calmly ascending love theme that has

---

** Written in 1933 by Jerome Kern and made a hit in 1959 by The Platters, "Smoke Gets in Your Eyes" was incidentally the same song Dreyfuss's classmates danced to in *American Graffiti*. Spielberg desperately wanted the Irving Berlin song "Always"—so much so that he named the film after it—but the songwriter stubbornly refused. Berlin died the very same month that John screened this film for the first time; ironically, John said he received a phone call from Berlin's office every year as he was planning the upcoming Pops season. "Don't forget Irving," they would say. "How could any of us forget Irving?" John replied. "It would be like forgetting who we are." (Dyer, "Irving Berlin Dead at 101," *Boston Globe*, September 23, 1989.)

heavenward aspirations; it plays softly on piano during their conversation that night, when Pete promises Dorinda he'll stop risking his life and become a flight instructor in Colorado. But, immediately, Pete gets one last emergency call. Dorinda's fears are empathized with a fraught haze of strings, but the score quickly shifts into action gear as she races to the runway, and the love theme taxis and takes off over a breathless rhythm when she passionately declares her love for Pete and he, for the very first time, shouts his love back—only she can't hear him over the engine's roar, which John punctuated with dramatic chord stabs. The doomed mission where Pete sacrifices himself while rescuing Al (Goodman) from an engine fire was notably unscored; John tiptoed in with a sympathetic string coda for the wordless scene of Al comforting Dorinda in the aftermath. For all the dubious criticism of flamboyance and manipulation they received over the years, John and Spielberg demonstrated genuine restraint and subtlety with the score for *Always*—from its sparse presence to its feathery texture.

Pete's sudden arrival in heaven—a burned-out forest with a small oasis of green grass and flowers—is met with celestial ambience created by harp, celeste, synthesizers, and strings. Out of this twinkling atmosphere, the love theme arises in an almost disembodied form as Hap sends Pete back to Earth to "inspire" another pilot—a handsome airhead named Ted. A while later, after ghost Pete has some fun messing with Ted's head, the love theme shivers when Pete sees a plane landing with Dorinda's signature wobbliness, the comedic tone instantly overtaken with heartache and a crying violin solo. Their melody becomes their spiritual connection after they can no longer see each other; Pete can't let Dorinda go, and as a result he keeps her in the prison of her own love for him, and this limbo stage is accompanied by otherworldly ambience and whispered quotes of their love theme spiked with sadness. Pete gets through to her one night as she hears his words in her sleep, and John wrapped the moment with a dreamy, cathartic bloom of their theme, deepened with a champagne piano solo and violins singing the painful beauty of their impossible love. Sent back to heaven for a kindly reprove from Hap, Pete is confronted with his duty: he has to set Dorinda free.

Time has passed on earth, and Ted is now an assured pilot working in the same forest where the action began. Another emergency call—a group of firefighters trapped in a deadly blaze and needing a path to the nearby river—stirs him into romantic action hero mode and causes Dorinda to race her bicycle to the airstrip, just like she did on the morning Pete died. This time, though, she steals Ted's plane and takes off on the mission herself, and John's music worries for her with a reprise of the mystical omen motif. But her resolve is met with a quiet build of the love theme, first on hornlike synthesizer, then actual French horn, carried upward by a gust of strings. The finale was shot and scored like a dream—with Dorinda flying into a fiery inferno and then up through heavenly heights. Gliding in the night sky, Pete sits behind her and is finally able to express all his feelings for Dorinda and release his hold on her heart. This cue, "Among the Clouds," was an extended meditation that tells its own tender story about saying goodbye, filled with lyrical solos for horn and woodwinds that deftly dive and dance around the dialogue—emphasizing important lines like

"The love we hold back," which John actually noted in his sketch. The orchestra lifts and lifts to the score's romantic apex and a higher plane of human understanding about grief and the hope-filled possibility of liberation *from* grief, a deep well of wisdom and feeling that this widower composer, of all people, could personally draw from. "His most poignant moments capture the tenderness and aspirations of the human spirit, sometimes gentle, sometimes soaring to lush heights," Spielberg wrote.[73]

Dreyfuss was critical of his performance in this climactic scene. "We did it 40 times, and Steven never said to change it, but he was clearly not happy with it," the actor said. "We just kept repeating it, and I ultimately think I just didn't get it, and he knew it. And that's my fault as an actor. I think my love for that movie, for the original, just fucked me up—just got in my way."[74] But whatever sins Dreyfuss feels he committed, the moment was made sublime with John's music. The film's coda does wobble and indulge in its own corn a little when Dreyfuss appears to Dorinda as a glowing apparition who takes her hand and leads her into the rest of her life. But the gorgeous, *religioso* denouement of their love theme redeems it. Whenever Spielberg wavered in his conviction, John provided the faith.

But not for film critics, who roundly dismissed *Always* when it opened in December. "There is little of [Spielberg's] trademark visual grandeur," complained Tom Matthews at *Boxoffice*, "and his pocket composer—John Williams—turns in one of his least distinctive scores to date. It's probably significant to note that at the close of the '80s—a decade which Spielberg ruled—the filmmaker has finally directed a movie which hardly matters at all."[75] Some found Spielberg still stubbornly childish in his first attempt at a romance; David Denby of *New York* magazine called the scene where Dorinda descends a staircase in a fancy dress "the most purely sexless moment in Spielberg's long, long career as a boy," and said it made him realize "to what extent sex in his movies is a matter of dreams and idealization."[76] Spielberg owned this critique when he admitted that, as an artist, he felt romance not for men and women together—but for the *past*, which he liked to "nostalgize." But looking back on the reception of *Always*, he said: "Some movies don't take off and there's a thousand reasons why.... It was a good experience for me to make that movie because it was all about human emotions. I have no regret at all."[77]

His next film would be savaged even more harshly.

* * *

Jenny Williams (Figure 11.1) was the spitting image of her mother. She, too, had married a film and TV composer—a New Yorker named Jay Gruska. After flirting with music and a brief attempt at an acting career, she pursued a master's degree in educational psychology and counseling from Cal State Northridge and found a job at the Maple Counseling Center in west Los Angeles, then started her own private practice in 1987—specializing in grief-recovery therapy. She was a self-described workaholic who was also starting a family with her husband in the Valley suburbs. John adored Jenny, but during this period he was often so busy that sometimes he wouldn't see her or his grandchild for a whole year at a time.

Figure 11.1. Joe, Jenny, and Mark Williams, ca. 1979 (Courtesy of John Williams).

On October 10, 1989, while giving birth to her second child—a boy named Ethan—Jenny had a massive stroke. She was lying in the hospital bed at Cedars-Sinai in Beverly Hills about 10 minutes after the birth, and her husband's friend laughed because she was having trouble finding simple words. Then she began shouting "Oh God!" and fell into a coma that lasted three days. While comatose, she had a series of seizures, and when she woke up she was paralyzed on her right side and had aphasia (the loss of speech from brain damage). She was able to mumble the word "stroke?" to Gruska, who said *yes*. Jenny was only 32. John was in the middle of recording his score for *Always*, a story about young and sudden death, and he was so overcome that he went into the hospital bathroom and wept. It was the first time in Jenny's life that she had ever seen him cry.[78] "It was terrifying," John said, "and certainly shocking, because my assumption immediately was, since her mother had passed from a similar kind of problem, this was something that had been a genetic inheritance in some way and that Jenny might be faced with this thing repeatedly, or it might have been more serious than it was."[79] It *was* serious: her doctor said she was going to be a vegetable for the rest of her life, *if* she survives. They said she would never work again, never *walk* again. She was given lifetime handicap parking, although the doctors doubted she would ever drive again.

But Jenny was *determined* to prove the doctors wrong, and was hellbent on getting back to her newborn son. (Gruska hired a wet nurse to help with Ethan in the aftermath.) In the course of a year, she made a defiant, miraculous, complete recovery, and became a positive force in the rehab ward among others who had suffered brain damage. With speech therapy, occupational therapy, and physical therapy, "I got everything back," she said proudly. "It took a long time for Ethan and I to bond," Jenny said. "That was the worst part of all." This dramatic episode was also a startling and painful echo of the aneurysm that had so viciously stolen Barbara—wife, mother, and heart of the Williams family—from their lives 15 years earlier.

They had all coped with that loss in different ways. Joe struggled with drug and alcohol abuse throughout his teen and adult life; he and Mark were incredibly close to their mother, so young when she was suddenly, invisibly ripped away. After Barbara died, Jenny was extremely worried about them: "I needed to be responsible for them, and that continued on for many, many years. They're both incredible people—the sweetest men you could ever meet—but they were really young and they needed help. I tried to do my best. I *still* kind of feel like I'm responsible."[80] In April 1990, just a few months after Jenny's stroke, Joe was arrested with two other people for the possession of 200 pounds of marijuana along with cocaine.[81] He was fired from Toto because, Joe admitted, "I had a cocaine addiction. Nothing abnormal. But as a singer, that's the one substance you can't do. It freezes your throat."[82] He and Mark had both gone into music, but professionally "it's always been challenging," Jenny said, "because it's hard to be *his* son."[83] On most of his solo albums, Joe wrote a song about or dedicated to his mother, "some sort of cathartic release for me in musical form," he explained.[84]

John did what he had always done: he put on the scuba gear of discretion and plunged to the depths of his musical ocean. Music, he admitted, can be "a hiding place. Other people do things for you, and you have excuses all the time that you're working. And that can make you an inattentive parent, possibly, which I think I would have to confess to being."[85] He never publicly mentioned Jenny's stroke. He still had to conduct the Christmas Pops in Boston that December, but he stayed close by during her recovery.

Jenny wrote about her stroke experience and shared that document with Michael Gorfaine—who encouraged her to show it to producers of TV movies.[86] In 1994, NBC aired *A Time to Heal*, which starred Nicolette Sheridan as "Jenny Barton" and a young Mara Wilson as her daughter Barbara, in a lightly fictionalized account of the traumatic event and Jenny's remarkable recovery; the movie was even scored by Gruska. The film's version of John, a character named "Don Peterson," was portrayed by actor Ken Jenkins. *John* channeled his pain and emotions into music; Jenny turned hers into a movie, which she saw as an extension of her therapy practice. "Tragedies can and do happen to young people," she said at the time. "Things happen. I know you can get past it and get on."[††][87] (Jenny later went on to receive a PhD in Health Psychology at the age of 60.)

* * *

[††] Also in 1994, Joe Williams made one of his most enduring contributions to pop culture: providing the singing voice for adult Simba in Disney's *The Lion King*.

Director Alan J. Pakula asked John to write "a sickening perfume melody" for his new film.[88] Pakula was behind some of the defining thrillers of the paranoid 1970s—*Klute, The Parallax View, All the President's Men*—and he frequently worked with New York composer Michael Small. But for his adaptation of a blockbuster novel by Scott Turow, *Presumed Innocent*—about a defense attorney accused of murdering his colleague—Pakula wanted John Williams. The project gave John a new and very different opportunity to accompany Harrison Ford, who dialed down his smirking charm to play the low-key Rusty Sabich—who may or may not have brutally killed his fellow attorney and partner in a torrid affair. Darker and sexier than his usual fare, John said simply: "It's a fantastic script."[89]

Like *The Accidental Tourist*, John wrote a score around an obsessive loop of the same theme on repeat. "She's dead, and you're still obsessing," Rusty's wife Barbara says early on, chastising her unfaithful husband and basically describing the main theme. Built on a hypnotic piano groove, the melody is a seductive, mysterious, dangerous torch song first introduced on French horn and then passed off to various instruments. The tune hovers like a perfume when Rusty pokes around Carolyn's empty office one night, when he's at her funeral and daydreaming of her lying in bed, when he flashes back to their hot-and-heavy covert courtship. When Rusty and Carolyn finally consummate their lust after a little courtroom foreplay, the attending quizzical keyboard and anxious, seasick strings are more threatening than sexy, and John accelerated the perfume theme more and more as their clothes come off, with rapid string runs sounding like alarms going off, the orchestra heaving and throbbing as he gets her on top of a desk and they go at it, climaxing with a wild string orgasm that doubles as a burst of violence when an image of her ecstasy face suddenly cuts to her bloody head in a crime scene photo. John's score was crucial for these flashbacks: Carolyn is already dead in the present and the music is her ghost, relentlessly haunting Rusty. The vortex of dangerous obsession that John swirled in this score recalls the work of Herrmann in scores like *Vertigo*—but unlike Herrmann, John spun off from his minimalistic mantra into a fully developed, singable melody.

The score's palette was loaded with the chilly, contemporary synths that John had been toying with in recent years. Perhaps he was bending to the fashion of electronic sounds that were so vogue now thanks to composers like Zimmer (who would use them liberally in *Regarding Henry*, another movie starring Ford as a lawyer). But they certainly fit the film's prevailingly bleak and cold mood, the gloomy shadows lensed by Gordon Willis, and the gruesome murder at the story's core. The only sweet relief comes in a family theme that accompanies Rusty and Barbara dropping their son off at school, a charade that everything is hunky-dory. The murder trial uncovers a web of corruption that goes all the way up to the judge, and shady tactics are used in Rusty's defense—ultimately getting the case dropped altogether. And just as everything seems to be okay, Rusty finds a hatchet in his toolbox with blood on it; strings churn along with his realization, growing queasily as he goes to the basement to wash off the blood, the perfume theme foaming into an intense adagio. *It was Barbara.* As his lamblike wife coolly confesses to the murder, icy keyboards twinkle underneath like cursed wind chimes and a solo violin plays an angular line on top of slow harp arpeggios. Rusty just stares at her and wells up as Barbara recounts the grisly scene; John's score retreats when she says "And life begins again," then returns when Barbara talks about how the trial made him suffer more than she realized. It was a stark, frigid finale to match the shocking reveal, and the music here was not so far from John's more unsettled concert music. After a concluding bit of narration, John closed the curtains with a full-blooded development of his perfume theme—complete with deep synth bass notes, bells, and rising intensity.

Critics mostly united to praise the film. Sheila Benson at the *L.A. Times* called it "one of those rare films where all the players seem to be in a state of grace, where the working of the machinery never shows and after it's over, one runs and reruns its intricacies with a profound sense of satisfaction."[90] Many reviews ignored the score altogether, although more than one critic jabbed that John ripped off the melody from "Norwegian Wood" by the Beatles.[91] It was a patently ridiculous claim: John never listened to the Beatles.

After recording *Presumed Innocent* in April 1990, John readied for another busy Pops season.‡‡ Spielberg was meant to attend opening night, but he stayed in L.A. for the birth of his new baby, Sasha.[92] John programmed music from a new Pops album: *The Spielberg/Williams Collaboration*, a robust celebration of their first 10 films together, which was recorded in May at Symphony Hall (one of the first albums recorded under the Pops' new contract with Sony Classical).[93] That summer, the Pops made history by inviting its first woman guest conductor, Marin Alsop, a protégé of both Bernstein and Ozawa; she was one of many guests working with the freelance Esplanade that season, since John took the main orchestra on another 10-city tour of Japan in the middle of the 1990 season. Once again, every concert was sold out, and this tour was "an experience beyond my capacity to describe," John said.[94] The prime minister of Japan, Toshiki Kaifu, attended one concert; John conducted both the Japanese and American anthems. "The audience listened to their own national anthem in silence," he said, "but there was warm, generous and spirited applause for ours." He was hesitant about performing Sousa's "The Stars and Stripes Forever," which every Pops concert ended with, but "when it came to the part where the audience in Boston always starts clapping, the Japanese audience started clapping right on cue." John marveled at the pin-drop silence in Japanese concert halls. "I particularly appreciated the audience's willingness to listen," he said. "That is something we miss sometimes in the garden-party atmosphere of the Pops at home with all the bottles and tables and talking." Normally he would keep to his hotel room on these tours, preserving his energy for the concerts—but on this trip, he ventured out to visit some of the ancient temples of Kyoto. "I am absolutely convinced that ghosts reside in those woods; it was absolute magic. At first the

---

‡‡ That spring, John also wrote and recorded new music for an *E.T.* theme park ride set to open at the brand-new Universal Studios in Orlando. *E.T. Adventure* opened in Hollywood the following year, and from this moment on, much of the music filling the air of Universal's theme parks around the globe was John's. It was, simply, everywhere.

conformity of so much we saw was a little off-putting, but then I began to understand the beauty of it too—it was like watching flocks of doves."[95] John brought with him a biography of William O. Douglas, the late Supreme Court Justice—"a man I have always admired," he said. "While I was in Japan I also picked up a history of modern Japan, which is feeding my infatuation with that very complicated and interesting society."[96] He was forever reading, learning, growing.

He was back in Boston in time for the traditional Fourth of July concert, where he premiered a new piece—*Celebrate Discovery*—written in advance of an international event in 1992 to mark the 500th anniversary of Christopher Columbus's arrival to the New World, which would feature replicas of the Nina, Pinta, and Santa Maria tracing the famous sailor's route from Europe.[97] After a rousing bugle fanfare, the piece has an oceanic swing with the motion of spraying waves, and a lyrical B section for strings and flitting flutes, steadily building without ever becoming bombastic—just an exciting ocean voyage. John was busy finishing his new clarinet concerto when a friend convinced him to check out a film in quick need of a composer—"and I just went dippy over the movie," John said. "It gave me the same feeling as *E.T.*, though it's a small picture, without that physical scope. I think the public is going to go crazy for this—it's a story about an eight-year-old outwitting some very Dickensian villains."[98]

* * *

Home Alone was not a project, in any conceivable way, with John's name on it. Writer John Hughes, moving away from the poppy teenage zeitgeist that made him famous, concocted the story around a simple premise: a young boy is accidentally left home alone at Christmas and has to defend himself against a pair of oily burglars. Hughes tapped Chris Columbus to direct the film on location in the suburbs of Chicago—a local high school was converted into the central, booby-trapped house interior—and he also suggested Macaulay Culkin, an adorable bundle of sassy wit and sweetness, to play the pint-sized hero, Kevin McCallister. Joe Pesci and Daniel Stern were cast as the bumbling but dogged bandits, Harry and Marv, and Catherine O'Hara brought humor and compassion to the part of Kevin's mother. It was essentially a live-action Road Runner cartoon, which Columbus helped nudge toward pathos by accentuating the arc of an old man next door who forges a surprisingly genuine bond with Kevin.

Bruce Broughton was hired to write the score—early posters and a teaser trailer listed his name in the credits—but when the schedule came into conflict with another project, Disney's animated film *The Rescuers Down Under*, he exited.[§§] Stranded without a composer in post-production, Columbus was already immediately moving on to his next film, *Only the Lonely* with John Candy, when he learned that John Williams was interested in seeing a rough cut of *Home Alone*. John screened the film at Amblin in August, and sent word to Columbus that he wanted to score it. "We were just completely overwhelmed," Columbus said. Here was a small, $18 million movie

---

[§§] "And the rest, as they say, is history," Broughton sighed. (Bruce Broughton to TG, December 8, 2015.)

that he and his producers were simply hoping would double its budget. He had no idea why John wanted anything to do with it—other than, *maybe*, because Columbus had built a strong temp score that featured Tchaikovsky's *Nutcracker*, Dave Grusin's score for *Murder by Death*, and Mannheim Steamroller's synthy take on "Carol of the Bells." "I think he probably saw the potential in that movie that even *I* didn't see," said Columbus, "because I was too close to it."[99] John was simply enchanted by the movie—and he also saw it as a chance to write some original Christmas carols, in the tradition of his late friend Alfred Burt. "Where else would I get such an opportunity?" said John, who proposed this idea to Columbus.[100] It was also John's suggestion to have his old friend Mel Tormé record a version of "Have Yourself a Merry Little Christmas" for the soundtrack. His enthusiasm for the project was bubbling over—he asked to spot the film twice—and when he got to work on it after Labor Day, he realized his ambitions were probably outsized for this little movie, but "if it moves you, or is something you care about, or something where your spirit resonates a little bit, it's easier to write music or poetry or anything else. When a composer looks at a film, if it speaks to you, it helps."[101]

Columbus thought the critical key in John's contribution was somehow blending the film's contrasting tones of slapstick, Three Stooges-esque comedy with its warm, Christmassy heart. "John just created this linear glue that held those two tones together," Columbus said, "which is *brilliant*."[102] John hadn't scored such a straight-up comedy since *1941*, and he suddenly remembered how exhausting the genre could be, where every millisecond matters in "these wonderfully burlesque—in the classic use of that word—comedy sequences that the orchestra accompanies so completely in the film, almost like a cartoon where every gesture that the orchestra makes is accompanied by some comedic action on screen."[103] He coordinated with the film's sound team and scored each violent vignette—Harry clutching a red-hot doorknob, Marv taking a paint can to the face—*right* up to the gruesome sound effect, then had the music stand down for the sizzling or thwacking payoff. "If the music had run all the way through, it would have been more cartoonish," explained music editor Michael Wilhoit.[104]

John had recorded the *Nutcracker* Suite with the Pops back in 1984, and he liberally borrowed Tchaikovsky's yuletide sauces for the flavor of *Home Alone*. Like he did with other classical composers, though, John converted the archetype into a thrilling new form of popcorn energy. The score opens with an homage to "Dance of the Sugar-Plum Fairy," setting an enchanted, slightly ominous mood with bells and twinkling Christmas lights, and introducing a theme of mischievous mystery. For the sequence where the McCallister family frantically packs in fast-motion, John remixed "Russian Dance" into his own whimsical "Holiday Flight." The film's main theme is forecasted right at the beginning, with synth bells ringing the first phrase like church bells calling us into the story. This melody was filled with the feeling of nostalgia and boyhood, with echoes of the old nursery rhyme "Rain Rain Go Away"—and of a glowing hearth with snow falling outside, especially when carried by sleigh bells and other wintry chimes. (Kevin seems to be living inside a Baby Boomer's ideal of Christmas—watching black-and-white noir movies, listening to golden oldies—which has the interesting side effect of making the film feel timeless.) This main tune became the carol "Somewhere in My Memory," with words by Leslie Bricusse.

The melody that formed the score's other carol, "Star of Bethlehem," is shrouded in religious mystery and it serves the sense of darkness and danger that Kevin is often in. John wrote a perky boy's adventure theme, usually performed by tuba, which accompanies Kevin's more carefree moments. For the self-proclaimed "Wet Bandits," John conceived an eely villain motif worthy of *Peter and the Wolf*, which stalks and slithers around in the lower end of the wind section. John was a grandfather by now, forever dignified, and as jarring as it is to hear his stately score in a slapstick movie with dialogue like "puke breath," "cheese face," and "I wouldn't let you sleep in my room if you were growing on my ASS"—it oddly makes sense to picture him weaving this fun musical story for his grandchildren, as if gathering them around the fire to read a modern-day *Oliver*, or *A Christmas Carol*. His score punctuates the comedy and shivers at the frights; when Culkin dramatically says, "Pack … my *suitcase*?," the line gets an exaggerated musical response. When old man Marley makes appearances in the early goings, hovering like the dreaded Ghost of Christmas Future, John manifests Kevin's terror with the melodramatic "Dies Irae." This is, unapologetically, story time at the library, where the only thing missing is the sound of kids booing at the villains. But it is also much, *much* more.

There is a real seriousness to the score—the scheming bad guy music has the artfulness of Prokofiev, and even the sneaking-around cues have musical integrity and structure. John's score nimbly dances with the pratfalls and springing traps, never leeching them of their primal, juvenile laughter, but also treating the film's stuntmen with the same dignity as the Martha Graham ballet company. Something in this conceivably crude, potentially stupid pantomime resonated with him—but he also simply couldn't help himself but handle it with care, as he did with everything. "A lot of composers can write sweeping, emotional material," said Columbus.

> Very few know how to write comedy cues. I think it's the most difficult thing in the world. Because you've seen so many comedies with a score that just speaks down to the film. I have had nothing but success when John is writing for comedy, because it's light on its feet in a certain way. It's not intrusive, and it's not telling the audience: "You need to laugh here." It's just being very playful. The comedy moments in *Home Alone*—the musical slapstick moments in the film—are just really beautiful in their simplicity.[105]

The real elevation, though, came in the tender and vulnerable moments that dot the narrative. John's two carols act as Kevin's guardian angels throughout his adventure: after Kevin's first brush with the bad guys, "Star of Bethlehem" sounds with seasonal resolve as he walks outside and declares out loud that he's not afraid anymore, and it sprints back into the house with him after he's spooked by Marley. John exploited this theme's gloomy side for Kevin's wild overreaction to seeing Marley in the drug store, then kicks it into a sleigh-driven action theme as he runs home. "Bethlehem" becomes even more fraught when Kevin recognizes Harry and hides from the bandits in a nativity scene, and John acknowledged the neighborhood church with a synthesized organ. "Somewhere in My Memory" is the bright sun to the other carol's melancholy moon, and John spread out a homey, Hallmark card version of it when Kevin finally feels sadness for wishing his family's disappearance. Likewise, as he walks home one night and sees other families gathering in cheer inside their own homes, the first choral performance of "Memory" is sung *Gently with nostalgia*. The film pivots when Kevin ducks into a cathedral and overcomes his fear of Marley to have a touching conversation about their respective family woes. A children's choir is shown singing a series of Christmas hymns in the background—and in the middle of "O Holy Night" and "Carol of the Bells" is "Star of Bethlehem," as if it were just another classic in the canon of yuletide carols. Truth be told: it qualified. This churchly calm is suddenly interrupted with a rock-like beat on synth drums invading "Carol of the Bells," which morphs into a steely combat version of "Bethlehem" as Kevin runs home to rig his house with an elaborate series of booby traps (John's nod to the Mannheim Steamroller temp track).

The film culminates with an escalating parade of pain inflicted on Marv and Harry, and John deftly varied the pace and intensity of his cartooning—with heavy use of pizzicato strings, triangle, and legato bass clarinets—to match the progression. "Memory" flips into action gear when Kevin thinks he's won and calls the cops (*why* he waited until now only makes sense in movie logic), and a horn heroically declares the "Bethlehem" tune as he braves a zip line out of a high window and into his treehouse. An accelerated, wobbly development of "Memory" hustles with Kevin across the street, the bad guys follow with their motif, and "Memory" grows increasingly frantic as Kevin goes in through the neighbor's flooding basement and runs up the stairs right into Harry and Marv. They talk about paying Kevin back torture for torture, but are suddenly knocked out by Marley—triggering a relieved crescendo of "Somewhere in Memory." Finally, on an impossibly beautiful white Christmas morning, "Memory" rings gently on bells and the orchestra picks up the melody, singing it with passion as Kevin runs downstairs in faith that his mom came home. The tune turns melancholy when he finds the house still empty and looks longingly outside, but then he hears the front door open and the sound of his mother's voice. "Memory" continues delicately as Mom admires Kevin's tree and decorations, then chimes over undulating, expectant strings when Kevin meets her with a frown—which he immediately replaces with a huge smile, and the orchestra wells up joyously as mother and son hug each other tightly. The film ends with a delicate bell ostinato introducing one last reprise of "Memory," played on a synth harpsichord, which is joined by the whole orchestra as Kevin looks out his window and sees Marley hugging his granddaughter, tears in his eyes as he waves to Kevin. For all of its physical comedy and Christmas wish fulfillment, the real reason multiple generations developed a powerful bond to *Home Alone* is because of these tearful moments—and because of John's sparkling, heartstring music.

"For John to be able to connect what I did in that movie," said Columbus, "not only propels the story forward, but from a narrative standpoint it's like he's taking the audience's hand and inviting them inside that world. It becomes immersive. That's what John's music does. Certain film scores almost keep the audience at bay, but John manages to *immerse* the audience in the warmth, or the terror, of the film." Columbus was shooting *Only the Lonely* in Chicago and wasn't able to attend the scoring sessions, which took place at Fox in October; so John sent him cassette tapes of each day's recordings via FedEx. "At lunchtime," Columbus said, "we'd pop in the cassette and listen to the cue. Everyone's jaws were dropping. By the time the score was finished—with not one note from me, by the way, it was all so perfectly done—we screened the film for the studio, and all of us were amazed at how much the score actually elevated the movie. I believe that to this day. The score gives the movie its emotional depth and complexity."[106] When George Lucas saw a crowd's reaction to the trailer for *Home Alone*, he told Fox chairman Joe Roth it was going to be a hit. "The movie business is binary," Lucas told him. "The light is either on or it's off."[107] But everyone involved was utterly dumbfounded when the film opened on November 16 and claimed the number one spot—for *12* weeks—generating $286 million and becoming the third-biggest hit in Hollywood history. "I don't know why it worked, why it was so popular," John admitted.

> If I did, I might have a different job these days. Still, it always seems that when the country is in recession, Hollywood is flying high. It's a very odd feeling to know that I wrote the scores to all of the top five grossing films, and to seven of the top ten—I try not to think about it, but it does say something about luck, doesn't it? I consider myself a very lucky man. And it's healthy to remind myself that I probably wrote scores to more than my share of the bottom seven films too—does anyone remember *Gidget Goes to Rome*?[108]

John was a central part of yet another cultural juggernaut, and once again, he was hugely responsible for *why* it won so many hearts. "A successful film is sometimes a happy accident," said Columbus, "and it's when everything is firing on all cylinders and everyone is working at their best level. John taught me to take myself more seriously as an artist, because I felt that he treated *Home Alone* with the same respect that he treated *Raiders* and *Close Encounters* and *Jaws*, and all of those great, great films. To be given a gift like that, to a young director, it instills you with some confidence, and makes you take yourself very seriously."[109] Both "Somewhere in My Memory" and John's score were nominated for Oscars—both lost—and John programmed his new carols and "Holiday Flight" at his next Pops Christmas concert. (Tormé was on hand to sing "Have Yourself a Merry Little Christmas.") Dyer acknowledged that "Memory" was "as sweet as a Christmas cookie," but "Williams gets away with it because he can't write insincere music, and he uses real sugar and real butter in his cookies."[110]

* * *

Leonard Bernstein died on October 14, 1990. "His departure creates an unfillable gap in our artistic and spiritual life," John said in a statement. "He leaves us at a moment when we seem to need him the most."[111] Bernstein was always "very sweet to me," John said. "He was like André: 'You shouldn't be doing those movies,' you know—that kind of thing." John witnessed "Lenny" ("You couldn't call him 'Maestro' or 'Mr. Bernstein,'" John said) in both his wildest behavior and his most sublime. "He drank way too much, wrecked his lungs with cigarettes and so on. Behaved very badly much of the time—all the girls in the office would go hide when Lenny was coming, because he would always grab them and kiss them on the mouth and start being crazy—but not hurtful. A great teacher. *Great* charisma. Nothing like it. He got on a podium or he'd get in a group of people, and suddenly there was only Lenny."[112]***

When the BSO acquired the Highwood estate in 1987 and absorbed it into the Tanglewood campus, Bernstein loved to retire to the Highwood mansion for drinks and supper after concerts—it was just a short walk from The Shed, through some woods—and John would often join him. One night, Bernstein entered the second floor and said, "Wait . . . this place is haunted. This ghost is crazy. It's haunted!" John had read somewhere that a traditional practice to get rid of unwanted spirits was to place a cup of white beans somewhere in the room, "so we used to have rituals up there with Seiji and others," he said, "put the white beans there and chase the spirits away and have a drink after the concert." The cooks and servers at Highwood were mostly Irish, and very superstitious, and when they heard Bernstein saying the place was haunted, they said, "Of course it's haunted. The cooks all know it." John learned that a farmhand on the property, long before it was Highwood, was killed when lightning struck a tree and it fell on him. The man was buried on the site, and his grave was recently moved when the new artists' parking lot was built. Bernstein made it a regular practice to dramatically walk around the upper room speaking to the ghost, or open a closet and say he felt warm air coming from nowhere.[113] Did he really believe it? "Well, he was pretty convincing," said Kim Taylor, neé Smedvig, the BSO's press liaison whose summer office was in Highwood, and who was often present at these dinners. "But then who knows with him! He had such a flair for the theatrical." One thing was clear to Taylor: "He was really excited to be with John. Oh, he thought John was amazing, and so remarkable and talented. He loved John."[114]

Six weeks after Bernstein's death, his friend Aaron Copland died. The *Hartford Courant*'s music critic wrote a column about the void now left with these two national treasures gone: "Today, with the music scene deeply fragmented, no single composer

---

*** In 1988, John was one of several composers who wrote a tribute piece for Bernstein by referencing "New York, New York" from his musical *On the Town*. Ozawa premiered John's short piece, *For New York (To Lenny! To Lenny!)* in the final Tanglewood concert that summer, and John programmed it in many future Pops concerts.

can hope for a wide enough consensus to claim anything like the 'dean-of-composers' mantle that Copland wore so lightly and without challenge."[115] A reader responded, nominating John Williams, and asked why the critic didn't even mention him in the article.[116]

By now, it was more than a valid question. Besides his stature on the national stage and heavy influence on popular culture, his composition of American anthems and his conducting presence in Boston and Lenox, John was also following in Copland's footsteps by writing a clarinet concerto. He had been working on it for three years, inspired by the LA Phil's Michele Zukovsky, who played in his concerts at the Bowl every year. "She didn't ask me for it," he said. "I just said, 'May I write you a clarinet concerto?' and she said yes."[117] Zukovsky had studied with the brother of John's early teacher, Sara Compinsky, and she always felt a kinship with him for that reason. "He's a *god* now, she said wryly, years later—"*then*, he was just still a human being. He struck me as being an old-fashioned gentleman. Everything was *slightly* formal, which seemed for him the best way to work."[118] Zukovsky went to John's house only once to hear him play through a few ideas on piano, and in April 1991 they premiered the concerto in the far-flung California city of Riverside (near his old Air Force base) with the Riverside Symphony. In July, he brought her to Tanglewood to perform it with the Pops. "It was not exactly what one expects of a Pops concert," complained Milton Cole of the *Daily Hampshire Gazette*, who thought Zukovsky's clarinet was too often swallowed by the sound of the orchestra. "When the audience of 12,825 applauded prematurely at a pause in the concerto, it seemed almost to be wishful thinking."[119]

It was an imposing, impressionistic work, much harder for a pops audience to swallow than the tuba concerto, with a lengthy cadenza for the instrument that read like a test for ears more accustomed to candy. The second movement ("Calmo") has the clarinet twisting around on a mysterious autumn wind that emanates from the string section, swirling around a loose melody with sister flute and brother horn. The final movement ("Con Brio") agitates the orchestra into a kind of demented, insistent rhythm, never giving the clarinet a safe or warm place to rest—all culminating in a clacking, chattering crash landing. At the time, John said: "It doesn't take itself too seriously, and it has tunes in it."[120] But there was no commercial recording, and he abandoned the work after that summer. When Zukovsky sent John a CD of the Riverside performance decades later, he wrote her back: "I haven't heard or seen a *note* of the Clarinet Concerto since Riverside. And listening to your recording quite blew me away. The most brilliant clarinet playing imaginable. The piece, with a few needed adjustments, will rest on whatever value it may have. But you are *invaluable*." "He did not like the finished product," Zukovsky said. "It's like he really does need a movie or a story, and when it's just abstract, it's harder for him. There was no story to connect to, and there was no movement for him to accompany. He was much more successful in the violin and bassoon concerto. But he was not happy with the clarinet concerto."[121] John continued thinking about how he would like to re-orchestrate the work for years afterward—if he could ever find the time.

* * *

Hook is either Spielberg's folly or one of his greatest adventures. It either represents everything fantastic about him as a director or it is the nadir of his worst instincts, either one last belch from the bloated, overindulgent 1980s—or a hearty, pixie-powered joyride. Here he was finally making his Peter Pan movie, and most critics wished he would just *grow up* already.

After having toyed with and discarding a straightforward musical about Pan, Spielberg was finally hooked by a script that posed a simple question, first raised by writer James V. Hart's son: *What if Peter Pan grew up?* The resulting story was about the yuppie, corporate generation, and a desperate need to rediscover and reclaim the spirit of childhood. Spielberg snatched it away from director Nick Castle, who had been developing the project for a year with Paramount.[122] He saw it as a perfect opportunity to finally tell the story of Neverland and the Lost Boys—but through the prism of a workaholic absent father. The production was a $70 million sandbox for big kids Robin Williams as Peter Banning (née Pan), Dustin Hoffman in a baroque wig and an English accent as Captain Hook, Bob Hoskins as the cockney sycophant Smee, Julia Roberts as tiny Tinkerbell, and a bunch of lost boys (and one lost girl). The enormous pirate ship set on the Sony lot attracted every celebrity under the sun, from Michael Jackson to Seiji Ozawa and his family. Spielberg had no desire to ever shoot a film on the open waters again, and his decision to make this a giant soundstage fantasy symbolized his entire concept for *Hook*: exaggerated, underlined, pantomimed make-believe. He said "he ended up making something that was akin to children's theater," recalled Bonnie Curtis, who became Spielberg's assistant just before production rolled. To that end, he also wanted the whole thing to be a lavish, roadshow musical. "There's always a fairy in Steven's ear wanting him to turn things into musicals," said Curtis. "We never explored it as far as we did on *Hook*."[123] John was just finishing up *Home Alone* with Bricusse when Spielberg asked the duo to dream up an entire songbook sprung from Hart's screenplay. With the exception of one leftover song, this was entirely separate from the work John had done for the abandoned Pan musical in 1985. Beginning in December 1990, Williams and Bricusse went wild composing a set of highly singable lullabies, ballads, and pirate shanties. "Spielberg's enthusiasm for the project was infectious and overwhelming," wrote Bricusse, who said he and John "were both caught up in the swirl of Steven's vision."[124]

For Granny Wendy, played by Maggie Smith, they wrote a reverie called "Childhood," which incidentally shared the opening notes of "Somewhere in My Memory." It was "the root song of the score," explained Bricusse, "since it represented the very heart of what the movie was about. Steven thought so, too. He loved it, called it a home run."[125] For Captain Hook they wrote a comedic recruiting song called "Stick With Me," and for the pirates, the jaunty "Low Below." There was an actual lullaby, "When You're Alone"; a serene and reflective ballad that Tinkerbell would sing about Peter's glory days in Neverland ("Believe"); and a tottery song for a grade school musical *within* the film, "We Don't Wanna Grow Up." John called Spielberg and producer Kathleen Kennedy into his bungalow at Amblin, where he and Bricusse demoed their fresh batch of songs at the piano. The film's lengthy production began on February 19, 1991, and the following month, several actors recorded their songs with pre-recorded instrumental accompaniment. "Maggie is not, alas, a singer," said Bricusse, so he called a favor from an old friend: Julie Andrews. "Trouper that she is, and a good pal of Maggie's, she learned the song overnight, drove over to the big recording stage at MGM on her lunch break, stood on the exact spot where Judy Garland had recorded 'Over the Rainbow' fifty years before, and sang 'Childhood' in the deliciously wavering voice of a ninety-year-old Wendy. It was perfection on the first take. She was with us maybe seven minutes. Steven shot Maggie doing the song at four o'clock that same afternoon."[126]

The most elaborate song sequence was a tour of the pirate town, with a huge cast of seamen singing "Low Below." First assistant director Bruce Cohen suggested hiring Vincent Paterson, who had just choreographed Madonna's performance of "Vogue" at the MTV awards. "We created this incredible piece," said Paterson, who also worked with Roberts on her fairy movement. "We spent at least a week shooting it. I had several days rehearsing, as well as working with John and going into the sound studio and taking some of the cast in with me." Somewhat spontaneously, Paterson even co-wrote a rap interlude with John:

> *This Peter Pan high boy*
> *Ain't no fly boy*
> *We'll take him and break him*
> *And shake him*
> *And bake him*
> *And make him give his propers to Hook ... Hook ... HOOK!!!*[127]

The film opens with a cast of schoolchildren singing "We Don't Wanna Grow Up" at a play where Peter is too busy taking business calls to pay attention to the female star: his daughter Maggie. Later, when Peter is in Neverland and training to duel Hook in order to reclaim his children, Maggie wistfully sings "When You're Alone" at night to a sea of sighing pirates. But Spielberg quickly began to doubt himself, and when he showed the "Low Below" footage to John on a flatbed KEM editor at his house one Sunday, "John lost all the color in his face," Spielberg said. "Doesn't have a lot of color to begin with, but he lost what he had. And he turned to me and said, 'This can't be a musical. You have to cut out this sequence and lose *all* the music.' And I did." Spielberg called everybody that day and said, "Hey, we're gonna save a million dollars! We're not gonna do any more musical numbers."[128] The director snipped the big song out seamlessly—Smee gets the hook for his boss, and just as quickly arrives at the ship door to give it to him with the pirates following behind and simply chanting a hold-over from the ditty: "Hook, hook, give us the hook." Bricusse was disappointed: "We were particularly heartbroken to lose 'Childhood,' but in the end it had to go, because there was simply no time or place for it." The lyricist thought they had an Oscar in the bag with that one in particular. "Beautiful song. Beautiful melody. Vintage Williams."[129]

The real legacy of that mostly discarded songbook was that, as John commenced scoring *Hook*, he already had a velvet bag overflowing with show tunes—and he decided to use them. Thus, *Hook* became the most musically theatrical score he ever composed, a "musical sans libretto," as Spielberg put it.[130] And because Spielberg's whole picture was *already* so theatrical, the music stuck to the material like Peter Pan's living shadow. John made "Childhood" the affectionate heart of his score, used "Believe" as a nostalgic leitmotif for Neverland, scored the goof-villainy of the pirates with "Low Below," and employed "When You're Alone" to represent Peter's kids. (Spielberg did leave the scene of Maggie singing her lullaby in his final cut.) From stem to stern, whether John was scoring an intimate conversation or a comedic ballet or a swashbuckling fight sequence, the *Hook* score is so infinitely, *tastily* singable that it's possible to whistle almost every single cue. This quality was as much catnip for children and John's fans as it was an allergen for some reviewers. "For once, a John Williams score seems indifferent to the action rather than attuned to it," wrote Ed Blank of the *Pittsburgh Press*.[131] In another pan of the film, the *Santa Fe New Mexican*'s Jon Bowman wrote that "Williams is in dire need of muzzling. His loud, brassy music runs roughshod over the action on the screen. Sometimes the dialogue is hard to pick out between the fanfare of trumpets and the wailing violins. At the least, the music telegraphs too much of the drama, spoiling the little suspense in this highly calculated affair."[132] The music did have a life of its own away from the picture, in part, because John was forced to start composing it before he saw a finished cut. Spielberg was racing to an early December release, and John's "only clue into the nature of what I was doing," Spielberg said, "was the screenplay and the first five reels (47 minutes) of edited film. These were not the ideal working conditions we had experienced over the course of an eleven-picture relationship. Yet remarkably, John has invented music with so much magic, delicacy, and simple beauty that the results have far outshone the process."[133]

The first substantial cue in the film sounds nothing like John Williams. Spielberg temped the scene of Jack's big baseball game, which his dad misses for work, with the 1980 Dave Grusin track "Mountain Dance." It fit the contemporary yuppie milieu—with Peter's mobile phone and corporate office, and the camcorder he sends to capture the game—and juxtaposes with the rest of the film's fairytale sound. John called pianist Mike Lang to help him figure out how to infuse the cue he wrote with Grusin's spirit, and Lang suggested getting some of the guys who normally played with Grusin to perform on it. They recorded "Banning Back Home" in a separate session, and "it sounded a lot like the 'Mountain Dance' record," Lang said, "but it was taking on a little funkier kind of thing." Lang had an impulse to pull his piano part a little away from a Grusin imitation, and into a slightly more gospel direction; they did a take, and John communicated from the booth: "Michael, that's totally wrong." Lang asked, "What do you mean?" John said, "It needs to be more like Mozart, like Poulenc." It was a strange note for a jazz track, but Lang knew exactly what he meant, "so I pulled back on the gospel stuff. It was very funny, his choice of words. He's very individual with his choice of language. It defines a lot of who he is when he's conducting."[134]

Leaving his all-important office, Peter reluctantly flies to London and the house where Wendy Darling adopted him as a boy, and it's here where the magic really begins. Granny Wendy stands at the top of the stairs and says, "Hello, boy," and the Childhood motif sounds gently, like a cradle mobile, reiterating as she insists on the one rule of the house: *no growing up*. Danger begins to brew when Peter visits the attic that night and briefly loses himself looking at a mural of Captain Hook—the dastard's theme rising eerily in the strings. From the cockeyed angles, moody lighting, and inexplicable sound of ship bells and seagulls in this scene, John and Spielberg made no bones about putting on a *show*. The tension between Peter's work addiction and his family crescendoes when he yells at his kids, and his wife Moira tosses his cell phone out the window. "We have a few special years with our children where they're the ones that want *us* around," she pleads with him. "After that, you're going to be running after *them* for a bit of attention. So fast, Peter. It's a few years, and it's over. And you are not being careful. And you are missing it." Suddenly the film isn't just a show—it has something serious and, for Spielberg, deeply *personal* on its heart. That message also hit John, who cited this monologue when he talked about his three grandchildren that winter: "I have not had a day off since early in the summer, and that made me crazy; I missed being around the youngsters more."[135] Reflecting on his experience as a working father, John later admitted that "it's a great privilege to be able to work in the way I work, but it is so intense that you neglect things. You can neglect people, you can neglect family. I have wonderful children. But it does so consume your life, this work—which it really shouldn't. A lot of the work that I do is certainly not that important. But the process of doing it is so all consuming—that is the truth of it. It isn't a *some*time thing. It's a full-time thing."[136]

John wrote a thrilling set piece for the surrealist breaking and entering of an unseen Hook kidnapping Jack and Maggie, heaving the sinister pirate theme with accelerating force and buccaneering brass. Like most of the score, this cue is full of highly choreographed hits to incidents—quilts flying off beds, Wendy's glass tipping over—and when Peter and Moira run frantically up the stairs, a melody runs up with them that seems to call out "Jack!" and "Maggie!" in unison. John sprinkles celeste fairy dust as Wendy tries to tell Peter about his past and who he really is, and when she emphatically says, "The stories are true," a low male choir rumbles with a wordless, ominous ooh-ing of the tune from "Low Below." Drunk in the attic that night, Peter's comical and gymnastic encounter with Tinkerbell is set to a Tchaikovskian ballet. Tink is given an extended treatment of her sugar-plum theme on celeste and orchestra as she pleads with Peter to go back to Neverland, but as he sneezes her into a dollhouse, and she realizes he *did* grow up, her theme grows depressed. In an echo of the scene in *E.T.* where the mom reads *Peter and Wendy*, John mimed Tink's exaggerated fall down the doll stairs as well as Peter's clapping to bring her back—and the scene crescendoes with a soaring, fantastic flight of "Childhood" as Tink carries Peter off to Neverland.

A groggy Peter wakes to the atmosphere of a bustling pirate town, scored with a jaunty pirate motif on Renaissance-style flutes, and "Low Below" bounces along in contrasting low and high woodwinds as Peter, in pirate disguise, follows Smee as he jigs along with the captain's hook. John scored Hook's theatrical entrance with a drum roll and a hit of the "Low Below" groove, which alternates with the darker, seafaring Hook motif introduced earlier in Wendy's nursery. Neither John, Spielberg, nor Hoffman really present Captain Hook as a serious menace; both the character and his music are mustache-twirling camp with just a hint of *he-might-actually-murder-someone* mystique. When Hook stares directly into Peter's middle-aged eyes, his motif slides on high, ghostly strings for an otherworldly effect. When Peter scrambles up to get a high view of Neverland—a stunning but unabashedly artificial vista—John introduces his nostalgic, aching aria for Neverland. Peter stumbles into the land of the Lost Boys, and John kept up with the ensuing chase in a highly animated ballet featuring a "Pomposo" romp for low tuba, trumpets, and timpani. He war-paints the boys' adventure-land with woodblock percussion, boo bams, and a synth voice which he described as "Neverland drums." It's all fun and games until Tink implores the boys to believe this doughy oldster *is* Peter Pan and to help him rescue his kids, supported with a melancholy quote of "Childhood." The boys' new leader, Rufio, draws a line in the sand forcing his crew to choose between him and Peter, and when an adorable boy called Pockets wanders over and closely studies Peter's face, John scored it like a holy moment. The music here was strongly inspired by another piece on the temp, a cue from the 1985 Georges Delerue score for *Agnes of God*—down to its harp arpeggios, initial chord progression, and a pensive melody on solo flute. Melodically, though, John diverted into a sacred song that he named "The Face of Pan."

The film keeps oscillating between extremes: one moment Peter is running from kids on skateboards and a sentient flower sniffing his privates, the next is a hushed fairy tale liturgy. It was an ambitious high-wire act for Spielberg to attempt, but as always, John helped him stick the landing by suffusing the walk with belief. From here, the story is split between the piratical hijinks of Hook and Smee, scheming to win the love of Peter's kids, and Peter's sweaty boot camp with the Lost Boys; John scored the two strands with vaudeville villainy and a jungle drum corps, respectively. Peter, sore and starving, smells the delicious "Never-Feast"—which John accompanied with a bouncy new processional theme, a wondrous piece of magic choreographed to shots of the boys chewing and handling invisible food. John bridged the space between Peter and his children with the sweetness of "When You're Alone," as a vulnerable Lost Boy asks Peter if he remembers his mother. Maggie's voice is heard softly in the distance singing the lullaby, then Spielberg cuts to her innocently serenading a bunch of dumbstruck pirates, her wobbly little voice buoyed with John's shimmering, bedtime orchestration. Hook takes Jack to his clock museum to destroy Peter's ticking stopwatch, and John's clocklike rhythm and Hook's flamboyant theme morph into the melancholy strains of "When You're Alone" as Jack starts to cry about how his dad never even tried to rescue him.

A baseball game staged just for Jack's pleasure is invaded by more of that lullaby when the pirate cheer squad accidentally chants "Run Home Jack" and begins to break the spell, but Jack snaps to and hits a home run, turning the lullaby into heroic triumph. Peter's heart is pierced when he sees Hook showing Jack the fatherly attention he has failed to do himself, and his sadness is empathized with "Childhood"—which persists with shaky determination as Peter tries to will himself to fly. He discovers his old treehouse and is flooded with boyhood memories; John's score dances with an emotional ballet, drawing on the Neverland theme, "Childhood," and a romantic interpretation of Tink's theme as she listens to Peter's story. The fullest development of "Childhood" yet comes as Peter recounts running away from home as a baby and feeling forgotten by his parents—then he suddenly remembers that he grew up because he wanted to be a *dad*, and the orchestra stirs from sadness to joy as he begins to levitate—an active version of "Childhood" takes off, and then a rapturous explosion of the Pan hero theme lets fly as a reborn Peter Pan goes for a joy flight. Swashbuckling jubilation turns *religioso* as Rufio kneels and hands Peter his sword, and a choir blesses this holy moment as the boys crowd around Peter and he crows triumphantly. As only John Williams could, he sells the majesty of this potentially ridiculous moment with the same sublime seriousness he gave *Empire of the Sun*.

The climactic "Ultimate War" is a nonstop smorgasbord of swashbuckling Korngold fanfare and bombast, another meticulously choreographed dance of sword parries and midair somersaults. It begins with a warlike stomp of the pirate theme—played "Militaire" style by anvil, field drums, and bass drum—and develops as a deliriously tuneful parallel play starring the score's major leitmotifs. The action is violently interrupted when Hook drives his sword through Rufio's heart, and John graces the moment with a dying horn version of the Neverland theme as Rufio dies in Peter's arms. The score oscillates between a victoriously active "Childhood," as Peter's kids convince him to take them home, and Hook's devious theme as he taunts Peter into dueling him. Swallowed by the (stuffed) crocodile with one last, slow gasp of his theme, Hook's defeat is celebrated by a merry splash of the Never-Feast motif. Having been redeemed, Peter knows he needs to return home with his kids; "The Face of Pan" repeats as Peter chooses his successor and says goodbye to the Lost Boys. Angelic women's voices sing haunting chords (marked "Slowly, with Reverence" and "Liturgico") as Peter flies off and the film rejoins Moira asleep in the attic, who weeps when she wakes to find her children back safely in their beds. A virtuoso flute solo directly matches a shot of the flute-playing Peter Pan statue in Kensington Garden, where Peter wakes to the sight of a man, suspiciously resembling Smee, sweeping up bottles and laughing at him. Tink's theme twinkles when she appears in the morning light and tearfully tells Peter: "You know that place between sleep and awake? That place where you still remember dreaming? That's where I'll always love you, Peter Pan. That's where I'll be waiting."[†††] Peter's boyish new version of fatherhood concludes

---

[†††] This line was one of many contributions by the film's punch-up screenwriter, Carrie Fisher. (Bruce Cohen to TG, November 15, 2021.)

the film, with Christmassy renditions of "Childhood" and "When You're Alone" as he reunites with his family and declares: "To live will be an awfully big adventure."‡‡‡

Hook opened on December 11. Most critics, who had followed the film's swollen budget and shooting schedule like it was another *Heaven's Gate*, were already lined up to clip its wings. Many harped on the film's stagey sets and Spielberg's theatricality. Time has both hardened the film's haters and fortified its admirers. At first Spielberg seemed to accept its judgment as a gigantic failure. "He's not a big fan of *Hook*," said James Hart, who for years tried to convince Spielberg to turn the material into a stage musical. "He's been very vocal about that."[137] Twenty years later, Spielberg said: "There are parts of *Hook* I love. I'm really proud of my work right up through Peter being hauled off in the parachute out the window, heading for Neverland. I'm a little less proud of the Neverland sequences, because I'm uncomfortable with that highly stylized world."[138] But as more than one generation vocally espoused their fondness for the film—including Spielberg's own children—he slowly accepted the love. He also said that John's score "is one of the best scores he's written for me."[139] For those who believe, *Hook* was a great game and an awfully big adventure—and one of the most enduring contributions from this pair of airborne storytellers.

* * *

As the Pops prepared for their Christmas concert in 1991, John made the announcement that he was going to retire as their conductor following the 1993 season. It was national news, and in Boston a front-page headline. "This year I turn 60 and I have been thinking very seriously about how I want to spend my time," John said. "I never thought I would become a professional conductor; composing has always been my first love." Reflecting on the message about priorities in *Hook*, he added: "I want to take the time to write some concert music, to travel less, and read, walk, and spend time with my grandchildren." He also told Dyer: "I want to devote more time to serious musical composition, but don't worry, I will always remember the advice of Vaughan Williams to a younger composer who had presented him with pages of crabbed counterpoint: 'Young man, if a tune should ever occur to you, don't fail to write it down.'"[140]

Approaching traditional retirement age, John seemed to suggest he might be entering the twilight of his career. But the movie gods just laughed. Two of his most important, eternal scores were just around the bend. And his concert life was *far* from over.

---

‡‡‡ John had a scary adventure of his own that July, when a flight from Boston to L.A. was forced to make an emergency landing due to a faulty light suggesting an engine fire. He was on board with Henry Mancini, and they had to take their shoes off and put their heads in their laps for the landing. Safely on the ground, when they slid down the inflatable slide John injured his foot. Just three months earlier, a friend of John's, Senator John Heinz of Pennsylvania, died in a grisly plane crash over an elementary school that claimed the lives of two children. John was scheduled to conduct a tribute gala concert in Pittsburgh that October, but was forced to bow out at the last minute because he was still frantically working on *Hook*, which he recorded at Sony that month.

12
Journey to the Island, 1991–1996

> *Conducting is instant gratification at the end of the night. Composing is a tougher job. Gratification comes once a year. I have always felt I was a composer first, conductor second.*
> —John Williams, 1992[1]

If Spielberg was tired of flying, figuratively, John was literally weary of air travel. He was jetting between Boston and Los Angeles a dozen times a year now, adding multiple-city tours with the Pops Esplanade; on top of that, Samantha had bought homes in Colorado and Santa Fe, New Mexico. Sitting on yet another airplane one day, he realized he wanted to spend more time on solid ground—which propelled his announcement to resign from the Pops. "I find traveling is less and less good for me," he said. "Also I wanted to find some more time to write a more thoughtful kind of music."[2] *Thoughtful*: he used that word several times when discussing his retirement, seemingly—and strangely—as an adjective in contrast to film work.

One flight in the spring of 1991 was to Dallas. He was there for a concert, but Oliver Stone took advantage of the opportunity and invited John to the Texas School Depository, where Lee Harvey Oswald supposedly fired all of the shots that cut down John F. Kennedy in the fall of 1963. "There's a museum on the third floor but the sixth floor, where Lee Harvey Oswald was, is closed," John said. "It was an eerie, spine-chilling experience to be up there and to look down on the grassy knoll and all of the other places that are burned in the memory of everyone who experienced that time."[3] After winning an Oscar for *Born on the Fourth of July*, Stone directed *The Doors*—a raucous film starring Val Kilmer as Jim Morrison, about the dog days of 1970s rock. "There was no point in going to [John] for that kind of movie," Stone laughed. But he wanted John for *JFK*. "Why not?" Stone said. "It made sense. His music came to stand for the American culture and a national pride."[4] *JFK* streamed from the same polluted wellspring of national lies and military overreach that shattered Stone's faith in America when he was in Vietnam. It followed *Platoon* and *July* in an ongoing series of films wrestling with the great American wound, inflicted by Kennedy's assassination, which spread and festered through the 1960s as the unwinnable war raged on. Never one to shy from controversy, Stone based his film on the theories of Jim Garrison, who was district attorney of New Orleans during the time of the assassination and who in 1969 put the official narrative—that Lee Harvey Oswald was the lone killer—on trial, hanging the full weight of an elaborate, alternative conspiracy theory on a Louisiana businessman named

Clay Shaw. Garrison summarized his arguments in a 1988 book, *On the Trail of the Assassins*, which found its way into Stone's hands while he was wrapping *July* in the Philippines. "It was a great gumshoe story," Stone said. "Garrison spins this tale out with international intrigue—a hell of a trail. As a dramatist, that excited me."[5] Stone cast Kevin Costner as Garrison—surrounded, in Stone fashion, by an elite ensemble including Sissy Spacek, Tommy Lee Jones, Gary Oldman, Jack Lemmon, Joe Pesci, and Donald Sutherland. He methodically deconstructed the "myth" put forward by the Warren Commission Report, simultaneously constructing his *own* myth through a new filmmaking style full of quick cuts, varying film gauges, faux-verité re-enactments, and subliminal techniques in a giant rushing tidal wave of montage cinema. In between more conventional moments of quiet dialogue and family drama, the film hurls one investigative argument after another, dramatized with rapid-fire collages of grainy flashbacks, doctored photos, real historical footage, and Hollywood sleight-of-hand. The end result was a breathless plunge into American history both real and imagined, culminating in a fiery sermon by Garrison about the nation's threatened soul.

John broke form and read the script. He also visited the set in New Orleans after the Pops season concluded, and watched about an hour of rough assemblage. But because of the film's tight post-production schedule and John's own commitments, he had to begin composing before he saw the finished film—before Stone even really started to edit.[6] "He already had strong notions about JFK of his own," said Stone. "He admired JFK. We never discussed how he was killed and all that, because it didn't need to be discussed. He just wanted to write an homage." John had personal connections to the Kennedys: Barbara was friends with the president's sister, Patricia, and she had followed "Jack's" progress in the Senate. But it was really the assassination on November 22, 1963—"my first recollection as an adult of weeping," John said[7]—that shocked him, "and I think the whole world," into a consciousness about the rest of the Kennedy family and "all of their ills and troubles and travails and successes, and so on, so that the whole family became *our* family."[8] The mission, said Stone, was for John "not only to convey the mystery and intrigue and the assassination, but bring out the human feeling of what Kennedy meant to the country—hope and future—and to create a bond for Garrison and the audience so that we'd like and understand Garrison ... an everyman caught in the midst of a whirlwind of facts and falsehoods." John had a strong response simply seeing the physical locations and rough footage: "I thought the handling of Lee Harvey Oswald was particularly strong, and I understood some of the atmosphere of the film—the sordid elements, the underside of New Orleans."[9] Working away from picture, he wrote and recorded six themes: one for Kennedy himself (titled "Prologue"), "The Motorcade," "The Conspirators," "Garrison's Obsession," "Garrison's Family Theme," and "Arlington"—each of them "reflecting different aspects of the film," said Stone, "to be used in the movie in various ways. He gave me that freedom, and I sometimes probably didn't use it the way he wanted. But, I don't know, he was a big man and he didn't have these petty problems at all."

John's noble melody for Kennedy was an optimistic inversion of the lament he wrote for *Born on the Fourth of July*, but once again he cast Tim Morrison's "American" trumpet in the part. The Kennedy theme is often introduced by a distinctive, Scottish-style snare tattoo—a recurring signature of the score befitting the late commander in chief, inspired by the Black Watch drum corps which John remembered hearing at Kennedy's funeral. The tune is elegantly aspirational, proud in its brass trumpet embodiment, and just a little melancholy. Like the fate of Camelot, it becomes a more fragile idea when played on solo piano, as when Garrison learns about Robert Kennedy's death and tells his wife he's scared. Most of the other themes rely on repetitive rhythmic, staccato patterns for the film's action and suspense, paranoia and intrigue. The Conspirators theme, which pulses with a clacking electronic heartbeat (created by Randy Kerber) and slides and slithers around on synthesizer, was copied by a dozen film composers in this film's wake. "There's a ticking metronome percussion," Stone said. "I never heard that quite the way it was used. That was sort of from his jazz background. It creates a feeling, for me, of continual scheming and intrigue." The Motorcade theme "spins out in a minimalistic way," John explained. "My hope was that Oliver Stone could be led into the pace of the sequence by the rhythms of the music. It is strongly kinetic music, music of interlocking rhythmic disciplines." Stone's montage-heavy approach enabled him to deploy these recorded suites—whether partial, in full, or even looped—wherever he saw fit. Editors Joe Hutshing and Pietro Scalia used them as tools to cut the picture. "A musical sequence that may have lasted seven minutes on the recording lasts a minute or two in the film," John remarked.[10] The resulting patchwork of endlessly repeating rhythms and melodic patterns fit the story's obsessive, endless rabbit hole. "It was really a great asset," Stone said. "I don't know why it's not more done."*

One of the casualties of Garrison's obsession is his family; his wife's tearful lament that he's missing out on his children's lives is reminiscent of the mother's speech in *Hook*. John responded with a gently downcast family theme, a minor-key lullaby for English horn over shimmering, childlike celeste. "You feel for his family," Stone said. "You feel there's a family lost in the movie, and that family lost is a disruption—not just *his* family, but the country." The sad soul of John's score is his Arlington theme, so named for the national cemetery where Garrison has a revelatory conversation with Donald Sutherland's mysterious Deep Throat character. This joined a long line of somber string adagios in Stone's films, and one can almost hear the heart of a country breaking in half, the strings keening for a leader executed—according to this film—by his own government. The adagio reprises in the courtroom finale, as Garrison details the government cover-up, quoting Hitler: "The bigger the lie, the more people will believe it." Historians, not for the first or last time, objected to Stone's vérité presentation

---

* This reverse approach, of a film being edited to an existing score, was more common in Europe—Sergei Eisenstein and Sergei Prokofiev famously worked this way—and in the 21st century it has become much more common in Hollywood, not only to accommodate musicians untrained in the technical skill of scoring to picture but also for the creative advantages of involving composers early in the process.

of many controversial "facts." John noted that the film grossed more than double outside of the United States as it did domestically, "indicating what I would have suspected, that the international audience remains fascinated with the Kennedys and with the America of the 1960s. I know that Oliver Stone is gleefully happy that there are discussions about opening the government files. Even if there is nothing in them, a kind of moral point will have been made. Although there are things in the film that some people could find objectionable," he added diplomatically,

> I think it was a valid work that caused people to think and rethink this great event in our history. And for young people who may not have paid that much attention to it in school, it was a real smack in the face. The film is made from a highly personal perspective and it is not to be taken seriously as history, but this is a valid subject for artistic presentation in the cinema.[11]

JFK and *Hook* were released within a week of each other in December 1991. The *JFK* score was nominated for an Oscar, but lost to Alan Menken's *Beauty and the Beast*—just as *July* had lost to *The Little Mermaid*. When John accompanied Yo-Yo Ma on piano in a soulful piece by Rachmaninoff at the John F. Kennedy Library that May—a performance for Soviet leader Mikhail Gorbachev, who was wrapping up a U.S. tour—Jackie Onassis, JFK Jr., Robert Kennedy's widow Ethel, and Senator Edward "Ted" Kennedy were among the attendees.[12] Rose Kennedy, the president's mother, often invited John down to Cape Cod for social occasions. "The conductor of the Pops is like the mayor of Boston," John said. "I didn't go, but they extended themselves." Jack's sister, Joan, was a regular presence at Symphony Hall, and when she wrote a book in 1992 called *The Joy of Classical Music*, John wrote the foreword. John also made contributions to several re-election campaigns for "Ted," JFK's youngest brother—and they became good friends.[13]

* * *

John's retirement from the Pops was nationwide news in a country where most symphony orchestras were now regularly performing his music—even if it *was* still in the ghetto of "pops" concerts. The announcement produced a steady drip of stock-taking and retrospective interviews and articles about John over the next two years as he completed his tenure, and it caused some to believe he was actually retiring from music altogether. John had nothing of the sort in mind, and he tired of people asking him how he felt about "the end." "To a healthy hypochondriac," he said, "the idea of retiring doesn't sound very good."[14] But he *was* anxious to slow down, and he had already begun declining offers to guest conduct. Untangling himself from the musical scene in Boston would be difficult, both logistically and emotionally, but he expressed total confidence about leaving his orchestra in good shape:

> I think we built a bridge between Arthur Fiedler and the present. I am a great believer in the positive aspects of change, and the orchestra and I both grew through

this experience. It's not all over tomorrow; we have two more seasons, and 18 months of opportunity to think about the future. Then there will need to be someone else to energize the Pops. The right kind of person can start building another bridge, to a different place.[15]

He was particularly eager to write more concertos. "At 60, you are not exactly creaking with age, but you have to be realistic about how much energy you have and where you want to put it. I am not leaving the Pops because I want to spend more time in Hollywood; I want to scale back there, too. I never thought of myself as a performer, and the best use I can make of my time and talent is to write music, and so I want to concentrate on that, to think about the pieces I am writing, give them time and breathing room."[16]

John was in Boston for the annual Christmas Pops in December 1991, but he skipped some of the festivities to meet with Ron Howard in New York and view footage from the director's new movie—tentatively titled *The Irish Story*. "It's a lyrical piece," John told Richard Dyer, "an immigrant story about a young man who comes to Boston in the 19th century and winds up making the rush for land claims in Oklahoma. I'm looking forward to the chance to write some Boston music."[17] The film, renamed *Far and Away*, was a passion project for Howard, whose ancestors came to America from Ireland and whose acting career—along with his father, Rance Howard—had started in westerns. In 1958, the four-year-old child actor flew to Ireland to shoot one of his first parts, for the war romance *The Journey*. "When I got out, one of the guys who was refueling the plane tousled my hair and said, 'You shouldn't get back on. You look like you belong here.'" That, he said, was the genesis of *Far and Away*, and it was later refueled when his great-grandmother showed him a scrapbook containing a news clipping from 1893 of the starting line of the Oklahoma Land Rush. She pointed to a man and said, "That was your grandpa Ralph. He got a racehorse so he could get out faster than the others." "Other people dismissed her," said Howard, "but I believed her."[18]

It was Irish *music* that finally lit the fuse in earnest. Howard saw the Irish folk group the Chieftains perform in Pasadena in 1984, and "there was one song they played about an emigrant going off to America that was bittersweet, romantic, and very Irish," he said. "You know how music somehow sets you thinking; I was daydreaming all the way home in the car about that song. Then I started making a few notes and plot ideas. That concert was the point of origin for the movie."[19] Howard knew he wanted the story to begin in Ireland and end in the American land race, but it would take several years, a proven success at the box office, the launch of his company Imagine Entertainment, several research trips to the Emerald Isle, and the help of screenwriter Bob Dolman to get the film off the starting line. He cast newlywed superstars Tom Cruise and Nicole Kidman as the leads: Joseph Donnelly, a headstrong farmer who dreams of having his own land, and Shannon Christie, the daughter of privilege who dreams of American modernity. The odd couple are thrust together by fate after Joseph tries to kill his greedy landlord, Shannon's father, and they run off to America together—where they evolve from reluctant roommates to lovers. The film began shooting in May 1991 in Montana, doubling as Oklahoma territory, then moved to Dublin and the nearby Irish coast. (The Dublin district of Temple Bar actually stood in for turn-of-the-century Boston.) Director of photography Mikhail Solomon shot it in 70mm, only the second film to do so since David Lean's *Ryan's Daughter* in 1970.[20] (Lean's widescreen vistas and sprawling historical epics were obvious inspirations for *Far and Away*.) At $60 million, it was the director's biggest and most expensive film to date.

Howard had known John since the 1970s, popping in to the occasional scoring session, and he had recently asked John for advice regarding his film about Chicago firefighters. Howard was casually feeling out if John wanted to score *Backdraft*, which John couldn't do, but when Howard mentioned the young composer he was considering, John assured him: "I really believe in Hans Zimmer." Howard also often worked with James Horner, "but there was something about the romance and sense of adventure that I wanted in *Far and Away*," Howard said.

> I wanted it to land emotionally, but I always thought there was a lot of humor in the movie, and it was almost a rom-com in the West in my mind. And without being cute, I wanted it to have a buoyancy, and a youthful spirit, and a sense of adventure. I certainly assumed that the Irish flavors would factor into it. But I just felt like John had such *range*, and could get both the emotion and the spirit of young love and also really come through in the land race and other action-driven sequences.[21]

John was a natural choice to fill the canvas of a Lean-sized epic, and Howard was further convinced when the Chieftains played with John and the Pops in May 1991. The Irish folk group was formed in 1962 by Paddy Moloney, a composer and performer from Dublin who specialized in the uilleann pipes and other native instruments, and by 1991 they had achieved international success and several Grammy nominations, and had also played on several films, including the Oscar-winning soundtrack for Stanley Kubrick's *Barry Lyndon*. "We needed Irish music played by Irish artists," said John. "These men are the best in the world—they're uniquely great. They just turn up, play their instruments and get on with it. In a way they remind me of Mozart as a child, always traveling on from one job to another."[22] It became a package deal—a chance to incorporate the band that sparked the film in the first place.

John had a deep love for Ireland, ancestral home of the Duffys (and, unknown to him then, the Nagles); he also traced his affections back to seeing *The Quiet Man* in 1952 when he was stationed in Newfoundland. "Something about it always stuck in my mind," he said. "This one has that same warm feeling as *The Quiet Man*, and that kind of comedy. I'm very excited about this girl, Nicole Kidman.... Great beauty, wonderful intelligence and humor; she's also a marvelous horsewoman and a wonderful athlete, all qualities that Miss O'Hara had; she really lights up the screen."[23] John had paid direct homage to *The Quiet Man* in *E.T.*, when the drunk alien catches the film on TV and watches John Wayne dramatically grab and kiss Maureen O'Hara. In his score, John braided an extra lush version of Victor Young's love theme with his own melody for E.T. to glorious effect. Thus, John said, *Far and Away* became a depository for a lot of "nostalgia and frustrated ambition."

Unlike Young, who adapted several traditional Irish folk tunes, here John felt compelled to write his own: "I wanted to manipulate them and bend them around with impunity."[24] He introduced many of these tunes in the film's opening scene, under an aerial approach to the coast of western Ireland, set in 1892. Moloney's uilleann pipes, an Irish cousin of the bagpipe, set the geographical stage with a minor-key wail, and then one of the score's primary themes timidly pokes through the orchestral fog on Moloney's lone penny whistle—a lyrical Celtic air for Joseph and his homeland, packed with pain, homesickness, and love all at once. In the opening cue, Moloney twisted and twirled the tune with deep feeling—the whole orchestra rising and rising with the melody before it descends back onto emerald ground. "I loved the music," Moloney said, but "just reading it, it felt a little bit static, so I said, 'John, is there any chance I could play this with my own style?' And he threw his arms around me and said, 'I thought you'd never ask!' Then he told the orchestra, 'You keep an eye on me, and I'll keep an eye on him.'"[25] Moloney and the Chieftains recorded some of their four cues separately in late March 1992—the actual first day of sessions booked at Sony was, fittingly, Saint Patrick's Day—and other cues with the full hundred-piece orchestra. (Cruise and Kidman attended at least one session.)

On the heels of that homeland theme comes a breathy pan flute playing John's main theme for *Far and Away*. It's really a love theme, both for the romance between Joseph and Shannon and the romance of Ireland, and it's another of John's simple, hummable melodies with a path so obvious to the ears that it feels centuries old. He was taken by the scope of the photography, which allowed him to explore his own Lean-sized ambitions. "The 70-millimeter scale suits this film," John said. "Ireland's magnificent topography is an inspiration in itself. A root source is Irish poetry that set the themes. Irish scales are older, modal. I put myself under their influence and listened with my soul's memory to feel these characters and their time."[26] Throughout the score, the love theme drifts from the loneliness of penny whistle or solo piano or flute, to sweeping, widescreen strings. It serves as a grand, heroic coda after Joseph goes on a victorious boxing streak, or when he hops off a train to claim his land in Oklahoma, and it's as delicate as a snowflake, surrounded by shimmering chimes, when Joseph and Shannon romantically heat up a cold, empty mansion. That scene features a field of starry, snowy notes that drift and float in the air, a passage that recalls the heavenly music from *Always* and *Heartbeeps*.

When we first meet Joseph, he's wrestling with a stubborn donkey and boxing with his brothers, and John wrote a "donnybrook" theme for these scenes and the later ones in Boston where Joseph earns money as a bare-knuckled prizefighter. This rambling jig is often performed by the Chieftains, lending the fight sequences a scrappy, barroom quality—you can practically smell the warm ale and tobacco. Their unique instruments included the *bodhrán*, a mallet-banged hand drum, and clinking "bones." When Joseph finds himself in a fog-covered duel with Shannon's suitor, the donnybrooking Chieftains are suddenly interrupted and counterpointed by the orchestra carrying the love theme, as Shannon whisks Joseph off in a getaway wagon. Another fight theme, which John titled "Blowing Off Steam," is a playful

Celtic scherzo. When Joseph and Shannon finally kiss, their love theme swells in the strings with a simple pan flute counterpoint—but the spell is suddenly broken when the house's owner storms in, and the orchestra panics and crescendoes as Shannon is shot in the back during their frantic escape. The love theme plays on frantic brass as Joseph runs down Boston's snowy streets with her, crying for help. A gentle, heartbreaking flute statement of the love theme plays over strummed harp as he tells her goodbye, and a ghostly rendition of the homeland theme, hovering over a churning string figure, ramps up with intensity and clacking percussion accompaniment—the orchestra pounding away as Joseph runs into the cold night, culminating in a smash cut to an exploding mountain out West.

The score subtly migrates in style from Ireland to America as the story progresses, and Copland-esque open fifths and the musical language of westerns meet the characters in Oklahoma. The land race cue is a showstopper: the epic visual of hundreds of eager landowners on horses and wagons, tumbling and toppling headlong over the sweeping plains of Oklahoma, gave John space to write a huge piece of bombastic pageantry much like the fanfares he wrote for the Olympics. Heralded by golden brass, a repeating string motor chugs along—punctuated by John's trademark timpani-cymbal "boom-TISH"; the donnybrook theme, love theme, and a new land race theme coalesce and collide with ornamental orchestration, constantly modulating upward with ratcheting suspense.[†] This theme was first heard in Boston during Joseph's climactic boxing match, teasing the promise of his future farm and future with Shannon. The introductory presentation of this fanfare, swept up by a jubilant bass line and flitting flute ostinatos, prefigured the festive arrival at *Jurassic Park*.

John spotted the film in Greenwich, Connecticut, where Howard cut the film. During a lunch break at a nearby restaurant, Howard asked John: "Why does music work? Why does it speak to us?" John said people have been asking that question forever, but the best guess he could offer was about how music taps into our atavistic cultural memories of thundering herds and birdsong and bubbling water. He explained his theory for 10 or 15 minutes, "but in the most unpretentious way," Howard said, "and almost like it's a miracle to him—almost as though he's humbled by the power of it, and *really* appreciative of his role in channeling that and using it and sharing that with people."

When Howard put John's score into a preview of the film, "our test scores and everything just really soared," the director said. "It wound up being one of my highest testing movies."[27] But *Far and Away* was a critical failure when it was released in May 1992, and it made a poor showing at the box office—a major heartbreak for Howard. Reviews were no less kind to the score. "The less said about composer John Williams' adaptation of Irish music and his 'triumphant' anthems, the better," David Armstrong snarked at the *San Francisco Examiner*.[28] Duane Byrge at the *Hollywood Reporter* was in a minority of admirers: "In big, bold combinations Mikael Solomon's sky-filled cinematography and John Williams' heartfelt score are far and beyond the easy excellencies of mere

---

[†] The land race cue was used in movie trailers for years afterward.

bigness—they are, like big dreams themselves, emblazoned by raw, small particulars."[29] Proud of his score, John started programming a suite in concerts. Even if the initial platform caved in, he could always rehouse tunes he liked in the concert hall.

* * *

John turned 60 in February 1992, but he was not planning to coast in his penultimate season with the Pops. There were six full weeks of concerts at Symphony Hall, and another tour. The season opened with actress Tyne Daly singing show tunes, and she was determined to coax her shy conductor into her act: "He's going to work with me as an actor," Daly said. "That's part of the deal."[30] She was persuasive; when Daly went into "Some People" from *Gypsy*, John bashfully delivered the father's line: "You ain't gettin' 88 cents from me, Rose." An emotional concert in July, captured for *Evening at Pops*, united folk singer Bonnie Raitt and her father, John Raitt. "It was one of the highlights of her life," said Susan Dangel, "because she'd never done a show with her father." It was a testament to "how much respect both of them had for John, and how excited they were to do it."[31] On July 13, Prince Philip, Duke of Edinburgh, paid a visit to Boston where, after receiving a 21-gun salute aboard the USS *Constitution*, he attended the "Nautical Ball" at Symphony Hall. Before dinner was served, the Pops welcomed the prince with a brass fanfare, *Aloft to the Royal Masthead!*, which John had composed for the occasion at the request of Boston Symphony patron Frances Fahnestock. The royal visitor asked John if he had invented the Boston Pops, and John said he did not. "Well, didn't you do *something*?" Prince Philip asked quizzically. John replied: "We jazzed it up a bit."[32]

In between the Pops series and appearances at Tanglewood, an 11-city tour with the Pops Esplanade took John from Washington, D.C., to the Hollywood Bowl—which served as his farewell U.S. tour as Pops conductor. "I don't like to travel," he reiterated, "but once I get to where I'm going, I enjoy being there." He admitted he did feel a sense of "schoolchildren on holiday" when he hung out with the orchestra on flights and in restaurants. "We develop our own little rituals," he said. "There's an opportunity to get to know each other a little better than we do back in Boston, when we all have our own lives to lead."[33] John continued to wrestle with just how much of his own music to program, conscious of not wanting to seem like a narcissist—but there were always complaints when he didn't play enough Williams music. "We came all the way from Des Moines to hear *Superman*," he heard one fan say.[34] But the gulf between the people and paid critics was as yawning as ever. In his *L.A. Times* review of the Bowl concert that August, Don Heckman said the program of John's music was "so ephemeral that had it gone on any longer, it might have floated away into the Hollywood sky."[35]

On the morning after that concert, John screened *Home Alone 2: Lost in New York*.[36] It was pure Hollywood logic that a sequel would follow the first slot machine, and the second film, again scripted by John Hughes and initially titled *Alone Again*, was a fairly bald carbon copy of the original: the new spin was letting Kevin loose in Manhattan, with its opulent hotels and glorious toy stores.[‡] But the basic gist

---

[‡] It also had the bizarre distinction of a cameo by future president Donald Trump.

was carried over in full: the McCallisters accidentally strand Kevin at Christmastime, he revels in the freedom of an adulthood playground, has to outwit the Wet Bandits through an increasingly inventive series of booby traps, and learns life lessons from an initially creepy but secretly wise elder—here a dowdy "pigeon lady." Everything was simply supersized: Macaulay Culkin, now 12, was paid $4.5 million to reprise the role of Kevin (after reportedly receiving $100,000 on the first film), the runtime was 20 minutes longer, and the fake noir movie used as a plot device was called *Angels with Even Filthier Souls*. "There is a franchise feeling about it. That's a new word that I've heard a lot in Hollywood recently," Chris Columbus said at the time, chewing on a term that would become all too familiar. "It's interesting, because I get offered scripts and they say, 'This can be a franchise,' and I'm like, 'Wait a second, in the old days it was supposed to be a great film.'"[37]§

Columbus had been previewing the film with a temp score made from the first movie, and John's mandate was: *more of the same*. Columbus defended the musical rehash: "It's like when you see *Raiders of the Lost Ark*; in the next Indiana Jones film you're going to want to hear the theme. Same with *Star Wars*. So for me it was a matter of recreating the score but not *imitating* the score. It didn't feel like John was doing an imitation."[38] One fresh opportunity was a chance for John to express musical affection for his native New York. He also wrote two new carols, "Christmas Star" and "Merry Christmas, Merry Christmas," again with Leslie Bricusse. The first is a dreamy, homesick ballad, the other a staccato sleigh ride—both catchy, but neither as indelible as their 1990 forebears. The majority of John's score was conspicuously cribbed from the original film—a reflection of the sequel's lack of originality, no doubt, but John was also just following orders. "*Home Alone 2* is, in some ways, a remake of *Home Alone 1*," said Columbus. "I can't deny that as the director." But Columbus also insisted that the score made it distinct: "John Williams kind of makes you forget that the first time you watch it. And we had extraordinary success with audiences when we were screening the film. Nobody seemed to mind. And for some reason, I think *Home Alone* is a better film, but I think *Home Alone 2* is funnier. I don't know why, except it makes me laugh harder—that's really it—and John's score may have something to do with that."[39] It was a score where the orchestra "babbles away vigorously," John said. "All the choreographed visual jokes are quite balletic. Really, part of the energy is the orchestra."[40]

Among the few novel passages are statements of his new carols—particularly the lovely "Christmas Star," which Kevin first hears sung by a choir in the lead-up to rigging his human Road Runner traps, and which provides a warm orchestral blanket for his reunion with Mom in Rockefeller Center (before "Somewhere in My Memory" returns, right on cue). The festal tune of "Merry Christmas, Merry Christmas" greets Kevin at Duncan's Toy Store. There is also a buoyant new theme

---

§ The first *Home Alone* marked the final time John worked with his friend and faithful orchestrator, Herbert Spencer, who died on September 18, 1992. "I must say my last years with John Williams have been the most enjoyable of all," Spencer said in 1988. (Carl Johnson, "An Interview with Herbert Spencer," *The Cue Sheet* 7, no. 3 [July 1990].)

for his arrival in New York—an homage to Gershwin—and Kevin's arrival at the Plaza Hotel is accompanied by a wide-eyed, winter wonderland theme reminiscent of the Never-Feast music from *Hook*. Tim Curry's wary concierge was given his own deliciously sinister motif for slithering low strings, "but again, it's not intrusive," said Columbus. "It's not hitting you over the head saying, *You need to laugh at this*."[41] For a scene where Kevin watches an orchestra concert at Carnegie Hall from the attic, John brought his Pops chops to bear—writing a medley of new arrangements of seasonal standbys "O Come, All Ye Faithful," "O Little Town Of Bethlehem," and "Silent Night," which act as underscore to an important conversation Kevin has with the Pigeon Lady.[**]

The film came out on November 20, 1992, and earned $136 million at the home box office—not the staggering statistic of the first movie but enough to become the fourth-highest grossing film of the year, well above *Far and Away* at number 22. Columbus's next project was a hit comedy with Robin Williams playing a man who goes undercover as a frumpy female nanny to spend time with his kids in the wake of a painful separation from his wife. "I desperately wanted John to do *Mrs. Doubtfire*," said Columbus, who called John before he even started shooting. It was another broad comedy with dramatic scenes, and he knew John could ace the assignment—but John wasn't available. "I can only imagine what his score would have been like," said Columbus,[††] who wasn't about to stop imagining John for future projects.[42]

* * *

John threw his back out in 1993. His final lap with the Pops collided with two major film assignments, both backbreaking in their own way: a modern-day dinosaur adventure and a sober Holocaust drama. Spielberg first heard about *Jurassic Park* in 1990 while Michael Crichton was working on the novel, and immediately wanted to turn it into a film. Crichton's fiction work (which included *The Andromeda Strain* and *Westworld*) was preoccupied with technology and nature run amok as a corrective to human hubris. His story about a wealthy tycoon who exploits a new science which lets him clone long-dead dinosaurs using preserved DNA, and the violent destruction his reckless theme park unleashes, was catnip for the wonder-striking director of *Jaws* and *Close Encounters*—a chance to awe and terrify a new generation with fantastically real-life monsters that have fascinated filmmakers since the birth of movies.

The screenplay by David Koepp wove a sweet story about a kid-wary paleontologist, Alan Grant (played by Sam Neill), and his fun, feminist partner Ellie Sattler (Laura Dern) into a plot about a prehistoric zoo on the loose; Spielberg gave plum roles to Richard Attenborough as park owner John Hammond, and Jeff Goldblum as the quipping chaotician Dr. Ian Malcolm. It also precipitated one of the biggest

---

[**] The onscreen musicians were actually filmed inside Chicago's Orchestra Hall where, years later, *Home Alone* would regularly screen with live accompaniment by the Chicago Symphony.

[††] The job went to Howard Shore, better known for his creepy crawly music for David Cronenberg and *Silence of the Lambs*.

special effects breakthroughs in movie history. John was thinking about the assignment as early as the summer of 1992, when Spielberg shot the film on location in hurricane-hammered Hawaii and then on soundstages near John's office at Universal.[43] ILM produced a stunning computer animation test of a T-rex chasing a flock of Gallimimus—which instantly killed Spielberg's original plan to use stop-motion puppetry, the means of conceiving these creatures since the days of *King Kong*. (As Alan says in the film: "The world has just changed so radically, and we're all running to catch up.") John went up to Skywalker Ranch in late February 1993 to watch a locked cut of the film. "The computer graphics of the dinosaurs are so beautiful," he told Dyer. "Never in your life have you seen what you're about to see. These creatures are so enormous, the texture and lighting of their skin, their movements, the integration with the live action—it is a staggering achievement. And to know that they aren't models but numbers in a computer blows my mind, which is a pre-computer mind!"[44] John also met with the film's sound effects crew to get a sense of their aural designs for the dinosaurs; he didn't want score and FX to be in competition—although at one point he did ask shakuhachi player Masakazu Yoshizawa to imitate the menacing howl of a dinosaur.[45]

The score's opening is almost deceptive: foreboding choir and that lone shakuhachi promise mystery and danger in an exotic locale. Those promises are delivered, of course—before long, the human visitors to Jurassic Park will be cowering and running for their lives from bloodthirsty behemoths. "It pumps away all the time," said John. "It's a rugged, noisy effort—a massive job of symphonic cartooning. You have to match the rhythmic gyrations of the dinosaurs and create these kind of funny ballets."[46] But this wasn't a monster movie score in any traditional sense. Instead of simply responding to the menace and mayhem, John endowed the film with a sense of majesty and religious awe.

This film *about* an amusement park was, in many ways, crafted *like* an amusement park—and the first thrill ride is the helicopter journey to Isla Nublar, which climaxes with a waterfall, some sudden drops, and a missing seatbelt. John introduced his first major theme on this ride: a singable anthem for the park. "High-spirited and brassy," he described it—"very thrilling and upbeat musically, very positive."[47] Hammond's grinning, portentous "welcome" to Jurassic Park is attended by a solemn pageant, as if announcing a great conqueror or king. John started playing around with the melody and its leaping fanfare as soon as the arriving party hops into their jeeps and rumbles across the island, with a sunny countermelody for this bright calm before the storm. This theme, cleverly, is how Hammond feels about his park.

Then, the moment of revelation. As Alan and Ellie gape, dumbstruck, at their first living dinosaur, John unfurled the score's other key theme: a hymn for the might and majesty of these ancient creatures newly risen from the dead. (The call of a brachiosaurus acts as a pleasing grace note.) For the first appearance of these "benign creatures," John said, he wanted to compose "some gentle *religioso* cantilena lines, music that tries to capture the awesome beauty and sublimity of the dinosaurs in nature."[48] This theme starts with short, reverent phrases on strings harmonized like church music, then gradually accelerates and flourishes into a triumphant, ornate salute full of wonder and glittering enchantment. This theme is how *Alan and Ellie* feel about the park's occupants. When the tour party comes upon a sick triceratops, the beast receives its own theme—another serene chorale for strings. The audience, again, is experiencing the animal the way Ellie does, with sympathy and profound respect. It was a masterstroke of subtly, emotionally bonding us to these creatures, so that when they begin to hunt humans, our feelings are a complicated cocktail of fear and love (a trick Max Steiner first established in *King Kong* in 1933). When Alan hides himself and the kids up in a tree overnight, unwittingly growing more comfortable in his fatherly role, John serenaded them with a lullaby on celeste that turns into a tender, twinkling statement of the main hymn. Meanwhile, a darker, sadder lullaby (also on celeste) underscores Hammond's weary recollections of Petticoat Lane, the far less dangerous marvel that started it all. Even when Alan makes the spine-chilling discovery of hatched raptor eggs, John complicates the audience's emotional response with an eerie choral passage shaded with piety.

There is, naturally, also plenty of mystery and mayhem—but John didn't let up on lyricism, even in the chase sequences and interstitial moments. The film starts with that sinister, four-note motto on shakuhachi (a minor-key cousin of the famous *Close Encounters* motto), which becomes a haunting shorthand for dino menace, and it charges on repeat when the relentless raptors attack. "I remember particularly the kitchen scene, which is one of the most terrifying scenes I think *I've* ever seen in a film," John said. "It's scored in a very operatic and dramatic way, and the gestures being operatic maybe made it a little larger than life—the whole idea was just that—so it was an opportunity for me to push the orchestral buttons to the limit."[49] In the aftermath of the T-rex assault, a frantic, spiraling motif—recalling the "Dies Irae" motif of death—gives expression to Ellie's panic and the intensifying danger, and it later picks up worried speed during the ticking time bomb sequence of Alan and the kids scaling an electric fence. Amid all of its scares and serenity, the film is also *funny*. For the park's animated educational video that starts the tour, John wrote the film's only real "cartoon" music (a cue he cheekily titled "Stalling Around," after legendary *Looney Tunes* composer Carl Stalling). In a wink of meta commentary, Hammond assures his guests: "This score is only temporary. It all has very dramatic music, of course—a march or something. It hasn't been written yet."

For the first time in their long history together, Spielberg wasn't able to attend the recording sessions. John auditioned his themes for Spielberg on his piano as usual, but when he gathered the orchestra at Sony in late March, the director was in Kraków, already weeks into shooting *Schindler's List*. "When I was happy with the picture," Spielberg said, "I locked the print. I literally said, 'This is a lock, this is the movie,' no more changes were done to it, and I turned it over to the post-production group."[50] Kathleen Kennedy oversaw the scoring sessions, and Universal rented satellite channels from a Warsaw television station so that Spielberg could review visual effects shots and music from afar. The score recordings were transferred to cassette and shipped to Eastern Europe, and the director "was really thrilled when the richness and the depth of that score just really filled my car ride to the location every day. I actually put the cassette into the car and listened to Johnny's score going to and from location in Poland."[51] This was one way Spielberg staved off the profound emotional stress of making *Schindler*. Meanwhile, John relinquished much of his conducting duties to Artie Kane—a longtime session pianist and husband of JoAnn Kane, who oversaw John's music preparation—because he was experiencing such severe lower back pain that his doctor told him not to conduct. He was recovered enough to start programming the new themes in concerts by summer. "I hope everyone's going to like it," he told Dyer in May. "You get caught up in the moment of creativity, with the chauvinistic spirit of everyone working on the film, but you can never really know what the public's going to do."[52]

At a cost of $60 million, *Jurassic Park* surpassed every possible measure of cinematic success when it came out on June 11, 1993—quickly becoming the highest-grossing film of all time. Not only were the digital creatures a breakthrough, marking the dawn of the computer effects age, it was also the first digital movie score in wide release. (Hundreds of theaters were equipped with the new DTS sound system, "The Digital Experience," in preparation for the film.) The movie spawned its own blockbuster franchise of sequels, videogames, parodies, and, aptly enough, a theme park ride. The score immediately found its way into marching bands and music rooms, and the main themes joined *Star Wars* and *Indiana Jones* as some of John's most recognized pop melodies; they were even used, perhaps with just a wink of irony, as wedding music. The soundtrack cracked Billboard's Top 50 album chart in 1993,[‡‡] and Goldblum, an amateur jazz pianist, often sang the tune at his shows with jokey lyrics ("In Jurassic Park, scary in the dark / I'm so scared that I'll be eaten"). "Music can do something, can't it, that storytelling, words, and pictures can't do," Goldblum said, reflecting on this score. "You have corresponding notes in your innards that it touches and plays upon."[53] Had this merely been a scary monster score, it would not have haunted anything past the film's background. But John went to church, and his deliciously divine tunes—like these prehistoric beasts—found a way to outlive their moment.

Some critics were unimpressed; one called it "generic adventure music."[54] But the score's power was undeniable. "It's both easy and fashionable to dump on John Williams, whose harmonious, orchestrally soaring pop scores have become as familiar and recognizable as the blockbuster movies they decorate," Sid Smith wrote in the *Chicago Tribune*: "With *Jurassic Park*, Williams may have turned out his finest work so far. As with *Jaws* ... Williams rises to this latest Spielbergian challenge with a majestic, stately theme that boasts a simplicity missing from the ornate pomposity of his score to George Lucas' *Star Wars*."[55] In 2012, *New York Times* classical critic Zachary Woolfe wrote a paean to the score, "which remains a wonder.

[‡‡] Twenty-two years later, when the ill-advised sequel *Jurassic World* came out with a new score by Michael Giacchino, John's reanimated main theme became a Top 10 hit.

There is no one better than Mr. Williams at drawing out delicious tension before laying down the big, unforgettable theme for the first time as the camera swoops toward the island park early on. Even more impressive, though, are the myriad ways in which he transforms the arching lines of that main melody, fragmenting and poisoning them as the mood turns from triumphant to ominous. The terse, tense music in *Jurassic Park* isn't fundamentally different from the soaring stuff.

Mr. Williams, for all his lyrical lavishness, is an expert at recycling, at making a given theme do many different things in the course of a film. This matches Mr. Spielberg's point in *Jurassic Park* that good and evil tend to arise from the same source. Passages like these are the ones you hear without really hearing—this is the film composer's true art—and Mr. Williams treats them with subtle, alert intelligence.[56]

The "John Williams Jubilee Season" at the Pops launched with an all-star gala tribute. Among the 2,000 attendees were Henry Mancini, Christopher Reeve, and Aretha Franklin, who sang "Respect" and "Bridge over Troubled Water" with the orchestra. Michael Dukakis and Boston's mayor, Ray Flynn, both tried their hands at percussion, and video tributes from Spielberg, Previn, and Bricusse filled the spaces between John's greatest hits, along with a biographical video tribute hosted by Richard Dreyfuss, the evening's emcee.[57] John's farewell season also included a concert with Linda Ronstadt and Rosemary Clooney. "This man knows how to follow a singer," Clooney said. "I just met him—and I love him."[58] The love from Boston had reached its apex, and John was certainly going out on a high.

In June, he took the Pops out for one final tour—a 2-week, 10-concert affair in Japan. Young Japanese women surrounded him for autographs, and his concerts—which mixed classic Ravel with originals like *Temple of Doom*—elicited foot stomping, whistling, and loud calls for encores. "Japanese audiences," said one attendee, "are typically much more reserved than this."[59] Each program opened with a new fanfare that John wrote (*Sound the Bells!*) for the June 9 wedding of Princess Masako, which he had composed the weekend before he arrived. It was the country's biggest social occasion since the last royal wedding in 1959, a three-day celebration that began with a highly secretive Shinto religious ceremony. Masako Owada was a commoner, the daughter of a Japanese diplomat who grew up in Boston while her father was teaching at Harvard in the 1980s. "We feel a great sense of pride that this lady spent so much time in Boston," John told local reporters. Asked what impressed him most about the private wedding in Shinto, he said: "The absence of music—though the quietude was a kind of music in and of itself." In contrast, his fanfare was a nuptial bell-clanging fireworks show for brass and orchestra. "I hope it's good, but I'm sure it's loud," he said, getting a laugh from the Japanese press.[60] "I don't think it sounds very Japanese," he admitted. "It is very festive and extroverted and Western. But it seemed like a good idea to celebrate a great event with the people of Japan."[61]

The *Jurassic Park* themes became the anthems for John's final Pops season. He conducted his new suite at the Fourth of July concert at Hatch Shell, where fans hoisted inflatable dinosaurs above a sea of 3,000 people.[62] The BSO surprised John by unveiling his name blazoned on the Shell, where it joined a host of other important composers. More than 14,000 turned out for his concert at Tanglewood in late July. "It was the warmest rapport between Williams and the Tanglewood Pops audiences in his thirteen years as Pops conductor," the *Daily Hampshire Gazette* reported. "The audience loved what they heard and loved John Williams, who played shamelessly to the crowd, raising his fist to the sky again and again and obviously enjoying the crowd's response of cheers and more applause."[63] That summer, Tanglewood reached an all-time attendance record: 336,862.[64]

In between Pops concerts, John was given his first-ever official "classical" program with the Boston Symphony. He conducted a cherished cello concerto by Edward Elgar, performed by Yo-Yo Ma, along with the Symphonic Dances from *West Side Story*. "Williams conducted with rare sympathy for the soloist and the piece, and waved his baton in jubilation when the concerto was over—this had obviously been as profoundly personal and meaningful an experience for him as he and Ma had made it for everyone else," Dyer reported.[65]

John was delighted when the BSO asked him to write an original concerto for Ma. "It seems to me that every living composer has written something for him," John said. "What he probably needs least of all in life is yet another piece from a composer floating around the Tanglewood woods. But my feeling for the instrument, and for Yo-Yo Ma and the cello repertoire, is such that I really want to try and see what I can do."[66] He would work on the piece sometime after scoring *Schindler's List* in the fall. After *Jurassic Park* and Japan, he was looking forward to a relaxing summer in Tanglewood, soaking up the music and trees between shows—but then Spielberg surprised him and said he needed *Schindler* several months earlier than planned, "so instead of my getting six weeks of equanimity and peace up here, I've had to write two minutes of music a day," John sighed. "The reason I haven't been around Tanglewood very much is that I've been bent over a writing table."[67]

* * *

John won his first Academy Award for *Fiddler on the Roof*, and in some kind of strange poetry, he won his last for *Schindler's List*. The two films could hardly be more different in tone and substance, but the pain and oppression of the Jewish people resonated strongly in both—and they each became fixtures of Jewish popular culture in the 20th century. Both were given their musical signature by a goyim from Hollywood, which would be amusing... if both scores weren't so great.

Schindler's Ark, published in 1982, was also written by a non-Jew. Thomas Keneally, an Australian author who descended from Irish Catholics and convicts, once told a reporter: "The old proposition that you should only write about what you know is wrong, because I believe that you don't know what you know until you've written about it."[68] Keneally discovered the story of Oskar Schindler—a German war profiteer who rescued 1,100 Jews during the Holocaust—in a fancy leather goods store in Beverly Hills. One of "Schindler's Jews" ran the shop and told Keneally the whole story. The author interviewed numerous survivors and spun his incredible true story into a historical novel, which became a bestseller and immediately drew Spielberg's attention; the director had just made *E.T.* at the time, and he was still using Nazis as cartoonish villains in the *Indiana Jones* pictures. Keneally wrote a screenplay draft himself as early as 1983, but it would be 10 years before Spielberg had a script that satisfied him—written by Steven Zaillian—and also felt sufficiently grown-up to do the story justice. Spielberg felt like an alien growing up, and "wanted to be a gentile with the same intensity that I wanted to be a filmmaker. I was so ashamed of being a Jew."[69] He ran from his heritage in both his personal life and his escapist fantasies, but with *The Color Purple* and *Empire of the Sun* he was gradually feeling his way toward a confidence to tell the hardest story of his life: the tragic story of his own people. Spielberg credited Kate Capshaw, who converted to Judaism when they married, with guiding him back toward his ancestry and also influencing the kinds of movies he wanted to make.[70] Truth began to upstage make-believe. "Now I'm filled with pride," the director said. "This film has kind of come along with me on this journey from shame to honor. My mother said to me one day, 'I really want people to see a movie that you make someday that's about us and about who we are, not as a people but as people.' So this is it. This is for her."[71]

Working with local crew members and extras, Spielberg shot the film in the spring of 1993 on sets and in the preserved streets and buildings of Kraków, abandoning his usual cinematic panache—including color photography and sweeping crane shots—to tell the story with as much reverence and verisimilitude as he knew it deserved. Liam Neeson played the womanizing, morally evolving Schindler, Ben Kingsley his Jewish bookkeeper Itzhak Stern, and Ralph Fiennes the sadistic Nazi officer Amon Goeth. With John's *Jurassic* music and weekly phone calls from comedian Robin Williams relieving some of his anguish, Spielberg plumbed the depths of his soul to emerge with the most unsparing, brutal, and passionate portrayal of the Shoah ever put on film. "Everyone's forgotten now," John observed a few years later, "but at the time a lot of people were sure that Spielberg couldn't film the Holocaust—he was far too glossy a director. What can one say about the Holocaust that wouldn't seem empty and banal?"[72]

John had actually started working on the project while Spielberg was in preproduction on both *Jurassic* and *Schindler*. "From the outset we knew there would be less music in this film than in our usual action film," John said. "The choice was to use music sparingly, which fits in with the choice to keep everything in black-and-white, lean and very simple; the photography would be very simple, straight on, flat, with no tracking shots, no dolly shots, nothing tricky. So there couldn't be anything like that in the music either."[73] Spielberg needed a lot of source music before filming— German dances and period recordings playing at parties, classical pieces coming from gramophones—and John helped make those selections. Carlos Gardel's tango "Por Una Cabeza" plays in the opening restaurant montage when Schindler works his charm on a gathering of Nazi bigwigs; during the liquidation of the Kraków ghetto, a Nazi soldier plays Bach's English Suite No. 2 in A minor on one of his victim's pianos, although—in one of the film's darkly comic bits—his comrade confidently identifies it as Mozart. Spielberg approved all of these selections, and John recorded them with a small period orchestra.[74] Two powerful moments in the film were scored with existing Hebrew chorales. After the liquidation of the ghetto—an excruciating sequence that features no music, only the sound of Nazis yelling, Jews wailing, and the jerk of gunfire—the song "Oyfn pripetshik" laments over a solo, schoolroom-style piano as the film's iconic little girl in red wanders through the smoldering war zone.[§§] In the film's modern epilogue, when the real Schindlerjuden pay a visit to Schindler's grave, a folk choir sings "Yerushalayim Shel Zahav (Jerusalem of Gold)" over simple acoustic guitar. (Spielberg licensed a recording of this song, written in 1967 by Naomi Shemer, that was made for the 1991 French film, *Pour Sacha*.).

But in strategic, special moments within this three-hour film, there would need to be original score. John did not read the script, nor did he steep himself in researching traditional Jewish music. "I find it a painful distraction to have to listen to music by other people while I am trying to organize things in my own mind," he said—and besides, he had delved deep into traditional Jewish music for *Fiddler* in 1971 and "the idiom has been part of my vocabulary ever since."[75] The script featured a Jewish violinist character who resents having to entertain his enemies, and John decided to write a main theme for solo violin even before the film was shot. (Ultimately, most of that character's scenes were never filmed.)[76] Even though Italians invented the violin, John noted, it "seemed the most direct way to express a certain aspect of Jewish life."[77] Itzhak Perlman, the Israeli virtuoso, had played with John and the Pops many times since 1981, and he was always in John's mind for *Schindler*. "Nobody in the world could play it better," John said.[78] (One of Perlman's mentors was Isaac Stern, John's fiddler on the roof.) "I find that John's writing for film, for me, is very classic," Perlman said. "When I hear his kind of music, it's one of those things where you really remember, and it affects you immediately as you watch the film. And I believe that's a sign of somebody who's really good at what they do."[79]

The initial main theme John wrote was a tune he called "Remembrances." He was going to stop there, "because I thought that would be enough thematic identification for the film," he said, "but I realized that it wasn't going to satisfy every requirement. It needed a slightly different flavor for some of the sequences, so I set about writing a completely different kind of melody, but in the same style."[80] This new idea, which became the "Theme from *Schindler's List*," was meant to sound like a "Hebraic lullaby," John said, "heard at your mother's knee." John preferred the former, but Spielberg insisted the latter should be the film's main theme. "There's a spiritual aspect to this one," Spielberg said.

Scoring this film "was a particularly daunting challenge," John admitted:

> Nothing could be good enough to meet a story like this. What I was most conscious of was a desire not to melodramatize; it is much more difficult to be restrained in your

---

[§§] The song was written by a Ukrainian poet and composer, Mark Warshawsky, and performed by the Li-Ron children's choir of Israel.

expression of intensity of feeling than it is to go out and hit hard. I felt this story required music that was gentle and loving. The orchestra of Richard Strauss, which was the orchestra of the period, would have been the wrong noise for a film like this.[81]

"All of us were terribly concerned that the film wouldn't slip over into kitsch or camp," he later reflected. "We were taking a terrible chance, because there are hundreds of thousands of survivors from the camps who could look at the film and say, 'This is Hollywood. This is not a representation of what I experienced.'"[82] Spielberg's plain, handheld camera work and colorless film stock lend the film a verité quality, as does the absence of score for the first 17 minutes. When John's music finally does arrive, it does so quietly, as a throng of exiled Jews cross a bridge of no return to the Kraków Ghetto on March 20, 1941. John introduced his main theme on solo French horn and strings in unison—a cradle song doubling as a dirge. The tune is a delicate commentary, a reminder of the innocence of childhood and a damning declaration of Jewish humanity in the face of the inhuman Shoah. "It was clear that part of the musical assignment," John said, "was to make a statement that even in these years of unspeakable tragedy there were loving aspects and beautiful aspects of Jewish life ... even then."[83] This theme plays on solo classical guitar when Schindler uses his watch to barter for the parents of a young woman in distress. Uneasy strings churn under a string statement of the theme as Stern helps Schindler make his list. In an almost panicked montage, as Schindler keeps saying "More, more!" the melody rises with mystery and optimism, horns pulsing underneath. When Stern realizes Schindler has in essence "bought" these people, his emotion is mirrored by a Perlman solo as he tells his boss: "The list is an absolute good. The list is life."

The "Remembrances" theme, another exquisitely lyrical elegy, is first heard on solo recorder as Spielberg's camera pans over mounds of family photographs and portraits in a warehouse filled with "Stolen Memories," John's title for the cue. This tune, as expressive and songlike as the other, mourns and waits with musical suspensions that only, ultimately resolve into a minor chord. After the Ghetto is emptied ("Nacht Aktion"), and Schindler looks in horror from his horse on high, flute and other winds sing this second lullaby as the little girl in red hides under a bed. A disquieted Hebraic clarinet solo skitters over a tense bed of strings as Nazis root out all of the stowaways—recalling slavery in Egypt and exile from Israel all over again.

The clarinet is often associated with traditional Jewish music, but actually came to it late. The ancient vernacular of "klezmer" music has its origins in early Jewish rituals—worship, weddings, and funerals—and was meant to imitate the human voice and the singsong nature of the given rites. Clarinet appears to have entered the equation in the 19th century in Russian-occupied Ukraine, and it became entwined with more popular forms of klezmer music in the 1900s. "When most of us think about Jewish music, we think in terms of the European experience of Russia, Poland, Germany and so on," John said. "*Schindler's List* is a good example of music that has a Jewish atmosphere, but it's from the European experience that we know so well."[84] (Clarinet was also, incidentally, Spielberg's instrument when he was a boy.)

There is a straightforward reprise of the main theme on strings as the families on Schindler's list report; full of anguished hope and mercy, the melody develops on winds as a host of familiar faces and names amass—and a solo French horn plays the secondary theme as they board the train. Perlman's anguished violin mourns and rages under the awful Auschwitz shower scene, intensifying with gathering stormcloud chords as the women scream, and a string orchestra takes over the melody as showers spray water down on the terrified survivors. In the midst of their startled relief, Perlman's violin continues in agony: the women watch as others go to their doom in the furnace. After Schindler's near-death rescue of a train full of "his Jews" heading to the wrong destination, strings play a relieved and somber reprise of the main theme as he leads them into the safety of his factory—a symbolic march of survivors—and Perlman provides an elegant counterpoint over the melody.

When the war finally ends and Schindler bids Stern farewell, the cue "I Could Have Done More" underscores the sadness of their parting with stilted fragments of the main theme. The gathered Jews pay their respects and give Schindler a letter with the signature of every worker, a moment accentuated by an eloquent statement of the Remembrances theme. Perlman's violin returns with the main melody as Stern hands Schindler a ring with an inscription in Hebrew: "He who saves a life, saves the world entire." The film's emotional climax, as Schindler fumbles and drops the ring, suddenly breaking into sobs as he points out all of his possessions that could have purchased another life, is scored with a statement of the secondary lullaby and a passionate violin cadenza. In the quiet aftermath, John himself played a somber piano rendition of the main theme under the end credits.[85]

For such a relatively short score, there are two other major highlights. John modeled a piece of hypnotic, Jewish-inflected minimalism, which plays under the montage of Schindler gathering his workforce, after the concert piece *Exodus* by Polish composer Wojciech Kilar. The clarinet-led work, which premiered in 1981, was inspired musically by Ravel's repetitious *Boléro* and narratively by the children of Israel's escape from Egypt through the Red Sea. This piece was in Spielberg's mind before production—he even used it in an early trailer[86]—and its unyielding determination, factory-like mechanics, and Jewish character made it a perfect fit for Schindler's operation; John honored its spirit while giving the new cue his own touch. A much more tragic cue is "Immolation," which accompanied the scene in April 1944 when German children play under a snowfall of human ash, and Jews are forced to dig mass graves. John wrote a heartrending elegy for strings and impassioned choir; Schindler spies the red coat without its wearer, and the orchestra grieves. The choir's words were taken from a Hebrew liturgy, supplied by Rabbi Bernard Mehlman from Temple Israel of Boston. "He very generously made a collection for me, with translations," John said. "I chose one of them because I loved the thought it expressed: 'With our lives, we give life.' From this kind of horror, this kind of sacrifice, life can come."[87]

John rented a house on Prospect Hill Road near Tanglewood to work on the score, and Ken Wannberg also moved in for the duration. Spielberg, who was editing his film in the Hamptons, sent over reels and all of the necessary video gear, and would occasionally come by to listen to material. "It all worked out so well that we want to try working this way again," John said. "I have to say that being in the Berkshires helped a lot with this particular score; it was a reflective, ruminative sort of period for me, and the glorious atmosphere there contributed a lot to the process of writing the music, I think."[88] The upside of this being a rush job meant that John could finally record a film score with the Boston Symphony. Partly as an accommodation for Perlman, the bulk of the score featuring his solos was recorded at Symphony Hall—most of it captured in a single day on September 20, 1993. "I think having an artist of Perlman's level involved, and the members of the Boston Symphony, contributed something very important to the spirit and tone of the film," John said. "During the recording, Itzhak and I could see the film, although the orchestra could not, so I invited everyone to come up and watch during the playbacks. Words couldn't describe how everyone was moved by what they were seeing, and of course that affected the kind of performance they brought to the music."[89] Sandy DeCrescent, John's longtime orchestra contractor, remembered that day above many others. Perlman, seated as usual,*** "could barely get through looking at the screen," she said. "It just ripped me apart. And he was so touched that he had tears coming down, and he asked to be moved so that he could see John but not the screen."[90]

John did several additional days of recording in Los Angeles the following week at Sony with his usual session players. DeCrescent asked studio cellist David Low, a onetime artistic director of the Jewish Brandeis-Bardin Institute in L.A., for his recommendations of klezmer musicians, and he resoundingly suggested Giora Feidman, "the finest klezmer player I have ever heard," Low said. A native Argentinian and former member of the Israeli Philharmonic Orchestra, Feidman was legally blind and played a translucent clarinet, and he showed up to Sony only 10 minutes before his session began. According to Low, the orchestra gave him a lukewarm reception, especially the other clarinetists, "who weren't familiar with his playing." The session began, and Feidman suddenly interrupted John after just a few bars and asked if the orchestra could play more quietly. John graciously took his suggestion and resumed conducting—and again Feidman stopped him. "The principal violinist looked at me in horror, assuming my career had just ended," said Low. "No one had ever stopped The Maestro." Feidman asked John if *he* could address the orchestra directly; John said yes, and Feidman instructed the strings to play with a single bow hair, giving barely a sound. After all, he explained, there were 60 of them and only one of him, and he wanted to play softly. "For the next three hours," Low recalled, "we experienced a sound and mood unlike anything I have heard in Hollywood. It was dark and deep—a true sound of death. The scenes on the screen were horrific and the sound of the clarinet amplified the mood with near silence." Feidman had been scheduled for the whole day, but they finished before lunch. "Most players were in tears at the end of the morning," said Low, "and by the time we finished we were all emotionally exhausted. Then we got in our cars," Low added dryly, "and went to play an evening session of the *Addams Family* film."[91]†††

*** Perlman contracted polio as a child, which left his legs permanently disabled.
††† John flew to Canada around Thanksgiving to record the score's choral pieces with the Toronto Mendelssohn Choir.

One of John's most frequently told stories—so frequent it grew stale—was about the day he first watched the film with Spielberg in the spring of 1993. "You need a better composer than I am," John said to Spielberg. "You're right," Spielberg replied: "But they're all dead."[92] When Spielberg relayed this anecdote, it was a comment on how John belongs with the greats; when John told it, it was self-deprecation. Maybe he kept repeating the story because it was funny—or maybe it was just a lighthearted way to deflect from the difficulty of summiting this emotional mountain. John admitted he wasn't typically in a corresponding state of emotion when writing emotional scenes for a movie, but for *Schindler's List* he often was.[93] He was so moved by the film that he summoned his most serious, despairing score to date—which, ironically, became one of his most popular. The themes were permanent fixtures at his live appearances—after the film came out, he wrote an extended, three-movement concert version—and Perlman immediately began performing it at his own concerts, "because that's what people want to hear," the musician said.[94]

The film was almost universally hailed by critics, and it won seven Oscars—including best picture and Spielberg's first for best director. "This is the best drink of water after the longest drought in my life," Spielberg said.[95] At the ceremony on March 21, 1994, all of the nominated scores were presented with a ballet choreographed by Debbie Allen; *Schindler* was paired with a pas de deux. When John took the stage at Dorothy Chandler Pavilion and accepted his fifth Oscar, presented by Goldie Hawn, he simply thanked Wannberg for his friendship, and Perlman and the Boston Symphony for their great artistry. "And for a man who always makes work fun and is a seeming, unending source of inspiration, Steven Spielberg." From the audience, his friend blew a kiss.[96]

Even a wary Stephen Holden at the *New York Times* expressed his admiration (mixed with condescension):

> John Williams, Hollywood's master of epic-scale musical pastiche, has reinvented himself almost as astonishingly as has the director Steven Spielberg. The composer, whose finest previous score was the grandiose parting-of-the-heavens music for Mr. Spielberg's *Close Encounters of the Third Kind*, has created for *Schindler's List* a soundtrack that is as haunting as it is unobtrusive. The main theme is a winding Eastern European-flavored tune that has a folk-dance pulse ingrained in its melodic swoops and dips, along with just the right touch of schmaltz. As played by Itzhak Perlman with an intense, almost gypsylike fervor, it mirrors the film's elegiac sadness and reinforces its historicity, ultimately becoming a wordless song of remembrance.... The score's darkest moment, its "Auschwitz-Birkenau" theme, owes no obvious debts. Against a distant rising and falling thunder of bass violins and drums, Mr. Perlman's solo violin conjures the naked human soul, shivering in the face of unspeakable degradation. The theme is astonishing for its delicacy and understatement.[97]

From the outset, John worried about being accused of turning the Holocaust into something "Hollywood." "Instead," he said, "the opposite happened.

Letters came to us from all over the world from people who had been in camps... saying that it was true and honest and that they embraced it. And Steven would be the first to say that [the] filming itself was miraculous. All the extras, for example, knew what they had to say, how to say it, how to hold their heads. It was as though the hand of God was directing the whole thing for all of us.[98]

Commenting on the two mammoth scores of 1993—which rivaled the global, long-term impact and stylistic breadth of his cosmic dyad from 1977—John said: "If you're really inspired about something, the music kind of writes itself. Then you just have to get out of the way and let it take over. *Schindler's List* was like this. It came out effortlessly. And with intensity. *Jurassic Park*, on the other hand, was at the other extreme. I had to forge and chisel out every note."[99] Spielberg suggested that there are certain assignments "where more of John comes out than other scores. I think the score where the essential John Williams came out, to me, was *Schindler's List*. I think that score defines him more than anything he's ever done for me." On any given day, it was the director's personal favorite. "I think it's the most important score he's ever written for one of my films. And the second most important score he ever wrote for one of my films is *Jaws*. There's a real yin and yang about those two films being my favorite scores of his."[100]

* * *

John and Spielberg both needed a break. "I'm just going to sit down and watch Court TV," the director joked. The trades reported that he was going to make *The Bridges of Madison County*, a romance, which Amblin optioned in early 1993—although Kathleen Kennedy denied that was ever really on the table. But John *did* mention the film as his next project, and he rented the same house with the intention of writing its score in the summer of 1994. "I loved watching my granddaughter rolling down the lawn on Prospect Hill in Stockbridge last summer," he said in December 1993.

> And I was delighted to learn that I could work there—I have chained myself to Hollywood all these years, and it turns out I didn't need to!... Telephones and fax machines have changed the world, and it was wonderful to look out on a Berkshire morning instead of having to confront a freeway in Los Angeles; writing the music felt so relaxed and easy. So I hope I get to do it all over again next summer. And when there is any free time, I intend to walk.[101]

Clint Eastwood, playing the lead, wound up directing the film himself, and John still planned on scoring it—he played golf with the actor occasionally, and it would have been a nice artistic reunion after *The Eiger Sanction* in 1975—but then John, too, bowed out.‡‡‡ Ultimately Spielberg took a break from directing for three whole years, and in the meantime, he launched the nonprofit Shoah Visual History Foundation

---

‡‡‡ Eastwood regular Lennie Niehaus composed the score.

to chronicle the testimonies of Holocaust survivors—he called it the most important job he'd ever done—as well as a new film studio, DreamWorks Pictures, with showbiz bigwigs Jeffrey Katzenberg and David Geffen.

John's final season as Pops conductor extended to the Christmas series, where he was joined by Tony Bennett and Kathie Lee Gifford. This "final" concert offered one last occasion for Dyer to take stock of John's legacy with the organization:

> The statistics on his tenure are pretty staggering: 13 seasons, more than 300 concerts, six national or international tours, 24 premieres and commissions, 28 CDs and nearly 50 television shows. Along the way, Williams has brought some of the leading artists of several musical worlds to the Pops—Isaac Stern, Itzhak Perlman, Jessye Norman, Yo-Yo Ma, James Galway, Leontyne Price, Marilyn Horne, Kiri Te Kanawa, Frederica von Stade, Kathleen Battle, Oscar Peterson, Sammy Davis Jr., Ray Charles, Sarah Vaughan, John and Bonnie Raitt, Tommy Tune, Joan Baez, Nell Carter, Roberta Flack, Rosemary Clooney, Linda Ronstadt, Whitney Houston, and Aretha Franklin....
>
> Williams took from Fiedler what worked: the shape of the program, the mix of music, putting the spotlight not only on celebrities but on members of the orchestra and young musicians. Williams improved discipline and morale and raised the standard of performance. He brought in guest conductors of competence and distinction, including a few from the concert world, and he took wary pride in the achievement of young protegees, like the assistant conductor, Ronald Feldman. He brought in lively new material, freshened up some old arrangements and shook up the repertory....
>
> He was a reluctant public figure, which was a source of his appeal. As a podium personality, Williams was initially a bit stiff, but it wasn't long before he started to enjoy making a spectacle of himself, once he got out there. Persuading John Williams to do anything can be a long process; once persuaded, there's no stopping him. The great strength of Williams' part-time commitment to the Pops was that it was whole-hearted. Williams came at the Pops from an unexpected direction, and every year he returned to it fresh. At the core of the extraordinary relationship Williams built both with musicians and audiences is their realization "he doesn't have to be doing this." He certainly doesn't need the money; he is not doing this out of personal motives, or to advance his career.[102]

John lost some weight and began doing daily sit-ups in response to his back pain. "The results show," Dyer said, "and he's proud of them."[103] Reflecting on the past 13 years, John said: "There are parts of us that are reserved and shy. The good thing about public performance is that you do have to reveal yourself. Along those lines, I thought, *Maybe I'll be a better composer if I do this*."[104] He was quite naturally asked whether, like Previn, he might now write a memoir. "I've never felt that I've done anything that warranted writing an autobiography," he said. "Still, funny things do happen now and then that make me remember how many things I've been able to do.

The other night, Samantha and I were watching Audrey Hepburn and Fred Astaire in *Funny Face* on television and suddenly I heard something familiar—I remembered scoring that scene, and that was 35 years ago! And the weight of it all suddenly strikes me."[105]§§§

Even with no films to score in 1994, the clock was ticking for John to finish his cello concerto for Yo-Yo Ma.**** John also agreed to act as "music adviser" for yet another Pops season while the BSO looked for a successor. "My love for the institution and Boston is such that I am just vitally interested in where the symphony is going," he said. "It's like my family, my friends."[106] In Los Angeles that March, John filled in for Henry Mancini at the last minute to emcee a banquet honoring Ennio Morricone, part of the annual conference of the Society for the Preservation of Film Music.[107] Mancini had cancer, but he was able to attend a 70th birthday bash in April at UCLA. John was there, along with Julie Andrews and Quincy Jones, and two million dollars were raised toward an endowment.[108] "I remember when Henry was close to dying, and he was on his way in an ambulance to UCLA," Ginny Mancini said; "I stopped by John's house to tell him how ill Henry was, and he started to cry. I mean, he loved Henry so much."[109] Mancini, one of the main cats from John's earliest days in the recording studio, died on June 14, 1994.

John's farewell at the Pops proved, like so many "farewell" tours of pop stars, impermanent. He was back in May to conduct nine concerts—including a 100th birthday tribute to Arthur Fiedler and a concert with Itzhak Perlman, who performed the theme from *Schindler's List*.[110] That score had immediately entered the concert repertoire around the country; Emanuel Borok, Russian-born concertmaster of the Dallas Symphony, asked John for a piano reduction so that he could perform it in recitals. "There's a musical twist in one of these pieces that is almost like an old Jewish song that I remember my mother singing, about a rabbi who sits in a house with a fire burning in a stove, and he's teaching the alphabet," Borok said. "If John wrote using just intuition, he made a perfect hit, because it's almost like a quotation from that song." Borok added: "Whether it will become a staple of serious violinists to be played other than encores, I don't know. We'll see."[111] John spent the summer orchestrating his cello concerto "around the clock," which was programmed for the opening of the new Seiji Ozawa Hall at Tanglewood on July 7. The piece was "a tribute to the expressive capabilities of the cello and to the human qualities Williams admires in Ma," Dyer wrote in his review.

> Some of Williams' concert music has seemed constrained, as if the composer were afraid to let himself do any of the things the world loves him for. This concerto has musical substance, density, weight—and it's as good as *E.T.* It also benefits from

---

§§§ John played piano on the score for *Funny Face* in September 1956; the composer was Adolph Deutsch.
**** Around this same time, flutist James Galway mentioned that "of all the composers hanging around, I wish John Williams would write a concerto for me. His music is very dramatic, and he writes great tunes." (Robert Croan, "James Galway Embraces Czech Composer's Music for Flute," *Pittsburgh Post-Gazette*, September 23, 1993.)

Williams' unrivaled savvy about sound—he is the luckiest of living composers because for decades he has had the opportunity to hear his newest music played back to him immediately by the best musicians. Williams is among the smartest of living composers because he has taken advantage of his luck. Ma's passionate performance was worthy of the piece.[112]

Ma had to compete with the sound of thunder and rain lashing against the hall on a wet, humid Thursday night. Spielberg and Capshaw were late to the concert because of the rainstorm; the concerto fittingly began with an orchestral thunderclap and then a sparkling river current in the strings and woodwinds. The cello twitches and writhes in the floodwaters, bellowing out a chaotic, animalistic theme that defiantly avoids any lyricism. (John once described the cello as "an animal that's beautiful, and not dangerous."[113]) As the four-movement work continues, though, Ma's instrument stretches out and begins to sing. In his program note, John explained that he cast the cello "in a kind of hero's role," and gave it a hero's theme that culminates in a "ruminative and virtuosic" cadenza. The second movement, "Blues," is a postmodern conversation with the ghosts of Duke Ellington and Billy Strayhorn, where "clusters in piano and percussion … form a frame within which the cello unveils its misty quasi-improvisations." In the "Scherzo" movement, "the music romps along in triple-time over treacherous landscape where athletic exchanges are periodically and suddenly interrupted by a series of fermati, as the orchestra and cello try to dominate and outdo each other." After so much anti-tuneful strife, John finally allowed for a "Song," his fourth movement, writing "long lyrical lines that would give the cello the opportunity to address the audience in the manner of a clear and direct soliloquy." Asked about the stark differences between John's film work and concert music, Ma asserted: "It's all the same person.... Everything has a construction behind it, but as an architect of music he's always serving people and the landscape, right? So in a piece of constructed music without a story, there's a story *behind* it. There's always a story behind it. It could be subconscious, it could be conscious, it could be fragments." For Ma, this concerto was about "different versions of struggle, and then reaching some form of epiphany at the end. It's implicit storytelling, not explicit storytelling."[114][††††]

John composed a short piece at Ozawa's request for the New Year of 1995. *Satellite Celebration*, which Ozawa premiered with the BSO on January 1 in Tokyo, was broadcast globally via satellite—hence the title—after a tour of the Far East. Way more melodious than the cello concerto, the piece begins as a lullaby round between solo instruments before swelling with tides of warm, humanist fervor. (Ma and Isaac Stern

---

[††††] John would continue to revisit and revise the cello concerto all the way up to a 2022 recording with Ma and the New York Philharmonic which improved the opening by replacing much of the thunder and lightning with more fluid, melodic orchestration. "The changes are not draconian," said John, who performed it with Ma in various cities over the decades. "It's a learning process, always, with these things. There have been cases where I've, like most writers, jumped at the first opportunity to record something that was premature to do. The violin concerto, for example, with Slatkin—it would have been better to have the performances, work the piece a little more with a little more honing and care. My advice to young composers is: don't release recordings before you should." (JW to TG, June 2, 2023.)

were among the soloists that day.) John later recorded this hopeful cantilena, which he renamed *Song for World Peace*. In February, he returned to Boston to (literally) pass the baton to newly appointed Pops conductor Keith Lockhart, who was recruited from Cincinnati to fill John's massive shoes. "It isn't often you get to look the future right in the face," John said at a photo op after the concert, hugging his successor.[115] John was immediately given the title of conductor laureate, and he returned in May to surprise the audience at Lockhart's first official Pops concert—joining guest stars Mandy Patinkin and Sylvia McNair at the piano and singing the Frank Loesser song "I Believe in You," with lyrics revised by John: "Send up a loud cheer / Lockhart is here / And it's spring at the Pops."[116] That summer he also drove his old "Rolls Royce" through a tour of Williams hits. "The audience was so glad," the *Globe* reported, "that one member, overcome by his feelings called out 'We love you, John!' Williams modestly acknowledged the spontaneous outburst of applause that followed, then turned back to his orchestra and the business at hand."[117]

When the New York Philharmonic turned 150 in 1992, the orchestra—under its new, forward-thinking executive director, Deborah Borda—ordered five new works to celebrate. Principal bassoonist Judith LeClair was invited to commission a concerto for her instrument, and it was her brother-in-law, Ronald Feldman—a cellist in the BSO who also served as assistant conductor to John in the Pops—who suggested John. She wrote him a "long shot" letter in early 1993, asking if he would consider writing a bassoon concerto. He wrote her back right away and said he would do it. "I was floored," LeClair said. "I couldn't believe it. You know, *why me?*" LeClair was not familiar with any of John's previous concert works, but she loved his film scores and particularly "the lyrical writing, the tunes, the melodies. I just thought, *God, what could he do for a bassoon?* We have Mozart, we have Weber, but nothing extraordinary." A few months later, the score was on her doorstep: "I brought it upstairs and I was so excited, and I played through it—and then I just burst into tears. Because I thought: *I can't play this. It's too hard. It's just too difficult.* I didn't really understand it yet."[118]

Thinking of the bassoon as a stick of wood, a former tree, John went back to Robert Graves's *The White Goddess*—the enigmatic book that he joked was nearly unreadable, that he wasn't sure if he understood, and that he had read many times over the past 25 years since discovering it in England. He based each of the concerto's movements on *The Five Sacred Trees* (his title for the work) of Celtic mythology. "*Eó Mugna*, the great oak, whose roots extend to Connla's Well in the 'otherworld,' stands guard over what is the source of the River Shannon and the font of all wisdom," he explained in his literary program note:

> The well is probably the source of all music, too. The inspiration for this movement is the Irish uilleann pipe, a distant ancestor of the bassoon, whose music evokes the spirit of Mugna and the sacred well. *Tortan* is a tree that has been associated with witches and as a result, the fiddle appears, sawing away, as it is conjoined with the music of the bassoon. The Irish Bodhrán drum assists. *The Tree of Ross* (or

Eó Rosa) is a yew, and although the yew is often referred to as a symbol of death and destruction, the Tree of Ross is often the subject of much rhapsodizing in the literature. It is referred to as "a mother's good," "diadem of the angels" and "faggot of the sages." Hence the lyrical character of this movement, wherein the bassoon incants and is accompanied by the harp. *Craeb Uisnig* is an ash and has been described by Robert Graves as a source of strife. Thus, a ghostly battle, where all that is heard as the phantoms struggle, is the snapping of twigs on the forest floor. *Dathi*, which purportedly exercised authority over the Poets, and was the last tree to fall, is the subject for the close of the piece. The bassoon soliloquizes as it ponders the secrets of the Trees.

LeClair might have been startled by how abstract and challenging *The Five Sacred Trees* was, "but it had the tunes in it that I was looking for," she said. "All the beautiful lines. Because I told him, 'I would love to expand the high register. I don't want it to just sound like a bassoon.' Some people write compositions for the bassoon and it's just hokey." (Among band kids, one derisive nickname for this instrument is the "farting bedpost.") "He wrote these beautiful, lyrical lines, and that's what I had wanted from him." LeClair worked on the piece for weeks with her husband, the pianist Jonathan Feldman, then flew out to visit John at his house in December. "I showed him what worked on the bassoon and what did *not* work," she said. "There were a lot of unplayable things technically—super unplayable—and some things that were repetitive. I was like, 'I just can't be up in that register that long, for such a long, exposed time.' It needed to be cut." LeClair laughed at her audacity: "You know, you tell John Williams, 'You need to cut some of your music.' But that's what amazed me the most: he didn't mind. He understood what was physically possible to play on the instrument and that he'd gone a little too far with extended solo lines. We changed it right there in his living room." John snipped 5–10 minutes' worth of passages, mostly in the final movement. "If I'd been working on it for months and *still* couldn't play it, then it had to be changed," LeClair said. "Because the whole point was to write a piece that's accessible to bassoon players. It still took me another year and a half to really get it totally the way I wanted it."[119]

LeClair premiered the concerto on April 12, 1995, at Avery Fisher Hall in Lincoln Center. It was conducted by Kurt Masur, the 67-year-old German music director of the Philharmonic, "and he just didn't want to have any part of it," said LeClair. "We didn't even rehearse it. We had to go double overtime on a rehearsal just so that we could get through it because he didn't want to spend any time on it at all. It was horrible—I've never seen John look so angry. I don't think I've had more stress in my entire life." Masur was not derisive of *this* piece or of John himself, LeClair explained; he was simply apathetic about contemporary music. John fumed as he helplessly watched the overtime rehearsal on the morning of the premiere—but when the baton finally went up that evening, the orchestra carried LeClair and the concerto into the air. "Glenn Dicterow played that big violin solo, and he was fantastic," LeClair said. "The whole orchestra was in love with John Williams, and they respected him so much. My colleagues just went overboard to make this piece happen. I'll never forget how supportive they were. Nobody really talked about if they *liked* it or not, but they were super supportive and played their butts off."[120] Reviewing *The Five Sacred Trees* for the *Boston Globe*, Anthony Tommasini heaped praise on LeClair, "who played every arching phrase and gesture with compelling character and plaintive tone," and he gave qualified kudos to John:

> Passages recall the Neo-Classical music of Stravinsky, the modal musings of Copland, the skittish counterpoint of Bartok; there are also postmodern murmurings and pungently dissonant, stacked-up Neo-Romantic harmonies. Williams' ear is acute; his borrowings are deftly done. The drawback is that the music can seem derivative. The most original episodes were the muted and delicate passages. The piece begins beguilingly, with an elegiac solo for bassoon. One by one instruments from the orchestra speak up, start dialogues, and arguments. Often the strings are used simply to provide a tremulous harmonic backdrop. Williams enriches his orchestra with sundry percussion and ethnic instruments.... And when he deploys them to create subtle effects and delicate colorings, the results are beguiling. Now and then, to provide dynamic contrast, Williams lets the full orchestra blare forth with brassy outbursts and arching string melodies. These moments were perhaps miscalculations. You get rustled from your meditative state by intimations of *E.T.*[121]

John was able to conduct the piece himself in San Francisco that November, and then "the whole thing was so much more easy and it was so much more enjoyable," LeClair said. "I felt safe when I played with him. When he conducted it, the piece took on a whole new meaning." They recorded the concerto with the London Symphony Orchestra the following June at Abbey Road, all in one morning. It was "one of the happiest days of my life," said LeClair. "It was in London, and we went out to dinner afterwards. I just remember staying up all night. I didn't want to go to sleep."[122]

The Five Sacred Trees was as abstract as it was programmatic, as bewitching as it was mystifying. The Celtic idioms were almost purer than the Irish music in *Far and Away*, more primal. The second and fourth movements are wild, untamed forests full of mischievous spirits, but the atmosphere and storytelling in them are utterly vivid. The three other movements are much more tuneful and reflective, lulling the listener into this enchanted cathedral of trees and conducting a seance with ancestors and stories from a long, long time ago—from the sleepy, melancholy conversation between harp and bassoon in "Eó Rossa" to the serene but strange sublimity of the finale. In this work John was a true *poet*, and more than any concert work since the first violin concerto, it was the most personally revealing. It was thorny but also poignant, it was lyrical—and magical. The "sacred tree" symbol was a resounding clue to John's philosophy about atavism and his nigromancy‡‡‡‡ of emotions. It was also the rare work that, without any qualifications, John himself thought was *good*.

* * *

---

‡‡‡‡ "Black magic." See: *Doctor Faustus*.

John finally returned to the movies, and he did so with Sydney Pollack. The actor-cum-director had his own "John Williams"—Colorado jazzman Dave Grusin, one of John's old Revue cellmates who scored nearly every Pollack film since 1974, including *Three Days of the Condor* and *The Firm*. But Pollack occasionally played the field: in 1985, he had asked John to score *Out of Africa*, a job that, when John declined for scheduling reasons, went to Englishman John Barry. For the retro romance that his new film required, he went to this master of romantic nostalgia—and a composer who had, decades earlier, scored several TV episodes of *Chrysler Theatre*, *Kraft Suspense Theatre*, and *Alcoa Premiere* that Pollack directed.

Sabrina Fair was a play written for Broadway in 1953, a modern-day romantic fable that delivered a gentle skewering of the one percent. Billy Wilder adapted it into a popular film a year later, starring Audrey Hepburn as Sabrina, William Holden as her dreamboat David Larrabee, and Humphrey Bogart as the elder Linus Larrabee, who eventually gets the girl. With films like *Tootsie*, Pollack showed a knack for making witty romances *like they used to*, but with a hip sensibility—and when the opportunity came to update this timeless story for the 1990s, he was an obvious fit. Still, it was initially "nerve-racking, downright stupid," Pollack admitted of remaking the beloved film. "But I got hooked on the idea of mixing '50s romanticism with the materialism, cynicism, and greed of the '90s—stealing the best parts of Billy Wilder and telling the story in a contemporary way."[123] Updates in *Sabrina* included the dollar amount of business mergers; Harrison Ford's Linus was also a little more ruthless and true-to-life for an electronics tycoon, and Julia Ormond's Sabrina a little more assuredly her own woman. Greg Kinnear, best known as a talk show host, was cast as David. Pollack shot the film in the spring of 1995 on sumptuous locations in New York, Martha's Vineyard, and Paris.

This picturesque film about high society gave John a chance to return to his roots as a jazz pianist, and it inspired one of his most purely romantic scores and a ballade for his own instrument—which, in a rare move, he performed himself on the recording. John said he wrote the theme imagining Audrey Hepburn, who once kissed him at a party at actor Roddy McDowall's house.[124] His right-hand notes sparkle and fizz like champagne over breezy jazz chords, and the melody of Sabrina's theme has just a hint of melancholy, or maybe wistfulness, as well as a whisper of magic. Sabrina has a bewitching effect on those around her—as Roger Ebert pointed out, this *is* a fairy tale.[125] The theme is first introduced while Sabrina narrates her situation with the Larrabees, even beginning with "Once upon a time...." Like the character, this tune begins timidly and eventually blossoms into grand, hypnotic beauty. The film's opening scene is an opulent party at the Larrabee "castle," and the theme's style matches the milieu of a tuxedoed pianist performing with an expensive orchestra on a bandstand as people sip bubbly and slow dance. (Later, Rachmaninoff's "Rhapsody on a Theme of Paganini" plays in the background of a swanky dinner with similar, piano-led romanticism.)

After young Sabrina flees from an embarrassing encounter with Linus, her melody rushes headlong from lush strings to accordion as she arrives in Paris. There, the theme's twinkling mystery accompanies her almost magical transformation from awkward bookworm into beautiful princess. Later, on the night Linus begins to fall for Sabrina over hand-spooned dinner at a Moroccan restaurant, her melody is picked up by solo acoustic guitar over dreamy, shimmering strings; the dialogue mostly drops out as we watch Linus begin to pay attention. There's no music when they finally kiss for the first time and she professes her love for him, because immediately Linus confesses to the ruse he's been playing: keeping her away from his brother in order to protect a jackpot merger. He's broken the spell. When the old man finally comes to his senses and flies to Paris to catch her, her theme seems to carry the plane, and the film ends almost exactly as it began—with Sabrina's fairytale narration and John's fairytale music. Linus has his own bouncy, comical theme for clarinet—often accented with upper-crusty harpsichord—and the themes in this romantic triangle often interplay as a *pas de trois*.

John also wrote two original songs: "(In the) Moonlight" and "How Can I Remember" are both introduced diegetically at the opening party, and the words— by Alan and Marilyn Bergman—are sung while David dances and romances. "Moonlight" becomes a kind of love theme for Linus and Sabrina, and "Remember" evokes the painful pining she experiences for David; both are poignant reminders of home and the way things were. In one glorious cue, which begins when Sabrina receives a letter from her father about David's engagement, a bell-like synth voice (familiar from the *Home Alone* scores) plays a mysterious repeating figure under a lone piano statement of "How Can I Remember." The picture blossoms into a love scene with her short-term Parisian paramour, the melody doubled on trombone (played by Mancini alumnus Dick Nash), then flute, with that repeating figure handed to the woodwinds. This montage of Sabrina's "transformation" swirls with fairy dust and a sparkling statement of "Moonlight," and the whole thing is a master class in orchestration and the story-driven development of themes. Both songs were recorded by lounge singer Michael Dees, and John also made several new orchestral recordings of loungey standards for the party source music. Sting, the Police rocker turned crooner, performed a swaying vocal version of "Moonlight" for the end credits, which he recorded at his studio in the south of England. That song earned John and the Bergmans an Oscar nomination, which came paired with a nomination for John's score.§§§§

John kept a special place in his heart for the amorous *Sabrina* score, even as the film's footprint dissolved faster than his much bigger hits. Another admirer was the pianist Emanuel Ax:

---

§§§§ He was actually nominated in *three* categories at the 1996 Academy Awards. In response to the monopoly that Disney established with the song scores for its hit animated films of the early 1990s, and a hunch that uninformed members were actually voting for the musical numbers rather than the actual *scores*, the Academy split the score category in two: "best musical or comedy score," and "best dramatic score." *Sabrina* was nominated in the former (Alan Menken's score for *Pocahontas* won), and *Nixon* in the latter. The double categories proved unpopular, Alan Menken's reign soon waned, and it went back to just one score award in 1999.

One of the things that totally gets to me is the very beginning, where the piano's doing these figurations. It's a little bit like the presentation of the rose in *Rosenkavalier*, where you have a beautiful tune and these *fabulous* chords underneath, which are just indescribably inspired. John gets this pattern, which is harmonically so fascinating and beautiful, combined with this tune. The underpinnings are what makes it for me.[126]

* * *

John's third, and final, film for Oliver Stone was *Nixon*—capping an informal trilogy set around the Vietnam War or, as one of the cues in *Nixon* describes it, "The 1960s: The Turbulent Years." "It was an accidental trilogy, if you want," said Stone, who continued to seek out "*the* American composer" for these epic national tragedies that took place in the prime of John's youth.[127] "I enormously enjoy working with this man," John said. "You don't have a feeling he's making films to earn a living or make money or to get big grosses."[128]

John referred to Stone as "quite a great man"—which is not how the director would have described Richard Milhous Nixon, the 37th president of the United States and a man whose specter haunted many of the director's films.[*****] Nixon was something of an obsession for Stone, who dedicated his 1995 biopic to his late father. Louis Stone was a stoic, emotionally withdrawn stockbroker and an Eisenhower Republican, and Oliver Stone—who co-wrote the Oscar-nominated *Nixon* screenplay with Stephen J. Rivele and Christopher Wilkinson—seemed to be searching for his father as much as for the former president. Several commentators noted that the director *himself* was rather Nixonian: ruthless, idealistic, an insider who always felt like an outsider and who inspired no shortage of haters. Billy Wilder reportedly asked Stone why on earth he wanted to make a movie about "Tricky Dick," the vilified crook and disgraced king. Because, Stone replied, "Nixon is the most important political figure in the second half of the 20th Century. He tore the country apart and nearly presided over a civil war."[129] And yet Stone's Nixon, as portrayed by an Oscar-nominated Anthony Hopkins, was no cartoon villain. Yes, he swears, drinks, glowers, bombs Cambodia without batting an eyelash, and rails against a host of "enemies," from the press to the commies to the hippies. At one point, he rings a bell to have his wife removed from the dinner table. But this Nixon is a complicated, tortured tangle of past wounds and possible glories: the resilient, ambitious survivor who lost two beloved brothers, a man who adored his saintly mother and doted on his daughters and never cheated on his wife, an inspiring leader and diplomat, a tragic figure of Grecian proportions who flew too close to the sun and scorched his entire country in the process. Surrounding Hopkins in the cast were Joan Allen as Pat Nixon, James Woods, Bob Hoskins, Ed Harris, Mary Steenburgen, and a host of top-shelf actors creating a full-color history alive with nuance and dimension and contradiction. The Nixon family nonetheless condemned

---

[*****] Immediately after *JFK*, Stone had made *Heaven & Earth*, about a Vietnamese woman and her plight during and after "Nixon's war," based on a true story and scored by the Japanese composer Kitarō.

Stone's film as "character assassination," and accused him of waiting for Richard and Pat to die (in 1994 and 1993, respectively) to "concoct imaginary scenes ... that are calculated solely and maliciously to defame and degrade President and Mrs. Nixon's memories in the mind of the American public."[130] But in both his soul-searching script and in casting Hopkins, an actor capable of sinister toughness as well as vulnerability and human warmth, Stone crafted a surprisingly empathetic portrait, one that accuses Nixon of dastardly deeds as it simultaneously reveals hidden virtues.

John's score followed suit: it was one of the most emotionally and *morally* complex compositions in his whole body of work. The beginning of the film plays almost like a monster movie, the camera pushing in on an empty White House at night, which is ominously shrouded in rain and lightning bolts. Stone modeled this on the opening of *Citizen Kane* (the first film assignment for Bernard Herrmann), and John scored it with low, sinister brass and cymbals crashing like thunderclaps. The prologue follows a text quotation from the gospel of Matthew: "For what is a man profited, if he shall gain the whole world, and lose his own soul?" which is musically accented with slithering strings and a low-end electronic effect that sounds like distant bombs—"this kind of thing where you almost don't hear it but you *feel* it, which is like a kind of napalm recollection, of something in Cambodia that perhaps hadn't even happened yet," John explained. "It's a kind of pre-lap into the future, and I think it can be very suggestive."[131]

One of John's primary themes for Nixon is an angular, minor-key march that some have compared, with great amusement, to Darth Vader's theme. It was the melody featured in an original score John composed for the trailer—"the story of Nixon's presidency in about five minutes of pounding music," marveled Stone, "that's full of evil at times, and beating with the drum of breaking news, and strangely, maybe defiantly and stubbornly, dignified in a twisted kind of way."[132] But as quickly as these dark storms gather, something more complicated—even noble—dares to shine through. John's empathy for the man, or at least the *character*, is unmistakable. One motif, a slowly rising surge of string chords, is rooted in Nixon's family home—in his mother's loving discipline and his father's stern lectures about hard work, remembered in black-and-white flashbacks. It's a tragic theme for Nixon's ascent, out of the tough soil of his father's lemon ranch, out of the blood of his prematurely dead brothers. "Dick" becomes like a frightened child when he's threatened with divorce; he promises Pat he'll never run for office again, and John's score takes him at his word. In that same scene, Nixon vocalizes why he fell in love with her in the first place, and a nostalgic, home movie–style montage of their Whittier courtship is scored with a lilting, lyrical melody on Tim Morrison's trumpet, touched with a hint of melancholy. "I came all the way from Boston to L.A. to play one solo!" Morrison said. But what a solo. "It was very beautifully written and captured the spirit of the moment in that film. Something John had an extraordinary feel for."

Morrison saw a side of John that had a shade of Nixon. "Oh yes, he can be polite, pleasant, and avuncular," Morrison said, "but when he feels disappointed, he can also be a bit of a Dutch Uncle as well. John is a serial perfectionist and he has resorted to less than personable measures in order to achieve those ends. At least I experienced that with him firsthand near the end of my playing career and collaborations with him. I guess it just comes as a bit of a surprise that someone so charming and affable could also be surprisingly cold and calculating given the right circumstances."[133] This was a rare vocalized complaint, but John himself admitted he could be a "Dutch Uncle"—one who gives "firm but benevolent advice"—and he would also tactically drum out musicians from his studio orchestra if he felt they were getting out of line, either through unprofessional behavior or an obvious lack of preparation. He was loyal to people, but he was *more* loyal to his vision of excellence.

Nixon is one of John's finest "adult" scores—full of passion and compassion, light and dark, *Sturm und Drang*, a bent and corrupted Americana in which idealism and nobility still poke through. "It's thematic, but in a more motivic way," John said, "which is to say that it's less sort of sing-song-y.

> It's not a melody that you sort of follow along in a kind of focused direction in terms of its nobility or its lack of nobility. It's full of contrasts and difficulties. *This* side of the orchestra's playing along in a kind of consonant way, where you have this kind of Shaker/Quaker, American roots solidity in it, and suddenly something happens in the other side of the orchestra which defuses that—a dissonant element that comes into it. So in musical terms, thematic terms, it's less simple, it's less easy to deal with. It's not just simply heroic. It's heroic one moment, and then it becomes—maybe perhaps *tortured* is too strong a word, musically, but that's sort of what happens.[134]

This score also features a designated theme for Nixon's famous meeting with Chairman Mao, a beautifully dreadful largo for strings that undercuts one of the president's greatest achievements with a feeling of mystery and melancholy. The scene's temp track was the "Aase's Death" suite from Edvard Grieg's *Peer Gynt*, and one of John's later orchestrators, Conrad Pope, always pointed to "The Meeting with Mao" cue as an example of John's genius: "I say, 'Go listen to 'Aase's Death,' now go listen to what John did, and you'll see this is the way to paraphrase the temp track.' People should learn it, because it's got the emotion of 'Aase's,' it has that sense of evolving, and the sort of sinuous, stringy... all that kind of stuff. And yet it's John Williams."[135]

"John really entered into the dark side of Nixon's character," Stone said, "and gave him grandeur.

> At the same time, [Nixon] could be petty and mean, but there was a grandeur theme that John addressed in a classical score that is reminiscent, for me, of the feelings evoked by the music of Mahler—a composer that Nixon himself admired.
>
> I was worried that the film would not hit an audience. And I was probably right, because it didn't. Although I love that film. It was a dark film that people could resist, because they can resist Nixon, and the music was in line with that. It wasn't as big and romantic as *Born*, or as flourishing and statement-oriented as *JFK*. But that was the nature of the film. When the three pieces were done, it was kind of like a perfect troika.[136]

All three tragic American scores were nominated for Academy Awards.††††† "Many people say the best film music is music that isn't noticed, that's so seamlessly a part of what you see and hear that you only feel it," John said, discussing the *Nixon* score. "I think what the audience gets from the music is some kind of emotional pull, hit, or tug in the gut, that the music puts there—that isn't there till we put the music in the scene."[137] It was a far cry from his loving paean to John F. Kennedy, but with this score John complexified an often-demonized American president and helped Stone reveal Nixon's humanity. Stone called John "the institution ... the gold standard," and he asked John to score other films after *Nixon*, but the scheduling never worked out. "I think I got three of the best pieces of music from John Williams that anyone ever got," Stone said. "I'm very lucky. They may not be the *Star Wars* kind of thing, but they were very distinctive to the films.... Each one was different in a very strong way."[138]

* * *

The Olympic Games returned to the States in 1996, and once again John's country asked him for an anthem. NBC had actively continued to use his 1984 "Olympic Fanfare and Theme" as the official music for their coverage of every Olympics since, forever associating John with the event right alongside Arnaud's *Bugler's Dream*. For the 1996 Summer Games in Atlanta, which also marked the centennial anniversary of the modern Olympics, John composed a triumphant piece called *Summon the Heroes*. "I remember seeing a photograph of a female athlete suspended above the ground, every fiber of her being stretching for a ball just beyond her reach," John said, "captured in a shot, freezing time and denying gravity. There is unquestionably a spiritual, non-corporeal aspect to an athletic quest such as this that brings us close to what art is all about."[139] He told the *New York Times* that his four-movement piece "has to be heroic, to have to do with the aspiration of nations to get along to compete. But there's also a theatrical aspect: we have to blow trumpets and bang drums to get people's attention. It's almost a call to nations. So the music has to be theatrical and heroic and inspirational, and what we get is a kind of flag-waving piece for heraldic brass."[140]

John dedicated the piece to Morrison, who performed the vaulting, lyrical solos when *Summon the Heroes* was recorded with the Pops in December 1995. It was previewed at a press conference in Atlanta, and John brought it to St. Louis in May, where he accompanied the torch passing through the Arch with the St. Louis Symphony. John kicked off the opening ceremonies on July 19 with the Atlanta Symphony, just as the sun went down on the new Centennial Olympic Stadium filled with 80,000 people.‡‡‡‡‡ Andrew Pincus at the *Berkshire Eagle* called it "a fanfare to end all fanfares. With its colossal brass opening, solo for trumpeter Tim Morrison and fireworks for percussion, it reflects what Williams describes as 'our awe at this incredible pursuit of athletic excellence and shared experience.'"[141] An enthusiastic crowd in

---

††††† *Nixon* lost to *Il postino* by the Argentine-Italian composer Luis Bacalov.
‡‡‡‡‡ Eight days later, Centennial Olympic Park was rocked by pipe bombs, injuring more than 100 people and killing two.

Atlanta that night in July, which included presidents Clinton and Carter, appeared to agree. John brought this heroic miniature to Tanglewood later that summer, then to London for three sold-out concerts at the Barbican Centre.[142] It was the star of an album (also called *Summon the Heroes*) that featured other Olympiad music, which spent 18 weeks at number one on Billboard's Classical Crossover Chart. For John, this six-minute "poem" was another evocation of our shared memory: "We remember the meaning of the trumpets and the conch shells and the shofars being blown to bring regiments together. The interval of the musical fifth we use to celebrate has been with us thousands of years."[143] The piece was unabashedly American and cardiovascular, a glowing love song for the human spirit.

* * *

Many filmmakers wanted John's magic, but not all of them got it. Director Victor Salva somehow convinced Disney to produce his screenplay about an albino man with magical powers—the movie *Powder*—and both John and Jerry Goldsmith expressed interest in scoring it. Music is "basically another character in your film," Salva said, so you obviously "want the Marlon Brando of film scoring." According to Salva, John's contractual option to back out after seeing a finished cut gave the studio concern, and they mutually decided not to proceed.[144]§§§§§

John was also offered *Mission: Impossible*, Paramount's first film adaptation of the popular 1960s TV series, which starred Tom Cruise and quickly became one of Hollywood's biggest franchises. John had not worked with director Brian De Palma since *The Fury* in 1978, and he was interested in doing the film, but said: "Would you mind if I change the theme?" according to editor Paul Hirsch. "The producers said, 'Oh, no, no, no—you can't change the theme.' He said, 'Well, never mind.' But I thought: hey, if John Williams wants to change the theme, I would be very interested to know what he would have come up with. He changed the theme for *Superman!*"******* After editing *The Fury* and the first two *Star Wars* films, Hirsch was disappointed not to have another chance to work with John. "I have known several artists who had an intuitive grasp of the audience, and they had this sort of unfiltered connection," Hirsch said. "I would include among those John Hughes, Stephen King, and John Williams—who connected with the audience in a way that huge numbers of people could relate to the emotions that he expressed through his music."[145]

The Hollywood trades also announced that John was going to collaborate, for the first time, with Roman Polanski[146]—the Polish Holocaust survivor who found Hollywood glory with films like *Rosemary's Baby* and *Chinatown* before earning international infamy for sexually abusing a 13-year-old girl in 1977. Polanski, now based in Europe, was starting production on *The Double*, a film adapted from a

---

§§§§§ Goldsmith scored *Powder*, which performed decently despite the bruising revelation ahead of its release that Silva had served time for child molestation.

****** "I think I probably would have said, 'Just go to Lalo,'" John later added. (JW to TG, June 2, 2023.) Danny Elfman scored the film, after Alan Silvestri's score was rejected, and he liberally quoted Lalo Schifrin's themes from the original TV series.

Dostoevsky novella about a man whose life is upended when his doppelganger turns up and begins to take over. But the film's star, John Travolta, immediately clashed with Polanski and walked off the project right before shooting was to begin in Paris; he was sued by Polanski, Travolta countersued, and the whole thing went up in flames.[147]

The next, actual recipient of John's genius was Barry Levinson, director of *Rain Man*, *The Natural*, and a loose trilogy of dramas set in Baltimore (*Diner*, *Tin Men*, and *Avalon*). Levinson had worked with a parade of great composers over the decades, including Randy Newman, Zimmer, and Morricone—preferring to make a new match based on the material at hand. "So much of the things that I do are not in any genre," Levinson explained, "so I kind of bounce around in that regard."[148] His new film, *Sleepers*, was based on a 1995 book by Lorenzo Carcaterra, purporting to be a factual memoir about the author's traumatic childhood. Its tale of a quartet of boys from Hell's Kitchen who get sent to a reform school, where they are repeatedly tortured and raped by sadistic guards—a crime that they tactically avenge as adults by way of murder and manipulating the legal system—was received with skepticism. But the book was a bestseller, and it caught Levinson's attention because "the idea of these reform schools, and some of the things that went on and were denied—the sexual abuse to these kids, etc.—I thought it was something that was a really tough subject to deal with, but I thought it was valid to do." Levinson adapted the screenplay himself, and assembled a starry cast that included Brad Pitt as one of the grown-up boys, Robert De Niro as their protective neighborhood priest, Dustin Hoffman as their alcoholic lawyer, and Kevin Bacon as an evil guard at the Wilkinson Home for Boys. The story spanned the 1960s through the 1980s, and Levinson used several nostalgic radio hits for the rosy boyhood section of the film.

When it came to original score, he wanted an orchestral opus in the vein of Leonard Bernstein. "Not that you're trying to copy it in any way," he said, "but it's New York, it has a certain kind of street quality to it." Levinson had approached John for another project years earlier ("I can't remember which one," he said)—but John wasn't available. For *Sleepers*, "I thought, *Well, this could be something that he might be interested in. I know he can do this.*" John agreed to score this grimly loaded story, after watching a rough portion of the film, while Levinson was still shooting. He took the Bernstein reference to heart and composed a dark, urban tone poem that evoked some of the same Americana anguish from Bernstein's only film score, *On the Waterfront*. His main theme wrests beauty from chromaticism, leaping to angular, unexpected intervals that trace the fissures of broken innocence. That innocence remains, even if only as a faint memory, in the tenderness of a solo flute and sympathetic strings. A lone French horn is a constant carrier of this melody, tapping into the same sour American palette of *Born on the Fourth of July* and *Nixon*. Levinson said he wanted John specifically because he knew that John could express the film's complexity of emotions—trauma, tragedy, fury—with a delicate hand and without ever slipping into melodrama. John could write music with tension that "doesn't release itself," Levinson said, "doesn't become sentimental in any way. I was thinking of Bernstein in that way—not to copy any of that, but somehow in that wheelhouse of emotion, and a certain kind of subtextual uneasiness."[149]

The *Sleepers* score was also marked by an unusually heavy electronic presence. An electric bass repeatedly descends under the main melody—a descent into the basement of memory, or hell itself—and the cold, mechanical sounds of a drum machine and synthesizers lend the score a harshness and modern beat that were an anomaly for John. Levinson did not recall requesting these electronics, but he thought they worked well in terms of evoking the time-spanning narrative. "We needed to somehow reflect some of that, so we don't feel like we're stuck in the early '60s," he said.

The Catholic church is both a backdrop and character in the film, personified by De Niro's Father Bobby—and John incorporated tolling bells and liturgical choir into a powerful scene where an adult Shakes (Jason Patric) goes to church one night and, as he touches a string of prayer beads, flashes back to a night in his boyhood that he spent gripping a rosary and praying while being raped. Levinson specifically desired a score that never "gets out in front," music that remains subtly integrated into the drama—but several sequences in the film are montages with no dialogue, only narration from Shakes, which gave music an outsized role. A pivotal football game at Wilkinson, in which the boys defeat their guards, leads to a savagely fatal beating of a Black boy named Rizzo (an event that later figures in the courtroom revenge plot). John wrote a high-stakes scherzo for the game that plunged the pattern of earlier action set pieces, like his playful "Scherzo for Motorcycle and Orchestra," into his 1990s ocean of darkness. Horns pump a syncopated Morse code rhythm over a low piano ostinato, with the added groove of a relentless drum machine beat.

A recurring ghostly motif—four notes falling—unites this moment of short-lived glory to the rest of an almost unrelentingly tragic score. Father Bobby is the final key to the plot that Shakes and Brad Pitt's character concoct after their two childhood friends murder Bacon's dastardly guard in 1981: they need the priest to provide a false alibi. To make their case, Shakes visits Father Bobby one night and finally reveals happened at Wilkinson. Levinson held the camera on De Niro's anguished face as he hears these horrors for the first time, but dropped out Patric's dialogue. Instead, John's score does the heavy lifting, with James Thatcher's solo horn playing the main melody, doubled with flute—providing its own haunted witness to these crimes. "I love that moment," Levinson said. "The camera just sits on Bob's face and it literally looks like his face is coming apart. Something has to take us away from just the starkness, otherwise [the audience is] going to be hearing the dialogue. So the music's got to be in there, but not in a way that we're just paying attention to music. I think that's where John really shines. That's what I mean where you can't get out in front. It's too tied to the emotion. It's one of my favorite scenes in the film."[150]

Sleepers was released on October 18, 1996, after premiering at the Venice Film Festival in August. It was not received well by critics or audiences, and its only Oscar nomination was for John's score. "The portentous yet slumberous-sounding *Sleepers* is the latest example of the Academy members' Pavlovian response to perennial winner John Williams' name," Ted Shen groused in the *Chicago Tribune*. "Fortunately, it doesn't stand a chance."[151] John indeed lost to Gabriel Yared's romantic score for *The English Patient*, and his score for *Sleepers* slipped into a cultural coma. It deserved a better fate: like *Nixon*, it was dark, complex, tragic, ultimately hopeful, and pregnant with melody. In many ways, John's film work was coming more and more in line with his thorny concert music. He was still growing—still pushing himself.

* * *

Yet another new concerto premiered just a few weekends before *Sleepers* opened. Trumpet player Michael Sachs grew up in Santa Monica and had always secretly longed to play on TV and movie soundtracks. Even without a music degree, he rose in the ranks of symphonic orchestra playing; he was actually a member of the Houston Symphony when John conducted his first violin concerto there in 1987. By now, he was principal trumpet in the Cleveland Orchestra where Tom Morris—former general manager of the BSO and the man responsible for bringing John to the Pops—was executive director. Morris wanted to commission a concerto for Sachs, and said they should each give some thought to *which* composer, then compare notes. When they met again, they both revealed that John Williams was their first choice. For Sachs, "this goes back to sitting in the theater as a 15-year-old when *Star Wars* came out, and just that first big B-flat major chord with Maurice Murphy, the principal trumpet from the London Symphony on his first day on the job, just coming out at you. He wrote so many iconic things for the trumpet and inspired so many of us to do what we do." Sachs considered the trumpet music in the end credits of *Born on the Fourth of July* "one of the most gorgeous things ever written." "I thought, if I could somehow get a trumpet concerto out of him, that would be like climbing Mount Everest. That would be the ultimate fantasy for me."[152]

John had been approached by other trumpet players about a concerto; Doc Severinsen, the longtime bandleader of *The Tonight Show with Johnny Carson*, once asked John for a "popular" concerto for his instrument.[153] It was an instrument John loved and knew intimately, so the opportunity to write a showpiece for Sachs's trumpet was an easy sell. John noted the early influence of Louis Armstrong, and how "in the '30s and '40s there were players like Harry James and Tommy Dorsey who really expanded the expressive capabilities of brass instruments," but there wasn't anything in the concert repertoire with "that kind of cantabile, expressive extension that these people introduced."[154] Sachs met with John for the first time in October 1993, flying through Los Angeles on his return from a tour in Japan. "I was taken by his immediate warmth and kindness," Sachs said.

> I mean, he's *John Williams*. For me, he's up in the highest ranks of the highest ranks of the highest ranks of what we do. I have so much admiration and respect for him. And he just could not have been nicer. Here's somebody who doesn't *need* to be that way. I've dealt with a lot of people in this business who are most definitely not that way, who the success has gotten to their head. But there's a humility about John, and an integrity about John that is unique to him, that immediately radiates from him when you meet him.[155]

John began sending Sachs "snippets" of ideas and thematic material a few months later, and Sachs would meet with John whenever he was in L.A. to play at John's home.

"Very early on I said, 'Look, I hope it's okay if I mention a couple things that, ergonomically, make it a little bit better,'" Sachs said, bracing for impact. "He's like, 'If this was good enough for Joachim and Brahms, it's good enough for me and you!'" Sachs was equally staggered by John's ear. One day he was at John's house practicing the piece, and John needed to make a phone call. "Listen," John said, "this is going to be about 20 minutes. But go ahead and play—you're not going to bother me. I'm in a different part of the house." "So I was noodling around," Sachs said,

> playing around with a few passages. He came back after the 20 minutes and he said, "That one passage in the first moment, you did *this* instead of *that*. You kind of went above before you came down, and you came *that* direction. Show that to me again." It was one of those things where I was just noodling around and it created something that actually became really challenging, but I came to realize that anything I was going to do, he was going to hear it. His awareness, and his radar, was so highly attuned, so attentive and intensive. It was just mind boggling to me how brilliant he was.[156]

At another point, Sachs was playing through the work-in-progress and John felt one section was too long. John said, "Play it again," and timed it with his stopwatch. The duration was approximately two minutes and 43 seconds, and John said, "It needs to be about 2:20. Okay, take this bar from that bar ..." and he started making cuts in real time. "Okay, try it again," he said, clicking his stopwatch. "Yeah, I like that a lot better," he said, after Sachs played it through. John looked down at his watch and said: "Yep. 2:20. Perfect."[157]

This concerto was a dialogue with the cultural history of the trumpet, opening with a shofar-like, ceremonial fanfare. "It almost harkens back to biblical times," said Sachs. "It's getting our attention," said John, "getting our hackles up, calling the heroes and all of the things associated with it."[158] In the first movement, John was looking for "the opportunity for the trumpet to sing," he said. "It led me more into a tonal, American romantic idiom."[159] The movement swells into action, casting the trumpet as an athletic hero running through an orchestral obstacle course before giving way to an extended cadenza. "The beginning of the cadenza, instead of it being this very flourishy, very pyrotechnical thing," said Sachs, "he all of a sudden goes to something that's very subdued, and very lyrical, and very introspective. You think he's going right and he goes left." The second movement is a lyrical ballad with terroir traces of the briary Americana fields John had tilled in *Nixon* and *Sleepers*, and it pairs the protagonist with several other instruments. "The trombone is a typical partner of the trumpet," Sachs said.

> English horn, referring to Copland's *Quiet City*. And then the flute is kind of an opposite. You have what can be a very powerful instrument juxtaposed against something seen as more of a delicate instrument, and showing how the trumpet and the flute can be very interwoven—that the trumpet can create that kind of delicacy

and intimacy. So creating these different partnerships within these different voicings, I felt like he was able to explore a very wide palette of the colors of the instrument.[160]

The final movement, "Allegro deciso," is a syncopated, staccato showcase for the star, with dramatic double and triple tonguing and, John explained, "scales, arpeggios, leaps, and all the great theatrics a great trumpeter can provide."[161]

Sachs considered this the first great American trumpet concerto; he premiered it at Cleveland's Severance Hall in late September 1996 with the orchestra's music director, Christoph von Dohnányi, conducting. The *Cleveland Plain Dealer*'s critic, Donald Rosenberg, described it as "an austere concert work of dignified personality, soloistic variety, and orchestral color" full of "luxurious and mysterious sonorities." But Rosenberg lamented the lack of "thematic ingenuity and vivid sense of drama—not to mention the humor—that pervade many of Williams' finest cinematic efforts."[162] It was an ongoing but shortsighted complaint.

* * *

Sabrina, *Nixon*, and *Sleepers* proved that not everything John touched turned to gold, at least not at the box office, and their lack of success further revealed just how important the Spielberg events and genre franchises were to John's popularity. Even during these quirky in-between years, though, his coolness refused to wane: when he conducted a show at the Hollywood Bowl in September 1995, critic Timothy Mangan sharply observed that "John Williams holds many distinctions, but perhaps the most impressive is that he's probably the only living composer who can draw more than 35,000 people to two concerts of his own music."[163] But these often overlooked scores are just as important to understanding John's talent, and they found him stretching forward in exciting ways.

The next year would be an incredibly momentous one, with opportunities to wade even further into this dark and dramatic musical sea, with new collaborators and two new films with Spielberg. Lucas, long dormant, would resurrect his *Star Wars* films, controversially filled with new special effects and story alterations. Lucas eagerly invited John to return to his popular galaxy, and the results offered a preview of a new trilogy soon to come. The end of the century—and the millennium—would yield a hymn for fallen soldiers, and a choral anthem about the fate of the galaxy.

John Williams was not retiring.

13
Duel of the Fates, 1997–1999

> *Who knows or can explain why things happen to each of us. We can only hope we become better and stronger from the experiences.*
> —**John Williams, 1997**[1]

In the early hours of February 23, 1997, police officers responded to a call from a woman hiding at her neighbor's house in a Los Angeles enclave above Coldwater Canyon. She had been in an argument with her husband, a big-time attorney for the Motion Picture Association of America, and threatened to leave with their infant twins. He brought out a gun. "Shortly after their arrival, officers heard several shots about 4:25 a.m.," the *Los Angeles Times* reported. "A SWAT team and crisis negotiators were called in soon afterward, but no officers entered the sprawling ranch house until 7:30 a.m. after they tried to contact Billick by telephone and over a bullhorn." When they entered, police found three bodies in the master bedroom. William Billick III had shot and killed his two babies—Alexandra Carolyn and Daniel Brand, both 18 months old—then himself.[2]

Their mother, Jacqueline Brand, was a violinist with the Los Angeles Chamber Orchestra who played on numerous film scores; her first with John was *Born on the Fourth of July*. A year after the murders, a memorial concert was held at Brand's temple, Kehillat Israel in Pacific Palisades, where her musician friends performed pieces by composers who knew Brand. John contributed a melody he had recently written for a film. He renamed it, simply, "Elegy."

If there was any theme, however unintentional, to the films John scored in the last few years of the twentieth century, it would be *violence and elegy*. From the horrors of slavery and lynchings to the carnage on the beach at Normandy, a pall of death and tragedy hung over the projects he chose to work on beginning in 1997. Even the *Jurassic Park* sequel he scored was almost cruel in its brutality. He responded with music that was percussively savage on one hand, and with solemn lamentation on the other.

* * *

Wynton Marsalis was hired to score *Rosewood*, an action-epic about a Black town in Florida that was decimated in 1923 after a white woman accused a Black man of rape and ignited a racial firestorm. Leaping up from smaller contemporary dramas about Black American life, director John Singleton conceived the film as a grand western, casting its fictional protagonist, played by Ving Rhames, as a solitary horseman who rides into town and has to choose whether to stay and help when the atrocities begin, or to ride on. In style, Singleton was influenced by the classical Americana films of John Ford, and in his depiction of ghastly, barbaric racism, Singleton took a page from *Schindler's List*. "I loved the way Spielberg structured his scenes and the way he used music and how he didn't make his antagonists one-dimensional. Even the Ralph Fiennes Nazi character was deeper, three-dimensional. And I didn't want to make the white characters all fire-breathing racists and the Black characters holier-than-thou, just singing in church and not shooting back when they're shot at."[3]

A venerated trumpeter and champion of jazz, Marsalis composed his score for a unique ensemble—with no string section—brimming with authentic blues, jazz, and church music true to Rosewood's time and place. "Wynton had an intellectual way to go about doing the score," said Bruce Cannon, Singleton's film editor, "and it really just didn't work emotionally. To me, I know, it felt really flat. It didn't bring out the life in the film or the power or the threat or the danger, or anything."[4] For a somber lynching scene, Marsalis contrastingly wrote an uplifting spiritual. "He was thinking of it as a higher, more abstract level of the history of the people," said music editor Lisé Richardson. "If you did a Broadway play about this story, the music would win a Tony because it was so amazing. I think because of the way [Singleton] shot the film, and how cinematic it was, there was just a little bit of disconnect."[5] Warner Bros. pressured Singleton to replace Marsalis's score, and his team joined the chorus. "We always talked about *what's best for the movie*," said Cannon. "And [Singleton] came to that conclusion—we all came to it together. But it was really hard to let go. He had Wynton on a pedestal. He had a lot of respect, and really was so happy to get Wynton, and it was actually a beautiful score—but it wasn't right for this movie." "It didn't pull out the emotion," Singleton agreed. "Wynton is a very accomplished musician, but he's not a film composer.... It was a very soulful, beautiful, jazzy kind of score, but it just didn't gel."[6]*

John heard about this intriguing project in need of a new score, and he agreed to screen it for the 29-year-old director—who was a major fan. In high school, Singleton would get ready in the mornings while blasting the throne room cue from *Star Wars*, and he would study to the music of *E.T.* and *Raiders*. "I could remember what action Indiana Jones was doing by the way the music changed and still get charged by his daring adventures," Singleton wrote.

> Sometimes I would close my eyes and visualize these movies which I'd seen so many times using the soundtracks as my guide. In doing so, I would feel the very soul of the film—the rhythm, the pace, the themes, all these would come to me in pure form without any visuals. As my collection of tapes accumulated I noticed that all of the film scores I had purchased were the work of one man—without realizing it I had grown up listening and studying the film music of John Williams.[7]

---

* Marsalis eventually released these recordings on his 1999 album, *Reeltime*.

John admired the craft and story of *Rosewood*, and after screening the film without any music at Warner Bros. in the fall of 1996, he told Singleton it reminded him of a Martin Ritt picture—which the young film nerd took as high praise.[8] *Rosewood* was pushed from its awards-minded December release, to February 1997, in order to accommodate John's schedule. John knew Marsalis, who had played with the Pops, and he called to explain the situation. "He said he had no objections," John recalled. "He said, 'You know that whole business in a way that I don't know.' He was very gracious about it, and just diffused any kind of feeling there may have been."[9] And even though Singleton worshiped John Williams, he *was* slightly concerned whether this old white guy could do justice to such a deeply Black story. "He wanted to write out some different hymns, gospel hymns," said Singleton, "and I was very nervous at first. But then again this is John Williams, and he says, 'Well, you know, I used to do arranging in the '60s—I arranged seven [sic] albums for Mahalia Jackson.'" That was all Singleton needed to hear.[10]

Of his own volition, John composed two original gospel songs—"Light My Way," an uplifting anthem, and "Look Down, Lord," a sorrowful, minor key petition—and in a most unusual gesture, he penned the prayerful words himself. "What very little I know about Black church music, or the little exposure I've had, I *treasure*," he said. "Because I always felt that that is *true* music, truly inspired, and truly unusual and unique to the group of worshipers."[11] John used the "Look Down, Lord" tune as an emotional anchor for his score, in orchestral settings as well as with the voice of gospel singer Shirley Caesar—who many felt had inherited Mahalia Jackson's mantle (*and* who had also performed on Marsalis's score).

John wove the bluesy atmosphere of a 1920s Southern milieu into an emotional, symphonic odyssey that begins in sweetness and lazy afternoons on the front porch, before descending into hell—then charging out of it headlong. He gave the Rhames character, Mann, a complex hero theme that yearns upward and drifts down chromatically, the feeling of hard-won triumph. Solo banjo, fiddle, and harmonica all twang motifs above a 70mm-scaled orchestra, which is occasionally joined by synths and electronic drums for a harsh, sinister effect. The score's palette and language were an outgrowth of John's disquieting work in *Sleepers* and *Nixon*, a continuation of the darkly beautiful chromaticism he used to convey the rotting underbelly of American society. But it also uniquely emanated from the soil and porches of *this* story, with the idiom of blues and spirituals informing the syntax of almost every cue.

A synthesized Fender bass solo opens the main titles in an emotionally ambiguous way. "It was very dark and fast," said Tommy Morgan, "and John asked if I would play bass harmonica and create a sound to go with what was written." So Morgan improvised a guttural *whoosh* with his instrument to punctuate the bass line by making "very low, very high-impact plosives," "and as I slowed down I hit them with *sforzando* with a flutter tongue. I had never played anything like that. I created it for that score."[12][†] Singleton took his time introducing the film's characters and its two towns—peaceful Rosewood and the "cracker" town of Sumner—before the inciting

---

[†] Among Morgan's previous scores with John was *Conrack*, which also starred Jon Voight.

incident, the false accusation of rape that uncorks a racial vendetta; John patiently filled the pre-fall paradise with his various character motifs, all delicately conversing with each other. The score's empathy for Jon Voight's widower, who becomes a kind of Schindler character, takes the form of a wandering clarinet line—a stark contrast to the chugging, dissonant guitar rhythm with snarling bass harmonica and jaw harp music for the posse of white predators that forms and foments a bloodbath of lynchings and cold-blooded murder.

Singleton's enthusiasm and heart are evident in every frame of the film, even as the storytelling wobbles between earnest social tragedy, guns-blazing western, and at times outright monster movie—but somehow John navigated the melodramatics and action with a score that nimbly slides from earthy anthropology to keening adagio to pitched-up Hollywood heroism without ever cracking into split personalities. The ideal expression of this story was found in his music. John announced the film's finale, a harrowing escape by train, with pounding timpani hits and Caesar's voice crying out the words of his central hymn ("Oh I've been weary and feeling tired, oh Lord"), the lyrics fitting to the action as Rosewood's refugees run toward a moving train ("I'm comin' home now") and climb aboard to safety. John "called me in and had me sing my two verses a capella," Caesar recalled. "When I finished, I looked at him and he was weeping."[13] Choir sings the upbeat "Light My Way" as Mann hops off the train in an understated, spiritual climax. "His score for this film is just so soulful, just so beautiful," Singleton marveled. "It just goes with every image of the film. He rides the film with his music."[14]

Rosewood had its world premiere at the Berlin Film Festival in February, where it was nominated for a Golden Bear, and there was a chorus of hosannas from critics. Duane Byrge of the *Hollywood Reporter* called it "a powerful and heartbreaking dramatization of that awful saga.... Head-and-shoulders above the usual, well-meaning, self-congratulatory folderol that makes it to the screen about racial injustice, *Rosewood* is a graceful evocation of a dignified community and a sobering insight into the madness of mob psychology." John's music, Byrge added, helps "kindle *Rosewood* to both its most warm and most incendiary moments."[15] But Warner Bros. struggled to market such a discomfiting film, and it disappointed at the box office—ironically getting wiped out on its opening weekend by the re-release of *The Empire Strikes Back*. Cannon felt that the studio abandoned the film—and that its poor showing altered the trajectory of Singleton's career. The director had ambitious plans to make epics about the Middle Passage and Emmett Till, and instead he made a *Shaft* remake and a *Fast and the Furious* sequel. Without question, Cannon said, the director would have worked with John again if he'd had the opportunity.[16]

"Working with Mr. Williams," the young director wrote in his liner notes, "I felt like a teenager again, privileged this time to not only hear, but to witness the process of his creativity. He is a consummate craftsman, writing music that magnifies the power of the film. I can truly say Mr. Williams' score embodies the soul of *Rosewood*."‡

* * *

---

‡ Singleton died in 2019 at the age of 51 after having a stroke.

Amidst the darkness of his present film projects, John was offered a little escapism to an entertainment from long ago and far away. George Lucas shook the cobwebs from his invented galaxy by redecorating the original *Star Wars* trilogy as a run-up to a new trio of prequels. "It's a pity," said Francis Ford Coppola, his one-time mentor, "because George Lucas was a very experimental crazy guy, and he got lost in this big production and never got out of it."[17]

Lucas made several alterations to his beloved films, taking advantage of the new computer magic unleashed by ILM, his company, with *Jurassic Park*. A computer-generated Jabba the Hutt could now share the screen with old deleted footage of Harrison Ford, and a CGI alien band sang a new rock song in Jabba's palace. In some cases, continuity was fixed—Ian McDiarmid replaced a forgotten actor who portrayed the Emperor in *The Empire Strikes Back*. In others, a perceived character flaw—like Han Solo shooting the buggy Greedo in cold blood—was "rectified." When each genetically modified film was shipped to theaters and effortlessly generated new millions of dollars, it was clear that *Star Wars* fever had never died. In the interim years, John's music had been repurposed in star-studded NPR radio dramatizations of the trilogy and, more recently, in popular flight simulator games from LucasArts. When author Kathy Tyers wrote her bestselling spinoff novel, *The Truce at Bakura*, she dedicated it to John: "I can't think of *Star Wars* without remembering the opening fanfare from its soundtrack. I can't imagine an Imperial Star Destroyer's long, triangular silhouette without hearing ominous triplet rhythms."[18]

One of the many things Lucas tampered with was the ending of *Return of the Jedi*. Besides adding new animated shots of the entire *Star Wars* galaxy celebrating the Empire's downfall, he wanted to replace the old Ewok song "Yub Nub" that originally concluded the film. So John composed a more serious but still triumphant piece called "Victory Celebration," which was modeled after the temp track song, "500 Nations," from Peter Buffett's 1994 world music album of the same name. John recorded his two-minute cue with a contract orchestra at Abbey Road in late November 1996; it was an appetizer for his imminent return to the world of *Star Wars*. "So much of what we do is ephemeral and quickly forgotten, even by ourselves," John said at the time, "so it's gratifying to have something you have done linger in people's memories."[19]

In 1997, *Star Wars* was reborn, celebrating the 20th anniversary of the movie that started it all with the release of Lucas's "Special Editions" and a host of fanfare.[§] Throughout the summer, John conducted concerts to commemorate the trilogy, including one piece that was synchronized to footage from the films. "What I didn't realize was that all aspects of the public would be entranced by it," he said, reflecting on the undying popularity of *Star Wars*. "Joseph Campbell taught me more about the film than I ever realized while I was working on it, why it had such resonance. It was

---

[§] As part of the promotion for the "Special Editions," John's three scores were given deluxe expanded releases by Fox and RCA Victor. There was an expensive ad campaign for the CDs, including TV spots on *The X Files* and sales teams dressed as *Star Wars* characters visiting movie theaters to hand out postcard ads and coupons. (Burlingame, "Energizer Jedi," *Hollywood Reporter*, January 15, 1997.)

a new experience for me to hear a major intellectual telling me the meaning of my work."[20] Much like Coppola with Lucas, John's friend André Previn just shook his head: "I keep telling him, 'For God's sake, stop writing for those cornball movies and go be a *composer*.'"[21]

* * *

Spielberg returned from his three-year hiatus with a one-two punch that recalled his dinosaur/historical epic duo from 1993—but this time punching below his weight. His first movie back was a misguided sequel to *Jurassic Park*; Spielberg considered *The Lost World* his first true *sequel*—the *Indiana Jones* films were more "serial adventures," he explained—and he later realized he should have listened to his own skepticism when he originally scoffed at the idea of making *Jaws 2*. "My sequels aren't as good as my originals because I'm too confident," Spielberg later admitted. "'This movie made a ka-zillion dollars,' which justifies the sequel, so I come in like it's going to be a slam dunk and I wind up making an inferior movie to the one before. I'm talking about *The Lost World*."[22]

His overconfidence was read by many critics as sheer boredom. Everything was just a bit off in *The Lost World*: Dean Cundey's vibrant cinematography was replaced with the gauzy luster of Janusz Kamiński (who never left Spielberg's side after *Schindler's List*); an overreliance on CGI exposed the still-young technology's growing pains; Jeff Goldblum was unsuccessfully transformed from wisecracking sidekick to action star and straight man, and he flailed for chemistry with the likes of Julianne Moore (playing his girlfriend Sarah) and Vince Vaughan as a photographer sent to document the animals roaming free on Isla Sorna. The magical alchemy of wonder, humor, and tenderness from the first film had curdled into a narrative mush that strained to hold together a parade of grisly set pieces.

And still John found inspiration in abundance. Seizing on the fact that this wasn't just a Xerox of *Jurassic Park*, he went down a very different musical path—writing the most primally percussive score of his career. "Steven's idea was that this was all taking place on an island someplace, in some Caribbean area," John said, "and that the music might be driven by some drums, if you like, or some sort of ethnic or jungle kind of texture or flavor."[23] His new main theme, replacing both the original celebratory anthem and religioso hymn, was a muscular, lumbering adventure tune that moves with the same jerky determination over uneven ground as the all-terrain vehicles traversing this new island. As Ian Malcolm and company venture warily toward Spielberg's version of *King Kong*'s Skull Island, orchestra plays the theme ("MISTERIOSO E MAGICO") over a blistering battery of tambourines, tam-tams, bass drums, timpani, and "jungle drums" for a dangerous but exhilarating effect. This theme crops up again after the rival, game-hunting team bags a bunch of dinos; the tune isn't *heroic* but simply an active evocation of the ancient wildlife. As the team's lead hunter Roland Tembo rallies the collection of survivors, his fantastic line—"Let's get this moveable feast underway"—kicks off a stately reprise of John's new theme with sparkling cascades.

The classic *Jurassic Park* anthem appears rarely and subtly in occasions when the first film is overtly referenced, resounding like a ghost when Vaughn's character, Nick, stumbles onto a mural advertising the park. But the core of this sequel score is ominous, queasy dread—like a jungle version of *Nixon*—or else a rumbling war path of drums. John found a variety of rhythmic patterns to motor these divergent expedition teams, accelerating from a determined trek to an endangered, anxious sprint. He steered clear of a lengthy sequence where Sarah and Nick bring a wounded T-rex baby into their trailer, drawing two adult T-rexes who batter the trailer halfway off a cliff. Score does not come back until Sarah perches precariously on a plate of cracking glass high above the ocean, with scurrying low strings accenting the fissures. The tempo picks up as their trailer starts to slide off the cliff, and bells toll as their teammate Eddie hears the T-rexes approaching; his gruesome death is acknowledged with freaked-out strings, followed by a moment of stoic relief as the survivors climb a rope and convene with the InGen hunting team. John punctuated the film's many other deaths with aleatoric, shrieking effects, high flute spasms, angry brass chords, and wild syncopated runs in his most postmodern, aggressive, rhythmic, and brutal score yet. When the transported T-rex stomps into urban southern California, the score stomps along with it, counterpointed by a minor key quotation of the classic *Jurassic* anthem, and then immediately followed by more frenzied orchestral mayhem.

As Ian and Sarah bait the monster with its baby to lure it back inside a cargo ship, the score is finally allowed a bit of triumph with a last thrilling burst of the *Lost World* theme and a weary coda. The epilogue features a lovely string statement of the theme as John Hammond speaks to CNN, followed by a solemn quote of the *Jurassic* hymn on solo piano. The film's last word belongs to the dinosaurs, reclaiming their island, and a rousing restatement of the beloved *Jurassic* anthem. Life finds a way again. "There's a little Max Steiner influence in some of John's score," said Spielberg,

> the *King Kong*-esque primitive jungle rhythm that he put into that. When I compare the scores, for me, all of John's work is equally ... blessed with genius. But I prefer the *Lost World* score, because it's much more complicated, musically, than the first one. It's got more themes. And when we do intone the *Jurassic Park* theme in the second movie, when they get into the visitor center which had been overgrown, you kind of have that little touch of nostalgia. In a way, it almost makes you miss the first movie while you're watching the second one.[24]

Most audiences agreed.

* * *

And just as they did in 1993, John and Spielberg went straight from Hammond's folly to historical trauma. *Amistad* was based on the true story of a group of kidnapped Africans who overthrew their captors on a ship heading for America, thereby posing a unique challenge to the legal system: were they people, or property? It was a promising subject for the filmmaker who had just done such justice to the Holocaust—but David Franzoni's script turned this premise into a convoluted history lesson, and Spielberg's instincts were both too insistent *and* too hesitant. He allowed himself many of the camera acrobatics and theatrical flair that he abstained from in *Schindler's List*, and his usually steady hand shook in the process. His depiction of the ocean transport of enslaved men, women, and children was effectively harrowing, but the majority of the film is a byzantine courtroom battle with a miscast Matthew McConaughey as attorney for the hero, Cinque (Djimon Hounsou), and his captured brethren. The white director had been stung by criticisms of sanitizing and sentimentalizing Alice Walker's *The Color Purple*, and yet his balance faltered once again under the weight of conveying the tragedy of Black Americans. In *Amistad*, their humanity was too sanctified and their plight too mythologized to reflect either the reality or the awfulness of their history.

Amistad opens with John's new logo music for DreamWorks, a fairytale fanfare for acoustic guitar and orchestra that accompanies the image of a little boy fishing off a crescent moon—an unintentional omen of the fabulist approach in the film to come. The film itself begins with a woman humming the melancholy theme for Cinque, a minor key lullaby at the heart of John's score. A semblance of realism is achieved in the opening sequence, as Cinque excruciatingly wriggles a nail loose and frees himself, then leads the bloody massacre of slavers aboard *La Amistad* in the middle of a huge storm—all without music—and yet the bizarre camera angles and Kamiński's otherworldly lighting create an almost comic book effect that undermines the scenario, and this prologue sets an odd tone for the rest of the movie. Cinque's motif recurs often throughout the next two and a half hours, sometimes with that unaccompanied female moan—like an absent mother's lament—and sometimes tenderly on a solo woodwind cushioned with string harmony. John baptized some of the jungle percussive rhythms from *Lost World* for a more sober depiction of African culture, possibly overstepping into Hollywood appropriation. There was no questioning his seriousness of purpose, but in this case, Spielberg's theatrics let John down.

Taken on its own, the score for *Amistad* is a stirring narrative of a noble African warrior caught up in tragedy and sorrow. Cinque's theme is a simple, singable melody full of heartbreak, and it never grows old throughout its variety of arrangements, whether carried by solo flute or chorus. A second theme carries Cinque's "Memories of Home," which uses the humming female vocal and African drums for a happier emotion. John also wrote a more hopeful theme which emerges when Cinque breaks through the noise in court (shouting "GIVE US US FREE")—an ascendant choral anthem in an African idiom. Susan Dangel, the Boston-based producer of *Evening at Pops*, had helped John find a text for *Schindler's List*;** she came through again on *Amistad*, this time sitting on the floor of the Cambridge Public Library and scanning poetry books. She found an ideal text in "Dry Your Tears, Afrika," a 1967 poem by Bernard Dadié, a literary anticolonial activist from Côte d'Ivoire. The poem wasn't in the public domain, "so I had to find the cultural attaché of Sierra Leone," Dangel said. "I went to

---

** She told John about the line in a Jewish prayer book, "With our lives, we give life." "He really liked that, so I said, 'Well, let me go to my rabbi and get it translated,'" Dangel recalled. "So I, with my Radio Shack recorder, went down to the rabbi—literally—and said, 'Could you record this?' He said, 'No, this isn't what you want. You want *this*.' 'No, no, no, I want this!'" (Dangel to TG.)

Washington and that guy translated it into Mende, and I recorded him reading it over and over again—slower, faster—into my Radio Shack recorder."[25] John took those syllables and fashioned them into his choral benediction, retaining the poem's title. The tune shows up again when John Quincy Adams (played by Anthony Hopkins) exhorts Morgan Freeman's character to discover who these *Amistad* Africans really *are*, and then it sings with serenity after Adams defends them in front of the Supreme Court.

Much of the score comprises noble patriotic music that John composed for Adams; once again, he used Tim Morrison's trumpet to invoke the better angels of this country, and the idiom associated with Aaron Copland (especially from works like *Lincoln Portrait*) to accompany this quirky old statesman and the lofty ideals he articulates in court. The long summation Adams gives in the film's climax is blanketed with score, and John diligently followed the turns in his speech: sourness as Adams reads a Southern politician's argument about the naturalness of slavery, rousing when he talks about the natural human desire for freedom—importing African music as Adams relays how Cinque called on his own ancestors to join him in court—then returning to Americana strings as Adams calls on his own "ancestors" (*literally*, in the case of his father, John Adams) by way of busts of the founding fathers inside the courtroom. The liberation and destruction of the slave fortress in Sierra Leone yielded the most extroverted celebration of "Dry Your Tears," launched in full with choir and modulating upward as a British naval ship fires cannons on the fortress. But the film ends on a conflicted note: a solemn choir trading Cinque's theme with a minor key version of "Dry Your Tears" as the freed Africans silently stand on a boat sailing back toward a home engulfed in its own civil war.

Hopkins was a regular visitor to the scoring sessions, which took place at Sony throughout October. Sally Stevens, a veteran session singer who became a vocalist contractor for John on this project, was tasked with finding a soloist to carry Cinque's theme—essentially providing the voice of Mother Africa. She heard about a mezzo-soprano opera singer, Pamela Dillard, and called Dillard on the road. "Sometimes you just get a feeling," Stevens said, "and just talking with her I felt like she was the right voice. And John loved her and ended up writing two more cues for her."[26] John conducted a 52-piece children's choir as well as a full adult choir, sometimes broken into cues for just men or only women. The choir was composed of about two-thirds Black singers, and a linguist was on hand to give instructions about correct Mende pronunciation. "There was a great effort made," Stevens said, "to make it as authentic and as honest and real as possible."

That didn't stop a few critics from crying foul. "'Dry Your Tears, Afrika' comes across somewhat slick and geographically confused (the vocals are more representative of South Africa than Sierra Leone)," Richard Harrington wrote in his review of the soundtrack for the *Washington Post*, "and Williams' use of supple percussive textures and tribal voices sounds like cultural shorthand rather than musical definition."[27] Mark Swed, a new classical critic at the *L.A. Times*, likewise protested that John "lets tribal music stand for the nobility of the African captives. But it only seems to contribute to the curious queasiness *Amistad* causes in some viewers, the feeling that a film intended to combat racism somehow ends up as part of the problem rather than the solution. When the music manipulates with patent contrivances, we start to question, rightly or wrongly, the sincerity of the film."[28]

Despite its flaws and tonal instability, *Amistad* reflected one of Spielberg's new obsessions: portraying the noble history of righting injustices. And it marked the beginning of his recurring enlistment of John to help him pay tribute to American glory.

* * *

The summer of 1997 was full of concerts. For an *Evening at Pops* show celebrating *Star Wars*, John sat down with Gene Shalit for an informal conversation about his work. "We wanted to have Gene," said Bill Cosel, the show's producer, "because he knows how to make John Williams laugh. It's a side of John the public doesn't see very often. He has a real funny bone, but once the cameras are on him, he develops a Presbyterian presence we have to crack open."[29] At Tanglewood, John recruited James Earl Jones to narrate *Lincoln Portrait* (with Seiji Ozawa conducting), and spent the month of August mentoring composer fellows. He never considered himself a teacher, but he was adequately comfortable "talking about their lives and problems—all musical concerns that composers have."[30]

The last in a staggering *four* new scores to debut that year was *Seven Years in Tibet*. John's music had traveled to the East before—most prominently in *Empire of the Sun*—and on its face *Tibet* offered a similar task: acknowledging an Asian environment but told from the perspective of a European protagonist. Brad Pitt played the real-life Austrian mountaineer Heinrich Harrer who, after escaping a British POW camp in the outbreak of World War II, found refuge in Tibet and forged an unlikely friendship with the young Dalai Lama. "But I didn't feel that it was appropriate to have too much 'fusion' music," said director Jean-Jacques Annaud, "because the score is not there to tell you *where* we are, but where we are *emotionally*."[31] The French filmmaker was known for his ambitious and exotic films set in distant times and foreign lands—among them *Quest for Fire* and *The Name of the Rose*; he spent a year in Vietnam to shoot his 1992 drama, *The Lover*. "I was very moved by the country," he said. "But when I came back, and after the success of the movie, I remember saying to my assistant, 'Please, let's find something that would allow me to understand the spirituality of Asia. There is something that I didn't get when I was shooting *The Lover*, and I want to understand what it is.'"[32]

He found what he was looking for in Harrer's 1952 memoir, *Sieben Jahre in Tibet*, and he spent six months and roughly a million dollars researching and scouting locations. The Chinese government, which was not represented favorably in the story, refused to let Annaud film in Tibet—so instead he shot in Argentina, going so far as bringing yaks into the country and using clandestine documentary footage of the real Tibet to flesh out his picture. An eleventh-hour controversy threatened to undermine the whole production, when a German magazine revealed that Harrer had been a member of the Nazi Party—something he failed to mention in his book. Annaud hastily added some new narration from Pitt to acknowledge this fact. The director met Harrer while he was planning the film, and told the 86-year-old that, in the early parts of the story, it would not be a very flattering portrait. Harrer said, "Ah, that's fine, because Tibet transformed me, and I even wrote it in my book. There is one line: 'Tibet transformed me.'" Annaud said: "That one line in your book is two hours of my movie."[33]

Annaud had previously used composers James Horner and Gabriel Yared, the latter having recently won an Academy Award for *The English Patient* (and subsequently becoming "a little more difficult to work with," according to Annaud). It was Peter Guber, the chairman of Mandalay Entertainment, who suggested John. Annaud met with John in Boston in May 1997 and showed him a rough cut of the film. "I love the man," Annaud said. "He was so polite." John discovered that Annaud was a music lover, so he invited the director to a Pops concert where John was conducting Simon Proctor's 1959 concerto for serpent, a strange baroque wind instrument that resembles a snake. John confided to Annaud that he was worried it would be out of tune. "And very fortunately it was very good," said Annaud, "and I remember he was very relieved. He's such a famous composer, famous conductor, a great classical music lover, and I was very charmed by the fact that he was worried about the interpretation of an unknown piece of baroque music with a serpent."

John chose to cast Yo-Yo Ma's cello in a starring role in his new score—but he called Annaud a few weeks into working on *Tibet* and expressed some misgivings. "Are you really sure that a cello is fine for this movie?" he asked, according to Annaud. "I remember saying, 'Yes, yes, absolutely.' But he was a bit afraid that it was going to be a bit too classical." During production, Annaud sourced several pieces of traditional music which he linked to onscreen ceremonies and performances at the Dalai Lama's palace: the harsh droning of long *dungchen* horns, gongs, chimes, and the exotic vocalizations of Buddhist monks—some from recordings he acquired, some of which he captured on location. This music would steep the audience in place and resonate with the mystery and beauty of the culture and its religion. What Annaud wanted from John was contrast: "The Buddhist music is very deep and profound, but does not necessarily convey the kind of emotion that we needed for the scenes. So sometimes I use it almost as score, but only in a few occasions."[34]

John's first theme introduced is an elegant, passionate string adagio, a lament for Harrer's pain—his fractured marriage and the son he unknowingly abandons. This sense of ache and loss pervades much of the film, sometimes crescendoing—as when a distraught Harrer receives divorce papers in prison and rages against barbed wire in the rain—and at other times very soft. But the film's main theme is a grand, romantic melody in the tradition of *Lawrence of Arabia*.[††] Over chromatically descending minor chords, this tune swirls and reaches upward in a way that suggests both aspiration and crying. Ma's interpretation often gives the theme its emotional personality,

---

[††] David Lean's 1962 film is echoed here in several ways, most visibly in Pitt's resemblance to Peter O'Toole's cocky, blue-eyed blond westerner in a foreign land. John saw the film in theaters with Barbara, and was a big fan of Maurice Jarre's iconic score.

lending it the cello's inherent melancholy. This theme accompanies Harrer's external adventure from a mountain expedition, carried on a quicksilver string rhythm—to solitary confinement in the camp, plucked delicately on solo harp—and into Tibet, performed on high flute as the Dalai Lama watches Harrer from afar. But it is equally adept at playing the *interior*, sometimes on a solo piano recorded to sound as distant as Harrer's son.

"A melody is something that very often is needed to sustain the emotion of the movie," said Annaud. "When you enter the theme, immediately it means something." For him, the main theme was about "fragility of a character. It's about redemption." And yet it was also capable of playing to the vastness of Tibet. When Annaud was scouting the region, his local guides said to him: "We are very bizarre people—we have strange thoughts. It's because of the thin air, and it's because of the solitude." "Look at those landscapes," said Annaud.

> It's very mineral, and the sky is extra blue—the rivers are extra blue as well. You could very quickly have a headache, and it gives you strange dreams. Therefore the scope is needed, the space. Even a large screen is not enough to explain the size, the dimension of those landscapes. Therefore, the solitude of a lonely little man. I always liked how man is small in the universe, and music can give that—specifically when it's composed by John Williams.[35]

John composed a motif especially for Tibet and the Dalai Lama, which slides along a pentatonic scale. There is also music of war. Then, at the *very* end of the picture, John briefly introduces a new theme for Harrer reuniting with his son Rolf—who initially wants nothing to do with him—back home in Austria in 1951. "Regaining a Son" (John's title for this cue) is a painfully beautiful elegy for cello and orchestra, with a slightly Viennese air, which begins as Harrer walks away from his young son's bedroom and carries over to the finale of Harrer helping an older Rolf climb a mountain. This melody is at once both hopeful and heartbreaking. *Elegy*, John said, "can be a wish or a prayer for condolences and the like, to assuage the grief of people who have lost. But it can be other things. It can be a wish and a prayer for wholeness, and forgiveness. These emotions, of all the instruments we have, are often best expressed by the cello, I think."[36]

When John rearranged this melody for the benefit concert honoring the slain children of Jacqueline Brand in early 1998, it was performed sparely by cellist John Walz and pianist Randy Kerber. "I was actually asked to go to his home and listen to the run-through, and I just couldn't," said Brand. "I regret now that I didn't, but I was like: *I can't. I can't go.*"[37] Three years later, John recorded his cello concerto with Ma along with a few other pieces—including this one, now reworked as an *Elegy* for Cello and Orchestra. The sessions took place at Sony in April 2001; John explained the backstory to Ma just before the recording, and told him that Brand was there in the orchestra. "I can tell you," Ma said, "there was a puddle on the floor by the time we finished."[38] Brand, now pregnant with a new baby girl, was overwhelmed. "To think that some of what happened in my life would matter enough for him to write that, and dedicate it to my children ... it's hard to find words for that honor. When children are taken senselessly, and before they have any chance themselves to make a life or to make an imprint, it gave their lives more imprint to me. And being Jewish, that's kind of a big thing. It is a beautiful memorial to them. It's important to me, emotionally, that they inspired anything like that."

Whenever she needed to go to a place to remember her lost children, Brand would drive up to her second house in Cambria and listen to *Elegy*, "and it kind of transforms me, seeing the ocean and the sun and all of that. It really is just such a gift. And my daughter is always like, 'Mom, why are you playing that piece?' Because she knows that I cry when I hear [it]. But for me it's a refuge, to feel. Because when you live with something like that, you can't walk around with it all the time." In Brand's mind, *Elegy* "starts out almost like a birth, very quiet and mysterious.

> Then you can hear heartache and pain in it, and almost like tears. Almost like the feelings I've had so many times of: *No, no, no.* And then somehow it resolves at the end, to me, where ... I know all of this is so symbolically cliché, but it almost resolves into like a rainbow or something that is very symbolic of heaven, or some transcendence. The piece is short—like their lives. It represents the whole experience of having these children, and then having their lives taken away—yet the beauty that they brought to me, and then the hope. It ends, to me, so high up and transcendent, just like trailing off to another realm that we hope we go to.
>
> How did he know all that? How did he know to work all of that in that piece? I think there's some communication going on from that other realm through him.[39]

Of the four films released in 1997, *Amistad* was the lone score to be nominated for an Oscar. Around the time of the ceremony, the Atlanta Gay Men's Chorus performed "Dry Your Tears, Afrika" in an evening of songs with Maya Angelou. David Puckett, the group's artistic director, saw the film over the holidays and "thought the piece was the most fabulous thing I'd ever heard," he said.[40] Like most of the nominees in every category that March, John lost to *Titanic*—which, ironically, *he* had been asked to score. "I wanted something that was more classically informed," director James Cameron said. "I said to Jon Landau, my producing partner on the film, 'I want the best composer in the world for this movie. Who is that?' And I think the obvious answer at the time would have been John Williams. And John was interested, *kind of*. But I wanted somebody that was more than *kind of* interested. So I said, 'Alright, who's next?'"[41] Cameron ultimately reunited with James Horner, whose score and song ("My Heart Will Go On") sunk all competition. John was so convinced he wouldn't win that he gave his seats to Jenny and her firstborn.‡‡

---

‡‡ Jenny's oldest child came out as trans in 2023. When Bobby Gruska broke the news to John, he was worried that his 91-year-old grandfather might be weirded out—but John took it in stride. John's nickname for Bobby had always been "Rooney." "You can still call me Rooney; I'm still the same person," Bobby said, to which John quipped: "Just in a lower register!" (Bobby Gruska to TG, January 16, 2024.)

No one knew it at the time, but Jenny had recently come out of the closet. "I always knew I was gay, but I didn't want to be," Jenny admitted.

> Because in those days, if you were gay you couldn't have kids. That was just the way it was. I remember when I was in college, I was in love with this girl, and I remember saying to myself: *Jenny, you can't do this, because you want kids. You like guys too—it's going to be fine. You should get married to a guy and have a family—that's what you want.* So it wasn't hard, and I didn't feel like I had to really push anything down very big. But it was a conscious *choice* to not be gay, because I actually had a lot of internalized homophobia. I didn't *want* to be gay. I felt like it was not okay.

After a rocky divorce from Jay Gruska, Jenny continued to date men—before she fell in love, at 40, with a straight woman. "The relationship, unfortunately, turned out to be somewhat of a disaster," said Jenny, "but it was a way for me to come out and to say: *This is Jenny. This is who I am.*" When she told her brother Mark, he said, "If our grandmother Lurene [Tuttle] was still alive and she heard this, she'd throw you a luncheon." When Jenny came out to her father, John said: "Fantastic. Wonderful. How great! It's funny, because when you say this it kind of makes sense, remembering how you were as a kid."[42]§§

* * *

There was never any doubt that John would score *Saving Private Ryan*. "His music still makes me break out in goosebumps," Spielberg said in February 1998. "I know I cannot find anybody better."[43] But the absence of music was a significant part of Spielberg's concept for his new project. On the heels of *Amistad*, this was another film that had the director's gaze fixed on the fluttering American flag, but this time he was much more in his element—paying tribute to his father's generation of soldiers, and the war that had possessed his imagination since he was a child. Spielberg pushed his craft farther than ever: in his opening sequence depicting the D-Day storming of Omaha Beach, he created the most visceral, urgent vision of combat that had ever been achieved on film. It was one of many battle sequences in the movie, and Spielberg opted to leave these raw, chaotic set pieces clear of score. "Sometimes the decision *not* to have music was as powerful as other scenes that audiences are familiar with *because* of the music," said Spielberg.[44] "The battle scenes were done in a realistic way," said John. "Music really struck the emotional part of it, and quieter scenes."[45]

The story was about a small band of soldiers led by Tom Hanks's Captain Miller, charged with tracking down Private James Ryan (Matt Damon), whose three brothers all died in action. The U.S. Army takes so much pity on their poor mother that it orders this quixotic rescue mission—a symbol, in Spielberg's mind, of finding decency within the hell of war. John's lean score opens the film with a solo French horn call, a

---

§§ After several "horrible" relationships, Jenny eventually found love with Joan Henehan, a banker she met through the board at her son Ethan's high school. They married in 2006.

snare tattoo, and a stoic but warm brass figure as a flag flaps in the wind and a family follows an old man into a military cemetery in the present day. Just as John found personal inspiration for music of pain and loss, he drew on his own feelings of earnest patriotism and memories of the Second World War. He was 12 in June 1944, and "more than any particular recollection of that specific day," he said, "what I of course carry with me is memories—a vivid memory of the period when the country was so focused and completely unified in its effort in the war, that brought people together in a way that, perhaps, it hasn't happened in our history."[46]

After Spielberg's long, graphic set piece depicting the nightmare of Normandy, a resolute requiem for strings and brass plays under a scene of secretaries typing letters of condolence to the families of soldiers killed in battle. John handled this moment with subdued but lyrical grace; quiet woodwinds provide the only commentary as Mrs. Ryan goes to her front door and falls to the ground when she sees an Army general and priest pulling up the drive. John's patriotic pastorale continues as generals discuss the fate of the surviving Ryan, and General Marshall responds by reading a letter that Abraham Lincoln wrote to a widow amidst the Civil War. (When the score was recorded by the BSO at Symphony Hall, John asked Tom Hanks to read this letter to the orchestra. "Tom, very sweetly, stood up in the balcony," John said, "and they were all enormously moved by it."[47])

Whenever John's score intermittently resurfaces in the film, it's an emotional catharsis after long stretches of tension or trauma. Strings rise with hope when Miller finds a deafened soldier who knows where Ryan is, offering a much-needed surge of joy, however muted, and a return of the American hymn as Miller makes a plan and his men see his hand shaking. There's no music for the grisly death of a medic played by Giovanni Ribisi—until he begins to call out for his mama, crying like a child: "I want to go home!" Dark chords attend this moment of desolation, with the repeating bassline from the chorale rising under beautifully troubled waters. John's weary horn motif sounds as Miller reads the medic's letter and hides his own convulsion of tears, halting chords empathizing with slightly ambiguous emotion—the composer showing tasteful restraint. Miller defuses a dangerously tense situation between his men by finally revealing his peacetime profession—he's a schoolteacher—and John scores this as a holy moment with tender, tired brass chords and strings rising with warm Americana as Miller says exactly what they need to hear at one of their lowest moments: "Just know that every man I kill, the farther away from home I feel." Piano joins strings in mystical chords as the men bury their comrade Wade's body at dusk. With John's score setting the tone, Spielberg's film is somehow both about the futility of war *and* the romantic mythicism of it—particularly the romance of camaraderie and sacrifice.

There is no score under the film's climactic battle, after Miller finally finds Ryan. In the aftermath of this long, grueling sequence, the rising bassline stirs and the chorale returns as Miller lies bleeding and Ryan looks around in a daze; strings join in as a soldier calls for the medic and planes fly overhead. Miller tells Ryan to "earn this," and his death is lamented by a brass elegy and solo trumpet singing a complicated melody under a documentarian wide shot of Ryan standing over Miller's body as men scurry around them. Arguably the film's lone misstep was its contemporary bookend, where Ryan's young face morphs into the old man from the prologue, and we realize he's standing at Miller's grave. But even as Spielberg erred slightly on the side of corn here, John scored the denouement with total dignity. Finally, under the end credits, John unveiled what was ostensibly the main theme from *Saving Private Ryan*.

He composed "Hymn to the Fallen" late in the scoring process, and he and Spielberg decided to use it as an emotional epilogue. In it, wordless voices hum a serene ode to the dead, and a passionate rhythm gradually drums up with fleet string counterpoint and snares in what amounts to a more reflective, battle-scarred version of his earlier patriotic pieces like *Liberty Fanfare*. "You had the sense that we needed a kind of requiem, almost, for the people lost in the film," John said. The goal was "to do that tastefully and discreetly and quietly, and hopefully elegantly."[48] There was a sense of gravity and purpose at the recording sessions in Boston, where the Tanglewood Festival Chorus joined the BSO. "Avoid anything grandiose or operatic," John told the musicians, "while still giving more." "Play it quietly—but loving it," he told the cellos at one point. "That's it. The color you just got is the thing."[49] Yet again, Morrison provided his American trumpet sound in numerous solos.*** Spielberg loved recording *Schindler's List* in Boston, and he felt it was important to have a familial band perform this particular score: "This is a movie about a company of soldiers, and it seemed appropriate to use an experienced company of musicians who are all virtuosos," he said. "Also we really wanted the sound of this room, Symphony Hall. On a soundstage you can get acoustically correct sound, but you don't hear the air. Here you get a rich, warm sound off the walls and ceiling, and you do hear the air; Symphony Hall is an instrument, too."[50]

Saving Private Ryan was praised from nearly every corner. Critics were in awe of the battle scenes and in shock at Spielberg's emotional restraint. "For once Spielberg pulls in the reins on composer John Williams," went one of several backhanded compliments, "whose abrasive overscoring has undermined many a picture. Here Williams delivers a developed soundscape of combat, occasionally giving way to an impressionistic internal strife where the subjective silence approximates shell shock."[51] Another critic wrote that John's self-control "matches everyone's on the project, from the actors' to Spielberg's. In fact, for all the grotesque violence, this is one of the director's least manipulative or emotionally weighted movies."[52] John's score was nominated for an Oscar—he lost to Nicola Piovani's score for the Italian Holocaust film *Life Is Beautiful*. And as much as some critics scoffed at John's now-annual nomination from his peers in the music branch (*New York Times* columnist Ty Burr jokingly called it a "secret Oscar bylaw"[53]), this very guarantee seemed to backfire against him when it came time for the rest of the body to cast their vote. His ubiquity was now assured—and for many Academy members, that was reason to give the award to someone else.

*** Morrison left the BSO the following month to pursue a full-time career in the Hollywood studios.

***

With his music, John had transformed into just about every conceivable character and culture—but it's hard to imagine a more radical skin for him to slip into than the experience of Black womanhood.

When Leonard Slatkin took over the National Symphony in 1996, he played matchmaker between John and former poet laureate Rita Dove, encouraging John to read her work and consider writing a song cycle. Slatkin also asked John to write a piece based on the words of John F. Kennedy. He "dove into all the speeches and everything that Kennedy wrote," Slatkin said, "and he came back, says, 'You know, I just can't find anything that I think I could do that's any better than the words that Kennedy spoke.' He just didn't feel worthy enough to do it, and so he turned that one down."[54] John was also reluctant to attempt a vocal work, perhaps with the jeers that met *Thomas and the King* still ringing in his ears. "I am *not* a vocal composer," he always insisted. But he loved poetry, a passion that was inflamed in the late 1960s in the midst of discovering *The White Goddess*. Poems inspired him, he said, through their sound, rhythm, meter, discipline, and "all of the memory traces buried in language that resonate with us," much like the sense of smell, and how a certain aroma can bring back the memory of what his mother wore when he was five years old.[55] In early 1997, John took a look at Dove's poem "Chocolate" and started flirting with a musical setting. The poem was "a very sexy thing" about making love, and he suddenly realized: "I don't want to do this cycle with Rita Dove. I *have* to do it. This is the most fun I've had in years."[56]

They began communicating by telephone. Dove said she didn't enter into it thinking, *Here is this older white man who's going to speak for me or speak for other Black women*.

> As we talked, and as we settled on what kind of a cycle, we did a lot of talk about the arc of the piece: *Is this going to be like a single thing?* And then it became a cycle, so it became almost inevitable that it was going to be about womanhood. I couldn't give him poems about being a man. And of necessity it's going to be about *Black* womanhood. My trust in him was there from the beginning. But of course I was cautious, as one should be about everything. But my trust in him increased and increased as we talked. I thought he was not going to do any harm. I thought it was going to be great. I really did.

"As a writer," Dove added, "I have written in the persona of slaves, and of men, and all sorts of things. This idea of appropriating another culture or gender, I think, becomes serious when the writer really has their own agenda and is not honest, and is not completely humbled to it. I don't have a problem with it as long as I can tell that the person is really, really being honest. He was!"[57]

Together, John and Dove settled on six of her poems. "Inadvertently we stumbled into a series of things that really added up to the curve, the outline, the gestalt—whatever—of a woman's life," said John, who was positively giddy when talking about the cycle.

"What can you say about a woman? A woman, I suppose, is to a man God's greatest creation. Man's body is made for work, but a woman's body is made for more noble, brilliant things. What a subject! The woman and her life—all the things that happen to her. And somehow accidentally, that's how this cycle came together."⁵⁸ John would call Dove and describe what he was thinking in terms of instrumentation. "I remember a couple of times where he said, 'I hate to tell you this, but this is a terrible word to end on for a singer,'" Dove laughed. "I'd go, 'You're right, you're right.'" John suggested the title *Seven for Luck*, which meant Dove needed to write one new poem for the series. The result, "Serenade," was a kind of tribute to John. "It is perhaps the most balladic of all of the poems," she said, "and the most deliberately musical in a traditional sense. And it was sort of like: 'John, thank you for what you do.' Because, of course, he's extremely melodic—in an age where a lot of composers grumble and say melody is saccharine and overstated and obvious. I'm thinking: *It takes a lot to make a good one.*"⁵⁹

John composed the cycle for soprano Kathleen Battle, an American opera star who had sung with the Pops, and performances with the National Symphony and New York Philharmonic were announced a year in advance. But at the last minute, Battle "decided she didn't want to sing it," Slatkin said. "It's very rare that somebody will have a piece written for them and then they refuse to perform it. To this day, I don't know why she didn't want to do it. Maybe she thought it wasn't something she could really learn, or maybe it didn't satisfy her music the way she wanted to."⁶⁰ (Battle still joined John in a gala concert opening the Hollywood Bowl in June, an event honoring Ernest Fleischmann.) Her withdrawal canceled the performances scheduled in New York and at the Kennedy Center. "But John still wanted to do it," said Dove, "which I'm eternally grateful for."

John conducted the cycle's premiere with the BSO at Tanglewood in July 1998—now with Cynthia Haymon, a seasoned American soprano.††† It wasn't the usual people-pleasing fare, but John was "one of the few conductors with enough personal cachet to lure the unwary concertgoer into listening to modern music," Susan Larson wrote in her review for the *Globe*—"and what's more, liking it." Dove wore a bright carmine gown, and she took the stage to read some of her words. Haymon "inhabited Dove's gorgeous poetry and Williams' high-flying melodies," Larson noted, "showing us a child's wonder at the world, a girl's sexual awakening as summer street lights 'ping into miniature suns'... Spontaneous and heartfelt applause followed every song, especially the Caribbean-lilting, food-lusting 'Chocolate'; the nervous-ironic confessions of 'Expecting,' the real skinny on being pregnant; and the quietly menacing 'Serenade,' introduced by Ann Hobson Pilot's eloquent harp solo."⁶¹ The *Berkshire Eagle*'s Andrew Pincus was equally delighted:

> Who could resist this opening line: "When I was young the moon spoke in riddles and the stars rhymed?" John Williams couldn't.... A romantic temperament and

---

††† Gil Shaham played John's violin concerto at this same concert, the first time it was performed by the BSO.

> a gift for melody, orchestration and atmosphere supplied the necessary talismans.... Dove's words, in the first place, are both the American language as it is spoken (sometimes with a black twist) and wonderfully evocative. On top of that, Williams is a master melodist, as his film scores show, and his luscious vocal lines float on a bed of gorgeous orchestral sound. The orchestrations, in fact, sometimes swamped the voice (though printed texts were a help). But in Cynthia Haymon, Dove and Williams had a soloist as funky and rapturous as their work. The BSO sounded fully in sympathy. Who would have guessed that the composer of *Star Wars* and *Superman* could be such a romantic—and a literate one at that—when he steps out of the studios?[62]

Even the *New York Times* was impressed: "Mr. Williams traces the poems' shifting moods with fine sympathy and precision, ranging from semi-speech to full, glorious song, all of which Ms. Haymon only enhanced with splendid and versatile vocalism," wrote James R. Oestreich. "She was as captivating drawling, 'But we can't do it—naw, because the wages of living are sin,' as she was suspending an exquisite pianissimo high note on the wondrous, childlike 'And I was older than I am today.' The composer turns a large orchestra to the various purposes in Mahlerian fashion, reducing it simply to flute and cello for the wistful 'Adolescence.'"[63]

John gushed over Dove—and even sang—in a taped conversation with her for an *Evening at Pops* program which previewed three of the songs. Explaining his thought process on the poem "Song," he told her: "What I've tried to do is make elisions in the words 'When ... I ... was ... young' to extend it a little bit through the technique of singing several notes for a one-syllable word, and have the singer conjure something of the past ... so she really has to take us back with her." "I think you've got something about what I was trying to do with the poem," Dove answered. "It's almost like an incantation. She wants to recreate the moment and call us back—but she's kind of pulling us in, too." It was a vibrantly mutual admiration society, two creators sparking off each other. "Well, I hope it's worthy of your great piece," John cooed.[64] From Mahalia Jackson to Shirley Caesar and now to Rita Dove, it was apparent that John had a gift for setting the voices of Black women. "I think John truly knew how to open himself to the voice in each of the poems," said Dove, "and to inhabit it. He does this for a living. But it isn't just a living—it's a real gift in him." Dove was especially struck by John's modesty: "When I say modest or when I say humility, I think I want to stress that here's a person who felt so secure or content in his being that he could open up to others, and let himself almost disappear if necessary. To bring something out of the other person. His largesse was incredible."[65]

John spent the fall working on another piece of art music—a French horn concerto. Over the years, he also had received several requests to write an opera: "I won't say it won't happen, but I'm 66," he said, "so I had better get at it pretty soon. And there is so much on my schedule for the next several years." Still, "I find writing concert music an antidote to the straitjacket demands of the film world," he said. "It has done more for my private interest and, hopefully, to lead to some growth as a composer." John felt compelled to offer a caveat:

> I have no particular pretensions about my concert pieces. When you think of Mozart's *Requiem* or Beethoven's Ninth, it's hard to have the gall to write music. Those works can humble all of us. When I was writing a cello concerto for Yo-Yo Ma, I told him of my feelings. He argued with me that if we all thought that way, none of us would do anything.[66]

* * *

Chris Columbus was in a jam. When he heard the score for his new film, a yuletide weepy about divorce and cancer, his heart sank. "It wasn't working," Columbus said. "It's the only time this has ever happened for me. But the score just wasn't … *emotional*. So this movie that we had taken out and previewed, and everyone is sobbing at the end of it, suddenly was flat."[67]

Columbus's mother died from the same type of cancer that Susan Sarandon's character has in the film, so "it was *very* personal to me." The score for *Stepmom* had been composed by Patrick Doyle, a Scotsman who regularly worked with Kenneth Branagh. In a cruel twist of irony, the 44-year-old composer was recovering from leukemia himself when he wrote the score, which was recorded at Sony in July. Columbus had been itching to work with John again, and his rejection of Doyle's score provided a chance; in the fall of 1998, John was both available and interested. "*Twice* he basically saved my ass," Columbus said, "on *Home Alone* and *Stepmom*. And he did it in such a major way. To use a baseball analogy, he hit two grand slams in terms of elevating the picture. So I was just like: *I want to work with this guy forever.* I couldn't imagine anyone else scoring my films."[68]

Julia Roberts played the stepmom-to-be, an attractive young photographer who's just moved in with Ed Harris; the resentment his two young children, Anna and Ben, feel toward her is fueled by their mother (Sarandon). No less than five screenwriters spackled together an overlong, overcooked tale out of that simple premise, and the film suffers from melodramatics and spelling out its many, many emotions in all-caps. But the actors gave winning performances, and where the movie succeeds most is in its Christmassy, New York fairytale feeling. "I obviously have a twisted obsession with Christmas," Columbus admitted. "It appears in a lot of films. And I think John is one of these people who, I don't know if he's *obsessed* with Christmas, but he creates a feeling of Christmas and the holidays without … hitting you over the head with it."[69]

John's score for *Stepmom* is a warm blanket, a delicate snowfall, a crackling fireplace—all cashmere and hot cocoa brimming with marshmallows. He tapped into the film's seasonal feeling of picturesque autumn turning to winter in an idealized Manhattan, and wrote a romantic tone poem for strings with twinkling celeste and piano, warm oboe and French horn lines, and a few featured solos for the classical guitarist Christopher Parkening. (Interestingly, Doyle's score had also spotlighted acoustic guitar.) He wrote two major themes, both legato and liquidy. The tune mostly associated with Isabel (Roberts) is a nocturne often performed on piano, a lyrical but somewhat roaming melody that floats above lightly bobbing string chords. The other is a more melancholy musing for Jackie (Sarandon) and the cozy cloud of woe that hangs over Columbus's narrative—played with dreamy sadness on solo woodwinds. But the themes aren't strictly assigned to these characters; instead they're used to express two different facets of motherhood, the joy and the sorrow.

A motif of simple, halting string chords italicizes Jackie's cancer. Ben, whose boyish attraction to magic presaged the next project that brought John and Columbus together, inspired *Home Alone*-esque sneak-around music. John wrote a few burlesque cues—a sprightly classical dance for Isabel's photoshoot of a horse and buggy with people in period costume, and an Americana ballet for Anna that plays under her soccer game and later when she theatrically tells a boy off at school. The film is simply smothered in John's music, which is pervasive under dialogue scenes and wordless moments alike, with transitions between scenes also often smeared with plush recitative. The score itself is a beautiful wintry landscape, and John evokes emotions with delicacy and understatement—it's enchanting—but Columbus's *use* and overreliance on music contributed to the film's heavy hand. There are simply too many hanky moments dripping with sentiment: Jackie taking Anna for a horseback ride through the snow in the early morning light and talking about remembering this "for always-always"; a montage of Isabel taking photos of Jackie and her kids during a postcard-perfect day; Jackie giving the children their final gifts on Christmas morning. Syrup oozes from every frame.

Columbus refuted any suggestion that this score was ever cloying:

> I think it's akin to comedy, in a sense. John treads lightly with comedy, and he never, ever makes the mistake of being too sentimental. It's a difficult thing to define, but a schmaltzy score … you just know it when you hear it. Just watch the Hallmark Channel and you understand why it's not working. John's scores connect to people in a very human way. The guy is a bit of a wizard in terms of his ability to get inside of you, the very soul of what the best music is. And it's never sentimental. It's always just right, just enough.

Columbus had temped his film with music by Thomas Newman, because of the inherent melancholy in those scores. "John embraced that sense of melancholy that I was going for," he said, and even though the score is absent of an extra-catchy signature theme, "there's an expansive quality to that score that moves me every time I see the film."[70]

Parkening debuted the end credits suite, "The Days Between," at a concert in Oregon a few weeks before the film's Christmas release. "I've been hoping John Williams will write a concerto for guitar and orchestra, and I'm looking forward to that someday," Parkening said.[71] Reactions to *Stepmom* were polarized—even some individual reviewers were self-divided. "As a critic, I found it a contrived and tired scenario that pits working woman against stay-at-home mom," wrote Carrie Rickey of *Knight Ridder News*. "As a moviegoer, I sobbed because it plays exposed nerves as though they were violin strings in the orchestra performing John Williams' insistent score. And as a stepmother I choked up, with tears and bile, at the film's depiction of the painful emotions experienced by at least two sides of the divorce triad."[72] Less conflicted was Kenneth Turan of the *L.A. Times*: "It may be unfair to ask a film like this not to be shamelessly manipulative, but wouldn't it be nice if audiences could be trusted to feel things more or less on their own without layers of unnecessary hokum entering the picture? ... It's not surprising that every teary situation imaginable is put through its paces and that all sensitive moments are trumpeted by John Williams' insistent score."[73] There was that word again: *insistent*.

Columbus stood resolutely behind John: "There is no question he earns the sentiment.

> And he basically services the actors' performances. He understands what's going on under their skin. I don't know how he does it—it's almost like he can read their minds. But that translates into a score that never gets in the way or tells you what to feel. I don't agree with those critics who say that John is telling you what to feel. He's just probably the greatest film composer we've ever had.[74]

* * *

It would be impossible to overstate the anticipation there was for a new *Star Wars* movie—and with it, a new John Williams score. A protracted, 15-year wait had been rewarded with the Special Editions, and fandom fire had never been hotter. When a trailer was released in November 1998, people bought tickets in droves to *Babe 2: Pig in the City* just to watch the two-minute commercial and then leave. Some camped out in multiplexes all day, running from one auditorium to another to watch the trailer dozens of times.[75] For Lucas, the film was years in the making; not only had he begun to conceive a prequel trilogy back when he was making the first series, but in the interim he had patiently been building the digital technology he thought was necessary to realize his vision.

But for all the forethought and ambition and time invested in it, *Episode I—The Phantom Menace* was an elegant belly flop. Lucas's hyper-realistic fantasyland was populated with robotic characters and overconfident computer animation. His human characters—Liam Neeson as Jedi master Qui-Gon Jinn, Ewan McGregor as young Obi-Wan Kenobi, Natalie Portman as Queen Amidala, Jake Lloyd as the moppet Anakin Skywalker—seem utterly stranded in a false environment, struggling to follow invisible scene partners with their eye lines and straining for chemistry with real ones, all while struggling to enliven leaden globs of plot exposition and spaceship-babble. The film is devoid of anything like Harrison Ford's charm, the original trilogy's beautifully tactile effects, Lawrence Kasdan's witty dialogue, or Irvin Kershner's assured direction. It was a multimillion-dollar pilot program for new digital effects technology and a rote, academic thesis about the plausible origins of characters and plot threads from a beloved film series. The first sentence in the title crawl was about the taxation of trade routes—a harbinger of the epic slog to come. (The crime of Jar-Jar Binks hasn't even been mentioned yet.)

But John could look beneath the flaws to find inspiration in the broader strokes of Lucas's story—of a young slave boy with special abilities who becomes separated from his mother, of sinister political machinations sowing the seeds of an evil empire, of a wise elder warrior at odds with his spiritual order. The film is filled with prophecies and omens, fertile territory for musical foreshadowing, and at its best when it sticks to world-building spectacle. "Audiences should find the increased complexity in the mythological aspects of the story as we go deeper into the past," John said, "back to the antecedents of the characters we know so well from the first three films."[76] He had certainly supported some awkward dialogue and chintzy visuals in the old trilogy, but by the time of the prequels, "Williams is going into sort of compensatory mode," said Frank Lehman, the preeminent *Star Wars* musicologist. "Actually, it's a great boon to his talents, because he's able to write music to fill in the gaps, to suggest a depth of feeling and poignancy to these relationships that's actually not really conveyed in the dialogue."[77]

John screened *Phantom Menace* on October 1, 1998, and he began composing a few weeks later—spending three months writing two hours of bustling, highly attentive music.[78] It had been a while since he attempted a storytelling score this dense; John watched a rough cut every day, absent layers of visual effects, and picked a scene to work on at his desk. He identified a few key sequences and characters who seemed to want their own leitmotifs. A lot of the fun was in taking established characters and deconstructing or "de-composing" their themes, he said, taking them apart and writing them, "in a sense, backward." Anakin's theme, for example, is subtly rooted in the Imperial March:

> It's the kind of theme you would have for a young boy, very innocent, lyrical and idealistic. But it's made up of intervals from Darth Vader's Imperial March. Which we know—be-bom-bom-BOM-bom-bom—an archetypical evil expression. I made Anakin's theme out of those intervals by inverting them or rearranging them rhythmically or accompanying them harmonically in a different way. It sounds familiar, very sweet. But if you listen to it carefully, there's a hint [of evil].[79]

The Emperor's theme is quoted much more plainly, *oohed* low by a male choir, since the character looks and sounds just as he did in *Return of the Jedi*. But when the film ends on shots of the "mysterious" Senator Palpatine, a victorious folk anthem full of pageantry and sung by children hides the villain's theme in plain sight. The Force theme and main *Star Wars* fanfare are treated traditionally, as are spare references to Yoda's motif. But John was proud that 90 percent of his two-hour score was completely original material.

The major new centerpiece of this *Star Wars* score was a demonic battle hymn for choir and orchestra which represented the new villain, Darth Maul, and a literal duel between good and evil. Once more, John turned to *The White Goddess*, where he found an old Welsh poem, *The Battle of the Trees*, that contained the line: "Under the tongue root, a fight most dread / And another raging behind, in the head." John had this translated into various ancient languages to set for his *Star Warsian* chorale, and went with Sanskrit "because I loved the sound of it," he said. "I condensed this into 'most dread inside the head,' which seemed both cryptic and appropriate. For the funeral scene, I had my own words, 'Death's long sweet sleep,' translated into Sanskrit too." When John told Lucas about this on the scoring stage, the director laughed: "Sanskrit! That'll give the fans something to figure out."[80] "Duel of the Fates" is a Stravinskian gale of pagan passion—sort of like the Emperor's Theme on performance-enhancing drugs. John intimates it throughout the film, having chorus whisper the lyrics as Maul and Palpatine's schemes are unspooled, but the theme doesn't really explode until the big showdown in a ship hangar on Naboo, as huge bay doors dramatically open to reveal Maul in all his red-faced, horned glory. Choir and orchestra bellow about this great battle during the film's dynamic set piece—although they keep getting interrupted by the Saturday morning cartoonery of Anakin's antics up in space and Jar-Jar's goofy ground battle amid Lucas's whiplash structure. John accompanied the plight of Amidala's squad with instrumental renditions of the hymn, suggesting that *many* different fates are waging war.

Chorus played a much larger role in *Phantom Menace* score than any previous *Star Wars* film; John said he felt it "might lend a ritualistic, quasi-religious quality ... to capture the magical, mystical force that a regular orchestra might not have been able to provide."[81] An impressionistic stream of voices paints a mystical seascape for the underwater Gungan city and of Qui-Gon and Obi-Wan's adventures below. After Qui-Gon dies at the hands of Maul, the London Voices attend his funeral pyre with a minor key lament that lends a sacred, mythical air to the film's emotional climax. John wrote a stoic, no-nonsense theme for Qui-Gon, ostensibly the film's main character, which isn't introduced until halfway through the picture. (It's first heard when the Jedi master goes back to gather Anakin after the podrace.) This tune is very loosely tied to the character in its application, and doesn't suggest much personality beyond masculine determination; Qui-Gon is just as often represented by a French horn playing noble but unthematic lines. Jar-Jar has his own whimsical, bouncy motif, and the droid army has a threatening action march. Shmi, Anakin's mother, is given a pensive melody—although it too isn't heard until she's saying goodbye to her son. Strangely, the important character of Queen Amidala did not earn a theme of her own. The overall score was, on one hand, more impressionistic and atmospheric than previous *Star Wars* chapters, but even when it is providing operatic narration, John's music is more ambiguously descriptive. "He was less specifically thematic than he had been in his earlier years," said Ben Burtt. "I noticed that when the music came in for *Phantom Menace* I could hardly guess where any cue went. It seemed like there were cases where the music written for a scene in reel two can easily be used in reel seven if you needed to change something or reshape it or something. I felt it was less specific to the actual action."[82]

John also transitioned to a new style of action scoring. Even though the Korngoldian brass continued to swashbuckle, instead of a poppy dance piece like "Here They Come" or "The Asteroid Field," many of *Phantom*'s chases and races are scored with busy, frantic string runs, runaway xylophone ostinatos, and hyperactive, stuttering, almost random-sounding energy. It was still methodically married to the onscreen action, but no longer doubling as a self-contained song. "It's a different approach to action music scoring," said Lehman—"more cellular, more minimalist in some ways. Which is not to say that there aren't little melodic hooks, though they may not be as immortal as something like the 'Asteroid Field.'" Lehman posited that the shift to digital filmmaking and digital editing brought about a "newfound flexibility in chopping up cues, and a faster editing pace just in general—number of cuts per moment in time. It's harder to write long, sustained, satisfying four-square melodies when there's a chance that you'll only hear three measures' worth of it, and then the rest will be tracked from some other part of the cue or will be discarded or buried under sound effects or whatever. So there's a more modern, optimized approach, which is ostinato driven, and textural, and a little less friendly to thematic writing."[83] Still, John managed to keep pace with Lucas's wild tone shifts and careening in and out of scenes, providing a linear adhesive that valiantly glued it all together and smoothed out the rough edges to give the picture a semblance of elegant order. The score was an elegant frosting, carefully made with the finest ingredients, on a very lopsided and disappointing cake.

Using his own unique force, John augmented and ennobled the film's emotional moments—never more so than when Anakin says goodbye to his mother. Conflicting currents of bittersweet feelings swim as Qui-Gon tells Anakin he's free; the Force theme quietly foreshadows the adventures of Anakin's future son, Luke, and the score is playful and magical as he runs off to pack his things, but then it suddenly turns sad on a plaintive, childlike recorder tune. After a jarring interruption featuring C-3PO, this cue culminates with one last run-back to his mom and their tearful goodbye, an oboe singing out Shmi's theme; then resolved brass chords sound behind Anakin when he promises he'll come back to free her. Shmi's melody gives comfort as she tells him to be brave and not to look back, and the scene climaxes with a dignified but devastating quote of the Force theme as the future Darth Vader marches toward his destiny. "John's music tells the story," Lucas said at the Abbey Road sessions in February 1999. "He also creates an emotional context for each scene. In fact you can have it both ways, because you can play a scene against the emotions that are in it because the music is there to tell you the truth. The music can communicate nuances you can't see; it says things the film doesn't say."[84]

Nine hundred pages of score were recorded across 16 three-hour sessions. Guests to the scoring stage included McGregor, McDiarmid, Anthony Daniels, and Spielberg. ("Look who's here," John told the LSO—"the man who tamed dinosaurs and taught them to speak and act.") The sessions were heady and nostalgic, and more than a little frazzled; John had to make many last-minute adjustments after Lucas (at Spielberg's advice) recut the final act. "If I were to have started all over again on the last reel, I would be ready to record in *July*, with the picture already in the theaters," John sighed. "So I've been making the music fit as we go along. That's why I'm constantly telling the players to drop measures 7 to 14." Some of these musicians had played on the original trilogy, while many of them *grew up* on those old scores; the principal horn player told John he was so excited that he hadn't slept for three nights. As always, John knew just what to say to get his desired performance: "Thank you," he said after one awkward read-through. "I have learned some more things that I needed to know. I think we can get it together better, and I know I can conduct it better." Later, he told the brass and percussion: "Let's see if we can make a more noble sound." Another time: "Could you menace without getting louder? The audience should *feel* this rather than hear it." "I'd love to take it that slowly," he said at one point, his eye on the projected movie, "but I can't."[85]

John's music was swept into the wild run-up to the film's opening day: May 19, 1999. He conducted the Las Vegas Philharmonic in his classic *Star Wars* theme at an annual convention for theater owners in March,[86] and Fox produced a music video for MTV using clips and behind-the-scenes footage choreographed to "Duel of the Fates." A cutting-edge videogame based on the film was filled with his score, an afterlife for John's music that was increasingly common. Thousands of groans were heard around the galaxy when the soundtrack album, released by Sony Classical two weeks before the film, spoiled a major plot point with the track titles "Qui-Gon's Noble End" and "Qui-Gon's Funeral." Dyer, who had dropped in on the scoring sessions (just as he'd done on *Empire Strikes Back*), reviewed the soundtrack glowingly for the *Globe*: "It's a stirring and far-reaching score, one of the most ambitious that Williams has ever crafted. In it one can hear the 20 years of additional experience in composing, recording, and conducting his music and that of others that Williams brought to this task.

> Wagner wrote the librettos for his *Ring* cycle backwards, adding the "back story" that would make sense of *Siegfried* and *Die Gotterdammerung*. But Wagner had the advantage of writing the music in order, and of knowing he was composing a vast, unprecedented cycle of works. Williams has had to work backward, so among other things, his score is a triumph of professional and imaginative craftsmanship. It is also remarkably fluid; Williams knows how to change musical character within a few beats, and how to develop themes and interweave them to achieve an emotional complexity that matches the way Lucas' primal images recur throughout the films, assembling and reassembling in the memory, and accruing a different resonance every time.[87]

Many other columnists and critics reviewed the album, and in their consistently inconsistent game of plagiarism whack-a-mole, some heard Prokofiev, others Stravinsky, some Bartok, others Elgar—but they all, it seemed, felt compelled to dismiss John as a serious composer. In a fiery defense for the *Philadelphia Inquirer*, Peter Dobrin countered:

> This is the kind of admission that puts music critics right into the classical-music doghouse, but I'll say it anyway: The score for the new *Star Wars* prequel is one of the most vivid soundtracks to come out of Hollywood in years. What's more,

it's real music.... Williams is derivative, you say? It's certainly true that his music is postmodern, a pastiche of Prokofiev, Saint-Saens, Vaughan Williams and, of course, Mahler: What composer, however, sprang whole from the head of Western music? Maybe Bach. But Brahms had Beethoven. Beethoven had Haydn. Even the firebrand Stravinsky had his roots in Rimsky-Korsakov. Why shouldn't Williams be allowed his influences?[88]

To that, Dyer added: "Out of his sources, George Lucas created a personal synthesis that is original, and Williams' music is original too."[89]

The album debuted in third place on Billboard's Top 200—the only soundtrack that had ever opened in the top five.[90] Many film critics gagged on *Phantom Menace*, and some dragged the score down with it, but most found John's classical, vivacious music the film's one bright spot. "Even if you're immune to *Star Wars* on screen, you've got to hand it to composer John Williams for showing some growth when he could have simply coasted on past triumphs," admired Fred Shuster at the *Los Angeles Daily News*. "The entertaining score ... is a fluid mixture of whimsical and adventurous elements that actually holds up on its own."[91] In a conflicted review, the *Chicago Tribune*'s Michael Wilmington admitted, "there is a warmth and glow to the images in *Phantom Menace* that imbue the whole film with a sense of exploration and joy that matches composer John Williams' soaring score."[92]

John programmed suites throughout his summer conducting schedule, premiering *Phantom Menace* music in late May with the Pops and then taking it to Chicago and Hollywood. Oddly, the score was completely ignored by John's peers in the film academy; *The Phantom Menace* was only nominated for its sound and visual effects. The film made almost a billion dollars, but it was a blockbuster sensation with a phantom at its center. No one seemed to actually *like* it.[‡‡‡] John did what he had always done with lackluster material: he ennobled it. And with two more prequels guaranteed in the works, it was clear that he wasn't about to leave *Star Wars* anytime soon—and that was just fine with his ever-growing legion of fans.

* * *

While celebrating his 25th season with the BSO, Seiji Ozawa announced he would be resigning in 2002. John commemorated the anniversary with a *magico* new concert piece, *for Seiji!*, written to highlight several soloists unique to the Boston ensemble: Jacques Zoon's flute, Richard Mackey's horn, Chester Schmitz's tuba, Geralyn Coticone's piccolo. "It's really more about the orchestra doffing their cap to their leader than it is a portrayal and sound of Seiji's character," John explained. He wrote it with Symphony Hall in mind, beginning in a sonorous D note because "when the orchestra strikes a beautifully pitched low D, the hall seems at its happiest." At rehearsal, John told the orchestra the piece was a *festschrift*, a word he borrowed from novelist John

---

[‡‡‡] Among children it was a different story; this author saw the film in theaters 10 times.

Updike, "which I gather is a collection of jottings, or writings, or ruminations—you know, put together for scholars. I just thought some of these jottings might be appropriate, I hope, and perhaps remotely deserving of this event.... Something for each section, at least, to be featured in the orchestra."[93] Ozawa premiered the piece himself in April. "Heaven-storming brass fanfares, fluttering flute riffs, piccolo duetting with harp, a shimmering pitched-percussion episode, a refulgently Mahlerian string tune, and many other dazzling effects had the entire band on its mettle—attacks razor-sharp, rhythm lethally pointed, dynamics turning on dimes," wrote Susan Larson. "The whole proceeding was as smart as paint, drawing bravos from the crowd."[94] John joined his friend on stage to share a bow.

John and Ozawa were an "unlikely duo," said Kim Taylor, "but they really had fun together" (Figure 13.1). One of the things they bonded over was baseball; the Japanese music director would always say his goal was to "conduct in the strike zone."[95] On October 16, the BSO played a new arrangement John wrote of the national anthem at a Red Sox game. Ozawa and John were frequently spotted together at games that fall—and each time they attended, the Red Sox won. Both men were private and serious, but unpretentious. "They just understood each other on different levels," said Taylor, "as only two artists of that stature really can."[96]

Figure 13.1. John and Seiji Ozawa with friends at Tanglewood, July 12, 1997 (Photo by Alan E. Solomon, Courtesy of John Williams).

* * *

Another friend of John's suffered an unspeakable tragedy that fall. Carl St.Clair had been an assistant at the Pops before taking over the Pacific Symphony in Orange County, California. In August, his 18-month-old son, Cole, drowned in a swimming pool; his wife was sitting in a nearby hot tub, but was unconscious from a diabetic seizure.[97] Two weeks later, St.Clair heroically returned to the podium to conduct a program of all John Williams music. The applause was potent when he opened with the *Olympic Fanfare and Theme*. "I knew when the music started, I'd be a lot better," St.Clair said, telling his audience that John's music "captures so vividly the many emotions experienced by mankind, from exaltation to the deepest sorrow."[98]

Sorrow suffused John's final film of the millennium. *Angela's Ashes* was a 1996 memoir by Frank McCourt about the author's miserable, impoverished Irish childhood, and Alan Parker's bleak, desaturated adaptation was one long slog of suffering. In the film, as in life, Frank's numerous child siblings die, his deadbeat dad drinks and disappears, and his mom is prostituted to her abusive cousin. Cramped quarters, buckets of human waste, and endless sheets of rain added to the mirthless carousel of despair, which McCourt gave his stamp of approval but most critics and audiences found intolerable. Still, it's not hard to understand John's attraction to the story—he *asked* if he could score the film, in fact, explaining that he loved the book and its "idiosyncratic prose."[99] His own Irish heritage and facility with melodic melancholia made him a square fit, and Parker's gray images practically begged for John's musical warmth.

The resulting score was "very subtle and restrained, and both of us, actually, were very keen not to go into the clichés of scores that are always associated with Irish films," said Parker, the English stylist behind *Midnight Express* and *Evita*. "We made a pact, John and I, very early on that there would be—from an instrumental point of view—no bodhrán drums and uilleann pipes…. The Riverdance mentality we were trying to avoid, quite frankly."[100] Instead, it should be "an emotionally direct score," John said. "I thought that probably was a right decision. I found the film to be a kind of chamber piece in the sense that you had the father and the mother and the children—four or five principal parts. Obviously, the music shouldn't be scaled on a Strauss opera; it would have been too big for the film." John's intimate chamber score features piano, harp, oboe, and cello, "set in front of a string orchestra."[101]

It is essentially an endless repetition and variation of two melodies, both parts of the same main theme. The principal tune is a minor key piano cantilena that sings over a slightly Irish piano motto rhythm. In its development throughout the score, John handed both strands to a variety of his featured solo instruments. His other theme is a keening, heaving adagio, which John gave to solo oboe in the beginning of the film—a tenderness offered to the young protagonist, Frankie. When Frankie's father fails—*and fails and fails*—to find work, John lamented the family's plight with the adagio on a solo cello. He alternately gave it to graceful piano and harp as well as impassioned full string orchestra, depending on the quietness of the moment.

The score is full of expressive solos of deep feeling, and these elegiac melodies underscore scenes but also just as frequently act as transitions, sometimes only for a few bars—emotional stitching for the tatty rags of Frank's wretched story. John wrote a second string adagio—or more specifically, a string *prayer*. "Angela's Prayer" has a more soaring, swirling, petitionary character, a close relative to some of the lamentations in *Schindler's List*. This adagio accompanies the McCourt family's initial ocean voyage to Ireland; later, mystical celeste and high string chords, aching with anticipation and suspension, hover over a grown-up Frank as he watches a lunar eclipse with his neighbors. After saying goodbye to the ghosts of his brothers and his life in Ireland, accompanied by a softly wrenching piano and cello duet of the adagio, Frank approaches the Statue of Liberty and a new life by boat, and John celebrates the film's one hopeful moment with a comforting new anthem for winds and strings—tagged with one final, redemptive brass intonation of the adagio theme as the anguish fades to black.

This was a dramatic bridge too far for *Associated Press* critic Matt Wolf, who found it "disconcerting to find generic emotions, with soaring music to match, replacing McCourt's idiosyncratic vision, as if composer John Williams were on Steven Spielberg duty."[102] (If *only* Spielberg had graced this material with his gift of dramatic balance.) "Parker's well-meaning adaptation is unrelentingly sodden," wrote the *Washington Post*'s Rita Kempley.[103] "Knowing the truth of *Angela's Ashes* doesn't make it in any way moving," Mick LaSalle burned in the *San Francisco Chronicle*. "It just makes the audience feel guilty for not caring. Here's some advice: Don't feel guilty."[104] Most reviews ignored the score altogether—the film's one saving grace—though *Salon* found it "mercilessly swelling."[105]

Parker only worked with John this one time, but he cherished the experience. "John Williams is *the* great maestro," the director said. "A sheer, sheer joy working with the man."[106] When *Angela's Ashes* earned John his 38th Oscar nomination, it distinguished him as the most Oscar-nominated person alive.

* * *

Paranoia about Y2K aside, the approach of a new millennium felt like a bright morning was dawning for the world. John was prepared to go in an exciting new direction—embracing modern minimalism and highly caffeinated Soviet influences, as well as the jazz of his youth—following Spielberg down unexpectedly dark visions of the future, Lucas down disappointingly plastic visions of the past, and joining forces with a boy wizard whose adventures would endear a whole new generation of children to John Williams. "With all its drawbacks," John said as the 20th century concluded, "I never forget that writing for the movies makes it possible for me to reach people and move them. That's one thing about which a film composer—if the film he scores is a success—does not need to worry."[107]

14
Where Dreams Are Born, 2000–2003

> *It's like when you smell bread baking and you think of your mother's kitchen. It's that kind of sensual connection, an aural memory. That's a successful score.*
>
> —John Williams, 2001[1]

As the new century dawned, John wrote a score appraising the prior one. *The Unfinished Journey* was a short documentary created by Spielberg from a collage of archival images and footage, with narration by the likes of Maya Angelou, Sam Waterston, and Bill Clinton, based on historical texts that were curated by historian Doris Kearns Goodwin. It premiered half an hour before the year 2000 in Washington, D.C., at an all-star New Year's Eve gala thrown by the Clinton White House. Everyone from actor Will Smith to opera singer Renée Fleming was on hand for the epic celebration, where Spielberg's film was projected onto giant screens on either side of the Lincoln Memorial.

John met Hillary Clinton at the White House around the release of *Amistad*, "and she talked to me about working with Steven Spielberg to create some special event for the millennium," he said. "A year went by and we heard no more about it, but early last year we got the go-ahead to develop a 20-minute film about America in the 20th century. The film is in several tableaux."[2] The chaptered montages—on Immigration and Building, The Country at War, Popular Entertainment, Arts and Sports, Civil Rights and the Women's Movement, and Flight and Technology—offered John a canvas to write a freestanding six-movement concert piece about the "American Journey," which is what he eventually renamed the work. For the premiere, he conducted a 100-piece orchestra along with the Army Herald Horns, choirs, and marching units of the U.S. Armed Forces.[3] "There is so much for Americans to be proud of," John said,

> even in some of our misfires and our outright failures. For example, in the fifth movement, "Civil Rights and the Women's Movement," you see the dogs and the water hoses and you also hear, combined with the music, the ennobling words of Dr. King. It gives us a sense that we have come through some hellish fire *together*. That was our take. We wanted to look at the good things and the bad things and frame them in such a way as to take heed, and to take heart at the same time, and have this be an uplifting experience.[4]

The concert was broadcast live on CBS. Everything had to be timed perfectly, with live picture accompaniment and multiple narration cues, and the piece ending *one minute* before midnight and a big fireworks show. There was a single dress rehearsal with everybody involved—everybody except Bill Clinton, because the president was busy. Someone stood in Clinton's place and read his lines, which accompanied the beginning and end of the 20-minute piece. "I was terribly worried," John said. "How is the president going to measure this out and be perfect?" John still hadn't seen Clinton before the performance, which took place in the freezing cold after 11 p.m., John's breath visible in the air. The music and picture started—and Clinton appeared at the podium reading his lines, right on cue. At an afterparty dinner in the White House, Clinton ran over and said, "John! I really nailed it, didn't I?" John said, "Yes sir, you did."[5]

American Journey became a fixture on John's concert programs, a full-scale concert work that expressed his own optimistic, romantic feelings about his country, without the constraints or caveat of a fictitious story. The piece begins with unfurling fanfare and pride and New England joie de vivre, then moves into the thunder and noble sorrow of wartime—an American hymn with echoes of *Born on the Fourth of July* and *Saving Private Ryan*. A rousing rodeo passage evokes Copland and Bernstein before a whimsical, syncopated dance celebrates athletics with several acrobatic solos moving around the orchestra. A gospel and blues rhythm marches under a yearning, searching melody in the work's highlight—the Civil Rights episode—which literally continues to *lift up*. The final movement paints a serene, pastoral portrait of American ingenuity and promise.

John's patriotic mood carried over into his first feature of the new millennium. "The American Revolution was a great event, but it seems most American schoolchildren don't know much about it," he said, when asked why he wanted to score *The Patriot*. "Also from a musical point of view, there were the demands of a large-scale action canvas."[6] Written by *Saving Private Ryan*'s Robert Rodat, *The Patriot* was directed by Roland Emmerich, the German fabulist who had recently blown up the White House in *Independence Day* and wrecked New York City with a computerized remake of *Godzilla*. This was the director's gambit at a more serious, dramatic epic, but even so, he was incapable of hiding his penchant for mythologizing and delighting in destruction.

Emmerich was a "super fan" of John's, having fallen in love with the music of *Jaws* and *Star Wars* like so many others. "I was a little bit starstruck when I first met him," the director said. "It's kind of like meeting one of your all-time legends."[7] Emmerich and his creative partner, Dean Devlin, had mostly worked with British composer David Arnold, who fully expected to score *The Patriot*. Arnold even composed a main theme at the beginning of production and recorded it with a full orchestra—but it was an audition for the job. "That was the first time that Roland had ever actually asked me to demo something," said Arnold, who based his theme on an old Welsh folk song. "I had the sense that something might be up." Within 10 minutes of Emmerich receiving the tape, Arnold got a call saying: "We're going with John Williams."[8] "That didn't go very well," Emmerich said. "I think he was pretty upset about it, too. But what can I do, right?"[9] In hindsight, Arnold had a dry sense of humor about it: "*I would bump me for John Williams.*"

John said he was excited to score a movie starring Mel Gibson, here playing a veteran of the French and Indian War, Benjamin Martin, whose own atrocities haunted him into becoming a pacifist opposing the fight against the British. But when a psychopathic Colonel Tavington, played by a snide Jason Isaacs, brings the fight to the doorstep of his South Carolina plantation and murders his teenage son, Martin pulls out his old hatchet and leads a savage guerrilla campaign of militiamen, terrorizing the King's Army into defeat. Heath Ledger played Martin's oldest son, Gabriel, in what was really a shameless saga of agitprop melodrama, a film which pitched the American Revolution as a *Braveheart*-style revenge story endowed with David versus Goliath righteousness. It was also, considering, a rather good one.

John spotted the film in March and composed throughout April. "It's a big assignment and a daunting job," he said. "It requires a lot of music. I'm not erudite on the topic of 18th century American music, although I know that William Billings was the most popular composer at the time. When I was at the Boston Pops we used to play some of his music." John didn't use any of Billings's work here, "but some of the folkloric thematic material I wrote was in the vein of what memory told me was the popular idiom of the day, adapted for the orchestra."[10] He created two major tunes: a heroic riding anthem with a strong blood tie to one of his themes from *American Journey*, and a love theme for young Gabriel and Anne that recalled American folk song, especially when played on solo fiddle by Mark O'Connor—a bluegrass star who made the hit album *Appalachia Waltz* with Yo-Yo Ma and bassist Edgar Meyer. "His sound has, for me, a very genuine and true ring of a development of the country music of Appalachia," said John, who also brought in 16 piccolos for some fife-style cues and a quicksilver countermelody to the main theme in his end credits suite.[11]

"We talked a lot about honor, because the Mel Gibson character has a lot of honor—but he also has a deep and dark past," said Emmerich. "Overall it was about creating an honorable person which has a dark undertone."[12] The film opens with a dark French horn motif for Martin's alter ego, "The Ghost," a nickname he earns for sneaking up and ambushing British troops, but also a reference to his grisly past. Early scenes of the Martin family's life on the farm before the war are presented with an idyllic, romanticized glow, and John wrote an overture of pastoral American paradise using his two main themes. (Even their freedmen and women servants seem blissful.) John wrote a string chorale that conveys Martin's love for his late wife, a theme he called "The North Star," which was a celestial metaphor for the children's absent mother. This motif reprises when Gabriel marries Anne and Martin gives his new daughter-in-law a North Star pendant that belonged to his wife.

The entire score is sumptuously melodic: weary trumpet solos attend Martin's lonely pacifism and worry for his children; there are abundant string adagios for the strong undercurrent of sadness and loss; the bloodthirsty British are treated with a drum rhythm like "The British Grenadiers" on steroids, along with a fleet fox hunt trumpet motif and low chugging cellos. When Tavington shoots young Thomas

Martin, John's subtle elegy for the scene helps it achieve genuine poignancy; likewise, when Gabriel is taken as a prisoner of the British army, who set the house on fire and take the help captive, John responded with a stunning immolation cue. (Another occurs later, when Anne and her fellow townspeople are locked inside a church set ablaze.) Gibson's eyes turn fierce and he runs inside the house for his gear; the score goes into a bleary-eyed brass frenzy as he emerges like a bloodthirsty John Rambo and enlists his sons to join him in going after the Brits. There's an inherent tension in the film: Martin keeps restating that violence is terrible and he has to live with the guilt of all the people he's murdered—John scored his first bloodletting with a slow movement of tragic Americana—but Emmerich's film also casts him as a badass action hero, who seems to single-handedly win the Revolutionary War. John's music elegantly threads this dichotomy, at turns scoring endangerment, noble sacrifice, and 18th-century American valor with equal conviction. Somehow, the earnestness of it all harmonizes into a consistent tone of pride and courage but at a terrible cost.

Spielberg's influence is heavy on the film: the carnage of battle sequences is captured with documentarian grit, Tavington stalks the Martin house like a velociraptor, and the horrific slaughter of helpless, screaming civilians channels the energy of *Schindler's List*. And it is all packaged within a devout love letter to America's better angels, a warm, three-hanky drama that, at its heart, is about family. John had no trouble getting on its wavelength, and the resulting score is an all-American paean. He excelled at these larger-than-life, mythical presentations of history—which caused some critics to recoil. Several took umbrage with "the excruciating finale, a righteous exclamation point," as Chris Garcia at the *American-Statesman* described it: "John Williams' score—all crashing cymbals and exultant trumpets—swells as Gibson runs in orgasmic slow-motion, carrying a shiny new flag through cannon smoke. I mean, how can you take this seriously?"[13]

"I was actually surprised when I made the movie how many Americans didn't know the intricacies of the Revolutionary War," said Emmerich.

> They always mixed it up with the Civil War—which drove me crazy. I said to John: "This was when the first democracy was created. This is a moment which we have to celebrate—without being on the nose, but you have to celebrate that." Because I also knew that this movie will be shown a lot in schools; and it actually *is* shown a lot in schools.... That's why I felt a certain responsibility, especially as a German. I questioned John a little bit about it, too, and it was also why he wanted to do this movie, because he thinks that the script captured this torn situation [when] farmers all of a sudden had to become soldiers again.[14]

John had plenty of opportunities to work a suite from *The Patriot* into concerts that summer. In June, he was honored with the first Hollywood Bowl Hall of Fame award, along with country singer Garth Brooks, in a gala concert conducted by John Mauceri. In his introduction of the award, Spielberg said: "No one knows how to write film music that goes straight to your heart and your soul better than John. I wouldn't be here if it weren't for him. He's as responsible for my career as me. He's my brother, father confessor, and my conscience."[15]

* * *

John also premiered a new concert work that summer. *TreeSong* was a violin concerto in all but name, written for Gil Shaham and inspired by a specific tree in Boston's Public Garden where John liked to go for walks. "I grew infatuated with this Chinese tree, the dawn redwood, which stands in the southwest corner," he said. "It not only looked lovely, but it seemed animate, even intelligent." One afternoon, he was walking through the local Arnold Arboretum with Dr. Siu-Ying Hu, a retired Harvard botanist, and "speaking to her about the tree I loved so much in the Public Garden when she stopped me. 'Is it like this one?' she asked, pointing to a nearby tree. I said it was, and she said, 'I planted them, back in the 1940s.'"[16] The Metasequoia was considered extinct, but when Hu came to the United States she brought over a pound of seeds from a small forest of the trees still growing in western China. "The tree became referred to as the 'living fossil,'" John said. "Standing before the tree one can sense its age and feel its wisdom." He named the first movement in *TreeSong* "Doctor Hu and the Metasequoia," and although the piece doesn't try to describe the tree "per se," John explained, "it does attempt, in my mind at least, to connect, to the degree possible, the great beauty and dignity of this magnificent conifer with the elegance and grace of Gil Shaham and his art."[17]

Shaham was a virtuoso born in Illinois but raised and trained in Israel, who had played with John many times before; he fondly remembered a concert at Tanglewood where a thunderstorm forced them all to huddle backstage and John talking sweetly to Shaham's young daughter, Ella. "He spoke to her a lot about trees," Shaham recalled. "He loves trees, and has a passion for them." The violinist was struck, like so many others, by John's modesty: "He says, 'Oh Gil, I don't really play violin, and maybe you have some suggestions.' And there were never any suggestions because his writing was really so fluent for violin. Every instrumentalist that I've spoken to about his music has said the same thing. Harpists: 'He writes so well for the harp.'" John was so self-deprecating about his conducting skills, Shaham said, that "you'd like to shake him."[18]

John's tree poem begins "Dreamily," in an enchanted forest of mystical broken chords and chimes, and the violin waking from a deep sleep. While the melody follows a jagged, dissonant path—like much of John's concert works—the orchestra's romantic atmosphere is more of a piece with his tonal film work. The forest erupts with activity in the second movement, a showcase for scurrying virtuosity on the violin; the orchestra swells to a magnificent, cinematic crescendo, then clears the floor for an extended solo. The initial broken chords slowly return on harp, and the final movement offers a song—John called it "The Tree Sings"—filled with desire and deep feeling, drifting back into the *magico* sylvan atmosphere of the opening. "He's always so modest about *TreeSong*," said Shaham.

> I think it's a great masterpiece, and I thought so from the moment I saw it. It's an incredibly moving melody, "The Tree Sings." Something very beautiful, and sort of

the perfect vehicle for a violin to sing. But he always is very modest. He's like, "Well, maybe I should revise that. Maybe I should tinker with it." "No, it's great! I love it."[19]

The concerto debuted at Tanglewood in July on the same program as John's antique *Essay for Strings*. "He has betrayed his druid's instincts before in a bassoon concerto, which he titled *Five Sacred Trees*," Andrew Pincus wrote in the *Berkshire Eagle*.

Lush, lyrical and all but mystical in its adoration, *TreeSong* unfolds quietly and slowly over an 18-minute span. In this, the work is a distant cousin of Chausson's *Poeme* for violin and orchestra. But *TreeSong* sings with Williams' personal brand of lyricism as the solo violin soars rapturously over an orchestra tinted by harp tones and delicate percussion. The music positively glows, as well it should in a performance under the composer's ministrations. That radiance may be a problem. *TreeSong* is such a deeply personal statement—such a retreat from the world of *Star Wars* and *Private Ryan*'s war—that its mysteries and beauties come to seem excess. The listener needs to be a bit of a mystic himself to enter into its raptures.[20]

The *New York Times*' James R. Oestreich compared the piece to Yo-Yo Ma's new polycultural venture, the Silk Road Ensemble: "It combines Western lyricism in the violin with fine, subtle Orientalizing in the orchestra, owing partly, no doubt, to Mr. Williams' cinematic sense."[21]

A few months later, the Los Angeles Opera announced that John was writing an original opera which would premiere in their 2004 season.[22] "It is true that I have discussed the possibility of writing an opera with Placido Domingo," John told Dyer, "but the matter is purely in the discussion phase at this point, and there is no commitment on my part or theirs, for that matter."[23] A spokeswoman for LA Opera confirmed that "nothing is definite," but insisted that Domingo, the company's artistic director, had cleared the announcement with John before the news conference. "He is such a respected composer and such a respected musician, and his music is loved throughout the entire world," said LA Opera conductor Kent Nagano. "So I felt that if his great gift for lyricism and for melody could be put into a framework of an operatic-like structure, this is something the whole world would notice."[24] John hedged, always quick to assert his discomfort in writing vocal music: "Better minds than mine have tried opera and not been successful—it is an art that has had difficulty renewing itself, especially in this country. Vanity being what it is, one is always tempted by these things, though—opera is a tantalizing prospect for any composer." He noted that Ozawa had asked him several times about writing an opera: "We never discussed the subject or the situation, whether it would be in Japan or Vienna or Tanglewood, but I'm very grateful to him for his continuing encouragement."[25]

It was Nagano's idea to have John compose an opera based on a short story by Woody Allen.[26] *The Kugelmass Episode*, published in the *New Yorker* in May 1977, was a whimsical tale about a disaffected married man who finds a magical cabinet that allows him to travel inside the world of novels; he chooses to enter *Madame Bovary* and begins an affair with its title character, with comically disastrous results.[27] (It was a foreshadow of the plot in Allen's 2011 film, *Midnight in Paris*.) Nagano secured permission from Allen, although Allen declined to adapt it himself ("He said he knew nothing about the theater," John explained), so Nagano contracted his old friend Michael Walsh, an American novelist who said that "since it was clearly both a comic opera and a French bedroom farce with fantastical elements, and since Williams was a Hollywood composer, and since Kent was at that time determined to bring the Opera and the Industry closer, I conceived it as a magic realism piece, using film as part of the overall production design to portray the sequences in the magic box and to heighten the contrast between Kugelmass' dumpy New York City apartment and Emma Bovary's life in 19th century Normandy." Walsh wrote a detailed treatment, and he and Nagano went to John's house to make a presentation—a congenial meeting that lasted for several hours.[28]

John loved the *idea* for the opera. He began to imagine a "Mozartian" ending, not in Allen's story, where six famous French novelists from the period gather together for "a vocalized complaint in counterpoint about why they haven't had an opportunity to go to New York and visit the Plaza Hotel."[29] But he called Walsh a few weeks later and said he felt the material wasn't right for him, "too Noo Yawk and urban for him to do it justice," in Walsh's memory. "Further, he said that writing an opera, something he had never done before, was a huge time commitment, and that if it failed he really didn't want that on his resume, so to speak. All very understandable. And that was that."[30] Mark Swed wondered if this project was always going to be dead in the water because of John's friendship with Previn and Mia Farrow, who were both enraged by Allen's tabloid-fodder affair with their young adopted daughter, Soon-Yi Previn, as well as his alleged molestation of Farrow's adopted daughter, Dylan. "André absolutely despised Woody," noted Swed,[31] and Farrow remained close friends with John, often joining him at Tanglewood every summer. "I don't know a better person," Farrow said. "And through all of the upheavals in my life, Johnny's been there. Without confronting anything head on. He just provides company. Company and comfort. And you can forget your woes, and admire the trees, and talk about what we're reading."[32]

Years later, John said he still thought the *Kugelmass* opera was a fabulous idea, but one that needed a libretto by Allen himself, or Mel Brooks—someone with a comedy vocabulary. But, he claimed it was mostly his insecurity that stopped him from pursuing the project any further. He told Domingo: "This opera thing is not my specialty. I'm not a vocal composer, and I'm 65 years old, and I don't know anything about the theater." Domingo laughed, and said, "I just asked [Tōru] Takemitsu"—the great Japanese composer—"to write an opera, and Takemitsu said, 'I'm not a vocal composer, I'm 65 years old, and I know nothing about the theater.'" On reflection, John said: "Takemitsu never wrote an opera—and nor will I."[33]*

The BSO's 2000 season opened with a fundraising gala to celebrate the 100th birthday of Symphony Hall, where John played a six-hand piano piece with Ozawa

---

* As of 2024, conductor Gustavo Dudamel was actively trying to convince John to write an opera. "It's my dream—because he would be amazing," Dudamel said. "He will do the opera of the 21st Century." (Gustavo Dudamel to TG, January 12, 2024.)

and Keith Lockhart.[34] The following February, Ozawa conducted John's revised cello concerto with the orchestra. "This is a very complicated piece," Ozawa said, "and very strong."[35] John always felt the concerto had been rushed for its premiere on that rainy night at Tanglewood in 1994: "I was in a frenzy to finish it in time. Once I heard it, one of the things I wanted to do was reduce the orchestration and adjust the balances." He was never content with the finale, so he rewrote it "putting in more extended lyrical themes, more opportunities for Yo-Yo to play singing, cantilena lines. I am now much happier about the piece."[36] John was always "fierce about re-examining his scores," said Ma. "In between performances of the concerto he would actually send me a new copy with slight changes, because he thought, *You know, I think this is a better way to express this.* So his connection to the craftiness of what he does is total.... And it's the ultimate mastery, but with humility. He's questioning: Is this good enough? Is this okay?"[37] Dyer was enamored of the revitalized concerto, which now "stands as a portrait of Ma's artistic personality. At the same time, it reveals more of Williams than his famous film scores do. The music is so personal that it is also a self-portrait—and a tribute to the music and kinds of music that Williams loves best."[38]

That same month, John's longtime friend at the BSO, Kim Smedvig, married singer James Taylor in a small ceremony at a Boston Church. It was John who inadvertently introduced the two, back when Taylor made his debut performance with the Pops in 1993. "I was quite nervous to perform with one of the world's best symphony orchestras my first time out, and John made me feel so welcome and at ease," said Taylor, who became a fixture with the Pops and at Tanglewood thereafter.[39] Smedvig had a meet-cute with Taylor in the green room—she broke her own rule of never entering before a performance, but she needed to confirm where Taylor was born because she was giving a pre-concert talk; the next day, the singer called her to inquire about his missing pocket watch, a gift from his grandfather, which had been stolen. Two years later, Taylor called Smedvig out of the blue, asked if she remembered him, and would she like to have dinner with him? They became inseparable and, eventually, engaged.[40]

Smedvig's parents were both gone by now, and she asked John to walk her down the aisle. Before the wedding, John was at the Four Seasons suite where Smedvig and her nieces were nervously getting ready; he sat down at the piano and calmly serenaded them with classical music. John often ate bananas for the potassium, and Smedvig asked if he could keep one in his coat in case she felt faint. "Of course, Angel," he said. At the intimate ceremony in Emmanuel Episcopal Church, their mutual friends Previn and Ma performed the music. John rarely called her "Kim": on one of their lengthy tours to Japan with the Pops, he learned about the diminutive "chan," a Japanese term of endearment affixed to names—usually children, or adorable pets. So he started calling her "Chan-Chan," essentially *Baby-Baby*. "It's sweet," she said. "He *always* calls me that."[41]

* * *

Spielberg had not written a screenplay since *Close Encounters of the Third Kind*. But after Stanley Kubrick died in 1999, Spielberg locked himself in a room for several weeks and emerged with *A.I. Artificial Intelligence*. It was a project that had obsessed Kubrick for decades; he recruited no less than five different writers to attempt an adaptation of a 1969 short story by Brian Aldiss, *Super-Toys Last All Summer Long*, about a future robot boy. Kubrick wanted to explore the story's mythical implications about creation and mothers, and he saw it as a powerful *Pinocchio* allegory—but he was never happy with the screenplays he tortured his writers to compose, and he was never sure technology could achieve what was inside his head. It was seeing *E.T.* that convinced Kubrick that he wanted a similarly sentimental approach, and it was *Jurassic Park* that convinced him the effects were now possible; he struck up a friendship and transcontinental conversation with Spielberg via phone and fax that lasted nearly 20 years. "At one point," John noted, "Kubrick said to him, 'You know, *you* should direct this picture.'"[42] When Kubrick died, Spielberg was compelled to honor his friend's wish.

The resulting film was a fascinating hybrid: Spielberg staged and shot it in ways that were more icily Kubrickian, and he retained most of the plot points and dramatic emphases he found in the story treatments and notes from his late friend; the movie's design was almost completely based on the hundreds of concept sketches that Kubrick commissioned from the British artist Chris Baker (aka Fangorn). Yet it was also a deeply personal story for Spielberg who, as John once joked, had "a *Pinocchio* fetish"—another story about a lost boy, abandoned by his parents, searching the skies for love and acceptance. *A.I.* was one of the director's most profound stories, beginning with an existential conversation about whether love that is programmed is real love, and the question: "Didn't God create man in order to love *him*?" It was also profoundly sad: a professor invents a robot child from the grief of losing his own son; an emotionally paralyzed couple agrees to "adopt" the robot, named David, because their biological son is in a coma; but when the robot, played by a beatific Haley Joel Osment, makes them too uncomfortable, he is left stranded in a forest and he sobs and begs as his mother drives away. Believing that he needs to find the Blue Fairy in order to become a real boy, David wanders the earth—through the purgatory of a "Flesh Fair," where humans kill robots for sport, and to his factory of origin where he confronts the meaninglessness of his own existence—then plummets into the ocean in despair. There, he finally finds the Blue Fairy, or at least her likeness, and petitions her to make him real in a hopeless prayer that lasts 2,000 years and into a new ice age. Awakened by highly advanced robots, David is given the chance to spend one last day with his mother—artificially resurrected using cloning technology. He falls asleep next to her, smiling, perhaps dying, in an ending that some critics found unforgivably sappy and a collapse into Spielberg's worst impulses. But it was, in fact, *Kubrick's* ending ... and a Rorschach test for viewers, many others of whom found it unbelievably tragic.

John responded to this heartbreaking fable with, in this author's opinion, the best score of his entire career. He met the future with icy atmospheres and modern minimalism, with techno brutality for the dystopian cities filled with sin and bloodlust. But for David he composed a lullaby, a melancholy song that captures the boy's innocent longing and questing for Mother's love. John wrote an angelic aria for the Blue Fairy, intoned by a wordless female voice over shimmering orchestration during David's long underwater prayer. Teddy, David's robot bear companion and Jiminy Cricket surrogate, has a sympathetic, curious motif for oboe. The score "is quite schizophrenic, at least in my mind," John confessed. "Very different from the things that Steven and I have done before—with the possible exception, maybe, of *Close Encounters*. I think it's closer to that in its timbral aspect."[43] It may have contained many personalities, but it was also deliriously free. "I felt like I had a finer set of brushes or opportunities and I was offered a considerable amount more freedom of musical expression," he added. "So much of what we have to do in film is restricted by the length of the scene or the texture and style of what the music needs to be to really marry with the scene itself. In the case of *A.I.* it was a broader canvas that offered the opportunity to stretch a little more than usual."[44]

Caught in the strange vortex of Kubrick and Spielberg, John approached David's odyssey with a fitting complexity, even contradiction. His leitmotifs, as catchy and hummable as anything he ever wrote, mirror the story like a fairy tale—John in heroic narrator mode—but within a musical current of impressionism and terrifying environment. He honored Kubrick's penchant for classical needle-drops, which famously included everything from Strauss waltzes to Ligeti choral nightmares, within the idiom and palette of his score—although the only explicit musical wish stated in Kubrick's *A.I.* jottings was to use Richard Strauss's 1911 opera, *Der Rosenkavalier*; John folded a piece of that Viennese chocolate into a scene where David and his companion, Gigolo Joe, arrive in Rouge City. "We don't know why he wanted it," John said, "but it's the one thing he stipulated."[45] Joe, a robot lover and David's unlikely father figure, is a walking jukebox who soundtracks his lovemaking sessions with romantic music. John selected a handful of songs from the 1930s, and wrote and recorded new orchestral accompaniments to original vocals by Dick Powell and Fred Astaire.

The heart-wrenching scene where David is abandoned in the woods received its own theme—an emotional storm, horror music for the heart that climaxes with loud, cascading piano runs. After the painful poignancy of David's long, unanswered prayer, the film's surprising fourth act features a hypnotic reprise of the Blue Fairy theme as David speaks to a simulation of the fairy, followed by an extension of the melody for solo harp and cello when the leader of the advanced Meccas—voiced serenely by Ben Kingsley—explains the limits of bringing back David's mother. David doesn't care that it can only be for one day, or that she'll be disoriented and possibly horrified. So the fairy-tale wish is granted, and David's final day with Monica, "The Reunion," is accompanied by John's emotional magnum opus—a yearning, resolved development of his lullaby theme. John said:

> I wrote half a dozen of these examples, not fully extended, and played them for Steven. We kept working on the last scene, the death of the mother, and I would play these themes on the piano and we would lay them against the film. And the one that we finally used seemed, to both of us, to be the right expression. It's very

simple, although it has its complexities. And it's also very direct. That scene is about seven minutes long—so it's a long stretch of material for a cantilena of that particular type. If it works, it's the result of our being able to make some kind of emotional connection with associations of lullaby, of a connection between a child and a mother. It seemed like the right solution.[46†]

Perhaps the conclusion of *A.I.* is a sweet, happy ending, or maybe it's unbearably bleak. Every human on earth is dead, after all, and David's long, miserable plight ends in a bed with his mother's corpse. But either way it's read, John, at least, provided David with musical salvation. "I think the thing that's unique about *A.I.*, for me at least, is the essential spiritual aspects of what it was examining," he said—

the idea that to be able to love someone is the thing that defines humanity in the end. The end of the film, when David—who's been looking for his mother and wanting to be human all these centuries now, and his mother has her final biological death ... he is able to die at the end of the film, and thereby achieving his humanity. By being able to die, he's proven himself to be human—which is the one thing we all share, we all eventually will do. So these are subjects that are abstract and spiritual and very personal, and they go right to where music *can* speak to. Music is really about this kind of thing at its core.[47]

A.I. baffled audiences and critics when it came out in June 2001. It was much darker than some expected, and much too saccharine for others. For his part, while he was editing the film Spielberg turned to producer Bonnie Curtis and said: "I don't care what anyone ever says: I just made a good movie."[48] *A.I.* earned $236 million worldwide, which was boffo box office for anybody but Steven Spielberg. "We didn't think it would be a big audience film, but I guess we were wrong," said John. "There's such an interesting mix of Stanley and Steven in it, and such powerful themes—the *Pinocchio* myth and love conquering death and time."[49]

John had the idea of converting his "Reunion" lullaby into a pop song, titled "For Always," with lyrics by Cynthia Weil—a Brill Building veteran who, with her husband Barry Mann, wrote several early rock hits. John had heard the debut album of Josh Groban, and he asked the young tenor to sing a duet with Belgium-born Lara Fabian, another trained singer swimming in the confluence between pop and classical. Groban was only 20, plucked from obscurity out of college and suddenly making a record with producer David Foster. Hearing that John was a fan was a "very validating thing at a time when I was feeling very, very, very scared about it all," Groban said. "Because I trusted his ear. I knew that he was not a flash in the pan kind of person, I knew that he was not a music biz, blow hot air kind of individual. He's the kind of person that I held

---

† At one point, Spielberg wanted to use the Beatles song "Golden Slumbers" for this finale, but the licensing cost was prohibitive. Perhaps the ghost of that song is in the gentle rhythm of John's opening piano notes. (Haley Joel Osment to TG, February 6, 2024.)

in this regard that I would hold someone like Stephen Sondheim.... The fact that he liked *me* made me like me a little better—at a time when I really didn't."[50]

Foster produced and arranged the duet, giving it some R&B radio attitude that was common in end credits songs at the time. Groban didn't feel good about his performance, but an hour after the recording session Foster told him: "John Williams is on the phone—he just loves it. He's just so happy. And Steven is so happy, and everybody's just so happy." "We always remember those first moments where you feel like somebody that you've idolized gives you a thumbs up," said Groban, who grew up adoring John's film scores and attending his concerts at the Bowl, sitting up in the nosebleed seats with his parents. Groban's grandmother was dying at the time he recorded "For Always," and he asked permission to burn the track onto a CD:

> The first person I ever played that song for was her. I went to Cedars-Sinai, drove over there with my mom, brought a little boombox. I just remember having the message of that song, the melody of that song, being able to play that for my grandmother, who was kind of in and out at that time. Music has such an incredible way of connecting with people and breaking through those things and those hardships.
>
> I just remember—and David doesn't know this, John doesn't know this, nobody knows that this happened—but that was one of the last moments I had with my grandmother, was being able to play that song for her, and play that message of that song for her. And so it will always have a very, very special place in my heart, personally, because it resonated so deeply with her, and with us in that room.[51]

* * *

It is, admittedly, hard to picture John Williams, 69, curled up with a hardcover of *Harry Potter and the Sorcerer's Stone*. But he had indeed read the uber-popular children's novel by J. K. Rowling ("because my kids were all reading the books," he explained) before he ever had any notion of scoring an adaptation. "I liked it very much," he said in 2001, "and it made me want to read on, especially now that people have told me that each book gets better than the one before."[52] Like everyone else on earth, Jenny also read the books, and "I said to him, 'Dad, you know what? *You're* Harry Potter.' And he goes, 'I think *you're* Harry Potter.' "[53] Ever since, they had a new pet name for each other: "Potter." Add to the suitable avatars for John from his own movies—which before now included Yoda and E.T.—a mild-mannered wizard with glasses, who casts spells and enchants the entire world.

The *Potter* series was a cultural phenomenon, outselling every other book in the United Kingdom and cracking the top of the *New York Times* bestseller list with millions of copies in print. Hollywood smelled a harvest, and Warner Bros. bought the rights to the first two books in 1998. The studio sought blockbuster names to direct—including Spielberg, who was rumored to be interested for months, but who now had many children with Kate Capshaw and decided to spend that next year and a half with his own young kids.[54] In the end, Chris Columbus was sorted as director, and an enormous, years-long film operation began, with opulent soundstage sets and Oxford locations, an avalanche of visual effects, and an adult cast of heavyweight British actors. Three unknown English children were cast in the lead parts, with the idea that they would grow up with their characters across seven films. Columbus was signed to direct the first two movies back to back, and one of his first phone calls, before he even began shooting, was to John:

> I wanted to make sure he was available, and he said yes immediately. *Harry Potter* was a no-brainer for either of us. *Home Alone* has a *little* action in it, but I had never really done a sweeping action movie with John, to utilize that side of him that Steven has used so many times. I particularly was dying to see what John would do with Quidditch. That, to me, was the moment I thought he could just bring alive, because you're talking about a sporting event that doesn't exist, that we have to *visually* invent anyway—even though it's been written for us in the book. I knew that John could write a *magical* score.[55]

Before he ever saw the film, John was asked to write the score for a short trailer. He very quickly came up with a theme for Harry's snowy owl, Hedwig. "Everyone seemed to like it, so I will probably use that music as one thread in the tapestry," he said.[56] The trailer music was recorded in L.A., even though the score itself was scheduled for a London orchestra. Hedwig's theme was an indication of the exceptionally busy, florid—and difficult to play—style that John was drawn to for this magical world. "I was sitting on the first stand," said Jacqueline Brand, who played the one-hour trailer session with a contract orchestra, "and that was the hardest thing I have ever been given to play in an hour. I was *gasping*—I was a little overwhelmed. And he was just like: 'Come come! Come come.' He always says that. And you just pull it out. I remember my heart was pounding."[57]

John spotted the film with Columbus in May, and immediately began writing a score that was as densely spotted as any *Star Wars* film—requiring 142 minutes of music in total. He took his leitmotif storyteller approach, but aimed at an even younger audience with cues that danced to every visual flourish. "There's a wonderfully childish aspect to *Harry Potter*," John said, "so I just thought the orchestral music should be colored in that way."[58] "*Harry Potter* exists through the eyes of Harry," said Columbus, "so I wanted the scenes where Harry first gets to Hogwarts, where the boats go across the lake, where Harry first walks into the great hall with the candles ... I wanted all of that to be driven by the music, because John could create that sense of awe and wonder from Harry's point of view. That was extraordinarily important to me."[59]

Most of the resulting, epic-length score is teeming and hyperactive, full of scurrying, fidgeting, cascading runs in the strings, woodwinds, and the score's signature instrument: celeste. For John, the celeste meant "something *innocent*, something that belongs to the spheres, something heavenly, if you like. It's a magical instrument—particularly when it's in tune. It's hard to get a good one, any musician will tell you."[60] He imported Randy Kerber from L.A. to sit with a contract orchestra, including several members of the LSO, for the many solos on this twinkling keyboard instrument, calling Kerber two weeks before the sessions to say, "There's a celeste part—you might want to take a look at it," Kerber recalled. "That was it. *I might want to take a look at it.* And he had never called before and said anything like that, so I was like: oh, I'll *definitely* be taking a look at it." Kerber was staying in a London hotel room with its own piano, because he was orchestrating another film score, and he "practiced like crazy." "And it's a good thing I did, because I had to play it with the orchestra on day one."[61]

From the opening bars under the studio logos, it sounds like a wild wind is blowing through the celeste—and the score continues to shimmer and bustle from then on. Even the main setting of Hedwig's theme, which John established as the film's principal melody, has spilling streams of celeste notes. "You really have to break the part up, because it's so fast," Kerber explained:

> You have to break it up between two hands. It doesn't necessarily lay that great *all* the time for the keyboard. So you have to play with one hand, and then grab this hand.... It's like you're going back and forth. So you work out the choreography between the hands, and then you get back to where it's smooth, and then you get it up to speed.

Kerber said there are two kinds of musicians when it comes to adrenaline on the day of a session: "You either *feed* off of that, and it heightens your performance and makes you *more* focused. Or you lose it, and you can't do it, and it's too much stress. But I liked the red light, and I like reading music a lot, and I love the challenge. I remember Artie Kane talking about that, too. He would almost *dare* people to write something that he couldn't play. He was fearless."[62]

Abandoning his incremental breadcrumb method from scores like *E.T.*, John laid the Hedwig theme out in full from the very beginning—and then repeated it over and over and over. The tune was instantly as memorable as his other signature popcorn themes, but wielded a bit more like a bludgeon. Its catchiness is truly remarkable considering how *chromatic* its leaps are. "It's a simple melody," said Kerber, "but the wonderful part is, where you think it will stay consonant he'll diminish the note by a half step, or augment by a half step in places. We're familiar with the shape of the melody, but the notes are slightly askew in places at the ends of the phrases. Anybody else would play the fifth and it would be what you've heard before. It's just slightly off in places—which I just love. That makes it so special."[63] There are many other character themes in the score, but none for the lead roles of Hermione or Ron. Harry's loneliness and longing for family elicited the score's most poignant melody, introduced on solo oboe as he sadly wishes himself a happy birthday. "I wanted John to bring that sense of loneliness and isolation to Harry's theme," said Columbus, whose films often dealt with people isolated from their families. "I just am obsessed with that, and I knew John could tap into that particular theme. What happens when you lose your family—and find a new one?"[64] After the battle is won and the film's adventure is over, this tune reprises with tender grace and triumph as Harry embraces his found family.

Hedwig's theme stands in for the entire wizarding world, flying and diving like the owl, but also carrying Harry's gaping reaction to the parade of incredible sights he witnesses from the moment giant Hagrid bursts through his door one rainy night. The celeste and other ornamentations lend the whole score a Christmassy, Sugar Plum Fairy quality, connecting it to John's previous scores for Columbus. A secondary magic theme has a more active, pumping pulse—a mysterious and mischievous dance draped in still more Christmas lights—heard first when Harry unwittingly frees a snake at the zoo. When Harry approaches Hogwarts by boat, the two themes connect to illuminate the majestic castle glowing in the night sky. (The mystical female choir here recalls the otherworldly spirits John summoned for films like *Family Plot* and *Close Encounters*.) A jaunty theme for Diagon Alley was orchestrated for recorders and bells and scratchy fiddling, as well as music for brass band—situating this world in the same general neighborhood as John's version of Neverland. There was a simple, ominous motto for the Sorcerer's Stone, and an oozing motif in the bass clarinets and contrabassoons for the unseen Voldemort. Gryffindor has its own school song cheer. A brassy sports fanfare heralds the flighty game of Quidditch.

The score spills over with minor motifs and melodic fragments, all choreographed like a hyperactive Russian ballet. John gave his sundry themes personalities distinct to sections of the orchestra, with the intention of creating a guide for children like the famous one by Benjamin Britten. When he arrived at AIR Studios in Lyndhurst that August, he actually carved out time to record an eight-movement suite arranged for the different sections which showed off the score's major themes. Past projects had offered John the chance to compose new Christmas carols, an original spiritual, or an opera's worth of leitmotifs; for this one, it was a musical curriculum for his grandchildren's generation.

Dyer was once again a fly on the wall at the closed-door sessions:

> Like every musician, Williams concerns himself with countless details of intonation, phrasing, dynamics, articulation, rhythm, and balance. Most of the subtleties he's after will escape the notice of the audience, but the audience would notice if they were wrong. Sometimes he turns to metaphor. During some slithering, chromatic Voldemort music he says, "Nasty, isn't it? Spidery. It should feel as if a spider is crawling all over you, and you can't get him off you." ("I love it when John crosses over to the Dark Side," exclaims [Ken] Wannberg.)
>
> The recording studio phase of the work is not a place for improvisation; it's for finishing as efficiently as possible the things you have scheduled yourself to do. But Williams delights in spontaneous impulse. This time he's concerned about a brief scene in which three ghosts sing a Christmas carol. This has been set up to "Deck the Halls," but Williams is not happy with this choice, even though it is a secular carol chosen to avoid giving offense to any religious group.
>
> "Why should there be anything from the Muggles world at Hogwarts?" he asks. So at night, he wrote a little tune for a new carol, and then he amused himself by producing the lyrics too.

> *Merry Christmas, Merry Christmas, ring the Hogwart bell,*
> *Merry Christmas, Merry Christmas, cast a Christmas spell*
> *Find a broomstick in your stocking, see the magic on display.*
> *Join the owls' joyous flocking on this merry Christmas day.*

Later he was delighted to learn that his lines would need to be translated into six languages. Williams was reluctant to set his own text until he learned that J. K. Rowling didn't want to write the words herself.

"Every day when I get here," Columbus told Dyer, "I am stunned at how wonderful the music is. It feels immediately familiar, but also wondrous and strange. I had taken out some shots because I felt they were slowing down the action, but when I heard the music, I put them back because John's work helped those scenes, improved them, and solved the problems."[65]

When it broomed into theaters that November, *Sorcerer's Stone* was heavily sauced in John's notes—it was the thickest and possibly most Mickey-Moused score he had ever composed. "I wanted to capture the world of weightlessness and flight and sleight of hand and happy surprise," he explained. "This caused the music to be a little more theatrical than most film scores would be. It sounds like music that you would hear in the theater rather than the film."[66] The movie was all but guaranteed to go gangbusters, and it did—but many adult critics resented the score: "The film's biggest offense is committed by composer John Williams," wrote David Kronke at the *L.A. Daily News*, "who frequently ladles on the bombast in his movie scores but just as often manages music of subtlety and power. This may be his most overblown work yet."[67] Other adjectives that appeared in reviews were "annoying," "pounding," "unending," "overpowering," "serviceable," "cloying," and "overwrought." The *Hollywood Reporter* condemned it as "a great clanging, banging music box that simply will not shut up."[68]

But for the happy hordes of children around the globe who lapped the film up like a goblet of Butterbeer, John's wondrous themes became the soundtrack of their dream world and their childhood, beloved and memorized and immortal. Schools and symphony orchestras took up the challenging but infectious tunes. In a second century, and for the third time, John Williams had snuck into the heads and hearts of an entire new generation.

* * *

On his 70th birthday, John bundled up in a heavy white sweater and a black kubanka-style cap and braved the 20-degree weather inside Rice-Eccles Stadium at the University of Utah in Salt Lake City. He had written new music for his fourth Olympic Games, and he conducted the Utah Symphony and the enormous Mormon Tabernacle Choir in a new anthem for the 2002 Winter Games: *Call of the Champions*. (There was a minor fuss when folks at home learned it was actually a pre-recorded track, owing to the freezing temperature.) "When you play for an audience as large as the Olympics or the millennium celebration, it becomes almost abstract," John said. "So I find that I focus on the very specific task at hand, which is to conduct the music properly. If you tried to think about anything more, it would be just overwhelming."[69]

He composed *Call of the Champions* not long after the September 11 terrorist attacks, but said a somber piece would not have been appropriate. "I wasn't consciously doing anything hymnal or choral that would put us in a ruminative mind. It's a heraldic and joyous piece, but it has something more serious at its core—not premeditated, but a reflection of the mood of the time. We are playing to billions of people, and the idiom of the piece wants to be fairly accessible in the best sense of that word, as we cross the culture gaps. We hope the heraldic, heroic aspects will be felt that way."[70] He was planning to use chorus as just a color, but then Susan Dangel suggested the old Olympics motto "Citius, altius, fortius"—Latin words for "Swifter, higher, faster." "I thought it would make a wonderful declamatory handle, just that triad of words sung in a very forceful way by the chorus," John said. "We had all 350 members of the Mormon Tabernacle Choir singing this and it was *electrifying*. It sounds like all the heroes coming down from Olympus and chanting together."[71] He felt the ending needed a *fourth* word, though, because "John has the syllables he's looking for," said Dangel, "the mood," so she found "some grad student at Harvard in the romance language department and said we needed a word like 'nobler,'" she recalled. The student came back with a Latin word, "clarius"—*clarity*.[72] The new anthem was included on the *American Journey* album along with *Song for World Peace*, *Jubilee 350*, and *Celebrate Discovery*—but none of these pieces had the same cultural afterlife as his original *Olympic Fanfare and Theme* from 1984.

Jenny and her kids came out to Salt Lake City to celebrate John's birthday with him, "so it turned out to be kind of a nice family event and a lovely way to mark the date for me," he said.

> Turning 70 doesn't feel any different than 40. The more you work in music, the more years you spend with it, the more in love with it you become. It's not like a job that's distasteful. It's the opposite of that—more seductive, more interesting. It's been a long journey, a greatly rewarding one in every way. An almost always happy one, and a continuing one. I don't feel any differently about the need to work, and to work well, than I ever did. I don't feel any differently about challenging every note I write any more now than when I was 35.[73]

Sony Classical released *Yo-Yo Ma Plays the Music of John Williams* that same month, a CD featuring the cello concerto, *Elegy for Cello and Orchestra*, and two new pieces that John had written for Ma. Three Pieces for Solo Cello was conceived to reflect the African American experience. "I thought that the cello might be especially well-suited to express the vernacular manner of musical speech and rhythmic inflection that characterize this most important 'root-source' of American music," John wrote in a liner note:

> In the first piece, "Rosewood," the cello groans under the crack of the work-gang whip and imitates the old steel-fronted guitar played by some of the early workers as they tried to ease the pain of their long hours in the field. The second movement,

"Pickin'," refers both to the art of banjo pickin' and the act of picking cotton itself. In this piece I also tried to capture some of the energy and drive of the old "side-slap" and "shoe-slap" dances that brought forth a natural exuberance that couldn't be quelled by the blanket of oppression.[74]

John named the third movement "The Long Road North," after a Rita Dove poem of the same name, which the poet had read during *The Unfinished Journey* concert at the Lincoln Memorial. "When she writes 'No more rockin' in Jim Crow's cradle,'" John said, "she describes the indomitable spirit that has always animated the long and inspiring African-American journey to freedom. The music also partly takes the form of a lullaby in which we might imagine a mother singing ... hush now child—don't cry ... someday ... someday!"[75] This notion of tracing a cultural history or journey through music was, in its way, cinematic, and it was a concept John would keep returning to in future concert pieces.

His fascination with musical ancestry was closely tied to his love of trees, and the other new work on the album—*Heartwood*—was inspired by a book of tree photographs a friend had given him. "Each tree pictured in the book conveyed a dignity and enduring strength that suggested a wisdom only attained after reaching great age. I was moved and impressed by these pictures, and I tried to capture something of their quiet majesty in the sketches I was writing." By calling it *Heartwood*, John added, he might also be describing "the cellular structure and spiritual core of the cello itself." John unconsciously channeled his father's old friend, Claude Thornhill, the dance band leader and orchestrator whose music was stored in the Williams attic when the composer went into the service during World War II, and which had remained in the attic of John's imagination. John thought he was evoking trees with the "deep vertical sonorities set out in the piece, particularly by the brass," "but as I listen now I realize how much they also recall and reveal an early enthusiasm of mine" for the "rich impressionistic harmonies favored by Thornhill which he usually presented in a reflective and moody setting."[76‡] John and Ma promoted their highbrow product in the most amusingly lowbrow way—by visiting a Costco superstore west of Culver City. For two hours, they signed autographs for an estimated 2,000 people. "This experience is all new to me," the very out-of-place composer said. "I've heard of this institution, but I've never been anywhere near it. Amazing to see what's done here."[77]

In March, John signaled a new life for film music by conducting his entire score for *E.T.* live to a screening of the film in celebration of its 20th anniversary. This was not the first time this sort of thing had been done—among other precedents, 10 years earlier Ozawa conducted Prokofiev's score for *Alexander Nevsky* in sync with the 1938 Sergei Eisenstein film. But advances in digital technology had finally made this musical tightrope walk much more feasible. Keeping in sync with picture, which was now facilitated by digital streamers and time codes, wasn't the only challenge of such

---

‡ John and Ma brought *Heartwood* to Tanglewood that summer, during a celebration of John's 70th birthday.

a concert, though; there was also the matter of finding whole film scores and their individual instrumental parts. This new frontier of presenting full scores with attendant screenings of their films became a project of historical preservation and restoration as much as it was about programming, but it would also become an important mode of film music evangelism—a new collective watching experience for beloved movies, and an economic and demographic boon for symphony orchestras.

It was a starry affair at the Shrine Auditorium in downtown Los Angeles. Not only were Spielberg and the stars of the film on hand, but a host of other celebrities, from Carrie Fisher to Ethan Hawke and Arnold Schwarzenegger, attended the screening and its afterparty, where the evening's diner was a replica of E.T.'s spaceship.[78] Spielberg had caught the same bug that compelled Lucas to revise his old *Star Wars* movies, and he "upgraded" some of E.T.'s puppet performance with CGI, added back in a deleted scene, and replaced firearms in the G-men's hands with harmless walkie-talkies. Unlike Lucas, he at least made the original cut available on a new DVD release.§ John conducted a 100-piece orchestra that included many of his regular musicians. Ralph Grierson played the shimmering end credits piano solo, just like he'd done back in 1982, at the end of a six-hour rehearsal the day before the event. It was pitch black in the auditorium, someone had left out a riser, and "I took a step into nothing," Grierson said, "and landed on my wrist—and ended my career. Just like that. I tell everybody it was a piece of cake: a couple years of psychotherapy and everything was fine." The rehearsal of that big *E.T.* piano solo was the last thing he ever played professionally. Several years later, Grierson bumped into John in the parking lot at a memorial service for a mutual friend. "John was like, 'Hey baby, how are you? How's the hand?'" Grierson recalled. "I said, 'Well, you know, it's about 85 percent.' He says, 'Oh great! I'll write something for you.' I said: 'John ... I, and every other person in a hundred-piece orchestra, have been there when one guy isn't 100 percent. I'm not going to be that guy.' He said, 'Oh yeah, baby, I think I understand.'"[79]

John was the musical director at the Oscars a few weeks after the *E.T.* concert, and as part of the Academy's maiden voyage inside the new Kodak Theater on Hollywood Boulevard, he conducted a medley he arranged of classic film scores—a *Tribute to Film Composers* that included selections from *Casablanca* through *Rocky* and *Titanic*. A few minutes later, his two nominated scores, for *A.I.* and *Sorcerer's Stone*, both lost to Howard Shore's inaugural *Lord of the Rings* score. Shore's staggering, sophisticated narrative of leitmotifs—which he built on with two subsequent films—was the closest film score project in ambition and scope since the *Star Wars* saga. Shore was an admirer of John's, though he said he wasn't directly inspired by those scores. New audiences formed a deep, emotional bond with the *Rings* scores, much like they had

---

§ Spielberg later repented: "I never should have done that," he said. "*E.T.* is a product of its era. No film should be revised based on the lenses we now are either voluntarily or being forced to peer through." (Zach Sharf, "Steven Spielberg Regrets Editing Guns Out of 'E.T.,' Says 'No Film Should Be Revised' for Today's Standards: 'That Was a Mistake,'" *Variety*, April 25, 2023.)

done with John's space operas. "That might have to do with the idea of storytelling and using a 19th century sound," Shore posited.

> The palette was so vast, you're able to tap into peoples' dreams, really, because it's just part of human culture—that sound we've all grown up with, this symphonic sound. You're talking directly to the audience in a way. Beyond the visual, beyond the film. You're saying things to them... it's like you're whispering in their ear.[80]

* * *

Attack of the Clones and the second *Harry Potter* adventure were both products of 2002, and they were the two blandest and least palatable sequels John had been saddled with since *Jaws 2*. Asked why he kept returning to the Skywalker well, especially after the critical drubbing of *Phantom Menace*, John answered with his trademark tact: "*Star Wars* is something I would like to complete if I can. I've enjoyed adding tunes to the collection of melodies and melodic identifications that go with the characters. But I would also say that there are sometimes commitments in life that are the result of relationships that are in place."[81]

Clones doubled down on the digital cluster from the first prequel, and its actors—trapped in airless bluescreen cages with invisible scene partners—had the air of hostages at gunpoint. Grown-up Anakin was played by Hayden Christensen as a whining, lovesick teenager with no impulse control, in what felt like an extended allegory about puberty. The plot is a tangled mess between a mystery investigated by detective Obi-Wan—something about Count Dooku and a clone army—and a *Romeo and Juliet* storyline for Anakin and Padmé which features juvenile dialogue and the sexual chemistry of a junior high play. Not even Anakin's return to Tatooine and descent into darkness—slaughtering a colony of Tusken Raiders in a rage after his mother dies—could spice up the soggy gumbo of poor writing and ugly computer artifice.

Besides finding some new ways to vary and quote his classic leitmotifs, John seized on one principal opportunity: "George said to me, 'Why don't you make a love theme that's like the old Hollywood movies, you know, when you could see Claudette Colbert in love with some handsome guy?'" John said.

> Meaning, I think, that what's expressed here musically is in the sort of traditional vein of a love theme. But it also has a sort of tragic aspect, I think. And the aspect of love that's eternal, really, is love that goes on beyond death. So it's "Liebestod," love-death, in a certain sense. Love as something that is infinite and goes on forever, and the music, I think, expresses that.
>
> You also have an aspect in *Episode II* of the lovers that's very similar to the classic love stories of Tristan-Isolde or Romeo-Juliet, where the lovers are separated by family—as they are in Romeo-Juliet—or by rank, as they are in *Episode II*. We have a queen and we have a soldier, a Jedi, and their ranks in the social structure of the way they live separate them and creates [sic] tension for them in their coming

together. And so the love theme expresses also this tragic aspect, of the things within social structures—even in the galactic world of George Lucas."[82]

The resulting theme, "Across the Stars," is an aching minor-key ballad that vaults and weeps with Golden Age Hollywood honey. It first stirs in a scene where Anakin cannot hide his attraction to Padmé while she packs for a hideout on Naboo, and it continues to serenade the would-be lovers as Lucas cuts back to scenes of their timid flirtation in daylight and agonized conversation by firelight. Its elegance and grandeur valiantly fight against the lousy romantic dialogue, straining under the stupidity of Anakin riding a giant CGI bug. The theme swells with tragic passion as the pair are wheeled into an arena where thousands of other giant insect creatures await their savage execution. Typically, the melody receives its full development in a concert suite version during the end credits.

There were other new themes—a motif for the conspiracy against Padmé's life, and another for the mysterious goings-on with the clone army—and a less anguished melody for the happy side of Padmé and Anakin's courtship. But nothing clicked with the ear or had quite the same bond with any particular character as was so reliably done in previous *Star Wars* scores. John all but abandoned his sweet boyhood theme for Anakin, and other legacy motifs are quoted with little character growth or exciting adaptation. Even the action scoring is chaotic and manic, moving away from the groove and melody-based set pieces of yore. John did push his aesthetic into new orbits by adding electric guitar to his cue for the opening chase on Coruscant, along with a ferocious percussion motor, and for the scene where Yoda feels the pain of Anakin's violent outburst, John imported some of the *misterioso* minimalism he was concurrently exploring in Spielberg's dark futurism. But much of the score simply lacks a sense of heart or enthusiasm, a situation made even worse by its reckless cut-and-pasting by Burtt, who was now acting as *film* editor. Burtt explained:

> Yes, the editorial process kept going on even after the film was scored, in big ways. And that created a necessity for a lot of recutting of the music to fit. I think that was probably very frustrating for Ken Wannberg, because they'd spotted with one version of the film, and George would keep cutting and changing and moving in some significant ways often, and changing things conceptually. And that would hurt the structure of the music—you'd now have to find a way to recut it to still have it fit as best as it could a given sequence.[83]

Nonetheless, the movie dutifully cloned hundreds of millions of dollars, even as critics let out a giant wheeze en masse. "I can't remember ever feeling so glad that a movie was finally over," Stephanie Zacharek wrote in *Salon*.[84] "The racial stereotype Jar Jar Binks is back, but with the volume turned way down," wrote John Griffin at *The Gazette* in Montreal. "Would the same could be said for composer John Williams, who must have been paid by the note."[85] One of the film's few admirers was the *Baltimore Sun*'s Michael Sragow: "This movie isn't mechanical; it's voluptuous," he wrote. "And with the help of co-writer Jonathan Hales and composer John Williams, [Lucas] taps an emotionalism that fuses the electric ingredients of the *Star Wars* saga, from the pioneer-clan feelings of John Ford westerns to the dystopian dread of Lucas' debut feature, *THX 1138*."[86]

Previn looked upon this dreck and despaired: "John is much too good a musician to stay satisfied with that forever. I hate to see him spend so much time doing, you know, *Home Alone* or whatever. It's so beneath him. But it's a pointless argument, because he likes doing it, and he does it very well."[87] When Dyer asked John about Previn's unending admonishment, John playfully shot back: "Maybe it's appropriate for me to tease him about returning to *his* old vineyards. I'd like to see him score at least one more film."[88] John worked "Across the Stars" into his summer concerts; in the blurb for a Pops show that May, the *Globe* advertised it with cheek: "Now that the consensus is that the latest installment is a dud, here's your chance to hear part of John Williams' score without sitting through the movie."[89]

Harry Potter and the Chamber of Secrets was equally disappointing—and somehow even more obnoxious. Rowling's book was a shameless dupe of her first, simply adding giant spiders, a giant snake, a magical phoenix, and a subplot about a haunted diary. The kid actors, with puberty coming at them like the Hogwarts Express, were hammier, the action duller, and the wide-eyed enchantment was starting to wear off. *Chamber* also introduced Dobby the House Elf—a wrinkled, digital abomination who vied with Jar Jar for the honor of being the most annoying "comic relief" character of the computer age. John was always planning to score the film for Columbus—but its inflexible production schedule competed with his work on *Catch Me if You Can*, so he took the unusual step of delegating the job.

William Ross, a California native who left his pre-med studies for a life in music, was a Hollywood utility player who composed his own scores but chiefly arranged and orchestrated for other film composers, including Alan Silvestri; he also worked with singers such as Barbra Streisand. John asked around for referrals on who might be able to adapt his first *Potter* score into a sequel effort while still completely retaining John's style, and everyone pointed to Bill Ross. The bashful arranger got a surprise phone call from Michael Gorfaine one day, telling him that John wanted to meet. John explained the situation to Ross, and said, "I hope adapting something isn't insulting to you. My first Oscar was an adaptation, and I consider it a true art form." Ross protested that, actually, he felt inadequate. "I don't see how I'm going to possibly be able to please you," Ross said. John gently told him, "Bill, I take pride in doing my homework."[90]

John still wanted to contribute new thematic material for the score; he spotted the movie with Columbus in London in May, and began writing new themes for Dobby and Fawkes the Phoenix. Dobby's theme is a bouncy, sweet motif that inspires far more tenderness than the ugly, self-flagellating creature itself. Fawkes was given a majestic theme that flaps ever upward with airborne grace. John also wrote a new theme for Kenneth Branagh's preening professor, Gilderoy Lockhart, which closely resembled the "No Tickets" cue from *Indiana Jones and The Last Crusade*. New action and mystery themes for the Weasley's flying car, the Hogwarts spiders, Moaning

Myrtle, and the titular chamber all have slightly less personality. The end result, with Ross judiciously applying music from the first score, was mostly a tired retread with only the occasional burst of fresh lyricism. As the recording sessions in London were approaching, John sent a package full of new music to Ross. "That night I actually called John and told him I was sending the music police to confiscate his pencil," Ross quipped. "I think he just couldn't stop writing. I was stunned by the amount of music he wrote. Some people get confused because they see my 'Music Adapted by' credit. That was something that John insisted on from our first meeting. The reality, however, is that *Chamber of Secrets* is a John Williams score beginning to end."[91] Perhaps so—but it wasn't anything from his top shelf.

Columbus insisted he "felt like I got 150 percent John Williams. I think that's a brilliant score. It's darker. It's creepier. He knew that the entire intention for *Potter* was always to get darker and darker." Columbus was scheduled to direct all seven *Harry Potter* films, but he bowed out after *Chamber*, utterly spent. As he left, he exhorted Warner Bros. to keep John on board for the rest of the series.[92]

* * *

John's priorities that year were clear: he offloaded the busy note masonry of *Harry Potter* to concentrate on Spielberg's far more rewarding adult fare. The director continued his bleak streak with another futuristic tragedy: *Minority Report* was based on a short story by Philip K. Dick, and like *Blade Runner* and *Total Recall*—two other films based on Dick's work—it spun a riveting, heart-racing yarn around the terrifying implications of advanced technology. It is the story of a trio of humans with the gift of precognition, who are harnessed to a new wing of law enforcement in Washington; John Anderton, played by Tom Cruise, is the lead detective, solving and stopping future murders … until his name comes up as a soon-to-be killer and he goes on the run from his own team—he's already running away from the death of his little boy, Sean—and in so doing, uncovers the inconvenient truth about the "precogs" and the whole Pre-Crime operation.

"I wanted to do this in a film noir kind of way," John said. "The grandparent of the score is the work of my old mentor and friend, Bernard Herrmann." Although the story takes place 50 years in the future, "Spielberg and I wanted the musical atmosphere of an old Bogart film like *The Maltese Falcon*. Some elements of the music are not tonal and depict the futuristic aspect of the film, but the movie is also about nostalgia and memory, and that's where the film noir element comes in."[93] Spielberg considered this John's first "black-and-white score." "For all nineteen of our collaborations, I think all of those scores have been in color. But this score is more experiential, it's more environmental—you *feel* it more than you hear it. It's not a tonal score. It's not full of melody, as *A.I.* was.… It's the music of suspense, a little bit like what Benny Herrmann used to do for Hitchcock."[94]

But there was still plenty of melody. Continuing in the bittersweet cantilena writing from *A.I.*, John wrote a theme for Sean that had some of the English lilt of *Jane Eyre*, which is first doled out over gently broken harp chords when a drugged-up Anderton watches old home movies of his son. It migrates from the human warmth of piano and oboe to a spectral synth, imitating a human voice, reflecting both the story's futurism and the haunting. A shorter motto for this ghostly synth voice cues the crucial memory of the day Sean was abducted. Sean's theme later returns with compassion when the central pre-cog, Agatha, feels his spirit in the house where Sean grew up and she tells Anderton and his wife about the man he would have become.

The score's other main melody is also a ghost—a keening wail for the murdered Anne Lively, who we eventually discover was Agatha's mother and whose killer was Lamar Burgess: Anderton's boss and the founder of Pre-Crime. There is something primal and almost Bedouin about the wail performed by singer Deborah Dietrich—Spielberg told Dietrich her performance got him "right in the giblets."[95] Wittingly or not, John was contributing to a trend that had infected Hollywood scores ever since Hans Zimmer asked singer Lisa Gerrard to wail melismas all over the *Gladiator* soundtrack in 2000. This "moaning woman" cliché evoked the Middle East at a time when a lot of stories were directly or indirectly obsessed with threats felt from Afghanistan and its environs, and for whatever reason—in a mystery story set in D.C. in 2054—John caught the virus. (Film music journalist Doug Adams said it was a little bit like "your grandpa buying a cell phone," but even when John used a trending trope "he doesn't just trot it out—he does something with it."[96])

But the bulk of John's score was "black-and-white" suspense, and a *lot* of running. The film's action was favorably compared to set pieces from the *Indiana Jones* series—acrobatic funhouses full of booby traps and daring escapes, which many Spielberg fans had been missing during his evolution into a serious historical filmmaker. In the midst of his own recent evolution as an action composer, John did score these sequences with some hyperactive mayhem and tossed-off syncopations, but he also laid a more consistent rhythmic track for the chases to groove on than in some of his recent escapades. A scampering staccato string figure spirals under Anderton's breakout on a busy vertical highway, and John spiced it with exciting brass runs reminiscent of Herrmann action in scores like *North by Northwest*—an essential template for stories about an innocent man on the run.

Despite the movie's dark tone and gloomy atmosphere, Spielberg gave its chase scenes—like Anderton crashing up through living room floors and landing upside down in a yoga studio—a winking sense of danger; John followed suit with a thrilling and sometimes humorous adrenaline. The page-turning coda to Anderton's lopsided fight and chase through a car factory, a woodwind duet like a breeze from the East, was pure Indiana Jones. An obsessive motif symbolizes the Pre-Crime operation in general and the story's central mystery; John took a page out of Herrmann's book of looping vortexes, but sped his up to a neurotic sprint. The conspiracy and countdown-ticking elements in this score harked back to John's paranoid thriller music for *JFK*, and he used a distant electronic explosion similar to the one in *Nixon*.

The suspenseful atmosphere in his score was offset by several classical source cues—another Kubrick homage by Spielberg—including Schubert's "Unfinished" Symphony in scenes of Anderton behaving as maestro of his high-tech computer system. The screenplay mentioned that Anderton liked classical music, but John's only personal selection was the use of a Haydn string quintet in the greenhouse of Dr. Iris Hineman. "It seemed to me to be the kind of thing a woman like this would play on the radio," he said.[97] The rest—including Bach's "Jesu, Joy of Man's Desiring" and Tchaikovsky's "Pathétique" Symphony—were chosen by Spielberg. After Anderton escapes his predetermined fate by choosing not to kill the man he believes murdered his son, escapes his prison sentence, and then exposes Burgess's crime and releases the pre-cogs—a new, serene pastoral theme concludes the film on a redemptive note.

John recorded the *Minority Report* score at Sony in April, and Cruise attended many of the sessions. "Tom is a very affable and appealing guy," said John. "From the time of *Born on the Fourth of July*, he's not only come to the recording sessions, but also shows up for the dubbing and mixing. I don't know whether it's because he wants to become a director himself, or whether he's just the kind of person who loves knowing everything there is to know about how movies are made."[98] Ramiro Belgardt went through many T-shirts drenched in sweat "because I was so nervous about it all," he said.[99]

Belgardt was a cellist from Michigan in his early 30s, who for the past decade had worked for the classical Delos Records company. A mutual friend referred him to Ken Wannberg, who needed help bringing John's music editing into the digital age. The most advanced piece of technology that Wannberg used was the Auricle Control System, a DOS-based program from the 1980s, housed on an old laptop, which essentially provided streamers and click tracks for recording sessions. Otherwise, John and "Wampi" still worked in exactly the same way they had done since the 1960s—but now music needed to be recorded and edited within a digital audio workstation like Pro Tools, and Wannberg "had no interest in learning how to do that," said Belgardt. So this young, tech-savvy musician came on board to shadow Wannberg's ancient process with John; he was *already* nervous before Cruise and Spielberg showed up and stood behind his computer, saying things like "Let's change this music around."

But Belgardt survived his trial by megastar, and became an irreplaceable part of John's team. Among John and Wannberg, he earned the nickname "Blossom" owing to his youth, and he proved to have the right lowkey temperament, seriousness, and also humor to harmonize with John's very tight, very established routine. "The whole point," Belgardt said, "was to try and not disrupt John's process as much as possible." Ironically, scoring a movie about a future with driverless cars and other plausible but radical technology, John was still working in the exact same way he did when he was scoring anthology TV shows at Revue: with pencil, paper, and a stopwatch. He never wanted to own or learn how to use computers; so "I'm his computer," Belgardt said.[100]

* * *

It was straight from the desaturated future of 2054 to the desaturated past of the 1960s. (Janusz Kamiński remained Spielberg's cinematographer, and every film took on a hazy, heavenly glow.) Spielberg was vacationing with his family when the script for *Catch Me if You Can* fell in his lap, a project with Leonardo DiCaprio already attached. "I needed this," he said after working for so long in the dark. "It sort of came along and rescued me."[101] John began working on his score in the summer of 2002, while Ross was simultaneously creating the *Chamber of Secrets* score, with John also multitasking by constantly sending Ross new *Potter* themes—and because Spielberg was in the Hamptons, John never auditioned his *Catch Me* themes on the piano. The recording sessions in September were the first time the director heard any of the music. "I have implicit trust," he told a visiting reporter.[102]

The true tale of Frank Abagnale, Jr., a young man who ran a staggering check fraud scheme and conned his way into becoming a pilot, a doctor, *and* a lawyer, took place in the swinging sixties. It was a time machine to John's own youthful exploits, and he was like a kid in a candy store. "It's really a sort of bon-bon, if you like," he said. "It's light, it's amusing, entertaining."[103] The setting and story allowed John, who continued to call his friends "baby," to write music with some "sixties swagger," a jazz-infused caper with echoes from his days in Mancini's band and scoring assignments like *Checkmate* and *How to Steal a Million*. It was a kind of "regressive loop," he said. "I think Charlie Parker would be very proud of him," said Spielberg.[104]

The opening titles, illustrated like an old Saul Bass creation, set the table with John's mysterious "Closing In" motif on vibraphone and saxophones, and musicians punctuating the tune with a voiced "shh" and finger snaps. John wrote this jazzy idée fixe for when Frank "begins to weaken and give in to his addiction," he explained, "almost like a drug addict going to the closet to find his fix, and they're returning unstoppably to do something they perhaps don't even want to do."[105] This music *sounds* improvised, especially in the walking swing section with upright bass and alto sax. Dan Higgins had no idea what awaited him that day.

"It was '10 to 5 Alto Sax at Sony,'" Higgins said. "I walk in and I don't know anything. I see the music, and I go, 'Oh, okay—it's gonna be fun. A lot to do.'" Higgins had been a session sax player since the mid-1980s, after a decade of gigging with jazz bands and touring with Sinatra. (His first session with John was *Presumed Innocent*.) "It wasn't like: *oh, I need to practice this for 12 hours because it's so awkward*," he said. "It just flowed. And many people comment to this day: they thought it was improvised. And I say, 'No, it's not improvised. Every note he wrote.' And the vibraphone was shadowing me a lot, so of course it's not improvised." Shadowing Higgins was Alan Estes, the brother of John's old high school bandmate, Gene. "But the flow of it," Higgins said, "he could capture that." John gave the opening titles the feel of improvisation by writing in grace notes and inflections, as well as mixing up the rhythm. "He knows what embellishments a good sax player would play, or an improvised saxophone player would add," said Higgins.[106]

This whimsical motif also stands in for the FBI, headed by Tom Hanks's Carl Hanratty, hot on Frank's trail. Its momentum is often frustrated, as when Carl bursts into Frank's Miami hotel room and Frank cons him into believing he's a Secret Service agent named Barry Allen. Spielberg constantly toggles between Carl's obsessive hunt and Frank's youthful joy ride, and John wrote a happy con theme that first starts to tingle when Frank receives his first checkbook from his father (Christopher Walken). This theme develops in fits and starts after Frank runs away from home and starts forging checks, slowly building confidence and learning tricks, and the syncopated dance—in a breezy 7/8—modulates and flowers with strings and chimes in an enchanting montage of Frank applying the Pan Am sticker from a toy airplane to his fake check—blooming with a shot of a bathtub full of soaking toys as Frank's operation explodes in scale. "Whenever he's conceiving of a new scam, a new trick, this magical little music is almost a little bit funny," said John. "That little musical trigger is always the same."[107] The happy con theme reprises when Frank forges a Harvard diploma and successfully inhabits the role of a physician, and then again as he takes a job as a lawyer and watches episodes of *Perry Mason* to learn the lingo.

There is an overwhelmingly playful buoyancy to Spielberg's direction of this story, filled with the awe of airplane travel and a scheme the FBI christens "The Float," and John's score is a stylish hepcat gallivanting and nimbly flying through a candy-colored world as wondrous as Harry Potter's. But Frank is also running—much like John Anderton—*away* from something. Spielberg's own Rosebud was his parents' divorce, and underneath all of this film's whimsy is a deep ache stemming from the marital breakdown of Frank's parents. Frank idolizes his father, a man who exudes cool confidence and charm; but as their happy home life crumbles, John introduces a lonely saxophone melody which he named "Recollections" and designated as the father's theme. Somehow it's the sound of heartbreak *and* running away, and it accompanies scenes of both. The Spielbergian disruption of a family idyll is felt keenly in this story, grounded in realism with no alien saviors to call for help. Frank does escape into a fantasy of his own making, and the perky con music stubbornly competes with this melancholy theme as Frank's hopes for saving his father's career and relationship keep running into the brick wall of reality. The father theme cuts sadly against Carl's laughter when Frank phones his pursuer on Christmas day, and Carl realizes the kid has nobody else to call. The tonal switches between playful escapade and tragedy are simply as smooth as Frank's cons, and John's music sells each facet with utter conviction, erasing any contradictions. The score is simultaneously a lighthearted "regression" to John's youth, and the empathy of an older man with access to deep pain.

The film came out in time for Christmas 2002. Several reviewers appreciated how "toned down" and different the score was from John's usual "pomp" and "sentimentality."[108] It was nominated for an Oscar, but lost to Elliot Goldenthal's Mexicano score for *Frida*. When Barbra Streisand announced the winner for Best Original Song that evening—"Lose Yourself" from *8 Mile*—John had to stand up to let rapper Eminem's co-songwriter Luis Resto, decked out in a Boston Celtics jersey and lots of bling, out of the aisle.[109] He was well accustomed, by now, to sliding over to let the Oscar winner get to the stage—but he kept going to the party anyway.

***

John rang in the year 2003 by participating in a 10-day festival at the Kennedy Center with Leonard Slatkin and the National Symphony, celebrating 100 years of film music. In addition to performances of his film and concert works, John wrote a piano duet that he and Slatkin performed together as accompaniment to silent film footage. "In the early days, someone would sit at the piano or organ and improvise something to go with the film, or grab themes from the standard classical repertoire," he explained. "I thought it would be fun for the audience to get a sense of what that was like." John wrote his piano score to accompany three classic scenes—the jeopardy of a lady tied to a railroad track; lovers in the desert; and the chases and pie fights of vintage comedies. "It's what we might have seen in 1910 and what we might have heard played on an upright piano," he said.[110]

He also brought this duet to Boston for some Pops concerts that summer, along with a concert version of *Catch Me if You Can* with Higgins performing his solos.[**] He had a very busy May: he was given the Olympic Order award by the International Olympic Committee, he conducted a gala concert for the LA Opera, threw out the first pitch at a Red Sox game, and helped dedicate a square in Boston to longtime Pops arranger Leroy Anderson. The National Symphony devoted their annual Fourth of July concert on the mall to John's classic film music; celebrating John Williams was now a national pastime.

John donated at least one million dollars to the building of a new home for the LA Phil, which had been in the works for a protracted 16 years.[111] Walt Disney Concert Hall was a great, gleaming silver sailboat on Grand Avenue, designed by John's friend, architect Frank Gehry. John composed carillon bell chimes for the new hall to signal audiences to the start of every concert, and at one of its three inaugural programs, on October 25, 2003, the LA Phil premiered a new commission: *Soundings* took those bells as "melodic beacons" for a conceptual piece that explored the acoustics of the new space and reflected its persona. "When I looked at the exterior of this building," John said, "I wondered what it would sound like if we played it." He wanted the piece to sound "as if the mother ship is singing to us." John had steel plates—smaller versions of the kind that flanked the hall—designed, cut, and tuned "so that I can return the sound of the sails to the hall."[112] It was a callback of sorts to the musical dialogue between humans and the mothership in *Close Encounters*. Gehry, who attended John's concerts at the Hollywood Bowl since the 1970s, said that John's compositions "get very architectural," "and they are very spatial." "It is a big space he creates in. It creates an emotion that you respond to. When you listen to it, you can't help but respond to the feeling of that space."[113]

Mark Swed rolled his eyes at the Hollywood stars who showed up for the party—Spielberg, Hanks, and Catherine Zeta-Jones acted as emcees—which he felt was shameless pandering to a film industry that hadn't bothered to donate to the hall's construction. As for John's new work: "If not strong on musical ideas," Swed wrote, *Soundings* "was strong on sound.

> It began in silence—a silence broken by the whirring noise of fans from the television lights (the PBS broadcast is Wednesday). Flutes and percussion then rustled to represent the hall awakening. As he is in film scores, Williams is most successful in creating a sense of expectation. Once wide-eyed, the hall, through Williams'

[**] At one of these concerts, Nancy Wilson sang "Make Me Rainbows," which she had recorded back in 1968.

score, quivered, trembled, pulsated, throbbed. There were eerie and extravagant effects I couldn't quite identify. Once it sounded as if a battery of glass harmonicas surrounded the audience. Williams cleverly created the amazing illusion of instruments traveling about this listening space. A deep electronic organ note made the ground on which we sat feel alive. (The real organ will be ready next year.)[114]

The rest of the program, co-conducted by John and LA Phil music director Esa-Pekka Salonen, placed John's music for *Close Encounters* next to selections from *King Kong*, *Vertigo*, and Jerry Goldsmith's *Planet of the Apes*. It was a fittingly filmic way to baptize Hollywood's local symphony orchestra, and a promise for how smart—and *classical*—a concert of film music could and should be. John was regularly asked about the divide between cinema and the concert hall, but he observed an increased "thawing" year by year. "In one sense, it's been an American thing," he said, "and I think it can be tied a little bit to our cultural inferiority complex, our obsession with the Eurocentric thing we've had about classical music.... I think now I can safely say that in the music departments of most of the major universities, composers want to study film music."[115]

He finished his horn concerto, which was commissioned for Dale Clevenger of the Chicago Symphony, and conducted it himself with the orchestra in November. The *Chicago Tribune*'s John von Rhein was unimpressed: "The composer's creative juices flow most freely when he has cinematic images to inspire him. His classical pieces tend to be episodic; the ideas feel manipulated rather than emerging spontaneously as in his best film scores." "Williams wrote the work in the middle of scoring of the third *Harry Potter* film, and it shows," von Rhein went on. "The disappointing thing about the score is how little it exploits Clevenger's virtuoso chops. Indeed, it sounds less like a concerto than a suite of tone-pictures for obbligato horn often accompanying the orchestra."[116]

Writing for a specific individual like Clevenger, John said, "replaces the film music cue sheet in my mind. My subject is now the person at hand. It's more liberating, at the same time more challenging."[117] The French horn, which John had favored in so many scores in solos and en masse, is the most "transportable instrument in the orchestra," able to blend with all of the other sections. But unlike any other instrument, he said, "it has the ability to evoke a nostalgia or bring us close to what we remember about antiquity. And it also can sound the call to battle, or it would sound the call to hunt, or the call to heroism or great deeds or even romantic ruminations." His concept for this concerto was to write a movement for each of the "dresses" the horn can wear. "It's probably less a concerto than a kind of suite," he admitted.[118]

The movement "Angelus" opens the concerto with "the distant pealing of the Angelus bell," John explained in his program note, "while the horn joins in, sending calls and signals to complete the picture." Then comes "The Battle of the Trees," the ghost of Graves persisting in John's imagination. Inspired by the Celtic poem that also spawned "Duel of the Fates," this movement imagines "groves of trees transforming themselves into warriors and led in battle by the brave oak. The horn enters the fray, as the percussion section creates sounds of trunks, branches, and twigs colliding in the struggle." In "Pastorale," the protagonist harmonizes with a solo oboe. "Nostalgia has been described as 'laundered memory,'" John wrote, "but our modern horn and oboe possess the power to produce it truly. They conjoin to 'dream backward' of a pristine glen." In "The Hunt," the horn plays its "traditional role, getting the blood up, exhilarating the spirit and animating the chase." The finale "Nocturne" depicts how "the day's end grants repose and a simple song is offered."[119] On first listen, the horn concerto—like most of John's concerti—can feel foreign, unknowable. For those who adore John's ear-tickling, heart-massaging film scores, it might seem frustratingly abstract, an exercise in 20th-century vanity.

But to spend time in this forest, to really get to know the piece, is to fall under its spell. There is as much drama and action in the concerto as any chase scene, only more primal and pagan. There is also a deep well of emotionality and lyricism, particularly in the "Pastorale" and "Nocturne" movements—just not the kind of melody that instantly grabs one's ear and beckons the listener to dance. It's a more ancient and mysterious melody, a whisper from Albion that hovers in the mists of this enchanted glen. One has to squint to get a good look at it, but to behold it is to become bewitched. The very sound of the French horn, John wrote, "conjures images stored in the collective psyche. It's an instrument that invites us to 'dream backward to the ancient time.'"[120]

This was music from *before* time—an area John seemed more and more interested in exploring as time marched on and death became a more frequent visitor.

15
Confluence, 2004–2008

> *One can admire a providentially given gift, but what you respect is someone who has all of it: the natural talent it all sits on, but also all the tools and technical expertise to bring it forward.*
>
> —John Williams, 2007[1]

Three film score giants died in 2004—Jerry Goldsmith, David Raksin, and Elmer Bernstein—all within weeks of each other. The film industry had changed dramatically since their respective heydays, and all three struggled to adapt and evolve with it. Raksin, the eldest, had been retired from scoring for decades and was a veteran teacher at USC. Bernstein's career waxed and waned, and one of his last big scores—for Martin Scorsese's *Gangs of New York*—had been thrown out and replaced. Goldsmith had recently reunited with *The Omen* director Richard Donner for the action film *Timeline*, but his score, too, was rejected. His final credit, *Looney Tunes: Back in Action*, was less than prestigious.

It was actually the most common thing for an aging film composer to be swept aside, forgotten, replaced. It happened to Bernard Herrmann and Max Steiner and Miklós Rózsa. It happened to just about everyone—except John Williams. He was now one of the last living links to the music of Old Hollywood, a wizened gentleman in his seventies ... and as eminent and busy—and popular—as he had ever been. Time had not passed him by, though some storylines were in the process of closing.

* * *

In the third chapter of John's latest blockbuster franchise, time was a major character. With an exhausted Chris Columbus tapping out, Warner Bros. recruited a more eccentric auteur to helm *Harry Potter and the Prisoner of Azkaban*—Alfonso Cuarón—in a move the *L.A. Times* found "both entirely reasonable and provocatively daring, especially for a studio that has played conservatively with the young wizard at every step."[2] The Mexican director of *Y tu mamá también* had also made the 1995 version of *A Little Princess* with Warners, which studio head Alan Horn said "confirmed to me that he could live in the world of fantasy and children and not be treacly and also be a little bit dark." Cuarón said: "I have to confess, I was a bit ignorant about the *Harry Potter* thing."[3]

The gambit paid off. Cuarón's vision, with the added advantage of Rowling's most inventive story, took the series into a bolder, more artful and idiosyncratic direction. The kid wizards were now young teens, starting to deal with romantic stirrings and existential angst but not yet full-blown hormones. The central mystery involved old friends of Harry's parents—his godfather, Sirius Black, is supposedly an evil murderer on his tail—which created opportunities for the hero to reflect on the ache of their absence. Hermione, we learn, has been using an enchanted "Time-Turner" to hop around the clock, and in the final act she and Harry go backward a few hours to alter destiny and save two lives. The twisty, melancholic story was shot on evocative locations in Scotland, lending the film a richer, more genuine atmosphere. "I was going into [their] teenage years, with a different kind of darkness," said Cuarón, who used a lot of handheld shots and naturalistic composition to ground the film in emotional reality. The studio was "a bit concerned at the beginning," he said, "because I wanted a new approach. It was important to bring fresh ideas and fresh eyes"—something he achieved with cinematographer Michael Seresin and other key artisans new to the *Potter* series. "But I don't think that John was ever out of the question," he said. "For me it was like: *What a dream!*"[4]

Cuarón was a serious fan, going all the way back to his childhood love for *Lost in Space* and *The Time Tunnel* and the early disaster films. He was also a keen listener to John's concert music. People only think of John as a post-romanticist, said Cuarón, who knew very well that John was far more flexible than that, and in fact "aligns to a new modernist approach. You can hear it in his early scores, the ones when I discovered him. Just because of the requirements of films, I think that there was a period in which we didn't hear that much." Cuarón felt that John had been reclaiming this voice with some of his scores in the late 1990s and early 2000s, and he knew John could go with him into a darker, stranger climate on *Azkaban*. "I was so lucky to find John in a moment in which he was eager to try different approaches." For his temp track, Cuarón advised music editor Thomas Drescher not to use any music from the first two *Potter* scores, and in fact *no* familiar film music at all. The result was a daring program of modern music by composers including Aulis Sallinen, Richard Danielpour, Erwin Schulhoff, Witold Lutosławski, Leonardo Balada, and George Antheil. "I think when he heard this," Cuarón said, "he was like, *Hmm, I like this*."[5]

John signed on to *Azkaban* in the summer of 2003 while the film was being shot. The very first thing he did was write an anthem for a Hogwarts choir, performed on screen, which he temporarily set to the famous witch incantation from *Macbeth* ("Double double / toil and trouble") at Cuarón's suggestion. The director also explicitly asked John to include something for the toads held by the choristers. "I shaped a little song," John said, "ending it with 'something wicked this way comes.' I sent it to Alfonso as a text and he loved it. He said, 'Let's not look any further; we don't have to hire a lyricist—we've got Shakespeare!'"[6] That chorale became a seed for the rest of the score, much of which has a minor-key Renaissance flavor with featured solos for recorder, penny whistle, lute, and harpsichord. "Alfonso had several scenes with a ghost character named Sir Cadogan, a fully dressed noble horseman who wafted through the castle," said John. "So the perfect thing to score this, we thought, was a kind of medieval band. I contacted a group in London who specialize in music of this period"—the Dufay Collective—"got their list of instruments and I was able to sprinkle the use of these instruments here and there with our concert orchestra."[7]

Part of Cuarón's new direction was to not wallpaper the film with music. "I told John that I didn't want descriptive music throughout," he explained. "I wanted the score to not just be a narrative device, but to capture the emotional undertone of the whole thing, almost like it's the conscience of Harry Potter."[8] John matured his palette and musical vocabulary for the wizarding world, underscoring the soul-leeching Dementors with Ligeti-like choir and quickening the far gloomier, rain-soaked Quidditch sequence with a dark, syncopated action fugato for horns and agitated strings. The emotional maturing of the characters yielded a wistful new family theme, which catches Harry on the precipice of childhood innocence and adult sorrow. The melody is played "Nostalgically" on solo recorder in scenes where Harry talks to Professor Lupin about his parents, and later when Harry dreams of living with his exonerated godfather. It twinges with the sadness of what was lost, but in the moment when Harry musters up his courage along with his father's Patronus avatar—a brilliant stag, and in doing so saving his own life—John handed the tune to a French horn and heavenly choir for a crescendo of mystical heroism. Cuarón and John spoke a lot about "the transition between innocence to experience, the journey of discovery," the director said. "That is also a journey that conveys a certain amount of pain—the pain of that other realm that you're leaving behind. But nevertheless, what is clear is that John refused to completely give up innocence. That is, I think, something that in many ways saved the film, benefited the film. Because *in* that darkness there are these constant glimpses of innocence."[9]

For as much as this film was more brooding and visually poetic than the previous chapters, it was still a quirky, kid-centric tale. John scored the sequence where Harry magically enlarges his cruel Aunt Marge with a sarcastic, Rossiniesque waltz, and he gave the wild Knight Bus sequence a crazed jazz tempo, "sort of a concerto for hubcaps and orchestra," he said. Cuarón had suggested: "What about something kind of like free jazz, almost like acid jazz?" John's eyes went wide and he replied, "Say no more!" For Cuarón, "the greatest moment I experienced was to witness John conducting the jazz orchestra. He was wired!"[10]* One of John's new motifs was a mysterious harpsichord motto for the Marauder's Map, an omniscient blueprint of Hogwarts with powers of surveillance. (The motif even sneaks in after the end credits like a little wink at the audience.) In keeping with Cuarón's narrative motif of birds flying through seasons to mark the passage of time, John wrote several fast-flitting flute runs; the very first cue recorded at Abbey Road was one of these quicksilver, very exposed flute solos, and the flutist Karen Jones had not seen the music before the session began. John told her she might want to take a look, but Jones said she was fine—"and performed it perfectly the first time," said the orchestra contractor, Isobel Griffiths. "John congratulated her. It was a good start."[11]

---

* This piece was a wild relative of the "Cantina Band" music from *Star Wars*—making it, one could say, *acid jizz*.

The film's visual centerpiece is Harry's joyful flight on the winged Hippogriff. John had already written so many memorable themes about the magic of flight, from *Superman* to *E.T.* to *Empire of the Sun*. Now he was tasked with creating still another—and he magically conjured a stunning new aerial showstopper. "Buckbeak's Flight" opens like a dramatic takeoff, with a visceral timpani heartbeat, then gets airborne with a string anthem (played "Exultantly") that fuses a rush of fear with a flood of adrenaline and thrill—dotted by little woodwind and brass rhythms and flourishes, dancing around this steady, wing-flapping tune. "We talked a lot about the expansive energy of getting into the teenage years," said Cuarón, "and then you see him flying and roaring into the skies—and from that release it's just such a poetic element that he did there that is almost ethereal."

John provided musical continuity from the other Potter films—Hedwig's theme and other threads are actively present—while ferrying the young wizards into an exciting new frontier. Cuarón was concerned about the film's emotional coda, its "aftertaste," "because we had very little time after the darkness," he said. When he shared his concern, John calmly said, "No, I recognize what you're talking about," and informed the director: "I'm going to use more music than what you have in your temp." Cuarón was astounded by the end result: "He knew how to take the audience—and me, the director—by the hand and just say: 'It's fine. Everybody's fine now,' without leaving behind that sense of melancholy for innocence lost. But at the same time allowing the wonder of what is to follow. He achieved that musically." Cuarón acknowledged that he and the cinematographer and the actors all took the film to a darker place—but "I have to say the tone of *Azkaban* was delivered by John."[12]

Prisoner of Azkaban remains the most artistically satisfying of the *Harry Potter* films, and it was as good a place as any for John to end his time with the boy wizard. The series continued with less visionary directors and a parade of other composers. Patrick Doyle, Nicholas Hooper, and Alexandre Desplat each reverently quoted Hedwig's theme in their disparate scores with varying success. "It was extremely frightening," said Desplat, the French-Greek composer whose desire to score films was lit by the original *Star Wars*. "I was not a kid, but still, I was impressed by the task in front of me because I knew that [John] had invented so many great moments in *Harry Potter*, and especially Hedwig's theme." He spent several weeks experimenting with that theme, "learning to play with it in any type of transcription or orchestration that I could think of before starting working." David Yates, director of the final two films in the series, eventually told Desplat he didn't want to rely on the theme so much, which the composer found liberating. But then the movies entered the cutting room and the editors were using John's music as temp. "It became hell," said Desplat, "because I don't write like John. *Nobody* writes like him."[13]

Unlike with *Star Wars*, John was content to take his hands off the *Potter* wheel and not worry about how his leitmotivic legacy would be handled. But Columbus was mad that Warner Bros. squandered their chance to retain John's services for the duration: "The concept that John wasn't used in subsequent *Potter* films has always troubled me," Columbus said. "I remember making a plea to some of the producers on the film and the studio—I was connecting it to *Raiders* and *Star Wars*—and I said, 'Who's better than Steven Spielberg? Why in God's name would you not want to continue with John Williams?'" For his part, John said he couldn't do the next film, *Goblet of Fire*, because the timing conflicted with his busy 2005 schedule. "Maybe John was too busy," said Columbus, "but I always thought that was the decision of the other directors—which I thought was a terrible mistake."[14]

John did say, to Mia Farrow's amusement, "I just don't think I can do any more *kid flying* movies."[15]

* * *

John was invited to serve as grand marshal of the Rose Parade on New Year's Day, 2004. He waved to the bundled masses along the route in Pasadena from a festooned car, wearing a Red Sox cap, with Samantha at his side. A few hours later, he stood on a high riser inside Rose Bowl Stadium to conduct the combined forces of the USC and University of Michigan marching bands in a jumbo-sized rendition of the national anthem ahead of the big college football game.[16]

It was an election year, and amidst scattered conducting gigs that spring he attended a fundraiser for an old friend of his from Boston, presidential hopeful John Kerry. It was Kerry's idea to throw a big concert at Symphony Hall in July, just hours after the Democratic National Convention. John conducted the Pops in a gala celebrating Senator Ted Kennedy's four decades of service, and he was joined by celebrities including Bono and Ben Affleck (who introduced himself as "just a constituent").[17] John had met Kerry in 1979 when he conducted the Pops for the first time, and his friendship with the senator's second wife, Teresa Heinz, dated back to John's early years in Pittsburgh. "We stand ready to do whatever we can to support them," John said.[18]

His 25th anniversary with the Pops was celebrated throughout the summer of 2004; he conducted several concerts himself, including an *Evening at Pops* program that paid tribute to Herrmann and Mancini. At Tanglewood, he resurrected the arrangements from his 1964 jazz album, *My Fair Lady Swings*, with singers Dianne Reeves and Brian Stokes Mitchell. John had encountered fans of these vintage charts over the years—"they all would know the music and know every note of the recording," he said with incredulity. Still, when the BSO's artistic administrator proposed doing them live for this anniversary season, John said: "You must be crazy!" John discovered that Shelly Manne's widow had the parts, and she gladly sent them over. "The scores were in my handwriting and the parts were more than legible," he marveled.[19] Spielberg and Scorsese came to Tanglewood for a Film Night concert in August; Scorsese waxed about their old friend Benny Herrmann, and Spielberg announced that a large tree was being planted in John's name on the grounds (along with trees for Seiji Ozawa and Leonard Bernstein).[20] For John, there could hardly be a higher honor.

He had just completed his latest score for Spielberg—which the director called "the feel good score of John's entire repertoire."[21] *The Terminal* is about a man named Viktor Navorski who arrives at New York's JFK airport only to find that Krakozhia, his fictitious

Eastern European country, is at war, and so he is temporarily *without* a country—which means he can't enter the United States. Thus commences a breezy situational comedy about a fish out of water, which turns into an inspirational comedy about an immigrant hero, which becomes a tender *romantic* comedy and finally crescendoes on a wave of bittersweet catharsis. Spielberg called it "a romantic adventure of the human spirit," and he cast America's most feel-good star as Viktor. Tom Hanks adopted a vaguely Bulgarian accent, channeling the work of Peter Sellers as he ambled around a gleaming capitalist dome packed with Burger Kings, escalators, and strangely empty gates, misunderstanding what those around him are saying and yet somehow rising to become a folk hero to the airport's multiethnic workers and a matchmaker for two attractive young Trekkies, as well as nearly winning the heart of a beautiful flight attendant named Amelia. Loosely based on a true event, *The Terminal* did feel good, as improbable as Viktor's rapid adoption of English or his ascent to the status of heartthrob architect artisan may have been. And yet, a strain of melancholy shot through the hijinks and warm smiles: Viktor's face is all suffering as he sees Krakozhia aflame on TV near the beginning, and it broadcasts his heartbreak after he loses Amelia in the end—and the entire reason he's even in New York, we discover, is because his father has died.

For John, it was "a love story, of course, in a way. But I also see this thing as kind of an Ellis Island poem, if you like. And so, musically, it's an opportunity to create music for Viktor that has an ethnic texture."[22] Thus, he gave Viktor a bouncing, spirited folk tune for clarinet and orchestra which evoked Eastern Europe with a little of the klezmer quality from his Jewish film scores. The theme is not invoked for quite some time, not until the airport is fully introduced along with the man in charge of customs, Frank Dixon, who hopelessly tries to explain Viktor's situation to him. The first piece of score in the film is actually John's anthem for Krakozhia—a stern Russianist march for the fictional country heard on a news report, which then transitions to ethereal synth voices as Viktor frantically runs around in a panic and the score plays with "GRAVE" urgency.

It is on Viktor's second day, when Dixon and his security team spot him wandering the terminal in his bathrobe, that the music begins to bounce. Viktor's theme is an amusingly defiant anthem, an ode to his resilience and resourcefulness and the consternation he causes the uptight Dixon. It plays when Viktor refuses to take Dixon's bait to leave the airport during a security lull, and again as he figures out how to return luggage carts for quarters, then later when he runs through the airport to Dixon's office after his pager goes off. In some ways, this is another "happy con" theme like the one in *Catch Me if You Can*, perfectly paired with Spielberg's Rube Goldbergian visual symphonies of escalating rewards. The clarinet theme takes on a "learning" variation, dancing with an inquisitive piano lick as Viktor teaches himself English using a New York tourist guidebook. Other airy dance themes accompany montages of Viktor looking for work in the airport, and also peppering the customs agent Dolores with questions from her admirer, Enrique. Viktor becomes a hero to the terminal workers after he rescues a fellow foreigner carrying medicine for his ailing father, and John anointed him with a theatrical hero theme which he called "A Legend Is Born."

John's love theme for Amelia and Viktor has a lightly jazzy personality, often performed on piano with upright bass—"a very kind of American sound," he said, "in contrast to Viktor's music."[23] It romantically blossoms in the moment when Viktor—inspired by the recurring facts that Amelia shares about Napoleon and Josephine—reveals the glittering water fountain he's built in the terminal just for her. Jazz is a significant plot point in the story: the peanut can that Viktor carries around contains a photograph full of jazz all-stars, a photo that inspired his father to write numerous clubs in America asking for each musician's autograph—all of which are in the can *except* for the lone player whose signature Viktor's father never received before he died: Benny Golson. This was a real photo, which John was well acquainted with, and one of the signatures belonged to Miff Mole; John revealed that "for many years I had his trombone. It was given to my father from that man, and given to me as a youngster when I was studying on that instrument."[24]

John assigned the score's many clarinet solos to Emily Bernstein, an L.A. session player who had been with his orchestra for years. One day when he was recording *The Patriot*, Bernstein was off the clock waiting for her ride—her partner JoAnn Turovsky, John's regular harpist—when John said he'd like to try one of his melodies on the clarinet. Bernstein had already put her instrument away and was eating licorice, with sticky fingers, and with no warning "they bring over this music," Turovsky recalled. "And that's the way it is with John: the lights go down, and it was *go*. She played perfectly—as usual, as always. He loved it, and that was what he ended up using in the movie."[25] From that point on, Bernstein was his principal clarinet. John did not know when he assigned her the prominent, virtuosic solos in *The Terminal* that Bernstein had terminal liver cancer. She was diagnosed in January; the sessions were in May. "She was already sick," said Turovsky. "It wasn't common knowledge yet, but she was already deep into chemo and all that. And so it was quite a feat for her."

Bernstein had a chance to rehearse her parts ahead of time, but on the big day, John decided to record some of her cues with a click—and much faster than she'd been practicing. "You're in tune to your partner," said Turovsky. "When I heard the click I thought, *oh my god!* We had just rehearsed it a couple of times at a different tempo, and then in pops the click and my heart skipped a beat there for a moment in sympathy." But Bernstein "just laid it down, and I think we did it two or three times—she never missed a note. I think the entire orchestra just erupted after she played it. It was incredible."[26] Spielberg insisted that Bernstein receive a special screen credit, and as a thank-you gift John gave her an inscribed book about Russian film music which he pulled off his own shelf. She received a lot of attention when the film came out, hearing from clarinetists around the world, including jazz great Eddie Daniels. "The whole experience with *The Terminal* has given me so much during a difficult time with my health," Bernstein said. "It has been a light in my life."[27]

Emily Bernstein died a few months later, on January 26, 2005. She was 46. "For a composer," John said, "there are two kinds of players: those who make you feel what you wrote isn't quite up to how you imagined it, or those who blow your mind when you hear what you've written, making you believe it's better than you ever imagined it could sound. Musicians in the second category bring other levels of meaning and depth to the music that perhaps you hadn't imagined were there."²⁸ In the end credits version of the theme, "you can hear [Emily] physically take a breath," said Turovsky, "and it's so poignant.... You hear her take this life-affirming breath right before she finishes this unbelievable solo."²⁹

* * *

John received a phone call from Ted Kennedy, personally letting him know that he was among that year's Kennedy Center Honorees. And so John found himself, in early December 2004, perched in the well-lit balcony of the D.C. opera house with a rainbow ribbon around his neck, sitting next to actors Warren Beatty, Ossie Davis, and Ruby Dee, singer-songwriter Elton John, and opera singer Joan Sutherland—as well as President George W. Bush and his wife, Laura—and receiving one of the country's highest prizes for an artist.

John actually knew the man who had helped conceive the prize. Nick Vanoff, a Greek-born dancer and producer of variety series and musical TV specials dating back to the 1950s, co-produced the first Kennedy Center Honors in 1978 with George Stevens, Jr.† John and Barbara were friends with Vanoff and his wife, Felicia—he always affectionately referred to Vanoff as a "gypsy," which for John meant "the people who put on the shows," said Bill Cosel, John's friend from Boston. "He doesn't see himself like that at all. He admires it, in a way, that they can do what they do—out of thin air."³⁰ Vanoff, who died in 1991, designed the annual Washington honors as a lavish television production—which somewhat bothered John. "I remember asking the late Senator Heinz about this," John said. "Why isn't this something that represents a government expression of appreciation, like the Medal of Honor or the Medal of Arts or those things? He said, 'No, no, there's no reason to change it. It isn't broken. Don't fix it.'"³¹

John did a round of press when the honors aired on CBS. He downplayed his success, as usual, attributing much of it to luck. Julie Chen, host of *The Early Show*, pushed back: "Five Oscars, seventeen Grammys, three Golden Globes, two Emmys, and now the Kennedy Center honor. That's not luck." "Maybe it's not luck," John conceded, chuckling. "It also makes me feel a little old." "No," Chen responded. "*Accomplished*." John accepted the word: "Accomplished. Thank you. *Mature*."³²

During John's portion of the ceremony, Spielberg paid tribute to his friend and introduced a biographical video featuring never-seen old photos and praiseful narration. Spielberg called John "a national treasure, as American as apple pie and"—gesturing up to the commander in chief—"President Bush's mom." Perlman performed the theme from *Schindler's List*, and the 70-person Marine Band played a suite of his greatest hits. John described the night as an out-of-body experience. "As glittery as the Oscars are, this seems even more so."³³

* * *

---

† The inaugural inductees included Fred Astaire and Richard Rodgers.

Why does tragedy inspire some of the best music? *Revenge of the Sith*, the final chapter in Lucas's prequel trilogy, concluded the story of Padmé and the Old Republic and turned Anakin into a corrupted apprentice to the revealed Sith lord and newly emperor, Palpatine. It sent Anakin's newborn children off to Alderaan and Tatooine, charging Obi-Wan with keeping an eye on young Luke and setting the table for the story that started it all in 1977. In between the digital cacophony of yet more star wars and star duels, the film is, at heart, a requiem.

It is also a dramatic improvement on *Clones* and easily the finest panel in this antebellum triptych. The poetry of ideas and parallels that Lucas attempted in this last act are strong: Anakin's lost innocence is symbolized by the wood carving he gave Padmé when he was a little boy, which lies in her hands during her funeral procession; the birth of their twins is juxtaposed against the sinister "birth" of Darth Vader. Narrative echoes and motifs from both trilogies ripple throughout, and *Sith* was also the darkest *Star Wars* film yet—with the entire Jedi order betrayed and mass executed, and Anakin massacring a roomful of terrified children. It is still hampered by much of the cinematic crud that preceded—the videogame visuals, Christensen's lack of gravitas, and still more cringey dialogue; Obi-Wan's adventures on a giant lizard inside the uncanny valley pull focus away from the intensifying human drama. Nevertheless, John dug deep and—aided by an aching performance from Natalie Portman—gave it the weight of grand tragedy and grown-up sadness.

He dutifully dispatched hyperactive battle music—the film opens with thunderous war drums and remains a constant flurry of activity. He wrote a new motif for the evil cyborg General Grievous, a hulking and sinister march sometimes juiced with chanting choir. There are martial and worried variations of the Force theme, brass palpitations and orchestral mayhem, off-kilter tribal music for the CGI lizard mount, and a new military march when the battle heats up (which foreshadowed John's theme for *Sunday Night Football*). But the heart of this score is heartbreak, and there are many passages where action pauses and John attends Padmé's intense sorrow and Anakin's nightmares about her dying. He interlaced introspective quotes of "Across the Stars" with a new lament for solo cello and an abundance of adagio string writing, and he turned the love theme into a swirling idée fixe that follows Anakin's descent into paranoia and ultimately the dark side. In one of the only poetically cinematic moments in the prequel series, a woman's anguished, desert-like wail hovers over an ominous pad as Padmé stares out her window at the setting sun while, across the city, Anakin does the same thing, and cries—fixated on her impending death.

Palpatine's final transformation into the Emperor is accompanied by familiar uses of the villain's classic theme from *Return of the Jedi*; when he tells Anakin about the Sith lord who learned how to cheat death, their conspiratorial conversation is scored with a haunting fog of throat singing. (Technically this was diegetic music for the giant bubble show they're attending, but the source of the music is never shown, and the mood is appropriately forbidding.) When the Emperor implements "Order 66," a montage of clone soldiers turning sides and executing their Jedi comrades is grieved with a deeply felt elegy for strings and choir. Yoda clutches his heart in emotional pain—the gravity of any given moment is constantly in tension with imagery that looks like a computer game cutscene—and the cue pivots from choral mysticism to tragedy as the scared younglings look to Anakin for help, and he responds by drawing his lightsaber for slaughter; meanwhile, Padmé sheds real tears and the skies blacken with smoke and sorrow. This was the closest Lucas ever came to earning the same level of poignancy that John brought to real historical atrocities. They spoke together about how the sequence "would be treated as a lamentation," John said. "It's the kind of thing that seems like a very good idea and I wrote it that way but it also has to be dubbed that way, and it has to be an across-the-board cooperation between dialogue, sound, and music, so that particular emotion of an elegy is put across despite some pretty horrific things that we're looking at."[34]

When John first recorded "Duel of the Fates" in 1999, Lucas hinted that he had secret plans for it in his final episode.[35] The anthem does appear in the climactic duel between Anakin and Obi-Wan on the lava planet of Mustafar, but for whatever reason, that piece was mostly abandoned and the main driver was a new choral war song which John called "Battle of the Heroes." An upward-sprinting string motor and some semiautomatic brass power the tragic theme, a warlike spin on Cinque's theme from *Amistad*. The battle rages on, climaxing with Obi-Wan chopping Anakin in half and leaving him in smoldering ruins. At last Ewan McGregor was unhindered by the acting straitjacket he had been in for the previous six hours, as he cries out with conviction, "You were my brother!" accompanied by another string threnody.

Loose ends are tied up with Yoda's theme and the Force theme, and John scored Padmé's birthing scene with a cryptic piece for celeste and flute. Interestingly, he brought back the music from Qui-Gon's funeral for Padmé's funeral procession. "I could have written another piece that might have as much impact or possibly more," John said, "but George and I felt it would be good to recapitulate themes where they would have the most impact for people—and that funeral cortège piece seemed to work equally well in this new piece, so all I had to do was extend it and reorchestrate it a little bit."[36] The film's finale bridged Lucas's new narrative with the beginning of the original *Star Wars*, and John quoted Leia's theme on French horn as Bail Organa offers to adopt the baby girl, and the Force theme when Obi-Wan agrees to take the boy to Tatooine; Padmé's cortège is counterpointed with the Imperial March, as Vader and the Emperor stare out at the Death Star under construction; Leia's and Luke's themes follow the respective infants, and this new trilogy crescendoes with a potent restatement of the classic "Binary Sunset" version of the Force theme, as Uncle Owen and Aunt Beru hold baby Luke and stare into the iconic twin suns. "I've never had an experience like this," John said, "where you're going back to do the third part of something that you did the fourth part of 20 years ago. I don't think it has been done anywhere."[37]

Revenge of the Sith came out in May 2005, earning much better notices than its two predecessors—even if the general feeling was a sigh of relief that this long cinematic war was finally over. The soundtrack album debuted in the top 10 of Billboard's album chart, and in his *Globe* review, Dyer said it contained the "most powerfully emotional music of the series."[38] A month earlier, the original *Star Wars* soundtrack was added to the National Recording Registry, alongside the Beach Boys' *Pet Sounds* and Neil Armstrong's first broadcast from the moon.[39] There was no question that *Star Wars* had become an indelible part of American culture, and it appeared that the epic space opera was now, at last, *complete*. But the marriage of greed and nostalgia is a powerful force indeed.

* * *

John scored no less than *four* films that year. "Even when Johnny was *hungry*, thirty years ago, he didn't do four movies in one year," quipped Spielberg, who gave John his second assignment of 2005.[40]

In a strange echo of 1977, John immediately followed a *Star Wars* film with a Spielberg epic about a close encounter of the third kind. "We can look back on our lives and think how profound sometimes even coincidence can be," John mused, "and we might even argue that all of us, as we go through life, become more and more conscious of things like that."[41] One major difference was that, in *War of the Worlds*, the aliens are not interested in making peaceful contact. In Spielberg's revision of the classic H. G. Wells story, the Martian invasion assumed the psychological trauma and explicit imagery from the 9/11 terrorist attack on the World Trade Center. It was only the second time in their 30-year history where, because of an unforgiving production schedule and special effects workload, John started scoring the film before Spielberg finished editing; only half of the 12 reels were complete. "John is writing the music in a semi vacuum," Spielberg said.

> He never saw the last 60 minutes of the movie! But he said he had enough of an experience in the first 60 minutes that he knew exactly how to write it. But I'll be absolutely blown away when I hear the first note, because I have no preconceptions about what the music's going to be like. Except John keeps reassuring me it's going to be really different than anything he's done before.[42]

It was. The only precedents were John's barbarically percussive music for *The Lost World*, his atonal atmospheres in *Images*, and his avant-garde concert music. He summoned a brutal, frenetic concerto for fear and orchestra to match the panic and destruction that Spielberg painted on a bleak but grand and visceral scale. After we meet Ray, a divorced dad played by a winning Tom Cruise, Spielberg tosses him right into the middle of an alien invasion at a New Jersey intersection—a patient filmmaking exercise in terror and suspense that escalates with Ray racing home while his neighbors are zapped into smithereens, covering him in gray human ash. "One of the most terrifying things I've ever seen," John said. "We have orchestral gestures and sound effects, but some of them also have a women's chorus—there are women making a kind of glissando that goes up almost like a shriek. The addition of something human, even though we don't exactly know that it's a women's chorus, gives us some feeling here that just a zap doesn't quite have. So you recognize some pain in it," he explained, even though the victims are gone before *they* can scream.[43]

A downed airplane and a wall of photos of the missing are just some of the other evocations of September 11, 2001—televised images that were so recently seared onto every American's brain. Besides displaying his absolute mastery of visual storytelling and balletic choreography of moving vehicles and action set pieces, Spielberg also bottled into cinema the sickening reality of a frightened mob—whether tearing through windshield glass with their bare hands or surging toward a departing ferry like a herd of frightened animals. John reused the women's shriek effect when victims are plucked up into roving tripods after the ferry is overturned, and he later employed male voices for a scene where Ray and his daughter Rachel hide out in a farmhouse basement. "If you dig really deeply into that soundtrack," John said, "there are men singing in that. It's even below the Russian bass. It goes into almost the register of Tibetan monks, which is the lowest kind of pitch that our bodies are able to make." The rest of his score was far more inhuman: a churning brass storm, savage Stravinskian and syncopated rhythms, high string clusters—all with a pounding, relentless pace of panic. "The role of the music and the role of the orchestra, really, as [Ray and his children] begin to drive away from the city, is to provide a propulsion that is pulling us forward and helping us to try to escape—although there isn't any escape," John said. In some places, a blaring brass punctuation recalls vintage monster movies. "We just sort of doff our cap, give a little referential nod to the genre."[44]

The basement scene, where Ray and Rachel fend off a creep played by Tim Robbins and a serpentine alien probe, is another Spielbergian monster horror sequence in the vein of the raptors in *Jurassic Park*'s kitchen or the spyders searching for John Anderton; John scored it with queasy suspense and an alarmed pulse. Ray blindfolds Rachel and has her sing "Hushabye Mountain" (written by the Sherman Brothers for the 1968 film *Chitty Chitty Bang Bang*) while he kills Robbins's character, and John's score pumps with a subtle heartbeat, punctuated by sounds of the lethal beating, then chugs and ramps up into a freak-out string cluster as the probe suddenly appears and Rachel screams; Ray hacks it apart to the strains of a Ligeti-like voice and string cluster, emerging from the monochromatic basement to find a landscape covered in red blood—like some gory remix of *The Wizard of Oz*. String elegies dot the soundtrack in moments of introspection and when Ray's son Robbie attempts to leave and join the army. John wrote a melancholy, battle-weary trumpet trio for the end credits, and Spielberg liked it so much that he used it again earlier, when Ray comes out of a destroyed house to find the fallen plane.

The film's denouement finally allows the first taste of musical relief, in the form of a stoic trumpet melody, lonely and strong, as Ray carries Rachel to her mom's townhouse in Boston and the family reunites amidst a flurry of autumn leaves; a solo piano wanders in a daze when Robbie emerges and finally hugs his father. The film begins and ends the same way: with Morgan Freeman providing narration from the book, scored with a shimmering, mysterious piece for an "electronically assembled group of sounds," as John described it.

"Selfishly, I feel the scariest music written for film was *Jaws*," Spielberg wrote in his liner note.

> For *War of the Worlds*, John reached for something not of this earth and composed a score that you feel on your skin, even before you become aware that you are actually hearing it. He has laid down a musical foundation of atmospherics and textural events, achieving a rhythmic propulsion that is so utterly primal it crawls up inside of you and makes you wonder how one composer could make such a radical departure in style from such masterworks of melodic phrasing as the flying theme from *E.T.*, to the enduring themes of the *Star Wars* series and come up with a new sound that gives *War of the Worlds* much of its ultra-realism.[45]

The dramatic differences between them, and the vital creative freshness of this score and *Sith*, were as awesome as the binary suns of 1997. Three decades later, age 73, John had done it again.

* * *

When he read Arthur Golden's *Memoirs of a Geisha* in 1997, John had immediately imagined a musical voice for its main character: solo cello. He even sent a copy of the book to Yo-Yo Ma with some vague dream of "setting the book to music," Ma said.[46] That suddenly became practical when Spielberg acquired the film rights, with plans to direct an adaptation immediately after *Saving Private Ryan*. But years went by, and when the project finally achieved liftoff in 2004, it did so with a new pilot—Rob Marshall, the dancer-choreographer who transitioned into directing musical films like the Oscar-winning *Chicago*.[‡] Ordinarily, John would jump ship on a would-be Spielberg film once it passed into other hands, as he had done on *Rain Man* and *Bridges of Madison County*. But he *really* wanted to score this story.

The debate about cultural appropriation, and about *who* gets to tell *whose* story, is an old one—and it would heat up in Hollywood even more intensely soon after. But even in 2005, the irony was not lost on critics that several white men were bringing this story about Japanese women to the screen. (Golden himself was a Jewish American from Tennessee.) Even the film's casting was controversial, with all three major female parts being played by non-Japanese stars of Chinese cinema.[47] For John, whose music had traveled from the shtetls of 1905 Eastern Europe to prisoner of war camps in 1940s China to a slave port in Sierra Leone, channeling the music of other cultures was an exciting challenge and a delicious opportunity. He had lightly touched on Japanese idioms in *None But the Brave* and *Midway*, had collaborated with Stomu Yamash'ta on *Images*, and his flute concerto was inspired by the Japanese shakuhachi. He had also been to Japan many times and followed his curiosities there. But he did even more concentrated

---

‡ Spielberg also considered directing a remake of *The Secret Life of Walter Mitty* starring Jim Carrey around this time. (Carol Beggy and Mark Shanahan, "Light Goes Dark Quickly; Williams Scores Again with 'Harry Potter,'" *Boston Globe*, June 3, 2003.)

reading about the culture's musical vocabulary and instrumentation before he set pencil to paper on *Geisha*, especially curious about how to write for the koto, a 13-stringed Japanese zither that featured in Golden's story, as well as the shamisen and biwa (both plucked lute-like instruments). "The challenge and the opportunity was [sic] to combine the modalities of Orientalism, that are pretty much understood internationally, with the broader emotional palette—I think I can put it that way—of the Western symphony orchestra," John said, "and bring them together in a very delicate and even fragile kind of setting, which *Geisha* certainly was, at least by contrast to me."[48] "Of course," he conceded, "every ear that's acculturated differently is going to hear it differently."[49]

He had never shaken the idea of representing Sayuri with a lone cello, "which is not Japanese particularly, and Yo-Yo is Chinese-American," John admitted. "But I think the biggest single mission perhaps of the filmmakers and myself is to try to seek universalisms in the story, in the music and in the emotions. The picture was given in English, not Japanese. So I did ring up Yo-Yo immediately and he said, 'Yes, yes, of course I'll come.'"[50] Ma was another musician who eagerly embraced and intermarried traditions of other cultures with his Silk Road Ensemble and other projects. "John is so incredibly curious, and he's humble," said Ma. "He needs to write what he's found out—about another person, about another story, about a discipline, about a science. He's going to try and find a way to put it through his mastery of composition, so that it comes out in some musical form, so those sounds can be reinterpreted as the thing that gave him the inspiration."[51]

Sayuri's theme is an Eastern-tinged heart song, marked "CANTABILE" in the score—a direction to play in a smooth singing style. Ma made *everything* sing, of course, and his empathetic embodiment of this solitary, searching tune gives the young girl—cruelly taken from her fishing village and sold into servitude—a soulful voice. This theme follows Sayuri from her lonely childhood to young adulthood, where she trains to become the most celebrated geisha in Japan, always with her vicious rival attempting to take her down. Often sad, her tune turns sweeter on solo erhu when the gentle Mameha (Michelle Yeoh) enters Sayuri's life. The theme's big showcase is a montage of Sayuri becoming a geisha—a stunningly photographed and choreographed sequence where Marshall's background as a musical theater director really shines. An uptempo harp arpeggio burbles under her theme, which is carried by combined strings and cello and ornamented with lots of little flourishes and instruments taking up fragments of the melody, which parallel the geishas' elegant dance; when it turns to the pain portion of Sayuri's training, the cue briefly detours into an athletic, aggressive solo for Japanese percussion before easing back into the theme. The drums here are "almost a suggestion of a sacrifice," John said, almost like "this child is being offered to a Mayan god somewhere."[52] The whole montage was scored, he said, like "the preparation of a princess."[53]

Essentially, Sayuri is a Japanese Cinderella—a pure-hearted orphan with mean mother and sister figures, derisively nicknamed "Pumpkin" and forced to clean and serve, and who falls in love with a handsome prince. Here, the prince is the much older Chairman, played with kindness by Ken Watanabe, who first meets her as a young girl on a bridge near a tree exploding with cherry blossoms—a moment that plants a seed and a prayer which power Sayuri through the rest of the story. John gave the Chairman a graceful, old world waltz for violin and orchestra, "a kind of *valse triste*, which is to say a sad waltz," he said, "but one that is imbued with a loving feeling."[54] He asked Itzhak Perlman to provide the character's "voice," further turning this score into "a kind of concerto grosso," he said, "for an assortment of solo instruments with string accompaniment."[55]

Sayuri and others are often shown playing koto onscreen, and John featured this plucked instrument prominently in his score. He hired two Japanese musicians, Masayo Ishigure and Hiromi Hashibe, "two lovely ladies who actually didn't read Western music," but who flawlessly imitated lines he demonstrated for them on the piano.[56] He often ghosted their koto lines with orchestral harp, "where you might have 70 percent of the energy coming from the koto and the rest coming from the harp," he explained. "But the combination of the two things gives the koto a kind of glow—it's different from a reverb; it's prettier than that. You could add any other instrument to do that, but the harp is very close to the koto, and it's fascinating because the koto's able to do a lot of things that the harp can't and vice versa because of the pedals and the tuning." He also had an army of local percussionists at the recording sessions in UCLA's Royce Hall, which took place in September, playing various kabuki instruments and taiko drums, as well as the Thai "nipple gong," tam-tam, and sundry. "It's all written out," John said. "And though we didn't do a lot of layering or overdubbing, we did some with the percussion, which gives it energy but also a kind of a glow."[57] He called on Masakazu Yoshizawa, the same shakuhachi player who imitated a dinosaur's cry on *Jurassic Park*, to provide some wild, atmospheric effects as well as emotion: when little Sayuri cries after being carted away from her family, the shakuhachi seems to be crying with her.

The film and score build to one of the most emotionally cathartic denouements in John's career, a cue he aptly titled "Confluence." After a life of hardship and rejection, both as a geisha before the Second World War and a laborer during the war, having pined for the Chairman from afar but never able to make contact, Sayuri is surprised by the older man on the same bridge from her youth, and he reveals that he always knew she was that little girl—and that he has been aiding her *and* carrying a torch for her this entire time. John serenaded their hushed conversation delicately with trembling quotes of Sayuri's theme on solo flute and English horn; Ma's cello wafts in and gains strength as the Chairman touches Sayuri's quivering face, and a small wood flute (played by Yoshizawa) cries with childlike joy when they kiss—the music blossoming into a grand string sweep and an emboldened, conclusive landing of Sayuri's theme on French horns. Marshall was elated with John's score. "It was a passion project for him," Marshall said. "I felt that from him, and he just poured his entire self into it in such a complete way, and such a full and passionate way. He understood it perfectly. He understood the longing, the sadness in the piece, but also the fragile nature of the character, and the beauty of the character, and understood her yearning and her desire and her angst."[58]

By and large, the film was reviewed as stylish but empty, a soap opera with fantastic production design. "The lavish kimonos, a sumo match, geisha dances, John Williams' lyrical East-meets-West musical score, and atmospheric cinematography by Dion Beebe emphasizing deep, dark colors all are hallmarks of classic Hollywood filmmaking," Kirk Honeycutt wrote in the *Hollywood Reporter*. "These are surface delights that might distract from Marshall's tendency to focus on melodrama over intimacy and emotional excess over restraint."[59] John was nominated for an Oscar and was demonstrably proud of the score, promoting it heavily along with Ma—they even performed the theme together on Jay Leno's *The Tonight Show*—and arranging a 25-minute suite for cello and orchestra, which he premiered at Tanglewood the following summer. Many musicians felt *Geisha* was far and away the best score of the year, and one of John's most incredible achievements—but his chances at the Academy Awards were perhaps diminished by also being nominated for his *next* assignment.

* * *

"John was very tired when he got to this picture," Spielberg said, referring to John's fourth assignment of 2005. "But he reached down deep and he pulled something wonderful out of his heart."[60] *Munich* is a grim, graphic, and startlingly cynical depiction of the 1972 killing of Israeli Olympic athletes by the Palestinian terrorist group Black September, and of Israel's response by sending a hit squad to assassinate the culprits by any means necessary.§ It was a provocative, mutual condemnation of the ceaseless cycle of violence in the Middle East, causing some to accuse Spielberg of anti-Zionism. The director insisted his goal was to exercise empathy for *all* players in this perennial conflict, and that fundamentally the film was a plea for peace.[61] He shot it like a spy thriller, paying homage to 1970s cinema with slow zooms and hand-held action as Avner (Eric Bana) and his team converse and conspire, debating morality and planting bombs. Production was executed like a mobilized army unit, with a scant nine weeks reserved for post-production; as Spielberg was shooting, editor Michael Kahn assembled scenes in a trailer that moved from location to location, then sent them off to Ben Burtt for sound design and John for score.[62] That, combined with John's year-end fatigue, partly accounted for a score that is both lean and mean—vacillating between moral weariness and a brooding pulse. The Frenchman who supplies Avner with intel effectively summarized this score in a line he delivers to the story's conflicted hero: "We are tragic men: butcher's hands, gentle souls."

The film opens with a melismatic motif wailed by singer Lisbeth Scott—one of the score's two central themes. "I think it might have been Steven's idea originally to have a woman singing a kind of cantilena," said John,[63] who was once more contributing (unintentionally) to the "wailing woman" trope that began with *Gladiator*. Scott sang the anguished lament not in Hebrew or Arabic, but in her own made-up syllables; like the film, John's music refuses to take a side. John conceived this theme for a climactic sequence which cuts between an agonized Avner having sex with his wife while experiencing vivid flashbacks to the athletes' death on the tarmac in Munich—an audacious medley of orgasm, violence, and sorrow.

---

§ The material recalled the subject of *Black Sunday*, albeit much less sensationalized; also, the historic events of *Munich* took place the same year that John met Spielberg.

The other major theme was for Avner himself, which John labeled "A Prayer for Peace." With its Hebraic accent, the melody is a melancholic psalm which bears relation to the Jewish lament in *Schindler's List* as well as to Israel's national anthem, "Hatikvah (The Hope)," which is actually heard, diegetically, in a TV news report of the attack before that elegiac piece gets transported into John's orchestral score. Avner's theme is conveyed by strings when he takes off on his first mission, imagining the terrorists killing his brethren, and then on warm acoustic guitar over a wordless montage of him bonding with his new crew—a brief scene that gave John a chance to expedite our emotional attachment to these five men. The tune is taken up by solitary clarinet when Avner's comrades begin to die one by one, and by solo cello, then piano in the film's downbeat finale as Avner questions all of the blood and peace he has sacrificed.

Spielberg ended the film with a politically freighted portrait of the New York skyline—the Twin Towers still hauntingly intact. As he did on *Saving Private Ryan*, Spielberg left most of the "battle" sequences without score, instead building suspense with the precisely orchestrated staging of cars and bodies and explosives. John supplied some of the tension with insistent electronic and percussive rhythms and low orchestral turbulence, recalling somewhat the plotting pulse in *JFK*. A deep electronic heartbeat flutters as the hit squad's first mark leaves a book lecture and goes shopping; a syncopated beat quickens after an oversized explosion goes off in a hotel. There are low rumblings on piano when Avner has another dream of the athletes, and chaotic smacking inside a piano as he anxiously scours his room for hidden explosives. John accented many of these throbbings and clouds of dread with instrumental colors from Persia and Armenia, including oud, duduk, and cimbalom. As opposed to the Eurocentric Jewish sound featured in *Schindler*, John said, "I felt what was needed was a different expression of the locale and ambience of Israel and Palestine itself."[64] After long stretches of musical absence for the film's nearly three-hour running time, John drew an emotional curtain with an expressive concert version of Avner's theme. At its core, the score channels "the enormous suffering and guilt and, eventually, paranoia that Avner experiences because of what he has been asked to do," John said. "The music, while it's quiet, digs pretty deeply into a lot of layers of grief that go with this film."[65]

The end of this marathon year also brought an end to one of John's longest partnerships—with the retirement of Ken Wannberg. "Wampi" moved up to Oregon, leaving his black binders filled with three decades of spotting notes behind in John's Amblin bungalow. Gone was John's wingman since 1967, from before John became famous and through his breathtaking ascent—the man who typed up detailed cue sheets, who was always working in the other room running a moviola, who sat in the recording booth at every scoring session, who made miracles out of forced music edits, and who fought for John in the final mix. Gone was the fellow soldier John could commiserate with and, after eight holes of golf, share a vodka on the rocks with—and laugh. "I would say that his whole life is music," Wannberg said of John.

> After he would do a cue and he'd play his golf and he came home and had dinner, he wouldn't go to bed—maybe he would start working on the next cue for the next

day, the one that he would be writing. So he would work all the time. He would be around music all the time.

"He's just John," Wannberg added of his friend. "I really think music takes over with everything. Music is everything to him—and it shows in his music."⁶⁶**

* * *

John decided to take a deserved hiatus from scoring, but he kept his dance card full. When NBC purchased the broadcasting rights for primetime Sunday night NFL games, a $600 million expense, the network asked John to write a suitably blockbuster-sized theme.⁶⁷ He had never been to a professional football game in his life, but felt he had enough of a grasp on the sport and its role in the American heart. "Football is a different kind of musical portrait," he said. "It's a tough test. It's a rugged, gladiatorial contest.... It's got a distinctly American character.... Football is about up-front linemen banging [into] each other." So he wrote a theme that was "rhythmically taut and strong and tough. It's brassy. It's not something you do with a lot of violins."⁶⁸ He wrote it in one month, along with several variations and bumpers. This syncopated martial anthem, reminiscent of the droid march from *Phantom Menace*, debuted on September 10, 2006, in a match between the Indianapolis Colts and the New York Giants. John later christened the theme *Wide Receiver*, and it continued to blast through television speakers every Sunday night for the next two decades.

The following October, he kicked off the 2007 World Series—a match between his beloved Red Sox and the Colorado Rockies—with a new arrangement of the national anthem, performed by a brass and percussion band plucked from the Pops. Booming through the PA system at Fenway Park, the announcer introduced John—wrapped in a Boston blue World Series jacket—as "the pride of Boston and the epitome of our culture." John's chart juiced the tune into a stirring call to battle and bent some of its familiar phrases into twisty new harmonies. Roger Catlin, TV critic for the *Hartford Courant*, complained that "it sounded a little off, as if the brass had warped like woodwinds in the Fenway rain."⁶⁹ Unlike the *Sunday Night Football* theme, this anthem did *not* become a staple.

John finally had ample time to spend on concert works, which he referred to as a "busman's holiday"—a droll British phrase he adopted from Previn.⁷⁰ He had attended a chamber concert at Tanglewood 10 years earlier in which BSO violist Michael Zaretsky and violinist Victor Romanul performed Bohuslav Martinů's "Three Madrigals." John told them how impressed he was by the rich sound of their combined instruments, and Zaretsky said: "Maybe you should write also for this combination." Years passed, and whenever John visited Boston he often told Zaretsky the idea was still in the back of his mind. Then, one day in October 2006, Zaretsky received an unexpected FedEx package with a finished, 13-minute Duo Concertante and a note saying that, if he liked it, he should give John a call. "Of course I called

---

** Wannberg later developed Parkinson's disease. He died in 2021.

him immediately," said Zaretsky. A week later, the two musicians joined John at his Blantyre cottage, and for three hours they discussed bowings and other string-centric notes—John with red pencil in hand. They agreed to debut the piece on a program with the Martinů duos, which had been an inspiration for John's concertante. "He always talked about how the two instruments played opposing each other, but at the same time played in unison," said the Russian-born Zaretsky. "Basically it was brilliance of both instruments he wanted to show."[71]

Tanglewood was ravaged by a biblical thunderstorm on December 1. Forces equal to a Category 1 hurricane tore through the grounds that John so loved to walk, grounds that he considered almost *sacred*, destroying 300 trees and causing $250,000 in damage.[72] One of the buildings most devastated was Seranak, the mansion where Serge Koussevitzky once resided. John was in the area composing at the time, and when he visited the campus to survey the scene, he compared it to General Sherman's march through Georgia. "It's hard to imagine a force so powerful," he said.[73] Clarence Fanto, a longtime reporter on Tanglewood for the *Berkshire Eagle*, got an alert that he would be receiving a call from John. "And sure enough, he came on the phone," Fanto said, "quite dismayed by the amount of damage. And he helped launch a fundraising effort, which I'm sure he was a major contributor to, for the restoration of the property there."[74] For John, Tanglewood was more than a summer home for music. "I'm still infatuated with it in the spiritual sense," he said.

> Perhaps that's naive on my part, but I still can sense Koussevitzky in this place, Bernstein in this place. It's especially meaningful for me—because I come from the commercial, profit-oriented film industry and music business—to come to a place where the spiritual, devotional idea of making music is still, at least for me, intact. I say to colleagues all around the country that I think the high place in American musical life is Tanglewood. This is a sort of Vatican.[75]

John's Duo Concertante was the most stripped-down chamber work he had ever written, and it premiered at Tanglewood the following August. At a rehearsal before the performance in Ozawa Hall, "we were playing the second movement of the piece, and John said to us, 'It's very intimate, like conversation between two people,'" Zaretsky recalled, in his Soviet-tinged English. "I sensed sadness in his presentation of this." Zaretsky mentioned his observation to Mark Volpe, the BSO's managing director, who softly told the violist that John had just lost his sister.[76] Joan Katherine died of congestive heart failure three days earlier, on August 14, 2007, at the age of 77. The second movement is "very, very deep," said Zaretsky, "and quite emotional music." Joan had been sick for a while—too sick, in fact, to attend her own mother's funeral the previous fall.[77]

Esther Williams (Figure 15.1) died in February 2006, just a few weeks before her 97th birthday. John said his Boston-native mother insisted that she lived so long "because she wanted to see the Red Sox win the World Series again. Once they did it in 2004, she felt she could pass on very happily."[78] John adored his gentle, long-suffering mother, his "Duck," and she could not have been prouder of her boy. John spoke at her

Figure 15.1. Esther and her son, ca. 1990 (Photographer unknown, Courtesy of John Williams).

funeral, a family-only affair, and in the parking lot after the memorial service several people came up and said, "I love your music!" "This is at his *mother's funeral*," said John's niece, Paula Arlich, "and you're coming up to him and talking about *Star Wars*? Are you kidding me right now? Give him a break." She began to notice how John would instinctively tense up, even around members of his own family—certain that everyone wanted a cup of his stardust. Arlich, Joan's daughter, made an appointment to visit him at his home one time to ask about her mother and their childhood haunts in New York. "He was a little standoffish," she said. "I guess maybe when people come to see him, he is always expected to give them something—which I think is sad."[79]

* * *

John was 75, and Spielberg and Harrison Ford were both in their 60s, when the gang got back together to make the misbegotten *Indiana Jones and the Kingdom of the Crystal Skull*. Lucas came up with a story about aliens, with Russian baddies replacing Nazis in the cold wartime of the 1950s; the extraterrestrial plot, while outlandish, is less of a problem than the talky script, subdued performances, and videogame visuals.

The whole operation feels like tired old men going through the motions. At the time, Spielberg took cover under the guise of populism: "John Williams and I have a word we use when we have something we think the audience will love," he said. "Maybe it'll be a little over the top, and we ask each other, 'Are we being too shameless?' In a way I think we've both grown kind of proud of being shameless."[80] But the "shamelessness" of past films like *E.T.* or even *Temple of Doom* was incandescent and full of faith—whereas this adventure had all the energy of a compulsory fire drill.

The fatigue extended to John's score, which does shamelessly recycle classic themes and travel music from the original trilogy without his usual spark of reinvention. When his 1989 theme for Henry Jones plays under a framed picture of Sean Connery's character, the moment reads as obligation.[††] John's new themes reflect the film's dour pace and spirit of their respective characters. The best is a noir-like saxophone melody for Irina Spalko, an icy femme fatale played by Cate Blanchett, which was inspired by movie music from the 1940s "where you would hear a slithering saxophone and certain harmonic progressions that would depict this dark side of sensuality and its power and its uses," John said.[81] For the crystal skull, he wrote a sleepy, repetitive incantation as an homage to science-fiction films of the 1950s. This new MacGuffin motif is sufficiently eerie and hypnotic, but less dramatically useful than, say, his vintage Ark of the Covenant theme from *Raiders* (which earns a cameo during the opening sequence where Indy helps the Russians locate the skull).

The score's thematic paucity is felt even further in a bouncy but forgettable action scherzo for Indy's wild motorcycle ride through his college campus with his new companion: Mutt. The young greaser, played by Shia LeBeouf and revealed to be Indy's secret son, was given his own uptempo adventure theme which was little more than an enthusiastic scale exercise. Mutt's theme takes off in the film's anticlimactic set piece where Indy, Mutt, and Marion Ravenwood—Mutt's mother—drive and duel against Spalko and the Russians through a jungle. As their respective themes parry and riposte, Mutt suddenly takes to the vines like Tarzan and swings into action with his up-and-down fanfare. "The combination of his sword fighting and swinging on these vines, and the heroics that he does, made me have some fun with the music," said John, who called the theme "Adventures of Mutt" in a nod to *The Adventures of Robin Hood*, one of Erich Wolfgang Korngold's most famous scores. "The music is not similar, but only in the sense that it is a swashbuckling theme for a young hero."[82] He referred to this theme as a "silly little piece," with "a certain particular jauntiness about it, maybe a hint of impertinence,"[83] but he liked it enough to keep it in rotation at his concerts long after most people forgot all about the character. The return of Marion occasions a reprise of her classic theme from *Raiders*, but again, the citations are mostly unvaried and literal—sapped of all their Nepalese barroom fire. The film culminates in a

---

[††] Connery turned down Spielberg's offer to come out of retirement to appear in this film. "It was not that generous a part," the actor said, "worth getting back into the harness and go for." (Ryan Parker, "Sean Connery Turned Down 'Indiana Jones 4' Because the Role Was Too Small," *Hollywood Reporter*, January 18, 2018.)

wedding between the senior citizens in a light-bleached chapel filled with characters we've never seen before—and even as Marion's enchanting theme flows into the stirring Raiders March, the whole film seems sentiently glad that it's over.

Most critics agreed that it was a mistake. James Mangold, the director of *Cop Land* and *3:10 to Yuma*, argued that the chief problem with *Crystal Skull* is that the earlier Indiana Jones pictures were such love letters to the fantastical, larger-than-life period of Golden Age Hollywood, and because the stories themselves were set in the 1930s and early 1940s, "all of it sits so happily within that period and coexists harmoniously," he explained, "because you have a driver's license to play. The period gives the music and everything else a sense of home against all the other elements." By moving the character into the 1950s, a period of modernism and grounded dramas like *On the Waterfront*, "you suddenly have this more challenging environment for these elements to play in," Mangold said, "which makes them feel slightly less authentic to what's happening onscreen, because they're a recall of another movie. It's just a different world, and it doesn't seem quite as right. And I don't mean just the music—I mean everything is just *off*."[84]

It appeared to be the final hurrah for this lovable old archaeologist—Spielberg was more than ready to retire his bullwhip and fedora—but instead, it was an arbiter for the troubling plague of nostalgia-mining on the horizon, when "intellectual property" would come to be more prized than intellectual sense. Hollywood was about to start fully gorging on its own tail, and John would have to decide whether he wanted to go along and just keep playing the hits.

* * *

Time kept ticking on, and there was no enchanted hourglass John could turn to reverse it. He needed a break, and he would technically not score another film for three years. But he wasn't ready to retire yet—not by a long shot. An action-packed decade awaited, one that not only yielded several new film scores and a flurry of concert works, but also an ascent in both American culture and the classical universe that John could never have imagined—and no other film composer had ever attained.

16
Simple Gifts, 2008–2014

> *Let high-art types gripe about Mr. Williams. Among those whose medium has been the orchestra, he is surely the best known, most popular, and richest composer in history.*
>
> —Anthony Tommasini, 2007[1]

After the brand new president-elect addressed the throng of 240,000 in Chicago's Grant Park, declaring to his hope-filled supporters "Yes, we can," Barack Obama stood and absorbed rolling waves of applause and joy while John's score for *The Patriot* poured from massive loudspeakers, lending the moment some extra cinematic gravitas.[2] John's sprightly fife dance for the American revolution had been conceived for a Hollywood movie; now it was celebrating the reality of the first Black president of the United States. John's music had been the backdrop of American life for Obama's generation—the new president was a teenager when *Jaws* came out—and now, on November 5, 2008, it was being claimed for ceremony on the biggest stage for one of the most significant nights in American political history.

Obama's inauguration "will be an event of historic proportion," said Senator Diane Feinstein, committee chair for the event. "It is appropriate that the program will include some of the world's most gifted artists from a wide range of backgrounds and genres."[3] The new president requested a performance by Aretha Franklin, the Queen of Soul, and for something classical he "very wisely selected Yo-Yo Ma to play," said John.[4] Ma was asked to put together a small chamber group to play a short piece, and Ma handpicked Itzhak Perlman, Gabriela Montero, a pianist from Venezuela, and clarinetist Anthony McGill to form a multiethnic, age-spanning quartet. Ma then called John to see "if I could either write a piece or organize something that might be appropriate for that moment," said John,[5] who was aware that Obama was particularly fond of Aaron Copland's music—but he also knew there was no Copland piece written for Ma's unique assembly of instruments. As a keen student of history, John knew that Copland's *Lincoln Portrait* was originally meant to be performed at Dwight D. Eisenhower's inaugural concert in 1953, only to be suddenly dropped from the program when a conservative congressman complained about Copland's liberal politics. Basing a new work around a Copland piece would be "a completed circle of events that is nice to think about," John said.[6]

But John was intimidated by the occasion, and nervous: "What possibly could be right and good," he said, "with enough virtuosity to show Itzhak and Yo-Yo and McGill?"[7] So he wrote four different pieces—some completely original, some based on an existing tune. One melody he toyed with was more contemporary: "Ashokan Farewell" was composed by folk musician Jay Ungar in 1982 and used as the theme for the popular Ken Burns documentary about the Civil War. John recorded his various options as "demos" with a quartet of top-shelf L.A. musicians in December 2008; some with a big applause ending, others a soft denouement.[8] Inside the rich American soil of Copland's 1944 ballet *Appalachian Spring* was an even older root of Americana: "The Gift to Be Simple," a Shaker hymn circa 1848. Simplicity, defined as "a Godly sincerity, and real singleness of heart, in all our conversation and conduct," was a virtue highly valued by the Shakers, a communal denomination born in England and transplanted to the American colonies in the 1770s.[9] John had previously recorded Copland's setting of the hymn for *The Green Album* with the Pops in 1992, swaddling the tune in lean lushness. Ultimately, he thought "a combination of the Shaker air, as a tribute to President Obama's affection for Aaron Copland, might be appropriate if I could combine it with some perhaps slightly hymnal idea, that might express in a very simple and not ostentatious way the solemnity and beauty of the moment, and the promise of the moment, and put it together for actually a kind of esoteric combination of instruments: violin, cello, piano, and clarinet."[10] John called this final piece *Air and Simple Gifts*.

As a young Black musician from Chicago, who went to the same high school as Michelle Obama, Anthony McGill was ecstatic to be part of the performance at this significant event. Rehearsals at Perlman's house on the Upper West Side in New York were "really intense and fun and awesome," McGill said. "It was such an important thing, and we spent so much time talking about it and thinking about it.... It felt like preparing for the Super Bowl." A few days before the inauguration, John joined the four musicians at John Philip Sousa Band Hall, the Marine Band's rehearsal facility in Washington, D.C., where they recorded *Air and Simple Gifts* as a safety. "It was so exciting," said McGill. "I think I was in shock, if you can be in shock before an event happens—like, not post-traumatic stress but pre-event excitement syndrome."[11]

It was a bitterly cold day on January 20, 2009—the wind chill made it feel even lower than 28 degrees when official proceedings began just before noon; 1.8 million people filled the city, with around 460,000 amassing on the National Mall for a glimpse, or an echo, of the activities on a platform in front of the United States Capitol.[12] In addition to former presidents Jimmy Carter, George H.W. Bush, and Bill Clinton, the starry guestlist included Spielberg, Oprah Winfrey, Tom Hanks, Samuel L. Jackson, Beyoncé, and Muhammad Ali. Evangelical pastor Rick Warren said an invocation prayer, Franklin sang "My Country 'Tis of Thee," and Vice President Joseph R. Biden was sworn in. Then, from a separate level above and behind the main dais, Ma's quartet launched into John's new chamber piece. (John had no reason to conduct, so he remained seated in the VIP section.)

The sound everyone heard emitting from loudspeakers was, in fact, that recording from Sousa Band Hall; at the eleventh hour, the decision was made *not* to broadcast a live performance, simply because it was too cold for the instruments to function properly. So Ma and Perlman put soap on their bows and Montero's piano was muzzled. When this fact later came out, it caused a minor fuss—no one likes being deceived—but as Ma said, "If we had played on the instruments that we had, we would have had a really terrible performance."[13] And McGill *insisted* they were all definitely still performing the notes there on the rostrum.

It "must have been the first time in history when an audience of hundreds of millions worldwide heard the premiere of a piece of chamber music," Mark Swed noted in the *L.A. Times*.[14] The nation's classical critics were mostly complimentary—Anthony Tommasini called it "a stylish and appealing four-minute work.

> He got the mood right, I thought, in this contemplative occasional piece. President Obama, it turns out, has a fondness for the music of Aaron Copland. So Mr. Williams fashioned a work that evokes the melancholic, calmly affirming, harmonically open-hearted world of Copland.
>
> The piece begins with a lacy, quietly searching melody for violin, soon accompanied by consoling modal piano chords. The cello joins in with a pensive melodic line that responds to the violin, while the piano gradually prods the music forward with undulant riffs. Soon the clarinet enters, playing the first two phrases of "Simple Gifts" ... using the melody as the theme for an elaborate set of variations. Though Mr. Williams riffs Copland variations closely, his treatment of the tune is distinct enough to come across as something genuine and personal. There is a jazzy episode, with pungent piano chords and flourishes for snappy clarinet. Then the instruments break into a burst of agitated, jubilant counterpoint, with the piano playing Bachian passages of busy 16th notes.
>
> Eventually the piece turns calm again, and the music becomes reflective, with wide-spaced harmonies and quizzical, halting melodic lines. *Air and Simple Gifts* does not end decisively but settles down and takes stock, for now. Befitting the occasion, it seemed like music of possibilities, with more to come.[15]

One critic noted that, "as the only American composer, post-Leonard Bernstein, to span the classical and popular divide in a big way, Williams was a natural choice for the job."[16] None of these pundits compared John's gifts to Copland's, even though no other composer had picked up the Americana mantle more faithfully and fervently.* But John had no need to hide behind Copland, and Obama's anointment made it official: John Williams was *the* American composer laureate. When Obama visited Japan that November, the Emperor Akihito was asked what he would like as a gift from the State Department: Akihito, a cellist, asked to have the original pencil copy of *Air and Simple Gifts*. Obama was excited to tell John about this the next time they saw each other, and "that's been a kind of a bond thing between us," said John.[17]

---

* It's doubtful anyone on the dais that day, or anyone listening at home, knew that John once played piano for Eugene Loring, the man who choreographed *Billy the Kid* for Copland.

McGill celebrated at a Mexican restaurant with his family after the inauguration ceremony; it had been an incredible day. More than a decade later, after Donald Trump's first presidency and all the political division and turmoil that fomented in the interim, McGill started to cry thinking back on John's piece: "The music encapsulated the feeling of hope at the time.

> Hope for our country, hope for humanity and for Black people and Americans. I think that music ... it sounds of Copland, it sounds of what makes America really, really wonderful. And that feeling of being united in that, and the kind of openness of that sound, and the chords he uses in the John Williams way—it was like the soundtrack for what America *could* be.[18]

* * *

In the three years between new film projects, John spent some of his spare time repackaging oldies. A smoke-and-lasers concert program called *Star Wars: A Musical Journey*—with echoes of the original laser concerts of 1978—had its premiere at the O2 arena in London in December 2008, then commenced an American tour the following October with Anthony Daniels, liberated from his stifling C-3PO costume, as narrator, and a traveling exhibition of *Star Wars* props and memorabilia. "We wanted to put it together with a symphony mentality but in an arena with the scope of a rock 'n' roll concert," said producer Gregg Perloff.[19] John was initially reluctant and skeptical of the concept, but he was eventually persuaded to supervise the musical assembly and even do some new orchestrations of themed highlights from his six-film opus. He exerted additional control by handpicking Belgian conductor Dirk Brossé to lead the 86-piece orchestra and 60-piece choir that took the circus from city to city.[20] "Whenever professional musicians tell me that they don't like the music of John Williams," Brossé said, "I tell them that they need to change professions." A few months earlier, *Harry Potter: The Exhibition* went on tour featuring props and costumes from the film series, with John's music playing on a loop.

John took advantage of his long busman's holiday by writing several new concert pieces. He added to his ever-growing concerto portfolio with a new work for an oft-neglected instrument: the viola.[†] He noticed the BSO's principal violist, Cathy Basrak, as one of the "fantastic virtuosi who sit there night after night, and we don't get a chance, even if we conduct them, to know them personally and know how really great they are."[21] After he heard Basrak's talent in an Alan Shulman piece for viola and orchestra, which he conducted with the Pops in 2003, John secretly began composing a concerto for her—and as he had done with several others before, he surprised her with the completed work at Tanglewood in 2007. He sent Basrak a note asking her to stop by his cottage at Blantyre. When she came inside, he had the score on his piano

---

[†] Prior to the 20th century, there were very few concerti written for viola; the instrument was both an overlooked butt of jokes among musicians as well as a difficult one to compose for. Hector Berlioz told Niccolò Paganini that in order to write for a virtuosic violist, the composer would really need to be able to play the instrument himself. (David M. Bynog, *Notes for Violists: A Guide to the Repertoire* [2021].)

and said: "So, I wrote this." Basrak's young daughter was with her, "and tearing around the place," she said. "I was like, *Oh my God, this was a mistake*." John was his typically timid self, telling Basrak: "We don't need to do anything about it. I just wanted you to have it. It's something that I did." "So I took that at face value," she said. "I took it and sat on it."[22] Later she asked Ann Hobson Pilot, the BSO's principal harpist, how to interpret John's cryptic comment; Pilot encouraged Basrak to learn the piece and play it for John, which she did the following summer.

Basrak grew up in the Chicago area in the 1980s avidly watching John on *Evening at Pops*, so it was a full-circle moment when she joined the BSO in 2000. She had always found him to be genuine, kind, and inquisitive, always asking about her children. When they agreed to premiere the concerto in the summer of 2009, she and John started exchanging letters. Knowing Basrak was married to the BSO's principal timpanist, Timothy Genis, John included a winking, extended "Family Argument" between viola and timpani in the second movement, a scherzo, which originally gave percussion the final word. "I don't know what your arguments are like at home, but I don't think that's really accurate," Genis joked.[23] So John revised it to let the viola win. The concerto ends with a lullaby passage—the married musicians had two young daughters at home—and a cadenza for viola and harp.

A few days before the concert, Basrak met with John in the conductor's room at Symphony Hall and played it through, making a few last-minute adjustments to bowings and articulation. She loved having direct access to John's brain; he instructed her to play the opening passage "sunnier," more optimistically than her original interpretation. But she never really knew what his intentions or the origins of the piece were, and she never asked him for an explanation. "Part of me likes that enigma about it," she said, "and likes that I didn't know that it was there, and I wasn't part of the process."[24] John sprung it on an unsuspecting Film Night audience at Symphony Hall on May 26, 2009. "The first movement offered Basrak taxing, unaccompanied passages all over the strings," the *Globe*'s Joel Brown reported, "with little bursts that touched on dissonance and long, still notes that hung in the air. In short, a showpiece."[25]

The introduction burbles like a gentle river under the heroine viola, which begins with a very lyrical melody that finds delicate dance partners with a flute and other solo wind instruments, and then gets imitated by the orchestra. But it's not long before the waters muddy and the emotions complicate, and that initial sunniness becomes a storm. There are extended cadenzas and impressive double stops that explore the whole range of the instrument, and then the river begins to flow once more. The viola becomes a buzzing bee in the jazzy scherzo movement, or perhaps an angrily chattering wife in its "argument" with the agitated timpani. The final movement is a return to the opening song and a mostly languid conversation between viola and harp. Basrak noticed in this and other works by John that the harp is "a voice he hears interactively," and that it seemed to have a magical and nostalgic quality for him.[26] She convinced Pilot to delay her retirement long enough to play the premiere, and John dedicated the third movement to the veteran harpist. The viola concerto ends "in Cathy's hands,"

John said in his introduction at the premiere, "in a mood of not only rumination but it seems to me, when I hear her play it, almost healing."

In a letter he wrote to Milton Babbitt, the Princeton professor of mathematics and composer of defiantly challenging serial music, John called his viola concerto "largely tonal and with 'tunes' of sorts ... certainly to be viewed as regressive by many ... but alas, it is too late for me to change.... Or improve, it seems."[27] John had met Babbitt at Tanglewood, and they became unlikely friends and pen pals. They bonded over a shared love of Jerome Kern and Irving Berlin—a shared love of *tunes*. Babbitt told John that he "was once a popular songwriter of songs that were never popular." "He loved Kern especially," John said, "and he was fascinated with my relationship to Benny Herrmann." Babbitt was also delighted when John told him how Conrad Salinger, who orchestrated for Kern, used to make up dirty lyrics to the tunes before they had any words. "They're unquotable, but unforgettable," said John. "Babbitt would say, 'Oh, you've got to give them to me!' No, I never had the courage to do it. I couldn't write it down, or certainly *speak* it."[28]

The viola concerto was never commercially recorded—although it was published by Hal Leonard—and Basrak never performed it with an orchestra after that debut. Still, John brought it up whenever he saw her. "My whole professional story changed," she said, "because now I have this concerto that's attributed to me, from him." The viola tends to be associated with doom and gloom, Basrak noted, whereas John really used the instrument's "middle register to be very soulful, and rhapsodic, and sometimes jazzy, and just ... *personal*."[29]

During John's annual Film Night concerts that same week, he debuted a new arrangement of his "E.T. and Me" theme, a virtuosic piece for solo harp and orchestra which he called *Stargazers*. It was another gift for the departing Ann Hobson Pilot, who had been with the BSO since before John's time—recruited to audition by Arthur Fiedler himself back in 1969. As a little Black girl growing up in Philadelphia, she always wanted to play the harp. "I worked hard, but what was I thinking?" she said. "The harp was considered to be the instrument of an angel, a white woman with flowing gowns."[30] She grew up in a family of musicians and became serious about the instrument as a teenager, graduating from the Cleveland Institute of Music to a spot with the National Symphony. When she became the BSO's assistant principal harpist, she was only the second African American ever to play in the orchestra. Her politics were as delicate as her instrument: "I was quiet. Still am. I didn't get into making a political presence. My statement was doing my job and showing that playing music well had nothing to do with color. If intelligent people looked at me, they'd acknowledge that."[31]

She was promoted to principal harpist in 1980, the same year John took over the Pops, and she remembered the early days when some of her fellow musicians let their own personal bitterness seep into their attitude toward John, which had culminated in his temporarily quitting. "It wasn't really a large group of people that didn't like John," Pilot said. "But it was enough at that particular time to make him—as a very sensitive man, I think—say, 'Well, see you later.'"[32] Pilot went on to become one of the country's premier harpists, and she was one of the only BSO principals who also played Pops concerts, which she never minded: "The orchestra sounded better under John than it had under Fiedler." She told James Levine, who had become the BSO's music director in 2004, that she wanted to retire in 2007. "My main goal was to leave before my playing went downhill. I feel that way about parties. I'd rather leave early than stay too long."[33] Levine begged her to stay for two more years, which she did, and he wanted to give her a retirement gift. She said it would be nice to have another harp concerto. Levine asked her who she would want to write it, and after thinking about it she said: "I'd like John Williams."

At first, John declined—the harp was just too difficult to write for, he told Pilot. "I kept saying, 'Ann, there are so many wonderful composers out there,'" to which Pilot replied: "John, if *you* can't write a harp concerto, who can?" "In the end," John said, "I found I couldn't resist her."[34] He donated the piece as a gift to Pilot and the orchestra. They corresponded by mail, "a few bars at a time," she said.

> He's right: the harp is a difficult instrument to write for, with the pedals and all, and unless you are a harpist ... any composer would not always know what works. Most of what he wrote worked. There was only one place in the cadenza where I would have needed a couple more hands and maybe a couple more feet in order to play that passage. He asked what could be done to revise it, and I gave him some ideas, and it was revised. There are some composers that if you criticize, or what they *consider* criticizing, their piece, they'll get defensive and all. But not John. He said, "Okay, we'll change it."[35]

Once again, John took his inspiration from trees. The first movement, "On Willows," refers to a verse in Psalm 137 that describes lyres hanging on willow trees; the music is full of color and glissandos. The second movement, with its tricky mixed meters, was inspired by a Robert Frost poem about a young boy hopping over birch branches, "so in the harp playing," Pilot said, "you can hear the guy hopping around." John described this movement as celebratory. "He wrote it to celebrate me, to celebrate my career," Pilot said. "Every time I would get to those places, *I* would feel like celebrating."[36] *On Willows and Birches* opened the BSO's regular season on September 23, 2009, with Levine conducting and Pilot playing from memory. The *Globe*'s Jeremy Eichler called it "a modest work in its musical substance and in its effect." The first movement "is slow, spare, and ruminative, with an undulating solo harp line drifting above a hazy orchestral landscape, creating a kind of spectral chamber music that seems to be heading somewhere it never quite reaches.

> The second movement ... is more chipper, caffeinated, and rhythmically emphatic, with an extended cadenza that puts the soloist's virtuosity squarely on display. And Pilot had plenty of it to show this appreciative audience. Her playing had impressive rhythmic clarity but also a keen sense of mood and color, not to mention

a fundamental graciousness and expressive warmth. As the crowd's ovation made clear, she will be missed.[37]

In another letter to Babbitt, John said he thought the concerto "proved to be an effective 'party piece' for Ann, whose personal brilliance and theatricality added to whatever qualities the piece may contain. Though a trifle to be sure, I'd love you to hear it if we can ever get it recorded."[38] Pilot, who did record the concerto a month later, said she admired John for "his kindness, his honesty, his compassion. There doesn't seem to be a mean bone in his body. He's just a warm, considerate human being. You can look at works like *Schindler's List* and tell that a person would have to be able to be compassionate, and all of those things that I just said, to write a piece like that."[39]

* * *

President Obama called John back to the White House on February 25, 2010, to collect a National Medal of Arts in a ceremony that also honored conductor Michael Tilson Thomas, John's old friend Jessye Norman the opera singer, and Elie Wiesel, author and Holocaust survivor. "Each has taken a different path to get here, each has made the most of different gifts," Obama said in a statement, "but all of them have reached the peaks of cultural achievement and all of them are a testament of the breadth and depth of human spirit."[40]

It was the first time a film composer had ever received this prestigious honor—with the caveat of Copland, who was in the second class of awardees in 1985. In his speech at a celebration dinner the night before the ceremony, playwright Tony Kushner touted "the openhearted, fantastically various, subtle, and grand film scores of a legendary composer we can consider, among other things, our country's culture's global reach, the way our nation resides in the world." Kushner (who became a frequent collaborator with Spielberg) also called for more government support and funding of the arts, which "can provide to government what in these times seems so calamitously lacking: the principles and tools of creation; taking pains, pausing for reflection, doubt, second-guessing, comfort with ambiguity and paradox, listening to the audience and to one's own soul."[41]

The new president inherited the worst economy in decades, a massive recession triggered by the housing loan crisis. Among those who suffered were symphony orchestras, and beginning in 2008 John ramped up his conducting appearances with the orchestras in Chicago, Pittsburgh, Fort Worth, and Detroit—every time donating his fee to their musicians' pension fund. The crisis in Detroit had begun even earlier, with the fallout of the automobile industry, and when Leonard Slatkin took over the wounded Detroit Symphony in 2008 "they needed to raise money, big time," he said.[42] Slatkin asked John if he would conduct a benefit concert with the orchestra, which John did in the midst of working on *Crystal Skull*. "Listen," said Mark Volpe, "you want to raise money? Have a fundraiser around John."[43] Slatkin repaid the favor by recording five of John's concertos—the tuba, bassoon, cello, horn, and violin—with his principals in Detroit. Every time, John would say, "I hope it's good enough." "I think he's insecure, a little bit, about his concert works," said Slatkin, who had given John's violin concerto its world premiere back in 1981.

> John has these feet in so many different worlds. And that's not so easy to do, it really isn't. None of us are going to be able to predict how his concert works will be thought of 50 years from now. We don't know. They're pretty good showpieces for the soloists—that gives them already some advantage. And because the name "John Williams" is attached, I think some of them will have life in the future. They won't just disappear.[44]

The 125th birthday of the Boston Pops in 2010 was accompanied by some hand-wringing in the *Globe* about whether the old institution might disappear in such uneasy times for orchestras and classical music. But John supplied a note of optimism: "There's a connection with a Boston audience that is so filled with pride and loyalty and tradition that is certainly unique in any American city I know about. And that pride and affection has been developed during decades. As popular culture, particularly in music, swings further away from the orchestras as a delivery system of music, we can also hope that it will swing back."[45] Still, he was candid in suggesting the orchestra's home—the hall his grandfather helped build—was a liability. For one thing, the stage was too shallow to do anything with a chorus or experiment on a grander scale. "Maybe we'll have to move out of the horseshoe-shaped box of Symphony Hall and into an area where we can have atmospherics and lights and so on," he said.[46] As the years went on, he sounded increasingly concerned about replacing the old hall.

* * *

Where the harp concerto meandered in a modern voice mostly unfamiliar to fans of John's popular film music, his concerto for oboe was sweet and songlike, with a graceful, tonal friend in the orchestra. The first movement is a playful exploration (marked "Exuberantly"), the third a puckish set piece reminiscent of his comedic action music, and the second a plaintive ballad and one of the most emotional and lyrical chapters of any concert work he ever wrote. Next to the tuba concerto, this bucolic beauty has the lowest barrier of entry for anyone curious to explore the concert music of John Williams.

Tokyo native Keisuke Wakao was 26 when Ozawa hired him to join the BSO in the spring of 1990. Ozawa told him: "I'm comfortable with you playing classical music, but now you have to play Pops."[47] The conductor knew Wakao was going home to Japan that summer, which he regularly did, and arranged for him to see the Pops on tour at Suntory Hall, exhorting him to understand what the Pops was—and to meet John. Wakao was instantly impressed by John's humility: "He's like Bill Gates in some ways, but he lives so modest. That amazed me more than anything. I went to his house twice—very simple." Wakao likened John to Andris Nelsons, the Latvian conductor who became music director of the BSO in 2014. "Very successful, super talented, has everything that many people wish to have. But they don't take that advantage. They just live every day same as anybody."[48] John was equally impressed, and he often complimented Wakao's playing. In 1999, Wakao recorded an album of John's film themes with a string quartet at the Colburn School in Los Angeles; John even accompanied him on piano for the theme from *Stepmom*. One day in the late 1990s, Wakao said to John: "Someday, if you think I deserve it ... if you write an oboe concerto I'd love to play it." Fifteen years later, John called Wakao at Tanglewood, out of the blue, and said: "It's ready." John had completed the first two movements and begun the third, and he had Wakao join him at Blantyre to read it through. Wakao was stunned: "This is what he said: 'If you don't like it, you don't need to play. I like to write for you, but if you don't like the piece, no problem. I can just take your name off [and] *not push*.' I said, 'How can I refuse him?' "[49]

Wakao flew to Los Angeles twice during the BSO's 2010–2011 season to rehearse with John. "It's a very difficult piece," he said. "It's not easy piece for oboe, but definitely not for me. It's a technical piece, in some ways, but you have to be very melodical. It's not just technique." Wakao thought it was beautiful: "The second movement is incredibly deep, and I hear some Asian music behind [it]—like in the beginning cello solo, it sounds like Japanese music a little bit."[50] The premiere at Symphony Hall, on May 25, 2011, was recorded and released by the BSO.

After this prolific burst of classical works, it would be almost a decade before John wrote another concerto. He stubbornly thought of these instrumental showcases as merely a *holiday*, "something to get away from," he said, "something to play with, some fabulous instrumentalists that I have the opportunity to work with and write for.

> If I had it all to do over again, I would have made a cleaner job of it—of having the film music and the concert music all being more *me*, whatever that is, or more unified in some way. But none of it ever happened that way. The film thing was a job to do, or an opportunity to accept. Writing a concert piece was a way of keeping myself busy if I had a month off, with little more than that as a motive.[51]

Could he really mean that? Stéphane Denève, a young French conductor mentored by Ozawa who became a passionate advocate of John's music, noticed that John only ever wrote music *for* someone else. Whether it was a film director, an event producer, or a concerto conceived for a specific player, he never seemed to write music just for himself—not since the days of his early symphony and sinfonietta. Every piece was an act of service or a dedication to a friend. Denève interpreted this, if nothing else, as John's complete lack of pretension. "I don't know *anybody* with this rich life that never speaks about himself," he said, "Never brags. It's fascinating."[52]

Now approaching 80, John was beginning to think more about his legacy—and even *that*, for him, was others-focused. He loved walking the verdant, tree-lined grounds of Tanglewood, and one day in 2005 he was on a stroll with Volpe and Ed Linde, chairman of the BSO's board of trustees, when they came across the area where Copland's ashes were spread in 1990. "He's not a hyper religious guy," said Volpe, "but he *is* a pretty spiritual guy. He says, 'I can feel Copland here.' "[53] John suggested creating a sculpture or bust of Copland to commemorate the composer's importance to Tanglewood—knowing full well that the BSO had a policy of refusing any visual art on the grounds. "We got approached by *so* many people saying, 'We want to do art,'" said Volpe. "And we said, 'No, no. It's a gestalt of nature and music.' We turned down *name* sculptors." So John was a bit sheepish when he asked Volpe, "Do you mind if we consider this?" Volpe said, "Well, I have the chair with me right here," gesturing to Linde. "Let's just do it."[54]

From that conversation, John formed the idea of commissioning, at his own expense, sculptures of three composers who had an outsized presence in the hills of Lenox: Copland, Bernstein, and Koussevitzky, the BSO music director who founded Tanglewood in 1940. "It amazed me that here on the campus there hadn't been any recognition or any reminder of these giants that are now lost to us in time," he said. "So I hope it is something that will not only adorn the campus but add to the richness of the experience that people have when they come here, add a spiritual dimension to the place."[55]

He began putting out feelers for a sculptor. One day he was walking in Manhattan when he passed a new statue of Eleanor Roosevelt in Riverside Park. *Whoever made that sculpture,* John thought, *he's my man!*[56] His "man" was in fact Penelope Jencks, a Boston-based artist who had actually been approached years earlier about creating a Copland sculpture. John made first contact with Jencks in 2006, they met for tea in Boston in 2007, then walked the grounds together after the Tanglewood season concluded that summer. "He is a lovely man," Jencks said, "a true gentleman, courteous, gentle, modest, soft-spoken, kindly, diffident, sweet natured, intelligent, and generous. A real gent! And he's the first 'real person' I have ever worked for. All my other clients have been groups or institutions of one sort or another."[57] At first, Jencks was nervous about working so closely with a "real person," especially after John started making detailed suggestions and requests for revisions. Her first attempt at Copland wasn't quite right—too youthful for John's liking—and he asked for something more "avuncular." That "was the first part that set me back a little bit," she said. "I was disappointed, because I wanted to make a different kind of sculpture. But I thought: okay, he's paying for this. And also, this is probably how he works when he's making music for a movie."[58] (When John described the act of composing a melody, he often compared it to sculpting.)

Jencks began working on the Tanglewood trinity all at once, and John had opinions about *everything*: their facial expressions, the size of bust, the type of stone used, the color of patina, the location for their installment. "Oh my god," said Volpe. "We were going to all the quarries all over western Massachusetts. And then he brought in horticulture people and a landscape architect to light it. I have no idea what he spent."[59] John ambled around Tanglewood in both the summer and wintertime with a tall stick so that Jencks could take reference photos for possible sites. She made multiple iterations of each figure, swapping phone calls and communicating through emails with Jamie Richardson—a personal secretary who began working with John in the early 2000s, and whose role expanded from aiding John on his travels to handling his correspondence and fielding interview requests, booking scoring stages, and eventually overseeing the Gorfaine/Schwartz agency's film concert empire. (Jencks referred to him as John's *amanuensis*.) "JW doesn't seem perturbed about costs," Jencks wrote in her journal.[60]

The Copland bust was unveiled in a private ceremony on June 30, 2011. John selected two pieces by the composer for a short concert, along with his own ode to Copland, *Air and Simple Gifts*. "I like to say if we're good, we can capture the magic of his music in concerts," he said, standing with Jencks in front of the new sculpture and addressing a small crowd, which included another Tanglewood fixture, James Taylor. "But what she's done, we can't do. She's captured his intelligence and his graciousness and his humility and his very special humanity in the piece, and that's a great gift to everyone, as it is to Tanglewood."[61] John kept one of the alternate bronze Copland busts for himself, which he displayed in his home.

The Bernstein and Koussevitzky sculptures took longer than either John or Jencks expected, mostly because John was unsatisfied with the sculptor's initial attempts. Her first bust of Bernstein depicted a blissful face with eyes closed, which she felt "captured Bernstein's propensity to throw himself into the music with enthusiasm and abandon." Her husband said it looked like he was having an orgasm. John felt the same—that it was too vulgar. "J.W. says that every conductor searches for the climaxes in each piece—and the big ones can even be orgasmic," Jencks wrote in her journal, "but in this sculpture it is 'all about Lenny, not about the music.'"[62] It's difficult, and amusing, to imagine John talking about orgasms with another person, and "he sort of was beating around the bush a little bit, because he didn't want to come right out and say it the way he did," Jencks said—although "I never got the impression that he was a *prude*."[63] John told Jencks he wanted Bernstein to look "more serious. Talmudic. Jewish. Thoughtful." For inspiration, he sent her a poem that Bernstein wrote in 1990 after learning he had a malignant tumor in his left lung. It began: "I made a deal with God. God, she was tough to deal with. Dealt me a tempting clause—Then a sharp zap to the kidney...."[64] In the end, John rejected *five* different versions of Bernstein, but eventually landed on one he liked. This bust was unveiled in 2014 inside Bernstein's former home-away-from-home, Highwood Manor House, where Bernstein had often theatrically exclaimed the presence of a ghost; the late composer's daughter Nina attended the ceremony.

After yet more trials and errors—and even a near stalemate—Koussevitzky's statue finally debuted in June 2019. Then John commissioned a fourth, of his old friend Seiji. At one point, Jencks told John: "Look, I would like to make a sculpture of *you* to go there, too." John said, "Oh, no, no.... That wouldn't be a good idea." Jencks thought: *It would be really nice to go for it, because he's alive! Maybe I could get him to pose for me in the life, rather than having to work from all these photographs.* "He's very retiring in his self," she noticed, "the way he puts himself forward. *Doesn't* put himself forward. Very modest."[65] Volpe also begged John—and Michael Gorfaine—to let the BSO add his likeness to these sacred woods. "I mean, he's *one* of the spirits of Tanglewood," said Volpe. "Fiedler passed through Tanglewood one day a year, so Fiedler's Boston, Boston, Boston. That's it. I say, 'We've got to have Penelope do a Williams bust,' and he shut it down. There was no ambiguity." Volpe noted that John wasn't completely allergic to recognition: he did not donate his multiple millions to Tanglewood anonymously, and his name was listed with other donors in the foyer of the Linde Center for Music and Learning on campus. But, Volpe added, "there's a Copland Library, there's obviously Bernstein Campus, a Koussevitzky Shed, an Ozawa Hall—and I strongly believe he's in the pantheon of that. But he's resisted."[66]

* * *

John was never *not* composing. "I developed from very early on a habit of writing something every day," he said, "good or bad.

> There are good days, and there are less good days, but I do a certain amount of pages, it seems to me, before I can feel like the day has been completely served. When I am working on a film, of course, it's a six-day-a-week affair, and when I'm not working on films, I always like to devote myself to some piece, some musical project, that gives me a feeling that I'm maybe contributing in some small way or, maybe more importantly, learning in the process.[67]

He had written very little chamber music. The music director of SummerFest, an annual festival put on by the La Jolla Music Society, invited John to write something after hearing his violin concerto in Aspen in 2004, but it took a few years of coaxing and completing. Finally, John produced a lengthy work that aligned with the 25th anniversary of SummerFest in 2011, and he gifted it to director Cho-Liang Lin. *Air and Simple Gifts* may have had a more massive audience, but with *Quartet La Jolla*, "Williams now has in his catalog a chamber music of more substance," Swed wrote—"a reflective, long-breathed half-hour quartet for the colorful combination of violin, cello, clarinet, and harp."[68] John rehearsed the musicians and gave feedback via Skype from Tanglewood, and John Bruce Yeh—principal clarinet with the Chicago Symphony—read a brief letter from John to the audience, affectionately imitating John's mild manner. Swed found the music similarly "genial." "Outside of the film studio, he does not appear to call attention to himself.

> The score, in five movements, has a French flavor, no doubt inspired by the harp. The second movement is an aubade, the old troubadour form that French composers love. The harp, Williams writes in his program note, is the score's spiritual center. The harp writing, however, is conventional. The allure was in the clarinet, highlighted by Yeh's fluent playing. The memorable movement is the fourth, titled Cantando, a sweet clarinet song touched by Bartók, Copland, and the blues.[69]

In an interview with the *New York Times* that summer, John talked about his writing habits and his antique tools. Asked if he ever experienced writer's block, he said no:

> For me if I'm ever blocked or I feel like I don't quite know where to go at the next turn, the best thing for me is to keep writing, to write something. It could be absolute nonsense, but it will project me into the next phase of thinking. And I think if

we ourselves as writers get out of the way and let the flow happen and not get uptight about it, so to speak, the muses will carry us along.

The wonderful thing about music is it never seems to be exhausted. Every little idea germinates another one. Things are constantly transforming themselves in musical terms. So that the few notes we have, 7, 8 or 12 notes, can be morphed into endless variations, and it's never quite over, so I think the idea of a block is something we need to work through.[70]

The pencil was always moving—but for John, there was something special about the inspiration he received from the visual and emotional stimulus of film.

* * *

War Horse opens with a deeply English tone poem. A solitary flute melody wheels above the English countryside of Dartmoor at sunrise, then comes a surge of pastoral string chords reminiscent of Ralph Vaughan Williams, which heave with deep sighs of affection for the place. John did not deny the influence. In his liner note, he wrote that "Edward Elgar, Ralph Vaughan Williams, Frederick Delius, George Butterworth, the Australian Percy Grainger, among others, all contributed to a rich literature that I've loved and admired for a long time. In a very real sense, 'Dartmoor, 1912' was written as an homage to these great men."[71] He said he didn't need to look at the scores of any of those composers to write in this idiom:

> Musicians know the modalities of these countries. Although in the case of Vaughan Williams I think I looked at his London Symphony *once*, many years ago. For *War Horse* I was thinking about how to get the atmosphere of Albion, the old country of England, and the green—going back to Henry Purcell and even earlier. It's not hard to do. It's certainly not hard to do for me.[72]

As the extended prologue continues, the country pub sound of an Irish harmonium accompanies the birth of a horse, and as the animal begins to run, a restless string orchestra churns with youthful energy; in the course of just a few minutes, several tunes are handed out like presents on Christmas morning. It was as if all of the enchanting, tonal populism that John had withheld in his recent concert works was spilling out in a flood of melody. "It was the first thing that I wrote in the score," John said. "It just seemed to me to be the place to go, the thing to do."[73]

Spielberg bought the rights to Michael Morpurgo's 1982 book, *War Horse*, after Kathleen Kennedy told him about the sensational new stage play on London's West End, which used life-size puppets to convey a horse's odyssey through the battlefields of World War I and the story of his long-lost human companion, Albert. Spielberg and screenwriter Richard Curtis departed from the play's narrative and abandoned Albert for much of the film, introducing Joey the horse to a successive series of British soldiers, German soldiers, and a little French girl and her grandfather—defying death many times before ultimately reuniting with Albert. "This is a story about connectivity between human beings, and there's this miracle animal that not only brings people closer to themselves but also brings warring nations closer together—in a symbolic way, not a literal way," Spielberg said. "I found that following Joey and encountering strangers, who do not remain strangers for long, that was the real challenge for all of us. How do you create memories in sequences with characters that you've never met before and those sequences only last seven or eight minutes on the screen? Making the characters unforgettable is the challenge."[74] The ace up Spielberg's sleeve, as always, was his faithful composer.

Other than the horse, John Williams is the one constant in this story, and he created an emotional musical companion that journeyed with the horse away from home, through mud and battle and into the depths of hell. "The *War Horse* score is so evocative of the land, place, the times, and the relationships between boy and horse," said Spielberg. John's themes "bond all of us together with this sound that made all of our work look like we had planned it.... He doesn't intellectualize his approach to scoring. It's what he feels, from scene to scene. And that's why he is who he is."[75]

John's opening overture introduces a theme for the land—so feelingly evocative of his own affection for England—as well as a coltish action motif performed "JOYOUSLY" by celeste and high woodwinds over a syncopated motor. After Albert makes contact with little Joey, he runs up a hill—time passing—accompanied by a heart-bursting love theme for the boy and his horse. A theme for the auction where Ted, Albert's father, bids for Joey against his landlord is like a sprightlier version of the family theme from *Prisoner of Azkaban*. (The landlord was played by David Thewlis, who portrayed Professor Lupin in that film.) When Ted brings Joey home and faces the ire of his long-suffering wife, who sent him to get a plow horse, a tipsy string motif plays to the moment's humor and Ted's unsteadiness. There's an immediate storybook quality to this film, and John's score is a constant lyrical narration. It also serves to woo us into love with Joey, forging an emotional bond that will soon be tested by separation and war. When Albert gently leads Joey to eat from a pail, John introduces a new theme for their bond—a noble folk tune that pines for home and family on "DOLCE" French horn. Of the score's many leitmotifs, this one emerges as its true heart.

"The film opens with a cinematic assault as audacious and unsparing as the Normandy landing in *Saving Private Ryan*," A.O. Scott wrote in his *New York Times* review.

> With widescreen, pastoral vistas dappled in golden sunlight and washed in music (by John Williams) that is somehow both grand and folksy, Mr. Spielberg lays siege to your cynicism, bombarding you with strong and simple appeals to feeling. You may find yourself resisting this sentimental pageant of early-20th-century rural English life, replete with verdant fields, muddy tweeds, and damp turnips, but my strong advice is to surrender. Allow your sped-up, modern, movie-going metabolism, accelerated by a diet of frantic digital confections ... to calm down a bit. Suppress your instinctive impatience, quiet the snarky voice in your head and allow yourself to recall, or perhaps to discover, the deep pleasures of sincerity.[76]

Pastoral majesty and equestrian romance are suddenly interrupted by the Great War, and that noble heart theme plays sadly as Albert says goodbye to Joey as he is led off to the front lines. The story segues to a darker chapter with stoic, martial music, frantic string gallops, storm clouds, and sadness. John introduces a weary battle motif on solo trumpet for this newly conscripted war horse after the kindly Captain Nicholls is cut down by German gunfire. The music, while occasionally rising with gentle hope, accompanies Joey as he meets several new humans, and mourns them when they die. A woodwind dance accompanies the montage of a little French girl, Emilie, training Joey to jump—but it quickly ends in glassy anxiety when German soldiers commandeer Joey back into the fray. The war horse trumpet motif reprises when Joey is tasked with carrying heavy cannons up a steep hill, thereby saving another horse named Topthorn.

A heartfelt string adagio laments Topthorn when he collapses, which will surely be Joey's fate if he doesn't escape, and a resolved, galloping action rhythm spurs on the trumpet motif as Joey runs through a night battle illuminated by exploding cannons and moonlight, finally getting tangled in a mess of barbed wire in the middle of No Man's Land. A concerned British soldier and a German soldier meet under a white flag to free this innocent prisoner, and for a few brief moments they laugh and join in shared purpose. After they cut Joey free, John's war motif plays as the British lad leads Joey into his trench and everyone gapes at this "remarkable horse"; the score then turns mystical when we see Albert, blinded by mustard gas, and it briefly hints at their bond theme as Albert hears about this miraculous horse who made it out of No Man's Land. But Joey is severely wounded, and an anxious cloud forms on brass and strings as a sergeant readies to put him down. Strings hold on a pregnant chord, and Albert's hopeful hand whistle triggers a phrase on a lone keyboard—not heard since a solo flute played it when Albert first connected with Joey. Albert blindly wanders through the parted soldiers, and a dam of tears bursts with the return of the tender bond theme for their hard-earned reunion.

The film's final act is scored with sustained, heaving sentiment that, depending on the perceiver, is either grotesque or utterly divine. A brass band plays the bond theme when an army doctor wipes Joey's forehead to reveal a white diamond that confirms his identity, and John concludes the scene with a spare, elegiac string theme that symbolizes the tears of both loss and joy that war precipitates. The bond theme cries when Albert is forced to say goodbye to Joey *again* after Emilie's grandfather wins the horse in an auction; a solo flute tune reminds us of the little girl, another casualty in the war, then gently nudges the old man to give Albert the horse that his granddaughter had loved so much. Finally, against a technicolor MGM sunset, Albert and Joey return home to the simple strain of the elegy theme on solo piano (played "REFLECTIVELY"). French horns and strings join as Albert crests the ridge and his mother runs to him, given voice by aching string relief. Brass band stoicism greets Ted, and strings sing as father and son shake hands and embrace. The last word is given to the stolid war horse theme on solo trumpet, as Joey stands alone.

This sumptuous, storytelling score was recorded in March, far ahead of the film's release date on Christmas day. "*War Horse* is the kind of musical score that is joyous," John said.

> This is a lyrical film requiring a lyrical response, not only in writing, but in performance from the orchestra—something else Steven understands instinctively and enjoys. So those recording sessions were more like playing a concert than they were recording the score for a film. It had to fit the film, obviously, and designed that way. But then we had to be off on a musical trail where we try to lose gravity, get everybody on the floor—all 90 musicians, as well as Steven—everybody's flying.[77]

The film and its score divided critics, between those who found in it the "perfect notes of triumph and tragedy" and those who felt grossly manipulated—like Gary Thompson at the *Philadelphia Daily News*, who brutally wrote that "there are moments when you wish Spielberg had never met composer John Williams."[78] Perhaps the film *was* "High Hollywood corn, expertly roasted," as the *Boston Globe*'s Ty Burr put it[79]—or perhaps it was an overwhelming tide of tragedy and spiritual exultation that no one but Spielberg and John could have pulled off. An admiring A. O. Scott connected it with the director's other stories about man's relationship with aliens, sharks, dinosaurs, and artificial intelligence—and the "nonhuman" characters, as they're so treated, in *Schindler's List* and *Amistad*: "Sometimes the nonhuman is a threat, at other times a comfort, but it always presents a profound ethical challenge based in a stark existential mystery: Who are we?

> Mr. Spielberg's answers to this question tend to be hopeful, and his taste for happy, or at least redemptive endings is frequently criticized. But his ruthless optimism, while it has helped to make him an enormously successful showman, is also crucial to his identity as an artist, and is more complicated than many of his detractors realize. *War Horse* registers the loss and horror of a gruesomely irrational episode in history, a convulsion that can still seem like an invitation to despair. To refuse that, to choose compassion and consolation, requires a measure of obstinacy, a muscular and brutish willfulness that is also an authentic kind of grace.[80]

Whatever his detractors thought of the film, Spielberg was effusive about the music: "The dramatic countryside of Dartmoor has inspired John Williams to compose a score of such beauty and quiet majesty that one might think the earth is speaking through him much as the heavens have done for nearly five decades."[81]

* * *

After a long absence, John's music filled multiplexes that Christmas. *The Adventures of Tintin* opened just four days after *War Horse*, "two diametrically opposite approaches to a musical representation of two diametrically opposite motion pictures," Spielberg said. "Which just shows that Johnny will fill a vessel, and take the shape of the vessel—that he is, as a composer, always in a liquid state of genius music-making. I don't know how he does it, and I don't know how he did it in the same year—but he did."[82]

John had never properly scored animation, with the odd exceptions of the Mr. DNA sequence in *Jurassic Park*, the opening of *A Guide for the Married Man*, and a few other in-film novelties. Slatkin once asked John if there was anything he *couldn't* do, and John said: "Yeah—cartoons." "Why not?" Slatkin asked. "It's too hard," John replied. "It's just constant activity."[83] An odd comment from a composer known for his hairpin choreography and "symphonic cartooning." He came close to scoring an animated feature in 2007, when director Pete Docter and producer Jonas Rivera visited John's bungalow to pitch Pixar's new film, *Up*. Randy Newman, Thomas Newman, and Michael Giacchino had created the distinct musical languages for Pixar's heartful, computer animated movies to that point, and *Up* would have given John something close to the classic Disney animated films he admired. He turned it down, which according to John was simply due to scheduling. "I would have been happy to do it," he later said. "It would have been a good thing to do."[84] Docter thought John was probably just being nice: "It's a bizarre pitch, right?" Docter said.

> You've seen the movie, but imagine it doesn't exist and I come in like: "There's an old man, he floats his house up, and he flies to South America." It's bizarre. Later he saw the film and he sent me a really wonderful letter, that I kept, about how much he enjoyed it, and he confessed that was the first Pixar film he had seen. So if you'd never seen [any of our films], you think: *Oh, it's cartoons. It's a weird man floating in his house....* I think he packaged it as "I'm too busy," but it just didn't hit him.[85]

But John jumped at the chance to accompany Spielberg's first foray into directing animation, the first in a proposed trilogy of films based on the popular *Tintin* comic series by the Belgian artist Hergé.[‡] Spielberg had been circling this idea since the early 1980s when a review compared Indiana Jones with the boy adventurer, and he now felt that computer animation and motion-capture performance technology could do the story's imaginative visuals justice. The entire process was new, liberating Spielberg from the laws of gravity as he staged hyper-realistic *oners* with meticulously choreographed action and coincidences using an airborne virtual camera. One knockout sequence has Captain Haddock receiving memories from his ancestor, Sir Francis Haddock, and Spielberg seamlessly cutting between past and present, between a bright modern desert and the swashbuckling high seas on a distant night. "This transgenerational experience that Haddock has is probably something we'd all like to have," John mused. "We could remember what our grandfathers were doing on a certain day in June, and actually feel it in the genetic swirl of things.

[‡] Producer Peter Jackson was to direct the sequel, but no further chapters were made.

Cutting back and forth is something we can actually do musically. You can hear Haddock's theme, you can hear Sir Francis' material, and actually mix them up and maybe suggest in Haddock's mind, or when he's on the screen, another suggestion of what Sir Francis was and what his energies were and so on. There can be a nice opportunity for music to transpose itself from one timeframe to another timeframe.[86]

The new filmmaking method also prompted a novel experience for John, who recorded part of his score very early, "when the graphics were just beginning to be drawn," he said. His goal for some of these action sequences was to recreate the "old Disney technique of doing the music first, and then having the animators animate to the silhouette of what the music is doing based on suggestions from the script," so he wrote some of the pirate action and comedic music for the Thompson twins "way back before we had anything more than a few little sketches."[87] Much of his score was recorded almost two years before the film was released, in the fall of 2009 and spring of 2010. Gustavo Dudamel, the young Venezuelan music director of the Los Angeles Philharmonic, made a surprise appearance at one session, and John handed Dudamel his baton to take the orchestra through a cue.

John wrote several options for the opening titles, and he wound up returning to his jazz roots again: the animated credits were reminiscent of the title sequence from *Catch Me if You Can*, and John responded with an even more offbeat overture that manically choreographs Tintin's visual activity in a piece that features harpsichord, saxophones, upright bass, and brush percussion. "We kept coming back to this 1920s, early 1930s European jazz," he explained.[88] The titles introduce John's main theme for Tintin, although that tune is swept up in a syncopated, caffeinated current that hinders it from becoming much of an earworm.

The score settles down more as the story begins, and John introduces a mysterious theme for the legendary ship, the Unicorn—a better *Indiana Jones* MacGuffin motif than the one from *Crystal Skull*, haunting and beautiful and developed into otherworldly grandeur. In fact, *Tintin* is largely scored more like a classic *Indiana Jones* adventure than a cartoon. There is a reflective, Indy-style quote of Tintin's theme when a merchant utters his name to the villainous Sakharine, and a vintage Indy moment when Tintin is chloroformed and shoved into a crate; the destination etched on the side, Karaboudjan, is dramatically revealed with exotically sinister muted trumpets. When Tintin and Haddock arrive in Bagghar, the glorious Eastern-tinged reveal sounds like a forgotten cue from *The Last Crusade*. The kid detective's melody might be bouncier and less memorable than the *Raiders* march, but John took it on a *Raiders*-sized adventure all the same, soaring it into the sky or flourishing it heroically as the story demanded.

John wrote a wobbly, Gallic motif for the bumbling Thompson Twins. "For whatever unconscious or intuitive reasons, I chose to feature a euphonium," he said of the tuba's smaller cousin, "accompanied by accordion for the Thompsons' theme. It can make a kind of silly sound, and at least in my terms of set of references, a period sound.... In the 1920s you might have heard a euphonium concerto." He wrote a light-footed theme for Snowy, Tintin's canine companion, which is adapted into a comical scherzo when the dog runs over and under a herd of cows to get to Tintin aboard a freighter ship. "Snowy's music is a quick dance," John said. "Snowy's a very contributive character in the piece.... For me he always provided a lightness and a tempo and a quickness—chasing the cat, over the fire engine, finding his way to Karaboudjan, all of this. Snowy lightens it right up for us."[89]

Haddock's introduction is scored like a sea shanty for eely, low-end woodwinds. It's a fitting theme for a sodden sea captain with an almost medical need for booze, and it calls to mind other seafarers and pirates from John's past—from *Jaws* (one could practically set Quint's signature "Farewell and adieu to you, fair Spanish ladies" to the tune) to *Hook*. The sequence in the desert, where Haddock's memories of Sir Francis spring to life, prompted the score's standout cue, with the mystical Unicorn theme growing like a storm cloud and exploding into a grand, swashbuckling set piece that blends Indiana Jones adventure with a quick-parrying action theme (which John later turned into a concert suite). His score for another virtuosic sequence in Bagghar, with Tintin chasing a bird who stole his scroll and nearly destroying the city in the process, prompts a busier, more Mickey-Moused approach that climaxes with a heroic version of Tintin's theme.

A rare bit of emotion sneaks into the score when Haddock tells Tintin he can never let failure defeat him, but it quickly bounces back into scurrying cartoon energy, culminating in another swashbuckling cue as Haddock duels Sakharine using giant shipyard cranes in a modern echo of their ancestors' swordfight. The themes for Haddock, Snowy, the Unicorn, and Tintin all take bows as the action concludes in the captain's newly claimed Marlinspike Hall, with promises of further adventures. John's delight was abundantly evident in the score's witty energy and inspired melodies, and even though there was a slight schizophrenia and mania in keeping with the visuals, Spielberg insisted that John's score pulled together the style and tone. "John is the bonding agent that unifies all the disparate, eclectic elements."[90]

At the beginning of a mostly negative review, the *Chicago Tribune*'s Michael Phillips praised Spielberg's title sequence—"scored, with a glancing touch, by his longtime mood generator, composer John Williams. It's always gratifying to hear what Williams can do when he's not in attack mode. Then comes the film proper, which is mostly in attack mode."[91] Critics either found the film "exhausting" and "an unplayable video game," or a sheer, kinetic delight. "Everything he did in live-action movies with rolling boulders and runaway convoys he does bigger and better—by a factor of ten—in every frame," raved *Vulture*'s David Edelstein. "At the end of two hours, my jaw ached from grinning."[92] *Tintin* grossed less in the U.S. than *War Horse*, but twice as much worldwide—and still both movies performed well below the director's heart-tuggers and adventures of yore. Spielberg's dino-sized blockbuster days, it seemed, might now be in the rearview mirror.

* * *

After reaching his own milestone birthday in February 2012, John celebrated the 100th birthday of Fenway Park by composing *Fanfare for Fenway*. He wrote this short piece in a week, and recorded it at Symphony Hall in March using six trumpets, six horns, five trombones, two tubas, timpani, and percussion from the BSO. "Obviously we couldn't have the Boston Symphony Orchestra on the outfield," he said—"it would damage the turf." He was thinking of his late Bostonian mother when he wrote it: "I heard about Fenway Park all my life from her, and I think when she was a little girl she would not have had the 35 cents to go.... There was also an emotional connection in my mind between Boston and Fenway Park and the Red Sox. You think of Boston, you think of Harvard and MIT as being the brains of the city, and Faneuil Hall might be the soul. But I think the beating, pounding heart of the city for Bostonians is Fenway Park."[93] He premiered his bright, sunny fanfare on April 20 in a ceremony attended by several veteran Red Sox players, preceding a game in which the home team lost to the Yankees. Musing further on the draw of Fenway, John said: "It looks like a hometown ballpark. It seems to be put together with nuts and bolts and old lumber.... It's maintained that old baseball yard feel and keeps in touch with a romantic past." He went on, and could just as well have been describing his own body of work: "It doesn't seem like a big, modern stadium. It doesn't seem fancy. It doesn't seem like a place that's expensive to go to. And it has a way of being in touch with the people; it connects to a strong nostalgia. It's a good, wholesome thing and reminds us of who we were and describes us as we are."[94]

John's 80th birthday was acknowledged throughout the year, from a balloon drop and giant cake shaped like Symphony Hall at a Pops concert in May, to a star-studded evening at Tanglewood in August with a crowd of 18,000.[95] John was surprised with video tributes from President Obama, Bill Clinton, George Lucas, Seiji Ozawa, and the Boston Red Sox. Jessye Norman and James Taylor both sang in a program that also featured movements from John's oboe, horn, and tuba concertos. Gil Shaham performed *Air and Simple Gifts* with Ma, McGill, and Montero. But one person was missing that night.

A lavish dinner party was being thrown at Seranak, the onetime summer home of Koussevitzky and his wife—the name was a portmanteau of Sergei and Natalie Koussevitzky—and the staff needed to confirm the guest list to make seating arrangements. Everyone kept asking, "Is Samantha coming?" and receiving conflicting answers, changing the seating around multiple times. John had a private plane ready for his wife, and the staff also needed to sort the logistics of where she would land. But she never came. "A little in us all died," said one attendee. "He didn't get angry. He just got depressed." It was a stark example of the toll that John's all-consuming work took on the ones around him. "There's a certain sadness about that," his friend said. "The few times we've talked about it, you can see the spirit dipping—and then he'll just shift to a different topic."

Samantha rarely ever joined John at concerts anymore, or at the Academy Awards. Jenny became his regular travel partner and "plus one," and in fact she was often misattributed as Samantha in photo captions. For the past decade, Samantha now lived in their second home in Los Olivos; located west of Santa Barbara and more than two hours from John's house in Holmby Hills—the house where Barbara had lived, the house John never left—it sat on 20 acres next to a horse ranch belonging to Monty Roberts, the celebrity horse trainer and friend of Queen Elizabeth II. Samantha "builds the most beautiful trellises and fences," John said admiringly. "She does it all by herself—except for the heaviest tree cutting and lifting, but she gets up in the oak trees. What she's doing married to a composer, neither one of us have any idea."[96] Samantha and John simply led independent lives, although they never divorced and they continued to show each other affection. He was giving her "little kisses" one day, and Samantha said, "You can kiss me—Audrey Hepburn kissed you!"[97]

Still, John's friends felt sadness for him, and they couldn't understand Samantha's remoteness. "Johnny's never been a complainer," said Mia Farrow.

> So, "Oh, you know, she loves her house up in Santa Barbara." And it was Santa Fe before that. "She's doing the work up there," kind of thing. I don't know whether it's that he doesn't need more and therefore it's okay? Is it just that, *well, that's just the cards he was dealt?* But one way or another, he's at peace with it.[98]

* * *

John used to compose for 10 hours a day, but by now he had cut that down to five or six.[99] Which was more than enough time to score one film per year—a leisurely schedule compared to his early career—and 2012 was devoted solely to Steven Spielberg and Abraham Lincoln. "When we're working together we're so much in the now, in this moment," John said of his working relationship with Spielberg. "There isn't a past, there isn't a future, you're so completely absorbed and concentrated. If you do that long enough, you suddenly realize, *my God, I'm 80 years old, what happened?* What happened was a well-spent, focused period of time."[100]

In March 2007, Liam Neeson was signed to play the 16th president of the United States, and Tony Kushner started writing a script based on the Doris Kearns Goodwin book, *Team of Rivals*.[101] In the interim, Neeson dropped out and was replaced by the English method actor Daniel Day-Lewis. Though dealing with the same basic subject matter of *Amistad*—Spielberg's new film focused on the passage of the Thirteenth Amendment, abolishing slavery—*Lincoln* was superior in almost every way, aided by Kushner's whip-smart dialogue and an impeccable cast. Spielberg confidently directed it as a word-centric film play, keeping the camera moving and creating attractive visual compositions with his actors, but favoring long takes and letting its many rich conversations breathe as if in real time. "I needed the audience to lean forward a little," he said.[102]

Abraham Lincoln was John's favorite historical figure as a boy, and he had already read Goodwin's book. (She was a friend.) His first thought "was that perhaps all the music should be only music that Lincoln had heard in his life." But he realized there wasn't enough known about that, "at least for my purposes, and so this led me to conclude that, in order for me to find what I needed for this particular scene or that particular scene, that I had to make it myself."[103] John said he wanted it to sound *genuine*: "To get it just right, I wanted the music to feel as if it was coming out of the bedrock of the American spirit—the soul, I guess.[104]" Most of his score, then, was imbued with the spirit of Copland's Americana—hymnal, plain, and wide open. And just as Copland had done with his own popular works, John located two wellsprings for his score: church music and Appalachian folk tunes of the 19th century. "It's all original," he said, "but that's the vocabulary."[105]

He began by scoring the last scene, when Lincoln delivers his second inaugural address, and used his discoveries there to inform the rest of his score. He and Spielberg took a lean approach to spotting: long sections unfold without any music, and the score often punctuates the conclusion of a monologue or scene by adding a warm or bittersweet coda to the topic at hand. John introduces a piano hymn—an aspirational tune with a staccato updraft, which he called "The American Process"—after a Black soldier recites the Gettysburg Address to its author, setting off the story's central dynamic and tone. Another more personal, subdued piano hymn plays when Lincoln finds his young son Tad sleeping by the fireplace.

The film isn't without humor, and John scored the montages where three rapscallion aids drum up votes with a bouncy folk tune for solo fiddle, upright bass, banjo, and orchestra. But the prevailing tone is a bone-weary but hopeful American reverence, culminating in the melancholy hymn for Lincoln's second inaugural address ("With Malice Towards None") which concludes the picture. John's original tunes are not strictly attached to any one character or theme, and therefore somewhat interchangeable. He wrote more cues than Spielberg ultimately used, and he also arranged multiple iterations of his tunes with different instrument ensembles: "Prayer" for brass, "Hymn" for strings, etc. He wanted to give Spielberg options, and in this case "there's not a ton of music," Ramiro Belgardt noted, "so he provides different orchestrations of the same tune. It's never a big, different approach, but he wants the melody on the clarinet, he wants it on the piano. That happened on *Lincoln* a lot."[106]

John suggested recording this score with the Chicago Symphony at their historic hall built in 1904. Not only was Lincoln *from* Illinois, but his home state was the first to ratify the Thirteenth Amendment. "Armed with that knowledge, Steven and I said to each other: 'They've earned the right to do this.'"[107] John's stately chorales were recorded over the course of three days in Orchestra Hall, which John felt had "a beautiful low end. I don't know if people watching this film think about these [kinds] of things, but the bass response in the orchestral recordings is particularly good."[108] John flew Randy Kerber out especially for the score's piano solos, and when the sessions were finished, Day-Lewis, who came to listen every day, thanked the musician "so sweetly and honestly and earnest," said Kerber. "I said, 'Well, I can't wait to see the movie.' And he said, 'Well, I really hope you like it.' And I swear he really meant that. He completely meant it! I was like: *wow*. There was this naivete, and this wonderful innocence."[109]

For the final goodbye, when Lincoln walks away from camera and his servant watches him go, "there was a whole discussion about: *What are we saying here?*" Belgardt remembered. "*Do we want a nobility?* which John had a solo trumpet for.

There was another version that had just a piano melody that was almost like a folk hymn, which would have given it more of a country home, back-to-his-roots kind of thing and not presidential as much. Steven had an idea, and John had an idea. Daniel Day-Lewis had an idea. We threw them all up on the stage." Ultimately, they went with the noble trumpet solo.[110]

Even Spielberg's usual detractors had trouble finding fault in his immaculate and stoic picture. "*Lincoln* is a grave and surprisingly subtle magic trick, conjuring the past and an almost ridiculously impressive figure in ways that transcend art direction and the right stovepipe hat," Michael Phillips wrote in the *Chicago Tribune*. "Last year's Spielberg film, *War Horse*, pushed the Old Hollywood artifice to a breaking point, and it had me wondering if Spielberg needed a change-up in terms of his longtime collaborators," Phillips added, specifically citing Kahn, Kamiński, and John. "All have returned for duty on *Lincoln*. And the results are exquisitely right. The picture does not go in for the hard sell."[111]

The *Lincoln* score was a seasoned addition to John's considerable corpus about the American dream—*Born on the Fourth of July*, *JFK*, *Nixon*, *Amistad*, *Saving Private Ryan*, *American Journey*, and *The Patriot*—but somehow delving even deeper into the core earthy roots of that dream. Many critics characterized it as a pastiche of Copland, who wrote his own *Lincoln Portrait* in 1942—but this charge irked John, "because it suggests that everybody who writes an Appalachian pastiche, like I did for *Lincoln*, is doing the same thing that Copland did, and that Copland's responsible for every Appalachian tune you hear orchestrated.

> In Copland's case, he didn't write his original pastiche. He took "Simple Gifts" right from the Shakers. As far as I know he didn't write his own. So the question is absurd on its face. Of course it's a pastiche! Has nothing to do with Copland at all. He doesn't own the Appalachian Mountains or the 19th century hymnbook of American folk song. So the question reveals a narrowness in the writer who writes these things.
>
> It's the root source, the same sources that Copland has looked at and others. Fair game for every American composer, and should be. It's like saying you can't write a twelve-bar blues anymore because W.C. Handy has already done that and copyrighted it. The idea that in some critic's mind *Lincoln* is derivative of Copland shows such a limited knowledge and view.[112]

John had carried this bullseye on his back ever since *Star Wars* put it there in 1977: *pastiche, forgery, imitation*. And although he maintained his demure, unflappable posture in interviews, this accusation clearly flapped his pride. Some people close to him thought it was partly what made him so guarded, so private, especially with journalists. Asked directly if the criticism of "plagiarism and hackery" wounded him, John said: "Mostly not really."[113] But those qualifying adverbs seemed pregnant with subtext.

John conducted music from *Lincoln* at a Fourth of July concert at the U.S. Capitol in the summer of 2013. He kept the patriotic feelings flowing with a new fanfare for The President's Own, the United States Marine Band. The elite ensemble celebrated their 215th anniversary in May at Wolf Trap, the summer music space in Virginia, where they premiered John's sparkling, cheerful miniature of brassy pageantry.[114] John developed a special relationship with the Marines, later returning to conduct The President's Own and recording an album of new arrangements of his film themes—and eventually being named an honorary Marine in a special ceremony. This was only strange insofar as John was an alumnus of the Air Force. "I have some missives from them," he said, "'Why don't you come and do something with us?' And I do feel a little remiss in not doing something with them. Can't do everything, I guess."[115]

* * *

John had always pondered the idea of a guitar concerto. He had a strong concept for a piece which would trace the instrument's history: "It's a Spanish-Italian instrument," he remarked, "but the hillbillies play, and the banjo players play, and the lead fronts of the Black slaves slapping it and so on."[116] When John wrote acoustic guitar solos for *Stepmom*, Christopher Parkening expressed his desire for a concerto from John. But the closest John ever got was in the summer of 2012, when the Spanish guitarist Pablo Sáinz Villegas premiered *Rounds* for solo guitar. John wrote the piece as a gift for the Parkening International Guitar Competition, and it was Parkening who suggested that Villegas—who won the competition in 2006—should play it as a finale of the competitive weekend in Malibu. The young guitarist went to John's house two days before, where John rehearsed the six-minute piece with him. "When I was a kid, I loved his music from *Superman*," Villegas said. "Thirty years later, when I visited him at his home in Los Angeles, I realized how much he understands the human condition. That's why he can transpose those emotions into wonderful melodies and harmonies. He is such an elegant, humble, true genius."[117]

Surprisingly, John had never written a classical piece for piano—not since his teenage sonata—and in this same year he wrote "a little encore piece" for Gloria Cheng to play at the end of her recital at Tanglewood in August. John's eccentric concept was a conversation between Phineas Newborn, Jr., a forgotten jazz pianist from Tennessee, and an enslaved woman named Mumbett who, with legal representation by a prominent attorney from Stockbridge, successfully sued the state of Massachusetts for her freedom in 1781. "What a fascinating conversation that might be," John said. "I wrote this piece with some thoughts and reflections as I had them of Phineas and some of his piano techniques, and speculated about the music that Mumbett might have heard in her life—which certainly would have been out of one hymnbook or another—and arranged a series of exchanges in these two modes."[118]

He had so much fun that he added three more movements inspired by imagined dialogues between his old hero Claude Thornhill and Thelonious Monk, Chet Baker and Miles Davis, and between Billy Strayhorn, Duke Ellington, and "Blind Tom" Wiggins, a piano phenomenon born into slavery in the 19th century. He called the piece, simply, *Conversations*. Writing for solo piano is very challenging, he admitted: "Every note has to count. Piano's a percussion instrument, of course, and the ability to sustain and maintain a lyrical line and a long tone is something that really constitutes an illusion if it can be done at all."[119]

Cheng had played on several of John's sessions since *Munich*, and she used *Conversations* as an excuse to commission short solo piano works by five other film composers: Randy Newman, Alexandre Desplat, Bruce Broughton, Don Davis, and Michael Giacchino. She premiered them on a program at the Colburn School of Music in November 2013, and turned the collection into an album and short documentary called *Montage*. Not too surprisingly, John started to think seriously about writing a piano concerto, which at one point he promised to Cheng. The two had become close, writing letters and sharing books about composers. "I do feel like I was a very special friend during this time," she said:

> I was just tickled that another letter from him would be waiting for me in my mailbox, a couple times a week often. And it was almost like a torrid correspondence, because I'd want to respond immediately. It was just nice, because we didn't talk on the phone—we did it this way. It was just lovely and old fashioned. I didn't feel particularly *privileged* by it. I just felt like: we have a connection that's *real*. Other people were sort of maybe wondering, you know, but ... we loved each other. I still do, but it's different now. His attention has turned to other things. I'm just grateful that we had that, and I have this beautiful trove of letters. We were special to each other.[120]

John dipped a toe into the concerto waters with a single-movement Scherzo for Piano and Orchestra, which was premiered in July 2014 by the young Chinese superstar, Lang Lang, in Beijing. The 10-minute piece was brash and turbulent, with an extended conversation—or really a heated argument—between the thundering piano and staccato timpani. At Cheng's request, John revised the scherzo and added a gentler, more inquisitive prelude, which she premiered in Barcelona some years later. But a full, proper concerto for piano would have to wait.

* * *

When John learned that 20th Century Fox was adapting the young adult novel *The Book Thief*, he wanted in. It had been nearly a decade since he'd scored a movie for anyone other than Spielberg, but he was touched by this story's notion "that words can save you, and that words could offer solace to you, and words could offer immortality to you."[121] Like *Schindler's Ark*, *The Book Thief* was a dramatized novel set during the Holocaust and written by an Australian—in this case Markus Zusak, weaving a tale about an Aryan German girl who helps hide a young Jewish man in her house. The film was shot on locations in Germany, with British director Brian Percival giving it some of the same handsome but glossy period quality he brought to the popular television series *Downton Abbey*.

"Brian Percival has said to me he wanted to make a small film," John said. "And I just said that I didn't think, in that respect, he'd been successful. It's really a big film, and it has a heart as big as this building we're in, and power and a force that's delivered quietly—but nonetheless with great power."[122] That was a nice way of describing a movie that was too knowingly beautiful and sanitized, and ultimately twee, for its grave subject matter. Playing the book-thieving protagonist, Liesel, the impossibly cherubic actress Sophie Nélisse is an American Girl doll version of Oskar Schindler as she harbors and bonds with a Jewish escapee, befriends a young Aryan Hitler youth, rescues a book from a Nazi bonfire, defiantly shouts aloud that she hates Hitler, and comforts her frightened neighbors with cute, made-up stories. "The years-spanning film, which observes traumatic historical events through Liesel's eyes, looks and tastes like a giant sugar cake whose saccharinity largely camouflages the horrors of the war," Stephen Holden wrote in the *New York Times*.

> Like a caring dentist reassuring a frightened child, it purveys a message: "Don't be afraid. I'll try not to hurt you, although you might feel a little pinch." ... I can't imagine that the creators of *The Book Thief* were aware of their movie's underlying message that it really wasn't that bad. John Williams's score—a quieter, more somber echo of his music for *Schindler's List*—lends the film an unearned patina of solemnity, for *The Book Thief* is a shameless piece of Oscar-seeking Holocaust kitsch.[123]

John nonetheless found ample inspiration in the film, which was framed like a children's book by an unseen narrator who turns out to be the Grim Reaper. "No one lives forever," the voice of Death coos. "Don't panic." John grounded this part of the movie with a piano motif that rises like a question, then slips into an inquisitive, bittersweet tune that is neither completely tragic nor melancholic, and which bore some resemblance to the searching solos in *Angela's Ashes*. John's locomotive score moves along two "tracks," he explained: "Literature, words, and writing offer solace and immortality; the other side of the track is the Voice of Death and that track also offers solace and immortality. These are two powerful notions that are highly original and poetic subjects for music to deal with."[124]

The film's opening cue chugs along on a string motor similar to the one in *Geisha*, accompanying the picturesque landscape of Germany in the winter of 1938. Liesel's baby brother dies on a train ride to Munich, where they are heading to be adopted by an older couple. As in *Angela's Ashes*, oboe and clarinet solos convey the hero's lonely sadness— although John swaddled this score in comforting strings and he scores the happy antics of Liesel and her friend Rudy with excited, syncopated dances. His theme for Liesel and the power of words is introduced in the prologue, and it comes into full bloom when she is invited into a book-lover's library owned by a mysterious woman named Ilsa—a "magical moment for her," John said.[125] "I think to myself: *what should this film sound like?* There's a piano melody or motif in *Book Thief* that is a kind of code, in a way, that has to do with the attraction and magnetism of books. And we hear it when Liesel is focused on the books—she sees them, and she's drawn to what's in them and the ideas that are there."[126] The piano nimbly skitters along, like Liesel's neurons of imagination, fluttering around a minor key string theme in waltz time. This idea persists as Liesel teaches herself to read, and recurs on harp when Max—the Jewish friend hiding in her basement—gives her a book full of blank pages for her to fill with her own words.

Max and Liesel's friendship is scored with a sweet, fragile song for solo oboe and strings. There are patches of darkness in corners of the score, but mostly it's a collection of warm, lyrical recitative and lovely arias that locate the inherent romance in tragedy—a byproduct of the film's fairy-tale tone, absent of almost all blood and brutality, where Death is given the personality of a wise and winking Dumbledore-like figure. At one point, Percival asked John: "Why can't death be beautiful?" John took the opportunity to share his anecdote about Hitchcock telling him that murder can be fun. The director, already starstruck, rubbed his head with his hand thinking: *he worked with Hitchcock as well?!*[127]

"If you press me about one single sequence that ... has the most power," John said, "it's the night of the bombing of Himmel Street"—a climactic scene in which most of the characters die.

> There's a theme that accompanies the voice of death—that's usually accompanied by strings in the orchestra, that is certainly melancholy, but it's hopeful also. The narration takes us across the sleeping families just before they're to be taken. All we hear are a combination of the voice and the orchestra itself. Musically it's painting this picture of a very lyrical, poetic, and beautiful, and peaceful end. It's, I think, an exceptional moment in a film that I've seen.[128]

Transcending the film's flaws, John delivered a gentle, singable lullaby score for death and the Nazi nightmare; it earned him his 49th Oscar nomination. The Academy hosted a high-class concert featuring selections from all of the nominated scores that year, a first, and John conducted a suite from *The Book Thief* at UCLA's Royce Hall. He lost the Oscar to Steven Price's thrumming, electronic-hybrid score for *Gravity*, an outer space thrill ride directed by *Azkaban*'s Alfonso Cuarón, and a striking contrast to the old-fashioned romantic score John had written for traditional symphony orchestra. With very few exceptions, John's way of scoring was an almost total anomaly. More and more, he was a man out of time.

* * *

"He's a good musician, and there's very little he doesn't know about the orchestra," Previn said in May 2014. "But he's been there too long. This is just my opinion. I say to him every once in a while: 'John, get the hell out of there.'"[129] At 85, Previn was *still* carping about Hollywood, still failing to see what John was doing as worthy of his talents.

What would have happened if John had listened to Previn or followed in his footsteps, burning the bridge to the studio lots and chasing classical prestige? More concertos, perhaps. A plum conducting job with a world-class orchestra? Unlikely. John admitted, even after all his experience, that he did not regard himself as a professional conductor.[130] The twin suns of popular cinema and John's genius gave him a platform and a presence that Previn could only dream of, and John knew better than to heed his friend's sour advice. In a written tribute for John's 80th birthday concert at Tanglewood, Dyer noted that John "took the Pops job, he said at the time, to win recognition for film music and all composers for film—not just himself. In reaching that aim he has been brilliantly successful. There is no need to 'legitimize' film music anymore; film music has an entirely different profile today, thanks mostly to him."[131] By now film music—and specifically *John's* film music—had been elevated to such a high status that, a few months after Previn's comment, the LA Phil devoted their season-opening gala to John's music. The audience included William Shatner, Frank Gehry, and Mayor Eric Garcetti. Perlman performed *Schindler's List*, the U.S. Army Herald Trumpets performed the *Olympic Fanfare* from the balconies, and the Los Angeles Children's Chorus sang "Dry Your Tears, Afrika."[132]

Addressing the night's big-ticket crowd, Dudamel said: "Musicians try to be close to composers like Mahler, Shostakovich. But in this opportunity we have the chance to be so close to this one, that is, John Williams." Dudamel recalled how, as a child, he would go to John's famous movies just to listen to the scores. Then, turning to John he said: "We are here tonight to pay homage to your genius and to your heart, because you are one of the best composers in our time. But the most important thing, you are a great human."[133] In a review, Swed noted the orchestra's long history with John, going back at least as far as Zubin Mehta's programming of *Star Wars*, but "Dudamel brings something new to the relationship," Swed wrote: "He is an unabashed Williams enthusiast." In response to Dudamel's interpretation of the Throne Room finale from *Star Wars*, the often disparaging Swed wrote: "Music that has become cliché felt renewed, as if Williams' score were what prodded the creative process. Williams' most lasting legacy is likely to be his influence on children. Dudamel is hardly alone. No composer in history has so infused young people with symphonic joy."[134]

John and Dudamel also became friends off stage. When the hotshot conductor was offered his first film-scoring assignment that year—for *Libertador*, the epic tale of Simón Bolívar, liberator of Venezuela from Spain and the namesake of Dudamel's hometown orchestra—he asked John for advice. Dudamel invited John to his house and "when he arrived, I was so afraid," the conductor said. "Even though we are very good friends, *very* good friends, I was really afraid to show him what I was writing."[135] Dudamel had been conceiving of his score as a symphony or an opera, and John quickly impressed on him that it had to be much more streamlined and economical than that. John said, "Wow, these two bars . . ." and then, "Can I sit at the piano?" He played the melody Dudamel had written and said, "This can go like *this*, and even if it's a battle, it can go like *this*. . . ." "And with the same melody, he played for me like *ten* different examples," Dudamel said. "The creativity, the imagination of John is *so* natural for him. It's so natural for him to see something and to put music to it."[136]

While John was now fully embraced by his hometown orchestra and its new music director, and welcomed into its hallowed temple during a regular subscription season, the friction between high and low art was still on display at that gala concert. After the children's choir sang, they ran off the stage theatrically screaming as the orchestra began the low notes of *Jaws*. When John took the podium to conduct the

Imperial March—what else?—he was interrupted by Darth Vader and a detachment of Stormtroopers. If John was annoyed by the invasion of childish populism into this serious tribute, he never let on. In fact, in an almost direct defiance of Previn's pleadings, he doubled down by committing to score the launch of a newly announced *Star Wars* sequel trilogy in the works. "I don't have a prejudice about, or I should say make a particular distinction between something that's high art and low art," John said.

> As Leonard Bernstein was always fond of saying, "There's good and bad." It could be the Beatles or it could be Béla Bartók. Music is there for everybody. It's a river we can all put our cups into and drink it and be sustained by it. So I have to say that I've never had any intellectual problem with that.
>
> I suppose if I was Beethoven, you may be able to be restricted in your sense of what's appropriate in art. But even Brahms greatly appreciated Johann Strauss, who one could say was at the level of high art and the other one a level of popular art. I am not in such an ivory tower in any respect that I need to worry about that in my own work. Whether I'm writing for concert or film, it's very simple. I just try to do the best I'm able to do. And other people will judge it for whether it's high, low, wide, or narrow—or whatever it may be. People want to hear it and want to play it . . . it just gratifies me. And as I listen, I think to myself: *I wish I could do better, and I'll try to do better the next time.*[137]

* * *

Death was the only thing that could possibly stop John from continuing to work. "Certainly my work days have shrunken," he admitted in 2015, "but it's still enough time to do the work. And I welcome doing it. Frankly, the alternative to working is *not* working, and that, I think for any of us, is not a healthy thing. 'Working' is maybe not the best word. Why don't we call it contributing?"[138] But Death is not always a beautiful, gentle narrator—and he came a little too close for comfort in early 2015 when John experienced atrial fibrillation and, because his blood pressure was low, his doctor recommended installing a pacemaker. ("By the way," John said, "if anybody ever tells you that you need one, don't hesitate."[139]) Complicating things even further, he was also suffering from horrendous back pain yet again. For the first time in 35 years, he had to miss Tanglewood that summer—and he also wasn't able to score Spielberg's next picture. John was 83, and it wasn't irrational to wonder if his days might be numbered.

17
Old Friends, 2015–2019

> *The true genius of John Williams is that these are mediocre works which John made great.*
> —George Lucas[1]

> *I'd be quite happy to have it go on indefinitely.*
> —John Williams, on *Star Wars*[2]

It was miraculous that as John entered his ninth decade, and Hollywood filmmaking evolved further and further into a digital manufacturing machine—completely hostile to pencils moving slowly on paper and romantic, symphonic development—he was still in demand. His contemporaries, with the rare exceptions of Ennio Morricone, Quincy Jones, and Lalo Schifrin, had mostly all passed on or certainly retired, and even the next generation was losing its standard-bearers. On June 22, 2015, James Horner died while piloting a small plane over the Los Padres National Forest near his home in Calabasas. The composer, who adopted John's general approach in everything from *Star Trek* to *Titanic*, was only 61. Even John's younger peers had watched as their working methods and styles were left in the dust—trampled over by composer factories that produced music by the foot in big steroidal blasts of sound, nondescript ambience, and endlessly chugging ostinatos. Any composers who did continue to look to classical, analog forms now had to spend precious time creating detailed synth mockups—long gone were the days of auditioning themes on a piano—and then contort their composition process to a never-locking picture, constantly being asked to rewrite cues to satisfy the director or studio and to make changes so as to accommodate the edit and visual effects delivery schedules. Somehow John, this self-proclaimed "antediluvian" dinosaur, without changing anything about his process, never went out of fashion.

Except … he *did*. There were really only two reasons why John's phone never stopped ringing in the last decade of his career: Steven Spielberg, and *Star Wars*. The two suns that set his career ablaze in the 1970s were the same ones still keeping it hot. The rest of Hollywood, from Marvel to *Moonlight*, had moved on. John's whole ethos, and the old system of making movies that allowed for it, was effectively extinct. His flame remained lit simply because Spielberg kept making films and had no intention of losing his most important collaborator—Howard Shore referred to Spielberg as John's "great patron"[3]—and because the Walt Disney Company, the corporate colossus that now owned *Star Wars*, recognized that it was worth bending over backward to retain the space opera's soul, its ennobling engine.

It was Kathleen Kennedy, Spielberg's longtime producer and the new steward of George Lucas's empire, who brokered the deal. *Star Wars* was the latest and greatest "IP" (intellectual property) to get gobbled up by a giant movie corporation when Disney bought Lucasfilm Ltd. and its sentimental treasures from Lucas in 2012 (for $4 billion) and made Kennedy president.[4] She wisely intuited that she should enlist as many of the actual intellects who helped make this property beloved in the first place, so even though *Star Wars: Episode XII—The Force Awakens* turned out to be an exercise in risk-averse, stockholder-friendly nostalgia regurgitation, at least the ship flew steady with the comforting presence of writer Lawrence Kasdan and actors Harrison Ford, Carrie Fisher, and Mark Hamill all on board.

Kennedy had a long-standing relationship with John; she was part of the "family," having been an assistant to Spielberg starting on *Raiders of the Lost Ark* and a producer for most of his extraordinary run, one of the few people allowed into Spielberg's scoring sessions and therefore "in that sort of rarefied inner circle," she said, where "everybody was just very comfortable and talking about things that I think normally you would never have access to, because it's just the vulnerability around the creative process." John's pet name for her was alternately "Angel face" or "Bubala" ("darling" in Yiddish).[5] "It's a good long time that I have been close to Kathy," John said. Shortly after assembling her core filmmaking team, she called "Johnny" up and asked if he would have dinner with her and the film's hot young director, J. J. Abrams, and John did not hesitate. "J. J. was wonderful with me," he said.

> We had a lot of fun. He was talking about what a fan of *Jaws* he'd been, and made a little poster or something when he was eight years old because he loved the music of *Jaws*, and how did I feel about coming on board to do the seventh installment of *Star Wars*? And I thought, *well, it would be a lot of fun*, and I saw no reason not to do it. I've always enjoyed doing them, and I was very anxious to see what he would do *with* it.[6]

So began a prolonged third wave of John's attachment to this faraway galaxy, in which "*Why not? It'll be fun*" was his modus operandi for working with new, young directors on a new trilogy of gigantic blockbusters, as well as creating new themes for spinoff movies, television series, and a new Disney land. *Star Wars* consumed the better part of John's ninth decade on Earth, requiring an outsized amount of his energy and time. Even after the critical bloodbath that had met the prequels, even after Lucas sold off his own creation to a board-directed entity that was the very antithesis of auteur artistry—Lucas referred to Disney as "white slavers" in a solecistic comment in the wake of the studio's new venture[7]—John never loosened his grip. Was it truly, simply a matter of "*Why not? It'll be fun*"? Or did *Star Wars* mean far, far more to John than he let on?

He did say he felt invigorated working with Abrams, who brought "a renewed energy, and a vitality, and a freshness that did not estrange any of the characters or any of the material from the texture and fabric of Lucas' creation, but revivified it. And one can feel that in J. J.'s energy. He's a young man. He's a very bright man. He travels at lightspeed in his thinking and in his actions."[8] Abrams was a disciple of Spielberg and now ordained as his blockbuster heir, and there was certainly no shortage of energy or enthusiasm in his approach to making the same kind of whizbang films he grew up on: he had brought Spielbergian wonder and camerawork to reboot the *Star Trek* series, and his 2011 film *Super 8* was an unabashed valentine to his idol. But too often, Abrams's reverent devotion to the aesthetics of his masters disguised a shortage of original ideas or personality. Like most of his films, *The Force Awakens* looks fantastic—and his emphasis on physical props and puppets and shooting on location redeemed much of the aesthetic magic lost in Lucas's prequel films. But Abrams and company basically took the proven pieces of *Star Wars* 1977 and recycled them with new names: the young nobody hero from a desert planet was now a girl named Rey; the Empire was now the "First Order," and the Rebel Alliance the "Resistance." There was a new dashing rogue pilot, a new weapon that destroys planets, and a new bad guy in a black helmet. Han Solo was reset to square one, roaming the galaxy with Chewbacca as a scrappy mercenary once more. The one truly novel wrinkle in the old fabric was Finn, a Black stormtrooper with a heart of gold. But like Kylo Ren worshiping at the altar of his grandfather's Darth Vader helmet, the film was fearfully beholden to its own nostalgia.

Thus, John found himself in a strange and creatively stifling situation. For all their flaws, the prequels had actually given him the stimulating task of "de-composing" his classic themes, and they also let him add a wilder, more ancient language to his neoclassical palette of the first trilogy. *The Force Awakens* and its sequels required much more of a straight copy of the original scores, or rather a copy of the essential fumes that persisted four decades later. John dutifully quoted his hits—the Force theme, Luke's theme, Leia's theme—as the callback-heavy plot prescribed. Everything additive was in a safely defined "Star Warsian" vocabulary—a term John coined to describe "a similarity in harmonic modalities, a similarity in stylistic intervallic choices for melodies and so on, similarities in orchestral textural presentations and the like"[9]—and perhaps for that reason, his new heroic-martial themes for Poe Dameron (Oscar Isaac) and the Resistance erred on sounding familiar to the point of generic. Kylo Ren's theme is similarly nostalgic, but missing the infectious singularity of John's previous bad guy tunes. Frank Lehman saw this as a feature, not a bug: "It's supposed to sound like a quasi, not quite fully realized evil motif in the style of Vader, but not actually living up to it. That's fitting for his character, as a shadow of a more memorable, memorably evil figure from his past."[10]

There are really two parts to Kylo's theme, John explained:

> There's a more ruminative part that is usually done softly. I don't think it portrays any particular weakness, but possibly hesitancy. But then there's the motif that's

often loud—*strong* might be a better word—that seems to be the embodiment of evil, almost in the same way that Darth Vader's motif originally made. I thought that it should be a relative of Darth Vader, but something entirely different also in terms of melody. In most cases it's presented in a very ominous, dangerous, dark way. It not only seems to fit what's happened to his character, but also the way he looks on the screen, the way he behaves.[11]

The strongest newcomer by far was John's theme for Rey—which was important, since she was going to be the central hero of three films. British actress Daisy Ridley gave her character as much nuance and personality as the script allowed—a mix of tomboyish pluck and steely sweetness. John was smitten: "I fell in love immediately," he said. "I think anybody would, man or woman. She is just a superstar born." But giving her a musical identity was a challenge, he said, "because her theme doesn't suggest a love theme in any way.

> It suggests an adventurer, a female adventurer, but with great strength. She's a fighter, she's infused with the Force, and it needed to be something that was strong but thoughtful. She's a very young girl, but she's a woman of diverse parts—and so there's a maturity, I think, about the approach, melodically, to her that I hope will fit her. It seemed particularly challenging, both in the scavenger section in the beginning and in the trip to the island to find Luke in the end, where her theme is pretty fully realized.[12]

Rey's theme arrives gently when we first meet her on Jakku, announced by a lonely flute and escorted by celeste and piano figures as furtive and fidgety as the young scavenger. Rey reminds the audience of both the fiery and beautiful young Leia and the heroic, questing young Luke, and John managed to pack a lot of those qualities into her theme: an exploring melody that is feminine and muscular, romantic and heroic, which he takes from the quietest moments of her staring innocently into the night sky to the heat of her battle with Kylo Ren as she unleashes the Force, where it victoriously erupts from the whole orchestra. It was completely unconscious on his part, John claimed, that the shape of Kylo's theme and Rey's theme were almost perfect mirrors of each other.[13]

The action cues and dramatic recitative are all fittingly grand and galactic, but there is an overall quality of ritual to the score—especially when it quotes old motifs without any variation or, more disappointingly, drops the needle directly on an old cue. The snowy forest climax between Rey and Kylo is heralded with the "Burning Homestead" rendition of the Force theme from John's original 1977 score. John was guided by a temp track constructed entirely from his earlier scores, which was a helpful tool for Abrams and a necessity in the new order of Hollywood effects films. The cut kept changing, VFX shots kept coming in, and a malleable temp track was part of the compromise John struck to score a newfangled film in 2015. Kennedy, old friend that she was, insisted from the outset that it was John's way or the highway: "I sat with each of the directors that came on board and said, 'This is how it's gonna go: we need to adapt to John, not the other way around.'"[14] Abrams, who clearly adored John and reveled working with him, happily agreed.

To accommodate his slow-cooked, analog process, Disney agreed to let John score finished reels and even individual scenes, record them with a full orchestra, then move on to score the next sequence when it was finished and record that—drawn across a period of five months from June to November for a total of 12 sessions. But this did not stop Abrams from making copious changes to his film or asking John for new cues, and when the dust settled, John wagered that he wrote an entire hour of music that was ultimately discarded or revised.[15]

Another casualty of this rambling schedule: it was the first *Star Wars* score not to be performed by the London Symphony Orchestra. The LSO had in fact been booked for *The Force Awakens*, for 15 to 20 sessions, and since the musicians were not salaried it was a real loss of income—nearly three weeks of work and thousands of pounds. They received notice just six weeks before the scheduled recording dates at Abbey Road. The reason given to Sue Mallet, planning director of the LSO, was that Abrams did not want to record in England[16]—but John admitted he did not want to go to London for the amount of time required, and the busy London orchestra simply could not have accommodated the start-stop marathon method adopted for this score. John was "absolutely mortified," said Mallet, who had been with the orchestra since 1967 and present for all of John's recording sessions with them over the decades. Ironically, the LSO was on a West Coast tour with Michael Tilson Thomas in March 2015 when the cancellation was announced, and John came to see them before their concert at Walt Disney Concert Hall to offer an apology in person. "That was very nice of him, to actually take the trouble," said Mallet. "A lot of people would not have done that."[17]

It was a heavy blow to the Brits—but fantastic news for John's L.A. players and a boon to the local musicians' union, at a time when so much scoring work was going overseas and L.A.'s few remaining stages sat empty for weeks at a time. When the Local 47 chapter of the AFM gave John a special Lifetime Contribution to Hollywood Award the following February, they estimated that the recording of *The Force Awakens* created jobs for 125 orchestra members, 23 singers, and more than 40 conductors, music contractors, and music preparation professionals. John credited Kennedy, Michael Gorfaine, and Jamie Richardson for working "so hard to convince the powers that this was in the best interest of the score and in the best interest of the film."[18] Recording in town also meant that John could invite Dudamel to Sony to conduct the iconic opening theme. "They played pretty well for me, but they played better for Gustavo," he quipped.[19] John was still recovering from crippling back pain, so he asked William Ross to help with some of the orchestration and even adaptation of cues, along with much of the actual conducting. The players learned about Horner's death in the middle of a session in June, and John said a few words in his honor. "I felt the best thing we could do is to dedicate the day to him," John said, "and make the best music we could."[20]

The other casualty of this score's demands on John's schedule, compounded by his pacemaker surgery and back issues, was that—for the first time in 30 years—he could not score Spielberg's latest film. *Bridge of Spies* was based on a true Cold War story about an American lawyer, played by Tom Hanks, hired to defend a Soviet spy. "Of course it kills both me and John," said Spielberg. "We are more than just collaborators—we are brothers."[21] But John did recommend someone special as his substitute: Thomas Newman, Alfred's youngest son. John had known "Tommy" since he was born, and Newman grew up hanging around the Fox scoring stage, sitting on ratty green couches and watching John record his score for *The Towering Inferno*.[22] Now he was a giant of his own generation, mixing a traditional symphonic approach with minimalism and studio experimentation to create memorable scores for popular films such as *The Shawshank Redemption*, *American Beauty*, and *Finding Nemo*. But subbing in for John Williams on a Steven Spielberg film was "very intimidating," Newman admitted. "There was no saying I could ever 'step in' and do what John does, but to step in and try to do what *I* do was what Steven had asked of me.... What else was I going to do? It'd be really hard to be John Williams."[23]

John gave all his energy to *Star Wars*, and Abrams could not have been happier with the results. "It was like hearing music from the gods," Abrams said.[24] While doing press for the film, he showed a reporter video from a session on his smart phone: "He's 83 and he's fucking incredible," the director gushed. "Dude, it was crazy."[25] *The Force Awakens* opened on a wave of hype not unlike *The Phantom Menace*, and it devoured more than $2 billion around the planet—breaking all previous box office records. A new generation fell in love with these variations on old archetypes, which immediately flooded the merchandise and theme park pipelines; Disney's galactic gamble had been handsomely rewarded.

The score earned John his 50th Academy Award nomination and put him in a balcony at the Dolby Theater next to Thomas Newman, ironically up for his Spielberg score, and the venerable Morricone who was there for his dread-filled western score for Quentin Tarantino's *The Hateful Eight*. When the 87-year-old Italian won his first competitive Oscar that evening in February, 2016—which elicited a lengthy standing ovation—he paid tribute to his fellow nominees, "and particular to the esteemed John Williams."[26] Morricone later praised John as a "complete musician," and "an exceptionally gifted composer whom I greatly respect."[27]*

* * *

John was the first composer to earn a lifetime achievement award from the American Film Institute. A host of his friends and admirers turned out on June 9, 2016, for another ceremony at the Dolby Theater. "How much of John Williams' music needs only to be heard?" Tom Hanks asked the audience rhetorically. "The visuals are nice, but not always necessary, because John's music has a singular authenticity that stirs our synapses. How much do you need? A few bars? Not even. A few *notes*." Hanks

---

* Morricone died on July 6, 2020, at the age of 91.

hummed brief phrases from *Jaws* and *Close Encounters* to prove his point. Harrison Ford dryly noted how he couldn't escape the Raiders March: "They play it every time I walk on a stage, every time I walk off a stage.... It was playing in the operating room when I went in for my colonoscopy." Lucas addressed John directly: "I had so many ideas for other movies, but I never got to them because you ensured that *Star Wars* would endure forever." Spielberg explained his and John's special working process to the audience, showing a snippet of the rough workprint of E.T. and Elliott taking flight without music, then showed some of his 8mm footage of John conducting that moment in 1982. He talked about the "arranged marriage of image and music" that causes audiences to fall in love with these movies, and after showing the final sequence of *E.T.* in all its glory, Spielberg rhapsodized:

> Without John Williams, bikes don't really fly, nor do brooms in Quidditch matches, nor do men in red capes. There is no Force, dinosaurs do not walk the Earth—we do not wonder, we do not weep, we do not believe. John, you breathe belief into every film we have made. You take our movies—many of them about our most impossible dreams—and through your musical genius you make them *real* and everlasting for billions and billions of people.

John was heralded to the stage by the victorious Throne Room march from *Star Wars*, and he mostly went for laughs and self-deprecation in his acceptance speech: "My first thought was: Actually, I'm really much too young for a thing like this," and he went on to list colleagues from the past who deserved this award, including his friends Alfred Newman and Bernard Herrmann:

> I owe a great deal to these men, and I owe a great deal to film, certainly. Music is like architecture, sculpture, and so on—*thousands* of years old. And film is the new kid on the block. A hundred years, *barely*. And though we will watch its evolution carefully, side by side with the art of music, I am enormously grateful, as all composers are, *to* film for giving us the broadest possible audience worldwide that any composer has ever enjoyed. I'm certain that Beethoven would have shunned it, but Wagner would have had his own studio out there in Burbank with a huge water tank with a "W" on it....
>
> Once I get over being stunned, I will treasure this night always. And tomorrow morning when I'm back at work, I will try to deserve all of this.[28]

The Spielberg-Williams magic on glorious display that night was largely missing from their next collaboration. One would have thought a lavish Disney movie based on a Roald Dahl fantasy about a big friendly giant and his little girl companion—from a novel written the same year *E.T.* came out, and a screenplay by *E.T.* scribe Melissa Mathison—would have all the makings of a vintage Spielberg fantasia.[†] Like *Tintin*,

---

[†] Mathison, who was often on set for *The BFG*, died suddenly from cancer before production wrapped.

The BFG slipped Spielberg from the surly bonds of earth's physics and allowed him to transpose his wildest dreams into cinema with the aid of motion-capture and modern digital effects. But that very unchecked liberation, while yielding some stunning visuals and weightless virtuosity, also stranded him in the uncanny valley that doomed so many of these pixelated pictures. (Ironically, his earthbound puppet from 1982 felt more real, and it has aged much more gracefully.)

John had actually met Dahl and his wife Patricia Neal at Robert Altman's house in the late 1960s. "He seemed to be a tweedy, literary type," John said.[29] "Bright. Sociable. It would be unfair to say he seemed to be a hard drinker—I can't say that—but it was a very *convivial* kind of atmosphere that Bob always had, with drinks and food buffet and lively company."[30] For John, *The BFG* offered a fun, fresh opportunity: "I kept saying to Steven, 'It's almost like a little child's opera, or a child's ballet where there are dances involved.'"[31] A scene where the BFG tries to catch dreams in a net reminded him of a Ray Bolger or Fred Astaire routine: "It's an amazingly musical and choreographic sequence, requiring the orchestra to do things that are more associated with musical films.... It's a bit more, at least in my mind, theatrical. You can almost feel that there's a curtain."[32]

The consequent score was emblematic of the tension between John's old, *E.T.*-style lyricism and his new restless "noteyness"—a hybrid of the Kern-loving tunesmith and the abstract concerto painter. Reacting to the white-water rapids of Spielberg's synthetic imagery, this music was an untethered stream of consciousness tone poem—lovely but slippery. The quicksilver, fairylike dreams inspired a lot of fleet, complicated solos for flute and staccato string carbonation—undoubtedly a "whizzpopper" to perform, but difficult for the ear, or the heart, to grab onto any kind of melodic or groove throughline. There is a noticeable evolution from John's Tinkerbell music in *Hook* to the magic-motored whimsy in *Harry Potter* to this—with each permutation becoming slightly more erratic, and progressively less hummable.

However, the BFG's theme is a dreamy, friendly waltz, which John first cloaks in playful mystery; but he quickly reveals its heart when the giant and the girl, Sophie, bond in his fairytale lair. The score is at its most beautiful in sleepy mode, rich with languid woodwind solos and *religioso* string chords, and Spielberg wisely carved out a few poignant moments of reflection and reverie. John wrote a dark waltz theme for jaw-dropping scenes of the BFG running and leaping across vistas from human civilization to Giant Country, and a comically oozing, *Home Alone*–style motif for the bigger, badder giants who torment him. After a fart-laden lunch with the Queen of the United Kingdom and a loud martial standoff between humans and the child-eating giants, John's score concludes on a solo piano version of the BFG theme—echoing similar, stripped-down finales in *War Horse* and *Lincoln*—a big friendly movie ending on a small, intimate note.

"*The BFG* is gonna be huge," declared *Variety*'s Peter Debruge after the film premiered at Cannes.[33] But the magic was gone. When the film opened in July, it earned a net positive response from critics but a paltry $55 million at the home box office. It grossed nearly three times as much internationally, but the grand total was still a dramatic decay from Spielberg's old business. This movie outlived the summer of 2016 only whenever John programmed a suite of his score in concert, a chance for the evening's principal flute to shine and the audience to catch a breath between themes, and movies, that they knew and loved.

* * *

The supreme success of *The Force Awakens* sealed Disney's investment in producing a new trilogy, and John was equally invested in seeing his nine-cycle space opera to completion. Director Rian Johnson was a USC film graduate who made an impression with striking episodes of *Breaking Bad* and the low-budget sci-fi film *Looper*, but he was a surprising pick to helm a *Star Wars* juggernaut, and he brought a very different attitude to Episode VIII, *The Last Jedi*—upsetting legions of fans (and even Hamill himself) by turning Luke into a cranky old hermit, revealing that Rey has no special ancestry, and literally burning the sacred Jedi texts, a metaphor for letting our obsession with the past die in order to create something new and interesting. Johnson's meta-textual screenplay was far more daring than Abrams's film, even as it was saddled with an almost crushing accrual of old Skywalker baggage and new Rey-Kylo-Finn-Poe-Hux ballast. A side quest to a casino planet with Finn and his new pal Rose, where they find a code-breaker who double-crosses them, is a cumbersome diversion, and the ever-present silliness—here including giant space cows, tiny birdlike Porgs, and a herd of galloping kangaroo horses—somewhat undermine Johnson's more sober and subversive intentions. But then, *Star Wars* was always a strange mélange of heroic myth, family drama, and goofy sideshows ... part religious parable, part toy commercial. Johnson's chapter had the undeniable asset of being something all too rare these days: unpredictable.

He normally worked with his cousin, composer Nathan Johnson, but they both grew up worshiping John's music, and the director was euphoric about collaborating with a real Jedi legend. "It's hard to talk about him without sounding like you're dedicating national park land or something," Johnson said. "It's hard not to just suddenly get into big, grand terms that start feeling ubiquitous and meaningless."[34] John *was* a national monument in Johnson's mind, a great edifice—that is, until the director went to John's house for the first time. There, beyond his holy awe at the leather-bound scores for *Close Encounters* and *Raiders*, Johnson marveled at the pencil-paper-piano setup and John's humble craftsman process. Johnson, a 1980s kid, used a pop culture reference from his youth to describe what happened when he met John:

> This is the skeleton key to me, to unlocking why all of his work feels so engaged and alive throughout, and the fact that he's done so much great work. You remember at the end of *Ghostbusters*, when the big demon dog has been turned into a statue and then Sigourney Weaver breaks out of it? There was this monumental statue in my head of John Williams, the *master composer*. And what broke out of that, once I got together with him and started working with him, was the childlike joy of invention, and the sharply tuned desire to break new ground and to engage with every single story as if it's the first score that he's doing.[35]

Johnson loved the leitmotivic opera music of Richard Wagner, and like many others, he assumed John did, too. "I thought I would totally impress him by talking Wagner," said Johnson. "I brought it up, and he just completely was disinterested and ignored it and moved the conversation on to baseball or something." Turning to the new *Star Wars* film, Johnson did not ask for any specific leitmotif references from prior scores, but they did talk a lot about Luke "and about the notion of the movie being Luke reclaiming his place as the hero," Johnson said.

> Recognizing that even as a human being with faults, he has to be a hero for the next generation—that's his role—and stepping into that role by the end of it ... but how Luke is kind of broken throughout a big chunk of the movie. So we talked about maybe, in that way, avoiding Luke's theme throughout the movie, or breaking it, and holding it off until the end to get that emotional catharsis when he does finally take the mantle and step up as the Luke Skywalker that we all want from our childhoods.[36]

Johnson offered to screen *The Last Jedi* without his temp track, which had been meticulously curated from other *Star Wars* films by Johnson's music editor, Joseph Bonn—but John said he was happy to hear it. "I like a lot of stuff in there," John said afterward. And then he went away, Johnson said, "and the first time I hear any of John's score is when the 200-piece orchestra is playing it on the Sony lot." This was a stark contrast to the *Force Awakens* workflow, and the complete opposite approach normally taken by Johnson and directors of his generation, an approach which he characterized as "collaborative to the point of granular detail." But he wanted to honor John's ancient method to the point of handing over, essentially, a locked cut and not making a million changes to the edit up until the premiere. "It just wasn't that kind of party for us," Johnson said proudly.[37]

John wrote a sweet and sunny tune for Rose, the new voice of class consciousness in the galaxy. More powerful was a new motif for Luke's stoic life on the island of Ahch-To—a syncopated, storm-beaten melody of flint and regret. But beyond an initial montage of craggy Luke's daily routine on the island, there wasn't much canvas for this theme until an exciting development in the end credits suite. The Canto Bight casino gave John a colorful new cantina scene, and he wrote an uptempo, Latin-style piece for steel drums and band. An unabashed film nerd, Johnson also dropped a piano quote of *The Long Goodbye* theme into the casino sequence. "I asked him if we could do that, and he giggled," said Johnson. "I think he was amused that *that* was the piece of score of his that I was obsessed with." (As a wrap gift for the director, John wrote his theme for Altman's 1973 film on a sheet of music paper.)[38]

The rest of John's score was perfectly functional *Star Warsian* recitative, expertly crafted orchestral activity with formal pronouncements of vintage themes—which now included those for Rey, Ren, and the Resistance. It was the same brand of leitmotif-heavy, heroic storytelling that John had always given *Star Wars*, but missing some of the live spark and hungry self-challenge. It was missing *risk*. Nothing in these sequel scores comes close to the operatic, youthful adventure of the first trilogy, or the heartbreaking elegy and primal howl in the second. Johnson begged to differ, pointing to his favorite musical moment in this score—for the climactic scene when Luke walks onto the battlefield of the salt planet Crait:

> It's completely unlike what we had temped. John did this amazing piece of score that has this massive rhythm backbone to it that just feels epic and builds to this insane, monumental, man-versus-a-row-of-machines climax. It's astounding.
>
> When we were recording it on the stage, the players—who have been working with him for decades and decades—were all just shaking their heads and coming up to me, saying, "This is like some *new shit*, man. People aren't writing this shit anymore. This is fucking great." It felt like great invention of somebody in their prime. It felt like when you watch that Beatles documentary and see them finding "Get Back."[39]

Johnson accepted the score that John presented almost completely—with one major exception. For a crucial scene where Kylo and Rey reach out from across the stars and touch hands, John initially wrote a cue that was "almost like a parent protecting Rey from Kylo," said Johnson. "He scored him reaching forward and their connection as *something bad is about to happen, and this is a threat*." Johnson thought it was beautiful, but the wrong emotional perspective:

> It wasn't like I was saying, "Oh, it should go *boom-ba-ba-boom*," or "It should be strings, not this . . ." It was talking on a bedrock level about the storytelling of the scene. My argument was just that we have to be in Rey's head at this moment, and the only way this moment works is if Rey doesn't perceive this as a threat but sees this as a genuine connection with somebody else—and she's very lonely, and this makes total sense. We have to play it straight, and thus it has to be played as romance.
>
> [John] was very protective of that character, and his instincts were very strong in that regard, so it took a lot of back and forth of conversations with him. And finally he was like, "Okay, I can see that." And I think what he turned over ended up working perfectly.[40]

Ross came to all of the sessions and did some conducting, although John was in much better shape than he was on the previous film. "He'd say, 'Hey Bill, you wanna pitch a few?'" Ross said. "We have a baseball analogy—he refers to me as 'the bullpen.'"[41] Johnson was so excited to have his very own John Williams score that he insisted a version of the film be released with an isolated score track. Of all the possible Williams scores to receive such an honor over the decades, *this* one was an odd choice—why did Spielberg never offer a similar feature?—but it is nonetheless a great demonstration of John's unwaveringly elegant craft and deftness at cinematic dramaturgy, as well as just how omnipresent his orchestral hustle and bustle is, and how critical it is to these movies actually feeling like *Star Wars*.

John attended the film's world premiere at the Shrine Auditorium on December 9, 2017; he also conducted a suite from his score at a concert for the year's Oscar nominees at Disney Hall.‡ One year earlier, after *The Last Jedi* was shot but before it was scored, Carrie Fisher died of sudden cardiac arrest, with traces of cocaine and heroin in her system.[42] The actress was always candid about her long and dangerous dance with drug addiction in several witty memoirs, and Fisher—whom John had known since she was a baby—was only 60. A special title card in *The Last Jedi*'s end credits, "In Loving Memory of Our Princess," was serenaded with a fragile statement of Leia's theme on piano. John's music was also present at Fisher's memorial service in March 2017 at the Forest Lawn cemetery, and he conducted her theme in tributes at several concerts that summer.

* * *

Kobe Bryant, the 18-time NBA All-Star, was an unexpected admirer of John's music: as a boy, Bryant would tie a towel around his neck and run around to the theme of *Superman*; as a player, he used the Imperial March to hype himself up before games; and as a father, he would rock his infant daughters to sleep on his chest listening to Hedwig's Theme.[43] The six-foot-six athlete from Philly could hardly have been less like John, but he recognized mastery when he heard it. "I asked myself a question," Bryant said: "What makes a John Williams piece timeless? How is he using each instrument? How is he using the space between them? How is he building momentum, and then how is he taking it away to build it again?"[44] As a basketball player, Bryant said he was "essentially conducting a game," "so I just wanted to talk to him about how he composed music and try to find something similar that I can then use to help my game as a leader and winning championships."

Bryant first contacted John for counsel just before the 2008 NBA season. "The first thing I told Kobe was, I'd never seen a basketball game," John confessed. "High school, college, professional, or television. And of course he laughed."[45] "But once I had told him my reason for reaching out to him," Bryant said, "he saw the connection immediately.... If we look in our same industry and we just look at things from that funnel, then you wind up essentially recycling information. So sometimes you look outside of that discipline to have a new point of view, a new perspective on it. [John] was digging it."

They continued to see each other over the years, with Bryant often visiting John backstage after shows at the Hollywood Bowl. When Bryant retired from basketball in 2016, he turned his attention to entertainment. He wrote a sentimental open letter, "Dear Basketball," as a retirement announcement, and one of his first post-game projects was turning that text into a short film. He wanted it crafted by undisputed masters of their fields, so he commissioned Disney animation veteran Glen Keane—who

---

‡ He lost the Oscar that year to Alexandre Desplat's *The Shape of Water*.

designed and animated Ariel in *The Little Mermaid*, among other achievements—and he asked John to write the score. The first thing John said to Bryant was, "I do classical pieces, and it's all by hand," almost as a warning. Bryant answered: "The piece will be hand-animated by Glen Keane, who is *you* in the animation space. I want it to have the human touch. I don't want it to be poppy, I don't want it to be hip-hoppy. I want timeless, classical music."[46]

Somehow, these three disparate artists—with two decades between each of them—hit it off. Keane was an avid fan of *Lost in Space* growing up in the 1960s, and when he told John how much he loved the music, John was completely embarrassed. "But it's wonderful, John!" Keane said. "It held the promise of wonder and excitement and fun and quirky and scary and dangerous, and it was all in this one score. And John—the roots of your entire career are in that score." Keane asked if he could play some of the old music. John said, "No, please don't!" "No, I really gotta play it for you," Keane insisted. "So I did."[47] The unlikely trio sat around a table in Keane's office "and we just talked," said Bryant. "John talked about how [the letter] made him feel, Glen how it makes him feel, and we all centered on the same thing, which is why I wrote it in the first place: the beauty of finding what it is that you love to do, and then finding the beauty of knowing that you will not be able to do that forever. Once they saw the nature of the piece, there was really nothing else to discuss."

Keane illustrated the five-minute film with graphite on paper, depicting the arc of Bryant's letter—from young Kobe tossing rolled-up tube socks, to NBA glory, to retiring at 37. John was equally inspired by Bryant's childlike enthusiasm and Keane's artisanal process. "The drawings have great fluidity and, in the best sense of the word, great simplicity," John said. "They really are gorgeous, not only to look at, but rhythmically they're fabulous." Keane always animated while listening to music, and for this story it was selections from *Empire of the Sun*. John used that score as a reference point, but initially he wrote something that was too big, "and he went back and he rewrote it for something that was more understated," said Keane, "in a similar way that Kobe's delivery, his narration, is very personal, uninflected, not trying to sell anything. More like *revealing*. Kobe's got a very quiet voice, and that also had a big impact in how we animated."

John took a short break from *The Last Jedi* and spent two weeks in March 2017 to write and record this short piece—a gift for Bryant. When the towering baller arrived at the Sony scoring stage, John said: "I hope that you like what I've written." Bryant just looked at John and said, "I feel pretty confident that it's going to be just fine." When Bryant heard John's piece for the very first time, emanating from a symphony orchestra, "Oh my God," he said. "I almost lost my mind. As soon as his hands went up and then the music started, I almost yelled out loud—but I had to remember that the red light was on and we're recording. . . . It was the most unreal experience I could ever have."[48] (Keane jotted a pencil sketch of the moment; Figure 17.1.) Bryant looked over "and just put his head on my shoulder," said Keane, "like, 'I can't believe it.' It was so beautiful. Then when it was done, John turned to us and said, 'I promise it's going to get better.'"[49]

It was one of the simplest, yet most inspired pieces John wrote during this decade: a brief journey taken by a humble, hummable tune that bottled a young boy's guileless dreams and aspiration for greatness and glory. His hymnal theme begins as a

Figure 17.1. Kobe Bryant listens as John records the score for *Dear Basketball*, 2017 (Illustration by Glen Keane, Courtesy of the artist).

gentle woodwind duet, which is passed to strings and then accelerates into soaring triumph to accompany Bryant's heyday. Then it grows small again, a lonely keyboard wandering a broken chord as Bryant's voiceover admits that his body can only play for so long. John's knack for noble flying music closes the loop, with heraldic horns and rolling timpani connecting Bryant's story to his music for American heroism—concluding with a bittersweet reprise of the theme on piano and an uplifting coda as the credits roll. Like the letter itself, the score is part valentine, part elegy—and John put his heart into it. He premiered it at the Hollywood Bowl in September, and Bryant surprised the audience by joining John onstage to narrate. The short film won an Oscar in March 2018—and then very shortly afterward, it became a poignant eulogy for Bryant when he died, age 41, in a helicopter crash on a foggy Sunday morning in Calabasas that also killed his 13-year-old daughter, Gianna. John's wistful, symphonic poem suddenly took on a new shade.

"It is elegiac, but it isn't weepy," John said of the film when he first scored it, never imagining the sudden. tragic fate of his young friend.

> It strikes its own manner of saluting the man and the game and the accomplishments with a lot of modesty, I think. It's very touching, and in the end that may be its highest achievement, that it's able to praise this man the way it does, without a lot of false vanity or hubris that could easily have spilled into it. That's my take on it in any case.[50]

* * *

Spielberg was in post-production on his new film when a very different project crossed his desk. Liz Hannah's script for *The Papers* told the story of Daniel Ellsberg and the Pentagon Papers, which revealed how American leaders bungled the war in Vietnam and lied about it, and about the team at the *Washington Post* who risked the wrath of Richard Nixon to publish them. *Ready Player One*, by contrast, was another motion-capture extravaganza—based on Ernest Cline's popular novel about virtual reality and pop culture. Spielberg had already locked his cut on the latter and was merely reviewing its voluminous effects shots, and he decided to use his brief window of availability to quickly shoot *The Papers*. "It spoke to me," he said. "There was an urgent contemporary political message in the material."[51] Urgent, because Donald Trump was the new president of a very divided United States, and journalism was under threat; the *Washington Post* had just changed its official slogan to "Democracy Dies in Darkness."

Variety announced that John would not be scoring *Ready Player One* due to the two post schedules overlapping, and that instead Alan Silvestri would be the latest composer allowed into Spielberg's increasingly open marriage.[52] It made sense: Cline's book was obsessed with the 1985 comic-sci-fi film *Back to the Future*, which Silvestri scored. "Like John," Spielberg said, "Alan understands the purpose of tailoring the themes you walk out of the movies humming, in order to identify characters and the epic movements in movies that are designed to be somewhat operatic."[53] But *The Papers*—which became *The Post*—only required a short, unfussy score that John could have cooked up in a week or two. The comparative mania and hypermedia of *Ready Player One* was more likely unappealing to John at this point in his life, and he was already exhausted from the two *Star Wars* sequels. Still, this was the second Spielberg film in three years that John did not score, and people began to ask: Who could the director possibly replace him with when he was gone?

The Post was another well-meaning, well-acted history lesson from Spielberg, stolid and smooth but just a little staid in its partisan righteousness. Starring Tom Hanks as *Washington Post* editor Ben Bradlee and Meryl Streep as the paper's owner, Katharine Graham,[§] its virtues included a recreation of the *Post*'s humble old newsroom and an unimpeachable cast performing good dialogue scenes about the power of journalism and holding power to account. Spielberg also whipped a few scenes and montages into will-they-or-won't-they-publish suspense and emotional catharsis. But it was an odd canvas for music, and did not ask for much.

Tone-wise, John split the difference between his paranoid obsession music for Oliver Stone and the brassy noir pulse in *Minority Report*; as Ellsberg xeroxes classified reports, John increases the heat with some chugging electric guitar and low electronics, sounds that tap into the milieu of longhair rebellion and Nixon's tech-driven surveillance. John had now scored two movies about Richard Nixon—here Spielberg

---

[§] John actually met Graham backstage after a concert at the Kennedy Center, where Yo-Yo Ma performed his cello concerto. "She said to me, 'Ah, Mr. Williams, I enjoyed your concerto very much—even though I don't like contemporary music,'" John recalled with a laugh. "I took that to mean my music was not very contemporary. I think she meant it to be a compliment." (JW interview for *The Post* electronic press kit [20th Century Fox, 2017].)

simply filmed a stand-in from behind who, with somewhat cartoonish gesturing, mimed along to actual taped recordings from the Oval Office. John's music mostly exists to goose suspense, either with ominous sustained strings or a thumping heartbeat—"where the orchestra does provide a rhythm, and even, you can say, an *atmosphere* of the printing process," he said.[54] Modulating clusters and alternating meters map the terrain of fraught sequences, as when Graham agonizes and then reluctantly decides to give the green light to publish.

The score is effective at quickening the pulse and accompanying the plot, but quickly evaporates from memory, and there were few opportunities for melodic reprieve. When Bradlee and his wife comment on a framed photo of the Grahams, a timid piano solo mirrors their sadness; the emotions that do seep through the newsroom machinations in *The Post* emanate from the tragic absence of Graham's husband, Philip, whose death by suicide forced a responsibility on her that she did not feel prepared for and now must either relinquish or seize. She has a conversation with her daughter late one night, and another gentle piano tune plays with string support as Graham cries and talks about how she never expected to be in this position. It's lovely and sad, but again, the melody wanders out of one's ear like a mist.

The score's sustained nervousness catalyzes into heroic action when Bradlee gives the order to run the story, and John introduces a rhythmic anthem for this democracy-saving mission with urgent staccato horn triads ascending over a string scherzo, which then turns to a major key as the historic papers emerge from the printing press. A noble horn attends Graham walking through the bustling newsroom, and an interlude of melancholy is broken when Bradlee shows her every newspaper from around the country publishing the documents in support, with exalted horns and soaring strings providing some tear-welling musical gusto. Tying this film to the judicial crescendoes in both *Amistad* and *Lincoln*, John scores the Supreme Court finale with patriotic dignity—swelling with pride for the founding fathers and the free press, then relaxing into the piano hymn for Graham and her newspaper, which her husband once called "the first rough draft of history." John said he wanted to convey "the simple respect and maybe even nostalgia for integrity and tradition, wrapped together ... quietly reflecting about a very powerful thing, the effective search for truth."[55]

Because of Spielberg's split attention on *Ready Player One*, he didn't hear any of John's score until the morning he arrived on the scoring stage. "I just sat there," Spielberg said, "and, as usual, loved every note John played."[56] It was recorded in a concise three days at the end of October—Hanks stopped by for a session—and John also wrote and recorded several easygoing lounge jazz source cues, a fun tonic to all the seriousness. *The Post* aptly premiered in Washington, D.C., in December. It was effective and sincere, as was its score—a handsome paean to the free press in a time when the economics of journalism, and the antagonism of another hostile president, were putting it in jeopardy. But the fruits of the Spielberg/Williams collaboration were increasingly becoming something that once would have been impossible to imagine: *unmemorable*.

* * *

John was not asked to score *Rogue One*, the first spinoff film in Disney's rapidly expanding *Star Wars* empire—Kennedy said they made a somewhat artificial delineation between the films that opened with a prefatory text crawl and the ones that did not—but he was privately disappointed with the application of his themes in Michael Giacchino's score. "He did feel very protective of *Star Wars*," one associate said. "He didn't like it when other people gave their take on it." John himself admitted that he would like his themes "to be what they are, and not be distorted or reworked."[57] That was motivation enough for him to compose a new theme for the next ancillary movie. *Solo* was a needless origin story of Ford's beloved character, and a troubled production from the start; actor Alden Ehrenreich struggled to find the right note between a Ford imitation and an organic character; Kennedy hired the irreverent filmmaking duo Phil Lord and Christopher Miller, fresh off the popular *The Lego Movie*, then fired them after four months of shooting in a creative clash over their tone of irreverence.[58] Ron Howard's steady hands were conscripted to try to save the movie.

On a list of potential composers for the job was John Powell, an affable Brit who emerged from Zimmer's camp to establish a unique voice that successfully merged old-school melodicism and modern minimalism, redefining Hollywood action music with his grooving techno scores for *The Bourne Identity* films, but also reviving classic traditions with his scores for animated films like *How to Train Your Dragon*. "I think there were probably people on the list who didn't want to do it because John was going to be involved," said Powell. "But I only wanted to do it *because* he was involved."[59]

A former violinist, whose father played tuba on many film scores in London, Powell idolized John and was well aware of John's influence on his own music in the more obvious ways—trumpet triads, certain harmonic shifts, telling a film's story with character leitmotifs. But John Williams is an iceberg, Powell said, and underneath the obvious orchestrational hallmarks is "an authoritative feeling as to where things are going, what the mood is, and what the tension and release of each scene into the next scene is.

> If you look at Korngold, [his music] has an energy to it, the way it changes all the time. But I always think that Korngold is just going off, so sometimes it sounds like he's searching for shit in the background. John Williams doesn't do that. He seems to keep the search limited until the movement is required. I think he's taken a very fluid type of music, which is a late 19th century, early 20th century approach to orchestral motion, and he's applied it way tighter to the story than anybody ever did.

When Powell got the *Solo* job, John called him and said: "I just want to be sure you're okay with doing this. Because you can write your own tunes—you don't need me." Powell laughed. He had already tried diving in and coming up with original material, and he felt completely stuck. "I said, 'Well, my role is surely to do the best thing I can for the film, and to say to you, 'No, I don't need you' would be the stupidest thing on earth, wouldn't it? Of course I need you!" Powell went even further, and asked the producers, "Can we have Yoda at the spotting session?"

John had never written a theme for Han Solo, although his love theme for Han and Leia somewhat served that purpose. The new anthem he wrote for *Solo* doesn't really sound like it belongs in the 1977–1983 era, but in a broad, *Star Warsian* way it channels the young rogue's street-racing, swashbuckling spirit of adventure. That's what he called it: "The Adventures of Han." It was actually two tunes combined into one substantial suite, which John first played for Powell on the piano at his house—"a hero tune being the A section plus a searching B section. I loved them both, obviously," said Powell. John recorded his suite with a full orchestra in L.A., along with several cues written to picture using the theme—these were his version of "demos." In a funny way, he found himself on the opposite side of the equation from when he was a young composer scoring movies like *Diamond Head* and *Valley of the Dolls* and tasked with adapting someone else's tunes. "He had to watch me take the stuff and change it and do different things with it and bend it and twist it," Powell said. But for the young padawan, "My heart just rose, because I realized: *now I know what we're doing....* It felt like he'd given us this link into the world of *Star Wars* that I felt was so authoritative. I knew that I wasn't going to go off track."

The two Johns bonded in an even deeper way when Williams acknowledged Powell's recent tragedy: his young wife, Melinda Lerner, died in 2016 in the wake of a transplant resulting from a rare bone marrow disorder. "He talked to me about losing my wife, because he'd lost his," Powell said, noting that Barbara's death happened "in a year just before he wrote some of the most amazing things in his life.

> He didn't go into great detail, but he was very kind about it. I remember thinking: It's interesting how it clearly either focused him more or made no difference. I reckon it focused him. I would say that I bet there's a connection between writing so well in the aftermath of such a tragedy ... the four last songs of Strauss being the most beautiful things he ever wrote, in a way. They're slow, but they are incredibly beautiful—and they seem to express something about the end of life.

Then came the most frightening moment for Powell, when John said: "Can I hear some of yours?" Powell was embarrassed by his messy composing process—piles of score papers sprawled with disordered fragments of ideas—but he was relieved when he learned that John's method was somewhat similar: "He has these big pieces of paper and there's scribbles of themes like that, and then—exactly the same as me— arrows. It's not perfectly written down.

> So I pull out this sheet, and I sit at the piano, and he sat there beside me—and I realized that I've called one of the tunes "Fuckety Fuck Fuck," or something like that. Because you get into a state when you're writing, you know, "Chewy Theme," "Chewy Theme 2," then like "Fuck Chewy," you know? I can't remember what it was, but it was just an endless title of embarrassingly awful words. I forgot to

rename it like "Chewy 3" or something like that. And I remember him saying, "Ooh, that's an interesting name." I said, "Yeah, I guess I was a bit frustrated when I wrote that one." He laughed.

So then I kind of honked my way through what I did—and I'm a terrible pianist as well. I think I gave him the out—I said, "And I shall play this as well as a viola player ever could," and then funked through it. One thing I played for him, and he went: "Oh, I think that's a bit too classical for them." And he was absolutely right. So I got a bit of feedback on the tunes there, but nothing that led me to kill myself—which was good. But also nothing that made me realize I'd cracked it either. He seemed to judge it very literally as to what needed to happen. And he was very kind about it.

Due to AFM stipulations, John's L.A. recordings could not be used in the film, so Powell had to faithfully transcribe and re-record them all in London along with the rest of his score. "But that was really good," Powell said. "I really had to understand what he'd written, and his orchestration and everything like that. There are loads of incredibly elegant things—just the way he puts motion in the orchestra and puts energy in the orchestra. I'd never really thought about how he was doing it before, and actually having to program it into [the music software] Logic just made me realize: okay, this is a really good technique. And I still use it now." Powell left the experience even more in awe of John than before: "We'll see the peaks of his career as musical fortresses of the best compositional rigor and best compositional effect that people can do. And then the rest of it we'll see as incredibly elegantly and beautifully written."

"We're lucky to have him," Powell added.

That was a sentiment more and more frequently expressed, in the form of honors and tributes to John. When he guest-conducted the orchestras in Cleveland, Philadelphia, and Chicago in 2018, the sold-out audiences in each city gave John standing ovations before he even started. Rapper Kendrick Lamar had just been awarded the Pulitzer Prize for Music when John went to Philadelphia, and the local classical critic, Peter Dobrin, noted amid his concert review that "if the Pulitzer judges wanted to open up to a wider range of American music ... the passing of two decades without awarding the prize to Williams says more about the judges than the master of this distinctly American art form."[60]

That March, John announced he was donating his complete library of film scores, concert music, and sketchbooks to Juilliard as a bequest.[61] In May, BMI (the performing rights organization that John belonged to) created a new lifetime achievement honor for their annual gala—and John was the inaugural recipient of the John Williams Award. "In the last year or two, awards seem to be coming along," he said at the ceremony. "It must have something to do with being so old, they must think now is the time." BMI had to twist John's arm to allow such an award to be named after him—and then only on the promise that they would not give it out again in his lifetime. "He's an artist, and I can't believe he doesn't actually, deep down, love the attention," said Doreen Ringer-Ross, who ran BMI's film music division for decades. "But

I think that he's very conscious about being cool and not being self-aggrandizing. And he's humble."[62]

Keith Lockhart and the Boston Pops devoted their entire 2018 season to John, recording an album of his greatest hits as well as some deep cuts, and taking the program on the road. John threw out the first pitch at a Baltimore Orioles game in June, temporarily trading his Red Sox gear for an orange Orioles jersey and cap. He was beginning to acknowledge the wear-and-tear of his film concerts by splitting baton duties with a co-conductor: when he celebrated his 40th season at the Hollywood Bowl on Labor Day weekend, he shared the podium with David Newman.

His lone concert premiere of the year was a playful miniature inspired by the famous ghost at Tanglewood. The occasion was Leonard Bernstein's centennial, which was celebrated all summer long at his beloved Berkshires haunt, and John used the anniversary as an excuse to turn his amusing memories—of Lenny's wild reactions and warding off the spirit with a cup of white beans at joyous dinner parties—into a piece for cello, harp, and orchestra called *Highwood's Ghost*. John cast Yo-Yo Ma and the BSO's principal harpist, Jessica Zhou, as jousting forces "having a mad duel," he said, "over who is going to be the ghost and who is going to be the ectoplasmic atmosphere."[63]

John had not conducted a concert in his beloved London in 22 years, and he was excited to return to the Royal Albert Hall for a weekend of concerts with the LSO in October, followed a week later by his first invitation to conduct the Vienna Philharmonic. Ever since Seiji Ozawa left Boston for the Vienna State Opera, his dream was for John to come to the cradle of western classical music and conduct at the storied Musikverein, a hall haunted by the ghosts of Bernstein and John's idol, Johannes Brahms.[64] But as soon as John landed in London, he was so sick that he went to the hospital, where doctors told him he needed to have his gallbladder removed immediately. John flew straight back to Los Angeles and had the surgery at UCLA Medical Center, canceling all of the European dates.[65] He listened to a livestream of the LSO concert from his hospital bed while his disappointed fans, many of whom had traveled from other countries and were never told the nature of John's illness, began to seriously worry about his health.

* * *

On February 28, 2019, André Previn died. John eulogized Previn with a formal statement: "In everything he did, he brought a keen intelligence, sharp wit, and an array of talents that was formidable. He was comfortably at home with Gene Kelly, Miles Davis, Mozart, and Mahler—a true renaissance man. And we have been fortunate indeed to have shared the light he brought to this sometimes dreary world for nearly 90 years."[66]

Previn had been one of John's dearest friends since the 1950s, a man who helped launch his career and who modeled the kind of manifold musical life—jazz pianist, arranger, pop record maker, film composer, classical composer, symphonic conductor—that John closely followed. Previn was John's entrée into the concert hall, the earliest champion and presenter of his classical efforts, his introduction to the

London Symphony, and his most vocal campaigner for the Boston Pops job. "I went to Boston," John admitted, for a "*silly* reason: I thought I wanted to be a conductor because André wanted me to be a conductor."[67]

Previn also never stopped harassing John for staying in Hollywood and scoring what he considered juvenile or artless movies, and he constantly needled John to get out. "I never met him and he didn't say, 'Stop writing that stuff!' " John laughed and ignored Previn's advice—or rather, he *adapted* Previn's advice by composing film scores worthy of the concert hall, and treating cinema like a canvas for serious music. He also increasingly poured his energies into concerti and other classical works, and in the process he eclipsed Previn not just in popularity but also prestige.

He certainly burned fewer bridges and showed less contempt for others. As time went on, Previn grew increasingly bitter. "The longest night in my life was with André," said Mark Volpe, who was president of the BSO in 1998 when Previn was awarded the Kennedy Center Honors, "and I was the one non-family member invited," Volpe said. "He had all his kids at one table, and then he had me with all his ex-wives [at the other]. It was just a nutty night. But André at the end was [saying things like], 'I didn't get my due.' And we had the awkwardness of [bringing] him back to Tanglewood— because he's such a great teacher, and could talk with the students—but I couldn't have him conduct the BSO anymore, because he physically couldn't. That was incredibly hard."[68] In his later years, Previn was financially impoverished and, according to Kim Taylor, "he was dying to do movies again. I think he really wanted to. So that was a complicated relationship, when he saw John's enormous success."[69]

But for John, "it was an amazing, lifelong friendship with someone who I looked up to greatly."[70] They continued to have phone conversations on Sundays, once or twice a month, all the way until Previn's death. Previn always called John "Babe." "Johnny's connection with André is a profound one," said Mia Farrow, one of the ex-wives whom John inherited as a friend.[71] "I miss him," John said.

* * *

Fisher's untimely death was one of many wrenches thrown into the next *Star Wars* film: *The Rise of Skywalker*. After attentively parting with Han in the first film and Luke in the second, this was to be Leia's grand finale. Kennedy and company had loved Rian Johnson and his audacious film, but the deafening fan backlash spooked Disney away from taking any more such wild swings. Colin Trevorrow, another young director seen as a Spielberg scion when his jumbo-sized sequel, *Jurassic World*, generated a billion dollars, had been hired to write and direct the third chapter of the new Skywalker trilogy—but he was suddenly dismissed after his modest passion project, *The Book of Henry*, opened to a critical drubbing and dismal box office.[72] And in the wake of *Solo*'s weak showing, Kennedy begged J. J. Abrams to come back and help her stick the landing with as few risky bumps as possible.

Abrams scrambled to weed out most of the weird seeds that Johnson had planted, and he attempted to appease a fundamentalist fanbase by resurrecting Emperor Palpatine as the heavy, revealing Rey to be Palpatine's granddaughter, calling in Billy

Dee Williams to reprise his Lando character, and somehow convincing Ford to cameo as a Force ghost. He also sidelined Rose, the Johnson-conceived character played by Kelly Marie Tran who was a particular target of angry fans, with more than a whiff of racism aimed at the American Vietnamese actor. Abrams awkwardly shoehorned Leia into a few scenes, using preexisting footage of Fisher and CGI. Dodging risk at almost every turn, he sabotaged each high stake that the story raised by immediately reversing it: Rey thinks she accidentally kills Chewbacca, but he's alive and well; C-3PO offers to have his memory permanently wiped (in order to translate an ancient Sith message) and says a tearful goodbye to his friends, but a few minutes later his memory is completely restored; Kylo dies, but he is immediately resurrected, and the same thing happens to Rey. In the midst of a doom-laden spectacle and possibly the best-*looking* film of the new trilogy, Abrams and Disney tried to be everything to everyone—and good intentions, zealous fandom, nostalgia, and corporate concerns all congealed into an attractive but disappointing simulacrum of that old Skywalker magic.

The finality of this final chapter did give Abrams an excuse to lure John in *front* of the camera. He devised a cameo for a junk shop scene where C-3PO says, "Don't mind us," and the camera pans over to John, wearing a brown cloak and a jeweler's eyepiece, polishing a doodad and shaking his head with annoyance. When Abrams suggested this idea, John reflexively said, "Oh no, no. That's too silly. I wouldn't possibly do that." But then he mentioned it to Samantha, and she said: "Oh, you HAVE to—that's more important than doing the score of the film!"[73] So John set aside a small piece of his dignity and came to set in costume, where he was greeted with a huge round of applause from the cast and crew—"We are in the presence of a supernatural genius," Abrams boyishly declared[74]—and sat down at a desk where he was surrounded by subtle nods to all of his 51 Oscar nominations: a metal book for *The Book Thief*, yellow barrels for *Jaws*, a whip for *Indiana Jones*, and even a clothes iron for *Home Alone*, all designed by the prop department to look like ancient galactic scrap.

Safely back at his writing desk, John was faced with all the same challenges that he had scoring *The Force Awakens*, and possibly more. Abrams sent him one reel at a time, like before, which John would then score and record—but then Abrams kept making changes to the cut as well as asking for alternate cues. "J. J. Abrams is an amazing director," said Powell, "but in a very different world—*very* different world.

> So I think it was hard, because changes were made in a way that were much more unexpected for John to have to adapt to. My understanding is that he definitely developed a technique for dealing with that through the last three. It's amazing how good those scores are, considered, and how brilliantly they work with the movie, considering the movie was kind of recut and so was the music. This meant he could do something, and then three weeks later he could do something else, and just pick it up and keep doing the changes. It's exhausting.

Even Kennedy admitted that this never-ending carousel of changes "created a lot of stress for John."[75] Abrams, who wrote some of his own theme music in the past and was used to a totally elastic, granular collaboration with his contemporary, Michael Giacchino, always has "just a lot of ideas," Kennedy said. "And John's not one to say, 'Stop having ideas.' That's really my job. I think J. J. didn't realize the gymnastics he was putting Johnny through, and after a while we had to go to him and say, 'Okay, you can't keep doing this, because you're forcing John into constant rearrangements and in some cases *rewriting*, and he just can't keep up with it.' So ... we adjusted."

Composed over the course of many months, John's score bombastically keeps pace with the relentless, overactive plot and its copious character references. At times it really does feel like an organist playing along to a silent movie in a highly reactive and literal way: we see Leia, cue Leia's theme; Kylo touches Vader's helmet, cue the Imperial March; someone is using the Force, enter the Force theme. John handled these quotations with elegance, but the Disney sequel scores all tend to be far less subtle and developmentally captivating than those in the previous trilogies. There are numerous citations of the Emperor's theme—in action, in eerie suspense, on solo oboe, and on galactically evil male choir. Many times, the temp track rises to the surface without apology: the ghostly finale of *Return of the Jedi* haunts Rey as she explores the bombed-out throne room from the 1983 movie; and when Luke force-lifts his old X-Wing out of the ocean, it triggers an exact statement of Yoda's theme from *Empire Strikes Back*. John attributed the latter idea to Belgardt, "and actually J. J. questioned it," John said, "but everybody said, 'Oh, yes—it has to be. The fans will all know.' So we went back to the score of *Empire Strikes Back* to get those bars exactly out of them."[76] Belgardt was adamant about it: "I was like, 'That's what it has to be!' I mean, obviously it's a callback ... and you want to hear that piece."[77]

If *anyone* knew how emotionally powerful music could be as a callback device, it was John Williams. "It's a little bit like how the olfactory system is wired with memory, so that a certain smell makes you remember your grandmother's cooking," he said, varying one of his go-to metaphors.[78] John never voiced any frustration about making literal copies of previous themes. "I think it's because he's very happy with what he did in the past," Belgardt offered, "and if it works in this film: 'Great. Let's do that.'"[79] Still, in prior sequel or prequel scores, John would usually rearrange or find brilliant new variations on familiar tunes, but in service to the nostalgia strip-mining of these Disney *Star Wars* films, his scores are often a lot of "Remember *this*? Remember *this*?"

"It *is* an exception," John admitted, "the use of something literal from an earlier film."[80]

Rey's theme receives the most satisfying development and growth of any melody in the score, tracking her journey from lonely Jedi training, to discovering her infamous lineage, to facing down the galaxy's most formidable monster. When she tells an alien, "I'm just Rey," and her theme echoes the sentiment, it is clear the melody has earned its place in the all-time *Star Wars* canon. John seemed to take the most delight in telling stories with her tune, which culminates in epic heroism as she and Ben, the good Jedi formerly known as Kylo Ren, take their stand against Palpatine, where it turns into a pas de deux with a redeemed variation of Ren's motif. "I could turn Ren's theme around—not upside down, but re-harmonize it," said John, "which was actually J. J.'s idea. He said to me, 'Can you make the trip from Ren to Ben on the same theme?' It worked out where his evil theme morphs brilliantly into a kind of a hero theme by a change of harmonic support."[81] John took Rey's inquisitive, questing melody all the way down to its most delicate piano chords when she helplessly watches the Resistance being obliterated in the sky above her and then hears the voices of all the famous past Jedi sending her courage. The saga's final scene has Rey traveling to Luke's old homestead on Tatooine, and before the poetic closing shot of the world's most famous binary sunset, John reprises her theme in its very first form as she slides down a sand dune—just like she did when the audience first met her.

The score's major new theme is a tender chorale for friendship: it sings *cantabile* during quiet moments among the trio of Rey, Finn, and Poe, and John mobilizes it into active duty when they storm a First Order ship to retrieve Chewie. He brings it back in the victorious finale, ennobled with brass and choir, as the galaxy—once again—celebrates the downfall of the Emperor and his empire. Other new motifs include a dark mass for the Sith and short melodic phrases for the story's MacGuffins, as well as Kylo Ren's knights.

John recorded some three hours of music in sessions that ran from July through November 2019, and much of it was sacrificed inside Abrams's editorial meat grinder. "As with *The Force Awakens*, things were [changing] considerably during post-production," Abrams said, "and I would always apologize that we were making adjustments, and John would always laugh and apologize that he hadn't written the right thing before. We were both just full of apologies to each other."[82] John did not complain, at least not publicly. "It was a wonderful way to spend six or eight months," he told *Variety*. "Each day I got up to work hard on difficult music. Yes, it was long, but I always had a sense of being grateful."[83]

He later confessed: "It is a challenge, of course, and it's not for everybody.

> It would drive you crazy if you let it. But I've often seen it as an opportunity to redo things that represent improvements also. I'm thinking back on the very first *Star Wars*, and there were a lot of changes in that. I remember Ken Wannberg going crazy trying to fit things together, and how much re-recording we did I don't remember—we must have done some. But in these recent ones with J. J. we were able, for whatever reason, to actually re-record a lot of things that were too badly cut up. But it's become part of the process. So easy for editors to change on their Pro Tools—half the time. Half of the cues you write you're told two or three days later, "This has all been changed," so you need to be able to sit down and either rewrite it or reassemble it or both.
>
> I would rather *not* do it, of course, and go on to something new. But I know that to be able to complete the process, one has to be able and willing to do that.[84]

The last yank of this tug-of-war came in the film's finale, in the moment when Ben resurrects Rey and they kiss. John wrote an old-fashioned, operatic rendition of Rey's theme for this scene, but Abrams kept asking for other options. "J. J. had such a hard time with that," said Belgardt.

> It was an 11th hour thing. It's midnight, and the thing has to go out at 6 a.m. *tomorrow*, and producers were involved and other music editors. I had people coming in for other options, like, "What do we do to make it work?" And in the end it ended up being what John originally wrote. John was like: "That's *Star Wars*. It's a weird anomaly for this kind of futuristic thing, but there's this old-fashioned music underneath it, and so that's what we're going to play."[85]

For Frank Lehman, the *Star Wars* sequel scores overcame the chaotic circumstances of their creation, and succeed in spite of their frequent cannibalization. "In a way," Lehman said, "rewriting or having music that evokes certain moods or idioms from those other movies actually gives it a more mythical throughline—which I think is marvelously effective—at the expense, perhaps, of having complete follow-through of every theme from all prior eight movies showing up in *Rise of Skywalker*, which did not happen.

> We were denied "Duel of the Fates," despite the fact that I think they recorded it, and there was quite a lot of choral music that hit the cutting room floor. It's still conversant with that style of the prequels, even if it's not deliberately referring to it. From start to finish, from "Imperial Attack" to "A New Home" in *Rise of Skywalker*, it's hard to find fault with what Williams has done.[86]

Sensing that this was the end of an epic 42-year journey, Spielberg joined Hamill, Kennedy, and Disney president Bob Iger on the last day of recording. A large BB-8 cake was wheeled out, and champagne toasts were given. "There were so many people crying, you couldn't believe it," one musician said. "And at the end the orchestra gave John an ovation that would not stop."[87] John said: "I felt so satisfied, and so complete in a way. Nine episodes in a great tale, beautifully done over many, many years. And that means that it's not an ending—that it's here with us, and will stay there, and it makes our lives part of that story.

"I'd be quite happy to have it go on indefinitely."[88]

* * *

He really meant it. Kennedy didn't have to twist John's arm very hard to coax him into composing a theme for Disney's new *Star Wars* theme land, Galaxy's Edge—although "there was a courtship period," according to Matt Walker, head of music at Walt Disney Imagineering.[89] Walker and the park's design team brought John in to look at models of the new land, and John asked why they couldn't just use some of his prodigious existing music. They argued that he had always written bespoke themes for new characters and even cities, and the newly conceived planet of "Batuu" should therefore have its own identity. Ross had adapted and repurposed John's *Star Wars* music for several Disney attractions, and he did the same with John's *Harry Potter* music for the wizarding world at Universal Studios. "But I think John couldn't resist the feeling of, *well, that needs its own special musical brand or musical theme*," Ross said. "It didn't have anything to do with money or legacy or anything. It was about: *Oh, there's some unfinished business there.*"⁹⁰ Disney only asked John for a theme, but he went off in the summer of 2019 and composed a five-minute symphonic tone poem filled with several new motifs. Ross recorded this suite with the LSO at Abbey Road, lending it some authentic vintage *Star Wars* cachet. But Walker and his team didn't want to just pump John's symphonic melodies into the land as indiscriminate background music, so instead, the suite was transformed into an ambient bed that blurred with insect chatter and naturalistic atmosphere. It only played in its full orchestral glory on board some of the land's new rides.⁹¹

Disney was determined to milk every last teat of Lucas's space cow, and they were now producing expensive television series for their new streaming service. *The Mandalorian*, a crowd-pleasing episodic western starring a Bounty Hunter With No Name and an adorable "Baby Yoda," took the first and biggest step outside of John's musical language when it premiered on Disney's new streaming service, Disney+, in November 2019. As he had done masterfully with Bill Conti's classic *Rocky* music in the *Creed* films, Swedish composer Ludwig Göransson metabolized John's style of orchestral, fanfaric majesty into an original Mandalorian theme that stands tall next to its predecessors, but also surrounded it with hip-hop beats, electronics, and his own hybrid classic-modern style. Göransson never learned what John thought of his music, but no news seemed like good news. John did ask Belgardt once what *The Mandalorian* sounded like; Belgardt played the score for about 10 seconds, and John said, "Okay, thank you."⁹²

After *Solo* sputtered and Disney decided to pump the brakes on its annual onslaught of theatrical features, a planned spinoff movie about Obi-Wan Kenobi was hastily converted into a six-part Disney+ series. Ewan McGregor was lured back to his character from the prequel films that he had previously distanced himself from, but which now had their own classic status among a younger generation. Composer Natalie Holt, a young Brit who had just scored the Marvel series *Loki*, was initially told she should steer clear of John's motifs in her score for *Obi-Wan Kenobi*; so she did. But then, at the last minute, Kennedy called John and asked if he would write a new theme for the series; he did so, and Ross and company came on board to heavily adapt this tune into the score alongside Holt's music.

Why couldn't he let *Star Wars* go? His personal loyalty to Lucas explained his dedication to the maligned prequels, but it became abundantly clear that John had some deep affection, or some paternal protectiveness, for this universe and its inhabitants. As Kennedy saw it, John was well aware of how many people expressed the idea that "he scored their lives" with the music of *Star Wars*, "and I think he feels a real responsibility to it, in a way," she said. "It's something he created, and as long as he feels he can continue to carry that on, he would much prefer that *he* do that and not pass it off if he doesn't have to."⁹³ John genuinely cared when other composers monkeyed with his themes, and he stayed on the crazy sequel train *despite* the circus of temp track addiction and piecemeal scoring and constant rewriting and the Pro Tools sausage machine. *Star Wars* did not become John's most prominent legacy because the fans imposed it on him; *he* willingly clung to it, *he* fanned the flame of association across four decades.

Perhaps it was no more complicated than the attraction of scoring a nine-cycle opera of extroverted, melodic, symphonic music that would then be heard and appreciated by millions of people and multiple generations. As little as Previn thought of this "cornball" material, it no longer seemed to diminish John in the eyes of classical orchestras—if anything, it endeared those serious musicians to John even more. Whenever John would launch into the Imperial March at any concert, anywhere in the world, the smiles on players' faces and the barbaric yawps from the audience were ample validation. When John co-conducted his annual concert at the Hollywood Bowl with Dudamel a few years later, the Venezuelan maestro—arguably now the most famous conductor in the classical world—came onto the stage with a toy lightsaber and began to duel with John to rapturous applause from a capacity crowd. John had enough savvy to know what would be demeaning to his reputation and what would not, and he had an innate sense of what the *volk* wanted.** Somehow, he had merged the popular admiration for his popcorn symphonies with the genuine appreciation of classical musicians. He had defeated the prejudice against his movie music and had earned the respect and admiration of the highest makers of music culture.

When the New York Philharmonic opened its newly renovated David Geffen Hall in the fall of 2022, one of the first concerts they gave was for the people who built the hall—"literally construction workers and those people," said Anthony McGill, the orchestra's principal clarinet. The program was a classical greatest hits, with popular pieces like the *William Tell Overture* by Rossini. "But the final piece, which was the encore, was where I actually knew that the hall was a total success," said McGill:

> When we started the theme from *Star Wars*, and played a little mini suite, we might as well have been playing the greatest piece of classical music ever written, because that's how serious that was. It felt like we were giving *that* as a gift to that audience, and you should have heard the applause after it. You should have heard it. I felt it, and it was the first time I could hear the applause of the people.
>
> That's what his music is. It's the music of *all* of us. It's humanity's soundtrack. Like, the *one* thing we can agree on is pretty much John Williams.[94]

** By contrast, he was adamant about music from *Jaws 2* not being programmed in concert. The name itself was an embarrassment.

18
Reunion and Finale, 2020–2024

> *Guess what? History will remember him as a great figure in music in the 20th century and early 21st century, and that's already written. I don't think we need to look into the future—that's already been established. And for people who don't know that, they will find out.*
>
> —Yo-Yo Ma[1]

The new decade dawned with great promise. In January 2020, John finally made it to Austria to conduct the Vienna Philharmonic—two nights of his greatest film hits—at the Musikverein, fulfilling the concerts that were canceled in 2018.

The historic importance of this occasion might have seemed overhyped; the fact that this European bastion of high art would invite *John Williams* to conduct his *film music* inside its sacred temple was interpreted by some as a kind of high culture coronation. Certainly Vienna was the fountainhead of a classical tradition and a classical elitism that, for a very long time, was even less likely to embrace movie music than its American counterparts. (Vienna was also, ironically, the birthplace of Hollywood music, giving the world Korngold and Steiner and a musical vocabulary that shaped the entire art form—John's work included.) If he had been asked to bring his *Star Wars* scores to the Musikverein in the 1970s or 1980s, it would have been front-page news in the classical world, maybe even a scandal. Now, in 2020, it was a different story. Like their peers around the globe, many of these conservatory-trained musicians grew up hearing and loving John's music. It wasn't some crucible of the soul for them to bring this American giant into their house—it was common sense. But it was perhaps the clearest signpost yet that the attitude among the classical guard about John's film music had totally transformed. The Vienna Philharmonic, "the most traditional orchestra on the planet," in Gustavo Dudamel's words, "play John's music, and they *love* it. I have talked to them.... [And] it's because it's very good music. There is the answer. It [has] changed completely."[2]

During intermission at one of the rehearsals, some of the players came up to John and said, "Maestro, can we play the Imperial March?" He said, "Well, certainly we can—if you have the music, I'd be happy to conduct it." "Oh, we have the music," they said—"we know it!"

> I told them I thought I'd already given them too much work for a two-hour concert, and they said, "Well, you have, but we want to play the Imperial March for you; it's

the new Radetzky!"* I've never heard it played so brilliantly, I must say. All the brilliant orchestras I've played it with have never been quite like this; it had a kind of force and power that was an expression of their own spirit and history. It was really quite thrilling.³

The review in Austria's newspaper, *Der Standard,* described "standing ovations and enthusiastic applause already at the first performance—as if God were welcomed by earthly disciples. And it's really true: the kindhearted John Williams is absolutely lovely, and in addition he is a god of film music."⁴ Anne-Sophie Mutter, the star virtuoso from southern Germany, joined John in Vienna to perform new arrangements of his themes for her solo violin and orchestra. "John was in heaven, the orchestra was in heaven, and so was the audience," Mutter said. "There was such joy, such appreciation and a feeling of camaraderie in music. Together with my debut with [Herbert von] Karajan this was the greatest musical moment in my life."⁵

John first met Mutter through Previn, her ex-husband, and she asked John to write "a few bars" for her, which turned into a short concert piece called *Markings*. Debuted at Tanglewood in July 2017, this was a "short, serene, very poetic, mostly lyrical piece," Mutter said at the time, "with a wonderfully witty and virtuosic center part. Sadly it is very short, and my hopes are still there that Mr. Williams, who is of course very busy, might find the time to add a few more bars."⁶ John mulled on the idea of turning his miniature into a larger piece, but in the meantime he was so besotted by Mutter and her violin that, again at her request, he devised an entire album of his classic themes interpreted by her 1710 Stradivarius. He took advantage of an unexpected three-month window that opened when Abrams delayed production on *Rise of Skywalker*, and crafted splendid solos for new concert arrangements of tunes from both obvious sources like *Star Wars* and *Harry Potter*, as well as less obvious ones—*Far and Away*, *Dracula*, and most obscurely, *Cinderella Liberty*. They recorded the album, *Across the Stars*, with John's studio orchestra in April 2019 on the old MGM soundstage where John and Previn once roamed as young men. Mutter had become John's muse, now a living connection to Previn, a virtuosic interpreter of his film music which she enthusiastically worshiped, and an inspiration for new music. He called her "The Princess," and she brought an extra cachet of classical music royalty to his Vienna debut.

Tom Morris, who had set John's conducting career in motion at the Pops in 1980 and had remained a friend, traveled to Vienna to witness this prestigious bookend at the Musikverein. Morris called it "one of the most incredible moments of my life.

> To see his rock star status with the audience, and with the Vienna Philharmonic, was just incredible. He has an iconic status as an American composer and an American conductor and an American musician which is, I think, unique. Copland never had that as a conductor. . . . Bernstein was an American conductor, but he was

---

* Johann Strauss composed the *Radetzky March* in 1848 for an Austrian military victory, and it became a tradition for the Vienna Philharmonic to perform on New Year's Day.

conducting mostly European repertoire. And here is John conducting American music … *his* music. All of a sudden, when you realize what he has written, and the quality of what he has written, and the variety of what he's written, and the fact that everyone knows all of it.... It's unprecedented.[7]

After the triumph in Vienna, John had a full slate of concert appearances on his calendar—when the entire world shut down.

* * *

"We look out the window—I look more now every day at the flowers, they're so beautiful," John said, speaking from his home in June 2020. "But particularly now, this quarantine, if you go outside and look at the sky above Los Angeles, it's a color blue that we almost never see. It's so very beautiful, this canopy of gorgeous blue above us."[8]

Like everyone else on planet Earth, John was forced indoors and into an extended sabbatical when the COVID-19 pandemic swept the world. He had already finished consulting on the score for *West Side Story*, Spielberg's new carbonated take on the Bernstein masterwork, which at last fulfilled the director's desire to make a big movie musical. It was mostly a ceremonial role for John, who recommended David Newman for the actual, heavily involved job of music direction. The film's release was indefinitely delayed because of the pandemic, and Spielberg spent *his* lockdown reflecting inward and developing a movie based on his childhood. For the first time in *decades*, John had no film to score and no concerts to conduct—although even a global pandemic couldn't stop him from being honored. In November, the Royal Philharmonic Society of London gave John their prestigious Gold Medal, announced in a digital broadcast. Instituted in 1870, previous winners of the award included Brahms, Britten, Shostakovich, and Bernstein. "I understand a little bit of the feel of British music history, and the great importance of this award," John said. "It's something indescribable for me and I'm very proud."[9]

He took full advantage of the Great Pause by starting a new violin concerto for Mutter. "The COVID period has given us all many things," he said, "a lot of discomfiture and concern and serious problems. But it also has given us time to think a little bit. For me, for my schedule, doing this for [her], it was perfect, because I had the time."[10] For Mutter, it was a *lifeline*:

> I couldn't do anything at all, other than study at home, because we basically had quarantine and we needed to stay for months, restricted. [The concerto] became a very dear friend on a daily basis. Having emails, and another version, or small details or information about change of tempi ... it gave me the time to really dig deeper than one usually can do in the hectic schedule of ... running around and having to perform standard repertoire while studying.[11]

"That's why," she said, "it is so deep ingrained in my heart." John's first violin concerto had been inspired by Barbara, emotionally dyed by the psychic rupture of her death. So it was strangely fitting that he said writing this second concerto for Mutter was "kind of a love affair." He punctuated his comment with a laugh, adding: "My wife will forgive me."[12]

John thought about using *Markings* as a middle movement, but he scrapped the idea after hearing Mutter's jazzy touch on his arrangement of "Nice to Be Around" from *Cinderella Liberty*. Previn once assured him that "Anne-Sophie can play anything. Don't worry—write it for her, she will play it." So John wrote a jazz-like idea, and in Mutter's hands "it becomes almost vocal—instead of note, note, note … it's word, word, syllable, syllable—some kind of elision, connection between note to the next note, which is a particular jazz thing. One note is here, another note is there, but there's something in the middle—always in all music, but particularly in jazz." He couldn't believe "this lady from Germany, who plays everything from Bach to Schoenberg and back again, would be doing this. And for me, once I discovered that, I thought: *ah, she can be very seductive. She can be with many languages*."[13]

With that jazz element established as what Mutter called a "stem cell," the concerto grew into a staggering four movements, and an odyssey through all of John's 70 years of writing music. It begins with a low string pedal and a curious harp solo, casting a spell of mystery and transporting the listener into another enchanted forest. In this dark beauty the violin emerges as a nervous spirit, looking around and then frantically trying to escape. John's principal theme strongly recalls his melody in both "Make Me Rainbows" from *Fitzwilly* and "Moonlight" from *Sabrina*, and it arrives in full in the second movement.† The violin quietly skims along a bubbling woodwind current and settles into a more optimistic quest, with the orchestra swelling to aid in its search. It grows restless and flighty again, with orchestral fairy dust and stomping timpani, and the third movement contains wild, mischievous fiddling answered by bells and chimes—a dance between the spirit and other monsters in the forest. The finale is quiet and languid: the violin sounds almost like it's melting, and it wearily sings the main theme over broken chords on harp. Still searching, still restlessly squirming through a scratchy theme from the second movement, it is subsumed by boiling drama in the orchestra before it finally insists on the theme in a dreamy reprise over the low pedal from the beginning and more harp arpeggios. The afterglow of the piece is mystical and peaceful, with two string chords repeating in a seesaw of cosmic wonder.

There was a bounty of tangible emotion expressed in this concerto, but John chose not to explain himself. "I've always believed that in the end, the music ought to be free to be interpreted through the prism of every listener's own personal history, prior exposures, and cultural background," he wrote in his program note. "One man's sunken cathedral might be another woman's mist at the dawning. The meaning must therefore reside, if you'll forgive me, in the 'ear of the beholder.'" Instead, he provided some non-emotional analysis, but he did explain that he imbued the concerto with a sense of improvisation, that Claude Thornhill—the band composer from

---

† John said any relationship to those melodies was purely accidental: "If it's in there, it's in there because it's somewhere down here in my right kidney." (JW to TG, March 9, 2023.)

his boyhood—haunted his pencil yet again, and that the piece's gentle resolution in A major "might suggest both healing and renewal."

John and Mutter premiered the concerto with the BSO at Tanglewood in July 2021, one of the very first timid returns to concertizing in the wake of a vaccine for COVID-19. It thus had the built-in advantage of falling on ears desperately thirsty for live music, although it was almost too much for listeners to take in for the first time. "No one could mistake this kitchen-sink concerto for film music," the *Globe*'s A.Z. Madonna wrote in a conflicted review.

> Many of Williams' signature elements (sonic textures deceptively simple in their fullness, distinctive and evocative timbres) were present in abundance, so much so that I sometimes felt like I was listening to several of his scores at the same time. However, absent were the memorable melodies that form the foundation of his most enduring works. At times, this approach was fascinating—almost a glimpse of what might have been had Williams' career played out in the concert hall rather than on the silver screen. More often, I noticed myself longing for leitmotifs.[14]

In his review for the *Berkshire Eagle*, Andrew Pincus complained that "the piece never quite seems to settle down.... Incident is piled on incident—crunching dissonances, rhapsodic flights, percussion outbursts, jarring rhythmic changes, soaring, cadenza-like improvisations—without apparent connection."[15]

John returned to Boston a few months later to help the orchestra reopen Symphony Hall after a year's long silence. It was something like religious ecstasy when BSO music director Andris Nelsons filled the great room with music again, starting with Beethoven's *The Consecration of the House* overture—and John's new concerto rode that feeling through to intermission. The audience had to show vaccine cards and negative COVID tests in order to attend, everyone was wearing masks, and in this surreal atmosphere of *memento mori*, where death was on everyone's mind and life had rarely felt more precious, John's piece seemed to tell a monumental story about existence, love, and loss. And though most concertgoers were not aware of it, Barbara's presence could be felt in the casting of the violin, in the painful passages, and in the work's complex beauty. In the many decades between his first and second concertos for Barbara's favorite instrument, John had lived an entire lifetime without her—and the music reflected that journey. This coda may have suggested "healing and renewal," but it was also clearly dark and introspective—and mysterious.

* * *

Another bastion of high art rolled out the red carpet when the Berlin Philharmonic welcomed John for three nights of sold-out concerts in October 2021. He had always been intrigued by Germany—he remembered coming to Hamburg with Barbara in 1968 and hearing Wagner for the first time, and the "spooky vibe" of the German audience's churchly relationship to music. Now he was ascending the podium at the Berlin orchestra's home, the Philharmonie. He was not only staggered by the history and the ghosts in the hall—he thought the Berlin Philharmonic was the best orchestra he had ever stood before.

It was another pilgrimage to the heart of classical music, and Mutter also arranged for John to visit nearby Leipzig and St. Thomas Church, where Johann Sebastian Bach was cantor in the 1700s. "I have always believed that no musician should die before going to Bach's gravesite in the church," John said. The head pastor gave him a tour of the church, and the organist went up and played a Bach prelude. "And then as we were leaving the church," John said, "I heard the strains of *Jurassic Park* coming out. I thought *what a blasphemy*, with Bach's remains having to listen to this."[16] He laughed at the memory—but after all, John had responded to the resurrected dinosaurs with, of all things, a *hymn*. To John's great surprise, Dudamel said the *Jurassic Park* theme moved him every time he heard or conducted it, and he likened the genius of its creation to Beethoven's *Pastoral* symphony. "You don't need only to think about dinosaurs when you listen to *Jurassic Park*," Dudamel said. "It's an anthem of humanity. It really brings my spirit to a level of pride, and in a very emotional way."[17] Movie music *was* the new church music, and here was another potent symbol: Williams and Bach, side by side in a Leipzig cathedral.

A few months later, John turned 90, and the entire year was a parade of celebrations and tributes. The *New York Times* ran an admiring profile on his birthday,[18] and John conducted the Philadelphia Orchestra in a concert at Carnegie Hall in April. The National Symphony spread their birthday party across three nights, performing both *E.T.* and *Jurassic Park* live to picture and throwing a lavish concert conducted by Stéphane Denève, with Mutter and Yo-Yo Ma performing and all-star guests including Spielberg and Daisy Ridley. The U.S. Army Herald Trumpets helped blast the *Olympic Fanfare and Theme*, and the evening concluded with the entire orchestra and audience singing "Happy Birthday."

The festivities continued at Tanglewood and the Hollywood Bowl that summer, and the LA Phil opened their fall season with the West Coast premiere of John's new violin concerto. Queen Elizabeth II died on September 8, and in one of her last official duties she approved the new list of cultural figures to be named honorary Knights of the British Empire. On that list was John, for his many years of "services to film music."[19]‡

He concluded his delirious 90th year by checking another orchestra and concert hall off his "bucket list," as Mark Volpe saw it—conducting the Filarmonica della Scala at the opera house La Scala in Milan, Italy, where operas by Puccini and Verdi premiered in the 1800s. An open rehearsal was held on the day before the concert in December, and anyone under 30 was invited to experience seeing John and the orchestra for free. Someone asked the young crowd how many of them had ever been in La Scala, or to *any* orchestra concert, "and I kid you not," said Mutter, "maybe 20, 30 raised their hands."[20] For the hundreds of others in attendance, it was their

---

‡ The award was formalized at an investiture ceremony in Washington, D.C., the following October.

first experience hearing a symphony orchestra, "and what better experience can you have than this one?" Mutter said. It was abundantly clear that John's music was perhaps the most powerful and effective gateway drug into the vast ocean of orchestra repertoire—even in a renowned classical place like Milan.

Volpe was staggered by how much John's music had infiltrated new generations in other cultures during the span of his career as an orchestra administrator. He had been traveling to Europe for almost half a century, and "I'm telling you," Volpe said, "30 years ago the film fanatics would know him, but not much more. Italy 30 years ago, you'd have to say '*Star Wars* composer.' Now, he goes to La Scala and they sell it out in 20 minutes."[21]

* * *

Spielberg's pandemic project was *The Fabelmans*, a thinly fictionalized memoir about his boyhood obsession with filmmaking and the foundational crack created by his parents' divorce. Communicating by Zoom video calls, as almost everyone did during the lockdown, Tony Kushner extracted anecdotes and details from Spielberg and spun them into a shaggy book of vignettes that had the ring of truth but, unfortunately, not the shape of a film story. Spielberg faithfully recreated his childhood homes and amateur 8mm moviemaking, as well as several events from his formative years that left a permanent mark. (John paid a visit to the set, a surreal time machine to his friend's boyhood.)

It was clearly an emotional exorcism of some of Spielberg's most haunting ghosts, but the tale was ultimately too close to his soul for him to see it clearly through an audience's eyes—and that myopia extended to the way it was scored. Spielberg heavily relied on source music, with the explanation that his juvenile home movies were soundtracked with Golden Age film scores and that his mom (Michelle Williams played the film's "Mitzi Fabelman") was an aspiring concert pianist. But vast stretches of the two-and-a-half-hour film unspool without any music at all, and in the end John only contributed about 20 minutes of original score. It felt like a broken contract: Spielberg, finally telling his own story, reneged on a promise to his audience, built across five decades, that John Williams was his full-time dance partner, his main squeeze—his "final rewrite."

Spielberg answered for the unusually spartan soundtrack thus: "When Johnny and I sit down to spot one of our films, the film kind of tells you where it needs music or where it would benefit without music."[22] John himself told Spielberg at the spotting session, "I don't think there should be that much music," and he admitted the choice was "certainly a glaring anomaly" in their body of work.[23] Because Leah Spielberg was a pianist, John said he thought it should be a small, piano-centric score, "and that probably it wouldn't have an orchestra, a big expressive delivery of music for a film like this that was so personal and introspective." It was personal for John, too, because he had known Leah and Arnold almost from the time he began working with their son. They often came to scoring sessions, and John would introduce them to the orchestra. John loved hearing Arnold's World War II stories, and Leah loved that her son's movie scores were played by the former concertmaster of the Philadelphia

Orchestra. "When [Steven's] scoring a movie," Leah once said, "he calls and says, 'Come over, we need your musical advice.' It's a crock, but I love hearing it."[24]

John wrote a simple piano tune for Mitzi and her son "Sammy," a tender, nostalgic lullaby with a descending bass line and just a whisper of melancholy. "A kind of evening piece," John said, "a serenade, an *aubade*." "Knowing Leah as I knew her, I think gave a sense of personal closeness to me in writing that little piece," John said. "It's not that I'm saying I was writing it for her—but in a sense I *was*." When he played it for Spielberg on the familiar Steinway in his Amblin bungalow, once more enacting their time-honored ritual, his 75-year-old friend wept. "I thought he was really upset," said John. "He really actually cried. He really loves his parents, deeply."[25] For Spielberg, this melody was a *gift*:

> That theme means how much John loved my mom, and how much John loves me. John knew my mom so well, and my mom adored him and he adored her. So the theme that he wrote, which appears for the first time in the last scene between Mitzi and Sammy in the kitchen, was something that he would have loved to have performed for her. She used to attend all of our scoring sessions, for dozens of films in the past. And this is one of the sessions, of course, she did not attend. And so *in memoriam* John composed this for her. And I think a bit for *me* as well. I think it's the most personal score John's ever written for any of our collaborations.[26]

There is no score at all for the film's first 10 minutes, not when little Sammy discovers the wonder of movies and constructs a train crash to film with his own camera, and not, ironically, as Mitzi enthuses about the beauty of music and surrendering to the classical score she's reading late one night. There is no score for the iconic shot of young Sammy watching his movie projected onto his open palms in a dark closet, nor when he pulls his mom inside and they watch it together in awe. This choice was not, like *Schindler's List* or *Saving Private Ryan*, because Spielberg approached the material in a stark, documentarian way. The shots, blocking, and visual poetry are all pure Spielbergian whimsy and wonder—only without any of the usual magical, emotional score in lockstep. These scenes, surely meant to evoke the marvel of the movies, thus feel strangely cold and detached. There is no music for the tornado scene, where everything else suggests it would normally be scored: the cuts, the dramatic camerawork, the emotion Mitzi is feeling, the fear, the nostalgia. "But where there is score," Spielberg argued, "it's extremely necessary, and it certainly heightens the emotion where emotion was required."[27]

Nearly 40 minutes into the picture, a glorious cue finally enters during the pivotal camping trip where, unbeknownst to anyone at the time, Mitzi is falling in love with her husband's best friend, Bennie, and she dances gracefully in front of the car headlights. While the two adult men gawk and Sammy captures the dance on camera, John introduces an Erik Satie–like waltz for celeste and chamber orchestra that is a bit woozy and drunken, like Mitzi, and also a bit in love with her, like Bennie and her husband Burt. John tried two different ideas for this scene: "The one we used, I think, was the first one that I did, that is more diaphanous and more fragile.

> Then a second version, which simply was too muscular and too orchestral. And the closer it got to a wafting dream, the better we seemed to be. A risky thing, suddenly having a kind of impressionistic orchestral piece in the middle of it, but I think—I hope—that it worked. It gave Mitzi a wonderful moment to put her dreamy personality on display, having been liberated by some little drink she had, that we could see Mitzi the dreamer, Mitzi the artist, Mitzi the one gliding through life with no gravity, just floating along like a ballet dancer.[28]

John reprised the theme several reels later, after the divorce, as Burt leafs through photos of Mitzi and his best friend, now happily married—salting the moment with an almost crushingly bittersweet flavor. "That's John's genius," said Spielberg. "That was not anything that I contributed to my own movie.

> John does it all the time. He'll basically use music to recall something that the audience remembers, and also to balance the story. I always like to say that John rewrites my films musically, and a callback like that is absolutely necessary, and so powerful, when Burt is looking at the pictures, in the last scene that Burt has with his son, Sammy, and he's suddenly overcome. It was John's idea.[29]

For the saddest scene in the film—a montage of Sammy filming his family as they explore their fancy new house—a trail of sad, spare piano notes is slowly joined by a haze of strings. Burt and Sammy's little sisters are so happy, but Mitzi looks into the lens with a forlorn expression. This heartbreaking cue carries into the tearful divorce announcement that follows, where Sammy can't handle seeing his little sister so distraught and so he dissociates, imagining himself capturing the moment with a camera.

The film ends with Sammy meeting his idol, John Ford—ingeniously played by David Lynch in an eyepatch—who gives the kid one piece of directing advice and then tells Sammy to "get the fuck" out of his office. As Sammy exits, stunned and happy, a jaunty Irish shanty accompanies his light steps away from camera and toward his filmmaking future. This cue sounds very much like "Out to Sea" from *Jaws*; that's because it almost *was*. "John's first pass at that was a much longer homage to *Jaws*," said Spielberg, "and we both felt that that was too on the nose and we didn't want to knock the fourth wall down." The film's final shot has Spielberg tweaking the actual camera to get a more interesting horizon—Ford's advice to his character in the film and Spielberg in real life—and he'd already broken the fourth wall in a scene where Sammy tells his high school bully he won't share the bully's secret "unless I make a movie about it someday." "I felt I could only afford two of those in the movie," said Spielberg, "not three."[30] John next tried an adaptation of "Rakes of Mallow," the Irish folk song used throughout Victor Young's score for *The Quiet Man*—which would have been several layers of meta commentary, considering it was one of the first film scores to make an impression on John when he was in the Air Force, and also that he quoted Young's love theme from the film in *E.T.* In the end, he split the difference, with allusions to both shanties. "I thought what we did would be missed by most people," John admitted.[31]

Belgardt said he and John actively searched for more places to apply score, "but if you look at it, where would you put music?" Belgardt argued. "It's not easy. Believe me, we did try to put it in a few spots. It never worked, because it felt manipulative. Sometimes Steven can be manipulative with John's music because it's so effective, and it starts to pull on your heartstrings. But a little restraint was welcome, I think, in this film. Everyone agreed. No one felt there needed to be more."[32]

Critics loved the film, but the public was mostly indifferent. It was nominated for seven Oscars, winning none. John received his 53rd nomination, and he lost to the far less traditional but far more prominent score for *All Quiet on the Western Front*. *The Fabelmans* is poignant and emotionally naked, a generous letter of love and forgiveness from Spielberg to his parents, and a kind of Rosebud that casts insightful new light onto so many of his other films and idée fixes. But it does not gel into a riveting yarn, as his work had so reliably done for so many years. This director, who forged an aesthetic where music was his coauthor, who regularly showed the opening set piece from *The Last Crusade* without score to demonstrate how slow and dull it was otherwise, had just committed a previously unthinkable sin—of telling his own life story without his most important weapon. "When I look at a film all put together, it's dead," Spielberg said in 1980.

> It's like lively death. The film moves, and it's action-paced, but there's sometimes nothing behind the eyes of the movie. And for me music has always brought out a kind of spirit, and the soul of the movie is evident once there was music to encourage it along. I've always felt that music was ... an integral part of movies, and I think in the 1960s people got away from that. They began to equate realism with *lack* of musical sound, the absence of music. And those were the days of the social commentary, when young filmmakers were afraid to be too theatrical or too sentimental.[33]

The Fabelmans was, as of the publication of this book, the last Steven Spielberg film John ever scored.

* * *

But it wasn't his final film score. When Disney purchased Lucasfilm, the company inherited Indiana Jones as well as *Star Wars*, and it wasn't long before Kennedy called the Nazi-fighting adventurer back into duty. Ford, on the cusp of 80, agreed to reprise what was arguably his most beloved role, and Spielberg agreed to produce but not direct. James Mangold was tapped for that task, as thrilling as it was impossible. "I had a movie fall apart, COVID was landing, and then this incredibly strange triumvirate of Kathy, Steven, and Harrison came to me about doing this," said Mangold, who openly admitted he knew it was "a fool's errand, in the sense that I'm *never* going to be able to do this on a level where there's not going to be people pissing about it."[34]

Mangold had directed one of the most critically respected comic book movies, *Logan*, which dealt with aging and mortality, and he felt the only honest way to make a new Indiana Jones movie starring an octogenarian hero was to confront the harsh realities of getting old. The main reason he couldn't resist taking this job, Mangold said, was the collaborators:

> Steven was a hero of mine since I was 12. John was a hero of mine since I was 12. Harrison has been a hero of mine since I was 12 or 13.... There's not a day I don't think about something about the work that these people have done. And the idea of actually getting a chance to collaborate with these people seemed to me to be a very private and personal gift that I would never obviously ever get again in my life. How often do we get to actually not just get to *know* or meet our heroes, but to *make* something with them?[35]

For his part, John wasn't so sure. After the three grueling *Star Wars* sequels, the idea of writing another two hours or more of densely orchestrated, highly choreographed action music sounded like a young man's game. "Steven called me and said, 'You know, John's not going to do scores anymore,'" Kennedy remembered.[36] John would not commit to scoring the film, and Kennedy told Mangold that John might just provide a new theme or two and that William Ross would likely adapt the rest from the existing Indiana Jones canon. Mangold grew up making Super 8 movies in the 1970s, and "John was making the sound of movies that inspired me to want to be a filmmaker," he said. He worshiped John's scores—not just for their famous themes, but the "granular filigree," the "fine, watchmaking work inside his scores," and for the audacity of John to reach back in time for a toolkit of romantic orchestration and unabashed melody to make something old seem completely new. *Indiana Jones and the Dial of Destiny*, which Mangold conceived with several other screenwriters, was about an old man dwelling on past adventures and presented with the possibility of going back in time. As a theme, it was almost too perfect for John at 90.

Mangold decided not to try to pressure John for a complete new score, or even bring it up, but to simply try to pique his creative interest. He explained his concept for the film, which opens with a long flashback of Indy during his World War II heyday, but mostly follows the retiring professor in the 1960s getting reluctantly back in the saddle to protect his goddaughter, Helena, and tangled up with an old Nazi nemesis who is searching for the Antikythera, an ancient time machine invented by Archimedes. His film used the latest de-aging technology to turn Ford into his younger self, and Mangold had a rough version of those effects in his three-and-a-half-hour cut of the film when he came back from shooting in England in early 2022— he jokingly called it "the *Berlin Alexanderplatz* of Indiana Jones movies"— which was the version he screened for John in his editing bay. Mangold sat behind John in awe at "the way he was just 100 percent locked in:

> At this point in my career, I've shown my movie in a cutting room to lots of different people—producers, studio heads, luminaries.... The stars come in. And I've never seen anyone walk in so entirely to a movie, in a way that I can only describe the way *I* feel when I watch it, meaning that everything goes away. But also that there was this permanent—I could even feel it [sitting] behind him—grin on his face as he was watching it. And I don't mean my movie was so good. I mean that he was giving himself so fully to the movie, and was just there to let the thing move through him and let whatever was going to process process.³⁷

John was immediately enthralled by Helena, Indy's goddaughter played by Phoebe-Waller Bridge, and wanted to write a theme for her. "I found her to be complex," John said. "She was a gambler and she was cosmopolitan, smoked, drank, was funny, witty—even, in a way, sexually ambiguous, or *broad* in her life in that sense—that it reminded me of Lauren Bacall. I might have said to myself: 'What would I write for Lauren Bacall?'"³⁸§ So he wrote a highly old-fashioned and very romantic heroine theme, full of swooning strings and stirred passions, with a trace of Marion's theme from *Raiders* to boot. Full of inspiration from that screening, he decided to write a few other themes: a new one for the Nazis as represented by Dr. Voller, a MacGuffin theme for the "dial" itself, and an ancient Greek war motif for the age of Archimedes. Again, one might wonder why this was worthy of his time. "Very frankly," he said, "I thought to myself: Well, I really don't want somebody else to do that. It was like when I was doing *Star Wars*. I thought: if I can possibly do it, I should try to do it."³⁹ John orchestrated his tunes as suites and recorded them at Sony, still with the goal of handing them over to Ross to adapt, much as they had done on *Harry Potter and the Chamber of Secrets*.

But then John started sketching cues while Ross worked on others. As with the recent *Star Wars* films, Kennedy and company arranged for John to have full orchestral recording sessions spread across months so that he could "demo" ideas while each effects-heavy reel was being finished. When Mangold heard John's lush Bacall suite for Helena, he had two immediate reactions: "What a magnificent piece of music it was. And two, I thought it was not right for the movie.

> My big note to him was: "It doesn't feel *naughty* enough." I felt like she's *trouble*. And this theme is just so in love with her that it doesn't reflect the sense, to me, that she's a bag of trouble. The example I always used, and I certainly used when I was *writing* Phoebe's character, was [Barbara] Stanwyck in *Lady Eve*. It's easy to fall in love with her, but it's going to be the death of you.⁴⁰

"I might have been the wrong composer for him," John admitted, shrugging, "who knows."⁴¹ Ironically, maybe John just had an antiquated sensibility. But he assured

---

§ When John first described *Raiders of the Lost Ark* in the spring of 1981, he said it was a "wonderful adventure film in the style of the '30s—like a Bogart-Bacall film set in the Middle East." (Dyer, "Williams Poised for Pops.")

Mangold these grand suites were just that, and that he could adapt Helena's theme to suit the action. "He never really paid attention to me," Mangold said, laughing at himself.

> I think he knew he had done something really wonderful. And what I realized was that John was doing something not unlike what I would do alone here writing, which is: he's just playing. And the fact that it's being played by an orchestra was creating too much of a platform for me. He's going to end up stealing and taking elements from this and twisting them in slyer fashions in different ways later as things evolve on the picture.[42]

As time went on, and when post-production was elongated because of reshoots, John kept writing more and more cues. "I had a lot more time than I normally would have had," he said, "and a lot less pressure." Mangold observed that, "not unlike me when I have an editor working on a scene separate from me, John comes in—and what Bill's done is fine, but John's like, 'No, no, no. Try inverting this.' And at some point I think he was just like, 'Give it to me!' and then runs back to write it himself. I saw that starting to happen, and I felt that I would end up getting what I wanted if I just stayed quiet and just kept giving my notes and letting things progress."

Ross had sketched a cue for the climactic nighttime chase on the airfield, where Voller has kidnapped Indy and is attempting to fly into the past (to kill Hitler and lead the Nazis to victory), relying on John's Nazi theme—a low and sinister brass chorale—to drive the action. Mangold was already starting to mix the film when he told John—who often came by the cutting room to discuss his score—that he felt the cue was too repetitive. So John went away and came back with a new five minutes of score, using Helena's theme as the melodic driver for the action. "I thought it was some of the best work in the movie," said Mangold. "He took her theme and let the brass play it and let it become a heroic romantic theme—because, interestingly, that's where … her character reveals her true romanticism."[43]

In all, there were eight scoring sessions from June 2022 to February 2023. Mangold was so happy with the score that, like Rian Johnson, he insisted an isolated score track be included on the film's Blu-ray release. *Dial of Destiny* came out in June 2023, a mixed bag likely always destined to be polarizing. The nostalgic thrill of seeing Ford looking like he did back in 1989 was offset by the uncanniness of the deep-fake technology and the general videogame look to a lot of the film. But Ford also gave one of the most vulnerable, tearful performances of his long career, completely investing in his aged Indy, full of pain and regrets. John's contribution, similarly, is both compromised and miraculous—between the blatant interpolations of temp track music (not just from other Indiana Jones films but also *The Adventures of Tintin* and *Minority Report*), and a genuinely fresh and exciting score with robust new melodies and an integrity of thematic development that harks back to his own glory days. Poetically, these two old adventurers were giving their very best, despite the modern, digital constraints pressing on them. Working with John, Mangold said, "I got to see how he *thinks*, and how he works, and how this stuff is born. And the innocence, and the great generosity of heart it comes from. I don't mean innocent like *naive*. I mean there's a beautiful purity to John and his love of music and movies, and the way they talk to each other.... In an age of nothing but cynicism, it's completely uncynical."[44]

* * *

John hinted that he might be done with film scoring in the *New York Times* profile that ran on his 90th birthday. "I don't particularly want to do films anymore," he told the reporter. "Six months of life at my age is a long time." When *The Fabelmans* and then *Dial of Destiny* came out, people kept asking about his "retirement," which he increasingly walked back. He certainly wasn't done writing *music*—only death could pry that from him—and if the right project or the next Spielberg film came along, his door was open.

He did not slow down, and his health remained remarkably robust, his mind sharp and his pencil moving. He wrote a muscular, optimistic anthem for ESPN college football, *Of Grit and Glory*, which premiered in January 2023. Then, an unusual commission came through Yo-Yo Ma, who had connected with the South African documentary filmmaker—Craig Foster—behind the Oscar-winning film, *My Octopus Teacher*. Ma wanted to learn more about and support the Sea Change Project, a conservation effort for the Great African Seaforest, and when Foster's friend and fellow nature documentarian commenced a new film project about the kelp forests, John Chambers knew he wanted to involve Ma somehow. A huge fan of John Williams, and one who knew just how important trees were to him, Chambers had the wild idea of asking Ma to ask John if he might consider writing an original composition that the filmmaking team could then synchronize their stunning underwater footage to; and to Chambers's utter shock, John said yes.

Once he finished *Dial of Destiny*, John turned to this blank canvas with the basic prompt and some information about the kelp forests—and he came back with a 15-minute tone poem for an idiosyncratic ensemble: Ma's solo cello, a chorus of eight other cellos, four harps, brass, winds, and keyboards—with no violins or violas. He consulted his underwater music from *A.I.* to see if it might give him any ideas, but he ultimately wrote an impressionistic, frequently dreamy water ballet that opens with a cantilena cello line and features a sumptuous, dark chocolate chorale for all the celli, swelling French horn chords, lots of playful interplay for the quartet of harps, and a mystical celeste finale. Liberated from the cue sheets and demands of a feature film, but equally unburdened by the traditions and form of a classical concerto, John swam joyously in a stream somewhere between his lyrical scene painting and his more abstract art music, for a piece inspired by a very different species of tree. He called it *Great Ocean Forests*.

He wanted to record a "demo" of the piece with his top-shelf orchestra at Sony, with LA Phil principal cellist, Robert deMaine, standing in for Ma. Wearing all black with a blue sweater draped around his shoulders, his hair a bit fluffy and amiss in the back, John created a genial atmosphere with his usual support team and his favorite players. "The first two notes don't have magic somehow," he told celeste player Joanne

Pearce Martin after the first full read-through. His directions were poetic—he told the orchestra one passage should sound like "little leaves lying on the water"—and his ears were as sharp as ever. He went into the booth at one point and had William Ross conduct just the four harps, and when he came back on the stage he said he heard discrepancies between their timbres: "Some are fleshy, some are metallic." After the first 10-minute break, he mischievously said: "Does anyone miss the violins?" Everyone laughed. After an especially good take, he told deMaine: "You're an angel." On the podium that afternoon, John truly looked like a wizard casting a spell, using spare, delicate, but very deliberate hand gestures—an old man with white hair and almost a century of wisdom—making magic *ex nihilo*, moving oceans and creating a picture with invisible paint, just the sound of moving air and vibrating strings.

He also, at last, wrote a piano concerto. Emanuel Ax was a kindly Polish luminary without an ounce of pretension, born in 1949 in the Soviet Union. He first heard about "Johnny Williams" through Previn, his friend and regular performance partner, and the first thing he ever learned about John was that he was a wonderful pianist. In fact, the first time he met John was while performing Mozart's Concerto for Three Pianos with him in a 1994 concert at Tanglewood conducted by Ozawa. Ax admired John "from a distance" over the proceeding decades, and when he read in the *New York Times* profile that John wanted to write his first proper piano concerto, Ax "took the bull by the horns" and wrote a letter to John, sent through Gorfaine, which said: "Look, if you're really serious about writing a piano concerto, I would *so* love to be involved in playing it." John wrote back the next day: "That's great. I'm going to work on it, and I will send it to you." "That's how it started," Ax said, chuckling at his temerity. "It's my fault. I was just very forward."[45]

For John, there was something almost biblical about writing for "Manny" (as everyone called Ax), because he could trace the pianist's pedigree back to the great kings of old. "You know the old saying that Bach is the beginning of all keyboard playing, and Liszt is the apex of technique, and together they make Beethoven possible?" John said. "So if you start with Beethoven: [Carl] Czerny was a student of Beethoven, Liszt was a student of Czerny, [Theodor] Leschetizky was a student of Liszt—Leschetizky taught everybody, including Georg von Lalewicz, who taught Mieczysław Munz—teacher of Manny. So Manny comes right directly from Beethoven."[46]

The concerto slowly took shape, day by day, during John's 92nd year on Earth. John sat at the Steinway in his house, which he christened "Stella," and also at the Steinway in his bungalow, where most of his beloved scores were written, and he strove to create a showcase for this giant wooden instrument of hammers and strings which he had been almost organically attached to since he was a child. John wrote a cadenza to open the work which he claimed he could never play himself, but which would give Manny "plenty of business to do." He explained that the concerto wasn't a "jazz piece," but that the first movement was Art Tatum, the second movement was Bill Evans, and the third movement was Oscar Peterson—all famous jazz pianists. "It only addresses their *sound*," he explained:

You and I have a piano that's 88 keys—Art Tatum's piano had about 120, maybe. That's in my head, there's no such thing, but the *sound* was like that. You thought, even if he's playing at the center of the keyboard, why did it sound like Rachmaninoff? It wasn't bangy or loud, it was just beautiful—and big. And the same thing with Bill Evans: it's velvety in the balance. And Peterson is, you know, *circus*—which may be the definition of a concerto finale. Everybody doesn't think so, and many end softly—including mine.[47]

In typical John Williams fashion, he shook his head and said, "Can you imagine the chutzpah of trying to add something to the canon of piano concerti?" He also added: "It's the *hardest* thing I've ever done."[48] John once remarked to Ax, who was constantly on the road: "Manny, you must be playing on some lousy pianos." Ax said, "No, every piano's my friend." John liked that. Asked what the piano meant to him, he answered: "I would say to you that the piano is my friend. My lifelong companion."[49]

* * *

For the better part of the 20th century, it was unfashionable and even unforgivable for a "real" composer to write music for Hollywood. In the doctrine of Classical Music orthodoxy and academia, film was commercial, populist, *cheap*, and its music was offensively tuneful, sentimental—*vulgar*. A high priest of avant-garde music was Pierre Boulez, one of its foremost composers, conductors, and adjudicators, and "the worst pejorative that Boulez ever had was to call something 'film music,'" said Mark Swed, longtime critic for the *Los Angeles Times*. "I remember him telling me he watched the broadcast of *Death of Klinghoffer*"—the 1991 opera by John Adams—"and he said, 'It's *film music*! It's not real music.'"[50]

These were the headwinds that John Williams flew into when he began his ascent as the greatest film composer of all time. Classical critics like Swed and his predecessors were indoctrinated to find John's joyful popcorn symphonies a pungent odor, and programmed to sniff out their classical influences and hear nothing *but*, to dismiss it all as kitsch or hacky pastiche—and to keep this music out of *serious* subscription concerts and in the *pops* sandbox where it belonged. Musicians, conductors, and administrators who were trained in postwar conservatories felt much the same. Those who ignored this edict, like Ernest Fleischmann at the LA Phil, were eyed with suspicion as must-be hucksters, exploiting the popularity of *Star Wars* for an easy buck.

Did John intentionally set out to change their minds? Was he on an active mission to elevate his film music and earn acceptance in their exclusive club? If so, he would never claim it. But in his unceasing quest for excellence, in his high art of composition and orchestration, he made sophisticated music that was worthy of the best orchestras in the world. And in pursuing a position as a public conductor, he secured a platform on which to make that case—with *music*, not with words—and to disseminate his evidence on a national, and then international stage. He did not bitterly rail against the critics or musicians who dismissed him. He did not write screeds or give lectures about why film music ought to be taken seriously. He simply held himself to a standard of exquisite perfection, treated musicians with kindness and collegial respect, and with his deeply heartfelt, sincerely stirring music he won the hearts first of everyday audiences, *volk*, then classical giants like Yo-Yo Ma and Gustavo Dudamel and Anne-Sophie Mutter—and in the course of four decades, he eventually converted or outlived most of those who rejected him. A robust online fandom developed. JWfan.com, founded in 1999 by a Spanish filmmaker named Ricard Befan, became the most active community for his fans around the world; they traded news, bootleg scores, gossip, insults, and genuine affection, and the undying intensity of their collective worship supercharged the religion that grew around John. Fans also entered *academia*, and a scholarly movement gradually grew in the new millennium, with more and more musicologists defying their predecessors and focusing their studies on John's music, leading to whole university courses, journals, and international conferences devoted to his work. He was revered not just by the small children and nostalgic adults waving their lightsabers at the Hollywood Bowl every summer, but by audiences of all ages and races and genders in Boston, New York, Cleveland, Philadelphia, and Chicago, in Vienna, Berlin, Milan, and Tokyo—and equally revered by the elite musicians in each of those cities.

And it wasn't just that they loved playing for *him*, although of course they did. But it was almost when other conductors began to interpret John's music that it became most evident that it belonged in the repertoire. For Swed, when Dudamel started conducting John's music, "I suddenly heard all kinds of stuff. And then as time went on, and Gustavo would *really* put work into these things, I heard a lot more happening than I had ever heard before."[51] Dudamel observed that John's film work is not the kind of music that only requires one rehearsal "because we have played this thousands of times. [There is] always something to get from the music—you know, *interpretation*. It's not static." Outside of their respective films, Dudamel said, John's music has "the dimension of an overture, or a symphonic poem, or a symphony." By the 2020s, the LA Phil had included some of John's scores in their audition material for new players. "There is Beethoven, Debussy, Stravinsky, Mozart—and John Williams," said Dudamel. "Imagine that."[52] One LA Phil musician offered that "his music will no doubt be in the orchestral canon along with Beethoven, Brahms, and Mahler for centuries in the future."

In the first half of his life, John ascended the highest peak of Hollywood's peculiar art form. By his twilight years, he had done something no other "film composer" had ever achieved: he had completely and decisively triumphed in "Tanglewood," the Vatican of classical music—and in the greatest halls on earth. "Just look at the 25 biggest orchestras of the U.S. next season," conductor Stéphane Denève said, emphasizing the point. "Who plays a piece of Boulez? I bet there is not one. All of them, the 25 orchestras—they will play music of John Williams."[53]

* * *

Epilogue: Heartwood

In October 2023, John traveled to Japan. Seiji Ozawa, the once vibrant, live-wire conductor, was now physically diminished and bedridden—the result of esophageal cancer, back problems, and a suite of other health issues. Ozawa had long wanted John to come and conduct his Saito Kinen Orchestra, the supergroup he formed in the 1980s (named after his mentor, Hideo Saito) that brought elite Japanese musicians from orchestras all over the world back home to play in a summer festival in the mountain city of Matsumoto, in central Japan. Denève visited Ozawa, his "precious mentor," at his Tokyo home in 2022, and Ozawa's young grandson Masaki (nickname "Bee") gave Denève a drawing of a sword that said: "John, I love your music, see you soon, from Masaki Ozawa." The French conductor promised he would hand deliver it, and when he saw John two weeks later for the National Symphony celebrations of John's 90th birthday, he reiterated how much Ozawa wanted John to visit Japan again, and Denève "also confided that Seiji was sadly not in great health, so that it was certainly urgent to do so."[1]

John, now 91, made the long journey out of respect for his old friend—and to see him one last time. It was the day of Ozawa's 88th birthday when John conducted the concert in Matsumoto, and John brought a Boston Red Sox jersey as a gift for his fellow baseball fan. He stood beside Ozawa's wheelchair backstage in the hall, surrounded by birthday balloons and stuffed sharks that Bee had signed for John, and he held his brittle friend's hands. "It was extremely moving," said Denève, who also came to Japan to share conducting duties with John. "Seiji was really very frail, he could not communicate anymore vocally, but his eyes showed excitement, gratitude, and joy. The two friends were reunited. It was nothing short of a miracle."[2] After the concert, Ozawa was wheeled onto the stage, wrapped in a red blanket (Figure E.1), and John firmly clasped his hands again as the Japanese audience exploded with applause.

Ozawa died six months later. His daughter Seira, who had been acting as his nurse for many years, wrote an essay about how the Japanese—and particularly Seiji—love snow. "Their idea is that snow falls to clean the world, makes it more beautiful," said John. "And they were so excited that morning, the day that Seiji died, when they had snow—the magic white that never comes, or so rarely comes in their climate. She took that as a sign that he was going to another realm that is washed and cleaned and prepared for him."[3]

John was, in many ways, alone now. He had Jenny and his two sons, of course; multiple grandchildren and even great-grandchildren. He had Samantha, a day trip away in Los Olivos. He had Steven Spielberg. He had his small, tightknit support team on

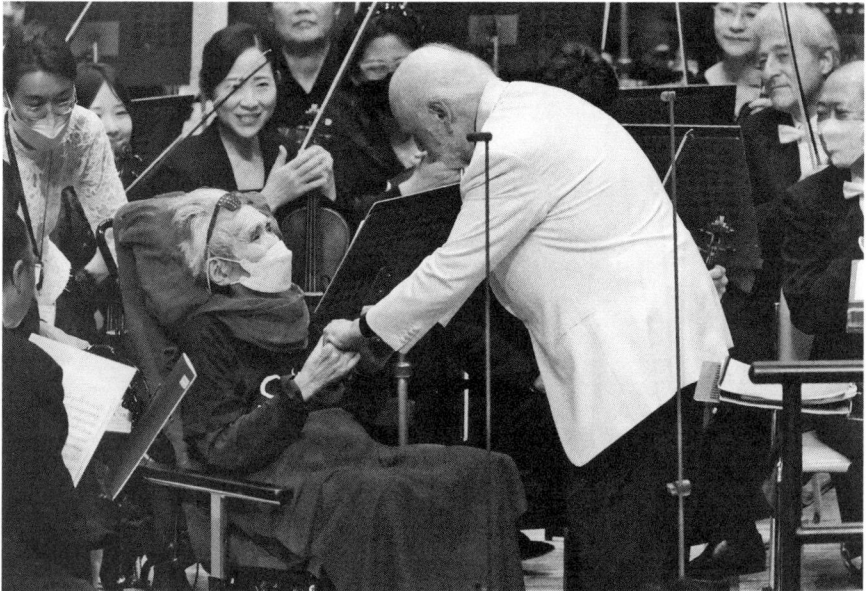

Figure E.1. John and Seiji Ozawa in Matsumoto, September 2, 2023 (Photo by Michiharu Okubo/©Michiharu Okubo/2023OMF).

the business side and on the music side. But his old friends, his comrades, were all gone: Seiji, André, Lionel. *Barbara*. "I'm alone," he admitted, "without my buddies."[4]

The second week of March 2024 ended with the Academy Awards, where John was nominated for his 54th Oscar for *Indiana Jones and the Dial of Destiny*. He did not win—he was *used* to not winning, and expected it—and at the last minute he decided not to attend the ceremony because of a cold. This same week began on Sunday, March 3: the 50th anniversary of Barbara's death. Fifty years since that horrible Sunday morning when John called Kathryn Altman and learned that his young wife was gone, stolen in the middle of the night while she was alone in a Reno hotel room. His childhood sweetheart, the mother of his children, the social force and cheerleader who set his professional life in motion—violently and suddenly ripped away just before his career really took off. "My whole life would have been hers," said John,[5] who still thought about Barbara, still missed her. (Figure E.2) When he spoke with Jenny on that anniversary Sunday, reflecting on the half-century that had passed since Barbara's death, John said he wasn't so much *sad* anymore ... he was angry.[6]

Figure E.2. John and Barbara with Delbert and Ann Mann, ca. 1972 (Courtesy of John Williams).

John's triumphs were undeniable and a great source of satisfaction, but at the core of his life there was still this gaping hole, this cosmic wound. He had summited the mountain of music and won the world's affection, but Barbara wasn't at his side to share in the joy.

* * *

And still he remained remarkably joyful, obstinately curious and perpetually stimulated. He earnestly said his ninth decade was his best one yet, and he kept expanding his mind, reading and learning about world history and current affairs; he even read Barbra Streisand's thousand-page memoir, cover to cover. He went on regular walks with Jenny in his neighborhood and on the golf course at Bel-Air Country Club, bumping into Barack Obama one day and asking the former president about his recent trip to Barcelona where Michelle got on stage and danced with Bruce Springsteen. He had regular meetings with Spielberg, and dinners with Dudamel and other friends in the classical gentry. He kept writing music every single day, kept eagerly taking the conducting opportunities thrown at his feet, making international travel plans and sucking the marrow from his one life. He kept *growing*. He read an opinion essay by David Brooks in the *New York Times* in which the columnist wrote: "I'm not an exceptional person, but I am a grower."[7] John resonated with that. "There's nothing extraordinary about me," he said, and how he got from being the kid in Flushing and the young jazzer making pop records (which now embarrassed him) and scoring clunky TV shows, to conducting the Berlin Philharmonic and writing concertos for Yo-Yo Ma and Emanuel Ax "has been some kind of *growth*, as a result of some intuitive proclivity of some kind," he said, "that I can't take credit for."[8]

"I think life is the greatest *possible* gift," John said, and he did not fear death. "Sleep is the godmother of death," he said, recalling a quote he read somewhere. "Sleep can be a wonderful relief. Sometimes you go to sleep, you don't even want to wake up. I don't think there's anything to fear at all."[9]

He had never been a religious man, but he certainly felt frequencies in the universe beyond the material. "If there's a spiritual element that we all have sensed since the Lascaux caves—we pray to the moon, or we sing to the sun, or we dance to make rain—we are under the suspicion that there is *something* spiritual in nature, some *it*," he said. "And the existence of *it* is what makes our razor-short earthly experience some significance of some kind that we don't understand, but we sense it." He always recapitulated the theme of atavism, and he put stock in Jung's idea of the collective unconscious: "Whatever the essence of art is, it is that shared memory. I think that we were all present at the Big Bang. We remember it. If you close your eyes at certain moments in life you can see it—whether it's the *moment d'extase*, for example, or other similar experiences that we have. Music is a path to that memory, and the reason we are moved by it is because it makes that connection."

He had a kind of spiritual communion with the great composers of the past, and he believed that people who had died—like Barbara—gave him strength and power. John admitted one day that he had developed his own eccentric religion. He insisted it was a joke, mere "silliness," but he had clearly given it deep thought. He had this "crazy" theory that however many neurons there were in the human brain—billions, possibly trillions—there was an equal number of objects in space. The two numbers are the same. "The brain is a model of the universe," he explained, "or the universe is a model of the brain," and that as our brains collectively, slowly acquire new objects—a new word, a new scientific discovery—they keep pace with each new planet or sun in the cosmos. "That's encouraging if it could be true," he smiled. But what is the ultimate acquisition? "What is the spiritual thing?" he asked. "Two things: *beauty* and *truth*. That's what we're looking for in art. That's all there is. And we can't find it yet because we're not *there* yet.

> They're telling us that about 150,000 years ago we got up and walked and the brain started to evolve. And at that time the cortex was probably the size of an orange, and the reptilian cortex the size of a walnut. It's taken 150,000 years of a rate of expansion to have the brain grow to the point that it is now. 150,000 years. Earth time, that's forever. Cosmic time, spiritual time, it's *nothing*—because the galaxy will move thousands of light years, and it only moves *this* much when we see it, but the distance is immeasurable. The speed of expansion from 150,000 years ago to now is the same speed of expansion of the universe. They match.

Thus, John concluded, if humanity can live another 150,000 years—"which is highly unlikely," he admitted—perhaps our brains will finally expand to meet the corresponding size of the universe and we will have, finally, "truth and beauty. No longevity anymore. None of that's there—just understanding of those two things."

John ran his quirky theory by a pathologist friend in Boston ... who immediately shot it down. "The anatomy of the human brain has great variation from individual to individual," the pathologist said—there's no uniformity. John laughed. "I know he's right, and I know I'm talking nonsense. *However*, if it only tells us that it's important that we survive long enough, we might understand what infinity is, what spirituality is. It's not religion—it's none of those things. It's simply *beauty* ... and *truth*."[10]

Acknowledgments

Close Encounters with the White Goddess

John Williams did not want me to write this book.

To be fair, he didn't want *anyone* to write his biography. Intensely private, extraordinarily modest, he has guarded his personal life like a fortress. Upon learning this, some outsiders assumed he must be hiding something. In some respects, he was—but not the tawdry or scandalous secrets they suspected. Mostly, there was pain, sadness, and some regret. There was also plenty of laughter and "silliness" and joy. But he didn't really talk about his home life or his private self with others, even friends he had known for decades. For John, there was something untoward or ungentlemanly about that. In an era of oversharing and social media, he was a man from another generation and another epoch of politesse. It simply wasn't *done*.

He was also, I think, a little suspicious of writers, having been misquoted or misunderstood many times in the past. Nor did he want some drooling fanboy who only cared about *Star Wars* and *Jaws* to write his life story; he was also tired of hearing the same tired criticism and derision of his film work as banal, or plagiarized.

He actually tried writing an autobiography once. He opened it with the first song he remembered hearing from his mother's lips, and he recounted stories about traveling to Europe with Barbara and putting on impromptu concerts with her in cafés. But he was insecure about the strength of his writing, and didn't make much progress. (He gave the unfinished attempt to Jenny.) Really, it was *insecurity* that made him wary of any kind of biographical project. He had read enough biographies of great composers and artists to know that theirs was usually a dramatic or "impressive" story. Whether they were self-taught or prestigiously educated, these composers' lives had *plots*. John thought his plot was, frankly, a little dull. "I didn't see the finish line—didn't have a finish line in mind," he told me. "I know it's a very pedestrian mindset to somebody who's writing a biography. It would have been easier for you to write if I had a fine classicist background in Greek or Latin or the Baroque classics that precede Bach...."

He didn't think his work was worthy of a book—he genuinely didn't! When John dismissed his musical achievements in interviews, one might naturally assume it was an act of false modesty. But there was nothing false about it. His fellow musicians, friends, and family members all attested that he was constantly minimizing his work, always doubting if it was any good, always saying things like, "Oh, nobody wants to hear from *me*." He always changed the subject from himself to something or somebody else. For a man as accomplished, renowned, successful, and beloved as John Williams, it was a staggering absence of ego and arrogance, a truly admirable character. But there may have also been an element of self-loathing in his self-abasement.

He always emphasized what little value there is in "our" (his) work, relative to the true masters. He might mention some way in which he related to Brahms—in his general posture toward the musical *past*, say—but then immediately emphasize that he should never be spoken of in the same breath as Brahms. Or how he saw a connection between himself and the self-educated Debussy, but rushing to add: "Debussy is a *god*—I'm just a cobbler."

But he also knew that the work he created was admired and worshiped by millions of people around the world. He knew that very well. And one day he admitted something revealing:

> There seem to be a lot of people around the world who enjoy my music—which is a *bonus*, because it started out to be *gebrauchsmusik* for a place in accompanying a film. And it's almost *better*, I think, that they don't know me. They don't know that I'm just an ordinary person who works. I felt that a kind of microscopic examination of my efforts in the past, to learn and to hopefully grow and do what I can do, was something better off in the private realm from the point of view of those who may want to enjoy the music.

"Why disabuse them?" he added. "Why *de*mythologize a person, so to speak?"

So how, then, did this book come about? I can equally attribute it to persistence, fanaticism, stupidity, incredible timing, and extreme luck. For two sweaty years, I traversed a long and scary "unauthorized" cavern, ducking many spinning sawblades and stepping out in faith onto a seemingly fatal chasm—and somehow I landed on solid ground and found John at an open, reflective moment in his 90th year. The door to his Amblin studio miraculously opened in the fall of 2022, very hesitantly at first—and then I spent 18 ecstatic months interviewing John on a regular basis, just the two of us, sometimes for hours.

These amounted to the most meaningful two years of my life, personally and professionally, and they radically transformed the nature of this book for the better. Because John decided to open up, to trust me with his story, the world can now understand much better and deeper the detailed contours of his life, education, career, and philosophy. There were still areas he kept private and off-limits, areas where I dared not poke too forcefully; there were also discoveries I made that I was not able to include here for various reasons.

If he wanted to remain unknowable and mythological, I believe he can still lay claim to such a feat. But until very recently, there was a universe where John Williams kept *everything* he knew and thought and experienced to himself, and to his grave—and that would have been a poorer universe indeed.

* * *

I have to thank my wife, Alison, above anyone else. At one point, she said this book was like my child from another relationship which she had to learn to love and care for—and she positively *thrived* in her role as its stepmother. She heard me talk about it basically nonstop (we had a rule of "no book talk" on Sundays, which I regularly broke), watched me disappear for hours, days, and weeks in my time-consuming devotion to it, went on research trips with me, went to *Tokyo* with me. She made John chocolate chip cookies for Christmas. (He was very taken with her, and mentioned her often.) She agreed to let me read the whole thing aloud to her and give me feedback. She lived the stress of the whole "unauthorized" odyssey, often more acutely and painfully than I did, and she was often nervous and scared about what I was doing and the potential fallout. But she supported me, encouraged me, and loved me—and my little book child—all the same. She deserves more than a paragraph, but I'll compensate for that in real life.

My parents and siblings were also incredibly supportive and encouraging; they were all there when my John Williams obsession began. My dad heard overly detailed updates throughout this journey on our Monday phone calls, and he offered advice and positivity. Adam, Libba, and cousin Laura all read parts of the book and gave constructive feedback. Thanks to my old friend Tim Compton for doing the same, and for plenty more. James Hughes deserves special thanks, not only for reading early chapters and providing comments, but for being a sounding board, a pen pal, and a writing inspiration. (In some ways, this project began when I contacted him about writing a biography of his father many years ago; no book came of that, but a wonderful friendship did.) To Taylor White: my true-blue pal, cheerleader, confidant, and the richest man in town. To Tim Page and Sasha Anawalt, my professors and two of the first true masters of the craft who believed in me. And to Steven Smith: you lit the fire with your Herrmann biography, which I read in Pittsburgh before my career began in earnest, and you responded so graciously to this green writer when I cold-emailed you and again when I moved to L.A., where we had regular lunches and you gave me pep talks and lots of good cheer; you directly precipitated this book with your Steiner biography, and then responded to endless emails and phone calls and questions and panics and laments and celebrations, all with unflappable wisdom, sincerity, and generosity. You freely opened your deep well of experience to me, as well as your heart and your home. Steven, you are a true mensch, and a treasured friend.

Thanks to the many "JWfans" and film score fans from around the world who answered the call and provided me with so many rare archival interviews, videos, recordings, and princely aid, particularly: Miguel Andrade, Maurizio Caschetto, Thor J. Haga, John Takis, Tim Burden, and Mike Matessino. I remember joining JWfan.com in 2003—user name "Maestro" (*how original*)—and reveling in finding a community of like-minded nerds; some became pen pals, others sent me rare score CDs from faraway countries. Internet fan groups can be toxic and nasty, but it's very special to still be connected to the best parts of that community, still receiving such gifts and companionship from its members. Special thanks also to Travis Elder, who helped me immensely with the ancestral research and the Nagle revelation, and to Jan Grabowski, a wizard of research and treasure-hunting who abundantly shared his hard work. Thanks to Deborah Falik for her time and efforts, and hopefully her forgiveness.

Thanks to inspirational, experienced authors Alex Ross and Nate Sloan for letting me bend your ear and answering many questions. Thanks to Joseph McBride, Richard Zoglin, Brian Jay Jones, and all of the other biographers I hounded with questions, and to my BIO support group; this was my maiden voyage and I needed all the help and counsel I could get. It was really nice not to feel alone. And to Alex Mansour—my whip-smart former "student," indefatigable (and unpaid) research assistant, coffee companion, musical problem solver, and extremely kind ally—this book could not have happened without you. I'm extra grateful for the friendship that came out of it.

To the librarians and archivists who assisted my research: Bridget Carr and Sarah Funke Donovan at the Boston Symphony Orchestra; Michele Beacham and Carolyn Conter at the Los Angeles Philharmonic; Amber Bertin and Dan Joseph Hassoun at the Black Film Center & Archive; Kelly Wallace at Los Angeles Public Library; Mary Kate Kwasnik at Patten Free Library in Bath; Betsy Paradis at Bangor Public Library; Molly Dohrmann and Elizabeth K. Batiuk at Vanderbilt University; Terry Brown at the Houston Symphony; Mary Beth Brown at the American Heritage Center, University of Wyoming; David Peter Coppen at the Sibley Music Library, Eastman School of Music. Thank you *so* much to Nikki Walsh and her team at Universal Pictures, and to Andie Childs at the American Federation of Musicians; apologies for the million emails! Thanks to Rose Doylemason at AFM Local 47. Scattered gratitude to Cheryl Pawelski, Mark Burford, Maro Chermayeff, Walter Podrazik, Ahmos Hassan, Gregg Sherman and Jeffrey Sherman, Doug Adams, Mark Burford, Vince Piazza, Erik Singer, Stéphane Lerouge and Universal Music France, Carlos Vega and Deutsche Grammophon, and to everyone else who gave of their time or provided me with valuable materials. Norm Hirschy: you are *the* reason this book exists. You have been so much more than an editor, and I could not ask for a greater champion during my first time in the arena.

Humongous thanks to Don Williams, Jenny Williams, Chris Cameron, and Paula Arlich—John's family members who gave so much to me, both materially and psychologically. I just hope I've given you and your families something valuable in return. I'm particularly grateful to James Newton Howard, one of my favorite composers and also a guy who asks probing questions and makes me feel like he cares about the answers; I know you helped turn the tide on this project. (Maybe I'll write *your* biography one day. I've already written your obituary!) To Louie Anderson: I'm sorry I didn't laugh harder at your jokes, and I'm sorry I can't send you an autographed copy of this book, or write a book *with* you. Your constancy and kindness helped make this happen, and I miss you a lot. Heartfelt gratitude to my loving and departed grandparents; and to my piano teacher, Mrs. Emeigh. To those who believed in me: David Kirschner, Jeff and Joan Beal, Uncle Tom and Aunt Barbara, Nathan Pickup, David Shire … and of course, *Mom*: I love you. To cousin Matt and the Hinelys: your hand-me-downs became my first cultural interests, and I discovered John Williams because of you.

Finally: John Towner Williams is the reason I fell in love with the orchestra and with movies; he is the reason I became interested in writing about film music and interviewing composers; his music was the imaginative and emotional fuel for most of my life; and getting to know him through this book was the Holy Grail of my career and time on this planet so far. I don't know if it can ever be topped. Thank you for your eternal melodies and ambrosia orchestration, for so many moments of transcendence and sublime beauty, for giving me a sense of purpose, and for overcoming your well-founded hesitations and opening up so unsparingly for this book, for becoming my professor, my Dutch Uncle John. I can never repay you, but hopefully this book expresses how much I love you. Your music will be *right here*, in my heart, for the rest of my own adventure on earth.

Tim Greiving
Summer 2025

Notes

Part 1

1. John Williams to TG, March 9, 2023.

Chapter 1

1. Ibid.
2. Henry Wilson Owen, A.B., *The Edward Clarence Plummer History of Bath, Maine* (1936).
3. Robert C. Toll, *Blacking Up: The Minstrel Show in Nineteenth-Century America* (1974).
4. "Best in Its History," *Bath Independent*, November 1, 1902.
5. "Duffy-Nagle," *Bath Independent and Enterprise*, April 27, 1904.
6. "Mrs. Richard Neagle," *Bath Independent and Enterprise*, June 30, 1906.
7. "New Theater Is Well Opened," *Ottawa Citizen*, October 25, 1910.
8. Robert M. Seiler and Tamara P. Seiler, *Reel Time* (2013).
9. "Tom Nagle, Crack Trap Drummer, Will Perform Next Week," *Calgary Herald*, September 16, 1922.
10. "A Fine Orchestra," *Calgary Herald*, May 25, 1914.
11. "Empress Theatre Opens Its Doors," *Calgary Herald*, April 3, 1915.
12. "Thomas Nagle," *Bath Independent*, July 6, 1918.
13. "Tom Nagle Visits Friends," *Ottawa Citizen*, August 10, 1918.
14. *The Sault Star*, Ontario, January 16, 1926.
15. Christine Cameron, text message to TG, January 31, 2022.
16. All quotes from Katherine Williams in this chapter are from "Johnny Williams, Bangor Boy, Taught Shirley Temple Drums," *Bangor Daily Commercial*, February 8, 1938.
17. Jenny Williams to TG, April 1, 2023.
18. Margaret Smith to TG, January 19, 2022.
19. "Johnny Williams Comes Home," *Bangor Daily News*, August 19, 1967.
20. "Crowd Will Dance at Chateau Tonight," *Bangor Daily News*, April 12, 1926.
21. Gary Giddins, *Bing Crosby: A Pocketful of Dreams* (2001).
22. "Conductor John Williams Discusses Symphony Hall, His Career and His Relationship with Spielberg and Lucas," WCVB, *On Chronicle*, August 12, 2011.
23. Susan Wilson, "As the Century Turned: Boston in 1900," in *Symphony Hall: The First 100 Years*, edited by Robert Kirzinger et al. (2000).
24. Barbara Walters, *Audition: A Memoir* (2008).
25. Abel, "Disc Reviews," *Variety*, September 4, 1929.
26. Marjory Adams, "Movie Facts and Fancies," *Boston Globe*, March 9, 1929.
27. Charles Wohlstetter, *The Right Time/The Right Place* (1997).
28. Abel, "Central Pk. Casino," *Variety*, August 28, 1929.
29. "The Week of a New Yorker," *Brooklyn Daily Eagle*, January 13, 1930.
30. Peter Duchin and Patricia Beard, *Face the Music: A Memoir* (2021).

31. Mordaunt Hall, "The Screen," *New York Times*, January 2, 1931.
32. JW to TG, October 28, 2022.
33. Giddins, *Bing Crosby*.
34. Steven C. Smith, *Music by Max Steiner* (2020).

Chapter 2

1. "Phuff?" *Time*, October 31, 1949.
2. JW to TG, March 7, 2023.
3. JW to TG, June 2, 2023.
4. JW to TG, March 7, 2023.
5. David Thomas, "Point Blank: John Williams (The Total Film Interview)," *Total Film Magazine*, September 1997.
6. Bob Colonna, *"Greetings, Gate!": The Story of Professor Jerry Colonna* (2007).
7. "Lay Cornerstone for New School," *Brooklyn Tablet*, May 2, 1936.
8. Irwin Chusid to TG, February 2, 2021.
9. "Johnny Williams Comes Home," *Bangor Daily News*, August 19, 1967.
10. JW to TG, March 7, 2023.
11. Michèle Wood, "The Men Who Made Music: Raymond Scott," from *The Swing Era: Vintage Years of Humor*, TIME-LIFE Records, New York (1971).
12. David Gates, "Artie Shaw: Swing and Loathing," *New York Times*, April 30, 2010.
13. Wood, "The Men Who Made Music."
14. Ibid.
15. JW to Stan Warnow, May 2008.
16. Wood, "The Men Who Made Music."
17. JW to Stan Warnow.
18. "Freak Draw," *Time*, April 19, 1937.
19. "Raymond Scott," *The New Yorker*, August 20, 1938.
20. Chusid to TG.
21. Jeff Winner to TG, February 3, 2021.
22. Irving Mills, "Phonograph Records: The New Talent Medium," *Billboard*, August 27, 1938.
23. Wood, "The Men Who Made Music."
24. Tom Nolan, *Three Chords for Beauty's Sake: The Life of Artie Shaw* (2010).
25. JW to TG, March 7, 2023.
26. Shirley Temple, *Child Star: An Autobiography* (1988).
27. David Thomas, "The King of Pop Corn," *Sydney Morning Herald*, October 25, 1997.
28. JW to TG, March 17, 2023.
29. JW to TG, October 9, 2023.
30. Kerry Lengel, "Composer Tunes in on Work with Spielberg," *Arizona Republic*, September 22, 2013.
31. JW to TG, April 14, 2023.
32. JW to TG, March 7, 2023.
33. Ibid.
34. "Trying It Out on the Dogs, Maestro's Idea," *Variety*, November 8, 1939.
35. "On Our Covers," *Leedy Drum Topics*, October 1939.
36. "Johnny Williams Delays," *Variety*, January 10, 1940.
37. "Kate the Great," *Time*, May 15, 1939.

38. "Kate Smith," *Variety*, October 11, 1939.
39. Ken Alden, "Facing the Music," *Radio and Television Mirror*, March 1940.
40. Tom Lord, *The Jazz Discography: Volume 3* (1992).
41. Michael J. Colburn, "John Williams Returns to Bands Where He Began 50 Years Ago," *The Instrumentalist*, June 2004.
42. JW to TG, March 7, 2023.
43. Paula Arlich to TG, January 24, 2023.
44. JW to TG, April 11, 2019.
45. Gail Jennes, "The Boston Pops Gets a Movie Composer Who Doesn't Chase Fire Engines as Its New Boss," *People*, June 23, 1980.
46. JW to TG, April 11, 2019.
47. JW interviewed by John Jacobson, *Music Express Magazine*, Hal Leonard (2012).
48. Richard Dyer, "Where Is John Williams Coming From?" *Boston Globe*, June 29, 1980.
49. Miles Davis and Quincy Troupe, *Miles: The Autobiography* (1989).
50. JW to TG, March 7, 2023.
51. JW to TG, October 9, 2023.
52. JW interviewed by Larry Lang, published June 7, 2016, on Air Force Bands website: https://www.music.af.mil/Multimedia/News/Article-Display/Article/861692/watch-interview-with-composer-john-williams/.
53. JW to TG, March 7, 2023.
54. Mark Warnow, "Your Hit Parade," *Billboard*, December 30, 1939.
55. "A Conversation with John Williams," Q&A compiled by Diane Read for replies to fan letters.
56. JW to TG, October 18, 2022.
57. Ibid.
58. JW transcript obtained from Bishop Loughlin Memorial High School.
59. "The Eyes," *Newsday* (Suffolk Edition), September 5, 1946.
60. JW to TG, June 2, 2023.
61. "Johnny Williams Comes Home," *Bangor Daily News*, August 19, 1967.
62. JW to TG, October 9, 2023.
63. JW to TG, March 9, 2023.
64. "A Conversation with John Williams."
65. Lengel, "Composer Tunes in on Work with Spielberg," 2013.
66. "Mark Warnow," *Broadcasting, Telecasting*, October 31, 1949.
67. Tom Link, *Universal City: North Hollywood: A Centennial Portrait* (1991).
68. "Seek Course in Auto Driving to Combat Accidents," *Los Angeles Daily News*, March 19, 1947.
69. JW to TG, March 7, 2023.
70. "A Conversation with John Williams."
71. Susan Sontag, "Pilgrimage," *New Yorker*, December 21, 1987.
72. Jane (Sullivan) Hemenez, "Hail North Hollywood," *Los Angeles Times*, September 27, 1992.
73. Richard Hein to TG, September 28, 2021.
74. Colonna, *"Greetings, Gate!"*
75. Vince Piazza to TG, February 27, 2021.
76. Perry Botkin, Jr., to TG, July 9, 2018.
77. Munch program obtained from Los Angeles Philharmonic.
78. *Music Express Magazine*.
79. "A Conversation with John Williams."

80. JW to Maro Chermayeff, March 26, 2000.
81. JW to TG, March 7, 2023.
82. Henry Roth, liner notes for *The American Scene Suite: Within the Piano World of Robert Van Eps* (Blue River Records, 1966).
83. Robert Van Eps, *The Physics of Piano Technique* (1954).
84. JW to TG, March 7, 2023.
85. JW to TG, March 9, 2023.
86. JW to TG, October 9, 2023.
87. "Personality of the Week," *The Arcade*, April 6, 1949.
88. "Teenagers Frolic at Low Cost," *Los Angeles Mirror*, September 6, 1949.
89. Austin Conover, "Teen-Age Dry Night Proves Popular," *Los Angeles Evening Citizen News*, June 30, 1949.
90. Piazza to TG, February 27, 2021.
91. Hedda Hopper, "Acting Came Easy, Opportunity Hard," *Baltimore Sun*, August 16, 1953.
92. *Time Magazine*, 1949.
93. JW to TG, April 11, 2019.
94. Leonard Slatkin to TG, April 30, 2020.
95. Alex Ross to TG, March 30, 2021.
96. JW to TG, April 11, 2019.
97. JW to Conrad Pope, April 24, 2020.
98. Jeff Bond and Ada Guerin, "Tune Talk," *Hollywood Reporter*, February 15–21, 2005.
99. Jerry Williams to TG, July 10, 2018.
100. Botkin to TG, July 9, 2018.
101. "Hopefuls for Commissioner of Safety," *The Arcade*, May 18, 1949.
102. Nancy Vaughn, "Beaver of the Week," *The Arcade*, November 18, 1949.
103. JW to TG, March 7, 2023.
104. Jerry Williams to TG, July 10, 2018.
105. JW to TG, March 7, 2023.
106. Louise DiTullio to TG, April 11, 2021.
107. JW to TG, March 7, 2023.
108. JW to TG, October 28, 2022.
109. Paul Galloway, "Airman Composes Way to Movie Musical Career," *The Beacon*, August 27, 1954.
110. Hein to TG, September 28, 2021.
111. Barbara Ruick MGM bio, June 10, 1953.
112. JW to TG, June 2, 2023.
113. Ibid.
114. JW to TG, October 9, 2023.
115. "John Williams in Air Force," *Valley Times*, January 18, 1951.

Chapter 3

1. Dyer, "Where Is John Williams Coming From?"
2. Jim Katzaman, "From Barracks to Tents to Dorms," *Airman*, February 1986.
3. Ibid.
4. JW to TG, March 7, 2023.

5. Ibid.
6. Ibid.
7. Bill Peterson to TG, May 12, 2023.
8. Ibid.
9. JW to TG, June 2, 2023.
10. JW to TG, March 7, 2023.
11. "Skinnay Ennis Is Featured at Club," *Tucson Citizen*, January 31, 1952.
12. JW to TG, March 7, 2023.
13. Ibid.
14. JW interviewed by Larry Lang, published June 7, 2016, on Air Force Bands website: https://www.music.af.mil/Multimedia/News/Article-Display/Article/861692/watch-interview-with-composer-john-williams/.
15. JW to TG, February 6, 2023.
16. JW to Larry Lang.
17. JW to TG, March 7, 2023.
18. JW to TG, March 9, 2023.
19. Derren Gilhooley, "John Williams on John Ford's 'The Quiet Man,'" *The Daily Telegraph*, June 1, 2002.
20. "G.I. Pens Music Score for Newfoundland," *Valley Times*, February 18, 1954.
21. Heather Barrett, "Star Wars Composer John Williams' First Score a 1952 Newfoundland Film," *CBC News*, September 30, 2015.
22. Paul Galloway, "Airman Composes Way to Movie Musical Career," *The Beacon*, August 27, 1954.
23. Michael J. Colburn, "John Williams Returns to Bands Where He Began 50 Years Ago," *The Instrumentalist*, June 2004.
24. Galloway, "Airman Composes Way to Movie Musical Career."
25. JW to TG, October 9, 2023.
26. "Two-Ring Ceremony Conducted," *Valley Times*, September 6, 1954.
27. JW to TG, March 7, 2023.
28. Carrie Goldsmith, *Deconstructing Dad: The Unfinished Life and Times of Jerry Goldsmith* (unpublished, ca. 2006), https://www.jerrygoldsmithonline.com/spotlight_biography_preview.htm/.
29. Jon Burlingame, "Music Mentor Ties Hollywood's Greats," *Variety*, October 23–29, 2000.
30. James Westby, "'Uno scrittore fantasma': A Ghostwriter in Hollywood," *The Cue Sheet*, January 1999.
31. JW to TG, March 7, 2023.
32. JW to TG, October 28, 2022.
33. Galloway, "Airman Composes Way to Movie Musical Career."
34. Hal Humphrey, "Colonna Takes the Plunge," *Los Angeles Mirror*, May 4, 1951.
35. Dwight Newton, "Day and Night with Radio and Television," *San Francisco Examiner*, May 17, 1951.
36. John L. Scott, "Barbara Ruick, 'Real Gone' Among Bop Set," *Los Angeles Times*, July 6, 1952.
37. Louella Parsons, "In Hollywood," *Camden Courier-Post*, December 4, 1951.
38. Carleton Carpenter, *The Absolute Joy of Work: From Vermont to Broadway, Hollywood, and Damn Near 'Round the World* (2016).
39. Parsons, "In Hollywood," *Bergen Evening Record*, August 26, 1953.

40. Dorothy Kilgallen, "Voice of Broadway," *Mansfield News-Journal*, March 3, 1953.
41. Ken Bloom, *Show & Tell: The New Book of Broadway Anecdotes* (2016).
42. JW to TG, March 7, 2023.
43. "Grey, Ruick Signed by CBS," *Billboard*, December 11, 1954.
44. Newton, "Day and Night with Radio and Television," *San Francisco Examiner*, January 19, 1955.
45. "20th Pacts Barbara Ruick," *Hollywood Reporter*, August 5, 1955.
46. "Columbia Inks Barbara Ruick," *Billboard*, August 27, 1955.
47. Parsons, "In Hollywood," *Camden Courier-Post*, August 8, 1955.
48. Winthrop Sargeant, "The Leaves of a Tree," *New Yorker*, January 12, 1963.
49. JW to Maro Chermayeff, March 26, 2000.
50. Ibid.
51. JW to TG, March 7, 2023.
52. Ibid.
53. Daniel Pollack to TG, April 22, 2021.
54. JW to Chermayeff.
55. Ibid.
56. Ibid.
57. JW to TG, March 7, 2023.
58. JW to Chermayeff.
59. S. Stephenson Smith, "The Economic Situation of the Performer," *Juilliard Review*, Fall 1955.
60. JW to Chermayeff.
61. "Three for Tonight," *Broadcasting, Telecasting*, June 27, 1955.
62. Information compiled by Åke Holm, https://www.harbel.one/inx-harbel.htm.
63. Chris Shull, "Blockbuster Guest," *Fort Worth Star-Telegram*, April 18, 2010.
64. JW to Chermayeff.
65. Vic Damone and David Chanoff, *Singing Was the Easy Part* (2009).
66. Kap., "Ambassador Hotel, L.A.," *Variety*, November 30, 1955.
67. Damone and Chanoff, *Singing Was the Easy Part*.
68. Edith Lindeman, "When Better Work Is Done, Gal's Name May Be Ruick," *Richmond Times-Dispatch*, February 19, 1956.
69. Shirley Jones, commentary on *Carousel* from *The Rodgers & Hammerstein Collection* (20th Century Fox, 2006).
70. JW to TG, March 7, 2023.
71. Parsons, "In Hollywood," *Camden Courier-Post*, September 24, 1956.
72. Jenny Williams to TG, March 10, 2023.
73. JW to TG, June 2, 2023.
74. JW to TG, February 13, 2024.
75. JW to TG, June 2, 2023.

Chapter 4

1. Jenny Williams to TG, March 10, 2023.
2. Ibid.

3. William Booth, "Shark Attack?! John Williams Liked the Sound of That," *Washington Post*, December 5, 2004.
4. "Legends: John Williams," CBS *Sunday Morning*, aired September 22, 2019.
5. Arthur Darack, "Tent Play Is Light and a Bit Zany Too," *Cincinnati Inquirer*, June 26, 1956.
6. Louella Parsons, "In Hollywood," *Camden Courier-Post*, September 24, 1956.
7. Albert Marx, liner notes for *World on a String* (Bethlehem Records, 1958).
8. *Personal Notes: André Previn and John Williams*, BBC, aired November 8, 1988.
9. Martin Bookspan and Ross Yockey, *André Previn: A Biography* (1981).
10. JW to TG, October 28, 2022.
11. Mia Farrow to TG, July 28, 2023.
12. JW to TG, June 2, 2023.
13. JW to TG, October 28, 2022.
14. JW to Jon Burlingame, USC composer forum, January 11, 2006.
15. Joshua Miller, *GoodTimes*, December 17–19, 1980.
16. JW to TG, August 21, 2023.
17. Phil Moore, *Things I Forgot to Tell You*, unpublished memoir (1986) from Phil Moore Collection, Indiana University Black Film Center/Archive.
18. Phil Moore story from JW to TG, December 1, 2022. I was never able to verify this session or its date with the American Federation of Musicians Local 47, and the recording was never commercially released. But JW insisted on the details about Radio Recorders, Helfer, and that Pete Candoli was playing trumpet. It's *possible*, he said, it was only a rehearsal and not a recording—but the whole orchestra was there.
19. JW to TG, March 9, 2023.
20. Most of the session date information in this book comes from the archives of the American Federation of Musicians Local 47.
21. JW to Alex Monty Canawati, September 15, 1990.
22. Gros., "Album Reviews," *Variety*, July 17, 1957.
23. Richard Dyer, "Where Is John Williams Coming From?" *Boston Globe*, June 29, 1980.
24. JW to TG, March 9, 2023.
25. JW to TG, June 2, 2023.
26. JW to Burlingame, USC, 2006.
27. *Personal Notes*, 1988.
28. Derek Elley, "The Film Composer: 3: John Williams," *Films & Filming*, August 1978.
29. Ibid.
30. Dyer, "Where Is John Williams Coming From?"
31. Micheline Keating, "The Editor Adventures in TV Land," *Tucson Daily Citizen*, March 22, 1958.
32. JW to TG, October 28, 2022.
33. JW to Steven C. Smith, September 6, 1984.
34. Ginny Mancini to TG, February 19, 2021.
35. Jack Curtis Dubowsky, *Easy Listening and Film Scoring 1948–78* (2021).
36. Jon Burlingame, *TV's Biggest Hits* (1996).
37. Scott Timberg, *Culture Crash: The Killing of the Creative Class* (2015).
38. Bookspan and Yockey, *André Previn*.
39. Ron Carter to TG, March 31, 2021.
40. Dan Higgins to TG, March 2, 2022.

41. Ronnie Lang to TG, March 13, 2021.
42. Leonard Slatkin, *Conducting Business: Unveiling the Mystery Behind the Maestro* (2012).
43. "Musicians Guild Cuts AFM Control in TV via Major Film Studio Deal," *Variety*, September 3, 1958.
44. Dennis McDougal, *The Last Mogul: Lew Wasserman, MCA, and the Hidden History of Hollywood* (1998).
45. John Caps, "Keeping in Touch with John Williams," *Soundtrack*, March 1982.
46. Leonard Feather, "From Pen to Screen: Stanley Wilson," *International Musician*, August 1970.
47. JW to Burlingame, USC, 2006.
48. JW always claimed it was a seven-year contract, and the dates of his TV work support that claim. Universal could not verify the date or provide a copy of the contract. It was reported that he "re-signed" with Revue in July 1962 ("On the Upbeat," *Variety*, July 11, 1962).
49. JW to Burlingame, USC, 2006.
50. Elley, "The Film Composer: 3: John Williams."
51. Burlingame, *TV's Biggest Hits*.
52. JW to TG, March 9, 2023.
53. Quincy Jones, *Q: The Autobiography of Quincy Jones* (2001).
54. JW to TG, March 9, 2023.
55. Burlingame, *TV's Biggest Hits*.
56. Jerry Goldsmith interview for Television Academy Foundation, May 8, 2002, https://interviews.televisionacademy.com/interviews/jerry-goldsmith.
57. "In Conversation with John Williams and Deborah Rutter: The John Williams 90th Birthday Celebration," https://www.youtube.com/watch?v=CKQTbpoH-d0.
58. JW to TG, October 9, 2023.
59. JW to TG, March 9, 2023.
60. Charles Stinson, "'Road Racers,' 'Daddy' Average Movie Fare," *Los Angeles Times*, June 12, 1959.
61. Dyer, "Where Is John Williams Coming From?"
62. *Personal Notes*, 1988.
63. JW to TG, March 9, 2023.
64. Edye Rugolo to TG, May 16, 2021.
65. Leonard Feather, "Noted Critic Takes Stock and Finds Valley Doesn't Swing," *Valley News*, April 5, 1962.
66. Leo Kovner, "Play Reviews," *Hollywood Reporter*, February 23, 1959.
67. JW to TG, June 2, 2023.
68. Jenny Williams to TG, March 10, 2023.
69. Rugolo to TG.
70. Bob Klein to TG, November 6, 2021.
71. Daniel Cariaga, "Williams Is 'Very Happy' at the Boston Pops Helm," *Los Angeles Times*, syndicated in *The Fresno Bee*, November 30, 1980.
72. JW to TG, October 9, 2023.
73. Dyer, "Where Is John Williams Coming From?"
74. JW to Pope.
75. Hank Grant, "On the Air," *Hollywood Reporter*, September 16, 1959.
76. Burlingame, *TV's Biggest Hits*.

77. Gene Cipriano to TG, March 13, 2021.
78. Jeff Eldridge, liner notes for *Checkmate/Rhythm in Motion* (Film Score Monthly, 2006).
79. John L. Hess, "Goddard Lieberson, Who Fostered LP's at Columbia Records, Dies," *New York Times*, May 30, 1977.
80. C. H. Garrigues, "They've Put New Life into the 1926 Hit 'Oh, Kay!' with a 1958 Cast," *San Francisco Examiner*, January 26, 1958.
81. JW to TG, March 9, 2023.
82. "L.A. Variety Operation Is Evident in Industry," *Santa Maria Times*, May 27, 1963.
83. "Reviews of This Week's Singles," *The Billboard*, December 31, 1960.
84. "Record Roundup: The Music from TV's 'Checkmate,'" *Tucson Daily Citizen*, August 26, 1961.
85. Lester Koenig, liner notes for *Shelly Manne & His Men Play "Checkmate"* (Contemporary Records, 1962).
86. Andrew L. Pincus, "Poetry in Movements," *Berkshire Eagle*, July 24, 1998.
87. JW to TG, July 20, 2023.
88. Dyer, "Where Is John Williams Coming From?"
89. Laurraine Goreau, *Just Mahalia, Baby* (1975).
90. JW to Jimmy Marino, 2003.
91. Dyer, "Where Is John Williams Coming From?"
92. Tube., "The Secret Ways," *Variety*, March 22, 1961.
93. James Powers, "'Secret Ways' Is Superior Film for Program Booking," *Hollywood Reporter*, March 21, 1961.
94. Howard Thompson, "'The Secret Ways,' Spy Film with Richard Widmark, Arrives," *New York Times*, May 25, 1961.
95. JW to TG, March 9, 2023.
96. Dyer, "Where Is John Williams Coming From?"
97. JW to Burlingame, USC, 2006.
98. Ibid.
99. Burlingame, *TV's Biggest Hits*.
100. Dyer, "Where Is John Williams Coming From?"
101. Mitchell Zuckoff, *Robert Altman: The Oral Biography* (2009).
102. Eldridge, liner notes for *Checkmate/Rhythm in Motion*.
103. Ibid.
104. David Shire to TG, February 24, 2021.
105. JW to TG, June 2, 2023.
106. Jenny Williams to TG, April 1, 2023.
107. Eliot Tiegel, "News of the World," *Billboard*, July 25, 1964.
108. Clarence Fanto, "All That Glitters Is Not Gold in John Williams' 1964 Jazz Arrangement of 'My Fair Lady,'" *Berkshire Eagle*, August 11, 2004.
109. James Powers, "'Diamond Head' Has Potent Ingredients, Name Values," *Hollywood Reporter*, December 26, 1962.
110. Tube., "Diamond Head," *Variety*, December 26, 1962.
111. Tube., "Gidget Goes to Rome," *Variety*, July 31, 1963.
112. Clu Gulager interview from 2002, included in *The Killers* (The Criterion Collection, 2015).
113. Don Siegel, *A Siegel Film: An Autobiography* (1996).

114. "20th Rushes 'Goldfarb' into Showcase; Columbia and Par Defer Releases," *Variety*, March 24, 1965.
115. Eldridge, liner notes for *Checkmate/Rhythm in Motion*.
116. Bosley Crowther, "The Screen: 'John Goldfarb' Arrives," *New York Times*, March 25, 1965.
117. JW to TG, March 9, 2023.
118. Ibid.
119. Jenny Williams to TG, April 1, 2023.
120. JW to TG, April 14, 2023.
121. Jenny Williams to TG, March 10, 2023.
122. Joseph Williams to TG, June 29, 2022.
123. Rugolo to TG.
124. Jenny Williams to TG, March 10, 2023.
125. JW to Stan Warnow.
126. Deborah Scott Studebaker to TG, February 7, 2022.
127. Allen Rich, *Valley Times*, February 22, 1965, p. 23.
128. "Catnaps for All: 'Cindy' a Blitz Job, Barbara Ruick Notes," *Dayton Daily News*, February 24, 1965.
129. Harvey Siders, "Exciting Season: Neophonic Finale: Lo-Cal Suite-ness," *Los Angeles Evening Citizen News*, March 31, 1965.
130. Mimi Clair, "The Jazz Scene: Neophonic Blows Hot, Cold," *Los Angeles Times*, March 31, 1965.
131. John Williams, program note for concerts on December 7–8, 1965, program obtained from Houston Symphony Orchestra.
132. Donald Steinfirst, "Barenboim-Previn in Tune: Pianist Brightens Brahms," *Pittsburgh Post-Gazette*, December 10, 1966.
133. Martin Bernheimer, "Philharmonic Goes Modern, Sort Of," *Los Angeles Times*, May 26, 1967.
134. Dyer, "Where Is John Williams Coming From?"
135. Bosley Crowther, "Screen: Sinatra Directs," *New York Times*, February 25, 1965.
136. Whit., "None but the Brave," *Variety*, February 10, 1965.
137. Carroll Newman to TG, April 15, 2021.
138. Dyer, "John Williams Is New Pops Maestro," *Boston Globe*, January 11, 1980.
139. David Newman to TG, April 6, 2021.
140. Burlingame, *TV's Biggest Hits*.
141. JW to TG, December 19, 2023.
142. Tommy Morgan to TG, April 30, 2021.
143. JW to TG, March 9, 2023.
144. Carroll Newman to TG.
145. John Williams eulogy for Lionel Newman, February 8, 1989.
146. Leslie Bricusse to TG, June 15, 2021.
147. Don Williams to TG, June 29, 2018.
148. JW eulogy for Lionel Newman.
149. Ray Bennett, "John Williams," *Hollywood Reporter*, March 8, 2000.
150. Timothy Mangan, "John Williams Interview," *Gramophone*, May 2006.
151. Whit., "Penelope," *Variety*, November 9, 1966.

152. K.W., "'Penelope' May Be Worst Film of Year," *The Record* (Hackensack, NJ), November 11, 1966.
153. Allen Macaulay, "Record Roundup: New Side of Merv," *The Morning Call*, February 4, 1967.
154. Mark Volman to TG, June 13, 2023.
155. Bennett, "John Williams."
156. Carl Johnson, "An Interview with Herbert Spencer," *The Cue Sheet*, July 1990.
157. Stephen Rebello, *Dolls! Dolls! Dolls!* (2020).
158. "News of the Movies," *The Daily News Leader* (Staunton, VA), December 20, 1967.
159. Rebello, *Dolls! Dolls! Dolls!*.
160. Jon Burlingame, "Kenneth Wannberg, Composer and Music Editor Who Worked with John Williams on 'Star Wars' Series and 50 Other Films, Dies at 91," *Variety*, February 3, 2022.
161. Ken Wannberg to TG, April 9, 2021.
162. John Takis liner notes for *Heidi* (Quartet, 2013).
163. Delbert Mann, *Looking Back . . . at Live Television and Other Matters* (1998).
164. Leonard Feather, "From Pen to Screen," *International Musician*, April 1969.
165. JW to TG, March 9, 2023.
166. Jenny Williams to TG, March 10, 2023.
167. JW to TG, March 9, 2023 and June 2, 2023.
168. Burlingame, *TV's Biggest Hits*.
169. Ibid.
170. Brogger letter to Mann, January 11, 1968.
171. Gene Lees, "In Memory of Mercer," *American Film*, December 1, 1977.
172. Mann, *Looking Back*.
173. Percy Shain, "'Heidi'—Brilliance a Classic Deserves," *Boston Globe*, November 18, 1968.
174. Mann, *Looking Back*.
175. JW eulogy for Lionel Newman.
176. Randy Newman to TG, August 30, 2023.
177. Jenny Williams to TG, April 1, 2023.
178. Carroll Newman to TG.

Chapter 5

1. JW to TG, March 9, 2023.
2. Leslie Bricusse, *Pure Imagination: A Sorta-Biography* (2015).
3. Francis Ford Coppola to TG, May 25, 2021.
4. Bricusse, *Pure Imagination*.
5. Petula Clark to TG, April 14, 2023.
6. Peter O'Toole interview on location for MGM publicity, included on *Goodbye, Mr. Chips* (Film Score Monthly, 2006).
7. Bricusse, *Pure Imagination*.
8. Petula Clark to TG.
9. *Personal Notes*, 1988.
10. JW to Steven C. Smith.
11. Program supplied by Houston Symphony Orchestra.

12. All correspondence from John during the production of *Chips* from "MGM Production Department files," collection at USC Libraries Cinematic Arts Library.
13. Abe Greenberg, "Barbara's Busted Beak or 'Boomtown or Bust'?" *Valley Times*, May 5, 1969.
14. Jenny Williams to TG, December 14, 2023.
15. JW letter to Lionel Newman, April 22, 1969.
16. JW to TG, March 17, 2023.
17. JW letter to Lionel Newman, April 22, 1969.
18. Mike Matessino, liner notes for *Goodbye, Mr. Chips* (Film Score Monthly, 2006).
19. John Grover to TG, January 28, 2022.
20. Matessino, liner notes for *Goodbye, Mr. Chips*.
21. Jenny Williams to TG, December 14, 2023.
22. Harvey Southgate, "Wind Ensemble Tests Eardrums," *Democrat and Chronicle*, May 1, 1969.
23. JW letter to Lewis Roth, April 17, 1969.
24. JW letter to Previn, April 18, 1969.
25. Mia Farrow to TG.
26. Details about Bergman lyrics and Schifrin's rejected score found in "CBS, Inc.," collection at UCLA Library Special Collections Performing Arts.
27. Robert Relyea, *Not So Quiet on the Set: My Life in Movies During Hollywood's Macho Era* (2008).
28. Mark Rydell to TG, April 29, 2021.
29. Charles Burr, liner notes for *The Reivers* (Columbia Records, 1969).
30. John Caps, "John Williams—Scoring the Film Whole," *Filmmusic Notebook*, 1976.
31. Rick., "The Reivers," *Variety*, November 26, 1969.
32. John Mahoney, "How Long Since You've Seen a Movie for Fun? Here's One," *Hollywood Reporter*, November 26, 1969.
33. Pauline Kael, "The Current Cinema: Americana," *New Yorker*, December 27, 1969.
34. John Caps, "John Williams: Scoring the Central Line," *The Cue Sheet* vol. 8, no. 3 (1991): 110–117.
35. JW to TG, March 17, 2023.
36. Dyer, "Where is John Williams Coming From?".
37. JW to TG, March 17, 2023.
38. Rydell to TG.
39. Dyer, "Sounds of Spielberg," *Boston Globe*, February 24, 1998.
40. Irwin Bazelon, *Knowing the Score: Notes on Film Music* (1975).
41. Barbara Isenberg, *Tradition! The Highly Improbable, Ultimately Triumphant Broadway-to-Hollywood Story of Fiddler on the Roof, the World's Most Beloved Musical* (2014).
42. Ibid.
43. "John Williams: Creating a Musical Tradition," feature on *Fiddler on the Roof* home video release (Metro-Goldwyn-Mayer, 2011).
44. Isenberg, *Tradition!*
45. "John Williams: Creating a Musical Tradition."
46. JW to TG, November 4, 2022.
47. Sandy DeCrescent to TG, February 9, 2023.
48. Jenny Williams to TG, March 10, 2023.

49. Mia Farrow to TG.
50. JW to TG, June 2, 2023.
51. Robert Graves, *The White Goddess* (1948).
52. Isenberg, *Tradition!*
53. Ibid.
54. Norman Jewison, *This Terrible Business Has Been Good to Me* (2004).
55. Isenberg, *Tradition!*
56. Elley, "The Film Composer: 3: John Williams.".
57. Mann, *Looking Back*.
58. Elley, "The Film Composer: 3: John Williams."
59. JW to TG, March 17, 2023.
60. Mann, *Looking Back*.
61. Edward L. Blank, "'Jane' Demonstrates the 'Eyre' of Delbert Mann's Ways," *Pittsburgh Press*, March 25, 1971.
62. Jamie Portman, "New Film Version of *Jane Eyre* a Vivid and Poignant Experience," *Calgary Herald*, January 30, 1971.
63. Karen Tyler, "What's Your Problem?" *Newsday* (Suffolk Edition), April 8, 1971.
64. Bazelon, *Knowing the Score*.
65. Tony Thomas, "A Conversation with John Williams," *The Cue Sheet* vol. 8, no. 1 (1991): 6–15.
66. JW to TG, March 9, 2023.
67. JW letter to Frederick Brogger, June 12, 1971, from "The Delbert Mann Papers" collection, Jean and Alexander Heard Library at Vanderbilt University.
68. "Dialogue on Film: Mark Rydell," *American Film*, June 1982.
69. Rydell to TG.
70. Morgan to TG.
71. Rydell commentary on *The Cowboys* home video release (Warner Bros., 2007).
72. Vincent Canby, "Screen: 'The Cowboys,'" *New York Times*, January 14, 1972.
73. Roger Ebert, "The Cowboys," *Chicago Sun-Times*, January 1, 1972.
74. "TV/Film Composers' Union Strike Demands Juicier Cut," *Billboard*, December 11, 1971.
75. Theodore Price, "Wind Ensemble Pulls Out Stops," *Democrat and Chronicle*, April 8, 1972.
76. Gerald Larner, "John T. Williams's First Symphony at the Nottingham Festival," *The Guardian*, July 10, 1972.
77. Peter Palmer, "Rousing Stuff as Previn Packs 'Em In," *Evening Post* (Nottingham), July 10, 1972.
78. JW to Steven C. Smith.
79. Elley, "The Film Composer: 3: John Williams."
80. "Final Concert of Season Announced by Symphony," *Valley News*, September 12, 1972.
81. "Hollywood Soundtrack," *Variety*, March 3, 1971.
82. David Thompson, *Altman on Altman* (2006).
83. Bazelon, *Knowing the Score*.
84. Stomu Yamash'ta to TG, December 13, 2021.
85. Graeme Clifford to TG, October 21, 2021.
86. "Imagining Images," feature from 2003, included on *Images* home video release (Arrow Academy, 2018).
87. "The Music Man," *Films Illustrated*, May 1972.

88. Lloyd Ibert, "Images," *Independent Film Journal*, June 8, 1972.
89. Jeanne Miller, "A Daring Attempt to Convey Madness," *San Francisco Examiner*, February 1, 1973.
90. Joe Baltake, "Altman's 'Images': A Film of Awesome Beauty," *Philadelphia Daily News*, September 12, 1973.
91. R. H. Gardner, "R. H. Gardner's Guide to the Movies," *Baltimore Sun*, June 26, 1973.
92. Micheline Keating, "'Images' Won't Let You Relax," *Tucson Citizen*, October 4, 1973.
93. "Stupids Expected at Fest, but Two Directors Pick Up Facts," *Variety*, October 24, 1973.
94. Zuckoff, *Robert Altman*.
95. Yamash'ta to TG.
96. JW liner notes for unreleased soundtrack album produced in *Images* (Quartet Records, 2021).
97. Christopher Palmer, "The Changing World of Film Music: Composer John Williams," *Crescendo International*, April 1972.
98. Alex Ross, "The Force Is Still Strong with John Williams," *New Yorker*, July 21, 2020.
99. https://www.youtube.com/watch?v=3ZK4e08uW1Y.
100. Norman Schwartz to TG, May 12, 2022.
101. Elley, "The Film Composer: 3: John Williams."
102. Howard Thompson, "'Pete 'n' Tillie,' Comedy, Opens at Baronet," *New York Times*, December 18, 1972.
103. Murf., "Pete 'n' Tillie," *Variety*, December 13, 1972.
104. Charles Champlin, "The Comedy 'n' Tragedy in Pete 'n' Tillie,'" *Los Angeles Times*, December 17, 1972.
105. Dale Munroe, "Pete 'n' Tillie," *Motion Picture Daily*, December 15, 1972.
106. Ronald Neame, commentary on *The Poseidon Adventure* home video release (20th Century Fox, 2000).
107. Jeff Bond, liner notes for *The Poseidon Adventure* (La-La Land Records, 2019).
108. Neame commentary.
109. JW to TG, December 19, 2023.
110. Caps, "Scoring the Central Line."
111. "The Poseidon Adventure," *Independent Film Journal*, December 11, 1972.
112. Whit., "The Poseidon Adventure," *Variety*, December 13, 1972.
113. Richard Dyer, *Nino Rota: Music, Film and Feeling* (2010).
114. David Thompson, *Altman on Altman*.
115. Zuckoff, *Robert Altman*.
116. *Johnny Mercer: "The Dream's on Me"* (Turner Classic Movies, 2009).
117. Zuckoff, *Robert Altman*.
118. Champlin, "A Private Eye's Honor, Blackened," *Los Angeles Times*, March 8, 1973.
119. Murf., "The Long Goodbye," *Variety*, March 7, 1973.
120. "Rip Van Marlowe," feature on *The Long Goodbye* home video release (MGM, 2002).
121. Pauline Kael, "The Current Cinema: Movieland—The Bums' Paradise," *New Yorker*, October 22, 1973.
122. Zuckoff, *Robert Altman*.
123. JW interview for *The Boys: The Sherman Brothers' Story* (ca. 2009).
124. Richard Sherman to John Takis, November 23, 2015.
125. Ibid.

126. Ibid.
127. JW, note for concerto from *John Williams: Concerto for Violin and Orchestra, Concerto for Flute and Orchestra* (Varèse Sarabande Records, 1983).
128. Sheridon Stokes to Maurizio Caschetto, January 2021, https://thelegacyofjohnwilliams.com/2021/01/18/sheridon-stokes-podcast/.
129. Richard Slater, "Williams' Work Given Premiere," *Los Angeles Times*, March 7, 1973.
130. JW to TG, October 28, 2022.
131. Ibid.
132. JW to TG, July 20, 2023.
133. John Mauceri to TG, May 24, 2023.
134. "New York Sound Track," *Variety*, August 22, 1973.
135. "Fox Out-Races Hounds of TV," *Variety*, September 19, 1973.
136. "A Women's Lib Oater," *Variety*, January 12, 1972.
137. "The Man Who Loved Cat Dancing," *Variety*, May 2, 1973.
138. Eldridge, liner notes for *The Man Who Loved Cat Dancing* (Film Score Monthly, 2002).
139. Morgan to TG.
140. Vincent Canby, "'The Man Who Loved Cat Dancing' Opens," *New York Times*, June 29, 1973.
141. Paul Williams to TG, March 25, 2021.
142. Don Lass, "Record Previews: Sinatra Is Back," *Asbury Park Press*, November 4, 1974.
143. Rydell to TG.
144. Ibid.
145. Paul Williams to TG.
146. Champlin, "Ponicsan Films Plumb the Depths of Navy Life," *Los Angeles Times*, December 9, 1973.
147. Murf., "Cinderella Liberty," *Variety*, December 12, 1973.
148. Gene Siskel, "Cinderella Liberty," *Chicago Tribune*, February 5, 1974.
149. Quincy Jones to TG, August 31, 2017.
150. Rydell to TG.
151. Rydell, commentary for *Cinderella Liberty* home video release (20th Century Fox, 2006).
152. Rydell to TG.
153. "20th-Fox Committed to Georgia Locale," *Boxoffice*, January 8, 1973.
154. Jay Samuels, "'Conrack' Rewards Moviegoers with Magic of Cinema," *Camden Courier-Post*, March 27, 1974.
155. Tony Macklin, "Jon Voight a Joy to Watch in 'Conrack,'" *The Journal Herald* (Dayton, OH), April 12, 1974.
156. Morgan to TG.
157. Caps, "Scoring the Central Line."
158. Jim Stingley, "Real 'Conrack': Evolution of a Country Boy," *Los Angeles Times*, April 12, 1974.
159. Zuckoff, *Robert Altman*.
160. Konni Corriere to TG, March 3, 2021.
161. Zuckoff, *Robert Altman*.
162. Joey Walsh to TG, August 15, 2023.
163. Edye Rugolo to TG.
164. Jenny Williams to TG, April 1, 2023.

165. Elliott Gould to TG, February 1, 2021.
166. Ibid.
167. Bobby Altman to TG, February 23, 2021.
168. Jenny Williams to TG, April 1, 2023.
169. Barbara's autopsy report provided by Washoe County, Nevada.
170. Linda Deutsch, "Composer Quincy Jones Survives Ballooning Brain Blood Vessels," *Reno Gazette-Journal*, October 16, 1974.
171. Corriere to TG.
172. Joseph Williams to TG.
173. JW to TG, March 9, 2023.
174. Jenny Williams to TG, March 6, 2024.
175. Jenny Williams to TG, December 14, 2023.
176. Ibid.
177. Carroll Newman to TG.
178. Panel discussion, "Behind the Score: The Art of the Film Composer," July 21, 2014, https://www.youtube.com/watch?v=_heFn4nmScI&t.
179. JW to TG, March 9, 2023.
180. Jenny Williams to TG, December 14, 2023.

Chapter 6

1. Steven Spielberg to TG, December 5, 2023.
2. Rebecca Keegan, "John Williams and Steven Spielberg Mark 40 Years of Collaboration," *Los Angeles Times*, January 8, 2012.
3. "Steven Spielberg & John Williams: The Adventure Continues," documentary by Laurent Bouzereau, included on *John Williams • Steven Spielberg: The Ultimate Collection* (Sony Classics, 2017).
4. Fred A. Bernstein, *The Jewish Mothers' Hall of Fame* (1986).
5. Spielberg to TG.
6. Ibid.
7. Ibid.
8. *Star Wars—Music by John Williams*, written and produced by David Buckton (BBC, 1980).
9. Joseph McBride, *Steven Spielberg: A Biography* (1997).
10. Ibid.
11. Spielberg to TG.
12. Elmer Bernstein, "What Ever Happened to Great Movie Music?" *High Fidelity*, July 1972.
13. McBride, *Steven Spielberg*.
14. Ibid.
15. Charles Fox to TG, January 24, 2024.
16. Spielberg to TG.
17. Dyer, "John Williams: New Horizons, Familiar Galaxies," *Boston Globe*, June 4, 1997.
18. McBride, *Steven Spielberg*.
19. Stephen Farber, "There's Something Sour About 'The Sugarland Express,'" *New York Times*, April 28, 1974.
20. Pauline Kael, "The Current Cinema: Sugarland and Badlands," *New Yorker*, March 18, 1974.

21. Bouzereau, "Steven Spielberg & John Williams: The Adventure Continues."
22. Spielberg, liner notes for *The Spielberg/Williams Collaboration* (Sony Classical, 1991).
23. Spielberg to TG.
24. T. R. Goldman, "'Toots' Thielemans, Master of the Jazz Harmonica, Dies at 94," *Washington Post*, August 22, 2016.
25. Mike Lang to TG, April 8, 2021.
26. Spielberg to Edith Bowman, *Soundtracking* podcast, December 13, 2021, https://edithbowman.com/2021/12/5667/
27. Spielberg to TG.
28. Tom Shone, "How to Score in the Movies," *The Sunday Times*, June 21, 1998.
29. Keegan, "John Williams and Steven Spielberg Mark 40 Years of Collaboration."
30. Bouzereau, "Steven Spielberg & John Williams: The Adventure Continues."
31. Spielberg to TG.
32. Ibid.
33. Kathleen Kennedy to TG, May 3, 2024.
34. Jenny Williams to TG, March 10, 2023.
35. Jones commentary.
36. Klein to TG.
37. Mancini to TG.
38. Edye Rugolo to TG.
39. Jenny Williams to TG, April 1, 2023.
40. JW to TG, October 9, 2023.
41. JW to TG, March 17, 2023.
42. Zuckoff, *Robert Altman*.
43. David Patrick Stearns, "Showcasing Classical Side of Titan of Film Score," *Philadelphia Inquirer*, April 26, 2016.
44. Stokes to Caschetto.
45. Jenny Williams to TG, April 1, 2023.
46. JW, liner notes for *Earthquake* (MCA Records, 1974).
47. Murf., "Earthquake," *Variety*, November 13, 1974.
48. Champlin, "Rattled by 'Earthquake,'" *Los Angeles Times*, November 15, 1974.
49. Champlin, "Oscar Race '75: Blockbusters Versus Gems," *Los Angeles Times*, January 12, 1975.
50. *Towering Inferno* ad in *Independent Film Journal*, May 15, 1974.
51. "'Inferno' Producer Sees No End to Crisis Films," *Boxoffice*, October 28, 1974.
52. Elley, "The Film Composer: 3: John Williams.".
53. "Dylan, Buffy, 'Inferno,' Manzarek, Baker Gurvitz, Hello, Sledge, Kiss, Brenda Patterson, Rifkin Top LPs," *Variety*, January 22, 1975.
54. Champlin, "'Inferno': How to Exceed in Disaster Films," *Los Angeles Times*, December 15, 1974.
55. Siskel, "The Year That Santa Said Oh! Oh! Oh!" *Chicago Tribune*, October 13, 1974.
56. Vernon Scott, "Clint Eastwood Finds Out About Himself—The Hard Way," *UPI*, syndicated in Kenosha News, May 17, 1975.
57. "Re-Scripted 'Eiger,'" *Variety*, February 13, 1974.
58. Clint Eastwood to TG, October 2, 2020.
59. JW to TG, December 19, 2023.

580 Notes

60. Kevin Thomas, "Eastwood Keeps Cool on the Eiger," *Los Angeles Times*, May 23, 1975.
61. Canby, "'Eiger Sanction,' Film of Climbing Spies," *New York Times*, May 22, 1975.
62. Frank Daley, "The Eiger Sanction May Be Year's Worst Film," *Ottawa Journal*, May 23, 1975.
63. Wayne Harada, "Predictable Eastwood," *Honolulu Advertiser*, June 18, 1975.
64. "Bruce, Focus, Giant, Taylor, Phillips, Buchanan, Kaempfert, Light, Leandros Top New LPs," *Variety*, September 3, 1975.
65. Charles Higham, "You May Not Leave the Movie House Singing Their Songs, But …" *New York Times*, May 25, 1975.
66. Most JW quotes about *Thomas and the King* from interview with TG, April 14, 2023.
67. Matessino, liner notes for *How to Steal a Million/Bachelor Flat* (Intrada Records, 2008).
68. All Sam Grossman quotes about *Thomas* from interview with TG, March 1, 2021.
69. All James Smillie quotes from interview with TG, February 14, 2021.
70. R. B. M., "Her Majesty's 'Thomas and the King,'" *The Stage and Television Today*, October 23, 1975.
71. Charles Lewsen, "Thomas and the King: Her Majesty's," *The Times* (London), October 17, 1975.
72. Klein to TG.
73. Dyer, "Reluctant Williams Remembers Early Stage Foray," *Boston Globe*, October 12, 2001.
74. "Major Theatrical Projects Revealed by Producer Witt," *Hollywood Reporter*, May 15, 1975. Don Black confirmed to TG on May 16, 2024: "I was very close to Peter Witt, who was a very colorful and excitable theater producer. He produced a musical of mine called Billy which I wrote with John Barry. I remember him saying that he could get John Williams to write the music for *Cashel Byron's Profession*, so I read it and was hoping this might happen. As you and I and the world knows, it didn't happen. Shame."
75. Tony Harrison, *Collected Film Poetry* (2007).
76. "Morning Pro Musica," radio program hosted by Robert J. Lurtsema (WGBH, June 23, 1983).
77. JW to Jim Svejda (KUSC), April 7, 2017.
78. Keegan, "John Williams and Steven Spielberg Mark 40 Years of Collaboration."
79. McBride, *Steven Spielberg*.
80. Keegan, "John Williams and Steven Spielberg Mark 40 Years of Collaboration."
81. Ben Hoyle, "We All Thought Star Wars Would Be Great for Three Weekends," *The Times* (London), May 10, 2019.
82. McBride, *Steven Spielberg*.
83. Spielberg, liner notes for *Jaws: Anniversary Collector's Edition* (Decca, 2000).
84. Burlingame, "John Williams Recalls Jaws," *Film Music Society*, August 14, 2012.
85. "Dialogue on Film: Verna Fields," *American Film*, June 1, 1976.
86. Spielberg liner notes, *Jaws*.
87. Hans Zimmer to TG, January 12, 2022.
88. Thomas Newman to Mark Forrest, Scala Radio, February 8, 2022.
89. Spielberg to TG.
90. Shone, "How to Score in the Movies."
91. Carl Gottlieb, *The Jaws Log: 30th Anniversary Edition* (2010).
92. Claire Noland, "Tommy Johnson, 71; Noted Tuba Player's Movie Work Boosted the Tension in 'Jaws,'" *Los Angeles Times*, October 25, 2006.

93. Ralph Grierson to TG, April 22, 2021.
94. Noland, "Tommy Johnson."
95. Ibid.
96. JW to Svejda, 2017.
97. Elley, "The Film Composer: 3: John Williams."
98. Ronnie Lang to TG.
99. Javier C. Hernández, "John Williams, Hollywood's Maestro, Looks Beyond the Movies," *New York Times*, February 8, 2022.
100. *Soundtracking*.
101. JW to Tommy Pearson, Classic FM, August 27, 2012.
102. https://www.billboard.com/artist/john-williams/chart-history/hsi/.
103. Slatkin to TG.
104. J. W. Rinzler and Lee Unkrich, *Stanley Kubrick's The Shining* (2022).
105. Mark Eden Horowitz, *Sondheim on Music: Minor Details and Major Decisions* (2003).
106. McBride, *Steven Spielberg*.
107. Bruce Dern, Christopher Fryer, and Robert Crane, *Bruce Dern: Things I've Said, But Probably Shouldn't Have: An Unrepentant Memoir* (2007).
108. JW to Steven C. Smith.
109. A. D. Murphy, "Bernard Herrmann, 64, Dies," *Variety*, December 31, 1975.
110. Dyer, "The Music Man," *Boston Globe*, October 7, 1990.
111. JW to TG, August 21, 2023.
112. Bennett, *Hollywood Reporter*, 2000.
113. Jack Sullivan, "Hitchcock and Music," in *A Companion to Alfred Hitchcock*, edited by Thomas Leitch and Leland Poague (2011),.
114. "Plotting Family Plot," documentary feature included in *Family Plot* home video release (Universal, 2013).
115. Richard Corliss, "Let Us Not Praise Famous Men," *New Times*, April 16, 1975.
116. Sullivan, "Hitchcock and Music."
117. Elley, "The Film Composer: 3: John Williams."
118. Morgan to TG.
119. Murf., "The Missouri Breaks," *Variety*, May 19, 1976.
120. "The Missouri Breaks," *Boxoffice*, May 31, 1976.
121. Mike Petryni, "'Missouri Breaks' Is Magnificent," *Arizona Republic*, May 26, 1976.
122. "The Score of Midway," feature on *Midway* home video release (Universal, 2013).
123. "Smight on 'Midway,'" *Variety*, March 19, 1975.
124. "The Score of Midway."
125. Joseph McBride, "Carl Foreman Muses on Mankind Obsessed by Terror Threats," *Variety*, June 16, 1976.
126. Bernard Drew, "John Frankenheimer: His Fall and Rise," *American Film*, March 1, 1977.
127. Scott Bettencourt, Mike Matessino, Jeff Eldridge, and Alexander Kaplan, liner notes for *Black Sunday* (Film Score Monthly, 2010).
128. Aljean Harmetz, "Frankenheimer Rides a Blimp to a Big, Fat Comeback," *New York Times*, April 10, 1977.
129. Arthur Knight, "Black Sunday," *Hollywood Reporter*, March 25, 1977.
130. Champlin, "Fuses Burning at All Ends in 'Black Sunday,'" *Los Angeles Times*, March 27, 1977.

131. Hoyle, "We All Thought Star Wars Would Be Great for Three Weekends."
132. Carroll Newman to TG.
133. JW to TG, November 8, 2023.
134. JW to TG, March 9, 2023.
135. Jenny Williams to TG, March 10, 2023.
136. Carroll Newman to TG.
137. Spielberg to TG.

Chapter 7

1. "Making Of" documentary included on *Close Encounters of the Third Kind* home video release (Columbia Pictures, 2017).
2. Matthew Robbins to TG, August 17, 2021.
3. J. W. Rinzler, *The Making of Star Wars* (2007).
4. Robbins to TG.
5. Mark Hamill to TG, May 10, 2017.
6. Paul Hirsch to TG, October 3, 2014.
7. George Lucas, interview with Leonard Maltin, included on *Star Wars* home video release (20th Century Fox, 1995), VHS.
8. Rinzler, *The Making of Star Wars*.
9. Elley, "The Film Composer: 3: John Williams.".
10. Rinzler, *The Making of Star Wars*.
11. Hirsch to TG.
12. Jon Burlingame, "Spielberg and Lucas on Williams," *Film Music Society*, February 8, 2012, http://www.filmmusicsociety.org/news_events/features/2012/020812.html.
13. Rinzler, *The Making of Star Wars*.
14. Ibid.
15. Marcia Lucas to TG, May 31, 2023.
16. Mangan, "John Williams Interview," 2006.
17. Alex Ross, *New Yorker*, 2020.
18. JW to TG, April 14, 2023.
19. Most JW quotes about *Star Wars* themes are from his liner notes for *Star Wars* (20th Century Records, 1977).
20. Ross, *New Yorker*, 2020.
21. Hamill to TG.
22. Rinzler, *The Making of Star Wars*.
23. JW liner notes for *Star Wars*.
24. "Morning Pro Musica," 1983.
25. Wannberg to TG.
26. Dale Pollock, *Skywalking* (1990).
27. Mark Swed, "'Blurred Lines' Verdict Would Rock Amadeus and Other Great Composers," *Los Angeles Times*, March 14, 2015.
28. JW to TG, November 8, 2023.
29. JW to TG, December 19, 2023.
30. Ross, "Listening to 'Star Wars,'" *New Yorker*, January 1, 2016.

31. Ross, "Scoring for Oscar," *New Yorker*, March 9, 1998.
32. Ross to TG, December 16, 2022.
33. Frank Lehman to TG, January 10, 2023.
34. JW to TG, March 9, 2023.
35. Stephen Williams, "The Force Behind the Pops," *Newsday* (Nassau edition), July 7, 1985.
36. JW to TG, March 9, 2023.
37. Laurie Winer, *Oscar Hammerstein II and the Invention of the Musical* (2023).
38. JW to TG, March 9, 2023.
39. Rinzler, *The Making of Star Wars*.
40. Ibid.
41. Hirsch to TG.
42. Wannberg to TG.
43. Ben Burtt to TG, November 16, 2021.
44. JW to TG, April 14, 2023.
45. Wannberg to TG.
46. Elley, "The Film Composer: 3: John Williams."
47. Ibid.
48. Harrison Ford to TG, December 16, 2021.
49. Hamill to TG.
50. Charles A. Barrett, "Fox Pressing to Meet 'Star Wars' Disc Demand," *Hollywood Reporter*, June 3, 1977.
51. Rinzler, *The Making of Star Wars*.
52. JW to TG, April 14, 2023.
53. https://www.billboard.com/artist/meco/.
54. JW quote on packaging for *Superman and Other Galactic Heroes* by Meco (Casablanca Records and Filmworks, Inc., 1979).
55. Colin Vaines, "The Unsung Virtues of the Music Men," *Screen International*, October 8, 1977.
56. Alexandre Desplat to TG, December 8, 2008.
57. Andrew Stanton to TG, May 24, 2022.
58. *Personal Notes*.
59. Ross, *New Yorker*, 2016.
60. Bob Balaban, *Spielberg, Truffaut & Me: Close Encounters of the Third Kind, an Actor's Diary* (2002).
61. Bruce Cook, "Close Encounters with Steven Spielberg," *American Film*, November 1, 1977.
62. McBride, *Steven Spielberg*.
63. Ibid.
64. "Making of" *Close Encounters*.
65. Elley, "The Film Composer: 3: John Williams."
66. Ian Lace, "The Film Music of John Williams" (1998), https://www.musicweb-internatio nal.com/film/lacejw.htm.
67. Julia Phillips, *You'll Never Eat Lunch in This Town Again* (1991).
68. Balaban, *Spielberg, Truffaut & Me*.
69. Ibid.
70. Richard Dreyfuss to TG, February 17, 2021.

71. Advertisement, *Variety*, December 2, 1977.
72. "Three Kinds of Close Encounters," featurette on *Close Encounters* (Columbia Pictures, 2017), Blu-ray.
73. Zimmer to TG.
74. JW to TG, July 20, 2023.
75. "Three Kinds of Close Encounters."
76. Elley, "The Film Composer: 3: John Williams."
77. JW to TG, October 28, 2022.
78. *Morning Pro Musica*.
79. Spielberg, liner notes for *Close Encounters of the Third Kind* (Arista Records, 1977).
80. Burlingame, "Spielberg and Lucas on Williams."
81. Michael Kahn to TG, April 6, 2021.
82. Howard Kazanjian to TG, April 7, 2021.
83. Paul Schrader to TG, March 25, 2021.
84. Janet Maslin, "Spielberg's Journey from Sharks to the Stars," *New York Times*, November 13, 1977.
85. Dyer, "Williams: On Record," *Boston Globe*, June 25, 1980.
86. Balaban, *Spielberg, Truffaut & Me*.
87. Ibid.
88. McBride, *Steven Spielberg*.
89. JW to TG, March 7, 2023.
90. Maslin, "Spielberg's Journey from Sharks to the Stars."
91. Michael Phillips to TG, February 25, 2021.
92. Spielberg liner notes.
93. Ross, *New Yorker*, 2016.
94. Spielberg to TG.
95. "Three Kinds of Close Encounters."
96. Zimmer to TG.
97. *Rock Center with Brian Williams*, July 26, 2012, NBC.
98. Dan Skartvedt, "Rock Fans Roar Approval at Symphony's Space Suite," *Long Beach Press-Telegram*, November 21, 1977.
99. Zubin Mehta to TG, August 8, 2022.
100. Heuwell Tircuit, "Smashing Success of 'Star Wars' and 'Close Encounters' Concerts," *San Francisco Examiner*, February 5, 1978.
101. https://www.laphil.com/about/watch-and-listen/the-la-phil-and-the-force.
102. "The Evening Program," hosted by Jim Svejda, Classical KUSC, April 7, 2017.
103. "Flexibility—That's the Name of the Game," *Stage and Television Today*, February 23, 1978.
104. "New York Sound Track," *Variety*, March 15, 1978.
105. William Livingstone, "John Williams and the Boston Pops: An American Institution Enters a New Era," *Stereo Review*, December 1980.
106. Charles A. Barrett, "Redgrave Draws Two Demonstration Groups to Oscars," *Hollywood Reporter*, April 4, 1978.
107. https://www.youtube.com/watch?v=zaJTETd_grg.

Chapter 8

1. Colin Vaines, "The Superman Film Composer," *Screen International*, July 29, 1978.
2. Zimmer to TG.
3. Elley, "The Film Composer: 3: John Williams.".
4. Maslin, "'The Swarm,' by Allen, Flies onto Screens," *New York Times*, July 15, 1978.
5. Canby, "Film: Altman Offers Apocalyptic Fantasy," *New York Times*, February 9, 1979.
6. *Morning Pro Musica*.
7. Vaines, "Meet the Man Who Loves Complications," *Screen International*, October 21, 1978.
8. Elley, "The Film Composer: 3: John Williams."
9. Hirsch to TG.
10. Elley, "The Film Composer: 3: John Williams."
11. *The Fury* (La-La Land Records, 2012).
12. Hirsch to TG.
13. Joseph Williams to TG.
14. Joseph Williams, interview, *Game Changers with Vicki Abelson*, June 5, 2024, https://www.youtube.com/live/mQzIRZ4SNKM.
15. Ron Pennington, "The Fury," *Hollywood Reporter*, March 10, 1978.
16. Kael, "The Current Cinema: Shivers," *New Yorker*, March 20, 1978.
17. "Spielberg Spanks Sequels as 'Cheap, Carnival Trick,'" *Variety*, October 29, 1975.
18. McBride, *Steven Spielberg*.
19. "John Williams: The Music of Jaws 2," feature on *Jaws 2* home video release (Universal, 2016).
20. John Cocchi, "Actor David Elliott Declares 'Jaws 2' Is Good 'Artistically, Technically,'" *Boxoffice*, February 13, 1978.
21. Michael Dempsey, "The Return of Jaws," *American Film*, June 1, 1978.
22. Arthur Knight, "Jaws 2," *Hollywood Reporter*, June 5, 1978.
23. "The Music of Jaws 2."
24. "Plenty of Teeth in MCA 'Jaws 2' Soundtrack Push," *Billboard*, June 10, 1978.
25. Champlin, "'Jaws' the 2nd Time Around," *Los Angeles Times*, June 16, 1978.
26. "The Music of Jaws 2."
27. "John Williams to Replace Ailing Fiedler at Hollywood Bowl," *Los Angeles Times*, July 22, 1978.
28. Lewis Segal, "John Williams Conducts at Bowl," *Los Angeles Times*, July 31, 1978.
29. Vaines, "The Superman Film Composer."
30. Liz Smith, "Denials Make the Heart Beat Faster," *Daily News* (New York), November 29, 1977.
31. David Wessel, "The Force Is with Him . . . ," *Boston Globe*, July 5, 1983.
32. Richard Donner to TG, July 31, 2014.
33. Elley, "The Film Composer: 3: John Williams."
34. Joseph Gelmis, "Gelmis / Getting Superman off the Ground," *Newsday* (Nassau edition), December 17, 1978.
35. Robbins to TG.
36. Matessino, liner notes for *Superman: The Movie* (La-La Land Records, 2019).
37. Ibid.
38. Donner to TG.

39. "Making Superman: Filming the Legend," feature on *Superman: The Movie* home video release (Warner Bros. Entertainment, 2001).
40. Donner to TG.
41. "Making Superman."
42. Paul Williams to TG.
43. All Bricusse quotes about *Superman* are from his memoir, *Pure Imagination*.
44. Hamill to TG.
45. Champlin, "Man of Steel, Feat of Clay," *Los Angeles Times*, December 15, 1978.
46. Kael, "The Current Cinema: The Package," *New Yorker*, December 24, 1978.
47. Ebert, "Superman: The Movie," *Chicago Tribune*, December 15, 1978.
48. Zimmer to TG, March 26, 2013.
49. Mike Matessino, Lukas Kendall, and Jeff Eldridge, liner notes for *Superman: The Music (1978–1988)* (Film Score Monthly, 2008).
50. Marilyn Beck, "Dick Van Dyke Likes Dramatic Roles, May Not Return to Comedy for Awhile," *Democrat and Chronicle*, January 19, 1979.
51. *Superman: The Music.*
52. JW to TG, March 9, 2023.
53. Vaines, "Tasting the Blood of Box Office," *Screen International*, January 20, 1979.
54. Ibid.
55. John Badham to TG, April 19, 2023.
56. Badham, liner notes for *Dracula* (MCA Records, 1979).
57. Badham to TG.
58. "The Revamping of Dracula," feature on *Dracula* home video release (Scream Factory, 2019).
59. Badham to TG.
60. Ibid.
61. John Bloom, interview feature on *Dracula* (Scream Factory).
62. Badham to TG.
63. Pennington, "Dracula," *Hollywood Reporter*, July 6, 1979.
64. Maslin, "Screen: Langella's Seductive 'Dracula' Adapted from Stage," *New York Times*, July 13, 1979.
65. Gary Arnold, "A 'Dracula' That Makes It Count," *Washington Post*, July 13, 1979.
66. Jack Garner, "Again—and Better," *Democrat and Chronicle*, July 14, 1979.
67. Badham liner notes.
68. McBride, *Steven Spielberg*.
69. Champlin, "Spielberg's Pearl Harbor," *Los Angeles Times*, December 14, 1979.
70. McBride, *Steven Spielberg*.
71. Ibid.
72. "The Making of 1941," feature on *1941* home video release (Universal, 2015).
73. Chris Hodenfield, "'1941': Bombs Away!" *Rolling Stone*, January 24, 1980.
74. "The Making of 1941."
75. Ibid.
76. Ibid.
77. Bob Gale to TG, April 7, 2021.
78. "The Making of 1941."
79. Ibid.

80. Matessino, liner notes for *1941* (La-La Land Records, 2011).
81. Elliot Tiegel, "Talent in Action," *Billboard*, November 10, 1979.
82. Hodenfield, "'1941': Bombs Away!"
83. Canby, "Film: California Goes to War in '1941,'" *New York Times*, December 14, 1979.
84. Ebert, "1941," *Chicago Tribune*, December 14, 1979.
85. Poll., "1941," *Variety*, December 19, 1979.
86. Hodenfield, "'1941': Bombs Away!"
87. Thomas Morris to TG, January 22, 2021.

Chapter 9

1. Martin Amis, "The World According to Spielberg," *The Observer* (London), November 21, 1982.
2. Caps, *Soundtrack*, 1982.
3. Dyer, "Mix Design and Mystery, You Get a Pops Maestro," *Boston Globe*, January 17, 1980.
4. https://muppet.fandom.com/wiki/Arthur_Fiedler.
5. Morris to TG.
6. Dyer to TG, May 1, 2020.
7. Morris to TG.
8. Ibid.
9. Harry Ellis Dickson, *Arthur Fiedler and the Boston Pops: An Irreverent Memoir* (1981).
10. Morris to TG.
11. Dyer, "Mix Design and Mystery, You Get a Pops Maestro."
12. Ibid.
13. Annalyn Swan, Abigail Kuflik, Lea Donosky, and Ron LaBrecque, "Boston Strikes Up the Band," *Newsweek*, January 21, 1980.
14. Kershner, commentary on *The Empire Strikes Back* home video release (20th Century Fox, 2013).
15. Mike Snider, "'Star Wars' Universe Revolves Around Vader," *USA Today*, April 22, 2005.
16. Alan Arnold, *Once upon a Galaxy: A Journal of the Making of Star Wars: The Empire Strikes Back* (1980).
17. Rinzler, *The Making of Star Wars: Return of the Jedi: The Definitive Story* (2013).
18. Arnold, *Once upon a Galaxy*.
19. Ibid.
20. Ibid.
21. *Star Wars—Music by John Williams* (1980).
22. Arnold, *Once upon a Galaxy*.
23. *Star Wars—Music by John Williams* (1980).
24. Dyer, "Williams Closeted in a Sci-Fi Setting as Pops 'Secret' Unfolds," *Boston Globe*, January 10, 1980.
25. Dyer to TG.
26. Dyer, "John Williams Bows In," *Boston Globe*, January 11, 1980.
27. Mary Campbell, "The New Man at the Pops," *San Francisco Examiner*, April 29, 1980.
28. Dyer, "John Williams Is New Pops Maestro," *Boston Globe*, January 11, 1980.
29. JW to TG, June 6, 2023.

30. Carl Apone, "Conductor Often Pops Up at Movie Award Time," *Pittsburgh Press*, April 5, 1981.
31. Dyer, "John Williams Bows In."
32. Stephen Farber, *The Dial*, July 1983.
33. Dyer, "Williams Closeted in a Sci-Fi Setting."
34. John Guinn, "Pops Plays On, Despite the Popcorn," *Detroit Free Press*, February 4, 1980.
35. Jennes, "The Boston Pops Gets a Movie Composer."
36. Ellen Pfeifer, *Boston Herald American*, January 11, 1980.
37. Ibid.
38. Jenny Williams to TG, April 1, 2023.
39. Robert Feldberg, "He Came to Fiddle at 'Heaven's Gate,' but Stayed to Score," *The Record* (Hackensack), February 1, 1981.
40. "Williams to Score 'Inchon!'" *Hollywood Reporter*, January 18, 1980.
41. Allan Bryce, "A Conversation with Jerry Goldsmith," *Soundtrack Magazine*, March 1981.
42. Bill Cosel to TG, April 2, 2021.
43. JW to TG, May 10, 2023.
44. JW to TG, June 2, 2023.
45. Pfeifer, *Boston Herald American*, April 28, 1980.
46. Jennes, "The Boston Pops Gets a Movie Composer."
47. Michael Knight, "Williams Opens Pops Season," *Berkshire Eagle*, May 1, 1980.
48. Yo-Yo Ma to TG, June 11, 2018.
49. Susan Dangel to TG, January 29, 2021.
50. Cosel to TG.
51. Dyer, "Q&A with John Williams," April 27, 1980.
52. M. R. Montgomery, "John Williams' Quiet Side," *Boston Globe*, March 18, 1981.
53. Morris to TG.
54. Dyer, "Williams Poised for Pops," *Boston Globe*, April 26, 1981.
55. Dyer, "Ch. 2's 25th in Song," *Boston Globe*, May 3, 1980.
56. Dangel to TG.
57. Livingstone, "John Williams and the Boston Pops."
58. George McKinnon, "Old Film's New End Puts Pops in Movies," *Boston Globe*, June 16, 1980.
59. Campbell, "The New Man at the Pops."
60. Thomas Sabulis, "Pops Takes on New a [*sic*] Look; Williams in Debut," *Boston Globe*, April 30, 1980.
61. Dyer to TG.
62. Sandy DeCrescent to TG, February 9, 2023.
63. Carroll Newman to TG.
64. JW to TG, March 9, 2023.
65. Carroll Newman to TG.
66. Apone, "Conductor Often Pops Up at Movie Award Time."
67. Carroll Newman to TG.
68. Farrow to TG.
69. Mancini to TG.
70. Rugolo to TG.
71. Slatkin to TG.

72. Steven North to TG, November 18, 2021.
73. Jenny Williams to TG, March 10, 2023.
74. "Obituaries," *Variety*, August 6, 1980.
75. Morris to TG.
76. Caroline Taylor, "John Williams on Parade," *Boston Globe*, August 8, 2010.
77. Spielberg, "Of Narrow Misses and Close Calls," *American Cinematographer*, November 1981.
78. Kazanjian to TG.
79. "AFI's Master Class: The Art of Collaboration," *Turner Classic Movies*, November 15, 2011.
80. "The Music of *Indiana Jones*," feature on *Indiana Jones* home video box set (Paramount Pictures, 2021).
81. Ibid.
82. Ibid.
83. Montgomery, "John Williams' Quiet Side."
84. "The Music of *Indiana Jones*."
85. Ibid.
86. Rian Johnson to TG, February 3, 2023.
87. "AFI's Master Class."
88. Ibid.
89. *Morning Pro Musica*.
90. Lawrence Kasdan to TG, May 24, 2022.
91. Dyer, "Pops Tradition Softens the Heart," *Boston Globe*, December 17, 1980.
92. *If These Walls Could Sing*, directed by Mary McCartney (Disney, 2022).
93. Trevor Jones to TG, February 5, 2024.
94. Kazanjian to TG.
95. JW to TG, March 9, 2023.
96. Douglas Brinkley, "Bob Dylan Has a Lot on His Mind," *New York Times*, June 12, 2020.
97. JW to TG, June 2, 2023.
98. "The Record Shelf," hosted by Jim Svejda, Classical KUSC, April 25, 2013.
99. Slatkin to TG.
100. Mark Peskanov to TG, January 23, 2021.
101. Stewart Oksenhorn, "The Man Who Loved Conducting: John Williams Makes Long-Delayed Aspen Debut," *The Aspen Times*, July 14, 2004.
102. Jenny Williams to TG, April 1, 2023.
103. J. G., "Classical Music Briefs," *Stereo Review*, May 1981.
104. Edward Rothstein, "Willliams [sic] Violin Concerto Has New York Premiere," *New York Times*, February 12, 1981.
105. *Stereo Review*, May 1981.
106. Peskanov to TG.
107. Apone, "Williams' New Concerto Flat; Violinist Saves Program," *Pittsburgh Press*, May 8, 1981.
108. JW to TG, July 20, 2023.
109. Andrew Farach-Colton, "Close Encounters in the Concert Hall," *Gramophone*, July 2022.
110. Kenneth Terry, *Down Beat*, March 1981.
111. Michael Ryan, *Boston Magazine*, July 1981.

112. "Ten O'Clock News," *Boston TV News*, July 1, 1981. https://bostonlocaltv.org/catalog/V_6OIPEM43A5JZJZY.
113. JW to TG, November 8, 2023.
114. Dyer, "Orchestrating a New Pops Season," *Boston Globe*, May 4, 1982.
115. "Whither Williams? Conductor of Pops Must Decide Soon," *Variety*, September 9, 1981.
116. Phillips to TG.
117. Allan Arkush to TG, February 18, 2021.
118. Phillips to TG.
119. Arkush to TG.
120. Michael Boddicker to TG, June 14, 2021.
121. Arkush to TG.
122. Phillips to TG.
123. Grossman to TG.
124. Livingstone, "John Williams and the Boston Pops."
125. McBride, *Steven Spielberg*.
126. Spielberg, liner notes for *E.T.: The Extra-Terrestrial* (MCA Records, 1982).
127. "The Music of *E.T.*," feature on *E.T.* home video release.
128. Gordon Emerson, *New Haven Register*, August 22, 1982.
129. Burlingame, "*E.T.* Turns 30," *Film Music Society*, October 10, 2012.
130. *Baxter v MCA, Inc.*, 812 F.2d 421 (9th Cir.), *cert. denied*, 484 U.S. 954 (1987), *on remand*, Case No. 88-6660 (C.D. Cal. 1988), *aff'd*, 907 F.2d 154 (9th Cir. 1990) [unpublished opinion].
131. JW interview for *The Boys: The Sherman Brothers' Story*.
132. Jack Sullivan, "Symphonic Storyteller," *Symphony*, Fall 2018.
133. Marian Zailian, "John Williams: Master of Movie Scores," *San Francisco Examiner*, July 18, 1982.
134. Richard Schickel, *Spielberg: A Retrospective* (2012).
135. McBride, *Steven Spielberg*.
136. Dyer, "Orchestrating a New Pops Season."
137. David Newman to TG.
138. *Morning Pro Musica*.
139. Grierson to TG.
140. Carol Littleton to TG, October 11, 2012.
141. George E. Turner, "Steven Spielberg and E.T. The Extra-Terrestrial," *American Cinematographer*, January 1983.
142. John Powell to TG, February 8, 2022.
143. Stéphane Denève to TG, September 4, 2023.
144. https://www.youtube.com/watch?v=ujC5ZWUDVf8.
145. "A Conversation with John Williams."
146. "The Evening Program," 2017.
147. Spielberg, liner notes for *E.T.*
148. Tom DiNardo, "Scoring Behind the Scenes: John Williams Talks About Making Movie Music," *Philadelphia Daily News*, July 14, 2003.
149. Vaines, "Making Successful Films," *Screen International*, May 26, 1979.
150. Cart., "Monsignor," *Variety*, October 27, 1982.
151. Lou Cedrone, "'Monsignor' Produces Laughter, But It's Not Intended to Be Funny," *Evening Sun* (Baltimore), November 3, 1982.

152. Gary Arnold, "'Monsignor': Unholy Success Story," *Washington Post*, October 23, 1982.
153. Dyer, "Orchestrating a New Pops Season."
154. JW, liner notes for *Monsignor* (Casablanca Records, 1982).
155. "100,000 'Extras' for MGM Film," *Back Stage*, July 3, 1981.
156. Cart., "Yes, Giorgio," *Variety*, September 15, 1982.
157. Maslin, "Screen: Pavarotti in 'Giorgio,'" *New York Times*, September 24, 1982.
158. Theodore W. Libbey Jr., "Disks Attest to the Versatile Talents of John Williams," *New York Times*, February 27, 1983.
159. Emerson, *New Haven Register*.
160. Rinzler, *The Making of Return of the Jedi*.
161. Kazanjian to TG.
162. Rinzler, *The Making of Return of the Jedi*.
163. Ibid.
164. Brian Jay Jones, *George Lucas: A Life* (2016).
165. Kazanjian to TG.
166. Rinzler, *The Making of Return of the Jedi*.
167. Thomas Newman to TG, October 13, 2015.
168. JW to TG, October 1, 2015.
169. Rinzler, *The Making of Return of the Jedi*.
170. Ibid.
171. Kazanjian to TG.
172. Ibid.
173. Wannberg to TG.
174. Kazanjian to TG.
175. Doug Adams to TG, April 12, 2021.
176. Robbins to TG.
177. Wessell.
178. Dyer, "Williams Renews Pops Pact," *Boston Globe*, December 21, 1982.
179. *Morning Pro Musica*.
180. Dangel to TG.

Part II

1. Andrew L. Pincus, "Pops' John Williams Finds His Musical 'Vatican,'" *Berkshire Eagle*, July 19, 1992.

Chapter 10

1. Peter Goodman, "A Great Little Visiting Band," *Newsday* (Nassau Edition), June 11, 1986.
2. Daniel Cariaga, "A Composer Who Takes It All in Stride," *Los Angeles Times*, April 21, 1983.
3. Martin Bernheimer, "Pop! John Williams on Philharmonic Podium," *Los Angeles Times*, November 12, 1983.
4. JW to TG, July 20, 2023.
5. Ernest Fleischmann papers (Collection 2293), UCLA Library Special Collections, Charles E. Young Research Library.

6. *Los Angeles Magazine*, October 1976.
7. Bernheimer, "A Close Encounter of the Painful Kind," *Los Angeles Times*, December 4, 1983.
8. "John Williams, Cont., II," *Los Angeles Times*, December 11, 1983.
9. "Last Word on Williams," *Los Angeles Times*, December 25, 1983.
10. "A Night with Sinatra Gets 3.5M for Cancer Research," *New York Daily News*, March 20, 1984.
11. JW to TG, December 19, 2023.
12. McBride, *Steven Spielberg*.
13. Bonnie Curtis to TG, May 14, 2021.
14. George McKinnon, "Williams Answers Spielberg's Call for Music," *Boston Globe*, May 13, 1983.
15. Rinzler, *Howard Kazanjian: A Producer's Life* (2021).
16. Burtt to TG.
17. Cart., "Indiana Jones and the Temple of Doom," *Variety*, March 16, 1984.
18. Arthur Knight, "Lucas-Spielberg 'Doom' Seems Destined for Boxoffice Glory," *Hollywood Reporter*, May 11, 1984.
19. Carroll Newman to TG.
20. *New Haven Register*, July 17, 1983.
21. Dyer, "Stars and Stripes Forever and Ever," *Boston Globe*, April 28, 1985.
22. *Patriot Ledger*, August 8, 1984.
23. Margo Miller, "The 'Tradition' That Cost Pops Its Conductor," *Boston Globe*, June 15, 1984.
24. Richard H. Stewart, "'We Didn't Drive Williams Away,'" *Boston Globe*, July 8, 1984.
25. Ibid.
26. Tim Morrison to TG, June 9, 2020.
27. Miller, "Williams to Resign as Pops Conductor," *Boston Globe*, June 14, 1984.
28. Cosel to TG.
29. Stewart, "Orchestra Management, Trustees Predict Notable Operation Change," *Boston Globe*, August 3, 1984.
30. "Crowd of 1 Million Views Hub Parade," *Berkshire Eagle*, July 5, 1984.
31. Richard Buell, "At the Pops: Williams' Farewell," *Boston Globe*, July 9, 1984.
32. Carroll Newman to TG.
33. Thomas Bonk, "It Wasn't the Only Game in Town," *Los Angeles Times*, July 29, 1984.
34. Mike Davis, "Futuristic Sendoff Wows Olympics Crowd," *San Bernadino County Sun*, August 13, 1984.
35. Richard Patterson, "Vilmos Zsigmond, ASC, and The River," *American Cinematographer*, November 1984.
36. Bob Grace, *Zest*, November 13, 1983.
37. Grierson to TG.
38. Marilyn Beck, "Company Becomes Two," *San Francisco Examiner*, January 17, 1984.
39. Glenn Rifkin, "Williams Will Return to Conduct Boston Pops," *Los Angeles Times*, August 3, 1984.
40. Dyer, "Sweet Music at the Pops," *Boston Globe*, August 3, 1984.
41. Cariaga, "Williams Talks About Pops Return," *Los Angeles Times*, August 4, 1984.
42. Dyer, "Sweet Music at the Pops."
43. Milton R. Bass, "The Lively World," *Berkshire Eagle*, August 9, 1984.
44. Ann Hobson Pilot to TG, April 13, 2021.
45. Dyer to TG.

46. Peter W. Kaplan, "John Williams Creates Themes for NBC News," *New York Times*, September 10, 1985.
47. JW, liner notes for *John Williams & "The President's Own"* (2021), https://express.adobe.com/page/MtAOvmGmJ8YRQ/.
48. Kaplan, "John Williams Creates Themes for NBC News."
49. Ibid.
50. Dyer, "Williams Is Ebullient on Pops' 100th," *Boston Globe*, April 28, 1985.
51. "Life in Double Time: A Rare Look at the Private and Public Worlds of Boston Pops Conductor John Williams," *Boston Herald Magazine*, April 28, 1985.
52. Kennedy to TG.
53. Louis Chunovic, "Spielberg Talks: Unveils Plans for 'Top Secret' 'Amazing' Show," *Hollywood Reporter*, September 11, 1985.
54. Ibid.
55. Richard Hack, "TeleVisions," *Hollywood Reporter*, October 1, 1985.
56. Aljean Harmetz, "'Amazing Stories' Tries New Tactics," *New York Times*, June 2, 1986.
57. Robbins to TG.
58. Pincus, "Boston Pops Drew Record Crowds on Recent Transcontinental Tour," *Berkshire Eagle*, August 16, 1985.
59. Donald Dierks, "All Good Music Sings to Williams," *San Diego Union*, July 28, 1985.
60. Dyer, "Williams Is Ebullient on Pops' 100th."
61. Ibid.
62. Chester Schmitz to TG, October 18, 2021.
63. Dyer, "Williams Is Ebullient on Pops' 100th."
64. Dyer, "Concerto Lets Tuba Reach New Heights," *Boston Globe*, May 9, 1985.
65. Anthony Tommasini, "Douglas Yeo Scores One for the Trombone," *Boston Globe*, May 27, 1991.
66. Schmitz to TG.
67. Marc Shulgold, "Williams' Tuba Concerto at Bowl," *Los Angeles Times*, September 9, 1985.
68. Bernheimer, "The Philharmonic Future: Enter Andre Previn," *Los Angeles Times*, October 28, 1984.
69. Derek Traub, "Mr. Previn Comes to Town," in *Past/Forward: The LA Phil at 100*, edited by Julia Ward and Robin Rauzi (2018).
70. "Hollywood Soundtrack," *Variety*, September 11, 1985.
71. Champlin, "46 Years Minding the Score at Fox," *Los Angeles Times*, September 12, 1985.
72. JW to TG, June 2, 2023.
73. JW to TG, December 19, 2023.
74. https://www.britannica.com/event/Challenger-disaster.
75. McBride, *Steven Spielberg*.
76. Harry Winer to TG, February 22, 2021.
77. Ibid.
78. Ibid.
79. JW to TG, March 7, 2023.
80. Winer to TG.
81. Jimmy Summers, "SpaceCamp," *Boxoffice*, August 1, 1986.
82. Winer to TG.
83. Marie Saxon Silverman, "Tommy Walker Applies Disneyland Know-How to Liberty Blowout," *Variety*, January 8, 1986.

84. Peter Goodman, "The Producers Celebrating Liberty '86," *Newsday*, June 11, 1986.
85. Tommasini, "'Liberty Fanfare' Premieres at Pops," *Boston Globe*, June 5, 1986.
86. Duane Byrge, "Scopus Award to Spielberg at Celebrity-Packed Dinner," *Hollywood Reporter*, December 16, 1986.
87. Jack Thomas, "Giving, the Mugar Way," *Boston Globe*, March 12, 1987.
88. Dyer, "Pride and the Pops," *Boston Globe*, May 5, 1987.
89. George Miller to TG, January 25, 2023.
90. Ibid.
91. Ibid.
92. Ian Underwood to TG, August 16, 2022.
93. Wannberg to TG.
94. Dangel to TG.
95. Miller to TG.
96. Ibid.
97. Maslin, "Film: The Witches of Eastwick," *New York Times*, June 12, 1987.
98. Jack Garner, "The Magic Is Missing in 'Witches,'" *Gannett News Service*, June 11, 1987.
99. Miller to TG.
100. Dyer, "Williams and the Pops March on to Japan," *Boston Globe*, November 13, 1987.
101. Dyer, "Their Championship Season," *Boston Globe*, July 28, 1987.
102. Dyer, "Williams and the Pops March on to Japan."
103. Myra Forsberg, "Spielberg at 40: The Man and the Child," *New York Times*, January 10, 1988.
104. Ibid.
105. Schickel, *Spielberg: A Retrospective*.
106. Spielberg to TG.
107. Shawn Murphy to TG, April 9, 2021.
108. Maslin, "Film: Spielberg's 'Empire of Sun,'" *New York Times*, December 9, 1987.
109. David Stratton, "Spielberg Gets Mystical," *Sydney Morning Herald*, March 10, 1988.
110. Byrge, "Empire of the Sun," *Hollywood Reporter*, December 1, 1987.
111. Canby, "Evoking Childhood Isn't Kid Stuff," *New York Times*, February 7, 1988.
112. Spielberg, liner notes for *The Spielberg/Williams Collaboration*.
113. Dyer, "Pops Japanese Tour: A Rousing Start," *Boston Globe*, November 28, 1987.
114. Ryo Jozuka, "Music Promoter Lifts Curtain on Backstage Antics of Major Stars," *Asahi Shimbun*, April 10, 2022.
115. JW to TG, May 10, 2023.
116. Dyer, "The Pops Leaves 'em Clapping," *Boston Globe*, December 4, 1987.
117. Dyer, "Williams and the Pops March on to Japan."

Chapter 11

1. Tony Thomas, "A Conversation with John Williams," *The Cue Sheet* 8, no. 1 (1991): 6–15.
2. Rick Carter to TG, February 16, 2024.
3. https://www.youtube.com/watch?v=H1tWKm9GsPg.
4. Zimmer to TG.
5. Paul Harvey, "The Orchestra as We Know It Is Dead," *Daily Spectrum* (Saint George, UT), March 5, 1988.

6. John Guinn, "William Bolcom: He Composes for Modern Ears," *Detroit Free Press*, May 22, 1988.
7. "People Watching," *Berkshire Eagle*, February 20, 1988.
8. Steve Metcalf, "Dickson-Dukakis: Pops Conductor on Family Ticket," *Hartford Courant*, July 17, 1988.
9. https://www.c-span.org/video/?c4453714/user-clip-john-williams-fanfare-michael-dukakis.
10. "Big Hit: 'Fanfare for Michael,'" *Spokesman-Review*, July 22, 1988.
11. John Powers, "When Worlds Collide," *L.A. Weekly*, August 4, 1988.
12. Peter Goodman, "Duke's Musical Connections," *Newsday* (Suffolk edition), July 22, 1988.
13. "Sundance to Fund Preservation of Classic Film Scores," *Hollywood Reporter*, January 21, 1988.
14. Dyer, "Williams Says Pops Well-Tempered for Upcoming Season," *Boston Globe*, May 1, 1988.
15. Bobby Gruska to TG, January 16, 2024.
16. Diane Read to TG, May 25, 2021.
17. Court testimony material for "Baxter v. MCA" trial (1988) reproduced in M. Fletcher Reynolds, "Music Analysis for Expert Testimony in Copyright Infringement Litigation" (PhD dissertation, University of Kansas, 1991), 180–241.
18. Michael Feinstein to TG, April 26, 2021.
19. JW to TG, May 10, 2023.
20. Dyer, "Williams Says Pops Well-Tempered for Upcoming Season."
21. Kasdan to TG.
22. NBC *Today*, March 27, 1989.
23. Kasdan to TG.
24. NBC *Today*, March 27, 1989.
25. David Newman to TG.
26. Kasdan to TG.
27. Leonard Feather, "Dave Grusin's Cruisin' with a Hit List," *Los Angeles Times*, May 7, 1989.
28. David Newman to TG.
29. Nancy Griffin, "Spielberg Gives His All Again," *South Florida Sun Sentinel*, May 24, 1989.
30. Dyer, "John Williams Begins 10th Year in Tune with Pops," *Boston Globe*, May 7, 1989.
31. Griffin, "Spielberg Gives His All Again."
32. Canby, "Film View: Spielberg's Elixir Shows Signs of Mature Magic," *New York Times*, June 18, 1989.
33. Daniel Buckley, "A Close Encounter with John Williams," *Tucson Citizen*, January 23, 1989.
34. Buckley, "Hollywood's Music Man," *Tucson Citizen*, January 21, 1989.
35. "Obituaries: Lionel Newman," *Variety*, February 8, 1989.
36. JW eulogy for Lionel Newman, February 8, 1989.
37. Ibid.
38. Spielberg to TG.
39. Cosel to TG.
40. Carroll Newman to TG.
41. Dyer, "Bernstein Celebrates His Reunion with Pops," *Boston Globe*, June 7, 1989.
42. Dyer, "John Williams Begins 10th Year in Tune with Pops."
43. Marian Christy, "John Williams' Pursuit of Excellence," *Boston Globe*, July 4, 1989.

44. Dyer, "John Williams Begins 10th Year in Tune with Pops."
45. "UA to Release Vietnam Story Starring Pacino," *Boxoffice*, June 12, 1978.
46. Oliver Stone to Bryant Gumbel, 1989 interview, included on *Born on the Fourth of July* home video release (Universal, 2012).
47. Oliver Stone to TG, May 22, 2020.
48. JW to TG, March 17, 2023.
49. Ibid.
50. Dyer, "You'll Be Hearing from Him," *Boston Globe*, August 31, 1989.
51. Gary Deeb, "'Born on the Fourth of July' Expands Out of Box Office," Post-Crescent (Appleton, Wisconsin), February 28, 1990.
52. Dyer, "You'll Be Hearing from Him."
53. Ibid.
54. Stone, commentary on *Born on the Fourth of July* home video release.
55. Ibid.
56. Stone to TG.
57. Randy Kerber to TG, March 9, 2022.
58. Stone, commentary.
59. JW to TG, March 17, 2023.
60. Stone to TG.
61. Holden, "The Pop Life," *New York Times*, February 7, 1990.
62. Daws., "Born on the Fourth of July," *Variety*, December 20, 1989.
63. Maslin, "Film View: Oliver Stone Takes Aim at the Viewer's Viscera," *New York Times*, December 31, 1989.
64. Holden, "The Pop Life."
65. Deeb, "'Born on the Fourth of July' Expands Out of Box Office."
66. Morrison to TG.
67. Deeb, "'Born on the Fourth of July' Expands Out of Box Office."
68. Chris Willman, "Keeping Score Behind Scenes," *Los Angeles Times*, March 21, 1990.
69. Stone to TG.
70. Jack Mathews, "No Southern Comfort," *American Film*, December 1, 1989.
71. Ibid.
72. Dreyfuss to TG.
73. Spielberg, liner notes for *The Spielberg/Williams Collaboration*.
74. Dreyfuss to TG.
75. Tom Matthews, "Always," *Boxoffice*, February 1, 1990.
76. David Denby, "Movies: Flying Low," *New York*, January 8, 1990.
77. Schickel, *Spielberg: A Retrospective*.
78. Jenny Williams to TG, March 6, 2024.
79. JW to TG, May 10, 2023.
80. Jenny Williams to TG, April 1, 2023.
81. Gary Gorman, "Ex-Rock Singer Arrested in Pot Raid in Oxnard," *Los Angeles Times*, April 26, 1990.
82. Paul Elliott, "The Secret History of Toto," *Classic Rock*, October 15, 2016.
83. Jenny Williams to TG, March 6, 2024.
84. Joseph Williams to TG.
85. JW to TG, February 13, 2024.

86. Jenny Williams to TG, March 6, 2024.
87. Mike Hughes, "Life Keeps Sheridan Swirling," *Gannett News Service*, April 18, 1994.
88. Michael Sragow, "Harrison Ford: 'Ferrari' Spins His Wheels," *San Francisco Examiner*, July 27, 1990.
89. Dyer, "Lending Snap to the Pops," *Boston Globe*, May 7, 1990.
90. Sheila Benson, "A Solid Case," *Los Angeles Times*, July 27, 1990.
91. John Griffin, "Movie Is OK, but Book Was Better," *The Gazette* (Montreal), July 28, 1990.
92. "No Pops for This Pop-to-Be," *Boston Globe*, May 8, 1990.
93. Dyer, "A New Recording Contract for Pops," *Boston Globe*, December 14, 1989.
94. Dyer, "Williams Talks of Pops' Past, Future," *Boston Globe*, July 19, 1990.
95. Ibid.
96. "Summer Reading Runs Dry to Breezy," *Boston Globe*, July 9, 1990.
97. Dyer, "Lending Snap to the Pops."
98. Dyer, "The Music Man," *Boston Globe*, October 7, 1990.
99. Chris Columbus to TG, March 23, 2021.
100. Dyer, "Gala Tonight Launches Pops' Star-Filled Season," *Boston Globe*, May 7, 1991.
101. *Home Alone* electronic press kit (20th Century Fox), 1990.
102. Columbus to TG.
103. *Home Alone* EPK.
104. James Hughes, "Holy Cow, Home Alone Is 25!" *Chicago Magazine*, November 10, 2015.
105. Columbus to TG.
106. Ibid.
107. Hughes, "Holy Cow, Home Alone Is 25!"
108. Dyer, "Gala Tonight Launches Pops' Star-Filled Season."
109. Columbus to TG.
110. Dyer, "Christmas Pops: Serious, Silly and Sweet," *Boston Globe*, December 20, 1990.
111. Beth J. Harpaz, "Leonard Bernstein Dead at 72," *Berkshire Eagle*, October 15, 1990.
112. JW to TG, December 19, 2023.
113. JW to TG, June 2, 2023.
114. Kim Taylor to TG, January 14, 2024.
115. Steve Metcalf, "With Bernstein and Copland Gone, Who Will Fill the Void in American Music?" *Hartford Courant*, January 6, 1991.
116. Stephanie J. Doerr, "Musical Void Filled," *Hartford Courant*, January 25, 1991.
117. Thomas, "A Conversation with John Williams."
118. Michele Zukovsky to TG, June 1, 2020.
119. Milton Cole, "Too Much Williams at Tanglewood Pops," *Daily Hampshire Gazette*, July 18, 1991.
120. Dyer, "Lending Snap to the Pops."
121. Zukovsky to TG.
122. McBride, *Steven Spielberg*.
123. Curtis to TG.
124. Bricusse, *Pure Imagination*.
125. Ibid.
126. Ibid.
127. Vincent Paterson to TG, February 24, 2021.
128. Spielberg to TG.

598   Notes

129. Bricusse, *Pure Imagination*.
130. Spielberg liner notes for *Hook* (Sony Music Entertainment, 1991).
131. Ed Blank, "Star-Filled Cast, Fine Acting Keep Spielberg's Hook Afloat," *Pittsburgh Press*, December 10, 1991.
132. Jon Bowman, "'Hook' Walks the Plank for Christmas," *Santa Fe New Mexican*, December 20, 1991.
133. Spielberg, liner notes for *Hook*.
134. Lang to TG.
135. Dyer, "Pops' Williams to Retire in '93," *Boston Globe*, December 20, 1991.
136. CBS *Sunday Morning*, September 22, 2019.
137. James V. Hart to TG, July 2, 2020.
138. Anthony Breznican, "Steven Spielberg: The EW Interview," *Entertainment Weekly*, December 2, 2011.
139. Spielberg to TG.
140. Dyer, "Christmas Pops: Serious, Silly and Sweet."

Chapter 12

1. Suzan Bibisi, "Hollywood Bowl Says Goodbye to Williams," *Los Angeles Daily News*, August 8, 1992.
2. Dyer, "John Williams Hits the Road," *Boston Globe*, July 24, 1992.
3. Dyer, "Gala Tonight Launches Pops' Star-Filled Season," May 7, 1991.
4. All Stone comments on the *JFK* score are from conversation with TG.
5. Robert Scheer, "Oliver Stone Builds His Own Myths," *Los Angeles Times*, December 15, 1991.
6. Dyer, "'Hook,' 'JFK' Are Latest Hits with the John Williams Touch," *Boston Globe*, January 19, 1992.
7. Dyer, "'Hook,' 'JFK' Are Latest Hits with the John Williams Touch."
8. JW to TG, April 10, 2024.
9. Dyer, "'Hook,' 'JFK' Are Latest Hits with the John Williams Touch."
10. Ibid.
11. Dyer, "Pops Opens in Style," *Boston Globe*, May 3, 1992.
12. David Nyhan, "Gorbachev's Soliloquy," *Boston Globe*, May 21, 1992.
13. JW to TG, April 10, 2024.
14. Pincus, "Pops' John Williams Finds His Musical Vatican."
15. Dyer, "Pops' Williams to Retire in '93." .
16. Ibid.
17. Dyer, "'Hook,' 'JFK' Are Latest Hits with the John Williams Touch."
18. Lawrence Christon, "Epic Picture, Epic Dreams," *Los Angeles Times*, May 17, 1992.
19. John Glatt, *The Chieftains: The Authorized Biography* (1997).
20. Christon, "Epic Picture, Epic Dreams."
21. Ron Howard to TG, October 6, 2023.
22. Glatt, *The Chieftains*.
23. Dyer, "Pops Opens in Style."
24. Ibid.
25. Matessino, liner notes for *Far and Away: Expanded Edition* (La-La Land Records, 2020).

26. Christon, "Epic Picture, Epic Dreams."
27. Howard to TG.
28. David Armstrong, "'Far and Away' from Luck of the Irish," *San Francisco Examiner*, May 22, 1992.
29. Byrge, "Far and Away," *Hollywood Reporter*, May 11, 1992.
30. Michael Blowen, "Names & Faces: It's Time for Tyne," *Boston Globe*, May 6, 1992.
31. Dangel to TG.
32. Dyer, "John Williams Hits the Road."
33. Ibid.
34. Pincus, July 19, 1992.
35. Don Heckman, "Lightweight Set from John Williams," *Los Angeles Times*, August 11, 1992.
36. Dyer, "John Williams Hits the Road."
37. Yardena Arar, "Happy Sequel: Director of 'Home Alone 2': Sometimes Love Can Buy Money," *Chicago Tribune*, November 26, 1992.
38. Columbus to TG.
39. Ibid.
40. Nancy Malitz, "'King of Pops' Says His Last Tour Is Really the Last," *Bellingham Herald*, August 5, 1992.
41. Columbus to TG.
42. Ibid.
43. Dyer, "Pops Opens in Style."
44. Dyer, "The Williams Whirlwind," *Boston Globe*, May 9, 1993.
45. Masakazu Yoshizawa to TG, August 12, 2006.
46. Thomas, *Total Film*.
47. Dyer, "The Williams Whirlwind."
48. Ibid.
49. "Return to *Jurassic Park*: The Next Step in Evolution," special feature on *Jurassic Park* home video release (Universal, 2013).
50. "The Making of *Jurassic Park*," 1995 special feature on *Jurassic Park* (Universal, 2013).
51. "Return to *Jurassic Park*."
52. Dyer, "The Williams Whirlwind."
53. Jeff Goldblum to TG, May 10, 2022.
54. Jerry Roberts, "Dinos Soar into Action in Big 'Jurassic' Classic," *Copley News Service*, June 17, 1993.
55. Sid Smith, "The Right Tracks: Hot Summer Movies Bring Along Some Great Music," *Chicago Tribune*, July 11, 1993.
56. Zachary Woolfe, "A Summer Blockbuster, Far from the Multiplex," *New York Times*, August 19, 2012.
57. Dyer, "Williams' Final Season Off to a Soaring Start," *Boston Globe*, May 13, 1993.
58. Dyer, "Clooney, Ronstadt Ignite Pops," *Boston Globe*, May 24, 1993.
59. Linda Cutting, "Boston Pops in Japan: Good, Loud and Popular," *Boston Globe*, June 16, 1993.
60. Ibid.
61. Charles A. Radin, "Pops in Tokyo: Ozawa Steals the Show," *Boston Globe*, June 11, 1993.
62. Dyer, "A Grand Final Fourth for John Williams," *Boston Globe*, July 6, 1993.

63. Milton Cole, "Love Affair Ignites, at Last, Between Williams and Pops," *Daily Hampshire Gazette*, July 22, 1993.
64. Clarence Fanto, "Tanglewood Attendance Sets Record," *Berkshire Eagle*, September 2, 1993.
65. Dyer, "Williams Makes a Stirring Debut with the BSO," *Boston Globe*, August 30, 1993.
66. Pincus, "BSO Honors Williams, Remembers Bernstein," *Berkshire Eagle*, August 22, 1993.
67. Ibid.
68. Emma Brockes, "The Monday Interview: A Wizard from Oz," *The Guardian*, October 30, 2000.
69. McBride, *Steven Spielberg*.
70. *Spielberg*, directed by Susan Lacy (HBO, 2017).
71. McBride, *Steven Spielberg*.
72. Thomas, *Total Film*.
73. Dyer, "John Williams: Making Movie-Music History," *Boston Globe*, March 20, 1994.
74. Ibid.
75. Ibid.
76. Ibid.
77. Thomas, *Total Film*.
78. Dyer, "The Williams Whirlwind."
79. Itzhak Perlman to TG, May 14, 2018.
80. Yann Merluzeau, "A Conversation with John Williams: From *Schindler's List* to the Cello Concerto," *Cantina Band* (Winter 1994).
81. Dyer, "John Williams: Making Movie-Music History."
82. Thomas, *Total Film*.
83. Ibid.
84. Jeff Bond, "Williams Tells," *Hollywood Reporter*, January 2006.
85. Dyer, "John Williams: Making Movie-Music History."
86. https://www.youtube.com/watch?v=v0RB-3sWbBA.
87. Dyer, "John Williams: Making Movie-Music History."
88. Ibid.
89. Ibid.
90. DeCrescent to TG.
91. David Low to TG, March 14, 2024.
92. Dyer, "John Williams: Making Movie-Music History."
93. JW to TG, March 9, 2023.
94. Perlman to TG.
95. https://www.youtube.com/watch?v=1HKTYYX50hQ.
96. https://www.youtube.com/watch?v=HYjit7CiUqM.
97. Holden, "Eloquent Movies with Eloquent Soundtracks," *New York Times*, January 30, 1994.
98. Thomas, *Total Film*.
99. Cheryl North, "Conductor John Williams Reflects on His Art and Inspiration," *Oakland Tribune*, November 20, 1994.
100. Spielberg to TG.
101. Dyer, "John Williams' Final Bow," *Boston Globe*, December 20, 1993.
102. Dyer, "Pops Star: The Legacy of John Williams," *Boston Globe*, December 12, 1993.
103. Dyer, "John Williams' Final Bow."

104. "Maestro Tops Off Pops Career," *Associated Press*, December 20, 1993.
105. Dyer, "John Williams' Final Bow."
106. "Boston Pops Director Returns to Podium," *Associated Press*, February 4, 1994.
107. Greg Jaklewicz, "Stars in His Ears," *Abilene Reporter-News*, April 3, 1994.
108. "Music Notes," *Hollywood Reporter*, March 16, 1994.
109. Mancini to TG.
110. Dyer, "Pops Season to Celebrate Arthur Fiedler Centennial," *Boston Globe*, April 28, 1994.
111. Laurel Ornish, "'Schindler' Music Making Encore Performances," *Fort Worth Star-Telegram*, May 4, 1994.
112. Dyer, "New Ozawa Hall Opens to Future," *Boston Globe*, July 8, 1994.
113. JW to TG, June 6, 2023.
114. Yo-Yo Ma to TG.
115. Dyer, "Spring Evoked with Wave of Baton," *Boston Globe*, February 7, 1995.
116. Dyer, "Lockhart and Pops Get Off to Rousing Start," *Boston Globe*, May 11, 1995.
117. Susan Larson, "John Williams Makes a Suite Return to the Pops," *Boston Globe*, May 13, 1995.
118. Judith LeClair to TG, June 19, 2023.
119. Ibid.
120. Ibid.
121. Tommasini, "Concerto Proves Williams Profound as Well as Prolific," *Boston Globe*, April 15, 1995.
122. LeClair to TG.
123. Robert W. Welkos and Elaine Dutka, "'Sense' Tops Globe Nod List with Six," *Los Angeles Times*, December 22, 1995.
124. JW to TG, December 19, 2023.
125. Ebert, "Sabrina," *Chicago Tribune*, December 15, 1995.
126. Emanuel Ax to TG, October 18, 2023.
127. Stone to TG.
128. JW interview on *Nixon Enhanced CD* (Hollywood Records, 1995).
129. Dutka, "Wrestling Nixon's Demons," *Los Angeles Times*, September 24, 1995.
130. Dutka, "Nixon Family Blasts Oliver Stone over Movie on President's Life," *Los Angeles Times*, December 19, 1995.
131. *Nixon Enhanced CD*.
132. Stone to TG.
133. Morrison to TG.
134. *Nixon Enhanced CD*.
135. Conrad Pope to TG, April 23, 2021.
136. Stone to TG.
137. *Nixon Enhanced CD*.
138. Stone to TG.
139. William K. Guegold, *100 Years of Olympic Music* (1996).
140. Neil Strauss, "The Pop Life: Meeting an Olympic Challenge," *New York Times*, May 16, 1996.
141. Pincus, "The Pops Goes to Atlanta," *Berkshire Eagle*, July 7, 1996.
142. Steven Poole, "Film Music: LSO / John Williams," *The Independent*, July 2, 1996.
143. "Williams Composes Torch Songs," *Associated Press*, July 16, 1996.

144. Victor Salva, "Jerry Goldsmith and Powder," May 8, 2009, https://pohocounty.blogspot.com/2009/05/jerry-goldsmith-and-powder.html.
145. Hirsch to TG.
146. Mark Kanny, "Pops Goes to the Movies," *Pittsburgh Post-Gazette*, March 7, 1996.
147. "Travolta Cleared to Sue over His 'Double' Trouble," *Hollywood Reporter*, November 5, 1996.
148. Barry Levinson to TG, May 12, 2020.
149. Ibid.
150. Ibid.
151. Ted Shen, "Handicapping the Film Scores," *Chicago Tribune*, March 23, 1997.
152. Michael Sachs to TG, June 12, 2023.
153. Mary Thornton, "The Trumpet Concerto of John Williams: From Commission to Concert," *ITG Journal* 21, no. 4 (May 1997).
154. Ibid.
155. Sachs to TG.
156. Ibid.
157. Ibid.
158. Donald Rosenberg, *Cleveland Plain Dealer*, September 22, 1996.
159. Thornton, "The Trumpet Concerto of John Williams."
160. Sachs to TG.
161. Thornton, "The Trumpet Concerto of John Williams."
162. Rosenberg, *Cleveland Plain Dealer*, September 27, 1996.
163. Mangan, "Williams, Philharmonic Please the Bowl Throng," *Los Angeles Times*, September 11, 1995.

Chapter 13

1. Dave Wilcox, "Crash Victim Turned Triumph into Trauma," *San Luis Obispo Tribune*, June 18, 1997.
2. Duke Helfand and Henry Weinstein, "Prominent Entertainment Attorney Kills Children, Self," *Los Angeles Times*, February 24, 1997.
3. Bernard Weinraub, "Stirring Up Old Terrors Unforgotten," *New York Times*, February 19, 1997.
4. Bruce Cannon to TG, July 8, 2020.
5. Lisé Richardson to TG, September 14, 2022.
6. John Singleton, commentary on *Rosewood* home video release (Warner Bros. Pictures, 2007).
7. Singleton, liner notes for *Rosewood* (Sony Music Entertainment, 1997).
8. Cannon to TG.
9. JW to TG, July 20, 2023.
10. Singleton, commentary.
11. JW to TG, July 20, 2023.
12. Morgan to TG.
13. *Dallas Morning News*, June 16, 1997.
14. Singleton, commentary.
15. Byrge, "Rosewood," *Hollywood Reporter*, February 10, 1997.

16. Cannon to TG.
17. Wendy Ide, "Francis Ford Coppola: 'I May Only Make One More Film,'" *Screen Daily*, December 8, 2015.
18. Kathy Tyers, *The Truce at Bakura* (1994).
19. Dyer, "John Williams: New Horizons, Familiar Galaxies," *Boston Globe*, June 4, 1997.
20. Ibid.
21. Burlingame, "A Career of Epic Proportions," *Los Angeles Times*, February 3, 2002.
22. Manohla Dargis, "A Word With: Steven Spielberg," *New York Times*, May 15, 2016.
23. "The Making of *The Lost World*," feature on *The Lost World* home video release (Universal, 2018).
24. Ibid.
25. Dangel to TG.
26. Sally Stevens to TG, February 24, 2022.
27. Richard Harrington, "'Titanic' Decked Out with Beautiful Music," *Washington Post*, January 25, 1998.
28. Mark Swed, "The Transcendent Sounds of 'Kundun,'" *Los Angeles Times*, January 9, 1998.
29. Dyer, "Conducting on TV," *Boston Globe*, June 22, 1997.
30. Mary-Jane Tichenor, "Conductor Loves the Berkshires," *Boston Globe*, July 12, 1997.
31. Jean-Jacques Annaud to TG, May 20, 2020.
32. Ibid.
33. David Kronke, "The High Price of Redemption: 'Tibet' Was a Welcome Challenge for Director Jean-Jacques Annaud," *Los Angeles Times*, October 16, 1997.
34. Annaud to TG.
35. Ibid.
36. JW, comments from concert with Berliner Philharmoniker, October 2021.
37. Jacqueline Brand to TG, April 1, 2021.
38. Ma to TG.
39. Brand to TG.
40. Susan Elliott, "Gay Men's Chorus Finds Voice with 'Songs of Freedom,'" *Atlanta Constitution*, March 4, 1998.
41. James Cameron to TG, September 12, 2016.
42. Jenny Williams to TG, March 10, 2023.
43. Dyer, "Sounds of Spielberg," *Boston Globe*, February 24, 1998.
44. Spielberg to TG.
45. "Music and Sound," feature on *Saving Private Ryan* home video release (Paramount, 2019).
46. Ibid.
47. Ibid.
48. Ibid.
49. Dyer, Sounds of Spielberg."
50. Ibid.
51. Brent Kliewer, "Shaken but Not Shattered," *Santa Fe New Mexican*, July 31, 1998.
52. Lawrence Toppman, "Film Succeeds in Taking the Tinsel Out of WWII," *Charlotte Observer*, July 24, 1998.
53. Ty Burr, "When Will Oscar Really Know the Score?," *New York Times*, March 1, 1998.
54. Slatkin to TG.
55. Pincus, "Poetry in Movements," *Berkshire Eagle*, July 24, 1998.

56. Ibid.
57. Rita Dove to TG, November 2, 2022.
58. Pincus, "Poetry in Movements."
59. Dove to TG.
60. Slatkin to TG.
61. Larson, "John Williams's Many Facets," *Boston Globe*, July 27, 1998.
62. Pincus, "Williams: From 'Star Wars' to Song," *Berkshire Eagle*, July 27, 1998.
63. James R. Oestreich, "Circling Back to a Time of Mystery and Wonder," *New York Times*, July 27, 1998.
64. *Evening at Pops*, PBS, July 27, 1998.
65. Dove to TG.
66. Tim Smith, "Composer Scores Hits on Screen and Podium," *South Florida Sun Sentinel*, April 5, 1998.
67. Columbus to TG.
68. Ibid.
69. Ibid.
70. Ibid.
71. Juanita Greene, "Virtuoso Guitarist to Open Series at Howard," *Herald-Palladium*, September 30, 2004.
72. Carrie Rickey, "Mama Drama," *The Gazette* (Montreal), December 24, 1998.
73. Kenneth Turan, "Stars Team for 'Step' Mother of all Weepies," *Los Angeles Times*, December 25, 1998.
74. Columbus to TG.
75. Terry Staunton, "Phantom Menace Mayhem," *Uncut*, January 1, 1999.
76. "Sounds of the Stars," *Reading Evening Post*, July 13, 1999.
77. Lehman to TG.
78. Bob Thomas, "The Music Man: Star Wars Composer Hits the Right Notes," *Associated Press/Winnipeg Sun*, May 13, 1999.
79. Ibid.
80. Dyer, "Making 'Star Wars' Sing Again," *Boston Globe*, May 28, 1999.
81. "Sounds of the Stars."
82. Burtt to TG.
83. Lehman to TG.
84. Dyer, "Making 'Star Wars' Sing Again."
85. Ibid.
86. Lewis Beale and Jack Mathews, "A New Glimpse of 'Phantom,'" *Daily News* (New York), March 12, 1999.
87. Dyer, "Williams Soars on New Score," *Boston Globe*, May 7, 1999.
88. Peter Dobrin, "'Phantom' Score Is Worthy Music," *Philadelphia Inquirer*, May 16, 1999.
89. Dyer, "Williams Soars on New Score."
90. "Star Wars: The Force Awakens Original Motion Picture Soundtrack from Oscar-Winning Composer John Williams Debuts at No. 5 on the Billboard 200 Chart," *PR Newswire*, December 29, 2015.
91. Fred Shuster, "John Williams. 'Star Wars: Episode I—The Phantom Menace' Soundtrack (Sony)," *Los Angeles Daily News*, May 21, 1999.
92. Michael Wilmington, "The Good," *Chicago Tribune*, May 18, 1999.

93. JW, interview with Brian Bell for premiere of "for Seiji!," WGBH, April 22, 1999.
94. Larson, "'For Seiji!' Captures Williams's Favorite BSO Sounds," *Boston Globe*, April 23, 1999.
95. JW to TG, June 2, 2023.
96. Kim Taylor to TG.
97. Mike Boehm, "St. Clair Chooses to Return with Crescendo," *Los Angeles Times*, August 27, 1999.
98. Meg James, "St. Clair Returns to Adoring Fans After Loss of Son," *Los Angeles Times*, August 29, 1999.
99. Bennett, *Hollywood Reporter*, March 8, 2000.
100. Alan Parker, commentary on *Angela's Ashes* home video release (Paramount Pictures, 2020).
101. Bennett, *Hollywood Reporter*.
102. Matt Wolf, "Film Version of 'Angela's Ashes' Not as Good as the Book," *Associated Press*, December 22, 1999.
103. Rita Kempley, "'Angela's Ashes': No Spark of Life," *Washington Post*, January 21, 2000.
104. Mick LaSalle, "It's All Downhill in 'Ashes': Irish Family's Suffering Is Unrelenting," *San Francisco Chronicle*, January 21, 2000.
105. Stephanie Zacharek, "Angela's Ashes," *Salon*, December 21, 1999.
106. Parker, commentary.
107. Stephen Wigler, "A Composer Who Knows the Score," *Baltimore Sun*, August 29, 1999.

Chapter 14

1. Jack Garner, "Symphonic Crusade," *Democrat and Chronicle*, April 27, 2001.
2. Dyer, "John Williams Listens to the Song of a Tree," *Boston Globe*, July 2, 2000.
3. Mark Helm, "Monster Party in D.C. for Y2K," *San Francisco Examiner*, December 13, 1999.
4. Jackson Braider, liner notes for *American Journey* (Sony Music Entertainment, 2002).
5. JW to TG, July 20, 2023.
6. Ray Bennett, "The Composers: First-Person Chronicles from Some of 2000's Best Original Score Hopefuls," *Hollywood Reporter*, January 2001.
7. Roland Emmerich to TG, May 12, 2021.
8. David Arnold to TG, November 21, 2017.
9. Emmerich to TG.
10. Bennett, January 2001.
11. Ibid.
12. Emmerich to TG.
13. Chris Garcia, "Playing 'Patriot' Games," *Austin American-Statesman*, June 28, 2000.
14. Emmerich to TG.
15. Patt Diroll, "Gala Aims to Keep L.A. on Its Toes by Bringing Dance Back Again," *Los Angeles Times*, June 27, 2000.
16. Dyer, "John Williams Listens to the Song of a Tree."
17. JW, liner notes for *TreeSong* (Deutsche Grammophon, 2001).
18. Gil Shaham to TG, April 30, 2021.
19. Ibid.
20. Pincus, "From 'Star Wars' to 'TreeSong' with John Williams," *Berkshire Eagle*, July 10, 2000.

21. Oestreich, "Freshness and Fire in a Tanglewood Idyll," *New York Times*, July 11, 2000.
22. Jan Breslauer, "The Domingo Factor: L.A. Opera's New Leader Outlines Strategy for Putting Company 'On the Map,'" *Los Angeles Times*, September 12, 2000.
23. Dyer, "John Williams Considers Prospect of Writing Opera," *Boston Globe*, September 15, 2000.
24. Mark Swed, "Determined to Be Daring," *Los Angeles Times*, September 16, 2001.
25. Dyer, "John Williams Considers Prospect of Writing Opera."
26. Michael Walsh to TG, February 17, 2023.
27. Woody Allen, "The Kugelmass Episode," *New Yorker*, May 2, 1977.
28. Walsh to TG.
29. JW to TG, March 9, 2023.
30. Walsh to TG.
31. Mark Swed to TG, February 16, 2024.
32. Farrow to TG.
33. JW to TG, March 9, 2023.
34. Julie Hatfield, "Key Players Turn Out at Gala," *Boston Globe*, October 16, 2000.
35. Dyer, "Ozawa Plans Firsts for BSO's 100th," *Boston Globe*, September 28, 2000.
36. Dyer, "John Williams Listens to the Song of a Tree."
37. Ma to TG.
38. Dyer, "Yo-Yo Ma, Williams Make Night Magical," *Boston Globe*, February 23, 2001.
39. Fanto, "A Musical 'Home Away from Home,'" *Berkshire Landscapes*, Summer 2022.
40. Ibid.
41. Taylor to TG.
42. Dyer, "John Williams Listens to the Song of a Tree."
43. "The Sound and Music of *A.I.*," feature on *A.I.* home video release (DreamWorks and Warner Bros., 2011).
44. Bond, "God Almighty!".
45. "The Sound and Music of *A.I.*"
46. Ibid.
47. Ibid.
48. Curtis to TG.
49. Dyer, "Williams's Touch on 'A.I.' Lingers," *Boston Globe*, July 6, 2001.
50. Josh Groban to TG, June 18, 2021.
51. Ibid.
52. Dyer, "The Wizard of Film Scoring Tackles 'Harry Potter,'" *Boston Globe*, May 18, 2001.
53. Jenny Williams to TG, March 10, 2023.
54. Zach Sharf, "Steven Spielberg Is 'Very Happy' He Rejected 'Harry Potter' Director Offer: 'I Sacrificed a Great Franchise to Be with Family,'" *Variety*, February 14, 2023.
55. Columbus to TG.
56. Dyer, "The Wizard of Film Scoring Tackles 'Harry Potter.' "
57. Brand to TG.
58. Matt Wolf, "Making 'Harry Potter's' Music Magic," *Associated Press*, November 14, 2001.
59. Columbus to TG.
60. JW to Brian Lauritzen, Classical KUSC, March 3, 2023.
61. Kerber to TG.
62. Ibid.

63. Ibid.
64. Columbus to TG.
65. Dyer, "Director Columbus Discovered the Right Composer for 'Harry Potter,'" *Boston Globe*, November 11, 2001.
66. Wolf, "Making 'Harry Potter's' Music Magic."
67. David Kronke, "Magic Broom Ride," *Los Angeles Daily News/Longview News-Journal*, November 15, 2001.
68. Kirk Honeycutt, "Harry Potter," *Hollywood Reporter*, November 12, 2001.
69. David Hinckley, "They Shoot, He Scores: Filmdom's John Williams," *New York Daily News*, January 8, 2002.
70. "Former Pops Conductor Puts Forth Olympic Effort," *Boston Globe*, February 7, 2002.
71. Braider, liner notes.
72. Dangel to TG.
73. Burlingame, "A Career of Epic Proportions."
74. JW liner notes for *Yo-Yo Ma Plays the Music of John Williams* (Sony Classical, 2002).
75. Ibid.
76. Ibid.
77. Gina Piccalo and Louise Roug, "The Classics at Costco," *Los Angeles Times*, February 26, 2002.
78. Piccalo and Roug, "Space for a Classic," *Los Angeles Times*, March 19, 2002.
79. Grierson to TG.
80. Howard Shore to TG, February 9, 2022.
81. Stephen Moss, "The Force Is with Him," *The Guardian*, February 3, 2002.
82. JW commentary, *Star Wars—Episode II: Attack of the Clones* home video release (Lucasfilm Ltd., 2013).
83. Burtt to TG.
84. Zacharek, "In Space, No One Can Hear You Groan," *Salon*, May 16, 2002.
85. John Griffin, "Send in the Clones," *The Gazette* (Montreal), May 16, 2002.
86. Sragow, "Universal Themes," *Baltimore Sun*, May 16, 2002.
87. Burlingame, "A Career of Epic Proportions."
88. Dyer, "Previn's Berlin Accent," *Boston Globe*, March 10, 2002.
89. "Williams Pops in," *Boston Globe*, May 26, 2002.
90. William Ross to TG, January 23, 2024.
91. Ford A. Thaxton, "William Ross on Adapting Harry Potter and the Chamber of Secrets," *Soundtrack Magazine* 21, no. 84 (2002).
92. Columbus to TG.
93. Dyer, "An Enduring Love for Music, Movies," *Boston Globe*, June 23, 2002.
94. "Sound and Score" feature, *Minority Report* home video release (Paramount, 2010).
95. https://valleycatmusic.com/Deborah-singer.html.
96. Greiving, "Moaning Woman," *Film Score Monthly Online* 14, no. 7 (July 2009).
97. Oestreich, "Schubertizing the Movies," *New York Times*, June 30, 2002.
98. Dyer, "An Enduring Love for Music, Movies."
99. Ramiro Belgardt to TG, January 25, 2023.
100. Ibid.
101. Rachel Abramowitz, "Spielberg Decides It's Time to Have Some Serious Fun," *Los Angeles Times*, November 3, 2002.
102. Ibid.

103. "Scoring: *Catch Me if You Can*," feature on *Catch Me if You Can* home video release (DW Studios, 2012).
104. Ibid.
105. Bond, "God Almighty!"
106. Dan Higgins to TG, March 3, 2022.
107. "Scoring: *Catch Me if You Can*."
108. Steve Persall, "Catch This One if You Can," *Tampa Bay Times*, December 24, 2002.
109. https://www.youtube.com/watch?v=klUAGK9Z-dg.
110. Tim Smith, "Maestros and the Movies," *Baltimore Sun*, January 19, 2003.
111. Christopher Reynolds, "Concert Hall Has Small Cast of Big Donors," *Los Angeles Times*, August 30, 2003.
112. Reed Johnson and Gina Piccalo, "Hollywood Has Fine Romance with Gehry's Sound Palace," *Los Angeles Times*, October 26, 2003.
113. Frank Gehry to TG, November 8, 2021.
114. Swed, "Williams Evokes Hall's Steel Beginnings in 'Soundings,'" *Los Angeles Times*, October 26, 2003.
115. "Sound and Image: John Williams and the Chicago Symphony," JW, interview with Phillip Huscher for Chicago Symphony Orchestra program, November 28, 2003.
116. John von Rhein, "Williams' Cinematic Journey Brings Wonder to CSO," *Chicago Tribune*, December 1, 2003.
117. JW, interview with Leonard Slatkin for *John Williams: Horn Concerto* recording by Detroit Symphony Orchestra (Naxos Portara, 2010).
118. Ibid.
119. JW, program note, November 29, 2003, and December 2, 2003, provided by Chicago Symphony Orchestra.
120. Ibid.

Chapter 15

1. Jack Sullivan, "Conversations with John Williams," *The Chronicle of Higher Education* 53, no. 19 (January 12, 2007).
2. John Horn, "Guiding the Growth of a Wizard," *Los Angeles Times*, January 18, 2004.
3. Ibid.
4. Alfonso Cuarón to TG, September 12, 2023.
5. Ibid.
6. Matessino, liner notes for *Harry Potter and the Prisoner of Azkaban*, from *Harry Potter: The John Williams Soundtracks Collection* (La-La Land Records, 2018).
7. Ibid.
8. Ibid.
9. Cuarón to TG.
10. Ibid.
11. Matessino, liner notes, 2018.
12. Cuarón to TG.
13. Desplat to TG.
14. Columbus to TG.
15. Farrow to TG.

16. T. J. Simers, "Now Everyone Will Say They're a Trojan Fan," *Los Angeles Times*, January 2, 2004.
17. Geoff Edgers, "Some Democrats Play Hooky to Attend Tribute to Kennedy," *Boston Globe*, July 28, 2004.
18. Pincus, "Williams Asks: Was It Really 25 Years?" *Berkshire Eagle*, July 30, 2004.
19. Ibid.
20. Dyer, "Williams Celebration Has a Surprise Ending," *Boston Globe*, August 17, 2004.
21. Spielberg, liner notes for *The Terminal* (Decca, 2004).
22. "In Flight Service: The Music of The Terminal," feature on *The Terminal* home video release (Paramount Pictures, 2014).
23. Ibid.
24. Ibid.
25. JoAnn Turovsky to TG, April 6, 2021.
26. Ibid.
27. "Pasadena Symphony Musician, Emily Bernstein, Loses Battle with Cancer," *Los Angeles Times*, February 4, 2005.
28. "John Williams: Writing the Soundtrack to Our Lives," *International Musician* 103, no. 7 (July 2005).
29. Turovsky to TG.
30. Cosel to TG.
31. JW to TG, March 9, 2023.
32. "John Williams: Movie Music Man," *CBS The Early Show*, December 15, 2004.
33. Kathy Blumenstock, "Six Stars Glitter Along the Potomac," *Washington Post*, December 19, 2004.
34. Bond, "Williams Tells.".
35. Dyer, "Making 'Star Wars' Sing Again."
36. Bond, "Williams Tells."
37. Ibid.
38. Dyer, "Latest 'Star Wars' Score Is an Emotional Adventure," *Boston Globe*, June 6, 2005.
39. "National Registry Adds 50 Recordings," *Associated Press*, April 6, 2005.
40. "Editing, Sound and Music," feature on *Munich* home video release (Universal Studios, 2015).
41. Bond, "Williams Tells."
42. "Scoring *War of the Worlds*," feature on *War of the Worlds* home video release (Paramount, 2020).
43. Ibid.
44. Ibid.
45. Spielberg, liner notes for *War of the Worlds* (Decca Records, 2005).
46. Nekesa Mumbi Moody, "Yo-Yo Ma Reunites with John Williams," *Associated Press/Philadelphia Inquirer*, December 21, 2005.
47. Justin McCurry, "Geisha Film Incenses Japanese," *The Guardian*, November 28, 2005.
48. Mangan, Timothy, "Composer for the Stars," *Gramophone*, May 2006.
49. Bond and Guerin, "Speaking in Tunes," *Hollywood Reporter*, February 17, 2006.
50. Mangan, "Composer for the Stars."
51. Ma to TG.

52. "The Music of 'Memoirs,'" feature on *Memoirs of a Geisha* home video release (Sony Pictures, 2007).
53. Bond and Guerin, "Speaking in Tunes."
54. "The Music of 'Memoirs.'"
55. "John Williams: Writing the Soundtrack to Our Lives."
56. Sullivan, "Conversations with John Williams."
57. Bond, "Williams Tells."
58. Rob Marshall to TG, July 28, 2014.
59. Honeycutt, "Memoirs of a Geisha," *Hollywood Reporter*, November 21, 2005.
60. "Editing, Sound and Music."
61. Ibid.
62. Ibid.
63. Ibid.
64. Bond, "Williams Tells."
65. Ibid.
66. Wannberg to TG.
67. J. A. Adande, "Pairing Williams with the NFL Is Sure to Be a Hit," *Los Angeles Times*, September 7, 2006.
68. Ibid.
69. Matthew Guerrieri, "Classical Notes: Striking Out?" *Boston Globe*, November 2, 2007.
70. JW to TG, October 28, 2022.
71. Michael Zaretsky to TG, September 13, 2021.
72. Fanto, "Tanglewood Hit," *Berkshire Eagle*, December 8, 2006.
73. Fanto, "Williams: Damage 'Devastating,'" *Berkshire Eagle*, December 9, 2006.
74. Clarence Fanto to TG, October 3, 2022.
75. Pincus, "Pops' John Williams Finds His Musical Vatican."
76. Zaretsky to TG.
77. Arlich to TG.
78. Jeffrey Gantz, "Williams Writes Tune for Fenway," *Boston Globe*, March 25, 2012.
79. Arlich to TG.
80. Terrence Rafferty, "Indiana Jones and the Savior of a Lost Art," *New York Times*, May 4, 2008.
81. Interviews with JW, Spielberg, and Lucas included on *Indiana Jones: The Soundtracks Collection* (Concord Records, 2008).
82. Ibid.
83. Janelle Gelfand, "John Williams Joins Pops, Remembers an Old Friend," *Cincinnati Enquirer*, August 1, 2010.
84. James Mangold to TG, August 18, 2023.

Chapter 16

1. Tommasini, "Come on with the Rain (Sharks and Ewoks Too)," *New York Times*, September 17, 2007.
2. https://youtu.be/jJfGx4G8tjo?si=V-bc3JcqJDR_KvHu.
3. Rob Hotakainen, "Aretha Franklin, Yo-Yo Ma to Play for Obama," *Miami Herald*, December 18, 2008.

4. JW, interview with Josephine Reed, National Endowment of the Arts, February 2010, https://www.arts.gov/stories/podcast/john-williams#audio-file.
5. Ibid.
6. Burlingame, "Williams' Music to Obama's Ears," *Variety*, January 15, 2009.
7. JW to TG, June 2, 2023.
8. Ibid.
9. Vicki J. Schaeffer, "An Historical Survey of Shaker Hymnody Expressing the Christian Values of Innocence and Simplicity" (PhD dissertation, Indiana University, 1992), 60.
10. JW, interview, NEA.
11. Anthony McGill to TG, November 11, 2022.
12. Tim Wallace, Karen Yourish, and Tony Griggs, "Trump's Inauguration vs. Obama's: Comparing the Crowds," *New York Times*, January 20, 2017.
13. Daniel J. Wakin, "Actually Live Debut Set for Inaugural Composition," *New York Times*, January 23, 2009.
14. Swed, "Music Review: A John Williams Premiere at SummerFest," *Los Angeles Times*, August 21, 2011.
15. Tommasini, "A New Williams Work for a Momentous Occasion," *New York Times*, January 20, 2009.
16. Arthur Kaptainis, "Concert Music Entertains Obama's Crowd," *Vancouver Sun*, January 21, 2009.
17. JW to TG, June 2, 2023.
18. McGill to TG.
19. John Horn, "'Star Wars' Concert: Coda with Yoda," *Los Angeles Times*, October 1, 2009.
20. Brossé to TG, November 4, 2009.
21. David Weininger, "Williams Salutes a Virtuosic Violist," *Boston Globe*, May 22, 2009.
22. Cathy Basrak to TG, September 18, 2023.
23. Weininger, "Williams Salutes a Virtuosic Violist."
24. Basrak to TG.
25. Joel Brown, "John Williams Takes Colorful Detour," *Boston Globe*, May 27, 2009.
26. Basrak to TG.
27. JW, letter to Milton Babbitt, September 4, 2007.
28. JW to TG, April 14, 2023.
29. Basrak to TG.
30. Edgers, "Groundbreaking Master of Angelic Instrument Set to Take Wing," *Boston Globe*, September 22, 2009.
31. Ibid.
32. Pilot to TG.
33. Edgers, September 22, 2009.
34. Ibid.
35. Pilot to TG.
36. Ibid.
37. Jeremy Eichler, "BSO Opens Season by Honoring One of Its Own," *Boston Globe*, September 24, 2009.
38. JW, letter to Babbitt, April 8, 2010.
39. Pilot to TG.

40. Christine Simmons, "Dylan, Eastwood Get White House Awards," *Associated Press*, February 26, 2010.
41. Kushner, speech for the President's Committee on Arts and Humanities dinner, National Museum of American History, February 24, 2010. (Shared by JW.)
42. Slatkin to TG.
43. Mark Volpe to TG, June 13, 2023.
44. Slatkin to TG.
45. Edgers, "'Pops' at 125: An Icon Evolves," *Boston Globe*, May 2, 2010.
46. Joan Anderman, "Endlessly Devoted to His Music," *Boston Globe*, May 11, 2010.
47. Keisuke Wakao to TG, September 21, 2021.
48. Ibid.
49. Ibid.
50. Ibid.
51. JW to TG, June 2, 2023.
52. Stéphane Denève to TG, September 4, 2023.
53. Volpe to TG.
54. Ibid.
55. James C. McKinley Jr., "John Williams Lets His Muses Carry Him Along," *New York Times*, August 19, 2011.
56. Penelope Jencks, *Three Sculptures at Tanglewood* (self-published, 2021).
57. Ibid.
58. Jencks to TG, October 14, 2021.
59. Volpe to TG.
60. Jencks, *Three Sculptures*.
61. Pincus, "United to Honor Copland," *Berkshire Eagle*, July 1, 2011.
62. Jencks, *Three Sculptures*.
63. Jencks to TG.
64. Jencks, *Three Sculptures*.
65. Jencks to TG.
66. Volpe to TG.
67. McKinley, "John Williams Lets His Muses Carry Him Along."
68. Swed, "Music Review."
69. Ibid.
70. McKinley, "John Williams Lets His Muses Carry Him Along."
71. JW, liner notes for *War Horse* (Sony Classical, 2011).
72. JW to TG, March 17, 2023.
73. "Editing & Scoring," feature on *War Horse* home video release (Touchstone, 2012).
74. Geoff Boucher, "Riding High," *Los Angeles Times*, December 15, 2011.
75. "Editing & Scoring."
76. A. O. Scott, "Innocence Is Trampled, but a Bond Endures," *New York Times*, December 22, 2011.
77. "Editing & Scoring."
78. Gary Thompson, "In This War, It's Horse Against Machine," *Philadelphia Daily News*, December 23, 2011.
79. Ty Burr, "Classic Hollywood Rides Again," *Boston Globe*, December 23, 2011.
80. Scott, "Innocence Is Trampled."

81. Spielberg, liner notes for *War Horse* (Sony Classical, 2011).
82. "Editing & Scoring."
83. Slatkin to TG.
84. JW to TG, May 10, 2023.
85. Pete Docter to TG, May 12, 2023.
86. "Tintin: The Score," feature on *The Adventures of Tintin* home video release (Paramount Pictures, 2012).
87. Ibid.
88. Ibid.
89. Ibid.
90. Ibid.
91. Michael Phillips, "'Tintin' Fake, Frantic, Tiring," *Chicago Tribune*, December 23, 2011.
92. David Edelstein, "The Bigger, Better *Adventures of Tintin*," *Vulture*, December 19, 2011.
93. Gantz, "Williams Writes Tune for Fenway."
94. Louise K. Cornetta, "Q&A: John Williams Talks Fenway, Red Sox," ESPN, https://www.espn.com/blog/music/post/_/id/98/composer-john-williams-talks-fenway-red-sox.
95. Eichler, "At Tanglewood, Pops and Friends Toast Williams," *Boston Globe*, August 21, 2012.
96. JW to TG, November 8, 2023.
97. JW to TG, December 19, 2023.
98. Farrow to TG.
99. Rebecca Keegan, "John Williams and Steven Spielberg Mark 40 Years of Collaboration," *Los Angeles Times*, January 8, 2012.
100. Ibid.
101. Carol Beggy and Mark Shanahan, "Names: Abe's Story on Hold for Indiana Jones," *Boston Globe*, March 27, 2007.
102. "In Lincoln's Footsteps," feature on *Lincoln* home video release (Touchstone, 2013).
103. Ibid.
104. Tim Smith, "Film Composer Williams in First Visit to Baltimore," *Baltimore Sun*, June 2, 2013.
105. Burlingame, "The Sounds of Cinema: 'Lincoln,'" *Variety*, February 8, 2013.
106. Belgardt to TG.
107. Burlingame, "The Sounds of Cinema: 'Lincoln.'"
108. "In Lincoln's Footsteps."
109. Kerber to TG.
110. Belgardt to TG.
111. Phillips, "A Political Animal of a Different Kind," *Chicago Tribune*, November 9, 2012.
112. JW to TG, March 9, 2023, and March 17, 2023.
113. JW to TG, March 9, 2023.
114. Smith, June 2, 2013.
115. JW to TG, July 20, 2023.
116. JW to TG, June 2, 2023.
117. John Wirt, "Part of a Purpose: Pablo Sáinz Villegas Shares the Romance of the Guitar at the Manship Theatre," *The Advocate* (Baton Rouge), October 27, 2019.
118. JW to TG, October 25, 2013.
119. Ibid.
120. Gloria Cheng to TG, February 1, 2023.

121. "The Legend and the Music," feature on *The Book Thief* home video release (20th Century Fox, 2014).
122. Ibid.
123. Holden, "A Refuge Found in Pages," *New York Times*, November 7, 2013.
124. Michael Ordoña, "The Scores: What Composers Hear," *Los Angeles Times*, December 10, 2013.
125. Ibid.
126. "The Legend and the Music."
127. Ibid.
128. Ibid.
129. David Ng, "André Previn's N.Y. State of Mind," *Los Angeles Times*, May 18, 2014.
130. JW to TG, April 10, 2024.
131. Dyer, "John Williams 80th Birthday Celebration," Tanglewood program, August 18, 2012.
132. Shalini Dore, "Darth Vader, Storm Troopers Crash Stage as L.A. Philharmonic Honors John Williams," *Variety*, October 1, 2014.
133. Ibid.
134. Swed, "Stars Align for John Williams," *Los Angeles Times*, October 2, 2014.
135. Gustavo Dudamel to TG, January 12, 2024.
136. Ibid.
137. JW to TG, December 17, 2015.
138. Ibid.
139. JW to TG, October 9, 2023.

Chapter 17

1. Lucas, comments at dedication of The John Williams Scoring Stage at the University of Southern California, April 26, 2011. https://cinema.usc.edu/news/article.cfm?id=11777
2. "The Maestro's Finale," feature on *Star Wars—Episode IX: The Rise of Skywalker* (Disney Plus, 2020).
3. Shore to TG.
4. Kim Masters, "The Force Is with Kathleen Kennedy," *Hollywood Reporter*, February 8, 2013.
5. Kennedy to TG.
6. JW to TG, December 17, 2015.
7. Liam Stack, "George Lucas Criticizes Latest 'Star Wars' Installment," *New York Times*, December 31, 2015.
8. JW to TG, December 17, 2015.
9. Ibid.
10. Lehman to TG.
11. JW to TG, December 17, 2015.
12. Ibid.
13. JW to TG, July 20, 2023.
14. Kennedy to TG.
15. Burlingame, "Film Score Icons Williams, Morricone and Horner Loom Large in Oscar Race," *Variety*, December 9, 2015.
16. Sue Mallett to TG, October 17, 2023.

17. Ibid.
18. Linda A. Rapka, "John Williams Receives Lifetime Contribution to Hollywood Award," AFM Local 47, https://www.afm47.org/press/john-williams-receives-lifetime-contribution-to-hollywood-award/.
19. Ibid.
20. JW to TG, July 20, 2023.
21. Spielberg, email to TG, March 23, 2018.
22. Thomas Newman to TG, October 13, 2015.
23. Ibid.
24. Seth Abramovitch, "Yes, I Did Say That!" *Hollywood Reporter*, August 28, 2015.
25. Brian Truitt, "The Force Awakens in J. J. Abrams," *USA Today*, December 13, 2015.
26. https://www.youtube.com/watch?v=8977YNfJdBU.
27. Alessandro De Rosa, *Ennio Morricone in His Own Words* (Oxford University Press, 2019).
28. "AFI Lifetime Achievement Award: A Tribute to John Williams," TNT, June 15, 2016.
29. Burlingame, "'Fantastic Beasts' and 'The BFG' Tap into Magical Musical Worlds," *Variety*, December 1, 2016.
30. JW to TG, May 10, 2023.
31. JW, interviews for *The BFG* electronic press kit (Disney, 2016).
32. Ibid.
33. Peter Debruge, "Cannes Film Review: Steven Spielberg's 'The BFG,'" *Variety*, May 14, 2016.
34. Rian Johnson to TG.
35. Ibid.
36. Ibid.
37. Ibid.
38. Ibid.
39. Ibid.
40. Ibid.
41. William Ross to TG, June 5, 2019.
42. Anthony McCartney, "Coroner: Cocaine Among Drugs Found in Carrie Fisher's System," *Associated Press*, June 19, 2017.
43. Kobe Bryant to TG, April 25, 2017.
44. Ibid.
45. JW to TG, April 27, 2017.
46. Bryant to TG.
47. Glen Keane to TG, May 2, 2017.
48. Bryant to TG.
49. Keane to TG.
50. JW to TG, April 27, 2017.
51. Josh Rottenberg, "Q&A: 'Ready Player One's' Steven Spielberg and Ernest Cline on Pooling Their Nostalgia to Tell a New Story," *Los Angeles Times*, March 23, 2018.
52. Burlingame, "John Williams and Alan Silvestri to Score Steven Spielberg's Next Films," *Variety*, July 7, 2017.
53. Spielberg, email to TG, March 23, 2018.
54. "Arts and Entertainment: Music for *The Post*," feature on *The Post* home video release (20th Century Fox, 2018).
55. Burlingame, "John Williams Is on Target to Set Yet Another Oscar Record," *Variety*, January 10, 2018.

56. "Arts and Entertainment."
57. JW to TG, July 20, 2023.
58. Brent Lang, "'Star Wars' Han Solo Spinoff: Lord & Miller Fired After Clashing with Kathleen Kennedy," *Variety*, June 20, 2017.
59. All Powell quotes in this chapter from Powell to TG, February 8, 2022.
60. Dobrin, "May the Force Be with Him," *Philadelphia Inquirer*, April 20, 2018.
61. "Academy Award-Winning Composer and Conductor John Williams to Bequeath Concert and Film Scores to Juilliard," https://www.juilliard.edu/news/131971/academy-award-winning-composer-and-conductor-john-williams-bequeath-concert-and-film.
62. Doreen Ringer-Ross to TG, April 28, 2021.
63. Burlingame, "John Williams Honored at BMI Film, TV and Visual Media Awards," *Variety*, May 10, 2018.
64. Taylor to TG.
65. JW to TG, October 9, 2023.
66. Deborah Vankin, "Andre Previn, Former L.A. Phil Music Director and Four-Time Oscar Winner, Dies at 89," *Los Angeles Times*, February 28, 2019.
67. JW to TG, June 2, 2023.
68. Volpe to TG.
69. Taylor to TG.
70. JW to TG, October 28, 2022.
71. Farrow to TG.
72. Chris Lee, "Colin Trevorrow's Firing from *Star Wars* Is Another Reminder That No Director Will Ever Be Bigger than the Franchise," *Vulture*, September 8, 2017, https://www.vulture.com/2017/09/star-wars-episode-8-colin-trevorrow-firing-explanation.html.
73. "The Skywalker Legacy," feature on *Rise of Skywalker* (2020).
74. Ibid.
75. Kennedy to TG.
76. "The Maestro's Finale."
77. Belgardt to TG.
78. Ross, The Force Is Still Strong with John Williams.".
79. Belgardt to TG.
80. "The Maestro's Finale."
81. Ibid.
82. Burlingame, "With 'Rise of Skywalker,' Composer John Williams Puts His Coda on 'Star Wars,'" *Variety*, December 18, 2019.
83. Ibid.
84. JW to TG, July 20, 2023.
85. Belgardt to TG.
86. Lehman to TG.
87. Burlingame, "With 'Rise of Skywalker.'"
88. "The Maestro's Finale."
89. Matt Walker to TG, May 16, 2019.
90. Ross to TG, June 5, 2019.
91. Greiving, "Star Wars: Galaxy's Edge Needed a Musical Score. Cue John 'Obi-wan' Williams," *Los Angeles Times*, June 12, 2019.
92. Belgardt to TG.

93. Kennedy to TG.
94. McGill to TG.

Chapter 18

1. Ma to TG.
2. Dudamel to TG.
3. Michael Beek, "John Williams on Composing for Film, His Concert Work—and the Vienna Philharmonic," *BBC Music Magazine*, February 23, 2021.
4. Stefan Ender, "Besuch vom Lieben Gott," *Der Standard*, January 19, 2020.
5. Beek, "John Williams on Composing."
6. Zoë Madonna, "Anne-Sophie Mutter on Williams, Nelsons, and the Silence of Nature," *Boston Globe*, July 16, 2017.
7. Morris to TG.
8. "At Home with Gustavo Dudamel and John Williams," Classical KUSC, June 30, 2020.
9. Beek, "John Williams on Composing."
10. *Great Performances*, "A John Williams Premiere at Tanglewood," aired November 12, 2021 on PBS, https://www.pbs.org/wnet/gperf/john-williams-anne-sophie-mutter-talk-composing-and-more-azi/13164/.
11. Ibid.
12. Ibid.
13. Ibid.
14. A.Z. Madonna, "At Tanglewood, a Showcase of John Williams's Strengths," *Boston Globe*, July 26, 2021.
15. Pincus, "Music Review: At Tanglewood, John Williams Premieres a New Concerto That 'Never Quite Seems to Settle Down,'" *Berkshire Eagle*, July 26, 2021.
16. JW to TG, October 9, 2023.
17. Dudamel to TG.
18. Javier C. Hernández, "John Williams, Hollywood's Maestro, Looks Beyond the Movies," *New York Times*, February 8, 2022.
19. Abbey White, "John Williams, Bob Iger Awarded Honorary Knighthood by Late Queen Elizabeth II," *Hollywood Reporter*, September 24, 2022.
20. Anne-Sophie Mutter to TG, August 11, 2023.
21. Volpe to TG.
22. Spielberg to TG, February 10, 2023.
23. JW to TG, February 6, 2023.
24. Bernstein, *The Jewish Mothers' Hall of Fame*.
25. JW to TG, February 6, 2023.
26. Spielberg to TG, February 10, 2023.
27. Ibid.
28. JW to TG, February 6, 2023.
29. Spielberg to TG, February 10, 2023.
30. Ibid.
31. JW to TG, February 6, 2023.
32. Belgardt to TG.
33. *Star Wars—Music by John Williams*.

34. Mangold to TG.
35. Ibid.
36. Kennedy to TG.
37. Mangold to TG.
38. JW to TG, November 8, 2023.
39. Ibid.
40. Mangold to TG.
41. JW to TG, November 8, 2023.
42. Mangold to TG.
43. Ibid.
44. Ibid.
45. Ax to TG.
46. JW to TG, November 8, 2023.
47. Ibid.
48. JW to TG, December 19, 2023.
49. JW to TG, June 2, 2023.
50. Swed to TG.
51. Ibid.
52. Dudamel to TG.
53. Denève to TG.

Epilogue

1. Denève to TG.
2. Ibid.
3. JW to TG, February 13, 2024.
4. JW to TG, November 8, 2023.
5. JW to TG, March 9, 2023.
6. Jenny Williams to TG, March 6, 2024.
7. David Brooks, "The Essential Skills for Being Human," *New York Times*, October 19, 2023.
8. JW to TG, November 8, 2023.
9. JW to TG, July 20, 2023.
10. JW to TG, March 7, 2023.

Index

For the benefit of digital users, indexed terms that span two pages (e.g., 52–53) may, on occasion, appear on only one of those pages.

Figures are indicated by an italic *f* following the page number.

1941, 239–42, 261, 265–66, 296, 342
2001: A Space Odyssey, 123, 134–35, 203, 216, 230–31
20th Century Fox, 35–36, 52, 66, 71, 74, 77, 78–79, 86, 95–96, 101–3, 108–10, 113, 116–17, 120–21, 128, 151, 153, 157, 179, 190, 200, 201, 203–4, 205, 210, 211–12, 214–15, 224–26, 236, 247–48, 257, 258, 286, 299, 300–1, 302, 308–9, 331, 345, 421, 503, 513

A.I.: Artificial Intelligence, 433–37, 444–45, 448–49, 548
Abbott and Costello, 39–40
Abrams, J. J., 509–10, 511–12, 513, 516, 528–30, 531–32, 536
Accidental Tourist, The, 321–23, 339
Adams, Doug, 448–49
Adams, John, 550
Adventures of Tintin, The, 494–97, 514–15, 547–48
Affairs of Dobie Gillis, The, 65
Air and Simple Gifts (concert work), 478–81, 488–89, 498
Akihito, Emperor of Japan, 480
Alcoa Premiere, 90–91, 96–97, 155–56, 384
Alien, 235
Allen, Debbie, 376
Allen, Irwin, 108–10, 151–52, 176–78, 179–80, 183, 223–24
Allen, Woody, 431–32
Aloft to the Royal Masthead (concert work), 363
Alsop, Marin, 340–41
Altman, Robert, 88, 97, 105, 142, 145, 146, 147–49, 153–55, 162, 163–65, 175, 176–78, 182–83, 189, 195n.††, 223–24, 237, 514–15, 517, 553
Always, 334–36, 337, 361
Amazing Stories, 295–97, 317
American Federation of Musicians (AFM), 68, 83–84, 512, 526
American Graffiti, 88–89, 158, 188, 202, 227–28, 334n.**
American Journey, aka *The Unfinished Journey* (concert work), 426–27, 428, 442
Amistad, 402–5, 408, 409, 426, 465, 494, 499, 501, 523
Andersen, Arthur Olaf, 58, 64

Andrews, Julie, 70, 106, 348–49, 379
Angela's Ashes, 424–25, 504–5
Anhalt, Edward, 97, 183–84
Annaud, Jean-Jacques, 405–7
Antheil, George, 64–65, 457
Apartment, The, 96, 115
Arkush, Allan, 265–67
Arlen, Harold, 37–38, 79–80, 98–99
Arlich, Paula, 474–75
Armstrong, Louis, 37, 393
Arnaud, Leo, 29, 52, 321, 389
Arnold, David, 427–28
Asimov, Isaac, 267
Astaire, Fred, 78, 81–82, 96–97, 179, 378–79, 435, 463n.†, 514–15
Atkinson, Bill, 46–47
Ax, Emanuel, 7–8, 385–86, 549–50, 554–55

Babbitt, Milton, 483, 485
Bach, Johann Sebastian, 41–42, 53, 55, 67, 158, 321–23, 371–72, 421–22, 449–50, 480, 538, 540, 549
Bacharach, Burt, 69, 134
Bachelor Father, 91
Bachelor Flat, 95–96
Badham, John, 192n.**, 235–38
Balaban, Bob, 214–15, 217–18
Bambridge, John, Jr., 58–59
Bambridge, John, Sr., 58–59, 99
Barber, Samuel, 126, 330
Barry, John, 192, 253–54, 295–96, 384
Basie, Count, 68–69, 85–86, 267–68
Basrak, Cathy, 481–83
Battle, Kathleen, 327, 378, 413
Baxter, Les, 77, 318–21
Beatles, The, 94–95, 98–99, 124–25, 234–35, 250–51, 261, 340, 436n.†, 507, 518
Because They're Young, 88–89
Beethoven, Ludwig van, 53, 67, 98–99, 157, 191–92, 208, 269, 330, 415, 421–22, 507, 514, 539, 540, 549, 551
Belafonte, Harry, 68–69
Belgardt, Ramiro, 450, 500–1, 530, 531–32, 533, 544
Bennett, Tony, 114n.§§§, 288, 378

Berg, Alban, 262–63
Bergman, Alan and Marilyn, 115, 126, 130–31, 150–51, 274, 288–89, 294–95, 385
Berlin, Irving, 37–38, 39–40, 52, 155, 334n.**, 483
Berlin Philharmonic, 539–40, 554–55
Bernheimer, Martin, 283–84
Bernstein, Elmer, 78, 82–83, 89–90, 92, 96–97, 142, 144, 170–71, 240–41, 243, 456
Bernstein, Emily, 462–63
Bernstein, Leonard, 8–9, 58, 77n.*, 96, 98–99, 157–58, 253, 257, 283–84, 305, 309, 317–18, 322, 327, 340–41, 346, 391, 427, 460, 474, 480, 487–88, 489–90, 507, 527, 536–37
BFG, The, 514–16
Billings, William, 428
Bishop Loughlin Memorial High School, 43–44
Black Sunday, 186–87, 197–98, 202–3, 471n.§
Bob Hope Presents: The Chrysler Theatre, 90–91, 97, 384
Boddicker, Michael, 266–67
Bolcom, William, 316
Book Thief, The, 503–5
Borda, Deborah, 381
Born on the Fourth of July, 328–32, 355–56, 357, 358, 391, 393, 396, 427, 450, 501
Borok, Emanuel, 252, 288, 379
Boston Symphony Orchestra, 25–26, 47–48, 242, 243, 244–45, 251, 257, 270–71, 290, 293–94, 303, 317–18, 329, 346, 363, 369–70, 374–75, 379, 380–81, 393, 410, 413–14, 422–23, 432–33, 460, 473–74, 481–82, 483–84, 486–88, 498, 527, 528, 539
Botkin, Jr., Perry, 47, 49, 52–53
Boulez, Pierre, 550, 551
Bradley, Desmond, 137–38
Brahms, Johannes, 6, 64, 98–99, 107, 137–38, 157, 189n.‡, 208, 303–5, 393–94, 421–22, 507, 527, 537, 551
Brand, Jacqueline, 396, 407–8, 438
Brando, Marlon, 82–83, 185–86, 195–96, 230–31, 390
Bricusse, Leslie, 113, 114–15, 123–25, 128–29, 149–50, 151–52, 165, 232–34, 294–95, 342, 348–50, 364, 369
Bridge of Spies, 513
Bridge Too Far, A, 203n.*
Bridges of Madison County, The, 377–78, 468
Britten, Benjamin, 60, 64–65, 193–94, 440, 537
Brossé, Dirk, 481
Broughton, Bruce, 321–22, 341–42, 502–3
Brown, David, 171, 172, 181, 187–88, 227–28. *See also* Zanuck, Richard D.
Browning, John, 67–68, 69
Bryant, Kobe, 8–9, 519–21
Burtt, Ben, 210, 275, 276, 278, 287, 419, 446, 471

Bush, George H.W., 297, 321, 479
Bush, George W., 463

Caesar, Shirley, 398, 399, 414
California Split, 163–66
Call of the Champions (concert work), 441–42
Cameron, James, 408
Campbell, Joseph, 400–1
Canby, Vincent, 143–44, 159–60, 223–24, 241, 313, 325
Candoli, Pete, 63–64, 80, 83, 98
Cannon, Bruce, 397, 399
Cantor, Eddie, 35–37
Capshaw, Kate, 285–86, 300–1, 302, 370–71, 380, 437–38
Carousel, 16, 66–67, 71, 78–79
Carpenter, Carleton, 65–66
Carson, Johnny, 66, 159–60, 191, 393
Carter, Jimmy, 162–63, 233, 389–90, 479
Carter, Ron, 83
Castelnuovo-Tedesco, Mario, 64, 83
Catch Me if You Can, 447, 450–52, 453, 461, 496
CBS Radio, 32–35, 36–37, 39–41, 42–43, 46–47
Celebrate Discovery (concert work), 341, 442
Central Park Casino, 28–29
Champlin, Charles, 154, 161, 179, 180–81, 198, 228–29, 234, 238–39
Chariots of Fire, 264, 270–71
Checkmate, 90–91, 92–94, 99, 155–56, 451
Cheng, Gloria, 502–3
Chicago Symphony Orchestra, 77, 297, 365n.**, 454, 500–1
Chieftains, The, 359–62
Chopin, Frédéric, 48, 53, 67, 78
Chusid, Irwin, 32–35
Cinderella Liberty, 160–63, 176, 536, 538
Cipriano, Gene, 83, 92
Clark, Petula, 121–22, 124–25
Cleveland Orchestra, 297, 393, 395, 526
Clevenger, Dale, 454
Cliburn, Van, 67–68
Clifford, Graeme, 146–47
Clinton, Bill, 389–90, 426, 427, 479, 498
Clinton, Hillary, 426
Clooney, Rosemary, 162, 288, 369, 378
Close Encounters of the Third Kind, 198, 213–22, 224, 230–31, 236, 238–41, 247–48, 250, 263, 264–65, 266–67, 268, 272–73, 290, 292, 315–16, 345–46, 365, 376, 433–35, 440, 453, 454, 513–14, 516
Colburn School of Music, 486–87, 502–3
Cole, Nat King, 80
Colonna, Jerry, 24, 26, 27–28, 32–33, 35, 39, 44, 51, 57–58, 60, 63–64, 65
Color Purple, The, 295, 305, 309–10, 370–71, 402–3

Index 621

Columbia Pictures, 45, 52–53, 56, 77, 82–84, 88–89, 100, 148, 164, 218, 254–55
Columbia Records, 66, 70–71, 92–95, 98, 99, 102–3, 134, 183–84
Columbus, Chris, 323–24, 341–43, 345–46, 363–65, 415, 416–17, 437–38, 439–41, 447–48, 456, 459–60
Compinsky, Sara, 47–48, 347
Concerto for Bassoon and Orchestra: *The Five Sacred Trees* (concert work), 347, 381–83, 431, 485–86
Concerto for Cello and Orchestra (concert work), 370, 379–81, 407–8, 415, 432–33, 442, 522n.§, 554–55
Concerto for Clarinet and Orchestra (concert work), 341, 347
Concerto for Flute and Orchestra: *Design* (concert work), 156–57, 178, 263, 298, 468–69
Concerto for Harp and Orchestra: *On Willows and Birches* (concert work), 483–85, 486
Concerto for Horn and Orchestra (concert work), 414–15, 454–55, 485–86, 498
Concerto for Oboe and Orchestra (concert work), 486–87, 498
Concerto for Piano and Orchestra (concert work), 502–3, 549–50, 554–55
Concerto for Trumpet and Orchestra (concert work), 393–95
Concerto for Tuba and Orchestra (concert work), 298–99, 347, 485–86, 498
Concerto for Violin and Orchestra (concert work), 123, 178, 202–3, 261–63, 283, 308n.§§§, 347, 380n.††††, 383, 393, 413n.†††, 485–86, 490, 537–38
Concerto for Violin and Orchestra no. 2 (concert work), 537–39, 540
Conrack, 162–63, 291, 332–33, 398n.†
Conversations (concert work), 502–3
Copland, Aaron, 25, 64–65, 91, 92–93, 108, 142, 172, 195–96, 250, 251–52, 257, 267, 346–47, 361–62, 383, 394–95, 404, 427, 478–79, 480–81, 485, 487–90, 499–500, 501, 536–37
Coppola, Francis Ford, 124, 160, 400–1
Cosel, Bill, 253, 289, 326, 405, 463
Courage, Alexander "Sandy," 78, 83, 117, 136, 149–50, 234–35
Cowboys, The, 110–11, 142–44, 145, 149, 152, 172, 195–96, 199, 229, 230–31, 252–53, 291, 332–33
Crane, Hart, 9
Crosby, Bing, 31, 47
Cruise, Tom, 315, 328, 329, 359–60, 390, 448, 450, 466–67
Cuarón, Alfonso, 456–59, 505
Curtis, Bonnie, 348, 436

Cutter, Murray, 52

Daddy-O, 88
Daddy's Gone A-Hunting, 127
Dadié, Bernard, 403–4
Dahl, Roald, 514–15
Daly, Tyne, 363
Damone, Vic, 69–71, 75, 92–94, 115
Dangel, Susan, 253, 254, 279, 308, 363, 403–4, 442
Darren, James, 88–89, 99–101, 105–6
Davis, Miles, 42, 68–69, 83, 150, 502–3, 527
Davis-Monthan Air Force Base, 58, 60, 325–26
Day, Doris, 65, 81–82, 98, 100n.***
Day-Lewis, Daniel, 499, 500–1
De Palma, Brian, 193, 201, 202, 224–26
Dear Basketball, 519–21
Debussy, Claude, 42, 52, 64, 72–73, 193–94, 228, 551
DeCrescent, Sandy, 255, 374–75
DeFranco, Buddy, 68–69
Delerue, Georges, 220–22, 317–18, 352
Delius, Frederick, 491
DeMille, Cecil B., 21, 267–68
Denève, Stéphane, 272, 487, 540, 551, 552
Denver, John, 297, 305
Desplat, Alexandre, 212, 459, 502–3, 519n.‡
Detroit Symphony Orchestra, 485–86
Deutsch, Adolph, 29, 78, 84–85, 96
Deutsche Grammophon, 119
Diamond Head, 99–100, 525
Dickson, Harry Ellis, 289–90, 293, 317
Dietrich, Deborah, 448–49
Dillard, Pamela, 404
Disney (company), 78, 132, 203–4, 213, 217, 219, 294–95, 295n.**, 312–13, 338n.††, 341–42, 385n.§§§§, 390, 495, 496, 508–9, 512, 513, 514–15, 516, 519–20, 524, 528–29, 530, 532–33, 544–45
Disney, Walt, 39–40, 155, 201–2, 213
Docter, Pete, 495
Dolan-DePetro, Gertrude, 26
Domingo, Placido, 431, 432
Donner, Richard, 229–35, 456
Dorsey, Tommy, 31, 46–47, 48, 240, 393
Dove, Rita, 412–14, 443
Downey, Morton, 32
Doyle, Patrick, 415–16, 459
Dracula, 225–26, 235–38, 536
DreamWorks Pictures, 377–78, 403
Dreyfuss, Richard, 188, 213, 215, 218, 220, 227–28, 333–36, 369
Dri-Nite Club, 49–51
Duel, 67n.**, 168, 170, 171, 227n.§
Dufay Collective., 457
Dukakis, Michael, 317, 321, 369

Duo Concertante for Violin and Viola (concert work), 473–74
Dvořák, Antonín, 202, 203, 205–6, 207, 306, 307–8
Dyer, Richard, 7, 243–44, 248–49, 255, 260–61, 294, 298, 306, 314, 327, 345–46, 354, 359, 367–68, 370, 378–80, 421, 422, 431, 432–33, 440–41, 447, 465–66, 505–6
Dylan, Bob, 98–99, 261

Earthquake, 178–79, 180
Eastman School of Music, 129, 144
Eastwood, Clint, 8–9, 181–82, 295, 377–78
Easy Rider, 123, 134
Ebbins, Milton "Milt," 65, 69, 71
Ebert, Roger, 143–44, 234, 241, 384
Eiger Sanction, The, 181–82, 273–74, 377–78
Elegy for Cello and Orchestra (concert work), 396, 407–8, 442
Elfman, Danny, 315–16, 332, 390n.******
Elgar, Edward, 193–94, 261, 298, 370, 421, 491
Ellington, Duke, 26–27, 34, 37, 42, 68–69, 89, 297, 327, 380, 502–3
Emmerich, Roland, 427–29
Empire of the Sun, 309–13, 325, 353, 370–71, 459, 520
Empire Strikes Back, The, 242, 244–49, 252–53, 275–76, 278–79, 399, 400, 421, 530
Essay for Strings (concert work), 106–7, 308n.§§§, 431
Estes, Gene, 47, 49, 451
Evans, Bill, 549–50
Evans, Robert, 197–98
Evening at Pops, 243, 251, 253–54, 279, 288, 289, 308, 363, 403–4, 405, 414, 460

Fabelmans, The, 541–44, 548
Fabian, Lara, 436–37
Fairchild, Edgar "Cookie," 37
Faith, Percy, 70–71
Family Plot, 192–95, 202–3, 216, 225, 230–31, 258, 273–74, 440
Fanfare, for the President's Own (concert work), 502
Fanfare for Fenway (concert work), 498
Fanfare for Ten Year Olds (concert work), 317
Far and Away, 359–62, 365, 536
Farrow, Mia, 75–76, 129–30, 136–37, 144, 255–56, 432, 460, 499, 528
Feidman, Giora, 375
Feldman, Ronald, 378, 381
Fiddler on the Roof (film), 135–36, 137–40, 141–42, 145, 149–50, 155–56, 186, 189, 196, 252–53, 262, 370, 372
Fiedler, Arthur, 25, 229, 242, 243–44, 250–51, 252, 253–54, 264, 288–89, 358–59, 378, 379, 483–84, 489–90

Fields, Verna, 188, 189, 266
Filarmonica della Scala, 540–41
Fisher, Carrie, 204, 223–24, 275, 353n.†††, 444, 509, 519, 528–29
Fitzwilly, 115, 117, 298, 538
Fleischmann, Ernest, 220, 243, 283–84, 299, 316, 413, 550
For New York (To Lenny! To Lenny!) (concert work), 346n.***
for Seiji! (concert work), 422–23
Ford, Harrison, 211, 220, 259–60, 268, 275, 324, 339–40, 384, 400, 417, 475–76, 509, 513–14, 524, 528–29, 544–45, 547–48
Ford, John, 61, 96–97, 396–97, 446–47, 543–44
Fosse, Bob, 65
Foster, David, 436–37
Foster, Stephen, 131, 182–83
Fox, Charles, 172
Frankenheimer, John, 197–99
Franklin, Aretha, 369, 378, 478, 479
Franklyn, Robert, 52
Freese's Department Store, 22–23
Funny Face, 64–65, 78, 378–79
Fury, The, 224–26, 390

Gale, Bob, 239–41
Galway, James, 378, 379n.****
Garcia, Jerry, 266
Garcia, Russell, 79–80
Garfield, Gil, 55–56
Garland, Judy, 36–37, 78, 116, 135n.§, 348–49
Garner, Pam, 93–94
Gehry, Frank, 453, 505–6
Gelb, Peter, 244–45
General Electric Theatre, 90–91, 96–97
Genis, Timothy, 482
Gershwin, George, 37–38, 52, 58, 70, 92–93, 96, 99, 327, 364–65
Giacchino, Michael, 368n.‡‡, 495, 502–3, 524, 529–30
Gidget Goes to Rome, 99–101, 152, 345
Gilligan's Island, 103
Godfather, The, 69n.††, 143–44, 151, 152–53, 158, 160, 178, 180–81, 197, 273–74
Goetschius, Percy, 41–42
Goldblum, Jeff, 365–66, 368, 401
Goldenberg, Billy, 67n.**, 170
Goldenberg, Morris "Mo," 67
Goldsmith, Jerry, 64, 81–82, 86–87, 90, 103, 117, 180–81, 199n.‡‡, 229–30, 235, 251–52, 285, 315–16, 317–18, 390, 454, 456
Golson, Benny, 462
Goodbye, Mr. Chips (1969 film), 121–22, 123–26, 127, 128–29, 130–32, 134, 137–38, 186
Goodman, Benny, 31, 162, 206, 240

Goodwin, Doris Kearns, 426, 499–500
Göransson, Ludwig, 533
Gorbachev, Mikhail, 358
Gorfaine, Michael, 299, 338, 447, 489–90, 512, 549
Gould, Elliott, 153, 154, 164–65
Graduate, The, 114–15
Graves, Robert, 5, 9, 137–38, 381–82, 454–55. See also *White Goddess, The*
Great Ocean Forests (concert work), 548–49
Green, Johnny, 28–29, 220–22
Grieg, Edvard, 388
Grierson, Ralph, 190, 271, 291–92, 444
Groban, Josh, 436–37
Grossman, Sam, 183–87, 267–68
Grusin, Dave, 86, 87, 114–15, 136, 153–54, 323, 341–42, 350–51, 384
Gruska, Bobby, 279, 336, 408n.‡‡
Gruska, Ethan, 337–38
Gruska, Jay, 278, 336–38, 409
Guide for the Married Man, A, 114–15, 132, 495
Guillermin, John, 196

Hamill, Mark, 201, 205, 211, 234, 252–53, 509, 516, 532
Hamlisch, Marvin 161, 187, 220–22, 253–54
Hammerstein, Oscar, II 16, 41n.†, 66, 106, 175, 209. See also Rodgers, Richard
Hanks, Tom, 8, 409–10, 451–52, 453, 479, 513–14
Hanson, Harold, 60
Hanson, Howard, 271–72
Harbert, James, 92–93, 98, 102–3, 183–85
Harry Potter and the Chamber of Secrets, 445, 447–48, 450–51, 546
Harry Potter and the Prisoner of Azkaban, 428–29, 456–60, 505
Harry Potter and the Sorcerer's Stone, 6, 437–41, 452, 481, 515, 532–33, 536
Hart, James V., 348, 354
Harvey, Paul, 316
Haymon, Cynthia, 413–14
Heartbeeps, 264–67, 361
Heartwood (concert work), 443
Heaven's Gate, 251–52, 354
Hedren, Tippi, 55–56, 96
Heidi, 117–20, 121–22, 129, 141, 203, 204–5
Hein, Richard, 47, 55–56, 130–31
Heinz, John, 354n.‡‡‡, 463
Heinz, Teresa (Kerry), 460
Helfer, Bobby, 78, 79–80, 136, 152–53
Hepburn, Audrey, 8–9, 78, 112–14, 334–35, 378–79, 384
Herlihy, Joe, 24, 25
Herrmann, Bernard, 29–30, 36–37, 82, 96, 126, 133, 140, 145, 149, 169, 193–94, 216, 224–26, 236, 253–54, 307n.‡‡‡, 339, 387, 448, 449, 456, 460, 483, 514
Higgins, Dan, 83, 451, 453
Highwood's Ghost (concert work), 527
Hirsch, Paul, 202, 203, 210, 224–26, 390
Hitchcock, Alfred, 8–9, 84, 96, 151, 169, 188, 192–95, 199, 215, 225, 258, 448, 505
Hollywood Bowl, 4, 220, 229, 243, 250, 283, 290, 299, 305, 318–19, 327, 347, 363, 395, 413, 429–30, 436–37, 453, 519–21, 527, 534, 540, 550–51
Hollywood Television Theatre, 199
Holocaust (Shoah), 43, 309–10, 365, 370–71, 376–78, 390–91, 402–3, 411, 485, 503, 504
Holst, Gustav, 202, 203, 207–8, 245–46, 283
Holt, Natalie, 533
Home Alone 2: Lost in New York, 363–65
Home Alone, 341–46, 348, 364, 385, 415, 416, 438, 447, 515, 529
Hook, 348–54, 357–58, 364–65, 497, 515
Hope, Bob, 24, 57–58, 60, 97
Hopkins, Anthony, 239–40, 386–87, 403–4
Horner, James, 296–97, 310n.††††, 360, 406, 408, 508, 512
Horton, Robert, 65–67, 91
Houston Symphony Orchestra, 106–7, 116, 126, 305, 308n.§§§, 393
How to Steal a Million, 112–13, 247–48, 326, 451
Howard, Ron, 359–60, 362, 524
Howren, Frank, 65–66
Hu, Dr. Siu-Ying, 430
Hughes, John, 341, 363–64, 390
Hymn to New England (concert work), 305–6

I Passed for White, 78, 89
Images, 127, 145–50, 152–53, 182–83, 188–89, 195–96, 307–8, 310–11, 466–67, 468–69
Inchon, 251–52
Indiana Jones and the Dial of Destiny, 545–48, 553
Indiana Jones and the Kingdom of the Crystal Skull, 475–77, 485–86, 496
Indiana Jones and The Last Crusade, 323–26, 332, 447–48, 544
Indiana Jones and the Temple of Doom, 285–88, 305, 323–24, 369, 475–76
Ingle, Don, 47, 49
Irving, Amy, 224–25, 257

Jackson, Mahalia, 8–9, 94, 398, 414
Jackson, Michael, 294–95, 348
Jacobs, Arthur P., 123, 124–25, 128, 155
Jamaica High School, 44
James Bond, 88–89, 112–13, 127, 136, 181, 186–87, 257–58, 286, 323–24
Jane Eyre, 139–42, 146, 181, 186, 229, 247–48, 448–49

Jarre, Maurice, 220–22, 253–54, 287–88, 317–18, 406n.††
Jaws 2, 226–29, 234–35, 245, 401, 445, 534n.**
Jaws, 123, 171–72, 174, 178, 180, 181, 182, 185–86, 187–92, 194–95, 196, 198, 200, 202, 213, 215–16, 226–28, 229, 240–41, 247–48, 257, 261, 298, 299, 313–14, 345–46, 365, 368, 377, 427–28, 468, 478, 497, 506–7, 509, 513–14, 529, 543–44
Jencks, Penelope, 488–90
Jewison, Norman, 135–36, 138–40, 149–50
JFK, 332, 355–58, 386n.*****, 388, 449, 472, 501
John Goldfarb, Please Come Home, 101–3
Johnny Staccato, 92
Johnson, Rian, 6–7, 259–60, 516–19, 528–29, 547–48
Johnson, Tommy, 190
Jones, Quincy, 86, 162, 166, 295, 317–18, 379, 508
Jones, Shirley, 66, 71, 92–93, 175–76
Jones, Spike, 34–35, 47
Jones, Trevor, 261
Juilliard School, The, 29–30, 56, 58, 59, 67–68, 73, 102–3, 130–31, 170, 262, 526–27
Jurassic Park, 321n.*, 361–62, 365–70, 371–72, 377, 396, 400, 401–2, 433–34, 467, 469–70, 495, 540

Kael, Pauline, 132, 154–55, 173, 226, 234
Kahn, Michael, 271–72, 501
Kahn, Roger Wolfe, 29, 78, 321
Kaifu, Toshiki, 340–41
Kamiński, Janusz, 401, 403, 450–51, 501
Kane, Artie, 367–68, 439
Kane, JoAnne, 367–68
Kasdan, Lawrence, 245, 260, 321–22, 323, 417, 509
Kasha, Al, 100–1, 152, 179, 180
Kazanjian, Howard, 216–17, 258, 261, 275–76, 278
Keane, Glen, 519–20
Kelly, Gene, 39–40, 78, 114–15, 165, 527
Keneally, Thomas, 295, 370–71
Kennedy Center Honors, 463
Kennedy, Edward "Ted," 8–9, 358, 460, 463
Kennedy, John F., 329, 355–58, 389, 412
Kennedy, Kathleen, 175, 295, 310n.††††, 348–49, 367–68, 377, 491–92, 509, 511–12, 524, 528, 529–30, 532–34, 544–45, 546
Kenton, Stan, 69, 106
Kerber, Randy, 223n.*, 330, 357, 407–8, 438–39, 500
Kern, Jerome, 6, 28–29, 37–38, 75, 76, 334n.**, 483, 515
Kerrigan, Nancy, 332
Kerry, John, 460
Kershner, Irvin, 97, 245, 417
Kilar, Wojciech, 374
Killers, The, 101

Klein, Bob, 90, 149n.****, 165, 175–76, 186–87
Klein, Manny, 29, 77
Kodály, Zoltán, 214–15
Korngold, Erich Wolfgang, 64–65, 169, 202, 205, 207–8, 209, 212, 253–54, 353–54, 419–20, 476–77, 524, 535
Korngold, George, 253–54, 263
Koussevitzky, Serge, 25, 132, 257, 474, 487–88, 489–90, 498
Kraft Mystery Theatre, 90–91, 97
Kraft Suspense Theatre, 90–91, 97, 384
Kubrick, Stanley, 134–35, 191–92, 202, 216, 360, 433–34, 435, 449–50
Kurtz, Gary, 203, 211–12, 220–22, 252–53
Kushner, Tony, 485, 499, 541

Lackland Air Force Base, 57–58, 117
Laine, Frankie, 65, 94
Landis, John, 238–40, 285
Lang, Jennings, 92, 125–26, 171–72, 174, 178, 181, 227n.§
Lang, Lang, 503
Lang, Mike, 171–72, 174, 350–51
Lang, Ronnie, 83, 92, 190–91
Lansing, Sherry, 257
Lear, Norman, 303
LeClair, Judith, 381, 382–83
Legrand, Michel, 29, 159, 234–35, 243
Lehman, Ernest, 192–94, 197
Lehman, Frank, 208, 418, 419–20, 510–11, 532
Lester, Richard, 234–35
Levine, James, 293, 483–84
Levinson, Barry, 315, 391–92
Lhévinne, Josef, 68
Lhévinne, Rosina, 56, 67–68, 69
Libertador, 506
Liberty Fanfare (concert work), 301–2, 303–5, 411
Lieberson, Goddard, 92–93, 94, 109–10
Ligeti, György, 216, 250, 435, 458, 467
Lincoln, 499–502, 515, 523
Littleton, Carol, 271–72
Lloyd, Norman, 199
Lloyd, Peter, 263
Lockhart, Keith, 380–65, 527
Loesser, Frank, 65–66, 380–81
London Symphony Orchestra, 144–45, 209, 212–13, 220–22, 234, 238, 246–47, 249, 261, 263, 278, 383, 393, 400, 420–21, 438, 491, 512, 527–28, 532–33
Loring, Eugene, 64–65, 480n.*
Los Angeles City College (LACC), 55–56
Los Angeles Opera, 431–32, 453
Los Angeles Philharmonic, 47–48, 107, 220, 229, 250, 283–84, 299, 316, 347, 454, 496, 505–6, 540, 548–49, 550, 551
Lost in Space, 109, 157, 457, 520

Lost World, The, 401–2, 403
Low, David, 375
Lucas, George, 6, 149, 158–59, 188, 197, 200, 201, 202–4, 205–8, 209, 210, 211, 213, 215, 216–17, 220–22, 224, 237, 245–46, 248–49, 257–58, 259, 261, 272, 275–76, 278–79, 285, 291–92, 295–96, 301, 302, 323–24, 345, 368, 395, 400–1, 417–21, 422, 425, 444, 445–47, 464–65, 475–76, 498, 508, 509–10, 513–14, 533–34
Lucas, Marcia, 201, 203–4, 285
Lustgarten, Edgar, 103–5, 137–38, 145
Lynch, David, 275, 543–44

M Squad, 85–86
M*A*S*H, 57–58, 145n.‡‡‡, 153
Ma, Yo-Yo, 5–6, 7–8, 252–53, 358, 370, 378, 379–81, 406, 407–8, 415, 428, 431, 432–33, 442, 443, 468, 469, 478–80, 522n.§, 527, 535, 540, 548, 550–51, 554–55
Mahler, Gustav, 118, 126, 168, 219, 388, 414, 421–23, 506, 527, 551
Mallet, Sue, 512
Man Who Loved Cat Dancing, The, 159–60, 163
Mancini, Ginny, 82, 90, 175–76, 255–56, 379
Mancini, Henry, 64, 80, 82–83, 89–90, 93, 101, 120, 171, 219–22, 243, 299, 330, 354n.‡‡‡, 369, 379, 385, 451, 460
Mangold, James, 477, 544–48
Mann, Delbert, 115, 117–18, 119–20, 127, 139–42, 176–78, 554f
Mann, Thomas, 9
Manne, Shelly, 83, 89–90, 92, 93, 98–99, 460
Markham, 90–91
Markings (concert work), 536, 538
Marquand, Richard, 275
Marsalis, Wynton, 288, 396–97, 398
Marshall, Frank, 258, 310n.††††
Marshall, Rob, 468, 469, 470–71
Marx, Albert, 79–80, 240
Marx, Chico, 55–56, 65
Marx, Groucho, 184
Maslin, Janet, 223–24, 238, 274, 309, 313, 331–32
Masur, Kurt, 382–83
Mathison, Melissa, 268, 514–15
Mauceri, John, 157–58, 309, 317–18, 429–30
McGill, Anthony, 10, 478–80, 481, 498, 534
McGovern, Maureen, 152–53, 162, 179, 233–34
McHale's Navy, 103
Meco, 212
Mehlman, Rabbi Bernard, 374
Mehta, Zubin, 107, 220, 283–84, 506
Memoirs of a Geisha, 468–71, 504–5
Menken, Alan, 332, 358, 385n.§§§§
Mercer, Johnny, 42–43, 113–14, 120, 141–42, 154
Meredith, Burgess, 131–32, 252–53
Merkur, Jacob Louis, 41

Meteor, 235
MGM, 28–29, 35, 48, 52, 55, 64, 65–66, 77, 78, 81–82, 85, 90, 123, 129, 164, 171–72, 270–71, 286, 287, 312–13, 325, 348–49, 493, 536
Midnight Cowboy, 134, 162
Midway, 196–97, 468–69
Milius, John, 238–41
Miller, George, 6–7, 210, 306–9
Miller, Glenn, 31, 81–82
Minority Report, 448–50, 522–23, 547–48
Mirisch, Walter, 115, 135, 196, 235–36
Mission: Impossible, 29, 130, 390
Mockridge, Cyril J., 86, 128
Mole, Miff, 462
Monsignor, 273–74
Montero, Gabriela, 478, 479–80, 498
Moore, Phil, 76, 78, 79–80
Morgan, Tommy, 109–10, 143, 159, 163, 195–96, 398–99
Moroder, Giorgio, 235, 290, 315–16
Moross, Jerome, 91, 96, 110–11, 142
Morricone, Ennio, 125–26, 317–18, 379, 391, 508, 513
Morris, Thomas, 242, 243–45, 253–54, 257, 262n.**, 293, 393, 536–37
Morrison, Tim, 329, 331, 332, 357, 387–88, 389–90, 404, 411
Mrs. Doubtfire, 365
Munch, Charles, 47–48
Munich, 471–72, 502–3
Murphy, Maurice, 393
Murphy, Shawn, 312–13
Music Corporation of America (MCA), 39, 78, 84–85, 129–30, 182, 191, 192–93, 228–29, 238, 321n.*, 332
Mutter, Anne-Sophie, 7–8, 154n.§§§§, 536, 537–38, 539, 540–41, 550–51
My Fair Lady, 70–71, 92–93, 99, 460
Mystery Science Theater 3000, 61–62, 88n.‡‡

Nagano, Kent, 431–32
Nagle, Thomas, 15–22, 360
National Medal of Arts, 463, 485
National Symphony Orchestra, 412, 413, 452–53, 483, 540, 552
NBC Nightly News, 294, 295–96
Nelsons, Andris, 486–87, 539
New England Conservatory, 25
New York Philharmonic, 10, 57, 284, 380n.††††, 381, 382–83, 413, 534
New York World's Fair (1939), 38, 39–40
Newman, Alfred, 46–47, 64, 74, 76, 78–79, 81, 86, 87, 108–9, 117, 120–21, 157, 163, 169–70, 205, 241, 276, 299, 513, 514, 537
Newman, Carroll, 108–9, 110, 121, 166–67, 199, 200, 255, 288, 290, 327

Newman, David, 108–9, 110, 270–71, 317–18, 323, 527, 537
Newman, Lionel, 5–6, 9, 64, 74, 78–79, 102–3, 105, 108–9, 110, 112–13, 117, 120–22, 128, 133, 134, 166–67, 175, 199, 201, 203, 220–22, 225–26, 241, 248, 253–54, 255, 257, 261, 275, 276, 288, 290, 299, 300–1, 312–13, 325–27
Newman, Marc, 121–22, 199, 244–45, 257
Newman, Randy, 64, 121, 299, 317–18, 333, 391, 495, 502–3
Newman, Thomas, 189–90, 276, 416, 495, 513
Nixon (film), 385n.§§§§, 386–89, 391, 392–93, 394, 395, 398, 401–2, 449, 501
Nixon, Richard, 121, 123, 158, 386–89, 522–23
None But the Brave, 107–8, 196, 284, 468–69
Norman, Jessye, 288, 378, 485, 498
North, Alex, 82–83, 134, 150, 169, 174, 256, 317–18
North Hollywood High School, 9, 31, 46–47, 49–51, 53, 54f, 55–56
Nostalgic Jazz Odyssey (concert work), 144
Not with My Wife, You Don't, 113–14

Obama, Barack, 3–4, 478–81, 485, 498, 554–55
Obi-Wan Kenobi, 533
O'Connor, Mark, 428
Of Grit and Glory (concert work), 548
Olympic Fanfare and Theme (concert work), 290–91, 293, 294, 301–2, 303, 321, 361–62, 389, 424, 442, 505–6, 540
Olympic Spirit (concert work), 317, 321
Onassis, Jackie (née Kennedy), 358
Ormandy, Eugene, 252
O'Toole, Peter, 112, 113, 121–22, 124–25, 129, 183–84, 233–34, 406n.††
Out of Africa, 297n.‡‡, 384
Owada, Masako (Empress of Japan), 369
Ozawa, Seiji, 8–9, 244–45, 253, 293, 317–18, 340–41, 346n.***, 348, 379, 380–81, 405, 422–23, 431, 432–33, 443–44, 460, 486–87, 489–90, 498, 527, 549, 552

Pakula, Alan J., 339
Paolucci, Robert, 46–47
Paper Chase, The, 158, 236
Parkening, Christopher, 415–17, 502
Parker, Alan, 424, 425
Paterson, Vincent, 349
Patriot, The, 427–30, 462, 478, 501
Pavarotti, Luciano, 274, 284, 307–8
Pell, Dave, 80
Penderecki, Krzysztof, 216, 236
Penelope, 114–15
Penn, Arthur, 81–82, 142, 195–96
Pepperrell Air Force Base, 60–64
Percival, Brian, 503–4, 505

Perlman, Itzhak, 262, 372, 373, 374–75, 376, 378, 379, 463, 469–70, 478–80, 505–6
Perry, Frank, 273
Peskanov, Mark, 262–63
Pete 'n' Tillie, 150–51, 332–33
Peter Gunn, 82–83, 92–93, 118, 171
Peter Pan, 268–69, 294–95, 295n.**, 309–10, 311, 348–54
Peterson, Bill, 58–59
Peterson, Oscar, 52–53, 162, 378, 549–50
Phillips, Julia, 213–14
Phillips, Michael, 213, 218, 264–65, 266, 267
Piazza, Vince, 47, 49–51
Pilot, Ann Hobson, 293–94, 413, 481–85
Pincus, Andrew, 389–90, 413–14, 431, 539
Pinocchio, 39, 128–29, 217–18, 254–55, 310, 433–34, 436
Pittsburgh Symphony Orchestra, 107, 220, 243, 253, 263, 354n.‡‡‡, 485–86
Plainsman, The, 111–12
Playhouse 90, 81–82, 92
Polanski, Roman, 390–91
Pollack, Daniel, 67–68
Pollack, Sydney 97, 142, 297n.‡‡, 384
Pollen, Sidney (Mel), 49, 58
Pope, Conrad, 388
Porter, Cole, 52, 75, 79–80, 98–99, 286, 316–17
Poseidon Adventure, The, 149, 151–53, 179, 188, 235
Post, The, 522–23
Powder, 390
Powell, Edward B., 52, 81
Powell, John 6, 271–72, 524–26, 529
Prelude and Fugue (concert work), 106, 109
Presumed Innocent, 339–41, 451
Previn, André, 5–6, 64, 75–76, 78, 79–80, 82, 90, 92–93, 96, 99, 105, 106–7, 113, 115, 116–17, 123–24, 126, 128, 129–30, 133, 136–38, 143–45, 146, 157–58, 175, 183–84, 209, 212–13, 216, 220, 243, 244, 249–50, 253, 263, 293, 299, 327, 369, 378–79, 400–1, 432, 433, 447, 473–74, 505–7, 527–28, 534, 536, 538, 549
Previn, Dory, 116, 123, 127
Prince, Hal, 184
Prince Philip, Duke of Edinburgh, 363
Prokofiev, Sergei, 52, 56, 60, 137–38, 148–49, 168, 204, 250, 267, 277, 343, 357n.*, 421–22, 443–44

Quartet La Jolla (concert work), 490
Queen Elizabeth II, 8–9, 61n.‡, 205–6, 220, 498–99, 540
Quiet Man, The, 61, 360, 543–44

Rachmaninoff, Sergei, 10, 29–30, 53, 57, 60, 75, 358, 384, 550

Index   627

Raiders of the Lost Ark, 139n.§§, 181, 240–41, 242, 258–61, 270–71, 274, 285, 301, 323–24, 345–46, 364, 397, 459–60, 476–77, 496, 509, 511–12, 513–14, 516, 546
Rain Man, 315, 468
Raitt, Bonnie, 363, 378
Raksin, David, 89, 241, 456
Rare Breed, The, 110–11
Ready Player One, 522, 523
Reagan, Nancy, 297
Reagan, Ronald, 84, 96–97, 101, 290, 303, 317
Redford, Robert, 96–97, 297n.‡‡, 323, 333–34
Reeve, Christopher, 231, 234–35, 273, 369
Reisman, Leo, 26–29
Reivers, The, 110–11, 130–34, 140, 142, 143, 145, 155–56, 162–63, 169, 170, 172, 182–83, 252–53, 291, 298, 332–33
Renard, Jacques, 25, 26–27, 36–37
Return of the Jedi, 275–79, 290, 298, 400, 418, 464–65, 530
Revue Studios, 84, 85–87, 90–91, 92, 97, 101, 102–3, 105, 109, 114–15, 136, 171–72, 258, 384, 450
Reynolds, Debbie, 51, 65, 204
Rhythm in Motion, 98, 99, 108–9
Riddle, Nelson, 46–47, 52, 64, 80
Rimsky-Korsakov, Nikolai, 41–42, 421–22
Ritt, Martin, 150–51, 162–63, 175, 176–78, 273, 332–33, 398
River, The, 291–92
Robbins, Matthew, 171, 192, 201, 230, 296–97
Roberts, Monty, 498–99
Robson, Mark, 116, 127, 178–79
Rodgers, Richard, 16, 37, 42n.‡, 66, 68–69, 79–80, 86, 106, 463n.†
Rogers, Pete, 24
Rogue One, 524
Romanul, Victor, 473–74
Ronstadt, Linda, 288, 369, 378
Rosewood, 396–99
Ross, Alex, 51–52, 208, 212–13, 218–19
Ross, William, 447–48, 450–51, 512, 518–19, 532–33, 546, 547, 548–49
Rossi, Max, 63–64
Rounds (concert work), 502
Rowling, J. K., 437, 441, 447, 456–57
Royal Philharmonic Society of London, 537
Rózsa, Miklós, 149, 169, 202, 241, 257, 317–18, 456
Rudin, Milton "Mickey," 71
Rugolo, Edye, 90, 105, 164–65, 176, 255–56
Rugolo, Pete, 82, 86, 90, 176
Ruick, Barbara (Williams), 47, 49, 51, 53–54, 55–56, 65–67, 69, 71, 74, 75, 78–80, 81–82, 89–90, 91, 92–93, 96, 98–99, 102–6, 110, 113, 117, 119, 127, 129, 130–31, 136–37, 139–40,

149n.****, 163–67, 171–72, 174–78, 193–94, 199, 200, 202–3, 204, 226, 242, 255–56, 262, 337–38, 356, 463, 498–99, 525, 537–38, 539–40, 552–54, 554f, 555
Rydell, Mark, 130–32, 134, 141–42, 143–44, 153–54, 160–61, 161f, 162, 176–78, 237, 291–92

Sachs, Michael, 393–95
Saint-Saëns, Camille, 37, 252, 421–22
Saito Kinen Orchestra, 552
Salinger, Conrad, 52, 65–66, 81, 86, 91, 483
Salkind, Ilya, 229–31, 234–35
Salonen, Esa-Pekka, 454
Salva, Victor, 390
Sanskrit (language), 286, 418–19
Satellite Celebration, a.k.a. Song for World Peace (concert work), 380–81, 442
Saturday Night Live, 191, 224n.†, 238–40
Saving Private Ryan, 409–11, 427, 468, 472, 492, 501, 542
Schaffner, Franklin J., 81–82, 274
Scherzo for Piano and Orchestra (concert work), 503
Schifrin, Lalo, 29, 130–31, 182–83, 234–35, 390n.******, 508
Schindler's List, 295, 309–10, 367–68, 370–77, 379, 396–97, 398–99, 401, 402–4, 411, 425, 429, 463, 471–72, 485, 494, 503–4, 505–6, 542
Schmitz, Chester, 298, 299, 422–23
Schoenberg, Arnold, 92–93, 157, 216, 538
Schrader, Paul, 213, 217
Schubert, Franz, 449–50
Scorsese, Martin, 193, 225–26, 295, 456
Scott, Lisbeth, 471
Scott, Raymond (and the Raymond Scott Quintette), 33–37, 45, 105–6
Scott, Ridley, 235, 315–16
Scott, Tony (musician), 68–69
Screaming Woman, The, 144, 295–96
Secret Ways, The, 95
Sendrey, Albert, 52
Sensurround, 178–79, 196–97
Seven for Luck (song cycle), 412–14
Seven Years in Tibet, 405–7
Severinsen, Doc, 393
Shaham, Gil, 413n.†††, 430–31, 498
Shalit, Gene, 252–53, 323, 405
Sheinberg, Sid, 187–88, 227, 258n.§, 268
Shemer, Naomi, 371–72
Sherman, Lee, 60, 67–68
Sherman, Richard and Robert, 149–50, 155–56, 467
Shire, David, 98, 182
Shore, Howard, 365n.††, 444–45, 508–9
Shostakovich, Dmitri, 56, 60, 271–72, 506, 537
Silvestri, Alan, 390n.******, 447, 522

Sinatra, Frank, 8–9, 42–43, 52, 66, 71, 78, 80, 82–83, 100n.***, 107–8, 159–60, 284, 326, 451
Sinfonietta for Wind Ensemble (concert work), 129, 487
Singleton, John, 396–99
Siskel, Gene, 161, 180–81
Skiles, Marlin, 77
Skinner, Frank, 59, 87–88
Slatkin, Eleanor, 83–84, 110, 190–91
Slatkin, Felix 83–84, 110
Slatkin, Leonard, 51–52, 83–84, 190–92, 249–50, 255–56, 262–63, 283–84, 380n.††††, 412, 413, 452–53, 485–86, 495
Sleepers, 391–93, 394, 395, 398
Smight, Jack, 144, 196
Smillie, James, 184–86
Smith, Kate, 39–40, 42–43
Solo, 524–26, 528, 533
Some Like It Hot, 84–85
Sondheim, Stephen, 185, 191–92, 253–54, 261, 436–37
Sontag, Susan, 9, 46–47
Sound the Bells! (concert work), 369
Soundings (concert work), 453–54
Sousa, John Philip, 169–70, 196–97, 303–5, 340–41, 479–80
South Pacific, 78–79, 82n.‡, 92–93, 117
SpaceCamp, 300–3
Spencer, Herbert, 86, 114–15, 128, 186, 210, 211, 238, 247–48, 363n.‡
Spielberg, Steven, 3–4, 67n.**, 85n.**, 134, 149, 152, 162, 164, 166, 168–70, 171–75, 176–78, 181, 185–86, 187–93, 194–95, 200, 201–2, 203–4, 209, 213–19, 220, 224–25, 226–28, 237, 238–42, 243, 247–48, 254–55, 257–60, 261, 265–66, 267, 268–73, 275–76, 278, 285–86, 287–88, 291–92, 294–97, 299, 300–1, 305, 309–12, 313, 314, 315, 323–24, 325, 326, 328, 329, 333–36, 340–41, 348–54, 355, 365–66, 367–69, 370–73, 374–78, 380, 395, 396–97, 401–5, 409–11, 420–21, 425, 426, 429–30, 433–38, 444, 446, 448–52, 453, 459–62, 463, 466–68, 471–72, 475–76, 477, 479, 485, 491–92, 494–95, 497, 499, 500–1, 503, 507, 508–9, 510, 513–16, 518–19, 522–23, 528, 532, 537, 540, 541–45, 548, 552–53, 554–55
St. Clair, Carl, 424
St. Louis Symphony Orchestra, 103–5, 107, 262–63, 389–90
Stalling, Carl, 367
Stanley & Iris, 332–33
Stanton, Andrew, 212
Star Spangled Banner, 340–41, 423, 460
Star Wars, 6, 109, 123, 143, 158, 166, 180, 196–97, 198–99, 200, 201–13, 215, 216, 218–22, 223–24, 229–30, 232, 234, 235, 245, 252–53, 257–58, 264, 266–67, 272–73, 275–77, 278–79, 283, 287, 299, 300–1, 302, 308n.§§§, 315–16, 319, 364, 368, 389, 390, 397, 400–1, 418, 419, 421, 422, 427–28, 431, 444–45, 446–47, 458n.*, 459–60, 465–66, 468, 474–75, 481, 501, 506, 508–10, 512, 513–14, 516, 517–19, 524, 525, 530–31, 532–34, 536, 541, 544–45, 546, 550
Star Wars: Episode I — The Phantom Menace, 417–22, 445, 473, 513
Star Wars: Episode II — Attack of the Clones, 445–47, 464
Star Wars: Episode III — Revenge of the Sith, 464–66, 468
Star Wars: Episode IX — The Rise of Skywalker, 528–32
Star Wars: Episode XII — The Force Awakens, 508–13, 516, 517, 529, 531
Star Wars: Episode XIII — The Last Jedi, 516–19, 520, 528–29
Star Wars: Galaxy's Edge, 532–33
Star Wars Special Editions, 400–1
Stargazers (concert work), 483
Steiner, Max, 29–30, 87, 149n.††††, 169, 189, 212, 287, 366–67, 402, 456, 535
Steiner, Nyle, 267
Stepmom, 415–17, 502
Stern, Isaac, 139, 149–50, 252–53, 262–63, 372, 378, 380–81
Stevens, Leith, 34–35, 169
Stevens, Sally, 404
Stewart, James, 96–97, 110–11, 239–40
Sting, 385
Stokes, Sheridon, 157, 178
Stoloff, Morris, 77, 80, 82–83, 107–8
Stone, George Lawrence, 25
Stone, Oliver, 108, 328–33, 355–58, 386–89, 522–23
Story of a Woman, 125–26
Strauss, Richard, 207–8, 230–31, 372–73, 435, 525
Stravinsky, Igor, 34, 88n.‡‡, 92–93, 113, 157, 168, 202, 207, 208, 219, 245–46, 250, 298–99, 383, 418–19, 421–22, 467, 551
Strayhorn, Billy, 380, 502–3
Streisand, Barbra, 184, 447, 452, 554–55
Sugarland Express, The, 162, 163, 171–75, 181, 188, 190, 230, 285
Summon the Heroes (concert work), 389–90
Sunday Night Football (*Wide Receiver*), 464, 473
Superman, 229–35, 237, 250, 254, 273, 363, 390, 413–14, 459, 502, 519
Svejda, Jim, 7–8, 220
Swed, Mark, 207, 404, 432, 453–54, 480, 490, 506, 550, 551

Symphony No. 1 (concert work), 126, 144–45, 202–3, 308n.§§§, 487
Szwarc, Jeannot, 227–28

Takemitsu, Tōru, 146, 432
Tales of Wells Fargo, 86–87, 90–91
Tanglewood, 25, 244, 254–55, 257, 264, 281, 286, 293, 305, 316–18, 346–47, 363, 369–70, 374–75, 379, 389–90, 405, 411, 413, 423*f*, 430, 431, 432–33, 443n.‡, 460, 470–71, 473–74, 481–82, 483, 486–90, 498, 502, 505–6, 507, 527, 528, 536, 539, 540, 549, 551
Tatum, Art, 549–50
Taylor, James, 488–89, 498, 549
Taylor, Kim (née Smedvig), 346, 423, 433, 528
Tchaikovsky, Pyotr, 203, 215–16, 257, 341–42, 449–50
Tedesco, Tommy, 163, 174, 292
Temple, Shirley, 35–36, 120–21
Terminal, The, 460–63
Thatcher, James, 392
Thielemans, Jean "Toots," 160–61, 162, 173–74
Thomas and the King, 183–87, 274, 412
Thornhill, Claude, 34–35, 42, 56, 106, 443
Three Pieces for Solo Cello (concert work), 442–43
Time to Heal, A, 338
Tiomkin, Dimitri, 76, 78, 81, 94, 128, 149–50, 169–70, 171
Titanic, 408, 444–45, 508
Tomlinson, Eric, 136, 220–22, 261
Tommasini, Anthony, 298–99, 303–5, 382–83, 478, 480
Tormé, Mel, 341–42, 345–46
Toto, 278, 290, 338
Towering Inferno, The, 179–81, 182–83, 196, 513
Towner, David, 25–26, 32, 486
Townsend, Irving, 92–94
TreeSong for Violin and Orchestra (concert work), 430–31
Truffaut, François, 213, 214–15, 220
Trump, Donald, 363n.‡, 481, 522
Turovsky, JoAnn, 462–63
Turtles, The, 114–15
Tuttle, Lurene, 47, 65, 127, 166, 176, 240n.***, 409
Twilight Zone: The Movie, 285

Underwood, Ian, 308
Universal Pictures, 3–4, 20–21, 37n.*, 46, 84–85, 86, 96, 111–12, 113, 125–26, 136, 168, 170, 171–72, 174, 187–88, 192–93, 196, 198, 202–3, 227–29, 265–66, 268, 295, 299, 340n.‡‡, 365–66, 367–68, 508
University of California, Los Angeles (UCLA), 49–51, 55–56, 65, 107, 120–21, 129, 146, 157, 317–18, 379, 469–70, 505, 527

University of Southern California (USC), 107, 127, 201, 239–40, 251, 456, 460, 516
Updike, John, 9, 306, 307, 309, 422–23

Valley of the Dolls, 116–17, 124, 127, 266–67, 317–18, 525
Van Eps, Robert (Bobby), 37, 48–49, 53–55, 59, 63–65, 67, 71–72, 76, 78, 87–88, 302
Vangelis, 315–16
Vanoff, Nick, 463
Varèse, Edgard, 149
Vaughan Williams, Ralph, 140, 193–94, 229, 298, 354, 421–22, 491
Vidor, King, 306
Vienna Philharmonic, 527, 535–37
Villegas, Pablo Sáinz, 502
Villeneuve, Denis, 216, 219
Volpe, Mark, 474, 485–86, 487–90, 528, 540–41

Wagner, Richard, 21, 119, 204–5, 219, 220, 236, 246–47, 267–68, 421, 514, 517, 539–40
Wagon Train, 65–66, 90–91, 155–56
Wakao, Keisuke, 486–87
Walsh, Joseph, 164
Walsh, Michael, 431–32
Walters, Barbara, 26
Walters, Louis, 26
Walton, William, 128, 193–94, 205–6, 208, 253–54
Wannberg, Kenneth, 111*f*, 117, 201, 203, 206–7, 210, 247–48, 278, 374–75, 376, 440, 446, 450, 472–73, 531
War, Korean, 55–56, 57–65, 73, 251–52
War, U.S. Civil, 15, 410, 429, 478–79
War, U.S. Revolutionary, 25–26, 43, 95–96, 427, 428–29
War, Vietnam, 59, 107–8, 123, 173–74, 197, 328, 329, 330, 331, 332, 355–56, 386
War Horse, 491–95, 497, 501, 515
War of the Worlds, 466–68
Ward-Steinman, David, 137–38
Warnow, Mark, 33–34, 37, 39, 42–43, 45
Warshawsky, Mark, 372n.§§
Warwick, Dionne, 116, 317–18
Waxman, Franz, 76, 96
Wayne, John, 61, 96–97, 142–43, 230–31, 239–40, 360
Weil, Cynthia, 436–37
Weiss, George David, 100–1
We're Lookin' Good (concert work), 305n.†††
West Coast Jazz, 79–80, 82–83, 130n.†, 301–2
West Side Story, 47, 67, 92–93, 95–96, 99–100, 135, 184, 370, 537
White Goddess, The, 74, 137–38, 381–82, 412, 418–19
Whiteman, Paul, 31

Wide Country, 90–91
Wilder, Billy, 84–85, 96, 384, 386–87
Williams, Donald, 54–55, 113, 208–9
Williams, Esther (née Towner), 25–26, 27*f*, 29, 31–32, 36–39, 41–43, 44, 46, 54–55, 87, 474–75, 475*f*, 498
Williams, Henry, 22–23
Williams, Jennifer "Jenny," 9, 22–23, 74, 75, 89–90, 98–99, 103–5, 118, 119, 121, 127, 129, 136–37, 164–65, 166, 167, 175, 176, 177*f*, 178, 184, 200, 204, 226, 240n.***, 251, 257, 262, 278, 279, 317–18, 336–38, 408–9, 437, 442, 498–99, 552–53, 554–55
Williams, Jerry, 35, 40*f*, 41–42, 46, 52–53, 54–55, 79–80, 98, 113–14, 174
Williams, Joan, 29, 32, 35–36, 40*f*, 41, 46, 63–64, 474–75
Williams, John
  accusations of plagiarism, 207–9, 376, 421–22, 501, 550
  becoming a father, 75
  becoming session pianist, 69, 77
  beginning of relationship with Spielberg, 168
  birth of, 30
  breakthrough film score, 112
  first composition, 56
  first concert as Boston Pops director, 243
  first concert work, 106
  first feature film as composer, 88
  first major screen credit as composer, 85–86
  first Oscar nomination, 116
  first public conducting appearance, 145
  grandparents of, 15, 19, 25–26
  health issues, 297, 313, 367–68, 378–79, 507, 512, 527
  hired to score *Star Wars*, 200
  joining the United States Air Force, 56
  major losses, 165, 300, 326, 474–75, 527
  major teachers, 41, 42, 45, 46–48, 58, 63–64, 67
  marriage to Barbara Ruick, 71
  marriage to Samantha Winslow, 255
  maturation of artistic style, 141
  moving to Los Angeles, 44
  parents of, 26
  relationship with London Symphony Orchestra begins, 144, 209
  relocating to London, 136
  retirement as Boston Pops director, 354
Williams, Johnny Francis (John Sr.), 4, 8–9, 15, 19, 22–24, 25, 26–29, 31–37, 39–43, 44–48, 49–51, 52–53, 54–55, 57–58, 63–64, 67, 77, 78, 87, 103, 106, 294, 300, 302, 321, 443, 462
Williams, Joseph, 89–90, 105, 119, 165, 166, 176, 226, 278, 301–2, 337–38, 337*f*, 338n.††
Williams, Katherine (Katie), 19, 22–24, 29, 32
Williams, Mark, 89–90, 105, 119, 127, 165, 166, 176, 226, 337*f*, 337–38, 409
Williams, Paul, 159–61, 161*f*, 232–33
Williams, Robin, 348, 365, 371
Williams, Samantha (née Winslow), 199–200, 252–53, 255–57, 264, 265*f*, 293, 297, 313, 316–18, 355, 378–79, 460, 498–99, 529, 552–53
Willis, Gordon 158, 339–40
Wilson, Nancy, 101, 453n.**
Wilson, Stanley, 85–87, 90–91, 92, 125–26, 127, 136
Winer, Harry, 300–3
Witches of Eastwick, The, 306–9
Woolfe, Zachary, 368–69
Wyler, William, 112, 113–14, 175, 189

Yamash'ta, Stomu, 146–47, 148–49, 468–69
Yared, Gabriel, 392–93, 406
Yes, Giorgio, 274
Yoshizawa, Masakazu, 365–66, 469–70
You Are Welcome, 61–63
Your Hit Parade, 39, 42–43, 44, 45, 48n.§, 52, 113–15

Zanuck, Richard D, 102–3, 116, 170n.*, 171, 172, 181, 187–88, 190, 227–28. *See also* Brown, David
Zaretsky, Michael, 473–74
Zemeckis, Robert, 239–40, 241
Zimmer, Hans, 189–90, 215–16, 219, 223, 234, 315–16, 332, 339–40, 360, 391, 448–49, 524
Zukovsky, Michele, 347